T U T O R I A L

COMPUTERS
for artificial intelligence
applications

Benjamin Wah and G.-J. Li

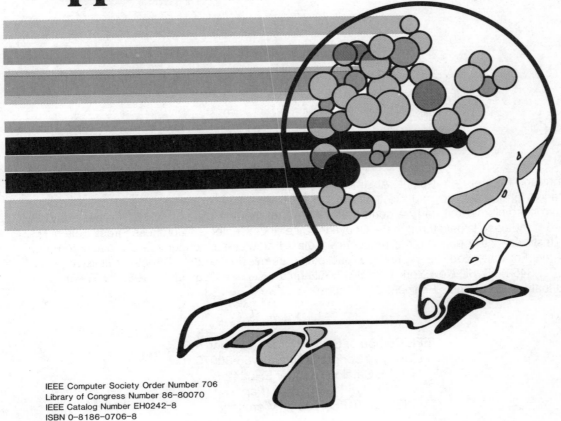

IEEE Computer Society Order Number 706
Library of Congress Number 86-80070
IEEE Catalog Number EH0242-8
ISBN 0-8186-0706-8

 IEEE COMPUTER SOCIETY

 THE INSTITUTE OF ELECTRICAL
AND ELECTRONICS ENGINEERS, INC.

IEEE

 COMPUTER
SOCIETY
PRESS

Published by IEEE Computer Society Press
1730 Massachusetts Avenue, N.W.
Washington, D.C. 20036-1903

COVER DESIGNED BY JACK I. BALLESTERO

IEEE Computer Society Order Number 706
Library of Congress Number 86-80070
IEEE Catalog Number EH0242-8
ISBN 0-8186-0706-8 (Paper)
ISBN 0-8186-4706-X (Microfiche)

Order from: IEEE Computer Society   IEEE Service Center
            Post Office Box 80452   44 Hoes Lane
            Worldway Postal Center   Piscataway, NJ 08854
            Los Angeles. CA 90080

 THE INSTITUTE OF ELECTRICAL AND ELECTRONICS ENGINEERS, INC.

Preface

This tutorial presents fundamentals in language-oriented and knowledge-oriented computer architectures for artificial intelligence applications, in short, AI architectures. As AI applications move from laboratories to the real world and as AI software grows in complexity, computational throughput, and cost are increasingly important concerns. Conventional von Neumann computers are unsuitable for AI applications because they are designed mainly for numerical processing. Although the idea of building intelligent systems is as old as the AI field itself, it is only in recent years that the design of special computer architectures for AI applications becomes feasible with the decreasing hardware costs, the advent in VLSI technology, and the experience gained with AI programming. Opportunities for increased efficiency in AI computations exist at every level, from improved instruction-set designs to parallel computer systems. A great amount of effort has been devoted to investigating and developing efficient AI architectures, and this topic is becoming more and more attractive for researchers and designers in the areas of computers and AI.

Solving a problem in AI, as well as many other problems, can be regarded as evaluating an algorithm. In general, the algorithm for solving any problem on a computer can be coded in software and executed on a conventional von Neumann computer. To cope with the increasing inefficiency and difficulty in coding algorithms in AI by using conventional languages, *declarative languages* have been developed. *Lambda-based* and *logic-based languages* are the two popular classes of declarative languages.

One of the starting points of the computer architect in supporting AI applications is the language rather than the algorithms. Of course, some primitive operations may be designed directly into hardware without first being translated by using a high-level language. This approach has been termed the *language-first approach*. A possible disadvantage of this approach is that each language may lead to a somewhat distinct architecture unsuitable for other languages, a dilemma in high-level-language computer architectures. In AI applications, the lambda-based and logic-based languages have been considered seriously by novel architects. Recent research lies in integrating the logic and lambda languages with procedural languages. The work on lambda- and logic-oriented architectures also provides useful guidelines for designing parallel architectures to support more advanced languages.

Another starting point for the computer architect is to design architectures to support the management of a large volume of knowledge. Recognizing that the major overhead lies in the search and manipulation of knowledge, the architect designs efficient storage mechanisms with distributed intelligence to support queries and updates of knowledge. The resulting architecture is strongly dictated by the knowledge representation schemes. A hybrid of the language-first and the knowledge-first approaches is of growing interest.

In spite of the growing importance of AI applications, the issues of designing these architectures have never been fairly and completely explored in a single publication. In fact, work in this area is so diversified that articles were published in other areas besides AI, ranging from psychology, medicine, manufacturing, computer architecture, software engineering, and database management to industrial engineering, electronics, theory of computation, communications, image processing, speech understanding, operations research, and the list grows. The literature search is also complicated by the fact that with the development of the Fifth-Generation Computer Systems, some work in this area is very recent and was published in many foreign countries. During our literature search to compile this tutorial text, we systematically went through over 60 different journals published in various countries and proceedings from over 50 conferences in the last 20 years and over 70 books. In view of this, the authors believe that a tutorial is urgently needed to promote more fruitful research efforts in this area.

The text of this tutorial is designed for engineers, programmers, graduate students, educators, and those involved in the research, development, and application of special-purpose computers for solving problems in AI. It is a tutorial in nature and provides a state-of-the-art survey. It is expected that this tutorial will serve as a guide for beginners, as well as a major reference for all professionals in computer engineering and AI. It is hoped that after reading the text readers will be able to understand the design issues, realize the limitations, write better programs, promote more research in this area, and trigger further creative designs for architectures and languages in AI.

The text is organized into nine chapters. A tutorial guide is provided at the beginning of each chapter to explain the underlying concepts and to annotate an up-to-date reference list. Each chapter, excluding Chapter 9, includes some reprinted articles to explain the design issues and to exemplify some recent developments.

Chapter 1 provides a general introduction to the problems and objectives in AI.

Chapter 2 discusses the motivations and design issues in designing specialized architectures for AI applications.

Chapter 3 explains the various declarative languages and programming techniques in AI, their developments, and their relationships to each other.

Chapter 4 focuses on the microlevel hardware architectures that include pattern matching, intelligent memories, and hardware unification units.

Chapter 5 investigates the macrolevel hardware architectures. Issues and designs on knowledge database machines and parallel searching are presented.

Chapters 6, 7, and 8 explore hardware architectures on the system level. Chapters 6 and 7 highlight architectures in general, while Chapter 8 presents architectures directly related to the Fifth-Generation Computer-System Projects in various countries.

Chapter 6 focuses on architectures for functional and lambda-based languages.

Chapter 7 concentrates on logic and knowledge oriented architectures. The architectures are divided into three classes and are directed toward logic programs, production systems, and semantic nets and distributed problem solving.

Chapter 8 discusses architectures of the Fifth-Generation Computer-System projects in England, the European Commission, Japan, and the United States.

Last, Chapter 9 exemplifies some architectures designed for applications in AI including speech recognition, image understanding, and computer chess.

We would like to take this opportunity to thank all the authors who have contributed to this tutorial text. We apologize to those authors whose valuable papers could not be included owing to page limitations and we also apologize to those authors whose shorter papers were selected in place of their longer and more comprehensive versions because of the page limitations. We tried to be as complete as possible in compiling the reference lists, which were based on contributions and accessibility of the work. We deeply regret any omissions and hope that they will be made known to us for use in future revisions. We would like to acknowledge the support of CIDMAC, a research unit of Purdue University, sponsored by Purdue; Cincinnati Milicron Corporation; Control Data Corporation; Cummins Engine Company; Ransburg Corporation; TRW; and the National Science Foundation grant DMC-85-19649 in preparing this tutorial text. Finally, we would like to thank sincerely Professor Chuan-lin Wu and the reviewers for their helpful criticisms, suggestions, and encouragement; Jo Johnson for her patient secretarial help; and Margaret Brown and her staff of the IEEE Computer Society Press for editing the text.

Benjamin W. Wah and Guo-Jie Li
University of Illinois, Urbana-Champaign

Table of Contents

*Professor Amar Mukhopadhyay has changed his name to Amar Mukherjee. His new address is Dept. of Computer Science, University of Central Florida, Orlando, FL 32751.

Chapter 7: Logic and Knowledge Oriented Architectures 347

7.A: Logic Programs

7.B: Production Systems

7.C: Semantic Nets and Distributed Problem Solving

Chapter 1: Introduction to Artificial Intelligence Applications

Artificial intelligence (AI) is a growing field that covers many disciplines [1-4]. There are many ways to define the field of AI [2,5-8]. As a science, essentially part of Cognitive Science [9,10], the goal of AI is to understand the principles that make intelligence possible [11,12]. As a technology and as a part of computer science, the goal of AI is to design intelligent computer systems that exhibit the characteristics associated with intelligence in human behavior; that is, understanding language and picture, learning, reasoning, solving problems, and so on [1,13-15]. Specializations in AI include knowledge representations, problem solving (search, automated reasoning, planning, and theorem proving), learning, natural-language (text or speech) understanding, computer vision, robotics, AI languages, expert systems, and several others (such as automatic programming, AI education). Many of these areas are related to each other. Research in the first three areas has focused on formal methods, while others emphasize applications.

Knowledge representation, a fundamental component of any AI system, is to encode information such as objects, goal, actions, and processes into data structures and procedures [16-18]. The most important current approaches are semantic networks [19,20], logic [6,21], frames [22], script [23], and production systems [24]. Representation schemes can be classified into declarative and procedural ones [23]. A procedural knowledge base is similar to a program and is difficult to understand and modify, while a declarative one generally requires wasteful searching. Most practical representations tend to be a hybrid of more than one category.

Problem solving and search, the earliest area of AI, explores a coherent theoretical foundation of intelligent mechanisms [6,7]. The general ideas of problem solving, such as state space, problem reduction [25-27], forward and backward reasoning [28,29], resolution rules of reference [30,31], planning [32-34], heuristic search [6,35-37], and pruning [38,39], have been widely applied to areas such as computer game playing [40-42], theorem proving [43-45], robotics, information retrieval, expert systems, and natural-language understanding. Much effort has been devoted to various heuristic-search algorithms and their complexity analysis [46-60]. Recently, nonmonotonic logic [61] and inexact reasoning [62-65] became interesting topics of research.

Machine learning, or knowledge acquisition, is the central but most difficult problem of AI research [66-69]. The field of machine learning can be organized around three primary research foci: theoretical analysis [70-77], task-oriented studies (engineering approach) [78-80], and cognitive simulation (cognitive modeling approach) [9].

There are many other problems in artificial intelligence. These issues will be discussed throughout the rest of this tutorial.

Two papers are included in this chapter. The origin of Lisp, using CAR and CDR, came from the seminal paper by McCarthy in 1960 [81] and is summarized in the next paper by McCarthy on the history of Lisp [82]. The second paper selected in this chapter, by Cercone and McCalla, highlights some issues in artificial intelligence [8]. The seminal paper by Newell and Shaw on the Logic Theory Machine [83] discusses the first AI language, IPL, and considers the problems in list structures. Owing to space limitations, this paper is not included here.

References

[1] A. Barr and E.A. Feigenbaum, *The Handbook of Artificial Intelligence,* vols. 1,2, and 3, William Kaufmann, Los Altos, Calif., 1981, 1982.

[2] D.G. Bobrow and P.J. Hayes, "Artificial Intelligence —Where Are We?," *Artificial Intelligence,* vol. 25, no. 3, pp. 375-415, 1985.

[3] A.L. Samuel, "AI, Where It Has Been and Where It Is Going?," *Proceedings of the 8th International Joint Conference on Artificial Intelligence,* pp. 1152-1157, William Kaufmann, Los Altos, Calif., Aug. 1983.

[4] B. Webber and N. Nilsson, eds., *Readings in Artificial Intelligence,* Tioga, Palo Alto, Calif., 1981.

[5] P.H. Winston, *Artificial Intelligence,* Second Edition, Addison-Wesley, Reading, Mass., 1984.

[6] N.J. Nilsson, *Principles of Artificial Intelligence,* Tioga, Palo Alto, Calif., 1980.

[7] N.J. Nilsson, "Artificial Intelligence: Engineering, Science or Slogan?," *The AI Magazine,* vol. 3, no. 1, pp. 2-9, Winter 1981-82.

[8] N. Cercone and G. McCalla, "Artificial Intelligence: Underlying Assumptions and Basic Objectives," *Journal of the American Society for Information Science,* vol. 35, no. 5, pp. 280-290, Sept. 1984.

[9] A. Newell and H.A. Simon, *Human Problem Solving*, Prentice-Hall, Englewood Cliffs, N.J., 1972.

[10] J.R. Anderson, "Cognitive Psychology," *Artificial Intelligence*, vol. 23, no. 1, pp. 1-11, 1984.

[11] H.A. Simon, "Artificial Intelligence System That Understands," *Proceedings of the 5th International Joint Conference on Artificial Intelligence*, pp. 1059-1073, William Kaufmann, Los Altos, Calif., Aug. 1977.

[12] D. Marr, "Artificial Intelligence—A Personal View," *Artificial Intelligence*, vol. 9, no. 1, pp. 37-48, 1977.

[13] E.A. Feigenbaum, "The Art of Artificial Intelligence—Themes and Case Studies of Knowledge Engineering," *Proceedings of the 5th International Joint Conference on Artificial Intelligence*, pp. 1014-1029, William Kaufmann, Los Altos, Calif., Aug. 1977.

[14] E.A. Feigenbaum, "Knowledge Engineering: The Applied Side," *Intelligent Systems: The Unprecedented Opportunity*, edited by J.E. Hayes and D. Michie, pp. 37-55, Ellis Horwood Ltd., Chichester, England, 1983.

[15] P.E. Hart, "Directions for AI in the Eighties," *SIGART Newsletter*, no. 79, pp. 11-16, ACM, New York, N.Y., Jan. 1982.

[16] R.J. Brachman and B.C. Smith, eds., "Special Issue on Knowledge Representation," *SIGART Newsletter*, no. 70, ACM, New York, N.Y., Feb. 1980.

[17] G. McCalla and N. Cercone, eds., "Special Issue on Knowledge Representation," *Computer*, vol. 16, no. 10, Oct. 1983.

[18] K. Niwa, K. Sasaki, and H. Ihara, "An Experimental Comparison of Knowledge Representation Schemes," *The AI Magazine*, vol. 5, no. 2, pp. 29-36, Summer 1984.

[19] M.R. Quillian, "Semantic Memory," *Semantic Information Processing*, edited by M. Minsky, MIT Press, Cambridge, Mass., 1968.

[20] S.C. Shapiro and G.H. Woodmansee, "A Net Structure Based Relational Question-Answerer," *Proceedings of the International Conference on Artificial Intelligence*, pp. 325-346, William Kaufmann, Los Altos, Calif., 1971.

[21] J.A. Robinson, "Logic Programming—Past, Present and Future," *New Generation Computing*, vol. 1, no. 2, pp. 107-124, 1983.

[22] M. Minsky, "A Framework for Representing Knowledge," *AI Memo 306*, MIT Press, Cambridge, Mass., June 1974.

[23] T. Winograd, "Frames and the Procedural-Declarative Controversy," *Proceedings of the International Conference on Artificial Intelligence*, pp. 151-157, William Kaufmann, Los Altos, Calif., 1975.

[24] A. Newell, "Production Systems: Models of Control Structures," *Visual Information Processing*, edited by W.G. Chase, Academic Press, Orlando, Fla., 1975.

[25] G. Ernst and A. Newell, *GPS: A Case Study in Generality and Problem Solving*, Academic Press, Orlando, Fla., 1969.

[26] D. McDermott, "Generalizing Problem Reduction: A Logical Analysis," *Proceedings of the 8th International Joint Conference on Artificial Intelligence*, pp. 302-308, William Kaufmann, Los Altos, Calif., Aug. 1983.

[27] D.R. Smith, "A Problem Reduction Approach to Program Synthesis," *Proceedings of the 8th International Joint Conference on Artificial Intelligence*, pp. 32-36, William Kaufmann, Los Altos, Calif., Aug. 1983.

[28] H.A. Simon, "Search and Reasoning in Problem Solving," *Artificial Intelligence*, vol. 21, no. 1-2, pp. 7-29, 1983.

[29] J.A. Robinson, "Logical Reasoning in Machines," *Intelligent Systems: The Unprecedented Opportunity*, edited by J.E. Hayes and D. Michie, pp. 19-35, Ellis Horwood Ltd., Chichester, England, 1983.

[30] J.A. Robinson, "A Machine-Oriented Logic Based on the Resolution Principle," *Journal of the ACM*, vol. 12, no. 1, pp. 23-41, 1965.

[31] R. Kowalski, *Logic for Problem Solving*, North-Holland, Amsterdam, The Netherlands, 1979.

[32] E.D. Sacerdoti, *A Structure for Plan and Behavior*, Elservier, New York, N.Y., 1977.

[33] R.E. Fikes and N.J. Nilsson, "STRIPS: A New Approach to the Application of Theorem Proving to Problem Solving," *Artificial Intelligence*, vol. 2, no. 3 & 4, pp. 189-208, 1971.

[34] B. Hayes-Roth and F. Hayes-Roth, "A Cognitive Model of Planning," *Cognitive Science*, vol. 3, no. 4, pp. 275-310, 1979.

[35] J. Pearl, "Some Recent Results in Heuristic Search Theory," *IEEE Transactions on Pattern Analysis and Machine Intelligence*, vol. PAMI-6, no. 1, pp. 1-13, Jan. 1984.

[36] J. Pearl, *Heuristics: Intelligent Search Strategies for Computer Problem Solving*, Addison-Wesley, Reading, Mass., 1984.

[37] A. Bagchi and A. Mahanti, "Search Algorithms Under Different Kinds of Heuristics—A Comparative Study," *Journal of the ACM*, vol. 30, no. 1, pp. 1-21, Jan. 1983.

[38] D.E. Knuth and R.W. Moore, "An Analysis of Alpha-Beta Pruning," *Artificial Intelligence*, vol. 6, no. 4, pp. 293-326, 1975.

[39] T. Ibaraki, "The Power of Dominance Relations in Branch-and-Bound Algorithms," *Journal of the ACM,* vol. 24, no. 2, pp. 264-279, April 1977.

[40] M.M. Newborn, "Recent Progress in Computer Chess," *Advances in Computers*, edited by M.C. Yovits, vol. 18, pp. 59-117, Academic Press, Orlando, Fla., 1979.

[41] D.S. Nau, "Decision Quality As a Function of Search Depth on Game Trees," *Journal of the ACM*, vol. 30, no. 4, pp. 687-708, 1983.

[42] M. Tarsi, "Optimal Search on Some Game Trees," *Journal of the ACM*, vol. 30, no. 3, pp. 389-396, July 1983.

[43] D. Loveland, *Automatic Theorem Proving: A Logic Basis,* North-Holland, Amsterdam, The Netherlands, 1978.

[44] C. Chang and R.C. Lee, *Symbolic Logic and Mechanical Theorem Proving*, Academic Press, Orlando, Fla., 1973.

[45] D. McDermott, "Deductive Inference: Question Answering/Theorem Proving," *SIGART Newsletter*, no. 63, pp. 2-6, ACM, New York, N.Y., June 1977.

[46] H.A. Simon and J.B. Kadane, "Optimal Problem-Solving Search: All-or-None Solutions," *Artificial Intelligence*, vol. 6, no. 3, pp. 235-247, 1975.

[47] V. Kumar and L.N. Kanal, "A General Branch and Bound Formulation for Understanding and Synthesizing AND/OR Tree Search Procedures," *Artificial Intelligence*, vol. 21, no. 1-2, pp. 179-198, 1983.

[48] T. Ibaraki, "Theoretical Comparisons of Search Strategies in Branch-and-Bound Algorithms," *International Journal of Computer and Information Sciences,* vol. 5, no. 4, pp. 315-343, 1976.

[49] C.A. Brown and P.W. Purdom, Jr., "An Average Time Analysis of Backtracking," *SIAM Journal of Computing*, vol. 10, no. 3, pp. 583-593, Aug. 1981.

[50] H. Berliner, "The B* Tree Search Algorithm: A Best-First Proof Procedure," *Artificial Intelligence*, vol. 12, no. 1, pp. 23-40, 1979.

[51] C.L. Chang and J.R. Slagle, "An Admissible and Optimal Algorithm for Searching AND/OR Graphs," *Artificial Intelligence*, vol. 2, no. 2, pp. 117-128, 1971.

[52] E.C. Freuder, "A Sufficient Condition for Backtrack-Free Search," *Journal of the ACM*, vol. 29, no. 1, pp. 24-32, Jan. 1982.

[53] J. Gaschnig, "Exactly How Good Are Heuristics?: Toward a Realistic Predictive Theory of Best-First Search," *Proceedings of the 5th International Joint Conference on Artificial Intelligence*, pp. 434-441, William Kaufmann, Los Altos, Calif., Aug. 1977.

[54] D. Gelperin, "On the Optimality of A*," *Artificial Intelligence*, vol. 8, no. 1, pp. 69-76, 1977.

[55] P.A.V. Hall, "AND/OR Graphs and Context-Free Grammars," *Communications of the ACM*, vol. 16, no. 7, pp. 444-445, July 1973.

[56] R.M. Karp and J. Pearl, "Searching for an Optimal Path in a Tree with Random Costs," *Artificial Intelligence*, vol. 21, no. 1-2, pp. 99-116, 1983.

[57] A. Mahanti and A. Bagchi, "AND/OR Graph Heuristic Search Methods," *Journal of the ACM*, vol. 32, no. 1, pp. 28-51, Jan. 1985.

[58] A. Martelli, "On the Complexity of Admissible Search Algorithms," *Artificial Intelligence*, vol. 8, no. 1, pp. 1-13, 1977.

[59] I. Pohl, "First Results on the Effect of Error in Heuristic Search," *Machine Intelligence 5,* edited by B. Meltzer and D. Michie, pp. 219-236, Elsevier, New York, N.Y., 1970.

[60] D.B. Lenat, "The Nature of Heuristics," *Artificial Intelligence,* vol. 19, no. 2, pp. 189-249, 1982.

[61] D.G. Bobrow and P.J. Hayes, eds., "Special Issue on Nonmonotonic Logic," *Artificial Intelligence*, vol. 13, no. 1 & 2, April 1980.

[62] L.A. Zadeh, "Approximate Reasoning Based on Fuzzy Logic," *Proceedings of the 6th International Joint Conference on Artificial Intelligence,* pp. 1004-1010, William Kaufmann, Los Altos, Calif., Aug. 1979.

[63] M. Ishizuka, "Inference Methods Based on Extended Dempster & Shafer's Theory for Problems with Uncertainty/Fuzziness," *New Generation Computing*, vol. 1, no. 2, pp. 159-168, 1983.

[64] P.R. Cohen and M.R. Grinberg, "A Theory of Heuristic Reasoning About Uncertainty," *The AI Magazine*, vol. 4, no. 2, pp. 17-24, Summer 1983.

[65] R. Giles, "Semantics for Fuzzy Reasoning," *International Journal of Man-Machine Studies*, vol. 17, no. 4, pp. 401-415, 1982.

[66] J.G. Carbonell, R.S. Michalski, and T.M. Mitchell, "Machine Learning: A Historical and Methodological Analysis," *The AI Magazine,* vol. 4, no. 3, pp. 69-79, Fall 1983.

[67] R.S. Michalski, J.G. Carbonell, and T.M. Mitchell, *Machine Learning: An Artificial Intelligence Approach,* Tioga, Palo Alto, Calif., 1983.

[68] T.M. Mitchell, "Learning and Problem Solving," *Proceedings of the 8th International Joint Conference on Artificial Intelligence*, pp. 1139-1151, William Kaufmann, Los Altos, Calif., Aug. 1983.

[69] D.B. Lenat, "The Ubiquity of Discovery," *Proceedings of the 5th International Joint Conference on Artificial Intelligence*, pp. 1093-1105, William Kaufmann, Los Altos, Calif., 1977.

[70] R.G. Smith, T.M. Mitchell, R.A. Chestek, and B.G. Buchanan, "A Model for Learning Systems," *Proceedings of the 5th International Joint Conference on Artificial Intelligence*, pp. 338-343, William Kaufmann, Los Altos, Calif., Aug. 1977.

[71] F. Hayes-Roth and J. McDermott, "An Interference Matching Technique for Inducing Abstractions," *Communications of the ACM*, vol. 21, no. 5, pp. 401-411, May 1978.

[72] J. Pearl, "On the Discovery and Generation of Certain Heuristics," *The AI Magazine*, vol. 4, no. 1, pp. 23-33, Winter/Spring 1983.

[73] J.G. Carbonell, "Experiential Learning in Analogical Problem Solving," *Proceedings of the National Conference on Artificial Intelligence*, pp. 168-171, William Kaufmann, Los Altos, Calif., 1982.

[74] P. Langley, "Learning Effective Search Heuristics," *Proceedings of the 8th International Joint Conference on Artificial Intelligence*, pp. 419-421, William Kaufmann, Los Altos, Calif., 1983.

[75] T.M. Mitchell, P.E. Utgoff, B. Nudel, and R. Benerji, "Learning Problem-Solving Heuristics Through Practice," *Proceedings of the 7th International Joint Conference on Artificial Intelligence*, pp. 127-134, William Kaufmann, Los Altos, Calif., 1981.

[76] P.D. Scott, "Learning: The Construction of a Posteriori Knowledge Structures," *Proceedings of the National Conference on Artificial Intelligence*, pp. 359-363, William Kaufmann, Los Altos, Calif., 1983.

[77] D.A. Waterman, "Generalization Learning Techniques for Automating the Learning of Heuristics," *Artificial Intelligence*, vol. 1, no. 1-2, pp. 121-170, 1970.

[78] A.L. Samuel, "Some Studies in Machine Learing Using the Game of Checkers II—Resent Progress," *IBM Journal of Research and Development*, vol. 11, no. 6, pp. 601-617, 1967.

[79] D.B. Lenat and J.S. Brown, "Why AM and EURISKO Appear to Work?," *Artificial Intelligence*, vol. 23, no. 3, pp. 269-294, 1984.

[80] G.D. Ritchie and F.K. Hanna, "AM: A Case Study in AI Methodology," *Artificial Intelligence*, vol. 23, no. 3, pp. 249-268, 1984.

[81] J. McCarthy, "Recursive Functions of Symbolic Expressions and Their Computation by Machine, Part I," *Communications of the ACM*, vol. 3, no. 4, pp. 184-195, 1960.

[82] J. McCarthy, "History of Lisp," *SIGPLAN Notices*, vol. 13, no. 8, pp. 217-223, ACM, New York, N.Y., 1978.

[83] A. Newell, J.C. Shaw, and H.A. Simon, "Programming the Logic Theory Machine," *Proceedings of the 1957 Western Joint Computer Conference*, pp. 230-240, IRE, New York, N.Y., 1957.

HISTORY OF LISP

John McCarthy
Artificial Intelligence Laboratory
Stanford University

1. Introduction.

This paper concentrates on the development of the basic ideas and distinguishes two periods - Summer 1956 through Summer 1958 when most of the key ideas were developed (some of which were implemented in the FORTRAN based FLPL), and Fall 1958 through 1962 when the programming language was implemented and applied to problems of artificial intelligence. After 1962, the development of LISP became multi-stranded, and different ideas were pursued in different places.

Except where I give credit to someone else for an idea or decision, I should be regarded as tentatively claiming credit for it or else regarding it as a consequence of previous decisions. However, I have made mistakes about such matters in the past, and I have received very little response to requests for comments on drafts of this paper. It is particularly easy to take as obvious a feature that cost someone else considerable thought long ago. As the writing of this paper approaches its conclusion, I have become aware of additional sources of information and additional areas of uncertainty.

As a programming language, LISP is characterized by the following ideas: computing with symbolic expressions rather than numbers, representation of symbolic expressions and other information by list structure in the memory of a computer, representation of information in external media mostly by multi-level lists and sometimes by S-expressions, a small set of selector and constructor operations expressed as functions, composition of functions as a tool for forming more complex functions, the use of conditional expressions for getting branching into function definitions, the recursive use of conditional expressions as a sufficient tool for building computable functions, the use of λ-expressions for naming functions, the representation of LISP programs as LISP data, the conditional expression interpretation of Boolean connectives, the LISP function *eval* that serves both as a formal definition of the language and as an interpreter, and garbage collection as a means of handling the erasure problem. LISP statements are also used as a command language when LISP is used in a time-sharing environment.

Some of these ideas were taken from other languages, but most were new. Towards the end of the initial period, it became clear that this combination of ideas made an elegant mathematical system as well as a practical programming language. Then mathematical neatness became a goal and led to pruning some features from the core of the language. This was partly motivated by esthetic reasons and partly by the belief that it would be easier to devise techniques for proving programs correct if the semantics were compact and without exceptions. The results of (Cartwright 1976) and (Cartwright and McCarthy 1978), which show that LISP programs can be interpreted as sentences and schemata of first order logic, provide new confirmation of the original intuition that logical neatness would pay off.

2. LISP prehistory - Summer 1956 through Summer 1958.

My desire for an algebraic list processing language for artificial intelligence work on the IBM 704 computer arose in the summer of 1956 during the Dartmouth Summer Research Project on Artificial Intelligence which was the first organized study of AI. During this meeting, Newell, Shaw and Simon described IPL 2, a list processing language for Rand Corporation's JOHNNIAC computer in which they implemented their Logic Theorist program. There was little temptation to copy IPL, because its form was based on a JOHNNIAC loader that happened to be available to them, and because the FORTRAN idea of writing programs algebraically was attractive. It was immediately apparent that arbitrary subexpressions of symbolic expressions could be obtained by composing the functions that extract immediate subexpressions, and this seemed reason enough to go to an algebraic language.

There were two motivations for developing a language for the IBM 704. First, IBM had generously undertaken to establish a New England Computation Center at M.I.T., and Dartmouth would be able to use it. Second, IBM was undertaking to develop a program for proving theorems in plane geometry (based on an idea of Marvin Minsky's), and I was to serve as a consultant to that project. At the time, IBM looked like a good bet to pursue artificial intelligence research vigorously, and further projects were expected. It was not then clear whether IBM's FORTRAN project would lead to a language within which list processing could conveniently be carried out or whether a new language would be required. However, many considerations were independent of this decision.

Apart from consulting on the geometry program, my own research in artificial intelligence was proceeding along the lines that led to the Advice Taker proposal in 1958 (McCarthy 1959). This involved representing information about the world by sentences in a suitable formal language and a reasoning program that would decide what to do by drawing logical consequences. Representing sentences by list structure seemed appropriate - it still is - and a list processing language also seemed appropriate for programming the operations involved in deduction - and still is.

This internal representation of symbolic information gives up the familiar infix notations in favor of a notation that simplifies the task of programming the substantive computations, e.g. logical deduction or algebraic simplification, differentiation or integration. If customary notations are to be used externally, translation programs must be written. Thus most LISP programs use a prefix notation for algebraic expressions, because they usually must determine the main connective before deciding what to do next. In this LISP differs from almost every other symbolic computation system. COMIT, FORMAC, and Formula Algol programs all express the computations as operations on some approximation to the customary printed forms of symbolic expressions. SNOBOL operates on character strings but is neutral on how character strings are used to represent symbolic information. This feature probably accounts for LISP's success in competition with these languages, especially when large programs have to be written. The advantage is like that of binary computers over decimal – but larger.

(In the late 1950s, neat output and convenient input notation was not generally considered important. Programs to do the kind of input and output customary today wouldn't even fit in the memories available at that time. Moreover, keypunches and printers with adequate character sets didn't exist).

The first problem was how to do list structure in the IBM 704. This computer has a 36 bit word, and two 15 bit parts, called the address and decrement, were distinguished by special instructions for moving their contents to and from the 15 bit index registers The address of the machine was 15 bits, so it was clear that list structure should use 15 bit pointers. Therefore, it was natural to consider the word as divided into 4 parts, the address part, the decrement part, the prefix part and the tag part. The last two were three bits each and separated from each other by the decrement so that they could not be easily combined into a single six bit part.

At this point there was some indecision about what the basic operators should be, because the operation of extracting a part of the word by masking was considered separately from the operation of taking the contents of a word in memory as a function of its address. At the time, it seemed dubious to regard the latter operation as a function, since its value depended on the contents of memory at the time the operation was performed, so it didn't act like a proper mathematical function. However, the advantages of treating it grammatically as a function so that it could be composed were also apparent.

Therefore, the initially proposed set of functions included *cwr*, standing for "Contents of the Word in Register number" and four functions that extracted the parts of the word and shifted them to a standard position at the right of the word. An additional function of three arguments that would also extract an arbitrary bit sequence was also proposed.

It was soon noticed that extraction of a subexpression involved composing the extraction of the address part with *cwr* and that continuing along the list involved composing the extraction of the decrement part with *cwr*. Therefore, the compounds *car*, standing for "Contents of the Address part of Register number", and its analogs *cdr*, *cpr*, and *ctr* were defined. The motivation for implementing *car* and *cdr* separately was strengthened by the vulgar fact that the IBM 704 had instructions (connected with indexing) that made these operations easy to implement. A construct operation for taking a word off the free storage list and stuffing it with given contents was also obviously required. At some point a *cons(a, d, p, t)* was defined, but it was regarded as a subroutine and not as a function with a value. This work was done at Dartmouth, but not on a computer, since the New England Computation Center was not expected to receive its IBM 704 for another year.

In connection with IBM's plane geometry project, Nathaniel Rochester and Herbert Gelernter (on the advice of McCarthy) decided to implement a list processing language within FORTRAN, because this seemed to the the easiest way to get started, and, in those days, writing a compiler for a new language was believed to take many man-years. This work was undertaken by Herbert Gelernter and Carl Gerberich at IBM and led to FLPL, standing for FORTRAN List Processing Language. Gelernter and Gerberich noticed that *cons* should be a function, not just a subroutine, and that its value should be the location of the word that had been taken from the free storage list. This permitted new expressions to be constructed out of subsubexpressions by composing occurrences of *cons*.

While expressions could be handled easily in FLPL, and it was used successfully for the Geometry program, it had neither conditional expressions nor recursion, and erasing list structure was handled explicitly by the program.

I invented conditional expressions in connection with a set of chess legal move routines I wrote in FORTRAN for the IBM 704 at M.I.T. during 1957-58. This program did not use list processing. The IF statement provided in FORTRAN 1 and FORTRAN 2 was very awkward to use, and it was natural to invent a function XIF(M,N1,N2) whose value was N1 or N2 according to whether the expression M was zero or not. The function shortened many programs and made them easier to understand, but it had to be used sparingly, because all three arguments had to be evaluated before XIF was entered, since XIF was called as an ordinary FORTRAN function though written in machine language. This led to the invention of the true conditional expression which evaluates only one of N1 and N2 according to whether M is true or false and to a desire for a programming language that would allow its use.

A paper defining conditional expressions and proposing their use in Algol was sent to the *Communications of the ACM* but was arbitrarily demoted to a letter to the editor, because it was very short.

I spent the summer of 1958 at the IBM Information Research Department at the invitation of Nathaniel Rochester and chose differentiating algebraic expressions as a sample problem. It led to the following innovations beyond FLPL:

a. Writing recursive function definitions using conditional expressions. The idea of differentiation is obviously recursive, and conditional expressions allowed combining the cases into a single formula.

b. The *maplist* function that forms a list of applications of a functional argument to the elements of a list. This was obviously wanted for differentiating sums of arbitrarily many terms, and with a slight modification, it could be applied to differentiating products. (The original form was what is now called *mapcar*).

c. To use functions as arguments, one needs a notation for functions, and it seemed natural to use the λ-notation of Church (1941). I didn't understand the rest of his book, so I wasn't tempted to try to implement his more general mechanism for defining functions. Church used higher order functionals instead of using conditional expressions. Conditional expressions are much more readily implemented on computers.

d. The recursive definition of differentiation made no provision for erasure of abandoned list structure. No solution was apparent at the time, but the idea of complicating the elegant definition of differentiation with explicit erasure was unattractive. Needless to say, the point of the exercise was not the differentiation program itself, several of which had already been written, but rather clarification of the operations involved in symbolic computation.

In fact, the differentiation program was not implemented that summer, because FLPL allows neither conditional expressions nor recursive use of subroutines. At this point a new language was necessary, since it was very difficult both technically and politically to tinker with Fortran, and neither conditional expressions nor recursion could be implemented with machine language Fortran functions - not even with "functions" that modify the code that calls them. Moreover, the IBM group seemed satisfied with FLPL as it was and did not want to make the vaguely stated but obviously drastic changes required to allow conditional expressions and recursive definition. As I recall, they argued that these were unnecessary.

2. The implementation of LISP.

In the Fall of 1958, I became Assistant Professor of Communication Sciences (in the EE Department) at M.I.T., and Marvin Minsky (then an assistant professor in the Mathematics Department) and I started the M.I.T. Artificial Intelligence Project. The Project was supported by the M.I.T. Research Laboratory of Electronics which had a contract from the armed services that permitted great freedom to the Director, Professor Jerome Wiesner, in initiating new projects that seemed to him of scientific interest. No written proposal was ever made. When Wiesner asked Minsky and me what we needed for the project, we asked for a room, two programmers, a secretary and a keypunch, and he asked us to also undertake the supervision of some of the six mathematics graduate students that R.L.E. had undertaken to support.

The implementation of LISP began in Fall 1958. The original idea was to produce a compiler, but this was considered a major undertaking, and we needed some experimenting in order to get good conventions for subroutine linking, stack handling and erasure. Therefore, we started by hand-compiling various functions into assembly language and writing subroutines to provide a LISP "environment". These included programs to read and print list structure. I can't now remember whether the decision to use parenthesized list notation as the external form of LISP data was made then or whether it had already been used in discussing the paper differentiation program.

The programs to be hand-compiled were written in an informal notation called M-expressions intended to resemble FORTRAN as much as possible. Besides FORTRAN-like assignment statements and go tos, the language allowed conditional expressions and the basic functions of LISP. Allowing recursive function definitions required no new notation from the function definitions allowed in FORTRAN I - only the removal of the restriction - as I recall, unstated in the FORTRAN manual - forbidding recursive definitions. The M-notation also used brackets instead of parentheses to enclose the arguments of functions in order to reserve parentheses for list-structure constants. It was intended to compile from some approximation to the M-notation, but the M-notation was never fully defined, because representing LISP functions by LISP lists became the dominant programming language when the interpreter later became available. A machine readable M-notation would have required redefinition, because the pencil-and-paper M-notation used characters unavailable on the IBM 026 key punch.

The READ and PRINT programs induced a *de facto* standard external notation for symbolic information, e.g. representing $x + 3y + z$ by (PLUS X (TIMES 3 Y) Z) and $(\forall x)(P(x) \vee Q(x, y))$ by (ALL (X) (OR (P X) (Q X Y))). Any other notation necessarily requires special programming, because standard mathematical notations treat different operators in syntactically different ways. This notation later came to be called "Cambridge Polish", because it resembled the prefix notation of Lukasiewicz, and because we noticed that Quine had also used a parenthesized prefix notation.

The erasure problem also had to be considered, and it was clearly unaesthetic to use explicit erasure as did IPL. There were two alternatives. The first was to erase the old contents of a program variable whenever it was updated. Since the *car* and *cdr* operations were not to copy structure, merging list structure would occur, and erasure would require a system of reference counts. Since there were only six bits left in a word, and these were in separated parts of the word, reference counts seemed infeasible without a drastic change in the way list structures were represented. (A list handling scheme using reference counts was later used by Collins (1960) on a 48 bit CDC computer).

The second alternative is *garbage collection* in which storage is abandoned until the free storage list is exhausted, the storage accessible from program variables and the stack is marked, and the unmarked storage is made into a new free storage list. Once we decided on garbage collection, its actual implementation could be postponed, because only toy examples were being done.

At that time it was also decided to use SAVE and UNSAVE routines that use a single contiguous public stack array to save the values of variables and subroutine return addresses in the implementation of recursive subroutines. IPL built stacks as list structure and their use had to be explicitly programmed. Another decision was to give up the prefix and tag parts of the word, to abandon *cwr*, and to make *cons* a function of two arguments. This left us with only a single type - the 15 bit address - so that the language didn't require declarations.

These simplifications made LISP into a way of describing computable functions much neater than the Turing machines or the general recursive definitions used in recursive function theory. The fact that Turing machines constitute an awkward programming language doesn't much bother recursive function theorists, because they almost never have any reason to write particular recursive definitions, since the theory concerns recursive functions in general. They often have reason to prove that recursive functions with specific properties exist, but this can be done by an informal argument without having to write them down explicitly. In the early days of computing, some people developed programming languages based on Turing machines; perhaps it seemed more scientific. Anyway, I decided to write a paper describing LISP both as a programming language and as a formalism for doing recursive function theory. The paper was *Recursive functions of symbolic expressions and their computation by machine, part I* (McCarthy 1960). Part II was never written but was intended to contain applications to computing with algebraic expressions. The paper had no influence on recursive function theorists, because it didn't address the questions that interested them.

One mathematical consideration that influenced LISP was to express programs as applicative expressions built up from variables and constants using functions. I considered it important to make these expressions obey the usual mathematical laws allowing replacement of expressions by expressions giving the same value. The motive was to allow proofs of properties of programs using ordinary mathematical methods. This is only possible to the extent that side-effects can be avoided. Unfortunately, side-effects are often a great convenience when computational efficiency is important, and "functions" with side-effects are present in LISP. However, the so-called pure LISP is free of side-effects, and (Cartwright 1976) and (Cartwright and McCarthy 1978) show how to represent pure LISP programs by sentences and schemata in first order logic and prove their properties. This is an additional vindication of the striving for mathematical neatness, because it is now easier to prove that pure LISP programs meet their specifications than it is for any other programming language in extensive use. (Fans of other programming languages are challenged to write a program to concatenate lists and prove that the operation is associative).

Another way to show that LISP was neater than Turing machines was to write a universal LISP function and show that it is briefer and more comprehensible than the description of a universal Turing machine. This was the LISP function *eval*[*e, a*], which computes the value of a LISP expression *e* - the second argument *a* being a list of assignments of values to variables. (*a* is needed to make the recursion work). Writing *eval* required inventing a notation representing LISP functions as LISP data, and such a notation was devised for the purposes of the paper with no thought that it would be used to express LISP programs in practice. Logical completeness required that the notation used to express functions used as functional arguments be extended to provide for recursive functions, and the LABEL notation was invented by Nathaniel Rochester for that purpose. D.M.R. Park pointed out that LABEL was logically unnecessary since the result could be achieved using only LAMBDA - by a construction analogous to Church's Y-operator, albeit in a more complicated way.

S.R. Russell noticed that *eval* could serve as an interpreter for LISP, promptly hand coded it, and we now had a programming language with an interpreter.

The unexpected appearance of an interpreter tended to freeze the form of the language, and some of the decisions made rather lightheartedly for the "Recursive functions ..." paper later proved unfortunate. These included the COND notation for conditional expressions which leads to an unnecessary depth of parentheses, and the use of the number zero to denote the empty list NIL and the truth value *false*. Besides encouraging pornographic programming, giving a special interpretation to the address 0 has caused difficulties in all subsequent implementations.

Another reason for the initial acceptance of awkwardnesses in the internal form of LISP is that we still expected to switch to writing programs as M-expressions. The project of defining M-expressions precisely and compiling them or at least translating them into S-expressions was neither finalized nor explicitly abandoned. It just receded into the indefinite future, and a new generation of programmers appeared who preferred internal notation to any FORTRAN-like or ALGOL-like notation that could be devised.

3. From LISP I to LISP 1.5.

a. Property lists. The idea of providing each atom with a list of properties was present in the first assembly language implementation. It was also one of the theoretical ideas of the Advice Taker, although the Advice Taker (McCarthy 1959) would have required a property list for any expression about which information was known that did not follow from its structure. The READ and PRINT programs required that the print names of atoms be accessible, and as soon as function definition became possible, it was necessary to indicate whether a function was a SUBR in machine code or was an EXPR represented by list structure. Several functions dealing with property lists were also made available for application programs which made heavy use of them.

b. Insertion of elements in lists and their deletion. One of the original advertised virtues of list processing for AI work was the ability to insert and delete elements of lists. Unfortunately, this facility coexists uneasily with shared list structure. Moreover, operations that insert and delete don't have a neat representation as functions. LISP contains them in the form of the *rplaca* and *rplacd* pseudo-functions, but programs that use them cannot be conveniently represented in logic, because, regarded as functions, they don't permit replacement of equals by equals.

c. Numbers. Many computations require both numbers and symbolic expressions. Numbers were originally implemented in LISP I as lists of atoms, and this proved too slow for all but the simplest computations. A reasonably efficient implementation of numbers as atoms in S-expressions was made in LISP 1.5, but in all the early LISPs, numerical computations were still 10 to 100 times slower than in FORTRAN. Efficient numerical computation requires some form of typing in the source language and a distinction between numbers treated by themselves and as elements of S-expressions. Some recent versions of LISP allow distinguishing types, but at the time, this seemed incompatible with other features.

d. Free variables. In all innocence, James R. Slagle programmed the following LISP function definition and complained when it didn't work right:

$testr[x, p, f, u] \leftarrow$ if $p[x]$ then $f[x]$ else if at x then $u[]$ else $testr[d u, p, f, \lambda :testr[d u, p, f, u]]$.

The object of the function is to find a subexpression of x satisfying $p[x]$ and return $f[x]$. If the search is unsuccessful, then the continuation function $u[]$ of no arguments is to be computed and its value returned. The difficulty was that when an inner recursion occurred, the value of u wanted was the outer value, but the inner value was actually used. In modern terminology, lexical scoping was wanted, and dynamic scoping was obtained.

I must confess that I regarded this difficulty as just a bug and expressed confidence that Steve Russell would soon fix it. He did fix it but by inventing the so-called FUNARG device that took the lexical environment along with the functional argument. Similar difficulties later showed up in Algol 60, and Russell's turned out to be one of the more comprehensive solutions to the problem. While it worked well in the interpreter, comprehensiveness and speed seem to be opposed in compiled code, and this led to a succession of compromises. Unfortunately, time did not permit writing an appendix giving the history of the problem, and the interested reader is referred to (Moses 1970) as a place to start. (David Park tells me that Patrick Fischer also had a hand in developing the FUNARG device).

e. The "program feature". Besides composition of functions and conditional expressions, LISP also allows sequential programs written with assignment statements and go tos. Compared to the mathematically elegant recursive function definition features, the "program feature" looks like a hasty afterthought. This is not quite correct; the idea of having sequential programs in LISP antedates that of having recursive function definition. However, the notation LISP uses for PROGs was definitely an afterthought and is far from optimal.

f. Once the *eval* interpreter was programmed, it became available to the programmer, and it was especially easy to use because it interprets LISP programs expressed as LISP data. In particular, *eval* made possible FEXPRS and FSUBRS which are "functions" that are not given their actual arguments but are given the expressions that evaluate to the arguments and must call *eval* themselves when they want the expressions evaluated. The main application of this facility is to functions that don't always evaluate all of their arguments; they evaluate some of them first, and then decide which others to evaluate. This facility resembles Algol's *call-by-name* but is more flexible, because *eval* is explicitly available. A first order logic treatment of "extensional" FEXPRs and FSUBRs now seems possible.

g. Since LISP works with lists, it was also convenient to provide for functions with variable numbers of arguments by supplying them with a list of arguments rather than the separate arguments.

Unfortunately, none of the above features has been given a comprehensive and clear mathematical semantics in connection with LISP or any other programming language. The best attempt in connection with LISP is Michael Gordon's (1973), but it is too complicated.

h. The first attempt at a compiler was made by Robert Brayton, but was unsuccessful. The first successful LISP compiler was programmed by Timothy Hart and Michael Levin. It was written in LISP and was claimed to be the first compiler written in the language to be compiled.

Many people participated in the initial development of LISP, and I haven't been able to remember all their contributions and must settle, at this writing, for a list of names. I can remember Paul Abrahams, Robert Brayton, Daniel Edwards, Patrick Fischer, Phyllis Fox, Saul Goldberg, Timothy Hart, Louis Hodes, Michael

Levin, David Luckham, Klim Maling, Marvin Minsky, David Park, Nathaniel Rochester of IBM, and Steve Russell.

4. Beyond LISP 1.5.

As a programming language LISP had many limitations. Some of the most evident in the early 1960s were ultra-slow numerical computation, inability to represent objects by blocks of registers and garbage collect the blocks, and lack of a good system for input-output of symbolic expressions in conventional notations. All these problems and others were to be fixed in LISP 2. In the meantime, we had to settle for LISP 1.5 developed at M.I.T. which corrected only the most glaring deficiencies.

The LISP 2 project was a collaboration of Systems Development Corporation and Information International Inc., and was initially planned for the Q32 computer, which was built by IBM for military purposes and which had a 48 bit word and 18 bit addresses, i.e., it was better than the IBM 7090 for an ambitious project. Unfortunately, the Q32 at SDC was never equipped with more than 48K words of this memory. When it became clear that the Q32 had too little memory, it was decided to develop the language for the IBM 360/67 and the Digital Equipment PDP-6 - SDC was acquiring the former, while III and M.I.T. and Stanford preferred the latter. The project proved more expensive than expected, the collaboration proved more difficult than expected, and so LISP 2 was dropped. From a 1970s point of view, this was regrettable, because much more money has since been spent to develop LISPs with fewer features. However, it was not then known that the dominant machine for AI research would be the PDP-10, a successor of the PDP-6. A part of the AI community, e.g. BBN and SRI made what proved to be an architectural digression in doing AI work on the SDS 940 computer.

The existence of an interpreter and the absence of declarations makes it particularly natural to use LISP in a time-sharing environment. It is convenient to define functions, test them, and re-edit them without ever leaving the LISP interpreter. A demonstration of LISP in a prototype time-sharing environment on the IBM 704 was made in 1960 (or 1961). (See Appendix 2). L. Peter Deutsch implemented the first interactive LISP on the PDP-1 computer in 1963, but the PDP-1 had too small a memory for serious symbolic computation.

The most important implementations of LISP proved to be those for the PDP-6 computer and its successor the PDP-10 made by the Digital Equipment Corporation of Maynard, Massachusetts. In fact, the half word instructions and the stack instructions of these machines were developed with LISP's requirements in mind. The early development of LISP at M.I.T. for this line of machines and its subsequent development of INTERLISP (nee BBN LISP) and MACLISP also contributed to making these machines the machines of choice for artificial intelligence research. The IBM 704 LISP was extended to the IBM 7090 and later led to LISPs for the IBM 360 and 370.

The earliest publications on LISP were in the Quarterly Progress Reports of the M.I.T. Research Laboratory of Electronics. (McCarthy 1960) was the first journal publication. The *LISP Programmer's Manual* by Phyllis Fox was published by the Research Laboratory of Electronics in 1960 and the *LISP 1.5 Programmer's Manual* by McCarthy, Levin, et. al. in 1962 was published by M.I.T. Press. After the publication of (McCarthy and Levin 1962), many LISP implementations were made for numerous computers. However, in contrast to the situation with most widely used programming languages, no organization has ever attempted to propagate LISP, and there has never been an attempt at agreeing on a standardization, although recently A.C. Hearn has developed a "standard LISP" (Marti, Hearn, Griss and Griss 1978) that runs on a number of computers in order to support the REDUCE system for computation with algebraic expressions.

5. Conclusions.

LISP is now the second oldest programming language in present widespread use (after FORTRAN and not counting APT, which isn't used for programming *per se*). It owes its longevity to two facts. First, its core occupies some kind of local optimum in the space of programming languages given that static friction discourages purely notational changes. Recursive use of conditional expressions, representation of symbolic information externally by lists and internally by list structure, and representation of program in the same way will probably have a very long life.

Second, LISP still has operational features unmatched by other language that make it a convenient vehicle for higher level systems for symbolic computation and for artificial intelligence. These include its run-time system that give good access to the features of the host machine and its operating system, its list structure internal language that makes it a good target for compiling from yet higher level languages, its compatibility with systems that produce binary or assembly level program, and the availability of its interpreter as a command language for driving other programs. (One can even conjecture that LISP owes its survival specifically to the fact that its programs are lists, which everyone, including me, has regarded as a disadvantage. Proposed replacements for LISP, e.g. POP-2 (Burstall 1968,1971), abandoned this feature in favor of an Algol-like syntax leaving no target language for higher level systems).

LISP will become obsolete when someone makes a more comprehensive language that dominates LISP practically and also gives a clear mathematical semantics to a more comprehensive set of features.

6. References.

Abrahams, Paul W. (1963), *Machine verification of mathematical proof*, thesis, MIT Computation Center, Cambridge, Mass.

Abrahams, Paul W., Barnett, J., et al., (1966), "The LISP 2 Programming Language and System", *Proceedings of the Fall Joint Computer Conference*, pp. 661-676.

Abrahams, Paul W. (1967), *LISP 2 Specifications*, Systems Development Corporation Technical report TM-3417/200/00, Santa Monica, Calif.

Allen, John (1978), *Anatomy of LISP*, McGraw Hill.

Berkeley, Edmund C. and Daniel Bobrow, eds. (1964), *The Programming Language LISP, its Operation and Applications*, Information International Incorporated, Cambridge, Massachusetts. (out of print).

Burstall, R.M., J.S. Collins and R.J. Popplestone (1968), *The POP-2 Papers*, Edinburgh University Press, Edinburgh, Scotland.

Burstall, R.M., J.S. Collins and R.J. Popplestone (1971), *Programming in POP-2*. Edinburgh University Press, Edinburgh, Scotland.

Cartwright, Robert (1976), *A practical formal semantic definition and verification system for typed LISP*, Stanford Artificial Intelligence Laboratory technical report AIM-296, Stanford, California.

Cartwright, Robert and John McCarthy (1978) "Representation of Recursive Programs in First Order Logic" (to be published). (Draft available as FIRST.NEW[W77,JMC] at SU-AI on ARPAnet).

Collins, G.E. (1960) "A method for overlapping and erasure of lists", *Communications of the ACM*, Vol. 3, pp. 655-657.

Church, Alonzo (1941), *Calculi of Lambda conversion*, Princeton University Press, Princeton, New Jersey.

Fox, Phyllis (1960) *LISP 1 Programmers Manual*, Internal paper, MIT, Cambridge, Mass.

Gordon, Michael (1973) *Models of Pure LISP*, Experimental Programming Reports: No. 31, University of Edinburgh, Edinburgh.

Gelernter, H., J. R. Hansen, and C. L. Gerberich (1960), "A FORTRAN-Compiled List Processing Language", *Journal of the ACM*, Vol. 7, No. 2, pp. 87-101.

Hearn, Anthony (1967), *REDUCE, a User-oriented Interactive System for Algebraic Simplification*, Stanford Artificial Intelligence Laboratory technical report AIM-57, Stanford, California.

Hewitt, Carl (1971), *Description and theoretical analysis (using schemata) of PLANNER: a language for proving theorems and manipulating models in a robot*, Ph.D. Thesis, MIT, Cambridge, Mass.

McCarthy, John (1958) "Programs with common sense", *Proceedings of the Symposium on the Mechanization of Thought Processes*, National Physiology Lab, Teddington, England.

McCarthy, J., Minsky, M., et al., (1959a), Quarterly Progress Report No. 52, Research Lab of Electronics, MIT, Cambridge, Mass.

McCarthy, J., Minsky, M., et al., (1959b), Quarterly Progress Report No. 55, Research Lab of Electronics, MIT, Cambridge, Mass.

McCarthy, John (1959c), Letter to the Editor, *CACM*, Vol. 2, No. 8.

McCarthy, J., Minsky, M., et al., (1960a), Quarterly Progress Report No. 56, Research Lab of Electronics, MIT, Cambridge, Mass.

McCarthy, John (1960b), "Recursive Functions of Symbolic Expressions and their Computation by Machine, part I", *CACM*, Vol. 3, No. 4, pp. 184-195.

McCarthy, J., Minsky, M., et al., (1962a), Quarterly Progress Report, Research Lab of Electronics, MIT, Cambridge, Mass.

McCarthy, J., Minsky, M., et al., (1962b), Quarterly Progress Report No. 64, Research Lab of Electronics, MIT, Cambridge, Mass.

McCarthy, John (1962c), *LISP 1.5 Programmer's Manual*, (with Abrahams, Edwards, Hart, and Levin), MIT Press, Cambridge, Mass.

McCarthy, J., Minsky, M., et al., (1963a), Quarterly Progress Report No. 68, Research Lab of Electronics, MIT, Cambridge, Mass.

McCarthy, J., Minsky, M., et al., (1963b), Quarterly Progress Report No. 69, Research Lab of Electronics, MIT, Cambridge, Mass.

McCarthy, John (1963c) "A Basis for a Mathematical Theory of Computation", in P. Braffort and D. Hirschberg (eds.), *Computer Programming and Formal Systems*, pp. 33-70. North-Holland Publishing Company, Amsterdam.

McCarthy, John (1963d) "Towards a Mathematical Science of Computation", *Proceedings of IFIP Congress, Munich 1962*, Amsterdam: North-Holland, pp. 21-28.

McCarthy, J., Minsky, M., et al., (1965), Quarterly Progress Report No. 76, Research Lab of Electronics, MIT, Cambridge, Mass.

McCarthy, J., Minsky, M., et al., (1966), Quarterly Progress Report No. 80, Research Lab of Electronics, MIT, Cambridge, Mass.

McCarthy, John and Carolyn Talcott (1979) *LISP with Proofs*, to be published. Versions of most chapters are available at the Stanford Artificial Intelligence Laboratory.

Marti, J. B., Hearn, A. C., Griss, M. L.and Griss, C. (1978) *Standard LISP Report*, University of Utah Symbolic Computation Group Report No 60, Provo, Utah.

The Mathlab Group (1977), *MACSYMA Reference Manual*, Laboratory for Computer Science, MIT Version 9, Cambridge, Mass.

Mitchell, R.W. (1964) *LISP 2 Specifications Proposal*, Stanford Artificial Intelligence Laboratory Memo No. 21, Stanford, Calif.

Moon, David A. (1974), *MACLISP Reference Manual*, Project MAC Technical Report, MIT, Cambridge, Mass.

Moses, Joel (1970) *The function of FUNCTION in LISP or why the FUNARG problem should be called the environment problem"*, M.I.T. Artificial Intelligence Memo 199, Cambridge, Mass.

Newell, A., and J.C. Shaw (1957) "Programming the Logic Theory Machine", *Proceedings of the 1957 Western Joint Computer Conference*, IRE.

Rulifson, J. et al. (1968), "QA4 - A Language for Writing Problem-Solving Programs", *Proceeding IFIP 1968 Congress*, TA-2, pp 111-115.

Stoyan, Herbert. Herbert Stoyan of Dresden, DDR has completed several chapters on the history of LISP.

Sussman, G. Winograd, T., and Charniak, E. (1970), *Microplanner Reference Manual*, AI Memo 203, AIL MIT, Camridge, Mass.

Teitelman, Warren (1975), *INTERLISP: Interlisp Reference Manual*, Xerox PARC Technical Report, Palo Alto, Calif.

Weisman, Clark (1967), *LISP 1.5 Primer*, Dickenson Press.

Many reports and memoranda of the M.I.T. and Stanford Artificial Intelligence Laboratories have dealt with various aspects of LISP and higher level systems built on LISP.

APPENDIX - HUMOROUS ANECDOTE

The first on-line demonstration of LISP was also the first of a precursor of time-sharing that we called "time-stealing". The audience comprised the participants in one of M.I.T.'s Industrial Liaison Symposia on whom it was important to make a good impression. A Flexowriter had been connected to the IBM 704 and the operating system modified so that it collected characters from the Flexowriter in a buffer when their presence was signalled by an interrupt. Whenever a carriage return occurred, the line was given to LISP for processing. The demonstration depended on the fact that the memory of the computer had just been increased from 8192 words to 32768 words so that batches could be collected that presumed only a small memory.

The demonstration was also one of the first to use closed circuit TV in order to spare the spectators the museum feet consequent on crowding around a terminal waiting for something to happen. Thus they were on the fourth floor, and I was in the first floor computer room exercising LISP and speaking into a microphone. The problem chosen was to determine whether a first order differential equation of the form $M dx + N dy$ was exact by testing whether $\partial M/\partial y = \partial N/\partial x$, which also involved some primitive algebraic simplification.

Everything was going well, if slowly, when suddenly the Flexowriter began to type (at ten characters per second)

"THE GARBAGE COLLECTOR HAS BEEN CALLED. SOME INTERESTING STATISTICS ARE AS FOLLOWS:"

and on and on and on. The garbage collector was quite new at the time, we were rather proud of it and curious about it, and our normal output was on a line printer, so it printed a full page every time it was called giving how many words were marked and how many were collected and the size of list space, etc. During a previous rehearsal, the garbage collector hadn't been called, but we had not refreshed the LISP core image, so we ran out of free storage during the demonstration.

Nothing had ever been said about a garbage collector, and I could only imagine the reaction of the audience. We were already behind time on a tight schedule, it was clear that typing out the garbage collector message would take all the remaining time allocated to the demonstration, and both the lecturer and the audience were incapacitated by laughter. I think some of them thought we were victims of a practical joker.

Artificial Intelligence: Underlying Assumptions and Basic Objectives

"Artificial Intelligence: Underlying Assumptions and Basic Objectives" by N. Cercone and G. McCalla from *Journal of the American Society for Information Science*, Volume 35, Number 5, September 1984, pages 280-290. Copyright © 1984 John Wiley & Sons, Inc. Reprinted by permission of John Wiley & Sons, Inc.

Nick Cercone
Computing Science Department, Simon Fraser University, Burnaby, British Columbia, Canada V5A 1S6

Gordon McCalla*
Department of Computational Science, University of Saskatchewan, Saskatoon, Saskatchewan, Canada S7N 0W0

Artificial intelligence (AI) research has recently captured media interest and it is fast becoming our newest "hot" technology. AI is an interdisciplinary field which derives from a multiplicity of roots. In this article we present our perspectives on methodological assumptions underlying research efforts in AI. We also discuss the goals (design objectives) of AI across the spectrum of subareas it comprises. We conclude by discussing why there is increased interest in AI and whether current predictions of the future importance of AI are well founded.

The news media, newspapers, and popular magazines are all clamoring to relate how computers in general and artificial intelligence (AI) in particular are about to revolutionize yet another aspect of life: "we'll soon be able to talk to (micro-) computers in English," "household robots are just around the corner," "the electronic office will make paper a thing the past," and so on and on and on. From these articles one might well conclude that the human species may soon be obsolete.

Let us assure you that the human being may yet persevere. Although AI *is* the key for making technology adaptable to people and AI *will* play a crucial role in the next generation of automated systems, scientists are a long way from discovering how to devise general purpose intelligent computers, i.e., machines which can behave with the full sophistication of the human mind. Computers can be made to play excellent chess, to diagnose certain types of diseases, to discover mathematical concepts, and, in fact, to excel in many other areas requiring a high level of human expertise. Paradoxically, scientists are not yet all that knowledgeable about how to make computers do the

sorts of things humans take almost for granted: seeing the world, manipulating objects, understanding "natural" languages such as English, navigating through the world, "commonsense" reasoning, and so on. These basic abilities of humans are necessary if we are ever going to talk to microcomputers in unrestricted English, to build a household robot, or to have a fully automated office environment.

In this article we present an overview of the subareas of artificial intelligence—the so-called "AI pie"—and discuss the methodological assumptions underlying much of AI. We do this by charting the activities, motivations, methods, and current status of research in each of the major AI subareas. We conclude with remarks on several major projects directly or indirectly related to AI which are now underway and we discuss their chances for success. First we introduce AI and briefly examine how it derived from a multiplicity of roots.

AI: An Interdisciplinary Field

Artificial intelligence is an interdisciplinary field. In Figure 1 we illustrate the multiplicity of roots from which AI derives, including contributions from psychology, philosophy, linguistics, electrical engineering, and computing science. The intersection between psychology and AI centers on the subareas known as cognitive psychology and psycho-linguistics. Philosophy and AI come together in the areas of logic, philosophy of language, and philosophy of mind. Intersections with linguistics include computational linguistics, psycho-linguistics, and socio-linguistics. Mutual concentrations between electrical engineering and AI include image processing, pattern recognition, and robotics. Finally, computing science overlaps AI proper and the related field of adaptive systems.

As well as being an interdisciplinary field, AI has many different subareas, Figure 2 illustrates our conception of the "AI pie." Major efforts into artificial intelligence re-

---

*Dr. McCalla is spending his 1983/1984 sabbatical year at Simon Fraser University.

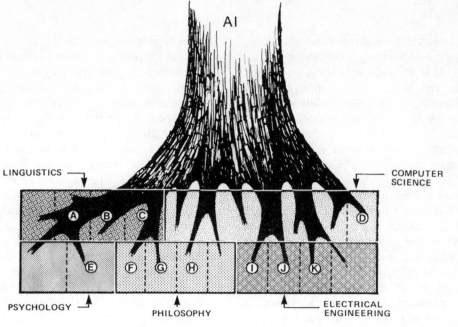

LINGUISTICS

COMPUTER SCIENCE

PSYCHOLOGY

PHILOSOPHY

ELECTRICAL ENGINEERING

Ⓐ PSYCHO—LINGUISTICS

Ⓑ SOCIO—LINGUISTICS

Ⓒ COMPUTATIONAL LINGUISTICS

Ⓓ ADAPTIVE SYSTEMS

Ⓔ COGNITIVE PSYCHOLOGY

Ⓕ PHILOSOPHY OF MIND

Ⓖ PHILOSOPHY OF LANGUAGE

Ⓗ LOGIC

Ⓘ ROBOTICS

Ⓙ IMAGE PROCESSING

Ⓚ PATTERN RECOGNITION

FIG. 1.   AI is an interdisciplinary field.

FIG. 2.   The AI "pie."

search have concentrated on natural language understanding, computer vision, learning, theorem proving and logic programming, search, problem solving, and planning, expert systems, knowledge representation, and other categories such as intelligent computer-aided instruction and tutoring, game playing, speech, automatic programming, and AI tools.

The methodological assumptions underlying research in artificial intelligence can be loosely categorized into *formal methods* and *writing programs*. In AI, as in many fields, it is important to have formal models. A variety of formal machinery has proven useful in AI, including first order logic (F.O.L.) and other logics, systems for formal semantics, e.g., Montague semantics, situational semantics, procedural semantics, and denotational semantics, and work on mathematics and grammars. But in AI it is not usually sufficient merely to prove things formally—building actively performing programs is also important. Usually AI systems are implemented in specialized symbolic languages such as LISP, PROLOG, production systems, or knowledge representation languages. Often the line between the two methodologies is unclear and we do not intend to imply that all AI research can be neatly separated into these two rough classifications. Much of the best work involves a judicious mixing of formal models and implemented systems.

Since the goal of artificial intelligence is to develop systems which behave intelligently, i.e., like humans, we outline design objectives that any ideal AI system should meet. An AI researcher should:

(1) develop a *working system* that actually behaves in an intelligent manner;
(2) *validate* the system's behavior through comparison with humans (external design objective);
(3) understand the *implications* of the system—its coverage, what it can do (internal design objective); and
(4) determine what can be *generalized* about the system, the lessons it teaches, the areas it impacts.

In the following subsections each subarea in the "AI pie" will be discussed including its successes and failures, its methodological assumptions, and how a typical system in the subarea meets the design objectives for an ideal AI system.

Natural Language Understanding

Automated natural language understanding has been a major research area since the earliest days of AI. Well-funded machine translation projects dominated research into natural language in the 1960s but their failure to account for meaning, context, and the many subtleties of language led to their ultimate demise. Innovative work of Winograd [1] and Schank [2] in the early 1970s addressed these issues and was largely responsible for bringing

natural language understanding researchers out of hibernation and this area has been flourishing ever since.

Understanding natural language involves three levels of interpretation: syntactic, semantic, and pragmatic levels. Syntactic processes "parse" sentences to make the grammatical relationships between words in sentences clear. Semantics is concerned with assigning meaning to the various syntactic constituents. Pragmatics attempts to relate individual sentences to one another and to the surrounding context. The boundaries separating these levels are not distinct. In particular, sentences need not pass through these levels of interpretation sequentially. Research continues into how to integrate information from any level when it is needed.

Vigorous research into all levels of natural language understanding is ongoing. Exploring alternative powerful parsing techniques is one major direction, e.g., augmented transition network parsers (Woods [3], Gazdar's [4] approach to parsing, etc.). Various schemes for explaining the semantics of natural languages include Montague's [5] intensional logic and the recently espoused theory of situational semantics (Barwise and Perry [6]). Much of the mainstream AI research of the 1970s and early 1980s has concentrated on modeling connected discourse and dialogue, especially focussing on pragmatic issues such as story structure (Wilensky [7], focus (Grosz [8]), reference (Hirst [9]), and so on. Another direction has been to build practical natural language systems, e.g., front-ends to database systems such as PLANES (Waltz [10]).

The methodology for most natural language understanding efforts has been writing programs using specific formal mechanisms (grammars, semantics) as their foundation. Considering the design objectives (in turn), we can say:

(1) Many of these systems (e.g., Schank's work, natural language "front-ends" to databases, etc.) actually behave in an "intelligent" manner. Some work is focussed less on surface behavior in which case performance is not a criterion.
(2) Seldom has the work in this area been well-validated; rather, intuitive feelings and judgments are substituted. Some natural language "front-ends" account for a wide variety of sentences but it is still difficult to say exactly where they succeed or fail.
(3) The syntactic components of most natural language systems are well understand. The implications for semantics are less well understood although a formal basis is developing with which to judge semantic theories. There is no generally accepted approach to understanding the implications of the various approaches to pragmatics, and an understanding of the basic pragmatics dimensions is still evolving.
(4) Several general lessons can be drawn from natural language research: (i) understanding language is a hard problem; (ii) there is a need for an integrated,

all-level approach; (iii) certain methodologies (in knowledge representation and parsing) are widely applicable in natural language understanding and the rest of AI; and (iv) research in this area has been influenced by (and should increasingly influence) computational linguistics, linguistics generally, philosophy of language, and socio-linguistics.

Computer Vision

The basic objective of computer vision research is to interpret pictures (rather than to generate pictures which preoccupies computer graphics). What "interpreting pictures" means differs depending upon the application to which the interpretation is to be put. For example, in interpreting satellite images it may be sufficient to roughly identify regions of forest blight or crop damage. Robot vision systems may find it necessary to precisely identify assembly components to accurately affix the components to the part under assembly.

In order to illustrate the basic dimensions involved in the computer vision task, it would perhaps be better to focus on "seeing" scenes in the "blocks world." The blocks world contains a number of simple blocks (boxes and pyramids) which can be stacked or unstacked by a robot arm connected to a television camera. Microworlds such as the blocks world provide a simplified but nontrivial microcosm of the "real" world in which the issues can be more easily studied and the lessons learned hopefully later generalized.

The computer vision task in the blocks world is to identify, starting with a television image, the objects in a scene and the relationships between them, e.g., "block A" is on top of "block B." The television picture is a digitized image, that is, an array of pixels (picture elements) that measure the intensity of light at each location in the image. Certain "low-level" techniques are needed to translate groups of pixels into similarly "shaded" lines or regions. Usually these are part of a given object. Ambiguities can arise in this stage of analysis due to occlusions between objects, due to anomalies of lighting, etc. The lines and regions must then be grouped into objects. Ambiguities are also possible at this stage once again due to occlusions, odd perspectives, shadows, and the like. The final stage is to identify relationships among the objects such as "in-front-of," "on-top-of," "inside-of." At this point the interpreted scene can be used, in conjunction with specialized reasoning techniques, to achieve the goals of the specific application.

The various components in this largely linear (low-level through high-level) approach to interpretation were developed principally in the late 1960s and early 1970s for the blocks world by Huffman [11], Clowes [12], Guzman [13], Waltz [14], Duda and Hart [15], and many others. Subsequent work by Montanari [16], Mackworth [17], and others has formalized and simplified many of these largely ad hoc techniques.

More recently, computer vision research has expanded beyond the blocks world into much more complicated domains. To handle these more complicated domains significant improvements must be made at all stages of the interpretation sequence. Work at the MIT vision laboratory under the direction of David Marr [18] on enhancing low-level vision algorithms established perhaps the major research direction of the last decade. These techniques illustrate that a large measure of success in interpretation can be achieved through exhaustive analysis of low-level phenomena. In contrast, a small but vigorous research effort is taking the opposite tack in attempting to bring "knowledge-based" high-level techniques to bear on interpretation, e.g., Havens and Mackworth [19]. Whichever approach (low-level or high) is followed, the strictly sequential nature of the interpretation process seems to be vanishing as information from all levels is integrated when needed.

To encapsulate the current state of computer vision research let us examine its standing in the four design objectives:

(1) Most computer vision systems are implemented. These implementations make use of programming languages such as MAYA, LISP, and Fortran, for high-level components and moreover can draw upon a plethora of mathematical techniques (differential equations, Fourier and other transforms, etc.) to aid low-level reasoning.

(2) Many of the computer vision systems exhibit surface level behavior which can be directly compared to human capabilities. Often this performance, although restricted to a narrow domain, is extremely impressive. As techniques are developed for more realistic applications this narrowness should gradually disappear.

(3) The inherent implications of any given approach to computer vision are not well understood in general. However, work by Montanari and Mackworth, for example, has illuminated the basic computational properties of many of the early vision algorithms. Minksy and Papert [20] in their book *Perceptrons* demonstrated fundamental limitations of certain localized syntactic methods for scene recognition. *Perceptrons* was extremely influential in reorienting computer vision methodologies to their current directions.

(4) Computer vision is perhaps the best crucible for illustrating both the power and limitations of local interpretation methods. It also shows that there is some similarity between vision and natural language in that morphological, syntactic, semantic, and pragmatic aspects can be identified in both. However, since the low-level vision algorithms are so specific to vision alone, not many of these algorithms are generalizable outside peripheral areas of AI such as image processing and pattern recognition. It is to be hoped that the more recent high-

level approaches will contain more lessons for AI generally.

Expert Systems

Expert systems are computer programs whose behavior duplicates, in some sense, the abilities of a human expert in his/her area of expertise. There are many examples of such programs from the fabled DENDRAL system [21] which performs automatic analysis of chemical spectroscopes through various medical systems such as the drug prescriber MYCIN [22] and the diagnosis program INTERNIST [23] to the geological PROSPECTOR [24] which recently discovered new mineral deposits.

While any design methodology can be used to build an expert system, the majority of these systems are implemented in production system architectures (Newell [25]). A production system is an ordered set of "if-then" or pattern-action rules whose action part is executed when the pattern part matches incoming data or data derived from previous rule execution. It turns out to be relatively easy to capture the expertise of many areas in such rules and through experimentation to "tune" them to behave appropriately. It is possible to view the creation of an expert system as a lengthy feedback cycle where sets of rules are formed and reformed to successively capture more and more of the reasoning of the expert. For this cycle to converge, it is crucial that the expert also progressively understand more and more of his/her own reasoning as it is made explicit in the expert system.

How do expert systems meet the design objectives?

(1) By definition an expert system is implemented and does behave intelligently in its narrow area of expertise.
(2) The design cycle ensures that an expert system will behave at the level of at least one human expert although it may not replicate the behavior of other experts in the same area.
(3) Not all of the interactions of the rules are clear for any given expert system. While the expert system seems to replicate the behavior of a human expert, in untested situations or new circumstances the rules might fail where the expert would not. There are no generally accepted validation techniques from which to infer the coverage of a set of expert system rules.
(4) While it is true that the production system architecture and "rule extraction cycle" work across a wide variety of domains, it is not clear that there are any general lessons to be learned for other areas of the AI pie. For example, it is an open question what (if any) worth expert system methodologies would have in helping to parse a sentence or represent the meaning of a sentence or a scene. It seems unlikely that a general purpose intelligence will consist entirely of a set of special purpose expert systems without additional machinery. Perhaps

the biggest worth of expert systems is their ability to promote AI as a potentially practical endeavor and not an academic frivolity with no long-term impact.

Search, Problem Solving, Planning

Problem solving refers to the ability of computers to automatically solve nontrivial problems. For example, if a mobile robot is asked to push a box off of a platform that it cannot get on top of directly, the robot should be able to deduce that moving a ramp up against the platform is a crucial prerequisite for gaining access to the box. How can the robot formulate such a plan?

First, the essential features of a given problem-solving situation are formulated by (i) ascertaining the important static attributes (the state) of the world, and (ii) finding the relevant actions (the operators) which can alter a state. In the mobile robot world the state would contain the names and locations of boxes, ramps, platforms, and the robot itself. The operators would correspond to real world actions such as "push box," "push ramp," or "move robot"; and would have the effect of transforming the state representation so as to reflect the resultant application of an operator in the real world.

The process of solving a problem then becomes the problem of automatically transforming some initial state to some desired goal state through the application of a sequence of operators. All relevant operators are applied to the initial state generating a set of successor states which are, in turn, "operated upon" to generate the next level of successor states, and so on until an entire "search tree" is formed. Eventually this search will terminate when a goal state is generated. The path from initial state to goal state contains the operators (in order) that constitute a plan which solves the problem.

An alternate approach to such "state-space" techniques is problem reduction search where a hard problem is broken down into successively simpler subproblems (generating an entire tree) until a level of trivially solvable problems is reached. The solutions to these solvable problems, when amalgamated, constitute a solution to the original problem. GPS [26] is the prime example of this approach.

Early work explored efficient methods of generating and searching such problem solving trees. Some of these methods work for any problem domain while others require the use of special purpose "heuristics" to prune the tree. In fact a whole theory of heuristic search was eventually elaborated by Nilsson [27].

Work by Sussman [28] and Sacerdoti [29] attempted to overcome some of the shortcomings of the traditional methods through a detailed examination of "blocks world" planning problems. Recent work has focussed on producing plans in more turbulent real world situations including dynamically changing worlds (McCalla, Reid, and Schneider [30]), worlds with many agents (Rosenschein [31]), and worlds where there are multiple goals (Hayes-Roth [32]).

The design objectives for AI have been met by problem-solving systems as followed:

(1) Most of the problem-solving systems have been implemented and show nontrivial behavior in a limited domain.

(2) Problem solving is the first area of the AI pie which we have encountered which explores a theoretical underpinning of intelligent behavior rather than surface behavior. Therefore it is difficult to externally validate any of the various approaches independent of the particular application which uses the approach. No formal studies have been initiated which contrast human problem solving with AI techniques for problem solving.

(3) The theory of heuristic search expounded by Nilsson [27] helps to determine the comparative powers of various search algorithms and suggests that there is a commonality among several ostensibly different forms of search. This theory is obviously useful for determining the properties of early approaches but more recent approaches have not been so formalized. Thus internal validation in these systems is largely ad hoc.

(4) Problem solving potentially underlies most areas of AI but is virtually unused in expert systems or computer vision research and only a few natural language systems have used problem solving methods directly. The areas to which problem-solving expertise have been most widely applied are computer game playing and robotics. Early approaches to problem solving taught the value and utility of microworlds. More recent planning approaches have also taught that once initial understanding has been gained it is important to leave the "microworld cradle."

Theorem Proving and Logic Programming

Theorem proving refers to the process of making logical deductions starting from a noncontradictory set of axioms specified in predicate calculus (firsts order logic). Robinson [33] showed how it was possible to totally automate this process using a method called *resolution*. The resolution principle underlies almost all theorem-proving research.

Any assertion that is to be proved using resolution theorem-proving techniques is first represented as a formula in the predicate calculus and then its negation is added to the set of axioms. A purely mechanical set of transformations can then be carried out by the theorem-proving program to put the axioms and negated assertion into so-called "clause" form. Any pair of these clauses can be "resolved" against one another in a matching process that results in the creation of a third clause (a "resolvent") that

logically follows from the previous two clauses. The resolution method automatically performs a series of such resolutions, eventually building a tree of clauses, resolvents, resolvents of resolvents, and so on. If eventually two clauses resolve to "nil," then the two clauses are contradictory which, in turn, implies that the initial set of clauses is contradictory and this implies, finally, that the assertion has been proved since its negation caused a noncontradictory set of clauses to become contradictory.

Much work in theorem proving has mirrored work in problem solving: working out more efficient searching techniques, adding heuristics to further constrain the search, and so on. It has even been demonstrated (Coles [34]) that most simple problem-solving tasks can be formulated and solved using a theorem-proving approach. One example of this is the use of theorem proving to form the basis of natural language question-answering systems (Green [35]). This led to early hopes that theorem proving would provide a universal "inference engine" for AI. These hopes have not come to fruition since the complexities of real world tasks seem to overwhelm the ability of theorem proving techniques to handle them without substantial additional machinery. In most practical problems there are simply too many clauses to keep the theorem prover from "combinatorially exploding," i.e., from entering into virtually infinite inference chains.

However, theorem proving is at the heart of the more recent development of logic programming. The programming language PROLOG (developed by Colmerauer et al. [36] and Kowalski [37]) has as its key original component a resolution theorem prover. An earlier language, Microplanner (Sussman et al. [38]; Hewitt [39]) had a nonresolution theorem prover at its core. Both languages encourage the programmer to state much of his/her problem in largely "declarative" nonprocedural assertions or formulae leaving most of the procedural inference to the automatic theorem prover embedded in the language. The recent explosion of interest in PROLOG and its ever widening use in AI suggests that this declarative style may be a very natural way of building large and intricate AI programs. It remains to be seen if PROLOG's mechanical theorem prover constitutes a potential "supernova" lurking within the language that will combinatorially explode when the programmer least expects it.

How do theorem proving and logic programming meet AI's design objectives?

(1) Theorem provers and logic programming languages are implemented, but do not attempt to behave intelligently. Instead they are tools for other, applications-oriented AI systems to use.

(2) It is obviously not appropriate to compare the performance of logic programming languages to human performance. It is also clear that humans do not prove theorems using resolution. The logical steps in a resolution theorem prover are simply too small to correspond to the steps in a proof by mathematicians; in fact, no useful original theorems

(i.e., in the human sense) have yet been proved by a resolution theorem prover.

(3) Resolution theorem proving is strongly founded on well developed formal principles of logic. As such, its implications are well understood—there are no hidden contradictions, although the methods are combinatorially explosive. Interpreters for logic programming languages have been implemented and tested using standard debugging and program analysis techniques.

(4) Logic programming seems to be a useful tool in many areas of AI. Theorem proving, apart from its use in PROLOG, has not proven so widely useful except for its adaptation to simple problem-solving tasks. Perhaps its biggest contributions to date have been to demonstrate the usefulness of taking a logical perspective to AI problems and to show that "weak" (underconstrained) inference methods need much knowledge to constrain the possibility of combinatorial explosion.

Knowledge Representation

For a system to be able to behave intelligently it must have knowledge of its domain of expertise. This knowledge includes facts and also rules for manipulating these facts. Over the years a number of different knowledge representation "paradigms" have emerged. One of the earliest such schemes represented knowledge in semantic networks where facts are stored at nodes, and relationships between the facts are represented by arcs. One of the most common relationships in semantic networks is the omnipresent "ISA" link which allows facts (e.g., dogs have tails) to be attached to classes of objects (e.g., dogs) and then inherited by specific objects in the class (e.g., Fido, Rover, etc.). Much research has gone into precisely specifying the meaning of semantic networks (especially the meaning of ISA, Brachman [40]) and elaborating different styles of networks; see Shubert, Goebel, and Cercone [41], Levesque and Mylopoulos [42], and others.

Another major school of thought about knowledge representation that has evolved is frames (or schemata); see Minsky [43]. Frames clump together relevant information about stereotypical situations that can be used to help recognize and reason about these situations. When understanding a story about restaurants or trying to understand a picture of a room, knowledge of stereotypical restaurants or canonical rooms allows many unstated assumptions to be inferred without difficulty. Frames have proven so useful that most programming languages for knowledge representation (e.g., KRL, Bobrow and Winograd [44]; KL-ONE, Brachman [45]) have explicit facilities for handling frames.

More recently, knowledge representation researchers have become increasingly concerned with the need to formally understand the expressive power and representational adequacy of various knowledge representation schemes. They have thus turned to logic to provide a basis for such reflection. When the various formalisms are "recast" in terms of logic, they can be compared and the strengths and weaknesses of logic for knowledge representation can be better understood. These investigations have led to a better understanding of knowledge representation and also to the development of new "non-monotonic" logics (Bobrow [46]) to handle incompleteness, default reasoning, and other unique requirements for knowledge representation.

A good overview of knowledge representation for the nonspecialist can be found in McCalla and Cercone [47]. A more specific treatment for researchers in knowledge representation is Brachman and Smith [48].

Knowledge representation is a fundamental component of any AI system so it is difficult, but instructive, to evaluate how it meets the general objectives of an AI system independently of the application.

(1) Much of the early knowledge representation work resulted in implemented systems ultimately culminating in knowledge representation programming languages. More recently, the concentration of effort has been on formal modeling without implementation.

(2) It is difficult to compare knowledge representation schemes to human performance, although some work has been done in attempting to justify semantic networks as the computer analogue of human associative memory (Collins and Quillian [49]).

(3) Implementing a knowledge representation language provides insights into the language and also the knowledge representation scheme that the language embodies. However, when the knowledge representation scheme has a formal logical basis these insights are much stronger. The recent fervor for such formal underpinnings in knowledge representation may be a harbinger for the rest of AI in the coming decades.

(4) The fact that knowledge representation applies so widely across AI is encouraging for those who believe that AI will discover general principles of intelligence. It is fair to say that non-monotonic logics will have an impact on logic generally, that the study of network formalisms and the integration of procedures with data will significantly affect other areas of computing science, and that eventual success in knowledge representation will provide structures that cognitive psychologists can use in their studies of human thinking.

Learning

Surprisingly, until recently, learning has not been a major concern for AI. Most AI researchers seem to have felt that it was first necessary to concentrate on how to make a program do something before figuring out how it could learn to do it. Still, a small cadre of "learning aficionados" have been attempting to explore the basic issues in learning, and learning has now begun to take on ever increasing significance in AI.

Samuel [50] built a checkers playing program which, by slowly modifying how it evaluated board positions as it gained experience, learned to play better than he did. Winston [51] built a program that could learn the description of various "blocks world" structures after being presented with a sequence of examples and "near-misses" (examples differing in only one attribute) of each structure. Lenat [52] constructed a program (AM) that used heuristic search techniques to "discover" (although not prove) many pivotal concepts in mathematics after starting from basic principles. A follow-up program, EURISKO (Lenat [53]), showed that similar methods could work in a wide variety of domains (e.g. fleet design, VLSI design, etc.). Mitchell's [54] LEX system learned heuristics and where to apply them when solving freshmen calculus problems. A series of programs called BACON (Langley [55]) were able to induce many fundamental "empirical" laws from raw data in a variety of scientific domains. A recent conference on machine learning (Michalski [56]) contains papers investigating generalization learning, learning by analogy, discovery learning, learning procedures, learning from observations, learning from examples, and many more. So, there are various approaches and a growing body of work in this ultimately crucial area of AI.

Learning is another of the "support" areas of AI, since it is an investigation into basic principles underlying intelligence rather than an application itself. Nevertheless, it can be judged according to AI's general design objectives.

(1) Most learning systems are implemented and tested. They do demonstrate interesting learning behavior, some of which (e.g., the checkers playing program or the AM discovery program) obviously challenges the performance of humans.
(2) Although human level learning capabilities are sometimes matched, there certainly is no attempt to make general claims about being able to learn as well as humans nor in the same way humans do (e.g., the checkers playing program learns quite differently from humans).
(3) Learning systems are not anchored in any formal bedrock. Thus, their implications are not well understood. Many of them have been exhaustively tested (Lenat's AM was run for literally hundreds of CPU hours) but exactly why they succeed or fail is never precisely clear.
(4) The one common thread running most AI approaches to learning (and distinguishing them from other non-AI approaches) is that learning in AI involves the manipulation of structures rather than of numerical parameters. It is fair to say that soon the different kinds of structure manipulation will be more rigorously categorized and that research on learning will become more directed. At

that time results in AI learning may also become crucial in related areas such as cognitive psychology, adaptive systems, and robotics.

Other Areas

There are a number of other areas that are often included in categorizations of AI research, including computerized game playing, AI approaches to education, tool building for AI, speech understanding, robotics and assorted other subdisciplines. Let's look very briefly at each of these in turn.

Today there are game playing programs that play near-master level chess, better checkers than any human, and excellent games of many other types. Interest in automating the game playing process has been manifest in AI since its inception as a field, not only for the obvious interest of getting a computer to play games well, but also because it was thought that the lessons learned by programming game playing strategies would generalize to the rest of AI. This latter goal, in fact, turned out to be supported by the realization that the kinds of search strategies utilized by game playing programs (to reason through the consequences of possible moves and counter moves) could be mapped directly onto the search strategies used for problem solving (see Nilsson [27]). However, more recently, as AI programs have become more "knowledge intensive," the so-called "weak, general" methods used in game playing have become less and less relevant. Although current game playing programs are extremely competent, game playing as a research area is now pursued more for its intrinsic interest than for the lessons it can give to other areas of AI.

Another "miscellaneous" area involves AI applications in education. There have been two main directions. The first is an attempt to bring AI techniques (especially from problem solving, knowledge representation, and natural language) to bear on producing intelligent tutoring systems that can behave with more subtlety and knowledge than traditional computer assisted instruction systems (see Sleeman and Brown [57] for a compendium of current pioneering efforts). This is clearly a hard AI applications problem which, to be solved in full generality, will need substantial progress in all areas of AI. The other major AI direction in education involves students exploring rich environments from which they can learn on their own initiative with the environment acting as a constraint that indirectly focusses their learning. A well known such environment is the LOGO (Papert [58]) "turtle graphics" programming system from which students can learn about programming and geometry. Other environments are now being built, as well, for the exploration of less "mathematical" subjects, e.g., Goforth [59].

A major endeavor for AI research has been "tool" building. This started very early in AI's history with the invention of the LISP programming language and timesharing by AI researchers at MIT, and has continued through to the more recent development of LISP machines,

SMALLTALK-80 and INTERLISP-D interactive programming environments, and the new knowledge representation programming languages. This will continue to be an area whose impetus will derive from the needs of other areas of AI and whose results will be crucial to success in these other areas.

In the mid-1970s three lavishly funded projects were carried out with computer understanding of spoken language as their goal. While no "talking typewriters" have yet emerged, these systems did achieve some success with limited vocabularies. Many of the issues of natural language understanding overlap speech understanding, and progress in speech understanding clearly depends on progress in natural language understanding research. The most important outcome of speech understanding research has been the development of architectures for speech understanding that are also useful for modeling distributed computation in general (HEARSAY II, Erman et al. [60]).

Robotics is an area that is often identified with AI, but most of the active research in robotics is not AI-based, but is instead involved in solving "lower level" manipulator control problems. However, work in computer vision is slowly starting to infiltrate robotics, and eventually planning will be absolutely crucial when brainier, more flexible, robots need to be built to work in less constrained situations than those faced by the current generation of factory robots.

A number of other areas are also identified with AI. These include automatic programming (getting the computer to program itself—which is now considered a formal area of computer science that is separate from AI), pattern recognition (whose aims are to be able to extract meaningful patterns from data, but without concern for AI issues), image processing (with similar goals to computer vision, but a much more engineering oriented methodology), and adaptive systems (an outgrowth of work on neural networks, McCulloch and Pitts [61], which is attempting to model mind at a neurological level rather than the higher level "mental structures" postulated by AI). Most of the practitioners in these fields and most AI people would agree that these areas are really separate from AI, although future collaboration cannot be ruled out.

Concluding Remarks

Computers are playing an increasingly important role in our jobs and in our daily lives. Conventional approaches to computer software and hardware, however, impose limitations to the computer's ability to meet the challenges presented by this increasing influence. In particular, the next generation of computer systems must be able to provide knowledgeable "decision support" for government and industry and must be usable by nonspecialists in the home and office. Artificial intelligence will play a crucial role in the development of these "intelligent" machines.

The Japanese were among the first to recognize that the next generation of machines would need to be substantially different from current machines. With the announcement of their "Fifth Generation" project in 1981, the future importance of AI was guaranteed since fifth generation machines will involve knowledge-based symbolic computation. This software will run on fifth generation hardware which will feature parallel processing in contrast to current sequential machine architectures. The Japanese predict that these machines will become available in the 1990s.

The Japanese interest in new ways of computing for the next generation of machines has found a sympathetic echo in much of the rest of the industrial world. Great Britain is embarking on a heavily funded project to build knowledge-based machines in the next decade. The ESPRIT project is a similar attempt by the European Economic Community. There are several defense-oriented projects in the U.S. which have a healthy dollop of AI involved. Many private U.S. companies have formed to build expert systems or support systems for AI as the market for such products increases. There is widespread corporate interest in building "human engineered" systems that make microcomputers accessible to naive users. Most other developed countries have substantially increased funding to AI so as not to be left behind in the development of the machines of the future.

Thus, AI is likely to become a major R&D effort for at least the next decade due to its imminent practical importance. Notwithstanding, there are more basic reasons for studying AI. The thought of building intelligent artifacts is intrinsically interesting and of obvious importance. Any theoretical insights that AI is able to achieve should illuminate longstanding problems in philosophy, psychology, logic, mathematics, sociology, education, and probably other disciplines as well. Within computer science AI may fundamentally alter the approach to database management, information retrieval, office automation, programming languages, and system design.

Is it likely that AI research will fulfill all of the promise envisioned for it? AI critics once roasted AI for having made many claims and predictions in the early days of the field that did not come to fruition.* There is a grave danger of similar over-optimism engulfing the field right now, especially since so many of the promises are being made by people from outside the field who do not realize how incredibly tough many of the unsolved problems in AI are. However, AI still brings to these tough problems a methodology that offers hope for their eventual solution. The

---

*In all likelihood these critics would never have been satisfied since whenever AI solves some problem, its "magic aura" disappears and it no longer seems to require intelligence. Historically, this "defining is defining away" problem has plagued most attempts to honestly evaluate AI's successes and failures (e.g., developments in time-sharing, symbolic integration, theorem proving, game playing, pattern recognition, programming languages, etc. have all been influenced by AI). It is encouraging, now, that practical results and well defined solutions can still be considered to be a part of AI.

computer is an incredibly powerful tool which helps researchers make their fuzzy ideas precise, which allows models of mind to be actually run and compared to human performance (and altered when such comparison is less than satisfactory), and which, most importantly, provides an amazing range of concepts concerning process and structure which did not exist before computer science elaborated them (see Minsky [62] for an interesting compendium of such concepts).

In conclusion, it is important to judge AI not as a unified discipline which understands everything about how to make computers behave intelligently. AI is a turbulent, exciting, audacious research area with a multitude of different approaches and influences that should continue to gain in credibility and importance in the years to come.

Acknowledgment

The authors would like to acknowledge the financial support of the Natural Sciences and Engineering Research Council of Canada and the Office of the Academic Vice-President of Simon Fraser University.

References

1. Winograd, T. *Understanding Natural Language*. New York: Academic; 1972.
2. Schank, R. C. "Conceptual dependency: A theory of natural language understanding." *Cognitive Psychology*. 3:552-631; 1972.
3. Woods, W. "Cascaded ATN grammars." *American Journal of Computational Linguistics*. 6(1):1-15; 1980.
4. Gazdar, G. "Phrase structure grammars and natural languages." *Proceedings of the International Joint Conference on Artificial Intelligence*. 556-565; 1983.
5. Montague, R. "The proper treatment of quanitification in ordinary English." In: R. H. Thomason, Ed. *Formal Philosophy*. New Haven: Yale University Press; 1974:247-270.
6. Barwise, J.; Perry, J. "Semantic innocence and uncompromising situations." In: P. French, T. Uehling, and H. Wettstein, Eds. *Midwest Studies in Philosophy VI*. Minneapolis: University of Minnesota Press; 1981:387-404.
7. Wilensky, R. "Why John married Mary: Understanding stories involving recurring goals." *Cognitive Science*. 2:235-266; 1978.
8. Grosz, B.J. "Utterance and objective: Issues in natural language communication." *AI Magazine*. 1:11-20; 1980.
9. Hirst, G. *Anaphora in Natural Language Understanding: A Survey*. Lecture Notes in Computer Science 119. Berlin:Springer-Verlag; 1981.
10. Waltz, D. L. "PLANES: An English language question answering system for a large relational database." *Communications of the ACM*. 21(7): 526-539; 1978.
11. Huffman, D. A. "Impossible objects as nonsense sentences." In: R. Meltzer and D. Michie, Eds. *Machine Intelligence 6*. New York: Elsevier; 1971: 295-323.
12. Clowes, M. B. "On seeing things." *Artificial Intelligence*. 2:19-116; 1971.
13. Guzman, A. "Computer recognition of three dimensional objects in a visual scene." Tech. Rep. MAC-TR-59, AI Laboratory, Massachusetts Institute of Technology; 1968.
14. Waltz, D. "Generating semantic descriptions from drawings of scenes with shadows." Tech. Rep. MAC-TR-271, Project MAC, Massachusetts Institute of Technology; 1972.
15. Duda, R. O.; Hart, P. E. *Pattern Classification and Scene Analysis*. New York: Wiley; 1973.
16. Montanari, U. "On the optimal detection of curves in noisy pictures." *Communications of the ACM*. 14:335-345; 1971.
17. Mackworth, A. K. "Consistency in networks of relations." *Artificial Intelligence*. 8(1):99-118; 1977.
18. Marr, D. *Vision*. San Francisco: W. H. Freeman; 1982.
19. Havens, W.; Mackworth, A. "Representing knowledge of the visual world." *IEEE Computer*. 16(10):90-96; 1983.
20. Minsky, M. L.; Papert, S. *Perceptrons; An Introduction to Computational Geometry*. Cambridge, MA: MIT Press; 1969.
21. Feigenbaum, E. A.; Buchanan, B.; Lederberg, J. "On generality and problem solving: A case study using the DENDRAL program." In: R. Meltzer and D. Michie, Eds. *Machine Intelligence 6*. New York: Elsevier; 1971:165-190.
22. Shortliffe, E. H. *Computer-Based Medical Consultations: MYCIN*. New York: Elsevier; 1976.
23. Pople, H. "The formation of composite hypothesis in diagnostic problem solving—an exercise in synthetic reasoning. "*Proceedings of the International Joint Conference on Artificial Intelligence*. pp. 1030-1037; 1977.
24. Duda, R. O.; Gaschnig, J.; Hart, P. E. "Model design in the PROSPECTOR consultation system for mineral exploration." In: D. Michie, Ed. *Expert Systems in the Micro-electronic Age*. Edinburgh: Edinburgh University Press; 1979:153-167.
25. Newell, A. "Production systems: Models of control structure." In: W. Chase, Ed. *Visual Information Processing*. New York: Academic; 1973:463-526.
26. Ernst, G.; Newell, A. *GPS: A Case Study in Generality and Problem Solving*. New York: Academic; 1969.
27. Nilsson, N. J. *Problem Solving Methods in Artificial Intelligence*. New York: McGraw-Hill; 1971.
28. Sussman, G. J. "A computational model of skill acquisition." AI Tech. Rep. 297, AI Laboratory, Massachusetts Institute of Technology; 1973.
29. Sacerdoti, E. D. *A Structure for Plans and Behavior*. New York: Elsevier; 1977.
30. McCalla, G.; Reid, L.; Schneider, P. F. "Plan creation, plan execution, and knowledge acquisition in a dynamic microworld." *International Journal of Man-Machine Studies*. 16(1):89-112; 1982.
31. Rosenschein, J. S. "Synchronization of multi-agent plans." *Proceedings of the Second National Conference on AI (AAAI-82)*. pp. 115-119; 1982.
32. Hayes-Roth, B.; Hayes-Roth, F. "A cognitive model of planning." *Cognitive Science*. 3:275-310; 1979.
33. Robinson, J. "A machine oriented logic based on the resolution principle." *Journal of the ACM*. 12:23-41; 1965.
34. Coles, S. "The application of theorem proving to information retrieval." Tech. Note 51, AI Center, Stanford Research Institute; 1971.
35. Green, C. "Theorem proving by resolution as a basis for question-answering systems." In: R. Meltzer and D. Michie, Eds. *Machine Intelligence 4*. New York: Elsevier; 1969:183-205.
36. Colmerauer, A.; Kanoui, H.; Pasero, R.; Roussel, Ph. "Un systeme de communication homme-machine en Francais." Research Rep. Groupe Intelligence Artifiicelle, Faculte des Sciences de Luminy, Marseilles; 1973.
37. Kowalski, R. "Predicate logic as a programming language." In: J. L. Rosenfeld, Ed. *Information Processing 74*. Amsterdam: North-Holland; 1974, pp. 569-574.
38. Sussman, G. J.; Winograd, T.; Charniak, E. "MICRO-PLANNER reference manual." AI Memo 203A, AI Laboratory, Massachusetts Institute of Technology; 1971.
39. Hewitt, C. "Description and theoretical analysis (using schemata) of PLANNER: a language for proving theorems and manipulating models in a robot." Rep. No. AI-TR-258, AI Laboratory, Massachusetts Institute of Technology; 1971.
40. Brachman, R. J. "What IS-A is and isn't: An analysis of taxonomic links in semantic networks." *IEEE Computer*. 16(10):30-36; 1983.
41. Schubert, L. K.; Goebel, R. G.; Cercone, N. "The structure and

organisation of a semantic network for comprehension and inference." In: N. V. Findler, Ed. *Associative Networks*. New York: Academic; 1979:122–178.

42. Levesque, H.; Mylopoulos, J. "A procedural semantics for semantic networks." In: N. V. Findler, Ed. *Associative Networks*. New York: Academic; 1979:93–119.

43. Minsky, M. "A framework for representing knowledge." In: P. H. Winston, Ed. *The Psychology of Computer Vision*. New York: McGraw-Hill; 1975:211–277.

44. Bobrow D. G.; Winograd, T. "An overview of KRL: A knowledge representation language." *Cognitive Science*. 1:3–46; 1977.

45. Brachman, R. J. "On the epistemological status of semantic networks." In: N. V. Findler, Ed. *Associative Networks*. New York: Academic; 1979:3–50.

46. Bobrow, D. G. (Ed.). Special issue on non-monotonic logic. *Artificial Intelligence*. 13(1,2); 1980.

47. McCalla, G.; Cercone, N. (Eds.). Special issue on knowledge representation. *IEEE Computer*. 16(10); 1983.

48. Brachman R.; Smith, B. Special issue on knowledge representation. *SIGART Newsletter No. 70*. 1980.

49. Collins, A. M.; Quillian, M. R. "How to make a language user." In: E. Tulving and W. Donaldson, Eds. *Organization and Memory*, New York: Academic; 1972.

50. Samuel, A. L. "Some studies in machine learning using the game of checkers." In: E. Feigenbaum and J. Feldman, Eds. *Computers and Thought*. New York: McGraw-Hill 1963:71–105.

51. Winston, P. L. "Learning structural descriptions from examples." Rep. No. AI-TR-231, AI Laboratory, Massachusetts Institute of Technology; 1970.

52. Lenat, D. B. "On automated scientific theory formation: a case study using the AM program." In: J. E. Hayes, D. Michie, and L. I. Mikulich, Eds. *Machine Intelligence 9*. New York: Halsted; 1977:251–286.

53. Lenat, D. B. "The nature of heuristics." *Artificial Intelligence*. 19(2):189–221; 1982.

54. Mitchell, T. M.; Utgoff, P. E.; Nudel, B.; Banerji, R. B. "Learning problem solving heuristics through practice." *Proceedings of the International Joint Conference on Artificial Intelligence*. pp. 127–134; 1981.

55. Langley, P. "Representational issues in learning system." *IEEE Computer*. 16(10):47–52; 1983.

56. Michalski, R. S. Ed. *Proceedings of the International Machine Learning Workshop*. Allerton House, Monticello, IL, 1983. Urbana-Champaign: Department of Computer Science, University of Illinois.

57. Sleeman, D.; Brown, J. S. *Intelligent Tutoring Systems*. New York: Academic; 1982.

58. Papert, S. *Mindstorms: Children, Computers, and Powerful Ideas*. New York: Basic Books; 1980.

59. Goforth, D. J. "LEPUS: An object oriented extension of turtle geometry." Tech. Rep. 83-9, Department of Computational Science, University of Saskatchewan; 1983.

60. Erman, L.; Fennell, R.; Lesser, V. R.; Reddy, R. "System organizations for speech understanding: implications of network and multiprocessor computer architectures for AI." *IEEE Transactions on Computers*. C-25(4):414–421; 1976.

61. McCulloch, W.; Pitts, W. "A logical calculus of the ideas immanent in nervous activity." *Bulletin of Mathematical Biophysics*. 5:115–133; 1943.

62. Minsky, M. "Form and content in computer science." *Journal of the ACM*. 17(2):197–215; 1970.

Suggested Readings

Barr, A.; Feigenbaum, E. A. *The Handbook of Artificial Intelligence: Volume 1*. Los Altos: William Kaufmann, Inc.; 1981.

Barr, A.; Feigenbaum, E. A. *The Handbook of Artificial Intelligence: Volume 2*. Los Altos: William Kaufman, Inc.; 1982.

Cohen, P. R.; Feigenbaum, E. A. *The Handbook of Artificial Intelligence: Volume 3*. Los Altos: William Kaufmann, Inc.; 1982.

Chapter 2: Introduction to
Computer Architectures for Artificial Intelligence

Many of today's computers are single-processor von Neumann machines designed for sequential and deterministic numerical computations [1-4], and are not equipped for AI applications that are mainly parallel nondeterministic symbolic manipulations [5-8]. Consequently, efficient computer architectures for AI applications would be sufficiently different from traditional computers [9-18]. These architectures have the following requirements.

Symbolic processing: In the microlevel, AI applications require symbolic processing operations such as comparison, selection, sorting, matching, logic set operations (union, intersection, and negation), contexts and partition, transitive closure, pattern retrieval, and recognition. In a higher level, these applications may require the processing of nonnumerical data such as sentences, speech, graphics, and images. Efficient computers designed for these applications should possess hardware for symbolic processing functions [19-21]. The most important ones are tagged mechanisms [20,22] and hardware stacks [23].

Parallel and distributed processing: Most AI problems are complex [24,25] and must be evaluated by high-performance computers. Owing to technological limitations of physical devices, parallelism is perhaps the only promising mechanism to further improve the performance of computers [8,10,26-29]. To prevent the bottleneck of a centralized controller, intelligence in such a system should be decentralized. In applying multiprocessing and distributed processing to solve problems with exponential complexity, which is typical for problems in AI, one must realize that multiprocessing is useful in improving the computational efficiency and *not in extending the solvable problem size* [30]. To extend the solvable problem space of such problems, the key is to find better models and more efficient heuristics.

Nondeterministic processing: Most AI algorithms are nondeterministic [31]; that is, it is impossible to plan in advance the procedures to execute and to terminate with the available information. Therefore, dynamic allocation and load balancing of computational resources are essential in AI architectures [10,32]. Further, an efficient interconnection network is needed to disseminate information for the scheduler. The trade off between the overhead of distributing the scheduling information and the overhead for the extra work needed without the scheduling information must be made. Moreover, efficient garbage collection is important for AI architectures owing to the dynamically allocated storage [32-34].

Knowledge base management: Since a very large amount of information has to be stored and retrieved in AI applications, large knowledge bases are inevitable [35-38]. An implementation using a common memory is inappropriate because of access conflicts. A decentralized memory system with distributed intelligence and capabilities for pattern matching and proximity search is required.

Software-oriented computer architectures: The efficiency of a computer system for an AI application depends strongly on its knowledge representation and the language used. An efficient AI architecture should be designed around the knowledge representations of the problems to be solved and the high-level AI languages to be supported. Further, the designed architectures should adapt to changes in granularity and data formats of various applications. Examples of these architectures are the dataflow machines [39,40], object-oriented architectures [41,42], Lisp machines [18,22], and Prolog-like machines, such as the Fifth-Generation Computer System [14].

Currently, extensive research is being carried out in designing efficient AI architectures. Many existing concepts in computer architecture, such as dataflow processing [43,44], stack machines [23], tagging [20], pipelining [27], direct execution of high-level languages [45-47], database machines [48], multiprocessing, and distributed processing, can be incorporated into future AI architectures. New concepts in computer architectures are also expected.

Four papers are included in this chapter. The first paper, by Boley, surveys computers for artificial intelligence up to 1980 and gives an extensive list of references [5]. The remaining three papers (Fahlman, Treleaven, and Hewitt and Lieberman) highlight the design issues in computer architectures for AI applications [6,8,10].

References

[1]   J.-L. Baer, *Computer Systems Architecture*, Computer Science Press, Rockville, Md., 1980.

[2]   J.-L. Baer, "Computer Architecture," *Computer*, vol. 17, no. 10, pp. 77-87, Oct. 1984.

[3]   H.S. Stone, *Introduction to Computer Architecture*, 2nd Edition, Science Research Associates, Chicago, Il., 1980.

[4]   G. Myer, *Advances in Computer Architecture*, John Wiley, New York, N.Y., 1978.

[5] H. Boley, "A Preliminary Survey of Artificial Intelligence Machines," *SIGART Newsletter*, no. 72, pp. 21-28, ACM, New York, N.Y., July 1980.

[6] S. Fahlman, "Computing Facilities for AI: A Survey of Present and Near-Future Options," *AI Magazine*, vol. 2, no. 1, pp. 16-23, Winter 1980-81.

[7] Arvind and R.A. Iannucci, "A Critique of Multiprocessing von Neumann Style," *Proceedings of the 10th Annual International Symposium on Computer Architecture*, pp. 426-436, IEEE Computer Society, Washington, D.C., June 1983.

[8] P.C. Treleaven, "The New Generation of Computer Architecture," *Proceedings of the 10th Annual International Symposium on Computer Architecture*, pp. 402-409, IEEE Computer Society, Washington, D.C., June 1983.

[9] M.F. Deering, "Hardware and Software Architectures for Efficient AI," *Proceedings of the National Conference on Artificial Intelligence*, pp. 73-78, William Kaufmann, Los Altos, Calif., Aug. 1984.

[10] C. Hewitt and H. Lieberman, "Design Issues in Parallel Architectures for Artificial Intelligence," *Proceedings of COMPCON S'84*, pp. 418-423, IEEE Computer Society, Washington, D.C., Feb. 1984.

[11] E.A. Feigenbaum, F. Hayes-Roth, D. Waltz, R. Reddy, and V. Zue, "The Building Blocks," *IEEE Spectrum*, pp. 77-87, Nov. 1983.

[12] D.I. Moldovan, "Survey of Computer Architectures for Artificial Intelligence," *Technical Report PPP-84-6*, University of Southern California, Los Angeles, Calif., July 1984.

[13] T. Moto-oka, et al., "Challenge for Knowledge Information Processing Systems," *Proceedings of the International Conference on Fifth-Generation Computer Systems*, pp. 3-89, ICOT, Tokyo, Japan, and North-Holland, Amsterdam, The Netherlands, 1981.

[14] K. Fuchi, "The Direction the FGCS Project Will Take," *New Generation Computing*, vol. 1, no. 1, pp. 3-9, 1983.

[15] H. Boley, "AI Languages and AI Machines: An Overview," *Proceedings of the German Workshop on Artificial Intelligence*, Springer-Fachberichte, Berlin, West Germany, 1981.

[16] D. Schaefer and J. Fischer, "Beyond the Supercomputer," *IEEE Spectrum*, vol. 19, no. 3, pp. 32-37, March 1982.

[17] D.A. Waterman and F. Hayes-Roth, *Pattern-Directed Inference Systems*, Academic Press, Orlando, Fla., 1978.

[18] M.F. Deering, "Architectures for AI," *Byte*, vol. 10, no. 4, pp. 193-206, April 1985.

[19] A. Mukhopadhyay, "Hardware Algorithms for Nonnumeric Computation," *IEEE Transactions on Computers*, vol. C-28, no. 6, pp. 384-394, June 1979.

[20] A. Hirsch, "Tagged Architecture Supports Symbolic Processing," *Computer Design*, vol. 23, no. 6, pages 75-80, June 1984.

[21] J. Campbell and J. Fitch, "Symbolic Computing with and without Lisp," *Record of Lisp Conference*, Stanford University, Menlo Park, Calif., 1980.

[22] M. Creeger, "Lisp Machines Come Out of the Lab.," *Computer Design*, vol. 22, no. 11, pp. 132-137, Nov. 1983.

[23] R. Doran, "Architecture of Stack Machine," *High-Level Language Computer Architecture*, edited by Y. Chu, Academic Press, Orlando, Fla., 1975.

[24] S.A. Cook, "An Overview of Computational Complexity," *Communications of the ACM*, vol. 26, no. 6, pp. 401-408, June 1983.

[25] J. Pearl, *Heuristics: Intelligent Search Strategies for Computer Problem Solving*, Addison-Wesley, Reading, Mass., 1984.

[26] L.S. Haynes, R.L. Lau, D.P. Siewiorek, and D.W. Mizell, "A Survey of Highly Parallel Computing," *Computer*, vol. 15, no. 1, pp. 9-24, Jan. 1982.

[27] K. Hwang and F.A. Briggs, *Computer Architecture and Parallel Processing*, McGraw-Hill, New York, N.Y., 1984.

[28] N.R. Lincoln, "Technology and Design Tradeoffs in the Creation of a Modern Supercomputer," *IEEE Transactions on Computers*, vol. C-31, no. 5, pp. 349-362, May 1982.

[29] J.P. Riganati and P.B. Schneck, "Supercomputing," *Computer*, vol. 17, no. 10, pp. 97-113, Oct. 1984.

[30] B.W. Wah, G.-J. Li, and C.F. Yu, "Multiprocessing of Combinatorial Search Problems," *Computer*, vol. 18, no. 6, pp. 93-108, June 1985.

[31] J. Cohen, "Non-Deterministic Algorithms," *Computing Surveys*, vol. 11, no. 2, pp. 79-94, June 1979.

[32] H.G. Baker Jr., "Optimizing Allocation and Garbage Collection of Spaces," *Artificial Intelligence: An MIT Perspective*, edited by P.H. Winston and R.H. Brown, vol. 1, pp. 391-396, MIT Press, Cambridge, Mass., 1979.

[33] J. Cohen, "Garbage Collection of Linked Data Structures," *Computing Surveys*, vol. 13, no. 3, pp. 341-367, Sept. 1981.

[34] H. Lieberman and C. Hewitt, "A Real-Time Garbage Collector Based on the Lifetimes of Objects," *Communications of the ACM*, vol. 26, no. 6, pp. 419-429, June 1983.

[35] E. Babb, "Functional Requirements for Very Large Knowledge Bases," *Proceedings of the ACM'84 Annual Conference*, pp. 55-56, ACM, New York, N.Y., Oct. 1984.

[36] M. Bartschi, "An Overview of Information Retrieval Subjects," *Computer*, vol. 18, no. 5, pp. 67-84, May 1985.

[37] G. Wiederhold, "Knowledge and Database Management," *IEEE Software*, vol. 1, no. 1, pp. 63-73, Jan. 1984.

[38] H. Sakai, K. Iwata, S. Kamiya, M. Abe, A. Tanaka, S. Shibayama, and K. Murakami, "Design and Implementation of Relational Database Engine," *Proceedings of the Fifth-Generation Computer Systems*, pp. 419-426, ICOT, Tokyo, Japan, and North-Holland, Amsterdam, The Netherlands, 1984.

[39] L. Bic, "A Data-Driven Model for Parallel Interpretation of Logic Programs," *Proceedings of the International Conference on Fifth-Generation Computer Systems*, pp. 517-523, ICOT, Tokyo, Japan, and North-Holland, Amsterdam, The Netherlands, 1984.

[40] N. Ito, H. Shimizu, M. Kishi, E. Kuno, and K. Rokusawa, "Data-Flow Based Execution Mechanisms of Parallel and Concurrent Prolog," *New Generation Computing*, vol. 3, pp. 15-41, 1985.

[41] M. Tokoro and Y. Ishikawa, "An Object-Oriented Approach to Knowledge Systems," *Proceedings of the International Conference on Fifth-Generation Computer Systems*, pp. 623-632, ICOT, Tokyo, Japan, and North-Holland, Amsterdam, The Netherlands, 1984.

[42] Y. Ishikawa and M. Tokoro, "The Design of an Object-Oriented Architecture," *Proceedings of the 11th International Symposium on Computer Architecture*, pp. 178-187, IEEE Computer Society, Washington, D.C., 1984.

[43] J.B. Dennis, "Data Flow Supercomputers," *Computer*, vol. 13, no. 11, pp. 48-56, Nov. 1980.

[44] P.C. Treleaven and I.G. Lima, "Future Computers: Logic, Data Flow, . . ., Control Flow?," *Computer*, vol. 17, no. 3, pp. 47-55, March 1984.

[45] Y. Chu, "Direct-Execution Computer Architecture," *Information Processing 77*, edited by B. Gilchrist, pp. 18-23, 1977.

[46] M. Yamamoto, "A Survey of High-Level Language Machines in Japan," *Computer*, vol. 14, no. 7, pp. 68-78, July 1981.

[47] M.J. Flynn, "Directions and Issues in Architecture and Language," *Computer*, vol. 13, no. 10, pp. 5-22, Oct. 1980.

[48] G.G. Langdon Jr., "Database Machines: An Introduction," *IEEE Transactions on Computers*, vol. C-28, no. 6, pp. 381-384, June 1979.

A PRELIMINARY SURVEY OF
ARTIFICIAL INTELLIGENCE MACHINES

Harold Boley
FB Informatik
Universitaet Hamburg
D-2000 Hamburg 13

This paper is a first attempt at a survey of concrete and abstract machines relevant to AI research, inspired by some recent developments in personal computers. In particular, we consider machines supporting higher-level programming languages used in AI, mainly LISP. The emphasis will be on gaining a global perspective on the emerging field of AI machines rather than on a detailed treatment of specific issues. Thus, readers who are specialists in one of the fields touched (e.g., in parallel and associative machines) will not learn anything new about their particular field (on the contrary, they may contribute additional AI-relevant material to later versions of the survey). However, particularly for AI researchers worrying about the efficiency of their systems, this survey may provide a quick access to this important new research areas. For more specific questions the references in the extensive topic-indexed bibliography should be consulted.

History

The idea of building intelligent systems in the form of special machines is as old as or even older than the AI field itself: Because the first conceptions of 'artificial intelligence' were shaped before programmable computers were available, they had to take the form of 'hardwired' machines.

However, the first thirty years of serious work in AI took place mostly above this machine level in the medium of programming languages [assemblers, list-processing languages such as LISP (McCarthy et al. 1962), pattern-directed systems like PLANNER (Hewitt 1971)]. Early machine designs for list-processing languages had little influence on subsequent AI research [(Shaw et al. 1958), (Hodges 1964), (Wigington 1963), (Bashkow et al. 1968)], or they were made outside of AI altogether [(Rice & Smith 1971), (Laliotis 1975)].

It was only in recent years that the design of special machine architectures for AI applications became feasible, mainly because of decreasing hardware costs, the advent of microprogrammable microprocessors, the arrival/return of personal computers, and the experience gained with interpreters/compilers for LISP-like AI programming languages. This chance was exploited by several projects which turned the long-existing abstract [mathematical or software] lambda-calculus [cf. TOPIC 1] and LISP [cf. TOPIC 5.2] machines [(Landin 1963), (McCarthy et al. 1962), (Reynolds 1972)] into concrete [hardware and microcode] machines for LISP. The most promising of these, the Greenblatt LISP machine [cf. TOPIC 5.3.1], also incorporates features of PLANNER-like languages (Greenblatt 1974).

In parallel to this development there spread a growing dissatisfaction [e.g. (Glushkov et al. 1974), (Haendler 1976), (Backus 1978), (Myers 1978), (Giloi 1980)] with the traditional von Neumann computer architecture (Burks et al. 1946), which led to the design of several kinds of non-von Neumann computers. The most relevant of these for applicative subsets of LISP-like AI languages seem to be reduction machines [cf. TOPIC 3].

LISP Machines and Non-Von Neumann Machines

LISP machines [cf. TOPIC 5] can be regarded as "high-level language computer architectures" (Chu 1975) for LISP, which share several features with non-von Neumann computers, the most important ones, perhaps being

1. Tagged architectures (Feustal 1973): The Greenblatt LISP machine, for example, makes use of the non-von Neumann feature of tagged machine words, e.g. for efficient list representation.

2. Stack machines (Doran 1975): Both the Greenblatt LISP machine and many non-von Neumann computers, such as the Berkling reduction machine (Berkling 1976), make us of hardware stacks.

However, there is a difference in attitude between these two recent developments: The LISP machine community attempts to go beyond the limits of time-shared computers for the execution of LISP, mainly beyond their speeds and their address spaces, thereby consciously keeping or even reinforcing certain aspects of the basic von Neumann architecture [e.g., the data/program equivalence which is characteristic of both LISP and von Neumann assemblers (Allen 1978), (Steele & Sussman 1979)]; the non-von Neumann community attempts to embody modern computational conceptions directly into unconventional machine structures, seeking a liberation from the long-established fundamental von Neumann architecture [e.g., by enforcing a data/program distinction at the hardware level (Organick 1973), (Giloni & Berg 1974)]. LISP machines and non-von Neumann machines can be viewed as complementary attempts at improving present-day computers: The former proceed 'bottom-up' from existing computers; the latter proceed 'top-down' from abstract models.

The Concept of AI Machines

While in the short run LISP machines as available today will be an adequate deviation from our traditional computers, in the long run more drastic changes in the machines used in AI may become necessary. The main reasons for this derive from the needs of still larger AI systems, which will become increasingly urgent as more practical production applications of research results are attempted. These AI needs include the following:

"A Preliminary Survey of Artificial Intelligence Machines" by H. Boley from *SIGART Newsletter*, Number 72, July 1980, pages 21-28. Copyright 1980, Association for Computing Machinery, Inc., reprinted by permission.

1. Need for special hardware realizations of heavily used non-numeric algorithms, today still programmed in symbol-manipulation languages [cf. TOPIC 7].

2. Need for large associative memories for [variable-length] complex data and for pattern-directed programs [cf. TOPIC 8].

3. Need for concurrent computations to assist in coping with combinatorial search explosions [cf. TOPIC 9].

4. Need for further unorthodox hardware and architectural means, mainly to obtain still better response times and larger fast storages [cf. TOPIC 10].

The changes in the von Neumann conception required to satisfy these needs will be drastic enough to justify a classification of the resulting architectures as non-von Neumann [even if they preserve the distinguished von Neumann characteristic of program/data equivalent, because this is also needed in many AI applications, e.g. when programs are automatically synthesized and immediately executed].

Therefore we propose to use the term 'machines for AI research' or 'AI machines' [as a counterpart of 'languages for AI research' or 'AI languages'] to cover the progressive series of LISP machines, machines for PLANNER-like and other AI languages, and those non-von Neumann architectures which contribute to the satisfaction of the AI needs mentioned.

By using the concept of AI machines the very large complement set to the set of von Neumann computers is narrowed down according to the practical needs of AI applications. It is probable that this subset of non-von Neumann computers will also be amenable to a more theoretical characterization.

Hardware, Software, and Semantics

The AI machine concept extends across the boundaries of the three fields of computer hardware, computer software, and formal semantics of programming languages: The boundary between software machines and hardware machines is crossed because of the intermediate microcode level ['firmware'] and, more importantly, because of the rise of high-level language computer architectures [cf. TOPIC 4]; the boundary between software machines and formal semantics is crossed because of the possibility of using "definitional interpreters" (Reynolds 1972) as operational semantics [cf. TOPIC 2].

For example, the AI machines for PLANNER-like languages existing today are mostly software interpreters, usually written in LISP [cf. TOPIC 6]. However, proceeding 'downward' from such LISP interpreters it will be possible to realize concrete [microcode and hardware] machines for these languages, as e.g., attempted with the PLANNER-like features of the Greenblatt LISP machine (Bawden et al. 1979); proceeding 'upward' from LISP interpreters it is possible to formalize abstract [mathematical] machines for these languages, as e.g., attempted with the PLANNER-like features of FIT (Boley 1979).

AI Language Directed Computer Design

The possibility of proceeding from software to hardware machines will probably become very important for AI, because it offers an ultimate [supplementary] means of making AI systems more efficient. More specifically, LISP directed computers permit AI programmers to worry about efficiency issues down to the level of LISP only, because efficiency issues below the LISP level are taken care of by the hardware.

It is therefore encouraging that "language directed computer design" (Worman 1972) has already been systematically investigated in computer architecture outside of AI (Myers 1978).

Of course, in the emerging field of 'AI language directed computer design' there will be difficult additional problems to solve, such as finding appropriate hardware realizations of AI language features like pattern-directed invocation and the non-determinism caused by it. However, the Greenblatt LISP machine may indicate a possible way toward such more concrete AI machines.

Greenblatt's Prototype AI Machine

Greenblatt's machine (Greenblatt 1974) is treated as a representative here, because it is well on its way to becoming a prototype for the coming generation of AI machines built in the form of personal computers.

1. It promises to be the best machine support for LISP, which is still by far the most important AI programming language.

2. It also provides for features of PLANNER-like languages, which hitherto have been defined on top of LISP.

3. It finally fulfills requirements which are also necessary for future AI machines, i.e., are not idiosyncratic to a particular language.

The Greenblatt machine supports "LISP machine LISP", an advancement of the MACLISP language (Moon 1974), which has been improved, e.g., by means of the following efficiently realized features:

1. Augmented arrays with 'leaders' for specifying combined data types consisting of arrays [items of the same type] and records [items of different types].

2. Functions with 'optional parameters' using automatic, user-controlled defaulting and with 'rest parameters'.

3. Functions with 'multiple-value-return' for conveniently yielding more than one expression [cf. (Friedman & Wise 1976), (Boley 1979)].

4. 'Closures' [functions together with bindings for free variables] used as datatypes to solve the "funarg problem" [cf. (Moses 1970), (Steele & Sussman 1976)].

5. 'Stack groups' as a substitute for "spaghetti stacks" (Bobrow & Wegbreit 1973a 1973b) for implementing coroutines, asynchronous processes, and generators [cf. (Boehm et al. 1977), (Fischler & Raulefs 1979), (Sussman & McDermott 1974)].

Furthermore, the Greenblatt LISP machine augments the usual interactive capabilities of LISP systems [cf. (Fischer & Laubsch 1980)] by the following:

1. A flexible software-implemented terminal with a raster scan TV driven by a 1/4 Mbit memory and refreshed at a rate of 67 Hz.

2. A mouse for conveniently pointing to parts of the display and for giving simple commands.

3. A keyboard with several levels of control/ shifting to facilitate single-keystroke commands.

4. A sophisticated real-time display-oriented editor with automatic pretty-print indentation, so that the user can always immediately see exactly what he is doing.

The machine has been designed in such a way that large LISP programs such as Woods' LUNAR English-language data-base query system can be executed very efficiently:

1. The swapping overhead is considerably reduced because each user has his own main memory [which retains frequently referred pages] and swapping hard disk [which uses fixed addresses].

2. The LISP machine is emulated by the microprogrammed microprocessor CADR, an advancement of CONS (Knight 1974), both of which have wide data and address paths and can extract/deposit any field in any register.

3. The list storage is compressed by representing lists as vectors of consecutive memory locations instead of using pointers to arbitrary memory locations whenever possible.

4. The garbage collector works real-time, incrementally, and in a compacting manner (Baker 1977).

5. LISP programs can be compiled directly into a large microprogram memory.

Greenblatt's LISP machine project therefore achieved the goal of creating a machine better suited for the execution of LISP than the time shared PDP-10 [DECsystem-10] computer, which for many years was the "workhorse of AI" (Bawden et al. 1979). The table below gives a rough comparison [e.g. all speed entries and the cost entries are approximations] between the Greenblatt LISP machine and the DECsystem-10. For both machines the table refers to the original processors, namely to the CONS processor [which is best documented] and to the KA 10 processor [which is most often used as a comparison basis for LISP machines], respectively. Of course, in the comparison the fact must be taken into account that the former is a 'small' personal computer [except for the shared file system and the hardcopy output] while the latter is a 'large' time shared computer.

Conclusion

In summary, we believe that the further development of AI machines would benefit by more 'interdisciplinary' communication across the various boundaries between

1. LISP machines and non-von Neumann architectures,

2. computer hardware, computer software, and operations semantics,

3. computer architecture and programming language design.

This communication might eventually yield a new synthesis of ideas which today are still isolated.

The Greenblatt LISP machine -- apart from its use for implementing large AI systems -- can play a dual role in the development of AI machines, namely the role of a prototype AI machine with which experience for future AI architecture may be gained and the role of an efficient vehicle for simulating higher-level AI machines.

Bibliography on AI Machines

The following bibliography has been compiled as a first step toward a unified perspective, the primary intention being to contribute to a continuous exchange of ideas on AI machines. The bibliography consists of a list of references, which is mostly indexed by topics. For the topics we don't use the obvious top-level breakdowns abstract|concrete machines or software|firmware |hardware machines because we want to emphasize the communalities across these boundaries. Instead, we use the more fine-grained breakdown lambda-calculus| definitional| reduction| high-level-language| LISP| PLANNER-like| more symbol-processing| associative[/parallel]| parallel| miscellaneous machines. In each topic we include the languages which are supported by the abstract or concrete machines listed.

Since the present interest in AI is in the LISP machines [[(Kurokawa 1979), (Lausch 19179)], a large percentage of references belongs to this important topic. The non-von Neumann architectures appear under more specific subtopics, which only contain references that are related to LISP machines or other wise seem to be already relevant to present-day AI. For example, analog machines are not yet included because the question of their [AI] relevance is still too controversial (Minsky & Papert 1971).

No claim of completeness is made for any of the topics--indeed we ask the reader to help us improve and expand this AI machines bibliography. In future issues of the Newsletter the bibliography may be continued, making use of the feedback obtained. In exchange, the actual state of the complete survey can be obtained on request.

Acknowledgement

I want to thank the following people for already having made valuable suggestions: Wilfried Brauer, Oskar Fuhlrott, Guenther Goerz, Eike Jessen, Dieter Kolb, Joachim Laubsch, Peter Raulefs, Frieder Schwenkel, Wolfgang Tietz, Wolfgang Wahlster.

Topics

1. LAMBDA-CALCULUS MACHINES

(Church 1941), (Landin 1963), (Reynolds 1972), (Wegner 1968).

2. DEFINITIONAL MACHINES

(Boley 1979), (Fischer 1977), (McCarthy et al. 1962), (Reynolds 1972), (Wegner 1968).

3. REDUCTION MACHINES

(Backus 1978), (Berkling 1971 1976 1979), (Hommes 1975 1977a 1977b), (Kluge 1979), (Mago 1979), (Organick 1979), (Treleaven & Mole 1980), (Vogl-Mildner 1978).

4. HIGH-LEVEL-LANGUAGE MACHINES

(ACM-IEEE 1973), (Carlson 1975), (Chevenance 1977), (Chu 1975), (Ditzel & Patterson 1980), (Fournier 1975), (Giloni & Berg 1974), (Snyder 1979), (Wortman 1972).

5. LISP MACHINES

5.1. Surveys

(Allen 1978), (Helmer 1979), (Kurokawa 1979), (Laubsch 1979), (Raulefs 1980), (Sloman et al. 1979).

5.2. Abstract Machines

(Allen 1978), (Gilmore 1963), (Juergensen 1974), (McCarthy et al. 1962), (Montenegro et al. 1975), (Moore II 1976), (Reynolds 1972), (Simon 1978), (Simon & Trademann 1977), (Steele & Sussman 1978), (Wegner 1968).

5.3. Concrete Machines

5.3.1. Greenblatt Machine-

(Baker 1977 1979), (Bawden et al. 1977 1979), (Greenblatt 1974), (Knight 1974), (Moon 1974), (Schoichet 1978), (Weinreb & Moon 1979).

5.3.2. Other Machines-

(Barbacci et al. 1971), (Bobrow & Clark 1979), (Chailloux 1978), (Deutsch 1973 1978), (Fiala 1978), (Goto 1974), (Goto et al. 1978), (Griss & Swanson 1977), (Guzman & Segovia 1976), (Kalhoff & Simon 1975), (Keller et al. 1978), (Luegger & Melenk 1973), (Nagao et al. 1979), (Steele & Sussman 1979), (Taft 1979), (Taki et al. 1979), (Williams 1978).

6. PLANNER-LIKE MACHINES

(Augenstein 1979), (Bobrow & Wegbreit 1973a 1973b), (Boehm et al. 1977), (Boley 1979), (Fischer 1977), (Fischer & Paulefs 1979), (Hewitt 1971 1977), (Hewitt et al. 1973), (McDermott 1975), (Montenegro et al. 1975), (Steiger 1974).

7. PLANNER-LIKE MACHINES

(Anderson & Gillogly 1976), (Bashkow et al. 1968), (Buchberger et al. 1979), (Griss & Kessler 1978), (Hodges 1964), (Hollaar 1978), (Lea 1977), (Learning Research Group 1976), (Laliotis 1975), (McGill 1977), (Mukhopadyay 1978), (Norman & Rumerhart 1975), (Rice & Smith 1971), (Sansonnet et al. 1980), (Shapiro 1972a 1972b), (Shaw et al. 1958).

8. ASSOCIATIVE [/PARALLEL] MACHINES

(Ahuja & Roberts 1980), (Ash & Sibley 1968), (Fahlman 1979), (Feldman & Rovner 1969), (Goto 1974), (Haendler 1976), (Jessen 1965 1975), (Love & Savitt 1971), (Lea 1977), (Lewin 1977), (McGill 1977), (Minsky & Papert 1971), (Minter 1972), (Parkami 1973), (Weicker 1974).

9. PARALLEL MACHINES

(Augensteain 1979), (Bobrow & Wegbreit 1973a 1973b), (Boehm et al. 1977), (Buchberger et al. 1979), (Despain & Patterson 1978), (Fischer 1977), (Fischer & Raulefs 1979), (Friedman & Wise 1978), (Giloni 1980), (Glushkov et al. 1974), (Guzman & Segovia 1976), (Haendler 1976), (Hewitt et al. 1973), (Keller et al. 1978), (Laliotis 1975), (Mago 1979), (Minsky 1979), (McGill 1977), (Moshell & Rothstein 1979), (Rice & Smith 1971), (Sullivan & Bashkow 1977), (Sullivan et al. 1977), (Treleaven & Mole 1980), (Vanaken & Zick 1978), (Williams 1978), (Zisman 1978), (Zuse 1958).

10. MISCELLANEOUS MACHINES

(Brown 1974), (Christaller & Metzing 1980), (Dennis & Misunas 1975), (Giloni 1980), (Haendler 1978), (Jessen 1975), (Myers 1978), (Organick 1973), (Sussman 1980), (Zisman 1978).

29

	Greenblatt LISP machine [CONS]	DECsystem-10 [KA10]	Improvement
LISP systems supported	LISP machine LISP [others adaptable]	MACLISP,INTER- LISP,UCILISP..	see text
microprogram memory	16K 48-bit-words	none	absolute
instruction set	LISP-directed	not high-level lang. directed	higher level
system language	LISP/microcode	MACRO-10	easier
program swapping	microprogrammed paging	macroprogr. core shuffling	micro paging
word length	32 bits	36 bits	no
virtual address space	24 bits [16,777,216 addr.]	18 bits [262144 addr.]	6 bits [64 fold]
cache ['pdl buffer']	1K words 200 nanoseconds	none	absolute
main memory	core/semiconductor 64K - 1 Mega words 1 microsecond	core 64K-256K words 1 microsecond	semicond. 0K-768Kw. no
swapping memory	hard disk 16 Mega words 25 milliseconds	drum/disk arbitrary	no
run time [relative times for LUNAR system]	ellapsed real time	virtual run time with time sharing delays	3 fold [MACLISP] 6-12 fold [INTRLSP]
cost	80,000 $	300,000 $	220,000 $

References

ACM-IEEE: Symposium on high-level-language computer architecture. University of Maryland, College Park, Maryland, November 7-8, 1973, ACM New York, IEEE Northridge, 1973.

Ahuja, S. & Roberts, C.: An associative/parallel processor for partial match retrieval using superimposed code. 7th Intern. Symp. Computer Architecture, May 1980.

Allen, J.: Anatomy of LISP. McGraw-Hill, New York, 1978.

Anderson, R. & Gillogly, J.: Rand intelligent terminal agent (RITA): Design philosophy. Rand, R-1809-ARPA, Feb. 1976.

Ash, W. & Sibley, F.: TRAMP: An interpretive associative processor with deductive capabilities. Proc. ACM 23rd Nat. Conf., Nevada, 1968, 143-156.

Augenstein, B.: Ein INTERLISP-Interpretierer fuer CSSA. Univ. Bonn, Institut fuer Informatik III, Memo SEKI-BN-79-01, 1979.

Backus, J.: Can programming be liberated from the von Neuman style? A functional style and its algebra of programs. CACM 21(8), August 1978.

Baker, H.: List processing in real time on a serial computer. MIT, AI Lab., Working Paper 139, 1977.

Baker, H.: Optimizing allocation and garbage collection of spaces. In: (Winston & Brown 1979).

Barbacci, M. et al.: C.ai (P.LISP), a LISP processor of C.ai. Carnegie-Mellon University, 1971.

Bashkow, T. & Kroft, D. & Sasson, A.: Study of a computer for direct execution on a list processing language. Columbia Univ., New York, AFCRL-68-0063, 1968.

Bawden,D. & Greenblatt,R. & Holloway,J. & Knight,T. & Moon,D. & Weinreb,D.: LISP machine progress report. MIT Memo 444, August 1977.

Bawden,D. & Greenblatt,R. & Holloway,J. & Knight,T. & Moon,D. & Weinreb,D.: The LISP machine. In: (Winston & Brown 1979).

Bell, C. & Newell, A.: Computer structures: readings and examples. McGraw Hill, 1971.

Berkling, K.: A computing machine based on tree structures. IEEE Trans. on Computers, Vol. C-20, No. 4, April 1971, 404-418.

Berkling, K.: Reduction languages for reduction machines. GMD Bonn, Internal Report ISF-GMD-76-8, Sept. 1976.

Berkling, K.: Answers to questions on the reduction machine. GMD Bonn, Internal Note, March 1979.

Bobrow, D. & Clark, D.: Compact encodings of list structure. ACM Trans. on Prog. Languages and Systems, 1, 1979, 266-286.

Bobrow, D. & Wegbreit, B.: A model for control structure for artificial intelligence programming languages. Proc. 3rd IJCAI-73, Stanford, August 1973a.

Bobrow, D. & Wegbreit, B.: A model and stack implementation of multiple environments. CACM 16(10), Oct. 1973b.

Boehm, H.-P. & Fischer, H. & Raulefs, P.: CSSA: Language concepts and programming methodology. Proceedings of the Symposium on Artificial Intelligence and Programming Languages. SIGPLAN Notices 12(8), Special Issue, August 1977.

Boley, H.: Five views of FIT programming. Univ. Hamburg, Fachbereich Informatik, IFI-HH-B-57/79, Sept. 1979.

Boulaye, G. & Lewin, D. [Eds.]: Computer architecture. Reidel Publ. Comp., Dordrecht, Boston, 1977.

Brown, P.: Macro processors and techniques for portable software. Wiley & Sons, 1974.

Buchberger, B. & Fegerl, J. & Lichtenberger, F.: Computer trees: a concept for parallel processing. Microprocessors and Microsystems 3(6), July/August 1979.

Burks, A. & Goldstine, H. & von Neumann, J.: Preliminary discussion of the logical design of an electronic computing instrument. Report to the US Army Ordnance Department. Reprinted in: (Bell & Newell 1971).

Carlson, C.: A survey of high-level language computer architecture. In: (Chu 1975).

Chailloux, J.: A VLISP interpreter on the VCMC1 machine. Univ. de Paris VIII - Vincennes, Reprinted in: Greussay, P. & Laubsch, J.: (LISP Bulletin). 2, July 1978.

Chevenance, R.: Design of high level language oriented processors. ACM SIGPLAN Notices, January 1977.

Christaller, T. & Metzing, D.: ATN-Grammatik 2, Einfuehrung, Anwendungen, Weiterentwicklungen. Einhorn-Verlag Berlin, 1979.

Chu, Y. [Ed.]: High-level language computer architecture. Academic Press, New York 1975.

Church, A.: The calculi of lambda conversion. Princeton University Press, 1941.

Despain, A. & Patterson, D.: X-TREE: A tree structured multi-processor computer architecture. SIGARCH 6(7), April 1978.

Dennis, J. & Misunas, D.: A preliminary architecture for a basic data flow processor. Proc. 2nd Annual Symp. Computer Architecture. IEEE Publ. No. 75CH0916-7C, 1975, 126-132.

Deutsch, P.: A LISP machine with very compact programs. Proc. 3rd IJCAI-73, Stanford, August 1973.

Deutsch, P.: Experience with a microprogrammed INTERLISP system. Proc. MICRO-11, Nov. 1978.

Ditzel, D. & Patterson, D.: Retrospective on high-level language computer design. 7th Intern. Symp. Computer Architecture, May 1980.

Doran, R.: Architecture of stack machines. In: (Chu 1975).

Fahlman, S.: NETL: A system for representing and using real-world knowledge. MIT Press, Series in Artificial Intelligence, 1979.

Feldman, J. & Rovner, P.: An Algol-based associative language. CACM 12(8), August 1969, 439-449.

Feustel, E.: On the advantages of tagged architectures. IEEE Trans. Computers C-22, 7, 1973, 644-656.

Fiala, E.: The Maxc systems. Computer 11(5), May 1978.

Fischer, G. & Laubsch, J.: LISP-basierte Programmentwicklungssysteme zur Unterstuetzung des Problemloesungsprozesses. In: Notizen zum Interaktiven Programmieren, Heft 3, FA 2 der GI, Darmstadt, Maerz 1980.

Fischer, H.: A defining VDL-machine for CSSA. Univ. Bonn, Institut fuer Informatik III, Memo SEKI-77-02, 1977.

Fischer, H. & Raulefs, P.: Design rationale for the interactive programming language CSSA for asynchronous multiprocessor systems. Univ. Bonn, Institut fuer Informatik III, SEKI-Projekt, Memo SEKI-BN-79-09, November 1979.

Fournier, S.: The architecture of a grammar-programmable high-level language machine. Ph.D. dissertation, Dept. of Computer and Information Science, The Ohio State University, June 1975.

Friedman, D. & Wise, D.: An environment for multiple-valued recursive procedures. 2me Colloque sur la Programmation, Paris, Springer Verlag, Berlin, 1976.

Friedman, D. & Wise, D.: Aspects of applicative programming for parallel processing. IEEE Trans. Computers 27(4), April 1978.

Gilmore, P.: An abstract computer with a LISP-like machine language without a LABEL operator. In: Braffort, P. & Hirschberg, D. [Eds.]: Computer programming and formal systems. North-Holland 1963, 71-86.

Giloi, W.: Rechnerarchitektur. Informatik Spektrum 3(1), Jan. 1980.

Giloi, W. & Berg, H.: STARLET - an unorthodox concept of a string/array computer. Proc. IFIP Congress-74, Stockholm, August 1974.

Glushkov, V. & Ignatyev, M. & Myasnikov, V. & Torgashev, V.: Recursive machines and computing technology. Proc. IFIP Congress-74, Stockholm, August 1974.

Goto, E.: Monocopy and associative algorithms in an extended LISP. University of Tokyo, Japan, May 1974.

Goto, E. & Ida, T. & Hiraki, K. & Suzuki, M. & Inada, N.: FLATS, a machine for · numerical, symbolic and associative computing. Proc. 6th IJCAI-79, Tokyo, Aug. 1979.

Greenblatt, R.: The LISP machine. MIT, AI Lab., Working Paper 79, Nov. 1974.

Griss, M. & Kessler, R.: REDUCE/1700: A microcoded algebra system. Proc. MICRO-10, 1977.

Griss, M. & Swanson, M.: MBALM/1700: A microprogrammed Lisp machine for the Borroughs B1726. Proc. MICRO-10, 1977.

Guzman, A. & Segovia, R.: A parallel configurable Lisp machine. University of Mexico, 1976.

Haendler, W. [Ed.]: Computer architecture. Workshop of the Gesellschaft fuer Informatik, Erlangen, May 1975, Informatik-Fachberichte Band 4, herausgegeben von W. Brauer im Auftrag der GI, Springer-Verlag 1976.

Helmers, C.: Returning to the tower of Babel, or ... some notes about LISP, languages and other topics ... Editorial, BYTE 4(8), Aug. 1979.

Hewitt, C.: Description and theoretical analysis (using schemas) of PLANNER: A language for proving theorems and manipulating models in a robot. Ph.D. February 1971, MIT.

Hewitt, C.: Viewing control structures as patterns of passing messages. Artificial Intelligence, Vol. 8, No. 3, June 1977.

Hewitt, C. & Bishop, P. & Steiger, R.: A universal modular ACTOR formalism for artificial intelligence. 3rd IJCAI-73, Aug. 1973.

Hodges, D.: IPL-VC, a computer system having the IPL-V instruction set. Argonne Natl. Lab., Appl. Math. Div. Argonne, Illinois, ANL-6888, 1964

Hollaar, L.: Rotating memory processors for the matching of complex textual patterns. Proc. 5th Annual Symp. Computer Architecture, SIGARCH 6(7), April 1978.

Hommes, F.: Simulation einer Reduktionsmaschine. Master-Thesis, Univ. Bonn, April 1975.

Hommes, F.: The internal structure of the reduction machine. GMD Bonn, Internal Report ISF-GMD-77-3, March 1977a.

Hommes, F.: The transformation of LISP programs into programs written in the reduction language. ISF-GMD-77-4, March 1977b.

Jacks, E. [Ed.]: Associative information techniques. Elsevier, New York, 1971.

Jessen, E.: Assoziative Speicherung. Elektronische Datenverarbeitung, Beiheft 5, Vieweg & Sohn, 1965.

Jessen, E.: Architektur digitaler Rechenanlagen. Springer-Verlag, Berlin, Heidelberg, New York, 1975.

Juergensen, H.: Zur Uebersetzbarkeit von Programmiersprachen. GI, 3. Fachtagung ueber Programmiersprachen, Kiel, Maerz 1974.

Kalhoff, B. & Simon, F.: Programmieren in LISP 1.5 - Benutzerhandbuch. Inst. f. Inform. u. Prakt. Math., Universitaet Kiel, Bericht 2/75, Juni 1975.

Keller, R. & Lindstrom, G. & Patil, S.: An architecture for a loosely-coupled parallel processor. Dept. of Comp. Sc., Univ. of Utah, UUCS-78-105, 1978.

Kluge, W.: The architecture of a reduction language machine hardware model. GMD Bonn, ISF-Report 79.03, August 1979.

Knight, T.: The CONS microprocessor. MIT, AI Working paper, No. 80, Nov. 1974.

Kurokawa, T.: LISP activities in Japan. Proc. 6TH IJCAI-79, Tokyo, Aug. 1979.

Laliotis, T.: Architecture of the SYMBOL computer system. In: (Chu 1975).

Landin, P.: The mechanical evaluation of expressions. The Computer Journal, Vol. 6, April 1963 - January 1964, 308-320.

Laubsch, J.: LISP-Aktivitaeten in den USA und Japan. Rundbrief der Fachgruppe Kuenstliche Intelligenz in der Gesellschaft fuer Informatik, Nr. 19, Dez. 1979.

Lea, R.: Associative processing of non-numerical information. In: (Boulaye & Lewin 1977).

Learning Research Group: Personal dynamic media. Xerox PARC, SSL 76-1, 1976.

Lewin, D.: Introduction to associative processors. In: (Boulaye & Lewin 1977).

Love, H. & Savitt, D.: An iterative-cell processor for the ASP language. In: (Jacks 1971).

Luegger, J. & Melenk, H.: Darstellung und Bearbeitung umfangreicher LISP-Programme. Angewandte Informatik, 6, Juni 1973, 257-263.

Lux, A.: Etude d'un modele abstrait pour une machine LISP et de son implementation. These de 3eme Cycle, Univ. de Grenoble, Mars 1975.

Mago, G.: A network of microprocessors to execute reduction languages, Part I. Int. J. Computer and Information Sc. 8(5), 1979.

McCarthy, J. & Abrahams, P. & Edwards, D. & Hart, T. & Levin, M.: LISP 1.5 programmer's manual. MIT Press, Cambridge, Mass., 1962.

McDermott, D.: Very large PLANNER-type data bases. AIM-339, AI Lab., MIT, 1975.

McGill, M. [Ed.]: Third workshop on computer architecture for non-numeric processing. Syracuse Univ., May 1977, SIGARCH 6(2), SIGIR 12(1), SIGMOD 9(2).

Meehan, J.: The new UCI LISP manual. Lawrence Erlbaum Associates 1979.

Minsky, M.: Computation: Finite and infinite machines. Prentice-Hall, London 1967.

Minsky, M.: K-lines: a theory of memory. MIT AI Lab. Memo No. 516, 1979.

Minsky, M. & Papert, S.: On some associative, parallel, and analog computations. In: (Jacks 1971).

Minter, J.: Associative memories and processors: a descriptive appraisal. Univ. of Maryland, Comp. Sc. Center, TR 195, July 1972.

Montangero, C. & Pacini, G. & Turini, F.: MAGMA-LISP: A "machine language" for artificial intelligence. Proc. 4th IJCAI-75, Sept. 1975, 556-561.

Moon, D.: Maclisp reference manual. MIT, Project MAC, April 1974.

Moore II, J.: The INTERLISP virtual machine specification. Xerox PARC, CSL 76-5, September 1976.

Moses, J.: The function of FUNCTION in LISP or why the FUNARG problem should be called the environment problem. SIGSAM Bulletin, July 1970, 13-27.

Moshell, J. & Rothstein, J.: Bus automata and immediate languages. Information and Control 40(1), January 1979.

Mukhopadhyay, A.: Hardware algorithms for nonnumeric computation. Proc. 5th Annual Symp. Computer Architecture, SIGARCH 6(7), April 1978

Myers, G.: Advances in computer architecture. Wiley, New York 1978.

Nagao, M. & Tsujii, J.-I. & Nakajima, K. & Mitamura, K. & Ito, H.: LISP machine NK3 and measurement of its performance. Proc. 6th IJCAI-79, Tokyo, Aug. 1979.

Norman, D. & Rumelhart, D. [Eds.]: Explorations in cognition. Freeman, San Francisco, 1975.

Organick, E.: Computer system organization: the B5700/6700 series. ACM Monograph Series, Academic Press, New York 1973.

Organick, E.: New directions in computer systems architecture. EUROMICRO Journal 5, 1979, 190-202.

Parkami, B.: Associative memories and processors: an overview and selected bibliography. Proc. IEEE 61, 1973, 722-730.

Raulefs, P.: Ergebnisse einer Umfrage zur Ermittlung des Bedarfs an Recheneinrichtungen fuer KI-Forschung in Deutschland. Rundbrief der Fachgruppe Kuenstliche Intelligenz in der Gesellschaft fuer Informatik, Nr. 20, Maerz 1980.

Reynolds, R.: Definitional interpreters for higher order programming languages. ACM Conference Proceedings 1972.

Rice, R. & Smith, W.: SYMBOL - a major departure from classic software dominated von Neumann computing systems. Proc. of the 1971 Spring Joint Computer Conference, Montvale, NJ, AFIPS 1971, 575-587.

Sansonnet, J. & Castan, M. & Percebois, C.: A list-directed architecture. 7th Intern. Symp. Computer Architecture, May 1980.

Schoichet, S.: The LISP machine. Mini-micro systems, June 1978, 68-79.

Shapiro, M.: A SNOBOL machine: a higher-level language processor in a conventional hardware framework. Dig. COMPCON 72, 1972a, 41-44.

Shapiro, M.: A SNOBOL machine: functional architectural concepts of a string processor, Purdue Univ., Lafayette, Indiana, Dissertation, 1972b.

Shaw, J. & Newell, A. & Simon, H. & Ellis, T.: A command structure for complex information processing. Proc. WJCC, 1958, 119-128. Reprinted in: (Bell & Newell 1971).

Simon, F.: Zur Charakterisierung von LISP als ALGOL-aehnliche Programmiersprache mit einem strikt nach dem Kellerprinzip arbeitenden Laufzeitsystem. Inst. f. Inform. u. Prakt. Mathem., Univ. Kiel, Bericht Nr. 2/78, Sept. 1978.

Simon, F. & Trademann, P.: Eine Beziehung zwischen consfreiem LISP und Stackautomaten. Inst. f. Inform. u. Prakt. Mathem., Univ. Kiel, Bericht Nr. 7705, 1977.

Sloman, A. et al.: Requirements for AI research - December 1978, A report to the Interactive Computing Facility Comittee of the Science Research Council, from the Artificial Intelligence Special Interest Group. AISB Quarterly, Issue 33, April 1979.

Snyder, A.: A machine architecture to support an object-oriented language. Lab. for Comp. Sc., MIT, MIT/LCS/TR-209, Ph.D., March 1979.

Steele, G. & Sussman, G.: LAMBDA: The ultimate imperative. MIT, AI. Lab., AI Memo 353, March 1976.

Steele, G. & Sussman, G.: The art of the interpreter or, the modularity complex (Parts zero, one, and two). MIT AI Memo 453, May 1978.

Steele, G. & Sussman, G.: Design of LISP-based processors, or SCHEME: a dielectric LISP, or finite memories considered harmful, or LAMBDA: the ultimate opcode. MIT AI Memo 514, March 1979.

Steiger, R.: Actor machine architecture. M.S. Thesis, MIT, 1974.

Sullivan, H. & Bashkow, T.: A large scale, homogeneous, fully distributed parallel machine, I. Proc. 4th Annual Symp. Computer Architecture, SIGARCH 5 (7), March 1977.

Sullivan, H. & Bashkow, T. & Klappholz, D.: A large scale, homogeneous, fully distributed parallel machine, II. Proc. 4th Annual Symp. Computer Architecture, SIGARCH 5 (7), March 1977.

Sussman, G.: What effect should cheap hardware have on AI research? Proc. 4th AISB-80, Amsterdam, July 1980.

Sussman, G. & McDermott, D.: The CONNIVER reference manual. MIT, AI Lab, Memo 259a, 1974.

Taft, S.: The design of an M6800 LISP interpreter. BYTE 4(8), Aug. 1979.

Taki, K. & Kaneda, Y. & Maekawa, S.: The experimental LISP machine. Proc. 6th IJCAI-79, Tokyo, Aug. 1979.

Teitelman, W.: INTERLISP reference manual. Xerox PARC, 1978.

Treleaven, P. & Mole, G.: A multi-processor reduction machine for user-defined reduction languages. 7th Intern. Symp. Computer Architecture, May 1980.

Vanaken, J. & Zick, G.: The X-PIPE: A pipeline for expression trees. Proc. of the 1978 Conf. on Parallel Processing, 1978.

Vogl-Mildner, K.: Recognizing data- and program-structures in a reduction language. ISF-GMD-78-3, March 1978.

Wegner, P.: Programming languages, information structures, and machine organization. McGraw-Hill, New York, 1968.

Weicker, R.: Turing machines with associative memory access. Automata, Languages and Programming, 2nd Colloquium, Saarbruecken 1974.

Weinreb, D. & Moon, D.: LISP machine manual. Second preliminary version. MIT, AI Lab, 1979.

Williams, R.: A multiprocessing system for the direct execution of LISP. Fourth workshop on computer architecture for non-numeric processing. Syracuse Univ., Aug. 1978. SIGIR 13(2), SIGARCH 7(2), SIGMOD 10(1).

Winston, P. & Brown, R. [Eds.]: Artificial intelligence: an MIT perspective. Vol. 2. The MIT Press, Cambridge, Mass. 1979.

Wortman, D.: A study of language directed computer design. Ph.D. dissertation, Stanford Univ., 1972, Reprinted as report CSRG-20, Univ. of Toronto, 1972.

Zisman, M.: Use of production systems for modelling asynchronous, concurrent processes. In: Waterman, D. & Hayes-Roth, F. [Eds.]: Pattern-directed inference systems. Academic Press, 1978

Zuse, K.: Die Feldrechenmaschine. MTW-Mitteilungen V, 1958, 213-220.

Computing Facilities for AI:

A Survey of Present and Near-Future Options

Scott Fahlman
Department of Computer Science
Carnegie-Mellon University
Pittsburgh, Pennsylvania 15213

At the recent AAAI conference at Stanford, it became apparent that many new AI research centers are being established around the country in industrial and governmental settings and in universities that have not paid much attention to AI in the past. At the same time, many of the established AI centers are in the process of converting from older facilities, primarily based on Decsystem-10 and Decsystem-20 machines, to a variety of newer options. At present, unfortunately, there is no simple answer to the question of what machines, operating systems, and languages a new or upgrading AI facility should use, and this situation has led to a great deal of confusion and anxiety on the part of those researchers and administrators who are faced with making this choice. In this article I will survey the major alternatives available at present and those that are clearly visible on the horizon, and I will try to indicate the advantages and disadvantages of each for AI work. This is mostly information that we have gathered at CMU in the course of planning for our own future computing needs, but the opinions expressed are my own.

Before going on, I should note this discussion will be limited to those machines and systems that are (or will be) in active use at one or more of the major established centers of AI research in the United States. This limitation is deliberate: in my opinion, it would be unwise for a new center to start from scratch with a machine or system that has not previously been used for serious AI research. To do so would be to take on a tool-building task that would delay the beginning of serious AI research for several years. Using an odd machine also tends to isolate the research group from the rest of the AI community. It seems a much wiser course to tie one's center in with others, so that tools and results can be shared.

Of course, this does not mean that one cannot do AI research on practically any machine if there is no other choice. Good AI research has been done on machines from Univac, Burroughs, Honeywell, and even IBM, using unbelievably hostile operating systems, and in languages ranging from Basic to PL-I. If corporate policy or lack of independent funds forces some such choice on you, it is not the end of the world. It should be noted, however, that the lack of first-rate facilities is very likely to lead to a lack of first-rate people, and will have a serious impact on the productivity of the people you do manage to attract. In this article, then, I will concentrate on the choices that might be made by centers that have a free choice in the matter and the funds to obtain facilities that will be dedicated to AI use.

One other warning must be given: this material will become obsolete very quickly. If you should encounter this article a year after publication, much of it will be out of date. If the time is two years after publication, it will be totally worthless.

Basic Computing Needs

What does an AI researcher want from his computing facility? What will make him most productive? Setting aside, for now, the very specialized needs of those doing signal processing or robotics, the needs of the rest are relatively straightforward to state, if difficult to satisfy. In fact, the needs of the AI researcher are not very different from the needs of any other researcher in computer science, except that facility-related problems seem to become acute in AI a few years sooner than they are felt in other research areas. The considerations are roughly as follows:

☐ AI programs tend to be very large because they contain, in one form or another, a lot of knowledge. It follows, then, that any machine used for AI must provide a large virtual address space in order to insulate the researcher from having to think about how to chop up his task into smaller tidbits and overlays. A 32-bit address space is comfortable for the forseeable future; a 24-bit (to the 32-bit word) address space is adequate for the next couple of years for most purposes; the 18-bit address space of the Dec-10/20 series is woefully inadequate and has seriously impeded the recent progress of AI. Don't even think about using anything smaller.

☐ Most AI programs burn a lot of cycles. If your machine is slow or is too heavily loaded, your high-powered researchers will be spending all of their time waiting for something to happen on their screens. They will spend this time plotting against the management and reading the help-wanted ads. To pack too many researchers onto a time-shared machine is a move of very dubious economic value.

☐ The operating system must be friendly. For AI, friendliness means flexibility. Protection and quotas must not get in the way, the utilities must be screen-oriented rather than paper-oriented, documentation must be on-line and easy to use, and individual users must have easy access to multiple processes so that some of the waiting time can be spent editing or doing other useful work. Most important, the system should stay up: when you have invested an hour of CPU time and eight hours of your own time in a computation, a crash can be very irritating. Since most AI researchers are experienced programmers, a user interface that is easy for beginners to use is relatively less important than on a machine for general use, but remember that you may want to export your results to an environment with less sophisticated users.

☐ Though AI researchers spend more of their time computing than most people in computer science, they still spend most of their time editing programs, editing text, formatting documents, and communicating with one another via computer mail. First-rate facilities for all these activities must be provided. My own working definition of "first-rate", among systems available today, would be the combination of Emacs and Scribe. Tastes may vary in this, but it is clear that the use of a teletype-oriented editor or a primitive text-processing system can waste a great deal of your researchers' valuable time.

☐ The programming done in AI is almost always of an experimental, evolutionary nature, and it is concerned mostly with symbol manipulation rather than arithmetic. This argues very strongly for the use of Lisp over other currently-available languages. An AI research center *must* provide a well-developed, well-maintained Lisp system; other languages are optional. The use of such languages as Sail for AI research seems to be declining rapidly now that good Lisps are widely available. It may be, as some researchers argue, that Smalltalk-like languages are the wave of the future, but that wave is still well over the horizon for most of us.

As I said, these requirements are simple to state, but hard and expensive to realize. To equip an AI center in a way that will help you to attract the best people, you should probably plan to spend something like $50K-$70K per researcher in computing equipment. (For serious work in robotics, plan to spend a lot more.) An established center can get by with less, but if you are trying to start a new center it will be very hard to recruit people to work with inferior facilities. There are many examples of well-intentioned efforts that never reached critical mass in people because the computing environment was wrong.

In providing these facilities, there are two basic approaches: time-sharing and the use of powerful personal machines connected by a high-bandwidth network. Time-sharing has been the mainstay of the field for over a decade and, as I write this, is still the only option available from commercial sources. The personal computing option is expected by most leaders in the field to be the dominant force of the next decade, starting very soon, but it will be a year or two before it is a practical option for users who do not want to do a lot of the development themselves. That is one of the reasons why the field is currently so unsettled: users must acquire enough time-sharing capacity to meet their present needs, but they want to save enough equipment money to allow for a quick move into the personal-computing world as soon as this becomes practical. We will consider the options in both of these worlds in the following sections.

Time-Sharing Options

Two families of time-sharing machines are used by the

vast majority of AI researchers: the Decsystem-20 (and its predecessor, the Decsystem-10), and the Vax, both products of the Digital Equipment Corporation. As I said earlier, it is possible to do AI on other machines, but anyone with a choice in the matter should probably stick with these two hardware families.

The Decsystem-20 Family

The Decsystem-20, available in a range of sizes, provides a mature programming environment and by far the largest selection of useful software. Unfortunately, an 18-bit address space is woven deeply into the instruction set of the Dec-20 family. When this family began with the old PDP-6, this must have seemed like an immense address space but, as we noted earlier, it is just too small to meet the needs of AI researchers in the 1980's. Some of the newer models of the Dec-20 extend the address space beyond 18 bits, but the additional address space is awkward to use and very little of the existing software can take advantage of it.

Despite the inadequate address space, there are some situations in which the Dec-20 may be the option of choice. In a crash project that will not be needing more than the available address space, the user amenities on the Dec-20 make it very attractive. In a situation where the research will consist mainly of using and extending existing AI systems, and where these systems run on the Dec-20, it is obviously the machine to use. In a large center, it may be advantageous to have users edit, process text, and do most of their program development on a large Dec-20 system, while big Lisp jobs are sent to one or more Vax machines for service. This option requires a very good local network if it is to be successful.

If you do use the Dec-20 hardware, you have a choice of two operating systems from DEC: Tops-10 and Tops-20. Tops-10 is an outmoded system that is totally unsuited to the needs of AI. Tops-20, based on the Tenex system developed at Bolt, Beranek, and Newman, is clearly superior since it provides demand paging, tree structured directories, multiple processes per user, flexible terminal handling, and the friendliest user-interface of any system that I have seen. (Some of these features have been tacked onto Tops-10 as afterthoughts, but in very clumsy forms.) All Tops-10 software runs on Tops-20, but the converse is definitely not true. Tops-20 users can run Interlisp, Maclisp, Emacs, Scribe, Tex, and most of the major AI programs that have been developed in the past decade. Some sites still run the older Tenex system; this is almost equivalent to Tops-20 in its features and available software, but users are on their own for maintenance.

While DEC states that they are not trying to phase out the Dec-20 in favor of the Vax, their pricing structure, especially for main memory, tends to make the Dec-20

family relatively unattractive. An option that some users may want to consider is a line of machines from Foonly, Incorporated. These machines execute the Dec-20 instruction set and can therefore run most of the same software. They tend to be substantially less expensive than the comparable machines from DEC, but they must run Tenex rather than Tops-20, and maintenance may be a problem in some areas. If you have the staff to do some of your own hardware and software maintenance, Foonly seems like a good option; if not, you should carefully explore the maintenance issues before buying.

In the Tops-20 world there are two major Lisp systems in use, both with fanatical adherents: Interlisp, developed at BBN and Xerox PARC, and Maclisp, developed at MIT. Interlisp contains a large number of built-in facilities to provide the user with a total programming environment -- arguably the best programming environment ever provided for any computer language. Everything from a built-in program editor to an indexing facility to a spelling corrector is provided as part of the system. All of this is documented and centrally maintained. Maclisp proponents point out that this wealth of features in Interlisp can often be more confusing than helpful and that little address space is left over for the users' programs.

Maclisp is a much leaner (some would say more primitive) system, in which efficiency has received the primary emphasis. Maclisp's compiler is able to produce very efficient fast-loading code, especially for arithmetic, which has traditionally been a weak area for Lisp. Many of Interlisp's more complex features are available in Maclisp as optional, user-loadable packages, but these are not considered part of the Maclisp system itself. Maclisp code is normally edited externally in the Emacs editor, which knows about Lisp syntax and pretty-printing; a special linkage between the two systems makes it easy to alter individual function definitions in the middle of a run. This external editing style has some advantages in dealing with comments and macros in the Lisp source; it can be awkward to handle these in an internal S-expression editor. It is also argued that it is easier for users to edit Lisp with the same editor that they use for everything else. Since several Tops-20 systems are now in use at MIT, I would expect future maintenance of Tops-20 Maclisp to be on a par with Interlisp maintenance. Documentation for Maclisp has been scandalously poor in the past, but the situation seems to be improving.

I have an opinion in the Maclisp vs. Interlisp debate, but I will not express it here. Both systems are very good programming environments. The dialect you use will be determined by the tastes of your people (a strong function of where they were educated) and by the language used by any collaborators you may have at other sites. It is relatively easy to transport most code between the two systems; it is harder to move users from one system to the other, since the user environments are very different.

The Vax Family

Digital Equipment's Vax family of computers is a newer design than the Dec-10/20 series, and its 32-bit virtual addressing solves the space problem for the forseeable future. It would appear that the Vax is destined to be the next major time-sharing machine for most of the computer science research community, including AI. If personal computing develops as quickly many of us believe it will, the Vax may well be the last time-sharing system that is in common use in the research community. At present, however, the Vax world is lacking many of the software amenities that are available on the Dec-20. The software situation on the Vax is being improved rapidly as Vaxes come into common use at major research sites. At some point, perhaps a year or so in the future, the Vax will become a nicer machine to work on than the Dec-20. Given comparable software, the Vax's large address space will certainly make it a superior machine for AI.

There are two major operating systems available for the Vax: the VMS system, supplied by DEC, and the Unix system, supplied by Bell Labs but extensively modified by members of the ARPA-sponsored research community. A third option, the Eunice package from SRI, is an emulator which disguises VMS to look like Unix to users and to programs.

DEC's VMS system is a curious mixture of strengths and weaknesses. Some of the system's internal mechanisms for paging, process scheduling and switching, and buffered disk I/O are very good, and are to some extent tunable to meet the needs of a particular installation. Unfortunately, the face that this system presents to users is an unpleasant one, obviously meant to appeal to the Fortran/Cobol market and not to those users who want a modern, flexible environment for editing and program development. Users can run only one job at a time, must contend with a very clumsy system of quotas and restrictions, must do all their I/O through a complex Cobol-ish record management system, and must deal with terminal drivers and system utilities that are strongly oriented toward the use of old-fashioned line editors. VMS is a large and complex system written mostly in assembler, and the sources for the system are expensive to obtain. This means that it is hard for users to modify the system except in the ways that DEC anticipated. Many of the VMS system's problems require only minor fixes, but users will have trouble making such fixes and DEC moves very slowly on such matters.

Unix also has its problems. The system was developed on the PDP-11 many years ago, and was moved to the Vax without much modification by Bell Labs. The system is full of concessions to the PDP-11's tiny address space and to the printing-terminal mentality that seems to have permeated Bell Labs until very recently. However, since it is very simple and is implemented in C, the Unix system is relatively easily modified to meet the needs of any given site or the opportunities presented by a new machine. It was largely because of this flexibility that Vax/Unix was chosen over VMS for use in the ARPA-sponsored VLSI and Image Understanding projects. This choice, in turn, has influenced many other research efforts to use Unix as well, and to try to coordinate the changes and improvements that they make.

A group at the University of California at Berkeley has taken the lead in this effort by adding demand paging and many other useful features to Vax/Unix. This group is responsible for VI, probably the best screen editor that is currently available on the Vax, though it lacks the flexibility of Emacs. They are also responsible for Franz Lisp, a nearly-compatible version of Maclisp that is written in C. At present, this is the only serious Lisp that runs on the Vax. Franz Lisp is still experiencing some growing pains and bugs, but its users at CMU seem to find it livable in its present state. It is slower than Maclisp on a comparable Dec-20, but it does make use of the Vax's large address space.

As I said, the Vax/Unix software world is improving rapidly. Franz Lisp and the Berkeley pager are being worked on to improve their efficiency. A group at USC/ISI is working on an Interlisp system for Vax/Unix, and expects to have a version available by the end of 1981. Scribe has just been moved to Vax/Unix, and a group at CMU has implemented an inter-process communication protocol that solves some long-standing difficulties with Unix pipes. In my opinion, the major items still missing from Vax/Unix are an editor with the power and flexibility of Emacs, a tree-structured information system to replace the present clumsy online manual, and a more intelligible interface to the operating system and the assorted utilities. (For some reason there is a tradition on Unix that programs should have two-letter names and meaningless single-character option switches. This was ugly but tolerable on a simple minicomputer system; it is quickly becoming intolerable in a diverse, software-rich research environment.)

Meanwhile, back in the Vax/VMS world, a group at MIT is working on NIL, a reimplementation of Maclisp with many added features. An emulator for NIL is now running on top of Maclisp, and the Vax/VMS version is nearing completion. The system may be ready for outside users in six months or so according to its developers. A version of EMACS is being written in NIL, and should be ready whenever NIL itself is. The NIL project has been plagued by delays, but when NIL is done it will offer more features and will probably be faster than Franz Lisp. Since NIL is a superset of Maclisp, it should be easy to move code from Maclisp or Franz Lisp into NIL.

The Eunice system from SRI is an attempt to get the best of both worlds by emulating the Berkeley-modified Unix system on VMS. I have not yet had a chance to observe Eunice first-hand, but it is said by its developers to run all Unix software without significant modification, and to do so at higher speed than on true Unix because of VMS's superior paging and file I/O. VMS and Eunice users can coexist on the same machine. Eunice is running now and has already been used to make Franz Lisp available to the VMS world. If all of these claims are true (and I have no reason to doubt them) then Eunice appears to be the best system for most users of the Vax: it is faster than real Unix and gives its users access to software developed for either of the other two systems. Unix retains some advantages in the area of user modifiability and simplicity, for users who need that.

In summary, I would say that Eunice or Berkeley Unix on the Vax looks like the right combination for most new AI centers to use. The Dec-20 is is a more comfortable system to use at present, but its address-space problem is fatal in the long run, and the Vax software situation is improving rapidly.

Personal-Computing Options

Time-sharing is based on the assumption that computers powerful enough to be useful for research, especially AI research, are so expensive that they must be shared among many users. Advancing technology is rendering this assumption obsolete. Every year the price of computers and memories comes down and personnel costs go up. The task of the past two decades was to find ways to use every precious computer cycle for productive work; the task of the 80's is to find ways to improve the researcher's productivity, even if some computer cycles are thrown away in the process. This change in the relative costs of machines and people provides the impetus for the move to powerful personal computers for AI research. The compromises inherent in time-sharing are just too wasteful of scarce human resources.

Two major research centers, Xerox PARC and the MIT Artificial Intelligence Laboratory, have taken the lead in exploring this new world using machines that they have built themselves, the Dorado and the Lisp Machine, respectively. From these two efforts, and from other efforts that are starting elsewhere, a consistent picture of the next generation of AI machines is emerging. Their features include the following:

- ☐ Each user has a machine whose speed is at least comparable to that of KA-10 processor, the workhorse time-sharing machine of an earlier era.

- ☐ Each machine has a high-resolution raster-scanned display, a keyboard, and a pointing device such as a "mouse". A color display and audio I/O are optional.

- ☐ Each machine has something like a megabyte of main memory and 100 megabytes of local disk storage, which is used as swapping space to provide a large virtual memory.

- ☐ The machines provide a large user-writable microstore, which is used to provide support for graphics, high-level languages, and sometimes to accelerate the user's critical inner loops.

- ☐ All of the machines are connected to one another by a high-bandwidth network -- an Ethernet or something comparable. This network also connects the individual machines to the printers, file-storage machines, and other shared resources.

The last component, the high-speed network, is an essential component of this technology. An important feature of the computing environments that were developed on time-sharing systems was the easy communication and the sharing of information and files among users. The high-speed network, along with appropriate software, allows us to bring this same ease of communication and sharing to the personal-computer world. It also allows for the sharing of the items that are still too expensive to replicate: printers, file systems, perhaps even a Cray-1 for the occasional job that wants to crunch lots of numbers.

By moving our research to personal computers, we obtain a number of advantages:

- ☐ Large, cycle-intensive programs can be run efficiently. In a time-sharing system, it is possible to meet the demands of the big AI programs or of a lot of users doing interactive editing, but it is very hard to satisfy both groups. On a personal machine, the system can be tuned to the task at hand.

- ☐ An interactive user interface of very high quality can be provided. This is due to the high-resolution display on each machine and to the instant availability of enough processing power to update that display when necessary. It is hard to provide such timely bursts of processing on a time-shared machine.

- ☐ The user has access to the full power of his machine, no matter what other users are doing. No more waiting until 4 a.m. to get cycles.

- ☐ Reliability is an inherent part of the personal machine environment. A failure in any one machine cannot bring down the others. The critical demonstration or production run can simply be moved to another machine.

- ☐ Some AI work requires the use of special, experimental processing hardware for such things as image-processing, knowledge-base searching, control of manipulators, and complex graphics. Such devices can easily be added to a personal machine, and can get the instant service that they may require. It can be very awkward, both technically and politically, to add experimental devices to a heavily used time-shared machine.

□ The computing environment can be extended in smaller increments than is possible on time-shared systems. If a few new researchers join the group, a few new machines can be added.

□ Any AI application systems that are developed on personal machines can be exported easily, simply by having the customers buy the same machines that they were used to develop the program.

Now for the bad news: as of today, you cannot go out and buy a personal machine of the typed described above. To date, the only research groups who have been able to use such machines are those who have built machines for themselves. Such machines will be marketed soon, but none have yet been delivered. So, despite all of the advantages noted above, you will have to live with time-sharing for another year or two. Still, it would be a mistake not to keep a close eye on the development of personal machines for AI, so that you can jump in when the time is right. In the remainder of this section, I will describe what I feel are the efforts that should be watched most closely.

Xerox PARC began the new era of personal computing with the development of the ALTO, a nice machine for some uses but too small for use in AI except as a graphics terminal. Xerox has recently developed a much more powerful machine called the Dorado. This machine is implemented in ECL and runs both Interlisp and Smalltalk. A slower and less expensive machine, the Dolphin, runs much of the same code as the Dorado and is coming into widespread use within Xerox. This machine is near the lower boundary of usefulness for AI— reasonable for many applications, but not for the large, cycle-intensive ones. Xerox seems to have no interest in producing the Dorado for outside sale, and is still trying to decide whether to sell any Dolphins to outsiders. For the near future, then, it appears that Xerox's contribution to AI and personal computing will be mostly in the form of ideas, not hardware.

The only other personal machine that has seen active service in AI is the Lisp Machine (sometimes called the CADR, since it is the second iteration of the design) from the MIT AI Lab. These machines have been in active use for about two years at MIT; to date, about a dozen have been built. The Lisp Machine is implemented in TTL, and it runs Lisp programs at a speed that is somewhere between that of a dedicated KA-10 and a KL-10. The Lisp system used on this machine is based on Maclisp, but it has many advanced features that depend critically on the Lisp Machine's micro-codability. In fact, aside from about 9000 words of custom

microcode, all of the code on the Lisp Machine is written in Lisp. The software includes a complete Lisp system with debugging aids and a compiler, graphics support, an Emacs-like editor, support for Smalltalk-like object-oriented programming, and a micro-compiler for turning some of the user's time-critical functions into Lisp Machine microcode.

After a number of false starts, there is now a company that is preparing to build and sell the Lisp Machine commercially. In fact, there are two such companies, reflecting a schism within the group at MIT. One company, Symbolics Incorporated, has signed up most of the Lisp Machine crew at MIT as employees or consultants and has re-engineered the MIT design for easier construction and maintenance. They expect to ship their first machines in the summer of 1981 for about $150K to $80K, is planned for introduction sometime around the summer of 1982; it is this machine that Symbolics hopes to sell in large quantities. Symbolics has a license to market all of the current MIT software, and plans to augment this software considerably in the coming months. The company appears to be quite well financed, with considerable business and manufacturing expertise, and the chances for their survival appear to be high.

The second company, Lisp Machines Incorporated, is primarily the creation of Richard Greenblatt, one of the key members of the original Lisp Machine group at MIT. LMI plans to offer the Lisp Machine and its software, exactly as it exists in the current MIT version, for about $80K per machine. This leaves LMI with a considerably smaller margin of profit than is traditional in the computer industry; they plan to compensate for this by requiring partial payment in advance and by selling mostly to "sophisticated" users who can handle some of the hardware maintenance themselves. LMI has received some firm orders and hopes to ship their first machine in February, 1981.

Three Rivers Computer Corporation has recently begun to ship their PERQ machines. These machines, priced around $30K-$35K, are considerably smaller than those discussed above, which makes them attractive as editing and office machines but not adequate for serious AI research. To be more specific, the PERQ at present offers only a 256K byte main memory, of which nearly 100K is dedicated to the display. The largest available local disk is is 24M bytes. The microstore is only 4K instructions, compared with 16K of more efficient microstore on the Lisp Machine. There is no hardware page map on the PERQ; memory mapping must be done in microcode. Three Rivers had plans to correct all of these deficiencies sometime in the future, but at present they are very busy trying to produce enough of the current machines to meet the demand for them. Whenever these extensions arrive, the PERQ will become a more interesting option for AI applications.

A group at Bolt, Beranek, and Newman has developed a personal machine called the Jericho. This machine is some-what less powerful than the Lisp Machine, but it is more powerful than the current PERQ: it can take any amount of main memory from .5 Megabytes to 2.5 Megabytes, comes with a 200 Megabyte disk, and offers a variety of display options, both monochromatic and color. The machine contains a hardware page map, but this is a simple, single-level map and provides only a 22 bit virtual address space (to the 32-bit word) in the current model. These machines are in use within BBN running PASCAL, and an Interlisp implementation is running but not yet polished. BBN will probably market these machines outside the company within the coming year, but this decision is still up in the air, as is the price.

The Spice project at CMU is an attempt to develop an integrated personal computing environment that will serve the needs of our entire computer science effort, including the traditional areas of CS as well as AI and robotics. One of the novel features of this work is our determination to use only commercially available hardware, and to make our software system portable to any machine that fits our general vision of what personal computers should be. In this way we hope to be able to take advantage of whatever hardware is most attractive at any given time, and to mix different hardware options in an integrated system that presents a consistent environment to the user. Another novel feature is that Spice supports multiple languages and multiple processes on each machine, and ties processes on the same or different machines together with a very flexible set of inter-process communication protocols. When it is complete, Spice will be a relatively portable software system containing a complete Lisp environment (similar to but simpler than Lisp Machine Lisp), a complete Ada programming environment, editors and text processing systems, a multi-media message system, software for a central file system, an extensive user-interface package, and many other features.

Our initial implementation of Spice will be on the PERQ, despite its present limitations for AI work. By the end of 1981, we hope to have a usable first version of Spice running, with an essentially complete (if rather slow) Lisp environment; development and improvement of Spice will continue for several years beyond that date. We plan to move Spice to a more powerful machine, more suitable for AI work, as soon as a few copies of such a machine are available to us. Some companies have expressed a desire to follow our work on Spice very closely; an industrial affiliates program is being set up facilitate the sharing of information with these firms.

A few words are perhaps in order about the specialized needs of workers in robotics and vision. Even more than most AI researchers, these people need the real-time response, the microcodability, and the good graphics interface that is provided by the personal machines. Until such systems can be obtained, the only good solution is to dedicate an entire Vax to the people who are doing this work, and to attach some sort of frame-buffer display to the Vax for work in vision. In the past, some of this work was done on dedicated PDP-11 systems or on local

PDP-11's tied to a larger time-shared processor. Such solutions are extremely awkward in practice. In addition, of course, robotics research requires a first-rate machine shop and an electronics shop, with people who know how to use these facilities properly.

One final consideration raised by the introduction of personal machines is the building that you put them in. For any AI research, it is important to have a building that is available (lit and heated or cooled) 24 hours per day, 7 days per week -- even when the contention for cycles is eliminated, many AI people will be nocturnal. But with personal machines on the way, it is important to have a building with adequate wiring and cooling throughout, and not just in a central machine room. It is not yet clear whether the personal machines will work best in offices, in clusters associated with a group of offices, or in a machine room with only the displays distributed around the building, but it would be unwise to lock out any of these options at this point. Rumor has it that IBM is piping Freon for cooling into every office in their new buildings -- can liquid helium pipes be far behind?

For More Information...

This brief survey has necessarily been superficial. Except in a few cases, I have not even tried to indicate prices, configurations, warranty and service information, or waiting times for delivery. In addition, users who are counting on items that are not available now will want to contact the organizations building these items for updates on the progress of the item in question. The following list should help you to find the right person to talk to, or at least someone who can tell you who the right person is. For readers on the Arpanet, I have also included netmail addresses where these exist. ■

For Vax/Unix:
Professor Robert Fabry
Department of Electrical Engineering
  and Computer Science
University of California
Berkeley, California 94720
(FABRY @ BERKELEY)

For Foonly machines:
Foonly, Incorporated
999 Independence Ave.
Mountain View, Ca. 94043
(415) 969-7815

For Franz Lisp:
Professor Richard Fateman
Department of Electrical Engineering
  and Computer Science
University of California
Berkeley, California 94720
(FATEMAN @ BERKELEY)

For Decsystem-20, Tops-20, Vax, and VMS:
Consult your friendly local DEC salesperson.
Interlisp is available through DECUS.

For Interlisp on VAX:
Mel Pirtle
University of Southern California
Information Sciences Institute
4676 Admiralty Way
Marina del Rey, California 90291
(PIRTLE @ ISIB)

For Maclisp and NIL:
Jon L. White
MIT Laboratory for Computer Science
545 Technology Square
Cambridge, Mass. 02139
(JONL @ MIT-MC)

For Eunice:
David Kashtan (technical questions)
Chuck Untulis (administrative questions)
SRI International
Computer Resources
333 Ravenswood Ave.
Menlo Park, California 94025
(KASHTAN @ SRI-KL, UNTULIS @ SRI-KL)

For Lisp Machines:

Russell Nofsker	Steve Wyle
Symbolics, Incorporated	Lisp Machines, Incorporated
605 Hightree Road	163 N. Mansfield Ave.
Santa Monica, Ca. 90402	Los Angeles, Ca. 90036
(213) 459-6040	(213) 938-8888

For PERQs:
Three Rivers Computer Corporation
720 Gross St.
Pittsburgh, Pa. 15224
(412) 621-6250

For Jericho:
Jim Calvin
Bolt, Beranek, and Newman
50 Moulton St.
Cambridge, Mass. 02138
(617) 491-1850 x4615
CALVIN BBN-TENEXG

For Spice:
Scott E. Fahlman
Department of Computer Science
Carnegie-Mellon University
Schenley Park
Pittsburgh, Pa. 15213
(FAHLMAN @ CMUA)

THE NEW GENERATION OF COMPUTER ARCHITECTURE

Philip C. Treleaven

Computing Laboratory,
University of Newcastle upon Tyne,
Newcastle upon Tyne, England

ABSTRACT

Four major areas of research are involved in attempting to identify the fifth generation of computers (cir. 1990). The investigation of: knowledge processing systems, data and demand driven computers, integrating communications and computers, and VLSI processor architectures. From these four areas, two approaches for the fifth generation are emerging: one "revolutionary" - a parallel logic machine supporting knowledge processing applications, and the other "evolutionary" - a decentralised control flow system consisting of a network of heterogeneous processors. This paper describes the above four areas of research and discusses how their computing technologies are converging to produce fifth generation computers. It then contrasts the revolutionary logic machine approach adopted by Japan's Fifth Generation Project, and favoured by the artificial intelligence community, with the evolutionary control flow computer approach favoured by the data communications and microelectronics communities.

1. INTRODUCTION

Since the International Conference in Tokyo in October 1981 when Japan launched its National Fifth Generation Project [10,17] there has been a growing acceptance in the computing science community that the traditional sequential control flow computers will be superceded in the 1990's by a new generation of general-purpose computers. The current approach adopted by Japan's Project, and one favoured by the artificial intelligence community, may be viewed as a parallel logic machine supporting knowledge-based expert systems applications [10,18]. However could the Japanese be right in their Project's aims but wrong in their logic machine approach?

Many factors support the adoption of a radically new generation of general-purpose computers. Firstly, computing is moving from a sequential, centralised world to a parallel, decentralised world in which large numbers of computers are to be programmed to work together in computing systems.

Secondly, the handling of non-numerical data such as sentences, symbols, speech, graphics and images is becoming increasing important. Thirdly, the processing tasks performed by computers are becoming more "intelligent", moving from scientific calculations and data processing, to artificial intelligence applications. Lastly, today's computers are still based on the thirty-year-old von Neumann architecture; essentially all that has happened is that the software systems have been repeatedly extended to cope with the increasingly sophisticated applications.

Important technological and social factors must also be considered. In technology, various separate areas of computing research are on the threshold of major advances [18]:

- artificial intelligence - methodologies to express "knowledge" and to infer from this knowledge, as seen in expert systems; and human-oriented input-output in natural languages, speech and pictures.

- software engineering - new programming languages and computational models; and programming environments building upon systems such as UNIX.

- computer architectures - distributed architectures supporting computer networks; parallel architectures giving high-speed computers for numerical calculations; and VLSI architectures to make full use of the potential of VLSI technology.

- VLSI technology - VLSI computer aided design systems including new methods for semi-automatic design of logic circuits; and new devices such as those using Gallium Arsenide and Josephson Junctions.

For social factors we should notice the progress of computing from scientific applications in the 1950's, through industrial and commercial applications in the 60's and 70's, and into consumer usage in the 80's and 90's. This marks the movement of the "focal-point" of computing from the current commercial applications into consumer applications. Thus, fifth generation computers are regarded as forming the corner-stone of so-called "intelligent" consumer electronics - sophisticated televisions, video recorders and learning aids etc. - the next

"The New Generation of Computer Architecture" by P.C. Treleaven from *The Proceedings of the 10th Annual International Symposium on Computer Architecture*, June 1983, pages 402-409. Copyright 1983, Association for Computing Machinery, Inc., reprinted by permission.

generation of wealth creating consumer products [10,12].

The implication of all these factors taken together is that von Neumann (control flow) computers, originally designed in the 1950´s for scientific computing, are no longer adequate for computation and that for the fifth generation a radical change in the theoretical concepts underlying computers is required. There are four major areas of research involved in attempting to identify this new generation of computers, namely the investigation of:

1. knowledge processing systems which embody "knowledge" bases and support problem-solving and inference functions;

2. data driven and demand driven computers that utilise parallelism with the aim of supporting novel (very high level) forms of programming;

3. communications & computers representing the fusion of wide-area networks, local area networks, and parallel computer architectures.

4. general-purpose and special-purpose processors specifically aimed at exploiting very large scale integration (VLSI).

Any one of these four research areas could provide the new generation of computers. But each area´s view of future computers seems very different, thus significantly affecting the style of future systems. Below, we examine each of these areas and assess their likely impact on the fifth generation.

2. KNOWLEDGE PROCESSING SYSTEMS

Knowledge information processing systems and processors are to support knowledge-based expert systems [3,4,21]. Knowledge-based systems embody modules of organised knowledge concerning specific areas of human expertise and support sophisticated problem-solving and inference functions, for the purpose of rendering the users intelligent advice on one or other specialised topics. An example would be a medical diagnosis system where a diagnosis is made in the same way as a physician, a surgeon, and a patient might co-operate to make a diagnosis. Knowledge in expert systems is often organised into IF-THEN rules of the form [3]:

```
IF     condition_1 and
       condition_2 and
       . . .
       condition_n

THEN   implication (with significance)
```

where if all the conditions are true then the implication is true, with an associated significance factor.

Two other important ingredients of knowledge processing systems are human-oriented input-output, and very high-level programming. Human-oriented input-output covers man-computer communication in natural language, speech, and picture images so

that information can be exchanged in ways natural to humans. Very high level programming languages provide improved programming methodologies, the best examples being logic (e.g. PROLOG) and functional (e.g. Pure LISP) languages. For example, in a PROLOG program [5,8] statements are relations of a restricted form called "clauses", and the execution of such a program is a suitably controlled logical deduction from the clauses forming the program. The following program [5]:

```
father (bill, john).
father (john, tom).
grandfather(X, Z)  :-  father(X, Y), father(Y, Z).
```

consists of three clauses. The first two defines that bill is the father of john, and john is the father of tom. The third relation uses variables X,Y,Z to express the rule that X is the grandfather of Z, if X is the father of Y and Y is the father of Z. Questions may be asked of the program, such as is john the father of tom:

```
father (john, tom)?
```

to which the machine would answer:

```
yes
```

or, using variables, WHO is the grandfather of tom:

```
grandfather (WHO, tom)?
```

to which it would respond:

```
WHO = bill
```

Knowledge processing systems are viewed as comprising three component machines [10,17]:

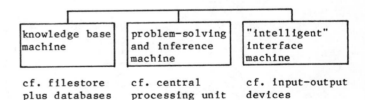

Figure 1: Knowledge Processing System

These machines, though serving specialised roles, will be linked by a common machine language and architecture usually thought of as being logic [10,18]. Knowledge processing systems, namely a parallel logic computer supporting knowledge-based applications, represents the artificial intelligence (AI) community´s view of future computers.

3. DATA DRIVEN AND DEMAND DRIVEN COMPUTERS

Data driven and demand driven computers [14] are machines that utilise parallelism with the aim of supporting very high-level forms of programming languages. They may be envisaged as "mainframe" (e.g. IBM 370) computers built from identical, powerful microcomputers, whose instruction execution is based on a parallel alternative to the traditional sequential control flow architecture. Various pairings of novel programming language styles and parallel architectures are being investigated [14]. Firstly, single-assignment languages (e.g. ID, LUCID, VAL, VALID) with data flow architectures. In a data flow computer the availability of input operands triggers the execution of the instruction which consumes the inputs. Secondly, applicative languages (e.g. Pure LISP, SASL, FP) with reduction architectures. In a reduction computer the requirement for a result triggers the execution of the instruction that will generate the value. Thirdly, object-oriented languages (e.g. SMALLTALK) with actor architectures. In an actor computer the arrival of a message for an instruction causes the instruction to execute.

As an illustration of these parallel computers we will briefly examine single-assignment and data flow. Single assignment languages are based on a rule stating: a variable may appear on the left-handside of only one statement in a program fragment. This allows the data dependencies in a program to be easily detectable and so statements, as below, may be specified in any order.

$$a := x * y$$
$$x := b + 1$$
$$y := b - c$$

These single-assignment statements would be represented by the following data flow machine instructions:

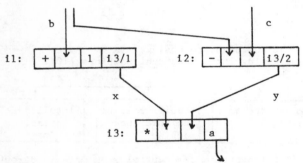

Figure 2: Data Flow Program

The most important properties of data flow are that instructions pass their results directly to all the consuming instructions and that an instruction is executed when it has received all its inputs - properties that affect the general-purpose nature of data flow. Since each architecture (i.e. data flow, reduction, actor) efficiently supports only a single programming style (i.e. single-assignment, applicative, object-oriented), it is essential in this area to decide which will be the most general-purpose architecture and which the dominant programming style of the future.

Data driven and demand driven computers are often based on a packet communication machine organisation [14]. This organisation consists of a circular instruction execution pipeline of resources in which processors, communications and memories are interspersed with "pool's of work", as

shown in Figure 3.

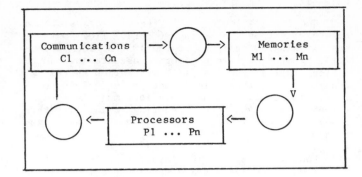

Figure 3: Packet Communication Computer

The organisation views an executing program as a number of independent information packets all of which are conceptually active, that split and merge. For a parallel computer, packet communication is a very simple strategy for allocating packets of work to resources. Each packet to be processed is placed with similar packets in one of the "pools of work". When a resource becomes idle, it takes a packet from its input pool, processes it and places a modified packet in an output pool, and then returns to the idle state.

Data driven and demand driven computers, namely a parallel machine supporting very high-level programming, represents the the academic computing community's view of future computers.

4. COMMUNICATIONS AND COMPUTERS

Data communications and computers (C&C) represent the fusion of wide area computer networks, local area computer networks, and parallel computer architectures to form a fully integrated computer-communications network. Data communications and computers, specifically computer networks and parallel computers, have in the past developed independently from each other, with advances in both technologies being sustained by the rapid development of semiconductor devices. However, the importance of fully integrating the following spectrum of decentralised systems has long been advocated [7]. To achieve this, it is clearly necessary for all component computers to conform to a common decentralised system architecture - allowing them to be programmed to co-operate in the communication of information and in the execution of a program.

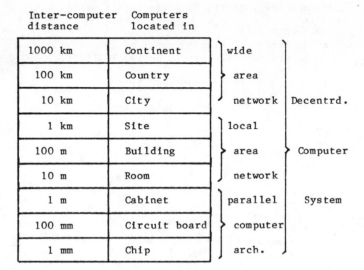

Inter-computer distance	Computers located in		
1000 km	Continent	} wide	
100 km	Country	} area	
10 km	City	network	Decentrd.
1 km	Site	} local	
100 m	Building	} area	Computer
10 m	Room	} network	
1 m	Cabinet	} parallel	System
100 mm	Circuit board	} computer	
1 mm	Chip	} arch.	

Figure 4: Spectrum of Decentralised Systems

These decentralised systems are usually based on control flow architectures enhanced with operating system concepts as illustrated by the Newcastle Connection distributed UNIX system. The Newcastle Connection [1] is the name given to a novel software subsystem added to a set of standard UNIX systems [11] in order to connect them together as a distributed system, initially using just a single Cambridge Ring . The resulting distributed system (which could employ a variety of wide and local area networks) is functionally indistinguishable at both the "Shell" command language level and at the system call level, from a conventional centralised UNIX system.

The secret of success is the hierarchical information and naming structure (for directories, files, devices, and commands) of UNIX. In the distributed system the structures of each component UNIX system are joined together as a single structure, in which each UNIX system behaves as a directory. This is illustrated by Figure 5.

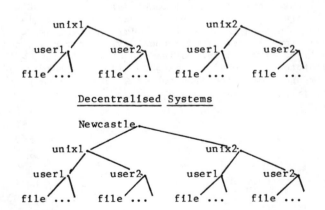

Figure 5: The Newcastle Connection of Unixes

The result is that each user, on each UNIX system, can inspect any directory, read or write any file, use any device, or execute any command, regardless of on which physical system it belongs. For example if a user "user1" wishes to copy "cp" a file "file1" to another file "file2", belonging to "user2", on the same machine he types the command:

        cp file1 /user2/file2

whereas on the decentralised system to copy the file "file1" to file "file2" of "user2" on machine "unix2" he types:

        cp file1 /../unix2/user2/file2

For those unfamiliar with UNIX, the initial "/" symbol indicates that a path name starts at the root directory, and the ".." symbol is used to indicate the parent directory. Perhaps the best analogy of the Newcastle Connection is with the naming structure of the international telephone network.

Communications and computers, namely a fully integrated computer-communications network, represents the data communications community's view of future computers.

5. PROCESSOR ARCHITECTURES EXPLOITING VLSI

Processor architectures to exploit very large scale integration (VLSI) define a new generation of VLSI building block to succeed the conventional microprocessor. Traditional microprocessors such as the Intel iAPX 432 containing over 100,000 transistors are starting to become commonplace. However, attempting to make larger-scale single processors in VLSI scaled to submicron dimensions becomes self-defeating, due to communication problems and the escalating costs of designing and testing such complex processors. One obvious solution (stimulated by the VLSI design philosophy of Mead and Conway [2,9]) is miniature microcomputers which can be replicated like memory cells and operate as a multiprocessor architecture. These novel general-purpose and special-purpose microcomputers are often implemented by only a few different types of simple cells, and use extensive pipelining and multiprocessing to achieve a high performance. Examples [16] range from special-purpose multiprocessors such as Kung's systolic arrays to general-purpose multiprocessors such as Caltech's Tree Machine built from 1024 identical chips.

In the future, VLSI architectures can be expected to be heterogeneous containing both general-purpose and special-purpose processors (see Figure 6).

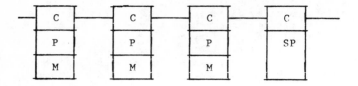

Notation:

    C   communications
    P   processor
    M   memory
    SP   special-purpose

Figure 6: VLSI Processor Architecture

Important design issues for VLSI architectures include communication and co-operation between processes and processors. The fundamental problem to be solved is how to orchestrate a single computation so that it can be distributed across the ensemble of processors.

One elegant VLSI architecture is embodied in the INMOS OCCAM programming language [13] and is based on concurrent processes (PROC) that communicate via channels (CHAN). A process - the fundamental working element - is a single statement, group of statements, or even a group of other processes performing a single task. A channel - the fundamental communication element - is an unbuffered structure allowing information to pass in one direction between two specific processes. Outputting to a channel is specified as "channel!variable" while inputting from a channel is given as "channel?variable". Communication behaviour corresponds to an asynchronous handshaking protocol employed by real electronic systems.

INMOS illustrates how OCCAM can even be used to simulate systolic array processors using a two-dimensional array for matrix multiplication [13]. One matrix enters the array from the left, while the other matrix enters from the top. As shown in Figure 7 two OCCAM program fragments are used to specify the two-dimensional array and an individual processing element. Each element "mult" has two input channels "up,left", whose values are multiplied "a*b" and accumulated "r", and two output channels "down,right".

```
CHAN vertical[n*(n+1)], horizontal[n*(n+1)]:
PAR i=[0 FOR n]
 PAR j=[0 FOR n]
  mult(vertical[(n*i)+j], vertical[(n*i)+j+1],
       horizontal[(n*i)+j], horizontal[(n*(i+1))+j])
```

a) two-dimensional array

```
PROC mult (CHAN up, down, left, right) =
 VAR r, a, b:
 SEQ
   r:=0
   SEQ i=[0 FOR n]
   SEQ
     PAR
       up?a
       left?b
     r:=r+(a*b)
     PAR
       down!a
       right!b:
```

b) processing element

Figure 7: OCCAM "systolic array" Program

In OCCAM, CHAN declares named channels "up..." or arrays of channels "vertical [...]", while SEQ and PAR define sequential and parallel blocks of processes respectively.

VLSI processor architecture, namely networks of miniature microcomputers, represents the microelectronics community's view of future computers.

6. FIFTH GENERATION COMPUTERS

The above four areas of research provide us with four seemingly different views of future computers, namely: knowledge processing systems, data and demand driven computers, integrated computer-communications, and VLSI processor architectures. However, the Japanese in their National Fifth Generation Computers Systems (FGCS) Project [10,17] as a starting point have attempted to integrate the views of the four research areas. Fifth generation computers will support knowledge-based expert system applications. Human interaction will involve natural language, speech and images. Programming will use very high level languages such as PROLOG. Architectures will support concurrency, utilising concepts such as data flow. Implementations will use the latest VLSI technology. And the systems will be highly decentralised at all levels with computers linked together in an integrated computer-communications network. This we attempt to illustrate in Figure 8.

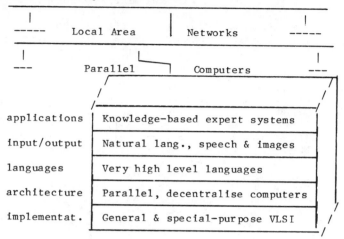

```
Wide Area Computer Networks

  |                                   |
 -----    Local Area    |  Networks    -----
                        |
  |                     |             |
 ---        Parallel         Computers   ---
```

applications	Knowledge-based expert systems
input/output	Natural lang., speech & images
languages	Very high level languages
architecture	Parallel, decentralise computers
implementat.	General & special-purpose VLSI

Figure 8: Fifth Generation Computer Systems

Given the technological and social factors (discussed in the introduction) supporting the adoption of a new generation of computers this "integrated" view of fifth generation computers would seem unquestionably correct.

Although the FGCS Project has identified this "framework" for fifth generation computers, there remains the important question of the computer's underlying theoretical concepts. These concepts will be determined by the choice of computer architecture (i.e. control flow, data flow, reduction, actor, logic) and by which of the four research areas (i.e knowledge processing, data & demand driven, communications & computers, VLSI) has the major influence on fifth generation computers. The five basic categories of computer architecture and their associated programming languages are shown in Figure 9.

Prog lang	convent.	single assignment	applicative	object-oriented	pred. logic
comp arch	control flow	data flow	reduction	actor	logic

Figure 9: Categories of Languages and Architectures

Regarding the style of fifth generation computers, two approaches, based on opposite ends of this spectrum, seem to be emerging: a "revolutionary" approach based on logic, and an "evolutionary" approach based on control flow. The former approach is taken by the artificial intelligence and academic computing communities, who are mainly concerned with supporting advanced applications and programming languages on a parallel computer, while the latter approach is taken by the data communications and microelectronics communities, who are mainly concerned with interconnecting heterogeneous processors in a decentralised system. Below we examine these two approaches to the fifth generation.

7. LOGIC APPROACH

Central to the logic approach is the design of a high-performance, parallel logic machine for knowledge information processing so as to support knowledge-based expert systems. The required maximum speed of such a machine is estimated to be 100M to 1G Logical Inferences per Second (LIPS) [10]. 1LIPS denotes one syllogistic inference operation per second (one invocation of a PROLOG clause), and corresponds to 100 to 1000 instructions per second for current computers.

To achieve this parallel logic machine three key items - currently the topics of vigorous international research - are necessary:

1. a parallel logic programming language

2. a parallel logic computer architecture

3. a symbol manipulation machine implementation

The current status of research into these three areas may be broadly equated as: programming languages - PROLOG [8]; computer architecture - the Edinburgh PROLOG Interpreter [20] written in assembler for the PDP-10; and machine implementation - the Sequential Inference Machine [18,19] (based on the Edinburgh Interpreter) currently being developed by the FGCS Project.

The Sequential Inference Machine (SIM) is a medium performance personal machine designed to support an extended version of PROLOG. SIM will consist of three hardware modules, namely a processor module, a memory module, and an input/output interface module. The processor is microprogrammable and contains special hardware such as registers and stacks to support logic unification and resolution. It also contains a cache and other virtual memory mechanisms. The memory employs a tagged architecture with each memory cell consisting of an 8 bit tag and a 32 bit data field. The logical address space is divided into 256 areas each of 16M words, which may be used as independent stack or heap areas. The input/output is composed of a bit-map display, Japanese character input/output devices, picture and speech input/output devices, and local network interfaces. SIM is designed to attain 20-30 KLIPS and will be implemented in TTL ICs. This PROLOG machine is to logic programming what LISP machines are to functional programming. The next stage of research is to identify a logic machine equivalent to a reduction machine.

In summary, the parallel logic machine approach is based on the following assumptions:

1. knowledge-based expert systems will be the important application area of the 1990's;

2. logic programming is the most effective machine language for expert systems;

3. parallel processing for high-performance is essential for knowledge processing; and

4.　fifth generation computing will be disjoint with conventional computing.

Given these assumptions the fundamental problem to be solved is the identification of a model of computation and machine organisation for the logic computer architecture.

8.　CONTROL FLOW APPROACH

Central to the control flow approach is the design of a "system" architecture for decentralised processing, extending the traditional von Neumann architecture. This decentralised architecture, we believe, has the following principles:

1.　nested organisation of variable-size memory cells (like the file structure of an operating system);

2.　contextual address space of cells (like telephone numbers);

3.　high-level machine language (as in LISP where instructions may be recursively defined);

4.　parallel, decentralised control of computation (as with UNIX commands);

5.　computer system (behaving as a processor and memory cell) is a network of computers.

In fact, these principles can already be recognised as providing the basis of operating systems such as UNIX [11]. Clearly modern operating systems are "virtual" decentralised systems whose principles reflect the environment in which people wish to program. Our task therefore is to isolate and refine this decentralised control flow model so that it may be incorporated into a programming language, computer architecture, and machine implementation.

The Recursive Machine proposal of Barton and Wilner [22] provides a good basis for decentralised control flow. In the machine, information is represented as nested delimited strings, where a delimited string is considered a variable-size memory cell. A string consists of two alphabets of characters, namely (i) delimiting characters left bracket "(" and right bracket ")", and (ii) data characters binary "0" and "1". Thus an array of the numbers 0 to 9 is encoded as:

$$(　(0)　(1)　(10)　(11)　(100) \dots　)$$

Addressing of information is based on a contextual address space in which each delimited string is considered a context relative to which a related string is identified by a selector. An address is a sequence of selectors specifying a path from the point of reference in the structure to the target string. Two classes of selectors are provided: relative "i", and superior "..". For instance, to access the whole of the above array from elsewhere in the surrounding context its selector, say "2", is used, whereas to access a subsidiary number "(100)" the address "2/5" is used.

$$2:(　1:(0)　2:(1)　3:(10)　4:(11)　5:(100) \dots　)$$
$$2　=　(　　(0)　(1)　(10)　(11)　(100) \dots　)$$
$$2/5　=　　　　　　　　　　　　(100)$$

Various developments at the University of Newcastle upon Tyne are based on decentralised control flow: the Newcastle Connection distributed UNIX system [1] mentioned previously; the interactive BASIX programming language [6]; and the LEGO multi-microcomputer system [15]. The BASIX language combines features of programming languages (e.g. BASIC, LISP) with features normally only found in operating systems (e.g. UNIX Shell). For example, BASIX has a single notion of object which serves the roles of variables, messages, programs, files and directories. The LEGO computer involves the implementation of a VLSI processor architecture from a network of miniature microcomputers that cooperate in the concurrent execution of a program. It implements delimited strings and contextual addressing.

In summary, the decentralised control flow system approach is based on the following assumptions:

1.　the communication and cooperation of heterogeneous processors (and processes) will be the most important task in the 1990's;

2.　recursive structuring of computer systems is essential for decentralised processing whether involving mainframe computers or miniature microcomputers;

3.　control flow is the most primitive and general form of computation;

4.　fifth generation computing will evolve from conventional computing.

Given these assumptions the most pressing problem is to refine the principles of the decentralised control flow computer architecture.

9.　CONCLUSIONS

Japan's FGCS Project, by its current research [18,19], apparently favours the revolutionary approach to the fifth generation of designing a parallel logic computer. However, we feel that the evolutionary approach of designing a decentralised control flow system is the more promising way of achieving many of the very ambitious goals characterising the FGCS Project. Our view is partly conservative in recognising the greater practicality in a world of existing systems and expertise, of persuading individuals and organisations to try out an evolutionary development. But we also believe that control flow is a more fundamental model of computation [14] than the four other models.

Highly parallel and decentralised computer systems will, and should, only supplant the traditional von Neumann computer if they can match the latter's generality and flexibility, as exemplified by the large variety of both conventional and very novel programming languages and styles that it supports with reasonable effectiveness. The important aspect of the von Neumann model which gives this flexibility is that it is a control flow model allowing the programmer (or compiler/interpreter) direct control over the low level operation of the target machine when this is necessary. Thus we would identify the key to the fifth generation as being some extended form of control flow which overcomes its deficiencies for decentralised concurrent systems, but retains its flexibility and generality.

ACKNOWLEDGEMENTS

Numerous people have contributed to the ideas presented in this paper. Firstly, I wish to thank members of Japan's Fifth Generation Project, Prof. Tohru Moto-oka and Dr. Shunichi Uchida, for explanations of their project. Secondly, I wish to thank my colleagues in the Computer Architecture Group at the University of Newcastle upon Tyne, in particular David Brownbridge, Isabel Gouveia Lima, Richard Hopkins, Roger Millichamp and David Mundy. Lastly, I wish to thank the Distributed Computing Systems Panel and the IKBS Architecture Study Group of the UK Science and Engineering Research Council for funding and encouraging Fifth Generation Computing Research in the UK.

REFERENCES

[1] Brownbridge D. et al: "The Newcastle Connection or UNIXes of the World Unite!", Software - Practice and Experience, vol. 12, (December 1982) pp. 1147-1162.

[2] Conway L. et al: "MPC79: A Large-Scale Demonstration of a New Way to Create Systems in Silicon", LAMBDA, Second Quarter (1980).

[3] Duda R.O. and Gaschnig J.G.: "Knowledge-based Expert Systems Come of Age", Byte (September 1981), pp. 238-281

[4] Feigenbaum E. A.: "Knowledge Engineering: The Applied Side of Artificial Intelligence", Memo HPP-80-21, Computer Science Dept., Stanford University, 1980.

[5] Ferguson R.: "PROLOG A Step Towards the Ultimate Computer Language", Byte (November 1981), pp. 384-399.

[6] Gouveia Lima I. et al: "Decentralised Control Flow - BAsed on unIX", Proc. ACM SIGPLAN 83 Conf. (to be presented).

[7] Kobayashi K.: "Computer, Communications and Man: The Integration of Computer and Communications with Man as an Axis", COMPUTER NETWORKS, vol. 5, no. 4 (July 1981). pp. 237-250.

[8] Kowalski R.: "Logic for Problem Solving", Elsevier-North Holland Publishing Company (1979).

[9] Mead C.A. and Conway L.A.: "Introduction to VLSI Systems", Addison-Wesley (1980).

[10] Moto-oka T. et al: "Challenge for Knowledge Information Processing Systems (Preliminary Report on Fifth Generation Computer Systems)", Proc. Int. Conf. on Fifth Generation Computer Systems, North-Holland Publishing Company (1982).

[11] Richie D.M. and Thompson, K., "The UNIX Time-Sharing System", Comm. ACM, vol. 17, no. 7 (1974) pp. 365-375.

[12] Servan-Schreiber J.J.: "The World Challenge", Collins (1981).

[13] Taylor R. and Wilson P.: "OCCAM Process-oriented language meets demands of distributed processing", Electronics (November 1982) pp. 89-95.

[14] Treleaven P.C. et al: "Data Driven and Demand Driven Computer Architecture", ACM Computing Surveys, vol. 14, no. 1 (March 1982) pp. 93-143.

[15] Treleaven P.C. and Hopkins R.P., "A Recursive Computer Architecture for VLSI", Proc. Ninth Int. Symp. on Computer Architecture, (April 1982) pp. 229-238.

[16] Treleaven P.C.: "VLSI Processor Architectures", IEEE Computer Magazine, vol. 15, no. 6 (June 1982).

[17] Treleaven P.C. and Gouveia Lima I.: "Japan's Fifth Generation Computer Systems", IEEE Computer Magazine, vol. 15, no. 8 (August 1982).

[18] Uchida S.: "Towards a New Generation Computer Architecture", Tech. Report TR/A-001, Institute for New Generation Computer Technology (July 1982).

[19] Uchida S. et al: "The Personal Sequential Inference Machine", Tech. Report TM-002, Institute for New Generation Computer Technology, (November 1982).

[20] Warren D.H.: "Logic Programming and Compiler Writing", Dept. of Artificial Intelligence, Univ. of Edinburgh, Research Report No. 44, (September 1977).

[21] Waterman D.A. and Hayes-Roth F.: "An Investigation of Tools for Building Expert Systems", Memo R-2818-NSF, Rand Corp., Santa Monica, California (June 1982).

[22] Wilner W.T., "Recursive Machines", Xerox Palo Alto Research Center, Internal Report (1980).

Design Issues In Parallel Architectures
for Artificial Intelligence

Carl Hewitt
Henry Lieberman

MIT Artificial Intelligence Laboratory
545 Technology Square
Cambridge, Mass. 02139

1. Abstract

Development of highly intelligent computers requires a conceptual foundation that will overcome the limitations of the von Neumann architecture. Such architecture should meet the following design goals:

* Address the fundamental organizational issues of large-scale parallelism and sharing in a fully integrated way. This means attention to organizational principles , as well as hardware and software.

* Serve as an experimental apparatus for testing large-scale artificial intelligence systems.

* Explore the feasibility of an architecture based on abstractions, which serve as natural computational primitives for parallel processing. Such abstractions should be logically independent of their software and hardware host implementations.

In this paper we lay out some of the fundamental design issues in parallel architectures for Artificial Intelligence, delineate limitations of previous parallel architectures, and outline a new approach that we are pursuing.

2. Introduction

Large-scale distributed systems are evolving rapidly because of

* The burgeoning growth of personal computers;

* The development of local and national electronic networks;

* The widespread requirement of arm's-length transactions among agencies.

The systems we envision share the following properties:

* *Continuous change and evolution.* Distributed artificial intelligence systems are always adding new computers, users, and software. As a result, systems must be able to change as the components and demands placed upon them change. Moreover, they must be able to evolve new internal parts in order to accommodate the shifting work they perform. Without this capability, every system must reach the point where it can no longer be expanded to accommodate new users and uses.

* *Absence of bottlenecks.* A bottleneck is a channel through which all communications must flow. In the von Neumann architecture, the single path between processor and memory acts as such a bottleneck. An adequate architecture for large-scale artificial intelligence systems cannot have such bottlenecks. A centralized decision making mechanism would inevitably become a bottleneck; therefore decision making must be decentralized.

* *Arms-length relationships.* In general, the computers, people, and agencies that make up distributed artificial intelligence systems do not have direct access to one another's internal information. For example, suppliers and their customers or competitors must deal with one another at *arm's length.* Arms-length relationships imply that the architecture must accommodate multiple computers at different physical sites that do not have access to each others internal parts.

* *Perpetual inconsistency among knowledge bases.* Because of privacy and discretionary concerns, different knowledge bases will contain different perspectives and conflicting beliefs. Thus all the knowledge bases of a distributed artificial intelligence system taken together will be perpetually inconsistent. Decentralization also makes it impossible to update all knowledge bases simultaneously. This implies that it is not even possible to know what kinds of information are contained in all the local knowledge bases in the system at any one time. Systems must thus have the capacity to operate in the presence of inconsistent and incomplete knowledge bases.

* *Need for negotiation among system parts.* In a highly distributed system, no system part directly controls the resources of another systems part. The various parts of the system must persuade one another to provide capabilities. A distributed artificial intelligence system's architecture therefore must support a mechanism for negotiation among parts.

Continuous growth and evolution, absence of bottlenecks, arm's-length relationships, inconsistency among knowledge bases, decentralized decision making, and the need for negotiation are interdependent and necessary properties for large distributed artificial intelligence systems.

Without a firm theoretical base, development of an architecture that is applicable to large-scale artificial intelligence systems will be much more difficult.

Reprinted from *The Proceedings of COMPCON S'84*, 1984, pages 418-423.

3. Foundational Issues

Large-scale artificial intelligence systems raise important issues for future architectures. Two that we are addressing are: the relationship between action, description, and reasoning; and the inadequacy of the closed-world hypothesis.

* *Integration of action, description, and reasoning.* Three kinds of computer languages have been developed; the descriptive, the action-oriented, and the reasoning or deductive. Descriptive languages represent knowledge using descriptions: languages that are based broadly on this approach include first order logic, KRL, NETL, Omega, and KL-ONE, etc. Action-oriented programming languages such as Fortran, Lisp and Ada implement processes that change objects. They tend to provide relatively weak descriptions of objects and the relationships among them. Reasoning languages plan, solve problems, or prove theorems. Logic programming languages (such Prolog [Kowalski 83]) are a subset of the reasoning languages that are limited by cumbersome description capabilities and by having inelegant mechanisms for taking action. Historically, languages strong in one of these kinds of capacities have tended to be relatively weak in the other. All three capabilities: action, description, and reasoning are necessary for large-scale artificial intelligence systems.

* *Inadequacy of the closed-world assumption.* The *closed world assumption* is that the information about the world being modeled is complete in the sense that exactly those relationships that hold among objects are derivable from the local information possessed by the system. Systems based on the closed world assumption (such as Planner [Hewitt 69] and Prolog [Kowalski 74]) typically assume that they can find all existing instances of a concept by searching their local storage. At first glance it might seem that the closed world assumption, almost universal in the artificial intelligence and database literature, is smart because it provides a ready default answer for any query. Unfortunately the default answers provided become less and less realistic as large-scale artificial intelligence systems become more distributed since less of the information is available locally.

* *Empirical Knowledge.* Algorithmic procedures are procedures, such as Gaussian Elimination, about which properties such as efficiency and correctness can be proved mathematically. In contrast Artificial Intelligence is mainly concerned with empirical procedures such as those required to drive from Palo Alto to Boston. In general empirical procedures make essential use of empirical knowledge and require interaction with the physical world in real time.

* *Dynamic Allocation.* An Artificial Intelligence architectures needs to dynamically allocate and re-allocate computational resources as required by ongoing empirical computations. Empirical computations require dynamic allocation because it is impossible to plan in advance which procedures will need to be run. Artificial Intelligence applications require that the highest priority be short latency (fast response time) in order to efficiently dynamically re-allocate resources as needed.

4. Scaling issues

Almost all other non von Neumann architecture projects are based on the unexamined assumption of *linear scaling*; (i.e., their announced goal is to build an architecture) in which *the speed of computation will increase in direct proportion to the number of computing elements without any reprogramming.* Almost all the non von Neumann architecture projects have uncritically accepted the assumption that simple linear scaling is possible.

Of course simple linear scaling is theoretically impossible because communication delay increases as as a machine becomes physically larger. As Chuck Seitz has pointed out, the cases in which linear scaling is *almost* achieved are pretty trivial involving rather special cases of crystalline (or systolic) regularity. For Artificial Intelligence applications, we feel that linear scaling is not directly achievable because increasing the number of computational elements in a system increases the complexity of the relationships among them. Use of the principles by which work is organized in large-scale human organizations is a powerful tool for making significant progress in architectures for Artificial Intelligence. The issues involved in the organization of work must be dealt with in the early stages of architectural design because it can have a significant impact on the kind of architecture that is useful. For example the architecture must support capabilities like having sponsors [Kornfeld 82, Barber 82].

To deal with this issue, we are working on the development of a *computational* theory of organizations and the organization of work [Barber, de Jong, and Hewitt 83]. An architecture that is capable of dynamic growth must be able to undertake major reorganizations of the work of a computation as it grows in size. In order to do this, the system must have an understanding of its own capabilities and limitations as well as an understanding of the goals and constraints of the computations being performed.

5. Limitations of Previous Architectures for Artificial Intelligence

Von Neumann machines, being sequential, are *inadequate* vehicles on which to base the development of large-scale artificial intelligence systems. We need architectures that are inherently parallel and sufficiently general to meet the requirements of distributed systems. Existing languages, which were designed for existing architectures, tend to be similarly inadequate. Languages designed for von Neumann machines are inherently sequential. Extensions to these languages restrict the amount of concurrency unnecessarily.

Artificial Intelligence systems need to organize information using *description lattices* that are the further development of early ideas on "semantic memories" [Quillian 68]. The consistency and completeness properties of first-order description lattices have been systematically explored in [Attardi and Simi 81]. One of the most important design criteria for a parallel architecture for Artificial Intelligence is to be able to store, retrieve, and reason about information in description lattices in parallel.

5.1. Applicative, Functional, and Reduction Architectures.

Applicative, functional, and reduction machine organizations are based on the mathematical theory of functions and function spaces. The underlying mathematical theory of the lambda calculus and the absence of assignment commands and state change facilitates parallelism and makes it easier to prove properties of procedures.

An important limitation is that these architectures do not support large-scale sharing of objects with a changing local state. Shared objects with a changing local state are required to support the allocation of resources and the implementation of cooperating and competing subsystems for artificial intelligence applications [Hewitt and de Jong 83a].

5.2. Data Flow Architectures.

Historically the term "data flow" is derived from trying to better structure the flow of communication signals between hardware modules. Modeling software in terms of communication between hardware modules has turned out to be limited because of the dynamic creation of objects that occurs in software. To cope with the limitation, Data Flow machine organizations are gradually evolving to have much in common with applicative, functional, and reduction machines.

Data Flow architectures exploit the nature of algorithmic procedures to plan and map algorithms efficiently onto the hardware before computation begins. As a result Data Flow architectures place highest priority on thruput as a criteria for efficient execution of the planned procedures. They were developed for running algorithmic rather than empirical procedures. As a consequence of focusing on algorithmic procedures, they place great emphasis on being able to plan the resource allocation for a computation before starting. They are weak in the capabilities for dynamic allocation of computational resources. In particular they are weak in parallel garbage collection [Lieberman and Hewitt 83]. Architectures for Artificial Intelligence require a more dynamic allocation of resources and greater emphasis on short latency (fast response time).

5.3. Logic Programming Architectures.

Logic programming is based on mathematical logic and the quantificational calculus. The quantificational calculus is a well defined powerful description language with solid elegant mathematical foundations. One of the major findings of our research is that logic programming architectures will not be adequate for distributed, parallel, artificial intelligence systems because they do not adequately deal with inconsistency [Hewitt and de Jong 83b, Hewitt 83]. Prolog [Kowalski 74] is based on essentially the same technology as Planner-like languages [Hewitt 69, Sussman, Winograd, and Charniak 70]. Prolog makes use of a flat data base of assertions that does not provide an adequate organization of the knowledge in the form of description lattices. A further problem is that logic programming confounds issues of description and action [Hewitt and de Jong 83a].

5.4. Blackboard Architectures.

The name "blackboard" brings to mind a group of agents communicating with a blackboard. This does not work work well in practice because the blackboard quickly becomes a bottleneck in reading and writing information. Introducing multiple blackboards quickly shifts the emphasis to some other architectural paradigm such as message passing.

5.5. SIMD Architectures.

Arrays of single instruction, multiple data (SIMD) stream computers are important for the early stages of visual, speech, and tactile processing. Thus an Artificial Intelligence architecture needs to be able to interface with such arrays on the periphery. SIMD architectures are designed to perform one operation at a time on a large array of data. Therefore they are not suitable of doing large-scale symbolic reasoning which requires multiple symbolic operations to performed in parallel for different symbolic structures.

5.6. Global Shared Memory Architectures.

A global shared memory is a single large shared structure which is used for interprocess communication. Global Shared Memory machine organizations communicate at a very low level reading and writing individual words of memory. Such architectures are inadequate for physically distant computers, because the central memory acts as a bottleneck. A global shared memory will become increasingly less attractive because the ratio of the average latency for accessing the global shared memory relative to the clock period will gradually increase over the course of time as communication time becomes the dominant efficiency consideration. For reasons discussed above, parallel artificial intelligence systems require a low relative latency (fast response time) for effective operation.

6. Actors

Actor theory [Hewitt and Baker 77, Clinger 81] provides a foundation for addressing the problems of constructing distributed, large-scale artificial intelligence systems. Actor theory treats issues of scaling information processing systems in an integrated fashion: It applies equally to large-scale multi-processing machines that reside in a single room, and to those in which the machines are geographically dispersed.

From what we have learned from this earlier work, we are now building an experimental system for practical applications. Message passing semantics is based on actors that are virtual computation units. Actors are inherently parallel. An actor is defined by its behavior when it receives communications. When an actor receives a message it can perform the following four kinds of primitive actions concurrently:

* Make simple decisions

* Create more actors

* Send more communications

* Specify its behavior in response to the next message received, thus characterizing its new local state

Conceptually, there is no *a priori* limit on the computational power of an actor. In practice, each actor tends to be relatively simple in order to keep systems modular. The power of actors stems from the ease with which systems of more specialized actors can be combined to accomplish larger tasks. The practical importance, utility, niceness, and versatility of actors stem from the following properties:

* *Actor systems are inherently parallel.* Because each actor responds to messages independently of other actors, systems of actors inherently have a high degree of parallelism. Different actors can be processing sub-tasks simultaneously, coordinating their activities by passing messages among themselves.

* *Actors have hardware generality.* Since actors are virtual computational units, their implementation is not dependent upon particular hardware configurations such as machine boundaries, the number of processors, or the physical location of machines. An actor can be implemented in hardware, in micro-code, or in software. Actors are organized at the hardware level by load-balancing between hardware processors to spread processing load, by migration between processors to relieve overcrowding and communication delays, and by efficient, real-time, distributed garbage collection.

* *Actors have software generality.* Being defined mathematically [Clinger 81], actors are independent of any programming language. Actors are very general with respect to the languages and language features they can support. In particular, they provide a uniform basis for description, action, and reasoning [Barber, de Jong, and Hewitt 83]. Actors support the parallel processing of lattice networks of descriptions (e.g., semantic networks), pattern-directed rules for reasoning, as well as procedures for taking action.

7. The Apiary Approach

The Apiary architecture is based on actor theory. The goal is to create an integrated, parallel hardware-software system that has the generality required for large-scale artificial intelligence systems. To date, much of the implementation work on the Apiary has centered around *simulation* of the Apiary on a network of current-generation sequential computers [Lieberman 83].

Most simulators for new machines perform at the level of *instruction sets* or *virtual machines*. The simulator implements a sequential interpreter for the instruction set in the host language, and programs written using the new machine's instruction set can be tested. Compilers translate higher-level languages into the instruction set. Instruction sets for conventional machines usually specify operations like loading and storing registers with fixed length bit strings. The instruction set level has the advantage that it is high enough to be convenient as the target for problem-solving languages, while low enough to experiment with the algorithms which will be needed to realize the computational model in hardware.

The Apiary as a whole has no "instruction set" since many computations can run concurrently. Instead, we can model the Apiary as a set of *workers*, each worker being analogous to a single computer executing instructions serially, together with its own memory, and the ability to communicate with other workers. The Apiary simulator must bridge the gap between programming sequential processors with modifiable state and a multi-processor system with no global state.

The primitive operations of the Apiary are not like those of conventional machines. Whereas instructions in Von Neumann machines manipulate the contents of registers, the Apiary must deal solely with actors and their responses to messages. Although an Apiary may be implemented at the lowest hardware level with transistors and wires, this must be hidden from Apiary applications. The four primitive capabilities mentioned earlier (creating actors, sending messages, making decisions, and changing behavior) form the backbone of a virtual machine for an Apiary worker, together with operations on primitive data types such as addition of numbers.

We have not yet taken the Apiary simulator down to the level of coding instructions as bit strings, defining memory formats, and specifying register sets. Though this will eventually be necessary for hardware implementation, the details will depend heavily on the particulars of implementation technology.

The Apiary is a parallel problem solving system, where users write programs whose computations may range over many processors. Artificial intelligence applications are characterized by their unpredictable nature. One cannot predict in advance how many concurrent activities will be necessary or desirable for solving a problem, how much memory will be needed, or how to best divide work among available processors. It follows that a parallel system for Artificial Intelligence must dynamically allocate all processor, communication, and memory resources in the system, without explicit intervention by applications programs.

This has some important consequences:

* *Actors may need to move from one worker's memory to another.* Actors may need to move even while the program is running. Care must be taken to assure this does not disturb running programs. One actor may need to communicate with an actor on another machine. When an actor moves from one worker to another, it is replaced with a *forwarding actor* on the local machine. The forwarding actor automatically forwards communications to the remote machine, so that movement of actors is transparent to running programs. To improve performance, the Apiary will want to spread out actors more or less evenly through the various workers, so that one worker's memory will not become a bottleneck.

* *Programs may need to move from one processor to another.* The number and kind of computational activities may vary in the course of a computation so that no static allocation of programs to processors may be used. To allow mobility of programs, we break up computations into very small units called *tasks*. A task represents the reception of a message by an actor, and encodes all the "machine state", so that moving a task from one worker to another is sufficient to assure the transfer of the computation. To improve performance, the Apiary will want to spread out tasks more or less evenly through the workers, so that as many processors as possible will be kept busy performing useful work.

The hardware will be composed of a changing number of physical processors, executing specific programs, each with its own local memory, yet we do not want programs to depend on the specifics of the hardware configuration. How do we create an illusion of flexible parallel computation from inflexible serial hardware?

Most of the work involved is the responsibility of a set of *housekeeping algorithms*, and much of the challenge of the implementation of the Apiary will lie in the creation of simple and efficient algorithms for these jobs.

* *Garbage collection.* Like traditional systems that support dynamic allocation of storage, the Apiary will require garbage collection. Garbage collection across multiple machines is facilitated by maintaining *interest tables*, which keep track of inter-machine pointers. Our preliminary thoughts on this important issue are spelled out in more detail in [Lieberman and Hewitt, CACM 1983].

* *Load balancing.* Each worker maintains a queue of tasks, representing all the concurrent computations that the worker is working on at each moment. If one worker becomes too overloaded with many tasks on its queue, it asks another worker to off load some of the work. In our simulator, each worker has a small number of *neighbors*, to which it is directly connected. Each worker is kept informed of the size of each of queue of its neighbors, so that underutilized workers can share some of the burden of the overloaded workers.

* *Migration.* Migration is the process of moving an actor from one worker's memory to another. When a task is moved during load balancing, all the actors it references will initially lie on the original machine, and actors will have to be transferred to the new machine as they are needed. Migration will also occur for performance reasons when the memory of one worker gets too full relative to its neighbors. There are two kinds of actors which need differing treatment during migration. *Unserialized* actors do not change their local state and can be copied from one machine to another as they are needed. *Serialized* actors can modify their local state, so each serialized actor must reside in one place only, and any other references to it from other machines must go through a forwarding actor.

8. Apiary Software Foundations

Prelude is the name of the software system we are developing for the Apiary. Prelude supports unified description, action, and reasoning systems that can exploit the large-scale parallelism made possible by VLSI. The hardware architecture for the Apiary accommodates two broad classes of machines: core machines and periphery machines. The core consists of high performance processors connected with high bandwidth, low latency communication links. The periphery consists of less powerful processors that are portable and do not require air conditioning.

Developing a new architecture for large-scale artificial intelligence systems is largely a software problem. Most of the super computers that are currently being designed and constructed will not be efficient for large-scale artificial intelligence applications.

We developed a number of experimental systems dealing with different aspects of the design of high-level actor-based language systems. First a basic actor programming language was developed for sending communications, creating actors, and making local state changes. Next a reasoning system that provides for reasoning about beliefs and goals in parallel was developed [Kornfeld and Hewitt 81, Kornfeld 82]. In parallel we developed a description language that incorporates the descriptive capabilities of logic in the in the context of lattices of descriptions. The description system was characterized axiomatically [Attardi and Simi 81]. Then the reasoning system was re-implemented to incorporate the use of the description system [Barber 82]. These languages and systems have been independently implemented in somewhat incompatible ways. In the course of the last year we have begun the integration of these various languages using Act2 [Theriault 83]. Currently Act2 integrates communication and local change capabilities with the lowest level descriptions in the description system. Being inherently parallel and having no assignment commands, Act2 has proven well suited for the implementation of asynchronous concurrent systems.

The generality of Act2 has been demonstrated by writing a metacircular description of Act-2 in Act-2 [Theriault 83]. Part of the demonstration consisted of constructing parallel applicative interpreters directly, such as one for Pure Lisp with parallel argument evaluation. This cannot be done using such applicative functional interpreters themselves, for they lack the ability to express the required local state changes. Thus, we discovered, through a concrete example, that Act-2 is more powerful than the purely applicative functional languages, like Pure Lisp.

In a related development, investigation of a shared-financial-account example confirmed the expectation that Act-2 is more suitable than the applicative functional languages for dealing with computational problems involving shared actors with changing local states. While working with the shared-financial-account example, we also conceived of and implemented a new approach to actor state changes [Hewitt and de Jong 83a]. From the perspective of this new approach, actors change state by transforming themselves into other actors.

Work is proceeding on the development of a source language debugging system for parallel systems called Time Traveler. The Time Traveler system builds on previous work on hardware debugging [Giaimo 75], debugging sequential programs [Balzer 69] and parallel simulation [Jefferson and Sowizral 82].

9. Conclusion

In this paper we have explored some of the fundamental design issues in parallel architectures for Artificial Intelligence, explained limitations of previous parallel architectures, and outlined the Apiary architecture that we are pursuing.

10. Acknowledgments

Much of the work underlying our ideas was conducted by members of the Message Passing Semantics group at MIT. We especially would like to thank Jon Amsterdam, Jerry Barber, Peter de Jong, Tim McNerney, Elija Millgram, Chunka Mui, Tom Reinhardt, and Dan Theriault. Valuable feedback was provided by Toni Cohen, Mike Farmwald, Morven Gentleman, Fanya Montalvo, Chuck Seitz, and Henry Sowizral. Comments by Toni Cohen, Peter de Jong, Elihu Gerson, Tom Reinhardt, Chuck Seitz, Charles Smith, and Leigh Star have been of fundamental importance in improving the organization and content of this paper.

This paper describes research done at the Artificial Intelligence Laboratory of the Massachusetts Institute of Technology. Major support for the research reported in this paper was provided by the System Development Foundation. Major support for other related work in the Artificial Intelligence Laboratory is provided, in part, by the Advanced Research Projects Agency of the Department of Defense under Office of Naval Research contract N0014-80-C-0505. We would like to thank Charles Smith, Mike Brady, Patrick Winston, and Gerald Wilson for their support and encouragement.

References

[Attardi and Simi 81] Attardi, G. and Simi, M. Semantics of Inheritance and Attributions in the Description System Omega. Proceedings of IJCAI 81, IJCAI, Vancouver, B.C., Canada, August, 1981.

[Balzer 69] Balzer, R.M. EXDAMS--EXtendable Debugging and Monitors Systems. Spring Joint Computer Conference, AFIP, 1969.

[Barber 82] Barber, G.R. Office Semantics. Ph.D. Th., Massachusetts Institute of Technology, 1982.

[Barber, de Jong, and Hewitt 83] Barber, G.R., de Jong, S.P., and Hewitt, C. Semantic Support for Work in Organizations. Proceedings of IFIP-83, IFIP, Sept., 1983.

[Clinger 81] Clinger, W.D. Foundations of Actor Semantics. AI-TR-633, MIT Artificial Intelligence Laboratory, May, 1981.

[Giaimo 75] Giaimo, E.C. III. The Program Monitor: A Programmable Instrument for Computer Hardware and Software Performance Measurement. Master Th., Massachusetts Institute of Technology, 1975.

[Hewitt 69] Hewitt C.E. PLANNER: A Language for Proving Theorems in Robots. Proceedings of IJCAI-69, IJCAI, Washington D.C., May, 1969.

[Hewitt 83] Hewitt, C. Some Fundamental Limitations of Logic Programming. A.I. Memo 748, MIT Artificial Intelligence Laboratory, November, 1983.

[Hewitt and Baker 77] Hewitt, C. and Baker, H. Laws for Communicating Parallel Processes. 1977 IFIP Congress Proceedings, IFIP, 1977.

[Hewitt and de Jong 83a] Hewitt, C., de Jong, P. Analyzing the Roles of Descriptions and Actions in Open Systems. Proceedings of the National Conference on Artificial Intelligence, AAAI, August, 1983.

[Hewitt and de Jong 83b] Hewitt, C., de Jong, P. Open Systems. Perspectives on Conceptual Modeling, Springer-Verlag, 1983.

[Jefferson and Sowizral 82] Jefferson, D., Sowizral, H. Fast Concurrent Simulation Using the Time Warp Mechanism, Part I: Local Control. Tech. Rep. N-1906-AF, RAND, December, 1982.

[Kornfeld 82] Kornfeld, W. Concepts in Parallel Problem Solving. Ph.D. Th., Massachusetts Institute of Technology, 1982.

[Kornfeld and Hewitt 81] Kornfeld, W.A. and Hewitt, C. The Scientific Community Metaphor. *IEEE Transactions on Systems, Man, and Cybernetics SMC-11*, 1 (January 1981).

[Kowalski 74] Kowalski, R.A. Predicate Logic as Programming Language. Proceedings of IFIP-74, IFIP, 1974.

[Kowalski 83] Kowalski, R.A. Logic Programming. Proceedings of IFIP-83, IFIP, 1983.

[Lieberman 83] Lieberman, H. An Object-Oriented Simulator for the Apiary. Proceedings of AAAI-83, AAAI, Washington, D.C., August, 1983.

[Lieberman and Hewitt 83] Lieberman, H. and Hewitt, C. A Real Time Garbage Collector Based on the Lifetimes of Objects. *CACM 26*, 6 (June 1983).

[Quillian 68] Quillian, M.R. Semantic Memory. In *Semantic Information Processing*, Minsky, M., Ed., MIT Press, 1968.

[Sussman, Winograd, and Charniak 70] Sussman, G.J., Winograd, T., and Charniak, E. MICRO-PLANNER Reference Manual. AI Memo 203, MIT AI Lab, 1970.

[Theriault 83] Theriault, D. Issues in the Design and Implementation of Act2. Technical Report 728, MIT Artificial Intelligence Laboratory, June, 1983.

Chapter 3: Artificial Intelligence Languages and Programming

One goal of computer scientists working in the field of AI is to produce programs that imitate intelligent behavior of human beings [1-5]. Von-Neumann-style programming that uses imperative languages, such as Fortran and Pascal, is inadequate because of its inability to specify parallel tasks and its unacceptable complexity [6-8]. To enhance programmers' productivity, a type of problem-oriented languages called declarative languages has been developed and widely applied in AI programming [9]. *Functional programming* [7,10,11] and *logic programming* [12-16] are the major programming paradigms of declarative languages.

Functional programming does not contain any notion of the present state, program counter, or storage. Rather, the "program" is a function in the true mathematical sense: It is applied to the input of the program, and the resulting value is the program's output. The terms *functional language, applicative language, dataflow language*, and *reduction language* have been used somewhat interchangeably [17-20]. Examples of functional languages are pure Lisp [21-25], Backus' FP [6], Hope [26], Val [27], and Id [28]. Interest in functional programming is steadily growing, because it is one of the few approaches that offer a real hope of relieving the twin crises of AI-oriented computing today: the absolute necessity to reduce the cost of programming and the need to find computer designs that make much better use of the power of VLSI and parallelism.

In its modest form, a logic program refers to the procedural interpretation of Horn clauses predicate logic [15,16]. The computer language Prolog [29-34] is based on logic programming. Generally speaking, logic programming is a reasoning-oriented or a deductive programming. In fact, some ideas of logic programming, like automatic backtracking, have been used in early AI languages QA3 [1], PLANNER, MICROPLANNER, and CONNIVER [3,35]. Logic programming has recently received considerable attention because of its choice by the Japanese as the core computer language for the Fifth-Generation Computer System Project [36]. Although it seems on the surface that logic programming is an independent and somewhat separate notion from function programming, an ideal AI-programming style should combine the features of both languages [96] and may be called "assertional programming" [13].

New languages and programming systems are being developed to simplify AI programming radically. It is expected that *object-oriented programming* [37] will be important in the 1980's as structured programming was in the 1970's. The language Smalltalk [38,39] is an example of object-oriented programming. Some ideas of object-oriented programming have been used in existing languages and systems, such as Simula, B5000, Lisp-AI notion of frame, ADA, and CLU. Other new object-oriented programming systems have also been developed [40-44].

AI programming languages have had a central role in the history of AI research. Frequently, new ideas in AI are accompanied by a new language that is natural for the ideas to be applied. Except for the widely used language Prolog, Lisp and its dialects, Maclisp [45], Interlisp [46,47], Qlisp [48], Common Lisp [49], Franz Lisp [50], etc., many other AI languages have been designed and implemented. Examples include IPL [51,52], PLANNER [53], CONNIVER [35], KRL [54], NETL [55], SAIL [56], POP-2 [57], FUZZY [58], and first-order logic. In general, three capabilities (namely, action, description, and reasoning) are needed for an AI language. Historically, languages strong in one of these capacities tended to be relatively weak in others. Prolog is a reasoning-oriented language that is limited by its inefficiency of description and action. Lisp, the second oldest programming language in present widespread use, retains some features of von Neumann programming. Some new languages, such as Loglisp [13] and QUTE [59], which amalgamate Prolog and Lisp in natural ways, have been developed. On the other hand, to explore parallelism, the parallel versions of Prolog and Lisp, such as Parlog [60], Concurrent Prolog [61,62], and Concurrent Lisp [63,64], have been proposed. Recent efforts are aimed at automatic programming that will allow the program to be generated from a simple specification of the problem [65-69].

Besides programming languages, it became apparent to the AI community since the mid-1960s that inference alone, even those augmented with heuristics, were often inadequate to solve real-life problems. To enhance the performance of AI programs, they must be augmented with knowledge of the problem domain rather than formal reasoning methods. This realization gave birth to *knowledge engineering* or *knowledge-based system*, the field of applied AI [70,71].

A knowledge-based expert system, or, in short, expert system, is a knowledge-intensive program that solves problems in a specific domain normally requiring human expertise [72-79]. An expert system consists of two parts: knowledge base and inference procedure. The knowledge base contains the facts and heuristics, while the inference procedure consists of the processes that search the knowledge base to infer solutions to problems, form hypotheses, and so on. What distinguishes an expert system from an ordinary computer application is that in a conventional computer program, pertinent knowledge and the methods for utilizing it are all intermixed. In an expert system, the knowledge base is separated from the inference procedure, and new knowledge can be added to the system without reprogramming.

Contemporary expert-system development techniques are shifting toward the use of software development tools that resemble a programming language, but include internal user-accessible databases and other high-level strategies for using knowledge to solve a class of problems [73,77,80,81]. Each tool suggests some additional design properties, such as rule-base and backward reasoning, for the knowledge-system architecture. Three of the most popular families of expert-system tools are (1) EMYCIN [82,83], KS300, and S.1; (2) HEARSAY-III [84] and AGE [85]; and (3) OPS which incorporates the MYCIN, HEARSAY-II, and R1 (XCON) expert-system families [86]. Other expert-system tools include LOOPS [87], ROSIE [88], RLL [89], MRS, and KMS. Some of these tools aim to provide a mixture of representations and inference techniques. Knowledge-acquisition tools such as TEIRESIAS [90], EXPERT [91], KAS [92], and learning tools such as META-DENDRAL [93] and EURISKO [94], have also been developed.

In this chapter, six articles are collected to introduce the various AI programming concepts and languages. Backus and Kowalski have, respectively, made pioneer contributions to functional programming and logic programming. Two of their articles are selected to show the broad view of the two basic AI programming methods [10,15]. As an example on the use of Lisp, the third paper, by Sheil, describes an exploratory programming environment [46]. In the fourth paper, the concept of object-oriented programming is introduced [37]. The last two papers present two parallel logic-programming languages, Clark and Gregory on Parlog [60] and Shapiro on concurrent Prolog [62]. Concurrent Lisp and related parallel architectures will be included in Chapter 6. The papers concerned with expert systems are not collected in this tutorial because of the page limitation.

References

[1]   A. Barr and E.A. Feigenbaum, *The Handbook on Artificial Intelligence*, 2, William Kaufmann, Los Altos, Calif., 1982.

[2]   E. Charniak, C. Riesbeck, and D. McDermott, *Artificial Intelligence Programming*, Lawrence Erlbaum Press, Hillsdale, N.J.,1980.

[3]   D. Bobrow and B. Paphael, "New Programming Languages for AI Research," *Computing Surveys*, vol. 6, no. 3, pp. 153-174, 1974.

[4]   E. Rich, "The Gradual Expansion of Artificial Intelligence," *Computer*, vol. 17, no. 5, pp. 4-12, May 1984.

[5]   P.H. Winston and B. Horn, *Lisp*, Second Edition, Addison Wesley, Reading, Mass., 1984.

[6]   J. Backus, "Can Programming Be Liberated from the von Neumann Style? A Functional Style and Algebra of Programs," *Communications of the ACM*, vol. 21, no. 8, pp. 613-641, Aug. 1978.

[7]   T. Winograd, "Beyond Programming Languages," *Communications of the ACM*, vol. 22, no. 7, pp. 391-401, July 1979.

[8]   B.D. Kornman, "Pattern Matching and Pattern-Directed Invocation in Systems Programming Languages," *Journal of Systems and Software*, vol. 3, pp. 95-102, 1983.

[9]   S. Eisenbach and C. Sadler, "Declarative Languages: An Overview," *Byte*, vol. 10, no. 8, pp. 181-197, Aug. 1985.

[10] J. Backus, "Function-Level Computing," *IEEE Spectrum*, vol. 19, no. 8, pp. 22-27, Aug. 1982.

[11] P. Henderson, *Function Programming, Application and Implementation*, Prentice-Hall, Englewood Cliffs, N.J., 1980.

[12] R. Kowalski, "Logic Programming," *IFIP Information Processing*, edited by R.E.A. Mason, pp. 133-145, Elsevier, New York, N.Y., 1983.

[13] J.A. Robinson, "Logic Programming—Past, Present and Future," *New Generation Computing*, vol. 1, no. 2, pp. 107-124, 1983.

[14] K.L. Clark and S-A. Tarnlund, eds., *Logic Programming*, Academic Press, Orlando, Fla., 1982.

[15] R. Kowalski, "Predicate Logic as a Programming Language," *IFIP Information Processing*, pp. 569-574, 1974.

[16] R. Kowalski, *Logic for Problem Solving*, North-Holland, Amsterdam, The Netherlands, 1979.

[17] R. Burstall, "Programming with Modules as Typed Functional Programming," *Proceedings of the International Conference on Fifth-Generation Computer Systems*, pp. 103-112, ICOT, Tokyo, Japan, and North-Holland, Amsterdam, The Netherlands, 1984.

[18] T. Ida and J. Tanaka, "Functional Programming with Streams—Part II," *New Generation Computing*, vol. 2, no. 3, pp. 261-275, 1984.

[19] D.A. Turner, "A New Implementation Technique for Applicative Languages," *Software—Practice and Experience*, vol. 9, no. 1, pp. 31-49, 1979.

[20] A.L. Davis and R.M. Keller, "Data Flow Program Graphs," *Computer*, vol. 15, no. 2, pp. 26-41, Feb. 1982.

[21] J. McCarthy, P. Abrahams, D. Edwards, T. Hart, and M. Levin, *Lisp 1.5 Programmer's Manual*, MIT Press, Cambridge, Mass., 1962.

[22] J. McCarthy, "History of Lisp," *SIGPLAN Notices*, vol. 13, no. 8, pp. 217-223, ACM, New York, N.Y., 1978.

[23] E. Sandewall, "Programming in an Interactive Environment: the Lisp Experience," *Computing Surveys*, vol. 10, no. 1, pp. 35-71, March 1978.

[24] M.L. Griss and E. Benson, "Current Status of a Portable Lisp Compiler," *Proceedings of the SIGPLAN Symposium on Compiler Construction*, pp. 276-283, ACM, New York, N.Y., June 1982.

[25] H.G. Baker, Jr., "Shallow Binding in Lisp 1.5," *Communications of the ACM*, vol. 21, no. 7, pp. 565-569, July 1978.

[26] R.M. Burstall, D.B. MacQueen, and D.T. Sannella, "HOPE: An Experimental Applicative Language," *Record of the Lisp Conference*, pp. 136-143, Stanford University, Menlo Park, Calif., 1980.

[27] J.R. McGraw, "Data Flow Computing: Software Development," *IEEE Transactions on Computers*, vol. C-29, no. 12, pp. 1095-1103, Dec. 1980.

[28] Arvind, K. Gostelow, and W. Plouffe, "An Asynchronous Programming Language and Computing Machine," *Technical Report 114a*, University of California, Irvine, Calif., Dec. 1978.

[29] A. Colmerauer, "Prolog in 10 Figures," *Proceedings of the 8th International Joint Conference on Artificial Intelligence*, pp. 488-499, William Kaufmann, Los Altos, Calif., 1983.

[30] W.F. Clocksin and C.S. Mellish, *Programming in Prolog*, Springer-Verlag, New York, N.Y., 1981.

[31] K.L. Clark and F.G. McCabe, "Prolog: A Language for Implementing Expert Systems," *Machine Intelligence 10*, edited by J. Hayes, D. Michie, and Y.H. Pao, pp. 455-471, Ellis Horwood Ltd., Chichester, England, 1982.

[32] A. Colmerauer, H. Kanoui, and M. Van Caneghem, "Last Steps Towards an Ultimate Prolog," *Proceedings of the 7th International Joint Conference on Artificial Intelligence*, pp. 947-948, William Kaufmann, Los Altos, Calif., Aug. 1981.

[33] B. Domolki and P. Szeredi, "Prolog in Practice," *IFIP Information Processing*, edited by R.E.A. Mason, pp. 627-636, Elsevier, New York, N.Y., 1983.

[34] D.H. Warren, L.M. Pereira, and F. Pereira, "Prolog—The Language and Its Implementation Compared with Lisp," *Proceedings of the Symposium on Artificial Intelligence and Programming Languages*, also *SIGART Newsletter*, no. 64, pp. 109-115, ACM, New York, N.Y., Aug. 1977.

[35] G.J. Sussman and D.V. McDermott, "From PLANNER to CONNIVER—A Genetic Approach," *Proceedings of the Fall Joint Computer Conference*, vol. 41, pp. 129-137, AFIPS Press, Reston, Va., 1972.

[36] T. Moto-oka and H.S. Stone, "Fifth-Generation Computer Systems: A Japanese Project," *Computer*, vol. 17, no. 3, pp. 6-13, March 1984.

[37] T. Rentsch, "Object Oriented Programming," *SIGPLAN Notices*, vol. 17, no. 9, pp. 51-57, ACM, New York, N.Y., Sept. 1982.

[38] A.J. Goldberg and D. Robson, *Smalltalk-80: The Language and Its Implementation*, Addison-Wesley, Reading, Mass., 1983.

[39] "Special Issue on Smalltalk," *Byte*, vol. 6, no. 8, Aug. 1981.

[40] Y. Ishikawa and M. Tokoro, "The Design of an Object-Oriented Architecture," *Proceedings of the 11th International Symposium on Computer Architecture*, pp. 178-187, IEEE Computer Society, Washington, D.C., 1984.

[41] F. Mizoguchi, H. Ohwada, and Y. Katayama, "LOOKS: Knowledge Representation System for Designing Expert Systems in a Logic Programming Framework," *Proceedings of the International Conference on Fifth-Generation Computer Systems*, pp. 606-612, ICOT, Tokyo, Japan, and North-Holland, Amsterdam, The Netherlands, 1982.

[42] N. Suzuki, K. Kubota, and T. Aoki, "SWORD32: A Bytecode Emulating Microprocessor for Object-Oriented Languages," *Proceedings of the International Conference on Fifth-Generation Computer Systems*, pp. 389-397, ICOT, and North-Holland, Amsterdam, The Netherlands, 1984.

[43] M. Tokoro and Y. Ishikawa, "An Object-Oriented Approach to Knowledge Systems," *Proceedings of the International Conference on Fifth-Generation Computer Systems*, pp. 623-632, ICOT, Tokyo, Japan, and North-Holland, Amsterdam, The Netherlands, 1984.

[44] D. Ungar, R. Blau, P. Foley, D. Samples, and D. Patterson, "Architecture of SOAR: Smalltalk on RISC," *Proceedings of the 11th Annual International Symposium on Computer Architecture*, pp. 188-197, IEEE Computer Society, Washington, D.C., 1984.

[45] D. Moon, *Maclisp Reference Manual*, MIT Press, Cambridge, Mass., 1974.

[46] B. Sheil, "Power Tools for Programmers," *Datamation*, vol. 29, no. 2, pp. 131-144, Feb. 1983.

[47] W. Teitelman and L. Masinter, "The Interlisp Programming Environment," *Computer*, vol. 14, no. 4, pp. 25-33, April 1981.

[48] E.D. Sacerdoti, R.E. Fikes, R. Reboh, D. Sagalo-wicz, R.J. Waldinger, and B.M. Wilber, "Qlisp—A Language for the Interactive Development of Complex Systems," *Proceedings of the National Computer Conference*, pp. 139-146, AFIPS Press, Reston, Va., 1976.

[49] G.L. Steele, Jr., "An Overview of Common Lisp," *Record of the 1982 Symposium on Lisp and Function Programming*, pp. 98-107, ACM, New York, N.Y., 1982.

[50] R. Wilensky, *Lispcraft*, W.W. Norton & Company, New York, N.Y., 1984.

[51] A. Newell, J.C. Shaw, and H.A. Simon, "Programming the Logic Theory Machine," *Proceedings of the 1957 Western Joint Computer Conference*, pp. 230-240, IRE, New York, N.Y., 1957.

[52] A. Newell, J.C. Shaw, and H.A. Simon, "Empirical Explorations with the Logic Theory Machine," *Computers and Thought*, edited by E.A. Feigenbaum and J. Feldman, pp. 109-133, McGraw-Hill, New York, N.Y., 1963.

[53] C. Hewitt, *Description and Theoretical Analysis (Using Schemas) of PLANNER: A Language for Proving Theorems and Manipulating Models in Robots*, Doctoral Dissertation, AI Laboratory, MIT, Cambridge, Mass., 1971.

[54] D.G. Bobrow and T. Winograd, "An Overview of KRL—A Knowledge Representation Language," *Cognitive Science*, vol. 1, no. 1, pp. 3-46, 1976.

[55] S. Fahlman, *NETL: A System for Representing and Using Real-World Knowledge*, Series on Artificial Intelligence, MIT Press, Cambridge, Mass., 1979

[56] J.F. Reiser, ed., *SAIL, Technical Report STAN-CS-76-574*, Computer Science Dept. Stanford University, Menlo Park, Calif., 1976.

[57] D. Davies, et al., *POPLER 1.5 Reference Manual*, University of Edingburgh, Edinburgh, England, 1973.

[58] R.A. Le Faivre, *FUZZY Reference Manual*, Computer Science Dept., Rutgers University, New Brunswick, N.J., 1977.

[59] M. Sato and T. Sakurai, "QUTE: A Prolog/Lisp Type Language for Logic Programming," *Proceedings of the 8th International Joint Conference on Artificial Intelligence*, pp. 507-513, William Kaufmann, Los Altos, Calif., Aug. 1983.

[60] K. Clark and S. Gregory, "Note on System Programming in PARLOG," *Proceedings of the International Conference on Fifth-Generation Computer Systems*, pp. 299-306, ICOT, Tokyo, Japan, and North-Holland, Amsterdam, The Netherlands, 1984.

[61] E.Y. Shapiro, "A Subset of Concurrent Prolog and Its Interpreter, *Technical Report TR-003*, ICOT, Tokyo, Japan, 1984.

[62] E.Y. Shapiro, "Object Oriented Programming in Concurrent Prolog," *New Generation Computing*, vol. 1, no. 1, pp. 25-48, 1983.

[63] K. Tabata, S. Sugimoto, and Y. Ohno, "Concurrent Lisp and Its Interpreter," *Journal of Information Processing*, vol. 4, no. 4, Feb. 1982.

[64] S. Sugimoto, K. Tabata, K. Agusa, and Y. Ohno, "Concurrent Lisp on a Multi-Micro-Processor System," *Proceedings of the 7th International Joint Conference on Artificial Intelligence*, pp. 949-954, William Kaufmann, Los Altos, Calif., Aug. 1981.

[65] D. Barstow, "A Perspective on Automatic Programming," *Proceedings of the 8th International Joint Conference on Artificial Intelligence*, pp. 1170-1179, William Kaufmann, Los Altos, Calif., Aug. 1983.

[66] E.J. Lerner, "Automating Programming," *IEEE Spectrum*, vol. 19, no. 8, pp. 28-33, Aug. 1982.

[67] D.R. Barstow, "An Experiment in Knowledge-Based Automatic Programming," *Readings in Artificial Intelligence*, edited by B.L. Webber and N.J. Nilsson, pp. 289-312, Tioga, Palo Alto, Calif., 1981.

[68] Z. Manna and R. Waldinger, "A Deductive Approach to Program Synthesis," *Proceedings of the 6th International Joint Conference on Artificial Intelligence*, pp. 542-551, William Kaufmann, Los Altos, Calif., 1979.

[69] D.R. Smith, "A Design for an Automatic Programming System," *Proceedings of the 7th International Joint Conference on Artificial Intelligence*, pp. 1027-1029, William Kaufmann, Los Altos, Calif., Aug. 1981.

[70] E.A. Feigenbaum, "Knowledge Engineering: The Applied Side," *Intelligent Systems: The Unprecedented Opportunity*, edited by J.E. Hayes and D. Michie, pp. 37-55, Ellis Horwood Ltd., Chichester, England, 1983.

[71] D.B. Lenat, "Computer Software for Intelligent Systems," *Scientific American*, vol. 251, no. 3, pp. 204-213, Sept. 1984.

[72] F. Hayes-Roth, "The Knowledge-Based Expert System: A Tutorial," *Computer*, vol. 17, no. 9, pp. 11-28, Sept. 1984.

[73] F. Hayes-Roth, "Knowledge-Based Expert Systems," *Computer*, vol. 17, no. 10, pp. 263-273, Oct. 1984.

[74] D.A. Waterman and F. Hayes-Roth, *Pattern-Directed Inference Systems*, Academic Press, Orlando, Fla., 1978.

[75] F. Hayes-Roth, D.A. Waterman, and D.B. Lenat, *Building Expert Systems*, Addison-Wesley, Reading, Mass., 1983.

[76] B.G. Buchanan, "New Research on Expert Systems," *Machine Intelligence 10*, edited by J. Hayes, D. Michie, and Y.-H. Pao, pp. 269-299, Ellis Horwood Ltd., Chichester, England, 1982.

[77] W.B. Gevarter, "An Overview of Expert Systems," *Technical Report NBSIR 82-2505,* National Bureau of Standards, Washington, D.C., 1982.

[78] D.S. Nau, "Expert Computer System," *Computer,* vol. 16, no. 2, pp. 63-85, Feb. 1983.

[79] R. Davis, "Expert Systems: Where Are We? And Where Do We Go From Here?," *The AI Magazine,* vol. 3, no. 2, pp. 3-22, Spring 1982.

[80] A.S. Cromarty, "What Are Current Expert System Tools Missing?," *Proceedings of COMPCON S'85,* pp. 411-418, IEEE Computer Society, Washington, D.C., 1985.

[81] V.P. Kobler, "Overview of Tool for Knowledge Base Construction," *Proceedings of the Data Engineering Conference,* pp. 282-285, IEEE Computer Society, Washington, D.C., 1984.

[82] W. Van Melle, E.H. Shortliffe, and B.G. Buchanan, "EMYCIN: A Domain-Independent System That Aids in Constricting Knowledge-Based Consultation Programs," *Machine Intelligence: Infotech State of the Art Report 9,* Infotech International, London, England, 1981.

[83] W. Van Melle, A.C. Scott, J.S. Bennett, and M. Peairs, "The EMYCIN Manual," *Technical Report HPP-81-16,* Computer Science Dept., Stanford University, Menlo Park, Calif., 1981.

[84] L. Erman, P. London, and S. Fickas, "The Design and Example Use of HEARSAY-III," *Proceedings of the 7th International Joint Conference on Artificial Intelligence,* pp. 409-415, William Kaufmann, Los Altos, Calif., 1981.

[85] H.P. Nii and N. Aiello, "AGE (Attempt to Generalize): A Knowledge-Based Program for Building Knowledge-Based Programs," *Proceedings of the 6th International Joint Conference on Artificial Intelligence,* pp. 645-655, William Kaufmann, Los Altos, Calif., Aug. 1979.

[86] C. Forgy and J. McDermott, "OPS—A Domain-Independent Production Systems Language," *Proceedings of the 5th International Joint Conference on Artificial Intelligence,* pp. 933-939, William Kaufmann, Los Altos, Calif., 1977.

[87] M. Stefik, D. Bobrow, S. Mittal, and L. Conway, "Knowledge Programming in LOOPS: Report on an Experimental Course," *The AI Magazine,* vol. 4, no. 3, pp. 20-30, Fall 1983.

[88] J. Fain and F. Hayes-Roth, et al., "Programming in ROSIE: An Introduction by Means of Examples," *Technical Note N-1646-ARPA,* Rand Corp., Santa Monica, Calif., 1982.

[89] R. Greiner and D. Lenat, "A Representation Language," *Proceedings of the First National Conference on Artificial Intelligence,* pp. 165-169, William Kaufman, Los Altos, Calif., 1980.

[90] R. Davis and B. Buchanan, "Meta-level Knowledge: Overview and Applications," *Proceedings of the 5th International Joint Conference on Artificial Intelligence,* pp. 920-928, William Kaufmann, Los Altos, Calif., 1977.

[91] S.M. Weiss and C.A. Kulikowski, "EXPERT: A System for Developing Consulting Models," *Proceedings of the 6th International Joint Conference on Artificial Intelligence,* pp. 942-947, William Kaufmann, Los Altos, Calif., 1979.

[92] R.O. Duda, J.G. Gaschnig, and P.E. Hart, "Model Design in the PROSPECTOR Consultant System for Mineral Exploration," *Expert System in the Micro-Electronics Age,* Edinburgh University Press, Edinburgh, England, 1979.

[93] B.G. Buchanan and E.A. Feigenbaum, "Dendral and MetaDendral: Their Applications Dimension," *Artificial Intelligence,* vol. 11, no. 1-2, pp. 5-24, 1978.

[94] D.B. Lenat and J.S. Brown, "Why AM and EURISKO Appear to Work?," *Artificial Intelligence,* vol. 23, no. 3, pp. 269-294, 1984.

[95] The Xerox Learning Research Group, "The Smalltalk-80 System," *Byte,* vol. 6, no. 8, pp. 36-48, Aug. 1981.

[96] D.G. Bobrow, "If Prolog Is the Answer, What Is the Question? Or What It Takes to Support AI Programming Paradigms," *IEEE Transactions on Software Engineering,* vol. SE-11, no. 11, pp. 1401-1408, Nov. 1985.

Software I

Function-level computing

A new programming method, linked to radically different architectures, may greatly simplify software development

Computer hardware has advanced tremendously in the last 25 years, going from vacuum tubes to very large-scale integrated circuits. In the same period neither the architecture of computers nor the programming languages used to control them have changed significantly. As a result, the expanding capabilities of VLSI are not being fully exploited and the costs of much-needed programs are soaring. Recognition of this fact has focused attention on a style of programming called functional programming, which offers the prospect of much cheaper programs and new machine architectures that exploit VLSI. The functional approach rejects the model of computing conceived by the mathematician John von Neumann and others. The von Neumann model is based on a computer consisting of a central processing unit (CPU), a store or memory, and a connection between them that transmits a single unit of data, or "word," between the CPU and the store. Because today's programming languages are modeled on such computers, programs are complex, concerned with the smallest data entities, and seldom reusable in building new programs.

The most unfortunate result has been the enormous cost of software. While computing power and hardware costs get cheaper every year, the writing of software becomes more expensive. The programs to make a given microprocessor useful may cost considerably more to develop than the microprocessor itself. Such costs and the expertise required to write programs discourage millions of people from using computers.

There are two functional programming styles, one—exemplified by the LISP language—was developed over 20 years ago. But while function definition is its central notion, LISP retains some features of von Neumann programming. The second style, called function-level programming, has been developed since the mid-1970s by a number of researchers, including this writer.

In this style, existing programs are put together with so-called program-forming operations to form new programs, which can again be used to build even larger ones. This approach allows parallel operations to be expressed easily; it suggests hardware designs built from large numbers of identical units that can achieve highly parallel operation, designs well suited to VLSI technology.

Function-level computing is still in its infancy; only relatively small resources are being devoted to its development. In part this is because it is more a revolutionary than an evolutionary approach to computing. Many theoretical and practical problems remain to be solved before it can become a reality in the

John Backus   IBM Research

marketplace. Nevertheless interest in function-level computing is steadily growing because it is one of very few approaches that offer a real hope of relieving the twin crises of computing today: the absolute necessity to reduce the cost of programming and the need to find computer designs that make much better use of the power of VLSI and of parallelism.

The von Neumann bottleneck

The key problem caused by the original design of computers is in the connection between the CPU and the store [see Fig. 1]. Since the huge contents of the store must pass, one word at a time, through this connection to the CPU and back again, one might call this the "von Neumann bottleneck."

This bottleneck blocks parallel operation and the effective use of more VLSI circuits, but, more critically, it is the model for serious drawbacks in programming languages. Programs in present languages alter the data stored in memory one word at a time. Variables in the programs are used to designate the storage cells, and one entire assignment statement is needed to alter the

---

The software challenge

The growth of computer use in the last few years has been fueled by the wide availability of cheap hardware, but it is becoming more and more clear that software is the limiting factor in putting raw computer power to use. Software packages may now cost more than the machines they run on, and even the several hundred thousand professional programmers in the United States cannot keep up with the demand. Programming, although it is becoming easier, is still too complex and tedious for the average computer user to pick up, and so the ultimate users of computing power—businessmen, accountants, scientists, and engineers—still require a middleman to communicate with their machines.

Some of the attempts at making programming easier and more efficient are aimed at relieving professional programmers of drudgery—by shifting repetitive tasks to the machine—while other attempts are aimed at simplifying and automating program generation so that nonprogrammers can set up complex tasks. These approaches are dealt with in the second and third articles in this special report, "Automating programming" [pp. 28–33] and "Programming for nonprogrammers" [pp. 34–38].

A more radical approach is presented by John Backus of IBM Research in San Jose, Calif., in "Function-level computing" beginning on this page. Mr. Backus, the originator of the Fortran computer language, believes that the problem lies in the basic architecture of current machines and current languages. He proposes that new basic designs for computers and corresponding new programming styles will make far easier the task of building complex programs from simple modules.

One thing is clear from these articles: while software automation is on the way, it is not yet here. Some simple tasks have been automated, but automatic generation of complex programs is still some way off.   —*Ed.*

Reprinted from *IEEE Spectrum*, Volume 19, Number 7, August 1982, pages 22-27. Copyright © 1982 by The Institute of Electrical and Electronics Engineers, Inc.

data for each variable. Thus programs consist of repetitive sequences of instructions, with control statements governing how many times and under what conditions the sequences of assignment statements are to be repeated.

If programming is to be really simplified, it is absolutely crucial to be able to build high-level programs from existing programs; and one must be able to do this knowing only the purpose of each constituent program without a lot of other details. [To understand how existing programming languages fail in this, see "The stores problem," p. 27].

A shift in focus in programming

Both von Neumann and LISP-style programs are more concerned with "object" building than with program building. For example, "average(x,y) = half(x + y)" defines an "object-level" program that transforms any pair of objects, x and y, into the desired result-object, their average. It uses object-forming operations (half, +) to build the objects x + y and then half (x + y). It says how to build an object, not how to build the program.

Function-level programming seeks to shift the focus and the level of programming from the combining of objects to the combining of programs (programs are now simply mathematical functions or mappings). The goal of this shift from object-level to function-level description of programs is to emphasize the main issue of programming: how programs are put together, rather than how objects are put together.

Instead of describing how to form the result-object for a program by applying object-forming operations to objects, the function-level style constructs the program directly by applying program-forming operations (PFOs) to existing programs. For example, the function-level description of average is "average = half ∘ + ". Here average is built from two simpler programs (half, +) with the PFO "composition," denoted by the small circle (∘), which means "do the right operation (+) first, then do the left one (half) to the result." Thus, average applied to a pair of numbers is simply the half of their sum.

In the function-level style half a dozen or more PFOs can be used to construct programs. In each case the meaning of a program built by a PFO is simply related to the meanings of the programs from which it is built. The program P ∘ Q always represents the composition of the purpose of P with that of Q, and P ∘ Q is always meaningful if it makes sense to apply P to the things that Q produces.

It is this ability to build up meaningful programs from either simple or complex ones that is the principal strength of the function-level style. It can describe programs that have no object-level counterparts; these tend to be concise, well structured and nonrepetitive.

Another program-forming operation is "construction," which is denoted by square brackets. The construction of two programs does both operations to its argument and returns a pair of results. Thus the program [half, double] applied to 4 gives $< 2,8 >$. If one now starts with three given programs P, Q, and R and builds the program P ∘ [Q,R], then its meaning is clear: first do [Q,R] to form a pair of objects, the first the result of applying Q, the second the result of applying R (a pair of objects is also an object). Then do P to that pair. P ∘ [Q,R] will be meaningful if it makes sense to apply P to pairs produced by Q and R.

In addition to the power that PFOs provide for building meaningful programs at all levels of complexity, they also have other important properties. For example, composition and construction satisfy the distributive law $[f, g] \circ h = [f \circ h, g \circ h]$, for all programs f, g, and h. Notice that the program on the right side can be made more efficient by transforming it into the one on the

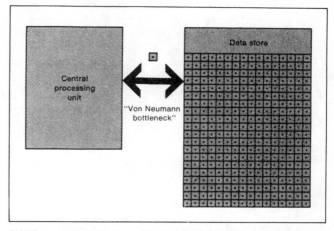

[1] The von Neumann machine operates on one word of data at a time, even when the same operation must be performed on thousands of words. Finding the location of a piece of data in memory and bringing it to the CPU therefore limits computational speed.

left, since the latter uses h only once. Thus even this simple law can be used to improve many programs. There are dozens of similar laws from which many theorems about programs can be derived; these can represent a large body of knowledge that can be used again and again to prove the correctness of programs and to guide their construction.

Some program-forming operations express parallel operations very naturally, whereas von Neumann programs are essentially sequential. When the program [P,Q] is executed, it makes no difference whether P or Q is done first or whether both are done together. This potential for parallelism in function-level programming, if incorporated into new computer architectures, would lead to a better use of VLSI.

To see why such languages may some day cut the cost of programming by a larger factor than Fortran achieved 25 years ago when it replaced machine languages, it may be helpful to contrast function-level programming languages with von Neumann languages in five major areas:

1. *Program domains*

Present programs map stores into stores, whereas their real purpose is to map objects into objects. The structure of data objects in the store is known only to the programs that use it; changing the size or structure of the data means changing the programs.

Function-level programs map objects into objects and thus a program directly represents the transformation that is its purpose. Objects can be numbers or symbols or even sequences of other objects. The structure of a data object is part of the object, rather than part of the program, so the same program can treat objects of different structure and size.

2. *Program building*

In the present approach, unless programs have a common data-storage plan, a composite program built from them is meaningless. In the function-level approach, programs can be freely built from others that have suitable purposes. The purpose of a program is simply related to those of the programs from which it is built.

3. *Program structure*

Present programs contain three kinds of structures: programs, expressions, and variables or constants. A program is built from

63

subprograms the simplest of which are the assignment statements (variable: = expression); these in turn are built from expressions (for example, $2x + y$), and expressions are built from variables and constants.

Function-level programs are built only from programs, and the simplest programs are given at the outset.

4. *Program-forming operations*

Present programs are built with three PFOs: composition, if-then-else, and while. Function-level programs can be built using six or more PFOs: composition, condition, construction, constant, apply-to-all, insert, and others [see "Function-level programming in action," below, for descriptions].

5. *Algebraic treatment of programs and correctness proofs*

With present programs, PFOs satisfy few algebraic laws. There are few general, practical theorems about programs; most apply only to a single program or a small class of programs (for

---

Function-level programming in action

Function-level programs consist of objects, functions, functional forms, definitions, and one operator called "application." Objects are numbers, symbols, words, or sequences. A sequence $< x_1, x_2, \ldots, x_n >$ of objects consists of x's which are either numbers, symbols, words, or sequences.

"Application" is the operation of applying a function to an object. For example, to apply the addition function $(+)$ to the object $< 1, 2 >$ we write:

$$+ : < 1, 2 > = 3$$

Primitive functions, like all functions, transform one object into another. Examples are:
1. Selector functions, which choose an element of a sequence:

$$1 : < x_1, x_2, \ldots, x_n > = x_1$$
$$2 : < x_1, x_2, \ldots, x_n > = x_2$$

2. Arithmetic functions, such as $+, -, \times, \div$, and so on.
3. Transpose:

$$\text{trans}: << 1, 2 >, < 3, 4 >> = << 1, 3 >, < 2, 4 >>$$

4. Distribution functions, such as distribute from the left:

$$\text{distl}: <x, <y_1, y_2, \ldots, y_n >> = <<x, y_1 >, <x, y_2 >, \ldots, <x, y_n >>$$

Functional forms are expressions denoting programs that are built from existing programs using program-forming operations (PFOs). Some examples of PFOs and simple functional forms built with them are:
1. Composition (of f and g):

$$(f \circ g) : x = f : (g : x)$$

In words: the composition of f and g, $f \circ g$, applied to x gives the result of applying f to the result of applying g to x. If f = arctan and g = sin, then $f \circ g$ is the arctangent of the sine.
2. Construction (of $f_1, f_2, \ldots, f_n$):

$$[f_1, f_2, \ldots, f_n] : x = < f_1 : x, f_2 : x, \ldots, f_n : x >$$

3. Condition (of p, f and g):

$$(p \rightarrow f; g) : x = f : x \text{ if } p : x \text{ is true;}$$
$$= g : x \text{ if } p : x \text{ is false}$$

4. Constant (of an object y; constant makes a constant-valued function out of an object):

$$\bar{y} : x = y \quad \text{for any x, the function y gives the result y}$$

5. Insert (of f):

$$/ f : < x_1, x_2, \ldots, x_n > = f : < x_1, / f : < x_2, \ldots, x_n >>$$

6. Apply-to-all (of f):

$$\alpha f : < x, x_2, \ldots, x_n > = < f : x_1, f : x_2, \ldots, f : x_n >$$

Definitions define new functions in terms of old ones. Thus **Def** $f = g \circ [h, k]$ means that f is to stand for the function $g \circ [h, k]$

The difference between function-level and von Neumann programs can be illustrated.

Vector inner product. The vector inner product is obtained by multiplying pairwise the elements of two vectors and adding these products. For example, in a billing system, a vector of the prices of all items would be multiplied by the vector of orders for each item to give the total bill.

(a) Von Neumann program:

```
c : = 0;
for i : = 1 step 1 until n do
    c : = c + a ( i ) × b ( i )
```

(b) Function-level program:

Define Inner Product = (insert +) ∘ (apply-to-all ×)
∘ transpose

Or in abbreviated form:

Def IP $= (/ +) \circ (\alpha \times) \circ \text{trans}$

This program is executed from right to left and can be expressed as follows: "The definition of inner product is: transpose the pair of vectors (pair their elements), multiply each pair together, and sum the resulting vector." A preprocessor or "translator" program would not have much trouble in translating language like the above into the FP definition.

To see this program in action, take the vectors $< 1, 2, 3 >$ and $< 4, 5, 6 >$ as an example and apply IP to this pair:
1. Composition gives:

$$(/ +) : ((\alpha \times) : (\text{trans}: << 1, 2, 3 >, < 4, 5, 6 >>))$$

2. Transpose gives:

$$(/ +) : ((\alpha \times) : << 1, 4 >, < 2, 5 >, < 3, 6 >>)$$

3. Apply-to-all gives:

$$(/ +) : < \times : <1, 4 >, \times : < 2, 5 >, \times : < 3, 6 >>$$

4. Multiply gives:

$$(/ +) : <4, 10, 18>$$

5. Insert gives:

$$+ : < 4, + : <10, 18 >>$$

6. Addition gives:

$$+ : < 4, 28 >$$

7. Another addition gives:

$$32$$

The von Neumann and functional programs for inner product have several differences:
1. The functional program is hierarchically built from three generally useful, preexisting programs ($+, \times$, trans). All the components (the two assignment statements and the 'for' statement) of the other program must be specially written for it alone.
2. The von Neumann program is repetitive—to understand it, one must mentally execute it, or use special mathematical tools. The FP program is nonrepetitive; if its components are understood, its meaning is clear.
3. The von Neumann program computes one word at a time by repetition. The functional program operates on whole conceptual units, not words, and does not repeat any steps.
4. The first program mentions the length, n, of the vectors; hence it lacks generality. The functional program is completely general.
5. The von Neumann program names its arguments—it will only work for vectors called a and b. The functional program can be applied to any pair of vectors without naming them.
—*J.B.*

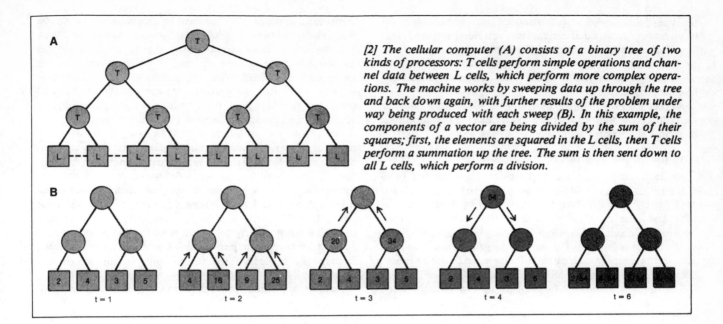

[2] *The cellular computer (A) consists of a binary tree of two kinds of processors: T cells perform simple operations and channel data between L cells, which perform more complex operations. The machine works by sweeping data up through the tree and back down again, with further results of the problem under way being produced with each sweep (B). In this example, the components of a vector are being divided by the sum of their squares; first, the elements are squared in the L cells, then T cells perform a summation up the tree. The sum is then sent down to all L cells, which perform a division.*

example, "Theorem: this program is correct").

With function-level programs, PFOs satisfy dozens of algebraic laws that yield many general theorems about program equivalence and about solving equations for programs. Proofs about large classes of programs are possible, and other proofs can be greatly simplified by drawing on standard general theorems, as in mathematics.

This comparison indicates that function-level languages have overcome many of the principle problems in von Neumann languages. However, these languages are very distant from the von Neumann model of computing, and this means that either many problems of optimization must be solved before they can be run on von Neumann computers with acceptable speed or else that new, non-von Neumann computers must be designed to execute function-level programs efficiently.

A non-von Neumann computer

A number of efforts are seeking to develop such a computer. Two projects are typical of these efforts. One is being led by Professor Gyula Mago at the University of North Carolina at Chapel Hill, the other by Professor Arvind at the Massachusetts Institute of Technology's Laboratory for Computer Science in Cambridge.

Prof. Mago's design is the more radical of the two, since the parallelism inherent in functional programs is carried out to the fullest in the structure of the computer, in which storage and processing units are intimately linked. The computer consists of an arbitrarily large number of cells, each of which is one of two types: leaf, or L, cells and tree, or T, cells [see Fig. 2]. The tree cells are connected to form a binary tree, with each cell communicating with one parent cell and two child cells. The leaf cells form the base of the tree, each cell being the child of a T cell; each L cell is connected to its two neighboring L cells in addition to its parent T cell. All L cells are identical, as are all T cells, so that the overall design of the computer is simple and well adapted to VLSI technology.

In operation, functional program expressions, including their data, are fed into the L cells. The T cells then partition the expression, breaking it down into independent subexpressions. Each subexpression is composed of a function and the data to which it is being applied; each can be evaluated at the same time as all the others. The partitioning of the T and L cells in this way divides the whole machine into a number of subtrees. Each subtree is a smaller machine applying its own program to its own data.

The L cells act both as storage units and as processors, while the T cells manage communication between the L cells. By its very structure, the cellular computer avoids the problem of addressing, since its operation ensures that when the moment comes to apply any subprogram, its data will be in the adjacent L cells to its right.

The operation of the computer consists of a series of upward and downward sweeps of information as increasingly large parts of the functional expression are computed. The process begins with the innermost parts, which can be calculated immediately, and ends when the entire expression has been evaluated.

The T cells distribute the microprogram required by each L cell to apply the operational part of the expression to data in neighboring cells. For example, a microprogram might instruct the L cell to send its contents to the T cells above that are working to evaluate the same expression. Thus, during each machine cycle, information will sweep up to the top of the subtree working on a given subexpression, and the information collected there will be sent down for further use by the L cells. At the end of each downward sweep, another stage in the evaluation of the subexpression will be completed.

Each cell of the machine is a fairly simple microprocessor containing both a CPU and a very small store. The L cells have a small store for microprograms, local storage for the symbol stored in the cell, its level of nesting in the expression, some condition registers, and a CPU.

The T cells are still simpler, basically containing only data registers and very simple processing units to direct the data and perform simple operations on it.

The basic simplicity of the cells and the fact that there are only two kinds means that the cost of designing and building such computers, even very large ones, should be manageable. Prof. Mago envisions computers with as many as a million cells, each with a few thousand circuits, with a number of cells on each VLSI chip.

Prof. Mago has made detailed calculations of the speed of operation of such computers. Performance of several billion instructions per second may be feasible in some applications. Yet, because of the simplicity of construction, such computers might be no more expensive that current large von Neumann machines. Since these machines implement both primitive programs and program-forming operations with microprograms, their machine language is a higher-level language than current so-called high-level languages.

At present, Prof. Mago is designing the elementary chips for the cellular computer and expects to produce the first prototype chips in a couple of years.

An alternative approach

An important alternative approach to implementing functional languages is the data-flow architecture of Prof. Arvind at MIT (data-flow ideas were first elaborated by Jack Dennis at MIT and later by Paul Kosinski at IBM Research Center, Yorktown Heights, N.Y.). Unlike the Mago machine, Prof. Arvind's design is intended for use with any functional language, not just the language we have been discussing. All such languages are compiled into a graphical data-flow language.

The Arvind machine itself consists of up to several thousand identical microprocessors connected by a packet communication network that allows any unit to send "tokens" to any other unit. Each token contains a piece of data and a "tag" telling to what processor the token is to be sent and with which other tokens its data is to be combined. When any processor receives a token, it matches it with its mate, performs the appropriate operation on the data of the token pair, forms a new token with the result, and sends it to the appropriate processor for further treatment.

Each processor has several sections [see Fig. 3]. A token normally arrives at the waiting-matching section, which contains tokens waiting for their mates. When a pair of matching tokens is formed, it is sent to the instruction-fetch section, which retrieves the needed instructions from its program memory and sends them with the data from the tokens to the arithmetic-and-logic unit (ALU). The ALU combines the data using the instructions to form a result. Finally this result is sent to the output section where it is incorporated into a new token whose tag is computed from the tags of the input tokens and from the addresses given in the instructions.

As much as possible, code related to a single loop within a pro-

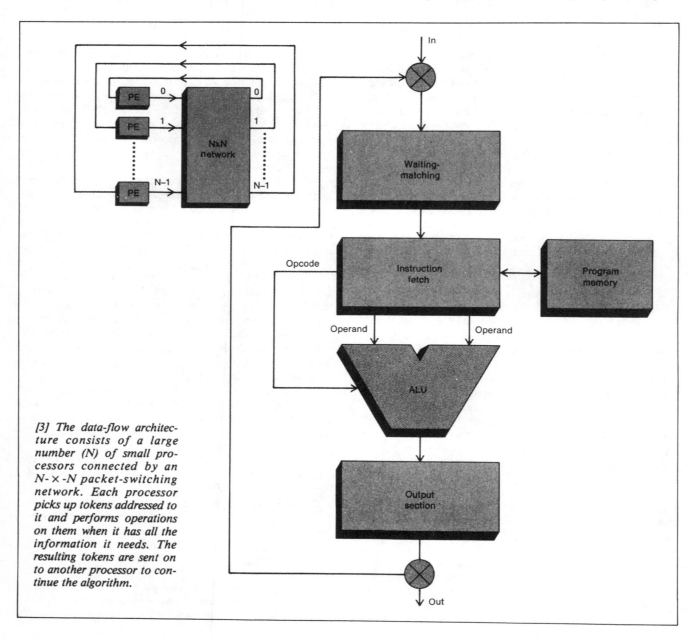

[3] The data-flow architecture consists of a large number (N) of small processors connected by an N-×-N packet-switching network. Each processor picks up tokens addressed to it and performs operations on them when it has all the information it needs. The resulting tokens are sent on to another processor to continue the algorithm.

The stores problem

Von Neumann programs depend on the details of the storage plan that positions their data in the store (a store is a set of named cells, each cell containing a word of problem data). Programs must also provide the structure for their data, which resides in the store as an unstructured set of words. Thus larger programs can be built only from smaller ones that share a common storage plan (where is the data and what is its structure?), with the result that they must all be planned and written together. This prevents building up large collections of programs that can be used over and over to make larger ones.

The word-at-a-time nature of programs is another important factor, along with the need for storage plans that interferes with their universal applicability.

The net result of these difficulties is that programming takes a great deal of time to learn and a great deal of time to do. In addition, prepackaged programs are often so inflexible as to severely limit their use, or they offer so large a catalogue of options and features that it is very difficult to learn how to use them. Thus the accomplishments of the vast army of programmers is not even cumulative.

One way to understand the basic problems of von Neumann programming languages is to observe that their programs always map stores into stores. However, the *purpose* of a program is to map objects into objects—for example, to map a matrix into its inverse, or a file of transactions into a file of responses. The purpose of a program is *never* to map stores into stores, yet this is what all von Neumann programs do. Thus the programmer must translate the purpose of his program—say, to map matrices into their inverses—into a mapping of stores in which the input matrix occupies certain cells and the results others.

This disparity between the purpose of a program, on one hand, and its actual store-to-store mapping, on the other, is the source of the difficulty in building von Neumann programs from smaller ones. Suppose there are two programs, one to invert matrices, the other to transpose them, but they have not been planned together. Now a program to calculate the inverse of the transpose of a matrix is desired. It would seem a simple matter to form the composition of the two program, which first does "transpose" and then does "inverse," to get the desired program. But unless both programs have a common storage plan (and independent programs generally do not), with the output cells of "transpose" coinciding exactly with the input cells of "inverse," the composition of the programs will not achieve the composition of their purposes: the resulting program will be meaningless.

It is possible to write special von Neumann programs called subroutines whose storage plans can be altered when they are *used*, rather than being fixed when they are written. Such subroutines can be reused more easily than ordinary programs but are less convenient for building larger programs than functional programs, which do not depend on storage plans.

—J.B.

gram is assigned to a physically related group of processors so that communication time between processors is minimized.

Prof. Arvind's group is now working on the detailed design of a 64-processor prototype machine, which they expect to be operating by the end of 1985.

It is too early to say which of these approaches to functional-style hardware will prove more fruitful, or whether some other approach may in the end be more suitable than either. Once prototypes are operating, it will be possible to compare the actual performance and costs of the various designs.

Problems remaining

A significant number of issues in functional programming need elaboration before commercialization can be considered. The most important relates to the handling of secondary and permanent storage. In addition, hardware must be built and tested, microprogramming systems elaborated, and problems run.

Before any of the projects developing parallel computers for functional programs have built a cost-effective model, some simple sequential computers for functional languages may evolve to fill the gap between today's computers and the parallel, non–von Neumann computers of tomorrow.

Were non–von Neumann computing to be widely adopted, its impact would likely be profound. Not only would programming time be reduced and repetitive programming of similar problems be largely eliminated, but programming of many applications could be simplified so that each one of millions of potential users could write programs for his own needs without the help of a professional programmer. Combined with the increased speed that would be possible with new computer architectures and VLSI design, a vast expansion of computer applications is entirely conceivable. Many tasks, such as visual recognition and computer graphics, involving many parallel computations could become much easier with such an approach. Finally, the design and manufacturer of hardware based on many identical parts could become much cheaper than current hardware. Overall, the possible advantages of non–von Neumann computing seem to justify

a much larger commitment of resources to its rapid development than is currently being made.

To probe further

The problems of conventional programming methods are discussed in "Can Programming Be Liberated from the von Neumann Style? A Functional Style and its Algebra of Programs," by John Backus, *Communications of the ACM*, August 1978, pp. 613–41. The difference between the function-level style and the LISP style of programming is elaborated in "Functional-level programs as mathematical objects," *Proceedings of the Conference on Functional Programming Languages and Computer Architecture*, October 1981, pp. 1–10, Association of Computing Machinery.

For a more complete description of the Mago machine see "A Network of Microprocessors to Execute Reduction Languages," Parts I and II, *International Journal of Computer and Information Sciences*, October and December 1979, pp. 349–85 and pp. 435–71.

"The U-interpreter," by Arvind and Kim P. Gostelow, *IEEE Computer*, February 1982, pp. 42–49, contains a description of the Arvind machine; a further description is found in "A multiple-processor data-flow machine to support generalized procedures," by Arvind and Zinod Kathail, *Proceedings of the Eighth*, *International Symposium on Computer Architecture*, IEEE and ACM, pp. 291–302.

About the author

John Backus is an IBM fellow at the IBM Research Laboratory in San Jose, Calif. He headed the group that produced the Fortran language and its first compiler. He also participated in the design of the international programming language Algol and proposed the language called Backus-Naur Form, or BNF, used to describe its syntax. A member of the National Academies of Sciences and of Engineering, Mr. Backus holds B.S. and A.M. degrees in mathematics from Columbia University. ◆

INFORMATION PROCESSING 74 – NORTH-HOLLAND PUBLISHING COMPANY (1974)

PREDICATE LOGIC AS PROGRAMMING LANGUAGE*

Robert KOWALSKI

*University of Edinburgh, Department of Computational Logic
Edinburgh, Scotland*

The interpretation of predicate logic as a programming language is based upon the interpretation of implications

$$B \text{ if } A_1 \text{ and } \ldots \text{ and } A_n$$

as procedure declarations, where B is the procedure name and $A_1, \ldots, A_n$ is the set of procedure calls A_i constituting the procedure body. An axiomatisation of a problem domain is a program for solving problems in that domain. Individual problems are posed as theorems to be proved. Proofs are computations generated by the theorem-prover which executes the program incorporated in the axioms. Our thesis is that predicate logic is a useful and practical, high-level, non-deterministic programming language with sound theoretical foundations.

1. INTRODUCTION

The purpose of programming languages is to enable the communication from man to machine of problems and their general means of solution.

The first programming languages were machine languages. To communicate, the programmer had to learn the psychology of the machine and to express his problems in machine-oriented terms. Higher-level languages developed from machine languages through the provision of facilities for the expression of problems in terms closer to their original conceptualisation.

Concerned with the other end of the man-to-machine communication problem, predicate logic derives from efforts to formalise the properties of rational human thought. Until recently, it was studied with little interest in its potential as a language for man-machine communication. This potential has been realised by recent discoveries in computational logic which have made possible the interpretation of sentences in predicate logic as programs, of derivations as computations and of proof procedures as feasible executors of predicate logic programs.

As a programming language, predicate logic is the only language which is entirely user-oriented. It differs from existing high-level languages in that it possesses no features which are meaningful only in machine-level terms. It differs from functional languages like LISP, based on the λ-calculus, in that it derives from the normative study of human logic, rather than from investigations into the mathematical logic of functions.

This paper deals only in a preliminary way with some of the issues raised by the consideration of predicate logic as a programming language. The semantics of predicate logic as a programming language is investigated in another paper with Maarten van Emden {5}. A more comprehensive investigation of the use of predicate logic for the representation of knowledge is in preparation. Hayes { 8 } and Sandewall {23} have also concerned themselves with topics related to the programming language interpretation of predicate logic. An earlier investigation with similar objectives was carried out by Cordell Green { 7 }.

2. SYNTAX

All questions concerning logical implication in first order logic can be replaced by questions concerning unsatisfiability of sentences in clausal form.

*This research was sponsored by a grant from the Science Research Council.

Such sentences have an especially simple syntax and lack none of the expressive power of the full predicate calculus. A sentence in clausal form is a set of clauses. A clause is a pair of sets of atomic formulas, written

$$B_1, \ldots, B_m \leftarrow A_1, \ldots, A_n$$

An atomic formula has the form $P(t_1, \ldots, t_k)$ where P is a k-ary predicate symbol and the t_i are terms. A term is either a variable $x, y, z, \ldots$ or an expression $f(t_1, \ldots, t_k)$, where f is a k-ary function symbol and the t_i are terms. The sets of all predicate symbols, function symbols and variables are any three sets of mutually disjoint symbols. Constants are 0-ary function symbols.

3. SEMANTICS

The semantics of sentences in clausal form is as simple as their syntax. Interpret a set of clauses $\{C_1, \ldots, C_n\}$ as a conjunction,

$$C_1 \text{ and } C_2 \text{ and } \ldots \text{ and } C_n .$$

Interpret a clause $B_1, \ldots, B_m \leftarrow A_1, \ldots, A_n$, containing variables $x_1, \ldots, x_k$ as a universally quantified implication,

for all $x_1, \ldots, x_k$, B_1 or $\ldots$ or B_m
is implied by A_1 and $\ldots$ and A_n.

The special cases where m = 0 or n = 0 deserve special readings.

If n = 0, read

for all $x_1, \ldots, x_k$, B_1 or $\ldots$ or B_m .

If m = 0

for no $x_1, \ldots, x_k$, A_1 and $\ldots$ and A_n.

If both m = 0 and n = 0, write the null clause,
□
interpreted as denoting falsity (or contradiction).

Methods for transforming arbitrary first-order sentences into clausal form are described in Nilsson's book {19}. It is our thesis, however, that clausal form defines a natural and useful language in its own right, that thoughts can conveniently be expressed directly in clausal form, and that literal translation from another language, such as full predicate logic, often distorts the original thought.

4. EXAMPLE: A PROGRAM FOR COMPUTING FACTORIAL

(F1) Fact(0,s(0)) ←
(F2) Fact(s(x),u) ← Fact(x,v),Times(s(x),v,u)

Regard the terms 0, s(0), s(s(0)),... as the numerals 0,1,2,.... Read Fact(x,y) as stating that the

factorial of x is y and Times(x,y,z) as stating that
x times y is z.   Read s(x) as referring to the
successor of x.   Given a program (or set of clauses)
for computing the Times relation, (F1) and (F2)
constitute a program for computing the factorial
relation.   To compute the factorial of the number 2,
we add to the program the clause

$$(F3) \leftarrow Fact(s(s0)),x)$$

which states that no x is the factorial of s(s(0)).
This contradicts (F1) and (F2) which logically imply
that the factorial of 2 is 2.   There exist proof
procedures which detect the contradiction by finding
the counter-instance s(s(0)) of x which is the
factorial of s(s(0)).   These proof procedures
compute the factorial of 2 without deriving any
logical consequences of (F1)-(F4) which do not belong
to the computation.

5. EXAMPLE: A PROGRAM FOR APPENDING LIST STRUCTURES.

(A1) Append(nil,z,z) ←
(A2) Append(cons(x,y),z,cons(x,u)) ← Append(y,z,u)

Interpret a term such as cons(x,cons(y,cons(z,nil)))
as a list $[x,y,z]$, as is done in such list processing
languages as LISP.   The constant term nil represents
the empty list.   Read Append(x,y,z) as stating that
z results from appending the list y to the list x.
The first clause asserts that the result of appending
any list z to the empty list nil is just z itself.
The second clause asserts that the result of appending
z to the non-empty list cons(x,y) is cons(x,u) where
u is the result of appending z to y.   To append the
list $[c]$ to the list $[a,b]$, we add to the program
the clause

(A3) ← Append(cons(a,cons(b,nil)),cons(c,nil),x)

which states that no list x results from appending
$[c]$ to $[a,b]$.   This statement contradicts (A1) and
(A2) which logically imply that $[a,b,c]$ results from
appending $[c]$ to $[a,b]$.   Any correct and complete
proof-procedure will prove the unsatisfiability of
the set of clauses $[(A1),(A2),(A3)]$.   Some proof-
procedures will do so by constructing the counter-
instance cons(a,cons(b,cons(c,nil))) of x, without
deriving logical consequences of (A1)-(A3) which do
not play an essential rôle in the construction.

6. HORN CLAUSES

The preceding two examples used only the Horn clause
subset of predicate logic.   Robert Hill has shown
that, in general, Horn clauses are adequate for
defining all relations computable over the domains of
Herbrand universes.   A Horn clause is a clause

$$B_1,\ldots,B_m \leftarrow A_1,\ldots,A_n$$

containing at most one disjunct in the conclusion,
i.e. $m \leq 1$.   In order to convert existing programs
into Horn clause programs (or, better, to reformulate
them) it is useful to bear in mind the procedural
interpretation of Horn clauses.   There are four
kinds of Horn clauses.

(1) $B \leftarrow A_1,\ldots,A_n$ (when neither n=0 nor m=0) is
interpreted as a procedure declaration.   The
conclusion B is interpreted as the procedure name.
The antecedent $\{A_1,\ldots,A_n\}$ is interpreted as the
procedure body.   It consists of a set of
procedure calls A_i.

(2) $B \leftarrow$ (when n=0) is interpreted as an assertion of
fact.   It can be regarded as a special kind of
procedure which has an empty body.

(3) $\leftarrow A_1,\ldots,A_n$ (when m=0) is interpreted as a goal
statement which asserts the goal of successfully
executing all of the procedure calls A_i.   A goal
statement can be regarded as procedure which has
no name.

(4) ☐ (when n=0 and m=0), the null clause is interpreted as a halt statement.   It can be regarded
as a satisfied goal statement, i.e. as a nameless

procedure with an empty body.

In the rest of this paper we will generally use the
term procedure in the wide sense which includes
assertions, goal statements and the halt statement as
special cases.

7. PROCEDURE INVOCATION

Useful inference systems for demonstrating the
unsatisfiability of sentences in clausal form can be
formulated without logical axioms and with just a
single inference rule called resolution $\{21\}$.   In the
procedural interpretation, resolution is interpreted
as procedure invocation.   For example, from the goal
statement

$$\leftarrow Fact(s(s(0)),x)$$

and from the procedure

$$Fact(s(x),u) \leftarrow Fact(x,v),Times(s(x),v,u)$$

resolution derives the new goal statement

$$\leftarrow Fact(s(0),v),Times(s(s(0)),v,x).$$

More generally, given a goal statement

$$\leftarrow A_1,\ldots,A_{i-1},A_i,A_{i+1},\ldots,A_n$$

and a procedure

$$B \leftarrow B_1,\ldots,B_m$$

whose name B matches the selected procedure call A_i
(in the sense that some most general substitution θ
of terms for variables makes A_i and B identical,
resolution derives the new goal statement

$$\leftarrow (A_1,\ldots,A_{i-1},B_1,\ldots,B_m,A_{i+1},\ldots,A_n)\theta .$$

Notice that treating variables as universally quantified within the clause in which they occur means that
all variable occurrences are interpreted as local to
the procedure in which they occur.

Procedure invocation, in the form of resolution, can
also be used to derive new assertions from old
assertions using procedures as antecedent theorems in
PLANNER $\{9\}$.   More generally, procedure invocation
can be applied to derive new procedures from old
procedures.   In its general form, given a selected
procedure call A_i in a procedure

$$A \leftarrow A_1,\ldots,A_{i-1},A_i,A_{i+1},\ldots,A_n$$

and given a procedure

$$B \leftarrow B_1,\ldots,B_m$$

whose name matches (with substitution θ) the selected
procedure call, resolution derives the new procedure

$$(A \leftarrow A_1,\ldots,A_{i-1},B_1,\ldots,B_m,A_{i+1},\ldots,A_n)\theta .$$

In this paper we concern ourselves primarily with the
use of resolution to derive new goal statements from
old ones.

8. COMPUTATION

The standard notion of computation, applied to Horn
clause programs, concerns the repeated use of procedure
invocation in order to derive new goal statements from
old ones with the ultimate objective of deriving the
halt statement.   More precisely, given a set S of
Horn clauses and an initial goal statement $C_1 \in S$, a
computation is a sequence of goal statements $C_1,\ldots,C_n$
such that C_{i+1} is derived by procedure invocation from
C_i using a procedure in S whose name matches some
selected procedure call in C_i.   A computation is
successful if it ends with the halt statement, i.e.
if $C_n = \Box$.   A computation terminates without success
if the selected procedure call in the end goal statement C_n matches the name of no procedure in S.

Fig. 1 illustrates the only successful computation
determined by the program (F1),(F2), activated by the
initial goal statement (F3), and employing the criterion of selecting procedure calls of the form Fact
(s,t) in preference to calls of the form Times(s',t',u').

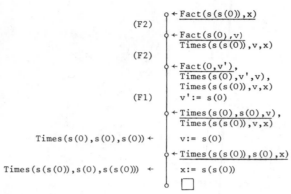

Fig. 1. A computation of the factorial of 2. In each goal statement, the selected procedure call is underlined. The arc, connecting C_i with C_{i+1} is labelled by the procedure used to derive C_{i+1} from C_i. The same arc is labelled by the assignment of terms to variables which is that part of the matching substitution which can be interpreted as passing output from the procedure name to the procedure call.

In the logic interpretation, computations are resolution derivations. The end goal statement of a computation is a logical consequence of the original set of sentences S. In particular, if the computation is successful, then it is a refutation of S, i.e. a demonstration of the unsatisfiability of S. Among existing theorem-proving systems, Loveland's model elimination [14], Reiter's ordered resolution [20] and our SL-resolution [10] are general purpose systems which, given a set of Horn clauses and an initial goal statement, admit the generation of no derivation which cannot be interpreted as a computation in the sense defined above. Kuehner's system [12] is special-purpose in that it is designed to deal only with sets of Horn clauses. However, his system has a bi-directional facility which can supplement the capability for generating new goal statements from old goal statements with a complimentary capability for generating new assertions from old ones. Our connection graph system [11] is a general purpose system which also provides bi-directional capabilities as well as providing facilities for deriving new procedures from old ones, as in macro-processing.

Except for the connection graph system whose completeness has not yet been demonstrated, all of these systems are complete and correct in the sense that a set of Horn clauses S is unsatisfiable if and only if the inference system admits a refutation of S. All of these systems avoid redundancy by selecting, for the application of procedure invocation, only a single procedure call in every goal statement. Other systems [14,15] which allow only the generation of new goal statements from old ones differ from these by admitting all the n! redundant sequences possible for selecting in turn n procedure calls from a goal statement $\leftarrow A_1, \ldots, A_n$.

In the sequel, we refer to proof procedures which derive new goal statements from old ones, using a selection criterion to avoid redundancy, as top-down procedures, to distinguish them from bottom-up procedures which derive new assertions from old assertions.

9. NON-DETERMINISM

Predicate logic is an essentially non-deterministic programming language. Non-determinism is due to the fact that a given program and activating goal statement may admit more than a single legitimate computation. Consider the following program for selecting an element from a list

(M1) Member(x,cons(x,y)) ←
(M2) Member(z,cons(x,y)) ← Member(z,y)

Fig. 2 illustrates the space of all computations determined by the program (M1),(M2) activated by the goal statement

(M3) ← Member(x,cons(a,cons(b,nil)))

which asserts the goal of finding an x which is a member of the list [a,b].

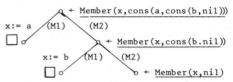

Fig. 2. The space of all computations determined by (M1)-(M3). The space contains two successful computations and one unsuccessfully terminating computation.

The non-determinism of predicate logic programs does not arise in the manner foreseen by McCarthy [16] and Floyd [6], through the addition to a deterministic language of an explicit amb or choice primitive. Predicate logic is essentially non-deterministic since it provides for the computation of relations, treating functions as a special kind of relation. As in PLANNER non-determinism is implemented by means of pattern-directed procedure invocation. It is the possibility that more than one procedure can have a name which matches a selected procedure call which gives rise to non-determinism.

The implementation of procedure call by pattern-matching has other consequences besides providing a tool for the implementation of non-determinism. In particular, the use of pattern-matching makes it unnecessary to use selector functions for accessing the components of data structures. Thus, for example, when using the cons function symbol for list processing it is unnecessary to use car and cdr functions for accessing the first and second components of pairs cons(s,t). A related use of pattern-matching is for the implementation of conditional tests on the form of data structures. This is illustrated, for instance, in the factorial example where pattern-matching implements a conditional test on the structure of the first argument t of a procedure call Fact(t,u). If t is 0 then the assertion (F1) responds. If t is s(x), for some x, then the recursive procedure (F2) responds. If t is a variable, then both (F1) and (F2) respond non-deterministically.

Predicate logic programs exhibit a second kind of non-determinism due to the fact that procedure bodies consist of a set of procedure calls which can be executed in any sequence. This kind of non-determinism is investigated in the section after next.

10. INPUT-OUTPUT

The generation and application, during procedure invocation, of the substitution θ which matches the selected procedure call A_i in a goal statement

$$\leftarrow A_1, \ldots, A_{i-1}, A_i, A_{i+1}, \ldots, A_n$$

with the name B of a procedure

$$B \leftarrow B_1, \ldots, B_m$$

has to do with the transfer of input and output. Instantiation of variables occurring in the procedure name B by terms occurring in the procedure call A_i corresponds to passing input from A_i to the body $B_1, \ldots, B_m$ of the procedure through the procedure name. The instantiated procedure body $(B_1, \ldots, B_m)\theta$ is the result of the input transfer. Instantiation of variables occurring in the procedure call A_i by terms occurring in the procedure name B corresponds to passing output (or, rather, partial output) back to the procedure call A_i which distributes it to the remaining procedure calls $A_1, \ldots, A_{i-1}, A_{i+1}, \ldots, A_n$. The instantiated residue $(A_1, \ldots, A_{i-1}, A_{i+1}, \ldots, A_n)\theta$

of the original goal statement is the result of this output transfer.

Fig. 3 illustrates the only successful computation determined by the program (A1),(A2) activated by the initial goal statement (A3). The assignments labelling the arc which connects consecutive goal statements C_i and C_{i+1} are the output components of the substitution generated in deriving C_{i+1} from C_i. Notice how the final output x:= cons(a,cons(b,cons (c,nil))) is the composition of the intermediate partial outputs x:= cons(a,x'), x':= cons(b,x"), x":= cons(c,nil). Computation of output from input is computation by successive approximation. In this example the successive approximations to the final output are x:= cons(a,x'), x:= cons(a,cons(b,x")) , x:= cons(a,cons(b,cons(c,nil))). Notice how the predicate logic notion of procedure differs from the usual notion of a procedure which initially accepts input and eventually returns output only upon successful termination.

(A2) ← Append(cons(a,cons(b,nil)), cons(c,nil),x)
      x:= cons(a,x')
(A2) ← Append(cons(b,nil),cons(c,nil),x')
      x':= cons(b,x")
      ← Append(nil,cons(c,nil),x")
(A1) x":= cons(c,nil)
      □

Fig. 3. Computation of output from input by successive approximation.

In fact, predicate logic programs do not explicitly distinguish between input and output. For this reason the rôle of input and output arguments of a procedure name can change from one procedure call to another. For example, in the goal statement

      (F4) ← Fact(x,s(0))

the second argument of Fact behaves as an input position whereas the first argument behaves as output position. In the goal statement (F3) the input and output positions are reversed. Fig. 4 illustrates the space of all computations determined by the program (F1),(F2) activated by (F4). Notice how changing the input-output positions of a procedure can turn a deterministic program which computes a function into a non-deterministic program which computes the function's inverse.

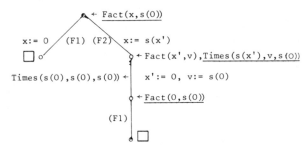

Fig. 4. The transformation of a 'deterministic' program into a non-deterministic one by changing the rôle of input and output arguments.

The ability to exploit the lack of explicit distinction between input and output is available also in the assertional programming languages ABSYS and ABSET {4}, which in other ways resemble predicate logic as a programming language.

11. SEQUENCING OF PROCEDURE CALLS

A procedure body consists of a set of procedure calls. Although a top-down proof procedure selects and executes procedure calls in some sequence, the specification of this sequence is not determined by the predicate logic program itself. The sequencing of procedure calls has no syntactic representation. Neither does it have a semantics, in the sense that sequencing does not affect the input-output behaviour of programs. This does not mean that sequencing is not important. Intelligent sequencing of procedure calls is a necessity for practical programming.

Consider the following program for sorting lists. This same program was also investigated for a similar purpose in {11}.

(S1) Sort(x,y)← Perm(x,y),Ord(y)
(S2) Perm(nil,nil) ←
(S3) Perm(z,cons(x,y)) ← Perm(z',y),Del(x,z,z')
(S4) Del(x,cons(x,y),y) ←
(S5) Del(x,cons(y,z),cons(y,z')) ← Del(x,z,z')
(S6) Ord(nil) ←
(S7) Ord(cons(x,nil)) ←
(S8) Ord(cons(x,cons(y,z))) ← LE(x,y),Ord(cons(y,z))
(S9) LE(1,2) ←   (S10) LE(1,3) ←
(S11) LE(2,3) ←   (S12) LE(x,x) ←

Here read Sort(x,y) as stating that y is a sorted version of the list x; Perm(x,y), that y is a permutation of x; Ord(y), that y is ordered; Del(x,y,z), that z results by deleting one occurrence of x from y; and LE(x,y), that x is less than or equal to y.

(S1) states that y is a sorted version of x if y is a permutation of x and y is ordered. If (S1) is interpreted by a top-down proof procedure which selects and completes the execution of the procedure call Perm(x,y) before activating Ord(y), and if in addition the first arguments of Sort, Perm and Ord are considered as input positions, then (S1) can be read as stating that

> (S1.1) in order to sort the list x, first generate a permutation y of x, then test that y is ordered; if it is, then y is a sorted version of x.

The meaning of the program does not change, however, if it is interpreted by a top-down proof procedure which selects and completes the execution of Ord(y) before selecting Perm(x,y). In such a case, still reading x as input variable, (S1) can be read as stating that

> (S1.2) in order to sort the list x, first generate an ordered list y, then test that y is a permutation of x; if so then y is a sorted version of x.

Clearly the difference in efficiency can be enormous, but the meaning, as determined by the input-output relation Sort(x,y), computed by the program, is the same. It is in this sense that the sequencing of procedure calls can be said to have no semantics.

The use of parallel processes and co-routines is a particular way of sequencing procedure calls. The possibility of independent parallel processing arises when, for example, different procedure calls in the same body share no variables. In such a case, the independent procedure calls can be activated simultaneously and, given a single processor, their execution sequences can be interleaved arbitrarily. On the other hand, the procedure (S1) in the sorting example illustrates a situation where two procedure calls can be executed semi-independently as co-routines. That the use of co-routines is possible in this example is due, in the first place, to the fact that partial output from the procedure call Perm(x,y) is transmitted to the latent call Ord(y) and secondly that such partially specified input can initiate computation as efficiently as totally specified input. Fig. 5 illustrates an unsuccessfully terminating computation determined by selecting for activation an instance of the procedure call Ord(y) before completing the execution of Perm(x,y). If (S1) is interpreted by a top-down proof procedure which selects the procedure call Perm(x,y) before

Ord(y) but interrupts the execution of Perm(x,y) activating Ord(y) in order to monitor the partial output of Perm(x,y), then reading x as input variable, (S1) states that

> (S1.3) in order to sort the list x, beginning with the empty sublist nil, first generate an initial sublist of a permutation of x, then test that the sublist is ordered. If it is not ordered, generate another sublist if there is any which has not been generated. If it is ordered but is not a complete permutation, then add another element to the sublist and test that the new sublist is ordered. If it is ordered and is a complete permutation of x, then it is the desired sorted version of x.

The equivalence of (S1.1),(S1.2) and (S1.3) can be demonstrated by noting that they differ only with respect to the different sequencing of procedure calls which they impose on the same program (S1).

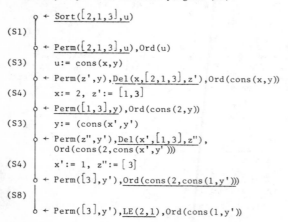

Fig. 5. An unsuccessfully terminating computation determined by the program (S1)-(S12) activated by the goal of sorting the list [2,1,3] incorporated in the goal statement ← Sort([2,1,3],u). Here the notation [2,1,3] is an abbreviation for cons(2,cons(1,cons (3,nil))). The computation terminates because no procedure name matches the call LE(2,1).

It is interesting that a sequencing of procedure calls which may be useful for one specification of input and output positions may be unusable for a different specification. Fig. 4 illustrates how a different sequencing of procedure calls is appropriate in (F2) when the second argument of Fact(x,y) is used for input rather than the first. For another example, suppose that the predicate symbols P and Q denote relations which are one-one functions. Consider the procedure declaration

R(x,z) ← P(x,y),Q(y,z).

Given a procedure call of the form R(t,z), where t contains no variables, the first argument position of the call acts as the input position and the second argument acts as output position. The selection of P(t,y) in preference to Q(y,z) in the instantiated procedure body leads to a deterministic computation. The unique output y:= t' of the procedure call P(t,y) is obtained and passed as input to the latent procedure call Q(y,z). The call Q(t',z) then succeeds with unique output z:= t". The alternative selection of Q(y,z) in preference to P(t,y) determines the much less efficient, non-deterministic algorithm which first generates pairs of output (t',t") for the procedure call Q(y,z) and then checks that P(t,t'). However, if the original procedure call has the form R(x,s), where s contains no variables, the first argument acts as output position and the second acts as input position. Efficient sequencing of procedure calls in the instantiated body ←P(x,y),Q(y,s) requires the activation of Q(y,s) in preference to P(x,y).

The viability of predicate logic as a programming language depends upon the eventual provision of an auxiliary control language which would provide a programmer with the ability to specify appropriate sequencing instructions to the interpreting proof procedure. Such a control language ought to be incapable of affecting the meaning of programs, influencing only their efficiency. Some day it may be possible to devise autonomous proof procedures which are able to determine for themselves efficient ways of sequencing procedure calls and of sequencing the application of procedures when more than one responds to a selected procedure call. In the meanwhile, it will not be possible to program effectively without the aid of an auxiliary control language. The importance and utility of such a control language has been argued by Pat Hayes {8}.

ACKNOWLEDGMENT

That sets of axioms are like programs, in the way that different formulations can have equivalent meanings but very different influences on efficiency, is a point of view which runs counter to the prevailing moods in symbolic logic and in artificial intelligence. In particular, the attacks by Anderson and Hayes {1} and by Minsky and Papert {17} against the utility of the theorem-proving paradigm depend upon the assumption that axioms convey meaning but not pragmatic information. Our contrary point of view was reinforced by joint research with Alain Colmerauer (reported in {11}) on axiomatisations of grammars, regarded as programs for syntactic analysis. Further reinforcement was provided by the work of Philippe Roussel {22}, who showed that many uses of the equality relation could be replaced by the more efficiently mechanisable identity relation. Roussel's experience encouraged us to abandon the equality relation altogether, replacing equalities, not interpretable as identities, by implications, as in the procedural interpretation of Horn clauses. The work of Colmerauer and Roussel has since resulted in the elaboration, at the University of Aix-Marseille, of the PROLOG language {3} based on predicate logic. The work of Hayes, arguing that control structures are needed to provide pragmatic information which cannot usefully be expressed by axioms, has now been reported {8}.

Another common impression about theorem-proving is that deduction is completely consequence-oriented and therefore unsuitable for goal-oriented problem-solving. Our contrary attitude was substantiated by our studies of Loveland's model elimination {13} and by our interpretation of model elimination as a goal-oriented resolution system {10}. Later, the discovery by Bob Boyer and J Moore {2} that certain ways of efficiently implementing theorem-provers resemble ways of implementing programming language interpreters, helped to suggest that theorem-provers can be regarded as interpreters for programs written in predicate logic. The work of Boyer and Moore led to the implementation of BAROQUE {18}, an experimental language with a LISP-like interpreter written in predicate logic and interpreted in turn by a resolution theorem-proving program written in POP-2.

The initiation of the work reported in this paper owes much to the profitable interactions we have had with Hayes, Colmerauer, Roussel, Boyer and Moore. In particular, the general thesis that computation and deduction are very nearly the same is due to Pat Hayes. This paper would not have been written, however, without the encouragement and enthusiasm for predicate logic programming of my colleagues David Warren and Maarten van Emden. We owe a special debt to Michael Gordon for his continuing interest and helpful criticsms, and to Aaron Sloman for his detailed and useful comments on an earlier draft of this paper.

This research was initiated during a visit to the University of Aix-Marseille, supported by C.N.R.S. It was continued with the aid of a Science Research Council grant to Bernard Meltzer.

REFERENCES

{1} D.B. Anderson and P.J. Hayes, The logician's folly, D.C.L. Memo No 54, University of Edinburgh, 1972.

{2} R.S. Boyer and J S. Moore, The sharing of structure in theorem-proving programs, *Machine Intelligence 7*, Edinburgh University Press, Edinburgh, 1972, 101-116.

{3} A. Colmerauer, H. Kanoui, R. Pasero and P.Roussel, Un système de communication homme-machine en français, Rapport preliminaire, Groupe de Researche en Intelligence Artificielle, Université d'Aix-Marseille, Luminy, 1972.

{4} E.W. Elcock, J.M. Foster,P.M.D. Gray,J.J.McGregor and A.M. Murray, ABSET, a programming language based on sets: motivation and examples, *Machine Intelligence 6*, Edinburgh University Press, Edinburgh, 1971, 467-492.

{5} M. van Emden and R. Kowalski, The semantics of predicate logic as programming language, D.C.L. Memo No 73, University of Edinburgh, 1974.

{6} R.W. Floyd, Non-deterministic algorithms, *J.A.C.M.* vol. 14, No. 4, 1967, 636-644.

{7} C. Green, Application of theorem proving to problem solving, *Proceedings of IJCAI*, Washington D.C., 1969, 219-239.

{8} P.J. Hayes, Computation and deduction, *Proceedings MFCS Conf.*, Czechoslovakian Academy of Sciences, 1973.

{9} C. Hewitt, PLANNER: a language for proving theorems in robots, *Proceedings of IJCAI*, Washington D.C., 1969, 295-301.

{10} R. Kowalski and D. Kuehner, Linear resolution with selection function, *Artificial Intelligence 2*, 1971, 227-260.

{11} R. Kowalski, A proof procedure using connection graphs, D.C.L. Memo No. 74, University of Edinburgh, 1973.

{12} D. Kuehner, Some special purpose resolution systems, *Machine Intelligence 7*, Edinburgh University Press, Edinburgh, 1972, 117-128.

{13} D.W. Loveland, A simplified format for the model-elimination theorem-proving procedure, *J.A.C.M.* vol. 16, 1969, 349-363.

{14} D. Loveland, A linear format for resolution, *Proceedings IRIA Symposium on Automatic Demonstration*, Springer-Verlag, 1970, 147-162.

{15} D. Luckham, Refinement theorems in resolution theory, *Proceedings IRIA Symposium on Automatic Demonstration*, Springer-Verlag, 1970, 162-190.

{16} J. McCarthy, A basis for a mathematical theory of computation, *Computer Programming and Formal Systems*, North Holland, Amsterdam, 1963.

{17} M. Minsky and S. Papert, Progress Report, Artificial Intelligence memo no. 252, M.I.T., January 1972.

{18} J S. Moore, Computational logic: structure sharing and proof of program properties, Part I, D.C.L. Memo No, 67, University of Edinburgh, 1973.

{19} N. Nilsson, *Problem solving methods in artificial intelligence*, McGraw-Hill, New York, 1971.

{20} R. Reiter, Two results on ordering for resolution with merging and linear format, *J.A.C.M.* vol 15, no. 4, 1971, 630-646.

{21} J.A. Robinson, A machine-oriented logic based on the resolution principle, *J.A.C.M.*, vol 12, 1965, 23-41.

{22} P. Roussel, Définition et traitement de l'égalite formelle en demonstration automatique, Thèse, U.E.R. de Luminy, 1972.

{23} E. Sandewall, Conversion of predicate-calculus axioms, viewed as non-deterministic programs, to corresponding deterministic programs, *Proceedings of IJCAI-3*, August, 1973, 230-234.

POWER TOOLS FOR PROGRAMMERS

by Beau Sheil

An oil company needs a system to monitor and control the increasingly complex and frequently changing equipment used to operate an oil well. An electronic circuit designer plans to augment a circuit layout program to incorporate a variety of vaguely stated design rules. A newspaper wants a page layout system to assist editors in balancing the interlocking constraints that govern the placement of stories and advertisements. A government agency envisions a personal workstation that would provide a single integrated interface to a variety of large, evolving database systems.

Applications like these are forcing the commercial deployment of a radically new kind of programming system. First developed to support research in artificial intelligence and interactive graphics, these new tools and techniques are based on the notion of exploratory programming, the conscious intertwining of system design and implementation. Fueled by dramatic changes in the cost of computing, such exploratory programming environments have become a commercial reality virtually overnight. No fewer than four such systems were displayed at NCC '82 and their numbers are likely to increase rapidly as their power and range of application become more widely appreciated.

Despite the diversity of subject matter, a common thread runs through our example applications. They are, of course, all large, complex programs whose implementations will require significant resources. Their more interesting similarity, however, is that it is extremely difficult to give complete specifications for any of them. The reasons range from sheer complexity (the circuit designer can't anticipate all the ways in which his design rules will interact), through continually changing requirements (the equipment in the oil rig changes, as do the information bases that the government department is required to consult), to the subtle human factors issues that determine the effectiveness of an interactive graphics interface.

Whatever the cause, a large programming project with uncertain or changing specifications is a particularly deadly combi-

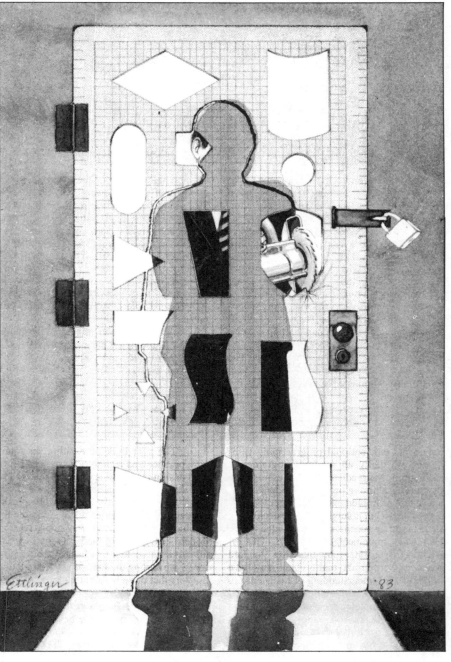

ILLUSTRATION BY DORIS ETTINGER

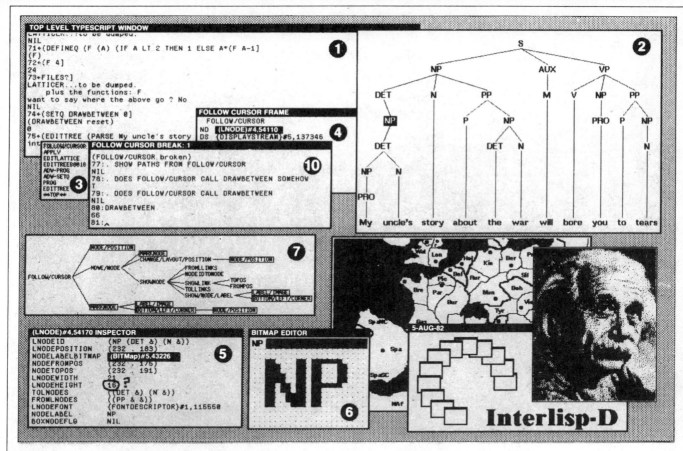

These two screen images show some of the exploratory programming tools provided in the Xerox Interlisp-D programming environment. The screen is divided into a series of rectangular areas or windows, each of which provides a view onto some data or process, and which can be reshaped and repositioned at will by the user. When they overlap, the occluded portion of the lower window is automatically saved, so that it can be restored when the overlapping window is removed. Since the display is bit-mapped, each window can contain an arbitrary mixture of text, lines, curves, and pictures composed of half-tones or solids. The image of Einstein, for instance, was produced by scanning a photograph and storing it digitally.

In the typescript window (labeled 1), the user has defined a program F (facto-rial) and has then immediately run it, giving an input of 4 and getting a result of 24. Next, in the same window, he queries the state of his files, finding that one file (LAT-TICER) has already been changed and one function (F) has been defined but not associated with any file yet. The user sets the value of DRAWBETWEEN to 0 in command 74, and the system notes that this is a change and adds DRAWBETWEEN to the set of "changed objects" that might need to be saved.

Then, the user runs the program EDITTREE, giving it a parse tree for the sentence "My uncle's story about the war will bore you to tears." This opens up the big window (2) on the right in which the sentence diagram is drawn. Using the mouse, the user starts to move the NP node on the left (which is inverted to show that it is being moved).

While the move is taking place, the user interrupts the tree editor, which suspends the computation and causes three "break" windows to appear on top of the lower edge of the typescript. The smallest window (3) shows the dynamic state of the computation, which has been broken inside a subprogram called FOLLOW/CURSOR. The "FOLLOW/CURSOR Frame" window (4) to the right shows the value of the local variables bound by FOLLOW/CURSOR. One of them has been selected (and so appears inverted) and in response, its value has been shown in more detail in the window (5) at the lower left of the screen. The user has marked one of the component values as suspicious by circling it using the mouse. In addition, he has asked to examine the contents of the BITMAP component, which has

nation for conventional programming techniques. Virtually all modern programming methodology is predicated on the assumption that a programming project is fundamentally a problem of implementation, rather than design. The design is supposed to be decided on first, based on specifications provided by the client; the implementation follows. This dichotomy is so important that it is standard practice to recognize that a client may have only a partial understanding of his needs, so that extensive consultations may be required to ensure a complete specification with which the client will remain happy. This dialog guarantees a fixed specification that will form a stable base for an implementation.

The vast bulk of existing programming practice and technology, such as structured design methodology, is designed to ensure that the implementation does, in fact, follow the specification in a controlled fashion, rathern than wander off in some unpredictable direction. And for good reason. Modern programming methodology is a significant achievement that has played a major role in preventing the kind of implementation disasters that often befell large programming projects in the 1960s.

The implementation disasters of the 1960s, however, are slowly being succeeded by the design disasters of the 1980s. The projects described above simply will not yield to conventional methods. Any attempt to obtain an exact specification from the client is bound to fail because, as we have seen, the client does not know and cannot anticipate exactly what is required. Indeed, the most striking thing about these examples is that the clients' statements of their problems are really aspirations, rather than specifications. And since the client has no experience on which to ground these aspirations, it is only by exploring the properties of some putative solutions that the client will find out what is really needed. No amount of interrogation of the client or paper exercises will answer these questions; one just has to try some designs to see what works.

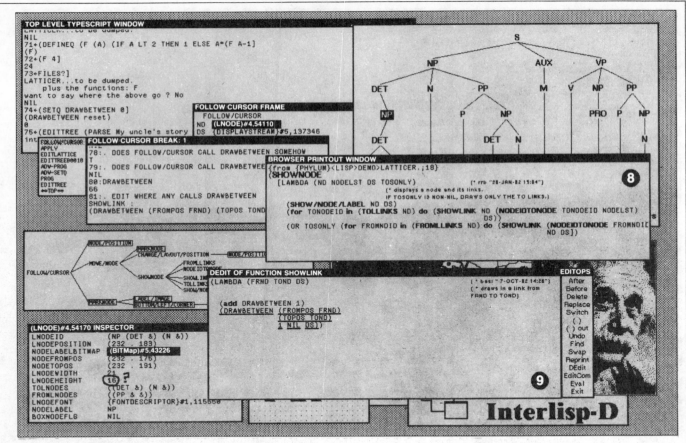

opened up a bitmap edit window (6) to the right. This shows an enlarged copy of the actual NP image that is being moved by the tree editor. Then, inside the largest of the three break windows (10) the user has asked some questions about the FOLLOW/CURSOR subprogram that was running when he interrupted, and queried the value of DRAWBETWEEN (now 66). The SHOW PATHS command brought up the horizontal tree diagram on the left (7), which shows which subprograms call each other, starting at FOLLOW/CURSOR.

Each node in the call tree produced by the SHOW PATHS command is an active element that will respond to the user's selecting it with the mouse. In the second image, the user has selected the SHOWNODE subprogram, which has caused its source code to be retrieved from the file (‹LISP›DE-

MO›LATTICER) on the remote file server (PHYLUM) where it was stored, and displayed in the "Browser printout window" (8) which has been opened at middle right. User functions and extended Lisp forms (like *for* and *do*) are highlighted by system-generated font changes.

By selecting nodes in the SHOW PATHS window, the user could also have edited the code or obtained a summary description of any of its subprograms.

Instead, the user has asked (in the break typescript window (10)) to edit wherever anybody calls the DRAWBETWEEN system primitive (which draws lines between two specified points). This request causes the system to consult its dynamically maintained database of information about user programs, wherein it finds that the subprogram SHOWLINK calls DRAWBETWEEN. It

therefore loads the code for SHOWLINK into an edit window (9) that appears under the "Browser printout window." The system then automatically finds and underlines the first (and only) call on DRAWBETWEEN. Note that on the previous line DRAWBETWEEN is used as a variable (the same variable the user set and interrogated earlier). The system, however, knows that this is not a subprogram call, so it has been skipped over. If the user were to make any change to this subprogram in the editor, not only would the change take effect immediately, but SHOWLINK would be marked as needing to be updated in its file and the information about it in the subprogram database would be updated. This, in turn, would cause the SHOW PATHS window to be repainted, as its display might no longer be valid.

The consequences of approaching problems like these as routine implementation exercises are dramatic. First, the implementation team begins by pushing for an exact specification. How long the client resists this coercion depends on how well he really understands the limits of his own grasp of the problem. Sooner or later, however, with more or less ill-feeling, the client accepts a specification and the implementation team goes to work.

The implementors take the specification, partition it, define a module structure that reflects this partitioning, freeze the interfaces between them, and repeat this process until the problem has been divided into a large number of small, easily understandable, and easily implementable pieces. Control over the implementation process is achieved by the imposition of structure, which is then enforced by a variety of management practices and programming tools.

USE OF INTERNAL RIGIDITY

Since the specification, and therefore the module structuring, is considered fixed, one of the most effective methods for enforcing it is the use of redundant descriptions and consistency checking. Hence the importance of techniques such as interface descriptions and static type checking, which require that multiple

statements of various aspects of the design be included in the program text. These statements allow mechanical checks that ensure that each piece of the system remains consistent with the rest. In a well-executed conventional implementation project, a great deal of internal rigidity is built into the system, ensuring its orderly development.

The problems usually emerge at system acceptance time, when the client requests not just superficial, but radical changes, either as a result of examining the system or for some completely exogenous reason. From the point of view of conventional programming practice, this indicates a failure at specification time. The software engineer

The implementation disasters of the 1960s are slowly being succeeded by the design disasters of the 1980s.

should have been more persistent in obtaining a fuller description of the problem, in involving all the affected parties, etc. This is often true. Many ordinary implementation exercises are brought to ruin because the consequences of the specification were never fully agreed upon. But that's not the problem here. The oil company couldn't anticipate the addition of a piece of equipment quite different from the device on which the specification was based. No one knew that the layout editors would complain that it doesn't "feel right" now that they can no longer physically handle the copy (even in retrospect, it's unclear why they feel that way and what to do about it), etc., etc., etc. Nor would any amount of speculation by either client or software engineer have helped. Rather, it would have just prompted an already nervous client to demand whole dimensions of flexibility that would not in fact be needed, leaving the system just as unprepared for the ones that eventually turned out to matter.

Whatever the cause, the implementation team has to rework the system to satisfy a new, and significantly different, specification. That puts them in a situation that conventional programming methodology simply refuses to acknowledge—except as something to avoid. As a result, their programming tools and methods are suddenly of limited effectiveness. The redundant descriptions and imposed structure that were so effective in constraining the program to follow the old specification have lost none of their efficacy—they still constrain the program to follow the old specification. And they're difficult to change. The whole point of redundancy is to protect the design from a single unintentional change. But it's equally well protected against a single intentional change. Thus, all the changes have to be made everywhere. (Since this should never happen, there's no methodology to guide or programming tools to assist this process.) Of course, if the change is small (as it "should" be), there is no particular problem. But if it is large enough to cut across the module structure, the implementation team finds that it has to fight its way out of its previous design.

Still no major problem, if that's the end of the matter. But it rarely is. The new system will suggest yet another change. And so on. After a few iterations of this, not only are the client and the implementation team not on speaking terms, but the repeated assaults on the module structure have likely left it looking like spaghetti. It still gets in the way (fire walls are just as impenetrable if laid out at random as they are when laid out straight), but has long ceased to be of any use to anyone except to remind them of the project's sorry history. Increasingly, it is actively subverted (enter LOOPHOLES, UNSPECs, etc.) by programmers whose patience is running thin. Even if the design were suddenly to stabilize (unlikely in the present atmosphere), all the seeds have now been sown for an implementation disaster as well.

EXPLORE DESIGN PROBLEMS

The alternative to this kind of predictable disaster is not to abandon structured design for programming projects that are, or can be made to be, well defined. That would be a tremendous step backwards. Instead, we should recognize that some applications are best thought of as design problems, rather than implementation projects. These problems require programming systems that allow the design to emerge from experimentation with the program, so that design and program develop together. Environments in which this is possible were first developed in artificial intelligence and computer graphics, two research areas that are particularly prone to specification instability.

At first sight, artificial intelligence might seem an unlikely source of programming methodology. But constructing programs, in particular programs that carry out some intelligent activity, is central to artificial intelligence. Since almost any intelligent activity is likely to be poorly understood (once a program becomes well understood we usually cease to consider it "intelligent"), the artificial intelligence programmer invariably has to restructure his program many, many times before it becomes reasonably proficient. In addition, since intelligent activities are complex, the programs tend to be very large, yet they are invariably built by very small teams, often a single researcher. Consequently, they are usually at or beyond the manageable limits of complexity for their implementors. In response, a variety of programming environments based on the Lisp programming language have evolved to aid in the development of these large, rapidly changing systems.

The rapidly developing area of interactive graphics has encountered similar problems. Fueled by the swift drop in the cost of computers capable of supporting interactive graphics, there has been an equally swift development of applications that make heavy use of interactive graphics in their user interfaces. Not only was the design of such interfaces almost completely virgin territory as recently as 10 years ago, but even now, when there are a variety of known techniques (menus, windows, etc.) for exploiting this power, it is still very difficult to determine how easy it will be to use a proposed user interface and how well it will match the user's needs and expectations in particular situations. Consequently, complex interactive interfaces usually require extensive empirical testing to determine whether they are really effective and considerable redesign to make them so.

While interface design has always required some amount of tuning, the vastly increased range of possibilities available in a full graphics system has made the design space unmanageably large to explore without extensive experimentation. In response, a variety of systems, of which Smalltalk is the best known, have been developed to facilitate this experimentation by providing a wide range of built-in graphical abstractions and methods of modifying and combining them together into new forms.

In contrast to conventional programming technology, which restrains the programmer in the interests of orderly development, exploratory programming systems must amplify the programmer in the interests of maximizing his effectiveness. Exploration in the realm of programming can require small numbers of programmers to make essentially arbitrary transformations to very large amounts of code. Such programmers need programming power tools of considerable capacity or they will simply be buried in detail. So, like an amplifier, their programming system must magnify their necessarily limited energy and minimize extraneous activities that would otherwise compete for their attention.

SOURCES OF DESIGN POWER

One source of such power is the use of interactive graphics. Exploratory programming systems have capitalized on recent developments in personal computing with extraordinary speed. The Xerox 1108 Interlisp-D system, for example, uses a large format display and a "mouse" pointing device to allow very high bandwidth communication with the user. Designers of exploratory programming environments have been quick to seize on the power of this combination to provide novel programming tools, as we shall see.

In addition to programming tools, these personal machine environments allow the standard features of a professional workstation, such as text editing, file management, and electronic mail, to be provided within the programming environment itself. Not only are these facilities just as effective in enhancing the productivity of programmers as they are for other professionals, but their integration into the programming environment allows them to be used at any time during programming. Thus, a programmer who has encountered a bug can send a message reporting it while remaining within the debugger, perhaps including in the message some information, like a back-trace, obtained from the dynamic context.

Another source of power is to build the important abstract operations and objects

Redundancy protects the design from unintentional change—but it's equally well protected against intentional change.

of some given application area directly into the exploratory environment. All programming systems do this to a certain extent; some have remarkably rich structures for certain domains, (e.g., the graphics abstractions embedded within Smalltalk). If the abstractions are well chosen, this approach can yield a powerful environment for exploration within the chosen area, because the programmer can operate entirely in substantively meaningful abstractions, taking advantage of the considerable amount of implementation and design effort that they represent.

The limitations of this approach, however, are clear. Substantive abstractions are necessarily effective only within a particular topic area. Even for a given area, there is generally more than one productive way to partition it. Embedding one set of abstractions into the programming system encourages developments that fit within that view of the world at the expense of others. Further, if one enlarges one's area of activity even slightly, a set of abstractions that was once very effective may become much less so. In that situation, unless there are effective mechanisms for reshaping the built-in abstractions to suit the changed domain, users are apt to persist with them, at the cost of distorting their programs. Embedded abstractions, useful though they are, by themselves enable only exploration in the small, confined within the safe borders where the abstractions are known to be effective. For exploration in the large, a more general source of programming power is needed.

Of course, the exact mechanisms that different exploratory systems propose as essential sources of programming power vary widely, and these differences are hotly debated within their respective communities. Nevertheless, despite strong surface differences, these systems share some unusual characteristics at both the language and environment level.

THE LANGUAGE LEVEL

The key property of the programming languages used in exploratory programming systems is their emphasis on minimizing and deferring the constraints placed on the programmer, in the interests of minimizing and deferring the cost of making large-scale program changes. Thus, not only are the conventional structuring mechanisms based on redundancy not used, but the languages make extensive use of late binding, i.e., allowing the programmer to defer commitments for as long as possible.

The clearest example is that exploratory environments invariably provide dynamic storage allocation with automatic reclamation (garbage collection). To do otherwise imposes an intolerable burden on the pro-

grammer to keep track of all the paths through his program that might access a particular piece of storage to ensure that none of them access or release it prematurely (and that someone does release it eventually!). This can only be done by careful isolation of storage management or with considerable administrative effort. Both are incompatible with rapid, unplanned development, so neither is acceptable. Storage management must be provided by the environment itself.

Other examples of late binding include the dynamic typing of variables (associating data type information with a variable at run-time, rather than in the program text) and the dynamic binding of procedures. The freedom to defer deciding the type of a value until run-time is important because it allows the programmer to experiment with the type structure itself. Usually, the first few drafts of an exploratory program implement most data structures using general, inefficient structures such as linked lists discriminated (when necessary) on the basis of their contents. As experience with the application evolves, the critical distinctions that determine the type structure are themselves determined by experimentation, and may be among the last, rather than the first, decisions to evolve. Dynamic typing makes it easy for the programmer to write code that keeps these decisions as tacit as possible.

The dynamic binding of procedures entails more than simply linking them at load-time. It allows the programmer to change dynamically the subprocedures invoked by a given piece of code, simply by changing the run-time context. The simplest form of this is to allow procedures to be used as arguments or as the value of variables. More sophisticated mechanisms allow procedure values to be computed or even encapsulated inside the data values on which they are to operate. This packaging of data and procedures into a single object, known as object-oriented programming, is a very powerful technique. For example, it provides an elegant, modular solution to the problem of generic procedures (i.e., every data object can be thought of as providing its own definition for common actions, such as printing, which can be invoked in a standard way by other procedures). For these reasons, object-oriented programming is a widely used exploratory programming technique and actually forms the basic programming construct of the Smalltalk language.

The dynamic binding of procedures can be taken one step further when procedures are represented as data structures that can be effectively manipulated by other programs. While this is of course possible to a limited extent by reading and writing the text of program source files, it is of much greater significance in systems that define an explicit

representation for programs as syntax trees or their equivalent. This, coupled with the interpreter or incremental compiler provided by most exploratory programming systems, is an extraordinarily powerful tool. Its most dramatic application is in programs that construct other programs, which they later invoke. This technique is often used in artificial intelligence in situations where the range of possible behaviors is too large to encode efficiently as data structures but can easily be expressed as combinations of procedure fragments. An example might be a system that "understands" instructions given in natural language by analyzing each input as it is received, building a program that captures its meaning, and then evaluating that program to achieve the requested effect.

A BASIC TECHNIQUE EXPANDED

Aside from such specialized applications, effective methods for mechanically manipulating procedures enable two other significant developments. The first is the technique of program development by writing interpreters for special purpose languages. Once again, this is a basic technique of artificial intelligence that has much wider applicability. The key idea is that one develops an application by designing a special language in which the application is relatively easy to state. Like any notation, such a language provides a concise representation that suppresses common or uninteresting features in favor of whatever the designer decides is more important.

A simple example is the use of notations like context-free grammars (BNF) to "metaprogram" the parsers for programming languages. Similar techniques can be used to describe, among other things, user interfaces, transaction sequences, and data transformations. Application development in this framework is a dialectic process of designing the application language and developing an interpreter for it, since both the language and the interpreter will evolve during development. The simplest way of doing this is to evolve the application language out of the base provided by the development language. Simply by allowing the application language interpreter to call the development language interpreter, expressions from the development language can be used wherever the application language currently has insufficient power. As one's understanding of the problem develops, the application language becomes increasingly powerful and the need to escape into the development language becomes less important.

The other result of having procedures that are easily manipulated by other procedures is that it becomes easy to write program manipulation subsystems. This in turn has two key consequences. First, the exploratory programming language itself can grow. The remarkable longevity of Lisp in the artificial intelligence community is in large part due to the language having been repeatedly extended to include modern programming language syntax and constructions. The vast majority of these extensions were accomplished by defining source-to-source transformations that converted new constructions into more conventional Lisp. The ease with which this can be done allows each user, and even each project, to extend the language to capture the idioms that are found to be locally useful.

Second, the accessibility of procedures to mechanical manipulation facilitates the development of programming support tools. All exploratory programming environments boast a dazzling profusion of programming tools. To some extent, this is a virtue of necessity, as the flexibility necessary for exploration has been gained at considerable sacrifice in the ability to impose structure. That loss of structure could easily result in a commensurate loss of control by the programmer. The programming tools of the exploratory environment enable the programmer to reimpose the control that would be provided by structure in conventional practice.

Programming tools achieve their effectiveness in two quite different ways. Some tools are simply effective viewers into the user's program and its state. Such tools permit one to find information quickly, display it effectively, and modify it easily. A wide variety of tools of this form can be seen in the two Interlisp-D screen images (see box, p. 132), including data value inspectors (which allow a user to look at and modify the internal structure of an object), editors for code and data objects, and a variety of break and tracing packages. Especially when coupled with a high bandwidth display, such viewers are very effective programming tools.

A WIDE VARIETY OF TOOLS The other type of programming tool is knowledge based. Viewer-based tools, such as a program text editor, can operate effectively with a very limited understanding of the material with which they deal. By contrast, knowledge-based tools must know a significant amount about the content of a user's program and the context in which it operates. Even a very shallow analysis of a set of programs (e.g., which programs call which other ones) can support a variety of effective programming tools. A program browser allows a programmer to track the various dependencies between different parts of a program by presenting easy to read summaries that can be further expanded interactively.

Deeper analysis allows more sophisticated facilities. The Interlisp program analyzer (Masterscope) has a sufficiently detailed knowledge of Lisp programs that it can provide a complete static analysis of an arbitrary Lisp program. A wide variety of tools have been constructed that use the database provided by this analysis to answer complex queries (which may require significant reasoning, such as computing the transitive closure of some property), to make systematic changes under program control (such as making some transformation wherever a specified set of properties hold), or to check for a variety of inconsistent usage errors.

Finally, integrated tools provide yet another level of power. The Interlisp system notices whenever a program fragment is changed (by the editor or by redefinition). The program analyzer is then informed that any existing analysis is invalid, so that incorrect answers are not given on the basis of old information. The same mechanism is used to notify the program management subsystem (and eventually the user, at session end) that the corresponding file needs to be updated. In addition, the system will remember the previous state of the program, so that at any subsequent time the programmer can undo the change and retreat (in which case, of course, all the dependent changes and notifications will also be undone). This level of cooperation between tools not only provides immense power to the programmer, but relieves him of detail that he would otherwise have to manage himself. The result is that more attention can be paid to exploring the design.

A key, but often neglected, component of an exploratory programming system is a set of facilities for program contraction. The development of a true exploratory program is design limited, so that is where the effort has to go. Consequently, the program is often both inefficient and inelegant when it first achieves functional acceptability. If the exploration were an end in itself, this might be of limited concern. However, it is more often the case that a program developed in an exploratory fashion must eventually be used in some real situation. Sometimes, the time required to reimplement (using the prototype program as a specification) is prohibitive. Other times, the choice of an exploratory system was made to allow for expected future upheaval, so it is essential to preserve design flexibility. In either event, it is necessary to be able to take the functionally adequate program and transform it into one whose efficiency is comparable to the best program one could have written, in any language, had only one known what one was doing at the outset.

The importance of being able to make this post hoc optimization cannot be overemphasized. Without it, one's exploratory programs will always be considered toys; the pressure to abandon the exploratory environment and start implementing in a real one will

be overwhelming; and, once that move is made (and it is always made too soon), exploration will come to an end. The requirement for efficient implementation places two burdens on an exploratory programming system. First, the architecture must allow an efficient implementation. For example, the obligatory automatic storage allocation mechanism must either be so efficient that its overhead is negligible, or it must permit the user to circumvent it (e.g., to allocate storage statically) when and where the design has stabilized enough to make this optimization possible.

Second, as the performance engineering of a large system is almost as difficult as its initial construction, the environment must provide performance engineering tools, just as it provides design tools. These include good instrumentation, a first-class optimizing compiler, program manipulation tools (including, at the very least, full functionality compiler macros), and the ability to add declarative information where necessary to guide the program transformation. Note that, usually, performance engineering takes place not as a single "post-functionality optimization phase," but as a continuous activity throughout the development, as different parts of the system reach design stability and are observed to be performance critical. This is the method of progressive constraint, the incremental addition of constraints as and when they are discovered and found important, and is a key methodology for exploratory development.

Both of these concerns can be most clearly seen in the various Lisp-based systems. While, like all exploratory environments, they are often used to write code very quickly without any concern for efficiency, they are also used to write artificial intelligence programs whose applications to real problems are very large computations. Thus, the ability to make these programs efficient has long been of concern, because without it they would never be run on any interesting problems.

More recently, the architectures of the new, personal Lisp machines like the 1108 have enabled fast techniques for many of the operations that are relatively slow in a traditional implementation. Systems like Interlisp-D, which is implemented entirely in Lisp, including all of the performance-critical system code such as the operating system, display software, device handlers, etc., show the level of efficiency that is now possible within an exploratory language.

The increasing importance of applications that are very poorly understood, both by their clients and by their would-be implementors, will make exploratory development a key technique for the 1980s. Radical changes in the cost of computing power have already made such systems cost-effective vehicles for

The programming languages used in exploratory systems minimize and defer constraints on the programmer.

the delivery of application systems in many areas. As recently as five years ago, the tools and language features we have discussed required the computational power of a large mainframe costing about $500,000. Two years ago, equivalent facilities became available on a personal machine for about $100,000, and a year later, about $50,000. Now, a full-scale exploratory development system can be had for about $25,000. For many applications, the incremental cost has become so small over that required to support conventional technology that the benefits of exploratory development (and redevelopment!) are now decisive.

One consequence of this revolutionary change in the cost-effectiveness of exploratory systems is that our idea of exploratory problems is going to change. Exploratory programming was developed originally in contexts where change was the dominant factor.

There is, however, clearly a spectrum of specification instability. Traditionally, the cost of exploratory programming systems, both in terms of the computing power required and the run-time inefficiencies incurred, confined their use to only the most volatile applications. Thus, the spectrum was

arbitrarily dichotomized into exploratory (very few) and standard (the vast majority). Unfortunately, the reality is that unexpected change is far more common in standard applications than we have been willing to admit. Conventional programming techniques strive to preserve a stability that is only too often a fiction. Since exploratory programming systems provide tools that are better adapted to this uncertainty, many applications that are now being treated as standard but which in fact seem to require moderate levels of ongoing experimentation may turn out to be more effectively developed in an exploratory environment.

We can also expect to see a slow infusion of exploratory development techniques into conventional practice. Many of the programming tools of an exploratory programming system (in particular, the information gathering and viewing tools) do not depend on the more exploratory attributes of either language or environment and could thus be adapted to support programming in conventional languages like FORTRAN and COBOL. Along with these tools will come the seeds of the exploratory perspective on language and system design, which will gradually be incorporated into existing programming languages

and systems, loosening some of the bonds with which these systems so needlessly restrict the programmer.

To those accustomed to the precise, structured methods of conventional system development, exploratory development techniques may seem messy, inelegant, and unsatisfying. But it's a question of congruence: precision and inflexibility may be just as dysfunctional in novel, uncertain situations as sloppiness and vacillation are in familiar, well-defined ones. Those who admire the massive, rigid bone structures of dinosaurs should remember that jellyfish still enjoy their very secure ecological niche.   ✱

Beau Sheil is on the research staff at the Palo Alto Research Center of the Xerox Corp., where he has been since receiving his PhD in computer science from Harvard University in 1976. His research interests include programming systems and the psychology of programming. Many of these ideas were first developed, and later polished, in discussions with John Seely Brown and other colleagues in cognitive and instructional sciences at Xerox PARC.

Object Oriented Programming

Tim Rentsch
Computer Science Department
University of Southern California
Los Angeles, California 90089-0782

Recently I had the opportunity to read the Intel manual introducing the iAPX 432 architecture. The manual is an amalgam of an informal overview of the hardware, a quick tutorial review of computer architectures in general, an introduction to the advanced concepts of the 432 in particular, and marketing hype proclaiming the advantages of the 432 over its competition. The 432's architecture has many interesting, unusual characteristics, and Intel is wise to introduce them in a form which is quickly assimilable. What most caught my interest is the claim that the 432 supports the "object oriented design methodology."

What is object oriented programming? My guess is that object oriented programming will be in the 1980's what structured programming was in the 1970's. Everyone will be in favor of it. Every manufacturer will promote his products as supporting it. Every manager will pay lip service to it. Every programmer will practice it (differently). And no one will know just what it is.

Surely there's a better way. I hope this paper will clarify object oriented programming by characterizing its more important aspects. These characterizations, while not a definition *per se*, should at least provide a better understanding, and ideally a commonly held one. Thus I hope we can avoid the deplorable and confusing situation just described.

History

The immediate ancestor of object oriented programming is the programming language Simula. The Smalltalk programming system carried the object oriented paradigm to a smoother model. Although other systems have definitely shown some object oriented tendencies, the explicit awareness of the idea – including the term "object oriented" – came from the Smalltalk effort. Furthermore, Smalltalk is still the strongest representative of object oriented programming in the sense of being the most unified under a single (object oriented) paradigm. Comments on some related efforts will be given in a later section. For now it is enough to note that object oriented programming arose when Smalltalk was developed and therefore the history of Smalltalk serves as the history of object oriented programming.

Smalltalk is the software half of an ambitious project known as the Dynabook. The Dynabook is a sort of computer holy grail, with the goal of being a truly personal computer. The Dynabook ultimately is expected to handle with equal facility any and all kinds of information management, and to be all (computer type) things to all people. Accordingly Smalltalk has to carry quite a burden of expressiveness and convenience.

Alan Kay is the man chiefly responsible for the vision of the Dynabook. In the late 1960's he did work on a preliminary version, known in that incarnation as the Flex machine. Then in the early 1970's he went to the Xerox Palo Alto Research Center and there formed the Learning Research Group. Alan's goal was still a truly useful personal computer, with the Xerox Alto being the interim hardware for the Dynabook, and with LRG doing Smalltalk as the software.

Smalltalk drew heavily from Flex, which in turn was an "Eulerized" version of Simula. While a LISP influence is clearly evidenced in the deeper structure of Smalltalk, the *class* notion from Simula dominated the design. The language became completely based on the notion of a class as the sole structural unit, with instances of classes, or *objects*, being the concrete units which inhabit the world of the Smalltalk system. Smalltalk did not completely give up its LISP heritage; rather that heritage is felt more as a flavor of the system than as specific ideas of the programming language.

Relationship of Smalltalk to Object Oriented Programming

More than a programming language, Smalltalk is a complete programming environment, all of which reflects the object oriented philosophy. Object oriented programming is so much a part of Smalltalk that it is difficult to tell where one leaves off and the other begins. While the entire Smalltalk system is worthy of investigation in its own right, we are now concerned only with object oriented *programming*, which is just a part of the Smalltalk system. A brief discussion will make clear the distinction and remove confusion about which term means what.

> Note: this paper is not a tutorial on the Smalltalk language. I will discuss the internals and specifics of Smalltalk only insofar as they relate to the topic at hand. Readers unfamiliar with Smalltalk may wish to read the references first, although I have tried to make this unnecessary. I suggest to the confused reader that he finish reading this paper, then consult the references to clear up any confusion, then (optionally) read this paper again.

Smalltalk may be thought of as comprised of four pieces, *viz.*, a programming language kernel, a programming paradigm, a programming system, and a user interface model. These pieces are fuzzily defined and not explicit within the actual Smalltalk system. They are basically hierarchical, though there is overlap and some convolution. Thus the user interface is built on the programming system, which is built following the programming paradigm and using the programming language kernel.

The *programming language kernel* is the syntax and semantics as determined by the Smalltalk compiler. The *programming paradigm* is the style of use of the kernel, a sort of world view or "meaning" attached to the entities in the kernel. The *programming system* is the set of system objects and classes that provides the framework for exercising the programming paradigm and language kernel, the things necessary to make programming possible and convenient. The *user interface model* is the use and usage of the systems building materials in order to present the system to the user – in other words, the given user interface plus the user interface "flavor." The combination of these four pieces is the Smalltalk system.

> Although I have represented the pieces as separate and independent, they are not, really. In fact they are inseparable and very interdependent. Not only could each piece itself not exist in a vacuum, the design for each piece influenced the design for all the other pieces, i.e., each design could not exist in a vacuum. A more faithful representation would be as interrelated aspects of the Smalltalk system. Following the note, however, I shall continue to consider them as "pieces" rather than "aspects."

Using this view of the Smalltalk world, imagine a line drawn within the programming system piece such that the objects and classes relating to the user interface model are on one side and the objects and classes relating to the programming paradigm and language kernel are on the other. We now find Smalltalk divided naturally into two parts: a user interface part, and another part. This other part is the object oriented programming aspect of Smalltalk. With the understanding that by "Smalltalk" I mean only as much of Smalltalk as is below the line of the user interface part, I shall henceforth use the terms "Smalltalk" and "object oriented programming" interchangeably.

Characterizing Object Oriented Systems

Object oriented programming is *not* programming using a Simula-like class concept, just as structured programming is not GOTO-less programming. Most of the definitions of structured programming fail to impart any real understanding of the term. We can do better by *characterizing* object oriented programming rather than giving a formal definition.

No explanation of object oriented programming could get off the ground without a discussion of objects. In characterizing such systems we are interested not in what an object is but in how an object appears. In what follows an object is always viewed from outside (the characterization of objects), not from inside (what objects "are").

It is no accident that in explaining object oriented programming objects are viewed from outside. The shift of viewpoint from inside to outside is itself an essential part of object oriented programming. In my experience this shift occurs as a quantum leap, the "aha!" that accompanies a flash of insight. In spite of this, I am convinced that the view from outside is the natural one – only my years of training and experience as a programmer conditioned me to "normally" view objects from inside. Probably due to the influence of formal mathematics, programmatic behavior was originally thought of as extrinsic. For understanding complex systems, however, intrinsic behavior provides a better metaphor, because people think that way (for example, children learn Smalltalk very quickly.) As Dijkstra cautions, we must be careful not to think something is convenient just because it is conventional. The first principle of object oriented programming might be called *intelligence encapsulation*: view objects from outside to provide a natural metaphor of intrinsic behavior.

Objects

The Smalltalk world is populated by items seen uniformly to be "objects." These "objects" are the sole inhabitants of an otherwise empty universe. This is not just a trick of nomenclature; the items are uniform in a number of ways, that uniformity producing the items' "objectivity." In what ways are objects uniform?

Objects are uniform in that all items are objects. An item found floating in the void of Smalltalk's universe is certain to be an amorphous blob. The blob has the properties of *objectness*: inherent processing ability, message communication, and uniformity of appearance, status, and reference. The item being amorphous means that no other properties are evident. The object may possess properties outside objectness, but these are made available by the whim of the object – any such properties are not visible to an outside observer.

Objects are uniform in that all objects are equally objectlike. What this means is that all objects communicate using the same metaphor, namely message passing. Objects send messages to communicate with objects. (Message sending is discussed later in the paper.)

Objects are uniform in that no object is given any particular status. Thus, "primitive" objects, such as integers, are objects just like any other. Also, "system" objects, such as class *Class*, are objects just like any other. Finally, user defined objects are objects just like any other. There are no "second class citizens."

Not only are objects themselves uniform, the means of referring to objects is uniform. An object is always dealt with as a whole, by using its (system internal) name; a given name may name any object, since all objects have the same kind of names. It follows that there is no way of opening up an object and looking at its insides, or updating ("smashing") its state. What is more important is that the concept of opening up an object does not exist in the language. (This is like trying to imagine that something is true that can't be thought of in the first place.)

Of course it is possible for the object itself to act as if it could be opened up. With suitable methods an object can choose to provide behavior that duplicates, say, a Pascal record. Pascal records can certainly have their insides looked at, or their state updated (or smashed). The distinction is that the object itself has chosen to provide this behavior – it is not part of the language. Furthermore, most objects do not normally provide such behavior. In a true object oriented system, this is as true of the system philosophy as of the actual mechanisms.

Processing, Communication, and Message Sending

For a processing system to be a useful one, processing activity must take place. In Smalltalk, the processing activity takes place inside objects. An object, far from being inert matter, is an active, alive, intelligent entity, and is responsible for providing its own computational behavior. Thus processing capability is not only inside the object, it is everpresent within and inseparable from the object.

The other property essential to a programming system is communication. An object in process may at times be entirely self sufficient, but when it is not it must have some way of interacting with objects outside of itself. Also, the user wants processing done to bring about his wishes. Both of these are needs of communication, and both are served by the mechanism of message passing.

Objects process and send messages to effect the user's desires as well as their own. A user asks an object to carry out some processing activity by sending to the object a message. The object may in turn ask other objects for information, or for some computational work to be done, by sending them messages, and so on.

Message sending serves as the uniform metaphor for communication in the same way that objects serve as the uniform metaphor for processing capability and synthesis. This uniformity is an important part of Smalltalk. In what ways is message sending uniform?

Message sending is uniform in that all processing is accomplished by message sending. The same mechanism serves to do addition, compute arctanh, request the most complicated file service operation, or provide whatever behavior is available from a user defined object. No other mechanism – such as "operating on data" – is available.

Message sending is uniform in that one message is just like another. By this I do not mean that all messages are identical, or that all messages have the same format, but that messages are sent the same way irrespective of the recipient. An example should clarify this: the message "+" to an integer, denoting addition, is sent the same way as the message "+" to a dictionary, (possibly) denoting adding an entry.

The distinction between communicating and accomplishing processing is a fine one in Smalltalk. Objects react to messages sent to accomplish processing by sending messages to accomplish processing. The buck has to stop somewhere (and indeed it does), but it seems as if it could be passed on indefinitely. A corollary of messages all being sent the same way is that each object potentially can respond to any message by sending other messages in turn. The principle as it applies to object oriented programming is: any object can accomplish processing requested by any message by directing message flow to other objects.

Messages

As the sending of a message is the only way of communicating, the message itself must be the information to be communicated. Conceptually a message is the text of the message-request. Additionally a message may be parameterized by sending along with the text one or more object names. The object name parameters are part of the language of discourse and are different from the text in that the text is constant whereas the parameters may vary. An object responds to a message with a *reply*, which is an object name.

A message serves to initiate processing and request information. The text of the message informs the object what is requested. The parameters supply any additional necessary information or computational ability. The reply confirms activity completed and returns the information requested.

There is a subtle but important distinction between a conventional procedure call, which denotes an action, and sending a message, which makes a request. In a typical procedural programming language it is hard to give up the notion that the caller of a procedure is somehow "in control." The caller and callee share a language, a set of procedural interfaces, by which the caller directs the callee to perform actions. In Smalltalk, on the other hand, a message is a request of what the sender wants with no hint or concern as to what the receiver should do to accomodate the sender's wishes. The sender, presuming all objects to be quite intelligent, trusts the receiver to do "the right thing" without worrying about exactly what the right thing is. Thus assured, the sender relinquishes control philosophically as well as actually, so that the interpretation of the message is left entirely up to its recipient. This notion, a sort of *call by desire*, is central to the object oriented philosophy.

Sharing

In order to meet the goals of the Dynabook project, Smalltalk must do more than provide computational activity *in situ*. A successful personal computer system will be understandable, usable, modifiable, and adaptable. All of these requirements can be met by a facility for *sharing*.

Sharing allows understanding because it is a good match to the way people think. For example, the earth and a basketball are different, yet each has the property *round*. There isn't one "round" that belongs to the earth and another that belongs to the basketball; the common attribute round is shared. People model the universe by collecting together archetypal attributes and allowing them to be shared by the things to which they are common.

Sharing makes for a usable system by facilitating *factoring*, the property of one thing being in only one place. Successful factoring produces brevity, clarity, modularity, concinnity, and synchronicity, which in turn provide manageability in complex systems. In a project as ambitious as the Dynabook, manageability is essential to usability.

Sharing increases the ease of making modifications. This may sound paradoxical, since changing shared parts increases the chance of producing unforeseen consequences. The paradox disappears on realizing that sharing is not a binary decision but a spectrum from totally shared to totally individual. One can choose an appropriate place for a modification by moving around in the sharing spectrum, whereupon consequently the level of detail is neither too great nor too trivial. To put this another way, you can concentrate on what must be changed, not what must be left alone. This is made possible by an explicit framework providing a spectrum of sharing.

Sharing provides for adaptation by being variable along another dimension, the dimension of individuality. What this means is that attributes can be shared by a group while allowing for individuals within the group to reinterpret some "shared" behavior *as it applies to the individuals themselves.* The previous sharing spectrum varies as to which objects share which collections of attributes; the dimension of individuality determines to what extent individuals within a given collection actually share the "common" attributes. The result of allowing individual variability is that, given something close to what you want, it is easy to produce exactly what you want by overriding shared behavior with individual behavior – to *adapt.* This situation of "I want something just like that, except ..." invariably arises in real use. Adaptation is supported by sharing in this form and is referred to as *differential programming.*

Smalltalk meets the goals of sharing by providing a framework of classing, subclassing, and superclassing, collectively referred to as *inheritance.* In relation to object oriented programming what is important is not the mechanism of classing and sub-superclassing but the provision for the merits of sharing. Inheritance is also an excellent paradigm – probably any particular framework would be – for *elucidation,* providing as it does a sort of road map for the system universe. The conclusion: object oriented systems provide an explicit framework for sharing so as to accrue the attendant advantages.

Notes on Related Systems

Smalltalk remains the model object oriented system. But no programming language is an island, and a mention of other systems is clearly called for. Following is a capsule summary of relevant systems. The point here is to view the work as it relates to object oriented programming, not to appraise the merits of the various systems.

A group of installations with Burroughs B220's used a clever scheme to insure portability of files from one installation to another, in order to get around the difficulty of not having operating systems. A file was arranged as a transfer vector with relative pointers, followed by actual B220 code, followed by data. Although the code and representation of data varied from installation to installation, the desired effect could be obtained by reading the file into a standard memory location and branching indirectly through the appropriate location in the transfer vector. This idea was later carried over into the operating system of the B5000. Indeed, the entire architectural concept of the B5000 pointed in this direction, offering the first hardware implementation of what are now known as capabilities. Unfortunately, the B5000 is almost legendary for being ahead of its time, unappreciated, and misunderstood, and so the impact of the earliest object oriented ideas was hardly felt.

The Sketchpad system of the early 1960's is an object oriented system that apparently was programmed using an object oriented style. But Sketchpad is a graphical interaction system, not a programming system. While Sketchpad was one of the earliest object oriented systems, its application to programming systems was not widely appreciated, perhaps because the object oriented philosophy was not explicit enough.

The programming language Simula is an ALGOL based simulation language which first introduced the class concept. Simula certainly can be used with a style which is highly object oriented. But old ideas die hard, and Simula's extensions over ALGOL were used in support of simulation features with traditional ALGOL style programming taking up the slack. In practice, Simula falls short of realizing object oriented programming for several reasons. One, primitive data types, system data types, and user data types do not all have equal status. Two, the extensions to ALGOL, while including the class concept, also included many "features" such as INSPECT and IN, which are contrary to the object oriented philosophy. Three, the object oriented metaphor has not really caught on in the Simula community, due to the roots of the language in ALGOL. Four, the typing mechanism in Simula often makes it difficult to realize the free-spiritedness of object oriented programming. If Sketchpad is an object oriented system without the language, Simula is an object oriented language which is rarely used in an object oriented fashion.

The LISP-AI notion of frames captures well the idea that behavior rides along with the thing whose behavior is being described. Also, the resemblance of the common/default mechanism of frames to the inheritance mechanism of Smalltalk is striking. I think of frames as an object oriented extension to LISP. Similar to Simula, however, the problem with frames is that the LISP notion very strongly remains, so that the inclination towards the object oriented philosophy is not nearly so strong, nor as clearly defined, as in a completely object oriented system.

The programming language Alphard is related but still in a rather uncertain state. After more use the character of Alphard will be clearer, but generally speaking Alphard centers on abstraction, which is roughly evenly divided between data encapsulation and abstract data types. If anything Alphard leans to the abstract data types side, though not so far as, for example, algebraic axiomatic specification. One clear oversight is that Alphard does not use inheritance in any strong fashion.

The programming language ADA, though still in the implementation stages, is clearly centered and focused on data encapsulation. The sense of operating on data is very strong in ADA, from syntax to operator overloading to separation of types from modules. Generic procedures capture some, but not nearly all, of the polymorphism inherent in object oriented programming, and ADA's facility for inheritance is weak at best. ADA has followed traditional (i.e., ALGOL style) language design principles so that the issues of implementation and usage would be clear at the outset. ADA is one of the few languages that was designed with extensive, specific requirements definitely given *a priori*; none of these requirements mentions object oriented programming.

The programming language CLU makes a serious effort in the object oriented direction. The sense of unification of reference mode is very strong in CLU, narrowing the distinction between different object categories. CLU falls a little short on the syntax side, which is still a conventional functional (i.e., data oriented) format. Also, the typing mechanism of CLU doesn't give a sense of freedom to the "receiver" of a message, since the particular response mechanism is specified by the type, which is known and explicit in the source at the call site. This restriction shifts the sense of control from the receiver (object oriented) to the sender (data oriented). Furthermore, CLU resembles Alphard and ADA in lacking a good inheritance mechanism. As with Alphard, CLU tries to balance abstract data types with data encapsulation by centering on abstraction, but CLU leans to the data encapsulation side more than Alphard does. Even so, CLU remains as the strongest "traditional" contender for supporting object oriented programming.

Conclusions

It is usual to understand new ideas in terms of familiar ones. Object oriented programming might be (and probably already has been) likened to abstract data types, data encapsulation, information hiding, and modularization. This may be more palatable to some audiences, but it ducks the issue. These comparisons neither do justice to, nor capture the essence of, the object oriented methodology. To quote Alan Kay:

> "Though Smalltalk's structure allows the techniques now known as data abstraction to be easily (and more generally) employed, the entire thrust of its design has been to supercede the concept of data and procedures entirely; to replace these with the more generally useful notions of activity, communication, and inheritance."

Object oriented programming holds great promise, but is not yet widely understood. In spite of object oriented programming just now becoming popular, the term of its use is already in danger of being overworked and misunderstood. My goal has been to argue for an understanding of object oriented programming, not just a dogmatic definition. Let us hope that we have learned our lesson from structured programming and find out what the term means *before* we start using it.

Acknowledgements

My thanks to all the people who have cheerfully let me express their ideas as though they were my own.

References

Dynabook and Related

Kay, A., "The Reactive Engine," Ph.D. Thesis, University of Utah, September, 1969

Kay, A., "A Personal Computer for Children of All Ages," ACM Nat'l Conf., Boston, Aug., 1972

Kay, A., and A. Goldberg, "Personal Dynamic Media," Computer, March, 1977

Kay, A., "Microelectronics and the Personal Computer," Scientific American, September, 1977

Other systems mentioned

Birtwhistle, *et al.*, *Simula Begin*, Petrocelli/Charter, 1975

Ichbiah, J.D., *et al.*, "Preliminary ADA Reference Manual," ACM SIGPLAN Notices 14, 6A, June, 1979

Intel Corporation, *Introduction to the iAPX 432 Architecture*, Manual Number 171821-001

Intel Corporation, *iAPX 432 Architecture Reference Manual*, Manual Number 171860-001

Liskov, B., *et al.*, *CLU Reference Manual*, MIT-TR 225, October, 1979

McKeag, R.M., "Burroughs B5500 Master Control Program," Queens University of Belfast, Northern Ireland, 1971

Roberts, B., and I. Goldstein, "The FRL Manual," MIT-TR 409, September, 1979

Sutherland, I., "Sketchpad," Ph.D. Thesis, MIT, 1963

Wulf, London, and Shaw, "An Introduction to the Construction and Verification of ALPHARD Programs," IEEE Transactions on Software Engineering SE-2, 4, 1976

Smalltalk

Byte special issue on Smalltalk, BYTE, August 1981 (primarily the following articles)
    Xerox Learning Research Group, "The Smalltalk-80 System"
    Robson, D., "Object-Oriented Software Systems"
    Tesler, L., "The Smalltalk Environment"
    Ingalls, D., "Design Principles Behind Smalltalk"
    Goldberg, A., and J. Ross, "Is the Smalltalk-80 System for Children?"

Ingalls, D., "The Smalltalk-76 Programming System: Design and Implementation," 5th Annual ACM Symposium on Principles of Programming Languages, January, 1978

PROCEEDINGS OF THE INTERNATIONAL CONFERENCE
ON FIFTH GENERATION COMPUTER SYSTEMS 1984,
edited by ICOT. © ICOT, 1984

NOTES ON SYSTEMS PROGRAMMING IN PARLOG

Keith Clark and Steve Gregory

Department of Computing, Imperial College
London SW7 2BZ, England

ABSTRACT

Several topics connected with systems
programming in the parallel logic programming
language PARLOG are discussed.

We argue that a parallel language needs a
much more elaborate metacall facility than the
simple succeed-fail metacall of PROLOG. In
order to program an operating system shell
which is failsafe, allows abort termination of
processes and which makes visible any incrementally constructed output of a user process,
a three-argument metacall primitive is needed
which always succeeds. The first argument is
the call to be evaluated, the second is the
status or result of the evaluation and the
third is an input argument which can be used
by some other process to control the evaluation of the call.

1 INTRODUCTION

1.1 Brief introduction to PARLOG

PARLOG (Clark and Gregory 1984a) is a
parallel logic programming language featuring
both and- and or-parallelism. For this paper
we need to use only the and-parallel subset of
PARLOG, which we shall briefly outline here.
This language, based on Horn clauses, differs
from PROLOG in three crucial respects: "don't
care non-determinism", parallel evaluation and
"mode" declarations to specify communication
constraints on shared variables. Each relation call can be evaluated as a separate process. The shared variables act as communication channels along which messages are sent by
incremental construction of streams, which are
lists of message terms.

1.1.1 Don't care non-determinism

A PARLOG clause takes the form

$r(t1,...,tk)$ <- <guard conditions> :
                <body conditions>.

where the : signals the end of the guard and
$t1,...,tk$ are argument terms.

Both the <guard conditions> and the <body
conditions> are conjunctions of relation
calls. There are two types of conjunction:
the parallel "and" (C1 , C2) in which the conjuncts C1 and C2 will be evaluated in parallel, and the sequential "and" (C1 & C2) where
C2 will only be evaluated when C1 has successfully terminated.

In the evaluation of a relation call
$r(t1',...,tk')$, all of the clauses for relation r will be searched in parallel for a candidate clause. The above clause is a candidate clause if the head $r(t1,...,tk)$ matches
the call $r(t1',...,tk')$ and the guard succeeds. It is a non-candidate if the match
fails or the match succeeds and the guard
fails. If all clauses are non-candidates the
call fails, otherwise one of the candidates is
selected and the call is reduced to the substitution instance of its body. There is no
backtracking on the choice of candidate
clause. We "don't care" which candidate
clause is selected. In practice, the first
one (chronologically) to be found is chosen.

During the search for a candidate clause,
no variables in the call are bound. There is
no output binding to variables of the call
until the evaluation commits to the use of
some clause. Because there is no backtracking
there is never any need to rescind a message
sent via a shared variable of the call.

The search for a candidate clause can be
controlled by the use of the ; operator between clauses. If a relation is defined by the
sequence of clauses

    Clause1.
    Clause2;
    Clause3.

Clause3 will not be tried for candidacy until
both Clause1 and Clause2 have been found to be
non-candidate clauses.

1.1.2 Modes

For every PARLOG relation definition
there is a mode declaration which states

whether each argument is input (**?**) or output (**^**). For example, the relation **merge(x,y,z)** has the mode (**?,?,^**) to merge lists **x** and **y** to list **z** (lower case identifiers are variables):

```
mode merge(?,?,^).
merge([u|x],y,[u|z]) <- merge(x,y,z).
merge(x,[v|y],[v|z]) <- merge(x,y,z).
merge([],y,y).
merge(x,[],x).
```

Concurrently evaluating relation calls communicate via shared variables; the modes impose a direction on this communication. Non-variable terms that appear in input argument positions in the head of a clause can only be used for input matching. If an argument of the call is not sufficiently instantiated for an input match to proceed, the attempt to use the clause suspends until some other process further instantiates the input argument of the call. For example, the first clause for **merge** has **[u|x]** in its first input argument position. Until the call has a list or partial list structure of the form **[u|x]** in the first argument position the first clause is suspended.

If all clauses for a call are suspended, the call suspends. A candidate clause can be selected even if there are other, suspended, clauses.

1.2 Concurrent PROLOG

Concurrent PROLOG (hereafter CP) (Shapiro 1983) is very similar to the and-parallel subset of PARLOG; the main difference is that CP uses read-only variable annotations on variables to specify the communication constraints, where PARLOG uses modes.

Because both PARLOG and CP are derivatives of the Relational Language of (Clark and Gregory 1981), they both feature don't care non-determinism, guarded clauses and the property that no bindings are made to a call until the evaluation commits to the use of some clause. (However, Shapiro has recently proposed a possible relaxation of this last property; we discuss this in section 8.)

1.3 Systems programming in PARLOG

In (Shapiro 1984), Shapiro develops in CP a failsafe Unix-like shell program to run foreground and background commands and handle **ABORT** interrupts for foreground commands. His approach relies on evaluating commands as conventional success-or-fail metacalls in the guards of the shell program. The fundamental problem with this approach is that the output of guard processes is not made available until the guard terminates. Hence, incrementally constructed output of a user process is not visible whilst the process is evaluating. This prevents interactive communication

between a user process and the user or between a user process and a filestore process, for example.

We follow through the examples of Shapiro's paper and show how they can be rewritten with user commands evaluated outside the guards, and hence with incrementally constructed data made visible, by using a three-argument metacall primitive that always succeeds. The first argument is the call to be evaluated, the second is the status or result of the evaluation (e.g. **SUCCEEDED**, **FAILED**) and the third is an input argument which can be used by some other process to control the evaluation of the call.

The use of this primitive not only allows interactive user programs but allows us to program a more powerful shell that allows the selective aborting of background processes as well as foreground processes. It also permits scheduling strategies to be imposed on processes.

As well as solving several problems in systems programming, the three-argument metacall subsumes certain PARLOG features such as negation as failure and the sequential "and", and allows us to reduce the or-parallel evaluation of the guards of alternative clauses to and-parallel evaluation. We contend that for these reasons the three-argument metacall is the natural metacall primitive for parallel logic programming languages like PARLOG and CP.

2 A SIMPLE SHELL

We begin by writing in PARLOG (Program 1) a simple shell that handles a stream of commands to run foreground and background processes without input or output. The relation **shell(cmds)** acts as a process which consumes a stream of commands **cmds** and invokes each as a process using the **call** metacall. The commands are labelled by **FG** (foreground) or **BG** (background).

```
mode shell(?).
shell([]).                          (S1)
shell([BG(proc)|cmds]) <-
    call(proc), shell(cmds).        (S2)
shell([FG(proc)|cmds]) <-
    call(proc) & shell(cmds).       (S3)
```

Program 1: a simple shell

Clause (S1) terminates the shell when the command list is closed. (S2) deals with a background command **BG(proc)** by invoking **proc** concurrently with resuming the shell to process the next command. (S3) is similar but handles foreground commands. It waits for the command process to terminate successfully before accepting the next command. This is due to the use of the sequential "and" (&) in place of the parallel "and" (,).

Program 1 is similar to the one given in (Shapiro 1984) except that, in the latter, foreground commands are evaluated in a guard as in clause (SS3).

```
shell([FG(proc)|cmds]) <-
    call(proc) : shell(cmds).          (SS3)
```

The use of the guard to enforce sequential execution is acceptable only if the foreground command does not produce any output, or if it is acceptable that all the output generated by the foreground process is only visible to the **shell** user when the process terminates. More realistically, the **shell** process should explicitly merge output streams from each invoked process so that messages from the processes can be displayed to the user or transmitted to other processes in the operating system.

3 A SHELL WITH OUTPUT

To make our shell program more useful we allow commands to produce stream output which is accessible as stream output of the **shell** whilst the process is running. This is implemented by Program 2, for the relation **shell(cmds,so)**. **cmds** is an input list of commands, as before except that a command is now of the form BG(proc,co) or FG(proc,co). **proc** is the process to be executed while **co** is the output stream of **proc** that should be passed out of the **shell** process via the **shell** output stream **so**. For example, a possible command is **BG(primes(x),x)** where **x** is the stream of primes to be displayed at the terminal.

```
mode shell(?,^).
shell([],[]).                          (OS1)
shell([BG(proc,co)|cmds],so) <-
    merge(co,nso,so),
    call(proc), shell(cmds,nso).        (OS2)
shell([FG(proc,co)|cmds],so) <-
    merge(co,nso,so),
    ( call(proc) & shell(cmds,nso) ).   (OS3)
```

Program 2: a shell with output from commands

Each time a command is received, the shell creates a new **merge** process to run concurrently with the command. (The **merge** in (OS3) could be replaced by **append** with no change to the behaviour.) Any output generated by the command process is merged onto the shell's output stream immediately. This is true of both foreground and background commands. If we were to follow Shapiro's method

of placing the call to **proc** in a guard in (OS3), any output generated by a foreground command would be invisible until the command terminated. This would make it impossible to run interactive foreground programs.

This example illustrates our point that the guard should not be used to enforce sequential evaluation; it is far too powerful. What is needed is the sequential **P & Q** construct which delays the evaluation of **Q** without delaying the output of **P**.

By running **shell** in conjunction with a message handler we can allow any sort of output message to be produced by a process, including requests for input via variables in the messages. Thus, a message of the form

```
filestore(GET,filename,x)
```

would be routed by the message handler as a **GET** request to the filestore. The retrieved file would be returned to the requesting process as the binding for the variable **x** which will be local to the sending process. In this way the processes being run by the **shell** can have input as well as output communication. For more details of the technique of two-way communication using variables in messages, which is due to Shapiro, we refer the reader to (Shapiro 1983) or to (Clark and Gregory 1984a).

4 PROCESS FAILURE

As Shapiro points out in (Shapiro 1984), the shell of Program 1 will crash if any of the commands fails since they are part of the same conjunction as the recursive shell invocation. To overcome this, he replaces the metacall **call(proc)** by **envelope(proc)** which always succeeds. The definition of **envelope** can be adapted to PARLOG as follows:

```
mode envelope(?).
envelope(proc) <- call(proc) :;
envelope(proc).
```

where we have used the sequential search operator ; between the clauses to ensure that the second clause is used only if the guard of the first clause fails.

This suffers from the same fatal flaw as that described in the previous section: since the command is evaluated in a guard its output will not be made available until it has successfully terminated.

4.1 A two-argument metacall

Our solution to this problem is to generalize the metacall primitive by adding a second argument:

```
call(goal?,status^)
```

Such a metacall evaluates its first argument **goal** and always succeeds with an output binding for **status**: **SUCCEEDED** or **FAILED** depending on the success or failure of **goal**. Any output generated by the evaluation of **goal** is available immediately, as it would be in a call **call(goal)**. The difference is that even if **goal** subsequently fails, the output generated up to the point of failure remains since the metacall succeeds.

The behaviour of a shell which evaluates commands (i.e. user programs) using this more general metacall seems to be what one would expect of a practical operating system. If a user program fails (resulting in a **FAILED** result from the metacall), the operating system will not crash. Moreover, output from a user program is incrementally available whether or not it ultimately fails. The output trace of a failed program is therefore available for debugging and other purposes.

A third possible value of **status** is **ERROR**, which will be issued if a run-time error occurs during the evaluation of a metacall. Again, the metacall itself will succeed in this case. We can now define a relation **terminated(status)** which succeeds when a metacall evaluation has finished:

```
mode terminated(?).
terminated(SUCCEEDED).
terminated(FAILED).
terminated(ERROR).
```

More generally, the **ERROR** message might be parameterized to include information about the type of error (invalid use of some primitive for example) and the call that resulted in the error. Finally, if the metacall is further generalized to accept inputs via bindings for variables in its error messages, we have a building block with which to implement error recovery.

4.2 Sealing the output stream of a terminated process

A program that fails or encounters an error (or even succeeds) before it has finished its output will leave a "dangling stream", i.e. a list with a variable as some tail sublist. The consumer of the output of a program evaluated by the two-argument metacall must therefore monitor the result of the program and close the dangling stream if the program terminates. For example, the second clause of Program 2 must be changed to

```
shell([BG(proc,co)|cmds],so) <-
    dmerge(status,co,nso,so),
    call(proc,status),
    shell(cmds,nso).                    (OS2')
```

Program 3 defines **dmerge** which is similar to **merge** except that it has an extra argument:

the **status** of the metacall process producing its first input stream. The extra fifth clause effectively closes this stream on the termination of its producer process by terminating the **dmerge** process when its **s** argument is **SUCCEEDED**, **FAILED** or **ERROR** and there is no output from the metacall waiting to be passed through (the **var** test). The **s** argument is acting as a termination message about the first input stream.

```
mode dmerge(?,?,?,^).
dmerge(s,[u|x],y,[u|z]) <- dmerge(s,x,y,z).
dmerge(s,x,[v|y],[v|z]) <- dmerge(s,x,y,z).
dmerge(s,[],y,y).
dmerge(s,x,[],x).
dmerge(s,x,y,y) <- terminated(s), var(x) :.
```

Program 3: a merge with a termination message

5 ABORTING PROCESSES

In (Shapiro 1984) Shapiro extends his shell program so that the current foreground process is aborted on receipt of an **ABORT** (or Control-C) interrupt on the command stream. His solution again relies on the execution of the command process in the shell's guard as in (SS3). He does this by having two clauses to handle foreground commands:

```
shell([FG(proc)|cmds]) <-
    call(proc) : shell(cmds).          (SS3)
shell([FG(proc)|cmds]) <-
    search(ABORT,cmds,ncmds) :
    shell(ncmds).                      (SS4)

mode search(?,?,^).
search(u,[u|x],x).
search(u,[v|x],y) <- u =/= v :
    search(u,x,y).
```

The command process of the metacall **call(proc)** runs in parallel with the process searching for an **ABORT** since both are in the guards of clauses and will be evaluated in parallel in the search for a candidate clause. The successful termination of either guard process aborts the other guard and the **shell** process is continued at the appropriate point in the input command stream.

For the reasons that we have already given regarding the need to access output of commands during their evaluation, we regard any solution that places a command evaluation in a guard as unsatisfactory. Moreover, the racing of guards will only allow abort termination of foreground processes, or of all processes.

5.1 A general metacall primitive

Our solution to the problem is once more to generalize the metacall to a three-argument form:

call(goal?,status^,control?)

The third argument **control** will normally be an uninstantiated variable. If it is bound to the term STOP by another process, the evaluation of **goal** will be terminated with **status** bound to STOPPED. We must now add another clause to our **terminated** relation:

terminated(STOPPED).

5.2 Aborting foreground commands

Program 4 gives our version of a shell that handles **ABORT** interrupts for foreground processes with an **ABORT** command given in the normal command stream. When a foreground command is received (AS3), the evaluation of the command and the search for an **ABORT** command are invoked as and-parallel metacalls, each of which can be prematurely terminated by a STOP message from the third process, **arb**.

The **arb** process monitors the results **s1** and **s2** of these metacalls: it STOPs the command process if the search for an **ABORT** is successful, or STOPs the search if the command process terminates. It also selects the appropriate command stream continuation point (**cmds** or **acmds**) depending upon whether the user process or the **ABORT**-seeking process has terminated first. This is then passed on to the recursive **shell** process which starts as soon as the **arb** process has terminated, either on a normal termination of the foreground process or on an **ABORT** being found.

```
mode shell(?), arb(?,?,^,^,?,?,^).

shell([]).                              (AS1)
shell([BG(proc)|cmds]) <-
    call(proc,s,c), shell(cmds).        (AS2)
shell([FG(proc)|cmds]) <-
    call(proc,s1,c1),
    call(search(ABORT,cmds,acmds),s2,c2),
    ( arb(s1,s2,c1,c2,cmds,acmds,ncmds) &
    shell(ncmds) ).                     (AS3)

arb(s1,s2,c1,STOP,cmds,acmds,cmds) <-
    terminated(s1) :.
arb(s1,SUCCEEDED,STOP,c2,cmds,acmds,acmds).
```

Program 4: a shell that handles ABORT
interrupts for foreground processes

5.3 Aborting background commands

Program 5 has an output stream for commands (as in Program 2) and allows the aborting of background commands. It does this by keeping a **procs** list of all the active background processes (those whose result variables have not yet been instantiated) identified by a **proc-id**. A message linking the command with its **proc-id** is output to the user when the process is invoked. When the special command **KILL(proc-id)** is received, the current **procs** list is searched by the **kill** process and the identified process is stopped by setting its **control** argument to STOP, using the assignment unification primitive :=. The **insert** process that adds a new record to the process list also generates the **proc-id** and may also garbage collect the current process list by deleting all the processes with a bound **status** variable.

The clause for **kshell** that deals with foreground commands has been omitted. It will be a slight modification of that in Program 4 to allow for an output stream merge. It need not add the foreground process to the process list and it can abort as before on an **ABORT** command.

```
mode shell(?,^), kshell(?,?,^),
    kill(?,?,^).

shell(cmds,so) <- kshell(cmds,[],so).

kshell([],procs,[]).                    (KS1)
kshell([KILL(proc-id)|cmds],procs,
        [KILLED(proc-id)|so]) <-
    kill(proc-id,procs,nprocs),
    kshell(cmds,nprocs,so).             (KS2)
kshell([BG(proc,co)|cmds],procs,
        [NEW-PROC(proc-id,proc,co)|so]) <-
    insert(PROC(proc-id,s,c),procs,nprocs),
    dmerge(s,co,nso,so),
    call(proc,s,c),
    kshell(cmds,nprocs,nso).            (KS3)

kill(proc-id,[],[]).
kill(proc-id,[PROC(proc-id,s,c)|procs],
            procs) <-
    c := STOP.
kill(proc-id,[PROC(p-id,s,c)|procs],
            [PROC(p-id,s,c)|nprocs]) <-
    proc-id =/= p-id :
    kill(proc-id,procs,nprocs).
```

Program 5: a shell that handles KILL
commands for background processes

6 PRIORITY SCHEDULING

6.1 Suspending evaluations

Our final refinement to the general meta-call primitive call(?,^,?) is to allow the evaluation of a metacall to be temporarily suspended and restarted by another process. The **control** argument can now be bound incrementally to a list of SUSPEND or CONTINUE messages, possibly terminated by the term **STOP**. Each time a SUSPEND message is sent on the **control** argument, the message is echoed on the **status** argument and the evaluation enters a suspended state. It can only be resumed by sending a **CONTINUE** message, which again is echoed on **status**.

6.2 A priority shell

In our previous shell programs, background processes continue running even when a foreground process is invoked. We might wish to give a higher priority to the foreground process, so that background processes run only when there is no active foreground process. This is implemented by Program 6.

```
mode shell(?), pri-shell(?,?).

shell(cmds) <- pri-shell(cmds,bgc).

pri-shell([],bgc).                         (PS1)
pri-shell([BG(proc)|cmds],bgc) <-
   call(proc,s,bgc),
   pri-shell(cmds,bgc).                    (PS2)
pri-shell([FG(proc)|cmds],bgc) <-
   bgc := [SUSPEND|bgc1] &
   call(proc,s,fgc) &
   bgc1 := [CONTINUE|nbgc] &
   pri-shell(cmds,nbgc).                   (PS3)
```

Program 6: a shell with priority to
foreground commands

Background commands are evaluated in parallel with the shell, as before, but share a common **control** argument. When a foreground command is invoked, a SUSPEND message is sent on this **control** argument, causing all background processes to suspend. When the foreground command terminates, a CONTINUE is sent, reactivating the background processes.

7 A PRIORITY SHELL WITH INPUT

We now treat the case of a foreground command taking input data from the shell's command stream. This input must be demand-driven: the command process will generate a stream of request variables, each of which will be bound to the next data item on the command stream when it is available. A com-

mand of the form **FG(proc,ci)** will invoke **proc** as a foreground process and treat **ci** as a list of variables to demand items from **cmds**. When the foreground command terminates, the remainder of **cmds** will be passed back to the shell.

As in Program 6, we shall give a foreground process priority over background processes. However, if a foreground process has to wait for input from the command stream, control can be relinquished to the background processes. This is implemented by Program 7, which gives a new fourth clause (PS4) to be added to the shell program of Program 6.

```
mode switch(?,?,^,^,?,?,^),
     sw(^,?,?,^,^,?,?,^).

pri-shell([FG(proc,ci)|cmds],bgc) <-
   bgc := [SUSPEND|bgc1],
   call(proc,s,fgc),
   switch(ci,s,fgc,bgc1,nbgc,cmds,ncmds),
   pri-shell(ncmds,nbgc).         (PS4)

switch(ci,s,fgc,[CONTINUE|bgc],bgc,
     cmds,cmds) <- terminated(s) :.
switch([req|ci],s,fgc,bgc,nbgc,
     [data|cmds],ncmds) <- var(s) :
   req := data,
   switch(ci,s,fgc,bgc,nbgc,cmds,ncmds).
switch([req|ci],s,[SUSPEND|fgc],
     [CONTINUE|bgc],nbgc,cmds,ncmds) <-
   var(s), var(cmds) :
   [SUSPEND|ns] <= s,
   sw(req,ci,ns,fgc,bgc,nbgc,cmds,ncmds).

sw(req,ci,s,fgc,bgc,bgc,cmds,cmds) <-
   terminated(s) :.
sw(data,ci,s,[CONTINUE|fgc],[SUSPEND|bgc],
   nbgc,[data|cmds],ncmds) <- var(s) :
   [CONTINUE|ns] <= s,
   switch(ci,ns,fgc,bgc,nbgc,cmds,ncmds).
```

Program 7: extensions to Program 6
to allow input

When a foreground command of the form **FG(proc,ci)** is received, a SUSPEND message is sent to the background processes, as in (PS3), and the command process is evaluated. A **switch** process monitors the status **s** of the evaluation and the stream of request variables **ci** that it generates.

There are three cases for **switch**. The first clause handles the termination of the foreground process: it sends a **CONTINUE** message to the background processes and passes back to the shell the current point in the (input) command stream and the (output) background process control stream. The second clause is a candidate if the foreground process has not terminated (the **var(s)** test in the guard) and there is a request for input on **ci** and data is available on the command stream (e.g. by type-ahead). In this case, the available data is assigned to the request variable.

The third clause for **switch** applies when the foreground process has not terminated and there is a request for input but no data is available on the command stream (the **var(cmds)** test). Now a **SUSPEND** message is sent to the foreground process, a **CONTINUE** sent to the background processes and the **switch** process enters a new state **switch1**. The call to <=, the PARLOG matching unification primitive, skips over the **SUSPEND** message that is echoed on the status stream of the foreground process.

While the foreground process is waiting for input there are two possibilities, handled by **switch1**. The first clause handles the termination of the process as before. The second clause is applicable if an item arrives on the shell's command stream. In this case, the item is assigned to the request variable, the background processes are suspended and the foreground process is resumed.

8 CONCLUDING REMARKS

8.1 Discussion

We have proposed the addition of a new metacall primitive **call(?,^,?)** into PARLOG and related languages to facilitate the writing of operating systems. The one-argument and two-argument forms of **call** can be defined in terms of this primitive:

```
mode call(?,^).
call(g,s) <- call(g,s,c).

mode call(?).
call(g) <- call(g,s,c), s = SUCCEEDED.
```

The metacall approach seems sound since operating systems are necessarily at a different level than user programs. An operating system program is not concerned with the details of user programs, only the results that they produce. In addition the system must be able to initiate, terminate and suspend the execution of user programs. The proposed primitive meets these criteria.

The suitability of the three-argument metacall as <u>the</u> metacall primitive is reinforced by the fact that it can be used to program two other control features of PARLOG: negation and the sequential "and", and to reduce the or-parallel evaluation of alternative guards to an and-parallel evaluation.

Program 8 defines negation as failure, and **&**, using the two-argument form of **call**. It evaluates **a & b** by executing a call to **a** in

parallel with a process which is input-suspended until the evaluation of **a** succeeds, whereupon **b** is called.

```
mode ~ ?.
~ a <- call(a,s), s = FAILED.

mode ? & ?.
a & b <- call(a,s), nextcall(s,b).

mode nextcall(?,?).
nextcall(SUCCEEDED,b) <-
    call(b).
```

Program 8: definition of negation and sequential "and"

PARLOG programs with clauses with non-empty guards can also be compiled into programs with a single guard clause in which the different guards are evaluated in and-parallel using three-argument metacalls in a manner similar to that used in Program 4. An arbitration process then monitors the results of these guard metacalls, selects the appropriate body, and explicitly kills the other guard metacalls. The details of this representation are given in (Clark and Gregory 1984b).

The general metacall primitive should be readily implementable on any architecture that properly supports PARLOG or similar languages. This is certainly true of ALICE (Darlington and Reeve 1981). All that is required is the ability to access the result of an evaluation (**SUCCEEDED, FAILED, ERROR**) and to terminate and suspend an evaluation.

The primitive has been implemented in the PROLOG-based PARLOG system (Gregory 1984). Copies of this system, for either micro-PROLOG or DEC-10 PROLOG, are available from the authors. It has been used to test all example programs presented in this paper.

8.2 Related work

"Write-early" variables have been proposed recently by Shapiro and described in (Furukawa et al. 1984) as a way of making the output of a guard visible before the guard has succeeded. A write-early annotation ^ placed on a variable in a goal signals that any bindings to the variable are made public immediately, even if they occur in clause guards. This feature can be used to partially implement the three-argument **call** as follows (CP syntax is used):

```
call(Goal,Status,Control) :-
    call1(Goal^,Status,Control?).
```

```
call1(Goal,stopped,stop).
call1(Goal,Status,Control) :-
    call(Goal,Status) | true.

call(Goal,succeeded) :- call(Goal) | true.
call(Goal,failed) :- otherwise | true.
```

The use of the write-early annotation is potentially very dangerous: it overrides the security of the elaborate and expensive unification of CP. This approach is an attempt to use the guard for purposes for which it is not intended. Our approach is to design the three-argument **call** as the primitive (it is a simple and flexible concept), and then use it to implement the guard as can be done in PARLOG.

The three-argument **call** has some similarities to the meta predicate **simulate** proposed for KL1 (Furukawa et al. 1984):

simulate(World,NewWorld,Goal,Result,Control)

This evaluates **Goal** relative to a local program **World** which can be updated to **NewWorld**. The **Control** argument here specifies some control strategy to be used, such as breadth-first or depth-first, while **Result** returns arbitrarily detailed information about the progress of the evaluation.

Like **call**, **simulate** can be used to obtain the success/failure result of an evaluation. It is not intended to allow an evaluation to be stopped or suspended, though there should be no difficulty in allowing this. As it is described in (Furukawa et al. 1984), it appears that an important difference between **call** and **simulate** is that the latter does not allow incremental communication between an evaluation ("object world") and the outside program ("meta world") unless write-early variables are used.

simulate is intended as a general purpose meta inference predicate having many different uses, some of which seem to require an interpretive evaluation. In contrast, we are proposing the three-argument **call** as a primitive of the language: one which is simple enough to implement efficiently but powerful enough to enable the programming of realistic operating systems.

ACKNOWLEDGEMENTS

This work was supported by the Science and Engineering Research Council under grant number GR/B/97473.

Many of the ideas germinated in discussions with Udi Shapiro and the members of the KL1 design team whilst the authors were visiting ICOT in October 1983. We would like to thank ICOT for inviting us and for providing a very stimulating research environment.

REFERENCES

Clark K.L. and Gregory S. (1981), A relational language for parallel programming. In *Proc. Conf. on Functional Programming Languages and Computer Architecture*, ACM, pp 171-178.

Clark K.L. and Gregory S. (1984a), PARLOG: parallel programming in logic. Research report DOC 84/4, Dept. of Computing, Imperial College, London.

Clark K.L. and Gregory S. (1984b), Notes on the implementation of PARLOG. Research report, Dept. of Computing, Imperial College, London.

Darlington J. and Reeve M.J. (1981), ALICE: a multi-processor reduction machine. In *Proc. Conf. on Functional Programming Languages and Computer Architecture*, ACM, pp 65-75.

Furukawa K., Kunifuji S., Takeuchi A. and Ueda K. (1984), The conceptual specification of the Kernel Language version 1. Technical report, ICOT, Tokyo.

Gregory S. (1984), How to use PARLOG. Unpublished report, Dept. of Computing, Imperial College, London.

Johnson S.D. (1981), Circuits and systems: implementing communications with streams. Technical report 116, Dept. of Computer Science, Indiana University.

Shapiro E.Y. (1983), A subset of Concurrent Prolog and its interpreter. Technical report TR-003, ICOT, Tokyo.

Shapiro E.Y. (1984), Systems programming in Concurrent Prolog. In *Proc. 11th ACM Symp. on Principles of Programming Languages*.

New Generation Computing, 1 (1983) 25-48
OHMSHA, LTD. and Springer-Verlag

Object Oriented Programming in Concurrent Prolog*

Ehud SHAPIRO
Department of Applied Mathematics,
Weizmann Institute of Science,
Rehovot 76100, Israel
Akikazu TAKEUCHI
ICOT Research Center
Institute for New Generation Computer Technology,
Mita-Kokusai Bldg. 21F, 4-28 Mita 1-chome, Minato-ku, Tokyo 108

Abstract   It is shown that the basic operations of object-oriented programming languages — creating an object, sending and receiving messages, modifying an object's state, and forming class-superclass hierarchies — can be implemented naturally in Concurrent Prolog. In addition, a new object-oriented programming paradigm, called incomplete messages, is presented. This paradigm subsumes stream communication, and greatly simplifies the complexity of programs defining communication networks and protocols for managing shared resources. Several interesting programs are presented, including a multiple-window manager. All programs have been developed and tested using the Concurrent Prolog interpreter described in.[1]

§1   Introduction

Concurrent Prolog[1] introduces an operational semantics of parallel execution to logic programs, thus allowing them to express concurrent computations. Concurrent Prolog can specify process creation, termination, communication, synchronization, and indeterminacy. This paper focuses on the object-oriented aspects of Concurrent Prolog. It is shown that the language lends itself naturally to the programming idioms and techniques of Actors[2] and Smalltalk.[3]

The paper is structured as follows. Section 2 reviews Concurrent Prolog.

---

*   Part of this research was carried out while Ehud Shapiro was visiting ICOT, the Institute for New Generation Computer Technology. Ehud Shapiro is a recipient of the Sir Charles Clore Fellowship.

Section 3 surveys the elements of object-oriented logic programming. Section 4 studies in detail a non-trivial Concurrent Prolog program : a multiple-window system. The system is operational on the DECSYSTEM-20 and VAX-11 for a VT100 terminal. Section 5 compares traditional object-oriented programming to object-oriented logic programming, and identifies two important programming techniques not easily available in the former : incomplete messages, and constraint propagation.

§ 2   Concurrent Prolog

An examination of the abstract computation model of logic programs suggests that they are readily amenable to parallel execution. A computation of a logic program amounts to the construction of a proof to a goal statement from the axioms in the program. The search space for a proof can be described by an And-Or tree, where an And-node corresponds to a conjunctive goal, and an Or-node corresponds to the different way to reduce a unit goal, using axioms in the program.

An abstract logic program interpreter searching an And-Or tree is assumed to make the **correct** non-deterministic choices at the Or-nodes and can traverse the And-nodes in an arbitrary order. The sequential Prolog interpreter, on the other hand, traverses And-Or trees in depth-first, left-to-right order : conjunctive goals are reduced from left to right, and if there are several alternative ways to reduce a unit goal, they are tried one by one, using backtracking.

One may attempt to search the And-Or tree in parallel, and two forms of parallelism are possible : Or-parallelism and And-parallelism. In Or-parallel execution several alternatives to reduce a unit goal are tried in parallel. In And-parallel execution the goals in a conjunction are reduced in parallel. Since goals in a conjunction may have logical variables in common, the processes attempting to prove each of the conjuncts are not independent and may interfere with each other by instantiating shared variables to incompatible (non-unifiable) solutions. Because of this dependency, one needs some means to coordinate the computations of And-parallel processes.

However, concurrent programming is more than attempting to parallelize the execution of code that can run sequentially : it must have the ability to respond in real-time to multiple events that occur concurrently. The emphasis on the declarative reading of logic programs in the past might have suggested that this formalism will be of no use to real-time application, such as the implementation of an operating system. Nevertheless, the contrary is suggested in the following.

Logic programming was founded on the dual reading of definite clauses. A definite clause

$$A :- B1, B2, \ldots, Bn. \qquad n \geq 0.$$

reads declaratively : A is true if $B1$ and $B2$ and ... and Bn are true. Kowalski's seminal paper[4] suggested a second reading to definite clauses, the procedural, or problem reduction reading : to execute the procedure call *A*, perform the procedure calls *B1* and *B2* and ... and *Bn*, or : to solve problem *A*, solve the subproblems *B1* and *B2* and ... and *Bn*. In the procedural reading, a unit goal is analogous to a procedure call, both in the way it is used and in the way it is implemented.

Concurrent Prolog[1] and its predecessors, the Relational Language of Clark and Gregory[5] and the language of van Emden and de Lucena,[6] employ a third reading of logic programs : the behavioral reading.

In the behavioral reading, a unit goal is analogous to a process, a conjunctive goal is analogous to a system of processes, and variables shared between goals function similarly to communication channels. A definite clause is read behaviorally : a process *A* can replace itself by the system of processes that contain *B1* and *B2* and ... and *Bn*. A prccess terminates by replacing itself with the empty system.

In the procedural reading, unification provides a mechanism for parameter passing, variable assignment, and data access and construction. In the behavioral reading it also provides a mechanism for message sending and receiving and an easy way of specifying the different actions to be taken upon the receipt of different messages.

In the behavioral reading, the actions a process can take are specified by the definite clauses in the program : all a process can do is to reduce itself to other processes. In the course of this reduction, variables shared with other processes may get instantiated via the unification of the process with the head of the reducing clause, thus achieving the effect of process communication.

To support process synchronization, Concurrent Prolog introduces a new syntactic construct, called read-only variables. Variables in a process can be annotated as read-only. A process suspends if every reduction of it requires the instantiation of a read-only variable.

Another construct in Concurrent Prolog borrowed from the Relational Language, the guarded-clause, is similar to Dijkstra's guarded-command in its effect. Together with the read-only annotations, guarded-clauses can specify a wide-range of indeterminate process behaviors.

The subset of Concurrent Prolog described and used in this paper was implemented in Prolog-10 on DECSYSTEM-20 and is described in[1], that paper also includes a full listing of the interpreter. With minor modifications, that interpreter can run in Pereira's CProlog on the VAX, under Unix and VMS. A listing of a Concurrent Prolog interpreter written in Waterloo Prolog for IBM / VM computers is available from the first author upon request.

The rest of this section provides a more detailed description of this subset of Concurrent Prolog.

2 . 1 Syntax

A Concurrent Prolog program is a finite set of guarded-clauses. A guarded-clause is a universally quantified logical axiom of the form

$$A :- G1, G2, \ldots, Gm \mid B1, B2, \ldots Bn. \qquad m,n \geq 0.$$

where the G's and the B's are atomic formulas, also called unit goals. A is called the clause's head, the G's are called its guard, and the B's its body. When the guard is empty the commit operator " $\mid$ " may be omitted. Clauses may contain variables marked read-only, such as $X?$. The Prolog-10 syntactic conventions are followed : constants begin with a lower-case letter, and variables with an upper-case letter. The special binary term $[X \mid Y]$ is used to denote the list whose head (car) is X and tail (cdr) is Y. The constant $[\ ]$ denotes an empty list.

2.2 Semantics

Concerning the declarative semantics of a guarded clause, the commit operator reads like a conjunction : A is implied by the G's and the B's. The read-only annotations can be ignored in the declarative reading.

Procedurally, a guarded-clause functions similarly to an alternative in a guarded-command. To reduce a process A using a clause $A1 :- G \mid B$, unify A with $A1$, and, if successful, recursively reduce G to the empty system, and, if successful, commit to that clause, and, if successful, reduce A to B.

The reduction of a process may suspend or fail during almost any of these steps. The unification of the process against the head of the clause suspends if it requires the instantiation of variables occurring as read-only in A. It fails if A and $A1$ are not unifiable. The computation of the guard system G suspends if any of the processes in it suspends, and fails if any of them fails.

The commitment operation is the most delicate, and grasping it fully is not required for the understanding of the example programs in this paper. It suffices to say that partial results computed by the first two steps of the reduction — unifying the process against the head of the clause and solving the guard — are not accessible to other processes in A's system prior to the commitment, and that after commitment all the Or-parallel attempts to reduce A using other clauses are abandoned.

The reduction of all processes in a system can be attempted in parallel, as can the search for a clause to reduce a process. Two restrictions prevent an all-out parallelism. Regarding Or-parallelism, only the guards are executed in parallel. Once a guard system terminates, the computations of other Or-parallel guards are aborted. Regarding And-parallelism, read-only annotations can enforce rather severe constraints on the order and pace in which processes can be reduced, as the example programs below show.

This completes the description of the subset of Concurrent Prolog used in this paper. One additional construct — otherwise — is introduced in Section 3. Our Concurrent Prolog implementation supports also the use of the system predicates of the underlying sequential Prolog, including arithmetic and external I / O.

It is worth mentioning that our Concurrent Prolog interpreter is more of a toy than a real implementation, since it is about 100 to 200 times slower than the underlying sequential Prolog implementation. It runs at approximately the same speed, 130 reductions per CPU second (LIPS), on a DECSYSTEM 2060 running Prolog-10 and on an IBM 4341 running Waterloo Prolog.

§3 Object Oriented Programming in Concurrent Prolog

Concurrent Prolog is capable of expressing modern programming concepts, including object-oriented programming. The concept of objects in Concurrent Prolog has close resemblance to that of Actor systems,[2] in that a computation is performed via the cooperation of distributed objects. First a general scheme for object-oriented programming in Concurrent Prolog is presented. It is then explained how objects can be created, and how they can cooperate in computation. A Concurrent Prolog programming technique, called filters, is then introduced, which achieves the effect of hierarchical definition of objects and property inheritance, a useful tool in other object-oriented programming languages. In addition to the usual object oriented features, Concurrent Prolog can provide new features that originate from the logical power of unification. One of them is computation by incomplete messages, and the other is implicit activation of objects, which is similar to a constraint network.[7,8,9]

3.1 Objects

Our view of objects is based on Hewitt's Actor model of parallel computation.

An object can be thought of as an active process that receives messages and performs action on its internal state according to the received message. During the computation, an object can send messages to other objects.

The general properties of objects are as follows:

(1) An object is a process that can have internal states. It becomes active when it receives a message.

(2) The internal state of an object can be operated upon from the outside only by sending it a message, which specifies the operation to be performed.

(3) An object can exchange messages with other objects during its computation.

(4) Any number of object-instances can be generated from a definition of an object.

3.2 Realization of Objects

The following shows how Concurrent Prolog realizes objects.

[1] **A (perpetual) object is a process that calls itself recursively and holds its internal state in unshared arguments**

The state of an object corresponds to the arguments of a process. Its internal state corresponds to arguments not shared by other processes. An object acts by reducing itself to other objects. A perpetual object survives by reducing itself to itself. A perpetual object changes its state by calling itself recursively with different arguments.

[2] Objects communicate with each other by instantiating shared variables
Since parallel processes are realized by And-parallelism, they can be linked by shared variables. These variables are used as communication channels among objects. Message passing is performed by instantiating a shared variable to a message. Because a shared variable can be referred to by multiple processes, a message can be sent to multiple objects at once. Successive communication is possible by the stream communication technique, that is, by instantiating a channel variable to the binary term ⟨*message*⟩. *X* (Prolog's counterpart of Lisp's dotted pair, usually written as [⟨*message*⟩ | *X*]) where ⟨*message*⟩ is a message to be sent and *X* is a new variable to be used in the next communication.

[3] An object becomes active when it receives a message; otherwise it is suspended.
The synchronization mechanism forces a process to suspend when it tries to instantiate read-only variables to non-variable terms. Since objects peek into their input stream in read-only mode, they are suspended if the next message is not available yet.

[4] An object-instance is created by process reduction
An object instance *B* is created when an object *A* is reduced via a clause
$A :- \ldots B \ldots$

[5] Response to a message
When an object sends a message which requires a response, the response can not be sent through the same shared variable, since logical variables are single-assignment. There are two techniques for sending a response to a message. One is to prepare another shared stream variable, in which the communication flows in the opposite direction. The other uses a technique called incomplete messages, which is explained more fully in Section 5.1. In this technique the sender sends a message that contains an uninstantiated variable and then examines that variable in a read-only mode, which causes it to suspend until this variable gets instantiated to the response by the recipient of the message. For example, a message *show* which asks a target object about its internal state is replaced by the message *show*(*State*), where the variable *State* is used as a communication channel that carries the response from the target object back to the sender. The sender will get the response in this variable sometime in the future, when the message is received and processed. So the sender must wait until the response variable is instantiated if it needs to refer to the response.

3.3 The *counter* Example
A simple example of how to describe an object is shown below.
   counter([*clear* | *S*], *State*) :−

counter(S ?, *0*).

counter([*up* | *S*], *State*) : −
  plus(*State*, *1*, *NewState*), *counter*(*S* ?, *NewState*).

counter([*down* | *S*], *State*) : −
  plus(*NewState*, *1*, *State*), *counter*(*S* ?, *NewState*).

counter([*show* (*State*) | *S*], *State*) : −
  counter(*S* ? , *State*).

counter([ ], *State*).   % *for temination.*

The object *counter* has two arguments. One is an input stream, and the other is its internal state. When receiving a *clear* message, it resets the state to 0. When receiving *up* and *down* messages, it increments or decrements its state by 1, respectively. The process $plus(X, Y, Z)$ suspends until at least two of its arguments are instantiated, then instantiates the third so that they satisfy the constraint $X + Y = Z$. If this constraint cannot be satisfied, *plus* fails. The implementation of *plus* is described in Section 5.2.

  When receiving a $show(X)$ message, *counter* unifies the variable X with the internal state *State*. The last clause terminates *counter* process, upon encountering the end of the input stream. Note that the stream variable is used recursively. In every reduction it is instantiated to a pair : the message and a new variable, to be used in the next communication.

3 . 4 Object-instance Creation

  Object-instance creation is accomplished by parallel-And. A new instance of an object *counter* may be created by executing the following code :

   terminal(X), *use_counter*(X ?, *C1*), *counter*(*C1* ?, *0*)

where *terminal* is an object that generates the stream of commands produced by a user at a terminal, *use_counter* is an object receiving commands from the terminal and passing the commands to the object *counter*, except for the *show* command, which, in addition to passing it to *counter*, causes the object *use_counter* to wait for the response from the object *counter* and then to output it to the screen. Note that the first argument of *use_counter* and the second argument of the object *counter* are treated as read only variables, because they are used only as input.

   use_counter([*show*(*Val*) | *Input*], [*show*(*Val*) | *Command*]) : −
    use_counter(*Input* ?, *Command*), *wait_write*(*Val*).

   use_counter([*X* | *Input*], [*X* | *Command*]) : −
    dif (*X*, *show*(*Y*)) | *use_counter*(*Input* ?, *Command*).

   wait_write(*X*) : − *wait*(*X*) | *write*(*X*).

$wait(X)$ is a Concurrent Prolog system predicate which is suspended if X is not instantiated, and succeeds otherwise. $dif(X,Y)$ is a system predicate that succeeds if and when it can determine that X and Y are different (i. e. not unifiable). Note that the stream variable is used as an object-instance name. Message passing is performed against the stream variable and not against the target object itself, because there are no global names in Concurrent Prolog, and the only information about an object that is accessible from outside are the communication channels to it.

As described before, a new object-instance is created using a definition in the program. However, object-instances created from the same definition are different and can be distinguished by the names of their communication channels. The example below demonstrates this. The object *use_many_counters* is similar to *use_counter*. It receives a command stream from the terminal. When it receives a *create(Name)* message, it creates a new object *counter* and saves its name and a communication channel to it in its internal state. Other messages must be the form (*Name, Command*), where *Name* specifies the name of an object *counter* to which the message *Command* should be sent.

> *use_many_counters*([*create(Name)* | *Input*], *List_of_counters*) :−
> > *couner(Com* ?, *0*),
> > *use_many_counters(Input* ?, [(*Name, Com*) | *List_of_counters*]).
> *use_many_counters*([(*Name, show(Val)*) | *Input*], *List_of_counters*) :−
> > *send(List_of_counters, Name, show(Val), NewList*) |
> > *use_many_counters(Input* ?, *NewList*), *wait_write(Val*).
> *use_many_counters*([*X* | *Input*], *List_of_counters*) :−
> > *dif(X, create(Y)), dif(X, show(Y)),*
> > *send(List_of_counters, Name, X, NewList*) |
> > *use_many_counters(Input* ?, *NewList*).

> *send* ([(*Name,* [*Message* | *Y*]) | *List, Name, Message,* [(*Name, Y*) | *List*]).
> *send* ([*C* | *List*], *Name, Message,* [*C* | *L1*]) :− *send(List, Name, Message, L1).*

The object *use_many_counters* has two arguments. One is an input stream from the terminal, and the other is a list of (*Name, Channel*) where *Name* is an identifier of the object *counter* given by the *create* command and *Channel* is the communication channel to that object. The object *send* takes four arguments. The first argument is the same as the second argument of *use_many_counters*. The second and the third arguments are an identifier of the object *counter* and

> *use_many_counters(In* ?, [ ])
> > *In* = [*create(c1)* | *In1*]
> *use_many_counters(In1* ?, [(*C1, X1*)]), *counter(X1*?, *0*)
> > *In1* = [*create (c2)* | *In2*]
> *use_many_counters(In2* ?, [(*c2, X2*), (*c1, X1*)]), *counter(X2* ?, *0*)
> > *In2* = [*create(c3)* | *In3*]
> *use_many_counters (In3* ?, [(*c3, X3*), (*c2, X2*), (*c1, X1*)]), *counter(X3* ?, *0*)

Fig. 1 Multiple object-instantiation

a message to be sent, respectively. The fourth argument is the updated list of counters. Figure 1 shows a situation in which three *create* commands were processed. Note that since there are no global variables in Concurrent Prolog, an object must keep channel variables associated with other objects in order to send messages to them.

The multi-window system described in Section 4 uses a similar technique to create processes and to associate with them windows and communication channels.

3 . 5　Default Programming, Filters, and Object Hierarchies

Some object-oriented languages, such as Smalltalk,[3] associate a hierarchy with objects. This hierarchy supports a very convenient form of default programming. Methods for responding to a message can be associated with an object high in the hierarchy, and an object-instance, receiving a message which it does not know how to respond to, can default to an object higher in the hierarchy to respond to the message. In addition to increasing the brevity of programs, such a mechanism also increases their modularity, since a code associated with a class of objects may occur only in the definition of the class, rather than with the definitions of its subclasses. This mechanism also encourages the programmer to identify useful abstractions, so it can be used.

Concurrent Prolog does not have special hard-wired mechanisms to support object hierarchies. However, a certain programming technique, called filters, together with a new Concurrent Prolog construct, *otherwise*, achieves a very similar effect. The resulting programs exhibit a behavior of an Actor-like cooperative group of objects.

Consider the following hierarchy of objects : a rectangular-area ; a window-frame, which is a rectangular-area with four border-lines ; a window-with-label, which is a window-frame with a label at the bottom of the window. These can be defined by a class-superclass hierarchy (see Fig. 2).

In a language that supports such hierarchies directly, the functionality of a rectangular-area is inherited by the window-frame, and the functionality of a window-frame is inherited by a window with a label. Operationally, an object

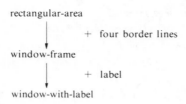

Fig. 2　Class-superclass hierarchy

that receives a message checks whether it knows how to respond to it. If it does not, then it defaults to its parent in the hierarchy to respond to it. In this sense every object in the hierarchy functions like a filter on a stream of message, and this is precisely how object hierarchies are implemented in Concurrent Prolog.

Every object in a hierarchy must have at least one designated input stream and one designated output stream, except the topmost object, which may have an input stream only. The hierarchical structure of the objects is reflected by the structure of the communication network that they form. An object A lower in the hierarchy has its output stream connected to the input stream of an object B next up in the hierarchy. If A receives a message that it cannot respond to, it simply defaults to B by passing to it the message.

The following Concurrent Prolog implementation of the window hierarchy demonstrates this technique. First a rectangular-area is defined.

> *rectangular_area*([*clear* | *M*], *Parameters*) :−
> *clear_primitive*(*Parameters*) |
> *rectangular_area*(*M* ?, *Parameters*).
> *rectangular_area*([*ask*(*Parameters*) | *M*], *Parameters*) :−
> *rectangular_area*(*M* ?, *Parameters*).

Parameters is a data structure consisting of four parameters (*Xpos Ypos, Width, Height*), where *Xpos* and *Ypos* are the coordinates of the upper-left corner of the area, and *Width* and *Height* are the size of the area. *clear_primitive* is a system defined primitive predicate which clears the screen area specified in its arguments.

From this *rectangular_area* object, a window-frame can be defined. The *frame* object can be viewed as a filter on the input stream of a *rectangular_area*. It filters two types of message, on which it knows how to respond : draw and refresh.

> *create_frame*(*M*, *Parameters*) : −
> *rectangular_area*(*M* ?, *Parameters*),
> *frame*(*M*?, *M1*).
> *frame*([*draw*|*M*], [*ask*(*Parameters*) | *M1*]) : −
> *draw_lines*(*Parameters*) |
> *frame*(*M* ?, *M1*).
> *frame*([*refresh* | *M*], [*clear* | *M1*]) : −
> *frame*([*draw* | *M*], *M1*).
> *frame*([*X*|*M*], [*X*|*M1*]) :−
> *dif*(*X*, *draw*), *dif*(*X*, *refresh*) |
> *frame*(*M* ?, *M1*).

The first clause specifies the initialization procedure, which creates a *rectangular_area* object by passing the parameters and an original *frame* object with the communication channel to the *rectangular_area*. The rest of the clauses specify the method for interpreting each message. On receiving a *draw* message, it asks the *rectangular_area* about the dimensional parameters and then draws four border lines. On receiving a *reflesh* message, it sends two messages, *clear* and *draw*, to the *rectangular_area* and self respectively. On receiving other messages, it only passes them to the *rectangular_area*.

To support default programming, a new construct is introduced to Concurrent Prolog, called *otherwise*. An *otherwise* goal that occurs in a guard succeeds if and when all other parallel-Or guards fail. Given the other clauses for *frame*, the last clause is equivalent to :

$$frame([X \mid M], [X \mid M1]) :-$$
$$otherwise \mid frame(M ?, M1).$$

It is not difficult to see that if all clauses for an object have empty guards, then *otherwise* can be implemented via a preprocessor that expands it to an appropriate sequence of calls to *dif*(_, _). If the guards are not empty, then *otherwise* can be implemented via a negation-as-failure primitive. In this sense *otherwise* does not increase the expressive power of Concurrent Prolog more than the addition of negation as failure does. However, an efficient implementation of *otherwise* requires a modification to the Concurrent Prolog interpreter.

Now, a window frame with a label is defined.

$$create\_window\_with\_label(M, Label, Parameters) : -$$
$$create\_frame(M1 ?, Parameters),$$
$$window\_with\_label(M ?, Label, M1).$$
$$window\_with\_label([change(Label) \mid M], OldLabel, M1) : -$$
$$window\_with\_label(M ?, Label, M1).$$
$$window\_with\_label([show \mid M], Label, [ask(Parameters) \mid M1]) : -$$
$$show\_label\_primitive(Label, Parameters) \mid$$
$$window\_with\_label(M ?, Label, M1).$$
$$window\_with\_label([refresh \mid M], Label, [refresh \mid M1]) : -$$
$$window\_with\_label([show \mid M], Label, M1).$$
$$window\_with\_label([X \mid M], Label, [X \mid M1]) : -$$
$$otherwise \mid$$
$$window\_with\_label(M ?, Label, M1).$$

The first clause defines the initialization procedure which creates the object *frame* with the parameters and a *window_with_label* with the communication channel to the object *frame*. The rest of the clauses define the methods to interpret messages. On receiving a *change* message, it changes the label. On receiving a *show* message, it asks the object *frame* about its parameters and displays the label in the appropriate position in the window, using the predefined predicate *show_label_primitive*. On receiving a *refresh* message, it sends two messages, *refresh* and *show*, to the *frame* and self respectively. On receiving other messages, it only passes them to the *frame*.

In the class-superclass hierarchy, a message which can not be processed by an object is passed to its superclass. In Concurrent Prolog such a hierarchy is simulated by a network of objects connected via communication channels, through which unprocessable messages are sent. A system like Flavor[10] and

Smalltalk-80[3] can permit objects to access instance variables of their superclass. However, in Concurrent Prolog, since a superclass of an object is also an object, such direct access to states of other objects is not possible. Instead of this, an object has to send a message asking about states to the object that plays the role of its superclass.

Table 1 shows the relation between objects and acceptable messages.

Table 1 Objects and acceptable messages

Objects		Messages	Process
rectangular_area	1	*clear*	clear the area
	2	*ask(X)*	instantiate *X* to parameters
frame	3	*draw*	draw four lines
	4	*refresh*	=1+3
		clear	send to *rectangular_area*
		ask(X)	send to *rectangular_area*
window_with_label	5	*change(Label)*	change the label
	6	*show*	display the label
	7	*refresh*	send to *frame*
		draw	send to *frame*
		clear	send to *frame*
		ask(X)	send to *frame*

In the case of an object *window_with_label*, there are two kinds of methods. One is an own method, and the other is a so-called generic method. Generic methods are invoked by sending messages to objects which play the role of a superclass.

In this cooperating objects approach, there is no difference between the class-superclass hierarchy and the part-whole relation. In other words, the role of an object in a group of cooperating objects is not determined from a structural description (such as superclass declaration and part declaration) but from a behavioral description in the form of a communication network. From this point of view, a *rectangular_area* can be seen both as a superclass of a *frame* and as a part of a *frame*. The essential point, however, is the behavioral role of the *rectangular_area* against the *frame*, and in this sense this approach is close to the Actor formalism.

More explanation is needed about the modularity of this approach. First, the internal states of an object can never be operated upon directly from a user of the object. All a user can do is to send a message that specifies the operation to be performed. Thus, the encapsulation of internal states is established. Second, there is no way to access directly component objects of an object from the outside, except by using incomplete messages, as explained in Section 5.1. Thus, the encapsulation of component objects is also established. By these properties of objects, it is possible to construct complicated objects from simpler objects in a modular way.

§4　Multi-window System

The following is a powerful and expressive example of a Concurrent Prolog implementation of a multi-windows system. The system is architectured after the MUF (Multi User Forks) program and the SM (Session Manager) program of the Yale Tools programming environment.[1] The Tools environment supports only multi-tasking but not multi-windows. Consequently, it does not support concurrent processes output to the screen, whereas this program does. On the other hand, Tools is a real, usable system, while this is still a toy.

The system can create processes dynamically, make them run concurrently and associate each process with a window that can display input and output of the process in the specified position on the screen. Terminal input is managed by the window manager, which can switch the connection between the terminal and a specified process. A user of this system can create several processes dynamically, make them run concurrently, and see concurrently the input-output behavior of each process in the window associated with it.

A window consists of a rectangular area, four border lines and a label field like the *window_with_label* defined above (see Fig. 3). It also has a text string as its internal states. A window has two modes. In normal mode it can fill the region with its text string, append a new string and display it by scrolling up if the window is full. In the other mode, called session manager, or sm mode, all the history of the input and the output since the window was created is displayed according to the commands the window receives, by scrolling up and down. In both modes, a window can also move to somewhere else on the screen, change its size, and so on. First the window object will be shown. General form of the window : :

$$window((Input, PI, PO), State, normal)　\text{in normal mode}$$
$$window((Input, PI, PO), State, sm)　\text{in sm mode}$$

The first argument of *window* is three communication channels : *Input* is input from the window manager, and *PI* and *PO* are output to the associated process and input from the process, respectively (see Fig. 4). The second argument, *State*, must be a data structure which represents the window's internal state : geographical parameters, contents (text string), and label. In the current implementation, it is represented as ($(X0, Y0, W, H)$, Y, *Contents*, *Label*) where $X0$ and $Y0$ are the coordinate of the upper-left corner of the window, W and H are width and height of the window respectively and Y points the current cursor position. The form of Contents is (*Tof*, *Top*, *Tail*, *Last*), where *Tof*, *Top* and *Tail* point the top of file (all the string), the head of the text currently displayed in the screen and end of text respectively. *Last* is used when entering the sm mode to save the current *Top*, which will be restored upon exit from sm mode. Text stings are represented as a bi-directionally linked list of lines, which can be constructed easily by unification with no occur-check. The varia-

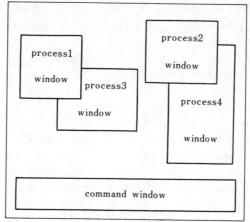

(a)   A sample screen of multi-window system

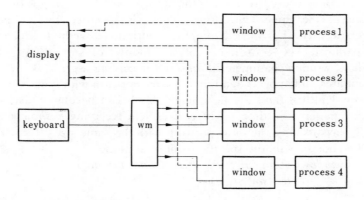

(b)   Total view of multi-window system
Fig. 3   Multi-window system

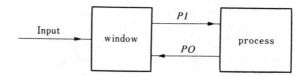

Fig. 4   A window object

ble *Label* is the label of the window. The fourth argument of *window* indicates the current mode of the window and must be sm or normal.

The window in both modes :

    window(([*erase* | *In*], *PI*, *PO*), *State*, *Mode*) : −
        erase_ window(*State*) |
        window((*In* ?, *PI*, *PO*), *State*, *Mode*).
    window(([*move*(*X*, *Y*) | *In*], *PI*, *PO*), *State*, *Mode*) : −
        erase_window(*State*), *set_parameters*(*xy*, (*X*, *Y*), *State*, *State1*) |
        window(([*show* | *In*], *PI PO*), *State1*, *Mode*).
    window(([*grow*(*W*, *H*) | *In*], *PI*, *PO*), *State*, *Mode*) : −
        erase_window(*State*), *set_parameters*(*wh*, (*W*, *H*), *Stfoe*, *State1*) |
        window(([*show* | *In*], *PI*, *PO*), *State*, *Mode*).
    window(([*show* | *In*], *PI*, *PO*), *State*, *Mode*) : −
        show(*State*) |
        window((*In* ?, *PI*, *PO*), *State*, *Mode*).

On receiving an *erase* message, the window erases the area specified in the *State* parameter, including border lines and label field. On receiving a *move*(*X*, *Y*) message, it erases the current area and appears in the new position, the xy-coordinate of the upper-left corner, which is specified by *X* and *Y*. *set_ parameters*(*xy*, (*X*, *Y*), *State*, *State1*) is a primitive method which changes the xy parameter (xy-coordinates of a window) ˙of *State* to *X* and *Y* and returns new window parameters *State1*. On receiving a *grow*(*W*, *H*), it erases the current area and appears again in the same position with a new size specified by the new width *W* and the new height *H*. It can become wider, narrower, longer or smaller according to *W* and *H*. On receiving a *show* message, it only redisplays itself in the same position with the same size.

    The code of window specific to normal mode : :

    window(([*sm* | *In*], *PI*, *PO*), *State*, *normal*) : −
        enter_sm(*State*) |
            window((*In* ?, *PI*, *PO*), *State*, *sm*).
    window(([*X* | *In*], [*X* | *PI*], *PO*), *State*, *normal*) : −
        fill_input(*X*, *State*, *State1*) |
            window((*In* ?, *PI*, *PO*), *State1*, *normal*).
    window((*In*, *PI*, [*X* | *PO*]), *State*, *normal*) : −
        fill_output(*X*, *State*, *State1*) |
            window((*In*, *PI*, *PO* ?), *State1*, *normal*).

On receiving an *sm* message, the window enters the sm mode. On receiving other messages, which must be messages to the associated process, it appends the messages to the current contents, displays it and passes it to the associated process. On receiving messages from the associated process, it also appends the messages to the current contents and displays it.

    The code the window executes only in sm mode is :

    window(([*up* | *In*], *PI*, *PO*), *State*, *sm*) : −

$show\_up(State, State1) \mid window((In?, PI, PO), State1, sm).$

$window(([down \mid In], PI, PO), State, sm) : -$
    $show\_down(State, State1) \mid window((In?, PI, PO), State1, sm).$

$window(([exit \mid In], PI, PO), State, sm) : -$
    $exit\_sm(State, State1) \mid$
    $window(([show \mid In], PI, PO), State1, normal).$

$window(([X \mid In], PI, PO), State, sm) : -$
    $window((In?, PI, PO), State, sm).$

On receiving *up* and *down* messages, the window scrolls up and down the screen respectively. On receiving an *exit* message, it exits from the sm mode and returns to the normal mode.

The window manager, wm for short, has two arguments.

$wm(Input, ListOfChannels)$

The first argument is the input command stream to the window manager, and the second argument is a list of pairs of a window label and an output channel to the associated process.

The window manager can accept three kinds of messages.

$wm([create(Label, Process, (PI, PO), (X0, Y0, W, H)) \mid Input], Processes) : -$
    $window(([show \mid In], PI, PO?),$
        $((X0, Y0, W, H), Y0, (C, C, C, C), Label), normal),$
    $Process,$
    $wm(Input ?, [(Label, In) \mid Processes]).$

$wm([resume(Label) \mid Input], Processes) : -$
    $find\_process(Label, Processes, PI, Processes1) \mid$
    $distribute([show \mid Input], PI, Input, PI1),$
    $wm(Input ?, [(Label, PI1 \mid Processes1]).$

$wm([close \mid Input], [(Label, []) \mid Processes]) : -$
    $wm(Input ?, [(Label, \_) \mid Processes1]).$

$wm([], Processes) : - close\_input(Processes).$

On receiving *create* $(Label, Process, (PI, PO), (X0, Y0, W, H))$ message, it creates a process *Process* and a window with label *Label* monitoring the process's input and output and sends a *show* message to the window. *PI* and *PO* are variables representing the primary input and primary output channels of the process respectively, and may appear in the goal *Process*. $X0, Y0, W$ and H are window parameters. On receiving the *resume*(*Label*) message, it finds the input channel to the process with a name *Label* from the list of processes *Processes* and connects the input stream of the window manager and the input channel of the process by creating the object *distribute*. At the same time, it picks up the process and places it in the top of the list of the processes. On receiving a *close* message, it closes the input channel of the process currently resumed. On reaching the end of the input stream, the window manager closes all the input channels of the processes and terminates.

The object *distribute* has four arguments. The first argument is an input channel from the terminal. The second and the third arguments are output channels to the window associated with the process currently resumed and to the window manager respectively. The fourth argument returns the updated input channel of the window when the connection is cut. The *distribute* object peeks ahead into the input, and if the input is a window manager command, then it returns the input stream and the window's input channel to the window manager and terminates. Otherwise it passes the input to the window process (Fig. 5).

$$distribute([X \mid Input], PI, [X \mid Input], PI) :-$$
$$\qquad member(X, [resume(\_), close, create(\_, \_, \_, \_)]) \mid true.$$
$$distribute([X \mid Input], [X \mid PI], Input1, PI1) :-$$
$$\qquad otherwise \mid distribute(Input?, PI, Input1, PI1).$$
$$distribute([], PI, [], PI).$$

find- process and close-input are written in the following way.

$$find\_process(Label, [Label, PI) \mid Processes], PI, Processes).$$
$$find\_process(Label, [PD \mid Processes], PI, [PD \mid Processes1]) :-$$
$$\qquad find\_process(Label, Processes, PI, Processes1).$$

$$close\_input([]).$$
$$close\_input([(\_, []) \mid Processes]) :- close\_input(Processes).$$

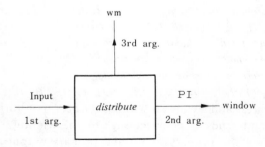

Fig. 5   A distribute object

§5   New Object-Oriented Programming Techniques in Concurrent Prolog

Concurrent Prolog supports several powerful object-oriented programming techniques not available easily in the Actor system and other object-oriented languages. These techniques heavily depend on properties of unification.

In object-oriented languages, a message is sent by specifying the name of the target objects. However, in Concurrent Prolog, objects are connected by shared variables, and a message is sent by instantiating a shared variable to it. Therefore, the name of the target object does not necessarily appear in the message passing phase. Furthermore, broadcasting becomes quite simple, because a message is sent to all the objects that share the variable at once. Generally, shared variables are made at the moment when a process creates a new system of processes, as in the following clause :

$$p(X) :- q(X, Y), r(Y?).$$

In the example above, Y is created and used as a communication channel from q to r. Shared variables can also be made dynamically by sending a variable as a part of a message. This means that a communication channel can be made dynamically and it can be sent to other objects as well. A message that contains variables is called an incomplete message. Section 5.1. explains this concept.

As described before, information can be sent implicitly to any number of objects without knowing who the receivers are by simply instantiating a shared variable to it. This can be seen also as if a sender and receivers of a message do not know each other beyond knowing that the variable is shared with some objects. All that the sender has to do is to instantiate a variable as soon as possible, and all that the receivers have to do is to wait until the variable becomes instantiated. This kind of implicit communication is useful for constructing a dependency network like Constraints,[7,8,9] as explained in Section 5.2.

5 . 1 Incomplete Messages

The concept of incomplete messages* is a new, encompassing programming paradigm, which includes the basic communication mechanism between objects, pipelined processing on stream data, and yields new object-oriented programming techniques. As in the Actor system, Concurrent Prolog is a model of parallel computation, and provides communication methods based on message passing through shared variables. A message is sent by instantiating a shared variable. A message that contains a variable is called an incomplete message. It makes a new variable shared between the sender and the receiver of the message, that is, it creates a new communication channel. Since once a variable is instantiated it will never be rewritten, it can carry only one message. In order to enable subsequent communication, generally a shared variable is instantiated to a pair of a message and a variable which will be used in a next communication, which gives the effects of a stream. Although pipelined processing on stream data usually requires adding new constructs to a language, it is subsumed naturally by the paradigm of the incomplete message.

A prime generator based on a Eratosthenes' sieve algorithm is a typical example of pipeline processing on partially obtained data.

$$primes :- integers(Z, I), sift(I?, J), outstream(J?).$$

---

* In TR-003[1] they are called *partially_determined_messages*.

$integers(N, [N \mid I]) :- N1\ is\ N+1 \mid integers(N1, I).$

$sift([P \mid I], [P \mid RI]) :- filter(I?, P, R), sift(R?, RI).$

$filter([N \mid I], P, R) :- 0\ is\ N\ mod\ P \mid filter(I?, P, R).$

$filter([N \mid I], P, [N \mid R]) :- M\ is\ N\ mod\ P, M>0 \mid filter(I?, P, R).$

$outstream([X \mid S]) :- write(X) \mid outstream(S?).$

The predicate *primes* is the top level goal which is invoked by a user first. It creates three objects : *integers*, which generates an infinite sequence of integers, *sift*, which sifts the integer sequence by the prime numbers obtained so far and *outstream*, which prints out the sequence of prime numbers one by one. All the communication among objects is carried by streams. For example, every time a new integer is obtained, the object *integers* sends it with a new variable which corresponds to a stream (not obtained yet) of integers larger than it. Another logic program implementation of this algorithm, which seems to require a more elaborate control mechanism, appears in.[12]

As in the case of a *show(X)* message to a *counter* object presented in Section 3.2, when a message requires a response, it is sent with a variable which will be instantiated by the receiver to the response, This is also an example of an incomplete message. However, this use of incomplete messages is different from streams, because the object that instantiates the .variable in the message is the receiver of the message, not the sender. Once a message is sent to an object, the sender and the receiver run independently as long as they can. If the response variable is not instantiated yet by the receiver when the sender refers to it, then the sender suspends.

This programming technique is extremely useful when implementing managers of shared resources. The following implementation of a queue manager demonstrates this. The queue manager handles the messages *enqueue(X)* and *dequeue(X)*, which represent requests to append X at the end of the queue and to return an element positioned at the head of the queue respectively. The predicate *qm* takes three arguments. The first argument is an input channel of requests from users, and the second and the third arguments are pointers to the head of the queue and the tail of the queue respectively. To ensure that the *qm* is invoked with an empty queue, these two pointers must be the same variable in the first invocation. For example, the situation where there are two user processes accessing the queue manager is described as follows.

$user1(X), user2(Y), merge(X?, Y?, Z), qm(Z?, Q, Q)$

user1 and *user2* are user processes sending requests to the queue. Those two request streams are merged into one stream by the object *merge* and the resulting stream is sent to the queue manager. The *merge* program is :

$merge([A \mid Xs], Ys, [A \mid Zs]) :- merge(Xs?, Ys, Zs).$

$merge(Xs, [A \mid Ys], [A \mid Zs]) :- merge(Xs, Ys?, Zs).$

The queue manager program is :

$qm([dequeue(X) \mid S], [X \mid Head], Tail) :- qm(S?, Head, Tail).$

$qm([enqueue(X) \mid S], Head, [X \mid Tail]) :- qm(S?, Head, Tail).$

On receiving a *dequeue*(X) message, it instantiates X to the top element of the queue. On receiving *enqueue*(X) message, it inserts X at the end of the queue. The behavior of *qm* is quite interesting when the queue is empty and the queue manager receives a *dequeue*(X) message. It never returns a negative response to the sender of the message. It only unifies the variable X with a variable which is located at the top of the queue. This variable will be instantiated to a queue element sometime in the future, when the *qm* will receive an enqueue message. After the unification, *qm* becomes free from the dequeue request and tries to serve the next request from the input stream. The point is that the interaction between the *qm* and the sender of a dequeue message is completed at the moment of the unification. The sender will not need to send another message to *qm* whether X is instantiated or not, and *qm* will never send any additional message to the sender. The response will be conveyed indirectly by instantiating X to an enqueued element when *qm* will receive an enqueue message.

The behavior of the *qm* is also interesting when it receives the message *enqueue*(X) with X uninstantiated. As in the case above, it unifies the variable X with the tail element of the queue and finishes the processing of the request. The object which will send a dequeue message in the future will receive the variable X if the object sending *enqueue*(X) will not have instantiated X at that time as in the case above. From the point of view of the sender of a *dequeue* message, the situation is the same as in the above example, and it will have to wait for the value of X when it will need to refer to it. The situation can be seen as the object sending *enqueue*(X) reserves the place to which it will really enqueue something only later (Fig.6).

From these observations, it is clear that the behavior of the object *qm* is only to connect logically the arguments of *dequeue* and *enqueue* messages, in their arrival order, and real information is sent from the enqueueing object to the dequeueing object directly. However the important point here is that this logical connection cannot be seen by the users of *qm*. All they can see is the *qm*

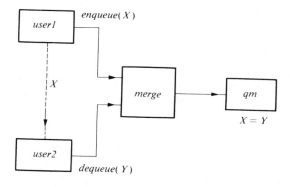

Fig. 6 The queue manager

object. This highly reduces the overhead on the resource manager because the manager will never be locked and request will never be refused. Using incomplete messages, we can create dynamically a new information path, which is hidden from the objects taking part in the message passing. This cannot be expressed in other object-oriented languages as simply as in Concurrent Prolog. This use of incomplete messages reduces message exchanging overhead and gives great expressive power to Concurrent Prolog.

5 . 2   Constraints

A constraint specifies a dependency relation among properties of objects. It is associated with procedures for satisfying it and can determine properties of objects if enough information about other properties of the objects are determined. There is no static input and output relation among the properties of objects ; rather, which property is input and which is output is determined dynamically, in an indeterminate way.

For example, the constraint $plus(X,Y,Z)$ specifies the relation,
$$X + Y = Z$$
where X, Y and Z are properties of some objects. Because the degree of freedom of this relation is two, it can find the value of an unknown property when two of the arguments are determined.

$$plus(2, 3, Z) \longrightarrow instantiate\ Z\ to\ 5.$$
$$plus(2, Y, 5) \longrightarrow instantiate\ Y\ to\ 3.$$
$$plus(X, 3, 5) \longrightarrow instantiate\ X\ to\ 2.$$

A constraint becomes active only when a sufficient number of its arguments are determined. Otherwise, it is suspended.

$$plus(X, 3, Z) \longrightarrow suspended$$
$$plus(X, 3, 5) \longrightarrow active\ and\ instantiates\ X\ to\ 2.$$

Constraints can form a dependency network over properties of objects. In the case of the *plus* constraints, it can represent simple equation systems, like :

$$plus(X,A,5) \qquad\qquad X+A=5$$
$$\&$$
$$plus(Y,1,X) \quad \Rightarrow \quad Y+1=X$$
$$\&$$
$$plus(Y,5,Z) \qquad\qquad Y+5=Z$$

In this network, each *plus* node plays the role of propagating values of properties of objects. For example, if the network receives 1 for A, it instantiates X,Y,Z to $4,3,8$ respectively, and if it receives 4 for X, it instantiates A,Y,Z to $1,3,8$ respectively, and so on.

Generally the representation of a constraint consists of methods to satisfy the relation. The constraint *plus* is defined in Concurrent Prolog simply as follows.

$$plus(X,Y,Z) :- wait(X),\ wait(Y) \mid Z\ is\ X+Y.$$
$$plus(X,Y,Z) :- wait(Y),\ wait(Z) \mid X\ is\ Z-Y.$$

$$plus(X,Y,Z) : - wait(Z), \ wait(X) \mid Y \ is \ Z - X.$$

where "X is Y" is a system predicate that evaluates an arithmetic expression Y and unifies the result with X. This definition shows that indeterminate computation is realized by Or-parallelism, and that the activation of a constraint is specified by *wait* predicates in guards. A dependency network of constraints can be formed by parallel-And and shared variables. For example, the equation system above is represented as follows.

$$plus(X,A,5), \ plus(Y,1,X), \ plus(Y,5,Z)$$

The behavior of this network is :: (Fig. 7)

> *Initially : All constraints are suspended*
> *A is instantiated to 1 externally*
> *then plus($X,A,5$) is now active and instantiates X to 4*
> *then plus($Y,1,X$) becomes active and instantiates Y to 3*
> *then plus($Y,5,Z$) becomes active and instantiates Z to 8*

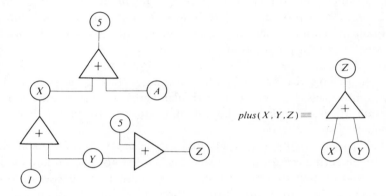

Fig. 7 The constraint network

The current implementation of constraints does not treat the methods for updating values of properties because logical variables are single assignment and can never be rewritten, and the dependency network cannot find the solution, even if there exists a unique solution, when the network contains some circular dependency, for example $plus(X,Y,5), \_plus(X,1,Y)$. However, this presents another example of the expressive power of Concurrent Prolog.

§6 Conclusion

The name of the game in designing a logic programming language is to find a control regime over logic programs that achieves a desired behavior. One is constrained by the requirements that any result of the computation must be a logical consequence of the axioms in the program, and that the control regime be both expressive and simple, to make the efficient implementation of algorithms possible without inducing too much runtime overhead. Sequential Prolog (side-effects excluded) is an example of such a logic programming language, designed to run efficiently on a von Neumann machine. Concurrent Prolog is another example.

Given these constraints, there was little freedom in choosing the target programming style when designing Concurrent Prolog. Hence it was an experimental finding, almost a surprise, that Concurrent Prolog lends itself most naturally to a very specific concurrent programming style, namely object-oriented programming. This paper has attempted to convey this finding via programming examples.

These examples have shown that the basic operations of object-oriented programming languages — creating an object, sending and receiving messages among objects, modifying an object's state, and forming class-superclass hierarchies — all correspond naturally to Concurrent Prolog programming techniques rather than to specialized programming language constructs. It is felt that showing that a programming technique in one language subsumes specialized constructs in another language is among the strongest evidence of the expressive power of a programming language.

In addition, a new object-oriented programming paradigm unique to Concurrent Prolog, called incomplete messages, has been presented. This technique subsumes stream communication and greatly simplifies the complexity of communication networks and the communication overhead usually associated with managing shared resources.

This paper provides only a glimpse of the potential of Concurrent Prolog to implementing constraint systems. The ability to determine dynamically the inputs and outputs of an object seems to be an invaluable asset for this task. A subsequent paper will explore further the application of Concurrent Prolog to this task.

Acknowledgements

The authors would like to thank Dan Ingalls for suggesting the problem of implementing a multi-window system as a generic object-oriented programming problem. We would also especially like to thank Kazuhiro Fuchi, Director of the ICOT Research Center, Kouichi Furukawa, Chief of the second research laboratory of the ICOT Research Center, and the other members of the ICOT staff, both for help with this research and for providing a stimulating place in which to work.

References

1) Shapiro, E. Y.: A Subset of Concurrent Prolog and Its Interpreter, ICOT Technical

Report, *TR-003* (1983).

2) Hewitt, C.: Viewing Control Structures as Patterns of Passing Messages, Artificial Intelligence, *8* (1977) .

3) The XEROX Learning Research Group: The Smalltalk-80 System, BYTE (Aug, 1981) .

4) Kowalski, R.: Predicate Logic as Programming Language, Proc. of IFIP 74 (1974).

5) Clark, K. L. and Gregory, S.: A Relational Language for Parallel Programming, Proc. of the ACM Conf. on Functional Programming Languages and Computer Architecture (1981).

6) van Emden, M. H. and de Lucena, G. J.: Predicate logic as a programming language for parallel programming, Logic Programming, (K. L.Clark and S. A. Tärnlund eds.) (Academic Press, 1982).

7) Steele, G. L.: The Definition and Implementation of a Computer Programming Language based on Constraints, MIT *AI-TR-595* (1980).

8) Borning, A.: The Programming Language Aspects of ThingLab, a Constraint-Oriented Simulation Laboratory, ACM Trans.on Programming Languages and Systems, *3, No.4* (1981).

9) Sussman, G. J. and Steele, G. L.: Constraints — A Language for Expressing Almost-Hierarchical Descriptions, Artificial Intelligence, *14* (1980).

10) Weinreb, D. and Moon, D.: Flavors: Message Passing in the Lisp Machine, MIT AI memo *no.* 602 (1980).

11) Ellis, J. R., Mishkin, N., van Leunen, M. and Wood, S. R.: Tools: An Environment for Timeshared Computing and Programming, Research Report, *232* (Department of Computer Science, Yale University, 1982).

12) Pereira, L. M.: Logic Control with Logic, Proc. of the 1st Int. Logic Programming Conf. (1982).

Chapter 4: Microlevel Architectures

The VLSI (very-large-scale-integration) technology has flourished in the past 10 years [1-5] and has resulted in the development of advanced microprocessors [6], semiconductor memories [7], and systolic arrays [8-12].

The microlevel architectures consist of architectural designs fundamental to applications in AI. In the design of massively parallel AI machines [13], some of the basic computational problems recognized are set intersection, transitive closure [8,26], contexts and partitions, best-match recognition, Gestalt recognition, and recognition under transformation. These operations may not be unique in AI and may exist in many other applications as well. Owing to the simplicity of some of these operations, they can usually be implemented directly in hardware, such as systolic arrays using the VLSI technology. Many other basic operations can also be implemented in VLSI. Examples include sorting [14-23] and selection [24,25], string and pattern matching [27-34], selection from secondary memories [35,36], dynamic programming evaluations [26,37,38], proximity searches [39], and unification [40-44].

Some AI languages such as Lisp differ from traditional machine languages in that the program/data storage is conceptually an unordered set of linked record structures of various sizes, rather than an ordered, indexable vector of numbers or bit fields of a fixed size. The instruction set must be designed according to the storage structure [45]. Additional concepts that are well suited for list processing are the tagged-memory [46,47] and stack architectures [48].

Two papers are included in this chapter. The first paper, by Mukhopadhyay, discusses hardware algorithms for database and string matching [31]. The second paper, by Vitter and Simons, presents parallel algorithms for the unification problem [43]. Readers may also want to refer to the paper by Douglas [40], which discusses the limitation of parallel processing, especially in the level of unification for logical inference systems and the match, select, and act phases of production systems. The tagged and stack mechanisms will be discussed with list processing in Chapter 6.

References

[1] C. Mead and L. Conway, *Introduction to VLSI Systems*, Addison-Wesley, Reading, Mass., 1980.

[2] B.P. Treleaven and C. Philip, eds., *VLSI Architectures*, Prentice-Hall, Englewood Cliffs, N.J., 1983.

[3] C.L Seitz, ed., *Proceedings of the Caltech Conference on Very Large Scale Integration*, Caltech, Pasadena, Calif., Jan. 1979.

[4] *Proceedings of the 2nd Caltech Conference on Very Large Scale Integration,* Computer Science Press, Rockville, Md., 1981.

[5] R. Bryant, ed., *Proceedings of the 3rd Caltech Conference on Very Large Scale Integration*, Computer Science Press, Rockville, Md., 1983.

[6] P.C. Treleaven, "VLSI Processor Architectures," *Computer*, vol. 15, no. 6, pp. 33-45, June 1982.

[7] T. Williams, "Semiconductor Memories: Density and Diversity," *Computer Design*, vol. 23, no. 9, pp. 105-116, Aug. 1984.

[8] H.T. Kung, "Let's Design Algorithms for VLSI Systems," *Proceedings of the Caltech Conference on VLSI,* ed. C.L. Seitz, pp. 65-90, Caltech, Pasadena, Calif., Jan. 1979.

[9] M.J. Foster and H.T. Kung, "The Design of Special-Purpose VLSI Chips," *Computer*, vol. 13, no. 1, pp. 26-40, Jan. 1980.

[10] J. Grinberg, G.R. Nudd, and R.D. Etchells, "A Cellular VLSI Architecture," *Computer*, vol. 17, no. 1, pp. 69-81, Jan. 1984.

[11] C.L. Seitz, "Concurrent VLSI Architectures," *IEEE Transactions on Computers*, vol. C-33, no. 12, pp. 1247-1265, Dec. 1984.

[12] J.A.B. Fortes, K.S. Fu, and B.W. Wah, "Systematic Approaches to the Design of Algorithmically Specified Systolic Arrays," *Proceedings of the International Conference on Accoustics, Speech, and Signal Proceedings*, pp. 8.9.1-8.9.4, IEEE, New York, N.Y., 1985.

[13] S.E. Fahlman and G.E. Hinton, "Massively Parallel Architectures for AI: NETL, THISTLE, and BOLTZMANN Machines," *Proceedings of the National Conference on Artificial Intelligence*, pp. 109-113, 1983.

[14] D. Bitton, D.J. DeWitt, D.K. Hsiao, and J. Menon, "A Taxonomy of Parallel Sorting," *Computing Surveys,* vol. 16, no. 3, pp. 287-318, Sept. 1984.

[15] J.D. Ullman, "Some Thoughts About Supercomputer Organization," *Proceedings of COMPCON S'84*, pp. 424-432, IEEE Computer Society, Washington, D.C., Feb. 1984.

[16] C.D. Thompson and H.T. Kung, "Sorting on a Mesh-Connected Parallel Computer," *Communications of the ACM*, vol. 20, no. 4, pp. 263-271, April 1977.

[17] C.D. Thompson, "The VLSI Complexity of Sorting," *IEEE Transactions on Computers*, vol. C-32, no. 12, pp. 1171-1184, Dec. 1983.

[18] C.C. Hsiao and L. Snyder, "Omni-Sort: A Versatile Data Processing Operation for VLSI," *Proceedings of the International Conference on Parallel Processing*, pp. 222-225, IEEE Computer Society, Washington, D.C., 1983.

[19] L.E. Winslow and Y.C. Chow, "The Analysis and Design of Some New Sorting Machines," *IEEE Transactions on Computers*, vol. C-32, no. 7, pp. 677-683, July 1983.

[20] M.A. Bonuccelli, E. Lodi, and L. Pagli, "External Sorting in VLSI," *IEEE Transactions on Computers*, vol. C-33, no. 10, pp. 931-934, Oct. 1984.

[21] G. Baudet and D. Stevenson, "Optimal Sorting Algorithms for Parallel Computers," *IEEE Transactions on Computers*, vol. C-27, no. 1, pp. 84-87, Jan. 1978.

[22] F.P. Preparata, "New Parallel-Sorting Schemes," *IEEE Transactions on Computers*, vol. C-27, no. 7, pp. 669-673, July 1978.

[23] C.P. Kruskal, "Searching, Merging, and Sorting in Parallel Computation," *IEEE Transactions on Computers*, vol. C-32, no. 10, pp. 942-946, Oct. 1983.

[24] B.W. Wah and K.L. Chen, "A Partitioning Approach to the Design of Selection Networks," *IEEE Transactions on Computers*, vol. C-33, no. 3, pp. 261-268, March 1984.

[25] A.C.C. Yao, "Bounds on Selection Networks," *SIAM Journal on Computing*, vol. 9, no. 3, pp. 566-582, Aug. 1980.

[26] L.J. Guibas, H.T. Kung, and C.D. Thompson, "Direct VLSI Implementation of Combinatorial Algorithms," *Proceedings of the Caltech Conference on VLSI*, pp. 509-525, Caltech, Pasadena, Calif., 1979.

[27] P.A.V. Hall and G.R. Dowling, "Approximate String Matching," *Computing Surveys*, vol. 12, no. 4, pp. 381-402, Dec. 1980.

[28] C. Hoffmann and M. O'Donnell, "Pattern Matching in Trees," *Journal of the ACM*, vol. 21, no. 1, pp. 68-95, 1982.

[29] A. Apostolico and A. Negro, "Systolic Algorithms for String Manipulations," *IEEE Transactions on Computers*, vol. C-33, no. 4, pp. 361-364, April 1984.

[30] J. Aoe, Y. Yamamoto, and R. Shimada, "A Method for Improving String Pattern Matching Machines," *IEEE Transactions on Software Engineering*, vol. SE-10, no. 1, pp. 116-120, Jan. 1984.

[31] A. Mukhopadhyay, "Hardware Algorithms for Nonnumeric Computation," *IEEE Transactions on Computers*, vol. C-28, no. 6, pp. 384-394, June 1979.

[32] S.R. Ahuja and C.S. Roberts, "An Associative/Parallel Processor for Partial Match Retrieval Using Superimposed Codes," *Proceedings of the 7th Annual Symposium on Computer Architecture*, pp. 218-227, IEEE Computer Society, Washington, D.C., May 1980.

[33] K. Goser, C. Foelster, and U. Rueckert, "Intelligent Memories in VLSI," *Information Sciences*, vol. 34, no. 1, pp. 61-82, 1984.

[34] S.L. Tanimoto, "A Boolean Matching Operator for Hierarchical Cellular Logic," *Proceedings of the Computer Society Workshop on Computer Architecture for Pattern Analysis and Image Database Management*, pp. 253-256, IEEE Computer Society, Washington, D.C., Oct. 1983.

[35] R. Gonzalez-Rubio, J. Rohmer, and D. Terral, "The Schuss Filter: A Processor for Non-Numerical Data Processing," *Proceedings of the 11th Annual International Symposium on Computer Architecture*, pp. 64-73, IEEE Computer Society, Washington, D.C., June 1984.

[36] H.C. Du, "Concurrent Disk Accessing for Partial Match Retrieval," *Proceedings of the International Conference on Parallel Processing*, pp. 211-218, IEEE Computer Society, Washington, D.C., 1982.

[37] D.P. Bertsekas, "Distributed Dynamic Programming," *IEEE Transactions on Automatic Control*, vol. AC-27, no. 3, pp. 610-616, June 1982.

[38] J. Casti, M. Richardson, and R. Larson, "Dynamic Programming and Parallel Computers," *Journal of Optimization Theory and Applications*, vol. 12, no. 4, pp. 423-438, Nov. 1973.

[39] P.N. Yianilos, "Dedicated Comparator Matches Symbol Strings Fast and Intelligently," *Electronics*, vol. 56, no. 24, pp. 113-117, 1983.

[40] R.J. Douglass, "A Qualitative Assessment of Parallelism in Expert Systems," *IEEE Software*, vol. 2, no. 2, pp. 70-81, May 1985.

[41] C. Forgy, A. Gupta, A. Newell, and R. Wedig, "Initial Assessment of Architectures for Production Systems," *Proceedings of the National Conference on Artificial Intelligence*, pp. 116-120, William Kaufmann, Washington, D.C., Aug. 1984.

[42] E. Tick and D.H.D. Warren, "Towards a Pipelined Prolog Processor," *New Generation Computing*, vol. 2, no. 4, pp. 323-345, 1984.

[43] J.S. Vitter and R.A. Simons, "Parallel Algorithms for Unification and Other Complete Problems," *Proceedings of the ACM'84 Annual Conference*, pp. 75-84, ACM, New York, N.Y., Oct. 1984.

[44] J.S. Vitter and R.A. Simons, "Parallel Algorithms for Unification and Other Complete Problems," *IEEE Transactions on Computers*, to appear 1986.

[45] G.L. Steele Jr. and G.J. Sussman, "Design of a Lisp-Based Microprocessor," *Communications of the ACM*, vol. 23, no. 11, pp. 628-645, Nov. 1980.

[46] E.A. Feustel, "On the Advantages of Tagged Architecture," *IEEE Transactions on Computers*, vol. C-22, no. 7, pp. 644-656, 1973.

[47] A. Hirsch, "Tagged Architecture Supports Symbolic Processing," *Computer Design*, vol. 23, no. 6, pp. 75-80, June 1984.

[48] R. Doran, "Architecture of Stack Machine," *High-Level Language Computer Architecture*, edited by Y. Chu, Academic Press, Orlando, Fla., 1975.

Hardware Algorithms for Nonnumeric Computation

AMAR MUKHOPADHYAY

Abstract—This paper is concerned with the design of hardware algorithms for nonnumeric computation. The subset of nonnumeric operations considered is derived from string processing languages such as Snobol or high-level database languages used in database management architectures. Being uniformly structured, the hardware could be implemented using LSI technology yielding an estimated pattern matching rate of about 100 million characters/s. The proposed nonnumeric processor will find applications in the environment of parallel (or associative) database management architectures, processing of large unstructured textual files, as a stand-alone microprocessor in digital communications which need simple search and update operations, or as a nonnumeric CPU that can be used along with the conventional CPU to expedite string processing operations.

Index Terms—Database management architecture, hardware algorithm, nonnumeric architecture, nonnumeric computation, parallel computation, Snobol, text retrieval.

INTRODUCTION

THE IMPORTANCE of nonnumeric computation as opposed to arithmetical computation was recognized by the early designers of computers in applications such as artificial intelligence, character recognition, information retrieval, language translation, weather forecasting, etc. [6]. In recent years nonnumeric computation has assumed a newer dimension because of its applications in the areas of large database management systems involving structured files of information as well as unstructured textual data, in digital communications involving simple operations on strings of characters, and in the development of string operation oriented languages for general purpose computers [4], [8], [18], [21], [28], [31], [33]–[35], [39], [40], [44], [46], [49], [50]. There has also been a similar upsurge of activity in nonnumeric computation involving finite graphs and in the development of efficient graph algorithms [10], [37]. A good fraction of computation time for most computer systems is expended in searching and sorting operations [24], [29]. In most artificial intelligence work, a significant part of the computation is concerned with dynamically varying nonnumeric information structures. With the proliferation of computers in all spheres of human civilization, most of what will be expected of future computers will be nonnumerical.

Manuscript received March 30, 1978; revised August 21, 1978. This work was supported by the National Science Foundation under Grant MCS76-04763. This paper was presented at the 5th Annual Symposium on Computer Architecture, April 3–5, 1978, Palo Alto, CA.

The author is with the Department of Computer Science, University of Iowa, Iowa City, IA 52242.

Existing computer architecture and hardware does not provide efficient nonnumeric computation. As Gimpel [16] points out, most machines are better at numerical computation by orders of magnitude than nonnumerical computation. There is no standardization at the machine level of any class of nonnumeric operations; a simple pattern matching, searching, deleting or retrieving operation when encoded at the machine level could look quite complicated compared to a reasonably complex arithmetical assignment statement. The designs of present day supercomputers [26] demonstrate a similar lack of elegance and efficiency in the implementation of nonnumeric operations. (The string pipeline in CDC STAR-100 is certainly a good attempt to remedy this situation.) During the last two decades, significant improvements have been attained in the size and speed of primary memory systems but because of the increase in the sizes of the data sets in practical applications most of the information must still reside in the secondary memory systems. It is expected that the current trend in development of block oriented storage organization, as found in rotating disk, will still continue to be true in newer technologies such as bubbles [45], CCD [3], and holographic [15] and electron-beam accessed memories [19]. The existing architectures of computers are inadequate to handle nonnumeric algorithms efficiently because of the need to transfer blocks of information back and forth from the CPU to secondary devices. The users of machine independent high-level language processors for nonnumeric operations have to depend, therefore, on expensive and time-consuming software systems.

The approach to overcome this difficulty of repeated block transfers is to employ parallel processing on different data blocks with associative processing in each block. Such an approach was proposed by Slotnick [39] and in recent years a significant amount of effort has been expended in the development of similar architecture in database applications. The idea of associative parallel processing needs to be reevaluated in the light of the recent upsurge in nonnumeric computation and in the context of a need to develop generalized nonnumeric machine architectures. In this paper we will be concerned with only one aspect of this architecture, that of designing an efficient nonnumeric processor for operations on strings and patterns that form the basis for Snobol-like and high-level database management languages. The proposed hardware will be sufficiently general to be applicable to any language oriented towards string computation. If the machine is to be employed for associative block processing with most of the information residing in serial access secondary devices, its overall organization will be as shown in Fig. 1, which also represents a general view of the architecture of some database machines [18], [33], [40]. The fundamental assumption is that the data are moving continuously from left to right over the read/write devices and the nonnumeric CPU performs its computation of pattern matching, retrieval and updating commands while the data are on the "fly." For some operations, more than one pass of data over the read/write head may be necessary.

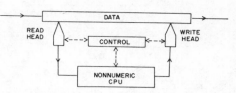

Fig. 1.   The organization of the nonnumeric processor.

IMPLEMENTATION OF PATTERN MATCHING OPERATIONS

A number of proposals for hardware implementation of pattern matching operations will be presented in this section. It is shown that uniformly structured cellular hardware which is suitable for LSI technology implementation [22], [30], [32] can be used to do most of the basic pattern matching operations. As a benchmark of these operations, we will pick a subset of Snobol pattern matching operations [16], [17]. Specifically, we will discuss cellular hardware for the implementation of pattern matching operations with alternation, concatenation, conditional and immediate value assignment, SPAN, BREAK, LEN, TAB, POS, ARB, ARBNO operations, string transformation and construction operations, and pattern matching with a class of pattern structures defined by regular expressions as a special case of unevaluated expression operator. Finally, implementation of DELETE, INSERT, and RETRIEVE operations applicable to database systems will be discussed. It should be clear that the proposed hardware algorithms could be used as subsystems for any nonnumeric processor. It should be noted, however, that in this paper we do not carry out the detailed logic design of the proposed hardware to the gate, pin connection, and LSI package level. Depending on the pattern matching operations, different configurations of cells, counters, registers, etc., are used. Obviously, it is not practical to design a system that requires separate interconnection structures for a distinct class of patterns. The total design of the machine might incorporate a microprogrammable control capable of reconfiguring the system for each class of patterns being matched, or it could employ a modular approach. The design of the total system will be the subject of future papers.

The Basic Cell

The basic cell for all the pattern matching operations is shown in Fig. 2. The cell contains a state flip-flop F (value 0 or 1) and a register X to hold the information of a single character X. The input symbol C is from a specified alphabet. The cell has a binary output f and a binary control input i and operates synchronously. The output function f at time t is defined as

$$f = 1 \quad \text{if } F = 1 \text{ and } C = X \text{ at time } t - 1$$
$$ = 0 \quad \text{otherwise.}$$

The state of F can be controlled by the input i as follows: the value of i at time t is taken by F at time t. At the beginning, F

is capable of being initialized to either value 0 or 1. Thereafter, its state is controlled by the input i.

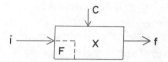

Fig. 2.   The basic cell for pattern matching.

Pattern Matching on a Single Pattern

A cascade of basic cells connected as in Fig. 3 will do the basic pattern matching operation. The input pattern to be matched is a string of characters $X_1 X_2 \cdots X_n$ and is placed in the registers of the cells. Each character of the text stream against which the pattern is to be searched is applied in parallel to all the cells. Notice that the input text stream is changing and can be scanned only once as in the case, for example, when a specific track from a rotating disk is read. All state flip-flops are initialized to 0.

If each character of the text stream is encoded as an 8-bit binary pattern, the input bus width for applying the text to the cascade is 8. A similar bus (not shown in Fig. 3) is shared among the cells of the cascade for the purpose of loading the pattern into the cascade; initialization of the state flip-flops can be done at the pattern loading time by adding an extra line to the bus which will be connected to the flip-flops. Since the cascade can be interpreted as an associative memory, each word of the memory being a single character, the sequential loading methods via a read/write buffer [13] can be used for this cascade. On the other hand, if the pattern length is bounded within a practical limit, an external register can hold the entire pattern. The logic of each cell will then only provide for comparison and control functions.

The input i to the entire cascade serves the purpose of "ANCHOR" in the Snobol sense. If $i = 1$ at time $t = 1$, the pattern matching is anchored with respect to the beginning of the input text. If the anchoring has to be done beginning at the kth character of the input text, the input i would be pulsed to 1 at time k. If during the application of the input text, the output f becomes 1, the pattern $X_1 X_2 \cdots X_n$ must occur in the input text. In general, if the output $f_k (1 \leq k \leq n)$ becomes 1 at time $k + 1$, the pattern $X_1 X_2 \cdots X_k$ matches the input text. If the pattern matching is done in the unanchored mode, that is, i is pulsed at every instant of time, multiple matches may take place which will be indicated by f becoming 1 a multiple number of times. If the pattern has a length k ($1 \leq k \leq n$), the pattern has to be placed right-adjusted and the anchor line should be connected to the $(n - k + 1)$th cell. This is indicated in Fig. 3 by the dotted

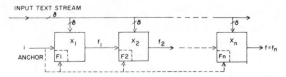

Fig. 3. The basic pattern matching device.

connection. Any subpattern which is a suffix of the given pattern $X_1 X_2 \cdots X_n$ can be matched by properly initializing the state flip-flops; for example, by setting $Fk = 1$ the subpattern $X_k X_{k+1} \cdots X_n$ could be matched. Simultaneous matching of several subpatterns is possible but one should apply caution in interpreting the results because $f = 1$ may imply several matches in the unanchored mode. For example, if the pattern is "abab" and the suffix subpattern is "ab," then with the text "ababab," $f = 1$ at time $t = 5$ will imply two matches. If the outputs f_i can be observed, arbitrary subpattern matching can also be implemented. The

Setting the anchor input to 1 provides the pre-cursor position (notice in Snobol this will correspond to anchor position 0); the propagation of the signal indicated by f_i denotes a partial match and an advancement of the cursor position. If $f = 1$, the cursor position has advanced by n, indicating a match. The input text remains unchanged throughout the operation. As an example, if the pattern "ALPHA" is set into the cascade and an input text "ALPHAL-PHALALA" is applied, the values of i and f for several anchor positions are as shown below for the duration of the input text.

TIME $\rightarrow$	1	2	3	4	5	6	7	8	9	10	11	12	13	14	
i	1	0	0	0	0	0	0	0	0	0	0	0	0	0	Anchored at 1
f	0	0	0	0	0	1	0	0	0	0	0	0	0	0	
i	1	1	1	1	1	1	1	1	1	1	1	1	1	1	Unanchored
f	0	0	0	0	0	1	0	0	0	1	0	0	0	0	
i	0	1	0	0	0	0	0	0	0	0	0	0	0	0	Anchored at 2
f	0	0	0	0	0	0	0	0	0	0	0	0	0	0	
i	1	0	0	0	1	0	0	0	0	0	0	0	0	0	Anchored at 1, 5
f	0	0	0	0	0	1	0	0	0	1	0	0	0	0	

subpattern

$$X_k X_{k+1} \cdots X_s \qquad (1 \le k \le n, 1 \le s \le n, s \ge k)$$

will match if Fk is set to 1 at time $s - k + 2$. If this subpattern matching facility is to be extended to the unanchored mode, the relevant flip-flops need to be pulsed by the ANCHOR line at every instant (as indicated by the dotted connection at the bottom).

Taking a conservative estimate (see the paper by Bloch and Galage [26]) of a 5 ns/logic stage for monolithic circuits and 10 stage delays per cell, pattern matching can be performed at the data flow rate of 20 million characters/s, which exceeds the data transfer rates of high-speed secondary devices by an order of magnitude. Using MSI or LSI, an estimated pattern matching rate of 33 million characters/s or 100 million characters/s can be achieved. A carefully designed pattern matching program will have a data handling rate of about 0.5 million characters/s.

The circuit of Fig. 3 can also be looked upon as performing a functional transformation of the input bit string at the anchor line to the output bit strings f_i. This interpretation fits Gimpel's definition of a pattern as a function operating on a cursor [16] as

(TEXT, PRE-CURSOR POSITION) PATTERN

$$= (\text{TEXT, POST-CURSOR POSITION}).$$

The string function COUNT($S1$, $S2$) which gives the number of strings $S2$ in $S1$ can be implemented by connecting the output f to a pulse counter and by operating the circuit in the unanchored mode. The counter has to be initialized to zero.

The cascade of Fig. 3 can also be interpreted as an associative memory, each word of the memory being a single character. Thus, the principle of operation of the array is based on associative parallel search—a concept first developed by Slade and McMahon [38] in 1956. The references on this topic are too numerous to mention [13], [42]. However, we would like to compare our scheme with some of the other apparently similar schemes.

In the early 1960's, Lee et al. [14], [27] proposed a cellularly organized information storage and retrieval system with distributed logic-in-memory one-dimensional cells. The text to be matched was statically held in this associative memory and the pattern to be matched was applied externally, symbol by symbol, under the control of an Unger-type [43] global control that issued the commands executed by each cell. String oriented machines based on Lee's idea have also been explored by others [47], [48]. In our scheme the situation is reversed: the pattern is held in the associative memory and the text comes from any random access or rotating secondary storage. In terms of practical implementation this should make a significant difference

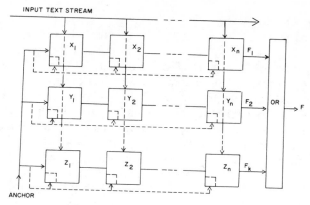

Fig. 4.   Pattern matching with alternation.

since the patterns could be limited to a maximum manageable size and the bulk of the information constituting the text could reside in conventional bulk memory.

String matching capabilities have also been implemented in a working machine CASSM [8], [40]. The "cellular" architectures of these machines implement a parallel search among the different tracks of a disk; the actual search operation being done sequentially by a set of commands which manipulate the data structures on the disk. Another database management machine RAP [33] which follows similar architectural principles as that of CASSM, does string manipulation operations in a similar track-parallel bit-serial fashion by an instruction set specially designed for it. We will deal with these machines later in the paper.

There is also a conceptual similarity between the pattern matching scheme of Fig. 3 and a scheme proposed by Karlowsky *et al.* [21]. In this scheme, the pattern to be matched is loaded into an associative memory as in our scheme, but rather than generating a hardware post-cursor signal, each match generates a fetch request to a machine instruction stored in a random access instruction memory. That instruction specifies what is to be done next, viz., mark the next cell in associative memory, ignore the following characters or indicate the end of match, etc. A similar scheme has been proposed by Zaky [46]. In both of these schemes additional control is needed for proper synchronization of the data and the memory cycles for fetching the instructions. Furthermore, these schemes do not address the problem of matching a complex pattern structure with a given text.

The pattern matching in Fig. 3 is done on-line and the total time is proportional to the length of the input text stream. It may be worthwhile to compare this with a mechanism that will translate a well known linear pattern matching algorithm [25] into hardware. For this algorithm we need only one comparator, not n as in Fig. 3. But we need n registers to hold n next(j) functions; furthermore, the input text has to be held statically in a buffer or for each mismatch the text needs to be dynamically skipped, depending on the value of next(j). This overhead is also present to the most recent modification of this algorithm as suggested by Boyer and Moore [5]. Rivest [36] has shown that the Boyer-Moore algorithm must have linear complexity at worst although the average complexity could be sublinear. The control

hardware involved in all these plus the preprocessing hardware for next(j) computations make the scheme more complex than that suggested in the simple cellular hardware of Fig. 3. Finally, the basic pattern matching scheme is easily adaptable to the case in which the alphabet of input characters could have some "DON'T CARE" symbols which could match with all symbols. If a "DON'T CARE" symbol θ occurs in the pattern, its realization as a cell is simply a "unit delay" box which advances the cursor position output by one cell. If θ appears in the text stream, the cells should be designed to match the symbols X_i or θ. Fischer and Patterson [11] have shown that the linear pattern matching algorithm of Morris-Knuth-Pratt breaks down if the alphabet has "DON'T CARE" symbols and they proposed a slightly worse than linear algorithm.

Pattern Matching with Alternation

As noted earlier the cascade of the previous section can be interpreted as an associative memory, each word of the memory being a single character. If each word contains k characters, simultaneous matching of k distinct patterns $p_1 = X_1 X_2 \cdots X_n$, $p_2 = Y_1 Y_2 \cdots Y_n$, $\cdots$, $p_k = Z_1 Z_2 \cdots Z_n$ against the input text stream is possible. If size of p_i is less than n, p_i should be placed right adjusted and the anchor line should be connected to the appropriate cell as explained in the previous section. This corresponds to an extension of the cellular hardware of Fig. 3 in two dimensions as shown in Fig. 4. The output F is the logical OR of the cascade outputs. If $F = 1$ during the application of the input text stream, then one of the patterns $p_1, p_2, \cdots, p_k$ must have occurred in the input text. This corresponds to the alternation operation in Snobol which is realized by a logical OR operation in our scheme. This circuit performs the following pattern transformation

$$(\text{TEXT}, c)(p_1 | p_2 | \cdots | p_k) = [c_1, c_2, \cdots, c_k],$$

where c is the pre-cursor position, c_i $(1 \le i \le k)$ is the post-cursor position for pattern p_i, and $|$ denotes the alternation operation.

If the patterns are placed right adjusted, the individual cascade output functions should become 1 at a time $c_i + 1$ if pattern p_i matches the text. If information about the cursor positions for a partial match is required the intermediate cascade outputs along the columns of the array have to be observed.

The circuit of Fig. 4 may be varied in many ways. The techniques for unanchored mode operation, subpattern matching, "DON'T CARE" symbols, and variable pre-cursor position anchoring, as described for a single cascade in the previous section, can be extended to this two-dimensional pattern matching device. Furthermore, a simple hardware modification can achieve what might be called *selective anchoring*. Let us say that the pattern p_i is to be anchored at pre-cursor position a_i. The k distinct pattern matching operations can then be denoted symbolically as

$$(\text{TEXT}, [a_1, a_2, \cdots, a_k])(p_1 | p_2 | \cdots | p_k) = [c_1, c_2, \cdots, c_k].$$

This can be achieved by connecting the anchor line to the appropriate cells within the different cascades. By incorporating additional "anchor control" logic it is possible to operate some subsets of cascades in the unanchored mode, subpattern matching mode, variable pre-cursor position mode, or a combination thereof. This could conceivably produce a rather complex pattern matching facility for future machines, surpassing the capabilities of Snobol or any other existing string processing language.

It is important to note that the difference between the unanchored and anchored mode of operation in this scheme is simply the presence or absence of a pulse at the anchor line. But this difference is tremendous in Snobol implementation because of the sequential nature of the matching process in which each failure is to be backed up by a readjustment of the pre-cursor position. The hardware scheme described here performs parallel computations for each possible anchor position.

The pattern matching is done on-line in Fig. 4 and it is worthwhile to compare this scheme with a mechanism that will translate into hardware a linear pattern matching algorithm of Aho and Corasick [1] (a generalization of Morris–Knuth–Pratt procedure [25]) with respect to a set of patterns or keywords. In this algorithm, the approach is to construct a finite state machine using the keywords and then apply the input text to the machine for possible matching. The construction of this machine in turn requires the construction of three other quantities called the "goto," "failure," and "output" functions, each of which takes a linear amount of processing time. The overhead involved in temporary storage, control functions for dynamically skipping portions of the text, and off-line preprocessing makes the scheme unattractive compared to the simple cellular hardware of Fig. 4.

Pattern Matching with Conditional and Immediate Value Assignment and Replacement

Whenever pattern matching over a set of patterns is done it is important to have conditional value assignment and immediate value assignment operations ($\cdot$ and \$ operators of Snobol) which identify the actual pattern being matched or the intermediate subpatterns for a partial match. Furthermore, in many string processing applications the matched part of the subject string ought to be replaceable by an object string. These operations can be done by the proposed hardware of Fig. 5. H is a shift register which holds m characters of input text coming from the text stream. With the arrival of each new character the contents of H is shifted one place to the right. The registers $R_1, R_2, \cdots, R_k$ hold the object patterns, that is, if the input text matches with pattern p_i, then the input text will be replaced by the contents of register R_i. (The case when the object string has a length greater than the matched string is treated later in the paper.) Thus, the network performs simultaneously the set of string functions [16]

$$\{\text{REPL}(\text{TEXT}, p_i, R_i)\}.$$

The register M holds the pattern being matched in the subject string at the time of replacement. Assume that the registers R_i and M can each hold m characters. When the output of the ith cascade F_i equals 1, the input string contains p_i ($1 \leq i \leq k$). Whenever $F_i = 1$, F is also 1, so the matched pattern held at H could be transferred to M through gates activated by F (indicated by small circles in Fig. 5). Then R_i is transferred to H through similar gating networks activated by F_i. The control part of the circuit must generate the appropriate timing signals to insure this sequence of events. Note that not more than one F_i could become 1 at the same time since it is assumed that the patterns $p_1, \cdots, p_k$ are distinct.

The implementation of the operation of immediate value assignment is complicated by the fact that F_i or F may not become 1 but a partial match can take place. Knowledge of the signals like $F_1, \cdots, F_k$ at each column position of the cellular array has to be made available to the control circuit in order that partial matches with the text string can be transferred out of H. A hardware scheme for this can be devised, but the details are left out.

String Transformations

The circuit of Fig. 5 could be easily adapted to the homomorphic string transformation operation

$$\text{REPLACE}(\text{TEXT}, S_1, S_2)$$

which substitutes in TEXT each character of S_1 by the corresponding characters of S_2 (S_1 and S_2 have the same length). To achieve this, the pattern matching array should hold the characters of S_1 in one column of cells and the characters in S_2 should be loaded in the registers R_i. If S_1 and S_2 denote two different alphabets of the same size, the circuit performs what is called a *transliteration* operation. Another string transformation operation TRIM is described below.

Trim Circuit

In Fig. 5 it has been assumed that the lengths of registers H, M, and R_i are the same. Usually, a design parameter will be their maximum length l and all registers will be of the same length l. In case an object string has length less than l, blank symbols will be introduced in the text stream. The following circuit, shown in Fig. 6, could be used to remove

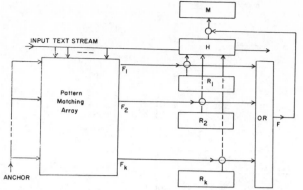

Fig. 5. Pattern matching with alternation, conditional assignment and replacement.

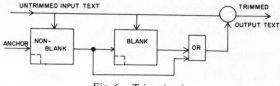

Fig. 6. Trim circuit.

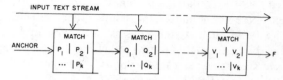

Fig. 7. Pattern matching with concatenation.

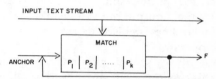

Fig. 8. Matching of repeated patterns.

unnecessary blank symbols from the output text stream. For that matter, this circuit can be used to remove blank symbols from any input string. It should be noted however that replacement and removal of blanks could not be done simultaneously on-line. The writing of the output text stream may have to be delayed by at least one rotation of the disk or equivalent time for other devices. The first cell is a comparator which produces an output 1 if the input character is nonblank. The second cell produces a 1 output if the input character is blank. The logical OR of these two outputs are used to gate the text string to an output buffer in which the trimmed text stream flows in. The anchor line is pulsed with the arrival of every new character. The output is assumed to be accumulated in a buffer which receives input only if the gating circuit (indicated by the circle) is open. Note that the trim circuit does not perform an exact analog of TRIM operation in Snobol where it is used to remove unnecessary blanks from the trailing edge of the card images.

By combining the replacement scheme of Fig. 5 and the trim circuit, it is possible to implement a positional transformation operation in which a sequence of single-character patterns $p_1 p_2 \cdots p_k$ is replaced by $t_1 p_{i_1} t_2 p_{i_2} \cdots t_k p_{i_k} t_{k+1}$ where t_i $(1 \leq i \leq k+1)$ is an arbitrary sequence of characters and i_s $(1 \leq s \leq k)$ is an integer from the set $(1, 2, \cdots, k)$ with the provision that $t_j p_{j_s}$ could be absent $1 \leq j \leq k$. The operation cannot be performed on-line since in general $t_j p_{j_s}$ and p_j will have different lengths. In the special case when $t_j p_{j_s}$ is absent, p_j is substituted by blank characters which have to be removed in a subsequent pass through a trim circuit.

If the requirement of on-line handling of the text stream is relaxed, hardware implementations of the string transformation functions such as ORDER, ROTATER, REVERSE, BLEND, LEXGT, and AGT can be devised involving such primitive operations as greater than or equal to comparison by the cells, circular shifts, sorting, merging, etc. The details of such schemes are omitted from this paper, as well as their definitions which can be found elsewhere [16], [17].

Pattern Matching with Concatenation

A hardware solution to pattern matching with alternation as well as concatenation is sketched in Fig. 7. Each rectangu-lar box in the diagram is a two-dimensional cellular array of the type shown in Fig. 4. The groups of alternations of patterns, viz., $p_1|p_2|\cdots|p_k$, $q_1|q_2|\cdots|q_k$, $\cdots$, $v_1|v_2|\cdots|v_k$ are loaded into the arrays initially. If the output $F = 1$ during the application of the text stream, the input text must contain a substring $p_i q_j \cdots v_s$ for some $1 \leq i, j, s \leq k$. If the sets of patterns are of unequal length, special connections (as explained earlier) of the anchor lines are needed.

It is important to recall that the implementation of pattern matching with concatenation and alternation in Snobol is a "bead diagram" algorithm which is essentially sequential and is rather expensive under FULLSCAN mode [17]. Several heuristics have been incorporated to improve the performance of the algorithm to obtain the QUICKSCAN mode operation [16]. The latest version of SPITBOL does not have any such heuristics since these make it possibly slower than FULLSCAN. The hardware implementation of Fig. 7 is essentially parallel and does away with the need to develop optimization heuristics since it always performs the equivalent of FULLSCAN matching.

As a special case of concatenation, if the set of patterns p_1, p_2, $\cdots$, p_k is concatenated to itself, a simpler scheme with a feedback connection will detect repetitions of the basic patterns p_1, p_2, $\cdots$, p_k in the text stream. This circuit is shown in Fig. 8. The anchor line is pulsed externally only at the beginning; it is pulsed thereafter by the output F. The input OR function is denoted by a simple connection. This means that whenever a pattern p_i is matched in the text stream a new search is initiated to detect another occurrence of p_i. This circuit will detect only the first of such repeated patterns. The circuit of Fig. 8 performs an operation similar to ARBNO of Snobol. This point will be treated later.

Implementation of the SPAN Operation

The idea of feedback employed in Fig. 8 for repeated patterns is useful for realizing the SPAN operation of Snobol.

The SPAN operation describes patterns like

a run of blanks	SPAN(' ')
a run of digits	SPAN('0123456789')
a run of letters	SPAN('ABC $\cdots$ XYZ').

The scheme is sketched in Fig. 9. The cell logic inside the cell marked ANY DIGIT matches with any incoming digit, the cell marked ANY LETTER matches with any letter, etc. The logical complexity of such match cells is not much more complicated than an ordinary match cell of Fig. 2, since groups of characters sharing certain properties get encoded in a special way as in EBCDIC or in ASCII codes. The input text is applied in parallel to all the cells. The span of characters matched is held in the shift registers whose gating is controlled by the 1 output of the logical OR network. Only one of the anchor lines is pulsed, depending on the argument of the SPAN operator.

A similar hardware scheme can do the BREAK operation of Snobol. In this case the input stream will be allowed to pass through until a match is found. The match signal will then inhibit further progress of streams of characters in the temporary register. For example, the circuit shown in Fig. 10 implements BREAK('ANY DIGIT') or BREAK('ANY LETTER') depending on the pulsing of the corresponding anchor line in unanchored mode. The NOT gate inhibits the flow of the text stream into the output register T when a match is found with respect to a single character. The anchor line E has to be pulsed with the arrival of every new character. If the text ends with END MARKER before break happens, the signal 'FLUSH T' will be used to empty the register T. If this signal is not used, the circuit implements the BREAKEM operation defined as

$$\text{BREAK}(\text{S}) \mid \text{REM}.$$

An adaptation of Fig. 10 with replacement hardware of Fig. 5 could be used to implement the BREAKX operation. The pattern matching would take place with respect to a string rather than a character. The match signal is then used for stopping the text stream as well as for replacing the matched part of the outgoing text by blank characters.

Implementation of LEN, POS, TAB, and Other Operations

The hardware implementation of these operations depends on some kind of counting operations. The definitions using only the cursor positions are given [16]:

$$c \, \text{LEN}(n) = c + n \quad \text{if } c + n \leq |\text{TEXT}|$$
$$= \varnothing \quad \text{otherwise}$$
$$c \, \text{POS}(n) = c \quad \text{if } n = c$$
$$= \varnothing \quad \text{otherwise}$$
$$c \, \text{TAB}(n) = n \quad \text{if } n \geq c$$
$$= \varnothing \quad \text{otherwise},$$

where $|\text{TEXT}|$ denotes the length of the input text stream and $\varnothing$ indicates the null post-cursor position, indicating no

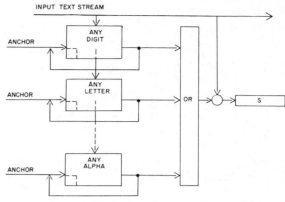

Fig. 9. SPAN operator.

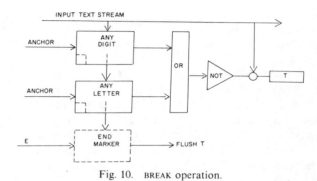

Fig. 10. BREAK operation.

match, which is depicted in our schemes by a 0 output of the pattern matching array.

The operation of LEN(n) can be implemented by the scheme shown in Fig. 11. The special symbol 'ENDMARKER' marks the end of any text stream. The counter is set to 0 at the beginning and it is incremented by 1 at the pulsing of the anchor line which is operated in unanchored mode. The output of the comparator is 1 as long as the counter number $x \leq n$. If the text stream is of sufficient length, it is gated to the output register R; a premature ENDMARKER generates a signal that can be used to flush the register R. The string function SUBSTR(TEXT, I, L) can be implemented by setting $n = L - I$ and by anchoring at a time when the Ith character of TEXT appears as the input.

Similar techniques can be used for POS and TAB operators. For POS, the text is gated out to R by separate control signals until the ANCHOR line is pulsed. The number of characters gated out up to the application of this pulse is compared with n. If these agree, R contains the legitimate part of the text, otherwise R is flushed. For TAB, the comparator decides whether n is greater than or equal to the number of characters passed at the anchor time. The gating process continues until n characters are passed; otherwise R is flushed. Premature ending of the text stream should always be used to flush R. The operators RPOS(n) and RTAB(n) (see [16] and [17] for definitions) can be implemented by similar techniques if the text stream can be held statically in a buffer. Since we are not making such an assumption we will omit such discussions from this paper.

Several other operators like REM, ANY, and NOTANY have

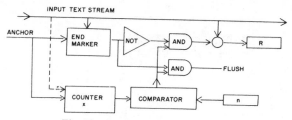

Fig. 11.   Implementation of LEN(n).

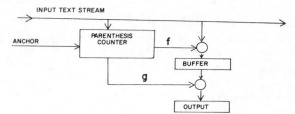

Fig. 12.   BAL operator.

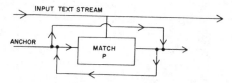

Fig. 13.   Implementation of ARBNO (or ARB).

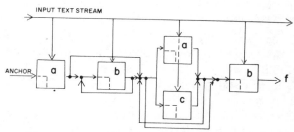

Fig. 14.   Pattern matching with regular expression.

obvious hardware solutions: REM is a control signal that allows the text stream to flow to the output register, ANY is the alternation circuit of Fig. 4 in unanchored mode where each pattern is a single character and NOTANY is ANY with output F complemented by a NOT gate. A hardware implementation of FAIL is not necessary since the circuit of Fig. 4 does pattern matching on all the patterns in parallel and FAIL can be simulated by operating the circuit in the unanchored mode. The operator SUCCEED is implemented by simply forcing the output F in Fig. 4 to be constant 1. An implementation of ABORT is simply a control signal that abandons the pattern matching circuit if $F = 0$.

Implementation of BAL Operator

An interesting Snobol pattern structure is BAL [16]. The BAL pattern matches all nonnull text streams which are balanced with respect to left and right parentheses starting from a given pre-cursor position. For example,

$$('a(b(\ ))cd', 0)\mathrm{BAL} = [1, 6, 7, 8]$$

which corresponds to the balanced strings 'a', '$a(b(\ ))$', '$a(b(\ ))c$', and '$a(b(\ ))cd$'.

A hardware scheme to implement the BAL operator is shown in Fig. 12. The box marked "parenthesis counter" receives the input text stream starting from the anchor time; it contains zero at the beginning. It has two binary outputs: $f = 1$ if the counter content is ≥ 0, otherwise $f = 0$; $g = 1$ if and only if the counter has value 0, otherwise $g = 0$. The counter counts up if it receives '(' and counts down if it receives ')'; it ignores any other symbol. If f is 0 it cannot change its value. Every time g is 1 a balanced string is gated into the output register from the buffer register which accumulates the character strings as long as $f = 1$.

The use of a counter in Figs. 11 and 12 implies that, in practice, an upper bound has to be set on the length of the input text stream as determined by the maximum possible number in the counter.

Pattern Matching with Pattern Structures Specified by Regular Expressions

The idea of feedback as employed in Figs. 8 and 9 combined with feedforward connections can be used very effectively to obtain hardware implementations of pattern matching operations with pattern structures specified by regular expressions [23]. Finnila and Love [53] have used similar connections for an actual implementation of a linear array processor. Regular expressions define sets of strings using Kleene star operator $\circledast$, union $(+)$, and concatenation (juxtaposition). In Snobol terminology, $\circledast$ is

equivalent to ARBNO(P), which is defined using unevaluated expression operator $*$ as

$$\mathrm{ARBNOP} = \mathrm{NULL} \,|\, \mathrm{P} * \mathrm{ARBNOP}.$$

This is equivalent to $P^{\circledast}$, where P is a set of patterns. A scheme to implement ARBNO is shown in Fig. 13. The anchor line is pulsed once at the beginning. The feedforward connection allows matching with respect to the NULL string. The feedback connection allows matching with respect to an arbitrary number of repetitions of patterns in P. Since union $(+)$ and concatenation operations are equivalent to alternation and concatenation as discussed earlier, any pattern structure denoted by a regular expression can be matched. As an example, the scheme to implement a pattern structure described by $ab^{\circledast}(a + c)^{\circledast}b$ is shown in Fig. 14. Note that the operator ARB, defined as

$$\mathrm{ARB} = \mathrm{NULL} \,|\, \mathrm{LEN}(1) * \mathrm{ARB}$$

can also be implemented as in Fig. 13, where P denotes alternation of all patterns consisting of single characters.

One should note that although regular expression pattern structure can be equivalently described by Snobol pattern structures with the unevaluated expression operator $(*)$, the converse is not necessarily true. For example, there is no regular expression pattern structure which is equivalent to $A = 'b' \,|\, 'a' * A'a'$. It should also be noted that pattern structure defined by extended regular expressions involving complementation $(\vdash)$ and intersection $(\wedge)$ operators [9] can also be implemented as these operations preserve the regularity of the resulting sets. Finally, for each distinct regular expression a separate interconnection of cells is necessary. In practice, it will be more convenient to specify a set of standard basic cells and to use a microprogrammed interconnection structure that will implement a given regular pattern structure.

Pattern matching algorithms for regular expression patterns have been developed by Thompson [41] and Aho–Hopcroft–Ullman [2] in the context of compilation. Pattern matching algorithms applicable to context-free pattern structures have also been developed using the principles of parsing algorithms for context-free languages. The development of a formal theory of pattern structures [12] is now an active field of research and it will be interesting to examine this theory with a view to developing hardware pattern matching algorithms.

Implementation of DELETE, INSERT, UPDATE, and RETRIEVE Operations

For general string processing applications it is useful to have operations that will modify, delete, and retrieve information following certain successful search operations. The replacement statement in Snobol is only a special case of these operations since the information that gets modified, dropped out, or retrieved may not necessarily correspond to the matched part of the text string. The assumption is that the subject text to be changed is placed contiguously with the key as might be the case for unstructured textual information files [20].

Let us define the operation DELETE(PATTERN, LENGTH) to be an operation that will erase from the text stream a number of characters equal to LENGTH immediately following a match with the given PATTERN. This could be implemented by replacing the normal stream of text immediately after a match by a stream of blank characters of length equal to LENGTH and then resuming the normal flow of the text. The output text stream is then allowed to flow through a trim circuit of Fig. 6. A schematic diagram is shown in Fig. 15. Because of the trim operation, DELETE cannot be performed on the fly. The operation RETRIEVE(PATTERN, LENGTH) could simply direct the flow of the text stream to an output buffer immediately following the pattern match for a duration of flow of number of characters equal to LENGTH. If we define the operation UPDATE(PATTERN, OBJECT TEXT) to be an operation in which the part of the subject text immediately following PATTERN is replaced by the OBJECT TEXT, complications will arise with respect to the length of the subject (s) and the length of the object (k) texts. If $k \leq s$, the hardware implementation is very similar to the replacement operation in Snobol (Fig. 5) except that the text immediately following the matched part of the subject text is replaced. Also, if $k < s$, the trailing end of the subject text part should be padded with blank symbols and then eliminated by a trim circuit as in the operation DELETE. Note that only when $k = s$ can the operation be performed on-line. The operation INSERT is the same as UPDATE with $s = 0$. It needs a text construction process that will temporarily halt the flow of the text stream (or have a sufficiently

long buffer to store it) and concatenate the object text with the subject text followed by the concatenation of the original text. The output stream is then written back to storage. For UPDATE operation with $k > s$, a similar procedure can be followed.

In general, for a text-oriented data management system more complex retrieval, update, and insert operations are needed and it may be more cost-effective to use an address mapping scheme followed by a match, as is done in several implemented systems [4].

APPLICATION TO DATABASE ARCHITECTURES

In this section we will briefly indicate the possible application of the nonnumeric processor in associative database computer architectures currently proposed in the literature [4], [8], [18], [21], [28], [33], [34], [40].

The general principles of organization behind all these architectures consists of providing a front-end computer which interfaces with a high-level database manipulation language. The structure of this language depends on the user's view of the data, that is, whether the data are unstructured textual information or structured information using a representation model (viz., hierarchical, relational, or network). The statements of this language are in the form of queries of different kinds of complex retrieval, update, insertion, deletion, set theoretic, and simple numerical operations. Most of these statements exhibit a natural parallelism on the data stored in a block of secondary storage. The front-end machine compiles these statements into a set of machine instructions for the associative processor which then operates on the data structure used to represent the data set. An examination of these operations reveals that they are fundamentally dependent on some pattern matching operations followed by certain modifications of control state information and/or updates of existing information. The nonnumeric processor discussed in the previous section could do these operations rather efficiently. Let us elaborate this point.

Bird, Tu, and Worthy describe an associative architecture for searching a very large textual base which is essentially unstructured. Their argument is that for a rapidly changing textual file as large as 5–50 billion characters, preprocessing, editing, and the use of a search surrogate may not be cost-effective since the surrogate itself might occupy 2 to 3 billion characters. Furthermore, the user may be interested in the raw textual data which preserve the full syntactic relationship. Their solution consists of a front-end machine

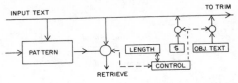

Delete (Pattern, Length)

Retrieve (Pattern, Length)

Update (Pattern, Object Text)

Fig. 15.   Delete, retrieve, and update operations.

called "query translator" which generates and feeds the "associative searcher" the keywords for search, which in turn accepts the stream of input text from a massive (50–1600 Mbytes) secondary storage and produces a hit list of addresses where the information corresponding to the keys is located. A third piece of hardware called the "query resolver" integrates this information with respect to a complex search specified in the original query and also decides how to respond to a specific user in a multiuser environment. The user then subsequently performs a retrieve, delete, or insert operation directly on the secondary device using the information supplied by the resolver. The contention of the proposal here is that the nonnumeric processor described in the previous section seems ideally suited to perform the task of the "associative searcher" since it performs a pattern matching operation on a stream of data on the fly. Furthermore, if necessary, the delete, insert, and update operations can also be performed on the data stream by methods discussed earlier without the need for an additional command from the user. This may necessitate a more complex query translator that will perform most of the functions of the query resolver and provide information for update, delete, and insert operations.

Another class of database management architectures is represented by the machines CASSM and RAP. The "cellular" architectures of these machines, as we have noted earlier, implement a parallel search among the different tracks of the disk. The actual search operations are performed sequentially by a set of content-addressed machine instructions which manipulate the formatted data in each track. The parallelism in these machines is due to the segmentation of the file into equal-length segments stored under the different heads of a "cylinder." In both of these machines the basic operations performed are searching for a pattern, marking some control bits, and altering existing information in different fields under the control of the marked bits. RAP uses a data format that corresponds to Codd's [7] relations whereas CASSM uses a more or less open-ended structure. The proposal in this paper is that the nonnumeric processor described earlier could perform the pattern-related operations of the "cells" of CASSM or RAP in a truly associative parallel fashion and at a much faster speed because of the use of built-in hardware algorithms.

The future impact of CASSM and RAP type architectures will of course depend on the development of cost-effective head-per-track devices. On the other hand, the adaptation of Bird–Tu–Worthy type architectures with the use of search surrogates developed using existing representational models seems reasonable and implementable using existing technology [51]. The design of a similar machine has also been reported by Masari et al. [52]. Because of the suitability of the nonnumeric processor in such architectures, it is hoped that the proposed hardware schemes in this paper will make an impact on future data base architectures.

References

[1] A. V. Aho and M. J. Corasick, "Efficient string matching algorithm: An aid to bibliographic search," vol. 18, no. 6, pp. 333–340, 1975.

[2] A. V. Aho, J. E. Hopcroft, and J. D. Ullman, *The Design and Analysis of Computer Algorithms*. Reading, MA: Addison-Wesley, 1975.

[3] G. F. Amello, "Charge-coupled devices for memory applications," in *AFIPS Conf. Proc.*, vol. 44, pp. 515–522, 1975.

[4] R. M. Bird, J. C. Tu, and R. M. Worthy, "Associative/parallel processors for searching very large textual data bases," presented at the 3rd Workshop on Computer Architecture and Nonnumeric Processing, Syracuse Univ., Syracuse, NY, May 17–18, 1977.

[5] R. S. Boyer and J. S. Moore, "A fast string searching algorithm," *Commun. Assoc. Comput. Mach.*, vol. 20, no. 10, p. 762, 1977.

[6] W. Buchholz, Ed., *Planning a Computer System*. New York: McGraw-Hill, 1962.

[7] E. F. Codd, "A relational model for data on large shared data banks," *Commun. Assoc. Comput. Mach.*, vol. 13, no. 6, p. 377, 1970.

[8] G. P. Copeland, G. J. Lipovsky, and S. Y. W. Su, "The architecture of CASSM: A cellular system for nonnumeric processing," presented at the 1st Annu. Symp. Computer Architecture, 1973.

[9] I. R. Copi, C. C. Elgot, and J. B. Wright, "Realization of events by logical nets," in *Sequential Machines*, E. F. Moore, Ed. Reading, MA: Addison-Wesley, 1964, p. 175.

[10] N. Deo, *Graph Theory with Applications to Engineering and Computer Science*. Englewood Cliffs, NJ: Prentice-Hall, 1974.

[11] M. J. Fischer and M. S. Paterson, "String matching and other products," Project MAC, Tech. Memo. 41, MIT, Jan. 1974.

[12] A. C. Fleck, "Formal models for string patterns," in *Current Trends in Programming Methodology*, vol. 4, R. Yeh, Ed. Englewood Cliffs, NJ: Prentice-Hall, 1978.

[13] C. C. Foster, *Content Addressable Parallel Processing*. Van Nostrand, 1976.

[14] R. S. Gaines and C. Y. Lee, "An improved cell memory," *IEEE Trans. Electron. Comput.*, vol. C-14, p. 72, Jan. 1965.

[15] A. K. Gillis et al., "Holographic memories—Fantasy or reality?" in *AFIPS Conf. Proc.*, vol. 44, pp. 535–539, 1975.

[16] J. F. Gimpel, *Algorithms in SNOBOL4*. New York: Wiley-Interscience, 1976.

[17] R. E. Griswold, J. F. Poage, and I. P. Polansky, *The SNOBOL4 Programming Language*. Englewood Cliffs, NJ: Prentice-Hall, 1968.

[18] L. D. Healy, G. J. Lipovski, and K. L. Doty, "The architecture of a context addressed segment sequential storage," in *Proc. Fall Joint Comput. Conf.*, p. 691, 1972.

[19] W. C. Hughes et al., "BEAMOS—A new electronic digital memory," *AFIPS Conf. Proc.*, vol. 44, pp. 541–548, May 1975.

[20] J. W. Hunt and M. D. McIllroy, "An algorithm for differential file comparison," Comput. Sci. Tech. Rep. 41, Bell Lab., Murray Hill, NJ, June 1976.

[21] I. Karlowsky, H. O. Leilich, and G. Steige, "A search processor proposal for data base applications," *Elektronische Rechenanlagen*, vol. 17, pp. 108–118, June 1975 (in German; abstract in *Computer Abstracts*, vol. 19, no. 9, p. 194, Sept. 1975).

[22] W. H. Kautz, "Programmable cellular logic," in *Recent Developments in Switching Theory*, A. Mukhopadhyay, Ed. New York: Academic Press, 1971.

[23] S. C. Kleene, "Realization of events in nerve nets and finite automata," in *Automata Studies*, C. E. Shannon and J. McCarthy, Eds. Princeton, NJ: Princeton Univ. Press, 1956.

[24] D. E. Knuth, *The Art of Computer Programming, Vol. 3, Searching and Sorting*. Reading, MA: Addison-Wesley, 1973.

[25] D. E. Knuth, J. H. Morris, and V. R. Pratt, "Fast pattern matching in strings," *SIAM J. Comput.*, vol. 6, no. 2, pp. 323–350, June 1977.

[26] D. J. Kuck, D. H. Lawrie, and A. H. Sameh, Eds., "High speed computer and algorithm organization," in *Proc. Symp. High-Speed Computer and Algorithm Organization*, Univ. of Illinois, Apr. 13–15, 1977.

[27] C. Y. Lee and M. C. Paul, "A content addressable distributed logic memory with applications to information retrieval," *Proc. IEEE*, p. 924, June 1963.

[28] C. S. Lin, D. C. P. Smith, and J. M. Smith, "The design of a rotating associative memory for relational data base applications," *ACM Trans. Data Base Systems*, vol. 1, p. 1, 1976.

[29] H. Lorin, *Sorting and Sort Systems*. Reading, MA: Addison-Wesley, 1975.

[30] R. C. Minnick, "A survey of microcellular research," *J. Assoc. Comput. Mach.*, vol. 14, pp. 203–241, 1976.

[31] N. Minsky, "Rotating storage devices as partially associative memories," in *Proc. ACM SIGFIDET Workshop on Data Description, Access, and Control*, 1972.

[32] A. Mukhopadhyay and H. S. Stone, "Cellular logic," in *Recent*

Developments in Switching Theory, A. Mukhopadhyay, Ed. New York: Academic, 1971.

[33] E. A. Ozkarahan, S. A. Schuster, and K. C. Smith, "RAP—An associative processor for data base management," presented at the Nat. Comput. Conf., 1975.

[34] B. Parhami, "A highly parallel computer system for information retrieval," in *Proc. Fall Joint Comput. Conf.*, 1972.

[35] J. L. Parker, "A logic per track retrieval systems," in *IFIP Congress*, 1971.

[36] R. L. Rivest, "On the worst-case behavior of string-searching algorithms," *SIAM J. Comput.*, p. 669, Dec. 1977.

[37] E. M. Reingold, Nievergelt, and N. Deo, *Combinational Algorithms*. Englewood Cliffs, NJ: Prentice-Hall, 1977.

[38] A. E. Slade and McMahon, "A cryotron catalog memory system," in *Proc. Fall Joint Comput. Conf.*, p. 120, 1960.

[39] D. L. Slotnik, "Logic per track devices," in *Advances in Computers*. New York: Academic Press, 1970.

[40] S. Y. W. Su, G. P. Copeland, and G. J. Lipovsky, "Retrieval operations and data representations in a context addressed disk system," in *Proc. ACM Programming Languages and Information Retrieval Interface Meeting*, 1973; also in "The architecture of CASSM," in *Proc. 1st Ann. Symp. on Computer Architecture*, 1973.

[41] K. Thompson, "Regular expression search algorithm," *Commun. Assoc. Comput. Mach.*, vol. 11, no. 6, p. 419, 1968.

[42] K. J. Thurber, *Large Scale Computer Architecture: Parallel and Associative Processors*. New York: Hayden, 1976.

[43] S. H. Unger, "A computer oriented toward spatial problems," *Proc. IRE*, vol. 46, p. 1744, Oct. 1958.

[44] Z. G. Vranesic and S. G. Zaky, "Nonnumeric applications of microprocessors," *Proc. IEEE*, vol. 64, no. 6, June 1976.

[45] J. E. Ypma, "Bubble domain memory systems," in *AFIPS Conf. Proc.*, vol. 44, pp. 523–528, May 1975.

[46] S. G. Zaky, "Microprocessors for nonnumeric processing," presented at the 3rd Workshop on Computer Architecture and Nonnumeric Processing, Syracuse Univ., Syracuse, NY, May 17–18, 1977.

[47] J. N. Sturman, "An iteratively structured general purpose computer," *IEEE Trans. Comput.*, vol. 18, Jan. 1968.

[48] G. R. Kane, "An iteratively structured information processor," in *Proc. 2nd Annu. Symp. on Computer Architecture*, Univ. of Houston, Houston, TX, Jan. 20–22, 1975.

[49] P. B. Berra, "Some problems in associative processor applications to database management," in *Proc. 1974 AFIPS Nat. Comput. Conf.*, vol. 43, pp. 1–5, 1974.

[50] R. J. Baum and D. K. Hsiao, "Date base computers—A step towards data utilities," *IEEE Trans. Comput.*, vol. C-25, Dec. 1976.

[51] L. A. Hollaar and D. C. Roberts, "Current research into specialized processors for text information retrieval," in *Proc. 4th Int. Conf. on Very Large Data Bases*, West Berlin, Germany, Sept. 13–15, 1978.

[52] A. El Masari, J. Rohmer, and D. Tusera, "A machine for information retrieval," in *Proc. 4th Workshop on Computer Architecture for Nonnumeric Processing*, Syracuse Univ. Conf. Cent., Syracuse, NY, Aug. 1–4, 1978.

[53] C. A. Finnila and H. H. Love, "The associative linear array processor," *IEEE Trans. Comput.*, vol. C-26, Feb. 1977.

Amar Mukhopadhyay received the D.Phil.(Sc.) degree from the Institute of Radiophysics and Electronics, University of Calcutta, in 1963.

He was a faculty member of Princeton University and Montana State University. He is now with University of Iowa, Iowa City, where he is a Professor of Computer Science since 1973. He held research positions with the Tata Institute of Fundamental Research, Bombay, and English Electric Research Laboratory, London, during 1965–1967. His earlier research interests were in switching theory, logical design, and cellular logic. He is the editor and coauthor of *Recent Developments in Switching Theory* (New York: Academic Press, 1971). His current interests include parallel and nonnumeric computer architecture, database machines, algorithms, and data structures. He was also an Associate Editor of IEEE Transactions on Computers during 1971–1974.

Reprinted from *IEEE Transactions on Computers*, Volume C-35, Number 5,
May 1986, pages 403–418. Copyright © 1986 by The Institute of Electrical
and Electronics Engineers, Inc.

New Classes for Parallel Complexity: A Study of Unification and Other Complete Problems for $\mathcal{P}$

JEFFREY SCOTT VITTER, MEMBER, IEEE, AND ROGER A. SIMONS

Abstract — Previous theoretical work in computational complexity has suggested that any problem which is log-space complete for $\mathcal{P}$ is not likely in $\mathcal{NC}$, and thus not parallelizable. In practice, this is not the case. To resolve this paradox, we introduce new complexity classes $\mathcal{PC}$ and $\mathcal{PC}^*$ that capture the practical notion of parallelizability we discuss in this paper. We show that four complete problems for $\mathcal{P}$ (nonsparse versions of unification, path system accessibility, monotone circuit value, and ordered depth-first search) are parallelizable. That is, their running times are $O(E + V)$ on a sequential RAM and $O(E/P + V \log P)$ on an EXCLUSIVE-READ EXCLUSIVE-WRITE Parallel RAM with P processors where V and E are the numbers of vertices and edges in the inputed instance of the problem. These problems are in $\mathcal{PC}$ and $\mathcal{PC}^*$, since an appropriate choice of P can speed up their sequential running times by a factor of $\Theta(P)$. Several interesting open questions are raised regarding these new parallel complexity classes $\mathcal{PC}$ and $\mathcal{PC}^*$. Unification is particularly important because it is a basic operation in theorem proving, in type inference algorithms, and in logic programming languages such as Prolog. A fast parallel implementation of Prolog is needed for software development in the Fifth Generation project.

Index Terms — Circuit value, completeness, computational complexity, depth-first search, fifth generation, parallel algorithms, path system, PRAM, RAM, random access, unification, union-find, WRAM.

I. INTRODUCTION

PARALLEL processing will be a key component of supercomputers of the future and will figure prominently in the Fifth Generation project. The speed of individual processors is improving year by year; however, the improvement is relatively slow. At the same time, the cost of processor hardware is decreasing. Parallel processing offers high potential for increased throughput by making use of several inexpensive processors cooperating on a common task.

This paper demonstrates that multiple processors can be used to great advantage in problems for which it was not thought possible. The problems in question are unification, path system accessibility (PSA), monotone circuit value (MCV), and ordered depth-first search (ordered DFS). The most widely encountered of these is unification, which arises in theorem proving [21], type inference algorithms [17] and

Manuscript received June 15, 1984; revised November 19, 1984. This work was supported in part by the National Science Foundation under Grants MCS-81-05324 and DCR-84-03613, an IBM research contract, IBM Faculty Development Award, Office of Naval Research Contract N00014-83-K-0146, and DARPA Order 4786.

J. S. Vitter is with the Mathematical Sciences Research Institute, Berkeley, CA, on leave from the Department of Computer Science, Brown University, Providence, RI 02912.

R. A. Simons is with the Department of Mathematics and Computer Science, Rhode Island College, Providence, RI 02908.

IEEE Log Number 8608211.

in Prolog compilers and interpreters [4], [23]. Unification is a basic operation in Prolog; an effective use of multiple processors could offer a tremendous improvement in program performance. This is especially important for the Fifth Generation project, since Prolog will play an integral role in software development.

The model of computation we use in this paper is the *uniform parallel random access machine* (PRAM) model discussed in [12], [24], and [28]. We denote the number of processors by P. All P processors individually execute a single program stored in common memory. The following PRAM models allow different degrees of concurrency when reading from or writing to the same memory location:

- *EREW PRAM Model* (EXCLUSIVE-READ EXCLUSIVE-WRITE): Neither concurrent reading nor concurrent writing is allowed.
- *CREW PRAM Model* (CONCURRENT-READ EXCLUSIVE-WRITE): Concurrent reading is allowed, but not concurrent writing.
- *CRCW PRAM Model* (CONCURRENT-READ CONCURRENT-WRITE): Concurrent reading and writing are allowed, but processors trying to write into the same memory location must be writing the same value, or else the program is illegal.
- *"Arbitrary" CRCW PRAM Model:* If several processors attempt to write into the same memory location, one arbitrary processor succeeds and the others fail.
- *"Priority" CRCW PRAM Model:* If several processors attempt to write into the same memory location, the processor with the lowest-numbered processor ID (highest priority) succeeds and the others fail.

The CREW PRAM model is sometimes referred to as the PRAM model, and the three CRCW PRAM models are sometimes referred to as WRAM models. The total amount of auxiliary memory (both shared and local) among the processors must be bounded by a polynomial of I where I is the size of the input. For a given RAM processor, each machine operation has arguments of size $O(\log I)$ and takes one unit of time. The running time of a PRAM is the maximum of the running times of its component RAM's. The restriction of the instruction arguments to size $O(\log I)$ is similar to that in the random access computer (RAC) model in [14].

The weaker the model, the easier it is to realize its assumptions via hardware. The five models above are listed in increasing order of strength; each model is a special case of the one below it. The EREW PRAM model, which is the weakest of these five models, suffices for all but one of the parallel algorithms in the paper.

Previous efforts at classifying problems as to their degree of "parallelizability" (that is, how well the problems can take advantage of multiple processors) have concentrated in one of two areas. One approach is to study time–space tradeoffs for parallelism in straightline programs. It is shown in [22] that tradeoffs of the form $ART = \Theta(n^2)$ exist for some problems such as the FFT computation where A is the number of parallel processors (accumulators), R is the amount of memory, and T is the time. With full parallelism (i.e., $A = R$), we have $R^2T = \Theta(n^2)$, which implies that a linear increase in processing power can cause a quadratic decrease in the running time. This has important implications for making effective use of supercomputers.

The second approach, which motivates this paper, consists of determining what problems can be solved in $O(\log^k I)$ time, for some constant k where I is the input size. The number of processors P is allowed to be very large, but must be bounded by a polynomial of I. This class of problems is called $\mathcal{NC}$ [19], [6] (for "Nick's Class"). We let $\mathcal{P}$ denote the class of problems that can be solved sequentially in time bounded by a polynomial of the input size. Clearly, we have $\mathcal{NC} \subseteq \mathcal{P}$.

The class of problems which are log-space complete for $\mathcal{P}$ (the "hardest" problems in $\mathcal{P}$, see [10]) is believed to be disjoint from the class $\mathcal{NC}$. It can be shown that if any problem which is log-space complete for $\mathcal{P}$ is also in $\mathcal{NC}$, then we would have $\mathcal{P} = \mathcal{NC}$, which is thought to be very unlikely. The four problems we discuss in this paper — unification, PSA, MCV, and ordered DFS — are each log-space complete for $\mathcal{P}$ [30], [7], [5], [11], [20], and [3]. This fact has been offered as evidence that these problems cannot make effective use of a PRAM.

In this paper, we show that unification, PSA, MCV, and ordered DFS can make effective use of PRAM's. We introduce complexity classes $\mathcal{PC}$ and $\mathcal{PC}^*$ to capture our practical notion of parallelizability, and show that these four problems are in $\mathcal{PC}$ and $\mathcal{PC}^*$. A problem in $\mathcal{P}$ is said to be in $\mathcal{PC}$ if its sequential RAM running time can be speeded up by more than a constant factor by using a CRCW PRAM with a polynomial number of processors. The class $\mathcal{PC}^*$ consists of those problems in $\mathcal{PC}$ for which the speedup is proportional to the number of processors.

Our notion of parallelizability is quite different from that used in connection with the class $\mathcal{NC}$. In order for a problem to be in $\mathcal{NC}$, there must be an algorithm for it that runs in $O(\log^k I)$ time, under the conditions explained above. Our notion of parallelizability does not require that the running time be reduced so dramatically; hence, problems (such as unification, PSA, MCV, and ordered DFS) that might not be in $\mathcal{NC}$, but can take advantage of a PRAM, can still be regarded as parallelizable. Another advantage of not requiring such a dramatic speedup is that the number of processors necessary for the parallel implementation might be more realistic; the number of processors needed to reduce the running time to $O(\log^k I)$ is often unreasonably large (say, I or I^2 or I^4), even though it is bounded by a polynomial of I.

The input to the unification, PSA, and MCV problems can be expressed in terms of a type of multigraph G with V vertices and E edges. Each of these four problems can be solved sequentially in $O(E + V)$ time, which is linear in the input size and is thus optimum. We show how to reduce the

running time to $O(E/P + V \log P)$ by use of an EREW PRAM with P processors. When the multigraph is not sparse, an appropriate choice of P cuts the running time by a factor proportional to P, thus taking full advantage of parallelism. The parallel time for PSA, MCV, and ordered DFS can be further improved by use of stronger PRAM models. We also investigate a practical almost-linear algorithm for unification and show how it can be parallelized. Our results are summarized in Table I. The symbol α denotes the functional inverse of Ackerman's function. The EREW PRAM time bounds in this paper represent a substantial improvement over the results in [29], in which the same bounds for unification, PSA and MCV, were obtained for a (stronger) model equivalent to the arbitrary CRCW PRAM model. (The model used in [29] was a CREW PRAM model augmented with a test-and-set instruction.)

II. Two New Computational Complexity Classes

It seems likely that neither unification, PSA, MCV, nor ordered DFS is in the class $\mathcal{NC}$ defined above. Many researchers take this as evidence that those problems are not parallelizable. However, we show in Sections IV–VIII that all four problems can benefit from parallel processing.

In this section, we establish alternative guidelines for determining which problems are parallelizable, in order to take into account these four problems. Problems in the class $\mathcal{NC}$ usually require many processors, typically I^2 or I^3, in order to achieve $O(\log^k I)$ parallel time. In many cases, such a large number of processors is not practical, even though it is bounded by a polynomial in I. We introduce the following new complexity classes $\mathcal{PC}$ and $\mathcal{PC}^*$, which do not force the number of processors to be unreasonably large. The class $\mathcal{PC}$ consists of those problems in $\mathcal{P}$ that can be speeded up by more than a constant factor by use of parallelism. The class $\mathcal{PC}^*$ is the stronger class in which the speedup is proportional to the number P of processors.

Definition 2.1: A problem $X \in \mathcal{P}$ is said to be in the class $\mathcal{PC}$ iff for every input size I, there is a corresponding number of processors $P(I)$ so that the following three conditions hold:
1) $P(I)$ is bounded by a polynomial in I,
2) $P(I) \rightarrow \infty$ as $I \rightarrow \infty$, and
3) the problem X can be solved in time $T_{\text{PRAM}}(I)$ by a program on a PRAM with $P(I)$ processors, such that, for any sequential RAM program that solves X, we have

$$\lim_{I \to \infty} \frac{T_{\text{PRAM}}(I)}{T_{\text{RAM}}(I)} = 0$$

where $T_{\text{RAM}}(I)$ is the running time of the sequential RAM program.

Definition 2.2: A problem $X \in \mathcal{P}$ is said to be in the class $\mathcal{PC}^*$ iff for every input size I, there is a corresponding number of processors $P(I)$ so that the following three conditions hold:
1) $P(I)$ is bounded by a polynomial in I,
2) $P(I) \rightarrow \infty$ as $I \rightarrow \infty$, and
3) The problem X can be solved in time $T_{\text{PRAM}}(I)$ by a program on a PRAM with $P(I)$ processors, such that, for any

TABLE I

Problem	Sequential Time	Parallel Time
Unification	$O(\alpha(2E,V)E+V)$	$O\left(\alpha(2E,V)\left(\dfrac{E}{P}+V\right)\right)$ ‡
	$O(E+V)$	$O\left(\dfrac{E}{P}+V\log P\right)$ ¶
PSA	$O(E+V)$	$O\left(\dfrac{E}{P}+V\log P\right)$ ¶
		$O\left(\dfrac{E}{P}+V\right)$ ‡
MCV	$O(E+V)$	$O\left(\dfrac{E}{P}+V\log P\right)$ ¶
		$O\left(\dfrac{E}{P}+V\right)$ †
Ordered DFS	$O(E+V)$	$O\left(\dfrac{E}{P}+V\log P\right)$ ¶
		$O\left(\dfrac{E}{P}+V\right)$ ‡‡

¶ = EREW PRAM
† = CRCW PRAM
‡ = arbitrary CRCW PRAM
‡‡ = priority CRCW PRAM

sequential RAM program that solves X, we have

$$\frac{P(I) \times T_{\mathrm{PRAM}}(I)}{T_{\mathrm{RAM}}(I)} = O(1), \quad \text{as } I \to \infty$$

where $T_{\mathrm{RAM}}(I)$ is the running time of the sequential RAM program.

The underlying parallel machine model can be chosen arbitrarily, but we prefer to use the CRCW PRAM (also known as WRAM) model, in which all processors involved in a write conflict must be writing the same value. All three types of CRCW PRAM's provide a mathematically elegant framework for the design and analysis of parallel algorithms, especially in light of the correspondence between parallel time and unbounded-fanin circuit depth [25]. The relative powers of the CRCW PRAM model and the (stronger) priority CRCW PRAM model are compared in [9]. Weaker and hence more easily implementable models of computation can simulate all models of PRAM's with little increase in time and space. For example, CREW PRAM's and all three types of CRCW PRAM's can be simulated by an EREW PRAM with an extra factor of $O(\log P)$ time and $O(P)$ processors [8] or with an extra factor of $O(\log^2 P)$ time and no extra processors [28]. All the PRAM models can also be simulated by an ultracomputer (bounded-degree network of processors with no global memory) in $O(\log P (\log \log P)^2)$ time per step and with no extra processors [27].

The general statements of the unification, PSA, MCV, and ordered DFS problems are given in Sections III and VI–VIII. The input for each problem consists of a type of graph with V vertices and E edges. We show in Sections V–VIII that each problem can be solved in $O(E + V)$ time sequentially and in $O(E/P + V \log P)$ time on an EREW PRAM with P processors. The $\log P$ term can be eliminated for PSA, MCV, and ordered DFS by using an appropriate CRCW PRAM model.

It is not known whether unification, PSA, MCV, and ordered DFS are in $\mathcal{PC}$, because, for sparse graphs, the parallel algorithms we have described for these problems perform no faster than the sequential ones. In order to specify when there is a speedup, let us use f to denote a monotone-increasing,

integer-valued function defined on the integers, which grows asymptotically faster than linearly, that is, $\lim_{n \to \infty} n/f(n) = 0$. We define the following restricted problems:

f-Unification

Same as unification defined in Section III, with the requirement that $E = \Omega(f(V))$.

f-Path System Accessibility

Same as PSA, as defined in Section VI, with the requirement that $E = \Omega(f(V))$.

f-Monotone Circuit Value

Same as MCV, as defined in Section VII, with the requirement that $E = \Omega(f(V))$.

f-Ordered Depth-First Search

Same as ordered DFS, as defined in Section VIII, with the requirement that $E = \Omega(f(V))$.

We can show easily that these restricted problems are log-space complete for $\mathcal{P}$. The next theorem shows that they are parallelizable as well.

Theorem 2.1: If the function f is integer-valued and monotone-increasing asymptotically faster than linearly, then f-unification, f-PSA, f-MCV, and f-ordered DFS are each in $\mathcal{PC}^*$.

Proof: The running times for each of these problems are $\Theta(E + V)$ [sequential], $O(E/P + V \log P)$ [EREW PRAM with P processors]. The input size is $\Omega(E + V) = \Omega(f(V))$. Since f is monotone-increasing asymptotically faster than linearly, then f^{-1} exists and is monotone-increasing asymptotically slower than linearly. Condition 3 of the definition of $\mathcal{PC}^*$ will hold if $I/P = \Omega(V \log P)$, or equivalently if $I/V = \Omega(P \log P)$. We have $I/V = \Omega(I/f^{-1}(I)) \to \infty$, as $I \to \infty$. Any sequence $P \to \infty$ chosen such that $I/f^{-1}(I) > P \log P$ will guarantee that Condition 3 of Definition 2.2 holds. For example, we could set $P := \lfloor I/(f^{-1}(I)(\log I - \log f^{-1}(I)))\rfloor$. ∎

There are several interesting open problems. For example, we have observed above that it is unknown whether the (general) unification, PSA, MCV, and ordered DFS problems are in $\mathcal{PC}$. The questions of whether $\mathcal{PC} = \mathcal{PC}^*$, $\mathcal{PC} = \mathcal{P}$, and $\mathcal{PC}^* = \mathcal{P}$ are fundamental open problems. We conjecture that the inclusions $\mathcal{PC}^* \subset \mathcal{PC} \subset \mathcal{P}$ are proper, that is, $\mathcal{PC}^* \neq \mathcal{PC} \neq \mathcal{P}$. (In order to rule out trivial proofs, we consider only problems in $\mathcal{P}$ that require the entire input to be read.)

It is clear that $\mathcal{NC} \subseteq \mathcal{PC}$; hence, proving that $\mathcal{PC} \neq \mathcal{P}$ is as hard as showing that $\mathcal{NC} \neq \mathcal{P}$, which is a long standing conjecture, as pointed out in Section I. We also conjecture that $\mathcal{NC} \neq \mathcal{PC}$, since it is a consequence of the conjecture $\mathcal{NC} \neq \mathcal{P}$ by the following argument: This paper shows that f-unification, f-PSA, f-MCV, and f-ordered DFS are in $\mathcal{PC}$, yet it can be shown easily that they are log-space complete for $\mathcal{P}$; thus, if $\mathcal{NC} = \mathcal{PC}$ then each of these three problems is in $\mathcal{NC}$ and is also log-space complete for $\mathcal{P}$, from which $\mathcal{NC} = \mathcal{P}$ follows as pointed out in Section I. It is also open whether $\mathscr{SC} = \mathscr{PC}$, where $\mathscr{SC}$ (for "Steve's Class") is the class of problems solvable in polynomial sequential time and in polylog space [12]. It might be interesting to develop the notion of reductions between problems in $\mathscr{PC}$ and to study the class of $\mathscr{PC}$-complete problems, under a suitable definition.

The comments at the beginning of the section on the impracticality of a large numbers of processors suggest that it would be interesting to consider other classes similar to $\mathscr{PC}$ and $\mathscr{PC}^*$, but with the added restriction that for any monotone-increasing sequence $g(I)$, we must be able to choose a sequence $P(I)$ that satisfies Condition 3 and which is bounded by $g(I)$. This essentially requires that the parallel algorithm for the problem should be asymptotically faster than the best sequential algorithm even when the number of processors grows arbitrarily slowly w.r.t. I.

III. The Unification Problem

Intuitively, the unification problem deals with determining if two given terms can be made textually identical by finding a set of substitutions for the variables in the terms and by replacing all occurrences of each variable by that variable's substitution. Terms can be defined recursively as follows:

Definition 3.1: The set of symbols consists of variable symbols $x, y, z, \ldots$ and function symbols $f, g, h, \ldots$. A term t either is a variable symbol or else it has the form $f(t_1, t_2, \ldots, t_k)$, for $k \geq 0$ where f is a function symbol and $t_1, t_2, \ldots, t_k$ are terms.

We represent an instance of the unification problem by a labeled directed acyclic multigraph G with V vertices and E edges. Each variable symbol is represented by a single vertex in the graph; the label of that vertex is the variable symbol. Each term of the form $f(t_1, t_2, \ldots, t_k)$ is represented as a unique vertex with label f and with directed edges to the vertices representing $t_1, t_2, \ldots, t_k$; the edge to t_1 is the *first* edge, the edge to t_2 is the *second* edge, and so on. The degrees of the vertices with the same function label are not required to be equal. Multiple edges are allowed, so E may be arbitrarily large w.r.t. V.

Definition 3.2: Designated vertices u_0 and v_0 are said to be *unifiable* iff for each variable there is a substitution term of finite length, such that, when the variables are replaced by their substitutions, the terms represented by u_0 and v_0 are textually identical.

For example, the terms $u_0 = f(x, y)$ and $v_0 = f(g(y, z), g(z))$ are unifiable, because the substitutions $x := g(g(z), z)$, $y := g(z)$ transform both u_0 and v_0 into $f(g(g(z), z), g(z))$. The graph for this example is shown in Fig. 1.

The terms $u_0 = f(x)$ and $v_0 = x$ are not unifiable because there is no substitution for x of finite length that can make u_0 and v_0 identical. The graph for this instance is given in Fig. 2. However, if Definition 3.1 is generalized to permit denumerably long terms, then the "infinite" substitution $x := f(f(f(\ldots)))$ does succeed in making both u_0 and v_0 identically equal to $f(f(f(\ldots)))$. In this case, we say that u_0 and v_0 are infinitely unifiable. Infinite unification can arise in the inference of recursive types [15] and in Prolog [4].

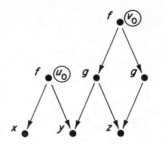

Fig. 1. Vertices u_0 and v_0 are unifiable.

Fig. 2. Vertices u_0 and v_0 are not unifiable, but are infinitely unifiable.

The problems can be formalized in the following way.

Unification

Input: A labeled, finite, directed acyclic multigraph G with V vertices and E edges and a pair of distinguished vertices u_0 and v_0.

Output: Are vertices u_0 and v_0 unifiable?

Infinite Unification

Input: (Same as above.)

Output: Are vertices u_0 and v_0 infinitely unifiable?

Strictly speaking, the output to these problems is merely a "yes" or "no" answer; but in practical situations, whenever the answer is "yes," we also wish to know a set of substitutions that unify u_0 and v_0.

We should point out that even though these definitions apply to problems in which only two specified terms u_0 and v_0 are being unified, the general case, in which several pairs of terms are to be unified simultaneously, can be reduced to the above problems easily. For example, if we wish to unify the pairs of terms $(u_1, v_1), (u_2, v_2), \cdots, (u_j, v_j)$, we can accomplish that by instead unifying the single pair of terms $u_0 = f(u_1, u_2, \cdots, u_j)$, $v_0 = f(v_1, v_2, \cdots, v_j)$.

Definition 3.3: If u_0 and v_0 are unifiable or infinitely unifiable, then a *most general unifier* (mgu) is a *minimal* set of substitutions that unify u_0 and v_0.

By minimal, we mean that each set of unifying substitutions can be derived from an mgu by further substitution. In the examples dealing with Figs. 1 and 2, mgu's have already been given. The set of substitutions $x := g(g(h(w)), h(w))$, $y := g(h(w))$, and $z := h(w)$ also unify u_0 and v_0 in the first example. This set of substitutions is not an mgu, but it can be derived from the mgu $x := g(g(z), z)$, $y := g(z)$ by the further substitution $z := h(w)$.

In the rest of this section, we summarize the previously known results regarding the unification problem and state our results. A recursive $O(E + V)$-time sequential algorithm for unification is given in [18]. We give a slightly modified version in Section V. We give an efficient $O(E/P + V \log P)$-time implementation on an EREW PRAM with P

processors in Section V-B. The authors in [18] mention the existence of nonrecursive $O(\alpha E + V)$-time algorithms, where α is the functional inverse of Ackerman's function, but to our knowledge no such algorithm has appeared in the literature. In the next section, we give our version of an $O(\alpha E + V)$-time sequential unification algorithm, and show how it can be parallelized on an arbitrary CRCW PRAM with P processors to run in $O(\alpha(E/P + V))$ time.

Unification is known to be log-space complete for $\mathcal{P}$. A restricted version, in which the terms u_0 and v_0 are represented as simple directed acyclic multigraphs, is also log-space complete for $\mathcal{P}$. By simple, we mean that only the leaves in the multigraph are allowed to have indegree greater than 1; in other words, the input size I is proportional to the length of a textual representation of u_0 and v_0. However, there are several restricted versions of unification that are in the class $\mathcal{NC}$ and thus can be solved in $O(\log^k I)$ time. One such case, in which v_0 contains no variables, is called *term matching*. Another example is the restriction in which v_0 does not contain more than one instance of each variable and there are no shared variables between u_0 and v_0. The results quoted in this paragraph are due to [7], [30], and [13].

IV. Parallelizing an Almost Linear Unification Algorithm

The fast unification algorithms in this paper are based on the following naive algorithm; its correctness is easy to verify. An equivalence relation (denoted by the symbol $\equiv$) is maintained to indicate vertices that have been unified. Initially, each vertex is in its own unique equivalence class. As the algorithm proceeds, each time a pair of vertices u, v are set equivalent by the statement "*Set $u \equiv v$,*" the equivalence classes of u and v are combined.

procedure *naive_unification*(u_0, v_0 : *vertex*);
begin
Set $u_0 \equiv v_0$;
while there is a pair of nodes (u, v) such that $u \equiv v$
    and u and v have corresponding sons u' and v'
    for which it is not yet known whether $u' \equiv v'$ **do**
        Set $u' \equiv v'$;
for each pair of nodes (u, v) such that $u \equiv v$ **do**
    if u and v have distinct function symbols **then**
        return('NOT UNIF. NOR INFINITELY UNIF.');
if the equivalence classes can be partially ordered
    by the directed edges of G **then**
        return('UNIFIABLE')
else return('INFINITELY UNIF., BUT NOT UNIF.')
end

The major inefficiency of this algorithm lies in dealing with each pair of vertices that must be made equivalent. The fast unification algorithms of Sections IV-A and V-A combine the first two loops of *naive_unification* and consider each pair of equivalent vertices only once. Those improvements alone do not speed up the algorithm sufficiently. The speed of these algorithms comes from their clever data structures for representing the equivalence relation.

The unification algorithm of Section IV-A is based on fast union-find algorithms, specifically path-compression with weighted union, as described in [1] and [26]. Its running time, for all practical purposes, is linear in the number of edges. More precisely, it runs in $O(\alpha(2E, V)E + V)$ time where V is the number of vertices, E is the number of edges, and α is the functional inverse of Ackerman's function. When $V < 2^{16} = 65,536$, we have $\alpha(2E, V) \leq 3$; in all reasonable situations, $\alpha(2E, V)$ is never larger than 4. We hereafter omit the arguments of α in order to remind the reader how much it resembles a constant. More details about the function α can be found in [26]. In practice, the almost-linear unification algorithm given here may actually perform faster than the linear algorithm of Section V because it does not have the overhead of recursive subroutine calls.

Section IV-B describes some techniques for parallelizing algorithms that are used in the remainder of this paper. In Section IV-C, we show how to make use of an arbitrary CRCW PRAM (also known as WRAM) with P processors to reduce the running time of the almost-linear unification algorithm to $O(\alpha(E/P + V))$. Recall that the arbitrary CRCW PRAM model we use resolves write conflicts by allowing an arbitrary processor to succeed.

A. The Sequential Algorithm

The authors in [18] mention the existence of nonrecursive $O(\alpha E + V)$-time algorithms, where α is the functional inverse of Ackerman's function, but to our knowledge no such algorithm has appeared in the literature. The following is our version of an $O(\alpha E + V)$-time sequential unification algorithm.

This algorithm unifies pairs of vertices by locating them and placing them in the same equivalence class, using *finds* and *unions*. For this algorithm, the equivalence classes are represented by union-find trees with *union* and *find* implemented using path compression and weighted union. If vertex r is the root of its union-find tree, then either *class_rep*[r] is a vertex equivalent to r whose label is a function or else *class_rep*[r] = *variable*. The label of each vertex v is assumed to be stored in *symbol*[v]. The list *unify* stores pairs of vertices whose union-find trees have been combined, but whose sons may still require processing. Initially, the only pair in the *unify* list is a new pair of vertices a and b, which are created to ensure that the designated vertices u_0 and v_0 are made equivalent in the first pass through the main loop.

In each pass through the main loop, a pair of vertices is removed from *unify,* and each pair of corresponding sons is made equivalent in the following way: First, the roots of the class representative of the two sons are found. If the roots r and s are distinct, then we test for compatability of their symbols. The symbols are compatible if at least one symbol is a variable or if the symbols are the same function symbol and have the same number of arguments. If the symbols are incompatible, then the unification cannot be completed and an error message is printed. Otherwise, the unification procedes by forming the union of the equivalence classes of r and s. If *class_rep*[r] or *class_rep*[s] is equal to *variable,* then a substitution for the mgu is printed, and the values of *symbol*[r] and *class_rep*[r] are updated if necessary; otherwise, both equivalence classes are represented by vertices labeled by a function, so the corresponding sons of r and s are marked to be unified by appending (r, s) to *unify*.

The main loop is able to check symbol compatibility, but it cannot detect the forming of a cycle of substitutions, as in Fig. 2. Such a cycle indicates that the two formulas are not unifiable, but rather infinitely unifiable. This unification algorithm contains a separate test for cycles that is performed at the end. An induced graph G' is formed from the original multigraph G; each vertex in G' represents one equivalence class. All directed edges in G from vertices in one equivalence class to vertices in a second are represented by one directed edge in G'. The test for cycles consists of a topological sort of the vertices of G'. If the vertices can be partially ordered, then u_0 and v_0 are unifiable; otherwise, they are infinitely unifiable.

In the code for *almost_linear_unification*, the function *recursive_symbol* is used to output the substitution in expanded form, for the benefit of the reader. It is not inherently part of the algorithm, and its code and running time are therefore ignored.

```
procedure almost_linear_unification(u_0, v_0 : vertex);
begin
{ Initializations }
Create new vertices a, b with the same function symbol;
Create new directed edges ⟨a, u_0⟩ and ⟨b, v_0⟩;
unify := ∅;   { list of pairs of vertices to be unified }
append((a, b), unify);

for each vertex v do
    if symbol[v] is a function then
        class_rep[v] := v
    else class_rep[v] := variable;

{ Main loop }
while unify ≠ ∅ do
    begin
    (u, v) := remove_front(unify);
    { Propagation loop }
    for i := 1 to outdegree[class_rep[v]] do
        begin
        u_i := the ith son of class_rep[u];
        v_i := the ith son of class_rep[v];
        r := find(u_i);  s := find(v_i);
        if r ≠ s then
            if (class_rep[r] ≠ variable)
            and (class_rep[s] ≠ variable)
            and ((symbol[class_rep[r]] ≠ symbol[class_rep[s]])
                  or (outdegree[class_rep[r]] ≠
                      outdegree[class_rep[s]])) then
                error('NOT UNIF., NOT INF. UNIF.')
            else begin
                { r and s are roots of union-find trees }
                union(r, s);
                if s is the root of its union-find tree
                    then r :=: s;   { Swap r and s }
                if class_rep[s] = variable then
                    print(symbol[s], '→',
                        recursive_symbol(r))
                else if class_rep[r] = variable then begin
                    print(symbol[r], '→',
                        recursive_symbol(s));
                    class_rep[r] := class_rep[s] end
                else append((r, s), unify)
                end
        end   { Propagation loop }
    end;   { Main loop }
```

{ Check for cycles }
Form the graph G' consisting of the root node from each union-find tree;
for each directed edge (u, v) in G **do**
  Create the directed edge $(find(u), find(v))$ in G' if it does not already exist;
Use topological sorting to check whether G' has a cycle;
if G' has a cycle **then**
    error('INFINITELY UNIFIABLE, BUT NOT UNIF.')
else return('UNIFIABLE')
end

Example: To illustrate this algorithm, we trace the execution of *almost_linear_unification*(u_0, v_0) for the graph depicted in Fig. 3. The terms being unified are $u_0 = f(g(y), x, g(y))$ and $v_0 = f(x, g(y), g(z))$. After (a, b) is appended to and then deleted from *unify*, the call *union*(u_0, v_0) is executed and (u_0, v_0) is appended to *unify*. When (u_0, v_0) is deleted from *unify*, three passes are made through the propagation loop. First, *union*(v_1, v_3) is performed. Depending on the implementation of *union*, either v_1 or v_3 will be the root of that union-find tree. In either case, the class representative of that root is v_1, and "$x \rightarrow g(y)$" is printed. In the second pass, performing *find*(v_3) yields the same root as *find*(v_1), resulting in $r = s$. In the third pass, *union*(r, v_2) is performed and (r, v_2) is appended to *unify* where r is the root of the union-find tree containing v_1. (As noted above, this r may be either v_1 or v_3, but in either case, we have *class_rep*$(r) = v_1$.) Thus, when (r, v_2) is deleted from *unify*, *union*(v_4, v_5) is performed, and either "$y \rightarrow z$" or "$z \rightarrow y$" is printed. ∎

Lemma 4.1: In the algorithm *almost_linear_unification*, the total running time of the propagation loop is $O(\alpha E)$.

Proof: Each iteration of the propagation loop runs in constant time except for two calls to *find*. Thus, it suffices to show that the total number of iterations of this loop is at most the sum of the outdegrees of all vertices. In each pass through the main loop, a pair (u, v) is removed from *unify* and the propagation loop iterates *outdegree*[*class_rep*[v]] times. Hence, it suffices to show that after (u, v) is removed from *unify*, *class_rep*[v] will never again be the class representative of any member of a pair removed from *unify*.

Except for the initial pair (a, b), a pair (r, s) of vertices is appended to *unify* only in the propagation loop after *union* has acted on that pair. In fact, when (r, s) is appended to *unify*, s is a son of r in its union-find tree, and hence s will never again be in a pair of vertices appended to *unify*. The conclusion now follows by the similar observation that whenever *class_rep*[s] is copied to *class_rep*[r], s is a union-find son of r, and hence s will never subsequently be in a pair of vertices appended to *unify*. ∎

Lemma 4.2: The total number of unions done in *almost_linear_unification* is less than V.

Proof: Initially, there are V sets. The *unions* are applied only to distinct root vertices and hence to distinct sets. Thus there can be at most $V - 1$ *unions*. ∎

Lemma 4.3: The total number of iterations of the main loop in *almost_linear_unification* is bounded by V.

Proof: The only pairs appended to *unify* are the specially created pair (a, b) and the pairs whose union-find trees

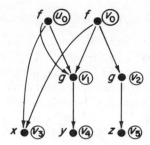

Fig. 3. Unify vertices u_0 and v_0.

have just been combined. Thus, by Lemma 4.2, the total number of pairs appended to *unify* is at most *V*. ∎

Theorem 4.1: The sequential running time of the algorithm *almost_linear_unification* is $O(\alpha E + V)$ where α is the functional inverse of Ackerman's function.

Proof: Each pass through the main loop, not counting the propagation loop, executes in constant time. By Lemma 4.3 and by inspecting the initializations, everything outside the propagation loop in the main loop runs in $O(V)$ time. The result now follows from Lemma 4.1. ∎

B. Techniques for Parallelization

The parallel algorithms in this paper are based on the PRAM models of computation described in the Introduction. First we shall describe some useful techniques for all the models. Later we shall describe techniques applicable to the stronger PRAM model.

For each of these algorithms, it is useful to partition the parallel time units into two distinct phases: the READ phase and the WRITE phase. Each processor's access to common memory is limited to reading during a READ phase and to writing during a WRITE phase. One advantage of this approach is that one processor will never attempt a read while another processor is performing a write, and vice-versa. All processors must be coordinated to cycle through these phases so that no two of them are executing instructions simultaneously in different phases. One method for implementing this, for example, is to have one or more processors serve as a common clock (with sufficiently long phases) that the other processors can consult.

All the parallel algorithms in this paper alternate between sequential mode and parallel mode. Changing from sequential mode to parallel mode can be done easily in constant time using concurrent reading: each idle processor can loop indefinitely, waiting for a special code to be written into common memory by the one active processor. Without concurrent reading, the changing from sequential to parallel mode can be done by having the one active processor broadcast that special code; the processors can pass the code to the others, as if they were nodes in a complete binary tree network, in $O(\log P)$ time. The change from parallel mode to sequential mode can also be done easily if each processor knows *a priori* when the other processors will finish the parallel section of code.

In the next section, such *a priori* knowledge is not always available. Instead, we use one of the CRCW PRAM models and introduce a third phase — the SYNCHRONIZATION phase —

which occurs between WRITE and READ phases. This phase allows the processors to communicate a completion signal to the processor that will proceed sequentially. Common memory access during the SYNCHRONIZATION phase is limited to updating the flag *all_processors_done,* which is initialized to **true** just before this phase begins. In each SYNCHRONIZATION phase, all processors still executing the current portion of the algorithm attempt to set *all_processors_done* := **false**. As long as at least one processor is still not done, the value **false** will be written; we will have *all_processors_ done* = **true** at the end of the SYNCHRONIZATION phase iff all processors have finished executing the code in question. This synchronization capability enables the parallel implementation of *almost_linear_unification* to alternate efficiently between sequential mode and parallel mode.

C. Parallelizing the Sequential Algorithm

This algorithm is described using the arbitrary CRCW PRAM model, in which simultaneous attempts by several processors to write into the same memory location are resolved by allowing one arbitrary processor to write successfully.

The propagation loop and the test for cycles in *almost_ linear_unification* are the only sections of code that are parallelized. Both are parallelized in similar ways; we shall illustrate the technique by considering the propagation loop only. For a given v, processor j executes the loop for each value of i in the range $1 \leq i \leq outdegree[class\_rep[v]]$ satisfying $i \bmod P = j \bmod P$. We shall call these values of i the *candidate* values for processor j. Each processor has either $\lfloor outdegree[class\_rep[v]]/P \rfloor$ or $\lceil outdegree[class\_ rep[v]]/P \rceil$ candidate values. For simplicity, we assume that each processor has exactly $C = \lceil outdegree[class\_ rep[v]]/P \rceil$ candidate values, by adding null candidate values to some processors, as needed.

The propagation loop is parallelized as follows: For a given v, the loop is iterated in parallel exactly C times. In the jth parallel iteration, each processor executes the loop for its jth candidate value. All the calls to *find* are performed to completion before any of the processors proceed with the rest of the loop. This is done using the synchronization mechanism described in Section IV-B. Parallel execution of *finds* is permitted because no harm is done when two or more processors try to compress the same portion of a path or when one processor is traversing a path that has been compressed by another processor.

Once all the calls to *find* are completed for the jth candidates, each processor executes the following code in parallel. This code replaces the "**if** $r \neq s$ **then** ..." clause of the sequential program given in Section IV-A.

```
{ r and s are local variables for each processor }
while r ≠ s do   { read phase #1 }
    begin
    if (class_rep[r] ≠ variable)
        and (class_rep[s] ≠ variable)
        and ((symbol[class_rep[r]] ≠ symbol[class_rep[s]])
            or (outdegree[r] ≠ outdegree[s])) then
                    { read phase #1 }
```

141

```
    return('NOT UNIF. AND NOT INF. UNIF.')
else begin
        {write phase #1}
        union_lock := processor ID;
        {read phase #2: was union lock acquired?}
        if union_lock = processor ID then
            begin
            union(r, s);   {write phase #2}
            {read phase #3}
            if s is the root of its union-find tree then
                    r :=: s;   {Swap r and s}
            if class_rep[s] = variable then
                    {write phase #3}
                    print(symbol[s], '→',
                            recursive_symbol(r))
            else if class_rep[r] = variable then
                    begin   {write phase #3}
                    print(symbol[r], '→',
                            recursive_symbol(s));
                    class_rep[r] := class_rep[s]
                    end
            else   {write phase #3}
                    append((r, s), unify)
            end
    end;  {else-clause}
{ At this point, the processor pauses if necessary
  until the beginning of read phase #1 for the
  next iteration of this while-loop}
r := father of r in its union-find tree;
s := father of s in its union-find tree;
end;  {while-loop}
```

The use of the union lock ensures that only one *union* is executed at a time. The comments at the right of the code indicate that the processor which acquires the union lock always completes the *union* operation and related housekeeping within three sets of READ/WRITE/SYNCHRONIZE phases, the time for which is bounded by a constant. After that, all active processors set r and s to be their respective fathers, in order to ensure that r and s are root vertices in the union-find tree. The resulting values of r and s will be equal for the processor that successfully acquired the union lock and for all other processors that were attempting to perform the same *union*. These processors are done and wait until the remaining *unions* are completed before proceeding to the next candidate value.

The following theorem asserts the parallel running time of this algorithm:

Theorem 4.2: The running time of the algorithm *almost_linear_unification* on an *arbitrary* CRCW PRAM with P processors is $O(\alpha(E/P + V))$.

Proof: There are at most $V - 1$ *unions,* each of which takes constant time because the parameters are roots of union-find trees. Thus, the "**while** $r \neq s$ **do**" loop above accounts for a total of $O(V)$ time. The rest of the propagation loop runs in $O(\alpha(E/P + V))$ time. The check for cycles at the end of the algorithm can be done in $O(\alpha(E/P + V))$ time using the same techniques as in the propagation loop. ∎

V. PARALLELIZING A LINEAR UNIFICATION ALGORITHM

A sequential unification algorithm with running time $O(E + V)$ is displayed in Section V-A. This algorithm is essentially the one given in [18]. The algorithm can determine whether G is unifiable, but cannot detect whether G is infinitely unifiable. Section V-B explains how to improve its running time to $O(E/P + V \log P)$ by using an EREW PRAM with P processors.

A. The Sequential Algorithm

This algorithm avoids the need for *unions* and *finds* by always handling roots of equivalence classes. The workhorse of the algorithm is the procedure *finish,* which processes its argument u after calling itself recursively to process the ancestors of u. We assume that each vertex has two adjacency lists: one for outgoing edges and one for incoming edges. The adjacency list of incoming edges can be constructed from the adjacency list of outgoing edges in $O(E)$ total time.

The algorithm constructs and uses an undirected graph G' with the same set of vertices as G. The presence of an edge in G' means that its endpoints have been made equivalent and are waiting to be processed. Each call of *finish* with argument u processes all the vertices equivalent to u by searching through the connected component of u in G'.

Processing a pair of equivalent vertices consists of testing for incompatibilities and, if none is found, either determining a substitution for the unification or making their corresponding sons equivalent. To test for incompatibilities, the value of *pointer*[w] is set to the vertex u that is equivalent to w and that has been passed to *finish* as an argument. If *finish* is called on different vertices in the same equivalence class, an incompatibility has been detected, so u_0 and v_0 are not unifiable. We should also note that the argument of *finish* will always be a vertex with a function label until only vertices whose labels are *variable* remain.

```
procedure linear_unification(u₀, v₀ : vertex);
begin
Create undirected edge (u₀, v₀) in G';
while there is a function vertex u do finish(u);
while there is a variable vertex u do finish(u);
return('UNIFIABLE')
end;

procedure finish(u : vertex);
begin
if pointer[u] is defined then error('NOT UNIFIABLE')
else pointer[u] := u;
Create a pushdown stack called stack;
push(end_marker, stack);
push(u, stack);

while (v := pop(stack)) ≠ end_marker do
    begin
    if (symbol[u] is not a variable)
        and (symbol[v] is not a variable)
        and ((symbol[u] ≠ symbol[v])
                or (outdegree[u] ≠ outdegree[v])) then
        error('NOT UNIFIABLE');
```

```
while v has some father t in G do finish(t);
while there is an undirected edge (v, w) in G' do
    begin
        if pointer[w] is not defined then
            begin
                pointer[w] := u;
                push(w, stack)
            end
        else if pointer[w] ≠ u then
            error('NOT UNIFIABLE');
        Delete undirected edge (v, w) from G'
    end;
    if v ≠ u then
        begin
            if symbol[v] is a variable then
                print(symbol[v], '→', recursive_symbol(u))
            else for i := 1 to outdegree[v] do
                begin
                    Let uᵢ denote the ith son of u in G;
                    Let vᵢ denote the ith son of v in G;
                    Create undirected edge (uᵢ, vᵢ) in G';
                end;
            Delete v and all directed edges out of v in G
        end
    end;
    Delete u and all directed edges out of u in G
end;
```

Example: To illustrate this, let us trace the execution of *linear_unification*(u_0, v_0) for the graph depicted in Fig. 3 in Section IV. The terms being unified are $u_0 = f(g(y), x, g(y))$ and $v_0 = f(x, g(y), g(z))$. Initially, undirected edge (u_0, v_0) is created to signify that u_0 and v_0 are to be unified. Suppose that *finish*(v_2) is called first. This is followed by the recursive call *finish*(v_0). Vertex u_0 is encountered via undirected edge (u_0, v_0) and is pushed onto the stack. When u_0 is popped off the stack, undirected edges (v_3, v_1), (v_1, v_3), and (v_2, v_1) are created, signifying that each pair of vertices is to be unified, and vertices u_0 and v_0 are deleted, along with all their incident edges. Then, *finish*(v_2) resumes by encountering v_1 via undirected edge (v_2, v_1) and pushing v_1 onto the stack. When v_1 is subsequently popped, v_3 is encountered via undirected edge (v_1, v_3) and is pushed, undirected edge (v_5, v_4) is created, and v_1 is deleted. When v_3 is popped, "$x \rightarrow g(z)$" is printed, and v_3 is deleted. Finally, v_2 is deleted, concluding the execution of *finish*(v_2). No more function vertices remain, so *finish*(u) is called with $u = v_4$ or $u = v_5$. Depending on which value of u is chosen, either "$z \rightarrow y$" or "$y \rightarrow z$" is printed, due to the presence of undirected edge (v_5, v_4). ∎

The following two lemmas are easy to prove.

Lemma 5.1: Each vertex does not get pushed onto the stack more than once.

Proof: A vertex w gets pushed onto the stack only if *pointer*$[w]$ is undefined, and *pointer*$[w]$ is given a value when w is pushed onto the stack. ∎

Lemma 5.2: The total number of (possibly duplicate) undirected edges created during the execution of *linear_unification* is at most E.

Proof: By Lemma 5.1, each execution of the "**if** $v \neq u$ **then**" clause is done for a different value of v. The number of pairs (u_i, v_i) processed during the execution of that clause is bounded by the outdegree of v. Hence, the total number of undirected edges created is bounded by E. ∎

The next theorem shows that the running time is linear.

Theorem 5.1: [18] The sequential running time of the algorithm *linear_unification* is $O(E + V)$.

Proof: Three loops are nested within the "**while** $(v := pop(stack)) \ldots$ **do**" loop, which iterates at most V times, by Lemma 5.1. Consider summing the total execution time of each of these loops during all its activations throughout a run of *linear_unification*. The first inner loop is "**while** v has some father t in G **do** *finish*(t)." It contains only overhead for looping and recursive calls, and runs in a total of $O(E + V)$ time. Each undirected edge (u, v) in G' can be created or deleted in constant time. Hence, by Lemma 5.2, the other two inner loops also execute in a total of $O(E + V)$ time. The rest of the algorithm clearly runs in $O(V)$ time. ∎

B. Parallelizing the Sequential Algorithm

Extra care must be taken in parallelizing the *linear_unification* algorithm. For example, if different processors work in parallel on calls of *finish* with different arguments, they may be handling vertices that should eventually be in the same equivalence class. In such a case, the processors might report an error condition due to different values of a *pointer*$[w]$ encountered. To preserve correctness, only carefully selected portions of this algorithm are done in parallel. After such a portion is completed, the processing of the algorithm is centralized again.

The rest of this section describes the EREW PRAM implementation and proves the following result:

Theorem 5.2: The parallel running time of *linear_unification* on an EREW PRAM with P processors is $O(E/P + V \log P)$.

In the parallel version of *linear_unification* we propose here, each of the following five code segments of the algorithm given in Section V-A are parallelized:

1) the creation of the adjacency list of incoming edges, as described at the beginning of Section V-A,
2) the function call "$v := pop(stack)$,"
3) the "**while** v has some father t in G **do** *finish*(t)" loop,
4) the "**while** there is ... **do**" loop, and
5) the "**for** $i := 1$ **to** *outdegree*$[v]$ **do**" loop.

The remaining parts of the code can be executed sequentially in $\Theta(V)$ time. Synchronizing from sequential to parallel execution mode takes $O(\log P)$ time per switch, as mentioned in Section IV-B. The time to switch from parallel mode to sequential mode takes constant time, since each processor knows *a priori* how long the other processors will execute. In the rest of this section, we indicate how to parallelize the above five code segments. Code segment 5 requires $O(E/P + V)$ parallel time, and code segments 1–4 each require $O(E/P + V \log P)$ parallel time on an EREW PRAM. We shall consider the five code segments in reverse order.

Code Segment 5: The last inner loop of *linear_unification* (code segment 5) creates undirected edges in parallel. Local, not global, data structures are used for this portion of code. Processor j executes this loop for each candidate value of i such that $i \bmod P = j \bmod P$. Each processor determines the ith sons u_i and v_i for the current candidate value of i that it is processing, and then creates a local copy of the undirected edge (u_i, v_i), as explained below. Note that the same undirected edge might be created more than once by the same processor and by different processors.

In order to get parallel speedup, every processor maintains locally for each vertex v a count and an adjacency list of the undirected edges (v, w) that it has created. This eliminates global contention. Each adjacency list is stored using consecutive slots in an array, so that access to the kth neighbor of v can be done in constant time.

By Lemma 5.2, there are at most E (possibly duplicate) undirected edges created in total, and by Lemma 5.1, there are at most V iterations of the "if $v \neq u$ then" clause. Since the creating of the undirected edges is split as equally as possible among the P processors, the number of undirected edges created by each processor is at most $E/P + V$. The total parallel time for code segment 5 is thus $O(E/P + V)$.

Code Segment 4: Parallelizing the "**while** there is . . . **do**" loop presents four problems. One problem is that, for the current vertex v, the undirected edges (v, w) must be divided evenly and efficiently among the P processors. If the total number of (possibly duplicate) undirected edges that have been created incident to v is U, then each processor is assigned $C = \lceil U/P \rceil$ undirected edges to process; the number of processors required is $P' = \lceil U/C \rceil \leq P$. We number these undirected edges as $1, \ldots, U$ as follows: first, we order the edges by the ID's of the processors that created them; within each processor, the edges are ordered by their placement in v's adjacency list. Processor j is assigned undirected edges $(j - 1)C + 1, \ldots, jC$ to process. (The P'th processor may have fewer than C edges to process.) We shall now show how $O(\log P)$-time preprocessing enables each processor to access each of its assigned undirected edges in constant time per edge.

In $O(\log P)$ parallel time using a communication pattern based on binary trees, each processor can determine how many undirected edges (v, w) were created by processors with a smaller processor ID. In the kth step, processor l, for $1 \leq l \leq P$, computes in constant time the number of undirected edges created by processors $l - 2^k, \ldots, l - 1$, by summing the numbers computed in step $k - 1$ by itself and processor $l - 2^{k-1}$. To avoid read and write conflicts, these results are stored in distinct locations according to the processor and step number. After $\lceil \log P \rceil$ steps, the final counts are determined. For each $1 \leq l \leq P$, processor l stores its final count in array location $count[l]$; we also set $count[P + 1] := U$.

Next, we initialize $location[j] := 0$, for $1 \leq j \leq P'$. For each l, processor l determines the minimum ID processor, if any, whose first assigned edge was created by processor l. Let us denote the ID of that processor, if it exists, by j_l; that is, j_l is the minimum integer such that $count[l] < (j_l - 1)C + 1 \leq count[l + 1]$. The value of j_l can be computed in constant time. Processor l sets $location[j_l] := l$. The remaining problem is to assign in $O(\log P)$ parallel time

the value l to $location[j_l + 1], \ldots, location[j_{l+1} - 1]$. This can be done by again using a binary tree communication scheme. In the kth step, processor j, for $1 \leq j \leq P'$, computes the highest ID j' in the range $j - 2^k + 1, \ldots, j$ such that $location[j'] \neq 0$, by examining the values computed in step $k - 1$ by itself and processor $l - 2^{k-1}$. The values $location[j']$ and $count[j']$ are also passed in each stage of the communication scheme. After $\lceil \log P \rceil$ steps, this computation is completed, and for each j, processor j sets $location[j] := location[j']$.

At this point, the value of $location[j]$, for $1 \leq j \leq P'$, is the ID of the processor that created the $((j - 1)C + 1)$st undirected edge, which is the first edge assigned to processor j. This edge is stored as the $((j - 1)C + 1 - count[location[j]])$st edge in processor $location[j]$'s adjacency list for v, and thus can be accessed in constant time. The remaining undirected edges assigned to each processor can be found by walking through the adjacency lists. When the end of an adjacency list is reached, the processor must "jump" to the next nonempty adjacency list. This "jump" information can be obtained with $O(\log P)$-time preprocessing using the above binary tree communication scheme. Hence, once all the preprocessing is done, which takes $O(\log P)$ time, each processor can access each of its C assigned undirected edges in constant time per edge.

The second problem in parallelizing Code Segment 4 involves the reading and writing of $pointer[w]$. In the parallel implementation, each processor maintains locally its own version of the array $pointer$; processor j's version of $pointer$ contains only changes made to it by processor j. Similarly, the "if $pointer[w]$" test is done only locally.

The third problem arises as a result of the local nature of $pointer$. Some global errors may go unnoticed, such as the case in which different processors assign different values to their own copies of $pointer[w]$, for some w. We shall see later that these errors can be detected in Code Segment 2. Another case is that w may be pushed onto the stack, even if w was popped from the stack earlier. This can be prevented by replacing the "if $pointer[w]$ is not defined" test with the stronger condition "if $pointer[w]$ is not defined **and not** $already\_popped[w]$." Code Segment 2 maintains the invariant that $already_popped[w] = $ **true** iff w has already been popped. In order to avoid read conflict, each processor stores its own copy of the array $already\_popped$; details on how this is done will be given in Code Segment 2.

A fourth problem is how to execute the calls to *push* in parallel. The order that vertices are pushed onto the stack is not important. What is important, though, is to avoid write conflicts. The solution is for each processor to push vertices onto its own local stack. Since there may be duplicate undirected edges, there may be duplicate vertices pushed onto the stacks. However, the "if $pointer[w]$ is not defined . . ." test guarantees that each local stack will not contain the same vertex twice.

We shall see below that each vertex is popped off the stacks at most once, even though vertices may be pushed onto the stacks more than once. Hence, the "**while** ($v := pop(stack)) \neq end\_marker$" loop iterates at most V times. Since at most E undirected edges are processed and they are processed in parallel, the total running time of Code Segment 4 is $O(E/P + V \log P)$.

Code Segment 3: The "**while** v has some father t in G **do** *finish*[t]" loop is parallelized by efficiently finding the next father vertex t to process. In the code for *linear_unification*, directed edges are deleted in groups at a time, each group consisting of edges with the same start vertex. When the outgoing directed edges of a vertex v are to be deleted, we "mark" vertex v as deleted, but do not physically delete the edges from the adjacency list of incoming edges, due to problems of write conflict. Thus, when searching for the next father t to process in Code Segment 3, the "marked" fathers must be skipped quickly. We assume that each processor keeps its own copy of the array *marked* in order to avoid read conflicts; when v's outgoing edges are deleted, each processor sets *marked*[v] := **true**.

The next unmarked father can be found efficiently using the following implementation of *get_next_father*, which is called sequentially for each remaining father of v. The array variable *last_processed*[v] points to the entry on v's adjacency list of fathers that was last returned by *get_next_father*(v); the initialization "**for each** vertex w **do** *last_processed*[w] := 0" is done at the beginning of *linear_unification*. In *get_next_father*, each processor keeps a local copy of *last_processed*[v] in order to avoid read conflicts. The variable *num_fathers* is equal to the original number of fathers on v's adjacency list.

The function *get_next_father* is called at most $2V$ times, since it never returns the same vertex more than once, but can return **null** V times. The main loop in *get_next_father* iterates $O(E/(P \log P) + V)$ times among all the calls to *get_next_father*, since each iteration either finds a father t or else skips $P \log P$ marked (already deleted) fathers. Each iteration can be done in $O(\log P)$ time. The "**if** some p_j exists $\cdots$" clause can be done using the binary tree communication scheme described above. The broadcasting can be done in $O(\log P)$ time in a similar way. The total execution time for Code Segment 3 is thus $O(E/P + V \log P)$.

Code Segment 2: We must parallelize a portion of the code for the function *pop*, because there may be as many as E vertices in total pushed onto the local stacks (counting duplicates), and we want the total running time to be $O(E/P + V \log P)$. We implement each local stack as a doubly-linked list of array slots; array slot v is in the list iff vertex v is on the stack. This data structure allows the vertices on the stack to be accessed sequentially; also, any vertex (by name) can be deleted from the stack in constant time. Note that each processor may have several local stacks, one for each call to *finish*. But the array slots used to implement the stacks can be shared by the processor, since each vertex is not pushed more than once by the same processor.

The code for *pop* is given below. We assume that *current* is set initially to 1 and that *already_popped*[v] is set initially to **false**. for each v.

```
function get_next_father(v : vertex) returns vertex;
{ For notation, we denote the jth processor by P_j and the value ⌈log P⌉ by logP. }
begin
loop
        Broadcast last_processed[v] to all P processors;
        for each 1 ≤ j ≤ P in parallel do
            begin
            Assign to P_j the (last_processed[v] + (j − 1) × logP + 1)st, ...,
                (last_processed[v] + j × logP)th fathers on v's adjacency list of incoming edges;
            p_j := minimum 1 ≤ p ≤ logP such that not marked[pth father assigned to P_j]
            end;
        if some p_j exists, for 1 ≤ j ≤ P then
            begin
            j' := minimum 1 ≤ j ≤ P such that p_j exists;
            t := p_j'th father assigned to P_j';
            last_processed[v] := last_processed[v] + (j' − 1) × logP + p_j';
            break loop
            end;
        { Get next block of P log P fathers of v }
        last_processed[v] := last_processed[v] + P × logP;
        if last_processed[v] ≥ num_fathers[v] then return(null)   { No fathers left }
end loop;

Broadcast t to all P processors;
for each 1 ≤ j ≤ P in parallel do
        marked[t] := true;
return(t)
end;
```

```
function pop(stack) returns vertex;
{ This "stack" is not required to act in a LIFO manner; order is not important.
  For notational purposes, we denote the jth processor by P_j. }
begin
if P_current's stack is empty then
      Find another processor with a nonempty stack;
  if there is no processor with a nonempty stack then return(end_marker)
  else current := ID of some processor with a nonempty stack;
  v := local_pop(P_current's stack);
  Broadcast v and P_current's value of pointer[v] to all P processors;
  for each 1 ≤ j ≤ P in parallel do
        already_popped[v] := true;   { the local copy of already_popped is used }
        if v is on one of P_j's local stacks then
           begin
           if (P_j's value of pointer[v]) ≠ (P_current's value of pointer[v])
                then error_condition[j] := true;
           Delete v from P_j's local stack
           end;
  return(v)
end;
```

In the above code, a processor with a nonempty stack can be found in $O(\log P)$ time using the binary tree communication scheme described earlier. The broadcasting of v and processor *current's* value of *pointer* [v] can also be done in $O(\log P)$ time in the same manner.

Among all the calls to *finish*, the total number of requests needed to determine another processor with a nonempty stack is bounded by $2V$, since each vertex is popped at most once; the overhead is $O(\log P)$ for the binary tree scheme, as explained above. In addition, each local stack contains at most $E/P + V$ vertices. Hence, the total time for Code Segment 2 is $O(E/P + V \log P)$.

If *error_condition* [j] = **true**, for any $1 \leq j \leq P$, then u_0 and v_0 are not unifiable. This can be checked in $O(\log P)$ time using a binary tree communication scheme after all the calls to *finish* are executed.

Code Segment 1: This code segment creates the adjacency list of incoming edges by processing the inputed adjacency list of outgoing edges. The adjacency lists are implemented as two-dimensional arrays, in which the endpoint to the ith edge in vertex v's list is stored in the (v, i)th slot in the array.

In the parallel implementation, each processor is assigned $(1/P)$th the outgoing edges, and creates a local incoming adjacency list for its assigned outgoing edges. For each vertex v, let $c_j(v)$ denote the number of edges incoming to v created by processor j. In $O(\log P)$ time using a binary tree communication scheme, each processor can determine $C_j(v) = \sum_{1 \leq k < j} c_k(v)$. Once $C_j(v)$ is determined, processor j knows where in the global adjacency list for v to deposit its $c_j(v)$ incoming edges. The total time required is thus $E/P + V \log P$.

This completes the proof of Theorem 5.2.

VI. THE PATH SYSTEM ACCESSIBILITY PROBLEM

In this section, we show how the standard $O(E + V)$-time sequential algorithm for the path system accessibility problem (PSA) can be parallelized to run in $O(E/P + V \log P)$ time on an EREW PRAM with P processors and in $O(E/P + V)$ time on an arbitrary CRCW PRAM with P processors. We begin by defining some terminology and stating an instance of the problem.

Path System Accessibility

Input: A finite set X of n nodes, a set of E "edges," which are ordered triples in the set $X \times X \times X$, and two sets $S, T \subseteq X$ of source and terminal nodes. For convenience, we let V denote the quantity n^2.

Output: Is there an *accessible* terminal node? A node $z \in X$ is accessible if $z \in S$ or if there exist accessible nodes x and y such that $\langle x, y, z \rangle$ is an edge.

We say that a node z is *adjacent* to the pair (x, y) if either $\langle x, y, z \rangle$ or $\langle y, x, z \rangle$ is an edge. For simplicity, we assume that the edges are stored in an adjacency list structure; all the vertices z adjacent to (x, y) are stored in a linked list. The algorithm for path system accessibility displayed below repeatedly appends nodes to the queue *reached* containing all accessible nodes found so far. The algorithm operates in *passes*, each pass consisting of one iteration of the **repeat** loop. Executing a pass involves collecting all nodes that are adjacent to a pair of accessible nodes where at least one member of the pair was collected in the previous pass, and appending them to the queue *newly_reached*. At the beginning of each pass, an end marker is placed in *newly_reached* to separate the nodes collected during the previous pass from those collected during the current pass. Whenever a node from *newly_reached* is about to be used to hunt for new adjacent nodes, it is removed from *newly_reached*. At the end of each pass, all nodes collected in the previous pass have been removed from *newly_reached,* and *newly_reached* contains only the nodes collected during the current pass. These nodes are copied into *reached* at the conclusion of each pass.

Before the first pass, all sources are placed in *newly_reached* and *reached*. Whenever a new node is reached it is tested for membership in T for a successful return. If no more nodes can be reached, then there is no accessible terminal node.

```
procedure path_system_accessibility;
begin
{ Initialize queues reached and newly_reached to empty;
  initialize each slot in array already_reached to false }
reached := ∅;
newly_reached := ∅;
for each node x do already_reached[x] := false;
for each x ∈ S do
    begin
    if x ∈ T then return('SUCCESSFUL', x);
    append(x, reached);
    append(x, newly_reached);
    already_reached[x] := true
    end;
repeat   { Start a new pass }
    { Mark the end of newly_reached }
    append(end_marker, newly_reached);
    while ((x := remove_first(newly_reached))
                              ≠ end_marker) do
        { Process next node in newly_reached }
        for each y in reached do
            for each z on the adjacency list
                of (x, y) or of (y, x) do
                if not already_reached[z] then
                    begin   { "Collect" z }
                    if z ∈ T then
                        return('SUCCESSFUL', z);
                    append(z, newly_reached);
                    already_reached[z] := true
                    end;
    { Add nodes collected during this phase to reached }
    for each x in newly_reached do append(x, reached)
until newly_reached = ∅;
return('UNSUCCESSFUL')
end
```

In the innermost loop, each edge is considered at most once and in constant time. Hence that loop executes in $O(E)$ time. Each of the loops outside the inner loop executes in $O(V)$ time. This proves the following theorem.

Theorem 6.1: The sequential running time of the above algorithm is $O(E + V)$.

A parallel version of this algorithm is based on the parallel processing of the inner **for** loop. All other parts of the algorithm are handled sequentially. The inner **for** loop is parallelized by having each processor execute it for $(1/P)$th the nodes z. The "**if not** already_reached[z]" test is ignored, so z is always appended to the queue. The queue newly_reached is implemented as a collection of local queues, in the same manner as the stacks in Section V-B. The calls to append are made to the local queues, one per processor. Each vertex z is appended at most once per queue. The duplicate z's can be removed when newly_reached is appended to reached. The function call remove_first is implemented in a way similar to

pop in Section V-B. The size of each local queue is at most $E/P + V$.

Theorem 6.2: The running time of the algorithm path_system_accessibility using an EREW PRAM with P processors is $O(E/P + V \log P)$.

Proof: The total time required for the inner loop is $O(E/P + V)$. Each local queue size is at most $E/P + V$, and the total number of vertices on newly_reached is at most V. Hence, the time required for all the calls to remove_first is $O(E/P + V \log P)$. The result follows. ∎

Theorem 6.3: The running time of the algorithm path_system_accessibility using an arbitrary CRCW PRAM with P processors is $O(E/P + V)$.

Proof: The $\log P$ factor can be eliminated from the time bound given in Theorem 6.2. The time to find a processor with a nonempty newly_reached queue can be reduced from $O(\log P)$ to constant time by having each processor with a nonempty queue attempt to write its ID into a specially designated global location. The processor that succeeds will be used. As long as there is at least one nonempty queue, some processor will succeed in writing. ∎

VII. THE MONOTONE CIRCUIT VALUE PROBLEM

This section begins with the usual $O(E + V)$-time sequential algorithm for the monotone circuit value problem (MCV), and a description of a parallel version that can run in $O(E/P + V \log P)$ time on an EREW PRAM with P processors and in $O(E/P + V)$ time on a CRCW PRAM with P processors. We begin by defining an instance of the problem.

Monotone Circuit Value

Input: A finite set of V vertices; for $1 \leq j \leq V$, vertex j is either an input (0 or 1), an AND-gate $AND(i_{j,1}, i_{j,2}, \cdots, i_{j,k(j)})$, or an OR-gate $OR(i_{j,1}, i_{j,2}, \cdots, i_{j,k(j)})$ where $1 \leq i_{j,1}, i_{j,2}, \cdots, i_{j,k(j)} < j$.

Output: Is the value of the expression represented by vertex V equal to 1?

This problem is solved by the following straightforward algorithm, which runs in time $O(E + V)$:

```
procedure monotone_circuit_value;
begin
for j := 1 to V do
    { Determine the value of vertex j }
    case type of vertex j of
        INPUT : v[j] := inputed value of vertex j;
        OR : v[j] := ⋁_{1≤ℓ≤k(j)} v[i_{j,ℓ}];
        AND : v[j] := ⋀_{1≤ℓ≤k(j)} v[i_{j,ℓ}];
    end;
return(v[V])
end
```

The key idea in the EREW PRAM implementation is to keep all processors calculating AND's or OR's of inputs to the same gate. This can be done by beginning each iteration of the **for** loop in sequential mode. Whenever an AND or OR gate is encountered, each of the P processors takes every Pth input vertex to that gate and calculates the AND or OR of those vertices accordingly. Using a binary tree communication scheme, the composite value can be computed from the P local values in $O(\log P)$ time. In order to avoid read conflicts, each processor must keep its own copy of the array v. Whenever $v[j]$ is computed, its value is broadcast to all P processors in $O(\log P)$ time. This proves the following theorem:

Theorem 7.1: The running time of the algorithm *monotone_circuit_value* using an EREW PRAM with P processors is $O(E/P + V \log P)$.

Theorem 7.2: The running time of *monotone_circuit_value* using a CRCW PRAM with P processors is $O(E/P + V)$.

Proof: The $\log P$ term can be eliminated because AND's and OR's of P values can be done in constant time. For example, to compute an AND of P values, one per processor, a global memory location is initialized to **true**; if any processor has a **false** value, it writes the value **false** into that global location. The final value is **true** iff all P values are **true**. ∎

VIII. The Ordered Depth-First Search Problem

In this section we apply our techniques from Section V to the standard $O(E + V)$-time recursive depth-first search traversal algorithm and show how it can be parallelized to run in $O(E/P + V \log P)$ time on an EREW PRAM with P processors and in $O(E/P + V)$ time on a priority CRCW with P processors.

Ordered Depth-First Search

Input: A finite, undirected graph G with V vertices and E edges, an integer $1 \le i \le V$, and a vertex w.

Output: Is w the ith labeled vertex in the ordered depth-first search ordering of the vertices of G starting with vertex 1 as the root?

By ordered, we mean that for each vertex, its children in the depth-first search forest are labeled in the same order as they appear on the vertex's adjacency list. The following straightforward algorithm computes the ordered depth-first search forest in $O(E + V)$ time, from which the above problem can be trivially solved:

```
procedure ordered_depth_first_search;
begin
for each vertex u do marked[u] := false;
for j := 1 to V do
    if not marked[jth vertex] then
        begin
        marked[jth vertex] := true;
        search(jth vertex)
        end
end;

procedure search(v : vertex);
begin
print(v);
for each z on the ordered adjacency list of v do
    if not marked[z] then
        begin
```

```
        marked[z] := true;
        search(z)
        end
end;
```

In the EREW PRAM implementation, for each recursive call to *search*, each processor keeps local values of the parameter v and the vertex z on v's adjacency list that was last searched. This can be done without read or write conflict by broadcasting, accounting for $O(\log P)$ time per call to search. The remaining difficulty is to show how to select quickly the next unmarked vertex on an ordered list. This arises in two places: once in *ordered_depth_first_search* and once in *search*. Without loss of generality, we shall show how to solve the latter instance, namely, choosing the next unmarked vertex on v's adjacency list. We use the function *get_next_father* in Section V, with some trivial modifications, such as replacing each instance of "father" with "neighbor." It finds the next neighbor in $O(t \log P)$ time where t is the number of executions of the outer loop. Each outer loop except for the last one processes $P \log P$ entries on the adjacency list, and there are at most $2V$ calls to the function. Thus, the total time required for all calls to *get_next_neighbor* is $O((E/(P \log P) + V) \log P) = O(E/P + V \log P)$. This gives us the following result.

Theorem 8.1: The running time of the algorithm *ordered_depth_first_search* using an EREW PRAM with P processors is $O(E/P + V \log P)$.

Theorem 8.2: The running time of *ordered_depth_first_search* using a priority CRCW PRAM with P processors is $O(E/P + V)$.

Proof: Each broadcast can be done in constant time using concurrent reading and writing. The function *get_next_neighbor* can be simplified considerably: The P processors are assigned in the order of priority to the next P neighbors on v's adjacency list. Each processor that is assigned an unmarked vertex tries to write its processor ID into a specially designated location. This continues until at least one processor has an unmarked vertex or v's adjacency list is exhausted. If a processor ID is written, the priority write mechanism guarantees that its vertex is the next unmarked neighbor on v's adjacency list. The total time required for all executions of *get_next_neighbor* is $O(E/P + V)$. ∎

If the depth-first search is not required to be ordered (that is, if the value returned by *get_next_neighbor* is some, but not necessarily the next, unmarked neighbor on u's list), then the priority CRCW PRAM model can be replaced by the arbitrary CRCW PRAM model. Care has to be taken to be sure that *last_processed* is not advanced unless there are no unmarked neighbors found among the P processors. An $O(\log^5 V)$-time probabilistic algorithm using a polynomial number of processors for the nonordered version of the problem has been developed [2].

Conclusions

We have shown in Sections IV–VIII that the unification, path system accessibility (PSA), monotone circuit value

(MCV), and ordered depth-first search (ordered DFS) problems can make effective use of parallel processing when the graphs are not sparse. The running times of the algorithms for these problems are $O(E + V)$ [sequential] and $O(E/P + V \log P)$ [EREW PRAM with P processors]. For the latter three problems the $\log P$ term can be eliminated by using the arbitrary CRCW PRAM model for PSA, the CRCW PRAM model for MCV, and the priority CRCW PRAM model for ordered DFS. For PSA, V is taken to be $|X|^2$ where X is the set of nodes. Our results are summarized in Table I.

We have introduced two parallel complexity classes $\mathcal{PC}$ and $\mathcal{PC}^*$, which offer broader criteria than does $\mathcal{NC}$ for determining whether problems are parallelizable. $\mathcal{PC}$ and $\mathcal{PC}^*$ contain several problems that are not likely in $\mathcal{NC}$, but which can make effective use of parallel processing. The nonsparse versions of unification, PSA, MCV, and ordered DFS considered in this paper require that $E = \Omega(f(V))$, for some function f that grows asymptotically faster than linearly. All four of these restricted problems are in $\mathcal{PC}$ and $\mathcal{PC}^*$, since they can attain $\Theta(P)$ speedup, with appropriate choices of P. On the other hand, these four problems are log-space complete for $\mathcal{P}$ and consequently are believed not to be in $\mathcal{NC}$.

It is a fundamental open problem whether or not the inclusions $\mathcal{PC}^* \subseteq \mathcal{PC} \subseteq \mathcal{P}$ are proper. It is also open whether there exists a linear-time sequential unification algorithm for the problem of infinite unification. By the results in Section IV, we know that f-infinite unification is in $\mathcal{PC}$ when f grows faster than the functional inverse of Ackerman's function, but it is still open as to whether it is in $\mathcal{PC}^*$. Other questions are posed in Section II.

The four problems we have studied represent typical problems that are log-space complete for $\mathcal{P}$. Our approach can be applied to several other problems in this class to get similar results. The big question is whether it is possible to get fundamentally better results. For unification, PSA, MCV, and ordered DFS, this is equivalent to determining if the sparse versions of the problems are in $\mathcal{PC}$.

References

[1] A. V. Aho, J. E. Hopcroft, and J. D. Ullman, *The Design and Analysis of Computer Algorithms*. Reading, MA: Addison-Wesley, 1974.
[2] A. Aggarwal and R. Anderson, "A parallel algorithm for the maximal path problem," personal communication.
[3] R. Anderson and E. Mayr, "Parallelism and greedy algorithms," Dep. Comput. Sci., Stanford Univ., Stanford, CA, Tech. Rep. STAN-CS-84-1003, Apr. 1984.
[4] W. F. Clocksin and C. S. Mellish. *Programming in Prolog*. New York: Springer-Verlag, 1981.
[5] S. A. Cook, "An observation on time-storage tradeoff," *J. Comput. Syst. Sci.*, vol. 9, pp. 308–316, 1974.
[6] ——, "An overview of computational complexity," *Commun. Ass. Comput. Mach.*, vol. 26, pp. 400–408, June 1983.
[7] C. Dwork, P. C. Kanellakis, and J. C. Mitchell, "On the sequential nature of unification," *J. Logic Program.*, vol. 1, pp. 35–50, June 1984.
[8] D. M. Eckstein, "Simultaneous memory access," Dep. Comput. Sci., Iowa State Univ., Iowa City, Tech. Rep. TR-79-6 1979.
[9] F. E. Fich, F. Meyer auf der Heide, P. Ragde, and A. Wigderson, "One, two, three, . . . , infinity: Lower bounds for parallel computation," in *Proc. 17th Annu. ACM Symp. Theory Comput.*, Providence, RI, pp. 48–58, May 1985.
[10] M. R. Garey and D. S. Johnson, *Computers and Intractability: A Guide to the Theory of NP-Completeness*. San Francisco, CA: Freeman, 1979.
[11] L. M. Goldschlager, "The monotone and planar circuit value problems are log space complete for P," *SIGACT News*, vol. 9, no. 2, pp. 25–29, 1977.
[12] D. S. Johnson, "The NP-Completeness column: An ongoing guide," *J. Algorithms*, vol. 4, pp. 189–203, June 1983.
[13] P. C. Kanellakis, personal communication, Feb. 1984.
[14] G. F. Lev, N. Pippenger, and L. G. Valiant, "A fast parallel algorithm for routing in permutation networks," *IEEE Trans. Comput.*, vol. C-30, pp. 93–100, Feb. 1981.
[15] D. MacQueen, G. Plotkin, and R. Sethi, "An ideal model for recursive polymorphic types," in *Proc. 11th Annu. ACM Symp. Principles Program. Lang.*, Salt Lake City, UT, Jan. 1984.
[16] A. Martelli and U. Montanari, "Unification in linear time and space: A structured presentation," Consiglio Nazionale delle Ricerche, Pisa, Italy, Internal Rep. B76-16, July 1976.
[17] R. Milner, "A theory of type polymorphism in programming," *J. Comput. Syst. Sci.*, vol. 17, pp. 348–375, Dec. 1978.
[18] M. S. Paterson and M. N. Wegman, "Linear unification," *J. Comput. Syst. Sci.*, vol. 16, pp. 158–167, Apr. 1978.
[19] N. Pippenger, "On simultaneous resource bounds," in *Proc. 20th Annu. IEEE Symp. Foundations Comput. Sci.*, San Juan, PR, Oct. 1979, pp. 307–311.
[20] J. Reif, "Depth first search is inherently sequential," Aiken Computation Lab, Harvard Univ., Cambridge, MA, Tech. Rep. TR-27-83, Nov. 1983.
[21] J. A. Robinson, "Computational logic: The unification computation," *Machine Intell.*, vol. 6, pp. 63–72, 1971.
[22] J. E. Savage and J. S. Vitter, "Parallelism in space–time tradeoffs," in *Proc. Int. Workshop VLSI: Algorithms Architectures*, Amalfi, Italy, May 1984; Amsterdam, The Netherlands: North-Holland.
[23] E. Y. Shapiro, "A subset of concurrent Prolog and its interpreter," Inst. New Generation Comput. Technol., Tokyo, Japan, Tech. Rep. TR-003, 1983.
[24] Y. Shiloach and U. Vishkin, "Finding the maximum, merging, and sorting in a parallel computation model," *J. Algorithms*, vol. 2, pp. 88–102, 1981.
[25] L. Stockmeyer and U. Vishkin, "Simulation of parallel random access machines by circuits," *SIAM J. Comput.*, vol. 13, pp. 409–422, May 1984.
[26] R. E. Tarjan, *Data Structures and Network Algorithms*. Philadelphia, PA: SIAM, 1983.
[27] E. Upfal and A. Wigderson, "How to share memory in a distributed environment," in *Proc. 25th Annu. IEEE Symp. Foundations Comput. Sci.*, West Palm Beach, FL, pp. 171–180, Oct. 1984.
[28] U. Vishkin, "Implementation of simultaneous memory address access in models that forbid it," *J. Algorithms*, vol. 4, pp. 45–50, 1983.
[29] J. S. Vitter and R. A. Simons, "Parallel algorithms for unification and other complete problems in $\mathcal{P}$," in *Proc. ACM 1984 Annu. Conf.: The Fifth Generation Challenge*, San Francisco, CA, Oct. 1984.
[30] H. Yasuura, "On the parallel computational complexity of unification," Yajima Lab., Kyoto University, Kyoto, Japan, Res. Rep. ER 83-01, Oct. 1983.

Jeffrey Scott Vitter (S'80–M'81) was born in New Orleans, LA on November 13, 1955. He received the B.S. degree in mathematics with highest honors from the University of Notre Dame, Notre Dame, IN, in 1977, and the Ph.D. degree in computer science from Stanford University, Stanford, CA, in 1980.

In 1980 he joined the faculty of Brown University, Providence, RI, where he is currently an Associate Professor of Computer Science. He is on leave this semester at the Mathematical Sciences Research Institute, Berkeley, CA. Prior to finishing graduate school, he worked as a computer performance analyst at Standard Oil Co. of California and as a Research Assistant and Teaching Fellow in the Department of Computer Science, Stanford University, Stanford, CA. His research interests include mathematical analysis of algorithms, computational complexity, parallel algorithms, software optimization, and interactive environments. He has written numerous articles and has been a frequent consultant. A patent application in the area of external sorting has been filed on his behalf. He was a Guest Editor of the

April 1985 special issue of IEEE Transactions on Computers on the subject of Sorting. He is coauthor of the upcoming books *Data Structures* (Science Research Associates, 1987) and *The Design and Analysis of Coalesced Hashing* (Oxford University Press, 1986).

Dr. Vitter has recently received an IBM Faculty Development Award, a National Science Foundation Presidential Young Investigator Award, and a Guggenheim Fellowship. He is a member of the IEEE Computer Society, Association for Computing Machinery, and Sigma Xi.

Roger A. Simons was born in Detroit, MI on May 11, 1943. He received the A.B. degree in mathematics, with honors, from the University of California, Los Angeles in 1964, the M.A. and Ph.D. degrees in mathematics (logic and Boolean algebras) from the University of California, Berkeley in 1966 and 1972, respectively, and the Sc.M. degree in computer science from Brown University, Providence, RI, in 1983.

In 1981, he joined the faculty of Rhode Island College, Providence, where he is currently an Associate Professor of Mathematics and Computer Science. From 1970 to 1981, he was on the faculty of the University of Wisconsin, Green Bay, rising to the level of Associate Professor. He has also been a Visiting Lecturer in mathematics at the University of Hawaii (1975, 1977, and 1985). In the summers of 1966 and 1967, he worked on program validation methodology at Aerospace Corp. of El Segundo, CA. And in the summers of 1983 and 1984, he consulted to Woodbury Computers Associates, NJ. His research interests include mathematical analysis of algorithms, computational complexity, parallel algorithms, circuit complexity, and applications of mathematical logic. He has written articles in computer science and mathematical logic as well as their applications to other fields including philosophy and regional planning. He is coauthor of the upcoming book *Data Structures* (Science Research Associates, 1987).

Dr. Simons is a member of the Association for Computing Machinery, American Mathematical Society, Association for Symbolic Logic, Pi Mu Epsilon, Sigma Xi, and the New York Academy of Sciences.

Chapter 5: Macrolevel Architectures

The macrolevel is an intermediate level between the microlevel and the system level. In contrast to the microlevel architectures, the macrolevel architectures are (possibly) made up of a variety of microlevel architectures and perform more complex operations. However, they are not considered as a complete system that can solve problems in AI applications but can be taken as more complex supporting mechanisms for the system level. The architectures can be classified into dictionary machines, database machines, architectures for searching, and architectures for managing data structures.

A dictionary machine is an architecture that supports the insertion, deletion, and searching for membership, extremum, and proximity of keys in a database [1-8]. Most designs are based on binary-tree architectures; however, design using radix trees and a small number of processors have been found to be preferable when keys are long and clustered [3].

A database machine is an architectural approach that distributes the search intelligence into the secondary and mass storage and relieves the workload of the central processor. Extensive research has been carried out in the past decade on optical and mass storage [9,10], backend storage systems [11], and database machines [12-21]. Earlier database machines developed were mainly directed toward general-purpose relational database management systems. Examples include the DBC, DIRECT, RAP, CASSM, associative array processors, text retrieval systems [12,13], and CAFS [18]. Nearly all current research on database machines to support knowledge databases assume that the knowledge database is relational; hence, research is directed toward solving the disk paradox [14] and enhancing previous relational database machines by extensive parallelism [22-25]. Commercially available database and backend machines have also been applied in knowledge management [26-28]. The relational database machines for the Japanese Fifth-Generation Computer System will be discussed in Chapter 8.

Searching is an essential to many applications, although unnecessary combinatorial searches should be avoided. The suitability of parallel processing to searching depends on the problem complexity, the problem representation, and the corresponding search algorithms. Problem complexity should be low enough such that a serial computer can solve the problem in a reasonable amount of time. Problem representations are very important because they are related to the search algorithms. Parallel algorithms have been found to be able to reduce dramatically the average-time behavior of search problems, the so-called combinatorially implosive algorithms [29-31].

A search problem can be represented as searching an acyclic graph or a search tree. According to the functions of nodes in the graph, the problem is transformed into one of the following paradigms: (1) AND-tree (or graph) search: all nonterminal nodes are AND nodes; (2) OR-tree (or graph) search: all nonterminal nodes are OR nodes; and (3) AND/OR-tree (or graph) search: the nonterminal nodes are either AND or OR nodes. A divide-and-conquer algorithm is an example algorithm to search AND trees; a branch-and-bound algorithm is used to search OR trees; and an α/β algorithm is used to search (AND/OR) game trees. Parallel algorithms for divide-and-conquer [32], branch-and-bound [33-40], and AND/OR-graph search [41-43] have been developed. Various parallel architectures to support divide-and-conquer algorithms [44,45] and branch-and-bound algorithms [46-56] have been proposed. Architectures to support searching logic programs and game trees will be discussed in Chapter 9.

Extensive research has been carried out in supporting dynamic data structures in a computer with a limited memory space. Garbage collection is an algorithm that periodically reclaims memory space no longer needed by the users [57-72]. This is usually transparent to the users and could be implemented in hardware, software, or a combination of both. For efficiency reasons, additional hardware such as stacks and reference counters are usually provided. Alternatives for supporting garbage collection are generally machine dependent and will be illustrated in the next chapter where the Lisp machines will be discussed.

Four papers are included in this chapter. The first paper, by Hawthorn and Dewitt, gives a performance comparison of several database machines including associative disks, RAP, CASSM, DBC, DIRECT, and CAFS [17]. Then Kellogg presents an example of a commercially available database machine and its application in knowledge management [27]. The third paper, by Wah et al., discusses issues and solutions to multiprocessing of combinatorial search problems [56]. Readers may also refer to the paper on implosive algorithms (not included here owing to space limitation) which discusses the speedup phenomenon of parallel algorithms [30]. The last paper, by Cohen, surveys garbage-collection algorithms and provide an extensive survey of references up to 1981 [57].

References

[1] M.J. Atallah and S.R. Kosaraju, "A Generalized Dictionary Machine for VLSI," *IEEE Transactions on Computers*, vol. C-34, no. 2, pp. 151-155, Feb. 1985.

[2] H. Schmeck and H. Schroder, "Dictionary Machines for Different Models of VLSI," *IEEE Transactions on Computers*, vol. C-34, no. 5, pp. 472-475, May 1985.

[3] A.L. Fisher, "Dictionary Machines with a Small Number of Processors," *Proceedings of the 11th Annual International Symposium on Computer Architecture*, pp. 151-156, IEEE Computer Society, Washington, D.C., June 1984.

[4] A.K. Somani and V.K. Agarwal, "An Efficient VLSI Dictionary Machine," *Proceedings of the 11th Annual International Symposium on Computer Architecture*, pp. 142-150, IEEE Computer Society, Washington, D.C., June 1984.

[5] T.A. Ottmann, A.L. Rosenberg, and L.J. Stockmeyer, "A Dictionary Machine (for VLSI)," *IEEE Transactions on Computers*, vol. C-31, no. 9, pp. 892-897, Sept. 1982.

[6] M.J. Carey and C.D. Thompson, "An Efficient Implementation of Search trees on O(log N) Processors," *Technical Report UCB/CSD 82/101*, Computer Science Division University of California, Berkeley, Calif., April 1982.

[7] C.E. Leiserson, "Systolic Priority Queues," *Proceedings of the Caltech Conference on VLSI*, Caltech, Pasadena, Calif., Jan. 1979.

[8] J.L. Bentley and H.T. Kung, "A Tree Machine for Searching Problems," *Proceedings of the International Conference on Parallel Processing*, pp. 257-266, IEEE Computer Society, Washington, D.C., 1979.

[9] S.W. Miller, ed., "Special Issue on Mass Storage Systems," *Computer*, vol. 18, no. 7, July 1985.

[10] S.W. Miller, ed., "Special Issue on Mass Storage Systems Evolution of Data Center Architectures," *Computer*, vol. 15, no. 7, July 1982.

[11] H.A. Freeman, ed., "Special Issue on Backend Storage Networks," *Computer*, vol. 13, no. 2, Feb. 1980.

[12] D.K. Hsiao, ed., "Special Issue on Database Machines," *Computer*, vol. 12, no. 3, March 1979.

[13] G.G. Langdon Jr., ed., "Special Issue on Database Machines," *IEEE Transactions on Computers*, vol. C-28, no. 6, June 1979.

[14] H. Boral and D. DeWitt, "Database Machine: An Idea Whose Time has Passed?," *Database Machines*, pp. 166-167, Springer-Verlag, New York, N.Y., 1983.

[15] F.J. Malabarba, "Review of Available Database Machine Technology," *Proceedings of the Conference on Trends and Applications*, pp. 14-17, IEEE Computer Society, Washington, D.C., 1984.

[16] J. Shemer and P. Neches, "The Genesis of a Database Computer," *Computer*, vol. 17, no. 11, pp. 42-56, Nov. 1984.

[17] P.B. Hawthorn and D.J. DeWitt, "Performance Analysis of Alternative Database Machine Architectures," *IEEE Transactions on Software Engineering*, vol. SE-8, no. 1, pp. 61-75, Jan. 1982.

[18] E. Babb, "Joined Normal Form: A Storage Encoding for Relational Databases," *ACM Transactions on Database Systems*, vol. 7, no. 4, pp. 588-614, Dec. 1982.

[19] D. Gajski, W. Kim, and S. Fushimi, "A Parallel Pipelined Relational Query Processor: An Architectural Overview," *Proceedings of the 11th Annual International Symposium on Computer Architecture*, pp. 134-141, IEEE Computer Society, Washington, D.C., June 1984.

[20] M. Kitsuregawa, H. Tanaka, and T. Moto-oka, "Application of Hash to Data Base Machine and Its Architecture," *New Generation Computing*, vol. 1, no. 1, pp. 63-74, 1983.

[21] D.E. Shaw, *Knowledge-Based Retrieval on a Relational Database Machine*, Ph.D. Dissertation, Stanford University, Menlo Park, Calif.; also as Technical Report, Columbia University, New York, N.Y., Aug. 1980.

[22] Y. Tanaka, "MPDC-Massive Parallel Architecture for Very Large Databases," *Proceedings of the International Conference on Fifth-Generation Computer Systems*, pp. 113-137, ICOT, Tokyo, Japan and North-Holland, Amsterdam, The Netherlands, 1984.

[23] K. Murakami, T. Kakuta, and R. Onai, "Architectures and Hardware Systems: Parallel Inference Machine and Knowledge Base Machine," *Proceedings of the International Conference on Fifth-Generation Computer Systems*, pp. 18-36, ICOT, Tokyo, Japan, and North-Holland, Amsterdam, The Netherlands, 1984.

[24] S. Shibayama, T. Kakuta, N. Miyazaki, H. Yokota, and K. Murakami, "A Relational Database Machine with Large Semiconductor Disk and Hardware Relational Algebra Processor," *New Generation Computing*, vol. 2, no. 2, pp. 131-155, 1984.

[25] H. Sakai, K. Iwata, S. Kamiya, M. Abe, A. Tanaka, S. Shibayama, and K. Murakami, "Design and Implementation of Relational Database Engine," *Proceedings of the Fifth-Generation Computer Systems*, pp. 419-426, ICOT, Tokyo, Japan, and North-Holland, Amsterdam, The Netherlands, 1984.

[26] C. Kellogg, "Knowledge Management: A Practical Amalgam of Knowledge and Data Base Technology," *Proceedings of the National Conference on Artificial Intelligence*, pp. 306-309, William Kaufmann, Los Altos, Calif., 1982.

[27] C. Kellogg, "Intelligent Assistants for Knowledge and Information Resources Management," *Proceedings of the 8th International Joint Conference on Artificial Intelligence*, pp. 170-172, William Kaufmann, Los Altos, Calif., 1983.

[28] P.M. Neches, "Hardware Support for Advanced Data Management Systems," *Computer*, vol. 17, no. 11, pp. 29-40, Nov. 1984.

[29] W.A. Kornfeld, "The Use of Parallelism to Implement a Heuristic Search," *Proceedings of the 7th International Joint Conference on Artificial Intelligence*, pp. 575-580, William Kaufmann, Los Altos, Calif., Aug. 1981.

[30] W.A. Kornfeld, "Combinatorially Implosive Algorithms," *Communications of the ACM*, vol. 25, no. 10, pp. 734-738, Oct. 1982.

[31] B.W. Weide, "Modeling Unusual Behavior of Parallel Algorithms," *IEEE Transactions on Computers*, vol. C-31, no. 11, pp. 1126-1130, Nov. 1982.

[32] E. Horowitz and A. Zorat, "Divide-and-Conquer for Parallel Processing," *IEEE Transactions on Computers*, vol. C-32, no. 6, pp. 582-585, June 1983.

[33] M.A. Franklin and N.L. Soong, "One-Dimensional Optimization on Multiprocessor Systems," *IEEE Transactions on Computers*, vol. C-30, no. 1, pp. 61-66, Jan. 1981.

[34] S.G. Akl, D.T. Barnard, and R.J. Doran, "Design, Analysis and Implementation of a Parallel Tree Search Algorithm," *IEEE Transactions on Pattern Analysis and Machine Intelligence*, vol. PAMI-4, no. 2, pp. 192-203, March 1982.

[35] E. Dekel and S. Sahni, "Binary Trees and Parallel Scheduling Algorithms," *IEEE Transactions on Computers*, vol. C-32, no. 3, pp. 307-315, March 1983.

[36] J.L. Baer, H.C. Du, and R.E. Ladner, "Binary Search in a Multiprocessing Environment," *IEEE Transactions on Computers*, vol. C-32, no. 7, pp. 667-677, July 1983.

[37] T.H. Lai and S. Sahni, "Anomalies in Parallel Branch-and-Bound Algorithms," *Communications of the ACM*, vol. 27, no. 6, pp. 594-602, June 1984.

[38] G.-J. Li and B.W. Wah, "Computational Efficiency of Parallel Approximate Branch-and-Bound Algorithms," *Proceedings of the International Conference on Parallel Processing*, pp. 473-480, IEEE Computer Society, Washington, D.C., 1984.

[39] G.-J. Li and B.W. Wah, "Coping with Anomalies in Parallel Branch-and-Bound Algorithms," *IEEE Transactions on Computers*, vol. C-35, no. 4, 1986.

[40] T.H. Lai and A. Sprague, "Performance of Parallel Branch-and-Bound Algorithms," *IEEE Transactions on Computers*, vol. C-34, no. 10, pp. 962-964, Oct. 1985.

[41] D.H. Fishman and J. Minker, " Representation: A Clause Representation for Parallel Search," *Artificial Intelligence*, vol. 6, no. 2, pp. 103-127, 1975.

[42] R.A. Finkel and J.P. Fishburn, "Parallelism in Alpha-Beta Search," *Artificial Intelligence*, vol. 19, no. 1, pp. 89-106, 1982.

[43] T.A. Marsland and M. Campbell, "Parallel Search of Strongly Ordered Game Trees," *Computing Surveys*, vol. 14, no. 4, pp. 533-551, Dec. 1982.

[44] F.J. Peters, "Tree Machine and Divide-and-Conquer Algorithms," *Lecture Notes CS 111 (CONPAR81)*, pp. 25-35, Springer-Verlag, New York, N.Y., 1981.

[45] M.R. Sleep and F. W. Burton, "Towards a Zero Assignment Parallel Processor," *Proceedings of the 2nd International Conference on Distributed Computing Systems*, pp. 80-85, IEEE Computer Society, Washington, D.C., April 1981.

[46] J.A. Harris and D.R. Smith, "Simulation Experiments of a Tree Organized Multicomputer," *Proceedings of the 6th Annual Symposium on Computer Architecture*, pp. 83-89, IEEE Computer Society, Washington, D.C., April 1979.

[47] M. Imai and T. Fukumura, "A Parallelized Branch-and-Bound Algorithm Implementation and Efficiency," *Systems, Computers, Controls*, vol. 10, no. 3, pp. 62-70, June 1979.

[48] B.C. Desai, "A Parallel Microprocessing System," *Proceedings of the International Conference on Parallel Processing*, p. 136, IEEE Computer Society, Washington, D.C., Aug. 1979.

[49] O.I. El-Dessouki and W.H. Huen, "Distributed Enumeration on Between Computers," *IEEE Transactions on Computers*, vol. C-29, no. 9, pp. 818-825, Sept. 1980.

[50] W.M. McCormack, F.G. Gray, J.G. Tront, R.M. Haralick, and G.S. Fowler, "Multi-Computer Parallel Architectures for Solving Combinatorial Problems," *Multicomputers and Image Processing Algorithms and Programs*, edited by K. Preston Jr. and L. Uhr, pp. 431-451, Academic Press, Orlando, Fla., 1982.

[51] M. Imai, Y. Tateizumi, Y. Yoshida, and T. Fukumura, "A Multicomputer System Based on the Binary-Tree Structure: DON(2)," *TGEC*, vol. EC83-23, no. 1, pp. 19-30, 1983.

[52] Q.F. Stout, "Sorting, Merging, Selecting and Filtering on Tree and Pyramid Machines," *Proceedings of the International Conference on Parallel Processing*, pp. 214-221, IEEE Computer Society, Washington, D.C., Aug. 1983.

[53] B.W. Wah, G.-J. Li, and C.F. Yu, "The Status of MANIP—A Multicomputer Architecture for Solving Combinatorial Extremum-Search Problems," *Proceedings of the 11th Annual International Symposium on Computer Architecture*, pp. 56-63, IEEE Computer Society, Washington, D.C., June 1984.

[54] B.W. Wah and Y.W.E. Ma, "MANIP—A Multicomputer Architecture for Solving Combinatorial Extremum-Search Problems," *IEEE Transactions on Computers*, vol. C-33, no. 5, pp. 377-390, May 1984.

[55] R. Finkel and U. Manber, "DIB—A Distributed Implementation of Backtracking," *Proceedings of the 5th International Conference on Distributed Computing Systems*, pp. 446-452, IEEE Computer Society, Washington, D.C., May 1985.

[56] B.W. Wah, G.-J. Li, and C.F. Yu, "Multiprocessing of Combinatorial Search Problems," *Computer*, vol. 18, no. 6, pp. 93-108, June 1985.

[57] J. Cohen, "Garbage Collection of Linked Data Structures," *Computing Surveys*, vol. 13, no. 3, pp. 341-367, Sept. 1981.

[58] E.W. Dijkstra, L. Lamport, A.J. Martin, C.S. Scholten, and E.F.M. Steffens, "On-the-Fly Garbage Collection: An Exercise in Cooperation," *Communications of the ACM*, vol. 21, no. 11, pp. 966-975, Nov. 1978.

[59] H. Lieberman and C. Hewitt, "A Real-Time Garbage Collector Based on the Lifetimes of Objects," *Communications of the ACM*, vol. 26, no. 6, pp. 419-429, June 1983.

[60] H.G. Baker Jr, "Optimizing Allocation and Garbage Collection of Spaces," *Artificial Intelligence: An MIT Perspective*, edited by P.H. Winston and R.H. Brown, vol. 1, pp. 391-396, MIT Press, Cambridge, Mass., 1979.

[61] H.G. Baker Jr., "List Processing in Real Time on a Serial Computer," *Communications of the ACM*, vol. 21, no. 4, pp. pp. 280-294, April 1978.

[62] H.C. Baker Jr. and C. Hewitt, "The Incremental Garbage Collection of Processes," *Proceedings of the Symposium on Artificial Intelligence and Programming Languages*, also *SIGART Newsletter*, pp. 55-59, Aug. 1977.

[63] J.J. Martin, "An Efficient Garbage Compaction Algorithm," *Communications of the ACM*, vol. 25, no. 8, pp. 571-581, Aug. 1982.

[64] D. Spector, "Minimal Overhead Garbage Collection of Complex List Structure," *SIGPLAN Notices*, vol. 17, no. 3, pp. 80-82, ACM, New York, N.Y., 1982.

[65] Y. Hibino, "A Practical Parallel Garbage Collection Algorithm and Its Implementations," *Proceedings of the 7th Annual Symposium on Computer Architecture*, pp. 113-120, IEEE Computer Society, Washington, D.C., May 1980.

[66] R. Fenichel and J. Yochelson, "A Lisp Garbage-Collector for Virtual Memory Computer Systems," *Communications of the ACM*, vol. 12, no. 11, pp. 611-612, Nov. 1979.

[67] J.M. Barth, "Shifting Garbage Collection Overhead to Compile Time," *Communications of the ACM*, vol. 20, no. 7, pp. 513-518, July 1977.

[68] H. Kung and S. Song, An Efficient Parallel Garbage Collection Systems and Its Correctness Proof, *Technical Report*, Department of Computer Science, Carnegie-Mellon University, Pittsburgh, Penn., Sept. 1977.

[69] L. Deutsch and D. Bobrow, "An Efficient Incremental, Automatic Garbage Collector," *Communications of the ACM*, vol. 19, no. 9, pp. 522-526, Sept. 1976.

[70] D. Bobrow and D. Clark, "Compact Encoding of List Structure," *ACM Transactions on Language and Systems*, vol. 1, no. 2, pp. 266-286, 1979.

[71] I.A. Newman and M.C. Woodward, "Alternative Approaches to Multiprocessor Garbage Collection," *Proceedings of the International Conference on Parallel Processing*, pp. 205-210, IEEE Computer Society, Washington, D.C., 1982.

[72] G. Steele, "Multiprocessing Compactifying Garbage Collection," *Communications of the ACM*, vol. 18, no. 9, pp. 495-508, Sept. 1975.

Reprinted from *IEEE Transactions on Software Engineering*, Volume SE-8, Number 1, January 1982, pages 61-75. Copyright © 1982 by The Institute of Electrical and Electronics Engineers, Inc.

Performance Analysis of Alternative Database Machine Architectures

PAULA B. HAWTHORN AND DAVID J. DEWITT

Abstract—The rapid advances in the development of low-cost computer hardware have led to many proposals for the use of this hardware to improve the performance of database management systems. Usually the design proposals are quite vague about the performance of the system with respect to a given data management application. In this paper we predict the performance of several of the proposed database management machines with respect to several representative INGRES queries. The systems analyzed in this paper include associative disks, RAP, CASSM, DBC, DIRECT, and CAFS. We demonstrate that no one database machine is best for executing all types of queries. We will also show that for one class of queries the degree of performance improvement achieved does not warrant use of a database machine.

Index Terms—Associative processors, backend computers, computer architecture, database machines, database management, parallel processors, performance evaluation.

I. INTRODUCTION

THE rapid advances in the development of low-cost computer hardware have led to many proposals for the use of this hardware to improve the performance of database manage-

Manuscript received November 6, 1980. This work was supported in part by the National Science Foundation under Grants MCS75-03839 and MCS78-01721, the U.S. Army Research Office under Contracts DAAG29-79-C-0182, DAAG29-79-C-0165, and DAAG29-80-C-0041, and the Applied Mathematical Sciences Research Program of the Office of Energy Research, U.S. Department of Energy, under Contract W-7405-ENG-48.

P. B. Hawthorn is with the Computer Sciences and Mathematics Department, Lawrence Berkeley Laboratory, Berkeley, CA 94720.

D. J. DeWitt is with the Department of Computer Sciences, University of Wisconsin, Madison, WI 53706.

ment systems. Usually, the design proposals are quite vague about the performance of the system with respect to a given data management application. In this paper we predict the performance of several of the proposed database management machines with respect to several representative INGRES [1] query streams. We will demonstrate that no one database machine is best for executing all types of queries. We will also show that for one class of queries the degree of performance improvement achieved does not warrant use of a database machine. We hope that these results will guide the design of future database machines so that a significant degree of performance improvement can be achieved for all classes of queries.

The term "data management machines" is used here to describe any special-purpose hardware built to enhance the performance of data management systems. The systems analyzed in this paper include both those actually built and those that remain designs on paper. The systems analyzed are associative disks [2]-[4], RAP [5]-[7], CASSM [8]-[10], DBC [11]-[16], DIRECT [17]-[20], and CAFS [21], [22].

Since most of the proposed designs are paper machines, we had to make certain assumptions about the characteristics of each machine in order to make the performance comparisons fair and consequently meaningful. These assumptions are discussed in Section II. Section III predicts and compares the performance of each machine when executing three benchmark retrieval queries. Because several of these systems have continued to evolve since our analysis began, the results presented may not reflect the performance characteristics of

TABLE I
DISK PARAMETERS AND VALUES

Parameter	Meaning	Value
BSIZE	block size	512 bytes
DROT	disk rotation time	.0167 seconds
DAVAC	average access time	.0300 seconds
DRATE	data rate to host	.0012 / block
DREAD	cell read time	.0008 / block
DCYL	# 512-byte blocks/cylinder	418 blocks

the latest versions of each design. The version of each system analyzed in this paper is based on the references cited.

While the analysis techniques we employ could be used for benchmarking the update performance of each machine, we have not done so in this analysis. This is because updates take a relatively short time to execute (compared to projections and joins) and basically consist of a retrieval operation followed by modification (or deletion) of the selected tuples.

The performance of a conventional computer system is also included in the comparison. Therefore, we are able to explore those design differences in the database machines that affect performance as well as the potential improvement of such machines over conventional systems. Our conclusions are presented in Section IV. The Appendix contains a brief description of the architecture of each machine.

II. SPECIFICATION OF DATABASE MACHINE CHARACTERISTICS

The performance analysis presented in Section III consists of an analytical comparison of the database machines. The comparisons are based on assumptions about the physical characteristics of the machines. These assumptions are discussed in this section.

A. Cell Storage Media

For the purposes of comparing the systems, it is assumed that each database machine except RAP and DIRECT uses moving head disks as the data cell storage media. Although associative disk machines and CASSM were designed for fixed-head disks, the use of the same media for all the systems helps make the analysis of the design differences independent of the storage media. Since RAP and DIRECT are caching systems, they are assumed to have the faster, but sequential, storage media that CCD's provide.

B. Physical Specifications for Disks

The physical specifications for the disks are assumed to be those of the Ampex 9200 disk drives. The rotation time of the moving head disk is denoted by DROT, which is assumed to be 0.0167 s. The average access time DAVAC is 0.030 s. The block size BSIZE is equal to 512 bytes. The data transfer rate of the disk, through the controller and channel, is DRATE = 0.0012 s/512 byte block. The time for a cell processor to read a block is not the same as DRATE because the block goes directly to the cell processor, instead of through the bus and the operating system protocols into the computer's main memory. This time, DREAD, for an Ampex 9200 disk would be 0.0008 s/block (0.0167 s/rotation/22 blocks/track).

DRATE is generally longer than DREAD in most computer systems due to channel and memory interference. DCYL, the number of 512-byte blocks per cylinder, is equal to 418 blocks (22 blocks/track * 19 tracks/cylinder). Table I summarizes these parameters.

C. CCD Physical Specifications

For the CCD[1] pages we assumed that both RAP and DIRECT use the high-speed smaller pages specified for DIRECT [17]. This assumption is made simply to keep the obviously changeable parameter of page size from entering the analysis. The size of the pages (CSIZE) is taken to be 16K bytes. The scan time for an entire page is CSCAN = 0.012 s for the CCD pages. These parameters are summarized in Table II.

D. Cell Processor Performance

Another assumption that we have made is that the cell processors are fast enough to keep up with the rotational speed of the cell storage media. Independent of the storage media, the cell processors must do the following.

1) Store the tuples in a buffer until the entire block is read and checked for errors.

2) If the query includes qualifications, compare the attribute values of each record in the block to the values in the query qualification.

3) If a tuple is a match, any of the following:

    a) perform any arithmetic functions specified in the query,

    b) transmit the tuple from the buffer to the host over a bus,

    c) transmit the specified attributes to the host.

In order to operate optimally, this work must be performed at the rotational speed of the cell. This rate is 0.0008 s/512-byte block on most standard disks. Therefore, the processors have 1.5 μs/byte to process the block. If the storage media is CCD or RAM pages, the time is 0.73 μs/byte. Assuming that it takes three instructions to examine a byte and that every byte must be examined, then a cell processor must be about a 2 MIP processor for the disk tracks and a 3 MIP processor for the CCD cells.

In practice, however, the performance requirements of the cell processors for both storage media can be significantly reduced through the following techniques.

1) All 512 characters in the block do not have to be manipulated. By storing the offsets of the attributes to be tested in cell-processor registers, then the only data that have to be examined by the cell processor are those attributes which are referenced in the query. If both the ratio of the number of bytes in the attributes involved in the qualification to the total number of bytes per block and the ratio of the number of successful comparisons to the total number of tuples are small, then the cell processors can be slower and

[1] This performance evaluation was initiated when CCD's were still considered to be a viable technology. Both of the cache-based systems (RAP and DIRECT) could also be implemented using RAM's. Furthermore, the performance of both systems using RAM's would not be significantly different from the results presented in this paper for CCD's.

TABLE II
CCD Parameters

Parameter	Meaning	Value
CSIZE	size of CCD page	16K bytes
CSCAN	page scan time	.012 seconds

TABLE III
Cell Parameters and Values

Parameter	Meaning	Value
NDCELL	Number of cells for CASSM, CAFS, DBC	19
NDRP	Number of cell processors in DIRECT	8
NDPAG	Number of data cells in DIRECT	16
NRCELL	Number of cells in RAP	16

still keep up with the cell cycle time. Furthermore, the data can be stored in the processor's memory through a DMA device, without taking processor time.

2) In [8] and [13] it is observed that very fast cell processors can be made inexpensively because they are simple single function devices and do not need the functionality (e.g., addressing and protection modes, interrupt handling, etc.) of a conventional processor. For example, [6] reported that the RAP cell processors were bound in speed by the data rate of the CCD pages, not the processor speed.

3) Finally, if the cell processor is not fast enough to complete query qualification in the time allotted, the next block will not be read into the cell processor's memory. In this case the cell processor must wait a full revolution of the cell storage media before reading the next block.

E. Number of Cells

Ampex 9200 moving-head disks contain 19 tracks/cylinder (the twentieth track is used as a timing track). Consequently, the number of cells for those database machines that are disk-resident, NDCELL, is assumed to be 19.

The number of 16K byte data pages in the CCD cache for RAP and DIRECT is assumed to be 16. Since RAP tightly couples the processors to the data cells, the number of cell processors for RAP, NRCELL, is also 16. This seems to be a fair assumption since the RAP processors are faster and slightly more powerful than those cell processors used for the database machines which can employ moving head disks.

The cells in DIRECT are not tightly coupled to the cell processors. To reflect DIRECT's usage of general purpose processors rather than the specialized less functional processors of the other systems NDRP was chosen to be 8. The results of [19] indicate that a data cell-to-cell processor ratio of 2:1 is sufficient for high performance. We have assumed, however, that all cell processors are 1 MIP processors (see Section III-D). It is important to keep in mind that DIRECT and RAP cannot process data directly on the disk, but instead rely on a disk cache constructed from CCD cells which must be loaded from the disk before processing can begin. We feel that reducing the number of cell processors available from 19 for the associative disk systems, to 16 for RAP, and 8 for DIRECT sufficiently compensates for the corresponding increase in functionality. Table III summarizes these assumptions.

F. Specification of a Conventional System

It is evident that an analysis based on the current INGRES implementation may not lead to general results due to the particular constraints of INGRES. Therefore, we have assumed that the conventional system supports a new high-performance INGRES which supports precompilation of queries. By inspecting the INGRES code it appears that the

CPU time per query would decrease by at least one half if queries were precompiled.

G. Host Time

The host for all the backend machines, and the entire system for the conventional machine, is assumed to be a DEC PDP 11/70. The host system must perform two functions for each of the backend systems: query compilation and communication with the backend. The former is denoted as "overhead," the latter "communication time."

1) Host Overhead: After the query is retrieved from the user's terminal, it is parsed and transformed into the appropriate form for the backend. The time required for this compilation is divided into two parts: OVCPU denotes the overhead CPU time, and OVIO denotes the overhead I/O time. In assigning numerical values to OVIO and OVCPU, we assume that the queries are precompiled, and that terminal communication time is so small that it can be disregarded.

The usual strategy for precompiling queries is that the user defines a query prior to execution time; the data management system parses, validity checks, and sets up a run-time module for the query. When it is executed, information about what the query depends upon (e.g., structure of the relation) must be checked. The minimal I/O time for such checking is one disk access per relation. Therefore, OVIO = DAVAC = 0.030 s/relation. This assumes that validity checking is done entirely in the host and does not involve the backend.

OVCPU is the CPU time required to perform this validity checking. In UNIX it takes 0.006 s of CPU time to request a memory-resident page from the operating system and transfer it into a user's address space [23]. In [24] it is shown that INGRES requires approximately 0.16 s of CPU time for validity checking and setting up a minimal query. Clearly, the time for the minimal value of OVCPU must fall between 0.006 and 0.16 s. Where it falls between these two values depends on the functionality of the validity checking: the amount of optimization present or possible, the level of security, etc. These two values shall be assigned to OVCPU as best case-worst case assumptions. It must be pointed out that this is an absolute minimum; in general there is much more work to do. If the database has changed, and the query must be recompiled, the extra work of creating the run-time module actually increases the overhead.

2) Host-to-Backend Communication Time: BCOM denotes the host CPU time to send a query to the backend system and receive the results. To assign a numerical value to BCOM, the following considerations must be taken into account. In UNIX, the measured interprocess communication time is 0.12

s for the 5 processes of INGRES to send messages to and receive messages from each other in a linear sequence [25]. This is 0.03 s for a send-and-receive transmission per process pair. The time, in UNIX, for a process to request a page of data from the operating system and to receive that page is 0.006 s if the page is in memory. Whether the time to communicate between the backend system is closer to the interprocess time or the page-transfer time depends on the design and the functionality of the interface. Rather than attempting to further narrow this value, the 0.006 s time is assigned as the "best case" time, and the 0.03 s time as the "worst case" time to perform a single communication with the backend system.

3) Host Data Processing Time: Each of the machines relies on the host to format the results for printing and move the results to the user's terminal. Some rely on the host to perform arithmetic functions. The amount of time required in the host is query and machine dependent. It is denoted by HDP, the host data processing time. The host parameters are summarized in Table IV.

III. Performance Comparisons

Each of the machines described is a cellular system: data are stored in cells, with a processor (in some cases dynamically assigned) per cell. Operations on the cells take place in parallel. While there are minor implementational differences between the machines, we have ignored them in this analysis since none of the machines is in volume production (see Section II). The purpose of our evaluation is to determine the effect of the major design differences on machine performance. The following list highlights some of the interesting differences between the machines which we shall examine.

1) Query-Processing Algorithms Implemented in the Machines: Each of the machines uses different algorithms for the join and project operators. For example, several designs depend on repeatedly scanning the database in order to perform a join operation.

2) The Performance of Caching Database Machines: RAP and DIRECT cannot process data directly on the disk, but instead rely on a CCD cache which is loaded from mass storage.

3) The Effect Upon Performance of the Transfer of Entire Tuples to the Host: The simpler database machines always must return the full tuple to the host.

In [24] three classes of relational queries are identified: overhead-intensive, data-intensive, and multirelational queries. In order to compare the performance of each database machine with each other and a "fast" version of INGRES, one query was chosen from each category. Query $Q1$ is an overhead-intensive query; $Q2$ is a data-intensive multirelation query (i.e., a join between two relations); and $Q3$ is a data-intensive query on a single relation which includes an aggregate operation.

Each of the three queries are actual queries and were chosen to reflect the "average" query of that type as reported in [24]. The database for the three queries is the University of California at Berkeley Department of Electrical Engineering and Computer Science's course and room scheduling database. This database contains 24 704 pages of data in 102 relations.

TABLE IV
Host Parameters and Values

Parameter	Meaning	Value best case -- worst case
OVIO	host overhead I/O time	.0300 seconds
OVCPU	host overhead CPU time	(.006--.1600) sec.
BCOM	host CPU time to communicate with backend	(.006--.0300) sec.
HDP	host time to format results for printing, perform math functions, etc.	query and database machine dependent

The data are information about courses taught: instructor's name, course name, room number, type of course, etc.

In the following section the total work and response times are calculated for each query on each machine. The total work is the sum of the time spent in all components of the machine. The response time is the sum of the component times that cannot be overlapped.

A. Q1–Short Queries

The query chosen for this analysis is as follows:

query $Q1$:
retrieve (QTRCOURSE.day, QTRCOURSE.hour) where QTRCOURSE.instructor = "despain, a.m."

QTRCOURSE contains 1110 tuples. Each tuple has 24 attributes and is 127 bytes long. The relation can be stored as a heap in 274 pages. The attribute "day" is a character field, 7 bytes long; "hour" is also a character field, and is 14 bytes long. Three tuples satisfied this query.

The following facts are relevant to the performance comparisons for this query.

1) The relation fits on one cylinder because the number of pages is less than DCYL, the number of disk blocks per cylinder.

2) Since there were only three tuples returned to the host, the time to process the retrieved data and send it to the user terminal is assumed to be 0. Also, since the hit ratio is so low, it is assumed that there is not a problem with bus contention or controller processor speed.

3) There is one relation in the query, so the host overhead CPU time OVCPU is a constant factor (0.006–0.160) s. OVIO, the host overhead I/O time, is 0.030 s.

1) Fast INGRES: The work to execute this query in a "fast INGRES" system is

FWORK = OVIO + OVCPU + DPIO + DPCPU.

When this query is executed by INGRES [25] there are 11 I/O references: three to the QTRCOURSE relation and eight to system relations. The references to QTRCOURSE are the data processing references. QTRCOURSE was hashed on instructor name. The worst case page reference time occurs when the three pages reside on separate cylinders. In this case there is one access per reference. The best case condition arises if they are on the same track in which case the reference time is one access and three block transfers. Thus, DPIO = (0.0336 best case–0.090 worst case).

For standard INGRES 0.12 s of CPU time are required to

process the query. Since the "fast INGRES" system is compiled (and not interpreted), the data processing CPU time will be half of the measured interpreted query. Therefore, DPCPU = 0.06 s.

The total work that a query incurs is a measure of the impact of the query on system performance. The total work for this query is

$$FWORK = OVIO + OVCPU + DPIO + DPCPU$$
$$= (0.13-0.34) \text{ s.}$$

Clearly, the overhead CPU and I/O times must be done serially since the one I/O reference contains information necessary for the validation of the query. However, the data processing I/O and CPU times can be overlapped. The response time is therefore

$$FRES = OVIO + OVCPU + \max [DPIO, DPCPU]$$
$$= (0.096-0.280) \text{ s.}$$

The best case is dominated by the CPU time to process the three pages, which at 0.06 s is almost half of the total best case work and almost two-thirds of the best case response time. The overhead CPU, at 0.16 s worst case, dominates the worst case work and response times.

2) Associative Disks and CAFS: For this query the associative disks and CAFS have the same functionality. The time required for either system is

$$AWORK = OVCPU + OVIO + BCOM + DAVAC + n*DROT.$$

There must be one disk access (DAVAC) to position the machine at the right cylinder. Then, since the data reside on a single cylinder and since the cell processors operate at the rotational speed of the disk, the data processing will take one revolution of the disk. Thus, $n = 1$. Then AWORK = (0.089-0.267) s. The response time is the same.

The major components of the best case time are the two disk access times: one to perform the overhead functions on the host and the other to position the disk arm for data processing. The worst case time is dominated by the host CPU overhead.

3) CASSM: First, the storage requirements for the QTRCOURSE relation on CASSM must be determined. There are 1110 tuples in the relation. Assuming a two-byte encoding of the relation name, 2220 bytes will be required to store the per-tuple relation name. There are 25 attributes per tuple. Assuming that each attribute name can be encoded in one 1 byte, then since the name is stored for each attribute of each tuple, 27 750 bytes are necessary to identify attributes. Each tuple is 127 bytes long; however, in CASSM no character fields over four characters long are directly stored. They are stored once, then pointers to the correct character string are stored in each tuple. Using that method for storing the relation requires 74 bytes per tuple, which includes 9 pointers to character strings. The nine attributes that are represented as character strings were measured to require 6417 bytes of storage. So the total storage required is 221 blocks, validating Langdon's conjecture that the extra storage required for the delimiters in CASSM is offset by the data encoding algorithm it uses [2]. These data will fit on one cylinder.

The work required to perform this query is

$$CWORK = OVCPU + OVIO + BCOM + DAVAC + n*DROT.$$

The number of rotations n is

1 rotation to mark all tuples
    for the relation QTRCOURSE
1 rotation to find the pointer to
    character string "despain, a.m."
1 rotation to mark all tuples with
    the pointer to "despain, a.m."
1 rotation to return all "day"
    attributes in marked tuples
1 rotation to return all "hour"
    attributes in marked tuples
$\overline{5.}$

It is assumed that CASSM sends the attributes to the host in their coded form, along with the necessary decoding information. Since the query only produces 3 tuples, the host CPU time required for decoding can be disregarded. The value for n for this query is therefore 5, and the work to process the query is CWORK = (0.156-0.334) s. The response time CRES is the same.

The best case time is dominated by the five rotations. The major component in the worst case is the same as in the previous systems, the host overhead CPU time.

4) DBC: The work required in the DBC for this query is

$$DBWORK = OVCPU + OVIO + BCOM$$
$$+ DCYL + DAVAC + DROT.$$

DBWORK differs from the associative disk case only in the time required to perform the DBC cylinder select DCYL. Although a significant part of the DBC design effort has been to make index selection and manipulation very fast, a time must be associated with cylinder selection. If it is assumed that the indexes reside in RAM, then the time to fetch and manipulate them is probably on the order of the time to fetch a memory-resident page in UNIX, 0.006 s. For this analysis it is assumed that DCYL = 0.006 s. Then DBWORK = (0.095-0.273) s. Since the cylinder selection must be done before the data processing can begin, it cannot be overlapped. DBRES, the response time, is therefore the same as DBWORK.

5) DIRECT: The work DIRECT must perform is

$$DWORK = OVCPU + OVIO + BCOM + DPIO + n*CSCAN.$$

CSCAN is the CCD page scan time; DPIO is the time to read QTRCOURSE from the disk.

The QTRCOURSE relation is 274 512-byte blocks long so it will fit in 9 of DIRECT's 16K byte data cells. In this query the cell processors will read from one data cell and write the requested attributes of the qualified tuples to another cell, thus forming a temporary relation. Assuming that no other queries are running, all 16 cells are available to hold the relation and thus the entire relation can be loaded from mass storage at once. Therefore, DPIO is one disk seek plus the transfer time. Of course, the best case I/O time is when the relation is already in DIRECT's buffers; in that case the time is zero.

DPIO = (0-(DAVAC + 274*DREAD))
     = (0-0.249) s.

Since nine data cells are required to store this relation, and there are only eight cell processors, two or three scan times are required to process this query. During the first scan each cell processor will read and process one data page. Qualifying tuples are placed in the processor's internal buffer which is written out to a CCD data cell only when it is either full or when all the input data pages have been examined. During the second scan, seven of the processors will each write their internal buffer into a new CCD page if their internal buffer contained any qualifying tuples. Also, during this second scan the eighth processor will read and examine the ninth data page. If after examining this page the processor has found any qualifying tuples, a third scan will be required to write its internal buffer to a CCD data cell. Since only 3 tuples satisfy this query, at most three processors will produce a new page. Thus, in the best case, two scans are required, and in the worst case, three.

The total work is

$$DWORK = OVCPU + OVIO + BCOM$$
$$+ (2*CSCAN-3*CSCAN) + DPIO$$
$$= (0.066-0.505).$$

In the best case the response time is the same as the total work because no overlapping is possible. If the pages must be read from secondary storage, as in the worst case, the data transfer time for the blocks entering the last data cell can be overlapped with the processing of the first eight. Since there are 32 512-byte blocks per data cell, the response time is

$$DRES = OVCPU + OVIO + BCOM + (1*CSCAN-2*CSCAN)$$
$$+ (CSCAN-(DAVAC + 242*DREAD + max (CSAN, 32*DREAD)))$$
$$= (0.066-0.490).$$

For both times, the best case is dominated by the scan times for the CCD data cells, and the worst case by the data transfer time from the disk.

6) RAP: For RAP the execution time of this query is

$$RWORK = OVCPU + OVIO + BCOM + DPIO + n*CSCAN.$$

QTRCOURSE, because it is 9 cells long, will completely fit in the sixteen RAP processor cells. If QTRCOURSE is already in the cache when the query begins, then DPIO is equal to 0. Otherwise, DPIO is the same as in DIRECT. Thus, DPIO = (0-0.249) s.

The number of cell scans n that must be performed for data processing is

1   to mark qualifying tuples in nine processor cells
1   to send marked tuples to host
―
2.

Thus,

$$RWORK = OVCPU + OVIO + BCOM + 2*CSCAN + DPIO$$
$$= (0.066-0.493) s.$$

The response time is the same.

7) Conclusion: While we have attempted to adjust the various system parameters (e.g., number of processors) in order to make the comparisons fair, one expects that a more complex system, where that complexity consists of added buffers, processors, etc., should result in faster response time and less system work. In Fig. 1 the system work for each of the systems is plotted. (We have not plotted the response times for each system since they are generally the same as the system work.) The systems are ordered along the horizontal axis on the basis of "increasing complexity":

1) INGRES, the "basic" system,
2) Associative Disks, CAFS—the cell processors are relatively simple,
3) CASSM—more intelligence in the cell and controlling processors,
4) RAP—very fast cell processors; CCD cells,
5) DBC—highly functional controlling processor: structure memory, index translation unit, etc.,
6) DIRECT—fast, general purpose cell processors, crosspoint switch.

This curve indicates that the increased complexity of the machines does not result in decreased system work or faster response times. While RAP and DIRECT exhibit the fastest best case times, they also have the slowest worst case times—in which case they are even slower than INGRES. This situation occurs because INGRES maintains QTRCOURSE as a hashed relation, and only reads three pages of it. The caching systems (i.e., RAP and DIRECT) had to serially read the entire relation. This seems to indicate that database machines which rely on caching do not perform satisfactorily on simple overhead-intensive queries. When compared with the performance of "fast INGRES" is it apparent that for this query the increased cost and complexity of the database machines do not result in a significant increase of performance.

B. Multirelation Queries

The second query chosen for our evaluation is the following multirelation query $Q2$:

```
retrieve  ( ROOMS.building, ROOMS.roomnum,
                ROOMS.capacity,
                COURSE.day,  COURSE.hour)
     where ROOMS.roomnum = COURSE.roomnum and
     ROOMS.building = COURSE.building and
         ROOMS.type = "lab"
```

The relation "COURSE" contains information about all the courses taught by the University of California at Berkeley Department of Electrical Engineering and Computer Science in the last four years. It contains 11 436 tuples in 2858 pages, and is stored in an ISAM storage structure, keyed on instructor name and course number. "COURSE" requires 130 tracks (seven cylinders) of disk space. The relation "ROOMS" contains information about every room that the EECS Department can use for teaching courses. It contains 282 tuples in 29 pages, and is hashed on room number. "ROOMS," since it is stored in 29 pages, can be stored on two tracks of one cylinder. The result of this query is a list which contains the build-

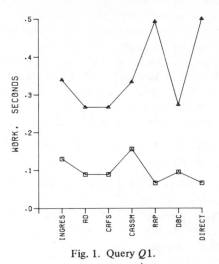

Fig. 1. Query $Q1$.

ing, room number, capacity, day, and hour of the use of any lab for the last four years.

Since the query is a two-relation query, we assumed that the overhead to for this query is double that of the single-relation queries. Thus, OVCPU the overhead CPU time is (0.012–0.32) s. The overhead I/O is 0.06 s.

1) Fast INGRES: It is assumed that the "fast INGRES" system uses the following algorithm for this query.

1) Form $R2$, the sorted, restricted projection of "ROOMS," retaining $R2$ in an in-memory array. $R2$ contains 22 tuples in two pages, and can easily be kept in memory.

2) Scan the "COURSE" relation and compare the join fields of each tuple in COURSE to each tuple in $R2$.

3) Output the required attributes of any matching tuples. Using this algorithm, the total work for fast INGRES is

$$FWORK = OVCPU + OVIO + RSORT + CCOMP + CDP + DPIO.$$

RSORT, the time to perform the sorted, restricted projection of ROOMS, will be calculated first. The work that must be performed to create $R2$ is as follows:

1) read the entire ROOMS relation, testing each tuple to determine if ROOMS.type = "lab",

2) for those tuples that are the correct type, write the building, roomnum, and capacity attributes to an in-memory array ($R2$),

3) sort $R2$ on "roomnum, building" and remove duplicates.

The CPU time to perform the above is composed of the time to sort $R2$ (which was measured to be 0.06 s on the 11/70) and the time to read ROOMS, which is equal to $0.006 * 29 = 0.174$ s. Therefore, RSORT = 0.23 s.

CCOMP, the time to compare the (roomnum, building) attributes in COURSE to those in $R2$, will be determined next. There are 22 tuples in $R2$, and 11 436 in COURSE. Since $R2$ is sorted, each of the COURSE tuples need be compared only until a "greater than" result is found. The (roomnum, building) attribute pair is 20 characters long. If for each COURSE tuple, on the average one half of the $R2$ tuples (11 tuples) are ex-

amined then the average number of comparisons that must be made per tuple in COURSE is $20 * 11$, or 220. Each character comparison requires at least three instructions: the comparison, the test for condition, and the loop control. Therefore, there are a minimum of 660 instructions for each of the 11 436 tuples in COURSE. This is about 7.5 million instructions. Since an 11/70 is a 1 MIP machine, 7.5 s will be required. This is a minimum time. It does not include the time to split the tuple into attributes, do type conversion, etc. The worst case time, however, should be no more than 15 s.

CDP, the time CPU time required to read the data, is calculated next. There are a total of 2887 pages read; the UNIX CPU time required to read a page is 0.006 s. Therefore, CDP = 17.32 s.

DPIO, the I/O time to read the data into memory consists of the I/O time to read the ROOMS (RIO) and COURSE (CIO) relations. Since the ROOMS relation is on two tracks of the same cylinder, the time to read it is RIO = DAVAC + DROT/2 + 29 * DRATE, where DROT/2 = the latency required to access the second track. The I/O time to read the COURSE relation is

$$CIO = DAVAC + 6*CYAVAC + (130 - 7) * DROT/2 + 2858*DRATE.$$

DAVAC is the average access time to begin reading the first cylinder. CYAVAC is the time to move the disk head from one cylinder to an adjacent one. For AMPEX 9200 disk drives, that time is 0.010 s. COURSE is stored in 130 tracks; the time to access the first track on each cylinder is included in the terms DAVAC and 6*CYAVAC; the time to access the remaining tracks is the average latency DROT/2. Finally, the time to transfer the data to memory is 2858 pages * DRATE.

Therefore, the total DPIO time is

$$\begin{aligned} DPIO &= DAVAC + ROT/2 + 29 * DRATE + DAVAC \\ &\quad + 6*CYAVAC + (130 - 7) * DROT/2 \\ &\quad + 2858*DRATE \\ &= 4.62 \text{ s.} \end{aligned}$$

The total work to process this query is

$$\begin{aligned} FWORK &= OVCPU + OVIO + RSORT \\ &\quad + CCOMP + CDP + DPIO \\ &= (29.74\text{–}37.55) \text{ s.} \end{aligned}$$

Since the data processing I/O can be overlapped with CDP, the response time is FRES = (25.12–32.93) s. Both times are dominated by the operating system overhead associated with reading the pages (CDP).

2) Associative Disks: It shall be assumed that the following algorithm is used in processing query $Q2$ in an associative disk system.

1) The sorted restricted projection of ROOMS ($R2$) is formed in the host.

2) The host issues 22 queries, one for each tuple in $R2$, to retrieve from the associative disk the tuples in "COURSE" with matching roomnum and building attributes as those in the query. These queries shall be denoted as the 22 subqueries, and are of the form

retrieve (COURSE.day, COURSE.hour)
where COURSE.roomnum = value1
and COURSE.building = value 2.

As matching tuples are returned, they are printed on the users's terminal.

The time to perform this query using the above algorithm is

$$AWORK = OVCPU + OVIO + RSORT$$
$$+ (n' + 1) * BCOM + RPROC + n' * CPROC.$$

RSORT, the CPU time to perform the sorted restricted projection of the ROOMS relation in the host, is the same as for fast INGRES. The number of communications required between the host and the associative disk (BCOM) is the number of subqueries ($n' = 22$) plus the one query to form the sorted restricted projection.

RPROC, the I/O time to process the restricted projection of ROOMS, is: $RPROC = DAVAC + DROT$. This is one average access time, plus one disk rotation time to perform the query (since the ROOMS relation resides on one cylinder).

The time to process each of the 22 subqueries CPROC is

$$CPROC = DAVAC + 6 * CYAVAC + 7 * DROT$$

which is the time to access each of the seven cylinders on which the COURSE relation resides and to perform the subquery on each.

Therefore, the total time is

$$AWORK = OVCPU + OVIO + RSORT$$
$$+ (n' + 1) * BCOM + RPROC + n' * CPROC$$
$$= (5.04\text{--}5.90) \text{ s.}$$

The response time is the same. The execution time of the 22 subqueries (4.55 s) dominates both the best and worst case times.

3) DBC: The key question in determining the performance of the DBC on this query is whether the search space in the seven cylinders used to store the "COURSE" relation can be narrowed to one or two cylinders by the use of attribute indices. The "COURSE" relation was clustered on course number, which is not mentioned in this query. Therefore, even if indexes existed for each of the "COURSE" attributes in this query, they would not narrow the search space because in the absence of any strong correlation between course number and the other attributes, it is to be expected that qualifying tuples will occur on each of the seven cylinders.

DBC handles single-relation queries only, and in [12] it was shown how joins are split into single-relation queries. Using the queries in [12] as a guide, we find that DBC will process query $Q2$ in exactly the same manner as the associative disk. Therefore, its execution time is the same as the associative disk.

4) CASSM: The algorithm which CASSM uses to implement joins is based on two bit-maps, one for each of the relations to be joined. First, a pass is made over the smaller relation (ROOMS), and the join attributes (roomnum, building) of qualifying tuples are used to hash to a bit-map to mark the presence of a value. Next, a pass is made over the second relation (COURSE) and a second bit-map is marked if the (roomnum, building) attribute pair hash to a location that is marked in the first bit-map. Also, if both bit-maps are marked, the tuple is itself marked for collection. Finally, a second pass is made over the first relation, and those tuples whose (roomnum, building) pairs hash to marked locations in both bit-maps are marked for output. The marked attributes from both relations are sent to the host processor to perform the actual join. This final step is required since the hash functions are most likely not perfect.

The time to execute this query in CASSM is

$$CWORK = OVCPU + OVIO + BCOM + HJOIN$$
$$+ n * RPROC + m * CPROC.$$

HJOIN is the amount of CPU time required in the host to perform the actual join. RPROC is the time required to scan the "ROOMS" relation and CPROC is the time to scan the COURSE relation. HJOIN will be computed first.

Using the above algorithm, 22 tuples of "ROOMS" and 422 tuples of "COURSE" are marked in both bit maps. Only the necessary attributes from those tuples are sent to the host. Those attributes require a total of 47 pages of storage. Because there are a small number of pages the host can complete the processing of this query by first sorting in memory the qualified tuples of the two relations and then merging the two sorted lists to match the correct tuples. The CPU time to sort the 47 pages is 14.1 s on the 11/70; therefore, HJOIN = 14.1 s.

The number of scans of the rooms relation (n) is

1	scan to mark bit map
1	scan to check COURSE's bit map and mark tuple
4	scans to return 4 attributes
6	n, total scans required of the ROOMS relation.

The number of scans of the COURSE relation (m) is

1	scan to mark map and mark qualifying tuples
4	scans to send attributes to host
5	m, the required number of scans of COURSE.

The total time to do this query is, therefore,

$$CWORK = OVCPU + OVIO + BCOM + HJOIN$$
$$+ n * RPROC + m * CPROC$$
$$= (15.50\text{--}15.83) \text{ s.}$$

The best and worst case times are dominated by the time to perform the join in the host. The response time is the same.

5) DIRECT: The DIRECT join algorithm works by joining each of n units in one relation (the outer relation) with all of the units in the other relation (the inner relation). If we consider a unit to be a page and there are n processors available, then each processor can join one page of the outer relation with the entire inner relation. (The granularity of a unit could be as fine as a tuple.)

For this query the COURSE relation will be the outer relation (in general, the outer relation is the larger of the two relations) and the ROOMS relation will be the inner relation. Each of the eight cell processors will first read the ROOMS relation, apply the restriction ROOMS.type = "lab", project over the desired attributes, and then sort the resulting 22 tuples. Each cell processor will keep these 22 tuples in an internal buffer for the duration of the query. Then each cell processor will join a subset of the COURSE relation with its own copy of the ROOMS relation using the same technique employed by "fast INGRES."

Using this algorithm, the work required is

$$DWORK = OVCPU + OVIO + BCOM + r*CSCAN$$
$$+ DSORT + c*CSCAN + DCOMP + DPIO.$$

The parameter r is the number of CCD page scans required by the cell processors to read the ROOMS relation. The time required by the cell processors to form the sorted restricted projection of ROOMS is DSORT. The parameter c is the number of scans of the COURSE relation required to execute the join. DCOMP is the CPU time required by the cell processors to compare the (roomnum, building) attributes in their subset of COURSE with the sorted, restricted projection of ROOMS. DPIO is the I/O time required to transfer the ROOMS and COURSE relations from mass storage to the CCD cells.

Since the entire "ROOMS" relation will fit on one CCD cell, only one scan is required by the cell processors to read the relation. Therefore, r equals 1. Forming the sorted restricted projection of the ROOMS relation takes 0.06 s on an 11/70. Since the DIRECT cell processors are assumed to also be 1 MIP processors, DSORT = 0.06 s.

Next, c will be calculated. The 2858 pages of "COURSE" correspond to 90 16K byte pages. Eight processors, each working in parallel, will require 12 scans of the COURSE relation to complete the join. Six cell processors will join their copy of the 22 tuples from the ROOMS relation with 11 16K pages of the COURSE relation; two cell processors will examine 12 pages of the COURSE relation. Each cell processor will process a distinct subset of the COURSE relation. One additional scan is required for each cell processor to write its output buffer to a CCD cell. Therefore, $c = 13$.

DCOMP is the CPU time required by the cell processors to compare the (roomnum, building) attributes in their subset of COURSE with the sorted, restricted projection of ROOMS. Since two cell processors must examine 12 pages of the COURSE relation, their execution time will be the limiting factor. For "fast INGRES" it was determined that, on the average, 220 comparisons must be made for each COURSE tuple examined and that each comparison requires 3 instructions. The two cell processors which examine 12 pages of COURSE will each examine 1525 tuples. This will require 1 million instructions at approximately 1 μs/instruction. Thus, DCOMP equals 1 s.

DPIO is composed of the time to read the ROOMS (RIO) and COURSE (CIO) relations into CCD memory. If the ROOMS relation is in CCD memory then RIO = 0; otherwise, RIO = DAVAC + 29 * DREAD. Thus, RIO = (0–DAVAC + 29 * DREAD).

Because the entire COURSE relation will not fit within the CCD cache the minimum value of CIO will occur when the first 15 16K byte pages are already loaded (along with the ROOMS relation): CIO = DAVAC + 5 * CYAVAC + 2378 * DREAD. If none of the COURSE relation is initially loaded, then CIO = DAVAC + 6*CYAVAC + 2858*DREAD. Thus,

$$CIO = (DAVAC+5*CYAVAC+2378*DREAD-$$
$$DAVAC+6*CYAVAC+2858*DREAD).$$

This formula assumes that the average access time must be used for only the initial access to the relation; the remaining scans will be for adjacent cylinders.

The total time is therefore

$$DWORK = OVCPU + OVIO + BCOM + r*CSCANS$$
$$+ DSORT + c*CSCANS + DCOMP + DPIO$$
$$= (3.29\text{--}4.07) \text{ s}.$$

For the best case 11/12 of the DCOMP time can be overlapped with the I/O time. For the worst case only 5/6 of it can be overlapped. Thus, the response time is

$$DRES = (2.37\text{--}3.24) \text{ s}.$$

It should be noted that DIRECT could achieve approximately the same level of performance on this query if it were constructed from 16 1/2 MIP processors instead of eight 1 MIP processors. Furthermore, the number of cell processors which could be effectively utilized could be increased to 90. However, doing so would decrease both the best and worst case execution times by at most 1 s (DCOMP equals 0) because the execution time for DIRECT is dominated by the time to load the CCD cache.

6) RAP: It is assumed that the algorithm used by RAP for this query is the same as the one which is used by the associative disk system. That is,
1) form sorted restricted projection of "ROOMS," holding it in memory,
2) perform 22 subqueries.

Since the RAP backend system does not include a general purpose computer, the sorted restricted projection of ROOMS must be performed in the host, which subsequently issues the 22 subqueries. The time required by RAP is

$$RWORK = OVCPU + OVIO + RSORT$$
$$+ (1 + n*c)*BCOM + r*CSCAN + n*(c*CSCAN) + DPIO$$

RSORT, the time to perform the sorted restricted projection, was calculated for "fast INGRES" to be 0.23 s.

The number of cell scans to produce the restricted projection of ROOMS (r) is

1	scan to mark tuple which satisfy the ROOMS restriction
1	scan to return marked tuples to the host
2	number of scans for ROOMS.

The number of scans of the COURSE relation ($n*c$) is calculated next. Because the CCD cache is not large enough to hold the entire COURSE relation (90 pages), this query will have to be processed as six separate phases ($n = 6$). Each phase will begin by first reading the next 16 pages into the cache and then applying the 22 subqueries. For each subquery one scan is required to mark the qualifying tuples and one is needed to return the marked tuples to the host. Thus, each phase will require $c = 2*22 = 44$ scans.

DPIO is the same is for DIRECT. The total work is therefore

$$RWORK = OVCPU + OVIO + RSORT + (1+n*c)*BCOM$$
$$+ r*CSCAN + n*(c*SCAN) + DPIC$$
$$= (7.06\text{-}14.18) \text{ s.}$$

Because the scanning of a cell in RAP cannot be overlapped with the loading of the data cells the response time is the same.

7) CAFS: CAFS handles joins in the same way as CASSM except that it does not mark qualified tuples, but passes them on to the host. To review the algorithm: there are two bit-maps, one for each of the relations to be joined.

1) First, a pass is made over the smaller relation (ROOMS), and the join attributes (roomnum, building) of qualifying tuples used to hash to a bit-map to mark the presence of a value.

2) A pass is made over the second relation (COURSE) and a second bit-map is marked if the (roomnum, building) attribute pair hash to a location that is marked in the first bit-map. Also, if both bit-maps are marked, the tuple is itself sent to the host.

3) A second pass is made over the first relation, and those tuples whose (roomnum, building) pairs hash to marked locations in both bit-maps are sent to the host.

The host must perform the actual join on the smaller relations passed to it.

The time to process query $Q2$ in CAFS is therefore

$$CAWORK = OVCPU + OVIO + BCOM + HJOIN$$
$$+ 2*RPROC + CPROC.$$

The time to perform the join in the host, HJOIN was discussed in the section on CASSM, and found to be 14.1 s.

RPROC, the time to scan the ROOMS relation and mark the first bit-map, is RPROC = DAVAC + DROT. CRPOC, the time to scan the COURSE relation, is

$$CPROC = DAVAC + 6*CYAVAC + 7*DROT.$$

The total time is therefore: CAWORK = (14.48-14.81) s. The response time is the same.

8) Conclusion: The results of this query are plotted in Fig. 2. The best performance is demonstrated by DIRECT. The associative disk and DBC systems also perform well because they do not rely significantly on the host. The CAFS and CASSM systems are handicapped by the fact that they must perform the join in the host.

The performance of RAP is very sensitive to whether the COURSE relation can be completely stored in the CCD data cells. In order to execute the join of the ROOMS and COURSE relations, RAP, like the associative disk and DBC systems, depends on rescanning the COURSE relation for each tuple of the ROOMS relation. While this approach limits the performance of the associative disk and DBC systems on join operations, it has a very significant impact on the performance of RAP when the size of the COURSE relation requires that the query be repeated for each section of the COURSE relation.

C. Aggregate Functions

An aggregate function is applied to a relation by first partitioning the relation based on the value of an attribute. Then

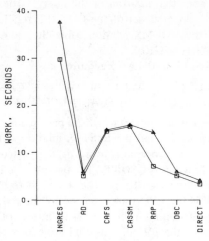

Fig. 2. Query $Q2$.

a function is applied to the tuples in each partition. The result is one value for each partition. The following query was chosen for the aggregate function query:

$Q3$: retrieve (GMASTER.acct, GMASTER.fund,
encumb = sum (GMASTER.encumb by
GMASTER.acct, G MASTER.fund)).

Relation GMASTER contains 194 tuples, 2 tuples per page, and resides on a single cylinder. There are 17 unique values for the (acct, fund) pair. The query returns to the user the 17 unique (acct, fund) pairs along with their associated sums.

The algorithm employed by INGRES for performing this query is to read the GMASTER relation once and retain in memory only the (encumb, acct, fund) attributes from each tuple. These are first stored in a temporary storage area and then sorted on (acct, fund). The sum is computed for each partition and the results are printed.

Since DIRECT utilizes simple, but general-purpose processors as cell processors, each cell processor can execute an algorithm similar to the one employed by INGRES. The entire query will be given to each cell processor which will perform the query on a subset of the GMASTER relation and report its partial results to the backend controller. After receiving the partial results from each participating cell processor, the controller will compute the final values for the 17 unique (acct, fund) pairs and return the results to the host for printing.

Since associative disks CAFS, DBC, and RAP do not directly support aggregate functions, either a host processor or backend controller must be used. The algorithm used by each of these machines is to first retrieve all the (acct, fund) pairs from the GMASTER relation and sort them to remove duplicates. This requires one backend communication and one pass over the data. Then the host (or backend controller) will issue the following query for each of the 17 unique values found:

Retrieve (GMASTER.encumb) where acct=value1
and fund=value2.

The host processor must then accumulate the sum and print it with the values of the acct and fund attributes on the user's terminal. This algorithm requires one backend communication and one pass over the GMASTER relation for each of the 17 unique values.

Since CASSM's cell processors are capable of summing attribute values, the host processor does not need to be used. The algorithm used is to find the first value of acct and set one of its mark bits to show it is participating in this sum and then mark every tuple that contains a pointer to that value of acct. This requires one pass over the data. During the next pass over the data, the first value of fund for the marked tuples is found and another mark bit is set. Then the CASSM cell processors will make another pass over the data in which the encumb attribute from each doubly marked tuple is summed. This algorithm continues by repeatedly finding the next unmarked value of the fund field for this value of acct. When all qualifying values of fund have been found, the algorithm is repeated until there are no more values of acct. In this particular query, the results are skewed because there was only one value for acct and 17 values for fund. Therefore, the algorithm takes one pass to mark all tuples for the one acct and then 34 passes for the 17 unique values of the fund field (two passes for each fund value).

Using the algorithms described above and similar techniques to those employed in Sections III-A and III-B, the performance of each database machine was evaluated for this query. The results are displayed in Fig. 3. From examination of this graph it is apparent that the CASSM and DIRECT machines give the best performance enhancement over a standard "fast INGRES" system. Even in the worst case (when the entire GMASTER relation must first be loaded into the cache) DIRECT is the fastest on this query. Notice, however, that RAP does not show the same degree of performance enhancement for this query. This seems to indicate that caching, when coupled with general purpose cell processors, works satisfactorily for this type of query. While DIRECT shows almost an order of magnitude improvement over INGRES on this query, that may not be too surprising since DIRECT has eight 1 MIP processors working on the query instead of just one. The results do indicate that parallelism can be successfully exploited to enhance query performance. The DBC also shows a significant degree of improvement. The associate disks, however, show almost no improvement for this query. This seems to be a consequence of the fact that the cell processors of these systems are not capable of summing attribute values and thus the host must handle each tuple twice.

IV. Conclusion

The purpose of this paper has been to gain insight into the possibility of the use of database machines and attempt a meaningful comparison between the different database machines which have been proposed.

Two query types previously defined are data-intensive and overhead-intensive queries. It has been shown [24] that database machines are not cost-effective if the application supported is mainly overhead-intensive queries.

In this paper it was shown that data-intensive queries can be performed very efficiently on database machines if the function performed on the data is a function the database

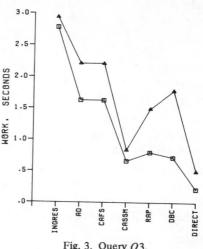

▲ WORST CASE TIME
☐ BEST CASE TIME

Fig. 3. Query $Q3$.

machine provides. For instance, if the function is a simple test for equality, the database machine can perform the query entirely in the backend system, thus causing a gain in the system's performance. However, if the queries are such that the function on the data is one that the database machine does not provide, as in the function of printing the data in query $Q1$, the host processor is heavily impacted and the database machine causes little gain in the system's performance.

The performance of DIRECT on queries $Q2$ and $Q3$ indicates that a database machine which employs a fast disk cache and general purpose query processors performs very well on nontrivial queries. The relatively poor performance of RAP on all three queries indicates that a caching database machine which relies on simple cell processors which must repeatedly scan the cache to perform the query is not a good design.

The poor performance of both DIRECT and RAP on query $Q1$ indicates that caching database machines are not a good design if the majority of transactions expected are simple retrievals from a single relation. For this case the associative disk and DBC systems are the best design. However, none of the proposed designs showed a significant performance improvement over the "fast INGRES" system. This seems to imply that if a database is structured so that the majority of simple queries can be processed quickly through the use of secondary indexes, then the benefits of a database machine may not be significant. However, for multirelation queries such as $Q2$ (for which INGRES employed a sophisticated join algorithm), the benefits of a database machine are very clear. One conclusion of this investigation is that more research is needed to marry the "on-the-disk-processing" of the associative disk, CASSM, and DBC systems for processing simple queries with an organization such as DIRECT for processing complex and multirelation queries.

One point which has not been covered in this paper is the effect of the SIMD (single instruction stream, multiple data stream) nature of all the database machines other than DIRECT. In [19] it is demonstrated that when a SIMD version of DIRECT is compared against a MIMD (multiple instruction stream, multiple data stream) version of DIRECT, the MIMD version of DIRECT outperforms the SIMD version by approximately a factor of four. The MIMD version of DIRECT permits several user queries to execute simultaneously. The significance of this is illustrated by query $Q2$ in which only three of DIRECT's cell processors were used to execute the query. In DIRECT the other five cell processors would at the same time be executing another query, thus improving overall system throughput.

APPENDIX
OVERVIEW OF PROPOSED DATABASE
MACHINE ARCHITECTURES

In this section each database machine is briefly described (for more details on each machine the reader is encouraged to examine the appropriate references) and its operation is illustrated with an example. That example is the following query QE:

retrieve (EMP.name, EMP.salary) where EMP.dept = 10.

Each machine is also illustrated with a figure. For comparison, Fig. 4 shows a standard computer system (i.e., one that does not include a backend machine). In that system the data blocks which are read are serially processed by the disk controller and the channel.

A. Associative Disks

Most earlier designs for hardware to enhance the performance of data management systems were associative disk designs. First proposed by Slotnik [4], the design is to attach a processor to each of the heads of a head-per-track device (disk or drum). Fig. 5 shows an associative disk system. The per-track processors are denoted as cell processors, and the processor that coordinates their activities is the controlling processor.

The cell processors can be loaded by the controlling processor with the value or values to search on, the search can take place in parallel, and the only data returned to the main computer are the records with the required values. As originally designed [4], the cell processors performed no arithmetic functions (e.g., sum, max, min, etc.). They were only search engines.

In Slotnik's associative disk system, query QE above would first be processed in the host machine and then a command would be sent to the associative disk to return all records in which the dept field = 10. The host processor would then format the tuples for printing, taking only the salary and name field from each tuple.

If all the cell processors attempt to return a value to the controlling processor at the same time serious performance problems can occur. There may be bus contention problems on the data bus from the cell processors to the controlling processor. If the system does not bottleneck at the bus, the controlling processor may have problems keeping up with the data rate of all of the cell processors transferring at once.

B. CASSM

CASSM (Context Addressed Segment Sequential Memory) is the data management machine developed at the University

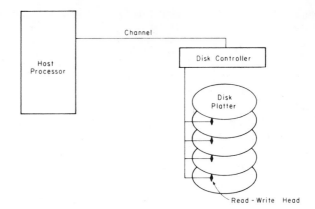

Fig. 4. Conventional system.

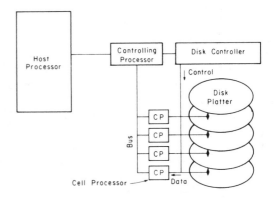

Fig. 5. Associative disks, CASSM, DBC.

of Florida. It was developed after associative disks, but before RAP, and represents a middle ground between them. CASSM is essentially a processor-per-head device, like an associative disk, but the processors have added capability in that they can perform a few arithmetic functions (integer sum, min, max).

The data are laid out in segments, where each segment is operated on by a single processor. The segments are not independent modules, however; data can freely migrate across segment boundaries. The processors operate under the direction of a separate controlling processor. On the fixed head disk, each segment is one disk track.

For our analysis we have assumed that CASSM is implemented on a moving-head disk. In this case its architecture closely resembles that of the associative disk, and is also represented by Fig. 5. The differences in the systems lie in the power and function of the cell and controlling processors.

In CASSM, the processors all execute the same function at the same time, where the functions are data-processing directives (search for, delete, add, etc.). The processors have a minimum of buffer space, and will only test for a single qualification on one attribute at a time. The system includes special-purpose functions for string searches, updates, inserts, and garbage collection. The processors also have the capability of following pointers within the records written on the disk, so the hierarchical and network data models can be supported as easily as the relational model. The capability exists to write instructions on the disk itself, to be read later by the processors to change their actions. This capability is used, for instance, to change the function performed after one pass over the data.

A significant feature of CASSM is that data are stored by attribute rather than by tuple or record. Each attribute is flagged with its name and attributes are grouped together in records. Each record is defined by delimiter fields and a record number. Groups of mark-bits are associated with both individual attributes and records. One of the mark-bits is a collection bit, which if set signifies that the CASSM processors should send the data to the host processor.

A data encoding algorithm is implemented in the hardware: each character-string value is stored only once, in a table of values. This table is stored as one of the segments. In the actual record, a pointer to the value is kept.

CASSM is limited in that only one attribute at a time may be tested or output. However, the testing of one attribute may be overlapped with the output of another.

The following explanation of the processing of a query in CASSM is based on a narrative of the execution of a similar query in [8]. To process QE, CASSM will, in the first cycle, mark all records that have the attribute-value pair (relation, EMP). Then in the next cycle, the attributes within the marked records are inspected and marked for collection if the record contains the attribute-value pair (dept, 10). The marked attributes "salary" are then returned to the host on the next cycle, while CASSM follows the name pointers in the marked attributes "name." The final cycle returns the name fields. The host machine must assemble the tuples to be printed by matching record numbers.

In the case that many values must be sent simultaneously to the controlling processor, the same performance problems occur as in the associative disk. CASSM deals with these problems by having the cell processors request the bus when they have a data item to transmit; if it is unavailable, the processor waits until it can transmit the data item it has before reading the next block. Therefore, bus contention problems may result in the query requiring several extra disk revolutions.

C. RAP

The relational associative processor (RAP) is similar to CASSM in that it was at first implemented by attaching multiple processors, one per head, to a fixed-head disk. However, RAP is very different from CASSM in that RAP supports only the relational data model.

There are three functional parts to the RAP design: the controller, the statistical unit, and the cells. On a fixed-head disk each cell is a disk track. There is one processor per cell. The controller communicates with the frontend computer and directs the actions of the cell processors and the statistical unit.

Fig. 6 shows the RAP system. The "controlling processor" box includes the statistical unit, and directs the functions of the cell processors. RAP is more powerful in function than CASSM because of the existence of the statistical unit, which performs more functions than the CASSM processors, and because each cell processor contains several comparator units, so several attributes can be tested simultaneously. RAP organizes data in relations which are stored in the data cells.

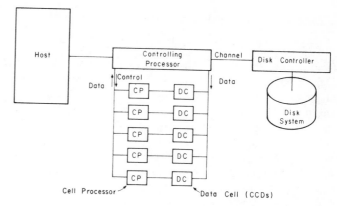

Fig. 6. RAP.

RAP, unlike CASSM and the associative disks, is a currently active research project. Subsequent implementations of RAP have used CCD's [6] and may eventually use random access memory [7] in place of the fixed-head disk. The version of RAP used in this discussion is that reported in [7]. It allows an individual cell to contain parts of several relations.

QE would be processed by RAP by passing the query to the RAP controller, which would determine which cells contain the "emp" relation, and direct the appropriate processors to return all tuples for which the dept = 10. The controlling processor would then pass these tuples to the host machine. In the case of bus contention the cell processors hold the data until the bus is free, thus potentially losing revolutions of the cells.

D. DBC

The data management machine being developed at Ohio State is called the Database Computer (DBC). Like CASSM, it is an attribute based system. It is a backend machine with seven major components, which are as follows.

1) The database command and control processor (DBCCP), which fields queries, communicates with the host machine, and controls the functioning of the other components.

2) The keyword transformation unit (KXU), which forms an encoded version of the keywords to send to the next unit.

3) The structure memory (SM), which takes the encoded keyword and looks it up in a directory to determine the positions (indices) of the matching attributes in secondary storage.

4) The structure memory information processor (SMIP), which performs set operations on the information from the structure memory.

5) The index translation unit (IXU) which decodes the information about the location of the attributes required in order to produce a physical address on the secondary memory.

6) The mass memory (MM), which is composed of moving head disks. Each disk has a processor per track (the track information processors) that will perform basic functions.

7) The security filter processor (SFP), which contains a capability list of who has permission to access what data.

In the block diagram Fig. 5, all of the above components except the MM are grouped together in the "controlling processor" box. The following explanation of the processing of query QE is derived from [11] and [12].

The DBCCP receives the command

Retrieve (name, salary) (relation = 'emp') & (dept = 10))

from the host processor. The predicate ((relation = 'emp') and (dept = 10)) is analyzed by the KXU, which determines if dept or relation are clustering keywords. In the case that they both are, the KXU transforms them into a coded, internal representation for look-up within the SM. The SM produces a series of index terms for relation = emp and for dept = 10 which are a coded representation of the cylinder numbers for the data. The SMIP performs a logical AND on the coded cylinder numbers so that only the coded cylinders for the data satisfying the predicate are passed to the next unit, the IXU. It transforms the internal coded representations into actual disk cylinder numbers, and passes the information to the DBCCP. The DBCCP then directs the MM to perform the given task on the proper cylinders (find those records with dept = 10 and relation = emp, and output the name and salary fields). The data go from the MM to the SFP which checks to determine if the access is proper. If so, the results are sent to the DBCCP, which sends them on to the host computer.

E. DIRECT

DIRECT is the backend data management machine under development at the University of Wisconsin—Madison (refer to Fig. 7). It is composed of a controller, an arbitrary number of query processors, a CCD cache consisting of a set of page frames, and mass storage. The page frames are connected through a special crosspoint switch [17] to the processors. This crosspoint switch permits each processor to read/write a different page simultaneously and two or more processors to read the same CCD page concurrently. The controller receives the query from the host computer and directs the processors to act on the proper pages. If the pages are not in the cache, the controller initiates a disk transfer and allocates page frames for them. Each processor can execute its instructions independently, so that it is possible that each processor can be executing a different query. The controller estimates the optimal number of processors to execute a query so that total system throughput is maximized. In [19] four alternative processor allocation strategies are analyzed.

To execute QE, DIRECT receives a compiled representation of the query from the host computer. After examining the query, the controller assigns a set of the available processors to work on the query. Through the use of the "next_page" operator [17], each processor examines a distinct subset of the EMP relation. After a processor makes a request to the controller for the "next_page" of the EMP relation, the controller returns the address of the appropriate page frame. The processor reads the page into its local buffer and scans the page for tuples which satisfy the query. Qualifying tuples are placed in an internal buffer. After the query processor finishes scanning a page of the source relation, it requests the next page from the controlling processor. When the query processor either fills its internal result buffer or receives a "no next page" notice, it writes the temporary relation page into a new CCD cell.

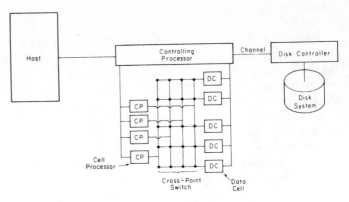

Fig. 7. DIRECT.

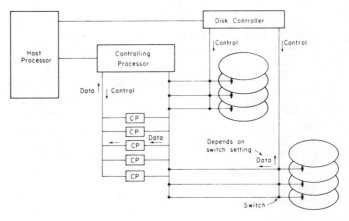

Fig. 8. CAFS.

F. CAFS

The content addressable file store (CAFS) consists of a filter box between the disks and the host computer. This box can simultaneously operate on 12 different data streams to allow only qualified tuples to pass through to the host. The system reported in [21] involves using disks whose track heads can be multiplexed to the CAFS box. They can also transfer data directly to the host, bypassing the CAFS system. Fig. 8 shows CAFS.

The first action by the host processor to run query QE with CAFS is to load the CAFS box with the search key (dept = 10) and to connect each of the disk tracks that contain the EMP relation to the box. Qualifying tuples will be passed to the host. Collisions that occur in CAFS will result in extra disk revolutions.

ACKNOWLEDGMENT

The authors would like to thank M. Stonebraker for his contributions to this paper.

REFERENCES

[1] M. Stonebraker et. al., "The design and implementation of INGRES," *TODS*, vol. 1, Sept. 1976.
[2] G. G. Langdon, "A note on associative processors for data management," *TODS*, vol. 3, pp. 148–158, June 1978.
[3] S. C. Lin, D.C.P. Smith, and J. M. Smith, "The design of a rotating associative memory for relational database applications," *TODS*, vol. 1, pp. 53–75, Mar. 1976.

[4] D. L. Slotnik, "Logic per track devices," in *Advances in Computers*, vol. 10, F. Alt, Ed. New York: Academic, 1970, pp. 291–296.

[5] E. A. Ozkarahan, S. A. Schuster, and K. C. Smith, "RAP—Associative processor for database management," in *AFIPS Conf. Proc.*, vol. 44, 1975, pp. 379–388.

[6] E. A. Ozkarahan, S. A. Schuster, and K. C. Sevcik, "Performance evaluation of a relational associative processor," *ACM Trans. Database Syst.*, vol. 2, June 1977; also, *Commun. Ass. Comput. Mach.*, vol. 17, July 1974.

[7] S. A. Schuster *et al.*, "RAP.2—An associative processor for data bases," in *Proc. 5th Annu. IEEE Symp. Comput. Arch.*, Apr. 1978.

[8] S.Y.W. Su and G. J. Lipovski, "CASSM: A cellular system for very large data bases," in *Proc. VLDB*, 1975, pp. 456–472.

[9] G. J. Lipovski, "Architectural features of CASSM: A context addressed segment sequential memory," in *Proc. 5th Annu. IEEE Symp. Comput. Arch.*, Apr. 1978.

[10] S.Y.W. Su, "Cellular-logic devices: Concepts and applications," *Computer*, pp. 11–28, Mar. 1979.

[11] J. Banerjee and D. K. Hsiao, "Performance study of a database machine in supporting relational databases," in *Proc. 4th Int. Conf. VLDB*.

[12] —, "The use of a nonrelational database machine in supporting relational databases," in *Proc. 4th Workshop Comput. Arch. Nonnumeric Processing*, Syracuse, NY, Aug. 1978.

[13] R. I. Baum, D. K. Hsiao, and K. Kannan, "The architecture of a database computer—Part I: Concepts and capabilities," Comput. Inform. Sci. Res. Cen., Ohio State Univ., Columbus, Tech. Rep. OSU-CISRC-TR-76-1, Nat. Tech. Inform. Service No. AD-A034-154.

[14] D. K. Hsiao and K. Kannan, "The architecture of a database computer—Part II: The design of structure memory and its related processors," Comput. Inform. Sci. Res. Cent., Ohio State Univ., Columbus, Tech. Rep. OSU-CISRC-TR-76-2, Nat. Tech. Inform. Service No. AD/A-035 178.

[15] —, "The architecture of a database computer—Part III: The design of the mass memory and its related components," Comput. Inform. Sci. Res. Cent., Ohio State Univ., Columbus, Tech. Rep. OSU-CISRC-TR-76-3, Nat. Tech. Inform. Service No. ADA-036 217.

[16] K. Kannan, "The design of a mass memory for a database computer," in *Proc. 5th Annu. Symp. Comput. Arch.*, Palo Alto, CA, Apr. 1978.

[17] D. J. DeWitt, "DIRECT—A multiprocessor organization for supporting relational database management systems," *IEEE Trans. Comput.*, vol. C-28, pp. 395–406, June 1979.

[18] —, "Query execution in DIRECT," in *Proc. ACM-SIGMOD 1979 Int. Conf. Management of Data*, May 1979, pp. 13–22.

[19] H. Boral and D. J. DeWitt, "Processor allocation strategies for multiprocessor database machines," *ACM Trans. Database Syst.*, vol. 6, June 1981.

[20] —, "Design considerations for dataflow database machines," in *Proc. 1980 ACM-SIGMOD Int. Conf. Management of Data*, May 1980.

[21] E. Babb, "Implementing a relational database by means of specialized hardware," *ACM Trans. Database Syst.*, vol. 4, pp. 1–29, Mar. 1979.

[22] G. F. Coulouris, J. M. Evans, and R. W. Mitchell, "Towards content addressing in databases," *Comput. J.*, vol. 15, no. 2, pp. 95–98, 1972.

[23] D. M. Ritchie, "A retrospective," *Bell Syst. Tech. J.*, vol. 57, part 2, pp. 1947–1969, July–Aug. 1978.

[24] P. Hawthorn and M. Stonebraker, "Performance analysis of a relational database management system," in *Proc. ACM-SIGMOD 1979 Int. Conf. Management of Data*, May 1979, pp. 1–12.

[25] P. Hawthorn, "Evaluation and enhancement of the performance of relational database management systems," Electron. Res. Lab., Univ. of California, Berkeley, Memo. M79-70.

Paula B. Hawthorn received the B.S. and M.S. degrees from the University of Houston, Houston, TX, in 1966 and 1974, respectively, and the Ph.D. degree from the University of California, Berkeley, in 1979.

Currently, she is a Research Computer Scientist at Lawrence Berkeley Laboratories, Berkeley, CA. Previously, she was with Britton-Lee, Inc., where she participated in the design of the first generally available database machine, the IDM 500. Her major research interests are in performance evaluation, distributed processing, and database machines.

David J. DeWitt was born in Akron, OH, on July 20, 1948. He received the A.B. degree in chemistry from Colgate University, Hamilton, NY, in 1970, and the M.S. and Ph.D. degrees in electrical and computer engineering from the University of Michigan, Ann Arbor, in 1971 and 1976, respectively.

Since 1976 he has been at the University of Wisconsin, Madison, where he is presently an Assistant Professor in the Department of Computer Sciences. His research interests include database management systems and computer architecture, particularly multiprocessor systems.

Dr. DeWitt is a member of Phi Beta Kappa and the Association for Computing Machinery.

INTELLIGENT ASSISTANTS FOR KNOWLEDGE AND INFORMATION RESOURCES MANAGEMENT

Charles H. Kellogg
System Development Corporation
Santa Monica, California

I   ABSTRACT

Work in Artificial Intelligence on knowledge based technology has produced a variety of practical applications while data management systems are used in almost every commercial enterprise of any significant size. Despite the advances in both data base and knowledge base technologies there is still a large gap between the capabilities of these tools and the "paperwork and information explosion" that faces modern society. Concern with this information access problem in the United States has lead to the creation of the new field of Information Resources Management and to Federal laws and executive orders aimed at reducing paperwork and promoting more effective management of information.

In this paper we outline the nature of this information management problem and describe certain AI and database technology that may help to close this information access gap. We introduce the notion of "Intelligent Assistants" for Information Resources Management(IRM) and describe how work on current approaches to "Knowledge Management" may lead to the technology necessary for the eventual creation of such intelligent assistants.

II   THE NEED

A. Information Resources Management

During the past 5-7 years considerable interest has arisen in managing information as a resource of large organizations. Generally the analogy is drawn with managing other, more traditional resources such as people, money, or facilities. Just as we plan, budget, and monitor the acquisition and disposition of those resources, so too should we manage the resources involved with collecting, storing, processing, transmitting, and using information. As a result, a new discipline of Information Resources Management (IRM) has appeared[2,3]. Many large organizations in government and industry are establishing corporate IRM programs to monitor information-related expenditures (including system development efforts) and to identify ways to improve the overall corporate position with regard to information resources.

In 1980 the U.S. Congress enacted the Paperwork Reduction Act of 1980 (P.L. 96-511)[4] which embraces the IRM concept openly and mandates that every Federal agency adopt the IRM approach. As a result, in attempting to implement the provisions of the Act, the Federal Government is beginning to grapple with some difficult management issues such as developing techniques for costing and valuing information, dealing with questions of data ownership, and locating potentially relevant information from vast data holdings collected by different parts of the organization for different purposes.

Several tools are under development to assist organizations in managing their information resources. The U.S. Office of Management and Budget is constructing a Federal Information Locator System (FILS) to serve as a central directory of information holdings throughout the Federal Government [5]. Other agencies and corporations are developing information resource directories which maintain pertinent data about the data elements, files, data bases, programs, systems, hardware, communication networks, people, funds, and other resources related to information [6,7,8,9,10,11]. Metadata bases such as these are the first steps in the potentially long process of providing support to the newly appointed information resources manager.

Concurrent with the development of the IRM approach, and in large part responsible for it, has been the development of distributed information systems and the decentralization of the systems development function.

B. Intelligent Information Resources Assistant

The IRM movement, in its relative infancy, has begun to address the need to identify and catalog the various information flows in helping the end-user identify what information is available. But providing assistance in understanding how to use the various resources effectively is a new problem which the IRM field has yet to address. Tools and mechanisms are needed to provide the user with a consistent, intelligent interface to the disparate information resources at hand. An Intelligent Information Resources Assistant (IIRA) is required to serve as librarian, research assistant, secretary, and staff member with regard to using information resources. The IIRA would help the end-user find relevant information, select suitable processing mechanisms, restructure the data for the selected processors, and combine the results from various sources or processes into meaningful information.

III   THE TECHNOLOGY

A.   A Knowledge Management System

An important if not essential tool for the development of an IIRA is a system for knowledge management. In "Managing Knowledge as a Corporate Resource"[12] Berry and Cook describe knowledge (as opposed to data or information) as a basic resource of an enterprise and outline a series of steps to achieve a corporate knowledge management capability. In "Knowledge Management: A Practical Amalgam of Knowledge and Data Base Technology"[13], Kellogg describes a strategy for transitioning from current Data Management to future Knowledge Management Systems.

At SDC we have constructed a series of increasingly more powerful and efficient Deductively Augmented Data Management (DADM) systems. The earliest system was described at the Very Large Database Conference in 1976[14].

Figure 1 illustrates the basic components of our system architecture. To a searching engine (preferably but not necessarily a relational data management system) and associated database we add a reasoning engine (deductive processor) and a knowledge base of application specific expertise. A user may access this combined system through a high level interface that accepts knowledge and questions in the form of logic statements and returns answers and explanations for those answers as derived facts and proofs respectively.

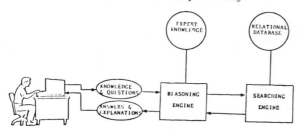

Figure 1.   The User/DADM Database Environment

The current version of our Knowledge Manager (KM-1) prototype is illustrated in Figure 2. KM-1 is composed of a logic-based deductive engine realized on a Lisp machine that plans and executes strategies for solution of deductive, database search, and compute problems related to answering a user's request for information. KM-1 can simultaneously access an external database and a local (Lisp machine) database to find and combine information necessary to create answers and explanations of those answers.

A user interacts with KM-1 via the Xerox 1100, bit-mapped display, mouse, and keyboard. A VAX 11/780 is used mainly as a file and print server for the 1100 and a Britton-Lee IDM-600 relational database machine is used to access large databases. The IDM-600 can provide access to as many as 50

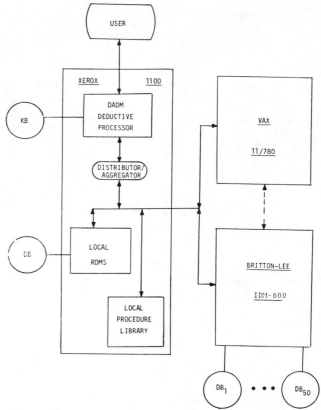

Figure 2.   Knowledge Manager (KM-1) System Environment

separate relational databases containing a maximum of 10 gigabytes of data. Communication between the Xerox-1100 and the VAX is by means of Ethernet. Direct communication between the 1100 and the IDM-600 is achieved by a serial RS-232 interface.

B.   An Intelligent Assistant for Managers

We will illustrate the operation of an application currently implemented within KM-1: The Manager's Assistant.

The Manager's Assistant consists of:

* A knowledge base comprising managerial expertise

* A manager-specific database of planned charges to projects

* A general MIS database of actual charges to projects

* A library of computable procedures for data analysis

Currently the Manager's Assistant contains knowledge about such concepts as "staffing", "plan/actual discrepancies", "personnel turnover" and many other notions that may be useful in assisting managers in their planning and project monitoring tasks.

Consider the case of a Manager who needs to find out if there are employees available who may be candidates for transfer from one particular project (PV) to another (CAD). This question may be input to the Manager's Assistant as follows:

(FIND EMP-1 IS ASSIGNED TO PV AND EMP-1
 CAN BE ASSIGNED TO CAD)

One employee is located (White) who meets these conditions. Figure 3 illustrates the information displayed on the Xerox 1100 as a result of deductively guided database search. To obtain this information the system first creates a "search/compute" plan consisting of thirteen constrained relations. Ten of the relations comprise a database access strategy that is distributed to the two database systems. The remaining relations are computed via Lisp procedures applied to tuples returned from database search.

The evidence tree shown in Figure 3

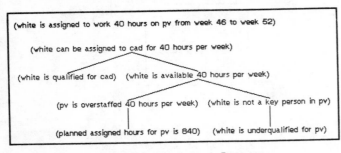

Figure 3. Manager's Assistant Response to the query "find employees assigned to PV who can be assigned to CAD".

displays the two top level conclusions (White is assigned to PV and he can be assigned to CAD) and lower level conclusions (White can be assigned to CAD because he is qualified and available; he is available because his project is overstaffed, he is not a key person on the project, and he is underqualified for his current position).

C. An Intelligent Assistant for Information Resources Managers

The manager's assistant described above includes expertise designed to support line managers in budgeting, planning, and project monitoring as well as staff assignment. An intelligent assistant for IRM will require similar expertise to support budgeting, planning, and monitoring of the use of information resources. Much additional expertise will have to be encoded about qualitative and quantitative attributes of various information sources to support reasoning about the value, credibility, and utility of those sources for meeting specific kinds of needs.

IV   SUMMARY

We have outlined some of the issues involved in achieving better computer-aided management of paperwork and other kinds of information resources.

Current approaches to knowledge management and deductive question answering provide the beginnings of a set of tools to support this enterprise but much remains to be done in capturing and utilizing the expertise necessary to create computer-based IRM assistants.

V   REFERENCES

[1] The Diebold Report: Information Resource Management, Infosystems, June, Oct., 1979.

[2] Information Resources Management: A Report of the Commission on Federal Paperwork, Government Printing Office, Washington, D.C.,052-003-00464-0, Sept., 1977.

[3] Horton, F. W., Information Resource Management: Concept and Cases, Association for Systems Management, Cleveland, Ohio, 1979.

[4] United States Public Law 96-511: The Paperwork Reduction Act of 1980, U.S. Congress, Dec. 11, 1980.

[5] United States Executive Order 12174: Paperwork, Nov. 30, 1979.

[6] An Information Management Study for Headquarters, Dept. of the Army, Arthur Young and Co. Washington, D.C., NTIS ADA 084841, June, 1979.

[7] The Design of an Information Management Program for Headquarters, Dept. of the Army, Arthur Young and Co. Washington, D.C., NTIS ADA 085936, Feb. 1980.

[8] Administration of Information Resources, Part I: Information Policy, Diebold Research Program, New York, Report 187S45, Sept. 1980.

[9] Administration of Information Resources, Part II: Implementing Computer Information Policy, Diebold Research Program, New York, Report 196S49, Feb. 1981.

[10] Meltzer, M., Information, The Ultimate Management Resource, AMACOM, New York, 1981.

[11] Horton, F. W. and Marchand, D.A., eds. Information Management in Public Administration, Information Resources Press, Arlington, Va. 1982.

[12] Berry, J.F., and Cook C.M., Managing Knowledge as a Corporate Resource, NTIS ADA029891, July, 1976.

[13] Kellogg, C., Knowledge Management: A practical amalgam of knowledge and database technology, in Proceedings of National Conference on Artificial Intelligence, Carnegie-Mellon University, 1982.

[14] Kellogg, C., Klahr, P., Travis, L., A Deductive Capability for Data Management, in Systems for Large Data Bases, Lockemann, P.C., Neuhold E.J., (eds.), North-Holland Publishing Co., 1976.

Multiprocessing of Combinatorial Search Problems

Benjamin W. Wah, Guo-jie Li, and Chee Fen Yu
Purdue University

Multiprocessor solutions to complex science and engineering problems require an effective representation of the problem and an efficient search. Functional requirements for search algorithms must open up a variety of architectures for any problem.

Multiprocessing refers to the concurrent execution of processes (or programs) in a computer hardware complex with more than one independent processing unit.[1] Conventionally, multiprocessing is defined as a centralized computer system with central processors, input-output processors, data channels, and special-purpose processors.

With the advent of VLSI technology, it has become cost effective to include a large number of general- and special-purpose processors in a multiprocessing system. The definition of *multiprocessing* has been extended to systems such as multiprocessors, systolic arrays, and dataflow computers. In this sense, parallel processing and multiprocessing can be considered synonymous. Examples of such systems range from the IBM 360 computers with channels, Illiac IV, Staran, Cm*, Trac, MPP, and the Cray X-MP to the latest fifth-generation computer system.

Major issues of multiprocessing

In using a multiprocessing system to solve a given problem, tremendous effort can be spent in designing a good parallel algorithm. The objective is to obtain an algorithm with a speedup proportional to the number of processors over the best available serial

algorithm. This must be done within the architectural constraints, and it involves trade-offs in computation time, memory space, and communications requirements.

The applicability of multiprocessing to the problem is also an important issue. The problem should be *polynomially solvable by a serial computer*. Intractable problems with complexity that is exponential in respect to problem size cannot be solved in polynomial time* unless an exponential number of processors are used.[2] This is, of course, technologically infeasible for large problems. For example, if the best serial algorithm requires 2^N microseconds to solve a problem of size N, it would require 2^{60} microseconds, or 366 centuries, to solve a problem of of size 60. Assuming that a linear speedup is possible, it would require 2^{50} processors to solve the problem in approximately one second, and 2^{40} processors to solve the problem in 20 minutes. For intractable problems, approximate solutions should be used in order to complete the algorithm in a reasonable time.

Multiprocessing is generally used to improve the computational efficiency of solving a given problem, *not to extend the solvable problem space of the problem*. Suppose that it takes N^k units of time to solve a problem of size N, where k is a constant (≥ 1) Assuming a linear speedup, a parallel algorithm with N processors in N^k units of time can solve problem of size $N^{(1+1/k)}$. For $k=3$, this size is $N^{1.33}$. Similarly, for a serial algorithm that takes k^N, $k>1$ units of time to solve a problem, the solvable problem size

---

*Saying that a problem is intractable with an exponential complexity implies that the best parallel algorithm cannot have a polynomial complexity with a polynomial number of processors. Supposing this is false, a serial simulation of this parallel algorithm can solve the problem in polynomial time, hence contradicting the fact that the problem has an exponential complexity.

Reprinted from *Computer*, Volume 18, Number 6, June 1985, pages 93-108. Copyright © 1985 by The Institute of Electrical and Electronics Engineers, Inc.

with N processors in k^N units of time is $N + \log_k N$. For a large N, this size is approximately N.

Search problems. This article examines the use of multiprocessing in solving combinatorial search problems. Combinatorial search problems involve the search for one or more optimal or suboptimal solutions in a defined problem space. They can be classified as *decision* problems, which find solutions satisfying a given set of constraints, or as *optimization* problems, which seek solutions satisfying the constraints and also optimizing an objective function. Examples include proving theorems, playing games, evaluating a logic program, solving a database query, designing a computer system, assigning registers for a compiler, finding the shortest path in a graph, solving a mathematical programming problem, and searching for a permutation order to sort a set of numbers. These problems occur in a wide spectrum of engineering and science applications, including artificial intelligence and operations research.

A search problem can be represented as an acyclic graph* or as a search tree. These representations are characterized by a root node with no edge entering it and by one or more terminal nodes with no exiting edges. In a search graph, one or more edges can enter any node except the root; in a search tree, each node except the root has exactly one edge entering it.

An edge in a search graph represents an assignment of value to an unassigned parameter. This can be illustrated by the 0/1 knapsack problem, in which N objects are to be packed into a knapsack. Object i has a weight w_i, and the knapsack has a capacity M. If object i is placed in the knapsack, then a profit p_i is earned. The objective is to fill the knapsack so as to maximize profit. The unassigned parameters are the set of objects that have not been considered. In expanding a node, an object, say i, is selected,

*An acyclic graph is one without cycles. In general, some graphs with cycles can be searched, but this topic is beyond the present scope.

and two alternatives are created: (a) object i is included in the knapsack, and (b) object i is not included.

The nonterminal nodes in a search tree can be classified as AND nodes and OR nodes. An AND node represents a (sub)problem that is solved only when all its children have been solved. An example of an AND node is

Search problems can be represented as acyclic graphs or search trees.

one that adds the solutions from all subtrees expanded from this node. In contrast, an OR node represents a (sub)problem that is solved if any one of its children are solved. (The definitions of AND and OR nodes are taken from Martelli and Montanari[3]; the roles of the AND and OR nodes in an AND/OR tree are reversed in Nilsson's definitions.[4]) Expanding a 0/1 knapsack problem by choosing an object to be included or excluded corresponds to transforming the problem from one state to another until the goal state is achieved. In this sense, the resulting tree contains only OR nodes.

To facilitate the design of multiprocessing systems for solving a search problem, the problem is transformed into one of the following paradigms according to the functions of the nodes.[4,5]

(1) *AND tree:* All nonterminal nodes in the search tree are AND nodes. An example is a divide-and-conquer algorithm that decomposes a problem into subproblems and solves the original problem by combining the solutions of the subproblems.

(2) *OR tree:* all nonterminal nodes in the search tree are OR nodes. Branch-and-bound algorithms that systematically prune unnecessary expansions belong to this class.

(3) *AND/OR graph:* The nonterminal nodes are either AND or OR nodes. Game trees and logic programs can be represented as AND/OR trees. Dynamic programming problems can be solved as acyclic AND/OR-graph searches.

A node is *active* if its solution value has not been found; otherwise, it is *terminated*. In a serial algorithm, the set of active nodes is maintained in a single list. A heuristic value defined by a heuristic function is computed for each node. The active node with the minimum heuristic value is always expanded first. A search is called a *depth-first search* if the negation of the level number is used as the heuristic function. In this case, the nodes in the active list are expanded in a last-in/first-out order. A search is called a *breadth-first search* if the level number is used as the heuristic function. In this case, the nodes in the active list are expanded in a first-in/first-out order. Lastly, a lower bound can be computed for each node in the active list. This represents the lower bound of the best solution that can be obtained from this node. By using the lower-bound function as the heuristic function, a *best-first search* expands the node with the minimum lower bound.

Dominance relations. To reduce the search space, unnecessary expansions can be pruned by dominance relations. When a node P_i dominates another node P_j, it implies that the subtree rooted at P_i contains a solution node with a value no more (or less) than the minimum (or maximum) solution value of the subtree rooted at P_j.

As an example, consider two assignments, P_1 and P_2, on the same subset of the objects to be packed into a knapsack in the 0/1 knapsack problem. If the total profit of the objects assigned to the knapsack for P_1 exceeds that of P_2 and the total weight of the objects assigned in P_1 is less than that of P_2, then the best solution expanded from P_1 dominates P_2.

A special case of the special class dominance tests is the class of *lower-bound tests,* which are used in branch-and-bound algorithms to solve minimization problems. If a solution with value v has already been found, then all active nodes with lower bounds greater than v can be terminated, since they would not lead to better solutions. The minimum of the solution values obtained at any time can be conveniently kept in a single location, called the *incumbent*.

Problem representation. A problem can be represented in multiple forms. For example, the knapsack problem can be represented in an OR tree and solved by a branch-and-bound algorithm[6] or formulated in dynamic programming and solved by an acyclic AND/OR-graph search. As another example, the search of the extrema from a set of numbers can be solved by either a divide-and-conquer (AND-tree) algorithm[7] or a decision-tree (OR-tree) search. In general, the search procedures for various representations are equivalent, in the sense that they generate the same solution(s). Kumar and Kanal have shown that various heuristic search procedures for state-space representations (e.g., A*, SSS*[4]), AND/OR-graph searches (e.g., AO*[4]), and game-tree searches (e.g., α-β[8]) are equivalent to branch-and-bound searches with dominance tests.[9]

Efficiency in solving a given problem depends on the representation. Although efficient search procedures have been established for some problems, the general question of deciding which representation leads to an efficient search is still open, especially in multiprocessing. Although combinatorial search algorithms have relatively large computational overheads, compared with the input-output overheads, efficient architectures for evaluating various search algorithms differ. It is difficult to map search algorithms to general-purpose architectures, since they have different architectural requirements.

Our objective is, therefore, *to obtain the functional requirements of various search algorithms.* Based on these requirements, a general-purpose architecture can be assessed as to whether it suits a given search algorithm and the most efficient way of mapping the algorithm can be developed. Special-purpose architectures can also be developed from the functional requirements.

In presenting the performance results in this article, we usually as-

sume synchronous models, although the search algorithm can be evaluated asynchronously. The performance results for synchronous models form a lower bound to those of asynchronous models. The article also covers the effects of heuristic and approximation functions on time and space efficiency and the important problems in selecting the nodes for expansion and defining the level of granularity.

Divide-and-conquer algorithms

The divide-and-conquer method is a well-known AND-tree representation that is used to solve many combinatorial search problems. Since a subproblem cannot be solved until all its descendants have been solved, divide-and-conquer algorithms can be viewed as bottom-up search procedures of an AND tree. There is no problem in deciding which node to evaluate in any step, as every node in the tree must be evaluated.

Studies conducted on parallel processing of divide-and-conquer algorithms can be classified into three types.

In the first, multiprocessors are connected in the form of a tree, especially a binary tree, to exploit the potential parallelism of divide-and-conquer algorithms.[10] A tree machine has a simple interconnection that is suitable for VLSI implementation. However, the root processor is often a bottleneck for such problems as merge sorting, and the fixed structure is not flexible enough.

The second approach uses a virtual tree machine[11] consisting of a number of processors with private memory. The processors are connected by an interconnection network, such as the binary *n*-cube, and a suitable algorithm to decide when and where each subproblem should be solved. The hierarchy of process communications in divide-and-conquer algorithms allows them to be mapped effectively onto this architecture.

The third type is a variation of the above approaches. Here, all processors are connected to a common

memory through a common bus.[12] Since data must be shared during execution, the memory or bus can become a bottleneck. Multimodule memory, augmented by caches, has been proposed to reduce the memory and bus contentions.

The functional requirement for evaluating an AND tree is, therefore, an interconnected conglomerate of processors. It is important to determine the *granularity of parallelism*—the minimum size of a subproblem that a processor evaluates in order to achieve optimal performance. The generally used criterion is processor utilization, KT^2, or AT^2, where K is the number of processors, T is the computational time, and A is the area of a VLSI implementation. If granularity is large, then the processors can be loosely coupled; otherwise, tight coupling, as in systolic arrays, might be necessary.

Studies of the complexity of divide-and-conquer algorithms in an SIMD model[12] and the conditions that assure optimal processor use[13] suggest, generally speaking, that a parallel search of an AND tree can roughly be divided into three phases: start-up, computation, and wind-down. In the start-up phase, the problem is split and the tasks diffuse through the network. During the computation phase, all processors are kept busy until the number of tasks in the system is less than the number of processors. In the wind-down phase, the results are combined, and some processors might be idle. Processor utilization depends on the ratio between the amount of time spent in the computation phase and that spent in the other phases. The time complexity of searching a binary AND tree of N leaves can be formulated in the following recursive equation:

$$T(N) = S(N) + 2T\left(\frac{N}{2}\right) + C(N) \quad N > 1$$
$$T(1) = O(1) \qquad (1)$$

where $S(N)$ and $C(N)$ are the complexity of the start-up and wind-down phases. The granularity that results in the optimal processor utilization is related to the complexity of $S(N)$ and $C(N)$. In finding the sum or the maximum of N numbers, $S(N) + C(N) = O(1)$; in using $N/(\log_2 N)$, processors achieve the maximum utilization.[14] In sorting N numbers, $S(N) + C(N) = O(N)$, and $\log_2 N$ processors should be used to maximize processor utilization. We have studied the *asymptotic processor utilization* and found that $N/\log_2 N$ is a threshold when $S(N) + C(N) = O(N)$.[15] For k (a function of N) processors, the processor utilization is one, between zero and one, or zero when the limiting ratio of k and $N/\log_2 N$ is zero, greater than zero, or approaching infinity, respectively.

Since processor utilization increases with a decreasing number of processors, it is not an adequate measure of the effects of parallel processing. A more appropriate measure is the KT^2 criterion, which considers both processor utilization and computational time. We have proven that the asymptotic optimal number of processors to minimize KT^2 in parallel divide-and-conquer algorithms is $\Theta(N/\log_2 N)$, when $S(N) + C(N) = O(1)$.[15] Simulations have verified that the optimal number of processors is either exactly $N/(\log_2 N - 1)$ or very close to this value.

Branch-and-bound algorithms

A branch-and-bound algorithm is a systematic search of an OR tree.[16] It is characterized by four constituents: a branching rule, a selection rule, an elimination rule, and a termination condition.

The selection rule examines the list of active subproblems (nodes) and selects one for expansion based on the heuristic value. For a serial search, the minimum number of nodes is expanded under a best-first strategy, provided all lower bounds are distinct.[16] This is achieved at the expense of increased memory space, as there are a large number of concurrently active subproblems. The algorithm is terminated when all active subproblems have been either expanded or eliminated.

The elimination rule prunes unnecessary expansions by means of lower-bound and dominance tests. For lower-bound tests, the incumbent z holds the value of the best solution found so far in the search. In minimization problems, a lower bound is calculated for each subproblem when it is created. A subproblem cannot lead to the optimal solution if its lower bound exceeds the incumbent; such subproblems can be eliminated from further consideration. This lower-bound test can be relaxed by defining an *allowance function,* $\epsilon(z)$. Subproblems with lower bounds greater than $z - \epsilon(z)$ are eliminated, resulting in a suboptimal solution that deviates from the optimal solution by at most $\epsilon(z_O)$, where z_O is the value of the optimal solution.[17] An example of an allowance function is the relative error deviation; a subproblem is terminated if its lower bound is greater than $z/(1 + \epsilon)$. An allowance function is very effective in reducing the computational complexity of branch-and-bound algorithms. We have found that for some NP-hard problems under best-first searches, a linear reduction in accuracy of the solution results in an exponential reduction in the computational overhead.[18,19]

Each of the four constituents of a serial branch-and-bound algorithm can be implemented by means of parallel processing.

(1) Parallel selection of subproblems: Multiple subproblems with the smallest heuristic values can be selected for expansion.

(2) Parallel expansion of subproblems.

(3) Parallel termination tests and update of the incumbent.

(4) Parallel elimination tests: These include the lower-bound and dominance tests.

We have studied the performance bounds of parallel branch-and-bound search, assuming (1) that only lower-bound tests are active, (2) that there is a single shared memory, (3) that no approximations are allowed, (4) that the subproblems are expanded synchronously, and (5) that the heuristic function is unambiguous.[20]

Let $T_b(k)$ (resp. $T_d(k)$) be the number of iterations required to obtain the optimal solution under a best-first (resp. depth-first) search with k processors. The following bounds have been derived:

(1) For a parallel best-first search, if the value of optimal-solution nodes differs from the lower bounds of other nodes, then

$$\left\lceil \frac{T_b(1)\text{-}1}{k} + 1 \right\rceil \leq T_b(k)$$

$$\leq \left\lceil \frac{T_b(1)}{k} + \frac{k\text{-}1}{k}h \right\rceil \quad (2)$$

where h is the maximum number of levels in the branch-and-bound tree.

(2) For a parallel depth-first search, if all solution nodes exist at level h, then

$$\left\lceil \frac{T_b(1)\text{-}1}{k} + 1 \right\rceil \leq T_d(k)$$

$$\leq \left\lceil \frac{T_d(1)}{k} + \frac{(k+1)\cdot(c+1)}{k}h \right\rceil \quad (3)$$

where c is the number of distinct incumbents obtained during the search. A similar equation can be also derived for parallel breadth-first searches. Equations (2) and (3) show almost a k-time reduction in the number of iterations when parallel processing is applied on the same search strategy and when $T_b(1)/k$ is large.

The best search strategy depends on the accuracy of the problem-dependent lower-bound function. Very inaccurate lower bounds are not useful in guiding the search; very accurate lower bounds prune most unnecessary expansions. In both cases, the number of subproblems expanded by depth-first and best-first searches does not differ greatly. A depth-first search is better because it requires less memory space, in proportion to the height of the search tree. When the accuracy of the

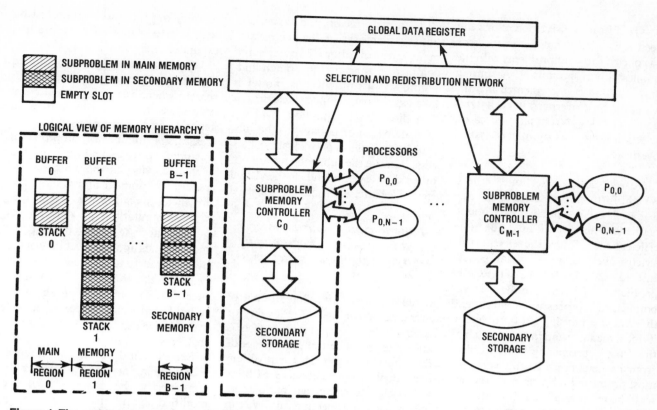

Figure 1. The architecture and logical structure of MANIP—a multiprocessor for parallel best-first search.

lower-bound function is moderate, a best-first search performs better. In this case, a good memory management system is necessary to support the memory space required.

Several architectures based on implicit enumeration have been proposed for parallel processing of branch-and-bound algorithms. These architectures delegate a subproblem to each processor, which reports to its parent processor when the evaluation is complete.[21] The limited degree of communication causes some processors to work on tasks that a better interconnection network would eliminate. Moreover, implicit enumeration is wasteful. Imai et al.[22] and El-Dessouki and Huen[23] have investigated parallel branch-and-bound algorithms based on a general-purpose network architecture with limited memory space and slow inter-processor communication. They used depth-first search, due to memory limitations.

Problems more efficiently evaluated by a parallel best-first search require more complex architectures. The de-sign problems are a selection of sub-problems with the minimum lower bounds and management of the required large memory space.

Manip – Multiprocessor for parallel best-first search with lower bound tests only. Figure 1 shows the architecture of Manip.[18,24] It consists of five major components: a selection and redistribution network, secondary storage, processors, global data register, and subproblem memory controllers.

The selection network selects sub-problems with the minimum lower bounds for expansion in each iteration and connects the memory controllers for load balancing. Secondary storage holds excess subproblems that cannot be stored in the memory controllers. The memory controllers manage the local list of subproblems, maintain the secondary storage, and communicate with other controllers through the selection and redistribution network. The processors are general-purpose computers for partitioning subproblems and evaluating lower bounds.

The global data register is accessible to all memory controllers and contains the value of the incumbent. To avoid contention during updates, this register can be implemented by a broadcast bus or a sequential associative memory. In the latter case, the minimum is found when the values of the feasible solutions are shifted out bit-serially and synchronously from all processors.

Two difficult issues must be solved in a parallel best-first search. First, the k subproblems with the smallest lower bounds must be selected from the N active subproblems in the system. Selection by software requires a time overhead of $O(N)$ in each iteration. A practical multistage selection network for selecting k elements from N elements requires $O(\log_2 N \log_2 k)$ time complexity and $O(N \cdot \log_2^2 k)$ hardware complexity.[25]

A single-stage selection network can also be used. One or more subproblems with the minimum lower bounds in each processor are sent to the neighboring processors and inserted into their local lists. A maximum of

$(k-1)$ shift-and-insert operations are needed to ensure that each processor has one of the k subproblems with the smallest lower bounds.[18] Assuming that insertion is implemented in software, the time overhead in each iteration is $O(k \cdot \log_2 N)$. In all these cases, selection represents significant system overhead.

No-wait policy. Selection overhead is high; furthermore, the selection rule is based on a fallible lower-bound heuristic. Therefore, it might be more efficient not to follow the selection rule strictly; We propose a no-wait policy. Instead of waiting for one of the k subproblems with the smallest lower bounds, each processor would expand the "most promising" subproblem in its local memory and initiate a fetch of the "most promising" subproblem from its neighbors. In this case, the most promising subproblem is the one with the minimum lower bound.

When the k most promising subproblems are randomly distributed among the processors, the average fraction of processors containing one or more of the most promising subproblems is at least 0.63,[18] resulting in a speedup proportional to $0.63k$. However, as expansion proceeds, the distribution might become nonrandom and require an interconnection network to randomize the distributions and balance the workload in the system. Experimental results on vertex-cover and knapsack problems have shown that the number of subproblems expanded increases by only about 10 percent when the above scheme replaces a complete selection. The performance is almost as good as that of a complete selection when the processors expand subproblems synchronously and perform one shift-and-insert operation for each subproblem expanded. The shift-and-insert operation can be overlapped with subproblem expansions and supported by a unidirectional ring network.

A second issue in implementing a best-first search lies in the management of the large memory space required. The multiprocessing model used to study this problem comprises a CPU, a main memory, a slower secondary memory, and a secondary-memory controller. The expected completion time of the branch-and-bound algorithm on this model is taken as the performance measure.

A direct implementation involving an ordered list of pointers to the subproblems results in poor locality of access, because the subproblems are not ordered by lower bounds in the virtual space. A better alternative is a special

Experimental results on integer and vertex-cover programming verify the algorithm's usefulness.

virtual memory that tailors its control strategies according to the locality of access.[26] However, this approach is inflexible, because the parameters of the control strategies are problem dependent. The inadequacies of these approaches are due, again, to strict adherence to the selection rule. We can also apply the no-wait policy here; it has resulted in the design of a modified branch-and-bound algorithm.[27]

A modified algorithm. In this modified algorithm, the range of possible lower bounds is partitioned into b disjoint regions (Figure 1). The subproblems in each region are maintained in a separate list. The top portion of each list resides in the main memory, and the rest resides in the secondary memory. Due to the high overhead of secondary-storage accesses, subproblems in a list are expanded in a depth-first manner. To implement the no-wait policy, the *modified selection rule* chooses for expansion the subproblem in the main memory with the smallest lower bound. Since subproblems within a list are not sorted, the *lower-bound elimination rule* has to be modified.

Assuming that the new incumbent lies in the range of list ℓ, all lists with indices greater than ℓ are eliminated. Subproblems in list ℓ with lower bounds greater than the incumbent are eliminated only when they are moved to the main memory during the expansion of list ℓ. As a result, it is necessary to carry out the lower-bound test on each selected subproblem before it is expanded.

When one list is used, the modified algorithm is identical to a depth-first search; when infinity lists are used, it is identical to a best-first search. In general, as the number of lists increases, the number of subproblems expanded decreases and the overhead of the secondary-memory accesses increases. The number of lists should be chosen to maximize the overlap between computations and secondary-memory accesses. This overlap, in turn, depends upon the accuracy of the lower-bound function and the access times of the main and secondary memories. The accuracy of the lower-bound function is problem dependent and can be estimated from sample problems of the same type.

Experimental results on integer-programming and vertex-cover problems verify the usefulness of the modified algorithm. For vertex-cover problems, the lower-bound function is very accurate, so a depth-first search results in the best performance. For integer-programming problems, the lower-bound function is less accurate. As a result, more stacks (two to three) achieve best performance. The improvement in paging overhead over a direct implementation of the best-first search can exceed a factor of 100.

Experience with Manip and prior studies show three functional requirements for efficient evaluation of branch-and-bound algorithms with only lower-bound tests: a loosely coupled interconnection of processors with load-balancing capability, a method of concurrent update, and broadcast of the incumbent.

Parallel dominance tests. When general dominance tests are used, it is necessary to keep the set of *current dominating nodes* (denoted by N_d) in memory. These are nodes that have been generated but not yet dominated. In general, N_d can be larger than the set of active nodes. A newly generated node, P_i, has to be compared with all nodes in N_d to see whether P_i or any nodes in N_d are dominated.

If N_d is small, it can be stored in a bank of global data registers. However, centralized comparisons are inefficient when N_d is large. A large N_d should then be partitioned into k subsets, $N_d^{20}, \ldots, N_d^{k-1}$, and distributed among the local memories of the k processors. A subproblem, $P_{i,j}$, generated in processor i, is first compared with N_d^i; any subproblems in N_d^i dominated by $P_{i,j}$ are removed. If $P_{i,j}$ is not dominated by a subproblem in N_d^i, it is sent to a neighboring processor and the process repeats. If it has not been dominated by any node in N_d, $P_{i,j}$ eventually returns to processor i and is inserted into N_d^i.

The functional requirements for implementing parallel dominance tests depend on the size of N_d and the structure of the dominance relation. When $|N_d|$ is small, broadcast buses or global registers carry important unstructured dominance tests, in which a dominance relation can exist between any pair of nodes. For structured dominance tests, it might be possible to partition the search tree and localize the dominance tests, but this poses additional complexity on the system architecture. On the other hand, when $|N_d|$ is large, it is necessary to partition N_d into subsets and to perform the dominance tests in parallel. This results in tight coupling of the processors, because the transfer of newly generated nodes between processors must be synchronized and overlapped with computations.

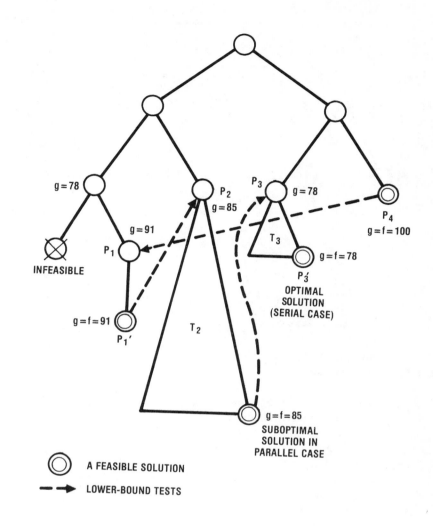

Figure 2. Example of a detrimental anomaly under a parallel depth-first search (allowance function $\epsilon = 0.1$).

Anomalies of parallelism in branch-and-bound algorithms. Since it is possible to overlap the communication overheads with computations for the various search strategies, the speedup of branch-and-bound algorithms can be measured by the ratio of the number of iterations of the best serial algorithm to that of the parallel algorithm under synchronous operations.

A k-fold speedup is expected when k processors are used. However, simulations have shown that the number of iterations for a parallel branch-and-bound algorithm using k processors can be more than the number of iterations of the best serial algorithm (this

phenomenon is a *detrimental anomaly*); less than one-kth of the number of iterations of the best serial algorithm (an acceleration anomaly); or less than the number of iterations of the best serial algorithm, but more than one-kth of the number of iterations of the best serial algorithm (a deceleration anomaly).[20,28,29]

It is desirable to discover conditions that preserve acceleration anomalies, eliminate detrimental anomalies, and minimize deceleration anomalies.

Figure 2 gives an example of a detrimental anomaly. Let $g(P_i)$ be the lower bound of subproblem P_i and $f(P_i)$ be the value of the best solution

that can be obtained from P_i. Suppose that the best serial algorithm for the problem is a depth-first search. In a serial depth-first search, subtree T_2 is terminated by the lower-bound test of P_1' as $f(P_1'/(1+\epsilon) \leq g(P_2)$, when $\epsilon = 0.1$. In a parallel depth-first search with two processors, a feasible solution, P_4, which terminates P_1 and P_1', is found in the second iteration. Consequently, P_2 is not eliminated, since P_1 is not generated and $f(P_4)/(1+\epsilon) > g(P_2)$. Subtree T_2 has to be expanded; this eventually terminates subtree T_3. If T_2 is much larger than T_3, the time it takes to expand T_2 by using two processors exceeds the time to expand T_3 by using one processor.

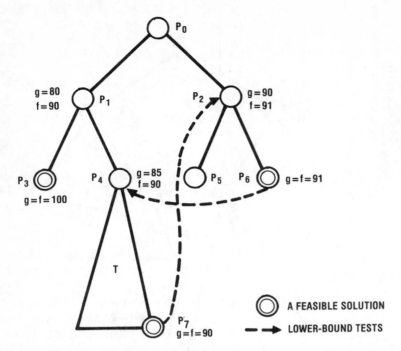

Figure 3. Example of an acceleration anomaly under a parallel depth-first search (allowance function $\epsilon = 0.1$).

Figure 3 shows an example of an acceleration anomaly. Subtree T will be expanded in a serial depth-first search, as $f(P_3)/(1+\epsilon) > g(P_4)$ when $\epsilon = 0.1$, but not in a parallel depth-first search with two processors, since P_2, and hence T, will be terminated by the lower-bound test with P_6: $(f(P_6)/(1+\epsilon) < g(P_4))$. If T is very large, an acceleration anomaly will occur.

A heuristic function is *unambiguous* if all nodes in the search tree have distinct heuristic values. An elimination rule (lower-bound or dominance tests) is said to be *consistent* with the heuristic function if the elimination of P_j by P_i implies that P_i is selected before P_j in a serial search. Anomalies are caused by a combination of reasons: (1) there are multiple solution nodes; (2) the heuristic function is ambiguous; and (3) the elimination rule is not consistent with the heuristic function.[2] These conditions cause the tree to be searched in a different order in the serial and parallel cases.

We have discussed the conditions sufficient for eliminating detrimental anomalies and the conditions necessary to preserve acceleration anomalies in a previous article[20]; a brief summary is given here. Assume that the same search strategy is used in serial and parallel cases. For branch-and-bound algorithms with dominance tests, only a best-first search with the following conditions guarantees that detrimental anomalies will not occur:

(1) The heuristic function is unambiguous.

(2) Approximations are not allowed.

(3) The dominance relation is consistent with the heuristic function.

Ambiguity in the heuristic function can be resolved by augmenting the original heuristic function with a tie-breaking rule, say, by level and left-right orientation. For most problems, dominance relations that are consistent with the heuristic function can be designed. Acceleration anomalies can occur in one of following cases: when a breadth-first or depth-first search is used; when some nodes have identical lower bounds; when the dominance relation is inconsistent with the heuristic function; when multiple lists of subproblems are used; or when a suboptimal solution is sought.

AND/OR-tree search

Searching an AND/OR tree is more complex than searching an AND tree or an OR tree. An AND/OR tree is searched in two phases. The first is a top-down expansion, as in searching an OR tree; the second is a bottom-up evaluation, as in searching an AND tree. Due to the existence of both AND and OR nodes, a parallel search algorithm should combine the features of AND- and OR-tree searches. The presence of OR nodes demands that a good selection strategy be developed. The granularity of parallelism, like that of parallel divide-and-conquer algorithms, is an important consideration. Specific restrictions on a given problem, such as pruning rules, must be considered. These rules are usually more complicated, as more information is involved in the process.

When two AND/OR subtrees are searched concurrently, more work than necessary might be performed if pruning information obtained from one processor is unavailable to the other processor. The extra work is called *information deficiency overhead*. Pruning information can be exchanged by messages or through a common memory. Increased communication overhead needed for pruning is called *information transfer overhead*. In general, a tradeoff exists between the information-deficiency and information-transfer overheads. A good parallel AND/OR-tree search should weigh the tradeoffs—the merits of parallel processing against the communications overhead of obtaining the necessary pruning information.

Parallel α-β search. A two-person game between players MAX and MIN can be represented in a game tree in which the moves of MAX and MIN are put in alternate levels of the tree. In the corresponding AND/OR tree, OR modes represent board positions resulting from MAX's moves and AND nodes represent positions resulting from MIN's moves. All nonterminal MAX nodes take the maximum score of their children, while nonterminal MIN nodes take the minimum score. This *minimax* procedure is used to find the best move for the MIN player represented as the root.[5]

A well-known technique to improve the efficiency of a minimax search is α-β *pruning.*[4] This technique uses two parameters, α and β, to define the search window. The α carries the lower bound of the MAX nodes; β represents the upper bound of the MIN nodes. The game tree has solution values defined for the terminal nodes only and is searched in a depth-first fashion.

In expanding a MIN node, if the value returned by any of its children is less than α, then this node can be pruned without further expansion. In this case, the value returned by this node to its parent—a MAX node—is less than α and another MAX node with value equal to α (according to the definition of α) already exists. The β is updated when a MIN node with a smaller value is found.

On the other hand, in expanding a MAX node, if the value returned by any of its children is greater than β, then this node can also be pruned. The α is updated when a MAX node with a larger value is found. The search is terminated when all nodes have been either pruned or expanded. The α-β search performs better when the initial search window is small.

The cost of searching a game tree depends on the distribution of values of the terminal nodes. The tree is said to have a *best-case ordering* if the first (or leftmost) branch from each node leads to the best value; it has a *worst-case ordering* if the rightmost branch from each node leads to the best value.

A number of parallel game-tree search techniques have been developed.[30] In the *parallel aspiration search,* the α-β window is divided into nonoverlapped subintervals, which are independently searched by multiple processors; Baudet reported that the maximum expected speedup is around five or six, regardless of the number of processors.[31] The speedup is limited because at least $W^{\lceil h/2 \rceil} + W^{\lceil h/2 \rceil} - 1$ nodes must be evaluated for a uniform

tree of depth h and constant width W, even when α and β are chosen to be the optimal minimax values.[8] Acceleration anomalies can also occur when the number of processors is small, say two or three.

Finkel and Fishburn have proposed a *tree-splitting algorithm* that maps a look-ahead tree onto a processor tree with the same interconnection structure.[32] The information-transfer overhead is small, due to the close match between the communications requirements and the interconnections. However, this is a brute-force

---

An efficient search method must involve AND and OR pruning.

---

search algorithm, and pruning is not considered in process assignments. The speedup drops to $\sqrt{k}$ under the best-case ordering, where k is the number of processors.

In the *mandatory-work-first scheme,*[33] the minimum tree searched in a serial algorithm is searched in parallel during the first phase. The resulting α-β window is used in the second phase, during which the rest of the tree is searched. This scheme performs better than the tree-splitting scheme under best-case ordering, but can be worse in worst-case ordering. In the latter case, many nodes pruned in the tree-splitting scheme might be visited in the second phase.

Another approach is to use a best-first search, such as the SSS* algorithm.[34] SSS* is effective in searching a randomly or poorly ordered tree, but requires more space and is not significantly better than an α-β search on strongly ordered trees. Kumar and Kanal have shown that the SSS* algorithm can be interpreted as a branch-and-bound procedure, and they have presented two parallel implementations of SSS*.[35]

Previous approaches to parallel game-tree search have emphasized reduction of the information-transfer overhead, but paid little attention to information-deficiency overhead. We

will consider the information-deficiency overhead in the illustrative context of the scheduling of parallel logic programs.

Parallel logic programs. Logic programming is a programming methodology based on Horn-clause resolution.[36] An example of a high-level language for logic programming is Prolog. Execution of a logic program can be considered as the search of an AND/OR tree.[35,37] The root represents the initial problem queried, the OR nodes represent (sub)goals, and the AND nodes represent clauses. All subgoals in the same body of a clause are children of an AND node. A (sub)goal (OR node) and its children display the choices of clauses with the same head. The terminal nodes denote clauses or subgoals that cannot be decomposed.

Searching an AND/OR tree for a logic program is quite different than searching other types of search trees. First, in contrast to extremum searches that find the best solution, solving a logic program corresponds to finding any or all solutions that satisfy the given conditions, the implicative Horn clauses, and the consistent binding of variables for the AND nodes. Second, the value of a node in the AND/OR tree for a logic program is either TRUE (success) or FALSE (failure). A node is usually selected for evaluation on the basis of a fixed order, such as the depth-first search. Third, a variable in a logic program can be bound to several values, and some subgoals might share a common variable.

An efficient search method must involve pruning. Two kinds of pruning exist here. In an AND pruning, if one of the children of an AND node is found to be FALSE, then all remaining children of this AND node can be pruned. Likewise, in an OR pruning, if one of the children of an OR node is found to be TRUE, then all remaining children of this OR node can be pruned. It should be noted that OR pruning applies only if the OR node shares no variables with its siblings.

Much research strives for parallel execution of logic programs. Conery

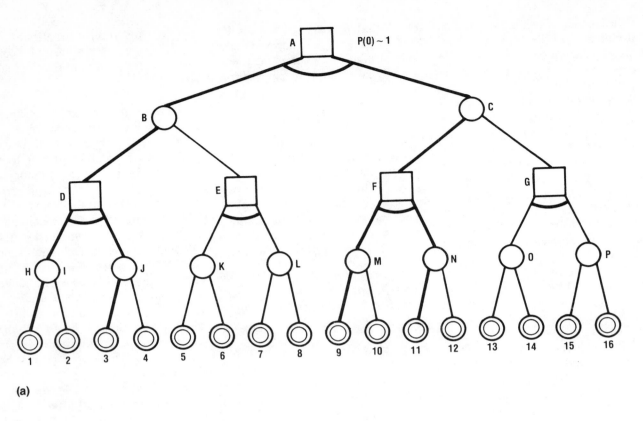

(a)

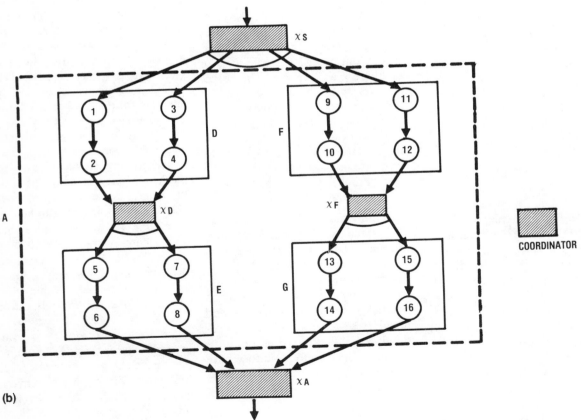

(b)

Figure 4. A binary AND/OR search tree (a) with high success probability and the corresponding fail-token-flow graph G_f. (b) AND nodes are represented as squared nodes; OR nodes are represented as circular nodes.

and Kibler[37] have classified four kinds of parallelism of logic programs: AND parallelism, OR parallelism, stream parallelism, and search parallelism; they have also investigated AND parallelism. Furukawa et al.[38] and Ciepielewski et al.[39] have discussed OR parallelism, while Lindstrom et al.[40] have addressed stream parallelism and pipelined Prolog processors.

However, very few studies have addressed processor assignment as a means to reduce information-deficiency overhead. Below, we present an algorithm that schedules searches of nodes according to estimated probabilities of a terminal node being true and does not distinguish AND and OR parallelism.

A new scheduling algorithm. Consider the case in which all terminal nodes have the value TRUE. For a binary AND/OR tree of height h (h is even and the root is at level 0), the solution tree is found after $2^{h/2}$ terminal nodes have been visited, as shown in Figure 4a. Once 1, 3, 9, and 11 have been visited, the root is determined to be true. In contrast, if all terminal nodes are FALSE, one can determine that the root is false by visiting $2^{h/2}$ terminal nodes (nodes 1, 2, 5, and 6 in Figure 4a). These observations imply that when most of the terminal nodes in a subtree are TRUE, searching the subtree by assuming that its root is TRUE is more efficient; otherwise, the subtree should be searched by assuming that its root is FALSE.

For the AND/OR tree in Figure 4a, we see that in a sequential search, if node 1 fails, then node 2 is examined; otherwise node 3 is examined next. That is, whether node 2 or node 3 is examined depends on the result of searching node 1. Similarly, the traversal of node 5 depends on the results of traversing nodes 1, 2, 3, and 4. A *fail-token-flow graph*, G_f, as depicted in Figure 4b for the tree in Figure 4a, can be drawn, according to this dependence information. A node (circle) in the graph is active only if it receives a fail-token from an incident edge. When a terminal node in the search tree is found to be false, a fail-token is

sent along the direction of the corresponding edge. The coordinator (shaded box) in the graph represents a control mechanism that coordinates the activities of the connected blocks. When a fail-token is received from any of the incident edges of a coordinator, fail-tokens are sent to *all* directly connected nodes. At the same time, any node searched in the block directly connected to this coordinator can be terminated, because it does not belong

The token-flow graph of AND/OR tree roots is modular and can be decomposed: subgraphs correspond to nonterminal tree nodes.

to the solution tree. For example, when node 1 is found to be false, a fail-token is sent to node 2. If node 2 is found to be false, a fail-token is sent to coordinator X_D. Any node concurrently searched in block D can then be terminated.

A simple parallel search strategy can be derived with the aid of G_f. To effectively search the tree, no more than $2^{h/2}$ processors are needed. A parallel depth-first search is applied in the first h steps by generating all children of a selected AND node, but only the leftmost child of a selected OR node. As an example, nodes 1, 3, 9, and 11 in the search tree are assigned to four processors in the fourth step. This corresponds to generating fail-tokens to activate these nodes in G_f (Figure 4b). If a node, say 3, is found to be FALSE, then a fail-token is generated and the idle processor is assigned to evaluate node 4. Close examination of Figure 4b shows that for each column of G_f there must be at least one node with the value TRUE if a solution tree exists. When a node is found to belong to the solution tree, all nodes on the path from the initial start node to this node in G_f must have failed. Processors for searching the AND/OR tree can be scheduled according to the state of execution in G_f at any time.

When the AND/OR tree is complete, and $Pr(h)$ (the probability that a

terminal node is TRUE) is constant, $Pr(0)$ (the probability for a solution tree is to be found from the root, which is assumed to be an OR node) can be shown to be close to one for $Pr(h) > 0.618$. The threshold is 0.382 ($= 1 - 0.618$) if the root is an AND node. In both cases, a node with the value TRUE can be found quickly in each column of G_f. As a result, the speedup is close to one.

On the other hand, if $Pr(h)$ is small, then the probability for a solution tree to exist at the root is close to zero and the above strategy is no longer suitable because a large number of nodes must be evaluated in each column of G_f. In this case, the scheduling should be done according to the *success-token-flow graph*, G_s. G_s is the dual of G_f, in the sense that a success token replaces a fail token and the columns in G_f are transposed to become the rows in G_s. Since searching for failure from an AND node is equivalent to searching for success from an OR node, the above scheduling algorithm can be extended with respect to G_s.

The token-flow graph obtained for the root of an AND/OR tree is modular and can be decomposed into modular token-flow subgraphs corresponding to all nonterminal nodes in the tree. If the probability of leading to a solution tree for a nonterminal node can be refined as the search progresses, the corresponding token-flow subgraph can be rederived. An idle processor can be scheduled according to the token-flow subgraph derived for the root of the given subtree. We have proposed a multiprocessor architecture, MALOP, which is based on an intelligent search strategy and effective scheduling.[41]

In summary, the important issues in parallel AND/OR-tree search are the granularity of parallelism, the parallel selection of nodes for evaluation, and the intelligent pruning of unnecessary nodes. Processors should know the global state of search in order to select the nodes for expansion and should be able to tell other processors to prematurely terminate their tasks, when necessary. The architecture should support dissemination of this information.

Figure 5. A graph with five stages and three nodes in each intermediate stage (a); an AND/OR-graph representation of the reduction in finding an optimal path in a three-stage graph (b). The problem in (b) is to find

$$\min \{a_{i,j} + b_{j,k}\};$$
$$i,j,k \in \{1,2\}$$

AND nodes are represented as squared nodes and indicate summations; OR nodes are represented as circular nodes and indicate comparisons.

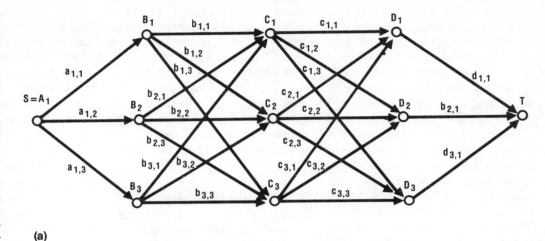

(a)

Dynamic programming

Dynamic programming, a powerful optimization methodology, can apply to many areas, including optimal control, industrial engineering and economics.[42] In general, DP transforms the problem into a form suitable for optimization, but it is not an algorithm for optimizing the objective function. One can represent a problem solvable by DP as a multistage problem, a divide-and-conquer problem, or an acyclic AND/OR graph-search problem. Various computational approaches can be used, depending on the formulation and representation. We discuss DP problems separately here because they illustrate the effects of representation on the design of the supporting multiprocessing system.

A DP formulation is characterized by a recursive equation whose left-hand side identifies a function name and whose right-hand side is an expression containing the maximization (or minimization) of values of some monotone functions. Depending on the form of the functional equation, a DP formulation can be classified into four types: *monadic-serial*, *polyadic-serial*, *monadic-nonserial*, and *polyadic-nonserial*. Monadic and polyadic DP formulations are distinct approaches

to representing various optimization problems; DP formulations can solve serial and nonserial optimization problems. *Serial optimization problems* can be decomposed into stages, and variables in one stage depend on variables in adjacent stages only. Problems such as sequential control, resource allocation, fluid flow, circuit design, and scheduling belong to this class. If variables in one stage are related to variables in other stages, the problem is a *nonserial optimization problem*. Examples include finding the optimal binary search tree and computing the minimum-cost order of multiplying a string of matrices.

To illustrate the concept of serial problems, consider the example of finding the shortest path in a multistage graph, as depicted in Figure 5a. Let $c_{i,j}$ be the cost of edge (i,j). The cost of a path from source S to sink T is the sum of costs on the edges of the path. Define $f_1(i)$ as the minimum cost of a path from I to T. The cost of getting from I to T via neighbor J is $c_{i,j} + f_1(j)$. To find $f_1(i)$, paths through all possible neighbors must be compared. Hence, the problem can be represented as

$$f_1(i) = \min_j [c_{i,j} + f_1(j)] \qquad (4)$$

This is a *forward functional equation*. The formulation is *monadic*; that is,

the cost function involves one recursive term only.

From Equation (4), $f(C_1)$, the minimum cost from C_1 to T is

$$f(C_1) = \min\{c_{1,1} + d_{1,1}, \; c_{1,2} + d_{2,1}, \\ c_{1,3} + d_{3,1}\} \qquad (5)$$

Equation (5) can be interpreted as an inner-product operation in respect to addition and minimization. If we define matrix multiplication in terms of a closed semi-ring $(R, \text{MIN}, +, +\infty, 0)$ in which MIN corresponds to addition and $+$ corresponds to multiplication in conventional matrix multiplications,[7] then equation (5) becomes $f(C) = C \cdot D$, where C is a cost matrix and D is a cost vector. It is easy to see that searching the shortest path in a multistage graph with a forward monadic DP formulation is equivalent to multiplying a string of matrices, i.e., $A \cdot (B \cdot (C \cdot D))$.

The same problem can be generalized to find the optimal path from any vertex i to any other vertex j. The functional equation is

$$f_2(i,j) = \min_k [f_2(i,k) + f_2(k,j)] \qquad (6)$$

where $f_2(i,j)$ is the minimum cost of getting from I to J. This cost function is polyadic because it involves more than one recursive term. A divide-and-conquer formulation is a special case of polyadic-serial formulations.

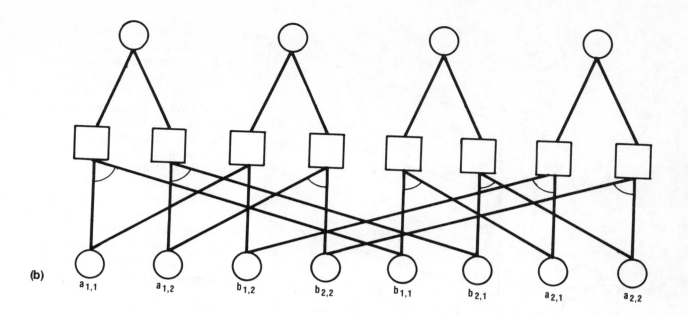

(b)

$a_{1,1}$ $a_{1,2}$ $b_{1,2}$ $b_{2,2}$ $b_{1,1}$ $b_{2,1}$ $a_{2,1}$ $a_{2,2}$

AND/OR graphs can also be used to represent serial DP problems. Basic operations in comparisons of partial solutions over all alternatives are represented as OR nodes. AND nodes represent operations involving computations of a cost function, such as summations. Figure 5b shows an AND/OR graph for reducing the search of the shortest path in a three-stage graph with two nodes in each stage. Gensi and Montanari have shown that formulating a DP problem in terms of a polyadic functional equation is equivalent to searching for a minimal-cost solution tree in an AND/OR graph with monotone cost function. [43]

A nonserial DP problem can be represented in monadic or polyadic form. [44] A monadic-nonserial formulation is an extension of equation (4) in which the dependence of the functional term involves variables in more than one adjacent stage. A polyadic-nonserial formulation is usually represented in the form of an acyclic AND/OR graph in which edges can extend between any two arbitrary levels of the graph.

Parallel processing has been applied to DP problems. Guibas, Kung, and Thompson have proposed a VLSI algorithm for solving the optimal pa-

renthesization problem, [45] for which linear pipelines have also been proposed recently. [46] Clarke and Dyer have designed a systolic array for curve and line detection in terms of a nonserial formulation. [47] However, these designs were directed toward implementation of a few special cases of DP formulations.

The choice of an architecture to support a serial DP problem depends on the formulation. First, if the problem is represented in a polyadic form and considered a divide-and-conquer problem, the architecture discussed above under the divide-and-conquer heading can be applied. For example, the problem of finding the shortest path in a multistage graph can be considered as the multiplication of a string of matrices, which can be decomposed into the multiplication of two or more substrings of matrices.

Second, equivalence between polyadic representations and AND/OR graphs allows various graph-search techniques to be translated into techniques for solving DP problems. Sometimes, when the AND/OR graph is regular, it can be mapped directly into a systolic array. [15]

Third, a problem can be represented in a monadic form and solved with a pipelining approach. This approach is suitable when many alternative partial

solutions must be compared. Below, we illustrate this approach for evaluating the multiplication of a string of matrices.

Figure 6 depicts a scheme for computing $(A \cdot (B \cdot (C \cdot D)))$ for the multistage graph in Figure 5a. An *iteration* is defined as a shift-multiply-accumulate operation in respect to the time at which a row or column of the input matrix enters a given processor in the systolic array. Note that the same iteration number is carried out at different times in different processors (iteration numbers are indicated in Figure 6a).

In the first three iterations, $C \cdot D$ is evaluated. The control signal FIRST is one; D, the input vector is serially shifted into the systolic array; and the result vector, $\{f(C_i), i = 1, 2, 3\}$, remains stationary. At the end of the third iteration, FIRST is set to zero. In the following three iterations, $B \cdot (C \cdot D)$ is computed. Note that matrix B is transposed, and the ith column of matrix B is fed into K_i. The input vector, $\{f(C_i), i = 1, 2, 3\}$, remains stationary, while the result vector $\{f(B_i), i = 1, 2, 3\}$, is shifted. At the end of the sixth iteration, the output vector $\{f(B_i), i = 1, 2, 3\}$, is formed. In the last three iterations, input vectors A and $\{f(B_i) \, i = 1, 2, 3\}$ are shifted into P_1 to form the final result.

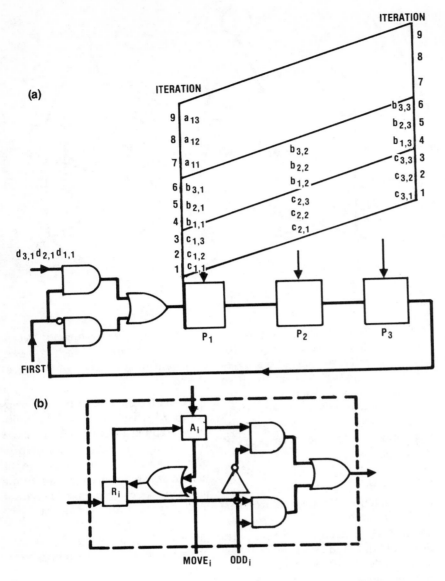

(a)

ITERATION

(b)

Figure 6. A pipelined version of a systolic array for multiplying a string of matrices (a); processor structure for K_i (b).

Few architectures solve nonserial DP problems directly. In an AND/OR graph representation of nonserial problems, edges may connect nodes at any two arbitrary levels. These graphs might have to be searched by an architecture with a flexible interconnection, such as a dataflow computer. Another approach is to transform the nonserial problem into a serial one and solve it with approaches developed for serial problems.[15] For problems in monadic-nonserial formulations, the dependence of variables can be removed by using one variable to represent the Cartesian product of several dependent variables. For problems in a polyadic-nonserial representation, such as an AND/OR graph, the dependence can be removed by replacing each edge that connects nodes not at adjacent levels with multiple edges that connect nodes at adjacent levels. This approach has been used in designing a systolic array for finding the optimal binary search tree.[15]

Research in problem solving usually aims at developing better algorithms. Unnecessary combinatorial searches should be avoided, because they do not contribute to the quality of the solutions. Evidence of this is clear in the efforts to design optimal algorithms and to understand the reasoning process in artificial intelligence. However, searching becomes inevitable when a good algorithm has been developed and is an essential to many applications.

In this article, we have investigated the limitations of multiprocessing in solving combinatorial searches. The suitability of multiprocessing depends on problem complexity, problem representation, and the corresponding search algorithms. Problem complexity should be low enough that a serial computer can solve the problem. Problem representations are very important because they are related to the search algorithms.

However, the question of deciding which representation leads to an efficient search remains open. Moreover, efficient architectures to evaluate various search algorithms differ. That

For the systolic array in Figure 6a, shifted data alternates between the input vector and the result vector every three iterations. The processor structure of K_i, depicted in Figure 6b, can control this alternation. R_i is a register that stores an element of the input vector, and A_i is the accumulator that stores the temporary result of an element of the result vector. Control signals ODD_i and $MOVE_i$ control the data paths. When the number of matrix multiplications is odd, ODD_i is one; hence, R_i is connected to the output and the input vector is shifted along the pipeline. When the number of matrix multiplications is even, ODD_i is zero, A_i is connected to the output, and the result vector is shifted. At the end of a matrix multiplication, the generated result vector becomes the input vector in the next iteration and is moved, by the control signal $MOVE_i$, from A_i to R_i.

In general, searching a multistage graph with N stages and k nodes in each stage takes $(N-1)k$ iterations with k processors. Because there are no delays between feedings of the input matrices into the systolic array, a processor utilization is very close to one when N and k are large.

is why we have developed functional requirements for a given search algorithm, requirements that allow efficient mapping of a search algorithm on a general-purpose multiprocessor and development of special-purpose processors for searching.

In this article, we have not attempted to list all possible cases, but to illustrate the different approaches through examples (Table 1). We hope these guidelines and examples can help designers select appropriate multiprocessing systems for solving combinatorial search problems. □

Table 1. Functional requirements of different paradigms of search algorithms. (The magnitudes of large and small granularities in various algorithms differ. Special interconnections include the tree architecture.)

ALGORITHM		FUNCTIONAL REQUIREMENTS	TASKS
Divide-and-conquer	Large granularity	Loosely coupled	Balance load
	Small granularity	Tightly coupled; special interconnections	Transfer control and data
Branch-and-bound	Lower-bound test only	Loosely coupled; broadcast capability	Balance load; share incumbent
	Dominance tests	Tightly coupled; shared memory	Balance load; share dominating nodes
Serial acyclic AND/OR-graph search	Large granularity	Loosely coupled; broadcast capability	Balance load; share state of evaluation
	Small granularity	Tightly coupled; special interconnections	Transfer control and data
Nonserial acyclic AND/OR-graph search	Large granularity	Dataflow processing	Share resources; coordinate tasks
	Small granularity	Map to serial AND/OR-graph search	Transfer control and data

References

1. A. C. Shaw, *The Logical Design of Operating Systems,* Prentice-Hall, Englewood Cliffs, N.J., 1974.

2. M. R. Garey and D. S. Johnson, *Computers and Intractability: A Guide to the Theory of NP-Completeness,* Freeman, San Francisco, Calif., 1979.

3. A. Martelli and U. Montanari, "Additive AND/OR Graphs," *Int'l Joint Conf. Artificial Intelligence,* 1973, pp. 1-11.

4. N. J. Nilsson, *Principles of Artificial Intelligence,* Tioga, Menlo Park, Calif., 1980.

5. A. Barr and E. A. Feigenbaum, *The Handbook of Artificial Intelligence,* Vol. 1-3, Kaufmann, Los Altos, Calif., 1981.

6. E. Horowitz and S. Sahni, *Fundamentals of Computer Algorithms,* Computer Science Press, Potomac, Md., 1978.

7. A. V. Aho, J. E. Hopcroft, and J. D. Ullman, *The Design and Analysis of Computer Algorithms,* Addison-Wesley, Reading, Mass., 1974.

8. D. E. Knuth and R. W. Moore, "An Analysis of Alpha-Beta Pruning," *Artificial Intelligence,* Vol. 6, 1975, pp. 293-326.

9. V. Kumar and L. Kanal, "A General Branch-and-Bound Formulation for Understanding and Synthesizing AND/OR Tree Search Procedures," *Artificial Intelligence,* Vol. 21, 1983, pp. 179-198.

10. F. Peters, "Tree Machine and Divide-and-Conquer Algorithms," *Conpar 81, Lecture Notes CS111,* 1981, pp. 25-35.

11. F. Burton and Huntbach, "Virtual Tree Machines," *IEEE Trans. Computers,* Vol. C-33, No. 3, Mar. 1984, pp. 278-280.

12. E. Horowitz and A. Zorat, "Divide and Conquer for Parallel Processing," *IEEE Trans. Computers,* Vol. C-32, No. 6, June 1983, pp. 582-585.

13. C. Tang and R. C. T. Lee, "Optimal Speedup of Parallel Algorithm Based on the Divide-and-Conquer Strategy," personal communication.

14. D. J. Kuck, "A Survey of Parallel Machine Organization and Programming," *ACM Computing Surveys,* Vol. 9, No. 1, Mar. 1977, pp. 29-59.

15. G.-J. Li and B. W. Wah, "Parallel Processing for Dynamic Programming," to appear *Int'l Conf. Parallel Processing,* August 1985.

16. E. L. Lawler and D. W. Wood, "Branch-and-Bound Methods: A Survey," *Operations Research,* Vol. 14, 1966, pp. 699-719.

17. T. Ibaraki, "Computational Efficiency of Approximate Branch-and-Bound Algorithms," *Mathematical Operations Research,* Vol. 1, No. 3, 1976, pp. 287-298.

18. B. W. Wah and E. Y. W. Ma, "MANIP—A Multicomputer Architecture for Solving Combinatorial Extremum Search Problems," *IEEE Trans. Computers,* Vol. C-33, No. 5, May 1984, pp. 377-390.

19. B. W. Wah and C. F. Yu, "Probabilistic Modeling of Branch-and-Bound Algorithms," *Proc. Compsac,* Nov. 1982, pp. 647-653; will also appear in *IEEE Trans. Software Engineering,* Oct. 1985.

20. G.-J. Li and B. W. Wah, "Computational Efficiency of Parallel Approximate Branch-and-Bound Algorithms," *Proc. Int'l Conf. Parallel Processing,* 1984, pp. 473-480.

21. B. C. Desai, "The BPU: A Staged Parallel Processing System to Solve the Zero-One Problem," *Proc. ICS 78,* Dec. 1978, pp. 802-817.

22. M. Imai, T. Fukumara, and Y. Yoshida, "A Parallelized Branch-and-Bound Algorithm: Implementation and Efficiency," *System Computer Controls,* Vol. 10, No. 3, 1979, pp. 62-70.

23. O. I. El-Dessouki and W. H. Huen, "Distributed Enumeration on Network Computers," *IEEE Trans. Computers,* Vol. C-29, No. 9, Sept. 1980, pp. 818-825.

24. B. W. Wah, G.-J. Li, and C. F. Yu, "The Status of MANIP—A Multicomputer Architecture for Solving Combinatorial Extremum-Search Problems," *Proc. 11th Ann. Int'l Symp. Computer Architecture,* June 1984, pp. 56-63.

25. B. W. Wah and K. L. Chen, "A Partitioning Approach to the Design of Selection Networks," *IEEE Trans. Computers,* Vol. C-33, No. 3, Mar. 1984, pp. 261-268.

26. C. F. Yu and B. W. Wah, "Virtual-Memory Support for Branch-and-Bound Algorithms," *Proc. Compsac,* Nov. 1983, pp. 618-626.

27. C. F. Yu and B. W. Wah, "Efficient Branch-and-Bound Algorithms on a Two-Level Memory Hierarchy," *Proc. Compsac,* Nov. 1984, pp. 504-514.

28. G.-J. Li and B. W. Wah, "How to Cope with Anomalies in Parallel Approximate Branch-and-Bound Algorithms," *Proc. Nat'l Conf. Artificial Intelligence,* 1984, pp. 212-215.

29. T. H. Lai and S. Sahni, "Anomalies of Parallel Branch-and-Bound Algorithms," *Comm. ACM,* Vol. 27, No. 6, June 1984, pp. 594-602.

30. T. A. Marsland and M. Campbell, "Parallel Search of Strongly Ordered Game Trees," *ACM Computing Surveys,* Vol. 14, No. 4, Dec. 1982, pp. 533-551.

31. G. Baudet, "The Design and Analysis of Algorithms for Asynchronous Multiprocessors," Tech. Rep., Dept. of Computer Science, Carnegie-Mellon University, Pittsburgh, Pa., 1978.

32. R. Finkel and J. Fishburn, "Parallelism in Alpha-Beta Search," *Artificial Intelligence,* 1982, pp. 89-106.

33. S. Akl, D. Barnard, and R. Doran, "Design, Analysis, and Implementation of a Parallel Tree Search Algorithm," *IEEE Trans. Pattern Analysis and Machine Intelligence,* Vol. PAMI-4, Mar. 1982, pp. 192-203.

34. G. Stockman, "A Minimax Algorithm Better than Alpha-beta?" *Artificial Intelligence,* Vol. 12, 1979, pp. 179-196.

35. V. Kumar and L. Kanal, "Parallel Branch-and-Bound Formulations for AND/OR Tree Search," *IEEE Trans. Pattern Analysis and Machine Intelligence,* Vol. PAMI-6, 1984.

36. R. Kowalski, *Logic for Problem Solving,* North Holland, New York, 1979.

37. J. Conery and D. Kibler, "AND Parallelism in Logic Programming," *Tutorial on Parallel Logic Programming, Int'l Conf. Parallel Processing,* D. DeGroot, ed., 1984, pp. 13-17.

38. K. Furukawa, K. Nitta, and Y. Matsumoto, "Prolog Interpreter Based on Concurrent Programming," *Proc. First Int'l Logic Programming Conf.,* 1982, pp. 38-44.

39. A. Ciepielewski and S. Haridi, "Control of Activities in OR-Parallel Token Machine," *IEEE Int'l Symp. Logic Programming,* 1984.

40. G. Lindstrom and P. Panangaden, "Stream-Based Execution of Logic Programs," *Proc. 1984 Int'l Symp. Logic Prog.,* Feb. 1984, pp. 168-176.

41. G. J. Li and B. W. Wah, "MALOP: a Multicomputer Architecture for Solving Logic Programming Problems," *Proc. Int'l Conf. Parallel Processing,* 1985.

42. R. Bellman and S. Dreyfus, *Applied Dynamic Programming,* Princeton University Press, Princeton, N.J., 1962.

43. S. Gensi, U. Montanari, and A. Martelli, "Dynamic Programming as Graph Searching: An Algebraic Approach," *J. ACM,* Vol. 28, No. 4, Apr. 1981, pp. 737-751.

44. U. Bertele and F. Brioschi, *Nonserial Dynamic Programming,* Academic Press, New York, 1972.

45. L. Guibas, H. Kung, and C. Thompson, "Direct VLSI Implementation of Combinatorial Algorithms," *Proc. Caltech Conf. VLSI: Architecture, Design, Fabrication,* 1979, pp. 509-525.

46. P. Varman and V. Ramakrishnan, "Dynamic Programming and Transitive Closure on Linear Pipelines," *Proc. Conf. Parallel Processing,* 1984, pp. 359-364.

47. M. Clarke and C. Dyer, "Systolic Array for a Dynamic Programming Application," *Proc. 12th Workshop Applied Imagery Pattern Recognition,* 1983.

Questions about this article can be directed to Benjamin W. Wah, School of Electrical Engineering, Purdue University, West Lafayette, IN 47907.

Benjamin W. Wah is an associate professor in the School of Electrical Engineering at Purdue University. His current research interests include parallel computer architectures, distributed databases, and theory of algorithms.

Wah received the BS degree in 1974 and the MS degree in 1975 in electrical engineering and computer science from Columbia University. He received the MS degree in computer science in 1976 and the PhD degree in electrical engineering in 1979 from the University of California, Berkeley. He has been a Distinguished Visitor of the IEEE Computer Society since 1983.

Guo-jie Li is a doctoral candidate in computer science and engineering at Purdue University. His research interests include parallel processing, computer architecture, and artificial intelligence.

Li graduated from Peking University in 1968 and received the MS degree in computer science and engineering from the University of Science and Technology and the Institute of Computing Technology, Chinese Academy of Science, in 1981.

Chee Fen Yu is a doctoral candidate in electrical engineering at Purdue University. His current research interests include computer architecture and artificial intelligence.

Yu received the BE degree in electrical engineering from the University of Malaya in 1980 and the MS degree in electrical engineering from Purdue University in 1983.

Garbage Collection of Linked Data Structures

JACQUES COHEN

Department of Physics, Brandeis University, Waltham, Massachusetts 02254

A concise and unified view of the numerous existing algorithms for performing garbage collection of linked data structures is presented. The emphasis is on garbage collection proper, rather than on storage allocation. First, the classical garbage collection algorithms are reviewed, and their marking and collecting phases, with and without compacting, are discussed. Algorithms describing these phases are classified according to the type of cells to be collected: those for collecting single-sized cells are simpler than those for varisized cells. Recently proposed algorithms are presented and compared with the classical ones. Special topics in garbage collection are also covered: the use of secondary and virtual storage, the use of reference counters, parallel and real-time collections, analyses of garbage collection algorithms, and language features which influence the design of collectors. The bibliography, with topical annotations, contains over 100 references.

Key Words and Phrases: garbage collection, list processing, marking, compaction, varisized cells, reference counters, secondary storage, parallel and real-time collection, analyses of algorithms, language implementation

CR Categories: 1.3, 4.10, 4.20, 4.34, 4.40

INTRODUCTION

Garbage collection—the process of reclaiming unused storage space—can be done by various algorithms. Since the late fifties and early sixties, when the first list-processing languages were implemented, many such algorithms have been proposed and studied.

Interest in garbage collection has increased considerably during the past decade with the introduction of records and pointers as data structures in new programming languages. The efficiency of programs written in these languages depends directly on the availability of fast methods for garbage collection. (Experience with large LISP programs indicates that substantial execution time—10 to 30 percent—is spent in garbage collection [STEE75, WADL76].)

Garbage collection has also become an important topic in data structures courses. Of the several books which have devoted entire sections to garbage collection [FOST68, KNUT73, BERZ75, ELSO75, HORO75, PFAL77, GOTL78, AUGE79, STAN80], Knuth's book, Section 2.3.5, is the most comprehensive. It contains detailed descriptions and analyses of some of the garbage collection algorithms that appeared prior to 1968, and, despite its age, it remains a standard reference for algorithms proposed before the seventies. Numerous papers have appeared since 1973.[1] However, no presentation has summarized and

[1] The book by Standish [STAN80], which appeared since this paper was submitted for publication, is a valuable reference on more recent work done in garbage collection.

Computing Surveys, Vol. 13, No. 3, September 1981

• *Jacques Cohen*

CONTENTS

———————◆———————

classified the work done in the area. The purpose of this paper is to provide such a presentation. More specifically, the objectives of this paper are

(1) to review the classical algorithms for collecting linked data structures;
(2) to provide a unified description of recent garbage collection algorithms and to explain how they relate to the classical ones;
(3) to survey the related topics of real-time garbage collection, analyses of garbage collection algorithms, and language features which influence implementation;
(4) to present a comprehensive bibliography on the subject.

Although storage allocation and garbage collection are interrelated, the emphasis of this paper is on garbage collection proper, that is, on reclaiming storage; buddy systems [KNUT73] and related work are not covered.

It is assumed that the reader is familiar with at least one list-processing language and has some understanding of its implementations. (This level of proficiency may be acquired by studying the initial chapters of Weissman's book [WEIS67] and the interpreter described in COHE72.) This paper

Computing Surveys, Vol. 13, No. 3, September 1981

should be useful to readers interested in data structures and their application in compiler construction, language design, and database management.[2]

A *cell* is a number (≥ 1) of contiguous computer words which can be made available to a user. Cells are requested by the user's program from a supervisory program known as the storage allocator. Since the number of available cells is finite, a time may come when no cells remain available. When this occurs, experience indicates that some of the previously requested cells will be *unused* and can therefore be returned to the allocator. A cell becomes unused, or "garbage," when it can no longer be accessed through the pointer fields of any reachable cell. It is the garbage collector's task to reclaim this unused storage space.

Garbage collection is usually triggered automatically either when the allocator runs out of space or shortly before. Higher level languages often contain primitives for requesting groups of words from the allocator. Garbage collection may be triggered when one of these primitives is executed. For example, in LISP, the function *cons* also calls the garbage collector.

A most vexing aspect of garbage collection is that program execution comes to a halt while the collector attempts to reclaim storage space. On modern fast computers, the program interruption is noticeable even to interactive users of dedicated processors. Users of time-sharing systems may experience interruptions lasting minutes. In extreme cases, successive collections may take place with little actual program execution between them, making continued execution impractical. Because of this necessary halt, until recently, languages allowing automatic collection of linked structures could not be used to write programs with real-time constraints.

Methods for garbage collection usually comprise two separate phases:

(a) Identifying the storage space that may be reclaimed.
(b) Incorporating this reclaimable space into the memory area available to the user.

---

[2] Collections in very large databases or file systems are not covered in this survey.

Phase (a) can be performed using one of two methods:

(a1) By keeping counters indicating the number of times cells have been referenced. Identification in this case consists of recognizing inaccessible cells (those whose reference count is zero).

(a2) By keeping a list of immediately accessible cells and following their links to trace and mark every accessible cell. This method of identification is usually called *marking*.

Phase (b) can also be subdivided into two classes:

(b1) Incorporation into a *free list* in which available cells are linked by pointers.

(b2) Compaction of all used cells in one end of the memory, the other end containing contiguous words which are made available to the allocator. There are various types of compaction, classified by the relative positions in which cells are left after compaction:

(b2.1) *Arbitrary.* Cells which originally point to one another do not necessarily occupy contiguous positions after compaction.

(b2.2) *Linearizing.* Cells which originally point to one another (usually) become adjacent after compaction.

(b2.3) *Sliding.* Cells are moved toward one end of the address space without changing their linear order.

It is also convenient to classify garbage collection according to the type of cells which are reclaimed. The early methods were applicable only to programs in which all cells were of the same size. With the introduction of records (or similar structures) into programming languages, it became important to perform garbage collection in programs involving cells of different sizes.

1. COLLECTING SINGLE-SIZED CELLS

1.1 Marking

LISP cells illustrate the problems involved in marking single-size cells. Each LISP cell has two fields: *left* (or *car*) and *right* (or

```
procedure mark(p); {p is a pointer that is called by
                    value}
begin
  if unmarked(p) then
    begin
      marknode(p);
      if nonatomic(p) then
        begin
          mark(left(p));
          mark(right(p))
        end
    end
end mark;
```

Figure 1

cdr). These fields contain pointers either to other cells or to atoms, special kinds of cells containing no pointers. Each cell also contains two Boolean fields (bits): one to help differentiate between atomic and nonatomic cells,[3] and the other to be used in marking.

The algorithm shown in Figure 1 is a recursive procedure for marking LISP lists (including atoms). It utilizes three auxiliary procedures:

nonatomic(p): Boolean function which tests whether the cell pointed to by p is nonatomic;

unmarked(p): Boolean function which tests whether the cell pointed to by p is unmarked;

marknode(p): Procedure which marks the cell pointed to by p by turning on its marking bit (marking bits are initially turned off).

Note the similarity of the marking algorithm in Figure 1 with the classical preorder tree-traversal algorithm [KNUT73]. The one in Figure 1, however, can handle general lists, including circular ones.

An efficient nonrecursive version of this algorithm uses an explicit stack which only stores pointers to the cells being marked. No return addresses need to be stacked. A pointer is pushed onto the stack just before marking the cell's right branch. The algorithm terminates when the stack is empty. Consequently, each node of the list is visited twice: once before marking the left field and once before marking the right field.

---

[3] Some LISP systems carry this information in the pointers to the cells.

The following predicament results from using the described algorithm in a collector operating exclusively in main memory: garbage collection is needed because of the lack of memory space; however, additional space is required by the stack of the marking algorithm. If the storage area consists of n LISP cells, the maximum depth required for the stack is then n. To reserve this much additional storage initially is uneconomical. Several algorithms have been proposed to circumvent this difficulty; all of them involve reducing the required storage by trading it for longer time needed in which to perform the marking.

The first of these algorithms (similar to Algorithm C, in KNUT73, p. 415) uses a stack of fixed length h, where h is substantially smaller than n. However, the pointers are stacked using mod h as the stack index. In other words, the stack can be thought of as being "circular," and when its index exceeds h, the additional information is written over previously stored information. The stack therefore only "recalls" the most recently stored h items and "forgets" the other ones.

First, the immediately accessible cells are marked. Marking then proceeds as in the algorithm in Figure 1. However, since some cells which should have been "remembered" have been "forgotten," the stack will become empty before the task is complete. When this happens, the memory is scanned from the lowest address, looking for any marked cell whose contents point to unmarked cells. If such a cell is found, marking resumes as before and continues until the stack becomes empty again. Eventually, a scan will find no marked cells referring to unmarked cells, and marking is complete.

Actually, the scanning need not start from the beginning of the memory each time. During marking, the algorithm can record the minimum address f of the forgotten nodes. The next scan will begin either just after the last address of the previous scan, or from f, whichever is smaller.

An elegant algorithm which dispenses with the use of a stack but which may require one additional bit per cell was developed independently by Deutsch and by Schorr and Waite (see SCHO67 and

KNUT73). The main idea of this algorithm is that the nodes of a tree or of a directed graph can be inspected without using a stack by reversing successive links until leaves (i.e., atoms) or already visited nodes are found. The link reversal can then be undone to restore the original structure of the tree or graph. (One can view the stack of the classical marking algorithm as "moved" into the cells by the link-reversal technique.) The additional bit per cell (called a *tag* bit) indicates the direction in which the restoration of reversed links should proceed (i.e., whether to follow the left or the right pointer). Knuth [KNUT73] suggests a method for avoiding using a tag bit by instead using the bit already necessary for testing whether a cell is atomic.

Veillon [VEIL76] has shown that it is possible to transform the classical recursive algorithm in Figure 1 into the Deutsch–Schorr–Waite algorithm. First, the parameter of the recursive procedure is eliminated by introducing the link reversal feature. The two recursive calls of the resulting parameterless procedure, needed to mark the left and right fields, are eliminated by introducing the tag bits to differentiate between the returns from the two calls.

Knuth (KNUT73, p. 591) proves by induction the correctness of the link-reversal marking algorithm of Deutsch–Schorr–Waite. An alternate proof may be obtained by noting that the transformations suggested by Veillon preserve correctness. Other proofs have recently appeared in GERH79, GRIE79, LEE79, KOWA79, and TOPO79. Yelowitz and Duncan [YELO77] present proofs of correctness of several marking algorithms. Their approach consists of first proving the correctness of a general abstract marking algorithm and then extending that proof to cover specific concrete algorithms derived from the abstract one.

Wegbreit [WEGB72b] proposes a modification of the Deutsch–Schorr–Waite algorithm which uses a bit stack instead of a tag bit per cell. In the light of Veillon's program transformation, one sees that Wegbreit's stack simply implements the returns from the parameterless recursive procedure derived from Figure 1.

In the algorithm of Figure 1, each cell is

visited twice. In the Deutsch–Schorr–Waite algorithm, the cells are visited three times. This additional visit and the overhead for restoring pointers and for checking and setting bits render this algorithm less efficient than the classical algorithm. (Benchmarks taken by Schorr and Waite showed that this is indeed true.) Schorr and Waite then proposed using a hybrid algorithm which combines a fixed-size stack with their link-reversal technique. It consists of using the stack algorithm whenever possible. If stack overflow occurs, the tracing and marking proceed by the method of link reversal (see KNUT73, p. 592).

Other marking algorithms which use a fixed-length stack have been proposed. The one by Kurokawa [KURO75] also uses a tag bit, but differently. When the fixed-length stack overflows, it is possible to remove some of the pointers from the stack and preserve the information by turning on the tag bit of the unstacked cells. These cells form a chain, the pointer to which is left on the stack. The removal of stack elements makes more space available for resuming the marking scheme. Later, when a pointer is unstacked, it is examined to determine whether the cell it points to is tagged. If so, the linked tagged cells are retraced. Kurokawa also proposes a variant of the algorithm which dispenses with the tag bits, using the mark bits instead.[4]

Peter Bishop has proposed a variant of Kurokawa's algorithm which deserves further investigation: When the stack overflows, its contents are "moved" into the cells according to the link-reversal technique. Marking then proceeds using the now-free area of the stack. If stack underflow occurs, an element can be popped (in the manner of the Deutsch–Schorr–Waite algorithm) from the portion of the stack stored in the cells. A careful comparison of Kurokawa's and Bishop's algorithms has not yet been done, nor has either yet been proved correct.

We have seen that, at most, three bits per cell are necessary to perform LISP's garbage collection. The first two are used in recognizing atoms and in marking; the third one is used as a tag bit, if needed by the algorithm. It should be pointed out that these three bits need not be located within or near their corresponding cells. Special areas of the memory (bit maps or tables) may be allocated for this purpose. Whether or not this should be done is, of course, machine dependent. Some LISP processors, for example, avoid the need for an (explicit) atom bit by placing atomic cells in a special region of the memory.

A convenient manner of implementing the tag bit in certain machines is described in COHE72. It takes advantage of the fact that all pointers refer to only odd (or only even) addresses, since two words are always used to implement a LISP cell. Turning on a tag bit can thus be accomplished simply by adding one to the address contained in the *right* part of the cell.

The algorithms described in this section can be generalized to cover cells of a single-size m, with $m > 2$. The generalized version of the algorithm in Figure 1 would involve recursively marking each of the m fields of the cell. A generalized variant of the Deutsch–Schorr–Waite algorithm would require an additional $\log_2 m$ tag bits per cell, the number necessary to represent m.

1.2 Reclaiming Marked Cells

The simplest method for reclaiming the marked cells (see phase (b1) of the Introduction) consists of linearly sweeping the entire memory. After turning off their mark bit, unmarked cells are incorporated into the free list administered by the storage allocator.

If compacting is preferred (phase (b2)), it can be performed by scanning the memory twice. In the first scan, two pointers are used, one starting at the bottom of the memory (higher address), the other at the top. The top one is incremented until it points to an unmarked cell; the bottom pointer is then decremented until it points to a marked cell. The contents of the marked cell are thereupon moved to the unmarked cell, a pointer to the new cell is placed in the old, and the mark bits are turned off. By the time the two pointers

---

[4] LIND74 had shown how marking can be done without tag bits or a stack, at the expense of additional processing time.

meet, all marked cells have been compacted in the upper part of the memory.[5]

The second scan is needed for readjusting the pointers: since some cells have been moved, it is essential to update any pointers to obsolete cell locations. This scan sweeps only the compacted area. Pointers are readjusted whenever they point to cells whose contents have been moved from the liberated area to the compacted area of the memory. Each of these pointers is replaced by the contents of the cell to which it was pointing. According to Knuth [KNUT73, p. 421], this method was first proposed by D. Edwards. LISP and ALGOL 60 programs describing in detail this method of compacting have appeared in HART64 and COHE67b. Note that the two-pointer compactor is of the *arbitrary* type; after compaction, cells which originally point to one another do not necessarily occupy contiguous positions of the memory.

1.3 Moving Collectors

An obvious algorithm for garbage collection would be to output all useful (i.e., reachable) data to the secondary storage area and then to read them back to the main memory. This, however, has several drawbacks:

(1) It may require additional storage equally as large as the main memory.
(2) The time overhead for transferring between memories is (usually) considerable.
(3) Unless special precautions are taken, shared cells would be output more than once, in which case the main memory may not be sufficiently large for reading back the information. (This situation becomes critical when the main memory contains loops of pointers.)

Minsky [MINS63] proposes an algorithm which eliminates the difficulties described in (3). His algorithm does not use a stack, but requires one marking bit per LISP cell. Each cell is traced and marked if unmarked. Triplets (the new address of a cell and the contents of its left and right fields) are computed and output to the secondary storage. The new address is also placed in the marked cell, and whenever a pointer to that cell is encountered, the pointer is adjusted to reflect the move. When the triplets are subsequently read back into the main memory, the contents of the fields are stored in the specified new address. Minsky's algorithm has the advantage of compacting the useful information into one area of the main memory. After compaction, list elements which are linked are positioned next to each other, making Minsky's algorithm a *linearizing* compactor. These two properties are very important when virtual memory is used, as will be discussed in Section 3.

In Minsky's algorithm, fields of the original list are used to store information about the output list; consequently, the original list is destroyed. In this respect, it is convenient to distinguish between the terms *moving* and *copying*. The former implies a possible destruction of the original structure, whereas the latter does not. Minsky's algorithm can be used to move lists in contexts other than garbage collection. Since its appearance, several other algorithms have been proposed to perform moving or copying. They can be used for garbage collection purposes as well. Most are designed to move or to copy lists without resorting to mark bits or to a stack.[6] As in Minsky's algorithm, (1) a forwarding address is usually left in the old cell, and pointers referring to that cell are readjusted accordingly, and (2) the moved lists are compacted in contiguous positions of the memory.

A few algorithms have been proposed for *copying* lists without using a stack or mark bits. They differ from the moving algorithms in that the altered contents of old lists are later restored to their original values. Lindstrom [LIND74], Robson [ROBS77], Clark [CLAR75, CLAR78a], and Fisher [FISH75] discuss the copying of trees and general lists.

Fenichel and Yochelsen [FENI69] suggest a variant of Minsky's collector which uses

---

[5] This type of compaction is similar to that performed in solving a problem proposed by Dijkstra (see the Dutch flag problem in DIJK76a).

[6] The similar but simpler problem of traversing trees without a stack or mark bits has been considered in SIKL72, DWYE73, LIND73, ROBS73, and LEE80. A recent book by Standish [STAN80] contains detailed descriptions of some of these algorithms.

an implicit stack but does not require mark bits. They divide the available memory into two areas called semispaces. At a given time, only one area is used by the allocator. When its space is exhausted, the reachable lists are moved to the other space in a linearized compacted form. The algorithm is intended for use in a paging environment.

Cheney's algorithm [CHEN70, WALD72], Reingold's algorithm [REIN73], and Clark's algorithm [CLAR76, GOTL78] all represent improvements over the previous algorithm: they require neither a stack nor mark bits. Cheney's algorithm is done by moving the list to a contiguous area; a simple test can establish whether a pointer refers to the old or the new region of the memory. Reingold's algorithm is achieved by using the Deutsch–Schorr–Waite link-reversal technique mentioned in Section 1.1. And Clark's algorithm moves a list into a contiguous area of the memory with the stack implicit in the list being moved. Clark shows that his algorithm is in most cases more efficient than both Cheney's and Reingold's.

Moving (or copying) algorithms may be classified according to the type of traversal used when inspecting the list being moved. Let us assume that most of the cells in a list are linked by their *right* fields, as is typical of LISP programs. A nonrecursive version of the marking algorithm of Figure 1 uses a list (stack) containing the addresses of cells whose *left* field has not yet been processed.[7] This list may be administered either as a true stack (on a "last-in, first-out," LIFO order) or as a queue (on a "first-in, first-out," FIFO order). According to this classification, the algorithms by Minsky, Fenichel–Yochelson, Reingold, and Clark use a LIFO order, whereas the one by Cheney uses a FIFO order. All of these algorithms move into adjacent locations the cells which originally were linked by the *right* field. These algorithms may therefore be classified as performing a linearizing type of compaction. Note that the algorithms which use a LIFO order will move closer together the cells corresponding to the sublists which terminate a list.

---

[7] This corresponds to calling *mark*(*right* (*p*)) before *mark*(*left* (*p*)).

```
procedure mark(p); {p is a pointer that is called by
                                                    value}
  begin integer i;
    if unmarked(p) then
      begin
        marknode(p);
        if nonatomic(p) then
          begin
            for i ← 1 until number(p) do
              mark(field (p, i))
          end
      end
  end mark;
```

Figure 2

2. COLLECTING VARISIZED CELLS

2.1 Marking

Figure 2 shows a marking algorithm similar to that of Figure 1, but applicable to varisized cells. Two additional auxiliary procedures are used:

number (*p*): an integer function yielding the number of contiguous words (items) in the cell to which *p* points (this information may be stored in the cell itself); and

field (*p, i*): a function yielding the *i*th item of the cell pointed to by *p*.

It is assumed that *p* always points to the first item of the cell. The algorithm can be modified to handle pointers to cell parts. If so, care should be taken to avoid collecting chunks of cells. Under the modified algorithm each item of the cell needs to be marked; thus bit tables are economical. (Note that bit tables would be less useful in conjunction with the algorithm of Figure 2.)

The algorithm in Figure 2, like that in Figure 1, requires stack storage space when none may be available. If the memory contains *n* cells of various sizes, the maximum depth required for the stack is *n*. When most of the cells contain several items, it might be worthwhile to reserve two additional fields per cell for distributing stack storage among the cells. Essentially, these fields contain the quantities *p* and *i* needed to implement the recursive calls of the procedure in Figure 2. A description of an algorithm of this kind appears in THOR72.

The marking algorithms of Section 1 which use a fixed-length stack can also be adapted to process varisized cells. They may then use a fixed-length stack of height h with stack index = mod h as before, but each stack position will contain information corresponding to p and i in the algorithm of Figure 2.

Variants of the Deutsch–Schorr–Waite link-reversal algorithm applicable to varisized cells are described in THOR72 and THOR76. Instead of using one tag bit, some of these algorithms use $\log_2 maxm$ bits per cell, where $maxm$ is the size of the largest cell. Other variants of the Deutsch–Schorr–Waite algorithm applicable when marking varisized cells have appeared in HANS77, MARS71, and WODO71.

2.2 Reclaiming Marked Cells

In opening, it should be mentioned that the method of compacting described in Section 1.2 is not applicable to varisized cells, since marked and unmarked cells cannot be swapped if they are of different sizes.

Several algorithms have been proposed for compacting varisized cells. One of the earliest is that of Haddon and Waite [HADD67, WAIT73]. This compactor is of the *sliding* type (see Section 1) and performs two scans of the entire memory. The objective of the first scan is to perform the compaction and to build a "break table," which the second scan uses to readjust the pointers.

The break table contains the initial address of each "hole" (sequence of unmarked cells) and the hole's size. An interesting feature of Haddon and Waite's algorithm is that no additional storage is needed to construct the break table since it can be proved that the space available in the holes suffices to store the table. However, from time to time the break table must be "rolled," that is, moved from one hole to a bigger one created through compaction. At the end of the first scan the break table occupies the liberated part of the memory. It is then sorted to speed up the pointer readjustment done by the second scan. Readjustment consists of examining each pointer, consulting the table (using a binary search) to determine the new position of the cell it used to point to, and changing the pointer accordingly.

The most unfavorable condition for Haddon and Waite's algorithm is when unit-size active cells alternate with unit-size inactive cells. It can be shown that the algorithm would take $O(n \log n)$ time, where n is the size of the storage (see FITC78).

Other compacting algorithms for varisized cells have been proposed. The LISP 2 garbage collection algorithm described in KNUT73, pp. 602–603, and those presented in WEGB72a and THOR76 have the following features in common.

Three (or more) linear scans are used. In the first scan the holes (inaccessible cells) are linked to form a free list. Two fields are reserved in each hole to store its size and a pointer to the next hole. A subsequent scan may combine adjacent holes into a single larger hole. The second scan consists of recognizing pointers and using the information contained in the free list to adjust them. This involves finding the ith hole whose address a_i is such that $a_{i-1} < p < a_i$, where p is the pointer being readjusted. The new value of the pointer can be computed by subtracting from p the sum of the sizes of the 1st, 2nd, $\ldots$, $(i-1)$th holes.[8] Once the pointers have been readjusted, a third scan takes care of moving the accessible cells to the compacted area. This compactor is therefore of the *sliding* type.

The second scan, which interpretively readjusts pointers, is the most time consuming of the three scans. Wegbreit [WEGB72a] proposes variants of this algorithm which make this scan more efficient. One variant consists of constructing a break table (called directory) which summarizes the information contained in the free list of holes. However, storage for the directory may be unavailable. Wegbreit suggests trying to use the largest hole for this purpose. When this is possible, binary search can speed up pointer readjustment.

Lang and Wegbreit [LANG72] suggest another variant of the algorithm, which subdivides the memory into a fixed number of equal segments. This variant requires a small additional area of memory to store the reduced break table, its initial address,

---

[8] It is therefore convenient to store these cumulative sums instead of recomputing them every time they are needed.

and its size for each segment. A first scan compacts each segment toward its lower address and constructs its break table. Whenever possible, that break table is copied into the liberated area of the segment; otherwise, marks are set to indicate that the reduced break table is stored in the liberated area of another segment. The second scan performs pointer readjustments using the information in the individual break tables. A third and final scan compacts the segments.

Another variant for collecting varisized cells was proposed in ZAVE75. It requires that each cell have an additional field. In the marking phase, all active cells are strung together using the additional field. This list of active cells is sorted by increasing addresses.[9] Pointers can then be readjusted by consulting the addresses in the list. The final scan compacts the active cells.

Terashima and Goto [TERA78] propose two algorithms for the compacting phase of the collection of varisized cells. In the first, pointers are readjusted by recomputing, for each pointer, the needed part of the break table. This computation is sped up by organizing the holes in a balanced binary tree, with the necessary pointers stored within the holes themselves. The balanced tree form minimizes computation of the readjustments. An intermediate scan is needed to construct the balanced tree from the linear list of holes obtained just after the marking phase.

The second compacting collector proposed by Terashima and Goto assumes that all elements of a cell are marked, and a separate bit table is used for marking. The memory is subdivided into a number of equal segments, each as long as the number of bits in a word of the bit table. Thus the size of the free space within a segment can be efficiently computed by counting the number of inactive bits in a word of the bit table. Pointer readjustment is based on these bit counts. This method is suitable for hardware implementation.

An interesting algorithm for readjusting pointers and compacting varisized cells

has recently been proposed by Morris [MORR78, MORR79]. It performs the compacting in linear time and it requires only one additional bit per pointer. No break tables are used. The algorithm is based on the following property: Assume that the contents of locations $a_1, \ldots, a_n$ point to location z. No information is lost if this tree structure with root z is transformed into a linear list by stringing together locations z, $a_1, a_2, \ldots$ and placing the contents of z in a_n. Once the new position of z, say, z', is known, it is simple to reconstruct the original tree by making the a_i's point to z'. The extra bit is used to process the tree structures.

Morris' algorithm is of the *sliding* type and requires two scans. The first only readjusts forward-pointing references. The second updates references pointing backward and performs the compaction. Although Morris proves the correctness of the algorithm, no data are available comparing its efficiency to that of other compacting algorithms. An algorithm similar to Morris' but requiring only forward scans and no additional bits has been proposed by Jonkers [JONK79].

Marking, pointer readjustment, and compacting can be made simpler if the list processing "preserves address ordering." This means that nodes are allocated sequentially, from low to high address: when a cell is created, its descendants have addresses which are always smaller than its own, and circular lists are therefore excluded. Under these conditions, marking can be performed in a single scan through the entire memory without using a stack. This scan also finds the number of active cells, which the second scan then uses for readjusting the pointers. The third and final scan performs the compaction which is of the sliding type. Details are given in FISH74.

Proposals have been made to try to postpone, as much as possible, the compaction of varisized cells [KNUT73, Section 2.5; PARE68]. This may be accomplished by keeping several free lists, one for each cell size commonly used in a program. These are called homogeneous free lists, or simply H-lists. In addition, another free list, the M-list, contains cells of miscellaneous sizes.

---

[9] This sorting may be expensive if the memory is fragmented.

The cells in the M-list are linked according to increasing addresses; the ordering in the H-lists is irrelevant. An unused cell is returned to one of the H-lists if possible. Otherwise, the cell is returned to its appropriate position in the M-list.

Requests for new cells are handled according to their size. If there is a nonempty H-list of the desired size, the new cell is taken from that list. If not, the cell is taken from the first M-list cell as large or larger than the desired size. If the M-list cell is larger than needed, it is split into two cells, with the first used to satisfy the request, and the second returned to one of the free lists.

If a cell of the requested size cannot be found in the M-list, a semicompaction is attempted. It consists of returning all elements of the H-lists to their appropriate positions in the M-list, and whenever two or more cells in the M-list are adjacent, combining them into a single larger cell. The test for adjacency is simple since the M-list is ordered by address. It is of course possible that even after semicompaction, a cell with the requested size remains unavailable. Standard (full) compaction may then be the only way to avoid program termination.

2.3 Moving Collectors

Some of the moving algorithms mentioned in Section 1.3 may be adapted to handle varisized cells. A representative of this class of algorithms [FENI69, CHEN70, BAKE78b] is described in the next section since it is particularly suitable for operation in virtual memory.

An algorithm for copying varisized cells is described in STAN80. It requires cells to have an additional field large enough to store an address. A first pass consists of linking all used cells via the additional field (see THOR72). A second pass copies each cell c_i in the linkage and inserts the copy, c_i', as the successor of c_i. The successor of c_i' becomes the cell c_{i+1}. After this copying, the odd-numbered elements of the new linkage contain the original cells and the even-numbered ones contain the copies. Finally, a third pass is used to readjust the pointers in each copied element and to sep-

arate the copy from the original. The degree of linearization achieved by this algorithm depends on the manner by which the cells are linked during the first pass. (Fisher [FISH75] and Robson [ROBS77] also describe algorithms for copying LISP cells which can be generalized for copying varisized cells.)

3. COLLECTING IN VIRTUAL MEMORY

The ratio of the size of secondary memory to the size of main memory is an important factor in designing collectors which operate in virtual memory. When this ratio is small, some of the algorithms described in the previous sections may be used. The methods described in this section, though, are suitable when the ratio is large.

The use of secondary storage through paging [COHE67a] changes the design considerations for implementing garbage collection algorithms in important ways. First, it is no longer necessary to try to avoid using additional storage for a stack, since the size of the available virtual memory in current systems is considerable.[10] Avoiding page faults and thrashing (caused by having structures whose cells are scattered in many pages), on the other hand, becomes a critical factor in improving the efficiency of garbage collection. Compaction is for this latter reason important when collecting in this environment. Cohen and Trilling [COHE67b] show that garbage collection with compaction brings about significant time gains in performance of LISP programs. They also found that a direct transcription of the classical garbage collection algorithms to a virtual memory environment can lead to unbearably slow collection times. CLAR79 contains additional useful information about the performance of compacting collectors operating in virtual memory.

Compaction of cells in virtual memory should not only eliminate unused holes but should also construct the compacted area so that pointers refer, if possible, to neighboring cells. As mentioned in Section 1.3,

---

[10] It is therefore doubtful that the link-reversal technique of Deutsch–Schorr–Waite should be used for marking.

Minsky's algorithm [MINS63] satisfies this requirement.

Measurements in actual LISP programs show that about 97 percent of list cells have just one reference to them [CLAR77, CLAR78b]. This property is important when designing garbage collection algorithms which operate in virtual memory.

Bobrow and Murphy [BOBR67] show that the use of a selective *cons* (the LISP function which requests a cell from the allocator) can improve the efficiency of subsequent processing and garbage collection. Basically, they advocate keeping one free-list per page. A new cell requested by a call of *cons*[x, y] is taken from the free area of a page according to the following strategy.

(1) First, if possible, take from the page containing the cell pointed to by `y`; otherwise,

(2) take from the page containing the cell pointed to by x; otherwise,

(3) take from the page containing the most recently created cell; otherwise,

(4) take from any page containing a fair number (say, 16) of free cells.

The purpose is to minimize page faults in manipulating linked lists. Additional information on garbage collection using virtual memory can be found in BOBR67, BOBR68a, BOBR68b, ROCH71, and BAEC72.

An important design consideration for implementing garbage collection algorithms in a paging environment is deciding when collection should be invoked. Since very large memories are currently available, it seems reasonable to collect whenever page faults render the program processing unbearably slow.

A class of algorithms suitable for use in virtual memory is the one described by Baker [BAKE78b]. It is based on the copying collector proposed by Fenichel-Yochelson [FENI69] and by Cheney [CHEN70] which was briefly described in Section 1.3. What follows is a more detailed presentation of this type of algorithm. Although it is applicable in collecting varisized cells, this presentation applies only to LISP cells.

The available memory is divided into two areas called semispaces. At a given time, only one is used by the allocator. During

```
pointer procedure move(p);
  begin
    if newspace(p)
      then return p
      else
        begin
          if old space(left[p])
            then left[p] ← copy(p);
          return left[p]
        end
  end move;
pointer procedure copy(p);
  begin pointer q;
    {The following statement assigns to q the address
     of a new cell taken from a contiguous area in the
     new space; as explained in the text this action
     implies incrementing the pointer B}
    q ← new;
    left[q] ← left[p];
    right[q] ← right[p];
    return q
  end copy;
```

Figure 3

garbage collection, the reachable lists are moved to the other space in a compacted form. The heart of the algorithm is the procedure *move* presented in Figure 3. The following description is based on Baker's paper [BAKE78b].

The procedure *move* moves a cell from the old semispace to the new one. The Boolean functions *oldspace*(p) and *newspace*(p) are used to test whether the cell pointed to by p is in the corresponding semispace. The auxiliary function *copy*(p) copies the cell whose address is p into the new semispace. After the copying, the procedure *move* stores the address of the new cell into the *left* field of the old cell.

The collector calls the procedure *move*(p) for all accessible cells p in the old semispace. This task is similar to that of marking, but in this case the cells are moved instead of marked. A stack is avoided by using two pointers, B and S, both of which initially point to the bottom of the new semispace. B points to the next free cell in the new semispace and is thus incremented by *copy*. First the immediately accessible cells are moved to the new semispace. The area between S and B now contains cells which have been moved into the new space but whose contents have not. This area is scanned (by incrementing S), and the contents of the area's cells are updated by calls to the procedure *move*. This in turn may result in incrementing B. Collection ends when S meets B.

In his dissertation, Bishop [BISH77] proposed an approach for designing collectors which operate in a very large virtual memory (of the order of 10^{12} bits). Even using the real-time approaches discussed in Section 5, it would be impractical to garbage collect the entire memory at one stretch. Since large portions of memory may remain unchanged during program execution, Bishop suggests collecting only in parts of the address space rather than in the entire space. (A similar approach is used in Ross' AED system [Ross67].) The memory is divided into areas which can be collected independently, and a variant of the Fenichel and Yochelson collector is used. This collector increases the locality of reference, an important factor in a paging environment.

Tracing and copying are performed only within a given area. The system keeps lists of all interarea references, both incoming and outgoing. Incoming references are modified to point to the area's new copy; they define the immediately accessible cells from which collection starts. Before discarding the old copy of an area, its useless outgoing references are removed from the corresponding lists of incoming references.

Bishop developed a method for maintaining the lists of interarea references and· indicated that this can be done automatically without incurring substantial run-time overhead. He advocates altering the virtual memory mechanism to cause traps when interarea references are stored into cells, and shows how virtual memory hardware can be constructed to perform this extra service efficiently.

4. REFERENCE COUNTERS

The use of reference counters (advocated by COLL60 and WEIZ63) has recently attracted renewed interest. An extra field, called *refcount*, is required for each cell to indicate the number of times the cell is referenced. This field has to be updated each time a pointer to the cell is created or destroyed. When *refcount* becomes equal to zero, the cell is inactive and can be collected. At least theoretically, *refcount* must be large enough to hold the number of cells in the memory and therefore must be as large as a pointer. The disadvantages of this approach are (1) the extra space needed for the counters, (2) the overhead required to update the counters, and (3) the inability to reclaim general cyclic structures.[11]

However, reference counters can conveniently be used to distribute garbage collection time as an overhead to processing. Every time a cell becomes inactive, it is pushed into a stack. When the cell is needed, it is popped from the stack and *then* the *refcounts* of its descendants are decremented. An advantage of this arrangement is that no new space is needed for the stack, since it can be simulated by stringing together the freed cells using the *refcount* fields. (Recall that these fields have to be big enough to hold a pointer.)

Deutsch [DEUT76], Knuth [KNUT73], and Weizenbaum [WEIZ69] suggest combining the reference counter technique with classical garbage collection. The former would be utilized during most of the processing time; the latter, being more expensive, would be performed as a last resort. This allows the use of small *refcounts* (thus reducing the storage requirements) because counters which reach their maximum value remain unmodified. Classical garbage collection, called when the free list is exhausted, starts by resetting all counters to zero. The counters of the accessible cells are restored during the marking phase of the collection by incrementing a cell's counter every time the cell is visited. The collection reclaims inactive circular list structures and cells with maximum *refcount* which have become unreachable. A recent paper [WISE79] shows that this restoration can be done efficiently when using Morris's compaction algorithm (see Section 2.2 and MORR78).

The hybrid approach suggested by Deutsch and Bobrow [DEUT76] is particu-

---

[11] BOBR80 and FRIE79 describe how reference counting can be used to manage certain classes of cyclic structures.

larly applicable to LISP. It is based on statistical evidence [CLAR77, CLAR78b] that in most LISP programs, most reference counts (about 97 percent) are one. The authors propose three hash tables (see BOBR75):

(1) The multiple reference table (MRT). Its key is a cell address and the associated value is the cell's reference count. Only cells whose reference counts are two or greater are listed in the MRT.

(2) The zero count table (ZCT) containing the addresses of cells whose *refcount* is zero. These cells may be of two types: those which are referred to only by the variables of a program (still active), and those which are truly unreferenced and can be reclaimed. It follows from (1) and (2) that if a cell's address is not in the MRT or the ZCT, its reference count is one.

(3) The variable reference table (VRT) contains the addresses of cells referred to by program variables (including the temporary variables in the recursion stack).

Deutsch and Bobrow note that there are three types of operations, called transactions, which may affect the accessibility of data. These are (1) allocation of a new cell, (2) creation of a pointer, and (3) destruction of a pointer.

Instead of updating the hash tables as the transactions occur, Deutsch and Bobrow propose storing them in a sequential file. The transactions are examined at suitable time intervals and then the tables are updated. This scheme has the advantage of minimizing paging overhead.

When a new cell is allocated, its address should be placed in the ZCT. Since this is usually followed by the creation of a pointer to the newly allocated cell (which implies removal from the ZCT), the pair of transactions can be ignored.

When a pointer is created, it is examined prior to its insertion into a cell or pointer variable. Three cases are possible:

(a) The pointer refers to a cell in the MRT. The corresponding *refcount* value is then increased by one if it has not already reached its maximum; otherwise, it is left unchanged.

(b) The pointer refers to a cell in the ZCT. The cell is then removed from that table, since its count becomes one.

(c) If tests (a) and (b) fail, the pointer refers to a cell having a *refcount* of one. It must then be placed in the MRT with a *refcount* of two.

When a pointer is destroyed (removed from a cell), two cases are possible:

(a) The pointer refers to a cell in the MRT. The cell's *refcount* value is decreased by one, except when it has reached its maximum, in which case it is left unchanged. If the new value of *refcount* is one, the cell is removed from the MRT.

(b) The pointer does not refer to a cell in the MRT. Its count is one by default, and should be reduced to zero. The cell is therefore entered in the ZCT.

The VRT is used when incorporating new cells into the free list. Since the stack is constantly being updated, the VRT is only computed periodically. A cell is reclaimed when its address is listed in the ZCT but *not* in the VRT. The ZCT is updated by eliminating the entries of reclaimed cells which are not pointed to by program variables.

Deutsch and Bobrow [DEUT76] designed their hybrid collector for operating in a paging environment, so that space availability is not at stake. For the classical collection they advocate using a variant of the two-semispace collector of Fenichel and Yochelson [FENI69]. The authors also point out that an auxiliary processor could speed up the collection. Its task would be to scan the ZCT and VRT tables to determine which cells could be incorporated into the free list.

Wise and Friedman [WISE77] propose a variant of the hybrid algorithm of Deutsch and Bobrow which is useful when only fast memory is available. Only one bit is assigned to the field *refcount*, and when that bit is one, the cell is referenced more than once. This is analogous to storing the cell in the MRT of the Deutsch–Bobrow algorithm.

Nodes whose reference counts are greater than two can be reclaimed only by a classical collection with a marking phase. An interesting feature of the one-bit *refcount* is that this bit can be re-used as a tag bit when using the link-reversal marking technique of Deutsch, Schorr, and Waite (see Section 1).

In order to delay the classical collection as much as possible, Wise and Friedman propose using tables to temporarily list cells whose *refcounts* are still one but are likely to be changed to two or zero. This situation occurs when performing assignments of the kind $r \leftarrow f(r)$, where r is a pointer. Assignments of this type are quite common in LISP, for example, $r \leftarrow cons(a, r)$ and $r \leftarrow right(r)$. The first often increases to two the *refcount* of the cell originally referred to by r. The second often reduces the count to zero. Unfortunately, no experimental data are available on the efficiency of the hybrid techniques described in this section.

Barth [BART77] considers reference counters in relation to shifting garbage collection overhead to compile time. He shows that savings in collection time are sometimes possible by carefully studying, at compile time, the program's assignments. For example, in the case of $r \leftarrow right(r)$, the cell originally pointed to by r may be incorporated into the free list if it is known that it will not be referenced by other pointers.

5. PARALLEL AND REAL-TIME COLLECTIONS

Two proposals have been made to circumvent the onerous garbage collection interruptions. The first is to allow garbage collection to proceed simultaneously with program execution by using two parallel processors: one is responsible for collection, the other for program execution. When collection actually takes place, it is bound by a known, tolerable, maximum time.

Minsky is credited by Knuth with initiating the development of algorithms for time-sharing garbage collection and list-processing tasks (see KNUT73, pp. 422, 594). If two processors are available, these tasks can be performed in parallel, with one of these processors, the collector, responsible for actual garbage collection, and the other performing the list processing and providing the storage requested by a user's program. Dijkstra [DIJK76b] calls this latter processor the *mutator*. The collector performs the basic tasks of marking and incorporating unmarked cells to a free list (see Section 1), during which time the mutator is active. The mutator may not, therefore, request cells until the collector makes them available.

The marking phase of Dijkstra's algorithm is more complex than the classical serial marking explained in Section 1. Two mark bits are required (instead of one) because a cell may be in one of three states. These states are represented by colors: *white* (unmarked), *black* (marked), and *gray* (indicating that the cell has been requested and used by a program). Intuitively, gray nodes are good candidates for becoming black. The mutator helps the marking phase of the collector by turning a white cell gray when the cell is requested and used by a program. The mutator is also responsible for triggering an interruption whenever the free list contains only one cell. Mutator processing resumes when the collector returns at least one more cell to the free list.

One of the collector's tasks is to mark the used cells, the cells in the free list, and any gray cells. This is done by initially graying the first used cell and the first free-list cell. Tracing proceeds by graying any cells linked to a gray cell c, and then blackening c. When the tracing ends, the white cells are incorporated to the free list and the black cells are whitened. As a result, inactive gray cells are first blackened by the collector and then whitened. During the *next* cycle of the collector these cells are incorporated into the free list.

France [FRAN78], Gries [GRIE77], and Muller [MULL76] provide detailed descriptions of Dijkstra's algorithm, but their main concern is to prove correctness. An extension of Dijkstra's algorithm with multiple mutators is considered in LAMP76.

Steele [STEE75] has independently developed a method for parallel garbage collection based on the Minsky–Knuth suggestion. He was one of the first to propose

Computing Surveys, Vol. 13, No. 3, September 1981

actual algorithms for collecting in parallel. Steel's collector makes exclusive use of semaphores and requires two bits per cell, which are used not only for marking but also for compacting and for readjusting pointers. Compaction is done using the two-pointer technique described in Section 1.2.

Comparing Dijkstra's to Steele's algorithm is difficult because these authors had different objectives. The former wanted to assure the correctness of his algorithm (regardless of its efficiency), whereas the latter had in mind an implementation using special hardware, possibly microcoded.

In a recent paper, Kung and Song [KUNG77] propose a variant of Dijkstra's method which uses four colors for marking and which does not need to trace the free list. The authors prove the correctness of the algorithm and show that it is more efficient than Dijkstra's. To this author's knowledge, none of the parallel garbage collection algorithms has been implemented, nor are any detailed results from simulation yet available.[12]

An alternative to using two processors is to have *one* processor time-share the duties of the mutator and the collector. Wadler [WADL76] shows (analytically) that algorithms for performing garbage collection with time-sharing demand a greater percentage of the processing time than does classical sequential garbage collection. This is because the collection effort must proceed even when there is no demand for it.

A second approach for avoiding substantial program interruptions due to garbage collection has been proposed by Baker [BAKE78a, BAKE78b]. His method is an interesting modification of the collector described in Section 3. Baker's modification is such that each time a cell is requested (i.e., a *cons* is executed) a fixed number of cells, k, are moved from one semispace to the other. This implies that the two semispaces are simultaneously active. In a paging environment, the extra memory required is of less significance than the possible increase in the size of the average working set. Since the moved lists are compacted, page faults are likely to be minimized.

The moving of k cells during a *cons* corresponds to the tracing of that many cells in classical garbage collection. By distributing some of the garbage collection tasks during list processing, Baker's method provides a guarantee that actual garbage collection cannot last more than a fixed (tolerable) amount of time: the time to flip the semispaces and to readjust a fixed number of pointers declared in the user's program. Thus his algorithm may be used in real-time applications.

A characteristic of Baker's real-time algorithm is that the size of the semispaces may have to be increased, depending on the value of k and the type of list processing done by the program. In other words, the choice of k expresses the trade-off between the time to execute a *cons* and the total storage required. For example, for $k = \frac{1}{3}$, a cell is moved every third time a *cons* is called. This would speed up the computation but increase the amount of storage required.

In his paper Baker offers an informal proof of his algorithm's correctness and shows how it can be modified to handle varisized cells and arrays of pointers. He also presents analyses of storage requirements of the algorithm and how they compare with those of other garbage collection methods. A LISP machine built at M.I.T. used Baker's approach [BAWD77];[13] its memory is subdivided into areas, and a list of outgoing references is kept for each. Those areas which do not change during program execution are not copied: tracing starts from their corresponding list of outgoing references. This approach, which has been further developed by Bishop (see Section 3 and BISH77), is a possible alternative for real-time collection. Another alternative is the use of an auxiliary processor as suggested by Deutsch and Bobrow [DEUT76] in their incremental garbage collection technique mentioned in the previous section.

---

[12] A simulation is briefly reported in KUNG77.

[13] This machine is a dedicated processor now in experimental operation. The builders report that, immediately following a semispace flip, the system performance may be degraded. This is due to the copying of objects from the old semispace into the new one. A variant of Baker's approach [LIEB80] is now being implemented in the MIT LISP machine.

*   *Jacques Cohen*

6. ANALYSES

Execution of a list-processing program typically involves many garbage collections. Let n be the average number of cells which are marked in one classical collection of single-sized cells. Let m be the total number of cells in the memory. Therefore, on the average, $m - n$ cells are recovered during one garbage collection. Collection time can be expressed by

$$\text{collection time} = \alpha n + \beta(m - n),$$

where α is the average time taken to mark (and subsequently unmark) a used cell and β is the average time taken to collect a free cell. Each inaccessible cell is inspected only once. Since the time for marking is much greater than the time for reclaiming inaccessible cells, it is not unreasonable to assume that β is considerably smaller than α. If compaction is used, the pointers of n cells may have to be readjusted, thereby increasing even more the ratio of the coefficient of n and $m - n$. Detailed estimates for α and β have appeared in KNUT73, p. 592, and in BAER77.

The cost of collection per collected word is

$$\text{collection cost per collected word}$$

$$= \frac{\alpha\rho}{1 - \rho} + \beta,$$

where ρ is the ratio n/m. If $\rho = \frac{1}{4}$, the memory is one-fourth full, and the cost is $\frac{1}{3}\alpha + \beta$. A larger value of ρ, for example, $\frac{3}{4}$, yields a larger cost $(3\alpha + \beta)$. This type of analysis, presented in KNUT73, shows how inefficient garbage collection can be when the memory becomes full.

Two new quantities N and T are now introduced. N stands for the total number of cells collected in the entire run of the program. T is the total time spent in useful program execution, excluding garbage collection. Then the total time for program execution is

$$\text{total program execution time}$$

$$= N \left(\frac{\alpha\rho}{1 - \rho} + \beta \right) + T.$$

Let γ be the ratio T/N, that is, the useful computing time per word collected. Hoare

[HOAR74] posits that the total cost of a program is proportional to the *product* of space and time:

$$\text{cost} = Nm \left(\frac{\alpha\rho}{1 - \rho} + \beta + \gamma \right). \quad (1)$$

This function reaches a minimum with respect to m when

$$\rho = \frac{1}{1 + r} \qquad \text{where} \quad r = \sqrt{\frac{\alpha}{\beta + \gamma}}.$$

Hoare's paper presents curves indicating how the cost varies with $1/\rho$ for various values of r. He points out that when $\alpha = 1$ and β is small compared to α, the extreme values of r are 1, and $\frac{1}{4}$. For these values of r, the cost curves are rather shallow around the optimum. Hoare suggests that a simple strategy for minimizing costs is to ensure that, after each collection, ρ lies between 0.6 and 0.8. If this does not occur, he recommends expanding or releasing the available memory so that ρ becomes approximately equal to 0.7. Hoare's analysis also indicates that the use of reference counters is justified only for programs whose value of r is close to one (i.e., γ is small).

Campbell [CAMP74] argues that Hoare's hypothesis of costs proportional to the product of time and space may be unrealistic. Campbell claims that, in certain large symbolic computations, *time*, rather than the product of space and time, should be minimized, since the amount of space needed to solve a problem is not subject to reduction. In these cases, the optimal strategy is to maximize the ratio of T to garbage collection time, that is,

$$\frac{\gamma}{\alpha\rho/(1 - \rho) + \beta}.$$

The above function has no extremum; according to Campbell, the recommended strategy is the "counsel of despair": choose m, the number of available cells, as large as possible.

Campbell also proposes a refinement of Hoare's analysis, that is, the one which minimizes the product of space and time. He notes that after a collection, a certain percentage, f, of the free list remaining from the previous collection is still free. Another percentage, g, of the rest of the storage

Computing Surveys, Vol. 13, No. 3, September 1981

204

corresponds to allocated but inactive cells. Let F_j be the size of the free list after the jth collection. Then

$$F_j = fF_{j-1} + g(m - F_{j-1})$$
$$= gm + hF_{j-1}$$

and

$$F_0 = m.$$

Campbell uses the above difference equation in connection with Eq. (1) to obtain optimal strategies similar to Hoare's but involving the quantities f and g. He claims that when $f = 0.4$ and $h = 0.2$, the optimal costs correspond to values of ρ below 0.6. Campbell then suggests that the best rule of thumb is to consider $\rho = \frac{1}{2}$—to insure that, after each collection, half of the total number of cells be available in the free list.

In the final part of his paper, Campbell proposes yet another variant of Hoare's analysis. This variant is applicable when a user knows the approximate total number of cells, W, the program will request during its execution. Campbell points out that there are several symbolic computations for which W can be estimated, and this may be used to develop optimal strategies for selecting ρ.

Arnborg's analytical study of optimal strategies [ARNB74] yields results similar to Hoare's. Arnborg considers the time to collect to be a linear function of n only, n being the number of marked (or active) cells. Like Campbell, he establishes difference equations which express storage availability between successive collections. Arnborg, however, uses smooth functions to approximate the difference equations. His results are obtained by minimizing an integral which expresses the total costs of collecting and actual computing. Arnborg's strategy, like Hoare's, is to determine the best size for storage after each collection. The strategy has been implemented in a SIMULA compiler running on a PDP-10. He claims that his strategy gave consistently better results than ad hoc policies designed for specific programs.

In a recent paper, Larson [LARS77] proposes still another method for minimizing garbage collection time by suitably choosing the size m of storage available. Collection time is expressed by

$$\text{collection time} = \alpha'n + \beta'm,$$

where α' and β' are quite similar to a and b as defined in the beginning of this section: α' is the time to mark, compact, readjust pointers, and unmark an active cell; β' is the time to inspect each cell. As indicated previously, α' is substantially greater than β'.

Larson measures the computation effort by the amount of data which are produced by a program. In LISP, for example, this corresponds to the number of *cons*. Larson proposes using a smooth function $n(x)$ expressing the number of active cells at the point in the computation at which x cells have been produced.

The total garbage collection time is expressed by an integral of a function of $n(x)$, α', β', and m. When α' and β' are independent of m, the minimization of the integral leads to a strategy identical to Campbell's: m should be as large as possible. The results are somewhat different when α' and β' vary with m. This occurs when virtual memory is used, since the values of α' and β' depend on the relative amounts of fast and slow memory available. Larson's strategy is summarized as follows: if the number of active cells n approaches the number of cells in the fast memory (m_0), minimization occurs when $m = m_0$, and it is therefore preferable to use fast storage only.

The cost of garbage collection when using very large virtual memories has been studied by Bishop [BISH77]. He argues that there are two components of the cost: the time to perform the collection, and the overhead caused by the increase in page faults when garbage is left uncollected. As seen previously, the first component increases linearly with the number of active cells. Bishop claims that the second component increases more than linearly with the amount of existing garbage. He expresses the second component in the form cx^a, where x is the number of uncollected cells and c and a are parameters. Another important variable is r, the rate at which garbage is generated by a program. Bishop assumes that garbage collection is performed periodically, and he minimizes the cost of collection with respect to the collection frequency. The optimal frequency is expressed as a function of the parameters a, c, r and the number of active cells n. Bishop's main result is that when $a \approx 1$ the cost of garbage collection (per cell collected) is proportional to n but inversely proportional to r, the rate of garbage generation. He then shows that the cost of collection can be reduced by segregating cells with different rates of garbage generation in separate areas of the memory.

Wadler [WADL76] presents two analyses of algorithms for real-time garbage collection. One applies to the Dijkstra–Steele method, which uses two parallel processors: the mutator and the collector. A *c-time* is defined by Wadler as the beginning of the collector's cycle. He also defines a *floating cell* as a cell which is marked by the mutator or collector at a *c-time* but is released before the beginning of the next cycle. Floating cells are momentarily useless since they are neither accessible by the collector nor available to the mutator. An extremely unfavorable situation for parallel garbage collection occurs when the only cells that are returned to the free list are the ones which were floating at a *c-time*. Even more unfortunately, Wadler's analytical study of the algorithm's average performance indicates that this unfavorable situation happens quite often.

Wadler then proceeds to define *power drain* as the ratio of the collector time to the mutator time. Using this definition, it is easy to show that the ratio of power drains between parallel and classical garbage collection can even be infinite: Consider, for example, the case where no cells are used or released. In classical garbage collection, the power drain is zero since the collector is never called. In parallel garbage collection, the power drain is one since the collector is kept busy even if it cannot retrieve any cells.

Wadler shows that when the two processors operate at maximum capacity,[14] the ratio of power drains is 2. This means that parallel garbage collection requires at least twice as much processing power as sequential garbage collection. He claims that with

___
[14] This maximum capacity is determined analytically.

the falling cost of processors, this drawback is amply offset by the advantage of avoiding garbage collection interruptions.

Wadler also analyzes the algorithm in which the tasks of the mutator and the collector are time-shared by a single processor. He finds that in this case also, the power drain is 2 if the collector is not wasting time attempting to do unnecessary garbage collection.

7. REMARKS ON LANGUAGE IMPLEMENTATION

Recursion is frequently utilized in programs which manipulate linked-list structures. A stack is indispensable for executing these programs. Therefore, separate regions for the allocated cells and for the stack must coexist in the memory. It is true that stacks can be "simulated" by linked lists, so that the memory stores only list structures. However, this is both space- and time-consuming, because an extra field is required to link together the data in the stack and more complex operations are needed for pushing and popping. It is therefore simpler to implement the stack in contiguous positions of the memory.

It has become current practice to divide the available memory into two areas which are allowed to grow from opposite ends. One of these is reserved for a stack using contiguous locations. The other, called the *heap*, is available to the allocator for providing new cells, also from contiguous locations. With this arrangement, a simple test can be used to trigger garbage collection. When the pointer to the next free stack position meets the pointer to the next available position in the heap, collection with compaction is invoked to retrieve space for new cells or for stacking. Therefore, the functions *push* and *new* (for requesting new cells) may trigger garbage collection.

In the case of LISP programs, the function *new* corresponds to a *cons*, and *push* is used internally by the compiler or interpreter. Collection can be started either by a *cons* or by a stack overflow caused by situations such as great recursion depth or reading long atoms (see BERK64 and COHE72).

Since the stack is used in implementing recursion, it usually contains pointers to active, useful cells. The marking algorithms of Section 1 are used to mark not only the structures referred to by the pointer variables of a program but also those structures which are referred to by pointers on the stack. Therefore, means must be provided to recognize whether a stacked quantity is a pointer (tag bits may be used for this purpose).

LISP processors sometimes allow a user to invoke the collector. This is useful when he has an idea of the most propitious time for triggering the collection. Also, the function *return* may be made available to the user. When a free list is used, the returned cells can be immediately incorporated into the list. However, when compaction is required (e.g., with the heap and stack arrangement), the returned cells may not be available to the allocator until after the next collection. Another problem with the function *return* is that a cell may be explicitly returned even though there is still a pointer to it. (This is sometimes called the *dangling reference* problem.) Thus care must be taken not to reuse the cell until there are no pointers to it.

Processors for languages like PL/I and PASCAL allow a user to call the function *new* and provide messages when storage is exhausted. The use of the functions *return* or *collect* is implementation dependent. This author is unaware of PASCAL runtime systems which perform fully automatic garbage collection. It is the user's responsibility to keep free lists of unused cells and to check whether a new cell may be obtained from a free list or must be requested from the allocator. The techniques for doing this kind of storage management are beyond the scope of this paper.

Arnborg [ARNB72] described the implementation of a SIMULA compiler designed to operate in a virtual memory environment. SIMULA is a language with block structure: variables declared in a block or procedure exist only when the block or procedure is activated. Although it would seem at first sight that one could collect the structures referred to by pointer variables upon exiting from the block in which they are declared, this is not the case. SIMULA also allows variables of such types as classes, arrays, and texts which may have longer life spans than their originating blocks; if these variables share linked structures with local block variables, collection cannot be done when exiting from a block.

Since Arnborg's proposed implementation operated in a paging environment, one of the objectives of the collection is to reduce the number of page faults. To perform the collection, Arnborg uses a variant of the method proposed by Fenichel and Yochelson [FENI69] described in Section 3. The variant can handle varisized cells rather than only simple LISP cells.

A SNOBOL implementation proposed by Hanson [HANS77] uses a variation of the garbage collection techniques for collecting varisized cells described in Section 2. It is assumed that additional space for the heap and for the stack can be requested from the operating system, although such requests should be kept to a minimum. An effort is made to reduce collection time by avoiding marking cells which are known to be used throughout the program's execution.[15] For this purpose the heap is subdivided into two areas of consecutive locations: *heap* 1 and *heap* 2. The first contains information which is constantly active and never needs to be marked; the second may contain inactive cells which can be collected. New cells may be requested from either area.

Collection is triggered when one of the heaps runs out of space. The phases of marking and compacting are applied only to the information in *heap* 2, although tracing and pointer readjustment in *heap* 1 may be necessary. A fourth phase, "*moving heap* 2," may be necessary to make room for *heap* 1 when an overflow of the latter triggered the collection. The allocator of the operating system is called when no cells can be collected from *heap* 2.[16]

Certain list processors, including SNOBOL and LISP, need to keep symbol tables which are updated at execution time when new atoms are read. These symbol tables

---

[15] Certain implementations of LISP's list of atoms may take advantage of this feature.
[16] Note that Bishop's technique of keeping lists of interarea links (see BISH77) could be used to administer these heaps.

often utilize hashing techniques and keep linear linked lists of identifiers (atoms) having the same hash value. The linear lists are stored in the heap, and means must be provided to reclaim inactive list elements. This reclamation may be crucial in applications which use a large number of atoms. A scheme for collecting these atoms is proposed in FRIE76. A related problem is that of collecting LISP atoms whose property lists are shared by other atoms. A method for collecting nonshared atoms and their property lists is described in MOON74.

Next to LISP, ALGOL 68 is the language for whose garbage collection implementation the most literature exists. This is not surprising, since ALGOL 68 allows for a variety of complex situations because of the interaction of such features as block structure, references that can point to different types of cells, linked structures that may reside in the stack or in the heap, and sharing of arrays (slices). Both the implementor and the user of the language can take advantage of some of these features to minimize collection time.

In ALGOL 68, each element of a cell must be marked since structures may share parts of cells. (A separate bit table may be used for this purpose.) Wodon [WODO69] suggests two possible approaches for marking varisized cells in ALGOL 68. One is the "interpretive" approach represented by the program of Figure 2. The parameter p is specified by two components: the pointer, and the type of the cell being pointed to. This latter information could be stored in the cell itself, but it is more economical to precompute, at compile time, *templates* which list the characteristics of each cell type: size and a bit pattern specifying which elements of the cell are pointers. Determining these quantities is more complex when a pointer can refer to cells of different types. (Templates may also contain pointers to other templates which describe the kind of cell referenced by each pointer.) This marking approach is called interpretive because the information in the templates may have to be processed several times during execution.

The second approach suggested by Wodon is to *compile*, for each program, a more efficient marking routine specific for tracing

the cells used in that program. Detailed descriptions (in ALGOL 68) of the interpretive and compiling approaches appear in BRAN71 and WODO71. It is believed that the compiling approach is more efficient than the interpretive one but requires additional storage for the local marking routines. The given references also propose using a compacting procedure requiring an external break table for readjusting pointers.

The collectors for ALGOL 68 proposed by Marshall [MARS71] and by Goyer [GOYE71] are also based on the classical techniques described in Section 2. The first uses the link-reversal technique for marking and Haddon and Waite's method [HADD67] for compaction and pointer readjustment. The second uses a stack for marking and a simplified version of Haddon and Waite's compacting procedure which requires an external break table. Note that the space used by the stack can be reused later by the break table. This additional space is needed only during garbage collection and can be returned to the operating system thereafter.

Baecker [BAEC70] makes recommendations on how to implement the ALGOL 68 heap in a computer with multilevel storage and which uses segmentation (i.e., addresses are given by an integer, referring to a segment, and an offset which specifies the location of a word within the segment). He also proposes introducing language constructs to allow a user to define different heap *areas* and to request that cells be allocated in specific areas of his choice [BAEC75].

8. FINAL REMARKS

Tables 1–5 summarize the characteristics of the main algorithms described in the corresponding Sections 1–5. The number of references presented in the bibliography bears witness to the importance of and interest in garbage collection. In spite of this activity, many facets of garbage collection remain to be investigated. In particular, no comparison has been made of the relative efficiencies of many of the algorithms described in Sections 1–5.

New developments in hardware are likely

Table 1

Algorithm	Main references	Auxiliary storage	Mark (M) or tag (T) bits	Complexity	Comments	Related work
Marking Single-Sized Cells[a] (n is the total number of accessible cells)						
Classical	KNUT73	Stack	M	$O(n)$	Stack may be as large as n	
Bounded workspace	KNUT73 (p. 415)	Limited-size stack	M	$O(n)$	Requires more time than the classical algorithm	KURO75, KURO79
Link reversal (Deutsch–Schorr–Waite)	SCHO67, KNUT73	No stack is needed	M and T	$O(n)$	As above (the tag bit may be replaced by the atom bit [KNUT73])	VEIL76, KOWA79, GERH79, GRIE79, LEE 79, TOPO79
Link reversal with bit stack	WEGB72b	Bit stack	M	$O(n)$	Similar to the above algorithm	SCHO67
Hybrid	KNUT73 (p. 592)	Limited-size stack	M and T	$O(n)$	Uses a combination of stack and link reversal	
Compaction of Single-Sized Cells (m is the total number of available cells)						
Two pointer	KNUT73 (p. 421)	None	None	$O(m)$	Only applicable to single-sized cells. Compaction is of arbitrary type[b]	HART64, COHE67b, DIJK76a
Moving Collectors of Single-Sized Cells (n is the total number of accessible cells)						
Minsky	MINS63	None	M	$O(n)$	Compaction of linearizing[b] type using LIFO traversal	
Fenichel-Yochelson	FENI69	Stack	None	$O(n)$	Uses two semispaces. Compaction of linearizing type[b] using LIFO traversal	MINS63
Cheney	CHEN70	None	None	$O(n)$	Compaction using FIFO traversal	WALD72
Reingold	REIN73	None	None	$O(n)$	Compaction using LIFO traversal and link reversal	SCHO67
Clark	CLAR76	None	None	$O(n)$	Compaction using LIFO traversal	

[a] These marking algorithms may be extended to mark varisized cells.
[b] See Section 1.

Table 2

Marking Varisized Cells (n is the total number of accessible cells)

Algorithm	Main references	Auxiliary storage	Mark (M) or tag (T) bits	Complexity	Comments	Related work
Classical	KNUT73	Stack	M	$O(n)$	Stack can be stored using an additional field of each cell	THOR72, WODO71
Link reversal	THOR72, THOR76	No stack is needed	M and several T's	$O(n)$	Requires log *maxm* bits per cell, where *maxm* is the size of largest cell	FENI71, MARS71, WODO71, HANS77

Compacting Varisized Cells (m is the total number of available cells)
All these compactors are of the sliding type[a]

Algorithm	Main references	Auxiliary storage	Mark (M) or tag (T) bits	Complexity	Comments	Related work
Rolling table (Haddon–Waite)	HADD67	None	None	$O(m \log m)$[b]	Break table (see Section 2.2) has to be rolled and sorted	FITC78
LISP 2	KNUT73 (p. 602)	Additional word per cell	None	$O(m)$	Requires three or more scans	WEGB72a, THOR76, LANG72, FITC78, TERA78
Morris	MORR78	None	T	$O(m)$	Requires two scans	JONK79, WISE79
Jonkers	JONK79	None	None	$O(m)$	Requires two scans	

Moving (Copying) Collectors of Varisized Cells (n is the total number of accessible cells)

Algorithm	Main references	Auxiliary storage	Mark (M) or tag (T) bits	Complexity	Comments	Related work
Variant of Fenichel–Yochelson and Cheney	BAKE78	None	None	$O(n)$	Moves cells in a breadth-first order	FENI69, ARNB72, CHEN70
Standish	STAN80	One field per cell	None	$O(n)$	Copies using three passes	THOR72

[a] See Section 1.
[b] Worst case.

Table 3. Collecting in Virtual Memory

Algorithm	Main references	Auxiliary storage	Comments	Related work
Baker	BAKE78	None	Uses two semispaces	FENI69, CHEN70
Bishop	BISH77	Space for keeping interarea lists	Designed for use in very large virtual memories	

Table 4. Reference Counters (m is the number of available cells)

Algorithm	Main references	Storage needed	Comments	Related work
Classical	COLL60, WEIZ63	An extra field (of size m) per cell	Cannot handle general circular lists	KNUT73, WEIZ69
Hybrid	KNUT73, DEUT76	An extra field (of size $m' \ll m$) per cell Auxiliary Tables	Combines reference counters with classical compacting garbage collection	WISE77

Table 5. Parallel and Real-Time Collection

Algorithm	Main references	Storage needed	Comments	Related work
Parallel (Dijkstra)	DIJK76b	No stack and two bits per cell	Main objective is to prove correctness; uses a free list	MULL76, GRIE77, FRAN78, KUNG77
Parallel (Steele)	STEE75	Stack, two bits per cell, and several semaphores	Designed to be microcoded; does compacting as well	WADL76, DIJK76b
Baker	BAKE78	Two semispaces whose sizes vary at execution time	Moving of accessible cells is done when a new cell is requested	MINS63, FENI69, CHEN70

to play an important role in speeding up collection. It has already been suggested that new machines should contain extra bits per word to be used for marking, tagging, or counting references. Machines with special hardware for segmentation and list processing have recently been constructed [BAWD77] and are now in experimental operation.

There has been an undeniable trend toward designing and implementing collectors for varisized cells stored in large virtual memories. No explicit guidance based on experimental evidence is yet available on how to do this collection efficiently or in real time. Two promising directions, discussed in Section 5, involve either using parallel processors or distributing some of the garbage collection tasks during the actual processing. It is hoped that this will allow the collection to be performed within a known, tolerable, maximum time.

Collection in very large virtual memories is another subject which will become increasingly important. The suggested approaches for these collections deserve further study [BISH77].

If these efforts in the direction of achieving efficient garbage collection succeed, they are bound to have an impact on the design of future programming languages.

ACKNOWLEDGMENTS

Joel Katcoff scrutinized every paragraph of the original and revised manuscripts. His stress on clarity and simplicity, coupled with his constructive remarks, was of great value in producing a better paper. The referees' and editor's comments made many other improvements possible. In particular, one of the referees, Peter Bishop, provided several pages of detailed suggestions on how to reorganize and make more precise the contents of the paper. A second referee also provided numerous constructive remarks. The author learned a great deal from these people, and this paper benefited greatly from their help. Carolyn Boettner's aid in preparing the final version of the manuscript is gratefully acknowledged. Finally, the author wishes to thank Jane Jordan for the care and patience with which she typed the text and its several revisions.

This work was supported by the National Science Foundation under grants MCS 74-24569 A01 and MCS 79-05522.

REFERENCES

The bibliography which follows includes a few references which are not explicitly mentioned in the text. Each reference is associated with a profile consisting of a sequence of letters between braces. The letters characterize the contents of the paper and their relationship to the topics covered in this survey.

A: Analysis
B: Benchmarks
C: Compacting
G: General
L: Language Features and Implementation
M: Marking
N: Reference Counters
P: Parallel and Real-Time Processing
R: Records or Varisized Cells
S: Copying and Secondary Storage
V: Virtual Memory

ARNB72   ARNBORG, S. "Storage administration in a virtual memory simulation system," *BIT* **12**, 2 (1972), 125–141. {CGLMRV}

ARNB74   ARNBORG, S. "Optimal memory management in a system with garbage collection," *BIT* **14**, 4 (1974), 375–381. {A}

AUGE79   AUGENSTEIN, M. J., AND TENENBAUM, A. M. *Data structures and PL/I programming*, Prentice-Hall, Englewood Cliffs, N.J., 1979. {GMN}

BAEC70   BAECKER, H.D. "Implementing the ALGOL 68 heap," *BIT* **10**, 4 (1970), 405–414. {GLV}

BAEC72   BAECKER, H.D. "Garbage collection for virtual memory computer systems," *Commun. ACM* **15**, 11 (Nov. 1972), 981–986. {BCMRV}

BAEC75   BAECKER, H.D. "Areas and record-classes," *Comput. J.* **18**, 3 (Aug. 1975), 223–226. {GL}

BAER77   BAER, J.L., AND FRIES, H. "On the efficiency of some list marking algorithms," in *Information processing 1977*, B. Gilchrist (Ed.), IFIP, North-Holland, Amsterdam, 1977, pp. 751–756. {ABM}

BAKE78a   BAKER, H.G. "Actor systems for real time computation," Lab. for Computer Science, MIT Rep. TR-197, M.I.T., Cambridge, Mass., March 1978 (see BAKE78b).

BAKE78b   BAKER, H.G. "List-processing in real time on a serial computer." *Commun. ACM* **21**, 4 (April 1978), 280–294. {ACGMNPRSV}

BART77   BARTH, J.M. "Shifting garbage collection overhead to compile time," *Commun. ACM* **20**, 7 (July 1977), 513–518. {LN}

BAWD77   BAWDEN, A., GREENBLATT, R., HOLLOWAY, J., KNIGHT, T., MOON, D., AND WEINREB, D. "Lisp machine progress report," Memo 444, A.I. Lab, M.I.T., Cambridge, Mass., Aug. 1977. {G}

BERK64   BERKELEY, E.C., AND BOBROW, D.G. (Eds.) *The programming language LISP*, M.I.T., Cambridge, Mass. 1974, 4th printing. {GL}

BERR78   BERRY, D.M., AND SORKIN, A. "Time required for garbage collection in retention block-structures languages," *Int. J. Comput. Information Sci.* **7**, 4 (1978), 361–404. {AL}

BERZ75   BERZTISS, A.T. *Data structures theory and practice*, 2nd ed., Academic Press, New York, 1975. {G}

BISH77   BISHOP, P.B. "Computer systems with a very large address space and garbage collection," Lab. for Computer Science, MIT Rep., TR-178, M.I.T., Cambridge, Mass., May 1977. {ACGLMRSV}

BOBR67   BOBROW, D.G., AND MURPHY, D.L. "Structure of a LISP system using two-level storage," *Commun. ACM* **10**, 3 (March 1967), 155–159. {V}

BOBR68a   BOBROW, D.G. *Storage management in Lisp, in symbol manipulation languages and techniques*, D. G. Bobrow (Ed.), North-Holland, Amsterdam, 1968. {CGMV}

BOBR68b   BOBROW, D.G., AND MURPHY, D.L. "A note on the efficiency of a LISP computation in a paged machine," *Commun. ACM* **11**, 8 (Aug. 1968), 558–560. {V}

BOBR75   BOBROW, D.G. "A note on hash linking," *Commun. ACM* **18**, 7 (July 1975), 413–415. {N}

BOBR80   BOBROW, D.G. "Managing reentrant structures using reference counts," *ACM Trans. Programming Lang. Syst.* **2**, 3 (July 1980), 269–273. {N}

BRAN71   BRANQUART, P., AND LEWI, J. "A scheme of storage allocation and garbage collection for Algol 68," in *Algol 68 implementation*, J. E. L. Peck, (Ed.), North-Holland, Amsterdam, 1971, pp. 199–238. {CGLMR}

CAMP74   CAMPBELL, J.A. "Optimal use of storage in a simple model of garbage collection," *Inf. Process. Lett.* **3**, 2 (Nov. 1974), 37–38. {A}

CHEN70   CHENEY, C.J. "A nonrecursive list compacting algorithm," *Commun. ACM* **13**, 11 (Nov. 1970), 677–678. {CRSV}

CLAR75   CLARK, D.W. "A fast algorithm for copying binary trees," *Inf. Process. Lett.* **9**, 3 (Dec. 1975), 62–63. {AC}

CLAR76   CLARK, D.W. "An efficient list moving algorithm using constant workspace," *Commun. ACM* **19**, 6 (June 1976), 352–354. {CRS}

CLAR77   CLARK, D.W., AND GREEN, C.C. "An empirical study of list structure in Lisp," *Commun. ACM* **20**, 2 (Feb. 1977), 78–86. {BV}

CLAR78a   CLARK, D.W. "A fast algorithm for copying list structures," *Commun. ACM* **21**, 5 (May 1978), 351–357. {ACRS}

CLAR78b   CLARK, D.W., AND GREEN, C.C. "A note on shared list structure in Lisp," *Inf. Process. Lett* **7**, 6 (Oct. 1978), 312–314. {B}

CLAR79   CLARK, D.W. "Measurements of dynamic list structure in Lisp," *IEEE Trans. Softw. Eng.* **SE-5**, 1 (Jan. 1979), 51–59. {BV}

COHE67a   COHEN, J. "Use of fast and slow memories in list-processing languages," *Commun. ACM* **10**, 2 (Feb. 1967), 82–86. {V}

COHE67b   COHEN, J., AND TRILLING, L. "Remarks on garbage collection using a two level storage," *BIT* **7**, 1 (1967), 22–30. {BCMV}

COHE72   COHEN, J., AND ZUCKERMAN, C. "Evalquote in simple Fortran: A tutorial on interpreting Lisp," *BIT* **12**, 3 (1972), 299–317. {CGM}

COLL60   COLLINS, G.E. "A method for overlapping and erasure of lists," *Commun. ACM* **3**, 12 (Dec. 1960), 655–657. {N}

DEUT76   DEUTSCH, L.P., AND BOBROW, D.G. "An efficient incremental automatic garbage collector," *Commun. ACM* **19**, 9 (Sept. 1976), 522–526. {CGLNV}

DIJK76a   DIJKSTRA, E.W. *A discipline of programming*, Prentice-Hall, Englewood Cliffs, N.J., 1976, Chap. 14. {G}

DIJK76b   DIJKSTRA, E.W., LAMPORT, L., MARTIN, A.J., SCHOLTEN, C.S., AND STEFFENS, E.F.M. "On-the-fly garbage collection: An exercise in cooperation," in *Lecture Notes in Computer Science*, No. 46, Springer-Verlag, New York, 1976; also appeared in *Commun. ACM* **21**, 11 (Nov. 1978), 966–975. {P}

DWYE73   DWYER, B. "Simple algorithms for traversing a tree without an auxiliary stack," *Inf. Process. Lett.* **2**, 5 (Dec. 1973), 143–145. {M}

ELSO75   ELSON, M. "Data structures," Science Research Associates, 1975. {CGMN}

FENI69   FENICHEL, R., AND YOCHELSON, J. "A LISP garbage-collector for virtual-memory computer systems," *Commun. ACM* **12**, 11 (Nov. 1969), 611–612. {CSV}

FENI71   FENICHEL, R. "List tracing in systems allowing multiple cell-types," *Commun. ACM* **14**, 8 (Aug. 1971), 522–526. {MLR}

FISH74   FISHER, D.A. "Bounded workspace garbage collection in an address order preserving list processing environment," *Inf. Process. Lett.* **3**, 1 (July 1974), 29–32. {CMR}

FISH75   FISHER, D.A. "Copying cyclic list structure in linear time using bounded workspace," *Commun. ACM* **18**, 5 (May 1975), 251–252. {CS}

FITC78   FITCH, J.P., AND NORMAN, A.C. "A note on compacting garbage collection," *Comput. J.* **21**, 1 (Feb. 1978), 31–34. {ABCR}

FOST68   FOSTER, J.M. *List processing*, Elsevier Computer Monographs, Elsevier-North Holland, New York, 1968. {G}

FRAN78   FRANCEZ, N. "An application of a method for analysis of cyclic programs," *IEEE Trans. Softw. Eng.* **4**, 5 (Sept. 1978), 371–377. {P}

FRIE76   FRIEDMAN, D.P., AND WISE, D.S. "Garbage collecting a heap which included a scatter table," *Inf. Process. Lett.* **5**, 6 (Dec. 1976), 161–164. {LM}

FRIE79   FRIEDMAN, D.P., AND WISE, D.S. "Reference counting can manage the circular environments of mutual recursion," *Inf. Process. Lett.* **8**, 1 (Jan. 1979), 41–45. {N}

GERH79   GERHART, S.L. "A derivation oriented proof of Schorr–Waite marking algorithm," in *Lecture notes in computer science*, vol. 69, Springer-Verlag, New York, 1979, pp. 472–492. {M}

GOTL78   GOTLIEB, C.C., AND GOTLIEB, L.R. *Data types and structures*, Prentice-Hall, Englewood Cliffs, N.J., 1978. {CGMR}

GOYE71   GOYER, P. "A garbage collector to be implemented on a CDC 3100," in *Algol 68 implementation*, J. E. L. Peck (Ed.), North-Holland, Amsterdam, 1971, pp. 303–317. {CLMR}

GRIE77   GRIES, D. "An exercise in proving parallel programs correct," *Commun. ACM* **20**, 12 (Dec. 1977), 921–930. {P}

GRIE79   GRIES, D. "The Schorr–Waite graph marking algorithm," *Acta Inf.* **11**, 3 (1979), 223–232. {M}

GRIS72   GRISWOLD, R.E. *The macro implementation of Snobol 4*, W. H. Freeman, San Francisco, 1972. {GM}

HADD67   HADDON, B.K., AND WAITE, W.M. "A compaction procedure for variable length storage elements," *Comput. J.* **10** (Aug. 1967), 162–165. {CR}

HANS69   HANSEN, W.J. "Compact list representation: Definition, garbage collection, and system implementation," *Commun. ACM* **12**, 9 (Sept. 1969), 499–507. {CGRS}

HANS77   HANSON, D.R. "Storage management for an implementation of Snobol 4," *Software: Practice and Experience* **7**, 2 (1977), 179–192. {BCMLR}

HART64   HART, T.P., AND EVANS, T.G. "Notes on implementing lisp for the M 460 computer," in BERK64. {C}

HOAR74   HOARE, C.A.R. "Optimization of store size for garbage collection," *Inf. Process. Lett.* **2**, 6 (April 1974), 165–166. {A}

HORO77   HOROWITZ, E., AND SAHNI, S. *Fundamentals of data structure*, Com-

JONK79   JONKERS, H.B.M. "A fast garbage compaction algorithm," *Inf. Process. Lett.* **9,** 1 (July 1979), 26–30. {CR}

KAIN69   KAIN, Y. "Block structures, indirect addressing, and garbage collection," *Commun. ACM* **12,** 7 (July 1969), 395–398. {L}

KNUT73   KNUTH, D.E. *The art of computer programming, vol. I: Fundamental algorithms,* Addison-Wesley, Reading, Mass., 1973. {ACGMNPRS}

KOWA79   KOWALTOWSKI, T. "Data structures and correctness of programs," *J. ACM* **26,** 2 (April 1979), 283–301. {M}

KUNG77   KUNG, H.T., AND SONG, S.W. "An efficient parallel garbage collection system and its correctness proof," Dep. Computer Sci., Carnegie-Mellon Univ., Pittsburgh, Sept. 1977. {AP}

KURO75   KUROKAWA, T. "New marking algorithms for garbage collection," Collection, in *Proc. 2nd USA–Japan Computer Conf.*, 1975, pp. 580–584. {BM}

KURO79   KUROKAWA, T. "A new fast and safe marking algorithm," Toshiba R&D Center, Kawasaki 210, Japan, Jan. 1979. {BM}

LAMP76   LAMPORT, L. "Garbage collection with multiple processes: An exercise in parallelism," *Proc. IEEE Conf. Parallel Processing,* Aug. 1976. {P}

LANG72   LANG, B., AND WEGBREIT, B. "Fast compactification," Rep. 25–72, Harvard Univ., Cambridge, Mass., Nov. 1972. {CMR}

LARS77   LARSON, R.G. "Minimizing garbage collection as a function of region size," *SIAM J. Computing* **6,** 4 (Dec. 1977), 663–668. {AV}

LEE79   LEE, S., DE ROEVER, W.P., AND GERHART, S. "The evolution of list-copying algorithms," in *6th ACM Symp. Principles of Programming Languages* (San Antonio, Tex.), Jan. 1979, pp. 53–56. {MS}

LEE80   LEE, K.P. "A linear algorithm for copying binary trees using bounded workspace," *Commun. ACM* **23,** 3 (March 1980), 159–162. {S}

LIEB80   LIEBERMAN, H., AND HEWITT, C. "A real-time garbage collector that can recover temporary storage quickly," MIT Lab. for Computer Science Rep. TM-184, M.I.T., Cambridge, Mass., July 1980. {PV}

LIND73   LINDSTROM, G. "Scanning list structures without stacks or tag bits," *Inf. Process. Lett.* **2,** 2 (June 1973), 47–51. {M}

LIND74   LINDSTROM, G. "Copying list structures using bounded workspace," *Commun. ACM* **17,** 4 (April 1974), 198–202. {CS}

MARS71   MARSHALL, S. "An Algol-68 garbage collector," in *Algol 68 implementation,* J. E. L. Peck (Ed.), North-Holland, Amsterdam, 1971, pp. 239–243. {CLMR}

MINS63   MINSKY, M.L. "A Lisp garbage collector algorithm using serial secondary storage," Memo 58 (rev.), Project MAC, M.I.T., Cambridge, Mass., Dec. 1963. {CS}

MOON74   MOON, D.A. "MACLisp reference manual," Project MAC, M.I.T., Cambridge, Mass., April 1974. {GM}

MORR78   MORRIS, F.L. "A time- and space-efficient garbage compaction algorithm," *Commun. ACM* **21,** 8 (Aug. 1978), 662–665. {CGR}

MORR79   MORRIS, F.L. "On a comparison of garbage collection techniques," technical correspondence, *Commun. ACM* **22,** 10 (Oct. 1979), 571. {C}

MULL76   MULLER, K.G. "On the feasibility of concurrent garbage collection," Ph.D. thesis, Tech. Hogeschool Delft, March 1976. {P}

OWIC81   OWICKI, S. "Making the world safe for garbage collection," in *Proc. ACM Symp. Principles of Programming Languages* (Williamsburg), Jan. 1981. {LP}

PARE68   PARENTE, R.J. "A simulation-oriented memory allocation algorithm," in *Simulation Programming Languages,* J. N. Buxton (Ed.), North-Holland, Amsterdam, 1968, pp. 198–209. {CL}

PFAL77   PFALZ, J.L. *Computer data structures,* McGraw-Hill, New York, 1977. {CGMR}

REIN73   REINGOLD, E.M. "A nonrecursive list moving algorithm," *Commun. ACM* **16,** 5 (May 1973), 305–307. {CS}

ROBS73   ROBSON, J.M. "An improved algorithm for traversing binary trees without auxiliary stack," *Inf. Process. Lett.* **2,** 1 (March 1973), 12–14. {M}

ROBS77   ROBSON, J.M. "A bounded storage algorithm for copying cyclic structures," *Commun. ACM* **20,** 6 (June 1977), 431–433. {CSR}

ROCH71   ROCHFELD, A. "New LISP techniques for a paging environment," *Commun. ACM* **14,** 12 (Dec. 1971), 791–795. {V}

ROSS67   ROSS, D.T. "The AED free storage package," *Commun. ACM* **10,** 8 (Aug. 1967), 481–492. {GR}

SCHO67   SCHORR, H., AND WAITE, W. "An efficient machine-independent procedure for garbage collection in various list structures," *Commun. ACM* **10,** 8 (Aug. 1967), 501–506. {MR}

SIKL72   SIKLOSSY, L. "Fast and read-only algorithms for traversing trees without an auxiliary stack," *Inf. Process. Lett.* **1,** 4 (June 1972), 149–152. {M}

STAN80   STANDISH, T.A. *Data structures techniques,* Addison-Wesley, Reading, Mass., 1980. {ACGMNPRSV}

STEE75   STEELE, G.L. "Multiprocessing compactifying garbage collection," *Commun. ACM* **18,** 9 (Sept. 1975), 495–508. {CGP}

TERA78   TERASHIMA, M., AND GOTO, E. "Genetic order and compactifying garbage collectors," *Inf. Process. Lett.* **7,** 1 (Jan. 1978), 27–32. {CR}

THOR72   THORELLI, L.E. "Marking algorithms," *BIT* **12,** 4 (1972), 555–568. {MR}

THOR76   THORELLI, L.E. "A fast compactifying garbage collector," *BIT* **16,** 4 (1976), 426–441. {CMR}

TOPO79   TOPOR, R. "The correctness of the Schorr–Waite list marking algorithm," *Acta Inf.* **11,** 3 (1979), 211–221. {M}

VEIL76   VEILLON, G. "Transformations de programmes recursifs," *R.A.I.R.O. Informatique* **10,** 9 (Sept. 1976), 7–20. {M}

WADL76   WADLER, P.L. "Analysis of an algorithm for real time garbage collection," *Commun. ACM* **19,** 9 (Sept. 1976), 491–500. {AP}

WAIT73   WAITE, W.M. *Implementing software for non-numeric applications*, Prentice-Hall, Englewood Cliffs, N.J., 1973. {GCR}

WALD72   WALDEN, D.C. "A note on Cheney's nonrecursive list-compacting algorithm," *Commun. ACM* **15,** 4 (April 1972), 275. {CS}

WEGB72a   WEGBREIT, B. "A generalized compactifying garbage collector." *Comput. J.* **15,** 3 (Aug. 1972), 204–208. {CGMR}

WEGB72b   Wegbreit, B. "A space efficient list structure tracing algorithm," *IEEE Trans. Computers* **C21** (Sept. 1972), 1009–1010. {M}

WEIS67   WEISSMAN, C. *Lisp 1.5 primer*, Dickenson Publ., Belmont, Calif., 1967. {G}

WEIZ63   WEIZENBAUM, J. "Symmetric list processor," *Commun. ACM* **6,** 9 (Sept. 1963), 524–544. {LN}

WEIZ69   WEIZENBAUM, J. "Recovery of reentrant list structures in SLIP," *Commun. ACM* **12,** 7 (July 1969), 370–372. {LMN}

WISE77   WISE, D.S., AND FRIEDMAN, D.P. "The one-bit reference count," *BIT* **17,** 4 (1977), 351–359. {GLN}

WISE79   WISE, D.S. "Morris' garbage compaction algorithm restores reference counts," *ACM Trans. Programm. Lang. Syst.* **1,** 1 (July 1979), 115–120. {CNR}

WODO69   WODON, P.L. "Data structure and storage allocation," *BIT* **9,** 3 (1969), 270–282. {CGLMR}

WODO71   WODON, P.L. "Methods of garbage collection for Algol 68," in *Algol 68 implementation*, J. E. L. Peck (Ed.), North-Holland, Amsterdam, 1971, pp. 245–262. {CGLMR}

YELO77   YELOWITZ, L., AND DUNCAN, A.G. "Abstractions, instantiations and proofs of marking algorithms," in *Proc. Symp. Artificial Intelligence and Programming Languages, Sigplan Notices* (ACM) **12,** 8 (Aug. 1977), 13–21.

ZAVE75   ZAVE, D.A. "A fast compacting garbage collector," *Inf. Process. Lett.* **3,** 6 (July 1975), 167–169. {CMR}

Chapter 6: Functional-Programming-Oriented Architectures

The origin of functional languages as a practical class of computer languages can perhaps be traced to the development of Lisp by McCarthy [1] in the early 1960s, but their ancestry went directly back to the lambda calculus developed by Church in the 1930s. The objective of writing a functional program is to define a set of (possibly recursive) equations for each function [2]. Data structures are handled by introducing a special class of functions called constructor functions. This view allows functional languages to deal directly with structures that would be termed "abstract" in more conventional languages. Moreover, functions themselves can be passed around as data objects. The design of the necessary computer architecture to support functional languages thus centers around the mechanisms of efficient manipulation of data structures (list-oriented architectures) and the parallel evaluation of functional programs (function-oriented architectures).

List-oriented architectures are architectures designed to efficiently support the manipulation of data structures and objects. Lisp, a mnemonic for list processing language, is a well known language to support symbolic processing. There are several reasons why Lisp and list-oriented computers are really needed. First, to relieve the burden on the programmers, Lisp was designed as an untyped language. The computer must be able to identify the types of data, which involve an enormous amount of data-type checking and the use of long strings of instructions at compile and run times. Conventional computers cannot do these efficiently in hardware. Second, the system must periodically perform garbage collection and reclaim unused memory at run time. This amounts to around 10-30 percent of the total processing time in a conventional computer. Hardware implementation of garbage collection is thus essential. Third, owing to the nature of recursion, a stack-oriented architecture is more suitable for list processing. Last, list processing usually requires an enormous amount of space, and the data structures are so dynamic that the compiler cannot predict how much space to allocate at compile time. Special hardware to manage the data structures and the large memory space would make the system more cost effective and efficient [3-6].

The earliest implementation of Lisp were done on the PDP-6 computer and its successors the PDP-10 and PDP-20 made by the Digital Equipment Corporation [1]. The half-word instructions and the stack instructions of these machines were developed with Lisp's requirements in mind.

Extensive work has been done for the DEC-system 10 and 20 on garbage collection to manage and reclaim the memory space used.

The design of Lisp machines was started at MIT's AI Laboratory in 1974. CONS, designed in 1976 [7-10], was superseded in 1978 by a second-generation Lisp machine, the CADR. This machine was a model for the first commercially available Lisp machines [11-13], including the Symbolics LM2, the Xerox 1100 Interlisp work station, and the Lisp Machine Inc. Series III CADR, all of which were delivered in 1981. The third-generation machines were based on additional hardware to support data tagging and garbage collection. They are characterized by the Lisp Machines Inc. Lambda supporting Zetalisp and LMLisp, [11-14], the Symbolics 3600 supporting Zetalisp, Flavors, and Fortran 77 [15-18], the Xerox 1108 and 1132 supporting Interlisp-D and Smalltalk [19-21], and the Fijitsu FACOM Alpha Machine, a backend Lisp processor supporting Maclisp [22,23]. Most of the Lisp machines support networking by using Ethernet. The LMI Lambda has a NuBus developed at MIT to produce a modular, expandable Lisp machine with multiprocessor architecture.

A single-chip computer to support Lisp has been implemented in the MIT SCHEME-79 chip [24-26]. Other experimental computers to support Lisp and list-oriented processing have been reported [27-36]. These machines usually have additional hardware tables, hashing hardware, tag mechanisms, and list processing hardware, or are microprogrammed to provide macroinstructions for list processing. Experimental multiprocessoring systems have been proposed to execute Lisp programs concurrently [37-43]. Dataflow processing is suitable for Lisp because these programs are generally data driven [44,45]. Other multiprocessing and dataflow architectures to support list processing have been proposed and developed [46-51].

Besides specialized hardware implementations, software implementations on general-purpose computers are also popular. The earliest Lisp compilers were developed on the IBM 704 and later extended to the IBM 7090, 360, and 370. Various strategies for implementing Lisp compilers have been proposed [52-57], and conventional microcomputers have been used to implement Lisp compilers [58-61]. Lisp is also available on various general- and special-purpose

217

work stations, typically based on multiple 68000 processors [58,61]. Lisp has been developed on Digital Equipment Corp. VAXstation 100, a MC68000-based personal graphics work station, and clusters of 11/782s running several dialects of Lisp and Common Lisp [62]. One dialect of Lisp, Franz Lisp, developed at the University of California, Berkeley, was written in C and runs under Unix and is available on many general-purpose work stations.

Architectures have also been developed to support object-oriented programming languages which have been extended from functional languages to additionally implement operations such as creating an object, sending and receiving messages, modifying an objects' state, and forming class-superclass hierarchies [63-65]. Smalltalk, first developed in 1972 by the Xerox Corp., is recognized as a simple but powerful way of communicating with computers. At MIT, the concept was extended to become the Flavors system. Special hardware and multiprocessors have been proposed to support directly the processing of object-oriented languages [66-69].

In *function-oriented architectures*, the design issues center on the physical interconnection of processors, the method used to "drive" the computation, the representation of programs and data, the method to invoke and control parallelism, and the optimization techniques [70]. Desirable features of such architectures should include a multiprocessor system with a rich interconnection structure, the representation of list structures by balanced trees, and hardware supports for demand-driven execution, low-overhead process creation, and storage management.

Architectures to support functional-programming languages can be classified as uniprocessor architectures, tree-structured machines, data-driven machines, and demand-driven machines. In a uniprocessor architecture, besides the mechanisms to handle lists, additional stacks to handle function calls and optimization for redundant calls and array operations may be implemented [25,71-74]. Tree-structured machines usually employ lazy evaluations, but suffer from the bottleneck at the root of the tree [75-80]. Dataflow machines are also natural candidates for executing functional programs and have tremendous potential for parallelism. However, the issue of controlling parallelism remains unresolved. A lot of the recent work is concentrated on demand-driven machines which are based on reduction machines on a set of load-balanced (possibly virtual) processors [47,81-90].

Owing to the different motivations and objectives of various functional-programming-oriented architectures, each machine has its own distinct features. For example, the Symbolics 3600 [18] was designed for an interactive program development environment where compilation is very frequent and ought to appear instantaneous to the user. This requirement simplified the design of the compiler and results in only a single-address instruction format, no indexed and indirect addressing modes, and other mechanisms to mini-

mize the number of nontrivial choices to be made. On the other hand, the aim in developing SOAR [69] was to demonstrate that a Reduced Instruction Set Computer could provide high performance in an exploratory programming environment. Instead of microcode, SOAR relied on software to provide complicated operations. As a result, more sophisticated software techniques were used.

Twelve papers are included in this chapter. These papers are meant to illustrate the concepts, but are not exhaustive to include all the proposed designs. Vegdahl surveys architectures for executing functional programming languages, which include some Lisp machines [70]. Greenblat et al. describe the Lisp machine developed at MIT [8]. The third paper, by Manuel, is a summary on the perspectives of Lisp and Prolog machines [11]. The next three papers describe three commercially available Lisp machines from Lisp Machine Inc. (Creeger), Symbolics (Moon), and Fujitsu (Hayashi et al.) [14,18,22]. The article that discusses another commercially available Lisp machine, the Xerox 1100 series, is included in Chapter 3 [91]. Then Sussman et al. discuss Scheme-79, a single-chip Lisp system [24]. The next paper, by Yamaguchi et al., presents the dataflow approach to Lisp processing [44]. The Eddy dataflow processor being developed at the Musahino Lab. implements extensions to Valid, a high-level functional language with recursion and parallel expressions for logic programming [49]. This will make it a Prolog as well as a Lisp machine and will be included in the next chapter. The ninth paper, by Ungar et al., shows the RISC architecture for implementing Smalltalk-80 [69]. The next two papers, by Mago and Keller et al., present example architectures for supporting functional programming languages. The first machine, MAGO, has a tree architecture [77], while the second machine is a reduction machine [88] (a longer version [87] is not included here). ALICE, a graph-reduction machine implementing Hope, Prolog, and LISP will be included in Chapter 8 [84,83]. Finally, Sugimoto et al. present a multi-microprocessor system for concurrent Lisp [43].

References

[1] J. McCarthy, "History of Lisp," *SIGPLAN Notices*, vol. 13, no. 8, pp. 217-223, ACM, New York, N.Y., 1978.

[2] J. Darlington, "Functional Programming," Chapter 5, *Distributed Computing*, edited by F.B. Chambers, D.A. Duce, and G.P. Jones, Academic Press, London, England, 1984.

[3] R. Fateman, "Is a Lisp Machine Different from Fortran Machine?," *SIGSAM Bulletin*, vol. 12, no. 4, ACM, New York, N.Y., 1978.

[4] J. Fitch, "Do We Really Want a Lisp Machine?," Proceedings of *SEAS/SMC Annual Meeting*, ACM, New York, N.Y., Jan. 1980.

[6] M.F. Deering, "Architectures for AI," *Byte*, vol. 10, no.4, pp. 193-206, April 1985.

[7] T. Knight, "The CONS Microprocessor," *AI Working Paper 80*, MIT, Cambridge, Mass., Nov. 1974.

[8] A. Bawden, R. Greenblatt, J. Holloway, T. Knight, D. Moon, and D. Weinreb, "The Lisp Machine," *Artificial Intelligence: An MIT Perspective*, edited by P.H. Winston and R.H. Brown, vol. 1, pp. 343-373, MIT Press, Cambridge, Mass., 1979.

[9] S.R. Schoichet, "The Lisp Machine," *Mini-Micro Systems*, vol. 11, no.6, pp. 68-74, June 1978.

[10] R.G. Greenblatt, T.F. Knight, J.T. Holloway, and D.A. Moon, "A Lisp Machine," *Proceedings of the 5th Workshop on Computer Architecture for Non-Numeric Processing*, pp. 137-138, ACM, New York, N.Y., March 1980.

[11] T. Manuel, "Lisp and Prolog Machines Are Proliferating," *Electronics*, vol. 56, no. 22, pp. 132-137, Nov. 1983.

[12] W. Myers, "Lisp Machines Displayed at AI Conf.," *Computer*, vol. 15, no. 11, pp. 79-82, Nov. 1982.

[13] T. Kurokawa, "Lisp Activities in Japan," *Proceedings of the 6th International Joint Conference on Artificial Intelligence*, pp. 502-504, William Kaufmann, Los Altos, Calif., 1979.

[14] M. Creeger, "Lisp Machines Come Out of the Lab.," *Computer Design*, vol. 22, no. 13, pp. 132-137, Nov. 1983.

[15] D. Weinreb and D. Moon, "Flavors, Message Passing in the Lisp Machine," *AI Memo 602*, MIT Lab, Cambridge, Mass., Nov. 1980.

[16] L. Walker, "Lisp Language Gets Special Machine," *Electronics*, vol. 54, no. 17, pp. 40-41, Aug. 25, 1981.

[17] A. Hirsch, "Tagged Architecture Supports Symbolic Processing," *Computer Design*, vol. 23, no. 6, pp. 75-80, June 1984.

[18] D.A. Moon, "Architecture of the Symbolics 3600," *Proceedings of the 12th Annual International Symposium on Computer Architecture*, pp. 76-83, IEEE Computer Society, Washington, D.C., June 1985.

[19] J. Moore, "The Interlisp Virtual Machine Specification," *Technical Report CSL 76-5*, Xerox PARC, Palo Alto, Calif., Sept. 1976.

[20] D.G. Bobrow, "The LOOPS Manual," *Technical Report KB-VLSI-81-13*, Xerox PARC, Palo Alto, Calif., 1982.

[21] B. Sheil, "Family of Personal Lisp Machines Speeds AI Program Development," *Electronics*, vol. 56, no. 22, pp. 153-156, Nov. 1983.

[22] H. Hayashi, A. Hattori, and H. Akimoto, "ALPHA: A High-Performance Lisp Machine Equipped with a New Stack Structure and Garbage Collection System," *Proceedings of the 10th Annual International Symposium on Computer Architecture*, pp. 342-348, IEEE Computer Society, Washington, D.C., June 1983.

[23] H. Akimoto, S. Shimizu, A. Shinagawa, A. Hattori, and H. Hayashi, "Evaluation of the Dedicated Hardware in FACOM Alpha," *Proceedings of COMPCON S'85*, pp. 366-369, IEEE Computer Society, Washington, D.C., 1985.

[24] G.J. Sussman, J. Holloway, G.L. Steel Jr., and A. Bell, "Scheme-79—Lisp on a Chip," *Computer*, vol. 14, no. 7, pp. 10-21, July 1981.

[25] G. Steel and G. Sussman, "Design of Lisp-Based Processor, or SCHEME: A Dielectric Lisp or Finite Memories Considered Harmful, or LAMBDA: The Ultimate Opcode," *AI Memo 514*, MIT, Cambridge, Mass., March 1979.

[26] G.L. Steele Jr. and G.J. Sussman, "Design of a Lisp-Based Microprocessor," *Communications of the ACM*, vol. 23, no. 11, pp. 628-645, Nov. 1980.

[27] M. Griss and M. Swanson, "MBALM/1700: A Microprogrammed Lisp Machine for the Burroughs B1726," *Proceedings of MICRO-10*, IEEE Computer Society, Washington, D.C., 1977.

[28] K. Taki, Y. Kaneda, and S. Maekawa, "The Experimental Lisp Machine," *Proceedings of the 6th International Joint Conference on Artificial Intelligence*, pp. 865-867, William Kaufmann, Los Altos, Calif., Aug. 1979.

[29] E. Goto, T. Ida, K. Hiraki, M. Suzuki, and N. Inada, "FLATS, A Machine for Numerical, Symbolic and Associative Computing," *Proceedings of the 6th International Joint Conference on Artificial Intelligence*, pp. 1058-1066, William Kaufmann, Los Altos, Calif., Aug. 1979.

[30] P. Deutsch, "Experience with a Microprogrammed Interlisp Systems," *Proceedings of MICRO-11*, IEEE Computer Society, Washington, D.C., Nov. 1978.

[31] M. Nagao, J.I. Tsujii, K. Nakajima, K. Mitamura, and H. Ito, "Lisp Machine NK3 and Measurement of Its Performance," *Proceedings of the 6th International Joint Conference on Artificial Intelligence*, pp. 625-627, William Kaufmann, Washington, D.C., Aug. 1979.

[32] N. Greenfeld and A. Jericho, "A Professional's Personal Computer System," *Proceedings of the 8th International Symposium on Computer Architecture*, pp. 217-226, IEEE Computer Society, Washington, D.C., 1981.

[33] J.P. Sansonnet, M. Castan, and C. Percebois, "M3L: A List-Directed Architecture," *Proceedings of the 7th Annual Symposium on Computer Architecture,* pp. 105-112, IEEE Computer Society, Washington, D.C., May 1980.

[34] J. Sansonnet, D. Botella, and J. Perez, "Function Distribution in a List-Directed Architecture," *Microprocessing and Microprogramming,* vol. 9, no. 3, pp. 143-153, 1982.

[35] J.P. Sansonnet, M. Castan, C. Percebois, D. Botella, and J. Perez, "Direct Execution of Lisp on a List-Directed Architecture," *Proceedings of the Symposium on Architectural Support for Programming Languages and Operating Systems,* pp. 132-139, ACM, New York, N.Y., March 1982.

[36] E. von Puttkamer, "A Microprogrammed Lisp Machine," *Microprocessing and Microprogramming,* vol. 11, no. 1, pp. 9-14, Jan. 1983.

[37] R. Williams, "A Multiprocessing System for the Direct Execution of Lisp," *Proceedings of the 4th Workshop on Computer Architecture for Non-Numeric Processing,* ACM, New York, N.Y., Aug. 1978.

[38] D. McKay and S. Shapiro, "MULTI—A Lisp Based Multiprocessing System," *Conference Record of the Lisp Conference,* Stanford University, Menlo Park, Calif., 1980.

[39] M. Model, "Multiprocessing via Intercommunicating Lisp Systems," *Conference Record of the Lisp Conference,* Stanford University, Menlo Park, Calif., 1980.

[40] C. Hewitt, "The Apiary Network Architecture for Knowledgeable Systems," *Conference Record of the Lisp Conference,* pp. 107-117, Stanford University, Menlo Park, Calif., 1980.

[41] A. Guzman, "A Heterarchical Multi-Microprocessor Lisp Machine," *Proceedings of the Workshop on Computer Architecture for Pattern Analysis and Image Database Management,* pp. 309-317, IEEE Computer Society, Washington, D.C., Nov. 1981.

[42] S. Sugimoto, K. Tabata, K. Agusa, and Y. Ohno, "Concurrent Lisp on a Multi-Micro-Processor System," *Proceedings of the 7th International Joint Conference on Artificial Intelligence,* pp. 949-954, William Kaufmann, Los Altos, Calif., Aug. 1981.

[43] S. Sugimoto, K. Agusa, K. Tabata, and Y. Ohno, "A Multi-Microprocessor System for Concurrent Lisp," *Proceedings of the International Conference on Parallel Processing,* pp. 135-143, IEEE Computer Society, Washington, D.C., 1983.

[44] Y. Yamaguchi, K. Toda, J. Herath, and T. Yuba, "EM-3: A Lisp-Based Data-Driven Machine," *Proceedings of the International Conference on Fifth-Generation Computer Systems,* pp. 524-532, ICOT, Tokyo, Japan, and North-Holland, Amsterdam, The Netherlands, 1984.

[45] Y. Yamaguchi, K. Toda, and T. Yuba, "A Performance Evaluation of a Lisp-Based Data-Driven Machine (EM-3)," *Proceedings of the 10th Annual International Symposium on Computer Architecture,* pp. 363-369, IEEE Computer Society, Washington, D.C., June 1983.

[46] W.K. Giloi and R. Gueth, "Concepts and Realization of a High-Performance Data Type Architecture," *International Journal of Computer and Information Sciences,* vol. 11, no. 1, pp. 25-54, 1982.

[47] P.C. Treleaven and R.P. Hopkins, "A Recursive Computer Architecture for VLSI," *Proceedings of the 9th Annual Symposium on Computer Architecture,* pp. 229-238, IEEE Computer Society, Washington, D.C., April 1982.

[48] M. Amamiya, R. Hasegawa, O. Nakamura, and H. Mikami, "A List-Processing-Oriented Data Flow Machine Architecture," *Proceedings of the National Computer Conference,* pp. 144-151, AFIPS Press, Reston, Va., 1982.

[49] M. Amamiya and R. Hasegawa, "Dataflow Computing and Eager and Lazy Evaluations," *New Generation Computing,* vol. 2, no. 2, pp. 105-129, 1984.

[50] H. Diel, "Concurrent Data Access Architecture," *Proceedings of the International Conference on Fifth-Generation Computer Systems,* pp. 373-388, ICOT, Tokyo, Japan, and North-Holland, Amsterdam, The Netherlands, 1984.

[51] G. Coghill and K. Hanna, "PLEIADES: A Multimicroprocessor Interactive Knowledge Base," *Microprocessors and Microsystems,* vol. 3, no. 2, pp. 77-82, March 1979.

[52] E. Sandewall, "Programming in an Interactive Environment: The Lisp Experience," *Computing Surveys,* vol. 10, no. 1, pp. 35-71, March 1978.

[53] J. Campbell and J. Fitch, "Symbolic Computing with and without Lisp," *Conference Record of the Lisp Conference,* Stanford University, Menlo Park, Calif., 1980.

[54] M. Deering, J. Faletti, and R. Wilensky, "PEARL—A Package for Efficient Access to Representations in Lisp," *Proceedings of the 7th International Joint Conference on Artificial Intelligence,* pp. 930-932, William Kaufmann, Los Altos, Calif., Aug. 1981.

[55] W. Teitelman and L. Masinter, "The Interlisp Programming Environment," *Computer,* vol. 14, no. 4, pp. 25-33, April 1981.

[56] M.L. Griss and E. Benson, "Current Status of a Portable Lisp Compiler," *Proceedings of the SIGPLAN Symposium on Compiler Construction,* pp. 276-283, ACM, New York, N.Y., June 1982.

[57] H. Samet, "Code Optimization Considerations in List Processing Systems," *IEEE Transactions on Software Engineering*, vol. SE-8, no. 2, pp. 107-113, March 1982.

[58] S. Taff, "The Design of an M6800 Lisp Interpreter," *Byte*, vol. 4, no. 8, pp. 132-152, McGraw-Hill, Aug. 1979.

[59] P. Deutsch, "ByteLisp and Its Alto Implementation," *Conference Record of the Lisp Conference*, Stanford University, Menlo Park, Calif., 1980.

[60] S.P. Levitan and J.G. Bonar, "Three Microcomputer Lisps," *Byte*, vol. 6, no. 9, pp. 388-412, Sept. 1981.

[61] T. King, "Expert Systems with 68000 and Lisp," *Microprocessors and Microsystems*, vol. 8, no. 7, pp. 374-376, Sept. 1984.

[62] W.D. Strecker, "Clustering VAX Superminicomputers into Large Multiprocessor Systems," *Electronics*, vol. 56, no. 21, pp. 143-146, Oct. 20, 1983.

[63] C. Hewitt, "Viewing Control Structure as Patterns of Passing Messages," *Artificial Intelligence*, vol. 8, no. 3, pp. 323-364, 1977.

[64] The Xerox Learning Research Group, "The Smalltalk-80 System," *Byte*, vol. 6, no. 8, pp. 36-48, Aug. 1981.

[65] M. Tokoro and Y. Ishikawa, "An Object-Oriented Approach to Knowledge Systems," *Proceedings of the International Conference on Fifth-Generation Computer Systems*, pp. 623-632, ICOT, Tokyo, Japan, and North-Holland, Amsterdam, The Netherlands, 1984.

[66] A. Plotkin and D. Tabak, "A Tree Structured Architecture for Semantic Gap Reduction," *Computer Architecture News*, vol. 11, no. 4, pp. 30-44, ACM SIGARCH, New York, N.Y., Sept. 1983.

[67] Y. Ishikawa and M. Tokoro, "The Design of an Object-Oriented Architecture," *Proceedings of the 11th International Symposium on Computer Architecture*, pp. 178-187, IEEE Computer Society, Washington, D.C., 1984.

[68] N. Suzuki, K. Kubota, and T. Aoki, "SWORD32: A Bytecode Emulating Microprocessor for Object-Oriented Languages," *Proceedings of the International Conference on Fifth-Generation Computer Systems*, pp. 389-397, ICOT, Tokyo, Japan, and North-Holland, Amsterdam, The Netherlands, 1984.

[69] D. Ungar, R. Blau, P. Foley, D. Samples, and D. Patterson, "Architecture of SOAR: Smalltalk on RISC," *Proceedings of the 11th Annual International Symposium on Computer Architecture*, pp. 188-197, IEEE Computer Society, Washington, D.C., 1984.

[70] S.R. Vegdahl, "A Survey of Proposed Architectures for the Execution of Functional Languages," *IEEE Transactions on Computers*, vol. C-33, no. 12, pp. 1050-1071, Dec. 1984.

[71] P.S. Abrahms, *An APL Machine*, Ph.D. Dissertation, Stanford University, Menlo Park, Calif., Feb. 1970.

[72] K.J. Berkling, "Reduction Languages for Reduction Machines," *Proceedings of the International Symposium on Computer Architecture*, pp. 133-140, IEEE Computer Society, Washington, D.C., 1975.

[73] D.A. Turner, "A New Implementation Technique for Applicative Languages," *Software—Practice and Experience*, vol. 9, no. 1, pp. 31-49, 1979.

[74] M. Castan and E.I. Organick, "M3L: An HLL-RISC Processor for Parallel Execution of FP-Language Programs," *Proceedings of the 9th Annual Symposium on Computer Architecture*, pp. 239-247, IEEE Computer Society, Washington, D.C., 1982.

[75] G. Mago, "A Network of Microprocessors to Execute Reduction Languages, Part I," *International Journal of Computer and Information Sciences*, vol. 8, no. 5, pp. 349-385, 1979.

[76] G. Mago, "A Network of Microprocessors to Execute Reduction Languages, Part II," *International Journal of Computer and Information Sciences*, vol. 8, no. 6, pp. 435-471, 1979.

[77] G. Mago, "Making Parallel Computation Simple: The FFP Machine," *Proceedings of COMPCON S'85*, pp. 424-428, IEEE Computer Society, Washington, D.C., 1985.

[78] R.M. Keller, G. Lindstrom, and S. Patil, "A Loosely-Coupled Applicative Multiprocessing System," *Proceedings of the National Computer Conference*, pp. 613-622, AFIPS Press, Reston, Va., 1979.

[79] A.L. Davis, "A Data Flow Evaluation System Based on the Concept of Recursive Locality," *Proceedings of the National Computer Conference*, pp. 1079-1086, AFIPS Press, Reston, Va., 1979.

[80] J.T. O'Donnell, *A Systolic Associative Lisp Computer Architecture with Incremental Parallel Storage Management*, Ph.D. Dissertation, University of Iowa, Iowa City, Ia., 1981.

[81] D.P. Friedman and D.S. Wise, "Aspects of Applicative Programming for Parallel Processing," *IEEE Transactions on Computers*, vol. C-27, no. 4, pp. 289-296, April 1978.

[82] W.A. Kornfeld, "ETHER—A Parallel Problem Solving System," *Proceedings of the 6th International Joint Conference on Artificial Intelligence*, pp. 490-492, William Kaufmann, Los Altos, Calif., 1979.

[83] J. Darlington and M. Reeve, "ALICE and the Parallel Evaluation of Logic Programs, *Preliminary Draft, Department of Computing*, College of Science and Technology, London, England, June 1983.

[84] K. Smith, "New Computer Breed Uses Transputers for Parallel Processing," *Electronics*, vol. 56, no. 4, pp. 67-68, Feb. 24, 1983.

[85] F. Hommes, "The Heap/Substitution Concept—An Implementation of Functional Operations on Data Structures for a Reduction Machine," *Proceedings of the 9th Annual Symposium on Computer Architecture,* pp. 248-256, IEEE Computer Society, Washington, D.C., April 1982.

[86] W.E. Kluge, "Cooperating Reduction Machines," *IEEE Transactions on Computers*, vol. C-32, no. 11, pp. 1002-1012, Nov. 1983.

[87] R.M. Keller and F.C.H. Lin, "Simulated Performance of a Reduction-Based Multiprocessor," *Computer*, vol. 17, no. 7, pp. 70-82, July 1984.

[88] R.M. Keller, F.C.H. Lin, and J. Tanaka, "Rediflow Multiprocessing," *Proceedings of COMPCON S'84*, pp. 410-417, IEEE Computer Society, Washington, D.C., 1984.

[89] T. Clarke, P. Gladstone, C. Maclean, and A. Norman, "SKIM—The S, K, I Reduction Machine," *Conference Record of the Lisp Conference,* Stanford University, Menlo Park, Calif., 1980.

[90] P. Treleaven and G. Mole, "A Multi-Processor Reduction Machine for User-Defined Reduction Languages," *Proceedings of the 7th International Symposium on Computer Architecture,* pp. 121-130, IEEE Computer Society, Washington, D.C., 1980.

[91] B. Sheil, "Power Tools for Programmers," *Datamation,* vol. 29, no. 2, pp. 131-144, Feb. 1983.

Reprinted from *IEEE Transactions on Computers*, Volume C-23, Number 12, December 1984, pages 1050-1071. Copyright © 1984 by The Institute of Electrical and Electronics Engineers, Inc.

A Survey of Proposed Architectures for the Execution of Functional Languages

STEVEN R. VEGDAHL

Abstract —Functional and imperative programming languages are characterized and compared with regard to *programming style* and *efficiency*. Machine design issues are characterized by interconnection topology, evaluation strategy, program and data representation, process management, and dynamic optimization techniques; short descriptions of a number of "functional" machines are given in terms of these issues. Multiprocessor issues and systems are particularly emphasized. Outstanding problems in the area are reviewed and an overall evaluation of proposed machines is given.

Index Terms —Computer architecture, data-driven architectures, data flow, demand-drive architectures, functional programming, multiprocessing, programming languages.

IN recent years, a number of scientists have advocated the use of functional programming (FP) as a means of increasing programmer productivity, enhancing the clarity of programs, and reducing the difficulty of program verification. A major drawback of using functional languages has been that they are perceived to run slowly on von Neumann computer architectures. This is a survey of architectures that have recently been proposed for executing such languages more efficiently. Also discussed are the major issues involved in designing such architectures, with particular attention given to parallel processing systems.

I. CHARACTERIZATION OF FUNCTIONAL LANGUAGES

The terms *functional language, applicative language, data flow language,* and *reduction language* have been used somewhat interchangeably in the literature to refer to languages that are based on function application and are therefore free of side effects. The term *functional language* is used throughout this paper for the purpose of clarity. This section characterizes functional languages by contrasting them with (traditional) imperative ones.

A. Imperative Languages

Imperative programming languages (e.g., Fortran, Pascal) have tended to be "high-level versions" of the von Neumann computer. Their principal operations involve changing the

Manuscript received January 25, 1984; revised July 16, 1984. This work was supported in part by the Fannie and John Hertz Foundation and in part by the Defense Advanced Research Projects Agency (DOD) ARPA Order 3597, monitored by the Air Force Avionics Laboratory under Contract F33615-78-C-1551.

The author was with Carnegie-Mellon University, Pittsburgh, PA 15213. He is now with the Computer Research Laboratory, Tektronix, Inc., Beaverton, OR 97077.

state of the computation in much the same way a machine-language program does [5].
- Program variables imitate machine words. Programmers think of them as locations in which a value can be saved.
- Control statements imitate jumps. For example *if–then–else* has the semantics: "Test the condition. If true, go and execute the 'then' statements; otherwise go and execute the 'else' statements."
- The assignment statement imitates fetch and store instructions of the underlying machine.

Central to an imperative model of computing is the concept of a *present state,* which encompasses the program counter, the values of all variables, the stack, etc. According to advocates of functional programming, thinking of program execution in terms of a *present state* has a number of undesirable consequences [5], [6].
- Two widely separated pieces of code may reference a common global variable and therefore have an "unanticipated" interaction. A programmer must also be concerned with issues such as aliasing, which can increase program complexity.
- A programmer concentrates on data manipulation, not on the essential algorithm.
- It is difficult to characterize parallel execution when several independent asynchronous processes can have side effects on one another.
- Program proof and transformation are more difficult because the imperative model does not lend itself to easy mathematical characterization. For example, a name in a given context can have different meanings at different times, due to the invocation of an operation that produces a side effect.

On the other hand, it may also be argued that many common computer applications (e.g., updating a database) are inherently imperative in nature, and that imperative programming languages are well suited to such tasks.

B. Functional Languages

Functional programs contain no notion of a *present state, program counter,* or *storage.* Rather, the "program" is a *function* in the true mathematical sense: it is applied to the input of the program, and the resulting value is the program's output. For example, if the "program" *Plus* computes the sum of two numbers, then 3 + 4 can be computed by applying *Plus* to the input $\langle 3, 4 \rangle$

$$Plus: \langle 3, 4 \rangle \rightarrow 7 .$$

Because a function's argument(s) and output value(s) may be

list structures, a function can define quite complex operations on its input.

Essential to functional programming is the notion of *referential transparency* [8], [46]: the value of an expression depends only on its textual context, *not* on computational history. The value of *Plus*: $\langle 3, 4 \rangle$ is determined only by the static definitions of *Plus*, 3, and 4.

Another way of viewing this is that the *output* is another form of the *function and input*; 7 and *Plus*: $\langle 3, 4 \rangle$ are simply different forms of the same object. The purpose of the computation is to *reduce* an *expression* to an equivalent *constant expression*.

The basic operation, then, in functional programming is function application. Data dependencies exist only as a result of function application, the value of a function being completely determined by its arguments. Notions such as *time dependence*, *side effect*, and *writable memory* do not exist.

Examples of functional languages are pure Lisp, Backus' FP [5], Hope [8], Val [58], Id [2], KRC [85], and ML [26]. Some, like Backus' FP, have no assignment statement. Others, such as Val and Id, are known as *single-assignment languages*, in which an "assignment statement" is simply a notational convenience for binding an expression to an identifier.

As an example of the functional style of programming, consider a functional program for computing the inner product of two vectors using a notation similar to that in [5]

$$IP = (Reduce\ Plus) \circ (Map\ Times).$$

Map is a functional form that applies an n-ary function to n vectors of equal length, resulting in a single vector of that length. *Reduce* is identical to the operator of the same name in APL. Thus,

$$IP: \langle \langle 2, 3, -2 \rangle, \langle 3, 1, 5 \rangle \rangle$$
$$= (Reduce\ Plus) \circ (Map\ Times): \langle \langle 2, 3, -2 \rangle, \langle 3, 1, 5 \rangle \rangle$$
$$= (Reduce\ Plus): \langle 6, 3, -10 \rangle$$
$$= -1.$$

Similarly, matrix multiplication may be defined as

$$MM = (ApplyToAll(ApplyToAll\ IP)) \circ Pair$$
$$\circ [First, Transpose \circ Second].$$

ApplyToAll applies a unary function to each element of a vector, resulting in a vector of identical length. *Pair* is a function that creates a matrix of pairs of elements of its two arguments; *First* and *Second* are functions that select the first and second elements of a vector, respectively. Thus, the multiplication of a 2×3 matrix and a 3×2 matrix

$$MM: \langle \langle \langle 0, 3, 2 \rangle, \langle 1, -4, 4 \rangle \rangle, \langle \langle 1, 0 \rangle, \langle 3, -2 \rangle, \langle 5, 1 \rangle \rangle \rangle$$

$$= (ApplyToAll(ApplyToAll\ IP)) \circ Pair \circ [First, Transpose \circ Second]:$$
$$\langle \langle \langle 0, 3, 2 \rangle, \langle 1, -4, 4 \rangle \rangle, \langle \langle 1, 0 \rangle, \langle 3, -2 \rangle, \langle 5, 1 \rangle \rangle \rangle$$

$$= (ApplyToAll(ApplyToAll\ IP)) \circ Pair:$$
$$\langle \langle \langle 0, 3, 2 \rangle, \langle 1, -4, 4 \rangle \rangle, \langle \langle 1, 3, 5 \rangle, \langle 0, -2, 1 \rangle \rangle \rangle$$

$$= (ApplyToAll(ApplyToAll\ IP)):$$
$$\langle \langle \langle \langle 0, 3, 2 \rangle, \langle 1, 3, 5 \rangle \rangle, \langle \langle 0, 3, 2 \rangle, \langle 0, -2, 1 \rangle \rangle \rangle,$$
$$\langle \langle \langle 1, -4, 4 \rangle, \langle 1, 3, 5 \rangle \rangle, \langle \langle 1, -4, 4 \rangle, \langle 0, -2, 1 \rangle \rangle \rangle \rangle$$

$$= \langle \langle 19, -4 \rangle, \langle 9, 12 \rangle \rangle$$

C. Programming in a Functional Language

According to Backus, programs are constructed in an imperative language by writing simple statements — such as the assignment statement — and "gluing them together" with control structures — such as *if–then–else;* programs in a functional language are composed by writing functions, and "gluing them together" with *functional forms*. The major components of his system are [5] the following.

1) A set of *objects*.

2) A set of *functions* that map objects into objects. These functions are analogous to built-in functions and operators in imperative programming languages.

3) A set of *functional forms* that combine existing functions or objects to form new functions. An example of a functional form is the *reduction* operator of APL.[1]

[1]Some functional languages [84] allow higher order functions — that is, functions that can be applied to functions — obviating the need for the notion of a *functional form*.

results in a 2×2 matrix.

The functional programming style can thus be characterized as the building of complex functions from simpler ones by using *functional forms;* the notion of the *state* of a computation is absent.

II. THE PROGRAMMER'S PERSPECTIVE

The use of functional languages has been advocated by a number of scientists [5], [24]. Claims have been made that the use of functional programs increases programmer productivity, program lucidity, and ease of verification. Morris *et al.* [61], however, raise the question: "Is applicative programming well-suited to someone who must make a living programming, or is it primarily for 'meta-programmers' who study programming?"

If functional programming is to become commonplace in the "real world," a number of issues must be resolved. Perhaps the most significant issue is whether real applications are suited to functional programming. Can a text editor, operating system, or video game be easily constructed in a functional language? If not, can the domain of its practicality be characterized?

Many argue in favor of functional programming languages by comparing them to conventional languages, such as Fortran or Pascal [5]. Included in such arguments, however, should be other "nonconventional" languages, such as Smalltalk [25], or CLU [53]. It may be the case that most of the high productivity attributed to functional programming is not due to referential transparency, but rather to other properties, such as abstraction, extensibility, higher order functions, and heap-allocated memory.

Finally, there is the question of whether functional languages can be mapped onto computer hardware and executed with reasonable efficiency, a topic that will be discussed in later sections.

A. Advantages of the Functional Programming Style

Proponents of functional programming claim that correct functional programs are easier to produce than equivalent imperative ones. Advantages cited include the following.

• Programs can be written at a higher level; a programmer can get the "big picture" rather than specifying a computation "a word at a time," as is typical in imperative languages [5], [6]. Time can be spent concentrating on the algorithm rather than on the details of its implementation.

• Its compact lucid notation allows more "algorithm" to be expressed per line of code. Evidence suggests that *number of lines of correct code per day* is roughly constant for a given programmer, independent of the language used [91]. A functional language would thus increase productivity because it takes fewer lines of code to express a desired concept in a functional language [84].

• Functional languages are free of side effects. A programmer can construct a program without being concerned about *aliasing* or "unexpected" modifications to variables by other routines. A consequence of this is that the procedure parameter passing mechanisms *call-by-value* and *call-by-name* have the same semantics [6], providing the computation terminates.

• Functional programs are easier to verify because proofs can be based on the rather well-understood concept of a function rather on the more cumbersome notion of a von Neumann computer [5].

• Functional programs often contain a great deal of implicit and easily detected parallelism [24]. Explicitly specifying parallelism on a von Neumann system can be quite difficult [41].

Programming experience seems to indicate that languages with FP features do in fact increase programmer productivity. APL has long been known as a language in which programs can be quickly constructed [54]. Poplar [61], a functional string-processing language, has been used by a number of people to create a report generation system, family budget maintainer, and a purchase order management system. The consensus among programmers was that the use of Poplar significantly decreased programming time. Users and designers of other functional languages have made similar claims about productivity [8], [84].

Although functional languages can be quite powerful, there is nothing "magic" about them. An "imperative" program can be written in a functional language by defining a structure that encodes the values of all variables and passing this structure as a parameter to every function, every function returning a modified version. Such modifications would correspond to changes in the values of variables in the imperative program.

B. Problems with the Functional Programming Style

One of the potential drawbacks of programming in a functional language is the difficulty — or at least the different approach — one encounters when programming an inherently sequential algorithm, such as one that consists largely of I/O operations. Consider an imperative program in which a file is opened and a pointer to it is passed among procedures, each reading a record from the file and then returning to the main program. A functional program, being free of side effects, would be somewhat awkward to write in this (imperative) style. If function *A* is to read a record from the input file, and function *B* is to read the next record, functions must be written so that *B* calls *A* (either directly or indirectly), and *A* must return both the *main result* and the *modified versions of all files it uses*. Performing I/O in this manner has much the flavor of simulating a von Neumann machine by "passing the whole machine state around from function to function."

The method of handling I/O that seems to have gained the widest acceptance among function programming advocates is that of using *streams*, which were originally proposed by Landin [51], and were later incorporated into a data flow language by Weng [95]. A stream is a representation of a list structure that is implemented by passing the elements sequentially; the use of streams can allow functional programs to be specified in a natural way, at least for simple input–output behavior. Examples have also been given in which streams can be used to model more complex sequential events in a functional language [4]. The question of whether the stream model is as general and as natural as its proponents claim will likely remain unanswered until a significant number of "real applications" are written in functional languages.

C. Debugging Functional Programs

The debugging of functional programs is another issue that requires further exploration. The experience of several scientists indicates that debugging may actually be easier when using a functional language [8], [61]. Although one cannot examine the state of the computation — there is no state — it certainly seems feasible to trace one or more paths down the "execution tree," examining the inputs and outputs of each function. This type of debugging seems well suited to functional programs since such a tree is a static object for a given input; an imperative program, on the other hand, has a state that changes with time. Debugging a functional program in a traditional way (setting break points, etc.) could be a confusing undertaking if *lazy evaluation* [32] (see Section IV-B-1) is employed because the order of evaluation may be nonintuitive [61].

The *equality assertion* feature of Poplar [61] seems well suited to functional programs and has been shown to be useful in allowing the compiler to aid in debugging. This feature allows the programmer to specify a *test input* for the function along with *values at intermediate points* of the computation and *the output value* for the chosen test input. The assertions act as comments, giving a reader an intuitive feel for what the program is doing. In addition, they are executed by the compiler to ensure that they are consistent with the actual code.

D. Conclusion

There is evidence that functional programs can be used to express a number of algorithms concisely and lucidly, requiring less effort than programming in an imperative language. Additional experience is required before it can be determined how much of the "functional programming advantage" is due to the lack of side effects, and how much is due to other features that are common to many functional languages.

III. EFFICIENCY CONSIDERATIONS

In the previous section, arguments were considered that programming in a functional language is better than programming in an imperative language. In this section, we explore efficiency considerations. Many FP proponents contend that whether or not functional programming increases programmer productivity, it produces programs that are highly suitable for parallel processing. On the other hand, functional programs have gained a reputation for running slowly.

A. Potential for Concurrent Execution

Functional programs often contain a great deal of implicit parallelism, making them attractive candidates for execution on parallel processors. Arguments of a function and distinct elements in a dynamically created structure can all be evaluated concurrently and independently [24]. In addition, a reduction (as in APL) with an associative operator can be evaluated as a tree rather than as a list, decreasing its running time from linear to logarithmic if sufficient processors are available [58], [87]. Finally, if the programmer/system is willing to spend computing time on results that may not be needed, all three clauses of a conditional expression can even be evaluated concurrently [67].

Proponents also argue that functional programs are also attractive for parallel processing because data dependencies are localized; the value of a function depends only on values of its arguments, giving rise to the possibility that communication overhead can be minimized by arranging for the evaluation of a function to occur "near" the evaluation of its arguments (but see Section III-B). Proposals for implementing this typically involve attempting to make the function hierarchy graph correspond roughly to the physical graph of processors.

B. Efficiency Problems

The power of parallel processing may be overshadowed by the apparently inherent inefficiencies of functional programs. Reasons cited for the lack of speed in functional languages have included the following [38], [62], [64], [88].

- The use of linked lists instead of arrays. A random access to an "array" element takes linear time rather than constant time.
- The high frequency of function calls and the resulting overhead for parameter passing, etc.
- Garbage-collection overhead.
- Lack of destructive updating. To return a modified version of a structure, it is necessary (logically) to return a new copy of the structure with the modification.
- Listful style. Some functional languages encourage the passing of intermediate list structures between composed functions. The use of such structures causes additional storage allocation and dereferencing operations to be performed, and adds to garbage-collection overhead.

Although several of the above points reflect the fact that functional languages are not as "close" to von Neumann computers as are imperative languages, others reflect only that many *implementations* have been inefficient. Fateman [22] points out that one of the reasons functional languages have their reputation for inefficiency is that they have typically been run interpretively rather than compiled. He presents an example in which a good Lisp compiler generates code as efficient as that produced by a Fortran compiler, by performing in-line expansion of common functions such as *car* and *cdr* and by eliminating tail recursion.

Although the use of linked lists is ideal for some operations, it is quite poor for array-like random accesses. It has been suggested that a tree representation of a sequential structure might be a good compromise between a linked list and an array [27], [44]; this would also allow destructive updating to be performed in logarithmic time. In some cases, the use of contiguous arrays is also appropriate.

Another problem is that most FP computations are performed on structures, not scalar values, diminishing the effectiveness of arranging for functions to compute their values "near" the evaluation of their arguments (see Section III-A). When a structure is represented by a pointer, accessing its elements may still require a large number of remote references.

1) The Impact of Programming Style on Efficiency: A more serious issue affecting efficiency is that the functional programming style encourages programmers to operate on large structures rather than "a word at a time." If A and B are arrays, an imperative programmer might write

$$A[i] + B[i]$$

while an APL programmer would likely write

$$(A + B)[i]$$

which, although more concise, causes a completely new array $A + B$ to be created when evaluated in a straightforward manner. Similarly, to compute the third largest element in a list L, an APL programmer might write

$$(Reverse\ Sort\ L)[3]$$

rather than running through a loop and keeping track of the three largest values. The general problem is that the evaluation of functions that operate on large structures can be inefficient. (The use of *lazy evaluation* [32] can lead to substantial improvement in some cases, at the cost of higher space and speed overhead (see Section IV-B-1).)

2) Recomputation of Values: Another potential inefficiency is the performing of the same computation repeatedly. Consider the recursive program to compute the *n*th Fibonacci number

Fib

$$= (Leq\ 1) \rightarrow Ident;\ Plus \circ [Fib \circ (Sub\ 1), Fib \circ (Sub\ 2)].$$

Although mathematically concise, this function takes exponential time when executed in the straightforward manner. The recursive program to determine whether a number is prime

$$IsPrime = (Reduce\ Or) \circ (ApplyToAll\ Divides) \circ Distl \circ$$

$$[(Filter\ IsPrime) \circ Upto \circ [2, Floor \circ Sqrt], Ident]$$

also invokes *IsPrime* multiple times for several values.

The fundamental problem seems to be that it can be quite difficult to detect at compile time when a function will be invoked with the same arguments, so that the result can be saved the first time it is computed, and *looked up* during subsequent calls [45]. An imperative program can explicitly save values that are known to be needed later. Keller and Sleep [46] have proposed a mechanism by which an FP programmer can specify when a result is to be cached. A totally automatic caching scheme introduces a number of implementation problems (see Section IV-E-2).

C. Compile Time Techniques for Improving Efficiency

Compiler optimization techniques can be used to solve some of the inefficiency problems of functional programs. Although not the subject of this paper, compiler techniques are a promising area of research, and are sometimes ignored by FP machine designers. Solving an efficiency problem by program transformation should at least be considered before a complex piece of hardware is designed.

Two approaches are being explored in the area of functional program transformation. *Discovery methods* employ a small number of transformations: a heuristic search is performed, applying the transformations in an attempt to improve the efficiency of the program. *Schema methods* employ a larger collection of transformations, but without searching.

Discovery methods [7], [45], [56], [74], [88] are generally variants of an unfolding–folding technique, which coalesces operations and attempts to minimize the number of intermediate list structures. A function is first *unfolded* by expanding some of its functions, replacing each with its definition. The goal is to extract "an atomic step" of a recursive function, and to transform the remainder of the function into an instance of the function itself. Tail recursion may often be eliminated to transform the function into iterative form [77].

Schema methods [48], [69], [87] do not perform heuristic searching; instead, a collection of predefined transformation templates are applied to transform the program. These methods are generally faster than discovery methods — no searching is done — but less general, as all transformations must be predefined.

Schemas have been developed for APL compilers that "understand" certain array manipulation/permutation operations such as transpose and sort, and can optimize such operations as

$$Reverse\ Reverse\ x \rightarrow x$$

and

$$(Sort\ x)[3] \rightarrow\ 'third\ smallest\ element\ in\ x'.$$

Compiler techniques for improving functional programs have generally concentrated on removing overhead such as intermediate list creation. While these techniques clearly improve performance on a von Neumann architecture, there is the possibility that such transformations may reduce the potential for parallelism. If it is necessary to perform a complex operation on each element of a list, performing the operations iteratively so that the list does not have to be physically created may not be the most efficient method on a multiprocessor architecture. The cost of storage management must be weighed against the potential speedup of concurrent evaluation. Such analysis by a compiler will not always be practical.

On the other hand, when an effective well-understood compiler technique is discovered to solve a particular efficiency problem, it should be used rather than building additional hardware to solve the problem. Hardware solutions should be applied only when compiler solutions are inadequate.

D. Conclusion

There is a great deal of inherent parallelism in many functional programs. Because of their freedom from side effects, they are attractive candidates for execution on parallel architectures. Efficiency problems, however, still exist. Some may be classified as "overhead" (e.g., intermediate list construction), while others are more fundamental (e.g., programming style). Whether parallelism and/or compiler techniques can compensate for or solve these problems remains an open research issue.

IV. DESIGN ISSUES FOR FUNCTIONAL PROGRAM MACHINES

This section compares and contrasts design decisions that have been made by architects of various FP machines along the following dimensions.

• The physical interconnection of the processors. These vary from uniprocessor systems to cube-interconnection networks.

• The method used to "drive" the computation.

• The representation of program and data. Most machines use a list or graph structure for both program and data. There are several design issues to consider even if a list structure is chosen.

• How parallelism is invoked and controlled. There are many issues here, including when to invoke parallelism, the mapping of processes to processors, and deadlock avoidance.

• Optimization techniques. Some proposed machines use evaluation strategies that attempt to avoid unnecessary and/or redundant computations.

Specific machines are examined with respect to these issues in Section V.

Not all machines discussed here were intended to execute purely *functional* languages. A number of them, particularly Lisp and APL machines, were designed for the execution of a nonfunctional language that contains a large functional subset; we refer to such languages as *quasi-functional*. Such machines are included to reflect points in the design space that would otherwise be overlooked. Although multiprocessors are the primary emphasis, a number of uniprocessors are included to present a richer view of the design space.

A. Physical Interconnection of Processors

The selection of a processor interconnection scheme in a multiprocessing environment is an important design decision. The subject has been one of great interest for designers of von Neumann multiprocessors [31], and the tradeoffs involved apply to FP multiprocessors as well.

Generally, a richer interconnection offers higher performance and flexibility at a greater hardware expense.[2] A complete interconnection is infeasible, however, because FP machine designers envision systems of hundreds or thousands of processors [9], [13]. At the other end of the spectrum are uniprocessor systems. While some have interesting features with respect to functional program implementation, they are not of particular interest in discussing interconnection strategies.

1) Shared Buses: The concurrent-Lisp processor [78] and Rumbaugh's data flow machine [73] each use a shared bus interconnection. The concurrent-Lisp processor has several memory banks, each attached to a single bus, with each processor directly connected to each memory bus, and processor communication done via the shared memory. Rumbaugh's system has two global memory banks—one for instructions and one for structure values—and local memories in each processor, used for caching. Bandwidth requirements make a shared bus approach feasible only for a small number of processors.

2) Ring: The *ZMOB* multiprocessing system [71] and the TI-data flow machine [39] each use a ring network in which data flow in one direction. Like shared bus architectures, bandwidth can become a bottleneck when the number of processors is large. The communication bandwidth of the 256 processor *ZMOB* network, for example, is only about one bit per microsecond per processor.

3) Tree: A number of designers have proposed tree-structured architectures [14], [43], [55], [65]. For a *reduction machine,* in which the problem can be decomposed into independent parallel subproblems, there is a natural mapping between the hardware (tree) and the software (tree of processes). Unfortunately, it is often necessary to copy data (e.g., parameter values) to each of a number of independent computations, making the bottleneck near the root of the tree a potentially serious problem. Sorting, for example, requires linear time on a tree, but can be performed in $O(\log^2 n)$ on a richer network [86]. Another problem is that the physical tree of processors has a finite depth, so that the resources at a leaf node may be insufficient for solving a large subproblem if the problem decomposes into a structure that is deeper than the physical tree.

A tree architecture may also be used in an SIMD manner, in which the tree is used as an associative memory and as a data shifter [55], [65]; lists may be stored across the leaves of the tree rather than in linked form. When insertion or deletion is required, some of the elements in the list are shifted to their neighbors; a single data shift among leaves of a tree may be performed in logarithmic time [70].

4) Hierarchical: A two-level system has been proposed for the ALICE multiprocessor [13] in which the processors are divided into tightly coupled *clusters,* which are then interconnected as a network. Parallelism unfolds dynamically, requiring the mapping of processes onto processors at runtime. The experience with the Cm* multiprocessor [41], also a clustered system but programmed imperatively, has shown that locality—important for good performance—is not easy to achieve. The performance of such a structure should be no worse than that of a tree, however, because a tree can be viewed as a special case of a hierarchical interconnection.

The U-interpreter [2] also uses a cluster strategy, with the clusters connected in a routing network (see next paragraph). Its designers intend to maintain a high degree of locality by requiring each cluster to work on a very closely coupled portion of the program, such as a single iteration of a loop.

5) Routing Networks: Several data architectures employ a routing network structure for communication between a set of processing elements and a set of memories [19]. The network used for Dennis' data flow project consists of $\log_2 N$ layers of N routers for an N-element system, each receiving packets at two input ports and transmitting them to one of two output ports. Two-way communication between processing elements and memories is achieved using a pair of tree routing networks. Although there is a rather large delay for a single memory access, such architectures are often designed primarily for total throughput. For large systems, however, network contention can easily degrade system throughput by 75 percent [68], although this can be improved by introducing buffering into the network [21].

6) Hypertorus: Hewitt [33] suggests a hypertorus interconnection—each processor being a member of n orthogonal ring networks where n is the dimension of the hypertorus—in which all processors contain local memory and are homogeneous. Attractive features of such a scheme are that the *maximum distance* between any two processors is proportional to the nth root of the number of processors, and that the interconnection structure is quite rich.

7) N-Cube: N-cube interconnections have also been suggested for FP architectures [2], [9], [13]. The connectivity of an n-cube is similar to that of a routing network, but each node contains a processor with memory rather than just a switch. The maximum distance between any two processors is logarithmic in the number of processors.

8) Conclusions: Although functional programs may exhibit a fair amount of locality, it is important for a processor to have reasonably efficient access to any other processor in the system if structures are to be shared. The shared bus, tree, and ring have bottlenecks that make them less desirable candidates. One-way routing networks cannot take advan-

---

[2]Richer interconnections may also give higher reliability, a topic that is beyond the scope of this paper.

tage of any locality, while the *cluster* approach has "arbitrary" locality boundaries with which the system must deal, although it appears to fit in well with the U-interpreter method of process-to-processor mapping. The *n*-cube and hypertorus give "gracefully degrading locality" and a rich interconnection structure, but still require the overhead of dynamic routing.

B. Method of Driving the Computation

Functions in an FP machine may be evaluated either top-down — where a function is evaluated when requested by another function that requires it as an argument — or bottom-

[23]. The infinite list of positive integer perfect squares, for example, may be expressed as

$$SquareList: 1$$

where *SquareList* is defined as

$$SquareList = Square \,\square\, (SquareList \circ (Plus \, 1))$$

where "$\square$" is a right-associative list construction operator (analogous to "cons" in Lisp). If the third element of the list is needed, lazy evaluation can invoke *SquareList* and *Square* until the third element is reduced

$$SquareList: 1 \rightarrow (Square: 1) \,\square\, (SquareList: 2)$$
$$\rightarrow (Square: 1) \,\square\, (Square: 2) \,\square\, (SquareList: 3)$$
$$\rightarrow (Square: 1) \,\square\, (Square: 2) \,\square\, (Square: 3) \,\square\, (SquareList: 4)$$
$$\rightarrow (Square: 1) \,\square\, (Square: 2) \,\square\, 9 \,\square\, (SquareList: 4) \,.$$

up — where a function is evaluated as soon as its arguments are available. The bottom-up approach is known as *data driven* computation, with each function (node) in a data flow graph being scheduled for evaluation as soon as its arguments arrive. Sequential and demand-driven evaluation are top-down — the arguments of function are not evaluated until a request is made that the function itself be evaluated.

1) Demand-Driven Evaluation: The *demand-driven* evaluation strategy makes use of the fact that *call-by-value* and *call-by-name* always return the same value in functional program (with *call-by-name* actually possessing better termination properties). A function's arguments are passed by name, and each is evaluated — again in a demand-driven fashion — the first time its value is needed; subsequent references to the argument use the already-evaluated form. This results in *unreduced* or *partially reduced* structures being passed among functions as arguments, each function application performing only the reductions necessary for its own evaluation. Demand-driven evaluation was used by Abrams [1] in his APL machine, and has been used in a number of implementations since [13], [43], [61]. It is also known as *lazy evaluation* [32] or *call-by-need* [63], [89].

Demand-driven evaluation generally introduces a fair amount of overhead. When a structure element is accessed, it must be determined whether it has already been reduced; if not, additional computation may be required. In a multiprocessor environment, several concurrent processes may simultaneously need the same structure to be reduced, requiring the synchronization and/or blocking [13]. The designers of Poplar note that in the cases where all elements of a structure were eventually required, lazy evaluation slowed programs in their implementation by a factor of about two [61]. In a multiprocessor system, communication and synchronization overhead may cause this factor to be even higher.

The advantages of the demand-driven evaluation include the potential for eliminating a vast amount of computation by evaluating only what is necessary for computing the result and the handling of infinite list structures in a natural way

Whether lazy evaluation may be — or must be — used depends on the semantics of the particular functional language.

2) Data-Driven Evaluation: A data-driven system incurs relatively little time overhead, with each operator node remaining inactive until *fired* — that is to say, when all its inputs have arrived. Parallelism is thus inhibited only by direct data dependencies; it is not inhibited because the result of a computation is not needed, as in demand-driven evaluation. Potential problems that appear in data-driven systems are the following.

• Too much parallelism might be generated. Memory could become swamped with partial results that are not yet used, causing deadlock. Decisions about suspending processes are more difficult because control passes from the bottom up.

• It is not possible to evaluate *structures* in a *lazy* manner because a data flow node only deals with fully evaluated structures; conceptually infinite structures therefore cannot be represented as data entities. Weng [95] applied the *stream* construct [51] to data flow computers, allowing conceptually infinite structures to be produced by sending them through data flow nodes one element at time. This requires the user/compiler to deal with two disjoint representations of the same concept: *structures* which can be manipulated efficiently, and *streams* which must be manipulated serially but can represent infinite objects.

• In a purely data-driven system all three subexpressions of a conditional statement would be evaluated in parallel, causing unnecessary computation to be performed. In practice, *switch* and *merge* nodes are inserted into the data paths of a conditional execution to delay the execution of the *then* or *else* expressions until after the condition is evaluated [19]. This amounts to lazy evaluation at the top level of a conditional expression, demonstrating that lazy evaluation can occur among function arguments — but not for structure elements — in a purely data-driven system.

In the example above, a data-driven system would completely evaluate *SquareList*: 1 before its result is passed to the node that uses the third element, requiring an infinite amount of computation.

3) Sequential Evaluation: The power and efficiency of sequential evaluation (in terms of both overhead and total computation) is closer to data-driven evaluation than to demand-driven. Treleaven *et al.* [82] argue that sequential evaluation is computationally equivalent to data-driven evaluation because both completely evaluate arguments before calling a function. Sequential evaluation does differ from data-driven evaluation in that it is top-down, so parallelism is more easily inhibited. There may be, however, more overhead because control must pass down the "computation graph" before results are passed up; in a data-driven scheme, the data (at the bottom of the computation graph) flow up the graph. Additionally, parallelism is not as natural to express in the sequential model.

4) Summary: Demand-driven evaluation requires more overhead than data-driven evaluation, but allows better control of parallelism, more selective evaluation, and a natural way of handling infinite structures. Data-driven evaluation is more efficient locally, but its "good performance" is limited to a narrower spectrum of computations, namely those which are data intensive and do not "blow up" when maximal parallelism is invoked. Sequential evaluation is similar to data-driven evaluation, but parallelism cannot be expressed as naturally.

C. Representation of Program Structures

Several methods have been proposed for representing programs and data in an FP system, the most common being graph and list structures. The most popular data representation is also a graph/list structure, but the decisions are largely independent.[3]

1) Program Representation and Execution Method: The representation of the program depends largely on the method used for program evaluation.

Sequential execution. In a (traditional) sequential program, code and data are separated, and instructions are executed sequentially; code can be considered an active agent that transforms the passive data. This method of execution is generally used primarily when the source language is quasi-functional.

Data flow. In this case, the data can be considered the active agents, moving through the "code graph" as they are transformed into the final result. The code representation is a data flow graph, possibly augmented by auxiliary data flow graphs that represent user-defined functions.

Reduction. A reduction machine takes the view that the *source-and-input* and *output* are merely two different forms of the same object, the output being the *reduced* form of the original program and input. An *object* in a reduction system is a structure the base elements of which are atoms and functions, a *reduced object* being one in which all base elements are atoms. The reduction process then consists of applying transformations to an object until it is in reduced form. Many reduction machines use graphs to represent structures and user-defined functions, although strings are sometimes used. Primitive functions — and sometimes even user-defined functions — are generally represented in machine code.

2) Traditional Machine Code: Several *quasi-functional* processors use traditional machine code for machine language [1], [28]. Such machines are usually uniprocessors that are microcoded for improved performance and are not truly functional in that they support global writable variables.

3) Graph-Structured Program Representation: Most of the current and proposed functional machines use some form of graph or list structure to represent the program, normally either list-structured machine code (reduction graph), a combinator graph, or a data flow graph.

Graph-structured machine code, often used in interpretive Lisp systems, is a variation of sequential code in which a graph structure is used to represent the program's structure. The machine executes instructions by traversing the list structure rather than by using a program counter. Reduction machines also use graphs of this form, but the mode of execution differs. In the former case, the environment is kept in a separate structure such as a display or association list, while in the latter case, the data become intermingled with the program as function definitions are inserted during the graph transformation.

A *combinator graph* is a version of the source program in which all variable and function references have been removed by applying combinator transformations [12]. Because there is no distinction between functions and data in a combinator system, function definitions are often *optimized* on the fly [83]. Such an optimization generally occurs when a function is defined in terms of two or more previously defined functions and the definitions are allowed to coalesce.

The combinator reduction proposed by Turner appears to require a large number of transformations, even for a simple program. Hughes [37] extended Turner's method by demonstrating that any function that satisfies two "functional" properties can be defined to be a combinator. Such "supercombinators" may then be compiled, increasing the speed of the object program when compared to Turner's method. Analysis by Jones [42] suggests that even without significant optimization, combinator-reduction outperforms lambda-reduction.

A *data flow graph* is similar to list-structured machine code with its pointers reversed to reflect bottom-up execution. The classical data flow program consists of a static graph that transform data as they pass through, recursive programs not being representable [39]. To allow recursive functions, the U-interpreter [2] replaces a *function node* with a copy of the definition whenever it is invoked, each copy having a *label* to identify it. Watson and Gurd [92] have constructed a machine that employs a similar strategy.

4) Token-String Program Representation: Berkling and Magó [6], [55] have proposed reduction machines that represent an expression by a string. The job of the processor(s) is to recognize patterns that can be reduced, and then to reduce them. Berkling's uniprocessor system evaluates polish prefix expressions using a stack, while Magó's tree-structured machine groups data segments by including parentheses in the token string.

---

[3]The use of list structures as program and data representation was introduced by McCarthy in the Lisp language. Having both program and data structures represented in the same way is considered to be one of Lisp's great strengths [57].

5) Data Representation Issues: The manner in which data are represented and accessed in a machine has a great bearing on the efficiency of a program. For accessing a structure, it is desirable to have the *random access* efficiency that an array representation would provide. On the other hand, data manipulations like concatenation and transposition — generally faster on list-structured data — should also be efficient.

Depending on the representation used, the question of whether to use monolithic data structures or pointers must also be resolved. A policy of always copying whole structures does not appear to be a good idea if large amounts of data are involved.

6) Methods of Representing Data: Traditionally, functional and quasi-functional systems have represented structures as linked linear lists of substructures. Although this has the advantage that many structure-manipulation operations can be done very quickly, *random access* to a structure element takes linear time. Another alternative, typically used in imperative languages, is to represent structures as arrays, allowing fast random access, but having the disadvantages that operations such as insertion take linear time and that memory can become fragmented when data blocks differ in size.

Some systems [28] use both lists and arrays under programmer control, giving the programmer some of the "best of both worlds" at the expense of requiring him to be concerned with another "programming detail." This method still does not solve the problem if a single structure must have both types of operations performed on it.

It has also been suggested that a tree be used to represent linear structures [27], [44], allowing most access and manipulation operations to be performed in logarithmic time. This approach has the disadvantage that the complexity of many simple access and data manipulation operations is increased, especially if the tree is required to remain balanced. Additional advantages of using a tree are that nondestructive updating of a structure can be performed in logarithmic time, and that reductions applying an associative operator can be performed in logarithmic time on a parallel architecture; a list structure requires linear time simply to access the elements in a list.

Some architectures represent all structures as token strings. This has the disadvantage that random access can be efficient only for the lowest-level structures, other data manipulation operations being expensive. An advantage in a multiprocessor system with distributed memory is that storage management can be simplified, as each processor can maintain its own address space.

7) Copying Structures: Tradeoffs exist between *copying pointers* and *copying data* strategies in a multiprocessor systems [66]. Copying large data structures among processors can be expensive in terms of time, bus contention, and memory utilization if only a few elements of a structure are needed. On the other hand, copying data incurs less overhead if all the data are eventually going to be used, and allows storage management to be performed at the individual processor level.

The decision whether to copy data or pointers is an instance of a general problem in FP systems: the program is written at a high enough level that the programmer is freed from — and the system is required to — make the decision. In an imperative program, the copying of data or pointers is generally specified explicitly.

Dennis [17] suggested a variation of the pointer-copying approach in which a pointer is cached in any processor to which it is copied, effectively building a copy of the structure in the remote processor as it is accessed. (Such caching is perfectly safe on a functional machine because a structure is never modified once it is created.) In the case where the remote processor has the only reference to a structure, it gradually migrates toward the remote processor, accessed portions of the structure in the local processor being reclaimed by the storage manager. Dennis suggested that this method might be used as a compromise between the "copy data" and "copy pointers" approaches, and that pointers (or atoms) might be sent in groups rather than singly to reduce communication overhead.

8) Storage Management: When pointers are used to implement structures, it is necessary to reclaim storage that has become unreferenceable. Reference counting may be used if graphs contain no cycles. Otherwise, a strategy such as marking or copying must be employed — possibly in conjunction with reference counting.

Although cycles are not necessary in data graphs — a purely functional language has no destructive operators — the optimization of certain graph representations can introduce cyclic list structures [13], [83]. In such cases the cost of garbage collection overhead must be weighed against the increased efficiency of structure access.

The drawbacks of a reference count strategy are that space is taken for a count field in each structure and that counts must be updated when pointers are copied or deleted. The advantage is that space can be recovered more quickly, and that reference counting is more easily performed asynchronously.

Halstead and Ward [29], [90] suggested a storage management strategy that uses *reference trees,* data structures linking together all references to a particular object in the system. Their approach allows garbage collection to occur on a local processor basis only, while finding global cyclic list structures through a strategy of migrating connected nodes to a common processor.

Magó's machine [55] necessarily approaches storage management in a different manner because there are no pointers; the problem in this case is what to do when the leaves of the tree become full. The method employed to alleviate the problem is to shift computations across the leaves of the tree — possibly quite expensive if large amounts of data are involved. If the entire tree becomes full, some computations are suspended, stored in secondary memory, and restarted at a later time.

D. Parallelism Issues

Design decisions about process communication, load balancing, control of parallelism, and other software issues vary substantially among multiprocessor FP systems. Although many systems are limited by the underlying architecture — a tree machine would not make good use of a global process list because efficient execution on a tree machine depends greatly on locality of reference [43], for example—there are generally many variations to consider.

1) Granularity of Parallelism: Many multiprocessor FP machines have a fine grain of parallelism, with every node in the program graph represented by a process containing small amount of state. A process node in the Dennis data flow machine [18] contains four words: an opcode, two data words, and the name of the successor instruction. Each node in the ALICE reduction machine [13] contains six fields: its name, the function name, argument list pointers, process state information, a reference count, and signal list for blocked processes. On such machines, a process tends to be active for a short period of time, performing a simple transformation.

Other methods of defining granularity include the following.

• Each node acts as a uniprocessor, reducing its own portion of the graph. When parallelism is desired (due to a function needing two operands evaluated, etc.), a new node may be created to perform the collateral evaluation [24].

• Each data item (as well as each operator) acts a process [33], [55].

• Require the user to program parallelism explicitly [78].

• Reducing the overhead of fine-grained parallelism by grouping several reduction nodes together and executing it as a single von Neumann process [47].

Although fine-grained parallelism is conceptually simple, it can lead to a great deal of process management and communication overhead. In particular, as the grain of parallelism becomes finer, less "intelligence" can be applied in making scheduling decisions. Fine-grained parallelism also generally leads to better load balancing [9]; again, this must be weighed against the increased overhead cost.

2) Mapping of Processes onto the Hardware: The mapping of processes onto a machine's processors involves attempting to attain several (sometimes conflicting) goals. On one hand, it is desirable to keep a process close to its data and to keep communicating processes close together. On the other hand, work should be shifted from overloaded processors to underloaded processors. This problem is compounded when the grain of parallelism is fine, and it is therefore not cost-effective to spend much computing time deciding where to execute a process.

Simple strategies at opposite ends of the spectrum are the uniprocessor approach in which all processes and data are kept in the same processor—clearly unacceptable in a multiprocessor system—and keeping a global list of processes from which an idle processor can choose a process to execute. The latter strategy spreads the workload evenly over all processors, but takes no advantage of locality.

Dataflow machines at the Massachusetts Institute of Technology [18] and Manchester [92] use routing networks in which the data (packets) and processors are separated. Locality is not an issue in process mapping on these systems because an instruction travels the same distance, once around the routing network, regardless of which processor it "uses."

Friedman and Wise [24] propose a strategy called *colonel and sergeants* that also uses a global process list. One process, the *colonel,* begins reducing the graph in *normal* order;

that is to say, performing depth-first traversal, visiting the leftmost son first. When the colonel reaches a point where parallelism could be invoked, a *sergeant* (if available) begins the secondary computation. The pending processes that are "close" to the colonel have the highest priority, so locality tends to be maintained in the sense that most processors in the system are working "close to one another."

A compromise between the *global list* and *uniprocessor* approaches involves the use of local lists of processes, either shared by a group of processors or unique to each processor. The *ZAPP* system [9] uses the latter approach, but allows a processor to "steal" a pending process from a neighboring processor when its own process list becomes empty. This strategy encourages processes to migrate to neighboring processors, and allows trees of processes to spread out all over the system while ensuring that no process is more than one processor away from its immediate offspring. The *Rediflow* system [47] uses a similar strategy, employing a "pressure model" to balance processor load among neighbors.

The tree architectures generally map the process tree directly onto the processor tree, resulting in a great deal of process locality. In AMPS [43], each leaf processor has its own list of pending processes, while in Magó's machine [55], each token resides in a unique leaf processor; tokens are mapped onto the sequence of leaf processors in the order in which they occur in the expression.

3) Invoking and Controlling Parallelism: Because functional programs tend to contain a great deal of implicit parallelism, the problem can arise that the system becomes swamped with processes. Another problem with excess concurrency is that it is possible that all memory might become tied up holding intermediate results for computations that are in progress, thereby creating a deadlock situation.

The conservative approach, of course, is never to invoke parallelism; this can be done on reduction machines by performing a *normal-order reduction* order—traversing the reduction tree in a depth-first manner, visiting leftmost son first. A common strategy is to invoke parallelism only on *strict* operators—those operators such as *plus* and *times* that require the evaluation of all their arguments—and to refrain from invoking it for *nonstrict* operators such as *if–then–else* and *cons*.[4] Maximal concurrency, of course, is obtained by evaluating expressions *eagerly*—invoking parallelism even for arguments of nonstrict operators. While such a strategy is optimal given an infinite number of processors, it is likely to cause a great deal of wasted computation, slowing down a system of finite capacity.

Systems that perform *eager evaluation* therefore generally constrain it in some way. The AMPS and ALICE systems [13], [43] allow the programmer to state explicitly whether a nonstrict operator is to be evaluated eagerly. ALICE additionally constrains eagerness by allowing it only when the compiler can determine that the eager computation will terminate [63].

The colonel and sergeants system [24] invokes parallelism

---

[4]Actually, *cons* may or may not be a strict operator, depending upon the semantics of the programming language and whether a *lazy evaluation* strategy is being employed.

232

whenever there is an idle processor available. This may require that a stray process be purged, in the case where it can be determined that the process is performing an unnecessary or divergent computation.

In the ZAPP [9] and Rediflow [47] systems, the amount of parallelism is determined by the processor load. Breadth-first expansion, which encourages parallelism, is employed when load is light, depth-first when it is heavy. This is implemented in ZAPP on a local basis by maintaining a list of processes, each ordered according to its depth in the computation tree, and giving shallow processes priority over deep ones only when the load is light. The amount of *eager* evaluation is constrained by allowing *unsafe* computations (computations that may never terminate) a limit on the amount of processing that they are allowed to perform [76]. A process may be terminated when it exhausts its "budget," presumably leaving behind a partially reduced graph that becomes subject to garbage collection; alternatively, the budget may be extended if system load is light enough, allowing the unsafe computation to continue, again with a (revised) bound on its computation time.

On data-driven machines, the evaluation of arguments is performed before the operator node is encountered, making it difficult to use properties of the operator in dynamically constraining eager evaluation. A possible solution would be to introduce top-down "demand tokens" [16], allowing parallelism to be controlled more finely at the expense of introducing more overhead.

4) Deadlock Avoidance: The problem of deadlock in FP multiprocessing systems seems to be more easily solved in demand-driven than in data-driven systems because parallelism is more easily constrained. ZAPP's strategy [9] of basing their expansion (depth-first versus breadth-first) on system load is part of its method of deadlock prevention. If the assumption is made that there is always enough memory in any processor to evaluate an expression in *normal order,* this strategy does in fact prevent deadlock by forcing each processor to act as a uniprocessor, evaluating an expression in normal order, when system load becomes extremely high. Such an assumption is valid in cases where the a computation tree remains small.

Another possible approach in concurrent FP systems is to wait until deadlock occurs, and then to free some memory by selecting certain process trees for purging. Because FP computations have no side effects, purging a partially completed computation means only that it may have to be recomputed later. In the extreme case, the computation tree would be pruned to the extent that a single process is active and is performing normal-order reduction.

E. Additional Optimizations

In Section IV-B-1, it was seen that *lazy evaluation* can potentially increase the efficiency of a functional program by reducing the amount of unnecessary computation. This section discusses two other dynamic optimizations that have been suggested. Compile time versions of each are also possible.

1) Avoiding Unnecessary Data Manipulations:

Operations such as transposition, rotation, and slicing can involve a great deal of data manipulation, yet occur frequently in functional programs. In designing his APL machine, Abrams proposed the use of a technique called *beating* [1], in which certain data manipulation operations are implemented by performing transformations on *array descriptors* rather than on arrays themselves. An array transposition might be implemented by exchanging indexes in the array descriptor, for example.

It is not clear that the generalization of this technique to linear list structures would be effective because the effectiveness of *beating* is diminished in the absence of *random access* to structure elements. In systems where arrays (or other structures with efficient random access) are present, optimizations similar to beating may be worthwhile.

2) Avoiding Redundant Computations: A potential source of inefficiency in functional programs is that their straightforward execution often causes the same computation to be performed repeatedly [46]. For example, although most evaluators would evaluate *Transpose*: x only once in

$$[Fcn1, Fcn2] \circ Transpose: x$$

it would probably be necessary for a compiler to discover the common expression in

$$[Fcn1 \circ Transpose, Fcn2 \circ Transpose]: x.$$

Even more difficult is the recognition that [*Fib*: 2] and [*Fib*: 1] (dynamically) occur more than once in

$$Fib: 4 \rightarrow Plus \circ [Fib: 3, Fib: 2]$$
$$Fib: 3 \rightarrow Plus \circ [Fib: 2, Fib: 1]$$
$$Fib: 2 \rightarrow Plus \circ [Fib: 1, Fib: 0]$$

In this particular case, dynamic recognition of common expressions could reduce an exponential algorithm to a linear one.

Most FP systems share the result of the common computation in the first case and could be augmented to do so in the second. Doing so in the third case probably requires some type of result caching, although combinator reductions sometimes recognize these in simple cases (not in *Fib,* however). As a result, the default strategy for result sharing tends be sharing in the first two cases but recomputing in the third.

The policy of saving the result if the common expression is easy to detect, and recomputing it otherwise is not always the most effective. The *Fib* example demonstrates that it is sometimes desirable to detect "difficult" common expressions. Conversely, it may sometimes be desirable to ignore easily detected common expressions. Consider the evaluation of an expression in which a list is traversed in different orders by two functions

$$[Traverses\text{-}forward, Traverses\text{-}backward] \circ$$

$$From\text{-}1\text{-}to\text{-}1\,000\,000$$

the cost of recomputing the common function *From-1-to-1 000 000* may be relatively small, while keeping its value in memory would use a large number (1 000 000) of cells. If *lazy* evaluation and an *appropriate* method of representing structures were used, the necessary number of cells might be reduced to a handful.

The profitability of sharing a computation thus seems to be somewhat independent of the ease of common-expression recognition. The only way of sharing results in a general manner appears to through caching [59], which introduces a number of new issues to consider [46].

• What results should be cached? If the result of every intermediate computation is cached, it seems that memory could be quickly swamped. If not everything is cached, on what basis does one decide what to cache?

• How should the cache directory be structured? How are the cached values mapped onto the processor(s)? How much extra interprocessor traffic will be generated by cache lookup requests? Can cache-lookup be made efficient enough that it does not slow up "fast" operations?

• What replacement algorithm should be used to determine what entries to purge when the cache becomes full? How much overhead does this algorithm introduce? Ideally, one would like to account for factors such as the complexity of the computation, the amount of storage it takes to cache results, the number of "recent" references, and whether there are outstanding computations waiting for the result. It is probably not desirable, however, to spend a great deal of time performing cache management.

• Should *easily detected* common expressions be subject to the same purging strategy as cached ones, so that a function like *From-1-to-1 000 000 does* effectively generate its elements twice if memory becomes scarce?

• Should cache lookup be done in parallel with computation? If this strategy is adopted, the process(es) performing the computation should be aborted if the cache lookup is successful.

The caching issue seems to be another instance of a potential efficiency problem due to the fact that an FP language is higher level than an imperative language. In a typical imperative language, the programmer has explicit control over the decisions about whether a value should be saved or recomputed, basing these decisions on the complexity of the computation, the likelihood of needing to reuse the value, etc. In a functional program, such issues are generally transparent to the user, the system being responsible for deciding whether to save a value. The most practical approach thus far proposed is that the programmer be responsible for specifying which results should be cached [46].

Harbison's analysis [30] of a von Neumann architecture that caches expression values suggest that a moderately sized cache (512 entries) can significantly improve performance. Caching in a functional multiprocessor architecture is likely to be complicated, however, by the cache being distributed over the entire system and by comparisons being performed on structure values rather than scalar values and variable names.

TABLE I
ABRAMS' APL MACHINE

Reference	[1]
Physical interconnection	uniprocessor
Representation of program	machine code
Representation of data	arrays with descriptors
Drive	demand
Avoiding redundant computations	beating (descriptor optimization)
Storage management	reference counts (on array descriptors)
Status	paper design only

V. OVERVIEW OF SPECIFIC ARCHITECTURES

This section is a collection of brief descriptions of a number of architectures for the execution of *functional* or *quasi-functional* languages. The first two sections present architectures with minimal interconnections, namely the uniprocessor and tree machines. The last three sections include *data-driven, demand-driven,* and "other" architectures that have richer interconnections.

A. Uniprocessor Architectures

The architectures in this section are single-processor machines. In many cases, the design goals did not include high performance, but rather demonstration of the feasibility of a particular evaluation strategy.

1) Abrams' APL Machine: Abrams' APL machine, while not a multiprocessor, is important historically because it introduced two important concepts: *beating,* which optimizes array operations, and *dragging,* a type of lazy evaluation. Minter's APL machine [60], which was based on Abrams' work, extended and improved his optimizations.

2) Berkling's Reduction Machine: The uniprocessor designed by Berkling has three stacks, two used for computing and one—the *system stack*—to handle control structure. Execution consists of the application of a handful of simple character-string reduction rules.

Limitations: Characters are the only form of data used, so the machine is quite inefficient when operating on large structures because the data structures must be copied and scanned character-by-character [82]. In addition, a great deal of character scanning is generally required to find instances of reduction rules.

3) Scheme-79: Scheme-79 is a single-chip lexically scoped Lisp machine. Two-level microcode is used to execute programs by traversing list-structured machine code. Interesting features of the architecture include the use of independent register assemblies to enable register parallelism, and the assignment of particular registers to specified hardware functions.

Limitations: The machine is not particularly fast; its compiled code runs at about the same speed as interpreted Lisp on a PDP-10. Its design goals, however, were oriented toward testing a design methodology and bringing up a working

TABLE II
BERKLING'S REDUCTION MACHINE

Reference	[6]
Physical interconnection	uniprocessor
Representation of program	character string
Representation of data	character string
Drive	sequential, with programmer-specified delayed evaluation
Avoiding redundant computations	local variable binding; programmer can specify call-by-name or call-by-value;
Storage management	stack
Status	operational

TABLE III
SCHEME-79

References	[36], [80]
Physical interconnection	uniprocessor
Representation of program	graph/list
Representation of data	graph/list
Drive	sequential
Avoiding redundant computations	Lisp static binding
Storage management	marking garbage collection
Status	operational

TABLE IV
LISP MACHINE

Reference	[28]
Physical interconnection	uniprocessor
Representation of program	machine code
Representation of data	graph/list, array
Drive	sequential
Avoiding redundant computations	Lisp dynamic binding
Storage management	incremental marking garbage collection
Status	operational

TABLE V
TURNER'S COMBINATOR REDUCTION MACHINE

Reference	[83]
Physical interconnection	uniprocessor
Representation of program	combinator graph
Representation of data	combinator graph
Drive	demand
Avoiding redundant computations	common parameter use, combinator optimizations, currying
Storage management	marking garbage collection
Status	operational (software interpreter)

TABLE VI
SKIM

Reference	[10]
Physical interconnection	uniprocessor
Representation of program	combinator graph
Representation of data	combinator graph
Drive	demand
Avoiding redundant computations	common parameter use, combinator optimizations, currying
Storage management	marking garbage collection
Status	operational

machine in a reasonably short period of time. A followup project, *Scheme-81*, is significantly faster [79].

4) Lisp Machine: The Lisp machine is a high-performance personal computer that is microcoded to handle Lisp operations, such as list manipulation and function call, efficiently. Structures may be stored in list or array form, the representation being specified by the programmer. An interesting feature of this machine is the existence of a two-bit *CDR code* for each list cell that saves a word of space in any cell in which the CDR is either *nil* or occupies the subsequent cell.

5) Turner's Combinator Reduction Machine: Turner's machine makes use of combinator logic to translate the functional language SASL into a combinator graph. Execution consists of performing normal-order reductions on the graph until it is completely reduced, except that certain reductions are delayed, causing evaluation to be done in a lazy manner. As implemented, reduction is performed in a destructive

manner; that is to say, when a subgraph is reduced, the memory location that its pointer occupies is overwritten with a pointer to the new structure. Because SASL is a functional language, such a technique is not only correct, but improves the performance of the system, as the reduction is reflected in all structures that (possibly indirectly) reference the reduced cell. The design of a combinator reduction machine (and associated compiler) that is potentially much faster has been reported by Johnsson [40] and Kieburtz [49].

Limitations: Although the design is an elegant one, there may be problems extending the architecture to multi-processor form. In particular, the combinator expressions used tend to obscure the *true structure* of the program, which could make process scheduling difficult.

6) SKIM: SKIM, a small combinator reduction machine patterned after that of Turner, is a standard uniprocessor architecture with 2K of microcode that performs combinator reductions as well as garbage collection and I/O. Its performance is described as similar to that of an interpretive system on a fairly fast processor.

B. Tree-Structured Machines

The tree machines all suffer from a bottleneck near the root. The first two architectures in this section attempt to alleviate the problem by performing redundant computations in different portions of the tree rather than to communicate results across the tree. The third architecture performs data-driven evaluation on a tree of processors, sending data results among tree elements whenever necessary. The final architecture mentioned, TALCM, uses the tree for performing SIMD operations.

TABLE VII
MAGÓ'S TREE MACHINE

Reference	[55]
Physical interconnection	tree
Representation of program	token string
Representation of data	token string, data copied
Drive	data (effectively)
Granularity of parallelism	one or more processes per reduction
Mapping of processes onto hardware	process tree maps onto physical tree
When to invoke parallelism	always
Avoiding redundant computations	never
Storage management	"shift register" to expand/contract process tree
Status	simulator operational

TABLE VIII
AMPS

Reference	[43]
Physical interconnection	tree
Representation of program	graph/list, array
Representation of data	graph/list, array
Drive	demand
Granularity of parallelism	each expression is a process
Mapping of processes onto hardware	demand list per processor; processors multiplex waiting for data; interior processors (of tree) do load balancing by shifting processes across tree
When to invoke parallelism	strict operators, but programmer can specify more eagerness
Avoiding redundant computations	common parameter use
Storage management	reference count
Status	simulator operational

TABLE IX
DDM 1

References	[14], [15]
Physical interconnection	tree
Representation of program	data flow graph
Representation of data	variable-length character strings
Drive	data
Granularity of parallelism	process per graph node
Mapping of processes onto hardware	recursive division among tree processors
When to invoke parallelism	all strict operators
Avoiding redundant computations	common parameter use
Status	operational

1) Magó's Tree Machine: Magó's tree architecture was one of the first multiprocessors designed for executing functional programs [5]. Both the program and data are represented by token strings, which reside in the leaf cells. Computation consists of reductions, each being performed by one or more interior nodes that transform the leaves. A computation *cycle* consists of an upsweep where data are sent from the leaves to the interior nodes and a downsweep where the leaf nodes are modified. The size of an expression may increase during the reduction process, giving rise to the possibility that an expression may "outgrow" its subtree during execution. When this happens, the *storage manager* shifts expressions among the leaf cells to make room for the growing expression.

Limitations: This architecture may be effective for certain classes of computations, but it has a couple of drawbacks for the general execution of functional programs. The first is the obvious bottleneck near the root of the tree. The second is that the system has no pointers, so all data movement must be performed by copying complete data structures; results are *never* shared, even in the simplest cases.

2) AMPS: AMPS is a reduction tree-machine proposed at the University of Utah in which the interior nodes perform process management and computation is performed in the leaf nodes. Computations are subdivided among the leaf nodes, which act as uniprocessors, each reducing its own portion of the computation. When it is necessary to fetch data from a remote processor, a request is sent across the tree. While waiting for remote data, a processor may choose another process from its process list on which to work. Interior nodes perform load balancing by attempting to keep all subtrees within predetermined load limits, shifting tasks from one subtree to another when necessary. Lazy evaluation is normally performed, but *eager evaluation* may be specified at compile time.

Limitations: Although the machine has the obvious bottlenecks of a tree-structured architecture, the designers claim that a great amount of locality can be maintained. Both the load-balancing scheme and the parameter-passing mechanism, however, promote nonlocality.

3) DDM1: The DDM1 architecture is a data-driven architecture that was developed at the University of Utah. Processing elements are organized into a tree structure, each pair of connected elements communicating via a data queue. Each processing element consists of an *agenda queue,* which contains firable instructions, an *atomic memory,* which provides the program memory, and an *atomic processor,* which performs execution.

Limitations: As with the architecture of Magó, this architecture has a bottleneck at the root of the tree, and does not allow pointers; hence, data must always be copied.

4) TALCM: TALCM is an architecture designed to execute Lisp in an SIMD (single instruction, multiple data) manner. Parallelism is invoked for associative searching and for list structure updates.

Limitations: Although certain operations can be performed faster than in a uniprocessor, such a machine would not take advantage of many of the opportunities available for parallelism in functional programs.

TABLE X
TALCM

Reference	[65]
Physical interconnection	tree
Representation of program	machine code
Representation of data	lists, represented as linear array
Drive	sequential
Granularity of parallelism	SIMD
Mapping of processes onto hardware	SIMD
When to invoke parallelism	during associative search or element shift
Avoiding redundant computations	Lisp dynamic scoping
Storage management	marking garbage collection
Status	simulator operational

TABLE XI
MASSACHUSETTS INSTITUTE OF TECHNOLOGY DATA FLOW PROJECT

References	[18], [20]
Physical interconnection	routing network
Representation of program	data flow graph
Representation of data	atoms (integers, reals, etc.)
Drive	data
Granularity of parallelism	process per graph node
Mapping of processes onto hardware	statically allocated instructions
When to invoke parallelism	except conditional where delay nodes are inserted
Avoiding redundant computations	common parameter use
Status	experimental model operational

TABLE XII
LAU

References	[11], [81]
Physical interconnection	shared/interleaved memory, accessed via switch
Representation of program	data flow graph
Representation of data	fixed-length tokens
Drive	data
Granularity of parallelism	process per graph node
Mapping of processes onto hardware	statically allocated instructions
When to invoke parallelism	all strict operators
Avoiding redundant computations	common parameter use
Status	operational

C. Data-Driven Machines

Data-driven (or data flow) processors have a tremendous potential for parallel processing. The first proposed data flow architectures were connected as routing networks, although more recent ones have different topologies.

1) Massachusetts Institute of Technology Data Flow Project (Dennis): The data flow multiprocessor designed by Dennis *et al.* at the Massachusetts Institute of Technology consists of four components.

• A set of *instruction cells* whose contents collectively represent the data flow program graph being executed.

• One or more *arbitration networks* that move firable instructions (i.e., functions whose operands have all arrived) to processing elements.

• A set of *processing elements* that perform the actual computation. A processing element transforms a firable instruction into one or more *result packets.*

• A *distribution network* that routes each result packet to its destination instruction in an instruction cell.

The execution of a program consists of firable instructions (packets) moving through the arbitration network to processing elements, being transformed into result packets which, in turn, move through the distribution network to update instruction cells, thereby creating more firable instructions.

Processors and memory are connected by a single routing network in which information flows in only one direction; there is therefore no locality. A design was considered in which each processor contained its own memory of instructions, but it was decided that an extremely intelligent compiler would be required to take advantage of the locality [18].

Limitations: The design does not allow recursive functions call of arbitrary depth, or structured data. Like all data-driven schemes, parallel execution occurs automatically, the system having little ability to limit it. Bottlenecking may also be a problem (see Section IV-A-5).

2) LAU: LAU is a data-driven architecture that consists of three major components. The *memory subsystem* is a set of memory banks in which all instructions are stored. The *control subsystem* contains three status bits for each instruction in the memory subsystem, denoting which of its operands have arrived and whether its execution has been completed. The *execution subsystem* consists of a set of processing elements that evaluate instructions that are read from the memory subsystem. Execution consists of an *instruction fetch processor* continuously scanning the control subsystem, placing the names of any firable instructions into a queue. This causes the named instructions to be read and queued up for execution by one of the processors in the execution subsystem, which reads its operands from the memory system, computes the result, and writes its data back into the memory subsystem. Finally, control bits are updated by an *update processor;* this may in turn cause additional instructions to become firable.

Limitations: As with the architecture of Dennis, recursive functions of arbitrary depth are not allowed, and structures are not easily handled because data items are fixed-length tokens. Additionally, communication being performed by a shared memory could lead to difficulty in increasing the size of the system.

3) Rumbaugh's Data Flow Multiprocessor: Rumbaugh's data flow architecture contains three classes of processors and two classes of memory. Three processors perform computing, one performs scheduling, and one, the *structure controller,* handles accesses to nonatomic data structures. *Instruction memory* contains the data flow instructions, and

TABLE XIII
RUMBAUGH'S DATA FLOW MULTIPROCESSOR

TABLE XIII
RUMBAUGH'S DATA FLOW MULTIPROCESSOR

References	[72], [73]
Physical interconnection	shared buses (processors separated from memory)
Representation of program	data flow graph
Representation of data	graph/list
Drive	data
Granularity of parallelism	process per user-defined function
Mapping of processes onto hardware	performed by scheduling processor
When to invoke parallelism	except conditional and user-defined function
Avoiding redundant computations	common parameter use
Storage management	reference count
Status	paper design only

TABLE XIV
TEXAS INSTRUMENTS' DATA FLOW MACHINE

Reference	[39]
Physical interconnection	ring (4 processors)
Representation of program	data flow graph
Representation of data	atoms (integers, reals, etc.)
Drive	data
Granularity of parallelism	process per graph node
Mapping of processes onto hardware	all nodes allocated statically
When to invoke parallelism	except on conditionals
Avoiding redundant computations	common parameter use
Status	operational

TABLE XV
MANCHESTER DATA FLOW MACHINE

References	[92], [93]
Physical interconnection	routing network
Representation of program	data flow graph
Representation of data	atoms (integer, real, etc.)
Drive	data
Granularity of parallelism	process per graph node
Mapping of processes onto hardware	processes move through network
When to invoke parallelism	except conditional and functional call
Avoiding redundant computations	common parameter use
Status	20-processor system under construction

structure memory, which is accessed only by the structure controller, contains all data structures. Each *computing processor* is directly connected to the *instruction memory*, the *scheduling processor*, and the *structure processor*.

Each structure is conceptually independent, although substructures are often shared to save computing time and memory space. Because structures in this system are acyclic, reference counts are used for storage management, as well as for structure optimization; modifications to a structure are performed in place whenever the reference count is *one*. Each processor contains a *structure cache*, which contains copies of substructures that are of current interest to the processor. Because functional programs are free of side effects, such caching is not difficult to implement.

Limitations: The processor–memory interconnection structure may make this architecture difficult to extend.

4) Texas Instruments' Data Flow Machine: The data flow machine implemented at Texas Instruments contains four microprogrammed processors in a ring and accepts static program graphs in which all instruction-processor mapping has been performed at compile time. Each processor has four major components.

• An arithmetic unit, which performs standard arithmetic and comparison operations.

• Memory, in which the instructions are stored.

• A hardware queue of pointers to *firable* instructions. The arithmetic unit executes these instructions sequentially.

• An *update controller*, which accepts data from other processors and inserts instruction pointers into the instruction queue.

Programs for this system are written in Fortran. A modified version of an optimizing Fortran compiler is used to create the data flow program graph.

Limitations: The machine does not allow structured data or recursive subroutines, and all subroutines must be expanded at link time. Although the ring could be a bottleneck, such an architecture seems feasible for a small number of processors. The authors [39] do not state how Fortran '66, a language with inherent side-effects (e.g., call-by-reference, common areas), is cleanly executed on a data flow machine.

5) Manchester Data Flow Machine: The Manchester data flow machine is similar to that proposed by Dennis in that it uses a routing networks to send packets between processing units and instruction store. It differs, however, in that there may be more than one logical instantiation of a single-instruction cell, allowing recursive invocations of a function and "unfolded" iterations. To ensure that a result packet arrives at the *correct* instance of an instruction, each instruction instance carries with it a *label,* and each result packet specifies both an instruction *and* a label name, the latter disambiguating among instances of an instruction. This is implemented by placing a *matching store* behind the instruction store; results for instructions with multiple inputs are collected in the matching store and sent to the instruction store as a unit after all results have arrived. A new label is created for each function invocation or loop iteration.

Limitations: Like other routing network data flow machines, parallelism may be difficult to control, and the network interconnection could be a bottleneck. The authors do not mention whether structures are handled, but adding them would not appear to be difficult. Although the matching store could be a bottleneck, there is no reason that multiple matching stores could not, in principle, be added.

6) U-Interpreter: The U-interpreter, a predecessor to Manchester data flow machine, also uses labeled packets to allow multiple instantiations of a single instruction. The major difference is that the U-interpreter uses a cluster architec-

TABLE XVI	
U-Interpreter	
References	[2], [3]
Physical interconnection	clusters of processors, connected by routing net
Representation of program	data flow graph
Representation of data	graph/list, stream
Drive	data
Granularity of parallelism	process per graph node
Mapping of processes onto hardware	assignment function
When to invoke parallelism	except conditional, function call
Avoiding redundant computations	common parameter use
Storage management	reference count
Status	under construction

TABLE XVII	
ALICE	
Reference	[13]
Physical interconnection	clusters of processors, each with one memory and ring buffer of processable packets; connection among clusters not decided
Representation of program	graph/list
Representation of data	graph/list
Drive	demand
Granularity of parallelism	process per node
Mapping of processes onto hardware	global (or per-cluster) process list
When to invoke parallelism	always when result is needed; and/or compiler can specify eager evaluation with the constraint that "safeness" is required
Avoiding redundant computations	common parameter use
Storage management	reference count (is considering marking garbage collection)
Status	simulator operational, hardware under construction

ture rather than a routing network. The clusters, each of which contains four processors with local memory, communicate via a routing network. The potential therefore exists for taking advantage of locality to reduce network traffic.

Because data flow programs are executed *bottom up*, a result packet would not necessarily know the location of the instruction instance (dataflow node) to which it is to deliver data. To resolve the problem, an *assignment function*, which computes a hash address from the instruction name and label, is defined that possesses the property that instructions having the same label execute in the same cluster. This gives programs a certain amount of locality, while allowing computation to spread throughout the system when user-defined functions are invoked or when iterations occur.

Limitations: As with all data flow machines, the issue of controlling parallelism remains unresolved. Effectively mapping processes onto hardware, particularly in a dataflow instruction-labeling scheme where two or more result packets must "find" the same destination instruction, could also be a difficult problem because the simplest solutions do not take advantage of locality.

D. Demand-Driven Machines

Demand-driven machines with rich processor interconnection structures show promise for evaluation of functional programs because support for *lazy evaluation* and *interprocessor communication* appear to be important features of a fast FP system. Judgment must be reserved, however, as none of the demand-driven processors has been completely implemented.

1) ALICE: In the ALICE system, several processors are connected via a shared bus to form a *cluster,* with clusters connected in a (yet unspecified) loosely coupled manner. ALICE is truly a *reduction machine:* each node in the original computation is specified by a packet. A packet requiring a subexpression to be reduced sets the *required* flag in the packet representing the subexpression and inserts it into the *packet pool* to be reduced. The parent process is awakened when the subexpression is totally reduced. Although eager evaluation is allowed, it must be specified at compile time,

the programmer/compiler being responsible for ensuring that divergent computations are not eagerly evaluated.

Limitations: The details of execution are given only for a single-cluster system, so process communication and migration, which are critical issues in a multicluster system, are not discussed. The fine granularity of parallelism is likely to create a great deal of process management overhead.

2) ZAPP: Normal mode of operation on the ZAPP system consists of each processor working on independent computation, adding processes to its local process list as it reduces a subgraph. When a processor is underloaded, it steals processes from neighboring processors, resulting in minimal movement of processes across the system when system load is heavy. When system load is light, however, processes tend to spread across the system in a manner similar to many of the tree architectures, but with the advantage that the "tree" in this case has no *a priori* depth, as a binary *n*-cube can be considered a "tree folded upon itself." Additionally, the cost of data communication is reduced (compared to a tree) because there is no bottleneck at the root.

Two other features of the system are noteworthy. The first is that system load determines the order in which computation is performed, reductions being performed depth-first when the system is loaded, and breadth-first otherwise (see Section IV-D-3). The second is the method of evaluating subexpressions that contain a nonstrict operator, and would therefore not necessarily be attempted during a *normal order* reduction because full evaluation of such expressions could cause the computation to diverge. Such an expression is allocated a "renewable budget" — an amount of computing it may apply toward the evaluation of the expression. When it exhausts its "budget," it is required to request additional processor time from the system, which will honor or reject the request, depending on factors such as system load.

TABLE XVIII
ZAPP

References	[9], [76]
Physical interconnection	binary n-cube
Representation of program	graph/list
Representation of data	graph/list
Drive	demand
Granularity of parallelism	process per graph node
Mapping of processes onto hardware	local process list on each processor; load balancing by allowing neighbors to steal processes;
When to invoke parallelism	invoked on strict operators, but unsafe nonstrict computations may run if "budgeted" processor load determines whether reductions are performed depth-first or breadth-first
Avoiding redundant computations	common parameter use
Storage management	marking garbage collection
Status	simulator operational

TABLE XIX
REDIFLOW

Reference	[47]
Physical interconnection	Two-dimensional array (or a "richer" connection)
Representation of program	graph/list, array
Representation of data	graph/list, array
Drive	demand, with programmer able to specify functions to be computed sequentially
Granularity of parallelism	one process per path in the computation tree
Mapping of processes onto hardware	local process list on each processor; load balancing by sharing processes with neighbors
When to invoke parallelism	strict operators, but processor load determines whether reductions are performed depth-first or breadth-first
Avoiding redundant computations	common parameter use
Storage management	marking garbage collection
Status	simulator operational

Limitations: Although processes representing connected nodes in the computation graph are usually no more than one processor apart, data structures can exist in remote processors because pointers are used. The question of whether the n-cube interconnection is rich enough to support communication also remains unanswered.

3) Rediflow: The Rediflow system is a followup to the AMPS project, differing particularly in processor interconnection, which is richer, and in the grain of parallelism, which is coarser. It is similar to ZAPP [9] in its load balancing strategy, in that a processors is allowed to "steal" processes from overworked neighbors. A "pressure" model is used to determine the flow of processes, in which each processor has an *internal pressure* (the load within the processor) and an *external pressure* (computed as a function of the pressures of

TABLE XX
FRIEDMAN AND WISE'S REDUCTION MACHINE

Reference	[24]
Physical interconnection	unspecified
Representation of program	graph/list
Representation of data	graph/list
Drive	demand
Granularity of parallelism	several reductions per process
Mapping of processes onto hardware	colonel/sergeants scheme
When to invoke parallelism	whenever sergeant processor is available; may have to kill wayward sergeants
Avoiding redundant computations	common parameter use
Storage management	unspecified
Status	paper design only

its neighbors). Load balancing is performed by distributing processes along *pressure gradients*.

The programmer is allowed to group computations into von Neumann processes. If this is done intelligently, a significant amount of fine-grained-parallelism overhead may be eliminated. The method for controlling parallelism is similar to that of ZAPP.

Limitations: As with ZAPP, the sharing of pointers potentially requires a large number of remote accesses; the problem of determining an acceptable interconnection structure is under investigation.

4) Friedman and Wise's Reduction Machine: The proposal of Friedman and Wise is that of an unspecified abstract multiprocessor, their design being primarily concerned with process scheduling. The key idea is that one processor executes a *colonel process* that is always running, and is reducing the program graph in normal order using *lazy evaluation*. All other processors run *sergeant processes*, which evaluate nodes in the graph that have been left suspended by the colonel, the highest priority sergeant processes being the ones that are "near" the colonel. In the event that a sergeant becomes "lost" performing a divergent computation, it is eventually recovered by the storage manager.

Limitations: Although the "nearness" metric is not well defined, it seems clear that only a small amount of computing time should be spent by a sergeant deciding which reduction to perform; otherwise, such time would dominate "useful" computing time, as sergeant tasks tend to be short. The scheduling strategy also does not seem to take advantage of *locality,* but rather tends to have all processors computing "near" one another (i.e., near the colonel); this is likely to cause contention among processors when common data structures are accessed.

E. Miscellaneous Machines

The machines in this section are being designed with artificial intelligence applications in mind. None has functional program execution as a principal goal, but it is expected that each will support one or more functional or quasi-functional languages.

TABLE XXI
CONCURRENT LISP ARCHITECTURE

Reference	[78]
Physical interconnection	shared buses (processors separated from memory)
Representation of program	graph/list
Representation of data	graph/list
Drive	sequential evaluation
Granularity of parallelism	explicitly programmed
Mapping of processes onto hardware	global process list
When to invoke parallelism	explicitly programmed
Avoiding redundant computations	dynamic scoping
Storage management	marking garbage collection
Status	simulator operational, with hardware under construction

TABLE XXII
ZMOB

References	[50], [71]
Physical interconnection	ring (20 MByte/s, 256 processors)
Representation of program	graph/list
Representation of data	graph/list, but copied as ascii strings
Drive	sequential evaluation
Granularity of parallelism	network of course processes
Mapping of processes onto hardware	statically
When to invoke parallelism	implementation-dependent
Avoiding redundant computations	dynamic scoping, common parameter use
Storage management	local marking garbage collection
Status	Several small (16–32 processor) versions are operational

TABLE XXIII
THE ARRAY

References	[33], [34], [52]
Physical interconnection	hypertorus, or any other mesh-connected network
Representation of program	actors
Representation of data	actors
Drive	responsibility of individual actors
Granularity of parallelism	responsibility of individual actors
Mapping of processes onto hardware	dynamic load balancing between neighbors; each processor multiplexes on actors
When to invoke parallelism	normally always, considering limits
Avoiding redundant computations	unspecified
Storage management	marking garbage collection
Status	preliminary version operational on local network; version running on a tightly coupled mesh-connected network under construction [35]

1) Concurrent Lisp Architecture: The concurrent Lisp architecture executes a version of Lisp 1.5 in which several of the destructive list operators have been removed and several parallelism operators added. The *slave processors,* which execute the user program, are scheduled by the *master processor.* There are four dedicated memory banks (process control, list structures, random access, and process stacks), each having a single bus, by which it is connected to each processor. Parallelism is explicitly programmed by the user.

Limitations: Because of the limited number of memory banks, it seems inevitable that system performance will degrade if more than a handful of processors is used.

2) ZMOB: The 256 processors in the ZMOB system are connected via a high-speed ring, so that a processor may communicate with any other in "unit time" where unit time is defined as the time it takes to send data once around the ring. It is intended to support a number of languages, including Lisp and Prolog, although there is no current Lisp effort [94].

Limitations: The coarseness of parallelism is greater than for most applicative architectures. Processors may not share pointers in the current system. While this simplifies garbage collection, it requires literal data to be copied when a (potentially large) structure is to be "shared." The ring architecture,

of course, causes system performance to degrade linearly as processors are added.

3) The Apiary: The Apiary is a multiprocessor actor system on which Lisp and other artificial intelligence languages are expected to run. The fundamental execution entity in the Apiary is the actor, which is an object that contains a small amount of state and can perform a few primitive operations: sending a message, creating another actor, making a decision, and changing its local state. Actors are divided into two classes, *rock bottom* and *scripted.* The actions taken by rock-bottom actors are specified by microcode; those of scripted actors are specified by a script, which is a program in a language such as Lisp. An actor physically runs on a *worker,* which is a collection of processors that define a node in the network. A worker typically consists of a communications processor, a storage management processor, and several *work processors.* Each worker has a *work queue* of actors on behalf of which it performs script-specified actions. If a worker becomes overloaded, it attempts to move some of its actors to neighboring workers.

Limitations: A number of issues relating to the execution of functional languages (e.g., limiting parallelism) have yet to be addressed.

VI. CONCLUSIONS

Can machines be built that will efficiently execute functional programs? Although many architectures have been built or proposed, it has yet to be demonstrated that functional programs can be competitive with von Neumann systems. The Lisp machine [28], which executes a quasi-functional language, is the only architecture considered here that has had widespread use for solving real problems.

A major issue in answering the above question is the high level at which functional programs are written, which may be a blessing during programming, but a curse during execution. The "system" is required to make many decisions that an imperative programmer — or his programming language —

would specify explicitly on a case-by-case basis, including the following.

- Should data be copied or should pointers be used?
- Should results be stored and reused or should they be recomputed?
- How should data be represented?
- When should parallelism be invoked?
- At what granularity should parallelism be invoked?
- How should processes be mapped onto processors?

For a language that is directly executed on hardware, these decisions are likely to be systemwide, and will clearly be "wrong" sometimes. Although it is possible for a compiler to make intelligent decisions in some instances, many questions are yet to be answered in this area as well [88]. Optimizations involving parallelism appear to be particularly difficult for a compiler to perform, as they often involve making use of dynamic information; difficult problems still remain in this area even for imperative languages [75]. On the other hand, other issues, such as synchronizing multiple list traversals, do seem well suited to compile-time analysis.

Allowing a compiler to make decisions about the manner in which data are represented also has ramifications with respect to separate compilation: What happens when two separately compiled programs expect data to be in different forms?

A. Desirable Elements of an FP Machine

What features would an "ideal" FP machine have? Based on the discussion in this paper, the following would be desirable.

- A multiprocessor system with a rich interconnection structure.

A multiprocessor allows the system to take advantage of the inherent concurrency in functional programs. A rich interconnection of processors seems to be essential if there is any hope of spreading work throughout the system, while maintaining moderately efficient access to remote data.

- Representation of list structures by balanced trees, if such does not add too much complexity to the system.

Although a tree is a more complex object than an array or list, the efficiency with which random access, structure manipulation, and destructive updating can be performed makes it an attractive candidate for data representation. This is particularly true if the compiler does not decide the type of data structure to be used.

- Hardware support for demand-driven execution.

Although demand-driven execution can often speed up a computation substantially, it has generated a great deal of overhead on currently built systems; hardware support to decrease this overhead is desirable.

- Hardware support for low-overhead process creation.

It is highly desirable that parallel execution be the norm, not the exception, when a functional program is being evaluated. If the mechanism for invoking parallelism is not efficient, program performance will be unacceptably slow.

- Hardware support for storage management.

The extensive use of structures in functional programs makes hardware support for storage management very attractive. If hardware/firmware support for storage management is not available, system overhead is likely to be markedly higher.

Of the architectures currently proposed, none meets all of the above criteria; most lack a rich interconnection structure or support for demand-driven execution. Of those remaining, ZAPP and Rediflow are the only architectures whose processor interconnections and process-to-processor mapping methodologies are well specified. Other systems such as ALICE and Apiary are worth considering, but are still in need of work in areas of concurrency control and/or interconnection structure.

B. Open Questions

The question of how efficiently functional programs can run on hardware is still largely unanswered. The following are some key issues that have been raised—but not fully answered—in the literature.

Compiler techniques: A major issue, which has not been addressed here, is that of compiler optimization. How much can program transformation and data structure selection improve program performance? Can compiler techniques be as effective when the program is to run on a multiprocessor?

Interconnection structure: What processor interconnections are most effective? N-cube and hypertorus machines have rich interconnection structures, yet have the potential to take advantage of locality. Given that pieces of a structure are likely to be distributed across the system, how much does locality buy? If not much, a routing network—or a routing network of clusters—may be more appropriate.

Controlling parallelism: How should parallelism be controlled? Data-driven architectures seem to be at a disadvantage here, but even those with demand drive have not demonstrated that the problem is solved. The method employed in ZAPP [9] and Rediflow [47] looks promising, but is largely untested.

Granularity of parallelism: Many proposed FP machines have a very fine grain of parallelism. Can hardware be built to support this efficiently, or will process creation and synchronization costs be unacceptably high? Perhaps a somewhat coarser granularity is more appropriate.

Tree representation of lists: Can lists be effectively represented by balanced trees? Are the logarithmic times for operations such as random access and insertion efficient enough that it is not necessary to consider using arrays and lists? How much overhead is involved in keeping trees balanced?

Caching: How big a problem is the recomputation of results? Are the current methods for handling it adequate? If not, can an effective caching scheme be developed?

C. Summary

There is promising evidence that programmer productivity can be increased for some classes of programs by the use of functional programming. Additionally, functional languages seem especially suited to parallel architectures because they lack side effects, giving rise to the possibility that functional programs may run more quickly than their imperative counterparts unless the imperative programmer is willing to program parallelism explicitly.

The efficient execution of functional programs on uniprocessor and multiprocessor systems is currently under active investigation. As of the time of this writing (July 1984), too few FP multiprocessors and compilers have been completely implemented, and hence it is not possible to answer the question until more experimentation is done.

ACKNOWLEDGMENT

The author wishes to thank A. Jones, R. Keller, J. Newcomer, G. Steele, P. Wadler, and W. Wulf for their valuable comments on earlier versions of this paper.

REFERENCES

[1] P. S. Abrams, "An APL machine," Ph.D. dissertation, Stanford Univ., Stanford, CA, Feb. 1970.
[2] Arvind, K. P. Gostelow, and W. Plouffe, "An asynchronous programming language and computing machine," Univ. California, Irvine, CA, Tech. Rep. 114a, Dec. 1978.
[3] Arvind and K. P. Gostelow, "The U-interpreter," IEEE Computer, vol. 15, pp. 42–49, Feb. 1982.
[4] Arvind and J. D. Brock, "Streams and managers," Computation Structure Group, Massachusetts Inst. Technol., Memo 217, June 1982.
[5] J. Backus, "Can programming be liberated from the von Neumann style? A functional style and its algebra of programs," Commun. ACM, vol. 21, pp. 613–641, Aug. 1978.
[6] K. J. Berkling, "Reduction languages for reduction machines," in Proc. IEEE Int. Symp. Comput. Arch., Jan. 1975, pp. 133–140.
[7] R. M. Burstall and J. Darlington, "A transformation system for developing recursive programs," J. ACM, vol. 24, Jan. 1977.
[8] R. M. Burstall, D. B. MacQueen, and D. T. Sannella, "HOPE: An experimental applicative language," in LISP Conf. Rec., Stanford Univ., Stanford, CA, 1980, pp. 136–143.
[9] F. W. Burton and M. R. Sleep, "Executing functional programs on a virtual tree of processors," in Proc. ACM Conf. Functional Programming Lang. Comput. Arch., 1981, pp. 187–194.
[10] T. J. W. Clarke, P. J. S. Gladstone, C. D. MacLean, and A. C. Norman, "SKIM—The S, K, I reduction machine," in LISP Conf. Rec., Stanford Univ., Stanford, CA, 1980, pp. 128–135.
[11] D. Comte and N. Hifde, "LAU multiprocessor: Microfunctional description and technological choices," in Proc. 1st Europ. Conf. Parallel Distrib. Processing, 1979, pp. 8–15.
[12] H. B. Curry and R. Feys, Combinator Logic. Amsterdam, The Netherlands: North-Holland, 1958.
[13] J. Darlington and M. Reeve, "ALICE—A multi-processor reduction machine for the parallel evaluation of applicative languages," in Proc. ACM Conf. Functional Programming Lang. Comput. Arch., 1981, pp. 65–75.
[14] A. L. Davis, "The architecture and system method of DDM1: A recursively structured data driven machine," in Proc. ACM Int. Symp. Comput. Arch., Apr. 1978, pp. 210–215.
[15] ——, "A data flow evaluation system based on the concept of recursive locality," in Proc. AFIPS Nat. Comput. Conf., 1979, vol. 48, pp. 1079–1086.
[16] A. L. Davis and R. M. Keller, "Data flow program graphs," IEEE Computer, vol. 15, pp. 26–41, Feb. 1982.
[17] J. B. Dennis, "First version of a data flow procedure language," in Lecture Notes in Computer Science. New York: Springer-Verlag, 1974, pp. 362–376; see also, Massachusetts Inst. Technol., Cambridge, MA, Tech. Rep. MIT MTMM-61.
[18] ——, "The varieties of data flow computers," in Proc. IEEE Int. Conf. Distrib. Syst., 1979, pp. 430–439.
[19] ——, "Data flow supercomputers," IEEE Computer, vol. 13, pp. 48–56, Nov. 1980.
[20] J. B. Dennis, G. -R. Gao, and K. W. Todd, "Modeling the weather with a data flow supercomputer," IEEE Trans. Comput., vol. C-33, pp. 592–603, July 1984.
[21] D. M. Dias and J. R. Jump, "Analysis and simulation of buffered delta networks," IEEE Trans. Comput., vol. C-30, pp. 273–282, Apr. 1981.
[22] R. J. Fateman, "Reply to an editorial," SigSAM Bull., vol. 25, pp. 9–11, Mar. 1973.
[23] D. P. Friedman and D. S. Wise, "Cons should not evaluate its argu-

ments," in Automata, Languages, and Programming, Michaelson and Milner, Eds. London: Edinburgh University Press, 1976.
[24] ——, "Aspects of applicative programming for parallel processing," IEEE Trans. Comput., vol. C-27, pp. 289–296, Apr. 1978.
[25] A. Goldberg and D. Robson, Smalltalk-80: The Language and Its Implementation. Reading, MA: Addison-Wesley, 1983.
[26] M. Gordon, R. Milner, L. Morris, M. Newey, and C. Wadsworth, "A metalanguage for interactive proof in LCF," in Proc. ACM Symp. Princ. Programming Lang., 1978, pp. 119–130.
[27] K. P. Gostelow and R. E. Thomas, "A view of dataflow," in Proc. AFIPS Nat. Comput. Conf., 1979, vol. 48, pp. 629–636.
[28] R. Greenblatt et al., "LISP machine progress report," Massachusetts Inst. Technol., Cambridge, MA, A. I. Memo. 444, Aug. 1977.
[29] R. H. Halstead, Jr., "Object management on distributed systems," in Proc. Texas Conf. Comput. Syst., Univ. Houston, Houston, TX, 1978, pp. 7-7–7-14.
[30] S. P. Harbison, "A computer architecture for the dynamic optimization of high-level language programs," Ph.D. dissertation, Carnegie-Mellon Univ., Pittsburgh, PA, Sept. 1980.
[31] L. S. Haynes, R. L. Lau, D. P. Siewiorek, and D. W. Mizell, "A survey of highly parallel computing," IEEE Computer, vol. 15, pp. 9–24, Jan. 1982.
[32] P. Henderson and J. H. Morris, "A lazy evaluator," in Proc. ACM Symp. Princ. Programming Lang., 1976, pp. 95–103.
[33] C. Hewitt, "The Apiary network architecture for knowledgeable systems," in LISP Conf. Rec., Stanford Univ., Stanford, CA, 1980.
[34] C. Hewitt and H. Leiberman, "Design issues in parallel architectures for artificial intelligence," in Proc. IEEE COMPCON, Feb. 1984, pp. 418–423.
[35] C. Hewitt, personal communication, 1984.
[36] J. Holloway, G. L. Steele, Jr., G. J. Sussman, and A. Bell, "The SCHEME-79 chip," Massachusetts Inst. Technol., Cambridge, MA, A.I. Memo. 559, Dec. 1979.
[37] R. J. M. Hughes, "Super-combinators: A new implementation method for applicative languages," in Conf. Rec. 1982 ACM Symp. LISP and Functional Programming, Carnegie-Mellon Univ., Pittsburgh, PA, Aug. 1982, pp. 1–10.
[38] R. D. Jenks and J. H. Griesmer, "Editor's comment," SigSAM Bull., vol. 24, pp. 2–3, Oct. 1972.
[39] D. Johnson et al., "Automatic partitioning of programs in multiprocessor systems," in Proc. IEEE COMPCON, 1980, pp. 175–178.
[40] T. Johnsson, "Efficient compilation of lazy evaluation," in Proc. ACM SigPlan Symp. Compiler Construction, June 1984, pp. 58–69.
[41] A. K. Jones, R. J. Chansler, Jr., I. Durham, P. Feiler, D. A. Scelza, K. Schwans, and S. R. Vegdahl, "Programming issues raised by a multiprocessor," Proc. IEEE, vol. 66, pp. 229–237, Feb. 1978.
[42] S. L. P. Jones, "An investigation of the relative efficiencies of combinators and lambda-expressions," in Conf. Rec. 1982 ACM Symp. LISP and Functional Programming, Carnegie-Mellon Univ., Pittsburgh, PA, Aug. 1982, pp. 150–158.
[43] R. M. Keller, G. Lindstrom, and S. Patil, "A loosely-coupled applicative multi-processing system," in Proc. AFIPS Nat. Comput. Conf., 1979, vol. 48, pp. 613–622.
[44] R. M. Keller, "Divide and CONCer: Data structuring in applicative multiprocessing systems," in LISP Conf. Rec., Stanford Univ., Stanford, CA, 1980, pp. 196–202.
[45] R. M. Keller and G. Lindstrom, "Applications of Feedback in functional programming," in Proc. ACM Conf. Functional Programming Lang. Comput. Arch., 1981, pp. 123–130.
[46] R. M. Keller and M. R. Sleep, "Applicative caching," in Proc. ACM Conf. Functional Programming Lang. Comput. Arch., 1981, pp. 131–140.
[47] R. M. Keller, F. C. H. Lin, and J. Tanaka, "Rediflow multiprocessing," in Proc. IEEE COMPCON, Feb. 1984, pp. 410–417.
[48] R. B. Kieburtz and J. Shultis, "Transformations of FP program schemes," in Proc. ACM Conf. Functional Programming Lang. Comput. Arch., 1981, pp. 41–48.
[49] R. B. Kieburtz, "The G-machine: A fast graph-reduction processor," Oregon Grad. Cen., Tech. Rep. 84-003, 1984.
[50] T. Kushner, A. Y. Wu, and A. Rosenfeld, "Image processing in ZMOB," IEEE Trans. Comput., vol. C-31, pp. 943–951, Oct. 1982.
[51] P. J. Landin, "A correspondence between Algol 60 and Church's lambda notation: Part I," Commun. ACM, vol. 8, pp. 89–100, Feb. 1965.
[52] H. Leiberman, "An object-oriented simulator for the Apiary," in Proc. AAAI Nat. Conf. Artificial Intelligence, Aug. 1983, pp. 241–246.
[53] B. Liskov et al., "CLU reference manual," in Lecture Notes in Computer Science, Goos and Hartmanis, Eds. New York: Springer-Verlag, 1981.

[54] E. P. Maclean, "The use of APL for production applications: The concept of throwaway code," in *Proc. ACM-STAPL APL Conf.*, 1976, pp. 303–307.

[55] G. A. Magó, "A cellular computer architecture for functional programming," in *Proc. IEEE COMPCON*, 1980, pp. 179–187.

[56] Z. Manna and R. Waldinger, "Synthesis: Dreams ⇒ programs," *IEEE Trans. Software Eng.*, vol. SE-5, no. 4, pp. 157–164, July 1979.

[57] J. McCarthy, "LISP — Notes on its past and future," in *LISP Conf. Rec.*, Stanford Univ., Stanford, CA, 1980, pp. v–viii.

[58] J. R. McGraw, "Data flow computing: Software development," in *Proc. IEEE Int. Conf. Distrib. Syst.*, 1979, pp. 242–251.

[59] D. Michie, "'Memo' functions and machine learning " *Nature*, vol. 218, pp. 19–22, Apr. 1968.

[60] C. R. Minter, "A machine design for efficient implementation of APL," Yale Univ., New Haven, CT, Res. Rep. 81, 1976.

[61] J. H. Morris, E. Schmidt, and P. L. Wadler, "Experience with an applicative string processing language," in *Proc. ACM Symp. Princ. Programming Lang.*, July 1980, pp. 32–46.

[62] J. H. Morris, "Real programming in functional languages," in *Functional Programming and its Applications. An Advanced Course*, Darlington, Henderson, and Turner, Eds. Cambridge, England: Cambridge Univ. Press, 1982.

[63] A. Mycroft, "The theory and practice of transforming call-by-need into call-by-value," in *Proc. 4th Int. Colloq. Programming*, 1980.

[64] ——, "Abstract interpretation and optimising transformations for applicative programs," Ph.D. dissertation, Univ. Edinburgh, Edinburgh, Scotland, 1981.

[65] J. T. O'Donnell, "A systolic associative LISP computer architecture with incremental parallel storage management," Ph.D. dissertation, Univ. Iowa, Iowa City, IA, 1981.

[66] J. K. Ousterhout, "Partitioning and cooperation in a distributed multiprocessor operating system: Medusa," Ph.D. dissertation, Carnegie-Mellon Univ., Pittsburgh, PA, Apr. 1980.

[67] R. L. Page, M. G. Conant, and D. H. Grit, "If-then-else as a concurrency inhibitor in eager beaver evaluation of recursive programs," in *Proc. ACM Conf. Functional Programming Lang. Comput. Arch.*, 1981, pp. 179–186.

[68] J. H. Patel, "Processor-memory interconnections for multiprocessors," in *Proc. IEEE Symp. Comput. Arch.*, 1979, pp. 168–177.

[69] A. J. Perlis, "Steps toward an APL compiler — updated," Yale Univ., New Haven, CT, Tech. Rep. 24, Mar. 1975.

[70] H. A. Presnell and R. P. Pargas, "Communication along shortest paths in a tree machine," in *Proc. ACM Conf. Functional Programming Lang. Comput. Arch.*, 1981, pp. 107–114.

[71] C. Rieger, R. Trigg, and B. Bane, "ZMOB: A new computing engine for AI," in *Proc. IJCAI*, Univ. British Columbia, Vancouver, B.C., Canada, 1981, pp. 955–960.

[72] J. E. Rumbaugh, "A parallel asynchronous computer architecture for data flow programs," Ph.D. dissertation, Massachusetts Inst. Technol., Cambridge, MA, May 1975.

[73] ——, "A data flow multiprocessor," *IEEE Trans. Comput.*, vol. C-26, pp. 138–146, Feb. 1977.

[74] W. L. Scherlis, "Expression procedures and program derivation," Ph.D. dissertation, Stanford Univ., Stanford, CA, Aug. 1980.

[75] K. Schwans, "Tailoring software for multiple processor systems," Ph.D. dissertation, Carnegie-Mellon Univ., Pittsburgh, PA, 1982.

[76] M. R. Sleep, "Applicative languages, dataflow and pure combinatory code," in *Proc. 20th IEEE COMPCON*, Feb. 1980, pp. 112–115.

[77] G. L. Steele, Jr., "Debunking the expensive procedure call myth, or, Procedure call implementations considered harmful, or, LAMBDA: The ultimate goto," in *Proc. ACM Annu. Conf.*, Oct. 1977, pp. 153–162.

[78] S. Sugimoto, T. Koichi, A. Kiyoshi, and Y. Ohno, "Concurrent LISP on a multi-micro-processor system," in *Proc. IJCAI*, Univ. British Columbia, Vancouver, B.C., Canada, 1981, pp. 949–954.

[79] G. J. Sussman, personal communication, 1984.

[80] G. J. Sussman, J. Holloway, G. L. Steele, Jr., and A. Bell, "Scheme-79 — Lisp on a chip," *IEEE Computer*, vol. 14, pp. 10–21, July 1981.

[81] J. C. Syre, D. Comte, and N. Hifdi, "Pipelining, parallelism and asynchronism in the LAU system," in *Proc. Int. Conf. Parallel Processing*, Aug. 1977, pp. 87–92.

[82] P. C. Treleaven, D. R. Brownbridge, and R. P. Hopkins, "Data-driven and demand-driven computer architecture," *ACM Comput. Surveys*, vol. 14, no. 1, pp. 93–143, Mar. 1982.

[83] D. A. Turner, "A new implementation technique for applicative languages," *Software — Practice and Experience*, vol. 9, pp. 31–49, Sept. 1979.

[84] ——, "The semantic elegance of applicative languages," in *Proc. ACM Conf. Functional Programming Lang. Comput. Arch.*, 1981, pp. 85–92.

[85] ——, "Recursion equations as a programming language," in *Functional Programming and its Applications. An Advanced Course*, Darlington, Henderson, and Turner, Eds. Cambridge, England: Cambridge Univ. Press, 1982, pp. 1–28.

[86] J. D. Ullman, "Some thoughts about supercomputer organization," in *Proc. IEEE COMPCON*, Feb. 1984, pp. 424–432.

[87] P. L. Wadler, "Applicative style programming, program transformation, and list operators," in *Proc. ACM Conf. Functional Programming Lang. Comput. Arch.*, 1981, pp. 25–32.

[88] ——, "Listlessness is better than laziness: An algorithm that transforms applicative programs to eliminate intermediate lists," Ph.D. dissertation (draft), Carnegie-Mellon Univ., Pittsburgh, PA, 1983.

[89] C. Wadsworth, "Semantics and pragmatics of lambda-calculus," Ph.D. dissertation, Oxford Univ., Oxford, England, 1971.

[90] S. Ward, "The MuNet: A multiprocessor message-passing system architecture," in *Proc. Texas Conf. Comput. Syst.*, Univ. Houston, Houston, TX, 1978.

[91] A. I. Wasserman and S. Gutz, "The future of programming," *Commun. ACM*, vol. 25, pp. 196–206, Mar. 1982.

[92] I. Watson and J. Gurd, "A prototype data flow computer with token labeling," in *Proc. AFIPS Nat. Comput. Conf.*, 1979, vol. 48, pp. 623–628.

[93] ——, "A practical data flow computer," *IEEE Computer*, vol. 15, pp. 51–57, Feb. 1982.

[94] M. Weiser, personal communication, 1984.

[95] K. S. Weng, "Stream-oriented computation in recursive data flow schemes," Massachusetts Inst. Technol., Cambridge, MA, Tech. Rep. MTMM-68, Oct. 1975.

Steven R. Vegdahl received the B.S. degree in mathematics from Stanford University, Stanford, CA, in 1976, and the Ph.D. degree in computer science from Carnegie-Mellon University, Pittsburgh, PA, in 1983.

He is presently working as a Research Computer Scientist at the Tektronix Computer Research Laboratory, Beaverton, OR. His research interests include algorithm animation, compilers, computer architecture, computational complexity, multiprocessing, object-oriented programming languages, microprogramming, and functional programming languages.

THE
LISP
MACHINE

ALAN BAWDEN
RICHARD GREENBLATT
JACK HOLLOWAY
THOMAS KNIGHT
DAVID MOON
DANIEL WEINREB

For many years, the PDP-10 computer has been the workhorse of Artificial Intelligence. But many factors conspire to make serious researchers want more than PDP-10s can provide. The Artificial Intelligence Laboratory's LISP machine is the way to satisfy these wants. Among its advantages are a large address space, hardware data types, a general, large microcode that can be compiled into talented pointer-manipulating instructions, a real-time garbage collector, a powerful editor, LISP used as a system implementation language, reasonable speed, and perhaps most important, a low price. Some of the inspiration for the LISP Machine project comes from the pioneering research into personal computing and display-oriented systems done by Xerox's Palo Alto Research Center. For a time, the LISP machine work was a joint project between the Artificial Intelligence Laboratory and the Laboratory of Computer Science.

Background

The LISP Machine is a computer system designed to provide a high performance and economical implementation of the LISP programming language.

The LISP language is used widely in the Artificial Intelligence research community and is rapidly gaining adherents outside this group. Most serious LISP usage has historically been on the DEC PDP-10 computer, and both INTERLISP at BBN/XEROX and MACLISP at MIT were originally done on the PDP-10.

Over the years, dramatic changes have taken place in the MACLISP implementation. At a certain point, however, modification and reimplementation of a language on a given machine can no longer efficiently gloss over basic problems in the architecture of the computer system. This is now the case on the PDP-10 and similar timeshared computer systems.

Timesharing was introduced when it became apparent that computers are easier to use in an interactive fashion than in a batch system, and that during an interactive session a user typically uses only a small fraction of the processor and memory available; often the computer can be multiplexed among many users while giving each the impression that he is on his own machine.

However, in the LISP community there has been a strong trend towards programs that are very highly interactive, very large, and use a good deal of computer time; such programs include advanced editors and debuggers, the MACSYMA system for mathematical manipulation, and various programming assistants. When running programs such as these, that spend very significant amounts of time supporting user interactions, timesharing systems such as the PDP-10 run into increased difficulties. Not only is the processor incapable of providing either reasonable throughput or adequate response time for a reasonable number of users, but the competition for main memory results in large amounts of time being spent swapping pages in and out (a condition known as "thrashing"). Larger and larger processors and memory, and more and more complex operating systems are required, with more than proportionally higher cost, and still the competition for memory remains a bottleneck. The programs are sufficiently large, and the interactions sufficiently frequent, that the usual timesharing strategy of swapping a program out of memory while waiting for the user to interact, then swapping it back in when the user types something, cannot be successful because the swapping cannot happen fast enough.

The LISP Machine is a personal computer. Personal computing means that the processor and main memory are not time-division multiplexed; instead each person gets his own. The personal computation system consists of a pool of processors, each with its own main memory, and its own disk for swapping. When a user logs in, he is assigned a processor, and he has exclusive use of it for the duration of the session. When he logs out, the processor is returned to the pool, for the next person to use. This way, there is no competition from other users for memory; the pages the user is frequently referring to remain in core; and swapping overhead is considerably reduced. Thus the LISP Machine solves a basic problem of timesharing LISP systems.

The user also gets a much higher degree of service from a LISP machine than from a timesharing system because he can use the full throughput capacity of the processor and the disk. Although these are quite inexpensive compared to those used in PDP-10 timesharing systems, they are comparable in speed. In fact, since disk access times are mainly limited by physical considerations, it often turns out that the disk used in a personal computer system is less expensive simply because of its smaller size, and yet has fully comparable throughput charactistics to the larger disk used by a timesharing system.

In a single-user machine, there is no penalty for interactiveness, since there are no competing users to steal a program's memory while it is waiting for its user to type. Thus the LISP machine system, unlike time sharing systems, encourages highly interactive programs. It puts service to the user entirely ahead of efficiency considerations.

Another problem with the PDP-10 LISP implementations is the small address space of the PDP-10 processor. Many LISP systems, such as MACSYMA and Woods' LUNAR program, have difficulty running in an 18-bit address space. This problem is partly the result of inefficiency in the compiling of PDP-10 LISP code: compilers for the PDP-10 produce only a limited subset of the large instruction set made available by the hardware, and they usually make inefficient use of the addressing modes and fields provided. It is possible to design instruction sets that enable much more compact compilations. This is an important fact in view of the likelihood that future programs will be quite a bit bigger; intelligent systems with natural language front ends may well be five or ten times the size of a PDP-10 address space.

The LISP Machine has a 24-bit virtual address space and a compact instruction set. Thus much larger programs may be used, without running into address space limitations. Since the instruction set is designed specifically for the LISP language, the compiler is much simpler than the PDP-10 compiler, providing faster and more reliable compilation.

The LISP machine's compact size and simple hardware construction are likely to make it more reliable than other machines, such as the PDP-10; the prototype machine has had almost no hardware failures.

The LISP Machine Implementation

A LISP Machine user has a processor, a memory, a keyboard, a display, and a means of getting to the shared resources. Terminals, of course, are placed in offices and various rooms; ideally there would be one in every office. The processors, however, are all kept off in a machine room. Since they may need special environmental conditions, and often make noise and take up space, they are not welcome office companions. The number of processors is unrelated to the number of terminals, and may be much smaller depending on usage patterns and economic circumstance.

The key to the system is the microprogrammed CONS processor [Steele]. CONS is a very unspecialized machine with 32-bit data paths and 24-bit address paths. It has a large microcode memory (16K of 48-bit words) to accommodate the large amount of specialized microcode to support LISP. It has hardware for extracting and depositing arbitrary fields in arbitrary registers, which substitutes for the specialized data paths found in conventional microprocessors. It does not have a cache, but does have a "pdl buffer" (a memory with hardware push-down-list pointer), that acts as a kind of cache for the stack, which is where most of the memory references go in LISP.

Using a very unspecialized processor was found to be a good idea for several reasons. For one thing, it is faster, less expensive, and easier to debug. Moreover, it is much easier to microprogram, which facilitates writing and debugging the large amounts of microcode required to support a sophisticated LISP system with high efficiency. It also makes feasible a compiler that generates microcode, allowing users to microcompile some of their functions to increase performance.

The memory is typically 64k of core or semiconductor memory, and is expandable to about one million words. The full virtual address space is stored on a 16 million word disk and paged into core (or semiconductor) memory as required. A given virtual address is always located at the same place on the disk. The access time of the core memory is about one microsecond, and of the disk, about 25 milliseconds. Additionally, there is an internal 1k buffer used for holding the top of the stack (the PDL buffer) with a 200ns access time.

The display is a raster scan TV driven by a 1/4 Mbit memory. Since characters are drawn entirely by software, any type or size of font can be used. Indeed, one of the advantages of having an unspecialized microinstruction processor such as CONS is that one can implement a flexible terminal in software for less cost than an inflexible, hardwired conventional terminal. The TV system is easily expanded to support gray scale, high resolution, and color. It is therefore very useful for both character display and graphics.

The keyboard has several levels of control/shifting to facilitate easy single-keystroke commands to programs such as the editor. The keyboard is also equipped with a speaker for beeping and a pointing device.

The shared resources are accessed through a 10 million bit/sec packet switching network with completely distributed control. The shared resources are to include a highly reliable file system implemented on a dedicated computer equipped with state of the art disks and tapes, specialized I/O devices such as high-quality hardcopy output, special-purpose processors, and connections to the outside world (e.g. other computers in the building, and the ARPANET).

As in a time sharing system, the file system is shared between users. Time sharing has demonstrated many advantages of a shared file system, such as common access to files, easy interuser communication, centralized program maintenance, and centralized backup. There are no personal disk packs to be lost, dropped by users who are not competent as operators, or to be filled with copies of old, superseded software.

The complete LISP Machine, including processor, memory, disk, terminal, and connection to the shared file system, is packaged in a single 19" logic cabinet, except for the disk, which is free-standing. The complete machine would be likely to cost about $80,000 if commercially produced today. Since this is a complete, fully-capable system (for one user at a time), it can substantially lower the cost of entry by new organizations into serious Artificial Intelligence work.

LISP as a System Language

In the software of the LISP Machine system, code is written in only two languages (or "levels"): LISP, and CONS machine microcode. The intermediate macrocode level, corresponding to traditional assembly languages, is not used for hand-coding, since it corresponds so closely with LISP; anything one could write in macrocode could be more easily and clearly written in the corresponding LISP. The READ, EVAL, and PRINT functions are completely written in LISP, including their subfunctions (except that APPLY of compiled functions is in microcode). This illustrates the ability to write "system" functions in LISP.

In order to allow various low-level operations to be performed by LISP code, a set of "subprimitive" functions exist. Their names by convention begin with a "%," so as to point out that they are capable of performing operations that may result in meaningless pointers. These functions provide "machine level" capabilities, such as performing byte deposits into memory. The compiler converts calls to these subprimitives into single instructions rather than subroutine calls. Thus LISP-coded low-level operations are just as efficient as they would be in machine language on a conventional machine.

In addition to subprimitives, the ability to do system programming in LISP depends on the LISP machine's augmented array feature. There are several types of arrays, one of which is used to implement character strings. This makes it easy and efficient to manipulate strings either as a whole or character by character. An array can have a "leader," which is a little vector of extra information tacked on. The leader always contains LISP objects while the array often contains characters or small packed numbers. The leader facilititates the use of arrays to represent various kinds of abstract object types. The presence in the language of both arrays and lists gives the programmer more control over data representation.

A traditional weakness of LISP has to do with functions that should be allowed to have a variable number of arguments. Various implementors have added mechanisms that allow variable numbers of arguments; these, however, tend to slow down the function-calling mechanism, even when the feature is not used, or to force peculiar programming styles. LISP-machine LISP allows functions to have optional parameters with automatic, user-controlled defaulting to an arbitrary expression in the case where a corresponding argument is not supplied. It is also possible to have a "rest" parameter, which is bound to a list of the arguments not bound to previous parameters. This is frequently important to simplify system programs and their interfaces.

A similar problem with LISP function calling occurs when one wants to return more than one value. Traditionally one either returns a list or stores some of the values into global variables. In LISP Machine LISP, there is a multiple-value-return feature that allows multiple values to be returned without going through either of the above subterfuges.

LISP's functional orientation and encouragement of a programming style of small modules and uniform data structuring is appropriate for good system programming. The LISP machine's microcoded subroutine calling mechanism allows it to also be efficient.

Paging is handled entirely by the microcode, and is considered to be at a very low level (a lower level than any kind of scheduling). Making the details of the virtual memory invisible to all LISP code and most microcode helps keep things simple. It would not be practical in a time sharing system, but in a one-user machine it is reasonable to put paging at the lowest level and forget about it, accepting the fact that sometimes the machine will be tied up waiting for the disk and unable to run any LISP code.

Microcoded functions can be called by LISP code by the usual LISP calling mechanism, and provision is made for microcoded functions to call macrocoded functions. Thus there is a uniform calling convention throughout the entire system. This has the effect that uniform subroutine packages can be written, (for example the TV package, or the EDITOR package) that can be called by any other program. (A similar capability is provided by the Multics system, but not by ITS or TENEX).

Many of the capabilities that system programmers create over and over again in an ad hoc way are built into the LISP language, and are sufficiently good in their LISP-provided form that it usually is not necessary to waste time worrying about how to implement better ones. These include symbol tables, storage management, both fixed and flexible data structures, function-calling, and an interactive user interface.

Representation of Data

A LISP object in MACLISP or INTERLISP is represented as an 18-bit pointer, and the datatype of the object is determined from the pointer: each page of memory can only contain objects of a single type. In the LISP Machine, LISP objects are represented by a 5-bit datatype field and a 24-bit pointer. (The LISP machine virtual address space is 24 bits).

The LISP Machine data types are designed according to these criteria: there should be a wide variety of useful and flexible data types; some effort should be made to increase the bit efficiency of data representation, in order to improve performance; the programmer should be able to exercise control over the storage and representation of data, if he wishes; it must always be possible to take an anonymous piece of data and discover its type; and there should be much type-checking and error-checking.

Symbols are stored as four consecutive words, each of which contains one object. The words are termed the PRINT NAME cell, the VALUE cell, the FUNCTION cell, and the PROPERTY LIST cell. The PRINT NAME cell holds a string object, which is the printed representation of the symbol. The PROPERTY LIST cell, of course, contains the property list, and the VALUE CELL contains the current value of the symbol (it is a so-called shallow-binding system). The FUNCTION cell replaces the EXPR, SUBR, FEXPR, MACRO, and similar properties in MACLISP. When a form such as (FOO ARG1 ARG2) is evaluated, the object in FOO's function cell is applied to the arguments. A symbol object has datatype DTP-SYMBOL, and the pointer is the address of these four words.

Storage of list structure is somewhat more complicated. Normally a "list object" has datatype DTP-LIST, and the pointer is the address of a two word block; the first word contains the CAR, and the second the CDR of the node.

However, note that since a LISP object is only 29 bits (24 bits of pointer and 5 bits of data-type), there are three remaining bits in each word. Two of these bits are termed the CDR-code field, and are used to compress the storage requirement of list structure. The four possible values of the CDR-code field are given the symbolic names CDR-NORMAL, CDR-ERROR, CDR-NEXT, and CDR-NIL. CDR-NORMAL indicates the two-word block described above. CDR-NEXT and CDR-NIL are used to represent a list as a vector, taking only half as much storage as usual. Only the CARs are stored; the CDR of each location is simply the next location, except for the last, whose CDR is NIL. The primitive functions that create lists (LIST, APPEND, etc.) create these compressed lists. If RPLACD is done on such a list, it is automatically changed back to the conventional two-word representation in a transparent way.

The idea is that in the first word of a list node the CAR is represented by 29 bits, and the CDR is represented by 2 bits. It is a compressed pointer that can take on only 3 legal values: to the symbol NIL, to the next location after the one it appears in, or indirect through the next location. CDR-ERROR is used for words whose address should not ever be in a list object; in a "full node," the first word is CDR-NORMAL, and the second is CDR-ERROR. It is important to note that the CDR-code portion of a word is used in a different way from the data-type and pointer portion; it is a property of the memory cell itself, not of the cell's contents. A "list object" which is represented in compressed form still has data type DTP-LIST, but the CDR-code of the word addressed by its pointer field is CDR-NEXT or CDR-NIL rather than CDR-NORMAL.

Number objects may have any of three datatypes: "fixnums," bit-arrays, and others. "FIXNUMs," which are 24-bit signed integers, are represented by objects of datatype DTP-FIX, whose "pointer" parts are actually the value of the number. Thus fixnums, unlike all other objects, do not require any "CONS"ed storage for their representation. This speeds up arithmetic programs when the numbers they work with are reasonably small. Other types of numbers, such as floating point, BIGNUMs (integers of arbitrarily big size), complex numbers, and so on, are represented by objects of the datatype DTP-EXTENDED-NUMBER that point to a block of storage containing the details of the number. The microcode automatically converts between the different number representations as necessary, without the need for explicit declarations on the programmer's part.

The most important other data type is the array. Some problems are best attacked using data structures organized in the list-processing style of LISP, and some are best attacked using the array-processing style of FORTRAN. The complete programming system needs both. LISP Machine arrays are augmented beyond traditional LISP arrays in several ways. First of all, we have the ordinary arrays of LISP objects, with one or more dimensions. Compact storage of positive integers, which may represent characters or other non-numeric entities, is afforded by arrays of 1-bit, 2-bit, 4-bit, 8-bit, or 16-bit elements.

For string-processing, there are string-arrays, which are usually one-dimensional and have 8-bit characters as elements. At the microcode level strings are treated the same as 8-bit arrays. However, strings are treated differently by READ, PRINT, EVAL, and many other system and user functions. For example, they print out as a sequence of characters enclosed in quotes. The characters in a character string can be accessed and modified with the same array-referencing functions as one uses for any other type of array. Unlike arrays in other LISP systems, LISP Machine arrays usually have only a single word of overhead, so the character strings are quite storage-efficient.

There are a number of specialized types of arrays that are used to implement other data types, such as stack groups, internal system tables, and, most importantly, the refresh memory of the TV display as a two-dimensional array of bits.

An important additional feature of LISP machine arrays is the "array leader." A leader is a vector of LISP objects, of user-specified size, that may be tacked on to an array. Leaders are a good place to remember miscellaneous extra information associated with an array. Many data structures consist of a combination of an array and a record; the array contains a number of objects all of the same conceptual type, while the record contains miscellaneous items all of different conceptual types. By storing the record in the leader of the array, the single conceptual data structure is represented by a single actual object. Many data structures in LISP Machine system programs work this way.

Another thing that leaders are used for is remembering the "current length" of a partially-populated array. By convention, array leader element number 0 is always used for this.

Many programs use data objects structured as "records;" that is, a compound object consisting of a fixed number of named subobjects. To facilitate the use of records, the LISP Machine system includes a standard set of macros for defining, creating, and accessing record structures. The user can choose whether the actual representation is to be a LISP list, an array, or an array-leader. Because this is done with macros, which translate record operations into the lower-level operations of basic LISP, no other part of the system needs to know about records.

Since the reader and printer are written in LISP and are user-modifiable, this record-structure feature could easily be expanded into a full-fledged user-defined data type facility by modifying read and print to support input and output of record types.

Representation of Programs

In the LISP Machine there are three representations for programs. Interpreted LISP code is the slowest, but the easiest for programs to understand and modify. It can be used for functions that are being debugged, for functions that need to be understood by other functions, and for functions that are not worth the bother of compiling. A few functions, notably EVAL, will not work interpreted.

Compiled LISP ("macrocode") is the main representation for programs. It consists of instructions in a somewhat conventional machine-language, whose unusual features will be described below. Unlike the case in many other LISP systems, macrocode programs still have full checking for unbound variables, data type errors, wrong number of arguments to a function, and so forth. Therefore it is not necessary to resort to interpreted code just to get extra checking to detect bugs. Often, after typing in a function to the editor, one skips the interpretation step and requests the editor to call the compiler on it, which only takes a few seconds since the compiler is always in the machine and only has to be paged in.

Compiled code on the LISP Machine is stored inside objects called (for historical reasons) Function Entry Frames (FEFs). For each function compiled, one FEF is created, and an object of type DTP-FEF-POINTER is stored in the function cell of the symbol that is the name of the function. A FEF consists of some header information, a description of the arguments accepted by the function, pointers to external LISP objects needed by the function (such as constants and special variables), and the macrocode that implements the function.

The third form of program representation is microcode. The system includes a good deal of hand-coded microcode that executes the macrocode instructions, implements the data types and the function-calling mechanism, maintains the paged virtual memory, does storage allocation and garbage collection, and performs similar systemic functions. The primitive operations on the basic data types, such as CAR and CDR for lists, arithmetic for numbers, reference and store for arrays, are implemented as microcode subroutines. In addition, a number of commonly-used

LISP functions, for instance GET and ASSQ, are hand-coded in microcode for speed.

In addition to this system-supplied microcode, there is a feature called microcompilation. Because of the simplicity and generality of the CONS microprocessor, it is feasible to write a compiler to compile user-written LISP functions directly into microcode, eliminating the overhead of fetching and interpreting macroinstructions. This can be used to boost performance by microcompiling the most critical routines of a program. Because it is done by a compiler rather than a system programmer, this performance improvement is available to everyone. The amount of speedup to be expected depends on the operations used by the program: simple low-level operations such as data transmission, byte extraction, integer arithmetic, and simple branching benefit the most. Function calling, and operations that already spend most of their time in microcode, such as ASSQ, will benefit the least. In the best case one can achieve a factor of about 20; in the worst case, maybe no speedup at all.

Since the amount of control memory is limited, only a small number of microcompiled functions can be loaded in at one time. This means that programs have to be characterized by spending most of their time in a small inner kernel of functions in order to benefit from microcompilation; this is probably true of most programs. There will be metering facilities for identifying such critical functions.

In all three forms of program, the flexibility of function-calling is augmented with generalized LAMBDA lists. In order to provide a more general and flexible scheme to replace EXPRs, FEXPRs, and LEXPRs, a syntax borrowed from MUDDLE [Galley and Pfister 1975] and CONNIVER [Sussman and McDermott 1974] is used in LAMBDA lists. In the general case, there are an arbitrary number of required parameters, followed by an arbitrary number of optional parameters, possibly followed by one rest parameter. When a function is applied to its arguments, first the required formal parameters are paired off with arguments; if there are fewer arguments than required parameters, an error condition is caused. Then, any remaining arguments are paired off with the optional parameters; if there are more optional parameters than arguments remaining, then the rest of the optional parameters are initialized in a user-specified manner. The REST parameter is bound to a list, possibly NIL, of all arguments remaining after all OPTIONAL parameters are bound. It is also possible to control whether or not arguments are evaluated.

Normally, such a complicated calling sequence would require an unacceptable amount of overhead. Because this is all implemented by microcode, and because the simple, common cases are treated specially, these advanced features could be provided while retaining the efficiency needed in a practical system.

Each macroinstruction is 16 bits long; they are stored two per word. The instructions work in a stack-oriented machine. The stack is formatted into frames; each frame contains a bunch of arguments, a bunch of local variable value slots, a push-down stack for intermediate results, and a header that gives the function that owns the frame, links this frame to previous frames, remembers the program counter and flags when this frame is not executing, and may contain "additional information" used for certain esoteric purposes. Originally this was intended to be a spaghetti stack, but the invention of closures and stack-groups, combined with the extreme complexity of spaghetti stacks, made us decide to use a simple linear stack. The current frame is always held in the pdl buffer, so accesses to arguments and local variables do not require memory references, and do not have to make checks related to the garbage collector, which improves performance. Usually several other frames will also be in the pdl buffer.

The macroinstruction set is bit-compact. The stack organization and LISP's division of programs into small, separate functions means that address fields can be small. The use of tagged data types, powerful generic operations, and easily-called microcoded functions makes a single 16-bit macroinstruction do the work of several instructions on a conventional machine such as a PDP-10.

The primitive operations that are the compiler-generated instructions are higher-level than the instructions of a conventional machine. They all do data type checks; this provides more run-time error checking than in MACLISP, which increases reliability. It also eliminates much of the need to make declarations in order to get efficient code. Since a data type check is being made, the "primitive" operations can dynamically decide which specific routine is to be called. This means that they are all "generic;" that is, they work for all data types where they make sense.

The operations that are regarded as most important, and hence are easiest for macrocode to do, are data transmission, function-calling, conditional testing, and simple operations on primitive types. These include CAR, CDR, CADR, CDDR, RPLACA, and RPLACD, plus the usual arithmetic operations and comparisons. More complex operations are generally done by "miscellaneous" instructions, that call microcoded subroutines, passing arguments on the temporary-results stack.

There are three main kinds of addressing in macrocode. First, there is implicit addressing of the top of the stack. This is the usual way that operands get from one instruction to the next.

Second, there is the source field. The source can address

any of the following: up to 64 arguments to the current function; up to 64 local variables of the current function; the last result, popped off the stack; one of several commonly-used constants (e.g. NIL) stored in a system-wide constants area; constants stored in the FEF of this function; and a value cell or a function cell of a symbol, referenced by means of an invisible pointer in the FEF -- this mode is used to reference special variables and to call other functions.

Third, there is the destination field, which specifies what to do with the result of the instruction. The possibilities are: ignore it, except set the indicators used by conditional branches; push it on the stack; pass it as an argument; return it as the value of this function; and make a list.

There are five types of macroinstructions, which will be described. First, there are the data transmission instructions, that take the source and MOVE it to the destination, optionally taking CAR, CDR, CAAR, CADR, CDAR, or CDDR in the process. Because of the powerful operations that can be specified in the destination, these instructions also serve as argument-passing, function-exiting, and list-making instructions.

Next we have the function calling instructions. The simpler of the two is CALL0, call with no arguments. It calls the function indicated by its source, and when that function returns, the result is stored in the destination. The microcode takes care of identifying what type of function is being called, invoking it in the appropriate way, and saving the state of the current function. It traps to the interpreter if the called function is not compiled.

The more complex function call occurs when there are arguments to be passed. First, a CALL instruction is executed. The source operand is the function to be called. The beginnings of a new stack frame are constructed at the end of the current frame, and the function to be called is remembered. The destination of the CALL instruction specifies where the result of the function will be placed, and it is saved for later use when the function returns. Next, instructions are executed to compute the arguments and store them into the destination NEXT-ARGUMENT. This causes them to be added to the new stack frame. When the last argument is computed, it is stored into the destination LAST-ARGUMENT, that stores it in the new stack frame and then activates the call. The function to be called is analyzed, and the arguments are bound to the formal parameters (usually the arguments are already in the correct slots of the new stack frame). Because the computation of the arguments is introduced by a CALL instruction, it is easy to find out where the arguments are and how many there are. The new stack frame becomes current and that function begins execution. When it returns, the saved destination of the CALL instruction is retrieved and the result is stored. Note that by using a destination of NEXT-ARGUMENT or LAST-ARGUMENT function calls may be nested. By using a destination of RETURN the result of one function may become the result of its caller.

The third class of macro instructions consists of a number of common operations on primitive data types. These instructions do not have an explicit destination, in order to save bits, but implicitly push their result (if any) onto the stack. This sometimes necessitates the generation of an extra MOVE instruction to put the result where it was really wanted. These instructions include operations to store results from the pdl into the "source," the basic arithmetic and bitwise boolean operations, comparison operations, including EQ and arithmetic comparison, instructions that set the "source" operand to NIL or zero, iteration instructions that change the "source" operand using CDR, CDDR, 1+, or 1- (add or subtract one), binding instructions that lambda-bind the "source" operand, then optionally set it to NIL or to a value popped off the stack, and finally, an instruction to push its effective address onto the stack.

The fourth class of macro instructions are the branches, that serve mainly for compiling COND. Branches contain a self-relative address that is transferred to if a specified condition is satisfied. There are two indicators that tell if the last result was NIL, and if it was an atom. The state of these indicators can be branched on; there is also an unconditional branch, of course. For branches more than 256 half-words away, there is a double-length long-branch instruction. An interesting fact is that there are not really any indicators; it turns out to be faster just to save the last result in its entirety, and compare it against NIL or whatever when that is needed by a branch instruction. It only has to be saved from one instruction to the immediately following one.

The fifth class of macro instructions is the "miscellaneous function" category. This selects one of 512 microcoded functions to be called, with arguments taken from results previously pushed on the stack. A destination is specified to receive the result of the function. In addition to commonly-used functions such as GET, CONS, CDDDDR, REMAINDER, and ASSQ, miscellaneous functions include subprimitives (discussed above), and instructions that are not as commonly used as the first four classes, including operations such as array-accessing.

The way CONSing together is done is that one first does a miscellaneous function saying "make a list N long." One then executes N instructions with destination NEXT-LIST to supply the elements of the list. After the Nth such instruction, the list-object appears on the top of the stack.

Another type of "instruction set" used with macrocode is

the Argument Description List, that is executed by a different microcoded interpreter at the time a function is entered. The ADL contains one entry for each argument that the function expects to be passed, and for each auxiliary variable. It contains all relevant information about the argument: whether it is required, optional, or rest, how to initialize it if it is not provided, whether it is local or special, datatype checking information, and so on. Sometimes the ADL can be dispensed with if the "fast argument option" can be used instead; this helps save time and memory for small, simple functions. The fast-argument option is used when the optional arguments and local variables are all to be initialized to NIL, there are not many of them, there is no data-type checking, and the usage of special variables is not complicated. The selection of the fast-argument option, if appropriate, is automatically made by the system, so the user need not be concerned with it.

Control Structures

Function calling is, of course, the basic main control structure in LISP. As mentioned above, LISP machine function calling is made fast through the use of microcode and augmented with optional arguments, rest arguments, multiple return values, and optional type-checking of arguments.

CATCH and THROW are a MACLISP control structure that will be mentioned here since they may be new to some readers. CATCH is a way of marking a particular point in the stack of recursive function invocations. THROW causes control to be unwound to the matching CATCH, automatically returning through the intervening function calls. They are used mainly for handling errors and unusual conditions. They are also useful for getting out of a piece of code when it discovered what value is to be returned; this applies particularly to nested loops.

The LISP Machine contains a data-type called "closure" that is used to implement "full funarging." By turning a function into a closure, it becomes possible to pass it as an argument with no worry about naming conflicts, and to return it as a value with exactly the minimum necessary amount of binding environment being retained, solving the classical "funarg problem." Closures are implemented in such a way that when they are not used the highly speed- and storage-efficient shallow binding variable scheme operates at full efficiency, and when they are used, things are slowed down only slightly. The way one creates a closure is with a form such as

```
(CLOSURE '(FOO-PARAM FOO-STATE)
    (FUNCTION FOO-BAR))
```

The function could also be written directly in place as a LAMBDA-expression, instead of referring to the externally defined FOO-BAR. The variables FOO-PARAM and FOO-STATE are those variables that are used free by FOO-BAR and are intended to be "closed." That is, these are the variables whose binding environment is to be fixed to that in effect at the time the closure is created. The explicit declaration of which variables are to be closed allows the implementation to have high efficiency since it does not need to save the whole variable-binding environment, almost all of which is useless. It also allows the programmer to explicitly choose for each variable whether it is to be dynamically bound (at the point of call) or statically bound (at the point of creation of the closure), a choice that is not conveniently available in other languages. In addition the program is clearer because the intended effect of the closure is made manifest by listing the variables to be affected.

Consider an example in which the closure feature is used to solve a problem presented in a paper by Steele [1977]. The problem is to write a function called

GENERATE-SQRT-OF-GIVEN-EXTRA-TOLERANCE,

which is to take as its single argument the factor by which the tolerance is to be increased, and to return a function that takes square roots with that much more tolerance than usual, whatever "usual" is later defined to be. The programmer is given a function SQRT that makes a free reference to EPSILON, which is the tolerance it demands of the trial solution. The reason this example presents difficulties to various languages is that the variable EPSILON must be bound at the point of call (i.e. dynamically scoped), while the variable FACTOR must be bound at the point of creation of the function (i.e. lexically scoped). Thus the programmer must have explicit control over how the variables are bound.

```
(DEFUN GENERATE-SQRT-OF-GIVEN-EXTRA-TOLERANCE (FACTOR)
    (CLOSURE '(FACTOR)
            (FUNCTION
            (LAMBDA (X)
                ((LAMBDA (EPSILON) (SQRT X))
                (* EPSILON FACTOR))))))
```

The function, when called, rebinds EPSILON to FACTOR times its current value, then calls SQRT. The value of FACTOR used is that in effect when the closure was created, that is, the argument to GENERATE-SQRT-OF-GIVEN-EXTRA-TOLERANCE.

The way closures are implemented is as follows. For each variable to be closed an "external value cell" is created, that is a CONSed up free-storage cell that contains the variable's value when it is at that level of binding. Because this cell is CONSed up, it can be retained as long as necessary, just like any other data, and unlike cells in a stack. Because it is a cell, if the variable is SETQed the new value is seen by all the closures that should see it. The association between the symbol that is the name of the variable and this value cell is of the shallow-binding type, for efficiency; an invisible pointer in the normal (internal) value cell supplies the connection, eliminating the overhead of searching stack frames or a-lists. If at the time the closure is created an external value cell already exists for a variable, that one is used instead of creating a new one. Thus all closures at the same "level of binding" use the same value cell, which is the desired semantics.

The CLOSURE function returns an object of type DTP-CLOSURE, that contains the function to be called and, for each variable closed over, locative pointers to its internal and external value cells.

When a closure is invoked as a function, the variables mentioned in the closure are bound to invisible pointers to their external value cells; this puts these variables into the proper binding environment. The function contained in the closure is then invoked in the normal way. When the closed variables happen to be referred to, the invisible pointers are automatically followed to the external value cells. If one of the closed variables is then bound by some other function, the external value cell pointer is saved away on the binding stack, like any saved variable value, and the variable reverts to normal nonclosed status. When the closed function returns, the bindings of the closed variables are restored just like any other variables bound by the function.

Note the economy of mechanism. Almost all of the system is completely unaffected by and unaware of the existence of closures; the invisible pointer mechanism takes care of things.

The retainable binding environments are allocated through the standard CONS operation. The switching of variables between normal and "closed" status is done through the standard binding operation. The operations used by a closed function to access the closed variables are the same as those used to access ordinary variables; closures are called in the same way as ordinary functions. Closures work just as well in the interpreter as in the compiler. An important thing to note is the minimality of CONSing in closures. When a closure is created, some CONSing is done; external value cells and the closure-object itself must be created, but there is no extra "overhead." When a closure is called, no CONSing happens.

The stack group is a type of LISP object useful for implementation of certain advanced control structures such as coroutines, asynchronous processes, and generators. A stack group is similar to a process (or fork or job or task or control-point) in a timesharing system; it contains such state information as the "regular" and "special" (binding) PDLs and various internal registers. At all times there is one stack group running on the machine.

Control may be passed between stack groups in several ways. A stack-group may be called like a function; when it wants to return it can do a %STACK-GROUP-RETURN which is different from an ordinary function return in that the state of the stack group remains unchanged; the next time it is called it picks up from where it left off. This is good for generator-like applications; each time %STACK-GROUP-RETURN is done, a value is emitted from the generator, and as a side-effect, execution is suspended until the next time the generator is called. %STACK-GROUP-RETURN is analogous to the ADIEU construct in CONNIVER.

Control can simply be passed explicitly from one stack group to another, coroutine-style. Alternatively, there can be a scheduler stack-group that invokes other stack groups when their requested scheduling conditions are satisfied.

Interrupts cause control of the machine to be transferred to an interrupt-handler stack group. Essentially this is a forced stack group call like those calls described above. Similarly, when the microcode detects an error the current stack group is suspended and control is passed to an error-handling stack group. The state of the stack group that got the error is left exactly as it was when the error occurred, undisturbed by any error-handling operations. This facilitates error analysis and recovery.

Note that the same scheduler-driven stack-group switching mechanism can be used both for user programs which want to do parallel computations, and for system programming purposes such as the handling of network servers and peripheral handlers.

One important difference between stack groups and other means proposed to implement similar features is that the stack group scheme involves no loss of efficiency in normal computation. In fact, the compiler, the interpreter, and even the runtime function-calling mechanism are completely unaware of the existence of stack groups.

Storage Organization

The LISP machine will use a real-time, incremental, compacting garbage collector. Real-time means that CONS and related functions never delay LISP execution for more than a small, bounded amount of time. This is very important in a machine with a large address space, where a traditional garbage collection could bring everything to a halt for several minutes. The garbage collector compactifies in order to improve the paging characteristics.

The basic algorithm is described in a paper by Baker [1977]. It is much simpler than previous methods of incremental garbage collection in that only one process is needed; this avoids interlocking and synchronization problems that are often very difficult to debug.

Storage in the LISP machine is divided into "areas." Each area contains related objects of any type. Since we do not encode the data type in the address, we are free to use the address to encode the area. Areas are intended to give the user control over the paging behavior of his program, among other things. By putting related data together, locality can be greatly increased. Whenever a new object is created, for instance with CONS, the area to be used can optionally be specified. There is a default working storage area that collects those objects that the user has not chosen to control explicitly.

Areas also give the user a handle on the garbage collector. Some areas can be declared to be "static," which means that they change slowly and the garbage collector should not attempt to reclaim any space in them. This can eliminate a lot of useless copying. All pointers out of a static area can be collected into an "exit vector," eliminating any need for the garbage collector to look at that area. As an important example, an English-language dictionary can be kept inside the LISP without adversely affecting the speed of garbage collection. A "static" area can be explicitly garbage-collected at infrequent intervals when it is believed that that might be worthwhile.

Each area can potentially have a different storage discipline, a different paging algorithm, and even a different data representation. The microcode will dispatch on an attribute of the area at the appropriate times. The structure of the machine makes the performance cost of these features negligible; information about areas is stored in extra bits in the memory mapping hardware where it can be quickly dispatched on by the microcode. These dispatches usually have to be done anyway to make the garbage collector work, and to implement invisible pointers.

An invisible pointer is similar to an indirect address word on a conventional computer except the indirection is specified in the data instead of in the instruction. A reference to a memory location containing an invisible pointer is automatically altered to use the location pointed to by the invisible pointer. The term "invisible" refers to the fact that the presence of such pointers is not visible to most of the system, since they are handled by the lowest-level memory-referencing operations. The invisible pointer feature does not slow anything down much, because it is part of the data type checking that is done anyway (this is one of the benefits of a tagged architecture). A number of advanced features of the LISP machine depend upon invisible pointers for their efficient implementation.

Closures use invisible pointers to connect internal value cells to external value cells. This allows the variable binding scheme to be altered from normal shallow binding to allocated-value-cell shallow binding when closures are being used, without altering the normal operation of the machine when closures are not being used. At the same time the slow-down when closures are used amounts to only 2 microseconds per closed-variable reference, the time needed to detect and follow the invisible pointer.

Invisible pointers are necessary to the operation of the CDR-coded compressed list scheme. If RPLACD is done to a compressed list, the list can no longer be represented in the compressed form. It is necessary to allocate a full 2-word cons node and use that in its place. But, it is also necessary to preserve the identity (with respect to EQ) of the list. This is done by storing an invisible pointer in the original location of the compressed list, pointing to the uncompressed copy. Then the list is still represented by its original location, preserving EQness, but the CAR and CDR operations follow the invisible pointer to the new location and find the proper car and cdr.

This is a special case of the more general use of invisible pointers for "forwarding" references from an old representation of an object to a new one. For instance, there is a function to increase the size of an array. If it cannot do it in place, it makes a new copy and leaves behind an invisible pointer.

The exit-vector feature uses invisible pointers. One may set up an area to have the property that all references from inside that area to objects in other areas are collected into a single exit-vector. A location that would normally contain such a reference instead contains an invisible pointer to the appropriate slot in the exit vector. Operations on this area all work as before, except for a slight slow-down caused by the invisible pointer following. It is also desirable to have automatic checking to prevent the creation of new outside references; when an attempt is made to store an outside object into this area execution can trap to a routine that creates a new exit vector entry if necessary and stores an invisible pointer instead. The reason for exit vectors is to speed up garbage collection by eliminating the need to swap in all of the pages of the area in order to find and relocate all its references to outside objects.

Results

As a demonstration of the system, and a test of its capabilities, two large programs have been brought over from the PDP-10.

William Woods's LUNAR English-language data-base query system was converted from INTERLISP to MACLISP, thence to LISP machine LISP. On the LISP machine it runs approximately 3 times as fast as in MACLISP on the KA-10, that in turn is 2 to 4 times as fast as in INTERLISP. Note that the LISP machine time is elapsed real time, while the PDP-10 times are virtual run times as given by the operating system and do not include the delays due to timesharing.

Most of the Macsyma symbolic algebraic system has been converted to the LISP machine; nearly all the source files were simply compiled without any modifications. Most of Macsyma works except for some things that require BIGNUMS. The preliminary speed is the same as on the KA-10, but a number of things have not been optimally converted. (This speed measurement is, again, elapsed time on the LISP machine version versus reported run time on the KA-10 time sharing system. Thus, paging and scheduling overhead in the KA-10 case are not counted in this measurement.)

LUNAR (including the dictionary) and MACSYMA can reside together in the LISP machine with plenty of room left over; either program alone will not entirely fit in a PDP-10 address space.

References

Guy L. Steele, *Cons*, not yet published (this is a revision of MIT AI Laboratory Working Paper 80, *CONS* by Thomas Knight).

Henry Baker, *List Processing in Real Time on a Serial Computer*, MIT AI Laboratory Working Paper 139, 1977.

Guy L. Steele, *LAMBDA - The Ultimate Imperative*, MIT AI Laboratory Memo 353, 1976.

Galley and Phister, *The MDL Language*, MIT Laboratory for Computer Science, 1975.

Gerald Sussman and Drew McDermott, *The CONNIVER Reference Manual*, MIT AI Laboratory Memo 259a, 1974.

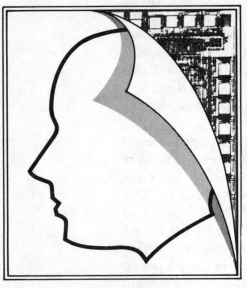

Lisp and Prolog machines are proliferating

New U. S Lisp machines are announced,
as Japan investigates Prolog and Lisp

by Tom Manuel, *Senior Editor, Information Systems*

What follows is part 1 of a two-part series on the commercial status of artificial intelligence. Part 1 delves into AI hardware systems now available, as well as reporting on several product-development projects close to fruition around the world. Prominent among the latter are projects under way in Japan, reported here in detail for the first time. These projects stem both from the fifth-generation computer project and from investigations into artificial intelligence.

Part 2 of the series, which will appear in the Dec. 1 issue, will be a close-up look at the software side of AI. Subjects to be covered will include AI programming languages, application development tools, and existing applications of knowledge-based (expert) systems and of natural-language processing.

The primary hardware tools available now for sculpting artificial-intelligence systems are computers designed to work with fast high-resolution graphics-programming work stations in order to optimize symbolic processing—the processing of the symbols standing for mental concepts, as opposed to numerical processing. The first of these computers were called Lisp machines because they were designed for efficient runnning of Lisp, the first and currently most popular language for AI work. Lisp was designed to easily write programs for the symbolic representation and processing of arbitrary objects and the relationships among them. The hardware tools of the AI trade available today are personal Lisp machines from three U. S. manufacturers, as well as emerging general-purpose work stations and a few mainframe computers, all with AI language support.

Advantages of the Lisp machines are the speed and efficiency gained from the fact that they are designed and tuned for symbolic processing. These work stations typically have large memories and virtual-memory management, plus advanced graphics. General-purpose work stations are not tuned for symbolic languages, but they have all the other advantages of the Lisp machines. Also, they can easily handle non-AI applications, such as the nu-

merical calculations required in computer-aided engineeering. Of course, the Lisp machines can be used for non-AI applications, too, and they are excellent programming development tools for all types of software. A couple of advantages of mainframe computers for AI work are, first, a company may already have them, and, second, AI applications developed for them can be integrated with other programs running on them.

Before Lisp machines came along, AI work was done on time-shared mainframe computers, primarily the DECsystem 10s and 20s, made by Digital Equipment Corp., Maynard, Mass. These machines are still in use for AI work, as are time-shared superminicomputers such as DEC's VAX-11 series. However, Digital has discontinued its project to build the successor to the DECsystem 20. Instead, it is concentrating its AI effort on its VAX superminicomputer line and specialized work stations.

From PARC and MIT

The earliest Lisp machines were designed at two research labs: the Laboratory for Computer Science at the Massachusetts Institute of Technology, in Cambridge, and Xerox Corp.'s Palo Alto (Calif.) Research Laboratory. In 1981 Xerox announced an Interlisp work station, the 1100. (Interlisp, one of the several dialects of Lisp, grew out of the original.) The 1100 was the first of a series—two other members are now available, the 1108 and the 1132 (see p. 153) Xerox plans to extend the 1100 series at both ends. At the low end will be a very low-cost work station with enough memory to execute a run-time version of Interlisp-D, which is the company's version of Interlisp. This computer would only run AI applications; it could not be used to develop them.

The entire 1100 series is compatible with Ethernet and the Xerox Network System architecture, and therefore customers can configure these work stations into systems with other XNS products, such as file, print and communications servers. The series is sold in Japan by Fuji Xerox and in Western Europe by Rank Xerox, while a similar machine is sold by Siemens in West Germany.

Another U. S. maker of personal symbolic computers is Symbolics Inc. in Cambridge, Mass. Formed in 1980 to commercialize symbolic-computing technology, the company was founded by members of the team that developed the MIT Lisp Machine and its operating system. Like Xerox, Symbolics introduced its first computer in 1981, the LM-2 being a commercial version of the MIT Lisp Machine [*Electronics,* Aug. 11, 1981, p. 159]. No sooner was this machine in production than Symbolics introduced its successor, the 3600 [*Electronics,* Aug. 25, 1981, p. 40]. This machine (Fig. 1), two to eight times more powerful than the LM-2, went into production in early 1983.

The third U. S. maker of Lisp machines is called, appropriately, Lisp Machine Inc., Culver City, Calif. It also shipped its first machine in 1981, the Series III CADR (CADR is a Lisp function that creates a new list starting at the second member of a previous list, and this was the second Lisp machine to be built). Lisp Machine's next-generation product is the Lambda [*Electronics,* Sept. 8, 1983, p. 196]. Like the Symbolics 3600, the Lambda (Fig. 2) comes with Ethernet capability.

The first practical Lisp machine made in Japan came from Fujitsu Ltd. [*Electronics,* March 24, 1983, p. 71]. The Alpha machine (Fig. 3) is a prototype back-end Lisp processor for a general-purpose computer. The company claims it will be the fastest Lisp machine around at 2.5 million to 3 million instructions a second when running simple programs. Lisp is also available on NEC Corp.'s ACOS series of mainframe computers.

Because AI machines are just starting to appear, no generally accepted set of benchmark programs for measuring and comparing their performance has been developed. Moreover, comparing machine-level rates in millions of instructions per second is misleading when evaluating high-level–language machines.

Performance numbers quoted in MIPS should only be used as broad guidelines, for the prospective buyer and user of these machines must consider many other features, particularly the set of software development tools offered and the particular dialect of Lisp available. Also to be taken into account are the availability of other programming languages, system reliability, and the level of hardware and software maintenance support being offered.

A comparison

To summarize the main features of the machines now available, the Xerox 1100 series has different models with a wide range of performance choices; Interlisp-D; Smalltalk-80, an object-oriented language; Loops, a programming tool that integrates four programming environments [*Electronics,* Sept. 8, 1983, p. 196]; and a well-tested network and server support system. The Symbolics 3600 has high performance; a very rich software development environment; Zetalisp, a derivative of Maclisp, which in turn is another dialect of Lisp; Flavors, an object-oriented language; Fortran-77; and Ethernet.

1. Symbol processor. The model 3600 computer from Symbolics Inc. is one of the class of systems commonly known as Lisp work stations. Designed for fast symbolic processing in Lisp, it is dedicated to a single user and features an interactive-graphics user interface.

The newest work station, Lisp Machine's Lambda also is fast. It has LMLisp, another child of Maclisp, with software development tools; a Lisp microcompiler and virtual control memory for easier tailoring of the machine intruction set; an optional MC68000 processor for running Berkeley Unix, C, Pascal, and Fortran-77; an 8088-based system diagnostic processor; and Ethernet facilities. DEC's VAX systems come in a wide performance range, from the new MicroVAX [*Electronics,* Oct. 20, 1983, p. 42] to clusters of 11/782s [*Electronics,* Oct. 20, 1983, p. 143]. They run much software, including several dialects of Lisp and a new Common Lisp, and offer Ethernet and DECnet. The 68000-based VAXstation 100 work station at $13,000 ($10,000 for the hardware and $3,000 for the software) adds the same kind of graphics-based user interface that the Lisp machines have.

General-purpose high-end work stations—typically based on multiple 68000 processors and offering the Unix operating system, virtual-memory management, large real memory, and advanced graphics-based user interfaces—could join Lisp machines and mainframes as hardware tools for AI development. One dialect of Lisp, Franz Lisp, developed at the University of California at Berkeley, is written in C and runs under Unix and presumably could be made available on the general-purpose work stations.

The AI machines on the market may come from the U. S., but Japan is investing much research and development effort in the field. The work there is both an investigation of artificial intelligence *per se* and also that included in the fifth-generation computer project.

The Japanese government's Electrotechnical Laboratory in Ibaraki has completed fabrication of a personal Lisp machine of roughly the same speed as the Symbolics 3600. If the software were refined by the addition of a full-fledged editor and command system it could be used for practical applications. The system has as its main processor the Pulce silicon-on-sapphire processor completed by Toshiba Corp. in 1978 as part of the government's pattern-information-processing project.

However, the single-processor machine is but the first step in the development of a data-driven Lisp machine named EM-3 for office automation, natural-language processing, knowledge-based systems, and other interactive applications. Yoshinori Yamaguchi, a senior researcher at the Ibaraki ETL, says that work is progressing on a parallel-processor hardware simulator using eight single-board 68000 processors.

In its final form, this system will have 80 to 100 very large-scale integrated processors of a yet-unknown type that the ETL researchers hope to design themselves. It may have to be made with gate arrays because silicon foundries are not readily available in Japan. Present plans call for the hardware simulator to be completed by the end of March 1984.

Key to the new machine, though, is the control mechanism, which will be developed during a one-year feasibility study starting next April. It is expected to be an advanced parallel-control mechanism that will be a natural extension of the data-driven scheme for function evaluation used in data-flow computers.

The primary programming language will probably be a Lisp-like language with Prolog features such as pattern invocation and backtracking, although Prolog is also being studied for possible use. Pattern matching also will be required in the language.

Beyond Lisp

Meanwhile, a group headed by Yasushi Hibino at the Nippon Telegraph & Telephone Public Corp.'s Musashino Electrical Communication Laboratory is building a Lisp machine that it expects to complete by the end of March. Multiple copies will be built for AI research.

The machine is being created as part of the so-called NUE project. NUE is the Japanese equivalent of the Chimera of Greek mythology, and the name is intended to indicate that the project is not language-restricted. It started off two years ago as a Lisp project, but it has now become a multilanguage project where procedural, functional, logical, and object-oriented languages will be developed with the syntax of Lisp but the semantics of other languages, including Lisp, Prolog, and Smalltalk.

The reasoning behind the NUE work is that AI problems cannot be solved with one programming style. Ideally, the execution system should work with the same efficiency for any style because the computational volume

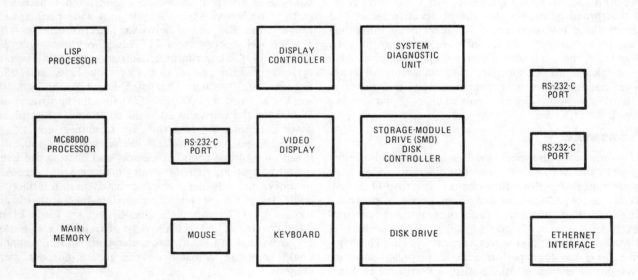

2. Lisp and more. The flexible, modular Nu Machine and Nubus architecture of this Lambda computer from Lisp Machine Inc. accommodates different processor types for different applications, such as a Lisp processor and an MC68000 in the same machine.

should be the same, but the programs will be easy or hard to write depending on the problem. With NUE, it should be possible to learn which styles are superior for which problems.

The name of the NUE machine is ELIS, from Electrical Communication Laboratory Lisp processor. Its speed in the interpreter mode is similar to that of Fujitsu's Alpha. Like experimental Lisp machines previously built in Japan, his machine makes use of microprogramming, he notes. ELIS has a 32-bit bus, using 24 bits for address and the remaining 8 bits as a tag. The address space is equivalent to a 27-bit address, because each address accesses an 8-byte cell, so a total of 128 megabytes can be addressed rather than the 16 megabytes that conventional 24-bit addresses can access.

Watch the pointers

Hibino says this configuration was selected because it provides the best performance: in Lisp, following the path of the pointers is more important than computation, so having two large pointer fields to the CAR and CDR instructions speeds up this operation. It could be considered extravagant, but, even when data is missing, memory usage is only double that of systems designed to conserve memory. Hibino also notes that memory conservation is no longer a primary concern, with 256-K chips permitting 4 megabytes of memory on a single board.

The processor has about half of its logic implemented in AMD2903 bit-slice chips and the remainder in Schottky TTL. The 2903 is not ideal for the application because of the vertical connections between the arithmetic and logic unit and the shifter. The vertical connections are superior in arithmetic operations such as add and multiply where shifting is part of the operation because it enables these operations to be performed in one clock cycle instead of two. But they slow down symbolic processing. However, the standard functions of the 2903 arithmetic and logic unit speed up standard data processing more than they degrade symbolic processing.

The ELIS hardware is in operation and the microprogram is working sufficiently well to measure performance. The firmware should be sufficiently refined that the system can be in use at the Musashino lab by April 1984, if the system software has been completed by that time. Hibino is not as yet able to say how many machines will be built or to disclose much else about future plans.

The first project in the Japanese fifth-generation computer effort is a

3. Symbolic helper. Fujitsu's Alpha is a back-end processor that provides users on a time-sharing computer with high-speed symbolic list processing. Connected to a Fujitsu mainframe, its instruction-processing unit executes the Utilisp variant of Lisp.

personal sequential-inference (PSI) computer for developing knowledge-processing software [*Electronics,* July 28, 1983, p. 101]. The PSI is intended for developing inferential symbolic processing programs at the Institute for New Generation Computer Technology (ICOT) and will have a sequential von Neumann architecture rather than the advanced parallel architectures planned for the eventual fifth-generation computers.

A cooperative effort

ICOT's functions are to design the hardware and software for fifth-generation subsystems and to build the software. The hardware production is being contracted out to computer companies. For example, the pilot model of the PSI (Fig. 4), is being fabricated by Mitsubishi Electric Corp. and Oki Electric Industry Co. Ltd. for evaluation by August 1984 and is to be made from conventional components. A later version will be made with custom VLSI circuitry.

Other ICOT-designed subsystems for the fifth-generation project will be manufactured by various Japanese computer companies. For example, NEC will fabricate a sequential-inference machine faster and larger than the PSI and scheduled for completion within the initial three-year phase of the project.

Also part of Phase One is a general-purpose parallel computer for maintaining and processing knowledge bases and relational data bases. Toshiba will build the basic engine for it, possibly using some very high-speed SOS technology. Hitachi Ltd. will be building a hierarchical memory subsystem—a memory that is organized as a hierarchy and is addressed by subject content at the appropriate level of the hierarchy—and a silicon disk to hold it (Fig. 5). NEC, Hitachi, and Fujitsu are expected to manufacture the parallel inference and knowledge-base machines that will be built during the second, or intermediate, phase of ICOT's fifth-generation project.

One of ICOT's software projects for the PSI is an enhanced version of Prolog. The PSI is being designed to optimize Prolog performance at no less than 20 klips—a fifth-generation performance term meaning a thousand

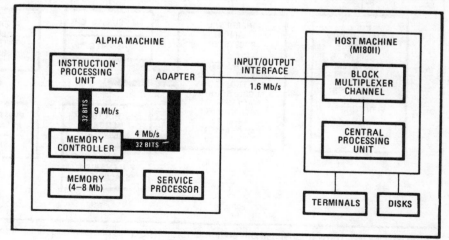

logical inferences per second. Lips is just a fancy term for the number of Prolog procedure calls per second. Since one procedure call averages from 100 to 300 machine instructions, 1 klips is roughly equivalent to 0.1 to 0.3 MIPS, thus giving the PSI raw instruction performance of 2 to 6 MIPS that is superior to the fastest Lisp machines currently available. This comparison, of course, must be taken with a grain of salt. It can only give a ballpark guess as to how the PSI will perform relative to the Lisp machines, because it is of little value to compare a Lisp procedure to a Prolog inference.

An inference machine

Meanwhile, at the University of Tokyo, Tohru Moto-Oka and a group of his graduate students are developing a parallel inference engine for a Prolog machine. An inference engine is a hardware system for reaching conclusions from facts and rules of inference stored in a knowledge base. This work is in cooperation with ICOT but receives some other funding and represents one of the several approaches—some not yet publicly revealed—toward development of fifth-generation architectures. In some ways, this work is the most advanced sector of ICOT's project because it will immediately jump into parallel processing, while ICOT is starting with a personal

sequential-inference machine. The group intends to build a system with 100 parallel high-speed processors, with the first usable system being completed in 10 years.

A simulator written in C has been completed, and the design of the core of the TTL hardware simulator will be completed by the end of this month. The first processor will be finished several months later, and by the end of March 1984, it should be in operation. Within two years after that, the group plan to build a 10-processor system and go on from there.

The Eddy data-flow processor being developed at the Musashino lab [*Electronics*, June 16, 1983, p. 114] will also be a type of Lisp machine. Extensions to Valid, the high-level functional language with recursion and parallel expressions for logic programming developed for this machine, will also make it a type of Prolog machine. The extensions will include pattern matching, making Valid suitable for simple, intuitive programming.

The present basic research phase at the Musashino lab will continue for another two or three years. If the work is continued to completion, a system suitable for user applications should be completed in seven to 10 years. This is roughly the same time scale as the ICOT project, for which this work provides an alternative.

Many observers note that the potential resources of the

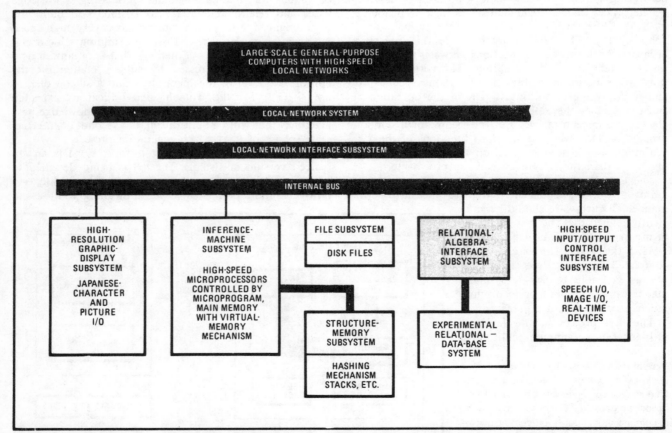

4. Fifth generation. The first Japanese fifth-generation prototype is this personal sequential-inference machine being developed by ICOT. Two major innovations are the inference machine and relational algebra subsystems. Software for the PSI represents the biggest effort.

four NTT Electrical Communication Laboratories—the Musashino ECL, the Ibaraki ECL, the Yokosuka ECL, and the Atsugi ECL—exceed by far those of ICOT. This is true even considering only the personnel and budget available for computer R&D, although the ECLs also have capabilities in semiconductor work and related fields. But the NTT labs each have many projects going, and there is no guarantee that management will continue work on all of them through to fruition at a high level.

Another major center of AI research is the UK, where work is under way on several flavors of Prolog machines. At the low end, there is a version of Prolog for Z80-based CP/M personal computers from Logic Programming Associates of London. It is intended for teaching basic Prolog and not for developing or running logic application programs.

Alice lives here

At the high end, a computer called Alice, for applicative language idealised computing engine, is being developed in a research project at London's Imperial College [*Electronics*, Feb. 24, 1983, p. 67]. It will be a parallel-processing machine designed for Parlog, a parallel version of Prolog, Lisp, and the college's own declarative fifth-generation language, Hope. Parallel architectures for nonprocedural languages like Prolog and Hope make sense because all the premises that might lead to a con-clusion in logic could be evaluated at the same time.

The Alice prototype will have 16 processors and 16 memory modules and a switch to connect any processor with any memory. The basic engine will be the transputer microprocessor chip from Inmos plc [*Electronics*, Sept. 22, 1982, p. 86], with 112 of them being used. Both hardware and software development are on schedule for completion by early 1985.

Hardware development is split into two parts: the communications ring carrying data packets, and the processing agents, each with multiple transputers. The communications ring is scheduled for completion in May 1984. A key element is a high-speed monolithic switch being built for Imperial College by Swindon Silicon Systems. The research group has been promised first samples as a Christmas present. From that point onwards, further progress will hang on the availability of transputer chips, which are just being formally unveiled (see p. 47).

For those seeking to experiment with Prolog programming, there are several options. Prolog versions are available from several sources for machines as diverse as Z80- and 68000-based microcomputers, PDP-11s, DEC20s, and VAX machines. There is even a version for the IBM/370 architecture available from the computer science department of Waterloo University, Waterloo, Ontario, Canada. And a new company, Silogic Inc. in Los Angeles, is now offering Prolog interpreters for a variety of machines, including the Z80 and MC68000 microprocessors, and is currently developing a Prolog compiler.

However, only the Japanese PSI computer is designed to be a Prolog-optimized machine the way the Lisp machines are for Lisp. There is the likelihood that efficient implementations of Prolog will soon become available on the U. S. Lisp machines. They may even outperform the PSI prototype and be available on the open market before it is running.

For instance, a version of Prolog from the University of Uppsala in Sweden is available now for Lisp Machine's Lambda. It is expected to deliver 4.5 klips initially and up to 20 to 25 klips when it is optimized with microcode. As for the 3600, Symbolics says that it is considering two strategies for Prolog: to provide it just as it would provide another language, such as Fortran, or to put the interesting aspects of Prolog into Zetalisp or to develop a Prolog with Lisp syntax.

Advanced, high-performance parallel AI architectures are being researched in the U. S. For example, at MIT, Robert H. Halstead Jr. leads a group that is constructing an experimental multiprocessor called Concert, which will combine 32 68000 processors. As one of its languages, it will run Multilisp, a multiprocessor version of Lisp that is being developed as part of the project. Another MIT project, funded by the Defense Advanced Research Projects Agency, plans to build a 64-processor machine using Symbolics 3600s. □

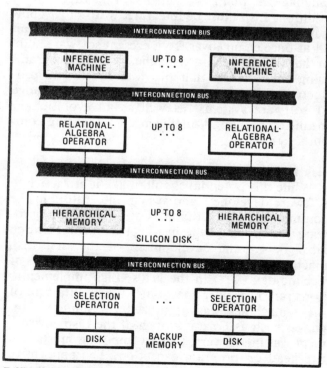

5. Hierarchical memory. A parallel relational–data-base machine using specially designed hierarchical memory on a silicon disk (fast semiconductor memory used like a disk drive) with a disk-drive backup is also part of Phase One of Japan's fifth-generation project.

Additional reporting came from Charles L. Cohen, Tokyo, and Kevin Smith, London.
This is the first part of a two-part special report. Reprints will be available for $6 each after part 2 is published in the Dec. 1 issue. Write to *Electronics* Reprint Dept., 1221 Ave. of Americas, N. Y., N. Y. 10020. Copyright 1983, McGraw-Hill Inc.

LISP MACHINES COME OUT OF THE LAB

No longer restricted to the research lab, artificial intelligence is becoming increasingly attractive to commercial users thanks to computer architectures designed to support the Lisp language.

by Mache Creeger

Artificial intelligence, defined as the science of enabling machines to reason, make judgments, and even learn, is often seen as a field whose practical benefits will be realized only at some future date. This is not entirely true. Artificial intelligence researchers have already contributed to the development of such techniques as timesharing, networking, and window systems—a part of the commercial computing world. However, a powerful software tool developed by the artificial intelligence community, the Lisp language, is just beginning to make an impact outside of the research labs.

The Lisp language deals with the complex and unpredictable data characteristic of the artificial intelligence (AI) field. It permits large, powerful programs that traditional programming techniques cannot handle to be written, tested, and modified. However, traditional computers (such as Digital Equipment Corp's system10 or VAX, and similar machines), cannot support Lisp so that it can become an efficient tool for commercial use. As a result, the power and productivity of the language

Mache Creeger is director of marketing at LISP Machine Inc, 3916 S Sepulveda Blvd, Culver City, CA 90230, where he is responsible for sales and marketing of the company's Lambda machine. Mr Creeger holds a BS and MS from the University of Maryland.

have remained in the research lab, where functionality, rather than speed, is the major consideration.

An efficient Lisp implementation requires an architecture optimized for the structure of the language, as well as very high storage capacity. In addition, Lisp must be integrated with other computing environments to eliminate the need for an all-at-once changeover from present software and/or hardware. Such a machine offers a programming environment that provides substantial productivity increases for the development of a range of software systems, as well as an evolutionary means of bringing "intelligence" to existing computer systems.

Lisp and the commercial world

While this potential should make it attractive to software developers and system integrators in the commercial world, the lack of appropriate hardware for the language has kept it in the research labs. Before the development of the first Lisp machines at the Massachusetts Institute of Technology (MIT) in the 1970s, Lisp implementations ran on mainframes. Since the architecture of these machines was optimized for numeric languages such as Fortran, much of the Lisp environment was in software, thereby imposing substantial overhead on program execution. The applicative and recursive nature of Lisp requires an environment that efficiently supports stack computations and function calling.

In addition, Lisp's memory requirements exceeded even the capacities of these large

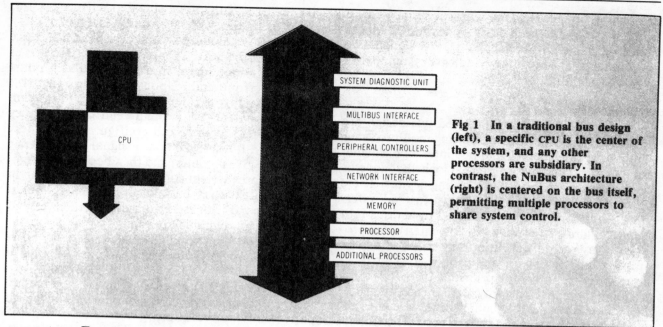

Fig 1 In a traditional bus design (left), a specific CPU is the center of the system, and any other processors are subsidiary. In contrast, the NuBus architecture (right) is centered on the bus itself, permitting multiple processors to share system control.

SYSTEM DIAGNOSTIC UNIT

MULTIBUS INTERFACE

PERIPHERAL CONTROLLERS

NETWORK INTERFACE

MEMORY

PROCESSOR

ADDITIONAL PROCESSORS

CPU

computers. Frequent stops for garbage collection made execution slow. Methods used to implement data-typing imposed another handicap. Lisp is a weakly typed language, meaning that functions can deal with a number of different data types (eg, fixed and floating point numbers) through a process called coercion, where a function recognizes the kind of data object it is dealing with and reacts accordingly. Traditional memory organizations require this process to be handled in a number of inefficient ways. Devoting fixed areas of memory to specified types causes memory fragmentation; other devices required extensive software overhead. Other problems were the language's poor arithmetic capabilities, since overcome by better compilers and hardware support, and its "stand-alone" nature. Because it was developed for use as a research tool by individuals or small groups, it did not integrate well into more traditional multi-user computing environments.

Lisp machine design

To illustrate how Lisp machine design overcomes these handicaps, consider the Lambda Machine from LISP Machine Inc. It is a lineal descendant of the original MIT Lisp machine, the CONS, which required mainframe support to operate. This machine was superseded by the CADR, which was later brought to the marketplace by LISP Machine Inc. The CADR was a personal, networked computer for programmers developing large, complex software systems. Drawing heavily on design experience gained from the CADR, the Lambda adds Lisp-oriented enhancements to the advanced high performance NuBus, also developed at MIT. Combining the Lambda processor with the NuBus architecture produces a modular, expandable Lisp machine with multiprocessor

capabilities. The Lambda offers an integral Multibus, Ethernet-II networking, and the Lisp Machine Lisp/Zeta Lisp operating environment.

NuBus's device-independent architecture, originally developed at MIT's Laboratory for Computer Science and now supported by Texas Instruments, centers on a 32-bit bus with a 37.5M-byte/s peak transfer rate. Important aspects are its ability to support multiple processors and the architectural flexibility furnished by the system diagnostic unit (SDU). Both of these distinguish it from traditional architectures (Fig 1).

Traditional bus architectures center on a single processor, with major subsystems arrayed around a specific central processing unit (CPU). In contrast, the NuBus is a communication-centered design that allows rapid interchange of data between a variety of devices within a 4G-byte address space. Input/output (I/O), interrupt, and memory signals are initiated uniformly over the bus, and transactions are based on a "master/slave" concept: any given device may control the bus and address another device as a slave for that transaction. A simple handshake protocol used between master and slave enables modules with different speeds to communicate. This arrangement allows a variety of processor combinations to be used.

NuBus architecture handles five functional classes of signals. Four card-slot identification signals assign a unique physical location to each of 16 boards, so that any system module can occupy any board location; no dual-inline package switches, jumpers, or special backplane wiring are necessary. Six control signals—CLOCK, RESET, START, and ACKNOWLEDGE for data transfers, and two transfer mode (TM) signals for type of transfer—perform all control functions. Modes include 8-, 16-, and 32-bit (full-word) transfers as well as block transfers of up to

16 words. Thirty-two signals carry a 32-bit address at the beginning of each clock cycle, and 32 bits of data in the remainder of each cycle. Five signals control bus arbitration, and two indicate system parity and parity validity.

Multiprocessor operations

Two elements of this high speed bus design are particularly important for supporting multiprocessor operations: the memory mapped interrupt scheme, and the distributed bus arbitration logic that governs the master/slave relationships among devices. There are no interrupt lines on the NuBus. Instead, interrupts are accomplished by write transactions into memory addresses monitored by the interrupted processor. Any memory location may be specified as an interrupt address for any processor. This technique specifies interrupt priorities in software by memory mapping the priority level of each interrupt, thus eliminating the difficulties otherwise encountered in systems using multiple processors with differing interrupt schemes.

Arbitration occurs each time control is transferred between bus masters, and is independent of data transfers. The winner of the arbitration controls the bus until an arbitration is won by another device, but control is not transferred until the losing bus master completes any current data transfer. The distributed bus arbitration logic provides fair bandwidth sharing between processors by organizing devices on the bus into logical groups. When several devices simultaneously request the bus, the highest priority device gains control, but no device can initiate new bus requests until all devices in the group have acquired the bus. This prevents high priority processors from starving those with lower priority.

A bus master that acquires the bus is automatically the highest priority device within its group; thus it can accomplish an undivided set of data transfers by continually arbitrating for, and winning, the bus. If no other processor requests the bus, the current bus master may continually initiate data transfers without rearbitrating for the bus each time. This scheme speeds up processing by relieving a bus master of unnecessary arbitration overhead.

The NuBus's modularity and device independence comes from the SDU. This 8088-based board serves both as an architectural supervisor and as a smart diagnostic front end. Upon power-up, the SDU verifies bus integrity, identifies boards in the system from the contents of a small read only memory (ROM) on each board, and configures the system accordingly. It tests each board, signals the presence of any defective modules, and then boots the system. The SDU stores system configuration information in a nonvolatile battery-backed complementary metal oxide semiconductor random access memory (CMOS RAM) and can dynamically change the system configuration on command. Two RS-232 serial ports serve either for remote diagnostics or as general purpose serial ports. The SDU is also the system clock source. Fig 2, a block diagram of the Lambda machine, illustrates the SDU's importance in system control and configuration.

The SDU also serves as the NuBus interface with the Multibus. The Multibus allows the Lambda to interface with numerous peripherals and board-level products. The two buses operate independently except during bus conversions, which are accomplished through a hardware mapping scheme that requires no participation by the 8088 processor. The Multibus's entire 1M-byte address space appears as one continuous block in the 4G-byte NuBus address space. Conversion from NuBus to Multibus is transparent; a NuBus processor can access data or execute a program from Multibus memory. Conversion from Multibus to NuBus is accomplished by a page-mapping scheme that uses the upper 10 bits of the Multibus address to reference a page-mapping table.

The 22-bit page-frame number obtained from the map is concatenated with the lower 10 bits of the Multibus address to yield a 32-bit NuBus address. Interrupts originating in the Multibus are mapped into NuBus interrupt addresses by the 8088 processor; interrupts from NuBus to Multibus are written by the NuBus to an addressable latch on the

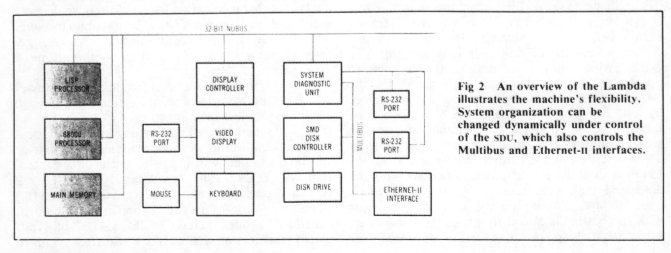

Fig 2 An overview of the Lambda illustrates the machine's flexibility. System organization can be changed dynamically under control of the SDU, which also controls the Multibus and Ethernet-II interfaces.

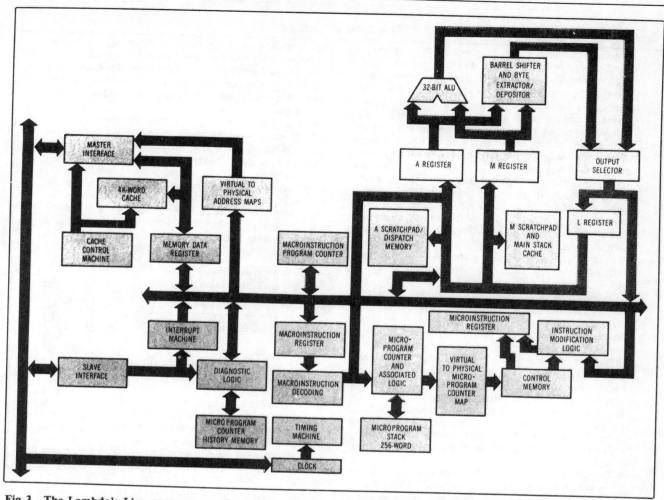

Fig 3 The Lambda's Lisp processor consists of four boards (not outlined in this diagram). Clockwise from the top left are the memory interface board, which interacts with the NuBus; the data paths board, where data manipulation takes place; the control memory board, which contains the microcode functions; and the random gates board, which includes several control and diagnostic functions.

SDU, which creates the appropriate Multibus interrupt. If both buses request each other simultaneously, the SDU prevents deadlock by giving priority to the slower Multibus-to-NuBus transfer, since NuBus-to-Multibus transfers can be rescheduled faster.

Another important aspect is Lambda's Ethernet-II interface, which executes the Advanced Research Projects Agency network (ARPANET) Transmission Control Protocol/Internet Protocol (TCP/IP). This interface facilitates resource sharing and interuser communication, easing the task of integrating a Lisp machine into an existing system. The Ethernet-II interface is controlled by another 8088-based board that provides the hardware interface and handles all network control protocols (NCPs). This frees the processor(s) from the overhead usually associated with NCPs, making protocol updates simpler and less time consuming.

Other hardware elements enhance NuBus operation. Memory boards in the NuBus system are self-contained memory controllers that support block transfers and error correction and logging. The memory holds 39-bit words: 32 bits of data and 7 bits of error-correction code. The video display system supports a high resolution (800 x 1024) display with two 1M-bit video buffers (useful when screen updates should not be seen), onboard logical functions, and a keyboard-mouse interface. Rounding out the generic aspects of the architecture are a disk controller that can handle four storage module device (SMD) drives, a 470M-byte Winchester disk drive, and a card cage with 21 slots: 13 for NuBus, 5 for Multibus, and 3 for either.

The Lisp processor

Four boards, utilizing high speed Schottky transistor-transistor logic (TTL) devices and communicating through a private bus on the backplane, constitute the Lisp processor. This general purpose 32-bit microprogrammable processor provides efficient pipelined execution of complex order codes. Although its optimal function is interpreting the Lisp compiler's bit-efficient 16-bit order code, the processor easily adapts to high level language execution as well as to specific

The Lisp language

The Lisp (List processing) language deals with arbitrary symbols—that can represent any concept—rather than numbers. The basic Lisp data structures are the atom and the CONS node. An atom, as its name indicates, is a data object that cannot be further broken down. A CONS node is a data structure that consists of two fields, each holding a pointer to another Lisp data object, which in turn may be an atom, another CONS node, or any other Lisp object, such as a string or an array. Any number of CONS nodes may be linked together to form data structures of arbitrary size and complexity; such structures prove ideal for handling unpredictable data such as natural-language representations. The list is one of the most important forms these complex data structures can take—hence Lisp's name.

Each Lisp atom has associated with it a property list, which gives additional information about the atom, including the atom's value (if it is a variable), its print name (a pointer to its character representation in memory), or any other property the programmer assigns. For instance, an atom that is an English word might have as a property its part of speech, its phonetic representation, or even its connotations.

Part (a) of the Figure illustrates Lisp's data structure. It represents a simple list—(THROW (THE BIG RED) BALL)—made up of six linked CONS nodes (the double squares) and seven atoms (each word in the list). NIL is a special atom used to mark the end of a list or sublist. This Lisp construct contrasts with a Fortran array shown in (b) containing the same list. In the Fortran array, parentheses indicate the beginning and end of sublists.

The Lisp list structure offers several advantages. For example, if a single sublist—such as "THE BIG RED"—appears in many lists, it need be represented in memory only once, and pointers in each main list can reference it. Moreover, the elements of a list need not be adjacent to each other within memory, allowing efficient use of storage space. Furthermore, elements can be easily added to or deleted from a list without affecting other data elements—only pointers need be changed. In contrast, many elements in a Fortran array must be moved up or down when one is inserted or deleted. In addition, Lisp allows sublists to be skipped during searches of main lists; as a result, Lisp can process large lists much faster and more efficiently than Fortran.

Productivity advantages stem from Lisp's functionally based programming style, its runtime nature, and its extensive editing and debugging facilities. In contrast to traditional programming, where a great deal of time is spent merely specifying application parameters that may not be fully known until the program is finished, a Lisp programmer can have a program up and running very quickly. It then can be modified to suit the needs of end users based on their actual experience with the software. As an example of Lisp's productivity enhancements, LISP Machine Inc devised a sophisticated Lisp-based CAD system that it in turn used to design its Lambda machine. The CAD system was completed in less than two man-years; if designed with traditional programming methods, completion would have required an estimated 50 to 100 man-years.

Lisp programs consist of a group of functions, in contrast to traditional languages, which consist largely of sequential instructions and attendant subroutines.

Lisp is thus a naturally modular language, and programmers can readily break down a function into many easily handled subtasks, or smaller functions. Lisp is highly recursive, allowing a function to call itself. This is a useful feature when a subtask is identical to the main task.

The language can either run interpretively or be compiled. In the interpretive mode, Lisp functions and data have the same structure; therefore, functions can manipulate or even create other functions. In modern Lisp machines, every bit of software, from the operating system to the editing and debugging utilities, is written in Lisp and can thus be easily customized to suit a programmer's needs. For example, a programmer can design applications software that creates a function in data-structure form, submits that structure to the system Lisp compiler (which is itself a Lisp pro-

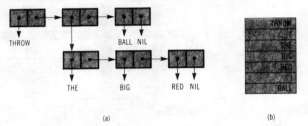

(a)　　　　　　　　　　　　　　　　(b)

gram), and then automatically executes the resulting compiled program as part of the applications software.

Lisp's runtime nature, which stems from its dynamic storage allocation and link-edit features, eases program generation by allowing programmers to defer decisions regarding the form of the final program. In contrast to traditional programming languages, Lisp does not require a declaration of required storage prior to writing the program. New storage is allocated during program execution as the program requires it. When the system senses that an area of memory can no longer be accessed by a program (eg, when a sublist's pointers are deleted from the main list), the inaccessible storage is automatically reclaimed and made available for new allocation through a process called garbage collection.

In addition, Lisp programs do not require a separate link-editing phase during compilation. Instead, functions are linked at run time and therefore can be easily changed even after compilation. Program modifications involve editing only those functions affected by the change and recompiling them—there is no need to recompile and link-edit the entire program.

Since Lisp has been the language of choice in the artificial intelligence field for many years, a powerful set of editing and debugging tools have been developed for it. Using such tools, a programmer can, for example, concurrently observe program source and execution, retrieve and modify any function, and recompile the modified function back into the program with very few keystrokes. Furthermore, because all of the programming utilities are written in Lisp, they can be easily incorporated into an applications program through Lisp's dynamic-linking capability. For example, the Lambda's Lisp Machine Lisp/Zeta Lisp environment includes an extensive window system, implemented by a message-passing feature called Flavors. This window system can be easily modified to serve as a user friendly interface for an applications program.

applications that rely on certain macroinstructions, which can be microcoded for faster execution. Main data paths of the processor are shown in Fig 3.

Four boards centralize related areas of the Lisp environment. Briefly, the data paths (DP) board contains the arithmetic logic unit (ALU), dispatch logic, scratchpad memories, and associated registers. The control memory (CM) board incorporates microcode functions and associated logic, and the microinstruction stack. The memory interface (MI) board, a NuBus master, contains cache, cache state machine, location counter, and diagnostic logic. Responsible for relations between the Lisp processor and the NuBus system, its operation is especially important for multiprocessor applications. Finally, the random gates (RG) board holds the macroinstruction decoder, statistics counter, history RAM, clock, matrix multiplier, and a slave NuBus diagnostic interface.

The Lisp processor's data paths are 32 bits wide: 24 bits for data and 8 bits for data-typing and other operations, giving the Lambda 67M bytes of address space (2^{24} 4-byte words). A 40-bit enhancement (planned for early next year) will expand the address space to 21.5G bytes. Since the number of bits used for data-typing will remain the same, little or no reprogramming will be necessary.

In addition to its large address space, the Lambda uses a technique known as CDR-coding to reduce storage demands of list structures by almost 50%, making the address space seem even larger. CONS (constructor) nodes (see the Panel) cannot be inserted into a list compressed by this technique. However, since the processor automatically reexpands the CDR-coding when the list is accessed for modification, the technique is transparent to the user.

Processor design aspects

Data are passed to and from the Lisp processor under control of the cache state machine, a specialized high speed processor. Using NuBus block-transfer capability, the cache state machine manages memory accesses in a look-ahead/look-behind mode based on the principle of set-local operations, or locality. Presuming that the next word to be accessed is nearby the last word requested, the machine transfers an entire block (up to 16 words) centered on the requested word into the cache.

To avoid the problem of one processor interfering with another's data and resulting inaccuracy of the data buffered in a processor's cache, the NuBus is monitored continuously. The cache state machine, in combination with the master interface, constantly checks the NuBus to determine whether any other processor is writing into a location represented in the cache. If so, it invalidates that location, thus both assuring reliable data and avoiding the need for cache sweeping—a fragile and unreliable method of cache verification.

Memory access occurs through a 2-level virtual paging system that employs three virtual-to-physical address maps to map 24-bit virtual addresses into addresses within physical memory in the NuBus. This paging implementation also supports an efficient garbage-collection algorithm, which reclaims static-memory areas less often than more volatile areas, thereby consuming less processing time.

The system's vectored interrupt system gives each device an address space in the interrupt slot, and assigns an address in software to each type of interrupt. Each interrupt's status is stored in a RAM, which is scanned to see if any device has requested an interrupt. When an interrupt request is found, scanning stops, thus preventing interrupts from being lost (new interrupts are still stored). No other interrupt is noted until the current one is serviced and cleared. Provision for both fast and slow interrupts provides a flexible interrupt environment.

Associated with the interrupt machine is the slave interface to the NuBus, used largely for diagnostic purposes. It communicates with the diagnostic logic. This logic includes a 4K x 16-bit microprogram-history RAM that holds the control memory addresses of the last 4096 microinstructions executed. For debugging, the system can be manually halted. It can also be programmed to halt in the event of a specified error or other condition, such as the execution of a given instruction a set number of times. At the time of the halt, the system's state is saved with no loss of information: the machine state is exactly as it was during the execution of the instruction that initiated the halt.

Diagnostic logic can then be used for unclocked transactions to trace machine state, or can single-step the system with user-generated clocks to track down possible timing problems. In combination with software debugging facilities, these diagnostic capabilities enable programmers to easily pinpoint and correct problems from the largest programs to the user-written microcode. The RG board also contains a high speed 16 x 16 matrix multiplier. This greatly speeds array referencing as well as simple arithmetic.

A macroinstruction program counter holds the address of the next macroinstruction to be executed. Since two consecutive instructions are usually used, two macroinstructions are fetched concurrently, packed into a single 32-bit word, and placed into the macroinstruction register. Macroinstruction decoding hardware allows a transfer to the appropriate microcode subroutine in a single operation, saving a significant amount of processing time.

Processor pipelining and virtual control store operation are governed by the microprogram counter and its associated logic. The logic tracks the options available when making or returning from a microinstruction subroutine call. This tracking prepares the machine for rapid execution of the next

COMPUTER DESIGN/November 1983

macroinstruction after it completes a microinstruction subroutine. A microcode subroutine-return stack, the 256-word microprogram stack, in addition to standard microinstruction addresses, contains extra control bits used to speed the execution of macroinstructions.

A virtual microcode paging implementation, the system's 64K x 64-bit virtual control store, is paged into a 16K x 64-bit physical control memory. A Lisp microcompiler allows programmers to write into the control store using Lisp, thus taking advantage of the language's productivity and editing facilities even while microprogramming.

The DP board performs actual data operations. Most significant design aspects for the execution of Lisp programs involve the scratchpad memory organization and some pipelining enhancements. The A scratchpad/dispatch memory holds multiway branch tables that are selected by a field in each dispatch microinstruction. In the M scratchpad memory, a 2K pointer-addressable RAM stores the top of the system stack, with hardware stack pointers. Due to Lisp's applicative, recursive nature, a large percentage of main memory references in the Lambda are to the stack, so this stack cache speeds up processing. Instruction modification logic associated with the control memory and microinstruction register supports relative addressing in the scratchpad memories. The L register stores information to be written back to the A or M scratchpad. This write is delayed until the beginning of the next microinstruction because of the Lambda's pipelined nature. If data in the L register are to be transferred from the A or M register (for use in the ALU) on that instruction, scratchpad memory is bypassed. Data are sent directly on and the scratchpad is updated from the L register.

Lisp as a tool

Multibus compatibility of the NuBus in the Lambda enables system integrators to take advantage of compatible products. Furthermore, the NuBus's multiprocessor capability aids in integrating Lisp into existing computing systems. An optional 68000-based processor, which implements a Berkeley-Unix environment, runs concurrently with the Lisp processor. The two computational environments are linked by a Streams/Pipes interface, based on the communication primitives of Lisp and Unix.

Serving as a backend processor to Lisp, the 68000 can allow current software to continue operating under the supervision of an evolving Lisp applications program. Conversely, the 68000 can act as a multi-user, multitasking front end to package and send requests to the Lisp processor, thus overcoming traditional limitations of the Lisp language.

The large programmable control store and the Lisp microcompiler allow the Lambda to be optimized for a given application by microcoding frequently called functions. This general purpose aspect of the Lambda design is likely to be extremely important to system integrators. For researchers, the microprogramming facilities are useful in emulating higher level language environments to aid in the design of advanced architectures. For example, the Lambda processor can be configured to perform Prolog-specific operations. (The Prolog logic programming language, based on Lisp, was chosen by the Japanese for their much publicized Fifth Generation Computer Project.) In addition, other machines' instruction sets can be emulated in microcode for efficient and flexible simulations.

Finally, the user of a device-independent bus such as the NuBus creates an open ended system. While a rigid computer architecture locks users into obsolescence, the NuBus's device independence concept permits processors, boards, and peripherals to be added as needs demand. Thus, Lisp machines can evolve along with user needs.

Architecture of the Symbolics 3600

David A. Moon
Symbolics, Inc.

Abstract

The Symbolics 3600 is a family of high-performance, single user computers optimized for the Lisp language and for interactive use. This paper briefly discusses some of the interesting aspects of the architecture, including the representation of data, the instruction set used for compiled code, the function calling discipline, and the way exception traps and interrupts are handled. The reader is assumed to have some previous exposure to the basic concepts of Lisp (4).

Introduction

The Symbolics 3600 is a family of high-performance, single user computers optimized for the Lisp language and for interactive use (1). The first 3600 was delivered in December 1982. The development of the architecture was based on experience with the original MIT Lisp Machine architecture (2) and a 2-year evaluation of the successes and failures of that pioneering architecture.

The 3600 is optimized for Lisp (3,4), but is designed to accomodate other languages as well, including symbolic languages such as Prolog, and conventional languages such as Fortran and Pascal. The architecture is designed to deliver performance comparable to a superminicomputer when running the conventional languages. Since the machine models assumed by the conventional languages are less powerful than the Lisp machine model, these languages are supported by a subset of the Lisp architecture. As an example, this paper briefly discusses the implementation of Pascal. The Prolog machine model is somewhat different; its architecture will be discussed in a companion paper (5).

Data are Object References

The fundamental form of data manipulated by any Lisp system is an *object reference*. The values of variables, the arguments to functions, the results of functions, and the elements of lists are all object references. An object reference designates a conceptual object. There can be more than one reference to a given object. Copying an object reference makes a new reference to the same object; it does not make a copy of the object.

Variables in Lisp and variables in conventional languages are fundamentally different. In Lisp, the value of a variable is an object reference, which can refer to an object of any type.

Variables do not intrinsically have types; the type of the object is encoded in the object reference. In a conventional language, assigning the value of one variable to another variable copies the object, possibly converts its type, and loses its identity.

A typical object reference contains the address of the representation in storage of the object. There can be several object references to a particular object, but it has only one stored representation. Side-effects to an object, such as changing the contents of one element of an array, are implemented by modifying the stored representation. All object references address the same stored representation, so they all see the side-effect.

In addition to such *object references by address*, it is possible to have an *immediate object reference*, which directly contains the entire representation of the object. The advantage is that no memory needs to be allocated when creating such an object. The disadvantage is that copying an immediate object reference effectively copies the object; thus immediate object references can only be used for object types that are not subject to meaningful side-effects, have a small representation, and need very efficient allocation of new objects. Small integers (traditionally called *fixnums*) and single-precision floating-point numbers are examples of such types.

In addition to immediate and by-address object references, the 3600 also offers *pointers*, a special kind of object reference that does not designate an object as such. A pointer designates a particular location within an object or a particular instruction within a compiled function. Pointers are used primarily for system programming (3).

In the 3600 architecture, an object reference is a 34-bit quantity consisting of a 32-bit data word and a 2-bit major data type tag. The tag determines the interpretation of the data word. Often the data word is broken down into a 4-bit minor data type tag and 28 bits used either as an address or as immediate data (see figure 1). Immediate object references are used for 32-bit integers, 32-bit floating-point numbers, and 28-bit characters. Addresses are 28 bits long. They designate 36-bit words in a virtual memory with 256-word pages.

Stored Representations of Objects

The stored representation of an object is contained in some

Reprinted from *The Proceedings of the 12th Annual International Symposium on Computer Architecture*, 1985, pages 76-83. Copyright © 1985 by The Institute of Electrical and Electronics Engineers, Inc.

Object References

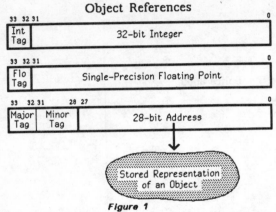

Figure 1

A String of Seven Characters: "Example"

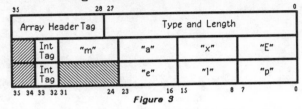

Figure 3

number of consecutive words of memory. Each word may contain an object reference, a *header*, a *special marker*, or a *forwarding pointer*. The data type tags distinguish these types of words. For example, an array is represented as a header word, containing such information as the length of the array, followed by one memory word for each element of the array, containing an object reference to the contents of that element (see figure 2). An object reference to the array contains the address of the first memory word in the stored representation of the array.

A *header* is the first word in the stored representation of most objects. A header marks the boundary between the stored representations of two objects and contains descriptive information about the object that it heads, which can be expressed as either immediate data or an address, as in an object reference.

A *special marker* indicates that the memory location containing it does not currently contain an object reference. Any attempt to read that location signals an error. The address field of a special marker specifies what kind of error should be signalled. For example, the value cell of an uninitialized variable contains a special marker that addresses the name of the variable. An attempt to use the value of a variable that has no value provokes an error message that includes the variable's name.

A *forwarding pointer* specifies that any reference to the location containing it should be redirected to another memory location, just as in postal forwarding. These are used for a number of internal bookkeeping purposes by the storage management software, including the implementation of extensible arrays.

Some objects include *packed data* in their stored

An Array of Three Elements: FOO, 259, BAR

Array Header Tag		Type and Length	
	Symbol Tag	Address ⟶ FOO	
	Int Tag	259	
	Symbol Tag	Address ⟶ BAR	

35   34 33 32 31   28 27   0

Figure 2

representation. For example, character strings store each character in a single 8-bit byte (see figure 3). This is more efficient than general arrays, which require an entire word for each element. Accessing the nth character of a string fetches the $n/4$th word of the string, extracts the $\mod(n,4)$th byte of that word, and constructs an object reference to the character whose code is equal to the contents of the byte. Machine instructions in compiled functions are stored in a similar packed form. For uniformity, the stored representation of an object containing packed data remains a sequence of object references. Each word is an immediate object reference to an integer, whose 32 bits are broken down into packed fields as required, such as four 8-bit bytes in the case of a character string.

A word in memory consists of 36 bits. 34 of these bits have already been explained. When a memory word contains a header or a machine instruction, the remaining two bits are used as an extension of the rest of the word. When a memory word contains an object reference, a special marker, or a forwarding pointer, the remaining two bits are called the *cdr code*. Conses and lists *(4, p.26)* are represented compactly by using the cdr code instead of a separate header to delimit the boundaries of these small objects and to encode common values of the CDR (see figures 4 and 5). The first word of the stored representation of a CONS contains an object reference to the CAR and a cdr-code that specifies the CDR, one of three values:

- cons: The second word contains an object reference to the CDR.
- next: The representation is one word. The CDR is a CONS whose representation is in the next memory

An Ordinary List of Two Elements

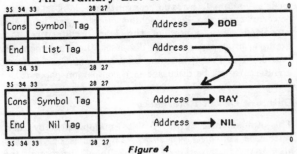

Figure 4

A Compact List of Two Elements

Next	Symbol Tag	Address ⟶ BOB
End	Symbol Tag	Address ⟶ RAY

35 34 33   28 27   0

Figure 5

location.

- end: The representation is one word. The CDR is NIL. If a CONS with a one-word representation is altered by the program in such a way that it now requires two words, a forwarding pointer redirects the original stored representation to the expanded representation.

Motivations of the Data Architecture

This system of object representation was designed to achieve the following goals:

Industry-standard 32-bit fixed-point and floating-point numbers are accomodated with a minimum of overhead (four bits). Floating-point numbers conform to the proposed IEEE P754 standard.

28-bit (rather than 32-bit) virtual addresses provide an adequate-sized virtual address space while freeing four bits for use as tags. The address granularity is a word, rather than a byte as used by many other machines, because the architecture is object-oriented and objects are always aligned on a word boundary. There is no undisciplined byte addressing of memory in this architecture; bytes exist only inside packed arrays. It is interesting to note that the 3600's 28-bit address can actually access the same number of usable words as the VAX's 32-bit address, because the VAX *(6)* expends two bits on byte addressing and reserves 3/4 of the remaining address space for the operating system kernel and the stack (neither of which is large).

Even when running Fortran, the 3600 deals strictly with tagged data. Other Lisp implementations have been complicated and slowed down by the need to deal with such untagged data as:

- *unboxed numbers* are numbers that occupy the entire machine word, with no tag bits left over. The 3600's 36-bit word accomodates a 32-bit number with room for a tag as well. The arithmetic hardware operates directly on this format, so there is no need ever to unbox a number.

- *alien structures* are untagged data structures defined by an operating system or an I/O device. Most I/O devices see the 3600 as a 32-bit machine; hardware automatically appends "fixnum" tags to the 32-bit word when accessing I/O buffers and memory-mapped I/O devices. The operating system is Lisp-based and always deals with tagged data. Alien structures such as directories in the file system are built out of 32-bit words and stored in memory with tags appended. The tags are not stored on the disk, so there is no loss of space efficiency.

- *compiled machine instructions*. The 3600 stores them with a "fixnum" tag.

- *the subroutine stack* is an alien structure in some systems, where it must conform to the conventions of a non-Lisp operating system or CALL instruction. That problem does not arise in the 3600, whose CALL instruction and operating system were designed for Lisp.

Tagging every word in memory produces these benefits:

- All data are self-describing and the information needed for full run-time checking of data types, array subscript bounds, undefined functions and variables, etc. is always available.

- It is possible to tell whether a data word contains an address or immediate data without referring to any context. Therefore a relocating garbage collector can easily change addresses as it moves objects, without changing numbers that were not intended to be interpeted as addresses.

- Given the address of any word in the stored representation of an object, by searching backwards for a *Header* tag or an *End* cdr code it is possible to recover the address and size of the stored representation along with an object reference to the object.

- It is possible to implement hardware to assist the garbage collector *(7)*, since the data structures it must understand are simple and local.

- The garbage collector can scan through memory for interesting object references without worrying about boundaries between stored representations of objects, nor about the particular types of objects represented.

- The garbage collector can relocate an object given only the address of any word in the stored representation of the object.

Instructions

The 3600 architecture includes an *instruction set* which is produced by the compilers and executed by a combination of hardware and firmware. All instructions are 17 bits long, consisting of a 9-bit *operation* field and an 8-bit *argument* field. Instructions are packed two per word.

Every instruction is contained in a *compiled function*, which serves as its static context. A compiled function has some fixed overhead, a table of constants, and compiled code consisting of a sequence of instructions (see figure 6). The table of constants contains object references to objects used

A Compiled Function

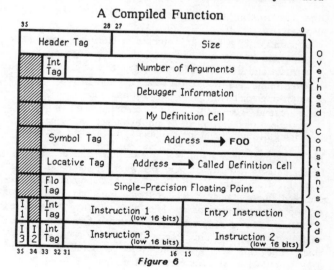

Figure 6

by the instructions, including LOCATIVE pointers to definition cells of functions called by this function. Indirection through the definition cell ensures that if a function is redefined its callers are automatically linked to the new definition.

The dynamic context of instruction execution is the *current stack frame*. The push-down stack is divided into frames; each function call creates a new frame. The current frame contains the arguments, local variables, and temporary storage of the current function. The top of the stack moves up and down as local variables and temporary results are allocated and deallocated. Instructions operate in a stack machine model: Many instructions pop their operands off the stack and push their results onto the stack. In addition to these 0-address instructions, there are 1-address instructions, which can address any location in the current stack frame. In this way the local variables of the current stack frame serve the purpose of registers in a general-register machine. The 1-address instructions include data movement instructions, which move data between the top of the stack and the addressed location, and multioperand instructions, which pop all of their operands except the last off the stack and take their last operand from a location in the current stack frame.

Instruction Classes

There are several classes of instructions; each uses *argument* in a different way. The first group of instruction classes develop a memory address by adding *argument* to a base address, one of:
- the beginning of the current stack frame.
- the end of the current stack frame.
- the beginning of the lexical parent's stack frame.
- the lexical parent's environment captured in a closure.
- the current function's constants table.
- the current function's constants table, with indirect addressing.
- an array used as a DEFSTRUCT structure.
- a flavor instance (with either direct or mapped indexing).
- the address of the current instruction.

Other instruction classes use *argument* for non-address purposes:
- to specify a byte field any number of bits wide, positioned anywhere within a 32-bit word. This specification takes ten bits and hence overflows into two bits of *operation*.
- as an immediate integer between -128 and 127.
- as an immediate integer between 0 and 255.
- to extend *operation*. Two distinguished values of *operation* use *argument* as an extended *operation* field, adding 510 additional instructions to the instruction set.

Many instructions are simply Lisp functions that are directly implemented by hardware and firmware, rather than being built up from other Lisp functions and implemented as compiled instructions. These Lisp functions and their corresponding instructions are known as *builtins*. They take a fixed number of arguments and return a fixed number of values on the stack. The arguments normally come from the stack, but the last argument can be specified by the *argument* field of the instruction as an immediate or as an address in the current stack frame, in some cases. Examples

of builtins are EQ, SYMBOLP, LOGAND (with two arguments), CAR, CONS, and MEMBER *(4)*.

Motivations of the Instruction Architecture

The goals of this instruction set design were three-fold, in descending order of priority: *functionality*, *simplicity*, and *performance*.

Functionality

The Symbolics Lisp language demands *generic* instructions. For example, the ADD instruction is capable of adding any two numbers regardless of their data types. User programs need not know ahead of time what type of numbers they will be adding, and users need no declarations to achieve efficiency when using only the fastest types of numbers. Automatic conversion between data types occurs when the two operands of ADD are not of the same type.

A flexible architecture, with plenty of spare operations in the instruction set and the ability to change the architecture at each major software release, leaves room to add support for non-Lisp languages and to make performance enhancements.

Compiler Simplicity

Making the compiler simple makes it fast, which is important in an interactive program development environment where compilation is very frequent and ought to appear instantaneous to the user. The architecture makes the compiler simpler by minimizing the number of nontrivial choices it has to make. The stack orientation avoids register allocation. Using only a single-address instruction format and avoiding the temptation of multiple ways to do the same thing presents the code generator with fewer choices.

We do use peephole optimization, which can be done quickly and without conceptual impact on the rest of the compiler, to make local choices. For example, the ADD instruction comes in three versions: with both operands on the stack, with the first operand on the stack and the second operand in an addressible location, and with the first operand on the stack and the second operand an immediate constant. The first version is the most general; the other versions are only known about by a peephole optimizer that is driven by a table of available instructions. Compilation of calls to builtin functions as instructions rather than function calls is also driven by peephole optimization.

Compiler simplicity is also enhanced just by using an instruction set designed for Lisp rather than adapting one designed for Fortran or for hand-crafted assembly language. 3600 instructions always check for errors and exceptions, so the compiler doesn't have to emit extra instructions to do that and then decide whether it is safe to optimize them out. Instructions operate on tagged data, so the compiler doesn't have to generate code to insert and remove tags. Instructions are generic, so the compiler doesn't have to keep track of declarations, select type-specific instructions, and translate between data formats.

Hardware Simplicity

The instruction architecture promotes hardware simplicity by having fixed length instructions, using only a single address, and having only four classes directly known to the hardware (*argument* contains immediate data, *argument* addresses the current stack frame from either end, and *argument* extends *operation*). There are no multiple fields to be decoded; instruction decoding is performed by a single microcode dispatch on the *operation* field. The instructions are designed to be executed by a short 3-stage pipeline.

The single-address instruction format sometimes entails extra data-movement instructions, for example to push operands on the stack before operating on them. Without a substantial amount of duplicate hardware, multiple-address instructions would require an extra clock cycle for each address. Since PUSH instructions are executed in a single cycle, the single-address architecture is just as fast. The compiler tries to avoid data movement through some simple optimizations, such as peephole optimizations and allocating a local variable to the place in the stack where its value is initially produced.

Unlike many machines, the 3600 does not have indexed and indirect addressing modes. These are replaced by structured, object-oriented operations such as subscripting an array and fetching the CAR of a list. This fits the instruction set more closely to the needs of Lisp and at the same time simplifies the hardware.

Performance

The performance goals for instructions are two: *code density* and *execution speed*. Dense code decreases paging overhead by making programs smaller and simplifies the memory system by decreasing the ratio of required instruction fetch bandwidth (in words/second) to processor cycle speed (in instructions/second). Packing two instructions per word provides adequate code density.

There are three categories of instructions in the 3600: *simple*, *memory-reference*, and *complex*, each with its own execution speed goal. Simple instructions such as data movement, arithmetic, logical, and byte-field instructions involve only one major hardware operation. They are executed in a single clock cycle (about 200 ns). Memory-reference instructions include Lisp operations such as CAR and AREF, nonlocal variable references, and branches. They are limited mainly by the speed of the memory; CAR (the fastest) takes four clock cycles. Complex instructions involve multiple major hardware operations. Examples are CALL, RETURN, the Common Lisp MEMBER function, certain housekeeping instructions, and simple or memory-reference instructions discovered to be complex at run time because of an exceptional condition such as the data type of the operands. Complex instructions invoke microcode subroutines; their speed depends on the number of microinstructions that need to be executed. A wide microinstruction word and fast microcode branching minimize this number.

The performance goal for simple instructions was not completely achieved in current members of the 3600 family. These machines do not simultaneously fetch and execute instructions, so a 1.25 cycle (average) instruction fetch delay must be added to the execution time of all instructions. The net decrease in performance is only about 30%, since typical programs spend most of their time executing the slower memory-reference and complex instructions. Future members of the family will fetch instructions from memory in parallel with execution of previous instructions.

Executing an Example Instruction

When executing a simple instruction, ADD for example, all of the following activities take place in parallel.

- The stack buffer fetches the two operands, from a register that always contains a copy of the top item in the stack and from a memory location calculated by adding *argument* to a base register.

- The fixed-point arithmetic unit computes the 32-bit sum of the operands and checks for overflow. This result is only used if both operands are fixnums.

- The optional floating-point arithmetic unit, if present, starts computing the sum of the operands and checking for floating-point exceptions. This result is only used if both operands are single-floats.

- The type-checking unit checks the data types of the operands.

- The stack buffer accepts the result from the fixed-point arithmetic unit, adjusts the stack pointer, and stores the result at the new top of the stack.

- The sequencer decodes the next instruction and produces the microinstruction that will control its execution. The sequencer diverts control to an exception handler if the selected arithmetic unit or the type-checking unit signals an exception or if the next instruction has not yet been fetched from memory.

When the operands of ADD are not both fixnums, executing the instruction takes more than one machine cycle and more than one microinstruction. In the case of adding two single-floats, the extra time is only required because the floating-point arithmetic unit is slower than the fixed-point arithmetic unit. In other cases, extra time is required to convert the operands to a common format, to do double-precision floating-point operations, or to trap to a Lisp function to ADD numbers of the less common types.

Function Call

Storage whose lifetime is known to end when a function returns (or is exited abnormally) is allocated in three stacks, rather than in the main object storage heap, to increase efficiency. The *control stack* contains function-nesting information, arguments, local variables, function return values, small stack-allocated temporary objects, and miscellaneous control information. The *binding stack* records dynamically bound variables *(4, p.55)*. The *data stack* contains stack-allocated temporary objects. This paper concentrates on the control stack, which is the most critical to performance.

The protocol for calling a function is to push the arguments onto the stack, then execute a CALL instruction which specifies the function to be called, the number of arguments, and what to do with the values returned by the function.

When the function returns, the arguments have been popped off the stack and the values (if wanted) have been pushed on. Note the similarity in interface between functions and instructions, especially builtin instructions.

Every time a function is called, a new stack frame is built on the control stack. A stack frame consists of the caller's copy of the arguments, five header words, the callee's copy of the arguments, local variables, and temporary storage, including arguments being prepared for calling the next function (see figure 7). The current stack frame is delimited by the frame-pointer (FP) and stack-pointer (SP) registers. FP contains the address of the first argument (in the callee's copy). SP contains the address of the last word in the stack frame. Since the current stack frame is always the topmost frame in the stack, SP also contains the address of the last word in the whole stack. The FP and SP registers are available as base registers in instructions that use their *argument* field to address locations in the current stack frame. The program-counter (PC) register always contains the address of the instruction currently being executed.

The header of a stack frame saves the registers of the caller (FP, SP, and PC) and describes the frame by specifying the function running in that frame, the number of arguments passed to the function and their arrangement in storage, where to put the return values (the *value disposition*), special actions to be taken when the function returns (the *cleanup bits*), and *instruction state* bits used by complex instructions executing in this frame. Note that the saved SP points below the caller's copy of the arguments, since they disappear from the stack when control returns to the caller.

To speed access to the control stack, the top several (up to four) virtual-memory pages of the stack are held in a dedicated fast-access memory known as the stack buffer. The stack buffer contains all of the current frame plus as many older frames as happen to fit. When the stack buffer fills up (during CALL), the oldest page spills into normal memory to make room for the new frame. When the stack buffer becomes empty (during RETURN), pages move from normal memory back into the stack buffer until the frame being returned to is entirely in the buffer. Associated with

the stack buffer are the FP and SP registers and the hardware for addressing locations in the current stack frame via the *argument* field of an instruction.

A compiled function starts with a sequence of one or more instructions known as the *entry vector*. The first instruction in the entry vector, the *entry instruction*, describes how many arguments the function accepts, the layout of the entry vector, and the size of the function's constants table (see figure 6), and tells the CALL instruction where in the entry vector to transfer control. The CALL instruction and the entry vector cooperate to copy the arguments to the top of the stack (creating the callee's copy), convert their arrangement in storage if required, supply default values for optional arguments that the caller does not pass, handle the &REST and APPLY features of Common Lisp, and signal an error if too many or too few arguments were supplied. The details are beyond the scope of this paper.

Function Return

A function returns by executing a RETURN instruction whose operands are the values to be returned. Abnormal exits from a frame, for instance via THROW *(4)*, also use the RETURN instruction but modify the caller's saved PC.

RETURN removes the current frame from the stack and makes the caller's frame current, by restoring the saved FP, SP, and PC registers. It then obeys the *value disposition* in the frame header, which says what to do with the values being returned. There are four possibilities:
- call for effect: discard the values.
- call for one value: push the first value on the caller's stack and discard the rest.
- call for multiple values: push all the values on the caller's stack and then push the number of values (as an object reference to an integer, of course). When control returns to the caller, it executes a TAKE-VALUES instruction, which converts the values to the form desired by the caller, typically by defaulting missing values or discarding excess values; an alternate form of TAKE-VALUES forms a list of the values.
- call for return: return all the values from the caller to its caller.

If the *cleanup bits* in the current frame are nonzero, special action must be taken before the frame can be removed. RETURN takes this action, clears the bit, and tries again. Cleanup bits are used to pop corresponding frames from the binding and data stacks, for UNWIND-PROTECT *(4)*, for debugging and metering purposes, and for internal housekeeping.

Motivations of the Function Call Discipline

The motivations for this particular function calling discipline are several:
- to implement full Common Lisp function calling efficiently
- to be fast, so that programmers will write clear programs
- to retain complete information for the Debugger
- to be simple for the compiler

To implement full Common Lisp function calling efficiently

A Stack Frame

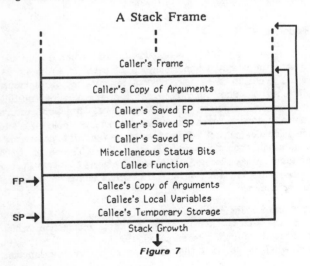

Figure 7

requires matching up the arguments supplied by the caller with normal function calling or with APPLY to the normal, &OPTIONAL, and &REST parameters of the callee, and generating default values for unsupplied optional arguments. The entry vector takes care of this. Common Lisp's &KEY parameters are implemented by accepting an &REST parameter containing the keywords and values, then using a TAKE-KEYWORD-ARGUMENT instruction to search the list for each &KEY parameter. Multiple values are passed back to the caller via the stack; the TAKE-VALUES instruction reconciles the number of values returned with the number of values wanted.

Function calling historically has been a major bottleneck in Lisp implementations, both on stack hardware and on specially-designed Lisp machines. It is important for function calling to be as fast as possible; if it is not, efficiency-minded programmers will distort their programming styles to avoid function calling, producing code that is hard to maintain and wasting a lot of time doing hand optimization that should have been taken care of by the Lisp implementation itself. The 3600's function call mechanism attains great speed (fewer than 20 clock cycles for a function call and return when no exceptions occur) by using a stack buffer to minimize the number of memory references required, by optimizing the stack frame layout to maximize speed rather than to minimize space, by arranging for the checks for slower exception cases to be fast (for example, RETURN simply checks whether the cleanup bits are nonzero), and by using the entry vector mechanism to simplify run-time decision-making.

The information that the Debugger can extract from a stack frame includes the address of the previous frame (from the saved FP in the header), the function running in that frame (from the header), the current instruction in that function (from the PC saved in the next frame), the arguments (from the stack; the header specifies the argument count and arrangement), the local variables (from the stack), and the names of the arguments and local variables (from a table created by the compiler and attached to the function).

The compiler is kept simple because there is only a single calling sequence. Any CALL can call any function, and the argument patterns are matched up at run time. Everything is in the stack and no register-saving conventions are required, since there are no general-purpose registers.

Exception Traps and Interrupts

Many exceptional conditions in the 3600 are handled by trapping to a Lisp function provided to handle the exception. Such exceptions include page faults, arithmetic operations on types of numbers that are not supported by hardware or firmware, transport traps for the garbage collector, stack overflows and other errors, debugging and metering traps, and I/O interrupts. Many of these conditions are detected in the middle of the execution of an instruction; how can the exception be handled cleanly and control be returned to the interrupted program afterwards?

The key is enforcing a clean separation between the microcode machine and the machine model seen by compiled

Lisp functions. The state of the microcode machine is backed up to a clean point, between Lisp instructions, as if the instruction that encountered the exception was never started. The PC and SP registers and the contents of the stack are restored to their values at the start of the instruction. This operation of backing up to a clean state is called *pclsring*, in a tradition derived from the ITS operating system *(8, pp.11-13)*. The word originally was an abbreviation for "restoring the program *(pc)* to user *(lsr)* state."

A page fault, for example, backs up the instruction to its beginning and calls the page fault handler function with two arguments, the address being referenced and whether it was read or written. When the handler returns, the instruction that faulted is retried. An ADD of two large integers is a different case, since retrying the instruction will do no good. The exception advances PC past the ADD instruction and calls the "bignum" addition function with the operands of the ADD as its arguments. When the exception handler returns, it pushes the sum on the stack and the desired effect of the ADD instruction has been achieved.

Such a simple and clean mechanism is not adequate for the complex instructions. These instructions typically make many memory references, and if the instruction were backed up to its beginning each time it got an exception, it might never run to completion. Therefore it is necessary to be able to interrupt a complex instruction in the middle while maintaining a clean interface. There are three ways to do this; an example of each follows.

Updating the Arguments

The builtin instruction MEMBER searches a list for a particular element. Each memory access might cause an exception, such as a page fault or a transport trap. The list might be circular, therefore it is essential to allow interrupts so that a runaway program can be stopped. MEMBER takes two arguments on the stack and pops them off when it is done, so the content of these stack locations while MEMBER is executing is not part of the instruction's contract. Each time MEMBER advances to a new element of the list, it updates its list argument to refer to the next part of the list. If the state of the instruction is backed up by a trap or interrupt, it will restart from the current element of the list, because the argument has been updated. This is a clean interface that requires no special care to restart the instruction after it has been interrupted.

Instruction State Bit

The BITBLT graphics operation (also known as RasterOp) modifies one array in memory as a function of its old contents and the contents of another array in memory. The inner loop of this operation is provided as an instruction that accesses memory in eight-word blocks for extra speed. The instruction is difficult to interrupt and restart because part of a memory block might have already been modified. This is solved by keeping a copy of the current memory block in a buffer on the stack and maintaining an *instruction state* bit, in the stack frame header, that says whether the buffer is valid. This bit is normally 0, but is set to 1 if the instruction is interrupted after a block has been copied into the buffer and modified in memory. Later, the instruction knows it is being restarted because the bit is nonzero, so it recovers its state from the buffer and clears the bit. A few other complex instructions also use this bit.

Completing the Instruction

The CALL instruction builds a new stack frame and then examines the type of function that was called and the number of arguments it accepts. In addition to errors, such as wrong number of arguments or stack overflow, a variety of recoverable exceptions, such as page faults and transport traps, can occur after the frame has been built. Backing up the instruction to its beginning would require undoing the building of the new frame, which would be complicated. Instead, CALL pretends that it successfully completed, but sets the PC to point to a special instruction, RESTART-TRAPPED-CALL, instead of the first instruction of the function that was called. When the exception handler returns, the RESTART-TRAPPED-CALL is executed; it continues the function-calling operation. The interface remains clean, because there is no special case in any exception handler for interrupting out of the middle of a function call. The complete state of the function call is encoded in the PC and the contents of the stack.

The Pascal Machine Model

The 3600 Pascal implementation maps into a subset of the machine model used by Lisp. We briefly discuss data representation, procedure calling, and instructions.

Pascal data types can be divided into four kinds: single-word scalars, multi-word scalars, composites, and packed data. Single-word scalars map directly into Lisp data types: INTEGER, subranges of INTEGER, BOOLEAN, and enumerated types map into Lisp integers. SHORTREAL maps into Lisp single-floats. Pascal pointers map into Lisp object references: arrays, LOCATIVE pointers to elements of arrays, or LOCATIVE pointers to local variables in the stack.

Multi-word scalar types include REAL, COMPLEX, and ROUTINE. These map into multiple Lisp objects; for example, a Pascal REAL variable is compiled as two Lisp variables containing integers. Each integer contains 32 bits of the 64-bit double-precision floating-point number.

Composites include arrays, records, sets, and strings. A large composite (longer than one word) maps into a Lisp array whose elements are its words. A small composite's single word stands alone, except in some subtle cases involving pointers and parameter passing. Thus a SET of 32 or fewer possible elements is an integer, while a larger SET is an array of integers with 32 bits in each. When a composite contains other composites, for example a record containing two arrays, the outermost composite maps into a Lisp array of sufficient size and the inner composites map into portions of that array.

Packed data inside composites are packed into integers, with up to 32 bits in each integer. Thus a string of more than 4 characters maps into an array of integers, with 4 characters in each.

Lisp integers that fit in 32 bits are implemented by immediate object references on the 3600. Hence if only the low 32 bits of each word are considered, Pascal's data representation is much the same as on a conventional machine. The tag bits add some advantages, such as uninitialized variable detection, automatic reclamation of unused storage, automatic bounds checking when heap-allocated storage is accessed, and very compact representation of debugging information used by tools in the Pascal programming environment.

Pascal uses Lisp storage allocation for its heap. A heap-allocated value is enclosed in a Lisp array with as many elements as there are words in the value. Thus Pascal's NEW is Lisp's MAKE-ARRAY and Pascal's DISPOSE is ignored, since the Lisp garbage collector takes care of that.

Pascal procedure and function calling map directly into Lisp function calling. The Lisp arguments are used like registers; thus passing a REAL by value takes two Lisp arguments. The display is passed as an extra argument, just as Pascal on a conventional machine would pass it in an extra register.

Pascal compiles into a subset of the instructions used by Lisp. The array-accessing instructions are used extensively for memory referencing. The byte-extraction instructions access packed data. The generic arithmetic instructions are used for arithmetic on INTEGERs and SHORTREALs; this gives Pascal the same arbitrary-precision integers as Lisp. Arithmetic on REALs uses subprimitive instructions that operate on double-precision floating-point numbers represented as pairs of integers.

References

1. *3600 Technical Summary*, Symbolics Inc, 1983.

2. R.D. Greenblatt et al. "The LISP Machine", *Interactive Programming Environments*, D.R. Barstow, H.E. Shrobe, E. Sandewall, eds. McGraw-Hill, 1984.

3. *Reference Guide to Symbolics-Lisp*, Symbolics Inc, 1985.

4. G.L. Steele. *Common Lisp*, Digital Press, 1984.

5. R.A. Cassels, D.A. Moon, in preparation.

6. *VAX-11 Architecture Reference Manual*, Digital Equipment Corporation, 1982.

7. D.A. Moon. "Garbage Collection in a Large Lisp System", *1984 ACM Symposium on Lisp and Functional Programming*, pp. 235-246.

8. D.E. Eastlake. *ITS Status Report*, AI Memo 238, MIT Artificial Intelligence Laboratory, 1972.

ALPHA : A HIGH-PERFORMANCE LISP MACHIE EQUIPPED WITH A NEW STACK STRUCTURE AND GARBAGE COLLECTION SYSTEM

HIROMU HAYASHI, AKIRA HATTORI, AND HARUO AKIMOTO

FUJITSU LABORATORIES LTD.
1015 KAMIKODANAKA,NAKAHARA-KU
KAWASAKI 211,JAPAN

ABSTRACT

ALPHA is a dedicated machine designed for high-speed list processing. In this article, we describe a highly effective stack which can support a value cache and virtual stack, and high-speed garbage collection algorithm for virtual memory. These new ideas have been studied in ALPHA. ALPHA is designed as a back end processor for a large computer under TSS. ALPHA allows TSS users to do more high-speed list processing than a large computer does.

Currently UTILISP is operating on ALPHA and runs several times faster than MACLISP on the DEC 2060.

INTRODUCTION

LISP has been widely used in the artificial intelligence area for quite some time. However many people have been frustrated by the response times when they develop application programs using LISP on a large TSS System. This is because LISP requires frequent list operations and a large cell space. To solve this problem, super personal LISP machines have been designed and shipped by some makers [1],[2],[3].

We are working to solve this same problem in the TSS system because it is necessary to use the existing software on a large system. The dedicated list-processing hardware is designed to be attached to a large computer system - a FUJITSU M-series machine. This machine is called "ALPHA". ALPHA differs from previously developed machines by having a new hardware stack and garbage collection method for virtual memory. The hardware stack can support high speed access to free variables and high-speed process switching.

The paper has three sections. We begin by describing an ALPHA hardware stack. We then discuss a new garbage collection method which is the most important point of this paper. Next, we present the details of ALPHA's hardware and performance.

The LISP language running on ALPHA is UTILISP[10], which was implemented by Tokyo University and is similar to MACLISP. UTILISP currently runs on ALPHA several times faster than MACLISP does on the DEC 2060.

STACK STRUCTURE

Stacks are very effective in high-level language machines. The stack structure used in block-structured languages - Algol, PL/I, Pascal, was described in detail by Organick[4]. In this section, the hardware stack structure used in ALPHA will be described. The stack is used for the environment save area and the functions work area. To use the hardware stack effectively in a LISP machine, the following problems must be solved.

(1) Fast evaluation of functions

There are many kinds of functions (list, macro code, micro code) in a LISP machine. Variables and arguments used in a function are stored in different locations of cell space or stack according to the function type. It takes a great deal of time to search for free variables in cell space, especially when the variables are deep-bound. To attain fast evaluation of functions, the variables must be located in stack, and must be searched for at high speeds.

(2) Supporting multi-processes

The multi-process mechanism is necessary for real time application and improvement of the user interface. Process switching time is the most important factor in implementing the multi-process mechanism. The use of only one hardware stack always requires swapping between the stack and main memory when process switching occurs. Thus,a one-stack architecture causes the process switching time to increase.

To solve these problems in ALPHA, the value cache and the virtual stack have been studied.

Value cache

The logical stack structure of ALPHA is shown in Figure 1. Several pointers are used for addressing the stack. STP(Stack Top Pointer) points to the top of the stack. A function is executed under its own frame where the machine control status and arguments are stored. The frame is generated when a function is called and is deleted when a function returns. Name(Function name),MPC(Micro Program Counter),FP(Frame Pointer), PC(Macro Program Counter) and arguments(number and value,or number,name and value) are saved and stored in the frame. FP indicates the start point of the current frame.

We consider the search mechanism for free variables in this stack structure shown in Figure 1. Functions F1,F2,and F3 are assumed to be nested as shown in Figure 2a. F1 calls F2 and F2 calls F3. Arguments X,Y and Z defined in F1 are used in F2 and F3. The stack structure is shown in Figure 2b when F3 is called, and the current frame is F3's. Variable X and Y are searched for through the Link Area, which means MPCS,FPS,and PCS. The values of X and Y are found in the frame of F1. As the nested level of functions is deeper, the time required to search for variables increases.

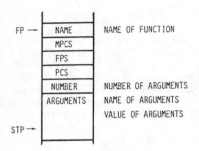

Figure 1. Stack Structure

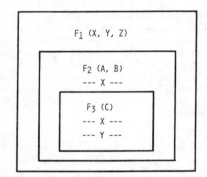

Figure 2a. Block Structure of Functions

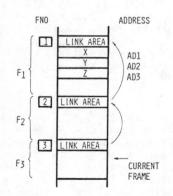

Figure 2b. Stack operation

To improve performance,a value cache has been introduced. A value cache is an associative memory with a special control mechanism. An entry in the value cache is illustrated in Figure 2c. V(Valid Bit) and FNO(Frame Number) control the value cache. The value cache control hardware is shown in Figure 2d. In searching for variables,the value cache is checked first. It is addressed by hashing hardware using the variable name. If a variable is found in the value cache, the value of the variable is obtained immediately. If the variable cannot be found in the value cache, all of the frames on the stack are searched. If the variable is found in a frame, the name,the frame number which indicates a function, and address pointer of the variable are stored in the entry of value cache, and the valid bit is set. When a new function is called, it checks whether names of the arguments and variables used in the new function are contained in the value cache. If the same name exists, the valid bit of the entry is reset. When a called function returns, the frame number of each entry is compared with the current frame number. If the current frame number is the same as the frame number of the entry, the valid bit is reset. The value cache is effective when deep-binding method is used, but is useless when shallow-binding method is applied. We can expect the high-speed evaluation of functions in ALPHA by means of a value cache.

V	FNO	NAME	ADDRESS
0			
1	1	X	AD1
1	1	Y	AD2
0			

V	: VALID BIT	(1 BIT)
FNO	: FRAME NUMBER	(6 BITS)
NAME	: NAME OF FREE VARIABLE	(19 BITS)
ADDRESS	: STACK ADDRESS OF VARIABLE	(16 BITS)

Figure 2c. Value Cache Entry

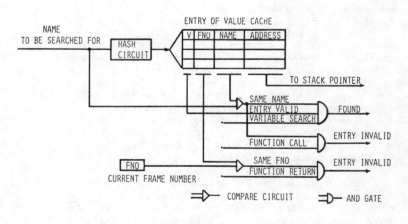

Figure 2d. Control Hardware of Value Cache

A value cache with eight entries has been designed for ALPHA. Currently,however,the value cache is not operating because UTILISP is implemented on ALPHA by the shallow-binding method.

Virtual stack

The hardware stack has many points of superiority compared with the cache memory:

(1) High speed access
(2) Simple control mechanism
(3) Reducing memory access

The one disadvantage is that it takes a lot of time to switch processes. This is caused by the swapping operation between the hardware stack (physical stack) and main memory (logical stack). To decrease the swapping overhead ,a virtual stack architecture was introduced in ALPHA. The hardware stack is divided into many blocks; each block can be shared by many processes, and blocks are assigned dynamically. Virtual stack operation is shown in Figure 3. In this situation, processes A,B,and C can be switched without any overhead. A virtual stack also has good performance when one process uses a large logical stack area. Most-recently-used logical blocks exist in the hardware stack. Swapping overhead appears only when frequent process switching and high-speed expansion and compression of the logical stack occur.

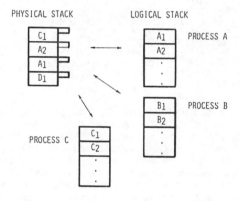

Figure 3. Virtual Stack Operation

The stack control circuit is shown in Figures 4a and 4b. Figure 4a illustrates the PTR(Stack Pointer) circuit and Figure 4b illustrates the logical-physical stack address translation circuit. A logical stack pointer is stored in the PTR before an actual stack operation occurs, and is checked to determine whether the address stored in the PTR is available on the physical stack. If the LN (Logical Block Number) of a logical stack pointer is the same as the LN in the PTR, V (Valid Bit) is set. V indicates whether the logical block indicated by the PTR is located in physical blocks. If the LN of a logical stack pointer is different from the LN already in the PTR, V is reset. This causes an interruption when the actual stack operation is issued.

The interrupt handler has a translation circuit start to get the PN (Physical Block Number) corresponding to the LN. The stack tag entry corresponds to the physical block. Each tag has V (Valid Bit), LSN (Logical Stack Number), and the LN. LSN is the process number. Once dynamic ad-dress translation is started, the current LSN and LN are compared with those in each tag, and V is checked. When there is no PN corresponding to the LN, the LRU (Least Recently Used) circuit generates a new PN and the interrupt handler starts the swapping operation. When the logical stack pointer decreases, and goes across the block boundary, the used logical block will be invalidated. ALPHA has four physical blocks; the block size is 2k words.

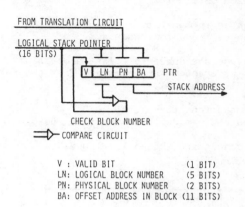

V : VALID BIT (1 BIT)
LN: LOGICAL BLOCK NUMBER (5 BITS)
PN: PHYSICAL BLOCK NUMBER (2 BITS)
BA: OFFSET ADDRESS IN BLOCK (11 BITS)

Figure 4a. Stack Pointer Circuit

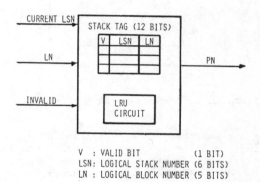

V : VALID BIT (1 BIT)
LSN: LOGICAL STACK NUMBER (6 BITS)
LN : LOGICAL BLOCK NUMBER (5 BITS)

Figure 4b. Translation Circuit

GARBAGE COLLECTION FOR VIRTUAL MEMORY

LISP performance is determined by the list processing speed and the efficiency of garbage collection. Real time garbage collection plays an important role, especially in real-time applications. Real time garbage collection methods are classified into three standard methods: one is the scheme using the trace-and-mark method [5], the copying method [6],[7],[8] and the reference count scheme [9]. The garbage collector described in [7] varies the rate of the copying operation according to the generation of the regions. In the method described in [8], the space is divided into subspaces and the copying operation on a subspace is executed by using a inter-subspace reference list for each subspace. However, these methods cannot reduce the overhead in a virtual memory system.

We have introduced a new garbage collection

method in which the cell space is divided into sub-spaces, and the reference count is used not for re-claiming each cell, but for reclaiming the sub-space. That is, the reference count is used only to identify the cells of the subspace directly referenced from outside the space.

To localize the garbage collection, the fol-lowing references are included in the reference count in each cell:

(1) References from cells in other subspaces
(2) References from atom-headers.

To reduce the burden of list processing, the following references are excluded from the refer-ence count in each cell.

(1) References from the stack
(2) References from cells in the same subspace

These references are showed in Figure 5.

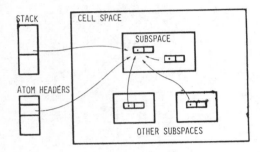

Figure 5. Reference Source to a Cell

When one subspace is reclaimed and a recalimed cell points to other subspace, the reference count of the target cell in other subspace must be decre-mented by one. If the pointed subspace is not in real memory, page-in operation is required. To lo-calize the garbage collection in real memory, a MRT(Multi-Reference-Table) has been introduced. It is used for delaying the update operation of the reference count of the target cell in secodary memory. The update amount of that reference count is placed in the MRT. This is added to the refer-ence count of the target cell when the subspace containing that cell is paged in real memory. The MRT is also used for containing the overflowed amount of the reference count as described in [9]. This method,thus,allows the garbage collection to run only on real memory, and page faults during the garbage collection do not occur. The marking and reclamation operation of this method is described in Appendix.

In this scheme, the active cells in a sub-space, can be traced and marked from the words on the stack which point into a subspace and from the cells in a subspace whose reference count is not zero. The garbage cells whose mark bit is off can be appended to the free list of a subspace. The garbage collector is started when the number of free cells in the free-page-list goes below a

specified value, or when there is no ready process because of I/O-wait, etc. Figure 6 shows the state transition of pages in a cell space. Once started, the garbage collector reclaims the first real page in the garbage-page-list, and the garbage collector appends the page to either the tail of the free-page-list, or to the tail of the garbage-page-list, according to the number of reclaimed cells, as shown in Figure 6. When reclaiming a virtual page in the garbage-page-list, the page is paged in and reclaimed. The function CONS gets a cell from the free-cell-list in the first page of the free-page-list. CONS appends the page to the tail of the garbage-page-list when it runs out of free cells.

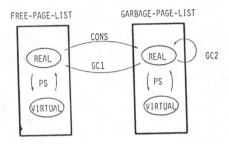

GC1: GARBAGE COLLECTOR RECLAIMING MORE CELLS
     THAN SPECIFIED NUMBER
GC2: GARBAGE COLLECTOR RECLAIMING LESS CELLS
     THAN SPECIFIED NUMBER
PS : PAGING SUPERVISOR

Figure 6. State Transition of Pages

It takes a great deal of time to swap pages in virtual memory. This is a critical factor when a garbage collector is operating. We use the RER (Reclamation Efficiency Ratio) and RTR (Reclamation Time Ratio) to evaluate the garbage collection method in virtual memory. Reclamation efficiency and reclamation time are defined as the number of reclaimed cells per unit time and the run time of one non-divisible garbage collection operation, respectively.

In this paper RER and RTR mean ratio of this proposed method to the trace-and-mark method. Their values vary according to the R/V (Ratio of Real memory size to Virtual memory size) and the ratio of active cells to total cells. The trace-and-mark method on virtual memory requires swapping each page twice. This method operates most effec-tively when the necessary cells are reclaimed only in real memory. This situation is presented by RER1. As the ratio of active cells increase, the reclamation operation causes a page to be swapped. RER2 presents this situation. The reclamation time is in proportion to the size of the cell space. RTR1 and RTR2 correspond to RER1 and RER2, respec-tively. These value are presented as follows.

$$PER1= \frac{Mt+2T(1-R/V)/N}{Mr}$$

$$PER2= \frac{Mt+2T(1-R/V)/N}{Mr+T(1-R/V)/N}$$

$$PTR1=S \times PER1$$

$$PTR2=S \times PER2$$

where Mt : References/cell in
            trace-and-mark method
       Mr : References/cell in
            the proposed method
       T : Disk access Time /
            Memory access time
       N : Cells in the subspace
       S : Subspace size
            (Total space/subspace)

RER and RTR are shown in Figure 7. These values were calculated under the condition that Mt=3, Mr=4, T=50,000, N=512, and S=4,000. Our proposed method shows that one unit operation of garbage collection is very short, and it is effective in real time application.

The advantages of this method are as follows.

(1) In the virtual memory, this garbage collector can select the subspace to reclaim among the real memory, so it can avoid page faults.
(2) Because it takes a short time to reclaim garbage cells in a subspace, real-time collection is enabled.
(3) Even when creating or modifying a list structure, it is unnecessary to update the reference count if the reference does not cross the subspace boundary. The overhead required to update the reference count is therefore reduced.
(4) There is no overhead to synchronize the list process and the garbage collector because the collector always reclaims subspace, one at a time.
(5) The marking operation can be executed on the stack whose depth is equal to at most the number of the cells in a subspace.
(6) Cyclic lists which are within a subspace can be reclaimed.

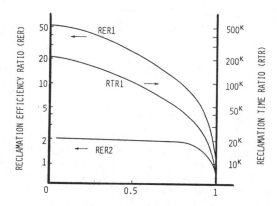

RATIO OF REAL TO VIRTUAL MEMORY (R/V)

$M_T = 3$ (REFERENCES/CELL)
$M_R = 4$ (REFERENCES/CELL)
$T = 50,000$ (DISK ACCESS TIME/MEMORY ACCESS TIME)
$N = 512$ (CELLS/SUBSPACE)
$RER1 = 0.75 + 50\ (1-R/V)$
$RER2 = \dfrac{3 + 200\ (1-R/V)}{4 + 100\ (1-R/V)}$
$S = 4,000$ (TOTAL SPACE/SUBSPACE)
$RTR1 = \{3 + 200\ (1-R/V)\} \times 1,000$

Figure 7. Reclamation Efficiency and Time

ALPHA HARDWARE AND CURRENT STATUS

This section describes the ALPHA hardware. ALPHA has been designed as a back-end processor that allows TSS users to do more high speed list processing than a large computer does. The LISP language on ALPHA is completely compatible with UTILISP on the FUJITSU M-series machine. UTILISP was implemented by Tokyo University, and is similar to MACLISP. The ALPHA system is shown in Figure 8. ALPHA is connected to a large M180II computer through the BMC (Block Multiplexer Channel), and has no I/O devices. It has an IPU (Instruction Processing Unit), an MSC (Main Storage Controller), an MSU (Main Storage Unit), an ADAPTOR and an SVP (Service Processor). The IPU executes high-speed list processing. The MSC controls memory access from the IPU and ADAPTOR. It has a dynamic address translation circuit for virtual addressing (16 MB). The MSU provides 8M bytes of real memory space. The ADAPTOR transfers data between ALPHA's main memory and the M180II. The SVP is used for controlling, testing, and maintaining ALPHA. ALPHA is implemented with 7700 STTL MSI chips, 30 STTL LSI chips (FUJITSU MB15K), 500 high speed 4K RAMs and 1200 dynamic 64K RAMs.

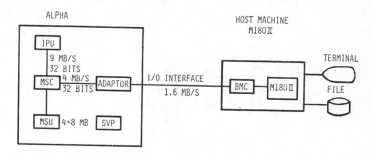

IPU: INSTRUCTION PROCESSING UNIT
MSC: MAIN STORAGE CONTROLLER
MSU: MAIN STORAGE UNIT
SVP: SERVICE PROCESSOR

BMC: BLOCK MULTIPLEXOR CHANNEL

Figure 8. ALPHA System

The hardware specifications of the IPU are listed in Table 1. The data section of the IPU is illustrated in Figure 9. There are three main buses (32 bits): Y-bus, A-bus, and B-bus. The IPU can execute ALU/Shifter and stack operations in one micro cycle. The use of only one PTR (Stack Pointer) allows the micro cycle to be fast in comparison to multi-PTR systems. A PTRS (PTR Save register) is used for effective multi-PTRs operation, and swapping of data between the PTRS and PTR can be executed independently of main bus operation. The IPU transfers data with the MSU through the M and W registers. The IBUF (Instruction Buffer) and IR (Instruction register) are used for macro instruction prefetch. Data type and operation code signals allow the IPU to execute multi-way micro instruction jumps.

The Micro sequence control section is shown in

Figure 10. There are many CS address sources: the MSTK (Micro stack), which is used for micro branch and link; the MPC (Micro Program Counter); multi-way jumps by data type; the OPM (Operation Memory), which indicates the macro instruction start address; return addresses saved in stack; micro function addresses stored in the atom-header; micro branch addresses indicated by the OPR (Micro Operation register); and fixed addresses used for interruptions.

Table 1. Hardware Specifications

1. Micro Instruction
   . Instruction Length   48 bits
   . Instruction Cycle   152 ns
   . Control Storage Size   16 KB
2. Main Memory
   . Virtual Address   16 MB
   . Page Size   4 KB
   . Real Memory   8 MB
3. Hardware Stack
   . Virtual Stack   4 Blocks * 2 KW
   . Block Swapping by LRU Algorithm
   . Value Cache
4. Other Features
   . Machine Instruction Prefetch
   . Hardware Multiplier / Divider

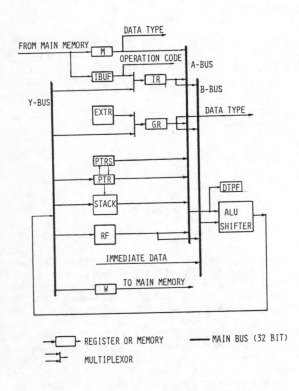

Figure 9. Data Section of IPU

At present, ALPHA is running with a 150-ns micro cycle. 4K bytes of data on ALPHA's memory is transferred to/from an M180 disk drive in 20 ms. UTILISP on ALPHA runs several times faster than MA-

CLISP on the DEC 2060. The ALPHA control system running on the M180II will be presented in other paper [11]. Using ALPHA, a user can execute a LISP program on ALPHA through an M180II terminal the same as he can on the M180II. The virtual stack and new subspace-oriented garbage collection system will be operating this summer. A LISP interpreter written in micro code and macro functions generated by compiler can run at high speeds using the fast stack operations, multi-way jumps by data type, macro instruction prefetch, and branch-on macro instructions.

CONCLUSION

A back-end type LISP machine, ALPHA, has been designed and implemented for list-processing. ALPHA has a highly effective hardware stack which supports both a value cache and a virtual stack. To satisfy real-time garbage collection on virtual memory, a new subspace-oriented garbage collection method has been introduced in ALPHA. This machine will be used for the development of artificial intelligence applications linked to software implemented on the M180II, for example, the Relational Data Base.

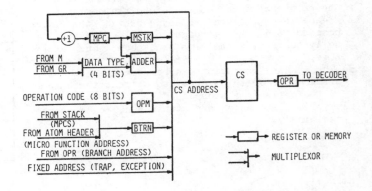

Figure 10. Micro Sequence Control Section

ACKNOWLEDGEMENT

The authors are very grateful to H.YAMADA and T. MIYAKAWA for their suggestions on the ALPHA project, to T. TANAHASHI and T. UYEHARA for their encouragement, and to M. NIWA, T. SHINOGI, A.SHINAGAWA, Y.KIMURA, and K. SATO for their help in developing the ALPHA machine. The ADAPTOR was designed by N. KAWATO, T. SAITO, S. HIROSE, and F. MARUYAMA.

APPENDIX

The marking operation from both the stack and the non zero RC(Refernce Count) cells in the subspace can be written as shown in function STACKMARK and NZRCMARK respectively.

Reclamation can be written as shown in function RECLAIM, where if a reclaimed cell points to other subspace, the RC of the target cell has to be decremented by one. Besides,as shown in function RCDECREMENT, if the target cell is in secondary memory, the entry for the cell must then be placed in the table MRT with a reference count of -1.

```
STACKMARK(PAGE)=
 prog(P)
  for each pointer P in the stack do
   if P points to the page PAGE
      then MARK(P)
    fi
   od
  end


NZRCMARK(PAGE)=
 prog(C)
  for each cell C in the page PAGE do
   if (RC of C = 0) and (MK of C = off)
      then MARK(C)
    fi
   od
  end


MARK(P)=
 prog()
  if MK of P = off
    then MK of P := on ;
     if CAR(P) points to the cell in PAGE
        then MARK((CAR(P))
      fi;
     if CDR(P) points to the cell in PAGE
        then MARK((CDR(P))
      fi
   fi
  end


RECLAIM(PAGE)=
 prog(COUNT,C)
  COUNT:=0;
  for each cell C in the PAGE do
   if MK of C = off
     then
       if CAR(C) points out of PAGE
         then RCDECREMENT(CAR(C))
       fi;
       if CDR(C) points out of PAGE
         then RCDECREMENT(CDR(C))
       fi;
       append the cell C
         to the free list in PAGE;
       increment COUNT
     else
       MK of C := off
   fi
  od;
  return COUNT
 end


RCDECREMENT(C)=
 prog()
  if cell C is in the real memory
    then decrement RC of C
    else
      if cell C is in the MRT
        then
```

```
            decrement the associated count
                in the MRT
      else
          place the cell C
              in the MRT with a count of -1
    fi
  fi
 end
```

REFERENCES

[1]   LISP Machine Inc. "Overview of the LMI Series LISP Machine".

[2]   D. Weinreb and D. Moon, "LISP MACHINE MANUAL", Symbolic inc.

[3]   B. W. Lampson and K. A. Pier, "A Processor for a High-Performance Personal Computer", Computer Architecture, 1980, pp.146-160.

[4]   E. I. Organick, "Computer System Organization", Academic Press, New York, 1973.

[5]   G. L. Steel, Jr, "Multiprocessing Compactifying Garbage Collection", Comm. ACM, 18, No.9, 1975, pp.495-508.

[6]   H. G. Baker, Jr, "List Processing in Real Time on a Serial Computer", Comm. ACM, 21, No.4, 1978, pp.280-294.

[7]   H. Lieberman and C. Hewitt, "A Real Time Garbage Collector that can Recover Temporary Storage Quickly", MIT AI Lab memo.

[8]   P. Bishop, "Garbage Collection in a Very Large Adress Space", MIT Lab for Computer Science report TR-178.

[9]   P. Deutsch and D. Bobrow, "An Efficient Incremental Automatic Garbage Collector", Comm.ACM,19,No.9,1976,pp.522-526.

[10] T. Chikayama,"UTILISP MANUAL", Tokyo University report METR 81-6.

[11] H. Akimoto and H. Hayashi, "Multi LISP Machine Control System", in preparation.

Reprinted from *Computer*, Volume 14, Number 7, July 1981, pages 10-21.
Copyright © 1981 by The Institute of Electrical and Electronics Engineers,
Inc.

*The Scheme-79 single-chip microcomputer implements an automatic
storage allocation system and an interrupt facility to support direct
interpretation of a variant of the Scheme dialect of Lisp.*

Scheme-79 — Lisp on a Chip

**Gerald Jay Sussman, Jack Holloway,
Guy Lewis Steel, Jr., and Alan Bell
MIT Artificial Intelligence Laboratory**

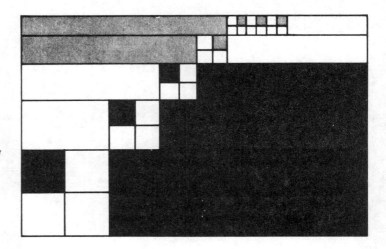

We have designed and implemented Scheme-79, a
single-chip microcomputer that directly interprets a
typed-pointer variant of Scheme,[1] a dialect of Lisp.[2] To
support this interpreter, the chip implements an automatic storage allocation system for heap-allocated data
and an interrupt facility for user interrupt routines implemented in Scheme. This article describes why Scheme
is particularly well suited to direct implementation of a
Lisp-like language in hardware, how the machine architecture is tailored to support the language, the design
methodology by which the hardware was synthesized, the
performance of the current design, and possible improvements to the design. We developed an interpreter
for Scheme written in Lisp. This interpreter can be viewed
as a microcode specification that is converted into actual
hardware structures on the chip by successive compilation
passes. To effect this we developed a language, embedded
in Lisp, for describing layout artwork. This language
allows procedural definition of generators for architectural elements, which are generalized macro components.
The generators accept parameters to produce the specialized instances used in a particular design. Our design
methodology made it possible to design and lay out this
chip in five weeks.

Why Lisp?

Lisp is a natural choice among high-level languages for
implementation on a single chip (or in any hardware,[3,4]
for that matter). It is a very simple language, in which a
powerful system can be built with only a few primitive
operators and data types. In Lisp, as in traditional machine languages, there is a uniform representation of programs as data. Thus the same primitive operators used by

a user's program to manipulate his data are used by the
system interpreter to effect control. We have added to the
traditional Lisp data types to allow representation of
programs in a form that can be efficiently interpreted by
our hardware.

Lisp is an object-oriented, as opposed to value-ori-
ented, language. The Lisp programmer does not think of
variables as objects of interest—bins in which values can
be held. Instead, each data item is itself an object to be
examined and modified, with an identity independent of
the variable(s) used to name it.

Lisp programs manipulate primitive data such as
numbers, symbols, and character strings. What makes
Lisp unique is that it provides a construction material,
called list structure, for gluing pieces of data together to
make compound data objects. Thus a modest set of
primitives provides the ability to manufacture complex
data abstractions. For example, a programmer can make
his own record structures out of list structure without
having the language designer install special features
explicitly for him. The same economy applies to procedural abstractions. Compound procedures defined by
the user have the same status as the initial system
primitives. The Lisp user can also manufacture linguistic
abstractions, because programs can be manipulated as
data and data can be interpreted as programs.[5]

We chose the Scheme dialect because it offers further
economies in the implementation of our machine. It is tail
recursive and lexically scoped. Tail recursion is a call-
save-return discipline in which a called procedure is not
expected to return to its immediate caller unless the immediate caller wants to do something with it after the
called procedure finishes. Tail recursion allows convenient definition of all common control abstractions in
terms of just two primitive notions, procedure call and
conditional,[6] without significant loss of efficiency.[7-9]

We also adopted lexical scoping of free variables, as in Algol-based languages. This is simpler to implement on the chip than the shallow dynamic binding schemes used in traditional Lisps, and it is more efficient than the alternative of deep dynamic binding.[10] In cases such as the rapidly changing environments in multiprocessing applications, lexical binding is more efficient than any dynamic binding strategy.

How the machine supports Scheme

All compound data in the system is built from list nodes, which consist of two pointers (called the CAR and the CDR, for historical reasons). A pointer is a 32-bit object with three fields: a 24-bit data field, a seven-bit type field, and one bit used only by the storage allocator. The type identifies the object referred to by the data field. Sometimes the datum referred to is an immediate quantity; otherwise, the datum points to another list node.[3,11,12] Figure 1 shows the format of a list node.

Lisp is an expression-oriented language. A Lisp program is represented as list structure, which notates what would be the parse tree in a more conventional language. Lisp expressions are executed by an evaluation process in which the evaluator performs a recursive tree walk on the expression, executes side effects, and develops a value. At each node of the expression, the evaluator dispatches on the type of that node to determine what to do. It may decide that the node is an immediate datum and is to be returned as a value, a conditional expression that requires the evaluation of one of two alternative subtrees based on the value of a predicate expression, or that it is an application of a procedure to a set of arguments. In the latter case, the evaluator recursively evaluates the arguments and passes them to the indicated procedure.

Lisp surface expressions are converted into machine programs, which are represented as list structure made of typed pointers. The type fields in our machine are analogous to the opcodes of a traditional instruction set. The dispatch to be made by the evaluator is encoded in the type field of the pointer to the translated expression. The transformation from Lisp to machine language preserves the expression structure of the original Lisp program. In the Scheme-79 architecture, the evaluator's recursive tree walk over expressions takes the place of the linear sequencing of instructions found in traditional computers. (The IBM 650[13] had an instruction set in which each in-

struction pointed at the next one. However, it was used to implement a traditional linear programming style, not to implement parse trees.) We call the machine language for our chip "S-code."

The S-code representation differs from the original Lisp expression in several ways. Particularly, it distinguishes between local and global variable references. A local variable reference is an instruction containing the lexical address of its value relative to the current environment structure. A global variable reference is a pointer that points directly at the global value of the symbol. A constant is a literal piece of data. When interpreted, a constant is an instruction that moves the appropriate data into the accumulated value. Certain primitive procedures (CAR, CDR, CONS, EQ, etc.) are realized directly as machine opcodes. Procedure calls are chains of instructions that accumulate the arguments and then apply the procedure. Control sequences (PROGN) are chains of instructions that direct the interpreter's tree walk. Conditionals are forks in a sequence chain.

In Figure 2, a simple Lisp program for appending two lists is represented in the S-code. The details of the S-code language are explained elsewhere;[14] this example is only to give an idea of what the S-code is like. A user of the Scheme-79 chip should never see the S-code.

At each step, the hardware evaluator dispatches on the state of the expression under consideration. The state of

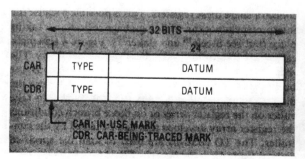

Figure 1. Format of a list node.

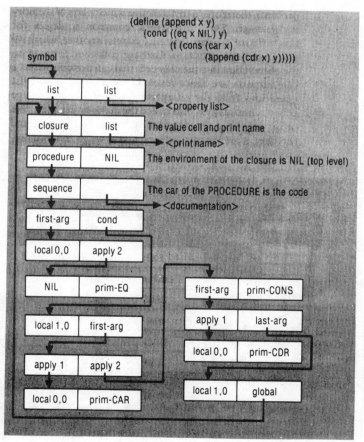

Figure 2. The S-code for APPEND.

the evaluator is kept in the set of registers shown in Figure 3. One register, VAL, holds the value of the last expression. EXP is a register for the current expression. If the current expression is a procedure call, the arguments are evaluated and built into a list kept in the ARGS register. When the arguments are all evaluated, the procedure is invoked. This requires the formal parameters of the procedure to be bound to the actual computed parameters. This binding is effected by changing the lexical environment register, DISPLAY, to point at the CONS of the ARGS register and the environment pointer of the closed procedure being applied. When evaluating the arguments to a procedure, the evaluator might have to recurse to obtain the value of a subexpression. The state of the evaluator must be restored when the subexpression returns with a value; this requires the state to be saved before recursion. The evaluator maintains a pointer to the stack of pending returns and their associated states in the register called STACK.

In our machine, data, programs, and even the stack are represented in list structure allocated from a heap memory. Neither the user nor the system interpreter is interested in how the memory is allocated, but memory is finite—and normal computation leads to the creation of garbage. For example, entries built on the stack during the evaluation of subexpressions are usually useless after the subexpression has been evaluated, but they still consume space in the heap. Thus the storage allocator must have means to reclaim memory that has been allocated but can no longer affect the future of the computation. The problem, therefore, is to determine which parts of memory are garbage. There are several common strategies for this.[15,16] One involves reference counts; another, which we use, is garbage collection. Garbage collection is based on the observation that the only cells that can possibly affect a computation are those reachable by a sequence of list operations from the interpreter's registers. Our garbage collection strategy is thus called the mark-sweep plan. We recursively trace the structure pointed at by the machine registers, marking each cell reached as we go. Eventually,

we mark the transitive closure of the list access operations starting with the machine registers; therefore, a cell is marked if and only if it is accessible. We then scan all memory; any location not marked is swept up as garbage and made reusable.

Usually, recursive traversal of a structure requires an auxiliary stack. This is unfortunate for our machine, for two reasons. First, it needs list structure to build stack; second, it is (presumably) garbage collecting because we ran out of room in which to build new list structure. Deutsch, Schorr, and Waite[17] developed a clever method of tracing structure without auxiliary memory; we use it. Our sweep phase has a two-finger compaction algorithm[11] that relocates all useful structure to the bottom of memory.

The chip also supports an interrupt system. The interrupt handlers are written in Scheme. Thus the user can, for example, simulate parallel processing or handle asynchronous I/O. The problem here is that the state of the interrupted process must be saved during the execution of the interrupt routine, so that it can be restored when the interrupt is dismissed. This is accomplished by building a data structure to contain the state of the relevant registers and pass it to the interrupt routine as a continuation argument.[18] The interrupt routine can then do its job and resume the interrupted process, if it wishes, by invoking the continuation as a procedure. The interrupt mechanism is also used to interface the garbage collector to the interpreter.

The Scheme-79 architecture

The Scheme-79 chip implements a standard von Neumann architecture in which a processor is attached to a memory system. The processor is divided into two parts, the data paths and the controller. The data paths consist of a set of special-purpose registers with built-in operators. The registers are interconnected with a single 32-bit bus. The controller is a finite-state machine that sequences through microcode and implements the interpreter and garbage collector. At each step, it performs an operation on some of the registers. For example, a sequence chain is followed by setting the EXP register to the CDR of the contents of the EXP register. The controller selects its next state on the basis of its current state and the conditions developed within the data paths.

There are 10 registers, each with specialized characteristics. To save space, the interpreter and the garbage collector share these registers. This is possible because the interpreter cannot run while a garbage collection is taking place (but see Steele[19] and Baker[20]). Figure 4 schematically shows the geometric layout of the register array. The registers and operators are all sitting on the same bus (the bus lines run vertically in the diagram). The arrows in the diagram depict control actions the controller can take either on the register array or on those branch conditions the register array develops that can be tested by the controller. The TO controls are used to load the specified register fields from the bus; the FROM controls are used to read the specified register onto the bus.

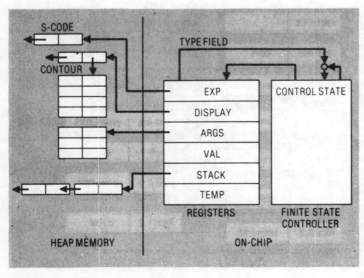

Figure 3. The hardware evaluator.

The division of storage words into mark, type, and data fields is reflected in the physical structure of most of the registers. On each cycle the registers can be controlled to gate one of the registers onto the bus and selected fields of the bus into another register. The bus is extended off the chip through a set of pads. The external world is conceptualized as a set of registers with special capabilities. The external ADDRESS register is used for accessing memory and can be set from the bus; the pseudoregister MEMORY can be read onto the bus or written from the bus. The actual access is performed to the list cell addressed by the ADDRESS register. The CDR bit controls which half of the cell is being accessed. One more external register, INTERRUPT (which can be read onto the bus), contains the address of a global symbol whose value (its CAR) is an appropriate interrupt handler.

The finite-state controller for the Scheme-79 chip is a synchronous system composed of a state register and the control map, which is a large piece of combinational logic. The control map is used to develop, from the current state stored in the state register, the control signals for the register array and pads, the new state, and controls for selection of the sources for the next sequential state. One bit of the next state is computed using the current value of the selected branch condition (if any). The rest of the next sequential state is chosen from either the new state generated by the control map or from the type field of the register array bus (dispatching on the type).

Including both the interpreter and garbage collector on the chip makes it difficult to create a compact realization of the map from old state to new state and control function. If we tried to implement this straightforwardly, using a programmed logic array, or PLA, for the map,

this structure would physically dominate the design and make the implementation infeasible. The map logic was made feasible by several decompositions; only a few of the possible combinations of register controls are actually used. For example, only one register can be gated onto the bus at one time. We used this interdependence to compress our register control. Instead of developing all of the register controls from one piece of logic (which would have to be very wide), we developed an encoding within the main map of the operation to be performed and the registers involved. This encoding was then expanded by an auxiliary map (also constructed as a PLA) to produce the actual control signals. This approach was inspired by the similar decomposition in the M68000,[21-23] which uses both vertical and horizontal microcode.

Unfortunately, this does not solve the problem. When examining the microcode, we found many microcode sequences to be nearly identical, differing only in the particular registers being manipulated. To take advantage of this regularity, we extended the previous decomposition to allow common short sequences to be encoded in the second-level PLA. Thus the Micro step consists of a one-(or more) cycle operation (Nano opcode) and a specification of registers to be used as source (from) and destination (to) operands. During the Micro step, the Nano PLA merges the specified source and destination registers into the extracted sequence.

Further savings were realized by taking advantage of the many identical sequences of microinstructions (except for renaming of registers) that contained no conditional branches. For example, to take the CAR of a specified source register and put it in a specified destination register takes two cycles: one to put the source out on the pads and

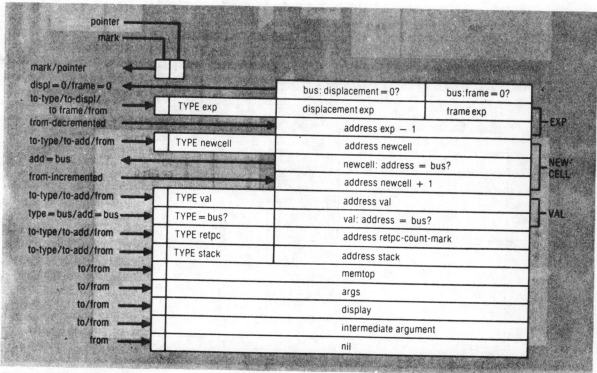

Figure 4. The register array.

tell the memory to latch the address and another to read the data from memory into the destination register. Since sequences like CAR are common, the microcode could be compressed by allowing a limited form of microcode subroutine. We did this rather painlessly by extending the horizontal (Nano) microcode map into a full-state machine (Figure 5). These common subsequences are then represented as single cycles of the Micro engine, which each stimulate several cycles of the Nano engine. To make this work, the vertical (Micro) sequencer must be frozen while the Nano sequencer is running. This mechanism was needed anyway, to make it possible for the chip to wait for memory response.

Still further savings were realized by subroutining common subsequences in the source microcode. Some of the common subsequences could not be captured by the Nano engine because they involved conditional branch operations, which the Nano engine was incapable of performing. They could, however, be subroutined in the source code by the conventional use of a free register to hold the return microcode address (Micro state) in its type field. Many microcode instructions were saved by this analysis.

Synthesizing the Scheme-79 chip

The major problem introduced by VLSI is that of coping with complexity—logic densities of over a million gates per chip will soon be available. The design of the Scheme-79 chip takes advantage of the techniques and perspectives gained in confronting the complexity problem in the software domain. Hardware design will increasingly become analogous to the programming of a large software system; therefore, we developed two languages embedded in Lisp to specify the behavior and the structure of our chip.

The first of these languages describes the algorithm to be embodied in the hardware. We chose Lisp as a convenient base language for embedding the description of the Scheme interpreter. By adding primitive operations that model the elementary hardware capabilities, we arrived at a form of Lisp (micro-Lisp) suitable for expressing our microcode. Although micro-Lisp has the structure of Lisp, its basic operations are ultimately for side effect rather than for value. They represent actions that can be performed on the registers on the chip. By using this form of Lisp, we can take advantage of such high-level language features as conditionals, compound expressions, and user macro definitions. For example, the following fragment of the on-chip storage allocator is written in micro-Lisp:

```
(defpc mark-node
    (assign *leader* (&car (fetch *node-pointer*)))
    (cond ((and (&pointer? (fetch *leader*))
                (not (&in-use? (fetch *leader*))))
           (&mark-car-being-traced! (fetch *node-pointer*))
           (&rplaca-and-mark! (fetch *node-pointer*)
                              (fetch *stack-top*))
    (go-to down-trace))
```

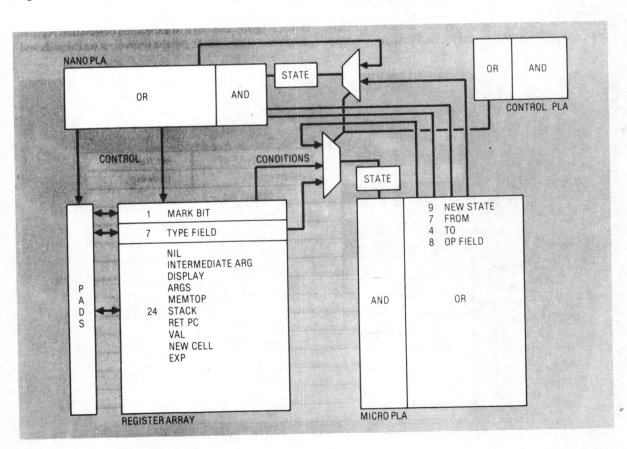

Figure 5. Scheme-79 architecture.

```
(t
    (&mark-in-use! (fetch *node-pointer*))
    (go-to trace-cdr))))

(defpc down-trace
    (assign *stack-top* (fetch *node-pointer*))
    (assign *node-pointer* (fetch *leader*))
    (go-to mark-node))
```

This example shows two subsequences of the microcode, labeled mark-node and down-trace. Down-trace is a simple sequence that transfers the contents of the machine registers *node-pointer* and *leader* into *stack-top* and *node-pointer*. Although the storage allocator was written as if it uses a set of registers distinct from those of the evaluator, there are micro-Lisp declarations that make these names equivalent to the registers used by the evaluator. The mark-node sequence illustrates the use of a compound expression that refers to the result of performing the CAR operation on the contents of the *node-pointer* register. The CAR operation is itself a sequence of machine steps that access memory. (This is an example of a Nano operation that performs a step to output the address to be accessed. A second step reads the data from the external memory into the *leader* register.) The compound boolean expression that tests the contents of the *leader* register as to whether it is a pointer to an unused cell is compiled into a series of microcode branches, which transfer to separate chains of microinstructions corresponding to the consequent and alternative clauses.

One benefit of embedding the microcode language in Lisp is that by providing definitions for the primitive machine operators that simulate the machine actions on the registers we can simulate the operation of the machine by running our microcode as a Lisp program. Micro-Lisp is also an easy language to compile.

Micro-Lisp is compiled into artwork by a cascade of three compilation steps. The first phase transforms micro-Lisp into a linear, sequential machine language. It removes all embedded structure such as the composition of primitive operators. This involves the allocation of registers to hold the necessary intermediate results. Conditionals are linearized and the compound boolean expressions are transformed into simple branches. The machine language is specialized to the actual target machine architecture by the code generators, which transform the conceptually primitive operators of micro-Lisp into single major-cycle machine operations, which can be encoded as single transitions of Micro (the vertical microcode state machine).

The second phase of the compilation process assembles the linear microcode into programming for the PLAs that control the Micro and Nano sequencers. The Nano PLA is constructed by selecting the needed nanocode from a dictionary of possible nano sequences. Nano instructions can be viewed as macros or subroutines invoked by Micro instructions. The operation field of the Micro instruction selects the Nano instruction; the Nano instruction can then selectively enable decoding of the from and to fields.

The third major phase of the compilation is performed by the PLA architectural element generator, an artwork synthesis procedure written in the layout language described below. This procedure has several parameters: one is the PLA specifications output by the previous phases; others control special details of the clocking, the order of bits in fields in the input and output wiring, the ground mesh spacing, and the option of folding the PLA for adjustment of the aspect ratio. These parameters provide flexibility in accommodating the PLA layout to the other structures on the chip.

The layout language

Current practice in chip design uses the idea of a *cell*, a particular combination of primitive structures that can be repeated or combined with other cells to make a more complex structure. The advantage of this approach is that a cell performing a common function is defined only once. More important, the cell encapsulates and thus suppresses much detail so that the problem of design is simplified. As in programming, we extend this notion (after Johannsen[24]) by *parameterizing* our cells to form compound abstractions that represent whole classes of cells. These classes can vary both in structure and function. We call these abstract parameterized cells *architectural elements*.

For example, a simple nMOS depletion load pullup comes in a variety of sizes. The particular length-to-width ratio of such a transistor is a simple numerical parameter. A parameterized pullup is a simple architectural element. It encapsulates the particular rules for constructing the pullup, including the placement of the contact from the poly to the diffusion layer and the placement of the ion implant. A more interesting architectural element is an n-way selector, which is parameterized by the number of inputs. In this case, such higher-level details as the means of driving the input lines and the particular logic by which the selector is implemented are suppressed. Small selectors may be more effectively implemented with one kind of logic, and large selectors with another.

These are still only simple parameters; we have developed much more powerful architectural elements. For example, a finite-state machine controller can be implemented as a PLA and state register. We have constructed a PLA generator parameterized by the logical contents and physical structure. This generator is used with a compiler that takes a program to be embodied in the state machine to produce the state machine controller, an architectural element parameterized by a program written in a high-level language. Although we have not completely parameterized it, we can think of our register array generator as an architectural element. In fact, an entire high-level language interpreter module can be accurately defined as an architectural element parameterized by the interpreter program augmented with declarations that describe how the interpreter data is represented in registers.

In our system, an architectural element generator is a procedure written in Lisp augmented by a set of primitive data-base and layout operators. This augmented Lisp is the layout language. (The layout language used in the design of the Scheme-79 chip has evolved substantially. It is described in Batali et al.[25])

The layout language primitives create representations of elementary geometric entities such as points and boxes on a particular mask layer. For example:

```
(PT 3 4)   is the point at location (3,4)
(THE-X (PT 3 4))   is 3
(BOX 'POLY 3 4 5 6) is a box on the poly layer from (3,4) to (5,6)
```

Sequences of connected boxes on a single layer can be conveniently constructed by specifying a width, an initial point, and a sequence of directions for proceeding along the desired path. The paths must be rectilinear; they are specified as a sequence of movements in either the *x* or *y* coordinate directions. Each movement can be either incremental or to an absolute position.

```
(BOXES (POLY 3) (PT 3 4) ( + X 20) (Y 35) (X 70))
    specifies a path in 3 wide poly from (3,4) to (23,4)
    to (23, 35) to (70, 35).
```

The layout language also provides, as primitives, certain common structures used in nMOS layouts, such as contact cuts between the various layers.

```
(CONTACT V POLY (PT 3 4)) makes a metal-to-poly contact which
    is vertically oriented and is centered at point (3, 4).
```

We can combine pieces of layout by instantiating each piece separately. We can then make compound cells by giving a name to a program that instantiates all of its pieces. The cell can be parameterized by arguments to the procedure that generates it. The following layout procedure creates a depletion-mode pullup of a given width and length. It encapsulates knowledge of the design rules by referring to globally declared process parameters.

```
(deflayout  general-pullup (length width)
    (boxes (diff width) (pt 0 −1) ( +Y ( + length 2)))
    (boxes (poly ( + ( * 2 *poly-overhang*) width))
        (pt 0 0) ( +Y length))
    (call (butting-contact))
    (boxes (implant ( + ( * 2 *implant-overhang*) width))
        (pt 0 ( − 0 *implant-overhang*))
        ( +Y ( + length ( * 2 *implant-overhang*)))))
```

A compound cell can be instantiated as part of a larger structure by invoking its name. The instance created by a call to a compound cell can be translated, rotated, and reflected to place it appropriately within the larger structure.[26] For example, we could put a pullup where we want it by writing

```
(call (general-pullup 8 2) (rot 0 1) (trans (pt 24 35)))
```

Each object can be given a local symbolic name relative to the larger structure of which it is a part. These names can be referred to by means of paths, which describe the sequence of local names from the root of the structure.[27] These symbolic names are attached to the coordinate systems of cells. They are useful for describing operations when creating artwork because they eliminate the need to explicitly write out the numerical values of the operands. For example, it is possible to place a driver cell at the end of a register so that its control outputs align with (and connect to) the control inputs of the first cell of the register column (think of the rows of the register array as bit-slices and of the columns as the individual registers). To effect this we call the drive cell generator to get an instance of the driver and then align the newly called-out instance so that the appropriate points coincide. We also can inherit names from substructure to make new local names.

```
(set-the 'exp-driver (call (regcell-driver)))
(align (the exp-driver)
        (the-pt end ph1-to ph2-driver exp-driver)
        (the-pt to-type-exp array))
(set-the 'to-type-exp (the-pt start sig to-driver exp-driver))
(set-the 'from-exp (the-pt start sig from-driver exp-driver))
```

A form (the-pt . . .) is a path-name: "the point which is the end of the ph1-to of the ph2-driver of the exp-driver (of me)."

Virtual instances of cells can be made. These do not actually create artwork, but they can be interrogated for information about such properties of the virtual artwork as the relative position of a particular bus metal or the horizontal pitch. In the following fragment, pullup-pair is made to be the local name of a virtual instance of the pullup-pair cell. This is used to extract parameters to control the elaboration of pullup-gnd so that it is compatible with the pullup-pair cell and can be abutted to it.

```
(deflayout pullup-gnd (gnd-width)
    (set-the 'v-pitch −10)
    (set-the 'pullup-pair
            (invoke* (pullup-pair gnd-width)))
    (set-the 'vdd
            (wire (metal 4)
                (pt (the-x end vdd pullup-pair) 0)
                (Y −10)))
    (set-the 'vdd2
            (wire (metal 4)
                (pt (the-x end vdd pullup-pair) −5)
                (X (the-x vdd2 pullup-pair))))
    (set-the 'gnd
            (wire (metal gnd-width)
                (pt (the-x end gnd pullup-pair) 0)
                (Y −10)))
    (boxes  (metal 4) (pt (the-x end gnd) −5)
        (X (the h-pitch pullup-pair))))
```

The layout language system is intended to be part of an interactive environment in which designs are developed by combining incremental modifications to and adaptations of existing fragments of design. Thus a layout procedure is not just a file transducer that takes an input design and cranks out artwork. Rather, it produces a data base that describes the artwork to be constructed. The output artwork is just one way of printing out some aspects of this data base. Other information contained in the data base embodies the user's conception of the structure of the artifact he is constructing, including mnemonic names for parts of his design. This data base can be interrogated by the user to help him examine his design, to annotate it, and to help produce incremental changes when debugging is necessary.

History

The project started with Guy Steele's painstaking hand layout of a prototype interpreter chip[28,29] as part of the 1978 MIT class chip project. The prototype differed from the current design in several ways. It used separate sets of registers for the storage allocator and evaluator processes, while our new design shares the same set of registers between them. Although this saves space by time multiplexing, it precludes the use of a concurrent garbage collector algorithm. The prototype chip was fabricated but never tested because a fatal artwork error was discovered (through a microscope!).

The design for the Scheme-79 chip began at the MIT Artificial Intelligence Lab in mid-June 1979. The first task was to construct the microcode we wanted the machine to interpret. We adapted a previous experimental implementation of the Scheme language (written in LISP for the PDP-10) by defining a storage representation and adding a garbage collector. We studied the microcode to determine which architecture would be effective for its implementation. The next step was to create a layout language in order to write procedures that would build the chip artwork. This was followed by the simultaneous construction of a compiler of the microcode to the PLA implementation and the layout of the register array. Complete preliminary implementations of the main structures of the chip were ready in our data base by July 8, 1979.

At this point we went to Xerox Palo Alto Research Center to use their Icarus automated draftsman program[30] to assemble and interconnect these pieces. This was the hardest part of the job; it took almost two weeks. The first completely assembled version of the Scheme-79 chip was completed on July 19, 1979. The implementation was done, except for the discovery of errors.

Some errors were discovered by the sharp eyes of people at Xerox and MIT. We had an 8×10-foot check plot with features of approximately 1/10 inch. Within a few weeks, we had discovered and corrected about 10 design-rule violations or artwork errors and two nonfatal logic bugs. At that point, a program was written by Clark Baker that extracted an electrical description (in terms of nodes and transistors) from our artwork. Baker's program discovered an implausible circuit fragment, which turned out to be an extra power pad superimposed on one of the data pads! This electrical description was then simulated with a program written by Chris Terman, which was based upon an earlier program developed by Randy Bryant.[31] The simulator helped find five additional serious logic errors, a rare PLA compiler bug, an invisible (1/8 minimum feature size) error introduced in the artwork conversion process, and an extraneous piece of polysilicon that had magically appeared during the repair of previous errors. The final simulations checked out a complete garbage collection and the evaluation of a trivial (450 microstep) user program. This experience indicates that efficient tools for checking both the physical and logical design are essential.

The chip went out for fabrication on December 4, 1979, as part of the MPC79 Multi-University Multiproject Chip-Set compiled by the LSI Systems Area of the System Science Laboratory at Xerox PARC. Using a process with a mininum line width of five microns (lambda = 2.5 microns), the Scheme-79 chip was 5926 microns wide and 7548 microns long, an area of 44.73 square millimeters. The masks were made by Micro Mask, Inc., and the wafers were fabricated by Hewlett-Packard's integrated circuit processing laboratory.

On January 9, 1980, we received four chips bonded into packages. By then, Howard Cannon had designed and fabricated a board to interface the Scheme-79 chip to the MIT Lisp Machine. This was a substantial project, which included an interface to allow our chip to access Lisp Machine memory. The interface board contains a map for chip addresses to Lisp Machine memory addresses, a programmable clock to allow the Lisp Machine to vary the durations of the clock phases and the interphase spaces, debugging apparatus to allow the Lisp Machine to set and read the state and internal registers of the chip, circuitry for allowing the Lisp Machine to interrupt the Scheme chip, circuitry to allow the Lisp Machine to single-step the chip, and an interface from chip bus protocols to Lisp Machine bus protocols. This interface project materially contributed to the success of the Scheme-79 chip project, because it allowed testing to begin almost immediately upon receipt of the chip.

The first chip we unpacked had a visible fatal flaw in the metal layer. The second one could load and read state but would not run. The third chip seems to work. It has successfully run programs, garbage collected memory, and accepted interrupt requests. We have found two nonfatal design errors that escaped our previous simulation and testing. One is a subtle bug in the garbage-collector microcode. It could cause rare disasters, but will never be a problem in the actual programs likely to be run by the chip. The other is a race condition in the logic associated with the pad used by the chip to signal the need for an interrupt to collect garbage. Luckily, this function is redundant and can be assumed by the interface.

Performance of the Scheme-79 chip

Three areas independently limit the performance of the machine: the algorithms embodied by the chip are not optimal; there are architectural improvements that can reduce the number of machine cycles per step in the interpreter; and there are electrical performance limits to the design.

The interpreter on the chip uses the heap memory system for all of its data structures, including the interpreter's stack. This becomes the dominant source of garbage produced by execution of a program; reclaiming this garbage is the dominant cost of execution. There are several ways to attack this problem.

We have estimated, by examining fragments of the microcode, that we allocate a heap cell for every 10 cycles of computation. The cost of allocating this cell is in two parts: approximately eight cycles are required to perform the allocation, and (assuming that half of the heap is reclaimed per garbage collection) 35 cycles are required to reclaim each cell. This, of course, implies that the current machine will spend 80 percent of its time in the storage allocator. The garbage collector itself has respectable performance. At a one-MHz clock rate, collection of a one-megabyte heap (128K Lisp nodes) takes less than six seconds. However, a copying collection algorithm[32,33] would generate a third as many memory accesses.

Of course, if the evaluator used a more traditional stack structure it would generate considerably less garbage. We chose not to do this because it would increase the complexity of many parts of the system. For example, there would have to be a mechanism for allocating nonlist structures in memory. Furthermore, the garbage collector would need to treat these structures specially and would have to mark from pointers stored in the stack. Also, a linear stack regime makes retention of control environments very complicated.[34] This impacts such user multiprocessing features as interrupts and nonlocal catch points.

Richard Stallman has observed that if we sequentially allocate the list nodes for our stack in a separate area, we can normally deallocate when popping, after making a simple check for retained control environments. Assuming that such retained control environments are rare in comparison to the usual uses of the stack, it will be almost as efficient as a normal linear stack on a conventional machine.

Interpreter performance can also be improved by optimizing use of the stack. This can be effected by exploiting the regularities of the stack discipline, which make many of the stack operations redundant. In the *caller-saves* convention (which the Scheme-79 chip implements), the only reason to push a register onto the stack is to protect its contents from being destroyed by unpredictable uses of the register during the recursive evaluation of a subexpression. Therefore, one source of redundant stack operations lies in the fact that a register is saved even if the evaluation of the subexpression does not affect the contents of that register. If we could look ahead in time, we could determine whether or not the register will retain its contents through the unknown evaluation. This is one standard kind of optimization done by compilers, but even a compiler cannot optimize all cases because the execution path of a program generally depends on the data being processed. Instead of looking ahead, we can try to make the stack mechanism lazy, in that it postpones pushing a register until its contents are about to be destroyed. The key idea is that each register has a state that indicates whether its contents are valuable. If a valuable register is about to be assigned, it is at that moment pushed. To make this system work, each register that can be pushed has its own stack, to allow decoupling of the stack disciplines for each of the registers. Each register-stack combination can be thought of as having a state that encodes some of the history of previous operations. The combination is organized by a finite-state automaton that mediates between operation requests and the internal registers and stack. This automaton serves as an on-the-fly peephole optimizer, which recognizes certain patterns of operations within a small window in time and transforms them so as to reduce the actual number of stack operations performed. We have investigated this strategy[35] and believe it can be implemented in hardware easily; it should substantially improve the performance of the algorithm. Pilot studies indicate that this technique can save three out of every four stack allocations in the operation of the interpreter.

Other trade-offs were made in the architecture of the chip. For example, our register array has a single bus. This forced the microcode to serialize many register transfer operations that logically could have been done in parallel. (A more powerful bus structure would result in a significant speedup.) We also decided to use simple register cells rather than buffered registers, which means that a register cannot be read and written at the same time. This is not usually a problem, because on a single-bus machine it is not useful to read out and load the same register. It does, however, cause increment and decrement operations to take two microcycles rather than one. This is significant because increment and decrement operations are in the innermost loop of the local variable lookup routine, and decrementing the frame and displacement field takes twice as long as is really necessary. Finally, we could have used more registers. In several cases, an extra intermediate would result in fewer register shuffles and CONSs to get something done. For example, special argument registers for holding the arguments for primitive one- and two-argument functions could make a serious dent in the storage allocated in argument evaluation and, ultimately, in the time taken to collect garbage. This optimization can be combined with our stack optimizer strategy (mentioned above). In fact, the entire argument about stack optimization can be thought of as an architectural issue because of the simple implementation of our peephole-optimizing automata in hardware.

We also made significant tradeoffs in the electrical characteristics of the Scheme-79 chip: the bus is not precharged; the PLAs are ratio logic, not precharged; there is a no on-chip clock generator; many long runs are made on poly and diffusion that should be made on metal; and some buffers are not sized to drive the long lines to which they connect. We also used a selector design with implanted pass transistors, an exceptionally slow circuit. Careful redesign of some of the circuitry on the chip would greatly improve performance.

The actual measured performance of our chip on a sample program is shown below. We calculated the values of Fibonacci numbers by the doubly recursive method. (This explodes exponentially; computing each Fibonacci number takes $(1 + \sqrt{5})/2$ times the time it takes to compute the previous one.) This is an excellent test program because it thoroughly exercises most of the mechanisms of the interpreter. Sums were computed using Peano arithmetic, which is the only arithmetic available on the chip. The program is as follows:

```
(define (+ x y)
   (cond ((zerop x) y)
         (t (+ (1− x) (1+ y)))))
(define (fib x)
   (cond ((zerop x) 0)                    ;If 0. result is 0.
         ((zerop (1− x)) 1)               ;If 1. result is 1.
         (t (+ (fib (1− x))
               (fib (1− (1− x)))))))
```

We computed (fib 20.) = 6765. with two different memory loadings, with a clock period of 1595 nanoseconds (not the top speed for the chip) and a memory of 32K Lisp cells. When the memory was substantially empty (so that garbage collection was maximally efficient), the Scheme-79 chip took about one minute to execute the program. With memory half full of live structure (a typical load for a Lisp system), the chip took about three minutes to execute the program.

We also compared this performance with that of our standard MacLisp interpreter on the same program, running on the DEC KA10 with a Scheme interpreter written in MacLisp. Lisp did not garbage collect during this operation, but it took about 3.6 minutes. The MacLisp Scheme interpreter (with unknown memory loading) took about nine minutes, with about 10 percent of the time spent in the garbage collector. ∎

Acknowledgments

We would like to thank Lynn Conway and Bert Sutherland of the Xerox Palo Alto Research Center System Science Laboratory and Jon Allen and Paul Penfield of MIT, for help, support, and encouragement. We would also like to thank all those people who gave us ideas and technical assistance, particularly Neil Mayle, Thomas F. Knight, Howie Shrobe, and Richard Zippel at MIT, and Lynn Conway, Jim Cherry, Dick Lyon, and Jerry Roylance at Xerox PARC. These people read and commented on designs, found bugs, and proposed patches. The resulting chip still had many bugs, which were found by sharp-eyed friends and by the simulation support provided by Clark Baker and Chris Terman of the MIT Laboratory for Computer Science. We would like to thank Howard Cannon for designing and constructing the apparatus for testing Scheme-79 chips on our MIT Lisp machines. Recently, we have had excellent suggestions for improving the next design from Richard Stallman and John Rees. Paul Penfield, Ron Rivest, Neil Mayle, John Batali, and Howie Shrobe have had good ideas about better design tools. We are sure that it would have been impossible to undertake so large a design without the extensive help provided by so many friends.

This article describes research done at the Artificial Intelligence Laboratory of the Massachusetts Institute of Technology. Support for the laboratory's artificial intelligence research is provided in part by the following sources: Advanced Research Projects Agency of the Department of Defense under the Office of Naval Research contract N00014-75-C-0643, National Science Foundation Grant MCS77-04828, and Air Force Office of Scientific Research Grant AFOSR-78-3593.

References

1. Guy Lewis Steele, Jr., and Gerald Jay Sussman, *The Revised Report on SCHEME: A Dialect of LISP,* MIT AI Memo 452, Cambridge, Mass., Jan. 1978.

2. John McCarthy et al., *LISP 1.5 Programmer's Manual,* MIT Press, Cambridge, Mass., 1962.

3. Alan Bawden, Richard Greenblatt, Jack Holloway, Thomas Knight, David Moon, and Daniel Weinreb, *LISP Machine Progress Report,* MIT AI Memo 444, Cambridge, Mass., Aug. 1977.

4. Eiichi Goto, Tetsuo Ida, Hiraki Kei, Masayuki Suzuki, and Inada Nobuyuki, "FLATS, A Machine for Numerical, Symbolic, and Associative Computing," *Proc. 6th Ann. Symp. Computer Architecture,* Apr. 1979, pp. 102-110.*

5. Guy Lewis Steele, Jr., and Gerald Jay Sussman, *The Art of the Interpreter; or, The Modularity Complex (Parts Zero, One, and Two),* MIT AI Memo 453, Cambridge, Mass., May 1978.

6. Guy Lewis Steele, Jr., and Gerald Jay Sussman, *LAMBDA: The Ultimate Imperative,* MIT AI Memo 353, Cambridge, Mass., Mar. 1976.

7. Guy Lewis Steel, Jr., "Debunking the 'Expensive Procedure Call' Myth," *Proc. ACM Nat'l Conf.,* Oct. 1977, pp. 153-162. Revised as MIT AI Memo 443, Cambridge, Mass., Oct. 1977.

8. Guy Lewis Steele, Jr., *LAMBDA: The Ultimate Declarative,* MIT AI Memo 379, Cambridge, Mass., Nov. 1976.

9. Guy Lewis Steele, Jr., *Compiler Optimization Based on Viewing LAMBDA As Rename Plus Goto,* MS thesis, MIT, Cambridge, Mass., May 1977; published as *RABBIT: A Compiler for SCHEME (A Study in Compiler Optimization),* MIT AI TR 474, May 1978.

10. Henry B. Baker, Jr., "Shallow Binding in LISP 1.5.," *Comm. ACM,* Vol. 21, No. 7, July 1978, pp. 565-569.

11. S. W. Galley and Greg Pfister, *The MDL Language,* Programming Technology Division Document SYS.11.01, Project MAC, MIT, Cambridge, Mass., Nov. 1975.

12. William R. Conrad, *Internal Representations of ECL Data Types,* Technical Report 5-75, Center for Research in Computing Technology, Harvard University, Cambridge, Mass., Mar. 1975.

13. *650 Data Processing System Bulletin G24-5000-0,* International Business Machines Corporation, 1958.

14. Jack Holloway, Guy Lewis Steele, Jr., Gerald Jay Sussman, and Alan Bell, *The SCHEME-79 Chip,* MIT AI Memo 559, Cambridge, Mass., Jan. 1980.

15. Wilfred J. Hansen, "Compact List Representation: Definition, Garbage Collection, and System Implementation," *Comm. ACM,* Vol. 12, No. 9, Sept. 1969, pp. 499-507.

16. Donald E. Knuth, *The Art of Computer Programming, Volume 1: Fundamental Algorithms,* Addison-Wesley, Reading, Mass., 1968.

17. H. Schorr and W. M. Waite, "An Efficient Machine-Independent Procedure for Garbage Collection in Various List Structures," *Comm. ACM,* Vol. 10, No. 8, Aug. 1967, pp. 501-506.

18. John C. Reynolds, "Definitional Interpreters for Higher Order Programming Languages," *Proc. 25th ACM Nat'l Conf.,* Aug. 1972, pp. 717-740.

19. Guy Lewis Steele, Jr., "Multiprocessing Compactifying Garbage Collection," *Comm. ACM,* Vol. 18, No. 9, Sept. 1975, pp. 495-508.

20. Henry B. Baker, Jr., "List Processing in Real Time on a Serial Computer," *Comm. ACM,* Vol. 21, No. 4, Apr. 1978, pp. 280-294.

21. Skip Stritter and Nick Tredennick, "Microprogrammed Implementation of a Single Chip Microprocessor," *Proc. 11th Ann. Microprogramming Workshop,* Nov. 1978, pp. 8-15.*

22. G. Frieder and J. Miller, "An Analysis of Code Density for Two Level Programmable Control of the Nanodata QM-1," *Proc. IEEE 10th Ann. Microprogramming Workshop,* Oct. 1975, pp. 26-32.*

23. A. Grasselli, "The Design of Program-Modifiable Micro-Programmed Control Units," *IRE Trans. Electronic Computers,* EC-11, No. 6, June 1962.

24. Dave Johannsen, "Bristle Blocks: A Silicon Compiler," *Proc. Caltech Conf. VLSI,* California Institute of Technology, Pasadena, Calif., Jan. 1979.

25. John Batali and Anne Hartheimer, *The Design Procedure Language Manual,* MIT AI Memo 598, Cambridge, Mass., Sept. 1980.

26. Carver A. Mead and Lynn A. Conway, *Introduction to VLSI Systems,* Addison-Wesley, Reading, Mass., 1980.

27. R. C. Daley and P. G. Neumann, "A General-Purpose File System for Secondary Storage," *AFIPS Proc. Conf.,* 1965 FJCC, Vol. 27, Part I, Nov. 1965, pp. 213-230.

28. Guy Lewis Steele, Jr., and Gerald Jay Sussman, "Storage Management in a LISP-Based Processor," *Proc. Caltech Conf. VLSI,* California Institute of Technology, Pasadena, Calif., Jan. 1979.

29. Guy Lewis Steele, Jr., and Gerald Jay Sussman, "Design of LISP-Based Processors: or, SCHEME: A Dielectric LISP; or, Finite Memories Considered Harmful; or, LAMBDA: The Ultimate Opcode," *Comm. ACM.,* Vol. 23, No. 11, Nov. 1980, pp. 629-645; also MIT AI Memo 514, Cambridge, Mass., Mar. 1979.

30. Doug Fairbairn and Jim Rowson, "ICARUS: An Interactive Integrated Circuit Layout Program," *Proc. 15th Ann. Design Automation Conf.,* June 1978, pp. 188-192.*

31. Randy Bryant, *The MOSSIM User Manual,* unpublished working paper, MIT Laboratory for Computer Science, Cambridge, Mass., 1979.

32. M. L. Minsky, *A LISP Garbage Collector Using Serial Secondary Storage,* MIT AI Memo 58 (revised), Cambridge, Mass., Dec. 1963.

33. Robert R. Fenichel and Jerome C. Yochelson, "A LISP Garbage Collector for Virtual-Memory Computer Systems," *Comm. ACM,* Vol. 12, No. 11, Nov. 1969, pp. 611-612.

34. Daniel G. Bobrow and Ben Wegbreit, "A Model and Stack Implementation of Multiple Environments," *Comm. ACM,* Vol. 16, No. 10, Oct. 1973, pp. 591-603.

35. Guy Lewis Steele, Jr., and Gerald Jay Sussman, *The Dream of a Lifetime: A Lazy Scoping Mechanism,* MIT AI Memo 527, Cambridge, Mass., Nov. 1979.

*These proceedings available from the Order Desk, IEEE Computer Society, 10662 Los Vaqueros Circle, Los Alamitos, CA 90720.

Gerald Jay Sussman is an associate professor of electrical engineering at Massachusetts Institute of Technology. His research interests are within the general area of using computers to model the intellectual processes of engineers. He is currently working on applying artificial intelligence techniques to computer-aided design of integrated systems, designing unusual architecture for the support of artificial intelligence programming, and investigating clean, modular styles in computer programming.

Sussman holds a BS and PhD in mathematics from MIT, obtained in 1968 and 1973, respectively. He is the author of the book *Computational Models of Skill Acquisition* as well as of numerous magazine and journal articles.

John T. Holloway is vice-president of technology at Symbolics, Inc., a company marketing Lisp machines, in Cambridge, Massachusetts. His research interests include special-purpose VLSI architectures for artificial intelligence applications and tools for computer-aided design.

Holloway has been associated with MIT's Artificial Intelligence Laboratory since its inception in 1965, participating in early robotics research and timesharing system development. From 1975 to 1980 he was instrumental in the design of "The Lisp Machine," a network-based scientific workstation developed as an alternative technology to timesharing. Most recently he was a principal research scientist in the Artificial Intelligence Laboratory's VLSI group; during that time he developed the Scheme-79 chip.

Guy Lewis Steele, Jr. is an assistant professor of computer science at Carnegie-Mellon University. His current research interests include programming language design and implementation, VLSI design, and computer architectures. Steele received his AB degree in applied mathematics from Harvard in 1975 and his SM and PhD degrees in computer science from MIT in 1977 and 1980. While at MIT, he worked within the Artificial Intelligence Laboratory. Steele is a member of ACM.

Alan Bell is a member of the VLSI systems research staff at the Xerox Palo Alto Research Center. His initial activities when he joined PARC in 1978 included being the primary architect and designer of the MPC VLSI silicon implementation system. His current activities center around VLSI design and the creation of an integrated wafer-scale framework in which many diverse, independently designed VLSI systems can communicate and interact with each other. Bell earned his BS in computer science at the University of California at Irvine.

PROCEEDINGS OF THE INTERNATIONAL CONFERENCE
ON FIFTH GENERATION COMPUTER SYSTEMS 1984,
edited by ICOT. © ICOT, 1984

EM-3: A LISP-BASED DATA-DRIVEN MACHINE

Yoshinori YAMAGUCHI,* Kenji TODA,* Jayanta HERATH,** Toshitsugu YUBA*

* Electrotechnical Laboratory
1-1-4, Umesono, Sakuramura, Niiharigun
Ibaraki 305, JAPAN

** Keio University
3-14-1, Hiyoshi, Yokohama 223, JAPAN

ABSTRACT

In this paper, a Lisp-based data-driven machine with a novel parallel control mechanism and its hardware prototype are presented. The proposed control mechanism is a natural extension of the data-driven scheme to the function evaluation and is achieved by packet communication architecture.

First, the control mechanism of the ETL data-driven machine-3 (EM-3) is overviewed. Next, the architecture of its hardware prototype is described. The hardware prototype designed accommodates eight processing elements which are connected via a communication network. Each processing element consists of a microprocessor and special hardware. The network is organized by several LSI router chips. Then the instruction set of the prototype and the design philosophy of a functional programming language for the data-driven machine are presented. Finally, the performance characteristics of the machine obtained by the software simulator are evaluated.

1. INTRODUCTION

For the next generation computers, a non von Neumann computer architecture and new software environments must be developed. The new computer architecture must be based on parallel processing and VLSI technology. Data-driven architecture is proposed as a new computation model [2,4]. It has parallel processing potential in both hardware and software; i.e., the maximum inherent parallelism in ordinary programs can be exploited at the architectural level of the computers. In this case, it is not necessary to specify parallel description of a program explicitly. Moreover, functional programming and logic programming styles are suitable for data-driven architecture.

The ETL data-driven machine-3 (EM-3) is a Lisp-based data-driven machine for non-numerical computations such as symbolic manipulations involved in knowledge based information processing systems. The primary goal of the EM-3 project is to study the feasibility of the practical data-driven machine for symbol manipulations. In recent years, there have been some attempts to construct new machines with data-driven architecture. However they have shown the potential of the data-driven architecture only in principle, since those machines are too small in scale to execute large programs.

The EM-3 aims at bringing out the intrinsic parallelism in ordinary programs which are written in EMLISP [15], a functional programming language. We have proposed an advanced control mechanism for the EM-3 using novel concepts such as pseudo-result, semi-result [16] and partial-result [13]. It has been proved that these notions cause new parallelism and accelerate program execution. We have advanced the data-driven concept to meet the challenge of producing the next generation computers.

The features of the EM-3 prototype are as follows:
(1) Multi-microprocessor implementation.
(2) Attached special hardware for the packet memory.
(3) Four by four router cell fabricated by gate-array LSI.
(4) Advanced control mechanism for function evaluation.
(5) Distributed list structure.
(6) Lisp-like data-driven language.

In this paper, the new control feature adopted in the EM-3 is first described briefly. Next, the hardware organization of the EM-3 prototype, instruction set and format of the communication packets used are described. Then the Lisp-like data-driven language, EMLISP, is outlined. Finally, a performance evaluation of the EM-3 prototype using the software simulator is presented.

2. Control mechanism of the EM-3

2.1 Pseudo-results and semi-results

EM-3 is a multiprocessing system with a number of identical processing elements (PEs) in which each PE is connected via a packet communication network. Figure 1 shows the functional organization of an EM-3 processing element. The functions of the sections are described in [12]. Each section of a PE processes received packets and sends the processed packets to the designated sections.

The function evaluation mechanism of the EM-3 belongs to the class of "full substitution" [10] for recursive programs. It can be observed that eager evaluation [3,5] and incomplete objects [11] belong to a similar class of computation. The difference is that our approach is a natural extension of the data-driven scheme to function evaluation, whereas the latter two approaches are based on the reduction scheme.

In order to achieve eager evaluation on the base of a data-driven scheme, the concept of a "pseudo-result" [12,16] is introduced. In the control mechanism of the EM-3, function execution causes the generation of a pseudo-result. The pseudo-result can invoke other operations and/or defined functions as the actual-result does. When and only when all argument values for a defined function become available, a pseudo-result is generated as the virtual result of the function execution.

Advanced control and pipelining are carried out using the concept of pseudo-results which increase the concurrency in multiprocessing environments. The proposed pseudo-result scheme relaxes the firing conditions of the data-driven scheme, and therefore the evaluation of a function is advanced, and the operations contained in the function can be executed concurrently with the evaluation of its successor. This allows a certain degree of overlapping of computation.

The lenient cons mechanism [1,9] can be implemented easily using this pseudo-result scheme. The sub structure obtained by executing a cons operation may include a pseudo-result, and this sub structure is a "semi-result". A cons operation accepts any combination of actual-result, semi-result and pseudo-result as its input, and generates a semi-result. A semi-result can fire operations and/or functions. When applying car/cdr operations for a semi-result, the output, which is not necessarily an actual-result, is obtained immediately. This allows advanced computation.

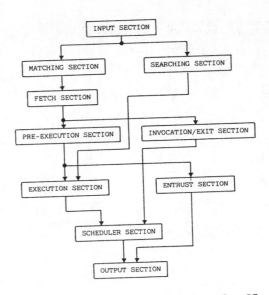

Fig. 1 Functional organization of a PE

2.2 Partial-result

The pseudo-result which is introduced in the control mechanism of the EM-3 can be regarded as a data type in the data-driven scheme. An operation manipulates a pseudo-result as an actual data. If an operation generates a new data type containing a pseudo-result, then all operations can evaluate it more eagerly. This new data type has an incomplete structure which resembles an intermediate form of the reduction mechanism. This incomplete structure is a "partial-result". In the reduction mechanism, the reduced form is rewritten by a new form until no rewriting can be applied, whereas in the partial-result mechanism, the partial-result can be manipulated freely. Therefore, if a partial-result contains any pseudo-result and if the value of this pseudo-result is a partial-result, it is possible to replace the old partial-result by a new partial-result. This process resembles the process of reduction. In the reduction mechanism, decomposition is invoked by a request, but in the partial-result mechanism, decomposition and evaluation are invoked concurrently.

Partial results are introduced here to evaluate add operation and/or multiply operation eagerly. Because the add operation and multiply operation hold the commutative law, we can calculate a series of add operation and/or multiply operations in any sequence.

The format of a partial result is assumed as follows.

(op, number-part, pseudo-result)

Here the op is + or *, which represents the operation for a partial calculation. The number-part represents the defined part of partial-result. The pseudo-result represents the undefined part of the partial-results which is designated as the value of the pseudo-result. For example, when an add operation is fired by the arrival of number 5 and pseudo-result #1, the output of the add operation will be a partial-result represented as (+, 5, #1).

We show the calculation of the partial-results by using an example. If the result of some function F is (+, 5, #1), a partial-result, and if the value of the pseudo-result part, #1 in this partial-result, is (+, 3, #2), another partial-result, then the new partial result of F is obtained by replacing #1, the pseudo-result part of the old partial-result, by (+, 3, #2). Then the present value of F is (+, 5, (+, 3, #2)) = (+, 8, #2), a new partial result. This replacement is carried out concurrently with the decomposition and generation of partial-results in the EM-3.

To execute partial calculation efficiently, two types of packets are introduced. One is a "request packet" which requests a further reduced form of a pseudo-result, and the other is a "reply packet" which gives the reply to the request packet. If the value of a reply packet is a partial-result, a new request packet for another pseudo-result, to replace the partial result, is generated. When the value of a reply packet is not a partial-result, the reduction process stops and substitutes the actual-result as the value.

Figure 2 illustrates the partial calculation of the recursively defined factorial function. It shows the computation process of the partial calculation, i.e., how the partial result is replaced and how the request or reply packet is sent or received. Note that the decomposition of the function invocation and the arithmetic operations are executed concurrently.

3. ORGANIZATION OF THE EM-3 PROTOTYPE

3.1 The structure of the EM-3 prototype

The purpose of the EM-3 prototype is
(1) To confirm the effectiveness of the EM-3 control mechanism.
(2) To measure different kinds of overheads to realize the data-driven machine.
(3) To evaluate the performance of a real data-driven machine by executing practical programs which cannot be executed on the software simulator.

Figure 3 shows the organization of the EM-3 prototype. The prototype consists of eight PEs, each of which is connected via a router network. A PE corresponds to the M68000 16-bit microprocessor with special hardware. The functions of a PE of the prototype are logically identical to those of the EM-3 which is shown in Figure 1. In the EM-3 prototype all PEs process packets in parallel, and each PE processes packets sequentially, because the function evaluation mechanism is realized by a control program in the microprocessor. The control program of the prototype is written in the C language.

```
        factorial(4) = #0

#0 = (*,4,#1)  ----> REQUEST for #1
               <---- REPLY  #1 = (*,3,#2)
    |
    v
#0 = (*,12,#2) ----> REQUEST for #2
               <---- REPLY  #2 = (*,2,#3)
    |
    v
#0 = (*,24,#3) ----> REQUEST for #3
               <---- REPLY  #3 = (*,1,#4)
    |
    v
#0 = (*,24,#4) ----> REQUEST for #4
               <---- REPLY  #4 = 1
    |
    v
#0 = 24
```

Fig. 2 Example -- partial-result calculation

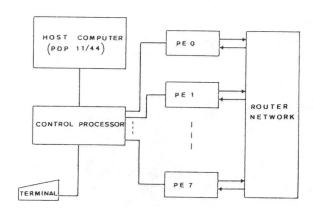

Fig. 3 Block diagram -- EM-3 prototype

There is no locality in the network. The communication packets pass from one PE to another PE via the network. Each PE is connected to the control processor via a 16-bit parallel interface. The control processor loads the user program from the host computer to all PEs, controls the status of each PE by using interruption and also controls the I/O functions.

The host computer, PDP-11/44, is used for software developments and file management. It includes the C compiler and the cross C compiler for the M68000 microprocessor. The control program of the prototype is debugged on the host computer.

Figure 4 shows the photograph of the EM-3 hardware prototype. This shows the control processor (top shelf) four PEs (each shelf contains two PEs), router network, another four PEs from top to bottom respectively. Each PE is composed of four 23cm * 25 cm boards. Router network is composed of a 35cm * 40cm board. Each PE is connected to a router network port and to the control processor by flat cables.

3.2 Organization of the PE

The organization of a PE is shown in Figure 5. The M68000 microprocessor is the main processor of a PE. The I/O interface connects the PE to the control processor. The packet memory control unit is the interface to the router network. Each unit is connected by the M68000 common bus.

Data-driven control of the EM-3 prototype is based on packet communication and packet processing. We focused our attention on the network and packet manager. The design issues of the hardware are:

(1) The communication cost of a packet must be cheaper than the cost of processing it.

The packet length is rather long (maximum 224 bits) and the total packet length is divided into packet segments in the router network. Each packet is 16 bits long. Therefore the maximum number of packet segments is 14. On average the router network can transfer a packet within 2 micro seconds. This is shorter than the packet processing time. The router network is described in section 4.

(2) The processing overhead for managing the packets must be reduced. The attached hardware, packet memories and its control unit are designed for this purpose.

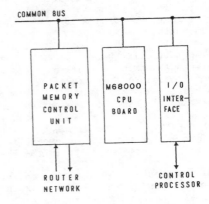

Fig. 5 Organization of a PE

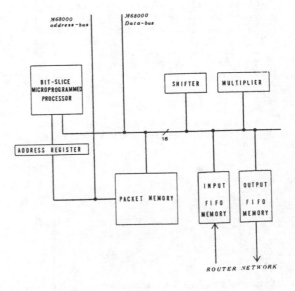

Fig. 6 Block diagram -- PMCU

Fig. 4 System hardware -- EM-3 prototype

Figure 6 shows the block diagram of the packet memory control unit (PMCU). This unit contains high speed memories to store communication packets. The memory size is 128 kbytes. This memory is divided into 4096 fields, so the length of each field is 256 bits. The packet memory organization is shown in the Figure 7. The first 16 bits of each field are used to implement a hash table for the matching memory. The next 16 bits are used to link the hash conflicts, link the free list of packets or link the input/output packet queue to packet communication network. The remaining 224 are bits used to store the body of the packets. Since these memories are allocated in the address space of the M68000 central processor, the processor and PMCU can read the information available in the packets or store any data to the packets. The M68000 and the PMCU run independently and concurrently. Hence it is possible for both units to access the packet memory simultaneously. In this case, preference is given to the M68000 accesses. PMCU can perform bit manipulation and simple arithmetic operations in the fields of a packet.

PMCU consist of two FIFO queues, a bit-slice microprogrammed microprocessor, an address register, a shifter and a multiplier. Input FIFO memory and output FIFO memory are used as an interface to the router network. A packet arrived from the router network is stored automatically in the input FIFO memory. A packet stored in the output FIFO memory is sent automatically to the router network. The microprogrammed processor can execute arithmetic or logical operations for the segmented fields of a packet. The shifter is used for field extraction and the multiplier is used to calculate the hash addresses. These functions are useful to reduce the overhead to process the matching function of the packets. The commands for PMCU are embedded in the address space of the main processor.

The PMCU reads the packet segments sequentially from top of the packet queue and stores then in the packet memory while associatively searching the set of packets

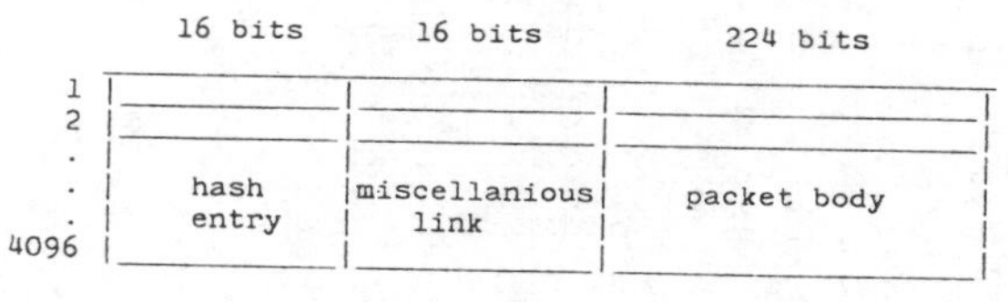

using hashing algorithms. Free space in the packet memory is managed by a free list pointer. Packet memories are accessible from both the main processor and PMCU. Hence, the main processor can read the required data from a packet in the memories, execute them and then write the result into the packet. In the main processor, a packet is represented by a pointer to the packet memory address in the PMCU where the packet management is carried out. Hence, there is no packet movement overhead in the PE.

It is easy to add new functional units to a PE of the EM-3 prototype by simply connecting the necessary add-on hardware to the common bus. For example, a new pseudo-result control unit will be suitable for the extension of functional units of the PE.

PMCU is constructed by using about 170 MSI chips on two boards. The length of the microprogram which controls the bit-slice processor is 64 bits long and its format is almost horizontal.

3.3 Organization of the network

The router network was adopted as the communication network of the EM-3. The packet communication network is organized as a router cell network. A special LSI chip was designed for this purpose. The router cell network is a multi stage interconnection network which consists of router cell LSIs. The router cell LSI has been designed as a general purpose element in the communication network.

The router cell LSI is a store and forward matrix switch with four input and four output ports. There are two buffers in each port to transfer series of data segments successively.

The specifications of the router cell chip are as follows.

(1) The router communication chip does not have a controller in it because of the pin limitation. This gives a generalized router network. A special controller can be designed for special applications, or the same chip can be added to the general router network to achieve the control feature.

(2) Each port of the router chip sends or receives messages by four parallel bits. Any number of router cells, in four bit increments, can be interconnected to form the network.

(3) The conflict of multi port destined to a single port is treated by a priority mechanism. The priority given to each port changes according to a round robin rule.

```
        16 bits       16 bits        224 bits
   1  |----------|--------------|-------------------|
   2  |----------|--------------|-------------------|
   .  |          |              |                   |
   .  |  hash    |miscellanious |   packet body     |
      |  entry   |  link        |                   |
4096  |----------|--------------|-------------------|
```

Fig. 7 Packet memory

(4) The whole router network system acts in a synchronous fashion. A central clock is supplied to all router chips and data transfers from chip to chip are executed during a single clock period.

(5) Packets are transferred through the router in pipeline fashion. A long packet is divided into packet segments and transferred as a sequence of packet segments. The end of the packet is designated by a special signal EOP.

(6) This LSI chip is composed of BI-CMOS gate array technology using 1357 gates. It can transfer one packet segment every 150 nano seconds.

The interconnection between the router cells is a modification of the delta network. The shuffle exchange network with eight input and eight output ports can comprise of two stages of four by four network cells with redundant half ports. In the implementation of the EM-3 prototype, these redundant ports are connected to implement redundant paths.

Figure 8 shows the layout for the interconnection of eight input and eight output network using two four by four router LSI chips. In the EM-3 prototype, 16 parallel bits can be dealt with using four router cells together.

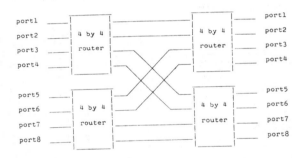

Fig. 8 Router network interconnection

Table 1 Format -- EMIL code

```
(opcode constant dest-list)
(call functionname no-of-arg no-of-ret dest-list)
(proc functionname no-of-arg dest-list)

where
  constant :: = (C-0 n) | (C-1 n)
  dest-list :: = {destination}*
  destination ::= (label { NIL | port-no |
                          { CONTROL | DATA }|(ARG u v)|
                          (RETURN no-of-ret) } )

  label ::= string
  no-of-arg ::= integer        no-of-ret ::= integer
  n ::= integer                u ::= integer
  v ::= integer                port-no ::= integer
```

4. INSTRUCTION SET

The EM-3 instruction set has a one-to-one correspondence with the intermediate language, EMIL code, used to represent data-driven graphs. Table 1 shows the format of the EMIL code. Each operation or function-name in the EMIL code represents a node of a data-driven graph and the dest-list represents the arcs of the graph. The set of data-driven operations are composed of Lisp-like primitives and a number of new operations specially constructed for the EM-3. The examples of the former operations are car, cdr, cons, atom, equal, plus, times, etc. Examples of the latter are the *distribute operation which distributes the input data to the corresponding nodes, the *switch operation which controls one input by the other input, and the *constant operation which always gives the constant data. When an operand of a operation is a constant datum, it is possible to place that constant datum in the constant field of the operation. The destination field consists of two sub fields. The label field represents the destination node name, and the other sub field represents the attribute of the node. For example, port-no represents the input port number of the operation where the operand is destinated and u in (arg u v) represent the argument number, in total of v arguments, of the function called. The instruction proc specifies the name of the function, the total number of arguments and the destination of each argument.

The EM-3 instructions are loaded to the instruction memory of all PEs by the loader. There is no instruction fetch conflict because all PEs have a copy of the instructions

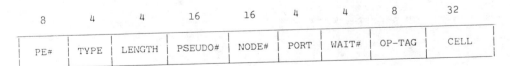

Fig. 9 Format -- result packet

5. PACKETS

A packet carries data or messages from one PE to another PE. The length of a packet varies with the packet type. There are six packet types used in the EM-3, the result packet, entrust packet, request packet, reply packet, incref packet and decref packet. The result packet carries data from one operation to the other operation and hence is used frequently in the data-driven environment. A result packet is 96 bits long; its format is shown in Figure 9. PE# represents the number of the destination PE. The PE# field is used by the router network to send a packet to the destined PE. TYPE represents the packet type number. These two fields are common to all packet types.

PSEUDO# is used to represent the environment in which the packet is generated. NODE# represents the node number of the data-driven graph for which the packet is destined. PORT represents the port number and WAIT# shows the number of inputs that can be accepted by a destination node. The OP-TAG represents miscellaneous information about the destination node, e.g. the destined node is a call instruction. The CELL field is composed of an eight bit tag field and 24 bit datum. In the router network, a result packet is divided into six 16 bit segments.

The usage of the entrust, request and reply packets are mentioned above and have different packet formats. The packet lengths are 128, 48 and 80 bits respectively. The incref packet(48 bit long) and decref packet (32 bit long) are used for collecting pseudo cable and heap garbage using the reference count scheme for storage management.

6. LISP-LIKE DATA-DRIVEN LANGUAGE

All EM-3 user programs EM-3 are written in the Lisp-like data-driven language, EMLISP. EMLISP is a high level programming language based on Lisp specially designed for data-driven computations. Parallel evaluation of an EMLISP program is based on the parallel execution of the arguments in a function and is drawn naturally when an EMLISP program is translated into a data-driven graph. The syntax and basic functions of EMLISP are similar to those of Lisp. Programs represented by S-expressions must be translated into the data driven graphs easily.

The design principles of the EMLISP are as follows:
(1) Pure functionality and the single assignment rule are adopted.
(2) Global and free variables are inhibited.

Table 2 Special features -- EMLISP

[Eliminated Functions]

Relatives of prog:	PROG, PROG2, PROGN
Flow of control:	GO, DO
Modifying list:	RPLACA, RPLACD, NCONC, ...
Relatives of array:	ARRAY, STORE, ...

[Appended Functions]

Blocking:	BLOCK
Parallel cond:	PCOND

(3) The functions replacing the existing list structure are inhibited.
(4) Loop constructs are inhibited.

Table 2 shows the functions which are deleted from and added to the conventional Lisp language. The new feature "block" is introduced to EMLISP to bring a procedural programming style such as "prog" in Lisp. Bound variables must be defined first in the block, whereas S-expressions can be written in any order. The linkages between S-expressions in the block are defind by the dependencies of the variables in the S-expressions. The single assignment rule must be followed in the block structure. The "pcond" structure is introduced to bring the guarded command feature. In the pcond structure, the propositional expressions are evaluated concurrently, then the corresponding forms are evaluated when the value of the conditional expressions are true. If the conditions are mutually exclusive, there is no need to execute the single assignment rule between the forms.

7. PERFORMANCE EVALUATION BY A SOFTWARE SIMULATOR

The performance of the EM-3 prototype is evaluated using a software simulator. The software simulator simulates the program behavior faithfully. In the EM-3 prototype, the functions of a PE are logically identical to those of the EM-3, but the input packets are processed sequentially. The simulation parameters assumed for this simulation are the same as those given in [12]. A router network is used for communication.

The following benchmark programs are executed in this simulation study:
1) q(n): The parallel version of the n queen problem giving all possible solutions.
2) qs(n): The Quicksort giving O(n) parallelism with a given n data.
3) fib(n): The Fibonacci function giving binary tree parallelism.

Fibonacci contains only numerical computations. All other benchmark programs executed contain numerical and non numerical computations. The execution times required to execute above benchmark programs in the EM-3 prototype simulator are measured by varying the number of PEs and plotted in Figure 10.

The ideal data-driven parallelism is obtained by modifying the EM-3 prototype software simulator. All result packets that can be executed simultaneously are counted before the execution. This gives the number of concurrent operations. It is assumed that the execution time is the same for all operations and an unlimited number of concurrent operations can be executed in one time step. Figure 11 shows the ideal data-driven parallelism variation over the time measured for above benchmark programs. Here the horizontal axis represents the time and the vertical axis represents the ideal data-driven parallelism. The data on the vertical axis is plotted by log scale based on 2. These figures show that the EM-3 prototype extract the concurrency embedded in the programs.

8. CONCLUSION

Our goal is to construct a prototype of a Lisp-based data-driven machine to execute more practical data-driven programs and simulate a data-driven machine architecture with a large number of PEs.

In [12] we have already shown the effectiveness of the control mechanism of the EM-3 for non-numerical computations. The EM-3 prototype will confirm this at a more practical level. There are many issues to be solved on data-driven architecture. We will continue our studies on those issues in a real environment.

The first version of the PE control program was implemented. It was written in the C language and compiled to the EM-3 prototype using a cross compiler. Few bench mark programs are executed on the EM-3 prototype. All software tools except the micro program and the environmemt of the C language are coded in the C language. We are planning to evaluate and improve the architecture of the prototype by executing a number of benchmark and application programs. We believe that many ideas for data-driven architecture should be tried out on the prototype and be tested by measuring and evaluating the performance of the prototype.

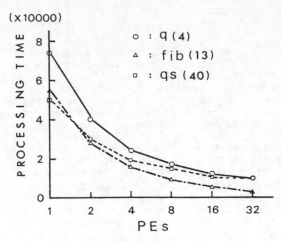

Fig. 10 Simulation results

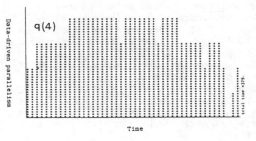

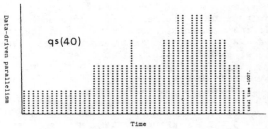

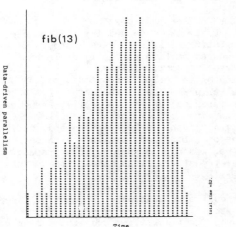

Fig. 11 Ideal data-driven parallelism variations over time

ACKNOWLEDGEMENT

We would like to thank Dr. Hiroshi Kashiwagi, Director General of Computer Systems Division, for providing the opportunity for the present study, and to the staff of Computer Architecture Section for their fruitful discussions.

REFERENCES

[1] Amamiya, M., R. Hasegawa, O. Nakamura and H. Mikami; A list-processing-oriented dataflow machine architecture, AFIPS NCC, 143-151 (1982).

[2] Arvind, V. Kathail and K. Pingali; A data flow architecture with tagged tokens, TM-174, Lab. Comp. Sci., MIT (Sept. 1980).

[3] Darlington, J. and M. Reeve; ALICE: A multi- processor reduction machine for the parallel evaluation of applicative languages, Proc. Funct. Prog. Lang. and Comp. Arch., 65-76 (Oct. 1981).

[4] Dennis, J.B., G.A. Boughton and C.K. Leung; Building blocks for data flow prototypes, Proc. 7th Ann. Symp. Comp. Arch., 1-8 (1981).

[5] Grit, D.H. and R.L. Page; Eager evaluation of functional programs and a supporting interconnection structure, Proc. 3rd Int. Dist. Comp. Sys., 811-816 (1982).

[6] Gurd, J. and I. Watson; Data driven system for high speed parallel computing -- part1: Structuring software for parallel execution, Computer Design, Vol.19, No.6, 91-100 (June 1980).

[7] Gurd, J. and I. Watson; Data driven system for high speed parallel computing -- part2: Hardware design, Computer Design, Vol.19, No.7, 97-106 (July 1980).

[8] Herat, J.; Performance evaluation of a data- driven machine using a software simulator, Masters thesis, Univ. of Electrocommunications, (March 1984).

[9] Keller, R.M., G. Lindstrom and S. Patil; A loosely-coupled applicative multi-processing system, Proc. NCC, 613-622 (1979).

[10] Manna, Z.; Mathematical Theory of Computation, McGraw-Hill, New York (1974).

[11] Peterson, J.C., W.D. Murray; Parallel computer architecture employing functional programming systems, Proc. Int. Workshop High-level Lang. Comp. Arch., 190-195 (May 1980).

[12] Yamaguchi, Y., K.Toda and T.Yuba; A performance evaluation of a Lisp-based data-driven machine (EM-3), Proc. 10th Ann. Aymp. Comp. Arch., 163 -369 (1983).

[13] Yamaguchi, Y. and T. Yuba; A partial caluculation for the numerical operations on data-driven machine EM-3, Proc. 27th Nat. Conv. IPS Japan, 7N-5 (Oct. 1983), in Japanese.

[14] Yamaguchi, Y., K. Toda and T. Yuba; The ETL data-driven machine EM-3: (1) Architecture, Proc. 26th Nat. Conv. IPS Japan, 5N-3 (Mar. 1983), in Japanese.

[15] Yuba, T., Y. Yamaguchi and T. Shimada; EMLISP: A Lisp-like language for a data-driven machine and its intermediate language, Proc. 24th Nat. Conv. IPS Japan, 7D-6 (Mar. 1982),in Japanese.

[16] Yuba, T., Y. Yamaguchi and T. Shimada; A control mechanism of a Lisp-based data-driven machine (EM-3), Inf. Proc. Lett., Vol. 16, No. 3, 139-143 (1983).

Reprinted from *The Proceedings of the 11th Annual International Symposium on Computer Architecture*, 1984, pages 188-197. Copyright © 1984 by The Institute of Electrical and Electronics Engineers, Inc.

Architecture of SOAR:
Smalltalk on a RISC

David Ungar, Ricki Blau, Peter Foley, Dain Samples, and David Patterson

Computer Science Division
Department of Electrical Engineering and Computer Sciences
University of California
Berkeley, California 94720

ABSTRACT

Smalltalk on a RISC (SOAR) is a simple, Von Neumann computer that is designed to execute the Smalltalk-80 system much faster than existing VLSI microcomputers. The Smalltalk-80 system is a highly productive programming environment but poses tough challenges for implementors: dynamic data typing, a high level instruction set, frequent and expensive procedure calls, and object-oriented storage management. SOAR compiles programs to a low level, efficient instruction set. Parallel tag checks permit high performance for the simple common cases and cause traps to software routines for the complex cases. Parallel register initialization and multiple on-chip register windows speed procedure calls. Sophisticated software techniques relieve the hardware of the burden of managing objects. We have initial evaluations of the effectiveness of the SOAR architecture by compiling and simulating benchmarks, and will prove SOAR's feasibility by fabricating a 35,000-transistor SOAR chip. These early results suggest that a Reduced Instruction Set Computer can provide high performance in an exploratory programming environment.

1. Introduction

The creators of Smalltalk have striven for a highly productive environment, and have demanded substantial computing support to achieve that goal. The Smalltalk-80 system is the result of a decade of work on programming environments and languages, and includes an editor, browser, and interactive graphics tools in addition to a compiler and debugger [GoR83, She83].

To increase the portability of the system, the Smalltalk-80 language is defined by a high-level virtual machine that is hidden from the Smalltalk programmer. Although a Smalltalk-80 program is compiled into virtual machine instructions, all interactions with the debugger use the source code. Smalltalk-80 achieves high programmer productivity in several ways:

FIGURE 1. Photograph of the Berkeley Smalltalk system [UnP83] running on a 68010 in the SUN workstation. The standard hardware configuration for Smalltalk-80 systems is a single-user computer with a bit-mapped display, pointing device (mouse), and several megabytes of main memory.

- by eliminating the need to specify the types of variables,

- by improving the speed of the compiler by linking subroutines on the fly, and

- by automatically managing dynamically varying data structures.

Unfortunately, Smalltalk has been hindered by slow or expensive implementations. The only Smalltalk-80 system that everyone agrees has adequate performance requires a Dorado. This is a powerful, single-user, 70ns ECL minicomputer with writable control store that costs over $100,000 [LPM81]. Smalltalk-80 needs that support because

- Smalltalk has no type declarations. The type of a variable cannot be determined until the program is run. Thus, the Smalltalk-80 virtual machine **must check the type of operands before performing arithmetic operations.**

- The Smalltalk approach to data abstraction results in programs that are composed of many small procedures. Therefore, Smalltalk-80 programs **have many more procedure calls** than traditional languages.

- The destination of a procedure call depends on the types of the operands and must be computed with a table lookup when the call is executed. Consequently, Smalltalk-80 **procedure calls are more expensive.**

- Dynamic data are created 10 times more frequently than on LISP systems [Ung84], so Smalltalk-80 **automatic storage reclamation is more frequent.**

Smalltalk-80 needs high performance at low cost, and one recent style of computer architecture, the Reduced Instruction Set Computer (RISC), claims to meet those demands for traditional programming systems [PaS81,PaS82]. In this style there is a much closer coupling between architecture and implementation.

To design a RISC,

- start with a fast and simple register-based instruction set similar to microcode in other machines, then

- identify the time-consuming operations in typical programs,

- and finally take the hardware saved by simplifying instruction execution and dedicate it to speeding up the time consuming operations.

RISC designs contrast with traditional high-level language computers that rely on long microcode sequences to provide complex functions "in hardware." Instead of microcode, RISC systems rely on software to provide complicated operations. Of course, software consumes memory, but we claim many would add memory to gain speed.

We are designing a machine that puts Smalltalk On A RISC (SOAR), and are evaluating the vigor of such an unusual hybrid. Berkeley Smalltalk [UnP83], a Smalltalk interpreter for the MC68010 that runs on the Sun workstation, has served as a test bed for many of our implementation ideas and as a source of information about the time-consuming operations required to support Smalltalk.

The SOAR project resulted from the third offering of the VLSI Computer Architecture course sequence at Berkeley. The first two offerings produced RISC I [PaS81] and the RISC Instruction Cache [PGH83].

In this paper, we introduce SOAR by describing our approach to four obstacles to building a fast Smalltalk-80 system:

- Type Checking,
- Interpretation,
- Procedure Calls, and
- Object Oriented Storage Management.

We then pay our respects to the architectural ancestors of SOAR, evaluate the performance consequences of the individual ideas in SOAR, compare the expected performance of SOAR to a fast ECL minicomputer, and describe the status of current SOAR implementations.

2. Type Checking

Since the operand types for an operation vary, types must be checked at runtime. For example, although the statement "c ← a + b" is usually integer addition [Bla83a], Smalltalk implementations must correctly handle other cases, such as scalar floating point addition. Previous implementations use microcode or software to check types before performing addition, penalizing the speed of the integer operation.

Traditional tag checking hardware checks data types to discover program errors. The purpose of tags in SOAR is to improve performance by guessing the types of the data and beginning the operation immediately, while simultaneously checking the tags to confirm the guess.

In the simplest and most common case, both operands are integers and the correct result is available after one cycle. If either operand is not an integer, SOAR aborts the operation and traps to routines that carry out the appropriate computation for the data types. The basis for type checking is a one-bit tag in each word indicating whether the word contains an integer or a pointer to a data structure with type-specific information. To reduce the cost of trapping, SOAR exploits *shadow registers* to catch the operands of the trapping instruction. These are inexpensive in single-chip processors–they are just two more registers on the data busses near the ALU. The shadow registers, simple instructions, and uniform instruction size speedup traps invoked by tag checks. Figure 2 shows the SOAR tags.

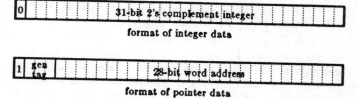

format of integer data

format of pointer data

FIGURE 2. SOAR supports two data types, 31-bit signed integers and 28-bit pointers. Pointers include a generation tag (as explained in section 4). SOAR words could have contained 32 bits of data plus one bit of tag for a total of 33 bits. The scarcity of 33-bit tape drives, disk drives, and memory boards led us to shorten our words to a total of 32 bits including the tag (31 bits of data).

The dynamic type checking of Smalltalk also influences the conditional branch instructions of SOAR. Architects have two choices in implementing conditional branches, explicit comparison instructions or condition code based branches. Condition codes can save a comparison instruction when the branch condition depends on comparing zero with the result of a previous arithmetic operation. This optimization fails with Smalltalk. The result of the operation cannot simply be compared to integer zero because the result's type will vary. Instead of condition codes, SOAR has compare-and-skip instructions that quickly perform integer comparisons. (A compare-and-branch instruction would not fit in one word.) Attempts to compare non-integer objects cause a tag trap to invoke a Smalltalk routine that performs the appropriate comparison operation. If the condition holds, there is a one cycle penalty for skipping an instruction. If the condition fails, the instruction following the skip is executed. This is normally a jump. SOAR jump instructions contain the absolute address of the target instruction. Because no address computation is required, SOAR eliminates the instruction prefetch penalty for jumps.

3. Interpretation

The Smalltalk-80 system is defined by a stack oriented virtual machine that is based on the Dorado Smalltalk-80 implementation [Deu83]. Each instruction is comprised of one to three bytes and generally corresponds to a token of the source program. These instructions are usually called *bytecodes*. This instruction set compacts object code but penalizes instruction decoding and execution. Bytecodes have the following advantages:

- The simple correspondence between source and object code simplifies the compiler and debugger.
- Smalltalk can be transported to a new machine by writing only the virtual machine emulator.

This approach has drawbacks too:

- Decoding such dense instructions takes either substantial hardware or substantial time. For example, the Dorado Instruction Fetch Unit consumes 20% of the CPU [Pie83]. Decoding simple bytecodes uses 70% of Berkeley Smalltalk virtual machine execution time.
- Some of the high level instructions require many microcycles to execute. These multicycle instructions must be sequenced by a dedicated control unit.

Following the RISC approach, we abandoned the instruction set of the Smalltalk virtual machine, and designed the SOAR instruction set from scratch to minimize the time and hardware needed to decode and execute instructions. SOAR instructions therefore resemble microinstructions. Although such an instruction set results in larger object code, we believe that the cost of additional main memory is offset by the gain in speed.

Each SOAR instruction occupies a 32-bit word, and most instructions take one cycle. The only exceptions are loads, stores, and returns, which take two cycles. The uniform length and duration of instructions simplify instruction prefetch. Figure 3 shows instruction formats:

A tagged architecture that lacks microcode must include instructions that manipulate and inspect tags. Because the Smalltalk system already relies on the compiler to ensure system integrity, we can allow the compiler to mix instructions that manipulate tags with instructions that are constrained by tags. Each SOAR instruction contains a bit that either enables or disables tag checking. Untagged mode (indicated by a % in the assembly language) turns off all tag checking and operates on raw 32-bit data. In untagged mode the tag bits are treated as data, and the complete instruction set can be used to manipulate this data. Finally, untagged instructions allow programs written in conventional languages such as C and

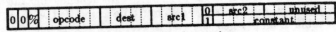

format of calls and jumps

format of other instructions

FIGURE 3. SOAR has two instruction formats. All instructions are tagged as integers to simplify storage reclamation. Jumps and calls contain a bit to enable process switches, a one bit opcode, and the absolute address of the target. Other instructions contain a bit to enable tag checking (%), a six bit opcode, the destination register (or condition specification for skips and traps), a source register, and either another source register or an immediate field.

Pascal to run on SOAR.

SOAR departs from RISC I by omitting byte-addressing. Instead, separate instructions insert or extract bytes from words. Byte-sized data are not needed because they do not exist as individually addressable entities in Smalltalk. Processors with byte-addressing incur a time penalty due to the alignment logic.

SOAR follows RISC in using register based expression evaluation instead of the stack model defined by the Smalltalk Virtual Machine.

Table I shows our instruction set.

4. Fast Calls

Smalltalk stresses program modularity, and relies exclusively on subroutines to achieve that goal. Programs consist of many small subroutines and consequently execute more call instructions than programs in other languages. In addition to being frequent, calls are also expensive because:

- To aid program debugging, Smalltalk-80 initializes all local variables on each call.
- One unfortunate consequences of Smalltalk-80's power is that the destination of a call is recomputed from the type of the first argument with a table lookup each time the call is executed.

The result is that many Smalltalk implementations (including Berkeley Smalltalk and Dorado Smalltalk) spend about half of their time on calls and returns [Deu81].

SOAR reduces the Smalltalk call/return overhead in several ways. First, SOAR avoids saving registers on each call by having many sets of registers reside on chip (Figure 5). This approach is similar to the register architecture in RISC I, but our measurements show that compared to C language subroutines, the shorter Smalltalk subroutines pass fewer operands and uses fewer local variables than C, and so need fewer registers. Each SOAR register window has eight registers instead of 12 for RISC.

opcode <28:23>₈	Instruction	Operands	Operation
			Table I. SOAR Instruction Set
10–17	[%]RET[I][N]	Rs,CONST	pc ← Rs+CONST
			Options as part of return:
			[%] Disables return address tag checking (non-LIFO context)
			[I] Enable Interrupts
			[N] Initialize R0,...,R7 .
40	[%]ADD	Rs,S2,Rd	Rd ← Rs + S2
42	[%]SUB	Rs,S2,Rd	Rd ← Rs - S2
44	[%]XOR	Rs,S2,Rd	Rd ← Rs xor S2
46	[%]AND	Rs,S2,Rd	Rd ← Rs & S2
47	[%]OR	Rs,S2,Rd	Rd ← Rs | S2
41	[%]SLL†	Rs,Rd	Rd ← Rs + Rs (Left shift)
50	[%]SRL	Rs,Rd	Rd ← Rs shift right logical 1 bit
52	[%]SRA	Rs,Rd	Rd ← Rs shift right arithmetic 1 bit
70	[%]INSERT	Rs,S2,Rd	Rd ← 0; byte S2<1:0> of Rd ← Rs<7:0>
71	[%]EXTRACT	Rs,S2,Rd	Rd<7:0> ← S2<1:0> byte of Rs; Rd<31:8> ← 0
60	[%]LOAD	(Rs)S2,Rd	Rd ← M[Rs + S2]
64	LOADC†	(Rs)S2,Rd	Rd ← M[Rs + S2]
62	%LOADM	(Rs)S2,Rd	t ← Rs − S2, x ← d;
			Repeat R[x] ← M[t];
			x←x−1; t←t − S2;
			until x=0.
30	[%]STORE	Rs2,(Rs)SCONST	M[Rs + SCONST] ← Rs2
32	%STOREM	Rs2,(Rs)SCONST	t ← Rs − SCONST, x ← S2;
			Repeat M[t] ← R[x];
			x←x−1; t←t−SCONST;
			until x=0.
20	[%]SKIP	COND Rs,S2	if COND(Rs,S2) pc ← pc+2
21–27	[%]TRAPi	COND Rs,S2	if COND(Rs,S2) R7 ← pc,
			pc ← Trap
00–37	[%]CALL	Addr	R7 ← pc, next
			pc←Addr, CWP←CWP−1.
40–77	[%]JUMP	Addr	pc ← Addr

†Separate opcode needed for trap handler.

I. Figure 4 shows the register organization of SOAR.

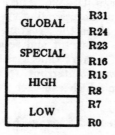

GLOBAL	R31
	R24
SPECIAL	R23
	R16
HIGH	R15
	R8
LOW	R7
	R0

FIGURE 4. Logical view of register file. The HIGHs hold incoming parameters and local variables. The LOWs are for outgoing arguments. The SPECIALs include the PSW and a register that always contains zero. The GLOBALs are for system software such as trap handlers..CE

When the number of activations on the stack exceeds the on-chip register capacity, SOAR traps to a software routine that saves the contents of a set of registers in memory. Unlike RISC I, SOAR has load- and store-multiple instructions to speed register saving and restoring. These instructions can transfer eight registers in nine cycles (one instruction fetch and eight data accesses). Without them, eight individual instructions would be needed that consume sixteen cycles (eight instruction fetches plus eight data accesses).†

The second way SOAR reduces Smalltalk-80 subroutine overhead is by eliminating the delay of local variable initialization. Instead of initializing each register with a separate instruction at the beginning of each subroutine, SOAR exploits VLSI and initializes all the registers of a window in parallel. This is done by the return instruction, concurrently with calculating the return address. This leaves the registers initialized for the next call.

The third way SOAR reduces subroutine overhead is by caching the result of the destination address table lookup in the instruction stream, as suggested by Peter Deutsch [Deu82]. Figures 6 and 7 illustrate this suggestion. This avoids the table lookup, but forces SOAR to support non-reentrant code. Since all Smalltalk processes

† In retrospect, these multi-cycle instructions added considerable complexity to the design, and the benefits may not prove to be worth the costs.

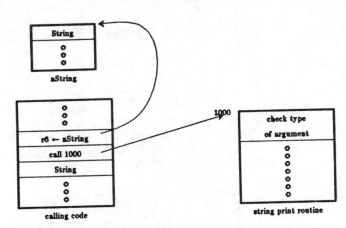

FIGURE 7. The next time the call is executed, control goes directly to the string print routine. A prolog checks that the current argument's type matches the contents of the word following the call instruction. This word contains the type that the argument had the previous time the call was executed. If the types match, control falls through to the string print routine, otherwise another lookup is needed.

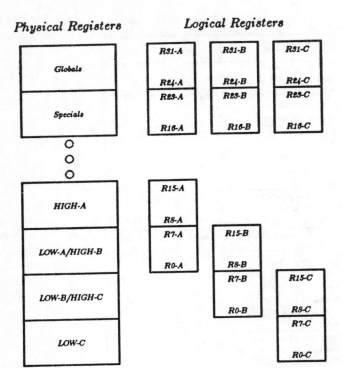

FIGURE 5. Like RISC I, SOAR has many physical sets of registers that map to the logical registers seen by each subroutine.

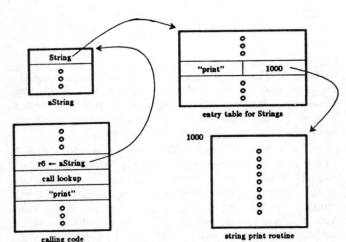

BEFORE

FIGURE 6. Caching the target address in the instruction stream: In this example, the print routine is called with an argument that is a string. (The argument is passed in r6.) The first time call is executed, the call contains the address of a lookup routine and the word after the call contains a pointer to the name "print". The lookup routine follows the pointers to the entry table for strings, and finds the entry for "print". It then overwrites the call instruction with a call to that routine and replaces the word after the call with the type of the argument (string).

share the same address space, process switches must be avoided in sections of code that modify or use the cached data. One approach would be to implement semaphores in software. This would be too expensive because each Smalltalk call executes a short non-reentrant section of code. The approach we followed was to add a bit to each instruction to disable process switches.

In Smalltalk, calls and jumps are so frequent that the virtual machine can defer a process switch until executing the next call or jump instruction. The SOAR call and jump instructions include a bit to specify when it is safe to switch processes [Deu82]. This bit enables a *software interrupt*. When the operating system desires a process switch, it sets a bit in the Program Status Word requesting the software interrupt and resumes execution of the same process. The next time a safe jump or call is executed, the software interrupt transfers control to the operating system which can then safely suspend the process.

5. Object-Oriented Storage Management

In Smalltalk-80, the data structures, or objects, are small (about 14 words for SOAR), and volatile. Smalltalk-80 systems face three challenges in managing storage for objects:

- **Automatic storage reclamation**—On average, 12 words of data are freed and must be reclaimed per 100 Smalltalk-80 virtual machine bytecodes executed; and
- **Virtual memory**—All objects must be in the same address space;
- **Object-relative addressing**—When a Smalltalk-80 subroutine is compiled, the objects it will manipulate are unknown. Only the offsets into the objects can be

compiled into the code.

Automatic Storage Reclamation. Traditional software and microcode implementations of object oriented systems rely on an object address table (Figure 8). Each word contains an index into this table, and the table entry contains the address of each object and its reference count. The reference count supports automatic storage reclamation by indicating when an object is no longer referenced. The indirection through the table also supports fast compaction.

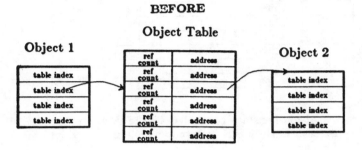

FIGURE 8. In traditional Smalltalk-80 systems, each pointer is really a table index. The table entry contains the target's reference count and memory address. The indirection through the table consumes base registers and time.

FIGURE 9. A SOAR pointer contain the virtual address of the target object. This is the fastest way to follow pointers.

SOAR supports Generation Scavenging [Ung84] to reclaim storage efficiently without requiring costly indirection or reference counting (Figure 9). Generation Scavenging is based on the observation that most objects either die young or live forever. Thus, objects are placed into two generations and only new objects are reclaimed. The algorithm requires that a table be updated whenever a pointer to a new object is stored in a memory location within an old object. Stores are so frequent that we provide hardware support for this check. SOAR tags each pointer with the generation of the object that it points to. While computing the memory address, the store instruction compares the generation tag of the data being stored with the generation tag of the memory address. 99.8% of the time, no table update is necessary and the store completes without trapping. Once again we rely on tags to confirm the normal case and trap in the unusual case.

Object-Relative Addressing. The indirection in

previous Smalltalk-80 systems required dedicated base registers for frequently accessed objects. These registers had to be updated for each procedure call or return. The direct object addressing in SOAR (and the Berkeley Smalltalk interpreter) obviates separate base registers. Instead, a single load or store instruction with an immediate offset suffices to access a field of an object.

Virtual Memory. SOAR's address space exceeds current Smalltalk-80 system sizes by several orders of magnitude. Thus, all the objects can fit in the address space, but SOAR must still somehow ensure that only active objects reside in main memory. The simplicity of paging address translation hardware makes this technique attractive. Since pages dwarf objects, objects that are used together must be grouped on the same page, otherwise much main memory could be wasted with unused portions of pages. Offline utility programs can regroup objects overnight and still maintain reasonable memory utilization; object groupings do not degrade quickly [Bla83b]. This software solution permits SOAR to enjoy the simplicity and performance of paging while making good use of main memory.

6. Architectural Heritage

Many machines inspired the ideas in SOAR, and we hereby pay our respects. The design philosophy, instruction set, and register architecture are indebted to RISC I [PaS82]. A related machine, the IBM 801 [Rad82], had a fast, one word call instruction like SOAR. MIPS–another machine with a simple instruction set–eschewed byte addressing, and SOAR follows that lead [HJB82]. The compare and branch concept has been used by many other machines–Von Neumann, for example, mentioned it in 1944 [BGV71].

The Burroughs 5000 is the original tagged machine, but to the best of our knowledge SOAR is the only machine that has tagged and untagged versions of each instruction. Many papers have proposed that data types could be checked in parallel with execution, but we have heard of only one other piece of hardware that implements it–the Symbolics 3600 Lisp machine [Roa83] uses tags to confirm the assumption that the second operand is the same type as the first operand, but it dedicates more bits to tags.

Peter Deutsch at Xerox PARC has proposed another approach to achieving efficient execution of a dense instruction set with simple hardware. When a subroutine is invoked, a translator routine converts it to the CPU's simpler, faster, and sparser native instruction set. A cache saves translated routines for reuse [DeS84].

7. Initial Performance Projections

The performance of Smalltalk systems is hard to measure without a complete system; infrequent but costly events can have a large impact. The Smalltalk-80 system includes two sets of benchmarks: macro-benchmarks, which exercise high-level operations such as compiling and text editing, and micro-benchmarks, which test low-level operations [McC83]. We have compiled seven

Table II. Relative Performance of Smalltalk-80 Micro-benchmarks					
Machine	Dorado	Dolphin	68000	VAX-11/780	SOAR
	(Xerox)	(Xerox)	(Tektronix)	(DEC)	(UCB)
year of introduction	1978	1978	1980	1978	1984
Technology	ECL	TTL	NMOS	TTL	NMOS
Cycle time	67 ns	180 ns	400 ns	200 ns	550 ns
virtual machine implementation	microcode			assembler	–
Object pointer size			16 bits	32 bits	
Benchmark	Relative speed: Dorado = 100%, larger is faster				
StringAtPut (replace char in string)	(100%)	11%	12%	8%	41%
StringAt (read char in string)	(100%)	11%	12%	7%	49%
ArrayAt (read element in array)	(100%)	11%	12%	8%	51%
ArrayAtPut (replace element in array)	(100%)	11%	10%	7%	51%
Size (read array size)	(100%)	12%	10%	7%	59%
ActivationReturn (call/return)	(100%)	14%	12%	6%	410%
3plus4 (3+4)	(100%)	7%	5%	2%	580%

micro-benchmarks by hand and run the SOAR object code on a simulator. In Table II we give the performance of SOAR relative to the Dorado. Smalltalk-80 was developed on the Dorado, which provides the best performance of any implementation. We also include figures for other implementations, taken from [McC83]. Alan Borning has projected that if the Intel iAPX-432, an object-oriented microprocessor were remicrocoded for Smalltalk-80, its performance would be about 20% of a Dorado [ABM83].

SOARs performance on these benchmarks ranges from 40% to 560% of a Dorado. Overall system performance of SOAR probably lies somewhere between the extremes. To quote from [McC83]:

"... it is a mistake to place a great deal of emphasis on micro-benchmark performance. It seems that there are only a few micro-benchmarks whose performance correlates strongly with global (macro-benchmark) performance. . . The activation/return benchmark correlates much more strongly with macro-level performance than do most other micro-benchmarks. So it appears that general system behavior is most strongly influenced by the speed of method activation and return. (This may be less true of machines with special stack hardware or other special hardware that would affect Smalltalk-80 bytecode performance in a non-uniform way."

While the final performance analysis awaits the running of the macro-benchmarks, we are encouraged by these initial results.

8. Implementation

The NMOS implementation of SOAR is 432 mils wide, 320 mils high, contains 35,300 transistors, and should be submitted for fabrication this summer. This chip uses the three-stage pipeline of RISC II: instruction prefetch, execution, and write result [KSP83]. The internal architecture contains a dual-ported register file with 72 32-bit registers connected to the ALU by two major busses. Each SOAR instruction cycle is broken into three phases:

1) bus precharge and register decode,
2) register read,
3) ALU operation and register write of result of previous instruction.

A CMOS version of SOAR is under investigation.

We are constructing the environment needed to embed the SOAR chip in a Smalltalk system. This effort includes building a compiler to translate Smalltalk-80 programs to SOAR instructions, a software simulator for running the compiled programs, and two circuit boards that explore different ways to integrate the SOAR chip into a SUN workstation. The first board provides an interface to memory boards that are dedicated to the SOAR chip. The second board relies on an on-board cache.

9. Conclusion

The SOAR architecture is one example of extending the RISC design philosophy to an object-oriented programming environment. What SOAR omits is as interesting as what it provides. It has no microcode, few multicycle instructions, and no fine-grained addressing hardware. The RISC design has been extended with parallel tag checking to allow the common case to execute at the same rate as RISC I, while trapping to software for the uncommon case. The simple instruction set, register windows, and shadow registers combine to reduce the cost of trapping. Our early performance studies suggest that a single chip SOAR can compete with an ECL minicomputer. If these predictions hold, we will conclude that Reduced Instruction Set Computers provide strong support for programming systems like Smalltalk-80.

10. Acknowledgements

Projects with the ambitions of SOAR need a lot of support, and we have been the fortunate recipients of substantial help from the Berkeley community.

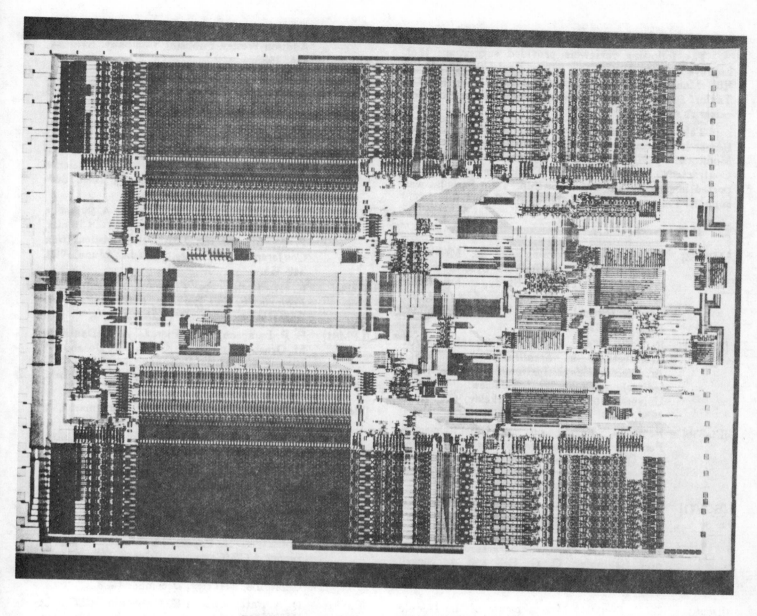

FIGURE 10. Checkplot of NMOS SOAR layout (*not a photograph of a chip*).

The original architecture experiments were conducted by the students of CS292R in the Winter of 1983. The courageous students are John Blakken, Richard Blomseth, Wayne Citrin, Bruce D'Ambrosio, Helen Davis, Mike Klein, James Larus, Carl Ponder, Richard Probst, Harry Rubin, Stuart Sechrest, and David Wallace. The students that worked on NMOS SOAR were Joan Pendleton, Shing Kong, Arthur Chang, Mike Klein, and Mike Remillard. The students working on CMOS SOAR were Mark Hopper, Grace Mah, Chris Marino, Peter Moore, Dave Wallace, and John Zapisek. Both projects have benefited from the hard working CAD groups at Berkeley. We would like to thank Richard Newton and Ken Keller for Hawk [KeN82,Kel84] and John Ousterhout, Gordon Hamachi, Bob Mayo, Walter Scott, and George Taylor for the Magic system [OHM84]. Paul Hilfinger is leading the SOAR Smalltalk-80 software support service, with Bill Bush and Jim Larus playing vital roles. Emil Brown and Frank Dunlap are completing the two boards for the SOAR chip. The first is a circuit board based on a design by Rich Blomseth, and the second is a Multibus-compatable board of his own design.

We would like to thank all the members of the Software Concepts Group at Xerox PARC for their help, suggestions, and inspiration. We want to especially thank L. Peter Deutsch who spent many afternoons explaining the intricacies of implementing Smalltalk-80. He also served as the official "exploratory programming environment implementation data base," explaining the advantages and disadvantages of each technique as well as the successes and failures of related projects.

The following reviewers provided suggestions that improved the quality of this paper: Paul Hilfinger, Mark Hill, Manolis Katevenis, Eduardo Pellegri, and George Taylor. Allene Parker prepared this paper for the camera's eye.

This work was sponsored by Defense Advance Research Projects Agency (DoD) ARPA Order No. 3803 Monitored by Naval Electronic System Command under Contract No. N00034-K-0251. David Ungar was supported in part by an IBM fellowship. Dain Samples was supported in part by a Bell Laboratories Scholarship.

11. References

[ABM83] G. Almes, A. Borning and E. Messinger, Implementing a Smalltalk-80 System on the Intel 432: A Feasibility Study, in *Smalltalk-80: Bits of History, Words of Advice*, G. Krasner (editor), Addison Wesley, September, 1983, 299-322.

[Bla83a] R. Blau, Tags and Traps for the SOAR Architecture, in *Smalltalk on a RISC: Architectural Investigations*, D. A. Patterson (editor), Computer Science Division, University of California, Berkeley, CA, April 1983, 24-41. Proceedings of CS292R.

[Bla83b] R. Blau, Paging on an Object-Oriented Personal Computer, *Proceedings of the ACM SIGMETRICS Conference on Measurement and Modeling of Computer Systems*, Minneapolis, MN, August, 1983.

[BGV71] A. W. Burks, H. H. Goldstine and J. VonNeumann, Preliminary Discussion of the Logical Design of an Electronic Computing Instrument, in *Computer Structures: Readings and Examples*, C. G. Bell and A. Newell (editor), McGraw-Hill, New York, NY, 1971, 92-119.

[Deu81] L. P. Deutsch, Measurements of the Dorado Smaltalk-80 System, Berkeley Computer Systems Seminar, Fall, 1981.

[Deu82] L. P. Deutsch, An Upper Bound for Smalltalk-80 Execution on a Motorola 68000 CPU, private communications, 1982.

[Deu83] L. P. Deutsch, *The Dorado Smalltalk-80 Implementation: Hardware Architecture's Impact on Software Architecture*, Addison Wesley, September, 1983.

[DeS84] L. P. Deutsch and A. M. Schiffman, Efficient Implementation of the Smalltalk-80 System, *Proceedings of the 11th Annual ACM SIGACT News-SIGPLAN Notices Symposium on the Principles of Programming Languages*, Salt Lake City, Utah, January, 1984.

[GoR83] A. J. Goldberg and D. Robson, *Smalltalk-80:*

The Language and Its Implementation, Addison-Wesley Publising Company, Reading, MA, 1983.

[HJB82] J. Hennessy, N. Jouppi, F. Baskett, A. Strong, T. Gross, C. Rowen and J. Gill, The MIPS Machine, *Proc. Compcon*, February 1982.

[KSP83] M. G. H. Katevenis, R. W. Sherburne, D. A. Patterson and C. H. Séquin, The RISC II Micro-Architecture, in *VLSI '83*, F. Anceau and E. J. Aas (editor), Elsevier Science Publishers (IFIP), North-Holland, 1983, 349-359.

[KeN82] K. H. Keller and A. R. Newton, A Symbolic Design System for Integrated Circuits, *Proceedings of the 19th Design Automation Conference*, Las Vegas, Nevada, , June 1982, 342-355.

[Kel84] K. H. Keller, *An Electronic Circuit CAD Framework*, U.C. Berkeley, March 1984. PhD Dissertation..

[LPM81] B. P. Lampson, K. A. Pier, G. A. McDaniel, S. M. Ornstein and D. W. Clark, The Dorado: A High Performance Personal Computer, CSL-81-1, Xerox PARC, Palo Alto, California, January 1981.

[McC83] K. McCall, The Smalltalk-80 Benchmarks, in *Smalltalk 80: Bits of History, Words of Advice*, G. Krasner (editor), Addison-Wesley, Reading, MA, 1983, 151-173.

[OHM84] J. K. Ousterhout, G. T. Hamachi, R. N. Mayo, W. S. Scott and G. S. Taylor, Magic: A VLSI Layout System, *Proceedings of the 21st Design Automation Conference*, Las Vegas, Nevada, , June 1984. Also appears in "A Collection of Papers on Magic," technical report UCB/Computer Science Dpt. 83/154, Computer Science Division, University of California, Berkeley, December 1983..

[PaS81] D. A. Patterson and C. H. Séquin, RISC I: A Reduced Instruction Set VLSI Computer, *Proc. Eighth International Symposium on Computer Architecture*, Minneapolis, Minnesota, May 1981, 443-457.

[PaS82] D. A. Patterson and C. H. Séquin, A VLSI RISC, *Computer 15,9* (September 1982), 8-21.

[PGH83] D. A. Patterson, P. Garrison, M. Hill, D. Lioupis, C. Nyberg, T. Sippel and K. S. Van Dyke, Architecture of a VLSI Instruction Cache for a RISC, *Proc. Tenth International Symposium on Computer Architecture*, Stockholm, Sweden, June 14-18, 1983.

[Pie83] K. A. Pier, A Retrospective on the Dorado, A High-Performance Personal Computer, *Proc. Tenth Annual Symposium on Computer Architecture*, Stockhom, Sweden, June, 1983, 252-269.

[Rad82] G. Radin, The 801 Minicomputer, *Proc. Symposium on Architectural Support for Programming Languages and Operating Systems*, Palo Alto, California, March 1-3, 1982, 39-47.

[Roa83] C. B. Roads, *3600 Technical Summary*, Symbolics, Inc., Cambridge, MA, 1983.

[She83] B. Sheil, Environments for Exploratory Programming, *Datamation*, February, 1983.

[UnP83] D. M. Ungar and D. A. Patterson, Berkeley Smalltalk: Who Knows Where the Time Goes?, in *Smalltalk-80: Bits of History, Word of Advice*, G. Krasner (editor), September, 1983, 189.

[Ung84] D. Ungar, Generation Scavenging: A Non-disruptive High Performance Storage Reclamation Algorithm, *ACM Software Eng. Notes/SIGPLAN Notices Software Engineering Symposium on Practical Software Development Environments*, Pittsburgh, PA, April, 1984.

Making Parallel Computation Simple:
The FFP Machine

Gyula Magó

Department of Computer Science
University of North Carolina at Chapel Hill

ABSTRACT

The FFP machine, a parallel computer now under development at the University of North Carolina at Chapel Hill, has ease and generality of programming, and high performance through parallelism as equally important objectives. This paper contains a discussion of these objectives and the means by which they are to be achieved.

INTRODUCTION

Motivated by a desire to exploit VLSI technology to gain speed, experimentation with parallel computers (or multiprocessors) is becoming more and more widespread. There are many projects under way, some of them already in, or approaching, prototyping phase, each with a different set of objectives, each trying to explore a different part of the design space.

Many of the projects could be characterized by the motto: "Speed at any price!" Such projects produce special purpose machines, or ones with limited programmability.

Other projects could be characterized by the motto: "Speed alone is not enough—ease and generality of programming are equally important!" Such projects aim to produce general purpose machines, i.e., ones that would be considered attractive for a large variety of applications. With these objectives, some speed may deliberately be sacrificed in order to get programmability—a general purpose system cannot be expected to match special purpose systems in their areas of specialization.

The FFP machine now under development at the University of North Carolina at Chapel Hill falls into the latter category. This paper contains an informal description of the central problems in constructing a viable programmable parallel computer, and the solutions proposed by the FFP machine to these problems. (This paper does not contain a description of the FFP machine. Such descriptions have appeared elsewhere[5,15,16,17].)

EXTENSIBILITY ("SCALABILITY")

A parallel computer[6,11] aims to achieve high performance by employing many processing elements (PEs) in executing programs—either a single large program, or a collection of smaller programs. (It is, of course, understood that in addition to this exploitation of parallelism the best available circuit technology would also contribute to achieving high performance.) Since the basic idea of parallelism is that more processors should be able to do more work, the ideal parallel computer is extensible: it is possible to add more and more processors to such a computer, and have it do proportionately more work as a result. Or as it is often said, the machine scales up. Consequently, an extensible parallel computer *does not have a predetermined size,* one could have more or less of it.

Extensibility has both structural and behavioral requirements. Certain interconnection structures are much easier to extend than others, especially if one requires that the machine be extensible in small increments. Another structural requirement is that the total amount of hardware should grow proportionately to the number of PEs employed. The demand that doubling the size of a parallel computer should double (or nearly double) its performance is a requirement concerning the behavior of the system. This is usually interpreted as follows: if a parallel computer already utilizes all parallelism in a program, then extending the machine will not make the same program (applied to the same data) run any faster. However, upgrading the system may allow the same program applied to larger data to take advantage of more parallelism.

The FFP machine aims to be extensible by means to be described in the following sections.

Locality

A large instance of an extensible parallel computer may contain processing elements that are arbitrarily far from each other. However, if such a computer is to work in an acceptable manner, most of the interactions within it should take place among processing elements that are close

Reprinted from *The Proceedings of COMPCON S'85*, 1985, pages 424-428.
Copyright © 1985 by The Institute of Electrical and Electronics Engineers, Inc.

(in some well defined sense) to each other. Such an exploitation of locality within computations *speeds execution* by reducing the average distance of communications and by reducing congestion in the interconnection network. Alternatively, it would permit use of a simpler interconnection network, thereby reducing the growth rate of the hardware structure.

The FFP machine preserves locality by keeping independent subcomputations (subprograms with their data) together. It uses a binary tree as an interconnection network. (Other networks may also be used: Kellman[13] described a version of the FFP machine that uses a sorting network.)

No advance planning by software

An extensible parallel computer should not rely on any planning (such as allocation of resources) to take place before execution, because such a planning (i.e., one processor planning certain aspects of the execution process for n processors, where n may grow beyond any bound) will become a bottleneck of the overall computation. To avoid such a bottleneck, the parallel computation should be able to develop freely at run-time, without any "compile-time" planning to aid or constrain it.

The FFP machine directly executes its machine language, without software planning any part of the execution process prior to execution.

MACHINE INDEPENDENT PROGRAMMING: NO ADVANCE PLANNING BY PROGRAMMER

If it is undesirable to have a piece of software do substantial planning for the execution of a parallel program, it is even more undesirable for the programmer to do such a planning.

Thus, an important desideratum is *machine independent programming* of a parallel computer. It could be described as one in which the programmer does not have to be concerned with (1) the number of processing elements (unless the program overflows the network), (2) the interconnection topology, and (3) the layout (or allocation) of program and data in the network of processors.

Admittedly, machine dependent programming is often tolerated when the objective is "speed at any price," but an argument against such planning is that it does not scale up (with the possible exception of some very regular computations). For machines that aim to be programmable, another argument often advanced is that new parallel architectures should allow—in addition to increased execution speed—programming that is no harder than that of the von Neumann computer, and preferably easier.

The FFP machine supports machine independent programming. The programmer need not concern himself with parallelism, which is implicit and therefore effortless.

DYNAMIC MAPPING OF PROGRAM AND DATA ONTO HARDWARE

The ideas of static and dynamic computations are familiar to most computer users. A *static computation* is one in which the shapes and sizes of data structures, and in the case of parallel computations also the degree of parallelism, remain constant during execution. A *dynamic computation* is one in which the same attributes change during execution. Static computations tend to be simple, regular and predictable; dynamic ones complex, irregular and unpredictable. Static computations tend to be more amenable to analysis, and therefore better understood than dynamic ones. Static computations may be viewed as special cases of dynamic computations.

We are accustomed to being able to execute both kinds of computations reasonably well on the von Neumann computer. It may be said, for example, that FORTRAN was meant for static computations (problems in scientific computing are usually thought to be static, although there are many exceptions), and LISP was meant for dynamic computations (AI computations tend to be dynamic).

A programmable parallel computer should aim for a degree of generality similar to that of the von Neumann computer by supporting dynamic computations efficiently. *Efficient support of dynamic computations* requires that all changes in program and data be allowed to take place freely. It is, therefore, important that parallel computers provide a mechanism to *map program and data onto the hardware dynamically,* or stated from the point of view of hardware: that there be a mechanism to *allocate machine resources dynamically.*

The cost of effecting changes in program and data should be as small as possible, but all changes—no matter how expensive—should be allowed to take place. If the designer of a parallel computer restricts this capability for the sake of high performance (however reasonable these restrictions may appear a priori), the ease and generality of programming will inevitably suffer. For this reason we believe that dynamic mapping of program and data onto hardware will come to be recognized as a requirement for programmability of parallel computers.

Moreover, to ensure extensibility, the changing program and data should be mapped onto hardware so as to *preserve locality within computations.* There is clearly a trade-off involved in deciding whether or not to preserve locality, especially, if only small instances of the parallel computer are planned. On the one hand, preserving locality will involve some overhead, but having locality will speed computations. On the other hand, if locality is not preserved, one will pay by slower execution. Only prototypes exemplifying these two fundamentally different approaches will be able to give us more quantitative information on this matter.

The FFP machine is a *reduction machine*: it rewrites FFP expressions with equivalent expressions at run-time, i.e., it maps FFP expressions onto the hardware dynamically. This mapping, called *storage management*[15], may be viewed as a generalization of dynamic allocation and garbage-collection on the von Neumann computer. It is a machine-wide process, which involves interrupting all computations in the machine, determining where resources are available or needed, and finally redistributing the available resources. By using global information in determining where resources and needs are located, the best allocation of resources is forced on the machine. In performing storage management, the FFP machine employs a great deal of parallelism and pipelining—large-scale parallelism is thus involved in executing not only user programs but also *operating system functions*.

High-level machine language

If one is to design into a parallel machine the ability to map program and data onto hardware dynamically, one must be able to specify *what* exactly is to be mapped onto the hardware at run-time. In other words, one must be able to foresee many important details of all parallel computations that the machine might be called to execute. This is why a top-down design of parallel computers is often advocated, with a sufficiently high-level "machine language" (e.g., a data flow language or a functional language[1]) as the starting point of the design.

The choice of language will obviously have far-reaching consequences for the resulting parallel machine. The language should have a high enough level so that it may give guidance for the design of the machine (e.g., it should express data structuring), and it should be flexible enough so that other languages may be translated into it conveniently.

The FFP machine was derived from the requirements of the FFP (Formal Functional Programming) language proposed by Backus[3]. FFP is in fact the machine language, since the FFP machine directly executes FFP programs. (There is a lower level language, in which the primitive operations of the FFP language are specified. Only in this language can message passing among PEs be specified, which is thus encapsulated into FFP primitives.) The FFP language, being a functional language, automatically takes care of synchronization of subcomputations.

Representation of program and data

Whereas a high-level machine language determines what to map onto hardware at run-time, choosing a representation for program and data determines in detail *how* this mapping is to be accomplished. The representation should be chosen so as to facilitate the efficiency of this dynamic mapping.

Flynn and Hennessy[8] give a good discussion of the importance of representation in distributed systems. In the case of the FFP machine, the representation of program and data has indeed proved to be the central design issue on which everything else hinges.

The FFP machine uses a *linear representation* for program and data: the FFP expression, a linear string of symbols, is mapped onto a linear array of PEs (cells) from left to right, typically one symbol per cell, possibly with empty cells interspersed. The mode of operation of the FFP machine is sometimes referred to as *string reduction*[21]. This linear representation enables the FFP machine to map its program and data onto the hardware at run-time, because it allows the *global storage management problem* to be *simply stated* (it is a one-dimensional problem[20]) and *rapidly solved* (in time proportional to the height of the machine tree[15]).

Furthermore, the representation employs no physical addresses, the expression in the machine is self-describing, and thus during storage management parts of the expression can freely be moved around.

Granularity of hardware

Besides what and how to map dynamically, the third issue that arises is how one provides the *processing power needed to carry out* efficiently the required dynamic mapping of program and data onto hardware.

A useful concept in discussing this is the granularity of a multiprocessor. Informally, in a *large-grain system* each processor is capable of performing nontrivial computations autonomously (each one is, in fact, a von Neumann computer), whereas in a *small-grain system* a processor would have to cooperate with other similar processors to do so. In hardware terms, each processor of a large-grain system typically contains a reasonably powerful ALU, a substantial instruction set and many thousand words of memory; each processor of a small-grain system would typically contain a bit-serial ALU, a small instruction set and a small amount of local memory. (There are other ways to define granularity, for example, in terms of the amount of hardware in the processing elements.)

Seitz[19] has recently noted that the generality of a multiprocessor system increases with its grain size. Indeed, most small-grain systems thus far have been special purpose systems (e.g., systolic processors[14]) or multiprocessors with limited programmability (e.g., SIMD machines[4,12,18,22]), whereas MIMD machines tended to be large-grain systems[2,7,9,10].

Although Seitz's observation is valid for existing systems, we do not believe that it expresses a general law. It is a central premise of the FFP machine project that *appropriately designed small-grain multiprocessors will prove superior to large-grain ones in supporting ease and generality of parallel computation*. The following are among the observations that support this hypothesis.

(1) A small-grain multiprocessor does not suffer from the separation of processing power and memory. For this reason it may be viewed as a "logic-in-memory" system, in which logic has been added to each memory location so that processing may be done within the memory itself.

(2) There is an abundance of processing power when compared with a large-grain system (as measured by the processing power/memory ratio). As a result, a small-grain system can afford to do a lot more copying and data movement than a large-grain one, and thus can better afford to map program and data onto hardware dynamically.

(3) In a small-grain system, maintaining full utilization of all processing elements is less important than in a large-grain system: one processing element represents only a very small fraction of the total processing power. A great deal of the complexity in large-grain multiprocessors is the result of trying to fully utilize all processing elements.

(4) Small-grain multiprocessors have the potential of exploiting fine-grain (expression level as opposed to procedure level) parallelism, simply because each memory location has an ALU close to it. Large-grain systems, by contrast, have inherent difficulties with exploiting fine-grain parallelism. The processing elements in a small-grain multiprocessor must be very good at communication and cooperation (including pipelining), because very little can be accomplished by a PE alone.

(5) The program decomposition problem (i.e., the problem of fitting program and data to the hardware—a difficult one for large-grain systems) can become trivial for small-grain multiprocessors, because they can instead fit the hardware to program and data. (The FFP machine provides an example of how this can be done.)

(6) An obvious advantage of small-grain multiprocessors is that they can have a higher degree of regularity—smaller building blocks used in larger numbers. This can mean lower engineering complexity, which has numerous derivative advantages.

The FFP machine is a small-grain system so that it would have the processing power needed to map dynamically program and data onto hardware. It is composed of two kinds of cells, T and L cells. These cells form a binary tree, the L cells being the leaf nodes, and the T cells being the internal nodes of the tree.

Fitting hardware to program and data dynamically is accomplished by a process called *partitioning:* the whole machine (a binary tree) is divided into a set of disjoint component binary tree machines such that each independent subcomputation (innermost FFP application) is contained in a separate component machine. Since partitioning and storage management—both machine-wide, global operations—must be done repeatedly during execution, the operation of the FFP machine is organized into cycles.

A consequence of the granularity of the FFP machine is that knowledge of most of the FFP language resides in software, in the definitions of the FFP operations, which are brought into the machine on demand. (This is because the cells are so small that they *cannot* know the FFP language.) The particular FFP language to which the machine responds is therefore easily changeable, making it simple to specialize the machine to different application areas.

SUMMARY

Achieving ease and generality in programming a parallel computer requires efficient support of dynamic computations. This in turn presupposes dynamic mapping of program and data onto hardware.

The FFP machine is a small-grain multiprocessor employing a linear representation for program and data in order to be able to carry out the required dynamic mapping of program and data onto hardware. It preserves locality in computations, and is therefore expected to scale up well. It can be programmed in a machine independent manner using the FFP functional programming language.

REFERENCES

1. ACKERMAN, W. B. Data flow languages. *Computer* 15, 2 (1982), 15–25.

2. AGERWALA, T. and ARVIND, Data flow systems. *Computer* 15, 2 (1982), 10–13.

3. BACKUS, J. Can programming be liberated from the von Neumann style? A functional style and its algebra of programs. *Communications of the ACM* 21, 8 (1978), 613–641.

4. BATCHER, K. E. Design of a Massively Parallel Processor. *IEEE Transactions on Computers* **C-29**, 9 (1980), 836–840.

5. DANFORTH, S. DOT, a distributed operating system model of a tree-structured multiprocessor. *Proceedings of the 1983 International Conference on Parallel Processing*, pp. 194–201.

6. DAVIS, A. L. Computer architecture. *IEEE Spectrum* **20**, 11 (1983), 94–99.

7. DENNIS, J. B. The varieties of data flow computers. *First International Conference on Distributed Computing Systems* (Huntsville, Alabama, October 1979), pp. 430–439.

8. FLYNN, M. J. and HENNESSY, J. L. Parallelism and representation problems in distributed systems. *First International Conference on Distributed Computing Systems* (Huntsville, Alabama, October 1979), pp. 124–130.

9. GAJSKI, D., KUCK, D., LAWRIE, D. and SAMEH, A. CEDAR—A Large Scale Multiprocessor. *Proceedings of the 1983 International Conference on Parallel Processing*, pp. 524–529.

10. GOTTLIEB, A. et al. The NYU Ultracomputer—Designing an MIMD Shared Memory Parallel Computer. *IEEE Transactions on Computers* **C-32**, 2 (1983), 175–189.

11. HAYNES, L. S., LAU, R. L., SIEWIOREK, D. P. and MIZELL, D. W. A survey of highly parallel computing. *Computer* **15**, 1 (1982), 9–24.

12. HILLIS, W. D. The Connection Machine. A.I. Memo 646, MIT A.I. Lab, Sept. 1981.

13. KELLMAN, J. N. Parallel execution of functional programs. Technical report UCLA-ENG-83-02, UCLA Computer Science Department, 1982.

14. KUNG, H. T. Why systolic architectures? *Computer* **15**, 1 (1982), 37–46.

15. MAGÓ, G. A. A network of microprocessors to execute reduction languages. Two parts. *International Journal of Computer and Information Sciences* **8**, 5 (1979), 349–385, **8**, 6 (1979), 435–471.

16. MAGÓ, G. A. A cellular computer architecture for functional programming. Digest of Papers, *IEEE Computer Society COMPCON* (Spring 1980), pp. 179–187.

17. MAGÓ, G. A. and MIDDLETON, D. The FFP Machine—A Progress Report. *International Workshop on High-Level Computer Architecture 84* (Los Angeles, California, May 23–25, 1984), pp. 5.13–5.25.

18. REDDAWAY, S. F. DAP—A Distributed Array Processor. *Proceedings of the First Annual Symposium on Computer Architecture* (1973), pp. 61–65.

19. SEITZ, C. L. Ensemble architectures for VLSI—a survey and taxonomy. *Proceedings, MIT Conference on Advanced Research in VLSI* (1982), pp. 130–135.

20. STANAT, D. F. and MAGÓ, G. A. Minimizing maximum flows in linear graphs. *Networks* **9**, 4 (1979), 333–361.

21. TRELEAVEN, P. C., BROWNBRIDGE, D. R. and HOPKINS, R. P. Data-driven and demand-driven computer architecture. *ACM Computing Surveys* **14**, 1 (1982), 93–143.

22. WAGNER, R. A. The Boolean Vector Machine. *Proceedings of the 10th International Symposium on Computer Architecture* (Stockholm, Sweden, June 13–16, 1983), pp. 59–66.

Rediflow Multiprocessing

Robert M.Keller
University of Utah
and
Lawrence Livermore National Laboratory

Frank C.H. Lin
University of Utah

Jiro Tanaka
University of Utah

Abstract

We discuss the concepts underlying **Rediflow**, a multiprocessing system being designed to support concurrent programming through a hybrid model of reduction, dataflow, and von Neumann processes. The techniques of automatic load-balancing in Rediflow are described in some detail.

1. Introduction

"Rediflow" is the name we give for a collection of ideas relating to multiprocessor system design and attendant software capabilities. The name is an elision of "reduction" and "dataflow", two models for evaluation of functional languages on multiple processors. As shall be seen, our conception also includes disciplined aspects of the "von Neumann" evaluation model as well.

1.1. Language and Software Issues

The motivation for use of functional languages stems from the fact that programs expressed in them usually contain a fair amount implicit concurrency, yet are **determinate**, or **speed-independent**, in that they are guaranteed to give the same results no matter how many processors are involved in their execution, and do so independently of the physical aspects of communication between those processors. As such, these languages seem to be ideal for the programming of multiprocessors when little concern over the distinctions between them and uniprocessors is desired. The determinacy criterion is essential for most applications, while intended exceptions can be handled with minor extensions to it. For example, we have successfully programmed distributed database applications, including those involving concurrent updating. Functional languages have other conceptual advantages, but space does not permit a lengthy discussion of them here. We claim that other types of languages, such as sequential languages and languages for logic programming, have an essentially functional character, and can be appropriately combined or embedded in them to share the advantages mentioned. One such combination is discussed herein.

This work has been supported by grants from the IBM corporation, National Science Foundation (MCS–8106177), Defense Advanced Research Projects Agency of the US Department of Defense (contract no. MDA903–81–C–0414) and, at LLNL, by U.S. Department of Energy (contract no. W–7405–ENG–48).

1.2. Hardware Issues

There presently seem to be no conceptual difficulties in interconnecting conglomerates of processors of arbitrarily-high peek processing capacities. Unfortunately, it is another matter to obtain useful work from such conglomerates. In order for a conglomerate to qualify as a **system**, it is necessary to provide linkages between the conception of problem solving and the hardware. Such techniques must be expressed in appropriate computer languages, which are then mapped for execution. Considerations of device technology being held invariant, it is the ease in performing this mapping which determines the relative success of a multiprocessing system.

The ease of mapping depends on the class of applications, the languages used, compilers, and the underlying hardware configuration. Clearly, for a fixed application, a special purpose machine can be designed which will out-perform all others on that application. Our goal here is not to address such machines, but rather to develop techniques which exploit multiprocessing power for a wide range of applications. A class of applications can be characterized by the **regularity**, **size span**, and **granularity** of its members.

Applications of high **regularity** contain many very similar operations which present similar computational demands. For these, approaches such as vector processors or cellular arrays may be most appropriate. The **static data flow** approach [6] also appears useful for applications of very high regularity, but less so for others, since it relies on a rather **balanced pipeline** approach to achieve speedup together with high utilization.

The **size span** characteristic of a set of applications relates to the extent the problem size is apt to vary over the lifetime of the system. While a particular array processor may be ideal for problems which can be contained in one array load, there may be extreme difficulties in "folding" larger problems to match the processor configuration. Even if such folding can be accomplished, it may result in significant unused processor cycles if not done with finesse.

Reprinted from *The Proceedings of COMPCON S'84*, 1984, pages 410-417.

The third differentiating characteristic mentioned is **granularity**. This term refers to the indecomposable units of work distributed to processors. Fine-grain operations would be on the level of bit operations, while slightly larger grains would be arithmetic operations. Large grains would be the level of processes or entire jobs. Rediflow is aimed at applications appropriate for **medium** (and larger) granularity, in which we intend to include irregularly-structured problems such as are found in, but not restricted to, the field of artificial intelligence. Other applications of medium granularity are certain adaptive numerical calculations, certain types of signal processing, and combinations of several application areas which interact in unpredictable ways.

2. Granularity considerations
Two areas of tradeoff which exist when considering granularity are communication overhead, and flexibility in load balancing. We first discuss communication. One reason why systems do not usually operate with peek speedup is that there must be some data communication between granules. This form of communication is minimal in the equivalent purely sequential computation. Therefore, attention must be given to reducing it in concurrent execution. For very small grains, the delay due to communication may exceed the delay of the operations themselves. For this reason, small granularity is not exploitable unless the regularity is so high that necessary communication paths are short and static, or unless there is little communication between grains. Widely distributing many small grains increases the likelihood that overhead due to communication will be large. Our conscious attempt at clustering small operations is one issue on which we seem to differ with other dataflow-related approaches (e.g. [28]). In summary, favoring large grains minimizes delay due to communication, but does so at the expense of loss of speedup due to concurrency.

As mentioned, another factor influencing the choice of granularity is **load balancing**, by which we mean the distribution of grains to the processing units. The ideal situation is a single initial expenditure involving sending equal-size grains to all processing units. However, it will seldom be possible to make such determinations a priori. Instead, many applications will present work loads which are data dependent, and thus not susceptible to static analysis. To fully exploit the available multiprocessing resources, thus attaining maximum speedup, we need to have the ability to **dynamically** distribute load. Here we must pay attention to the tradeoff which favors small grains for the **ability** to balance more evenly, but which favors larger ones to minimize the total effort in actual distribution.

An area of concern often mentioned in relation to granularity is that of **context switching**, i.e. saving a processor's registers when it switches its attention from one unit of work to another, before the former unit is complete. This is therefore a technique for effectively reducing the grain-size, particularly if there is need to vary priority among large grains which may become temporarily inactive due to data dependencies (e.g. a process waiting for an i/o request to complete). As such, it seems fair to lump this overhead with that of load balancing.

3. System organization issues
In addition to intended application granularity, multiprocessing systems can be classified according to processor-memory structure. At one extreme, we have "dancehall" configurations, wherein one can imagine the system as having processors lined up along one side of a large dancehall, and memories along the other, with a network of switches in between. At the other extreme are "boudoir" configurations, in which each processor is closely paired with a memory, and a network of switches is used to communicate between such pairs.

Dancehall configurations appear to provide a uniform time access of any processor to any memory. However, this uniformity may disappear if there is significant contention at individual switches. Unfortunately, this delay also becomes uniformly longer with increasing numbers of processors and memories. It is possible to introduce caches which are coupled closely with processors and which retain local information for faster access, however this introduces the difficult problem of "coherence"(cf. [7, 24]): when one processor wishes to update information which has been cached by another, the latter must be invalidated, which entails additional communication overhead. Any machinery introduced to overcome this problem has a diluting effect on the useful capacity of the system. Boudoir configurations avoid this problem, since each processor has exclusive control over its own memory. This control also obviates introduction of special instructions for multiprocessor memory access, such as test-and-set and its derivatives [10].

4. Locality
The connection of a single processor with its memory has been pejoratively called the "von Neumann bottleneck" [1]. However, we are convinced that it is a powerful device, to be exploited as much as possible. A large number of such "bottlenecks" operating concurrently gives a very high aggregate bandwidth, much higher than a dancehall configuration with the same number of processors and memories, and with less attendant latency of memory accesses. Of course, these processor/memory pairs do not usually operate in isolation; however, if the communication between the components of the pair occur much more often than communication between pairs, in which case we say there is a high **locality**, then the boudoir configuration will be superior. It is conjectured that applications of medium grain and larger usually **do** possess sufficient locality to make the boudoir approach attractive.

When using large numbers (hundreds, to tens of thousands) of processors, it is not attractive to employ a centralized task queue from which processors seek work. One reason for this is that such a queue creates a bottleneck, and is contrary to reliability considerations. A second, more subtle, reason is that such a queue tends to destroy locality, in that it homogenizes the distribution of data. As an alternative, we propose in Section 8 a method in which not only is the work distributed to the processors, but in which the method itself is also distributed.

5. Evaluation models

Several evaluation models have been suggested as the basis for multiprocessor execution. The most conventional of these entails extending the sequential von Neumann execution model to "processes" which run concurrently, but with various forms of communication between them. This method is a large-grain one, and has been most successful when processes are preassigned to physical processor-memory pairs [9]. Related, but much finer-grained are "dataflow" approaches, in which operations such as arithmetic are distributed to multiple function units and operands streamed through logical locations which feed such units. These have a potentially very high degrees of concurrency, but care must be taken, lest potential speedup be absorbed by communication overhead.

Another type of models is called "reduction", in which both the program and data are treated as an integrated, but distributed data structure. The spreading of this structure over the available processors permits its concurrent transmutation at many sites. A fine-grain string-reduction multiprocessor has been described by Mago [23]. Another string-reduction multiprocessor, of medium granularity, is presented in [20]. A medium-grain multiprocessor based on graph reduction is described in [14]. The approach of Rediflow is an extension of the latter.

In the reduction model of evaluation, no resident registers are employed, so cost of context switching is kept to a minimum, enabling rapid multiplexing of existing processor load in an effort to generate more load for concurrent execution. On the other hand, when the system is sufficiently loaded, such multiplexing should be abandoned in favor of more conventional sequential execution. One means of achieving this effect will be discussed later.

5.1. Evaluation by Graph Reduction

Our particular reduction evaluator can be derived from the lambda-calculus as a theoretical basis [4]. If one begins with a simple lambda calculus evaluator operating on string substitution, and introduces optimizations such as the use of pointers to sub-expressions rather than manipulating sub-expressions themselves, one is lead to a graphical, rather than string, representation. Attempts to make efficient the copying (which arise out of function applications, or equivalently "beta-reductions") inherent in this graph representation lead to the use of a linearized segment representation, in which the operator nodes of the graph correspond to words in the segment, and lists of addresses relative to the beginning of the segment represent arcs from the corresponding nodes. Values of "free" variables are imported in vectors, rather than

employing an "association list" which must be searched repeatedly. More details on such representations may be found elsewhere [14, 5, 15]. It is worth noting that so-called **combinator** implementations [27] are also a form of fine-grained graph **reduction**.

A computation in this model begins as a single graph, with the result of one node "demanded" The demand then propagates to other nodes, some of which are primitive operators and others of which are defined by graphs of their own. The latter are expanded by virtually replacing the nodes with the defining graphs. A scheme similar to one described in [14] is employed for performing this virtual replacement through global address linkages.

As an example, suppose there is a tree-structured database distributed in the memory layer. This database may have been generated by some prior program, or explicitly loaded. Suppose further that we have a number of functions f1, f2, f3, ... each a "specialist" in performing a certain kind of search on the database. For example, one function might produce a certain "view" of the database, a sub-tree of nodes with a pre-specified property. A second might compute an aggregate function on the database, such as the number of positive nodes. A third might produce a transformed copy of the database, which is structurally the same, but having node values defined according to some mapping on individual nodes. All these functions could be performed concurrently on the database, each potentially recursively splitting into other function instances, perhaps creating its own data, which is made available for higher-level instances of the functions or for output. It is also possible for one function to be using another's output **while** the latter is being computed, rather than after it is computed. Such phenomena have all been demonstrated in Rediflow.

An advantage inherent in the reduction model is that **all** synchronization for the above activities is **implicit** in the underlying functional language implementation. This removes a considerable burden from the programmer. Whenever "strict" functions are involved (functions which require all of their arguments), the spawning of the necessary activities takes place automatically. This is a strong contrast to process-oriented models, in which there are three separate endeavors: setting up processes, synchronizing them, and using their values.

6. Integration of von Neumann Processes

Despite the advantages of the reduction model mentioned above, there remain aspects of applications which cannot exploit its inherent concurrency, synchronization, etc. It is not uncommon to find segments of applications which have a high peak concurrency, but have many internally **sequential** embedded segments. Such phenomena have been known since the earliest discussions of concurrent computation.

The effect of applying machinery powerful enough for concurrent computation to inherently sequential segments is dilution of overall speedup. For example, a major difficulty with the reduction model is its memory intensiveness. It imitates an elegant mathematical model of functional languages, in which data values are never modified in place; they are only created, and destroyed (by storage reclamation). To do this for every conceivable operation means that much time is spent recycling storage. Although a certain amount of this can be done concurrently with other processing, the overhead seems to remain significant. A desirable goal is therefore to combine the load-spreading potential of reduction with other methods which are not so storage intensive. The approach taken in Rediflow entails what we call "von Neumann processes". These are encapsulated sequential processes which communicate with their environment in special ways. Externally, they appear as a form of "dataflow" functions, an observation made by Kahn [13]. Internally, von Neumann processes are ordinary sequential programs; operations appearing to be file input and output ("get" and "put") are used to communicate internal data values to and from the environment in the form of "tokens" moving on channels.

A key difference between our implementation of von Neumann processes and the suggestion of Kahn is that our implementation does not automatically supply **unbounded** buffers as channels. Instead, infinite buffers which can be attached to channels are naturally implemented in the reduction portion of the model, the operations of which are based on data structures rather than token passing. The interface from a von Neumann process to a reduction-implemented function solidifies a stream of token values into a stream data structure, while the interface from a reduction-function to a von Neumann process does the opposite. These functions are quite similar to ones which are used for external stream i/o in implementations of the reduction model [19].

Software networks of only one type of function can be connected together arbitrarily, the interface functions being used to connect networks of different types. The integration of the two models is done in such a way that what would have been merely **arcs** in distributed data structures can function as logical communication channels between processes. As such, the integration combines the "structure" and "token" models described in [5]into one unified system. Further details are given in [26].

As an example of the use of von Neumann processes, consider a function which performs the "APL-reduction" of a sequence (assumed non-empty) by a binary operator g (assumed non-associative), i.e. if the sequence is [x1, x2, ..., xn] the result is g[....g[g[x1, x2], x3], xn]. A pure reduction implementation would likely use an "accumulating" function such as (expressed in our language FEL [19])

```
reduce[g, x] =
  {
    result red1[head:x, tail:x]

    red1[accum, y] =
     if y =[ ]
        then accum
        else red1[g[accum, head:y], tail:y]
  }
```

Such an implementation would create n-1 instances of red1. This is inefficient, even with a built-in "tail recursion" optimization, since a von-Neumann process could evaluate the same function by the following sequential program:

```
reduce[g, x] =
  {*
   var y, accum;
   accum := head:x;
   y := tail:x;
   while y <> [ ] do
       begin
       accum := g[accum, head:y];
       y := tail:y
       end;
   return accum;
   *}
```

The above example does not demonstrate the use of channels. If the sequence were tokens from a channel, rather than components of a data structure, the corresponding von Neumann process might be

```
reduce[g, x] =
  {*
   var y, accum;
   accum := get:x;
   while more:x do
       accum := g[accum, get:x];
   return accum
   *}
```

Evaluation of the effectiveness of von Neumann processes is demonstrated in [26]. It should be noted, however, that they would not be superior if the operator g were associative, and data structures used for the sequence permitted easy concurrent decomposition (cf. [16]). In this case, a **divide and conquer** approach could be used, and for such, the reduction model seems well-suited.

7. Physical Configuration
As mentioned earlier, Rediflow currently assumes a configuration in which a number of processor-memory pairs are interconnected via a switching network. The combination of such a pair with an appropriate packet switch for information transfer will be called an **Xputer**, a primitive sketch of which is shown in Figure 7-1.

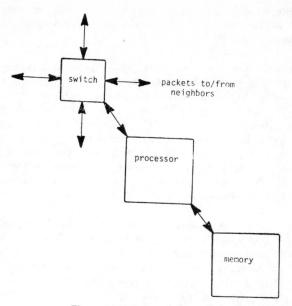

Figure 7-1: Sketch of an Xputer

The exact form of the Xputer network is not too important in this exposition. For a small number of nodes, say up to a few hundred, a rectangular **grid** interconnection should be adequate (see Figure 7-2). Input/output devices, which are not shown, may be attached at any nodes. For larger numbers of nodes, an interconnection topology with a lower worst-case delay is attractive. The concepts expressed in this paper can be used in such a system without modification.

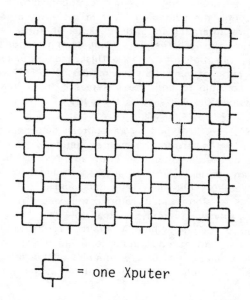

= one Xputer

Figure 7-2: Sketch of an Xputer network

We can think of an Xputer grid as forming a plane surface, with the switches, processors, and memories each forming logically parallel **layers**. The layers need not be physically parallel. Interconnection exists only at the switch layer, while the memories in the memory layer have a combined

globally addressable address space. If one Xputer needs to access the memory of another, it forms a request packet containing the address to be accessed. That packet is then routed within the switch layer to the Xputer containing the addressed location. A result packet is then formed, which is then routed to the requesting Xputer. This request/return mechanism is integrated with the demand-drive mechanism of reduction evaluation, so that remote triggering of function evaluations can take place.

8. Load distribution and balancing

The refusal to rely upon a centralized queue for the distribution of work load means that other distribution methods must be used. As stated earlier, the smaller the grain, the more effective load balancing can be made. To avoid granularity so small that communication delays become significant, we aim at "medium" granularity. The approach taken in Rediflow is based on the contention that, ideally, grains behave as molecules of fluid being poured over a "surface" of processor-memory pairs. The reduction model enables this granularity, but we still need a means of making the fluid model work. We use the analogy of **pressure** to explain how this is done.

As with most multiprocessor organizations, queues are used to hold the backlog of work. In our case, the items on these queues are called **chares** (small tasks). Among several other queues to be described, each Xputer has a queue called the **apply queue** which is the reservoir of **migrable chares**. Chares on this queue represent function-instances which may be done on **any** available Xputer, due to the granularity and addressability assumptions stated earlier. Each such chare carries a "closure" which points to both a block representing the code of the function and a tuple of "imported" values, in addition to the actual argument, which may also be a tuple. Pure copies of such code blocks are cached locally in an Xputer, following an initial fetch from secondary or resident storage. There is no a priori correspondence between logical code and physical Xputer, and the same function may be executed in many different Xputers.

The number of chares on an Xputer's apply queue, weighted together with other resource utilization measures such as memory usage, can be thought of as defining its **internal pressure**. For the moment, assume that the Xputer can sense not only this pressure, but also the pressures of its neighbors, some function of which is called the **external pressure**. When the internal pressure sufficiently exceeds the external, some chares from the apply queue may issue forth into the interconnection network, where they are distributed to Xputers with lower pressures. In fact, Rediflow employs a moderately-intelligent switch, which is capable of directing chares along pressure **gradients** to find such low points. When a chare reaches an Xputer with a local pressure minimum, it is absorbed into its apply queue. This tends to raise the pressure of that Xputer, and lessen the likelihood that it will receive more chares, until its internal pressure becomes lower due to completion of work.

The phenomenon of **saturation** occurs when all Xputers are sufficiently busy that any attempt to migrate apply-chares would be futile, despite pressure differentials. An additional aspect of the Rediflow load balancing mechanism is the detection of such saturation. When external pressure is sufficiently high, migration attempts cease.

Obviously, pressure of Xputers is continually changing. Accordingly, it is necessary to continually update each Xputer's sense of its environmental pressure. This is done through a sampling process, in which the switch of each Xputer computes **transmitted pressure** as a function of transmitted pressures of its neighbors. One heuristic which seems to work well is to define the transmitted pressure to be 0 if the Xputer's internal pressure is below a certain threshold, and 1 + the **min**imum of the neighbor's transmitted pressures otherwise, with an absolute maximum on the order of the diameter of the network. This has the desired effect of permitting chares to flow toward the least loaded node.

9. Throttling

As mentioned earlier, an advantage of the reduction model of computation is that concurrently-executable work is easily spawned for migration to other processors. In effect, a "tree" is grown which corresponds to a single expression from which the "output" of the running program is extracted on a continuing basis. The default mode of servicing each Xputer's apply queue is FIFO, which traverses the tree **breadth first** and thus has the virtue of reaching concurrently executable nodes earlier. However, when saturation conditions exist, an Xputer switches to LIFO to give **depth first** traversal, in order to **throttle** its rate of chare production. This is helpful for avoiding queue overflows and for reducing the possibility of over-commitment of memory space, which could result in a kind of deadlock. (This suggestion was also made in [3].) In saturated mode, operators which would normally demand arguments concurrently are changed to demand them sequentially. This is easy to do within the reduction model. Finally, certain **eagerness** operators are normally compiled into the reduction code to cause anticipatory demands to components of suspended data structures [8] for added concurrency [17]. Eagerness operators are ignored in saturated mode.

10. Garbage collection

Distributing addressable memory across many modules, as is done in Rediflow, necessitates a distributed garbage collector. Although there are several candidates which suggest themselves, our current approach is to use a **copying** garbage collector [2]. In our distributed variation of this approach, the entire address space is divided in half, which appears as a halving of the memories in each Xputer. Allocation takes place within each Xputer from **successive** locations of its half-space. (Incidentally, the occupation level of this half-space contributes to the Xputer's internal pressure.) When all space is used up, accessible records are copied to the other half-spaces in

the same Xputers. In this way, the distribution of data which is necessary for concurrent processing is maintained.

Distributed copying can be achieved by packets, enabling all Xputers to have an active role in garbage collection concurrently. (This packet-oriented implementation is not present in our current simulator). A related approach is used in Halstead's "Concert" [11], although he uses a "real-time" collector which tries to compact to one Xputer, rather than preserving the data distribution. Our approach can be converted to a real-time one, using methods similar to those described in [12], however we have not yet worked out these details.

Another aspect of garbage collection to be exploited concerns load balancing when von Neumann processes are involved. Due to their constantly regenerating nature, the latter are typically much larger-grained than functions evaluated by pure reduction, and therefore somewhat of a hindrance to dynamic load-balancing. Nonetheless, their contribution to Xputer pressure can be assessed by the presence of their components on internal queues, and they can be shifted from one Xputer to another with reasonable ease during garbage collection, when addresses are remapped anyway. The simulation of this form of balancing is currently not done.

11. General Packet Flow

A rough overview of the organization of an Xputer as explained above may be found in Figure 11-1. This diagram assumes that pressure sampling information is sent through the switching layer in the form of **packets**, which are intermingled with packets of other varieties (containing apply chares, data requests and responses, and garbage collection messages). This assumption has been used in most of our simulation results so far. However, it is also possible to dedicate a separate serial channel to the transmission of pressure information.

A **fetch** packet is issued by an Xputer which needs to get a datum from a location in another Xputer. It contains the address of the datum, and a return address. When a fetch packet arrives at the other Xputer's in-queue, the location is checked for containing valid data, and if so, a **forward** packet is created which returns the value to the first Xputer. However, it may be that the data have not yet been produced, in which case the return address is reserved in the second Xputer until such a time as the data are available. Also, if production of the data has not yet been demanded, it will be demanded at that time.

Because all result data have pre-allocated globally-addressable locations, it is not necessary to use any form of "token matching" [28] to get the data to their destinations. Thus, fast von Neumann-style memory is internally exploited in each Xputer. The use of addressing also permits routing tables to provide the shortest possible route to be chosen through the switching layer.

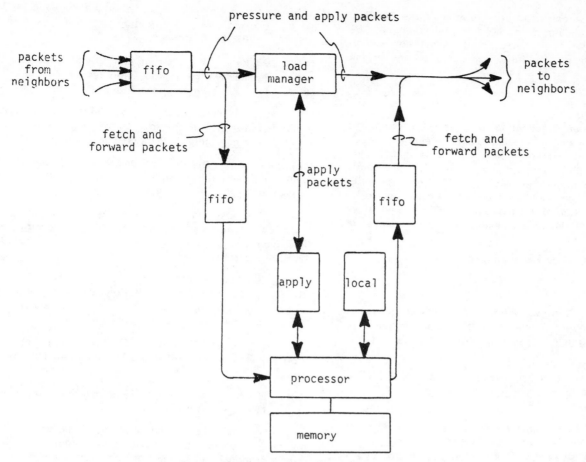

Figure 11-1: Packet flow within a Rediflow Xputer

12. Performance evaluation

The performance of the Rediflow architecture is being evaluated using simulation. As with most studies in their formative stages, we have begun evaluating speedups using an **introspective** model, i.e. one in which speedups are measured against a single processor with the same technological assumptions, architecture, and evaluation model as the multiprocessor. Due to certain needed improvements in our model, we are not yet ready to begin challenging existing sequential processors for applications with low degrees of concurrency. However, if the potential concurrency is high, then we believe Rediflow can exploit it with a demonstrated speedup.

We have been running two kinds of benchmarks. One consists of "toy" programs which exhibit a single kind of activity, such as pure "divide and conquer". The other consists of more "realistic" applications which combine a number of activities, in the areas of simple database searching and updating, and correlative signal processing. To briefly summarize, we have measured speedups in the range of 1 to 8 for the realistic applications, with fewer than 32 Xputers, and of up to 30 with the toy programs with as many as 128 Xputers. Memory space in our simulator is currently a principal limiting factor. In the

process, we have demonstrated that the load distribution techniques designed for Rediflow apparently work well. They do exploit locality, in that typically over 50% of the data packets, and 80% of the apply packets, traverse paths of length at most 2. Usually fewer than 15% of all operations performed need to communicate outside one Xputer. We have also observed that the switches hypothesized for Rediflow do not seem to be a bottleneck under current technological assumptions.

13. Future Work

In addition to continuing our on-going evaluation and improvement of the basic Rediflow system, we are widening the investigation of application areas. For example, we and colleagues are in the process of including means of concurrently evaluating logic programs (cf. [22, 25]).

We also intend to engage in studies of reliability. An added feature of the mathematical model underlying functional evaluation is that data are never destroyed, making such a model a natural candidate for expressing a recovery model [18, 21]. This, coupled with our contention that physical configuration is apt to be more gracefully degradable than a dancehall configuration, make Rediflow an attractive candidate for a reliability investigation. We hope to prove this, and other concepts discussed, through one or more physical multiprocessor realizations in the next few years.

14. Conclusions

We have presented a collection of ideas being integrated into a multiprocessing system called Rediflow, which employs a packet-switching network to implement higher-level programming abstractions aimed at efficiently running medium-grained applications with high degrees of concurrency. We have discussed a technique for load-balancing in an essentially-distributed system. Finally, we have explained preliminary results on performance of Rediflow.

References

[1]   J. Backus. Can programming be liberated from the von Neumann style? A functional style and its algebra of programs. Communications of the ACM 21(8):613-641, August, 1978.

[2]   H.G. Baker, Jr. List processing in real time on a serial computer. Communications of the ACM 21(4):280-293, April, 1978.

[3]   F.W. Burton, M.R. Sleep. Executing functional programs on a virtual tree of processors. In Functional programming languages and computer architecture, pages 187-195. October, 1981.

[4]   A. Church. The calculi of lambda-conversion. Princeton University Press, 1941.

[5]   A.L. Davis and R.M. Keller. Dataflow program graphs. IEEE Computer 15(2):26-41, February, 1982.

[6]   J.B. Dennis. Data flow supercomputers. IEEE Computer 13(11):48-56, November, 1980.

[7]   M. DuBois and Faye A. Briggs. Effects of cache coherency in multiprocessors. IEEETC C-31(11):1083-1099, November, 1982.

[8]   D.P. Friedman and D.S. Wise. CONS should not evaluate its arguments. In Michaelson and Milner (editors), Automata, Languages, and Programming, pages 257-284. Edinburgh University Press, 1976.

[9]   E.F. Gehringer, A.K. Jones, and Z.Z. Segall. The Cm* testbed. Computer 15(10):40-49, October, 1982.

[10]   A. Gottlieb, et al. The NYU Ultracomputer-Designing an MIMD shared memory parallel computer. IEEETC C-32(2):175-189, February, 1983.

[11]   Robert Halstead. private communication, MIT, 1983.

[12]   P. Hudak and R.M. Keller. Garbage collection and task deletion in distributed applicative processing systems. In Proc. Conf. on Lisp and Functional Programming, pages 168-178. ACM, ACM, August, 1982.

[13]   G. Kahn. The semantics of a simple language for parallel programming. In Information Processing 74, pages 471-475. IFIPS, North Holland, 1974.

[14]   R.M. Keller, G. Lindstrom, and S. Patil. A loosely-coupled applicative multi-processing system. In AFIPS Conference Proceedings, pages 613-622. June, 1979.

[15]   R.M. Keller and G. Lindstrom. Hierarchical analysis of a distributed evaluator. In Proc. International Conference on Parallel Processing, pages 299-310. August, 1980.

[16]   R.M. Keller. Divide and CONCer: Data structuring for applicative multiprocessing. In Proc. 1980 Lisp Conference, pages 196-202. August, 1980.

[17]   R.M. Keller and G. Lindstrom. Applications of feedback in functional programming. In Conference on functional languages and computer architecture, pages 123-130. October, 1981.

[18]   R.M. Keller and G. Lindstrom. Approaching Distributed Database Implementations through Functional Programming Concepts. Technical Report, University of Utah, Department of Computer Science, 1982.

[19]   R.M. Keller. FEL (Function Equation Language) Programmer's guide. 1982.AMPS Technical Memorandum No. 7.

[20]   W.E. Kluge. Cooperating reduction machines. to appear in IEEETC , 1983.

[21]   Frank C.H. Lin. A distributed load balancing mechanism for applicative systems. December, 1983.PhD Thesis Proposal, Department of Computer Science, University of Utah.

[22]   Lindstrom, G. and Panangaden, P. Stream-Based Execution of Logic Programs. In Proc. 1984 Int'l. Symp. on Logic Programming. February, 1984. (to appear).

[23]   G. A. Mago. A Network of Microprocessors to Execute Reduction Languages, Part I. International Journal of Computer and Information Sciences 8(5):349-385, March, 1979.

[24]   C.V. Ravishankar and J.R. Goodman. Cache implementation for multiple microprocessors. In Compcon '83, pages 346-350. IEEE, March, 1983.

[25]   U.S. Reddy. Transforming Logic Programs into Functional Programs. In Proc. 1984 Int'l. Symp. on Logic Programming. February, 1984. (to appear).

[26]   J. Tanaka. Optimized concurrent execution of an applicative language. PhD thesis, University of Utah, Department of Computer Science, December, 1983.

[27]   D.A. Turner. A new implementation technique for applicative languages. Software - Practice and Experience 9:31-49, 1979.

[28]   I. Watson, J. Gurd. A practical data flow computer. IEEE Computer 15(2):51-57, February, 1982.

A MULTI-MICROPROCESSOR SYSTEM FOR CONCURRENT LISP

Shigeo Sugimoto*, Kiyoshi Agusa*, Koichi Tabata**, Yutaka Ohno*

* Department of Information Science
Kyoto University
Kyoto 606, JAPAN

** University of Library and Information Science
Yatabe-cho, Niihari-gun
Ibaraki 305, JAPAN

abstract

Recent advances of VLSI technologies have made multi-microprocessor systems feasible to construct. This paper presents a multi-microprocessor system for a LISP-based concurrent programming language, Concurrent LISP. Concurrent LISP is designed for user oriented concurrent programs, especially for artificial intelligence programs. The authors had developed Concurrent LISP on single processor systems. The multi-microprocessor system proposed here is constructed on the basis of these experiences. The multi-microprocessor system is constructed using general purpose microprocessors and it has the language oriented system configuration.

The multi-microprocessor system presented has the nine processor elements and the large common memory area. Reflecting the types of the data to be stored and their access mechanisms, each processor element has the specialized memory interface circuits, and the common area is separated into three sub-areas. The system software is distributed to all the processor elements and has the hierarchical configuration. The system software, especially the operating system, is simplified well to reduce the system overhead.

1 Introduction

This paper describes a multi-microprocessor system which has specialized memory interface circuits for list processing and multiprocessing. We have developed a LISP-based concurrent programming language, called Concurrent LISP (C-LISP) [5]. C-LISP has been developed to make use of multi-process description mechanism for the artificial intelligence problems instead of conventional description mechanisms such as backtracking and coroutines. C-LISP is user oriented, and it has simple yet flexible facilities to describe concurrent processes. We had developed the C-LISP interpreter on a large scale computer (FACOM M-200) [5] and on an MC68000 system [3]. Based on the experiences on these interpreters, we are at work on the development of a C-LISP machine composed of multiple 16-bit microprocessors (nine MC68000's) and a large common memory area (8 MB) [4].

C-LISP has flexible facilities to describe explicit parallelism. A typical example program is a multi-process search program for a game problem: multiple cooperative processes search their own paths in the search space for the game. During the execution of C-LISP programs, many concurrently executable processes are normally created. C-LISP programs need large computation power, as most of LISP programs need much computation capacity rather than I/O capacity. Multi-processor system configuration is fruitful for C-LISP, since in such configuration every processor element will be utilized well by C-LISP processes.

The multi-microprocessor system presented is an MIMD type system consisting of two different types of processor elements and a very large common memory area. C-LISP programs are stored on the common memory area and executed by the processor elements in parallel. The two types of processor elements are Master Processor (MP) for the management of the whole system and Interpreter Processors (IP's) for interpretation of C-LISP programs. The system monitor is distributed to MP and IP's. Each IP has the interpreter which is controlled by the system monitor. All IP's have the same program and have no data of processes except certain portion of processes.

We paid our attentions to two key problems for designing our system. One problem is to make the processor elements be dedicated to interpretation of C-LISP programs. Since many concurrent processes are normally created, all the processor elements are fully utilized by the processes. The other problem is the well balanced design of the system software and hardware. On the general purpose system, the software bridges the gap between the speciality of the applications and the generality of the system. Therefore, the overhead of the software is usually heavy. On the other hand, we may get powerful C-LISP system if we can construct the machine using special hardware architecture or firmware. However, it is expensive and time consuming to construct such specialized systems. We designed this system using general purpose microprocessors with small scale additional hardware.

2 Overview of the System

2.1 Concurrent LISP

Concurrent LISP is a concurrent programming language based on LISP 1.5. C-LISP completely includes LISP 1.5 as its sequential part. C-LISP has simple yet powerful concurrent functions to create a process explicitly and to write inter-process communication. The definition of a process of C-LISP is:

Reprinted from *The Proceedings of International Conference on Parallel Processing*, 1983, pages 135-143. Copyright © 1983 by The Institute of Electrical and Electronics Engineers, Inc.

"A process is a self-contained entity which evaluates a given form."

Processes are activated at top-level and at STARTEVAL functions. The process activated at top-level is called the main process, and other processes activated at STARTEVAL functions are called sub-processes. A process which creates a new process is called the parent process of the created process. On the contrary, the created process is called the son process. Processes have properties such as identifiers, relationships among processes, status, mailboxes, evaluation results and so on.

The concurrent functions include three primitive concurrent functions, which are STARTEVAL for process activation, CR and CCR for interprocess communication, and also includes the basic functions for manipulation of process properties. All of these functions are designed to be fruitful for the language feature of LISP.

This definition allows users to use processes as program components in their programs like variables and procedures. Since C-LISP is designed for writing problem solving programs which require flexibility of both control and data structure, C-LISP is useful not only for writing application programs in itself but also for constructing application oriented languages on it.

The primitive concurrent functions STARTEVAL, CR and CCR are presented below. The language feature is described in detail in the references [4][5].

* starteval[$proc_1$;$proc_2$; $\cdots$;$proc_n$]
  $proc_i$ = list[$name_i$;$form_i$;$shared_i$],
  $name_i$ = name of i'th son process,
  $form_i$ = form to be evaluated by i'th son process.
  $shared_i$ = shared variables available for i'th son process.

When a process executes STARTEVAL, the process may activate n son processes. Each son process has its own name specified by name and evaluates form. The value of STARTEVAL is a list of names of son processes;
  starteval[$proc_1$;$proc_2$; $\cdots$;$proc_n$]
    = list[$name_1$;$name_2$; $\cdots$;$name_n$].
* cr[var;form]
A process evaluates form with the exclusive right to access the variable var. During evaluation of form, the process keeps the right. The value of cr[var;form] is the value of form;
  cr[var;form] = form.
* ccr[var;condition;form]
A process waits until condition is neither NIL nor F, and evaluates form with the exclusive right to access the variable var shared among processes. The value of ccr[var;condition;form] is the value of form;
  ccr[var;condition;form] = form.
C-LISP processes communicate with each other via shared objects. These two primitives guarantee mutual exclusion for the shared objects among the processes. (The shared objects are variables shared among processes, certain properties on property lists, and mailboxes of processes.)

The following example program shows a program for Fibonacci number. This program is not a typical one but includes several concurrent

functions in a few lines. This function also shows processes can be activated recursively.

```
(FIBONACCI (LAMBDA (N)
  (COND ((LESSP N 2) 1)
    (T
      ((LAMBDA (X)
        (PLUS (FIBONACCI (SUB1 N))
          (CCR X (TERMP X) (PROCVAL X))))
      (CAR
        (STARTEVAL
          ((GENSYM)(FIBONACCI (SUB2 N)) NIL)))))
)) )
```

The meaning of this function is as follows:
If n<2 then fibonacci[n]=1.
Otherwise, create a new process which executes fibonacci[n-2]. The new process is given a name generated by gensym[] and no shared variables in the initial environments. The creating process computes fibonacci[n-1] by itself. The creating process waits until the created process terminates. (termp[x] becomes true if process x has terminated.) The creating process gets the result of the created process by procval[x]. The creating process adds these values and returns it.

2.2 Overview of the System Configuration

2.2.1 C-LISP Interpreter

Fig.1 shows the overview of the configuration of the interpreter on single processor systems [3][5]. The interpreter has two program modules, the schedule module and the interpret module. The former manages all processes, i.e., management of process activation, process switching and process termination. The latter interprets given C-LISP programs under the control of the former. For quick process switching, the interpret module is designed to load no private data of processes in itself. We call this feature "transparency" of the interpret module. Each process has its own private data on the process control block (PCB), the control stack, and the environment realized using association list (A-list) method. For the realization of the multiple control stacks and environments, linked structure is utilized well in the interpreter. Though continuous memory allocation is usually more efficient in both

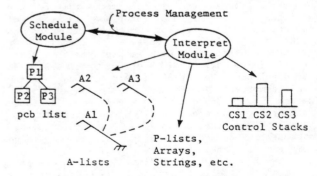

Fig.1 Overview of the C-LISP Interpreter

aspects of access speed and memory size than the linked structure, it is difficult to arrange the data of multiple processes into continuous memory space. The performance of the interpreters already developed is not so high because of the memory management task for multiple processes. The interface circuits described in this paper are designed to solve this problem.

Based on the configuration of the interpreter, we determined the basic design of the multi-microprocessor system. The followings are the basic concepts for the design.
1. C-LISP processes should be loaded on one common space.
2. Processors which interpret programs should be transparent for processes, i.e., C-LISP engine.
Consequently, followings are the basic problems which must be solved.
1. The bus bottleneck problem must be solved to connect considerable number of processors to the common bus.
2. The access methods for specialized memory areas should be reflected on the hardware configuration to improve the access speed.
3. Each processor should determine its tasks by itself to reduce overhead for the processor-processor interaction.

2.2.2 The Hardware Configuration

The multi-microprocessor system consists of nine 16-bit microprocessors, MC68000 (M68K), and a large common memory area (8MB). The processor called Master Processor (MP) manages the entire system, and other eight processors called Interpreter Processors (IP's) interpret C-LISP programs under the control of MP (Fig.2). According to the access method and access frequency, the common memory is separated into three parts, each of which has the independent common bus, to avoid the bus bottleneck.

Each processor element consists of the processor part and interface part. The former is designed as a general purpose single board computer with one M68K (8 MHz), RAM (256 KB), ROM (2/4 KB), one communication port, and IEEE 796 bus interface. Each processor has its own programs on the local memory, i.e., the system monitor functions, the garbage collectors, and interpreter functions. The latter includes intelligent interface circuits to the common memory areas, and interrupt interface circuits between processor elements. The interface circuits play the very

important role in this system because they bridge the gap between the specialized information structure of C-LISP and the general purpose microprocessor.

The three common memory areas are as follows.
1. Control Stack area: Control stacks of all processes are stored. The control stacks contain control information of processes such as return address and temporary variables. The stack area is divided into 1 KB blocks. Each process has logically continuous control stack space which is composed of one or more physical blocks.
2. List Cell area: List cells are stored. This area is designed to have 1 Mega Cells. Each cell has 48 bits, 20 bits each for CAR and CDR, and 8 bits for attributes.
3. PCB and Random Access (PCB & RA) area: Non list data, such as character strings and arrays, are stored. C-LISP system also uses this area as working space for system management.

In the case of a multi-M68K system with one common bus, no more than two processors can be connected to the bus, since 62.5 % of one machine cycle is necessary for memory access. In our system, all M68K programs are stored on local memory, whose access time is shorter than the common memory, to decrease the access frequency to the common area to half or less.

For inter-processor communication, this system has the interrupt signal lines between MP and IP's, i.e., star-connection configuration whose center is MP. The interrupt lines are used for synchronization of the processors, and the communication messages are put on the interrupt message buffers on the PCB & RA area. The usage of the interrupt lines are restricted to several purposes, which are described in the later section, because of the overhead for the synchronization.

2.2.3 The Software Configuration

The software which works on the multi-micro-processor system is composed of
1) User Programs,
2) Interpreter,
3) Garbage Collector, and

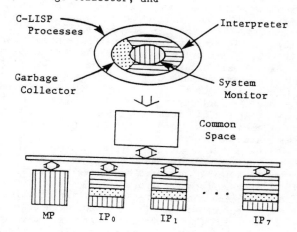

Fig.3 Layered Configuration of the Software

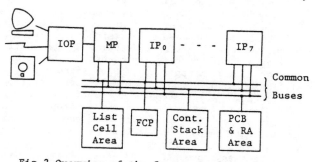

Fig.2 Overview of the System Configuration

4) System Monitor.
Fig.3 shows the layered configuration of the software and the relationships bewtween the software components and hardware components.

1) User Programs

User programs are put on the list cell area. During their execution, the interpreter creates and puts information necessary to execute user processes on the common memory, i.e., association lists and property lists on the list cell area, control stacks on the stack area, and arrays, strings, large numbers and process control blocks on the PCB & RA area.

2) Interpreter

The interpreter on every IP executes users' programs on the common memory. The interpreter should not possess data of user processes on the local memory for quick process switching. This feature is called "transparency" of the interpreter.

3) Garbage Collector

This system has the garbage collectors for every common memory area. The garbage collectors are invoked by the events indicating shortage or exhaustion of memory cells. The PCB & RA area garbage collector squeezes garbages out of allocated area, and reclaims free area. The stack area garbage collector is invoked by exhaustion of the stack blocks, and finds the garbage blocks among the allocated ones. The list cell area garbage collector is invoked by the FCP interrupt which indicates that the exhaustion of list cells will come soon.

List cell area garbage collection is designed to be performed by all processors in parallel. We use a modified mark-and-collect algorithm for our system. The garbage collection is performed in two phases: in the first phase, each IP marks active cells from the roots of the processes allocated to itself, and in the second phase, each IP collects unused cells in its allocated portion, which is an eighth part of the whole area. MP arranges the synchronization of these activities at each phase, and restores the collected cells to FCP. All IP's execute their tasks in parallel under the control of MP. In both phases, the load of the tasks is distributed to all processor elements, so that the response time of the garbage collection is improved. Since no bad effect is caused by overwriting marks on the same cells, IP's need not access cells exclusively for marking and may mark the same cells twice or more. As the exclusive access usually takes a long time, this is an advantageous feature. The on-the-fly garbage collection algorithm [2] is not introduced, because it obliges IP's to load no roots for marking at all. Such complete transparency is considered harmful for the system performance.

4) System Monitor

The functions of the system monitor (or the operating system) are distributed to MP and IP's. MP portion mainly performs housekeeping tasks, and IP portion performs monitoring of user processes. The MP portion manages state transition of waiting and suspended processes, receives requests from IP's and IOP (I/O Processor), and executes the requested functions. On the other hand, the IP portion selects a process and executes it.

Communication between these portions, i.e., intra-OS communication, is performed via either interrupt interfaces between MP and IP's or message buffers on PCB & RA area. The key problem for the design of the system monitor is to let IP's work as freely as possible. Therefore, the direct intra-OS communication via the interrupt interfaces should be restricted only to real time communication to stop or to suspend execution of running processes. The strategies to manage processes and processors are presented in another section.

3 Intelligent Interface Circuits

The multi-microprocessor system is composed of general purpose microprocessors. Though memory area is separated to avoid bus bottleneck, we must provide specialized interface circuits between the processors and the common memory components because objects stored in the common memory have specialized data structure and access mechanism which may be different from those of the conventional microprocessor.

3.1 List Cell Interface

3.1.1 Basic Idea

The followings are the basic requirements for the C-LISP machine for efficient list cell access.

Address Translation: Since a list cell usually has three portions in it, CAR, CDR and attributes, the length of a cell is rather longer than the bus width of processors. A list cell should be accessed using cell address to decrease the overhead for address translation by processors.

Quick List Read/Write: Quick list read/write operation is indispensable for quick access to a variable on an association list (A-list) and fast list manipulation. For quick list manipulation, the overlapped list read operation, i.e., list pre-fetching, will work well, since the next cell to be operated may be found on the interface registers.

Free Cell Pointer Circuit (FCP): The pointer to the top of free cell list must be accessed exclusively. Since heavy overhead is inherent in the arbitration of the pointer by software, we should provide special purpose circuit, which always possesses the current top of the free cell list and automatically updates it to avoid the overhead.

Quick list cell manipulation is important for the C-LISP system to reduce the system overhead for the memory allocation problem. In sequential LISP systems, continuous data structures are used for efficiency, e.g., CDR-coding [1], shallow binding and deep binding implemented using stacks. However, to manage continuous structures is difficult in the case of multiple process/processor systems. For example, our system uses A-list method to make environments of processes. Though A-list method is said inefficient compared with other sophisticated methods, it is considered more efficient to put multiple environments on the common area. Moreover, if we can get quick list access facilities, we can make other components of the interpreter in the form of lists because of the flexibility of list structure.

3.1.2 the List Cell Interface Circuit

The cell interface circuit has 16 IFR's, the sequence control logic, and bus interface logic. Fig.4 shows the concepts of the overlapped operation and the configuration of the interface circuits. The width of an IFR is 24 bits consisting of 20 bits cell address (i.e., up to 1 MCell) and 4 bits attributes. Since one cell consists of 48 bits, two IFR's are occupied by one cell. The IFR's are composed of high speed TTL memory chips. The cell interface command is encoded as an absolute address in the M68K's memory space. Fig.5 shows the instruction schema. The cell command has two attributes and four IFR fields. The first IFR field, i.e., to-CPU field, specifies the IFR to/from which M68K transfers data. The second field, i.e., Cell-Address field, specifies the IFR which contains the cell address

to be accessed. The third and forth fields, i.e., CAR and CDR fields, specify IFR's to/from which CAR and CDR data are transfered from/to the list cell area. The R/W field specifies the direction of data transfer between IFR's and the list cell area. (R/W=R means that data is read from the list cell area, and R/W=W means the reversed direction.) The M/N field specifies that the attributes of a half cell are masked at the data bus buffer of the local bus. (M/N=M means "mask", and M/N=N means "no-mask".) The following example is an M68K's move instruction used for data transfer on the list cell interface circuit.

MOVE.L [N,R,1,2,3,4],destination

The meaning of this instruction is:

The contents of IFR1 is moved to the destination, and CAR and CDR data of the cell specified by bit

23 – 20	19	18	17–14	13 – 10	9-6	5-2	1,0
Sel.Cell	M/N	R/W	to-CPU	Cell-Addr.	CAR	CDR	00

23-20 – Select Cell Area
19   – Mask or Non-mask
18   – Read or Write
17-14 – To-CPU Register Field
13-10 – Cell Address Register Field
9 – 6 – Car Register Field
5 – 2 – Cdr Register Field
1 – 0 – Always zero for long word operation
 * If zero, no data is transfered between IFR's and cells.
 ** If zero, Test-and-Set operation is executed on the target cell.

Fig.5 Instruction Schema of the List Cell I/F

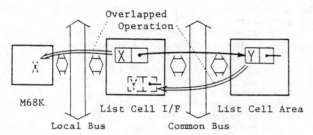

a. Concepts of the Overlapped Operation

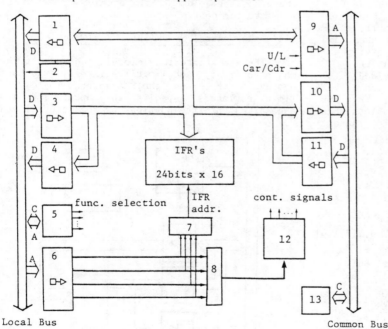

1.Interrupt Address Buffer
2.Interrupt Signaling Logic
3.Local Output Buffer
4.Local Input Buffer
5.Local Bus Control Logic
6.Local Address buffer
7.Register Address Multiplexer
8.Zero Detecter
9.Common Address Buffer
10.Common Output Buffer
11.Common Input Buffer
12.Sequence Control Logic
13.Common Bus Control Logic

Note:
*U/L=Upper word/Lower word
*Both buses satisfy IEEE 796 bus specification.
*A=Addr.,D=Data,C=Command

b. Block Diagram of the List Cell Interface Circuit

Fig.4 The List Cell Interface Circuit

IFR2 are read and moved to IFR3 and IFR4 respectively.

The interface register 0 (IFR0) has the special role. If to-CPU field contains zero, it means Test-and-Set operation is executed on the cell specified by the Cell-Address field. If other fields contain zeroes, it means those fields are not used in the operation. In Fig.6, several instructions are presented. In those instructions except the Test-and-Set instrusction, the operation on the common bus starts just after the operation on the local bus has finished. Thus, this interface manages the overlapped operation of data transfer on the local bus and the common bus.

This interface circuit has the update-interrupt facility which is provided to detect an update event on a shared variable. The address of the updated cell is passed to M68K. The system monitor receives this event and executes the relevant tasks.

3.1.3 the Free Cell Pointer Circuit

This system is designed to have only one free cell list in the common cell memory. The exclusive access to the top of free cell list should be maintained to deliver a new free cell to each processor consistently. We provide the FCP circuit for quick CONS operation. It is the simplified circuit which has the register holding the next free cell address, the register holding the remaining free cell number and the interrupt logic. (Fig.7 shows the configuration.) The former register is called the free cell pointer register (FCPR) and the latter register is called the free cell counter (FCC). At each time a processor element reads FCPR to get a new cell, FCP automatically updates FCPR just after the read operation. This schema is guaranteed by giving the highest priority of the list cell bus to FCP. FCC and the interrupt logic are provided for initiating the list cell garbage collection. FCP decrements FCC whenever FCPR is read. When FCC indicates that the remaining cells are less than certain amount, FCP interrupts MP to request

garbage collection. Exhaustive use of free cells is inhibited to guarantee correct response for read FCPR operation. FCP activities are summarized as follows:
1. arbitration for exclusive access to the top of the free cell list,
2. automatic update of the top of the free cell list, and
3. detection of shortage of the free cells.

These activities are simple but heavy if executed by software. Since CONS operation and the list cell garbage collection are primitive operations of LISP and CONS is executed frequently, FCP is indispensable for our system.

3.2 Control Stack Interface

3.2.1 Basic Idea

Since the access frequency to control stack is quite high, for example about 1/5 of the whole memory access in the C-LISP interpreter on the single M68K system [3], efficient access mechanism is indispensable for this system.

The stack area is divided into 1 KB blocks, which are allocated to processes block by block. In the interpreter on the single M68K, since this memory management is performed by software, it has quite heavy overhead to test illegal access to outside area of allocated blocks. Therefore, we need memory management facilities on the processor elements to provide logically continuous space for each process. In addition to the memory management problem, local buffer memory should be provided on the processor elements to accelerate the access speed to the control stacks.

3.2.2 the Control Stack Interface Circuit

The stack interface circuit consists of three major portions; the limit registers, the buffer memory (4 KB), and the DMA control logic. The limit registers specify the upper and lower boundaries of the portion of the control stack

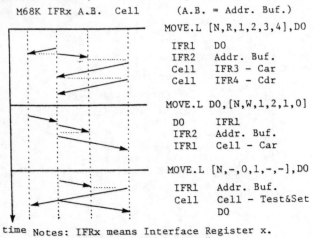

M68K IFRx A.B. Cell   (A.B. = Addr. Buf.)

MOVE.L [N,R,1,2,3,4],D0

```
IFR1    D0
IFR2    Addr. Buf.
Cell    IFR3 - Car
Cell    IFR4 - Cdr
```

MOVE.L D0,[N,W,1,2,1,0]

```
D0      IFR1
IFR2    Addr. Buf.
IFR1    Cell - Car
```

MOVE.L [N,-,0,1,-,-],D0

```
IFR1    Addr. Buf.
Cell    Cell - Test&Set
        D0
```

time Notes: IFRx means Interface Register x.
"-" means "don't care".

Fig.6 Flow of Data on the List Cell Interface

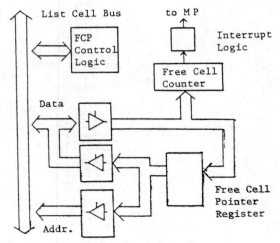

Fig.7 Free Cell Pointer Circuit

loaded on the buffer. The DMA controller transfers blocks between the buffer and the stack area. Fig.8 shows the concepts of the operation and the configuration of the stack interface circuit.

Each process is given its logically continuous stack space. The interpreter accesses to a control stack of a process using the logical address. The accessed location is always found on the stack buffer. This is guaranteed by the guard areas located at the both ends of the loaded portion on the buffer. (When either of the guard areas is accessed, the system monitor makes the next block available on the buffer.) When the system monitor transfers a block from the buffer to the common memory, it allocates a physical block to a logical block. Consequently, the interpreter is freed from the heavy overhead for stack manipulation. We use this pseudo-page-fault manipulation mechanism, since M68K has no page-fault facilities. Our method has the restriction that the processor cannot access distant location from the location accessed currently. (Since we assume the width of the guard area is 256 bytes, the processor cannot access the location whose

offset from the location accessed currently is more than 255 bytes.) However, this restriction has little effect on the software, since the control stack space has the very strict locality.

As described above, the stack interface circuit has two major functions, i.e., memory management for the logical stack spaces of processes and buffering of the active portion of the stacks for the common memory. The former feature is indispensable to realize the multiple process environments, i.e., virtualization of the users' memory spaces. The latter has the buffering effect but it disrupts the transparency of IP's. By this disruption, process switching overhead becomes rather heavy to swap out/in blocks. However, if processor elements have no buffer on the interface, the low access speed to the stack area will cause severe effect on the system performance since access frequency of the stack area is quite high. In addition, the process switching overhead is negligible, because it needs about 2 ms to switch processes while switching interval is designed to be long. (Notes: DMA controller consumes 0.5 ms to transfer one block, and four blocks are transfered in the average for each process switching. LISP interpreter usually consumes long CPU time, so that we assume one or more seconds for the interval timer which triggers process switching.)

3.3 Example Procedures

Fig.9 presents an APPEND and a SASSOC procedure, which are typical procedures for list manipulation. These procedures utilize the interface circuits well.

4 System Monitor

This system has the distributed system monitor. The tasks of the monitor are process management, processor management, and memory management. I/O management, which is one of the major tasks of operating systems, is executed by

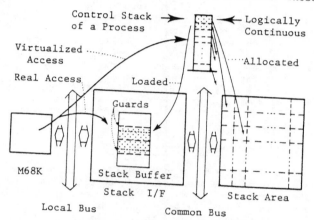

a. Concepts of the Stack I/F Operation

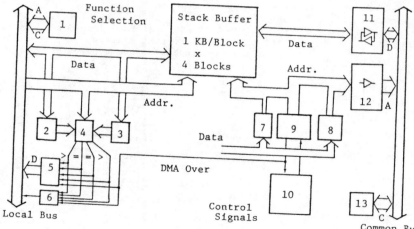

1. Local Bus Control Logic
2. Lower Limit Register
3. Upper Limit Register
4. Address Comparator
5. Interrupt Vector Register
6. Interrupt Control Logic
7. Buffer Block Addr. Reg.
8. Common Block Addr. Reg.
9. DMA Counter/Addr. Reg.
10. DMA Controller
11. Data Buffer
12. Address Buffer
13. Common Bus Control Logic

b. Block Diagram of the Stack Interface Circuit

Fig.8 The Stack Interface Circuit

343

the I/O processor (IOP), so that it is excluded in this paper.

4.1 State Transition of C-LISP Processes

Fig.10 shows the state transition diagram of C-LISP processes. All processes are monitored and moved from state to state by the system monitor. To move a process from the waiting state to the ready state, the system monitor must test the waiting condition written in C-LISP: the system monitor evaluates the second parameter of CCR by itself. Therefore, the state transition diagram from the system monitor's view is different from the users' view as shown in Fig.10.

```
      MOVE.L   a,[M,-,1,0,-,-]       ; read list a
      MOVE.L   [-,R,n,1,2,3],dummy   ; load first elem.
A1:MOVE.L   [M,R,2,3,2,3],A7@-    ; move elem. to CPU
      CMP.L    #NIL,[M,-,3,0,-,-]    ; end of list ?
      BNE      A1
      MOVE.L   b,[M,-,3,0,-,-]       ; set b on IFR3
A2:MOVE.L   A7@+,[N,-,2,0,-,-]    ; move elem. of a
      MOVE.L   FCP,[M,-,1,0,-,-]     ; get a cell
      MOVE.L   [M,W,1,1,2,3],[N,-,3,0,-,-]
                          ; CONS & set current list top on IFR3
      CMPA.L   #BOTTOM,A7            ; termination test
      BEQ      A2
      finished

a. Append - append list b to a.

      MOVE.L   a,[M,-,1,0,-,-]       ; set A-list
      MOVE.L   [-,R,n,1,3,4],dummy   ; get first pair
S1:CMP.L    #NIL,[M,R,4,3,1,2]    ; termination test
      BEQ      S2
      CMP.L    [M,R,1,4,3,4],x       ; variable match ?
      BNE      S1                    ; not match
      MOVE.L   [N,-,2,0,-,-],value   ; get value
      finished
S2:CMP.L    [M,R,1,0,-,-],x       ; last var. match ?
      BNE      error                 ; not match -> error
      MOVE.L   [N,-,2,0,-,-],value   ; get value
      finished

b. Sassoc - find a dotted pair whose CAR is x in a.
         ("-" means don't care.)
```

Fig.9 Example Procedures

Created   6   Pending   3   Terminated

Ready   2   Run
         1

5   4

Cond.   9   Wait
Test

      8   C.T.   7
          Ready   Waiting
                          (Users' View)

1.Selected for execution   2.Timeout
3.Suspended for I/O, etc.   4.CCR wait
5.Condition satisfied   6.I/O completed, etc.
7.Shared var. updated, etc. 8.Selected for testing
9.Condition unsatisfied

Fig.10 State Transition Diagram of User Processes

4.2 Allocation of Processes to Processors

C-LISP processes are created by MP and reside in the common memory area. For the process management task, the system monitor has process queues and process pools for every state. Fig.11 shows the relationships of those queues and the system monitor. It shows that MP executes the housekeeping tasks, and IP's execute the interpretation tasks. MP creates new processes, watches events, moves a process from pending/wait to ready/condition-test-ready, and monitors process termination, and IP's select processes and execute them.

4.3 Inter-process Communication

C-LISP processes communicate with each other via shared objects. All the shared objects are put on the common memory, so that they are always visible from MP and IP's. Communication messages are, therefore, buffered on the objects, and no direct communication between processor elements is necessary. Mutual exclusion for the shared objects is controlled by flags located at the shared objects: whenever IP's interpret CR or CCR, they test-and-set those flags.

The system monitor synchronizes the processes for the inter-process communication. The synchronization operation is triggered by event messages put on the request message queue. IP's put the event messages on the queue when they recognize the local events such as update events of shared objects and release events of shared objects.

4.4 Inter-processor Communication

Since the system monitor is distributed to MP and IP's, the components communicate with each other for cooperation. As this communication is performed inside the system monitor, it is called Intra-OS communication. This system has two types of the intra-OS communication; the indirect communication via the request message queue and the direct communication via the interrupt interface circuit. (Fig.12 and Table 1 summarize the intra-OS communication.) The former is mainly used to transfer request messages of processes and event messages to MP. This type of communication

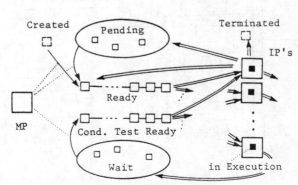

Fig.11 Process Management

is one directional, since MP directly replies to the relevant processes. The latter is used for very restricted purposes, while the former is used for many purposes. To let IP's be dedicated to interpretation, the direct communication is used only for the messages which must be transfered as soon as possible.

4.5 Memory Management

The memory management is very simple because no protection mechanism is needed. This system has the simple memory allocation and reclamation facilities. Each common area has memory allocation status descriptor which has the master information necessary for memory management, e.g. FCP. C-LISP processes get memory cells under the control of the managers of these descriptors. On the other hand, the system has the garbage collection facilities to reclaim the garbages in the allocated area as described earlier.

5 Discussion and Conclusion

In this paper, we presented the special purpose machine which comprises general purpose microprocessors. C-LISP was designed to apply multi-process description techniques to artificial intelligence problems instead of the conventional techniques such as backtracking and coroutines. From the experience on the interpreters developed earlier, the authors found that C-LISP programs usually have enough parallelism for implementing them on multiprocessor systems, in addition to the fact that LISP programs usually require very large computation power.

The hardware configuration of this system strongly reflects the language feature of C-LISP. However, our system includes several key problems common among multi-microprocessor systems, such as the bus bottleneck problem and the multiprocess environment problem. We chose general purpose microprocessors, since it was considered expensive and time-consuming to make special purpose processors by hardware or by firmware. Thus, the system is constructed using the general purpose microprocessor with small yet powerful circuits for special purposes.

Special purpose multi-processor systems consisting of general purpose processors will become more popular. We consider specialized small scale circuits may bridge the gap between the generality of the processors and the speciality of users' application on such multi-processor systems.

Acknowledgements

The authors thank Mr.N.Sonobe, Mr.A.Yamamura and Mr.T.Okada of Kyoto University for their contribution to this paper. The authors also thank Mr.T.Fukuda, Senior Engineer of Nihon Denki Kagaku Inc. for his help and contribution to this research.

References

[1] CLARK, D.W. and GREEN, C.C., An empirical study of list structure in LISP, Comm. ACM Vol.20, No.2, Feb. 1977
[2] DIJKSTRA, E., LAMPORT, L., MARTIN, A.J., SCHOLTEN, C.S., and STEFFENS, E.F.M., On-the-fly Garbage Collection: an exercise in cooperation, Language Hierarchies and Interfaces (Lecture Note on Computer Science 46) Springer-Verlag, 1976
[3] SONOBE, N., SUGIMOTO, S., AGUSA, K., TABATA, K., and OHNO, Y., Concurrent LISP on a Personal Computer, 24th Annual Convention of IPSJ, Mar. 1982 (in Japanese)
[4] SUGIMOTO, S., TABATA, K., AGUSA, K., and OHNO, Y., Concurrent LISP on a Multi-Micro-Processor System, IJCAI 81, Aug. 1981
[5] TABATA, K., SUGIMOTO, S., and OHNO, Y., Concurrent LISP and Its Interpreter, Journal of Information Processing, Vol.4, No.4, Feb. 1982

Table 1 Intra-OS Communication

Direct Communication (Interrupt Driven Com.)
From MP to IP
Synchronization request for Garbage Collection
Kill request of running processes
From IP to MP
Synchronization acknowledgement of G.C.
Process termination report
G.C. request (intentional G.C.)
Indirect Communication (Buffered Communication)
From MP to IP
none
From IP to MP
I/O request
Pending report of CR and CCR
Event messages (Release shared objects, Update shared objects, and etc.)

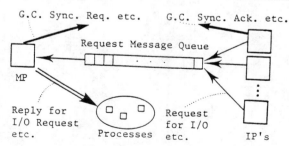

G.C. Sync. Req. etc.   G.C. Sync. Ack. etc.

Request Message Queue

MP

Reply for I/O Request etc.   Processes   Request for I/O etc.   IP's

Fig.12 Intra-OS Communication

Chapter 7: Logic and Knowledge Oriented Architectures

In logic and knowledge oriented architectures, the ideal goal is for the user to specify the problem in terms of the properties of the problem and the solution (logic or knowledge), and the architecture exercises the control on how the problem is to be solved. This goal is not fully achieved yet, and users still need to provide small but undue amounts of control information in logic programs, partly by ordering the clauses and goals in a program and partly by the use of extra-logical "features" in the language.

Knowledge and logic oriented architectures can be classified according to the knowledge representation schemes. Besides incorporating knowledge into a program written in a functional programming language, some of the well-known schemes are logic programs and semantic networks. According to the search strategy, logic programs can further be classified into production systems and logical inference systems [1-6]. Computer systems to support functional programming languages have been discussed in the last chapter. In this chapter, computer systems to support logic programming languages and semantic nets will be highlighted. Systems related to the Fifth-Generation Computer Systems Project will be shown in the next chapter.

Substantial research has been carried out on parallel computational models of utilizing AND parallelism, OR parallelism, and stream parallelism in logical inference systems [7-22], production systems [23-25], and others.[26] The basic problem on the exponential complexity of logic programs remains open at this time.

Sequential Prolog machines using software interpretation [27,28], emulation [29,30], and additional hardware support such as hardware unification and backtracking [31-33] have been proposed. Single-processor systems for production systems using additional data memories [34] and a RISC architecture [4] have been studied.

New logic programming languages suitable for parallel processing have been investigated [35]. In particular, the use of predicate logic [36], extensions of Prolog to become Concurrent Prolog [37-43], Parlog [44], and Delta-Prolog [45], and parallel production systems[46] have been developed. Concurrent Prolog has also been extended to include object-oriented programming [41] and has been applied as a VLSI design language [42]. One interesting parallel language is that of systolic programming, which is useful as an algorithm design and programming methodology for high-level-language parallel computers [47].

Several prototype multiprocessor systems for processing inference programs and Prolog have been proposed, some of which are currently under construction. These systems include multiprocessors with a shared memory [39]; ZMOB, a multiprocessor of Z80's connected by a ring network [48-52]; AQUARIUS, a heterogeneous multiprocessor with a crossbar switch [53]; and MAGO, a cellular machine implementing a Prolog compiler that translates a Prolog program into a formal functional program [54]. Techniques for analyzing Prolog programs such that they can be processed on a dataflow architecture have been derived [55-58]. DADO is a multiprocessor system with a binary-tree interconnection network that implements parallel production systems [59-62]. An associative processor has been proposed to carry out propositional and first-order predicate calculus [63].

It has been recognized that a combination of Lisp, Prolog, and an object-oriented language such as Smalltalk may be a better language for AI applications [64]. Computers of this type that implement a combination of the AI languages may use microprogramming to emulate the various functions. Prolog is also available as a secondary language on some Lisp machines. A version of Prolog interpretor with a speed of 4.5 klips has been developed for Lisp Machine's Lambda [65]. Some of the prototype multiprocessors, such as ZMOB [48-52] and MAGO [54], were developed with a flexible architecture that can implement object-oriented, functional, and logic languages. FAIM-1, a multiprocessor connected in the form of a twisted hex-plane topology, implements the features of object-oriented, functional, and logic programming in the OIL programming language [66].

Besides representing knowledge in logic, it can also be represented in terms of semantic nets. Proposed and experimental architectures have been developed. NETL [67-69] consists of an array of simple cells with marker-passing capability to perform searches, set-intersections, inheritance of properties and descriptions, and multiple-context operations on semantic nets. Other proposed architectures include THISTLE with value-passing capability and the BOLTZMANN Machine with value-passing capability and probabilistic processing elements. Thinking Machine's Connection Machine is a cellular machine under construction with 65536 processing elements. It implements marker passing and virtually reconfigures the processing elements to match the topology of the application semantic nets [71,72]. Associative processors [73,74] and dataflow architectures [88] for processing semantic nets have also been proposed.

With the inclusion of control into stored knowledge, the resulting system becomes a distributed problem-solving system. These systems are characterized by the relative

347

autonomy of the problem-solving nodes, a direct consequence of the limited communication capability [75-77]. With the proposed formalism of the Contract Net, contracts are used to express the control of problem solving in a distributed processor architecture [78-80]. Related work in this area include Petri-net modeling [81], distributed vehicle-monitoring testbed [82,83], distributed air-traffic control system [84], modeling the brain as a distributed system [85,86], and distributed task allocation system [89].

This chapter has three parts. Part 1 is on parallel processing of logic programs and contains nine papers. The first four papers, by Ciepelewski and Haridi, DeGroot, Conery and Kibler, and Li and Wah, present parallel models of computation of logic programs [12,14,21,18]. The next five papers, by Tick and Warren, Weiser et al., Despain and Patt, Amamiya et al., and Davis and Robison, show parallel architectures for logic programs: a pipelined Prolog processor [33], ZMOB [51], Aquaris [53], dataflow execution of logic programs enhanced with functional constructs [87], and FAIM-1 [66].

Part 2 is on parallel processing of production systems and has three papers. Forgy et al. analyze the feasibility and present simulation results on designing architectures for production systems [4]. Then Tenorio and Moldovan present schemes for mapping production systems to multiprocessors [25]. The last paper, by Stolfo and Miranker, shows DADO, an experimental prototype under construction [61].

Part 3 is on architectures to support semantic nets and distributed problem solving and contains six papers. The first three papers (Fahlman, Fahlman and Hinton, and Hillis) present NETL, THISTLE, and the BOLTZMANN Machine [69,70], and Thinking Machine's Connection Machine [71]. The next paper (Corkhill and Lesser) shows an example of the distributed vehicle monitoring testbed [82]. (Readers may want to refer to a survey in this area by the same authors [83].) Then Smith presents the Contract-Net framework of distributed problem solving [79]. Last, the paper on LOCO discusses distributed task allocation in AI processing [89].

References

[1] H. Boley, "AI Languages and AI Machines: An Overview," *Proceedings of the German Workshop on Artificial Intelligence,* Springer-Fachberichte, Berlin, West Germany, 1981.

[2] D.G. Bobrow, "If Prolog Is the Answer, What Is the Question?," *Proceedings of the International Conference on Fifth-Generation Computer Systems,* pp. 138-145, ICOT, Tokyo, Japan, and North-Holland, Amsterdam, The Netherlands, 1984.

[3] R.J. Douglass, "A Qualitative Assessment of Parallelism in Expert Systems," *IEEE Software,* vol. 2, no. 2, pp. 70-81, May 1985.

[4] C. Forgy, A. Gupta, A. Newell, and R. Wedig, "Initial Assessment of Architectures for Production Systems," *Proceedings of the National Conference on Artificial Intelligence,* pp. 116-120, William Kaufmann, Los Altos, Calif., Aug. 1984.

[5] D. Schaefer and J. Fischer, "Beyond the Supercomputer," *IEEE Spectrum,* vol. 19, no. 3, pp. 32-37, March 1982.

[6] D.A. Waterman and F. Hayes-Roth, *Pattern-Directed Inference Systems,* Academic Press, Orlando, Fla., 1978.

[7] H. Ogawa, T. Kitahashi, and K. Tanaka, "The Theorem Prover Using a Parallel Processing System," *Proceedings of the 6th International Joint Conference on Artificial Intelligence,* pp. 665-667, William Kaufmann, Los Altos, Calif., Aug. 1979.

[8] S.I. Nakagawa and T. Sakai, "A Parallel Tree Search Method," *Proceedings of the 6th International Joint Conference on Artificial Intelligence,* pp. 628-632, William Kaufmann, Washington, D.C., Aug. 1979.

[9] C. Smith, "The Power of Parallelism for Automatic Programming Synthesis," *Proceedings of the 22nd Annual Symposium on Foundations of Computer Sciences,* IEEE Computer Society, Washington, D.C., 1981.

[10] M.J. Wise, "EPILOG = Prolog + Data Flow: Arguments for Combining Prolog with a Data Driven Mechanism," *SIGPLAN Notices,* vol. 17, no. 12, pp. 80-86, ACM, New York, N.Y., Dec. 1982.

[11] S. Umeyama and K. Tamura, "A Parallel Execution Model of Logic Programs," *Proceedings of the 10th Annual Symposium on Computer Architecture,* pp. 349-355, IEEE Computer Society, Washington, D.C., June 1983.

[12] A. Ciepielewski and S. Haridi, "Execution of Bagof on the OR-Parallel Token Machine," *Proceedings of the International Conference on Fifth-Generation Computer Systems,* pp. 551-560, ICOT, Tokyo, Japan, and North-Holland, Amsterdam, The Netherlands, 1984.

[13] H. Yasuhara and K. Nitadori, "ORBIT: A Parallel Computing Model of Prolog," *New Generation Computing,* vol. 2, no. 3, pp. 277-288, 1984.

[14] D. DeGroot, "Restricted AND-Parallelism," *Proceedings of the International Conference on Fifth-Generation Computers,* pp. 471-478, ICOT, Tokyo, Japan, and North-Holland, Amsterdam, The Netherlands, Nov. 1984.

[15] L. Bic, "A Data-Driven Model for Parallel Interpretation of Logic Programs," *Proceedings of the International Conference on Fifth-Generation Computer Systems,* pp. 517-523, ICOT, Tokyo, Japan, and North-Holland, Amsterdam, The Netherlands, 1984.

[16] T. Khabaza, "Negation as Failure and Parallelism," *Proceedings of the International Symposium on Logic Programming,* pp. 70-75, IEEE Computer Society, Washington, D.C., Feb. 1984.

[17] G. Lindstrom and P. Panangaden, "Stream-Based Execution of Logic Programs," *Proceedings of the International Symposium on Logic Programming,* pp. 168-176, IEEE Computer Society, Washington, D.C., Feb. 1984.

[18] G.-J. Li and B.W. Wah, "MANIP-2: A Multicomputer Architecture for Evaluating Logic Programs," *Proceedings of the International Conference on Parallel Processing,* pp. 123-130, IEEE Computer Society, Washington, D.C., June 1985.

[19] J.H. Chang, A.M. Despain, and D. DeGroot, "AND-Parallelism of Logic Programs Based on A Static Data Dependency Analysis," *Proceedings of COMPCON S'85,* pp. 218-225, IEEE Computer Society, Washington, D.C., 1985.

[20] J.S. Conery and D.F. Kibler, "Parallel Interpretation of Logic Programs," *Proceedings of the Conference on Functional Programming Languages and Computer Architecture,* pp. 163-170, ACM, New York, N.Y., 1981.

[21] J.S. Conery and D.F. Kibler, "AND Parallelism and Nondeterminism in Logic Programs," *New Generation Computing,* vol. 3, no. 1, pp. 43-70, 1985.

[22] D.A. Carlson, "Parallel Processing of Tree-Like Computations," *Proceedings of the 4th International Conference on Distributed Computing Systems,* pp. 192-198, IEEE Computer Society, Washington, D.C., May 1984.

[23] M.D. Rychener, "Control Requirements for the Design of Production System Architectures," *Proceedings of the Symposium on Artificial Intelligence and Programming Languages,* also *SIGART Newsletter,* pp. 37-44, ACM, New York, N.Y., Aug. 1977.

[24] K. Oflazer, "Partitioning in Parallel Processing of Production Systems," *Proceedings of the International Conference on Parallel Processing,* pp. 92-100, IEEE Computer Society, Washington, D.C., 1984.

[25] M.F.M. Tenorio and D.I. Moldovan, "Mapping Production Systems into Multiprocessors," *Proceedings of the International Conference on Parallel Processing,* pp. 56-62, IEEE Computer Society, Washington, D.C., 1985.

[26] B.V. Funt, "Whisper: A Problem-Solving System Utilizing Diagrams," *Proceedings of the 5th International Joint Conference on Artificial Intelligence,* pp. 459-464, William Kaufmann, Los Altos, Calif., Aug. 1977.

[27] J.P. Adam, et al., "The IBM Paris Scientific Center Programming in Logic Interpreter: Overview," *Report, IBM France Scientific Center,* IBM, Paris, France, Oct., 1984.

[28] Y. Igawa, K. Shima, T. Sugawara, and S. Takagi, "Knowledge Representation and Inference Environment: KRINE—An Approach to Integration of Frame, Prolog and Graphics," *Proceedings of the International Conference on Fifth-Generation Computer Systems,* pp. 643-651, ICOT, Tokyo, Japan, and North-Holland, Amsterdam, The Netherlands, 1984.

[29] M. Yokota, et al., "A Microprogrammed Interpreter for Personal Sequential Inference Machine," *Proceedings of the International Conference on Fifth-Generation Computer Systems,* pp. 410-418, ICOT, Tokyo, Japan, and North-Holland, Amsterdam, The Netherlands, 1984.

[30] W.F. Clocksin, "Design and Simulation of a Sequential Prolog Machine," *New Generation Computing,* vol. 3, no. 2, pp. 101-120, 1985.

[31] M.S. Johnson, "Some Requirements for Architectural Support of Software Debugging," *Proceedings of the SIGPLAN Symposium on Compiler Construction,* pp. 140-148, ACM, New York, N.Y., June 1982.

[32] N. Tamura, K. Wada, H. Matsuda, Y. Kaneda, and S. Maekawa, "Sequential Prolog Machine PEK," *Proceedings of the International Conference on Fifth-Generation Computer Systems,* pp. 542-550, ICOT, Tokyo, Japan, and North-Holland, Amsterdam, The Netherlands, 1984.

[33] E. Tick and D.H.D. Warren, "Towards a Pipelined Prolog Processor," *New Generation Computing,* vol. 2, no. 4, pp. 323-345, 1984.

[34] D.B. Lenat and J. McDermott, "Less Than General Production System Architectures," *Proceedings of the 5th International Joint Conference on Artificial Intelligence,* pp. 923-932, William Kaufmann, Los Altos, Calif., 1977.

[35] C.J. Hogger, "Concurrent Logic Programming," *Logic Programming,* edited by S.-A. Tarnlund and K. Clark, pp. 199-211, Academic Press, Orlando, Fla., 1982.

[36] M.H. van Emden and G.J. de Lucena-Filho, "Predicate Logic as a Language for Parallel Programming," *Logic Programming,* edited by S.-A. Tarnlund and K. Clark, pp. 189-198, Academic Press, 1982.

[37] E.Y. Shapiro, "Subset of Concurrent Prolog and Its Interpreter," *Technical Report TR-003,* ICOT, Tokyo, Japan, 1983.

[38] A.J. Kusalik, "Serialization of Process Reduction in Concurrent Prolog," *New Generation Computing,* vol. 2, no. 3, pp. 289-298, 1984.

[39] P. Borgwardt, "Parallel Prolog Using Stack Segments on Shared-Memory Multiprocessors," *Proceedings of the International Symposium on Logic Programming,* pp. 2-11, IEEE Computer Society, Washington, D.C., Feb. 1984.

[40] K. Ueda and T. Chikayama, "Efficient Stream/Array Processing in Logic Programming Languages," *Proceedings of the International Conference on Fifth-Generation Computer Systems,* pp. 317-326, ICOT, Tokyo, Japan, and North-Holland, Amsterdam, The Netherlands, 1984.

[41] E. Shapiro and A. Takeuchi, "Object Oriented Programming in Concurrent Prolog," *New Generation Computing,* vol. 1, no. 1, pp. 25-48, 1983.

[42] N. Suzuki, "Concurrent Prolog as an Efficient VLSI Design Language," *Computer,* vol. 18, no. 2, pp. 33-40, Feb. 1985.

[43] A. Taueuchi and K. Furukawa, "Bounded Buffer Communication in Concurrent Prolog," *New Generation Computing,* vol. 3, no. 2, pp. 145-155, 1985.

[44] K. Clark and S. Gregory, "PARLOG: Parallel Programming in Logic, *Research Report DOC 84/4,* Imperial College, London, England, 1984.

[45] L.M. Pereira and R. Nasr, "Delta-Prolog, A Distributed Logic Programming Language," *Proceedings of the International Conference on Fifth-Generation Computer Systems,* pp. 283-291, ICOT, Tokyo, Japan, and North-Holland, Amsterdam, The Netherlands, 1984.

[46] L.M. Uhr, "Parallel-Serial Production Systems," *Proceedings of the 6th International Joint Conference on Artificial Intelligence,* pp. 911-916, William Kaufmann, Los Altos, Calif., Aug. 1979.

[47] E. Shapiro, "Systolic Programming: A Paradigm of Parallel Processing," *Proceedings of the International Conference on Fifth-Generation Computer Systems,* pp. 458-470, ICOT, Tokyo, Japan, and North-Holland, Amsterdam, The Netherlands, 1984.

[48] C. Rieger, R. Trigg, and B. Bane, "ZMOB: A New Computing Engine for AI," *Proceedings of the 7th International Joint Conference on Artificial Intelligence,* pp. 955-960, William Kaufmann, Los Altos, Calif., Aug. 1981.

[49] R. Trigg, "Software on ZMOB: An Object-Oriented Approach," *Proceedings of the Workshop on Computer Architecture for Pattern Analysis and Image Database Management,* pp. 133-140, IEEE Computer Society, Washington, D.C., Nov., 1981.

[50] U.S. Chakravarthy, S. Kasif, M. Kohli, J. Minker, and D. Cao, "Logic Programming on ZMOB: A Highly Parallel Machine," *Proceedings of the International Conference on Parallel Processing,* pp. 347-349, IEEE Computer Society, Washington, D.C., Aug. 1982.

[51] M. Weiser, S. Kogge, M. McElvany, R. Pierson, R. Post, and A. Thareja, "Status and Performance of the ZMOB Parallel Processing System," *Proceedings of COMPCON S'85,* pp. 71-73, IEEE Computer Society, Washington, D.C., Feb. 1985.

[52] S. Kasif, M. Kohli, and J. Minker, "PRISM: A Parallel Inference System for Problem Solving," *Proceedings of the 8th International Joint Conference on Artificial Intelligence,* pp. 544-546, William Kaufmann, Los Altos, Calif., 1983.

[53] A.M. Despain and Y.N. Patt, "Aquarius—A High Performance Computing System for Symbolic/Numeric Applications," *Proceedings of COMPCON S'85,* pp. 376-382, IEEE Computer Society, Washington, D.C., Feb. 1985.

[54] A. Koster, "Compiling Prolog Programs for Parallel Execution on a Cellular Machine," *Proceedings of the ACM'84 Annual Conference,* pp. 167-178, ACM, New York, N.Y., Oct. 1984.

[55] L. Bic, "Execution of Logic Programs on a Dataflow Architecture," *Proceedings of the 11th Annual International Symposium on Computer Architecture,* pp. 290-296, IEEE Computer Society, Washington, D.C., June 1984.

[56] R. Hasegawa and M. Amamiya, "Parallel Execution of Logic Programs Based on Dataflow Concept," *Proceedings of the International Conference on Fifth-Generation Computer Systems,* pp. 507-516, ICOT, Tokyo, Japan, and North-Holland, Amsterdam, The Netherlands, 1984.

[57] K.B. Irani and Y.F. Shih, "Implementation of Very Large Prolog-Based Knowledge Bases on Data Flow Architectures," *Proceedings of the 1st Conference on Artificial Intelligence Applications,* pp. 454-459, IEEE Computer Society, Washington, D.C., Dec. 1984.

[58] N. Ito, H. Shimizu, M. Kishi, E. Kuno, and K. Rokusawa, "Data-Flow Based Execution Mechanisms of Parallel and Concurrent Prolog," *New Generation Computing,* vol. 3, no. 1, pp. 15-41, 1985.

[59] S.J. Stolfo and D.E. Shaw, "DADO: A Tree-Structured Machine Architecture for Production Systems," *Technical Report,* Columbia University, New York, N.Y., March 1982.

[60] A. Gupta, "Implementing OPS5 Production Systems on DADO," *Proceedings of the International Conference on Parallel Processing,* pp. 83-91, IEEE Computer Society, Washington, D.C., 1984.

[61] S.J. Stolfo and D.P. Miranker, "DADO: A Parallel Processor for Expert Systems," *Proceedings of the International Conference on Parallel Processing,* pp. 74-82, IEEE Computer Society, Washington, D.C., Aug. 1984.

[62] S.J. Stolfo, "Five Parallel Algorithms for Production System Execution on the DADO Machine," *Proceedings of the National Conference on Artificial Intelligence*, pp. 300-307, William Kaufmann, Los Altos, Calif., Aug. 1984.

[63] W. Dilger and J. Muller, "An Associative Processor for Theorem Proving," *Proceedings of the Symposium on Artificial Intelligence*, pp. 489-497, IFAC, New York, N.Y., 1983.

[64] I. Takeuchi, H. Okuno, and N. Ohsato, "TAO—A Harmonic Mean of Lisp, Prolog, and Smalltalk," *SIGPLAN Notices*, vol. 18, no. 7, pp. 65-74, ACM, New York, N.Y., July 1983.

[65] T. Manuel, "Lisp and Prolog Machines Are Proliferating," *Electronics*, vol. 56, no. 22, pp. 132-137, Nov. 1983.

[66] A.L. Davis and S.V. Robison, "The FAIM-1 Symbolic Multiprocessing System," *Proceedings of COMPCON S'85*, pp. 370-375, IEEE Computer Society, Washington, D.C., 1985.

[67] N.V. Findler, *Associated Network*, Academic Press, Orlando, Fla., 1979.

[68] S. Fahlman, *NETL: A System for Representing and Using Real-World Knowledge*, Series on Artificial Intelligence, MIT Press, Cambridge, Mass., 1979.

[69] S.E. Fahlman, "Design Sketch for a Million-Element NETL Machine," *Proceedings of the 1st Annual National Conference on Artificial Intelligence*, pp. 249-252, William Kaufmann, Los Altos, Calif., Aug. 1980.

[70] S.E. Fahlman and G.E. Hinton, "Massively Parallel Architectures for AI: NETL, THISTLE, and BOLTZMANN Machines," *Proceedings of the National Conference on Artificial Intelligence*, pp. 109-113, William Kaufmann, Los Altos, Calif., 1983.

[71] W.D. Hillis, "The Connection Machine: A Computer Architecture Based on Cellular Automata," *Physica*, pp. 213-228, 1984.

[72] Thinking Machines Corporation, "The Connection Machine Supercomputer: A Natural Fit to Application Needs," *Technical Report*, Thinking Machines Corporation, Waltham, Mass., 1985.

[73] D.I. Moldovan and Y.W. Tung, "SNAP: A VLSI Architecture for Artificial Intelligence Processing, *Technical Report PPP 84-3*, University of Southern California, Los Angeles, Calif., 1984.

[74] D.I. Moldovan, "An Associative Array Architecture Intended for Semantic Network Processing," *Proceedings of ACM'84 Annual Conference*, pp. 212-221, ACM, New York, N.Y., Oct. 1984.

[75] R. Davis, "Report on the Workshop on Distributed Artificial Intelligence," *SIGART Newsletter*, no. 73, pp. 43-52, ACM, New York, N.Y., 1980.

[76] R. Davis, "Report on the Second Workshop on Distributed Artificial Intelligence," *SIGART Newsletter*, no. 80, pp. 13-83, ACM, New York, N.Y., 1982.

[77] M. Fehling and L. Erman, "Report on the Third Annual Workshop on Distributed Artificial Intelligence," *SIGART Newsletter*, no. 84, pp. 3-12, ACM, New York, N.Y., 1983.

[78] R.G. Smith, "The Contract Net: A Formalism for the Control of Distributed Problem Solving," *Proceedings of the 5th International Joint Conference on Artificial Intelligence*, p. 472, William Kaufmann, Los Altos, Calif., Aug. 1977.

[79] R.G. Smith, "A Framework for Distributed Problem Solving," *Proceedings of the 6th International Joint Conference on Artificial Intelligence*, pp. 836-841, William Kaufmann, Los Altos, Calif., Aug. 1979.

[80] R.G. Smith and R. Davis, "Frameworks for Cooperation in Distributed Problem Solving," *IEEE Transactions on Systems, Man and Cybernetics*, vol. SMC-11, no. 1, pp. 61-70, Jan. 1981.

[81] J. Pavlin, "Predicting the Performance of Distributed Knowledge-Based Systems: A Modeling Approach," *Proceedings of the National Conference on Artificial Intelligence*, pp. 314-319, William Kaufmann, Los Altos, Calif., 1983.

[82] D.D. Corkill and V.R. Lesser, "The Use of Meta-Level Control for Coordination in a Distributed Problem Solving Network," *Proceedings of the 8th International Joint Conference on Artificial Intelligence*, pp. 748-756, William Kaufmann, Los Altos, Calif., Aug. 1983.

[83] V.R. Lesser and D.D. Corkill, "The Distributed Vehicle Monitoring Testbed: A Tool for Investigating Distributed Problem Solving Networks," *The AI Magazine*, vol. 4, no. 3, pp. 15-33, Fall 1983.

[84] S. Cammarata, D. McArthur, and R. Steeb, "Strategies of Cooperation in Distributed Problem Solving," *Proceedings of the 8th International Joint Conference on Artificial Intelligence*, pp. 767-770, William Kaufmann, Los Altos, Calif., Aug. 1983.

[85] A.S. Gevins, "Overview of the Human Brain as a Distributed Computing Network," *Proceedings of the International Conference on Computer Design: VLSI in Computers*, pp. 13-16, IEEE Computer Society, Washington, D.C., 1983.

[86] W. Fritz, "The Intelligent System," *SIGART Newsletter*, no. 90, pp. 34-38, ACM, New York, N.Y., Oct. 1984.

[87] M. Amamiya and R. Hasegawa, "Dataflow Computing and Eager and Lazy Evaluations," *New Generation Computing*, vol. 2, no. 2, pp. 105-129, 1984.

[88] L. Bic, "Processing of Semantic Nets on Dataflow Architectures," *Artificial Intelligence*, vol. 27, no. 2, pp. 219-227, Nov. 1985.

[89] V.M. Milutinović, J.J. Crnković, L.Y. Chang, and H.J. Siegel, "The LOCO Approach to Distributed Task Allocation in *Aida* by Verdi," *Proceedings of the 5th International Conference on Distributed Computing Systems*, pp. 359-368, 1985.

Execution of Bagof on the Or-parallel Token Machine

Andrzej Ciepielewski and Seif Haridi
Dept. of Telecommunication and Computer Systems
Royal Institute of Technology
10044 Stockholm, Sweden

ABSTRACT

In order to achieve efficient parallel execution of
logic programs new computer architectures and new
ways of controlling execution of programs must be
deviced. In this paper we discuss one aspect of Or-
parallel execution. We describe mechanisms necessary for parallel execution of the bagof construction and show how their implementation is supported
on a parallel token machine consisting of a limited
number of processors, a token pool and a storage. In
the context of Or-parallel execution the bagof construction is not only a way to collect alternative
solutions of a relation in a list (bag). It is also a way
to control parallelism, because the search tree of a
program becomes smaller when the bagof is used.
Besides, the bagof has been proposed as an interface
between pure Or-parallelism and a form of And-
parallelism. The main problems encountered during
distributed implementation of the bagof are: control of termination of subcomputations looking for
the alternative solutions to a program, and merging
of the solutions into the environment of the computation waiting for the results. The decentralised
mechanisms we propose here are also of interest
outside the domain of pure Or-parallelism.

1. Introduction

In order to achieve efficient parallel execution of
logic programs new computer architectures and new
ways for controlling execution of programs must be
deviced. In our research we have concentrated on
problems of Or-parallel execution of logic programs,
partly because they are easier than the problems of
combined And-Or-parallelism, and partly because
their solutions are part of the solutions to the more
general problem.
We have defined a process model for Or-parallel execution and a storage model for managing multiple,
simultaneous bindings produced during the execution
[1,2]. We have also defined a mechanism for aborting
unnecessary processes [2,3]. Finally we have designed
a parallel token machine supporting Or-parallel execution, abortion mechanism, and the storage defined

by the model [2,3,4].
In this paper we describe mechanisms necessary for
parallel execution of the bagof construction, and
show extensions to the token machine supporting
implementations of the mechanisms.
The bagof is a construction for collecting solutions
to a relations in a list. The construction can be
invoked anywhere in a program. In the context of
parallel execution the bagof has an important side-
effect of controlling parallelism, because the search
tree of a program becomes much smaller when bagof
is used.
The bagof construction we use is analog to the ones
described in [5,6,7].
The rest of this paper is organised as follows. First,
to make the paper self contained, we give an overview of the token machine with the model of storage
for maintaining multiple, simultaneous bindings of
variables, and introduce shortly the semantics of the
bagof. Afterwards, we describe the problems of a
parallel implementation of bagof, and present the
mechanisms necessary for solving them. Finally we
show the extensions that must be done to the token
machine in order to support implementation of the
mechanisms, and show a small example.

2. Overview of the Or-Parallel Token Machine model

An Or-parallel computation can be visualised as an
unlimited number of independent processes, one for
each alternative nondeterministic branch in the
search tree of a program, sharing a storage for
binding environments and programs (see Figure 1).

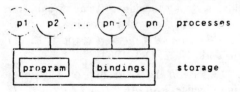

Figure 1. An or-parallel computation model.

In the Or-Parallel token machine model, the unlimited
number of processes is mapped onto a finite number

of processors. On this conceptual level the machine, as depicted in Figure 2, consists of a token pool, a set of processors and a storage. The storage is divided into a static memory for programs and a dynamic memory for the binding environments and other management information. Tokens in the pool represent processes which are ready for execution but are not allocated a processor. Processors execute processes as prescribed by the tokens and create new tokens. Processors communicate with the storage to access program and data.

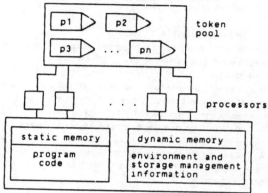

Figure 2. The Or-Parallel Token Machine model.

The state of a process consists of a list of goals and a binding environment. Such a state is represented in our machine by a token residing in the token-pool or in one of the processors, a binding environment residing in the dynamic memory, and by a, possibly empty, list of continuation frames also residing in the dynamic memory.

A token consists of the following fields:
1. Literal reference (L),
2. Context name (C),
3. Environment reference (E),
4. Continuation-Frame reference (CF)
5. Term list reference

A binding environment of a process consists of contexts for storing values of variables in literals. A new context is created each time a literal is invoked. A context name refers to a context in a given environment. During Or-parallel execution each variable may be bound to several values, still each process must have access to just one value, the one in its environment.

There are several methods for maintaining a separate address space for each binding environment. In this paper we present a simplified version of the storage model described in [1,2]. Other models are described in [8,9,10].

The storage for binding environments consists of two types of storage: directory storage and context storage. A directory, stored in the directory storage, consists of references to contexts stored in the context storage. Each process has a private

directory. The binding environment of a process consists of all the contexts referred from its directory. Variables in the environment of a process are accessed and updated through the unique name, a triple: <environment reference, context name, variable name>, where environment reference is the address to the directory of a process, context name is the offset of an entry in the directory, variable name is the offset in the context addressed by the entry.

When a process creates two or more offsprings each gets a private directory. The new directories are created from the old one in the following way. Each context referred from the old directory is investigated. If it does not contain unbound variables - we say it is committed, then the reference to it is placed in all the new directories at the same offset as in the old one. If the context contains unbound variables - we say it is uncommitted, then a copy of the context is made for every new directory, and the reference to one copy is placed in each directory at the same offset as in the old one. By making copies of uncommitted contexts we ensure that alternative values will be given to variables in separate contexts belonging to different environments. At the same time we utilise the single assignment property of logic variables by allowing sharing of committed contexts.

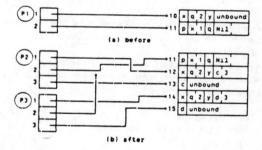

Figure 3. Snapshot of the storage before and after creation of two processes and duplication of the environment. At (b) context 11 is shared between the new environments, context 10 has been copied into contexts 12 and 14, where y has got different values.

An improved model in which investigation of all entries in the directory of a process is avoided, when new directories are created, is described in [1,2].

A continuation frame has the following fields:
1. Literal reference (L),
2. Context name (C) and
3. Continuation-Frame reference (CF).

Continuation frames are read-only data objects that are usually shared among several tokens.

The pair <L,C>, either in a token or a continuation frame, represents a goal; the L-field identifies a static literal and the C-field identifies the context, in a given environment E, containing the values of the variables occurring in the literal L. Literals of a clause are selected form left to right. This implies that the head of the goal-list is always the current goal and the tail consists of the remaining goals. The pair <L,C> of a token represents the current goal, whereas its continuation frames represent the remaining goals. Below, when the machine instructions are outlined, the L-field in tokens and continuation frames will be a reference to an instruction.

A processor execution cycle proceeds as follows. The processor fetches a token from the token pool, fetches the referred instruction from the static storage, and finally decodes and executes the instruction. A result of an instruction is zero, one or more tokens. No more tokens means that this branch of the search tree has terminated, either with success or with failure. One token means that the current branch is continued. More tokens means that a nondeterministic point has been encountered and a fork into new branches has occurred.

Horn clauses are translated into an abstract machine code. Below we show only sequences of generated instructions; the machine representation of terms is given in [11].

We use the following metavariables, which may be indexed, to range over basic syntactic entities:

    Terms: t, q, r, s.
    Literals: R, S.

By #t and #R we mean a reference to the representation of the term t and to the relation (clause) R respectively.

A program consist of an initial call and relations. An initial call having n terms containing m distinct variables as parameters:

    $R(t_1, ..., t_n)$

is translated into:

    INIT-CALL m #R (#t1 #t2 ...#tn)
    DISPLAY

Execution of the first instruction initialises a computation. The initial token transfers the control and the parameters to the relation R. The initial continuation frame points to the following DISPLAY instruction. This instruction will be executed by all computations which will complete R successfully.

An assertion having n terms containing m distinct variables as parameters:

    $R(t_1, ..., t_n)$

is translated into:

    #R -> ENTER-UNIFY m (#t1 #t2 ... #tn)
    RETURN

A token invoking a relation (assertion or implication) carries the context name and the parameters of the caller. Before the unification is executed ENTER-UNIFY creates a new context. When the code of an assertion is executed no new goals are created, after the unification has finished successfully the control is transferred to the caller. If an assertion has been called by an initial call the next instruction

to be executed after RETURN is DISPLAY.

An implication having n terms containing m distinct variables as parameters:

    R(t1,...,tn) <-
        S1(q1,...,qm1) &
        S2(r1,...,rm2) &
        :
        SI(s1,...,sml)

is translated into:

    #R -> ENTER-UNIFY m (#t1 ... #tn)
        FIRST-CALL #S1 (#q1 ... #qm1)
        CALL #S2 (#r1 ... #rm2)
        :
        LAST-CALL #SI (#s1 ... #sml)

The instructions of an invoked implication are always executed in the same context. When a relation, invoked by a FIRST-CALL instruction or a CALL instruction, terminates, the next instruction to be executed is identified by the continuation frame created during that call. On the other hand a LAST-CALL instruction does not create any continuation frame, and therefore when a relation initiated by a LAST-CALL terminates, control is returned to the caller of the implication. This leads to tail recursion optimisation.

A Relation R consisting of several clauses, C1 C2 ... Cn, is translated into:

    #R -> PAR-CHOICE (#C1 #C2 ... #CN)
    #C1 -> DUPLICATE   #CN -> DUPLICATE
      Code for ...   Code for
      clause C1   clause Cn

PAR-CHOICE results in a number of new subcomputations. Each will start by creating a copy of the current environment.

The following description of the instructions, is relative to the token being interpreted, so "Remove first continuation frame" actually means to remove the first continuation frame from the list associated with the interpreted token.

Another abbreviation we use is "transfer control and parameters to X", it means: create a token referring to X and its parameters and send it to the token pool.

(1)   INIT-CALL m #R (#t1 #t2 ... #tn) :
    Create the initial environment; create, in the new environment, a context for m variables; create a continuation frame, save address to the next instruction in it and link it first in the continuation frame list; transfer control and parameters to R;

(2)   DISPLAY
    Display values of the variables in the context corresponding to the initial call.

(3)   ENTER-UNIFY m (#t1 #t2 ... #tn) :
    Create a context for m variables in the current environment. Execute a unification step; the callers parameters are referred to by a secondary field in the interpreted token.

(4)   RETURN :
Return control to the caller. A reference to the next instruction to be executed is stored in the first continuation frame.

(5)   FIRST-CALL #S (#t1 ... #tn) :
Create a continuation frame referring to the next instruction and link it first in the continuation frame list; transfer control and parameters to S.

(6)   CALL #S (#t1 ... #tn) :
Remove the first continuation frame; create a new continuation frame referring to next instruction and link it first in the continuation frame list; transfer control and parameters to S.

(7)   LAST-CALL #S (#t1 ... #tn) :
Remove the first continuation frame; transfer control and parameters to S.

(4)   PAR-CHOICE (#C1 #C2 ... #Cn) :
Create n tokens sharing environment of the interpreted token; The created tokens share also the continuation frame list of the interpreted token.

(9)   DUPLICATE
Duplicate the environment of the interpreted token; Transfer control to the next instruction. This instruction, as well as the other storage operations, is described in detail in [1,2].

The complete specification of the basic machine is presented in [2,4].

3. Semantics of Bagof

Invocation of a predicate with the help of Bagof will have the following format: bagof(b-variable, term, predicate). There are two constraints: b-variable must not occur in the term or the predicate following it, and all variables occurring in the term must also occur in the predicate following it. The above constraints are introduced to enforce the intended use of Bagof (see below).

Let us show an example of an implication containing a bagof call.

primefactors(lpf,x) <-
bagof(lpf,u,primedivisor(u,x)).

The initial call primefactors(lpf,10) will produce, assuming the function primedivisor is properly defined, the list lpf=<2,5>.

Bagof(s,t,P) is logically equivalent to:

$$s = <u \mid \exists y_1,...,y_k (u = t \wedge P)>$$

where $y_1,...,y_k$ are variables occurring only in P and t (local to bagof). The bagof can only be used to produce a binding for s, it cannot be used to test if some list satisfies a condition or to generate values for any non-local variables. To satisfy the last assumption, and still be able to have an efficient implementation, we require all non-local variables to be ground.

Bagof(s,t,P) invokes a relation with the same name as the name of P, and produces a list s, where each element is an instance of t with variables bound by an alternative solution of P. The invoked relation is exe-

cuted in Or-parallel mode, as described earlier. The list of terms is produced only if execution of the invoked relation terminates.

Let us show two more examples.

A program

initial call: motherofchildren(Eve,ch).
relation: motherofchildren(m,ch) <- female(m) & bagof(ch,q,childof(q,m)).

with properly defined relations female and childof, will produce the list,ch, of all children of Eve.

And a program

initial call: bagof(list-of-pairs,Pair(s,l),p(s,l)).
relation: p(s,l) <- student(s) & bagof(l,u,takes-course(s,u)).

with properly defined relations student and takes-course, will produce a list of pairs: a student, all courses taken by the student.

The examples above are taken from [5].

Alternative definitions of bagof are possible [6], but in the context of Or-parallel execution the one above seems to be the only reasonable one, since invocation of a relation finds all solutions to it (all sets of bindings making it true).

4. Implementation Problems

When a relation with several statements is invoked a set of independent computations is started, each working on its own binding environment. Each computation branches into several subcomputations etc, until the successful leaves (empty goal list) of the search tree are reached. A successful leave of a tree contains a final binding environment. To be used, each result (binding of a set of variables) must be extracted from a final environment.

When a relation p is invoked by bagof(s,t,p) in an environment E0, an ordinary Or-parallel computation is started for p, except that its initial environment is a copy of E0, i.e. contains all bindings created prior to the invocation. When the execution of the relation p is ready, the results from the final environments must be transferred to the environment E0, and the list s constructed, consisting of the instances of the term t with different bindings. We will illustrate the problem by a schematic example. In the schematic examples below, we will use a notation similar to the one used in the preceeding sections but extended with notation for the bagof construct and bagof goals.

Variables: x,y,z
Terms: t,q,r,s
Literals: P,Q,R,S
Bagof construct: bagof(x,t,P)
Ordinary goals: <P>,<R>,<S>
Bagof goal: <bagof(P)><&>

Notice that the goal corresponding to the bagof construct consists of two goals: a proper goal for the literal invoked by bagof, and a "&" (Collect-) goal, which will be explained shortly.

Consider the following schematic program P. The program consists of the initial call P and the following relations:

(1) P <- Q & bagof(x,t,R) & S
(2) Q <- Q1
(3) Q <- Q2
(4) R <- R1
(5) R <- R2

S is an assertion

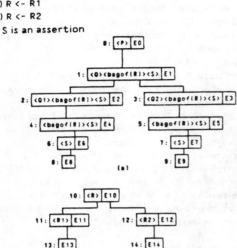

(a)

(b)

Figure 4. Search trees for the program P. (a) shows the search tree for P without the search subtree for an invocation of bagof(R) ("main" tree), and (b) the search tree for an invocation of bagof(R) ("auxiliary" tree). A node in a search tree consists of a list of goals and an environment reference. Variables in bagof are not shown. Collect goals are ignored in this figure.

Consider Figures 4a and 4b. When the goal <bagof(R)> in e.g. node 4 is executed, the traversal of the branch in the main tree containing this node is suspended, until the auxiliary search tree for the goal <R> is traversed. Traversal of the auxiliary search tree is started. The initial binding environment in the root of the search tree for R (node 10), is a copy of the environment E4. When all the leaves of the auxiliary tree are reached, construction of the suspended branch can continue. The environment E6 is constructed from E4, and the results extracted from E13 and E14. The goals in the branch beginning with node 6 can use all the results created during the execution of bagof(<R>) and gathered in the list x.

There are two problems to be solved: synchronisation of the final subcomputations of a bagof goal, and merging of the results from the environments of the final subcomputations into the environment of the suspended computation.

Let us first consider the synchronisation problem.

5. Synchronisation Mechanism

When a leaf in an auxiliary search tree is reached, it must be known if all other leaves in the tree have been reached (termination problem), and which goal is to be executed next.

To solve the termination problem, we introduce a collect goal and a counter. The collect goal is part of a bagof goal, and the counter is associated with the suspended node of the main tree. When a leaf in a auxiliary tree is reached, the next goal to be invoked is the collect goal following the bagof proper goal, which had invoked traversal of this auxiliary tree. Conceptually, for every subcomputation in the auxiliary tree, the list of remaining goals consists of the goal list in the current node and the goal list in the suspended node in the main tree. When a successful leaf in an auxiliary tree is reached, then the next goal to be solved, is the first goal on the list in the suspended node. When a goal in a node of an auxiliary tree fails, all the remaining goals in this node must be skipped, and the first goal in the suspended node should be invoked. To achieve this, we introduce references from nodes in an auxiliary tree to the goal to be taken in the suspended node. The problem arises because even failures must be counted in order to know when the execution of a bagof goal terminates.

The synchronisation mechanism works as follows. The counter is initialised to 1 when the proper goal of a bagof is invoked, and is increased by n-1 when n descendants of a node in an auxiliary tree are created. The counter is decreased each time when the collect goal of the bagof goal is invoked. The collect goal is executed every time a final leaf in the auxiliary tree is reached, even in the case of a failure. The construction of the main tree continues (the goal following the collect goal is invoked) when the counter reaches zero.

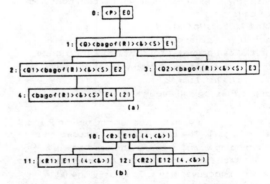

(a)

(b)

Figure 5. Initial levels of the trees from Figure 4 augmented with the control information. (4,<&>) is a reference to the collect goal in the node 4, (2) is the value of the counter.

Consider Figure 5. The bagof goal in node 4 was executed and the traversal of the auxiliary tree was started. The counter associated with node 4 is 2 and there are two leaves in the auxiliary tree. The continuation point after the construction of the auxiliary tree is the goal <&> in node 4.

In parallel systems it is not good to have centralised resources, like the counter we have just defined, accessed by many computations, because access to such resources creates potential bottle-neck. Having a common counter would lead to memory contention.

Instead of having a one counter we propose a tree of counters. The shape of a counter tree corresponds to the shape of the associated auxiliary search tree, that is, each node of a counter tree corresponds to a node with more than one descendant in the associated auxiliary tree. A node in the auxiliary tree has a reference to the corresponding node in the counter tree.

A counter tree is managed as follows.

- The root of a counter tree is created when the first node in the auxiliary tree having more then one descendent is reached. The counter in the root is initialised to the number of descendants of the node in the auxiliary tree. All descendant nodes will refer to the created counter tree node.

- A descendant to a node in the counter tree is created when a node in the auxiliary tree, referring to this counter node and having more than one descendant, is reached. The counter in the new node is initialised to the number of descendants of the associated node in the auxiliary tree. All descendant nodes of the node in the auxiliary tree will refer to the created counter tree node. If a node in an auxiliary tree has just one descendant, the descendant inherits parent's reference to a node in the counter tree.

- The counter in a counter tree node is decreased when one of the final leaves referring to it is reached, and the following collect goal is invoked. When the counter in a node reaches zero, the counter in its ancestor node is decreased recursively. When the counter in the root reaches zero, i.e. when all the leaves of an auxiliary tree are reached, the construction of the suspended branch in a main tree can continue.

Consider Figure 5 again. The counter tree for this example consists of just one node, and it is thus reduced to a single counter.

Let us show a more complex example.

    initial call: T
    relations: T <- bagof(x,t,P) & Q

        P <- R & S
        R <- R1
        R <- R2
        S <- S1
        S <- S2
        S <- S3
        Q,R1,R2,S1,S2,S3 are assertions.

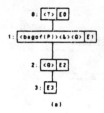

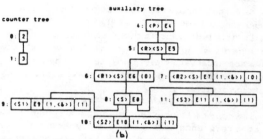

Figure 6. (a) shows the main search tree for the program T. (b) shows part of the auxiliary tree and the associated counter tree. (1,<&>) is a reference to the collect goal in node 1 of the main tree, (n) is a reference to node n in the counter tree. The continuation information is shown only in the leaves of the auxiliary tree.

Consider Figure 6. Node 0 in the counter tree was created when the goal <R> in node 5 was invoked. Node 1 in the counter tree was created when the goal <S> in node 8 was invoked. Say, <R2> in node 7 is invoked and fails. Then the counter in node 0 is decreased, and when goals <S1>, <S2>, and <S3> get ready in any order, the counter in node 1 is decreased and when it reaches zero the counter in node 0 is decreased, and also becomes zero.

Let us now consider the problem of merging the results from the environments of final subcomputations into the environment of a suspended computation.

6. Merge Mechanism

When a goal of the form <bagof(s,t,P)> is executed, a list s is constructed, consisting of instances of term t with the variables bindings provided by the alternative solutions to the relation P.

Consider Figure 7. s is bound to a data constructor List with the variable bindings in the context with name 2 and address 10. Components of List are t(y,z,w), and the auxiliary variable x. The bindings of y and z are the solutions to P, and the binding of x links two solutions to P. Context 10 contains values of y and z provided by the first solution, the value of s, and the value of x referring to the second solution. Context 40 contains values of y and z provided by the second solution, and the value of x, being in this case Nil. Contexts 30 and 50 contain the rest of the binding trees of x and y provided by solutions 1 and 2 respectively.

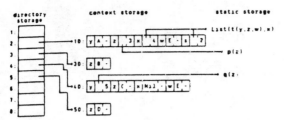

Figure 7. The storage representation of a possible solution to bagof(s,t(y,z,w),P(y,z)): s=List(t(A,p(B),E),List(t(q(D),C,E),Nil)). We have assumed that P(y,z) have two solutions and that w is a non-local variable. The offsets in the directory and the addresses in the context storage are chosen arbitrarily.

When a bagof computation is started it gets a private copy of the current binding environment, and the reference to the current environment is saved. Each Or-parallel subcomputation executes in its own environment. When a subcomputation successfully terminates, the results provided by it, must be copied from its environment to the saved one. A result is the binding for variables in the term t, in a bagof call.

The binding of a variable consists of a tree of values (provided there are no circular bindings). Each value is a pair <Term, ContextName>, where ContextName is a reference to an entry in an environment directory. When a value is copied from a context in one environment to a context in another environment, the Term field remains unchanged, but the ContextName field gets a new value, because the corresponding entry will get a different offset in the new directory, than in the old one.

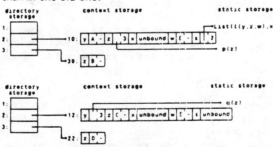

Figure 8. Content of the storage after both solutions shown in Figure 7 are ready, but only the first solution has been copied. (a) shows the saved environment with the incomplete list of solutions. (b) shows the environment of the second solution.

Consider Figure 8. Bindings provided by the second solution, see (b), will be copied to the saved environment and linked to the first solution, see (a). During the copying, the dynamic part (ContextName) of the value of y in context 22 is changed, the result is shown in Figure 7. Notice that only the relevant contexts in a result environment are copied to the saved environment, and that the variables have the same

offsets before and after copying.
Notice also, that the requirement about the non-local variables being ground has been done to make efficient copying of values between environments possible.
Copying of solutions between the environments is done independently for each subcomputation, the cooperation is needed only when a solution is linked into the list of solutions. The cooperation is achieved by associating with the suspended computation a reference to the currently last element on the list of solutions. When a solution is copied the saved reference is replaced by the reference to the new solution, and the new solution is linked last in the list.
Consider Figure 7. When the first solution is ready, the context name 2 (referring context 10) is associated with the suspended computation. When the second solution is ready and copied, it is linked in the list by binding x in context 10 to the second solution. Was it not the last solution then the context name 5 (referring context 40) would be associated with the suspended computation.

7. Implementation of the mechanisms on the token machine

In order to support the bagof construction the basic machine must be extended to handle the information associated with the described mechanisms. Two new types of frames, collection frames and counter frames, and some new instructions are introduced, and two instructions are modified. Tokens are extended with three fields, Collection-Frame reference, Counter-Frame reference, and Type, and consist of the following fields:

1. Literal reference (L),
2. Context name (C),
3. Environment reference (E),
4. Continuation-Frame reference (CF)
5. Collection-Frame reference (CL)
6. Counter-Frame reference (CN)
7. Type
8. Term list reference (T)

Collection frame reference identifies a list of collection frames associated with the token. The head of this list corresponds to the most recently invoked bagof goal, since bagof calls can be arbitrary nested. Counter frame reference identifies a list of counter frames associated with the token. The head of this list corresponds to the most recent node of the auxiliary search tree having more than one descendant node. The type field indicates if a token represents a failed or a successful computation. Continuation frames are unchanged.
Collection frames have the following fields:

1. Literal reference (L)
2. Destination context name (DC)
3. Result context name (RC)
4. Context name (C),

5. Environment reference (E),
6. Continuation-Frame reference (CF)
7. Collection-Frame reference (CL)
8. Counter-Frame reference (CN)

A collection frame is created for each invocation of a bagof goal proper. The fields of a collection frame are used in the following way. Literal reference and Continuation-Frame reference are used to find the continuation point when a computation terminates. On a successful computation the same information may be found in the first continuation frame pointed by the token. Destination context name, Result context name, Context name and Environment reference are used to transfer bindings between environments, and to link the alternative solutions. Besides, Environment reference and Context name are used to build a new token when all computations invoked by the corresponding bagof call proper have terminated. A result context name identifies the context containing variables of the term t in a bagof goal, this name is the same for all solutions. The destination context name identifies the solution most recently appended to the list of solutions. The fields Collection-frame reference and Counter-Frame reference are necessary for nested invocations of the bagof construct. The nested bagof calls are implemented by the same technique as the nested calls in general, i.e. by linking frames, in this case collection frames.

Counter frames have the following fields:
1. Counter
2. Counter-Frame reference

A counter frame is created each time a goal in a node with more than one descendant is executed. The Counter field records the number of non terminated branches.

Both collection and counter frames are shared data objects which must not be duplicated.

The execution cycle of processors is unchanged. Horn clauses without the Bagof construct are translated and executed as before. An implication containing m unique variables and having a bagof call in its body, but not in the first or last call position, with other calls of any type:

R(t1,...,tn) <-
     :
bagof(s,t,P(q1,...,qk)) &
     :

is translated into:
#R -> ENTER-UNIFY m (#t1 ...#tn)
     :
BCALL #Pi(#q1 ... #qk)
COLLECT m-1 #s #t #x
     :

where m is the number of distinct variables in the clause plus link variable x, where x is an auxiliary variable necessary for constructing a list of solutions. A similar implication with a bagof call first in the body, and other calls of any type, is translated into:

#R -> ENTER-UNIFY m (#t1 ...#tn)
FIRST-BCALL #Pi(#q1 ... #qk)
COLLECT m-1 #s #t #x
     :

And finally, a similar implication with a bagof call last in the body, is translated into:
#R -> ENTER-UNIFY m (#t1 ...#tn)
     :
BCALL #Pi(#q1 ... #qk)
COLLECT m-1 #s #t #x
IMPL-RETURN

The synchronisation and merge mechanisms are implemented as follows. When a bagof goal proper is invoked, the information about the suspended node in the main tree is saved in a collection frame, which contains also a reference to the instruction to be taken when a subcomputation fails and the information needed by the merge mechanism. The counter trees are built of counter frames. A collection frame is created when BCALL, FIRST-BCALL, or INIT-BCALL is executed. Its Destination context name field is updated when a COLLECT instruction is executed. A collection frame is released when the associated counter tree becomes empty. A counter frame is created, and its counter initialised, when a PAR-CHOICE instruction is executed. The counter is decreased when a COLLECT instruction is executed, and the frame released when the counter reaches zero.

Two instructions of the basic machine, ENTER-UNIFY and PAR-CHOICE, are modified. The new and the modified instructions are described below. As before, the description of an instruction is relative to the token being interpreted.

(3') ENTER-UNIFY m (#t1 #t2 ... #tn) :
Create a context for m variables in the current environment; execute a unification step; the callers context name and parameters are referred to in the interpreted token; if the unification succeeds, transfer control to the next instruction; if the unification fails and it is a computation working on a solution to a bagof goal, i.e. the token refers to a collection frame, transfer control to the instruction saved in the first collection frame.

(9') PAR-CHOICE (#C1 #C2 ... #Cn)
If it is a computation working on a solution to a bagof goal, create a counter frame with the counter equal to n and link it first in the list of counter frames; create n tokens sharing the binding environments and all the frame lists of the interpreted token.

The above named instructions BCALL, INIT-BCALL, and FIRST-BCALL are very similar, for this reason and for the lack of space we show just BCALL.

(10) BCALL #S (#t1 ... #tn) :
Remove the first continuation frame; create a continuation frame referring to the next instruction and link it first in the continuation frame list; duplicate the current environment; create a

359

collection frame and save in it: the current context name and the environment reference, the address of the following COLLECT instruction and the address of the current continuation frame, name of the context for variables in S, the reference to a node in the current counter tree; link the created collection frame first in the collection frame list; S will execute in the new environment.

(11)   COLLECT I #d #t #x

If the type of the current token is not a failure: add a solution to the bag s, i.e. allocate in the environment saved in the first collection frame, a new context for all variables in the clause except for s, save its name in the first collection frame, copy the bindings of variables in the term t from the current environment to the saved environment, and link the new solution last in the list of solutions (the list is empty in case all subcomputations failed); independently of the type of the current token, decrement the counters recursively, starting from the first counter frame; if the resulting counter tree is empty: close the list of solutions, and restore the part of the token saved in the first collection frame (context name, environment reference, continuation frame reference, collection frame reference, counter frame reference); transfer control to the next instruction; the next instruction will execute in the restored environment.

(12)   IMPL-RET:

Remove the first continuation frame; return control to the caller. A reference to the next instruction to be executed is stored in the continuation frame which has become first.

The complete specification of the extended machine is presented in [2].

8. An Example

Before discussing the results presented in this paper, we will show search trees and the code for one of the programs mentioned in Section 3.
The program:
    initial call: mother-of-children(Eve,children).
    relations: mother-of-children(m,ch) <-
        female(m) & bagof(ch,q,childof(q,m)).
    female(Eve). female(Marie).
    childof(Jack,Eve), childof(Jane,Eve),
    childof(Daniel,Eve), childof(Mark,Marie)
In the trees below, we replace the variables textually, where possible, by the terms to which the variables become bound, instead of showing the contents of environments.
In contrast to the schematic examples presented earlier, we show explicitly that a goal consists of a literal and a context name.
The main search tree:

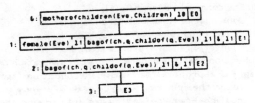

The auxiliary search tree for the bagof goal in node 2 of the main tree, and the counter tree corresponding to a situation when nodes 1, 2 and 3 of the auxiliary tree has just been reached:

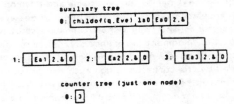

The code:

```
0: INIT-CALL 1 #motherofchildren #Eve #children
1: DISPLAY
#motherofchildren -> 2: ENTER-UNIFY 4 m ch
3: FIRST-CALL #female #m
4: BCALL #childof #q #m
5: COLLECT 3 #ch #q #x
6: IMPL-RETURN
#female -> 7: PAR CHOICE 8 11
8: DUPLICATE
9: ENTER-UNIFY 0 #Eve
10: RET
11: DUPLICATE
12: ENTER-UNIFY 0 #Marie
13: RET
#childof -> 14: PAR CHOICE 15 18 21 24
15: DUPLICATE
16: ENTER UNIFY 0 #Jack #Eve
17: RET
18: DUPLICATE
19: ENTER UNIFY 0 #Jane #Eve
20: RET
21: DUPLICATE
22: ENTER UNIFY 0 #Daniel #Eve
23: RET
24: DUPLICATE
25: ENTER UNIFY 0 #Mark #Marie
26: RET
```

With the information shown above the reader should be able to simulate execution of the program, in order to discover that the final result of the execution is children = <Jack,Jane,Daniel>. We restrain from showing execution snapshots, because of the lack of space.

PROCEEDINGS OF THE INTERNATIONAL CONFERENCE
ON FIFTH GENERATION COMPUTER SYSTEMS 1984,
edited by ICOT. © ICOT, 1984

RESTRICTED AND-PARALLELISM

Doug DeGroot
IBM Thomas J. Watson Research Center
P.O. Box 218
Yorktown Heights, New York 10598

ABSTRACT

A method of compiling Prolog clauses into single execution graph expressions is presented. These graphs are capable of expressing potential and-parallelism in the clauses. The run-time support is minimal: simple and efficient tests suffice to detect potential and-parallelism and no recalculation of the execution graphs is required. Some parallelism may, however, be overlooked. An execution model is presented which hopefully overcomes these limitations.

AND-PARALLELISM

And-parallelism in logic programming involves the simultaneous execution of subgoals in a clause. Whereas or-parallelism attempts to achieve increased speed by investigating many possible solutions in parallel, and-parallelism attempts to achieve increased speed by investigating the subparts of a particular solution in parallel. Many models of parallel logic programming attempt to exploit both of these forms of parallelism.

Because subgoals within a clause can share variables, variable binding conflicts can arise in and-parallelism if all subgoals within a clause are allowed to execute unconstrained and if two concurrently executing subgoals attempt to instantiate (bind) a shared variable to two different values. Clearly these binding conflicts must be prevented. Two major approaches have generally been taken to solve this problem. The most common approach, perhaps, involves some method of annotating variables, as in Parlog [Clark], IC-Prolog [Clark2], Concurrent-Prolog [Shapiro], and Epilog [Wise]. In these schemes, variables are annotated in a variety of ways to indicate which subgoals can bind values to specific variables and which cannot. In particular, only one subgoal is allowed to bind a value to each variable. Such subgoals are called "producers" of those variables. In contrast, Conery describes a sophisticated, non-annotated, process-structured system that dynamically monitors variables and continually

develops data dependency networks to control the order of execution of subgoals, never allowing two potential producers for the same variable to execute in parallel [Conery]. In this scheme, a particular subgoal may be a producer of a variable in one invocation and a consumer of that variable in another.

Without the benefit of variable annotations, and-parallel execution of logic programs can lead to highly-complex coordination problems at run-time. Because of these problems, parallel logic programming schemes that implement non-annotated and-parallelism generally incorporate sophisticated control mechanisms to ensure that these problems either do not arise or are corrected. If these control mechanisms are not compiler-related but instead are code segments that must be repeatedly executed while interpreting a logic program, they may detract from the performance gains achieved by the and-parallelism, and could even produce negative gains. It is important, therefore, to search for methods of achieving and-parallelism which rely mostly on compiler-related technology instead of run-time technology. This paper presents one such method.

NON-ANNOTATED AND-PARALLELISM

In this section, problems with achieving and-parallelism without annotations are described. The main problem is the possibility of creating binding conflicts for variables. Given a clause such as

f(X) <- p(X) & q(X).,

if f is called with an unbound variable argument, then X remains uninstantiated when we invoke both p(X) and q(X) in parallel. During execution, p and q may produce solutions with two different values of X. Clearly we cannot return either value of X as the result of f(X) until one of the values has been proven by the other goal. But this may be impossible for either of the two values, and it may be necessary to reinvoke both p and q in order to derive new values of X. In general, this scheme might be viewed as repeatedly reinvoking both p and q, deriving two complete sets of answers - one for p and one for q.

The value of f then is the intersection (join) of the two sets that are produced by p(X) and q(X). It is significant that this set can be computed either dynamically or statically, and that if it is computed dynamically, the sets of answers produced by all goals in the computation can be "streamed" back as they are computed, forming a pipelined computation mechanism.

If the set of answers for p(X) is small and contains the solution X=a but the set of answers for q(X) is very large and does not contain X=a, then this "join" scheme may waste processor time by producing the entire large set for q, while f(X), the parent goal, waits to see if q(X) is ever going to produce the value X=a. Instead, as the set of values for p(X) is produced, we can forward each value from p(X) to q(X), making sure that q works only on values produced by p. The set of answers returned by f(X) will then be the set of answers returned by q(X). The potential for execution economies is significant. In addition, this "forwarding" technique can effectively take advantage of goal reordering to achieve further economies [Warren], whereas the "join" technique cannot. This scheme of "forwarding" values from subgoal to subgoal has been extensively proposed and studied.

Notice that now subgoals within a clause do not produce conflicting sets of variable bindings. Parallelism occurs because while one goal is operating on its argument, the preceding goal is "preproducing" a subsequent value to be tested if necessary. But unfortunately, if a program consists mostly of deterministic procedures and clauses, little parallelism will be exhibited by this "forwarding" technique. In this case, the "join" technique would appear to exhibit greater parallelism as well as higher efficiency. If many answers exist, however, the "join" technique exhibits great parallelism but low efficiency. In practice, the "join" technique may prove impractical [Conery].

Notice that in the "forwarding" scheme, for a given potential solution only one subgoal is ever in execution at any one time. Many subgoals within a clause may be in execution at the same time, but if so, they will be working on different potential solutions. Consequently, production of a single, specific solution is always the result of a sequential execution. This is the reason simple "forwarding" schemes exhibit little parallelism when executing largely deterministic programs. To derive parallelism within the production of a single solution, some way must be found to decompose the list of subgoals into sets of parallel subgoals.

Conery's method does exactly this. His method involves a set of elaborate run-time algorithms which dynamically compute parallel execution graphs based on data dependencies between subgoals. It can execute in parallel both deterministic and non-deterministic programs. While Conery's scheme nearly always achieves optimal and-parallelism, it does so at considerable expense because of the complexity of the supporting run-time algorithms. This expense may be so high as to render the scheme impractical. However, if techniques can be found to shift more of the algorithmic burden to the compiler and to significantly reduce the amount of run-time computation, and-parallel "forwarding" schemes may prove to be a practical solution to the problems of and-parallelism.

VARIABLE BINDING CONFLICTS

When considering a program clause such as

$$f(X) <- p(X) \text{ \& } q(X).,$$

it is generally impossible at compile time to determine whether or not p(X) and q(X) can execute in parallel without creating a binding conflict. If f is called with a ground argument (any term not containing a variable), such as in the call "f(4)", then the two subgoals become at run-time p(4) and q(4). Since the argument to f contains no variables, no binding conflicts can arise by the parallel execution of p and q. If however f is called with an unbound argument or with a non-ground argument (a term containing one or more variables), then p and q will share at least one variable, and hence the potential for binding conflicts exists if p and q are executed in parallel. Consequently, in this case, p and q must execute sequentially. The important point is that some sort of run-time test is needed in order to determine whether p and q can execute in parallel or if they must execute sequentially.

Consider now the clause

$$f(X,Y) <- p(X) \text{ \& } q(Y).$$

Here it appears that X and Y are independent variables and that p and q can execute in parallel. This is far from certain, however. For suppose a call to f is made similar to one of the following:

$$f(Z,Z).$$
$$f(Z,g(Z)).$$
$$f(g(Z),h(2,Z)).$$

Then at run-time X and Y will be aliases of each other or will have values that share at least one variable. If p(X) and q(Y) execute in parallel, then the potential for binding conflicts exists. Run-time tests again become necessary.

The situation can be even more complicated. Consider the clause

$$f(X) <- p(X) \text{ \& } q(X) \text{ \& } s(X).$$

If at run-time f is called with a ground argument, as in the call "f(4)", then all three subgoals can execute in parallel. But if f is called with a non-ground argument, p(X) must first execute while q(X) and s(X) wait. Upon completion of p(X), if p has instantiated X to a ground term, then q(X) and s(X), the two remaining subgoals, can execute in parallel. But if X is still non-ground after completion of p, then q(X) and s(X) must execute sequentially. Thus depending on the call and execution, three different execution graphs result. Figure 1 illustrates the three graphs.

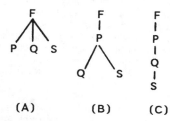

Figure 1. EXECUTION GRAPHS

Conery uses five run-time algorithms to monitor execution of subgoals in a clause and to dynamically determine the execution graphs: the Literal Ordering Algorithm, the Forward Execution Algorithm, the Backward Execution Algorithm, the And-process Algorithm, and the Or-process Algorithm. Although these algorithms are quite expensive, they do achieve nearly optimal detection of and-parallelism.

In the next section, a method is presented which determines a much more restricted form of and-parallelism. An important advantage of this method is that it requires much simpler run-time support. It will, however, occasionally fail to detect some potential for parallelism due to the fact that it computes only one execution graph, and this is done at compile-time using incomplete information. Later it will be argued that this may in fact be an advantage. Several simple algorithms are used in this scheme, the most complex of which is performed only at compile-time; the run-time tests are quite simple. Each is described below.

THE TYPING ALGORITHM

This section describes a simple algorithm for determining when two or more terms are independent (share no common variables) or are interdependent (share at least one common variable). Actually, the algorithm can only accurately determine when two or more terms are clearly independent. Otherwise, the algorithm will assume, perhaps incorrectly, that the terms are interdependent. How this af-

fects the parallel execution of a program is described later.

Each term is allocated a special type field. A term can have one of three types:

1 - a ground term (contains no variables; this type includes integers, strings, and complex ground terms)

2 - a non-ground, non-variable term (i.e., a term with a known principle functor but which contains at least one inner variable)

3 - a variable (i.e., an uninstantiated variable)

These types and the special type field are in addition to any other type or tag fields usually found in data representations, such as integers, lists, strings, etc. [Warren2]. Most terms appearing in the source program can easily have their type codes preset by the compiler. For instance, all integers, constants, and complex ground terms can have their type codes preset to 1; local variables (those not appearing in the head of a clause) can be preset to type 3; and finally, all structured source code terms containing one or more variables will be preset to type 2. In a structured term, not only is the term itself preassigned a type, but so are all components of the term at all levels. Note that all variables appearing in the head of a clause cannot have their types determined at compile-time since their values will not be known until run-time. Variables in queries, however, will be preset to type 3.

Determining the type of a term at run-time is slightly more difficult. We clearly cannot afford the run-time expense of traversing several entire structures on each procedure invocation or exit in order to determine if a structure is ground or if two structures share a common variable. Instead, an efficient approximation technique is desired. Such a technique is now presented.

First, consider how variables (type 3) can inherit type 1 or type 2 codes. Consider the following program for append:
    append(nil,L,L).
    append(X.Y,Z,X.L) <- append(Y,Z,L).
and the call
    append(nil,a.b.c.nil,R)?.
The compiler will have preassigned type code 1 to both nils and to the list a.b.c.nil and type code 3 to the variables R and L. Since the call unifies with the first append clause, R becomes bound to the list structure through unification, and the type code of R is then changed from 3 to 1. This example shows how output variables can inherit type 1 or type 2 codes from input variables through the normal unification procedure.

Now consider the call
        append(a.nil,b.c.nil,S)?.
This call unifies with the head of the second
append clause, with substitution
        (a/X,nil/Y,b.c.nil/Z,X.L/S).
The compiler will have preset X.Y and X.L
to type 2. At run-time X, Y, and Z will all
inherit type codes of 1 and S will inherit a
type code of 2. As terms are being constructed or decomposed in unification, any
whose type code is still 2 after unification
(meaning non-ground) has its address placed
in a special "pending" list. Following the
successful termination of all subgoals in the
clause, all structures on the pending list are
investigated to see if they have become
ground terms. This is done simply: the type
codes of all the top level components in a
pending structure are checked to see if they
are ground (or have become ground) terms
(have type codes of 1). If so, then the
structure on the pending list has also become
ground, and its type code is now set to 1.

In the append example above, it is easy
to see that when the subgoal completes, L
will be bound to "b.c.nil", and since this is
a ground term (whose type code was preset
to 1 by the compiler), L will inherit a type
code of 1, as in the first example. Before
returning control from the top-level call to
append, the argument S, whose address has
been placed on the pending list and whose
value is X.L, will be checked. Now, because
both X and L will have type codes of 1, the
type code of S is changed from 2 to 1,
meaning it is now ground. The fact that the
list "b.c.nil", the value bound to Z, is
ground and has type code 1, could not only
have been the result of a compile-time determination but also the result of an input action
or a similar term construction sequence.

Consider this example of "finishing" a
constructed symbol table, as described in
[Warren]:

        finish_st(nil).
        finish_st(sym(S,Lson,Rson)) <-
                finish_st(Lson) &
                finish_st(Rson).

Here the leaves of the tree will all be set to
nil upon completion of the program. As execution of each clause completes, the subtree
represented by the head of the clause will
have become ground, and the type code of
the structure can be set to 1. Upon completion
of the procedure, the entire tree will be
ground, have a type code of 1, and contain
only components whose type codes are 1.

It is of course possible that some structures might be constructed which are at first
non-ground but which later become ground
and yet which escape detection. For example

consider:
        f(X) <- find_a_var(X,V) & V=nil.
Here, assume that X has a variable in it several layers deep and that find_a_var binds
it to V. When V is set to nil, we exit. X is
taken off the pending list and its top level
components are inspected. The top level
component which contains V will still have a
type code of 2 (non-ground) and so the type
code of X will not be changed to 1, even
though now X is ground. It is possible that
later some traversal program might discover
that X is in fact ground and so set the type
code to 1, but this is far from certain. This
escape of X's might result in some loss of
parallelism, as will be explained below. However, due to the way goals are distributed
for parallel execution, this loss is anticipated
to be low, perhaps even insignificant.

THE INDEPENDENCE ALGORITHM

Given the clause
        f(X) <- g(X) & h(X) & p(X).,
a compiler might assume all three subgoals are
interdependent and so must be executed sequentially. However, to see if the three
subgoals can be executed in parallel, all that
must be done is to check at run-time whether
or not the actual parameter to f is ground and
thus has a type code of 1. If so, then g,
h, and p can all execute in parallel. If not,
then we assume that they must execute sequentially. However, after execution of g(X),
we can again check the type code of X. If it
is now 1, then we can execute the two remaining subgoals in parallel.

Consider the clause
        f(X,Y) <- g(X) & h(Y).
Here, the compiler would identify g(X) and
h(Y) as being potentially independent
subgoals and emit appropriate type checking
code which at run-time attempts to verify the
independence of X and Y. If they are independent, then g(X) and h(Y) can execute in
parallel. If the test fails, then g and h are
executed sequentially. The Algorithm used to
test for the independence of two parameters
is shown in Figure 2. Tests for more than
two variables are similar but involve $O(n2)$
tests, where n is the number of arguments
appearing in the clause head. Because n will
usually be very small, and because the test
algorithm is so very simple, the actual overhead is minimal.

    IF TYPE(ARG1) = 1 OR TYPE(ARG2) = 1
        THEN INDEPENDENT ELSE
    IF TYPE(ARG1) = TYPE(ARG2) = 3 AND
        ADDRESS(ARG1) ¬= ADDRESS(ARG2)
        THEN INDEPENDENT ELSE
    (ASSUME) DEPENDENT;

    Figure 2. INDEPENDENCE ALGORITHM.

PROGRAM EXECUTION GRAPHS

Two utility predicate routines are provided for testing terms at run-time: GPAR(X1,...,Xn) and IPAR(X1,...,Xn). The value of GPAR(X1,...,Xn) is true if all of the arguments to GPAR are ground terms (type code 1). If any argument is non-ground, the value of GPAR is false. Similarly, the value of IPAR(X1,...,Xn) is true if all its arguments are mutually independent; but if any two are interdependent, the value of IPAR is false. GPAR simply checks the type code of each of its arguments to ensure that they are all 1; IPAR uses the Independence Algorithm. Both take an arbitrary number of arguments; but IPAR requires at least two.

Six types of execution expressions are allowed:

1. G
2. (SEQ E1 . . . En)
3. (PAR E1 . . . En)
4. (GPAR(X1,...,Xk) E1 . . . En)
5. (IPAR(X1,...,Xk) E1 . . . En)
6. (IF E1 E2 E3)

G is an arbitrary goal (procedure call). An SEQ expression indicates that the following expressions are to execute sequentially, in presentation order, while a PAR expression indicates that they are to execute in parallel. A GPAR expression indicates that if all the arguments of the GPAR function call are ground terms, then the following expressions are all to execute in parallel; but if any one of the arguments is not ground, then the expressions are all to execute sequentially, in order. Similarly, an IPAR expression indicates that if all the arguments of the IPAR call are mutually independent, then the following expressions are all to execute in parallel; but if any two arguments are interdependent, then the following expressions are to execute sequentially, in order. The IF expression chooses between two alternative actions based on the evaluation of the boolean expression E1, choosing E2 if true and E3 if false.

All program graphs will be constructed from these six expression types. Consider the clause

$$f(X) <- p(X) \& q(X) \& s(X).$$

This clause can be compiled into several different program execution graph expressions, some of which are:

$$f(X) = (SEQ\ p(X)\ q(X)\ s(X)).$$

$$f(X) = (GPAR(X)\ p(X)\ q(X)\ s(X)).$$

$$f(X) = (GPAR(X)$$
$$p(X)$$
$$(GPAR(X)\ q(X)\ s(X))).$$

The first allows no possibility of parallelism and is equivalent to execution graph c of Figure 1. The second allows all three subgoals to execute in parallel if X is ground, and therefore to achieve execution graph 1a; but if X is not ground, execution reverts back to graph 1c. If X is ground, the third expression will achieve the maximal parallelism of graph 1a. If X is not ground, however, this third expression will first execute p(X) and then retest X. If X is now ground, q(X) and s(X) will execute in parallel, as in 1b; otherwise they will execute sequentially, as in 1c. Thus the third expression is capable of achieving any of the three execution graphs of Figure 1.

Several important points should be noted:

1. First, only one execution graph expression is created for the clause. This graph is created at compile-time. No reordering of goals occurs at run-time which can lead to the need to dynamically create an alternative execution graph. The tests made by IPAR and GPAR and the typing algorithm are all very simple and inexpensive.

2. To achieve execution graph 1a, the third expression above actually makes a redundant test to see if X is ground. Fortunately, the amount of additional overhead introduced by this redundant test is small since the GPAR(X) test is so simple.

3. Even though under ideal circumstances the third expression can achieve maximal parallelism, it may occasionally fail to find parallelism due to the approximation technique of the typing algorithm. Consequently, in this scheme, all three goals might execute sequentially while in Conery's scheme they would execute in parallel.

As another example, consider the clause

$$f(X,Y) <- p(X) \& q(Y) \&$$
$$s(X,Y) \& t(Y).$$

The compiler will produce the following execution graph expression:

$$(GPAR(X,Y)$$
$$(IPAR(X,Y)\ p(X)\ q(Y))$$
$$(GPAR(Y)\ s(X,Y)\ t(Y))\ )$$

If X and Y are independent at run-time but not ground, the execution graph of Figure 3 will be achieved. Conery's scheme will also achieve this same execution graph. But

Conery's scheme has one advantage - as soon as q(Y) completes, t(Y) can begin execution, even if p(X) is incomplete. In the scheme presented here, t(Y) will have to wait until the first two subgoals complete. This is a result of the definition of an SEQ expression. This loss of parallelism is due to the limited execution graph expressions and is not a result of the approximation technique of the typing algorithm. Consequently, there are two ways in which the and-parallelism of a clause may be restricted.

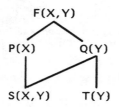

Figure 3. EXECUTION GRAPH

Finally, consider the following quicksort program and the compiled execution expression:

```
qksort(L,SL) <-
    partition(L,L1,L2) &
    qksort(L1,SL1) &
    qksort(L2,SL2) &
    append(SL1,SL2,SL).


(SEQ
    partition(L,L1,L2)
    (IPAR(L1,L2)
        qksort(L1,SL1)
        qksort(L2,SL2) )
    append(SL1,SL2,SL) )
```

A PARALLEL EXECUTION MODEL

In this section a parallel execution model is presented for executing the graph expressions. The model is intended to run on a tightly-coupled parallel architecture with each processing element containing its own large, local memory. Each processor is assumed to have a copy of the entire program resident in its memory (or at least to have rapid paging access to the program).

When all processors are busy executing pieces of a large program, it is not necessarily beneficial for one processor to decompose its own piece of work into two or more pieces since it may end up having to execute them both anyway. The busier the processors are, the less beneficial a task decomposition is likely to be. We adopt the following views in the model:

1. When all processors are busy doing useful work, it is not necessarily beneficial to distribute work among them.

2. When a processor executes a clause, it assumes it will have to execute all subgoals in the clause by itself (that is, it assumes all other processors are busy doing useful work).

3. Subgoals will be distributed to other processors only when those processors have volunteered to help (when they have asked for work). This will usually occur only when the requesting processor is idle (has no goals to execute) or at least is lightly loaded (perhaps all its goals are suspended).

4. Before distributing a subgoal set, we try to ensure that it is nontrivial.

Because it may frequently prove non-beneficial to dynamically decompose a task when all processors in the system are busy, it may similarly prove non-harmful if an occasional opportunity for parallelism is not detected. Consequently, the loss of maximal detection of parallelism due to the approximation technique of the typing algorithm and as a result of the limited execution graph expression types is believed to be acceptable. The return is in the extreme simplicity of the run-time component of the model.

Each processor maintains two expression stacks - a sequential stack and a parallel stack. The sequential stack contains expressions that must be - or have been decided to be - executed sequentially; the parallel stack contains expressions that can be executed in parallel. When a user query is read, it is converted into an execution graph expression and placed on the sequential stack of some processor. Each processor checks the top of its sequential stack to obtain its next piece of work. If the expression on top of the stack is a goal, that goal is executed as in normal Prolog systems. If it is an IPAR or GPAR expression, the specified test is performed, and if the result is true, the following subexpressions are all placed on the parallel stack. If the result is false, the sub-expressions are all placed on the sequential stack. An SEQ expression simply puts the following list of sub-expressions back on the sequential stack, while a PAR expression puts its sub-expressions on the parallel stack. The actual entries on the stacks will, of course, be pointers to expressions and not the expressions themselves.

If the sequential stack becomes empty, the processor takes an expression off the parallel stack and executes it. However, if the parallel stack is also empty, the processor can volunteer to help some other busy processor.

When a busy processor receives an offer to help from some idle processor, the busy processor can, if it wants, check to see if it has any entries on its parallel stack. If it does, it can select any one of these and assign it to the volunteering processor. It should be clear that entries on the parallel stack can be executed in any order in parallel. Entries on the sequential stack, however, must be executed sequentially, in order, in a "last-in, first-out" manner.

As the system becomes busy, requests to help from volunteers will decrease, and the number of entries on each processor's parallel stack will tend to increase. If a parallel stack reaches some "high" level, the processor may opt to process a potentially parallel expression sequentially. By so doing, any extra overhead in performing the test, decomposing the expression, pushing sub-expressions onto the parallel stack, and popping them back off at some later time can be avoided. Further, by executing a group of several related subgoals, instead of a string of separate subgoals, the architectural and software implementations can potentially take advantage of the many aspects of program locality (e.g., [Tick]).

BACKTRACKING

Backtracking will behave as described in [Chang]. Space limitations prevent a detailed description of the scheme here. A very important advantage shared by this scheme is that all backtrack points can be computed at compile-time. Each goal can have at most two backtrack points. Goals in SEQ or PAR expressions have a single backtrack point; but goals in IPAR and GPAR expressions have two - one used when the IPAR or GPAR expression is executed in parallel and one for when the expressions are executed sequentially. This particular backtracking scheme achieves some of the efficiency of intelligent backtrack schemes [Pereira].

USER-SPECIFICATION OF PARALLELISM

Because of the limitations of the execution graph expressions, certain clauses may be compiled into sequential graphs when with only minor changes they could be compiled into parallel graphs. For example, the following clause will be compiled into the given execution graph expression:

    f(X) <- g(X) & h(X)

    (GPAR g(X) h(X))

This expression will execute in parallel only if X is ground. If the clause is rewritten as
    f(X) <- g(X) & h(Y) & X=Y.,
the following expression is compiled
    (SEQ (PAR g(X) h(Y)) X=Y).

The second clause clearly has potential performance and semantic dif- ferences from the first. But if the programmer is aware of these differences and considers them non-harmful, he may choose the second clause in an effort to establish greater parallelism at run-time. This second clause can achieve parallelism irrespective of whether X is ground or non-ground.

As another example, consider the following, more efficient quicksort program. This program uses difference lists to avoid the calls to the append program.

    qksort(L,SL-Rest) <-
           partition(L,L1,L2) &
           qksort(L1,SL-T) &
           qksort(L2,T-Rest).

Unfortunately, the restricted and-parallel method presented here will fail to detect any potential for parallelism. But if the program is changed to

    qksort(L,SL-Rest) <-
        partition(L,L1,L2) &
        qksort(L1,SL-T1) &
        qksort(L2,T2-Rest) &
        T1=T2.

then the following parallel execution graph is obtained:

    (SEQ partition (L,L1,L2)
        (IPAR (SL,Rest,L1,L2)
             qksort(L1,SL-T1)
             qksort(L2,T2-Rest))
       T1=T2)

How frequently the programmer will be able to assist the compiler with this type of change remains to be seen.

SUMMARY

A method for obtaining restricted and-parallelism in logic programs has been presented. The method involves the compile time creation of a parallel execution graph expression for each program clause. Only one expression per clause is created. The run-time algorithms involved are simple and inexpensive. Due to the limitations of the graph expressions and to the approximation technique of the typing algorithm, an opportunity for parallelism may occasionally be missed. However, a parallel execution model that utilizes demand-driven distribution of work may provide efficient, parallel execution of the graphs in a manner that renders these misses harmless.

BIBLIOGRAPHY

[Chang]   "And-Parallelism of Logic Programs Based on Static Data Dependency Analysis," Jung-Herng Chang and Doug DeGroot, in preparation.

[Clark]   "PARLOG: A Parallel Logic Programming Language," Keith L. Clark and Steve Gregory, Research Report DOC 83/5, Imperial College, March 1983.

[Clark2]   "The Control Facilities of IC-Prolog," Keith L. Clark and Frank McCabe, in Expert Systems in the Microelectronic Age, D. Michie, editor, Edinburgh Univ. Press, 1979.

[Conery]   The AND/OR Process Model for Parallel Execution of Logic Programs, John S. Conery, Ph.D. dissertation, Univ. of California, Irvine, Tech. Report 204, Information and Computer Science, 1983.

[Pereira]   "Selective Backtracking," Luis Moniz Pereira and Antonio Porto, in Logic Programming, Keith L. Clark and Sten-Ake Tarnlund, editors, Academic Press, 1982, pp.107-114.

[Shapiro]   "A Subset of Concurrent Prolog and Its Interpreter," Ehud Y. Shapiro, ICOT Tech. Report TR-003, February, 1983, Tokyo, Japan.

[Tick]   "Towards a Pipelined Prolog Processor," Evan Tick and David H.D. Warren, Proc. of the 1984 International Symposium on Logic Programming, IEEE, pp. 29-40.

[Warren]   Applied Logic - Its Use and Implementation as a Programming Tool, David H.D. Warren, Ph.D. dissertation, Dept. of Artificial Intelligence, Univ. of Edinburgh, 1977.

[Warren2]   "An Abstract Prolog Instruction Set," David H.D. Warren, Technical Note 309, October 1983, SRI International.

[Wise]   "A Parallel Prolog: the Construction of a Data Driven Model," Michael J. Wise, Univ. of New South Wales, Australia.

New Generation Computing, 3 (1985) 43-70
OHMSHA, LTD. and Springer-Verlag

AND Parallelism and Nondeterminism in Logic Programs

John S. CONERY
Department of Computer & Information Science,
University of Oregon,
Eugene, OR 97403-1202, USA
Dennis F. KIBLER
Department of Information & Computer Science,
University of California,
Irvine, CA 92717, USA

Received 10 September 1984

Abstract   This paper defines an abstract interpreter for logic programs based on a system of asynchronous, independent processors which communicate only by passing messages. Each logic program is automatically partitioned and its pieces distributed to available processors. This approach permits two distinct forms of parallelism. OR parallelism arises from evaluating nondeterministic choices simultaneously. AND parallelism arises when a computation involves independent, but necessary, subcomputations. Algorithms like quicksort, which follow a divide and conquer approach, usually exhibit this form of parallelism. These two forms of parallelism are conjointly achieved by the parallel interpreter.

Keywords : Nondeterminism, Process Model, AND Parallelism, OR Parallelism, Intelligent Backtracking

§1 Introduction

In 1980, we started our investigation into the possibility of using a logic programming language for programming highly parallel, dataflow style multiprocessors. At that time, it was not at all clear that there was any parallelism in logic programs beyond the "obvious" parallel tree search.[1] Our initial goals were to:

▷ Identify potential sources of parallelism in logic programs.
▷ Define the parallelism in terms of an abstract interpreter which would be independent of any particular hardware organization (*i.e.* do not base the interpreter on any existing or proposed dataflow machine, or assume the processors will have access to a common, shared memory).
▷ Define the parallelism for "pure logic programs," as opposed to Prolog programs; Prolog has too many features that rely on the semantics of a von Neumann architecture.
▷ Make the interpreter work for any pure logic program; for any version of the interpreter, there may be some parallelism that is not exploited, but any program should be successfully interpreted, sequentially if necessary.

In particular, we wanted to be able to exploit parallelism in nondeterministic programs.

▷ Exploit the parallelism automatically, *i.e.* do not force a programmer to add control annotations to his or her program to identify portions that can be executed in parallel; rather, have the system determine automatically how the program should be executed.

Our first interpreter, which was written in DEC-10 Prolog, exploited only OR parallelism.[2] Later, the model was expanded, and a form of AND parallelism was incorporated.[3] In this paper, we will summarize the main features of our basic model, and present a more detailed account of our implementation of AND parallelism. Complete details of the model can be found in Conery's thesis.[4]

The distinguishing feature of our model, which is called the AND/OR Process Model, is that any pure logic program will be interpreted correctly. By this we mean that given an infinite number of processors and an infinite amount of time, all deducible answers will be found. Contrast this with the standard depth-first interpreter, which loops on some inputs even though deducible answers exist. Furthermore with a finite number of processors our interpreter is guaranteed to return all answers that the standard depth-first interpreter does. Many other models accept only deterministic programs, which we feel is too restrictive. Nondeterminism is a major advantage of logic programming. Our interpreter maintains a correct interpretation of nondeterminism while performing both AND and OR parallelism. Moreover the method for achieving AND parallelism has some of the properties of *intelligent backtracking* so new processes are not spawned promiscuously.

We begin this paper by defining several different ways of achieving parallelism in logic programs. Then we briefly describe our basic AND/OR process model. The next four sections develop our mechanism for achieving AND parallelism, giving specific algorithms and underlying data structures. We use the map coloring example of Pereira and Porto and matrix multiplication to illustrate simple AND parallelism. In the last sections we discuss the difficult case of backtracking while in the midst of AND parallelism. Again we use the map coloring example to illustrate how the various data structures are updated. Finally we summarize our contribution and suggest some future work.

§2   Sources of Parallelism

An interpreter of logic programs starts with a goal statement such as

$$\leftarrow p(X) \wedge q(X) \wedge r(Y).$$

and tries to derive the null clause through a series of resolutions. The interpreter must *solve* each subgoal in the goal statement, by finding a clause in the program with a head that matches the subgoal, and then forming a new goal statement from the remaining subgoals and the body of the selected clause. When there are many possible clauses in the program with heads that match a subgoal, a tree of derived goal statements is defined. A typical (sequential) implementation, such as a standard Prolog interpreter, performs a depth-first search of this tree. The initial goal of our research was to identify the steps in the interpretation that can be done in parallel.

One possibility is a parallel search of the tree of derived goal statements: at each choice point, distribute the goal statements at descendant nodes to interpreters running on independent computers. For example, if p(X) in the above example matches the heads of two clauses C1 and C2, have one processor solve the goal statement consisting of $q(X) \land r(Y)$ and the body of C1, and have another processor solve the goal made from $q(X) \land r(Y)$ and the body of C2. The expected speedup in execution will be obtained if one of these interpreters derives the null clause more quickly than an interpreter that performs a simple depth-first search.[1] The amount of time required in such a system (ignoring inter-computer communication times) will be directly proportional to the length of the shortest path in the search tree from the root to a null clause. The amount of time required by a depth-first interpreter is proportional to the sum of path lengths in all branches to the left of the first branch that contains the null clause.

However, this form of parallel search will not yield any speedup for programs that are implementations of deterministic functions. The main characteristics of deterministic programs are that there is just one answer, and the search tree is deep and narrow, often just a single path with no choice points. A good example is a program to compute the product of two matrices. One of our major goals was to obtain the same speedup in execution for deterministic programs that is possible in dataflow or functional programming while at the same time exploiting parallelism in nondeterministic programs. For example matrix multiplication can be done in parallel in the the dataflow language Id in time $O(n)$ instead of $O(n^3)$.[5]

Four other sources of programming were defined in.[2] *Search parallelism* comes from being able to do a parallel search for clauses with heads that match a selected subgoal. Here the results of the parallel search are passed to a uniprocessor inference mechanism. This form of parallelism will be useful for distributed database types of applications. Examples of search-parallel systems include the work of Warren,[6] Taylor,[7] and Minker.[8]

OR parallelism is exploited when a system can perform parallel computations based on the fact that a subgoal matches the heads of more than one clause. The parallel tree search is one form of OR parallelism; the interpreters of Haridi[9] and Furukawa[10] are also based on this form of parallelism. The mechanism for OR parallelism of the AND/OR process model is slightly different, as will be explained in the next section.

AND parallelism arises when two or more subgoals from a single goal statement are solved in parallel. This can be quite complicated. Referring to the example above, $p(X)$ and $q(X)$ have a variable in common, and the system must ensure that the processes that solve these subgoals bind X to the same value.

Stream parallelism is sometimes identified with AND parallelism, as described by Kowalski,[11] Clark,[12] and Shapiro.[13] This comes from viewing the processes that solve subgoals as coroutines that communicate via shared variables. Referring back to the example clause, subgoals $p(X)$ and $q(X)$ could be solved simultaneously by viewing the shared variable X as a stream. One of the subgoals will be the producer of values for the stream, the other will be the consumer. Execution of producers and consumers proceeds simultaneously on different processors. The interpreters of Clark and Gregory[14] and Shapiro[13] are implementations of what we call stream parallelism.

The important distinction between our implementation of AND parallelism and stream parallelism is that current implementations of stream parallelism restrict their inputs to deterministic programs. On the other hand, our implementation of AND parallelism requires the sequential solution of subgoals such as $p(X)$ and $q(X)$, which have a variable in common; some parallelism is lost, and communication costs may be higher in some architectures if the shared variable is bound to a very large term.

§3 The AND/OR Process Model

In the AND/OR Process Model, goal statements are solved by sets of processes that communicate only via messages. There are two types of processes: AND processes and OR processes. A process is created to solve some portion of the logic program. At any time, a process may decide to divide its input problem into subproblems and create descendant processes to solve those subproblems. Processes communicate only with their parents or descendants. The set of processes and their communication paths form a dynamic AND/OR tree that is constantly changing as processes are created, executed, and then terminated.

During execution, a process undergoes a series of state transformations. A transformation is considered to be an atomic event, triggered by receipt of a message. Our processes are quite similar to the serialized actors of the ACT I language of Hewitt and Attardi.[16]

The kinds of messages sent by processes are

▷ success:
This message is sent from a process to its parent, indicating that the subproblem was solved. Success messages carry information about variable bindings that were made in order to solve the subproblem.

▷ fail:
This message is also sent from a descendant to a parent; it indicates that the subproblem was not solvable.

▷ redo:
Sent by a process to a descendant that has already sent at least one success; this message tells the descendant to compute another answer for subproblem.

▷ cancel:
This message is sent by a parent to a descendant when the parent knows it does not need any more answers from that descendant.

An AND process is created to solve a goal statement, such as the one given in the previous example. It solves the goal statement by creating descendant OR processes for each subgoal, and waiting for success messages from each. AND parallelism arises when an AND process is able to create more than one such descendant at any one time.

The subproblem for an OR process is always exactly one subgoal. This goal comes from its parent's goal statement. The OR process can solve this subgoal in one of two ways: the subgoal may match the head of a unit clause, in which case the OR process immediately sends a success message, or the subgoal may match the head of a nonunit clause, in which case the OR process creates a descendant AND process to solve the body of the matching clause. OR parallelism is exploited when more than one AND descendant is active at any time. In alternative approaches to OR parallelism, a process is given the entire context of the problem solving state. If successful, such a sprouted process reports back to the top level goal. In our approach an OR process receives only a single goal and reports back to its immediate parent. This reduces the size of messages and set-up time for OR processes. For a fuller description of comparison of this form of OR parallelism with the goal tree search described in Section 2, see Conery's thesis.[4]

§4 Parallel AND Processes

A *sequential* AND process solves its subgoals one at a time; it can mimic a sequential interpreter by solving the subgoals from left to right. The transmission of redo messages to previously solved goals is equivalent to backtracking. A *parallel* AND process is one that can solve more than one subgoal at any time. AND parallelism in the AND/OR process model is achieved by creating more than one OR process simultaneously. The rules for state transitions in parallel AND processes are much more complex than the rules for sequential AND processes, as the parallel processes must react to success and fail messages from more than one active descendant.

Whether the AND process is sequential or parallel, it can be viewed as a tuple generator. The denotational semantics of logic programming define the meaning of a goal statement of N variables to be an N-ary relation.[17] A logic programming interpreter must therefore generate the required N-tuples of terms needed to solve an input goal.

The brute force method for AND parallelism is to immediately create a process for every subgoal. There are three reasons why this will not be effective; all three reasons are based on the fact that the solution of one subgoal often binds variables that are arguments in other subgoals.

The first drawback to brute force parallelism is that the AND process must ensure that solutions for the different subgoals bind common variables to the same terms. For a relatively simple clause like

$$f(A, C) \leftarrow p(A, B) \wedge q(B, C).$$

it may be possible to compute the tuples $\langle A, C \rangle$ by using some form of parallel join algorithm on the relations defined by p and q with respect to variable **B**. In the general case, however, this may be quite difficult. In the clause

$$f(A, B, C) \leftarrow p(A, B) \wedge q(B, C) \wedge r(C, A).$$

the AND process must compute tuples $\langle A, B, C \rangle$ where all three subgoals are satisfied at the same time.

A second argument against solving all subgoals at once is that by waiting until some of the variables of a subgoal **G** are bound via the solution of other subgoals, the OR process created to solve **G** may be more efficient: there are often fewer solutions, and fewer fruitless choices made in constructing those solutions.[9]

Finally, and of most practical importance, some subgoals *fail* if an attempt is made to solve them before a sufficient set of variables are instantiated; these are the subgoals with *mode declarations*.[18] For example, in the goal statement

$$\leftarrow length(L, N) \wedge X \text{ is } 5 * N.$$

the goal of multiplying **N** by five fails unless **N** is instantiated to an integer in the solution of the first subgoal. In some systems, **X is 5 * N** is written sum(**X**, **5, N**), which is not solvable until any two of the three arguments are bound to integers. This subgoal named **sum** is said to have a *threshold* of two.[15]

An effective method for achieving AND parallelism is thus a problem of correctly ordering the subgoals, of deciding which subgoals must be solved sequentially and which can be solved in parallel. The implementation of AND parallelism defined in Conery's thesis[4] has three major components. There is an *ordering algorithm* that automatically decides the order in which the subgoals should be solved, a *forward execution* component which creates the descendant OR processes in the proper order, and a *backward execution* component to handle fail and redo messages and decide which subgoal(s) must be re-solved before resuming forward execution.

§5 Ordering of Subgoals

The basis for the ordering of subgoals in the body of a clause is the sharing of variables. Whenever two or more subgoals have a variable in common, one of the subgoals will be designated the *generator* for that variable, and it will be solved before the others, which are now *consumers*. The solution of the generator is intended to bind the shared variable to some value. After the generator has been solved, the consumers may be scheduled for solution.

Note that a subgoal can be the generator of some variables and a consumer of others. This is especially true when the subgoal represents function call, *i.e.* where some of the arguments are input arguments (which must be fully instantiated) and other arguments must be uninstantiated variables that will be bound by the execution of the function. Such a subgoal is a consumer of variables in the input positions, and a generator of variables in the output positions.

It is possible that the solution of a generator will not bind its variable, or it may bind the variable to a nonground term. In this case the consumers still share a variable in common. When that happens, one of the consumers must take on the role of generator and be solved before the other consumers. This situation is discussed in detail in a later section; for now, we will make the simplifying assumption that the solution of a generator binds the shared variable to a ground term.

Generators and consumers are similar to the lazy producers and eager consumers of IC-Prolog.[12] The term "generator" is used here, since their action is more closely related to generators in other languages (see, for example, Alphard[19]), in that they produce a *sequence* of independent terms. The producers of IC-Prolog create a single complex term through a series of partial bindings.

§6 Dataflow Graphs

Generator and consumer relationships within a single clause can be shown pictorially as a *dataflow graph*. In these graphs there is one node for each subgoal, including the head, and a set of directed arcs to indicate generator/ consumer relationships. For each variable there will be an arc from its generator to each subgoal that consumes the variable. An *immediate predecessor* of a subgoal G is defined to be a subgoal that is a generator for one of the variables in G. A predecessor, in general, is either an immediate predecessor or a predecessor of an immediate predecessor.

The head of the clause is a special case. It is considered to be the generator of every variable that is bound when the AND process is created. The ordering algorithm of the next section requires this information, so the head of the clause (*i.e.* the subgoal being solved by the parent OR process) is included in the state information of a parallel AND process. The head is also the consumer of variables that are not instantiated when the AND process is created. Where it is important, the head will be included in the pictures of dataflow graphs in later sections.

§7 The Ordering Algorithm

The ordering algorithm must designate a generator for every variable in the goal statement. It does this automatically, without relying on control annotations supplied by the programmer. Logically, any subgoal can be the generator of any variable that appears as one of its arguments. The only exceptions are determined by evaluable predicates or user defined procedures with mode declarations. The ordering algorithm is used primarily to ensure that mode constraints are not violated, and secondarily to produce an efficient ordering. Another constraint on the form of the graph is that the graph must be acyclic; the reasons for this will be obvious when the forward execution algorithm is explained in the next section.

There are a number of rules one can use to identify generators. The first, mentioned above, is that the head of a clause is the generator for all variables that are instantiated when the clause is invoked.

Second, some of the subgoals in the body may have I/O modes. These subgoals may be evaluable predicates, for which the system already knows the modes, or they may be user-defined functions, in which case the user can specify a mode declaration. A good example is the evaluable predicate is from DEC-10 Prolog, which has the mode declaration

$$\leftarrow \text{mode is}(?, \, +).$$

This declaration shows that is has two arguments. The question mark means that terms in that argument position can be either variables or nonvariable terms. The plus sign means that the corresponding argument *must* be a ground term: it must not contain any uninstantiated variables by the time the subgoal is selected for solution. Another possibility (not shown in this example) is a minus sign, which means that the corresponding argument must be an uninstantiated variable, and that as a result of the procedure call the variable will be instantiated. If there is a minus sign in the mode declaration for a predicate, then the ordering algorithm knows that a subgoal with this predicate symbol *must* be the generator for any variables used in that argument position. A plus sign means the subgoal can *never* be the generator for any variables occurring in the corresponding argument position. The above mode declaration indicates that a subgoal is(X, Y) can never be a generator for any variables occurring in an expression in the second argument position, but might be the generator of a variable that is the first argument.

The two rules just described—that the head is the generator of variables that are bound when the procedure is called and that mode declarations cannot be violated—are the only two rules that are strict, in the sense that if they are broken an incorrect ordering will be constructed. By themselves they are not sufficient to designate generators for every variable in the body of a clause. There are a number of heuristic rules that could be used in conjunction with these two rules in order to make sure all variables have generators and the resulting ordering is relatively efficient.

The only heuristic currently implemented in the ordering algorithm is the *connection rule*. Briefly, when the connection rule is applied in order to find a generator for a variable V, it looks for a subgoal that (1) contains V as an unbound variable, and (2) consumes variables for which generators are already known. The connection rule is stated more concisely as step 3.a of the ordering algorithm Fig. 1. The basis for using this rule is that, in general, a subgoal will have fewer possible solutions, and thus be more easily solved, when some of its variables are bound.[9]

The ordering algorithm uses the following variables:
B The set of literals in the body. Initialized to contain every literal in the body ; when a literal is designated as a generator, it is removed from B.
S The set of variables for which generators have been specified.
U The set of variables for which generators are not known yet. Note that the union of S and U contains every variable in the clause.

The algorithm :
1. Identify as many generators as possible using mode declarations; remove those literals from B, and initialize S to be the variables generated by these literals.
2. Add to S the variables instantiated in the head of the clause; the head is the generator of these variables. Initialize U to be the set of all remaining variables.
3. Repeat until $B = []$ or $U = []$:
   a. Make a set LS with every literal in B that has at least one variable in U and one variable in S {note: if S is empty, LS will also be empty}.
   b. If LS is empty after step (a), find the leftmost literal in B that has a variable in U and add it to LS {LS contains just this one literal}.
   c. For every literal L in LS, assign L as the generator of any variables in U that occur in L. Remove these variables from U and add them to S. Remove L from B.

Fig. 1 The literal ordering algorithm.

Finally, if a variable is not assigned a generator through application of the previous three rules, the leftmost subgoal in which the variable occurs is designated as the generator for that variable. This rule, called the "leftmost rule," is simply a default, and is included to make sure that every variable will have a generator. It is most often invoked when there are no bound variables in the head. In these cases, the leftmost rule is applied once, and then the connection rule finds generators for the remaining variables.

Note that since mode declarations are known before a clause is called, the second rule can be applied when clauses are compiled or first loaded by the interpreter. The other rules are applied at runtime, once the pattern of variable instantiation in the clause is known. As an optimization, our current interpreter keeps dataflow graphs for clauses in a cache, indexed by the pattern of variable instantiation in the head. Whenever a new AND process is created, this cache is searched to see if an existing graph can be used. This optimization is quite effective, especially when recursive clauses are being interpreted.

§8 Examples of Subgoal Orderings

The ordering algorithm will be illustrated by four examples. The dataflow graphs produced for these examples are shown in Figs 2(a)~2(d).

8.1 Disjoint Subgoals: Fig. 2(a)

In the clause

$$f(X, Y) \leftarrow g(X) \wedge h(Y).$$

the two subgoals in the body are clearly independent. The graph pictured in Fig. 2(a) is the case when neither X nor Y is instantiated when the process is created. The leftmost rule was used to designate $g(X)$ as the generator of X and $h(Y)$ as the generator of Y. Note that if there are N_g solutions for $g(X)$ and N_h ways of solving $h(Y)$, then $N_g \times N_h$ pairs of X and Y values may have to be constructed by the AND process. The remaining pairs, after the first, will be created in response to redo messages; the method used to enumerate all pairs is described later in the section on backward execution.

Clause: Call:

$f(X, Y) \leftarrow g(X) \, \& \, h(Y).$ $\leftarrow f(X, Y).$

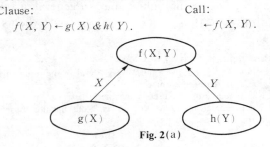

Fig. 2(a)

8.2 Shared Variable: Fig. 2(b)

In the clause

$$query(P, I) \leftarrow author(P, X) \land loc(X, I, D).$$

the two subgoals have the local variable **X** in common, and no call to query can ever cause **X** to be instantiated when the clause is selected. When the AND process is created, if **I** is instantiated but **P** is not, then the connection rule specifies that loc(X, I, D) should be the generator of **X**. Otherwise, author(P, X) is designated, either by the connection rule (**P** is instantiated but **I** is not) or by the leftmost rule. The graph pictured in Fig. 2(b) shows the case for when **P** is bound when the AND process is created, and author(P, X) is chosen as the generator for **X**. This is an example of where the connection rule implements the optimal ordering, in the sense that the solution of either author(P, X) or loc(X, I, D) will be more efficient if **X** is bound.

Clause:
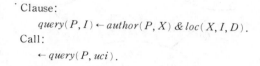

Call:

$$\leftarrow query(P, uci).$$

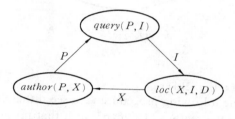

Fig. 2(b)

8.3 Deterministic Function: Fig. 2(c)

The following clause illustrates the general form of a deterministic function, in this case an implementation of a divide and conquer algorithm.

```
solve(P, Q) ←
    divide(P, P1, P2) ∧
    solve(P1, Q1) ∧
    solve(P2, Q2) ∧
    combine(Q1, Q2, Q)
```

On every call to solve, **P** will be bound to a term representing the input problem. As a result, **Q** will be bound to a term representing the output of the function. The optimal ordering of subgoals is: divide problem **P** into independent subproblems **P1** and **P2**; then solve **P1** and **P2** in parallel via the recursive calls, thereby instantiating **Q1** and **Q2**; when both are done, construct answer **Q** from partial answers **Q1** and **Q2**. This sequence of events is implied by the picture in Fig. 2(c); exactly how it is achieved is described in the next section, on forward execution. This graph can be produced by repeated application of the connection rule, so mode declarations are not required. In general, however, mode declarations will be required when ordering the subgoals in the body of a clause that implements a function.

377

$$solve(P, Q) \leftarrow divide(P, P1, P2) \: \& \: solve(P1, Q1) \: \&$$
$$solve(P2, Q2) \: \& \: combine(Q1, Q2, Q)$$

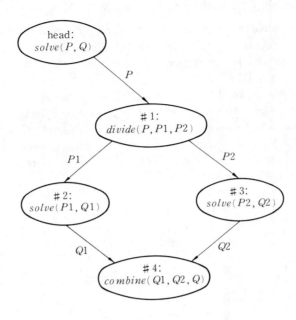

Fig. 2(c)

8.4 Map Coloring : Fig. 2(d)

The goal of the following procedure is to see if there is an assignment of one of four colors to the regions of a map* such that no two adjacent regions have the same color:

```
color(A, B, C, D, E) ←
    next(A, B) ∧ next(C, D) ∧
    next(A, C) ∧ next(A, D) ∧
    next(B, C) ∧ next(B, E) ∧
    next(C, E) ∧ next(D, E).
    next(red, blue) ←.
    next(red, green) ←.
    next(blue, green) ←.
        ⋮
```

The calls to **next** will succeed only if the arguments have been (or can be) instantiated to terms representing different colors. There is one call to **next** for each border in the map. This Prolog solution of the map coloring problem was originally given by Pereira and Porto in their papers on intelligent backtracking.[20]

When the AND process for the body of this clause is established, none of the variable in the head will be instantiated. The subgoal ordering shown in the figure was produced by first using the leftmost rule to designate **next(A, B)** as the generator for both **A** and **B**, *i.e.* the solution of this subgoal assigns colors to regions **A** and **B**. The connection rule was used to identify the three subgoals in the middle row of the dataflow graph as generators of the other three

---

* The map to be colored by this clause is shown in Fig. 6, along with procedure code and other information used by the interpreter.

$$color(A, B, C, D, E) \leftarrow next(A, B) \& next(C, D) \& next(A, C) \& next(A, D) \&$$
$$next(B, C) \& next(B, E) \& next(C, E) \& next(D, E)$$

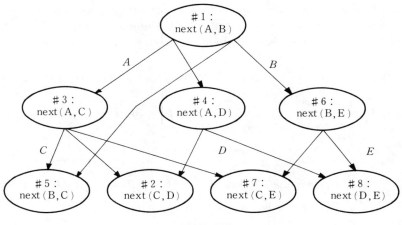

Fig. 2(d)

variables. That leaves the remaining four subgoals as consumers. The role of these consumers in this problem is to verify that colors assigned by generators are valid for the rest of the map.

Not unexpectedly, when this problem is interpreted, the generators in the middle row first create a combination of values that is unacceptable to some of the consumers on the bottom row. There are a number of difficult problems presented by this example, as the AND process tries to coordinate the four generators in order to create, eventually, every five-tuple of colors that satisfy the constraints of this goal list. Many of the problems arise from the relative timing of the arrival of fail and success messages. The general principles will be explained in the section on backward execution. A detailed trace of the parallel solution of this problem is presented at the end of this paper.

§9   Forward Execution

Subgoals in the body of a parallel AND process will always be in one of three states: *blocked*, *pending*, or *solved*. A subgoal is in the blocked state when an OR process has not yet been created for it. A subgoal is in the pending state when an OR process has been created for it, but the process has not yet sent back either a success or fail message. Finally, a subgoal is in the solved state after the OR process that was created for it has sent back a success message.

Forward execution is essentially a graph reduction procedure. Whenever the AND process receives a success message from a descendant, it means the corresponding subgoal can be resolved away from the body of the clause; in the dataflow graph, the node for the subgoal and all arcs leaving it are removed from the graph. The AND process succeeds after a success message has been received from every descendant, *i.e.* after the graph has been completely reduced. Recall that a success message from an OR process created to solve a subgoal **G** has the general form **success(G**θ**)**, where **G**θ is a copy of **G** with (possibly) some variables bound. The graph reduction step is accomplished by resolving **L** with the current set of subgoals in the body of the clause. If **G** is a generator of a set of variables, then some of those variables may be instantiated in **G**θ. Envision values flowing from **G** to the consumers, as the resolution of **G**θ with the remaining subgoals causes those variables to be bound in the resolvent.

379

The criterion for deciding when to start an OR process for a subgoal is that a subgoal is ready to be solved only when all of its predecessors have been solved, *i.e.* when the corresponding node in the dataflow graph has no incoming arcs. If the graph is acyclic, and each subgoal can be solved, then eventually a process will be started for every subgoal. A more formal presentation of the forward execution algorithm is given in Fig. 3. Figure 4 shows the parallel solution of two sample goal lists as sequences of graph reductions.

1. When the start message is received, initialize a list B to be the complete set of literals to be solved.
2. Repeat until B is the empty list:
   a. Apply the ordering algorithm to the literals in B to make a dataflow graph G.
   b. Start an OR process for every literal in G that has no incoming arcs and that does not already have a process.
   c. Wait for a message from an OR descendant.
   d. If the message is *fail*, call the backward execution algorithm (Section 5.3).
   e. If the message is *success(Lθ)*, resolve B with $\neg L\theta$, making a new body B {note: B now has one less literal, and bindings in θ have been applied to all remaining literals}.

Fig. 3 Forward execution algorithm.

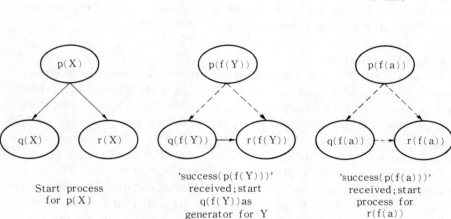

Fig. 4 Sequences of graph reductions.

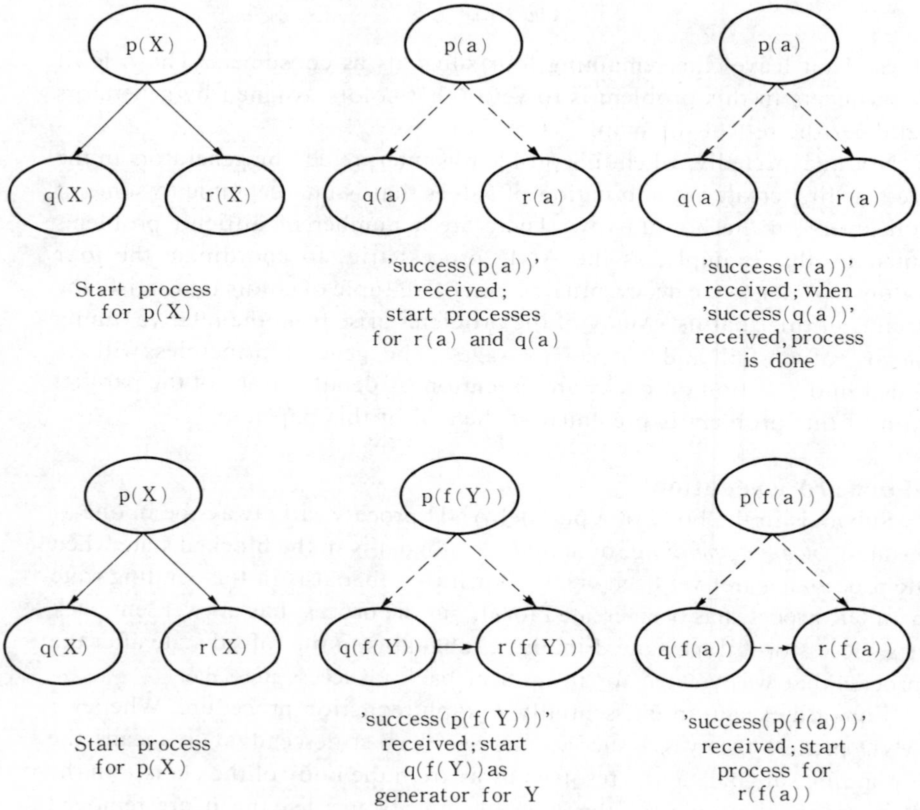

This figure shows two possible sequences of graph reductions during forward execution for the goal statement.

$\leftarrow p(X)\ \&\ q(X)\ \&\ r(X).$

Nodes and arcs drawn with dotted lines have been removed. In the first sequence, $p(X)$ generates the ground term a, and $r(a)$ and $q(a)$ can be solved in parallel. In the second sequence, X is bound to $f(Y)$, making the remaining literals $r(f(Y))$ and $q(f(Y))$. The literal ordering algorithm must be called to decide on a generator for Y; then that generator will be solved before the other literal.

Figure 3 shows that the ordering algorithm will be applied after every success message is received. This is necessary for those cases when a generator binds its variable V to a non-ground term containing a new variable V'. If there is more than one consumer of V, they will then have a common variable in V'. Since subgoals with variables in common are not solved in parallel, and since every variable must have a generator, the ordering algorithm must be called again to specify a generator for V'. When the generator binds V to a ground term, which contains no variables, then step 2.a can be omitted.

The combination of the ordering algorithm and the forward execution strategy is sufficient for parallel solution of clauses that define deterministic functions. The distinguishing characteristics of these clauses are that the subgoals in the body are also deterministic functions, meaning they all have mode declarations, and for every combination of inputs there is just one output value for each output variable. Barring system failure, deterministic functions are guaranteed to succeed when given legal inputs, meaning the AND process for one of these clauses will never have to respond to fail or redo messages.

Matrix multiplication is a good example of such a function. One way of writing this function as a logic program is shown in Fig. 5. The head of the procedure is mm(A, B, C). When called, A and B will be bound to terms representing matrices, and after the call, C will be instantiated to their product. A row in a matrix is represented as a list of integers, and a matrix is a list of rows

Interpreter Measurements:

N	Number of Processes	Number of Steps	Time	Steps/Time	Number of Messages	Message Size
1	13	25	21	1.19	13	382
2	46	91	35	2.60	46	1630
3	121	241	49	4.91	121	4822

/*To multiply two matrices, transpose the second, then form all inner products.*/

$mm(A, B, C) \leftarrow transpose(B, BT)$ & $mmt(A, BT, C)$.

/*Multiply all rows of A with entire matrix B. */

$mmt([ ],\_,[ ])$.
$mmt([A1 | An], B, [C1 | Cn]) \leftarrow mmc(A1, B, C1)$ & $mmt(An, B, Cn)$.

/*Multiply all columns of B with row A. */

$mmc(\_,[ ],[ ])$.
$mmc(A, [B1 | Bn], [C1 | Cn]) \leftarrow ip(A, B1, C1)$ & $mmc(A, Bn, Cn)$.

/*Form the inner product of two vectors. */

$ip([ ], [ ], 0)$.
$ip([A1 | An], [B1 | Bn] C], \leftarrow ip(An, Bn, X)$ & C is $X + A1 * B1$.

/*To transpose a matrix, call 'columns' to divide it into two parts: the first column and the rest of the columns; then transpose the rest. */

$transpose([[ ] | \_],[ ])$.
$transpose(M,[C1 | Cn]) \leftarrow columns(M, C1, Rest)$ & $transpose(Rest, Cn)$.

$columns([ ], [ ], [ ])$.
$columns([[C11 | C1n] | C], [C11 | X], [C1n | Y]) \leftarrow columns(C, X, Y)$.

/*Mode declarations, required for proper ordering.*/

$mode(is, [?, +])$. $mode(mmt, [+, +, -])$.

$mode(mm, [+, +, -])$. $mode(mmc, [+, +, -])$.

Fig. 5 Matrix multiplication program.

(*i.e.* a list of lists; see Fig. 5).

The top level of the function is simply a call to transpose one argument, followed by a call to a procedure that actually multiplies the matrices. BT is the transposed version of B; it is a list of columns instead of a list of rows. After transpose succeeds, the problem is to distribute all possible pairs of rows of A with columns of BT to the inner product function. This is done by the two auxiliary functions mmt and mmc. The internal structure of these two procedures is identical: there are two subgoals in the body of each; one subgoal is a call to a lower level function with the first element of the input list, while the other subgoal is a recursive call with the remainder of the list. The dataflow graphs for both functions show that the subgoals are independent, and can be solved simultaneously. The inner product function shown here is sequential in nature, since the results of the multiplications are be summed serially.

Analysis of the bodies of mmt and mmc shows that since the recursive call can be done at the same time as the call to the lower level function, the time required to solve a problem of size n is proportional to the time required to solve the largest subproblem, rather than proportional to the sum of times to solve both subproblems. The time required to compute the product of the two matrices is thus the time required to distribute the last of the row/column pairs to the process that performs an inner product, plus the time required to do that inner product. For the multiplication of $n \times n$ arrays, this time is $O(n+n+n)$, *i.e.* $O(n)$.[5]

The table in Fig.5 shows the results of some simulations of matrix multiplication, giving number of steps required, and the simulated time used. The results support the claim that parallelism in deterministic functions can be exploited by the AND parallelism of the AND/OR Process Model.

§10 Backward Execution

The purpose of backward execution is to coordinate the actions of the generators in their production of terms for the variables of the goal list. If there are n variables in its goal list, an AND process is expected to construct as many n-tuples of terms as possible. A subset of these n-tuples belong to the relation defined by the clause the AND process is interpreting.

A straightforward model for generating tuples is provided by the nested loops of a procedural language, such as Pascal. For example, a nested loop implementation of the previously defined map coloring problem is of the form:

baselineskip = 14pt

```
for A := Red to Blue do
    for B := Red to Blue do
        for C := Red to Blue do
            for D := Red to Blue do
                for E := Red to Blue do
                    if Next(A,B)and . . . and Next(D,E) then
                        Writeln('success(A,B,C,D,E)');
```

An abstract description of the working of this model is as follows: Initial values (red) are assigned to all variables. The initial tuple ⟨red, red, red, red, red⟩ is tested by the boolean expression in the body of the loop. The next tuple is created by assigning the innermost variable, E, its next value. Eventually, the last value (blue) is assigned to the innermost variable. The next tuple is obtained by *resetting* the variable E to its first value while making the second value of the next-innermost variable D. In general, whenever there are no more values for a variable, the previous (outer) variable is given a new value, and whenever a variable is set to a new value, all later variables (all those closer to the body of the loop) are reset to their initial values.

Nested generators can also be used to describe the overall behavior of the sequential Prolog interpretation. However, since the same predicate that *tests* adjacent colors is also used to *generate* colors, the Prolog implementation has the advantage that it never constructs any obviously wrong tuples. In the Pascal implementation, all 5^4 5-tuples of colors are generated. The first 3^4 of these have the general form ⟨red,red,C,D,E⟩, which can never work because **A** and **B** cannot be the same color. In Prolog, next(A,B) is the generator of **A** and **B**, and it never instantiates both **A** and **B** to the same color, thus effectively the construction of a large number of useless tuples.

This simple model for generating tuples has been for use in parallel AND processes as a way of coordinating the transmission of redo messages to descendant OR processes. It is not a very elegant model of tuple generation, but it is straightforward, and complete (meaning it constructs all possible tuples as

$$color(A, B, C, D, E) \leftarrow next(A, B) \,\&\, next(C, D) \,\&\, next(A, C) \,\&\, next(A, D) \,\&$$
$$next(B, C) \,\&\, next(B, E) \,\&\, next(C, E) \,\&\, next(D, E).$$

$next(red, blue) \leftarrow .$ $next(red, yellow) \leftarrow .$ $next(red, green) \leftarrow .$
$next(blue, red) \leftarrow .$ $next(blue, yellow) \leftarrow .$ $next(blue, green) \leftarrow .$
$next(yellow, red) \leftarrow .$ $next(yellow, blue) \leftarrow .$ $next(yellow, green) \leftarrow .$
$next(green, red) \leftarrow .$ $next(green, blue) \leftarrow .$ $next(green, yellow) \leftarrow .$

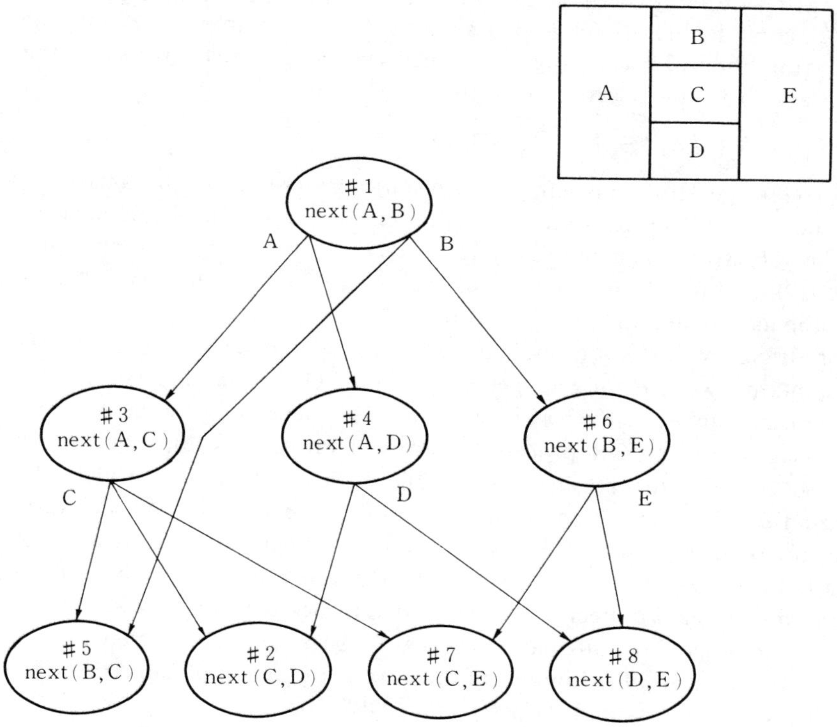

A map with five regions, the coloring problem as a list of eight borders, and the dataflow graph created by the ordering algorithm. This method of solving a map coloring problem in logic was originally used by Pereira and Porto[20] to illustrate intelligent backtracking.

Fig. 6 The map coloring problem.

long as the domains of the generated variables are finite), and inherits the same efficiency of the Prolog version of the nested loop model.

§11 Data Structures for Backward Execution

Adoption of the nested loop model for constructing tuples of terms in a parallel AND process requires a *linear ordering* of subgoals and implementation of a *reset* operation. These will be defined in this section; the actual sequence of events carried out in backward execution will be described in the next section. Examples will refer to the clause and dataflow graph of Fig. 6.

Many of the data structures require a means for identifying a particular subgoal in the body of a clause. The technique used is to refer to a subgoal by a term of the form #N, where N is the place the subgoal occupies in the text of the clause. With respect to the example of Fig. 6, the term #2 refers to next(C, D), the second subgoal in the body.

Recall that in the nested loop model, after a generator G has assigned its last value to a variable, the previous (next outer) generator assigns a new value, and G is reset. In a parallel AND process, we cannot use textual ordering to decide the relative position (inner vs. outer) of generators. The solution is to define a linear ordering of subgoals, independent of the textual ordering in the original program, and use the linear ordering to decide when to reset a generator with respect to other generators.

For reasons that will be explained later, the linear ordering is actually an ordering of all subgoals, not just the generators. The only constraint on the relative position of any two subgoals in the linear ordering is that a generator must always come before all subgoals that consume its variable. In the current implementation, the linear ordering is obtained via breadth first traversal of the dataflow graph. The linear ordering of the subgoals of Fig. 6 is

$$[\#1, \#3, \#4, \#6, \#5, \#2, \#7, \#8]$$

The reset operation must effectively restart a generator, so that a variable takes on the same set of values once again. The generator does not have to produce the values in the same order after a reset; the only requirement is that a variable is bound to all the same values again. Also, a reset may occur before the generator has created all possible values.

For efficiency, resets are implemented using lists of answers. The AND process maintains two lists for each generator, called U, for "used" answers, and UU, for "unused" answers. Each is initially []. Whenever a value arrives in a success message from the OR process for the generator, it is appended to U. When a reset is called for, all answers but one from U are copied to UU. The remaining answer becomes the new current value of the variable. As the AND process again requires additional answers, it takes them from UU instead of sending a redo message to the OR process for the generator. Only when UU is empty (all answers having been transferred to U) does the AND process send another redo message. Although this appears to be a time/space tradeoff, by keeping answers instead of recomputing them we avoid a complicated protocol between the AND process and its descendant OR processes.

Backward execution also often requires cancel messages to be sent to descendant OR processes. After a parent sends a cancel message, it can ignore any subsequent messages received from the descendant. This situation may arise when a descendant sends a message, but the message has not yet been processed by the time the parent decides to send the cancel message. In the discussion below, *replacing* a process P means sending P a cancel message, creating a new process P′ for the same subgoal, and using the process ID of P′ in place of P.

When an AND process receives a fail message from the OR process for a subgoal G, one of the generators that precedes G in the linear ordering must produce a new value. If that generator cannot generate a new value (*i.e.* it returns a fail message in response to the redo message), one of the other generators that precedes G must be sent a redo. In choosing generators to reset, we do not simply choose the one closest to G, but instead choose a generator that creates values that are consumed—directly or indirectly—by G. This is an optimization over the sequential nested loop model. If a failed subgoal does not consume a variable V, there is no sense in obtaining a new value of V via a redo to the generator of V; instead, obtain a new value for a variable consumed by G.

Associated with each subgoal is a *redo list*. The redo list determines which generators will be sent redo messages and in what order redo message will be sent. The redo list for a subgoal G contains G and every predecessor of G, sorted according to the linear order (with subgoals that are earlier in the linear order occurring later in the redo list). Redo lists are created at the same time the linear ordering is made. Redo lists for the subgoals of the example problem are shown in Fig. 6.

Finally, an AND process maintains a structure called the *failure* context to keep track of the failed subgoals and decide exactly which generator should be sent the next redo message. The failure context is initially the empty list, and as fail messages are received, subgoal numbers are added to this list.

§12   Processing of Backward Execution

An overview of backward execution is that when a fail message is received, the backward execution algorithm is called to trace out a path in the dataflow graph that extends back from the failed subgoal toward the root of the graph. The failure context reflects the current state of this path. When a generator is encountered along this path, it is sent a redo message. This path should eventually include every predecessor of the failed subgoal, if required. If the failure context ever grows to extend beyond a subgoal with no predecessors, or to include the head of the clause, then the AND process fails.

The desired backward path is simply the redo list for the failed subgoal. This list contains every predecessor of the subgoal, *i.e.* it contains every generator that could possibly affect the set of values consumed by the subgoal. An AND process will always be able to determine which generator to re-solve when it first receives a fail message, since all it has to do is send a redo message to one of the immediate predecessors of the failed subgoal. However, once the backward execution algorithm has embarked on a backward path, subsequent failures from subgoals not on this path can cause difficulties. This is known as a *multiple failure*; rules for handling multiple failures are described later.

Sending a redo message to the OR process for a generator is the analog of incrementing a variable in the nested loop model. In that model, inner variables were set to their first values. Similarly, whenever a generator is sent a redo message, *all generators that appear later in the linear ordering must be reset*.

When a fail message is received, the AND process appends the subgoal number of the failed subgoal to the failure context list. Then the AND process searches for a redo list R such that the new failure context is a prefix of R. The first subgoal in the resulting suffix identifies which predecessor of the failed subgoal should be sent a redo message.*

Referring to Fig. 6, if the process for #2 sends a fail message, the failure context is set to list [#2]. [#2] is a prefix of the redo list [#2, #4, #3, #1], and the suffix after this match is [#4, #3, #1], so the OR process for subgoal #4 is sent a redo message. Looking ahead, suppose the process for #4 fails; this means there are no more values for that variable. The failure context becomes [#2, #4], the suffix after the match is [#3, #1], and the process for subgoal 3 will be sent a redo message.

Whenever a generator is sent a redo message, the corresponding subgoal is moved from the solved state to the pending state, since process for the generator is again trying to construct an answer. When any generator is sent a redo message, a number of other subgoals will be effected. First, all generators that are later in the linear ordering are reset; this is the step that correlates most directly with the nested loop model. Generators that are reset after being solved are still considered to be solved, since there will be one answer left in the list U that can be used as the current value of the variables generated. Second, some consumer processes will have to be canceled. If a subgoal consumes a variable that is generated by any generator that was either sent a redo or reset, then that subgoal must be canceled, since it consumes values that are being changed. The processes for these subgoals will be replaced when all of their predecessors are once again in the solved state. Note that a subgoal might have a new process created immediately, in the case that all of its generators were simply reset.

The processing of success messages has to be modified slightly, in order to accommodate the failure context. When a success message is received, and the forward execution algorithm starts a set of new processes, the subgoals corresponding to the new processes must be removed from the failure context list. Thus the failure context list grows and shrinks as generators are sent redo messages and then respond with additional answers. The failure context shrinks all the way back to the empty list when a new process is started for the subgoal that originally failed. A more concise presentation of the backward execution algorithm is in Fig. 7.

1. When a fail message from process ↑L is received, change the state of #L from pending to blocked {note: the process that was created for #L failed and no longer exists; L is now blocked until a predecessor is re-solved}.
2. Append #L to the failure context.
3. Unify the updated failure context with a prefix of one of the redo lists. The failure context is of the form [#F1, ..., #L], and the matched redo list is of the form [F1, ..., #L | X].
4. The unification of the previous step may succeed when the failure context is exactly the same list as one of the redo lists, *i.e.* X is the empty list. If this is the case, the AND process fails.
5. If the list X from step (3) is not empty, it must be of the form [#G | Xn]. #G is the generator that is to be redone. If #G is the head of the clause, the AND process fails. Otherwise, send ↑G a redo message, and change the status #G from solved to pending.
6. Whenever the OR process for a literal #G is sent a redo message, the AND process may have to reset or cancel some literals to the right of #G in the linear ordering:
   a. For every generator later than #G in the linear ordering, perform a reset operation. These generators remain in the solved state, since their consumers can immediately (re)use the first value. The variables generated by these generators and the variable generated by #G are called the modified variables.
   b. For every literal #L later than #G in the linear ordering, cancel ↑L and change the state of #L to blocked if it consumes any modified variable. It does not matter if #L is a

---

* This operation is concisely expressed in Prolog with the concat procedure: concat(A, B, C) means that C is the concatenation of lists A and B, or, equivalently, that A is a prefix and B a suffix of the list C. If F is the current failure context, and R is the redo list, then concat(F, [X | Y], R) asks "is F a prefix of R? If so, unify X with the first element of the list that must be concatenated with F to make R." X is the subgoal which should be sent a redo message.

generator or not or if it was previously solved or pending; if it consumes a modified variable, its process ↑L must be canceled.

7. It is possible that some of the OR processes canceled in the previous step can be replaced immediately (since if the variables they consume were reset, the corresponding generators are still in the solved state), so the forward execution algorithm is invoked to start a set of new OR processes.

8. When a new process is started for a literal #N that is currently in the failure context, remove #N and any literals to the right of it from the failure context {note: this step must be taken by the forward execution algorithm as well, after a success message causes a set of new processes to be created}.

Fig. 7 The backward execution algorithm.

§13 Map Coloring Example

The complete parallel solution of the map coloring problem is presented in this section. This very complicated example has three parts. First, we show the forward execution phase as the first tuple of colors was created. Next, we show what happened during backward execution. In the current implementation of the parallel interpreter, the final solution was obtained very quickly, with few redo messages to processes for generators. The third part of the example shows what might happen with a slightly different sequence of events, when a multiple failure would occur. In this example we again use #N to denote subgoals and ↑N to denote the OR process created to solve subgoal N.

When the AND process was first created, and after the subgoals were ordered, the only subgoal for which an OR process could be started was #1: next(A, B). Eventually, this sent back success(next(red, blue)), binding A to red and B to blue. Next, processes for the three generators in the middle row of the graph were started. All three succeeded, and as the success messages arrived, the following occurred:

▷ ↑3 sent success(next(red, blue)), setting C to blue. Since all predecessors of #5 were solved, a process for this subgoal (at that time next(blue, blue)) was created.

▷ ↑4 sent success(next(red, blue)), setting D to blue, enabling the creation of a process for #2, next(blue, blue).

▷ ↑6 sent success(next(blue, red)), binding E to red. Processes for the remaining two subgoals, #7 and #8, both next(blue, red), were started.

At this point, the status of the AND process was: subgoals #1, #3, #4, and #6 solved; subgoals #2, #5, #7, and #8 pending; failure context empty. The processes for subgoals #2 and #5 are about to send fail messages, while the other two are about to succeed. The transitions explained next describe what happened when the fail message from ↑5 was read first; then the transitions that would have occurred if the fail from ↑2 arrived first will be explained. In either case, the AND process will go into the same state eventually. The only difference in the sequences of state transitions is that if the message from ↑2 arrives first, the number of transitions required to reach the state in which the first success is sent is longer.

13.1 Case 1: #5 fails first

The variable context was set to [#5], which is the prefix of the redo list [#5, #3, #1]. The suffix is [#3, #1], and a redo message was sent to ↑3. The subgoals to the right of #3 in the linear ordering, and the actions taken for each, were,

▷   #4: Reset.
▷   #6: Reset.
▷   #2: Canceled (will be replaced when new C arrives from ↑3).
▷   #5: Already terminated.
▷   #7: Canceled (will be replaced when new C arrives).
▷   #8: Replaced with new process (since D, E modified by resets).

Again, as an implementation detail, the reset of a generator that has sent only one value really has no effect, and the replacement of a process such as that for subgoal #8 can be avoided when its variables do not change values. The state of the AND process after this transition: subgoals #1, #4, and #6 solved; subgoals #3 and #8 pending ; subgoals #2, #5, and #7 blocked; failure context [#5].

The fail message from the original process for subgoal #2 then arrived. Since that process had been canceled, this message was ignored. The successes from the original processes for #7 and #8 arrived, and they also were ignored. Note that even though there is a process for #8 at this time, it has a different ID than the original process. The AND process always ignores messages from processes it has canceled.

The success· from #3 arrived, with next(red, yellow), binding C to yellow. New processes for #2, now next(yellow, blue), and #5, now next(blue, yellow), and #7, now next(yellow, red), were created. Since there is a new process for #5, it was removed from the failure context. The state of the AND process: subgoals #1, #3, #4, and #6 solved; subgoals #2, #5, #7, and #8 pending; failure context [].

Finally, all of the pending processes sent success messages; the order is irrelevant. In particular, note that ↑8 could have sent its success message before the success from ↑3 in the previous paragraph. After the last was received, the AND process sent its parent the message

success(color(red, blue, yellow, blue, red))

13.2   Case 2: #2 fails first
When the state of the AND process had subgoals #1, #3, #4, and #6 solved, with the remaining subgoals pending and an empty failure context, two fail messages were on the way. The next sequence of transitions shows what would have happened had the failure from ↑2 arrived first. This sequence involves multiple failures.

The fail message from ↑2 arrives, the failure context is set to [#2], which is the prefix of the redo list [#2, #4, #3, #1]. ↑4 is sent a redo message, and then the remaining subgoals in the linear ordering are handled as follows:

▷   #6: Reset.
▷   #2: Already failed.
▷   #5: Not affected.
▷   #7: Canceled (since E was reset),replaced with a subgoal that has same values for variables.
▷   #8: Canceled, will be replaced when new D arrives from ↑4.

The failure context is [#2]; solved subgoals are #1, #3, #6; pending subgoals are #4, #5, #7, and #2 and #8 and blocked.

The fail message from ↑5 arrives. #5 is pending, not canceled, so the AND process has to handle this message. #5 is appended to the failure context, making [#2,#5]. This does not match any redo list. The processing of this failure is *postponed* until the failure context is reset to the empty list. The state remains the same, except #5 is now blocked and not pending as before.

A success from the process for #7 will arrive (either now or after the success from #4; either way, it has no effect on what follows). The message success(next(blue,yellow)) arrives from ↑4. Start processes for the goals #2, next(blue,yellow), and #8, next(yellow,red). Remove #2 from the failure context, which becomes the empty list. This means the failure of #2 has been completely handled.

Now we come to a new situation, the processing of the (postponed) failure of #5. There is one postponed failure, from the original process for subgoal #5. This process was never canceled during the backward execution behalf of #2, so a failure context is created for it now. From this point, the AND process behaves as if it had just received the fail from ↑5: the failure context is [#5], the matching redo list is [#5,#3,#1], ↑3 is sent a redo message, and the subgoals to the right of #3 are:

▷ #4: Reset (D is once again blue).
▷ #6: Reset (E is still red).
▷ #2: Canceled, will be replaced when new C arrives from ↑3.
▷ #5: Already canceled.
▷ #7: Canceled, will be replaced when new C arrives.
▷ #8: Canceled (since D,E reset), replaced by new process for original D and E.

The state of the AND process is now: subgoals #1, #4, and #6 solved; subgoals #3 and #8 pending; subgoals #2, #5, and #7 blocked; failure context [#5]. The current values of the variables are A = red, B = blue, C unbound, D = blue, and E = red. Note that this is the same state as earlier (in case 1), when #5 and #2 were failures and the fail message from #5 arrived first.

§14 Conclusion

In this paper we have shown an effective procedure for translating logic programs into a collection of communicating processes. Furthermore we have defined an abstract interpreter for these processes which permits both AND and OR parallelism. Neither technique for achieving parallelism makes any additional assumptions about the logic program and both types of parallelism operate conjointly on the same logic program. The details of achieving AND parallelism with semi-intelligent backtracking are complicated and rest on ideas about goal ordering and dataflow. All of the essential algorithms and data structures have been presented in this paper.

Parallel solution of the body of a clause is essentially an attempt to create a dataflow graph from the body, and then solve the subgoals in the order specified by the graph. This attempt is successful when the subgoals all succeed, which is often the case when the clause implements a deterministic function. However, in nondeterministic functions and relations, it is not always the case that subgoals can be solved on the first attempt. When a subgoal fails, an interpreter must re-solve a previously solved subgoal, hoping the next solution creates new variable bindings that allow the failed subgoal to be solved.

Backward execution is the name of the mechanism in parallel AND processes that determines which subgoals must be re-solved in response to failures. The mechanism is quite complicated, and requires a large overhead in terms of data structures to represent the state of each subgoal and the state of the process as a whole. Fortunately, the overhead does not interfere with forward execution; it is only when subgoals fail that the rather awkward backward execution mechanism is invoked.

There are a number of improvements that can be made in the definition and implementation of backward execution. Many descendant processes may be canceled needlessly, sequential processing of multiple failures is very conservative, and the nested loop model itself may not be the best abstract model of tuple generation. The philosophy has been to define a method that is sufficient to coordinate the subgoals that bind variables to values, so that eventually as many tuples of values are created as possible.

Rather than spending time in fine tuning the backward execution mechanism, it is time to move on to the next step, and show how the parallel processes may be efficiently implemented on a non von Neumann system. The long term goal of the research is the design of a non von Neumann computer architecture for parallel execution of logic programs. More explicitly this means that one must define a mapping from the set of processes into a finite set of processors.

References

1) Conery, J. S., Morris, P. H. and Kibler, D. F., "Efficient Logic Programs : A Research Proposal," *Technical Report 166*, Department of Information and Computer Science, University of California, Irvine, April, 1981.

2) Conery, J. S. and Kibler, D. F., "Parallel Interpretation of Logic Programs, "*Proceedings of the Conference on Functional Programming Languages and Computer Architecture*, pp. 163-170, ACM, October, 1981.

3) Conery, J. S. and Kibler, D. F., "AND Parallelism in Logic Programs." in *Proceedings of the Eight International Joint Conference on Artificial Intelligence*, pp. 539-543, 1983.

4) Conery, J. S., "The AND/OR Process Model for Parallel Interpretation of Logic Programs," *Ph.D. Thesis*, University of California, Irvine, 1983. (Available as *Tech. Report 204*, Department of Computer ane Information Science, UC Irvine)

5) Gostelow, K. P. and Thomas, R., "Performance of a Simulated Dataflow Computer," *IEEE Transactions on Computers, C-29(10)*, pp. 905-919, October, 1980.

6) Warren, D. S., Ahamad, M., Debray, S. K. and Kale, L. V., "Executing Distributed Prolog Programs on a Broadcast Network." in *1984 International Symposium on Logic Programming*, pp. 12-21, 1984.

7) Taylor, S., Lowry, A., Maguire, Jr., G. Q. and Stolfo, S. J., "Logic Programming Using Parallel Associative Operations," in *1984 International Symposium on Logic Programming*, pp. 58-68, 1984.

8) Eisinger, N., Kasif, S. and Minker, J., "Logic Programming : A Parallel Approach," *Proceedings of the First International Programming Conference*, pp. 1-8. Faculté des Sciences de Luminy, Marseille, Sept., 1982.

9) Ciepielewski, A. and Haridi, S., "Formal Models for OR-Parallel Execution of Logic Programs," *CSALAB Working Paper 821121*, Royal Institurte of Technology, Stockholm, Sweden, 1982.

10) Furukawa, K., Nitta, K. and Matsumoto, Y., "Prolog Interpreter Based on Concurrent Programming," *Proceedings of the First International Logic Programming Conference*, pp. 38-44. Faculté des Sciences Luminy, Marseille, ., '., 1982.

11) Kowalski, R. A., "Predicate Logic as a Programming Language," *iFi* 74.

12) Clark, K. L. and McCabe, F., "The Control Facilities of IC-1 log," in *Expert Systems in the Microelectronic Age* (D. Michie, ed.), Edinburgh University Press, 1979.

13) Shapiro, E. Y., "A Subset of Concurrent Prolog and Its Interpreter," *ICOT Technical Report TR-003*, Institute for New Generation Computer Technology, Tokyo, Japan, 1983.

14) Clark, K. L. and Gregory, S., "A Relational Language for Parallel Programming," *Proceedings of the Conference on Functional Programming Languages and Computer Architecture*, pp. 171-178. ACM, October, 1981.

15) Zara, R. V., "A Semantic Model for a Language Processor," *Proceedings of the A. C. M. National Meeting*, pp. 323-339, 1967.

16) Hewitt, C. and Attardi, G., "Act 1 for Parallel Problem Solving," *Technical Report*, MIT.

17) van Emden, M. H. and Kowalski, R. A., "The Semantics of Predicate Logic as a Programming Language," *JACM, 23(4)*, pp. 773-742, October, 1976.

18) Pereira, L. M., Pereira, F. C. N. and Warren, D. H. D., "Users Guide to DECsystem-10 Prolog," *Technical Report*, Department of Artificial Intelligence, University of Edinburgh, September, 1978.

19) Wulf, W. A. and Shaw, M., "Abstraction and Verification in ALPHARD: Defining and Specifying Iteration and Generators," *CACM, 20(8)*, pp. 553-564, August, 1977.

20) Pereira, L. M. and Porto, A., "Intelligent Backtracking and Sidetracking in Horn Clause Programs—the Theory," *Report 2/79*, Departamento de Informatica, Universidade Nova de Lisboa, Portugal, October, 1979.

MANIP-2: A MULTICOMPUTER ARCHITECTURE FOR EVALUATING LOGIC PROGRAMS

Guo-jie Li and Benjamin W. Wah

School of Electrical Engineering

Purdue University

West Lafayette, IN 47907

ABSTRACT

Logic programs are conventionally evaluated by brute-force depth-first search. To avoid unnecessary searching, an intelligent search strategy that guides the search by heuristic information is desirable. In this paper, the evaluation of a logic program is modeled as the search of an AND/OR tree. A heuristic function using the ratio of the success probability of a subgoal to the estimated overhead of evaluating the subgoal is found to be useful in guiding the search of logic programs. An optimal search strategy that minimizes the expected overhead is proposed and analyzed. The optimal strategy requires a large run-time computational or storage overhead. An efficient heuristic search strategy that can be implemented on a multiprocessor architecture is presented.

INDEX TERMS: AND/OR tree, AND parallelism, heuristic search, logic programming, OR parallelism, pruning, success probability.

1. INTRODUCTION

Logic programming is a programming methodology based on Horn-clause resolution [Kow79]. The efficiency of solving a logic programming problem depends strongly on the many ways of representing the logic program. Evaluating a logic program can be considered as the search of an AND/OR tree [Kow79,CoK83]. The root is labeled by the initial problem to be queried; the OR nodes represent (sub)goals; and the AND nodes represent clauses.[*] All subgoals in the same body of a clause are children of an AND node. A (sub)goal (OR node) and its children display the nondeterministic choices of clauses with the same head. The terminal nodes denote clauses or subgoals that cannot be decomposed. Figure 1(a) shows an example of the AND/OR-tree representation of a logic program. In general, a logic program without any inference loop can be viewed as an acyclic AND/OR graph. A finite AND/OR tree is obtained from the AND/OR graph by duplicating common descendent nodes.

The AND/OR tree in Figure 1(a) can be represented more clearly in Figure 1(b) as a high-level OR tree involving the selection of all combinations of clauses, and multiple low-level AND trees representing the solution tree resulted from clauses selected in the OR tree. Parallel processing can be applied to evaluate the multiple solution trees in parallel (OR-parallelism), or can be applied to search a solution tree in parallel (AND-parallelism). Note that the number of edges in

---

Research supported by CIDMAC, a research unit of Purdue University, sponsored by Purdue, Cincinnati Milicron Corporation, Control Data Corporation, Cummins Engine Company, Ransburg Corporation, and TRW.

International Conference on Parallel Processing, 1985.

---

[*] The definitions of AND and OR nodes are taken from [MaM73]. The roles of the AND and OR nodes are reversed in Nilsson's definition [Nil80].

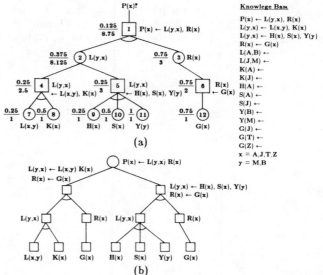

Figure 1. (a) An example of a logic program represented as an AND/OR tree. (OR nodes are represented as circular nodes; AND nodes are represented as squared nodes. In the logic program, P: happy; L: like; R: rich; K: kind; H: handsome; S: strong; Y: young; G: goodjob; A: Ares; B: Betty; J: John; M: Mary; T: Tom; Z: Zeus. The numbers outside each node are the ratio of success probability to expected search cost.) (b) The same logic program represented as a hierarchy of OR tree followed by AND trees.

this representation could be much large than that of an AND/OR-tree representation.

AND-parallelism involves the simultaneous execution of subgoals in a clause. Since subgoals within a clause can share variables, the binding of variables of concurrently executing subgoals must be coordinated to avoid conflicts of a shared variable being bound to more than one value. AND-parallelism is limited by the measures to avoid conflicts. One approach to avoid conflicts is to annotate variables to indicate which subgoals can bind values to specific variables and which cannot [CIG83]. In particular, only one subgoal, called *producer*, is allowed to bind a value to a variable. Conery proposed a complex, non-annotated, process-structured system that dynamically monitors variables and continually develops data dependency networks to control the order of execution of subgoals, never allowing two potential producers for the same variable to execute in parallel [CoK83]. DeGroot described a method to obtain restricted AND-parallelism by compile-time creation of a parallel execution-graph expression for each program clause [DeG84].

Reprinted from *The Proceedings of the International Conference on Parallel Processing*, 1985, pages 123-130. Copyright © 1985 by The Institute of Electrical and Electronics Engineers, Inc.

In OR-parallelism, all subgoals are independent of each other, and consistency checks for shared variables needed in AND-parallelism are avoided [Kow79,Mot84]. However, an OR-tree representation is inefficient due to the large number of branches needed as compared to that of an AND/OR tree. Given an initial query, ← A,B, with n ways of solving A and m ways of solving B, the OR tree contains n×m branches, whereas an AND/OR tree contains n+m. To improve the efficiency of an OR-tree search of logic programs, several models that modify pure OR-parallelism, such as introducing process bundles [YaN84] and bagof [CiH84], are proposed.

In this paper, we study parallel processing for an AND/OR-tree representation and exploit both AND-parallelism and OR-parallelism. The search strategy developed can be extended to the corresponding AND/OR-graph representation. The search algorithm is generally considered different from an AND/OR game-tree search for the following reasons. First, in contrast to combinatorial-extremum searches that find the best solution, solving a logic program corresponds to finding any (or all) solution(s) satisfying the given conditions, the implicative Horn clauses, and the consistent binding of variables for the subgoals. Second, the value of a node in the AND/OR tree for a logic program is either TRUE (success) or FALSE (failure). The selection of a node for evaluation is usually based on a fixed order, and heuristic information to guide the search is not available. Third, a variable in a logic program can be bound to several values, and some subgoals may share a common variable. For example, in Figure 1, some subgoals share variable x, and x can be bound to any of Ares, John, Tom, and Zeus. For a particular variable in a subgoal, a subset of its possible values may be allowed. In contrast, the nodes in a game tree are independent. Lastly, pruning rules for evaluating the AND/OR tree of a logic program are different from α-β pruning due to the binary values returned by the terminal nodes.

Since the search space of a logic program is large, an intelligent search strategy that guides the search is very important [Pea84]. Parallel processing is not useful here because it is generally used to improve the computational efficiency of solving a given problem, but *not to extend the solvable problem space of the problem*, especially when the problem space is exponentially large [WLY85]. The efficiency of a search strategy can be improved by guiding the search with heuristic information, and reducing the search space by pruning.

Heuristic information to guide the search, such as the success probability of each subgoal or clause and the estimated overhead (or *cost*) of searching a subgoal or clause, remain an open problem. In this paper, a heuristic search based on the information of the ratio of success probability to estimated cost is studied. This search strategy is aimed to minimize the expected search cost and the dynamic run-time overhead of evaluating logic programs.

Pruning is used to eliminate unnecessary expansions when it is determined that a solution tree cannot be found from a subgoal or clause. Two kinds of pruning exist. In *AND-pruning*, if one successor of an AND node for a given binding of values to variables is known to be FALSE, then all its remaining successors for the same binding can be pruned. Likewise, if one solution is sought, then *OR-pruning* can be applied to prune other successors of an OR node once one of its successors is known to be TRUE. In this paper, it is assumed that one solution tree is sought from an AND/OR-tree representation of a logic program, and hence both AND-pruning and OR-pruning can be applied.

Pruning and parallelism are conceptually illustrated in Figure 2(a). In a sequential depth-first search, if Node 1 fails, then Node 2 will be examined next, otherwise Node 3 will be examined. Similarly, the traversal of Node 5 depends on the results of traversing Nodes 1, 2, 3, and 4. This dependence

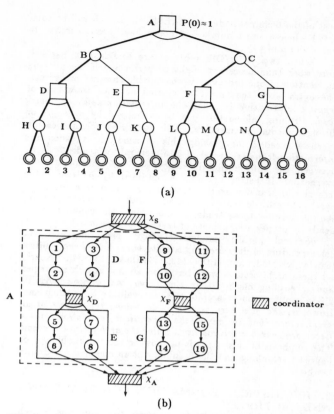

(a)

(b)

Figure 2. (a) A binary AND/OR search tree with high success probability (circular nodes represent OR nodes; squared nodes represent AND nodes). (b) The corresponding fail-token-flow graph, G_f.

information can be represented in a *fail-token-flow graph*, G_f, as depicted in Figure 2(b) for the tree in Figure 2(a). A node (circle) in the graph will be active only if it receives a fail-token from an incident edge. When a terminal node is found to be FALSE, a fail-token is sent along the direction of the corresponding edge. The coordinator (shaded box) in the graph coordinates the activities of the connected blocks. When a fail-token is received from any incident edge of a coordinator, fail-tokens are sent to *all* directly connected nodes. At the same time, any node searched in the block directly connected to this coordinator can be terminated because it does not belong to the solution tree. For example, when Node 1 is found to be FALSE, then a fail-token is sent to Node 2. If Node 2 is found to be FALSE, then a fail-token is sent to Coordinator χ_D. At this time, any node concurrently searched in Block D can be terminated. When a solution tree is found, there is one node in each column of G_f that returns TRUE. G_f can be used to represent pruning in AND-parallelism when the success probability is high and most of the terminal nodes are TRUE.

On the other hand, when the success probability of the goal is low, most of terminal nodes are FALSE. The search for the inexistence of a solution tree in OR-parallelism can now be represented by the *success-token-flow graph*, G_s. G_s is the dual of G_f in the sense that a fail-token is replaced by a success-token, and the columns in G_f are transposed to become the rows in G_s. Referring to Figure 2(a), Nodes 1, 2, 5, and 6 are assigned to four processors. If any of Nodes 1, 2, 5, and 6 succeeds, then a success-token is generated, and the next connected node is assigned to an idle processor. Since most of the terminal nodes are FALSE, the search will be completed when a small number of nodes have been searched in each column of G_s.

When two AND/OR subtrees are searched in parallel, more work than necessary might be performed if the pruning information of one processor is unavailable to other processors. The extra work that must be carried out due to a lack of pruning information is called the *information-deficiency overhead*. Pruning information can be exchanged by messages or through a common memory. This increased communication overhead needed for passing this information is called the *information-transfer overhead*. In general, a tradeoff exists between the information-deficiency and information-transfer overheads. If better pruning is obtained by increasing the information-transfer overhead, then the information-deficiency overhead will decrease. A good parallel search algorithm should consider these tradeoffs and reduce the run-time overheads by proper assignments of tasks to processors.

Several parallel models of logic programs and the corresponding multiprocessing architectures have been studied [FuN82,KKM83, Mot84,DeG84,CiH84,HaA84,StM84]. Nearly all these architectures were based on ad hoc search strategies and scheduling methods. In this paper, we propose MANIP-2**, a multicomputer architecture to evaluate logic programs. However, *the goal here is not in describing the details of an architecture, but in giving the theoretical foundation of the necessary search algorithm upon which the architecture is based.* The emphasis of this paper is in showing the reasonableness of heuristic searching and the feasibility of an effective scheduling method.

2. HEURISTIC INFORMATION FOR SEARCHING AND/OR TREES

The useful heuristic information to guide the search include the predicted success probability of a solution tree being found from a subgoal or clause, and the associated average cost of finding the solution tree.

The success probability of a node (or alternatively a branch) in an AND/OR-tree representation of a logic program is an a priori probability that reflects the possibility of finding a solution tree over all unifications from this node. These probabilities are used to guide the search initially, and will be improved after more dynamic pruning information is obtained.

For a terminal node with variable x, its success probability is $m(x)/n(x)$, where $n(x)$ is the total number of values that variable x can acquire, and $m(x)$ is the number of values acquired by x in this terminal node. It is assumed that all values in the domain of a variable are equally likely to be assigned to a subgoal. When a subgoal shares more than one variable with other subgoals, its success probability can be computed as the product of the success probabilities of the variables if all variables are independent. In general, the success probability of a node cannot be directly determined by the success probabilities of its immediate descendents, which may be correlated (the descendent nodes may contain shared clauses or subgoals that renders them dependent). It may have to be evaluated from actual information in the knowledge base. For example, in Figure 1(a), four values can be bound to x, and two can be bound to y. For the eight combinations of values of x and y, only two of them exist in the knowledge base. Hence, the success probability of L(x,y) is 0.25.

Assuming that a nonterminal node K has two immediate descendents, K_1 and K_2, let $P(\cdot)$ be the a priori success probability of a node. Then

$$P(K) = \begin{cases} P(K_1) \cdot P(K_2 \mid K_1) & (K \text{ is AND}) \\ P(K_1) + P(K_2) - P(K_1) \cdot P(K_2 \mid K_1) & (K \text{ is OR}) \end{cases} \quad (1)$$

Eq. (1) can be generalized to nodes with more than two descendents. The computation of the a priori conditional probabilities can be complex due to the shared variables.

The success probabilities of a logic program can also be either assigned initially by the designer, or determinated by statistic collected during execution. In the latter case, no a prior probability is available before the program is executed, and all branches are assumed to have equal possibility of success. A deterministic search strategy, such as a depth-first search, has to be used initially. For example, in Figure 1, the success probability of the clause L(y,x)←L(x,y)·K(x) is the probability that both L(x,y) and K(x) succeed. However, L(x,y) and K(x) are dependent, and the success probability of L(y,x) would be difficult to compute. Statistic collected show that the success probability is 0.25. Other success probabilities in Figure 1 were computed by enumerations of all combinations of binding of variables.

Since unification has a linear complexity [PaW78, MaM82], the search cost can be defined by the number of nodes traversed before a solution tree is found to exist or not exist. The cost for searching a subtree depends on the structure and dependence of the subtrees, the query used, and the partial search results already obtained. One way is to define an average search cost based on the estimated probabilities of success. For node K with descendents K_1 and K_2 and assuming that K_1 is searched first, the average search cost is

$$C(K) = C(K_1) + \begin{cases} C(K_2 \mid K_1) \cdot P(K_1) & (K \text{ is AND}) \\ C(K_2 \mid K_1) \cdot (1 - P(K_1)) & (K \text{ is OR}) \end{cases} \quad (2)$$

Simulations have shown that the average search cost depends on the structure of the tree, but is quite insensitive to changes in the success probability. A complete binary AND/OR tree with unitary search cost at the terminal nodes was assumed. The simulation results depicted in Figure 3 indicate the relationship between the success probabilities of the root of trees with height 12 and 16, respectively, and the associated average search cost. The average cost is the smallest when p is either zero or one, and is maximum when p is around 0.5. Moreover, the difference between the maximum

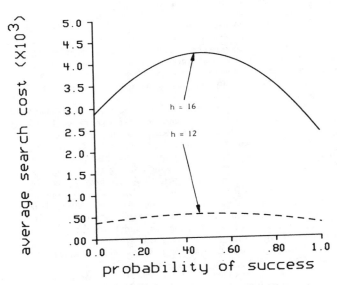

Figure 3. A plot of the search cost versus the success probability of the root.

** MANIP is a multicomputer architecture proposed earlier to evaluate parallel branch-and-bound algorithms with a best-first search, which is an OR-tree heuristic search guided by lower bounds of subproblems [WaM84].

and the minimum costs is relatively small, reflecting the insensitivity of the expected search cost with respect to the success probability.

The average search cost of a subgoal is difficult to be formulated mathematically because it is related to the dependence of descendent subgoals (due to the shared clauses and subgoals). Moreover, the average search cost depends on the search strategy and the order that values are bound to variables, which in turn are driven by the average search costs. Hence the search costs would have to be initially estimated from statistic collected by a given search strategy. As better search costs are obtained, the search will become more efficient, and better estimates on the search costs can be obtained. For example, in Figure 1, the average search cost for $L(y,x)$ was computed by averaging the search cost to verify the result of $L(y,x)$ for all combinations of values of x and y. The search strategy used in computing the costs in Figure 1 assumed a left-to-right traversal of the descendents.

The expected search cost of a subgoal represents an average over all possible queries, all possible paths leading to this subgoal, and all possible combinations of values of variables for a given search strategy. However, when the path leading to a given subgoal is known, the minimum cost and the associated success probability of obtaining a solution tree are better measures to guide the search. Of course, this will result in an enormously large amount of stored information for each subgoal that renders the scheme impractical.

3. HEURISTIC SEARCH FOR LOGIC PROGRAMS

Let $P(x)$ and $C(x)$ be the probability of success and the associated average search cost for node x. Define the criteria Φ_a and Φ_o for any node x as

$$\Phi_a(x) = \frac{P(x)}{C(x)} \quad \text{(x is descendent of an OR node)} \quad (3)$$

$$\Phi_o(x) = \frac{1-P(x)}{C(x)} \quad \text{(x is descendent of an AND node)} \quad (4)$$

Simon and Kadane have studied the optimal OR-tree search and have proved that the search sequence $b = b_1, ..., b_n$ is optimal iff $\Phi_a(b_i) \geq \Phi_a(b_{i+1})$, where the b_is are descendents of an OR node b with precedence relationships [SiK75]. Barnett has extended their results to optimal search from AND nodes with the assumption that all immediate descendents are independent [Bar83]. Garey has proved that the optimal sequence of performing a set of tasks until one of them fails or all tasks are fulfilled is in descending order of Φ_o [Gar73].

For a pure OR-tree or AND-tree search, the search order is well defined by a single heuristic function. However, when an AND/OR tree is searched, there are two criteria, Φ_a and Φ_o, to order the AND and OR nodes, respectively. Hence a complete order cannot be defined for all active nodes. To resolve this problem, we can decompose an AND/OR tree into a hierarchy of a single OR tree, each terminal of which is an AND tree (Figure 1(b)). The following theorem relates the criteria Φ_a and Φ_o and defines an optimal search order for an AND/OR tree with dependent nodes.

Theorem 1: Suppose that an OR node K has n immediate descendent AND nodes, $K_1, ..., K_n$, and that the AND node K_i, $1 \leq i \leq n$, has i_m immediate descendent OR nodes, $K_{i_1}, ..., k_{i_m}$. If $\Phi_a(K_i) \geq \Phi_a(K_{i+1})$, then the expected search cost $C(K)$ is minimum when all descendents of K_i are searched before K_{i+1}.

Proof: Suppose that K_{i_1} is found to be TRUE, then the conjunction of the remaining subgoals of K_i, namely, $K_{i_2}, ..., K_{i_m}$, forms a new AND node, K_{i_2}'. The conditional probability of $K_{i_2}, ..., K_{i_m}$ being TRUE, given that K_{i_1} is TRUE is

$$P(K_{i_2}') = P(K_{i_2}, ..., K_{i_m} \mid K_{i_1}) = \frac{P(K_i)}{P(K_{i_1})} \quad (5)$$

To get the optimal strategy, we need to compare the probability-to-cost ratios in respect to node K_{i_2}' and K_{i+1}. Using Eq's (2) and (5),

$$\Phi_a(K_{i_2}') = \frac{P(K_{i_2}')}{C(K_{i_2}')} = \frac{P(K_i)/P(K_{i_1})}{C(K_{i_2}, ..., K_{i_m} \mid K_{i_1})} \quad (6)$$

$$\geq \frac{P(K_i)}{C(K_i)} \geq \frac{P(K_{i+1})}{C(K_{i+1})} = \Phi_a(K_{i+1})$$

Eq. (6) implies that the remaining subgoals $K_{i_2}, ..., K_{i_m}$ should be unified first before K_{i+1}. If subgoal K_{i_2} is found to be TRUE, then the above proof can be applied again to show that the remaining subgoals of K_i should be unified before K_{i+1}. □

Theorem 1 shows that the optimal strategy of searching an AND/OR tree is to select the most promising solution tree with the largest Φ_a value among all possible solutions trees, and to examine AND nodes in this solution tree in descending order of Φ_o values. The search is switched to the next best solution tree (with the next largest Φ_a value) if the first solution tree fails.

The key issue in performing the above optimal strategy is to find the most promising solution tree with the largest Φ_a value, and for the solution tree selected, the node with the largest Φ_o value. If h, the height of a complete AND/OR tree, is taken as a measure of the problem size, then it is unlikely that a polynomial-time algorithm exists for finding the most promising solution tree. Let B_o and B_a be the numbers of branches of each OR and AND node, respectively. If $B_a = 1$, then there are $B_o^{h/2}$ possible solution trees, each of which consists of one node. To get the maximum Φ_a over all solution trees, at least $B_o^{h/2} - 1$ comparisons are needed. This is the lower-bound complexity for computing the largest Φ_a when $B_a = 1$. In general, if $B_a > 1$, then before Theorem 1 can be applied, the AND/OR tree has to be transformed into a hierarchy of an OR tree, each terminal of which is an AND tree. The number of terminal nodes in the transformed tree has a lower bound of $O((B_o^{B_a})^{B_a^{h/2-1}})$. Hence to select the largest Φ_a and Φ_o values would require an exceedingly large amount of computational time. Another approach is to store these values associated with each node in the AND/OR tree and to retrieve the decisions in real time. Unfortunately, this would require a large amount of storage space with a lower bound of the same complexity as stated above. Therefore, it is unrealistic to apply the optimal search strategy in respect to an AND/OR-tree search.

Owing to the intractable complexity of propagating the Φ_a and Φ_o values of all terminal nodes to the root in implementing the optimal AND/OR-tree search, an efficient top-down heuristic search is proposed here. As stated in Section 2, each node in the AND/OR tree can be assigned an estimated success probability and the associated expected search cost. These values, together with the information of the path leading from the root to this node, can be used to compute a heuristic value for the node. The search will be guided by the heuristic values.

A *solution tree* is a tree such that all nonterminals are AND nodes and all terminals are OR nodes. To minimize the search effort for a *solution tree*, it is necessary to first find one of the FALSE terminals in this tree, since the search can be terminated once this node is found. This method will be used to compute the heuristic values for AND nodes. From the duality between AND and OR nodes, a *failure tree* is a tree such that all nonterminals are OR nodes and all terminals are AND nodes. A failure tree is the dual of a solution tree, such that the entire AND/OR tree is FALSE if all nodes in the

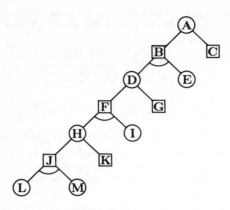

Figure 4. Computation of the heuristic values (OR nodes are represented as circular nodes; AND nodes are represented as squared nodes).

failure tree are FALSE. To stop the search of a failure tree as early as possible, it is necessary to verify that one of the terminals is TRUE. This method will be used to compute the heuristic values for OR nodes.

Referring to the partial binary AND/OR tree in Figure 4, suppose that AND-node F is to be searched. For the goal to be TRUE, Nodes E and F must be TRUE. This is the information that can be extracted directly from the path leading from the root to F. The heuristic value of Node F will be the ratio of the probability of verifying Node A to be TRUE to the associated search cost. This can be computed as the ratio of the probability of success of Nodes E and F to the total average search cost of verifying that Nodes E and F are TRUE or any of them is FALSE. Note that Nodes E and F may be dependent. Other information, such as nodes searched from E, would be also crucial to computing the heuristic value for F. However, this information cannot be extracted directly from the path, and would require a high run-time overhead to maintain, hence will not be considered here. Similarly, the heuristic value of AND-node J is based on information about Nodes E, I, and J. In general, the heuristic value $\Phi_a(x)$ of an AND node x is based on information extractable from the path leading from the root to x such that the goal can be verified to be TRUE. The information on the complete path from the root to any AND node must be maintained with each AND node.

To compute $\Phi_o(x)$ for an OR node x, the information extractable from the path leading from the root to x such that the goal can be proved to be FALSE will be used. Complete information on the path from the root must also be maintained for each OR node. Referring to Figure 4, in computing the heuristic value for OR-node H, the goal will be FALSE if Nodes C, G, and H are FALSE. Note that these nodes may be dependent.

The following heuristic-search algorithm, BAO, is a top-down best-first search algorithm that uses heuristic information about a particular set of solution trees for a given AND node and a particular set of failure trees for a given OR node. It is assumed that the values of Φ_a are available for each set of clauses with the same head (an OR node) in the logic program. Similarly, the values of Φ_o for each subgoal in a clause (an AND node) are also available. It is further assumed that the values bound to a variable are independent and in a fixed order, and that the values of Φ_o and Φ_a are applicable to all instantiations. The following procedure is applied iteratively by binding each variable to a constant value (or to a set of constant values that could be the domain of the variable) until the goal is proved to be TRUE or FALSE. There is an Active List containing tasks in decreasing order of heuristic values.

Without loss of generality, assume that the goal node, S, is an OR node.

BAO--Heuristic Search Algorithm for one solution tree:

(1) (*Initialization*): Initiate search from S. If S is known to be TRUE or FALSE, then stop. Otherwise, create a task for S with the information that S is an OR node, and compute its heuristic value. The task is inserted into the Active List.

(2) (*Decomposition*): Select a task T from the Active List with the maximum heuristic value. If T is a ground node, then go to Step 3. If T contains a variable that is not bound, a constant value (or a set of constant values that could be the domain of the variable) is bound to the variable. Decompose the task (an AND or OR node) into its immediate descendent tasks. The new tasks, with their heuristic values, the information about the path from S, and the values bound to variables are inserted into the Active List in the proper order. Go to Step 2.

(3) (*Pruning*): For Task T under consideration, the following steps will be carried out based on values returned by the ground node.
   (a) The subgoal or clause (T_n) on the path from the root to T that is nearest to the root and becomes TRUE or FALSE is found.
   (b) The information on T_n is incorporated into all tasks in the Active List. Subtasks in some tasks can be removed based on T_n. If all subtasks within a task W are removed, then pruning will be carried out recursively on W.
   (c) The values successfully or unsuccessfully bound to variables are broadcast to all active tasks.
   (d) The heuristic values for all active tasks are updated. The active tasks are reordered if necessary.

(4) (*Termination*): If S is terminated, then return success with the bound values. If S cannot be bound to any new value, then return failure. Otherwise, go to Step 2.

There are several considerations when Algorithm BAO is implemented. First, a single list of active tasks is kept, and the AND and OR nodes are not distinguished. Depending on the heuristic values and whether the node concerned is an AND or OR node, the objective is to either prove that the goal is TRUE or prove that it is FALSE. Second, pruning performed in Step (3) requires a large overhead because the entire Active List has to be updated and reordered. However, the merits on the number of tasks eliminated and the better heuristic values generated are doubtful. To avoid this run-time overhead, pruning can be performed after a task is selected from the Active List (Step 2). In this case, all pruning information will be recorded in a common list. Of course, this may result in some unnecessary tasks in the Active List. Third, the computation of the heuristic values could be complex when all dependency of subgoals and variables are considered. In practice, some simplifying assumptions may be made in combining the heuristic values together. For example, a heuristic function to compute the success probability and cost of a conjunction of subgoals could be the product of the success probabilities and the sum of the associated costs of the subgoals. Lastly, the algorithm investigates many possible solution trees in parallel by switching from one to another based on the heuristic information obtained. This results in a large number of tasks in the Active List, which is a fundamental problem in heuristic searches. To reduce the storage space required, static analysis can be performed to arrange the clauses with the same head and the subgoals in each clause in a proper order, and to use a depth-first strategy to search the AND/OR tree. Of course, the order defined will be based on the average over all possible queries and all possible ways of reaching a particular subgoal.

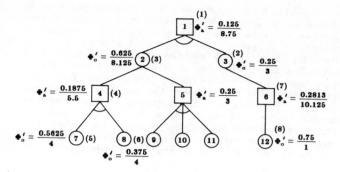

Figure 5. Illustration of the BAO procedure using the same example shown in Figure 1. (OR nodes are represented as circular nodes; AND nodes are represented as squared nodes. The number in parenthesis outside each node shows the order that this node is examined in the BAO procedure.)

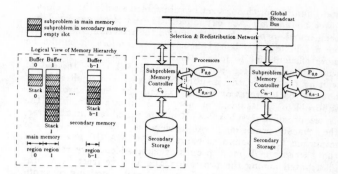

Figure 6. The architecture of MANIP-2, a multiprocessor for parallel heuristic search of logic programs and AND/OR graphs.

The BAO algorithm is illustrated in Figure 5 by explaining snapshots of solving the logic program in Figure 1. The cost of each unification is assumed to be unity. The query is "Who is happy?" Node 1 is unified first. For simplicity, suppose that all successful bindings are equally likely, and that x is first bound to John. Let the updated heuristic values be Φ_a' and Φ_o', respectively. After decomposition, subgoals L(y,x) (Node 2) and R(x) (Node 3) with the corresponding heuristic values are inserted into the Active List. Since $\Phi_o'(3) > \Phi_o'(2)$, Node 3 is selected, and Node 6 is created. In computing $\Phi_a'(6)$, the goal is expected to be TRUE, implying that Node 2 and 6 are TRUE. Hence the heuristic information of Node 2 must be included. The correlation between Nodes 2 and 6 may be complex. For simplicity, Nodes 2 and 6 are assumed to be independent. $P'(6)$ (resp. $C'(6)$), the new success probability (resp. new average cost) of Node 6, is the product (resp. summation) of the original success probabilities (resp. original average costs) of Nodes 2 and 6. $\Phi_a'(6)$ becomes 0.2813/10.125. As $\Phi_o'(2) > \Phi_a'(6)$, Node 2 is selected in the next iteration, and Nodes 4 and 5 are created. Intuitively, Node 6 is likely to be TRUE, but to terminate the search for the goal as soon as possible, the active node that may fail first should be investigated. In computing $\Phi_a'(4)$ and $\Phi_a'(5)$, the heuristic information on Node 3 must be included. For example, $\Phi_a'(4)$ is computed as $(0.75 \times 0.25)/(2.5 + 3)$. Suppose that variable y is first bound to Mary. Node 4 is next selected, as $\Phi_a'(4)$ is the largest among all active nodes. This means that the possible solution trees involving Node 4 is the most promising. Nodes 7 and 8 are inserted into the Active List in Iteration 4. Note that in computing $\Phi_o'(7)$ and $\Phi_o'(8)$, $\Phi_a(5)$ rather than $\Phi_a'(5)$ is used. The reason for this is that the goal is expected to be FALSE if Node 7 or 8 is selected, and the failure probability and cost of Node 5 are needed in this case, but the information on Node 3 (which is included in $\Phi_a'(5)$) does not affect the decision on Node 7 or 8. $\Phi_o(7)$ is computed as $(0.75 \times 0.75)/(1 + 3)$. Once Nodes 7 and 8 are instantiated in Iterations 5 and 6, respectively, Node 2 is known to be TRUE by values returned from the ground terms. Node 5 can thus be pruned by OR-pruning if a single solution tree is sought. In the last two iterations, Nodes 6 and 12 are unified, and the solution is "John is happy."

4. PARALLEL HEURISTIC SEARCH OF LOGIC PROGRAMS

In this section, we study the problems associated with the parallel processing of the AND/OR-tree representations of logic programs. By minor modifications of MANIP [WLY84],

parallel heuristic search of logic programs can be carried out efficiently. The architecture of MANIP-2 is shown in Figure 6.

The first problem in parallel processing is the unification of shared variables. When AND-parallelism is involved, variable binding conflicts must be prevented. A lot of efforts have been devoted to solving this problem [ClG83,CoK83,DeG84,Sha83]. We do not attempt to propose a new method to overcome this problem. Instead, we assume one or more of the following conditions: (a) that the subgoals do not share variables; (b) that the shared variables are uninstantiated; (c) that a producer subgoal has bound one or more values to a shared variable and forwards them to many consumer subgoals. In any of these cases, processors can carry out tasks independently.

The second problem is the granularity of parallelism. If the granularity is small, then the information-transfer overhead will be high. In contrast, if the granularity is large, then the information-deficiency overhead will be high, and the degree of parallel processing may be small. The proper granularity depends on the capacity of the communication network, the number of processors, and the relative overhead between the top-down unification of variables and the bottom-up return of solution values. In searching a logic program, if the cost of a subgoal selected is smaller than the defined granularity, then the subgoal is considered as an indivisible operation and processed by a single processor.

Once the granularity is determined, the next problem is to determine the scheduling of the k parallel processors. Given a list of active tasks ordered by decreasing probability-to-cost ratios, the problem is to determine the number of processors to evaluate each task in parallel. To minimize the expected completion time, the problem can be formulated into a complex integer-programming optimization problem. Moreover, the processors have to be rescheduled again once a given solution tree is found to be TRUE or FALSE. Considering the facts that the scheduling algorithm is complex and that static scheduling is not feasible, we decide to assign a free processor to each task in the Active List. When a task has reached its minimum granularity, it will be processed by a single processor until completion.

Another problem is on resource sharing. For a set of processors evaluating a solution tree, it is necessary to search those subtrees with the largest failure-probability-to-cost ratios. Likewise, for sets of processors examining different solution trees, the possible solution trees with the largest success-probability-to-cost ratios must be evaluated. Further, load balancing must be carried out to keep all processors busy. The ring network in MANIP is adequate for load balancing the processors.

The parallel selection problem has been studied thoroughly in MANIP. In the parallel evaluation of branch-

and-bound algorithms, a set of subproblems with the minimum lower bounds must be expanded. The selection overhead has been found to be high; furthermore, the selection rule is based on a fallible lower-bound heuristic. Therefore, it might be more efficient not to follow the selection rule strictly. A no-wait policy has been proposed [WaM84,WLY85]. Instead of waiting for one of the k subproblems with the smallest lower bounds, each processor would expand the "most promising" subproblem in its local memory and initiate a fetch of the "most promising" subproblem from its neighbors. In this case, the "most promising" subproblem is the one with the minimum lower bound. Evaluations for MANIP have shown that, when the k most promising subproblems are randomly distributed among the processors, the average fraction of processors containing one or more of the most promising subproblems is at least 0.63, resulting in a speedup proportional to 0.63k. Further, with occasional redistribution of subproblems with small lower bounds using a ring network, the performance is almost as good as that of a complete selection.

The no-wait policy can be applied here to schedule processors for evaluating subgoals in its local memory. Subgoals with large failure-probability-to-cost ratios (resp. large success-probability-to-cost ratios) and a suitable granularity can be sent to neighboring processors connected on the ring network when AND-parallelism (resp. OR-parallelism) is considered. Load balancing is, therefore, carried out automatically with the shuffle and selection of subgoals.

Yet another problem is on the communication of pruning information from one processor to another processor. When the result on a common subgoal is found, it must be communicated to other processors to stop the processing of a subset of the eliminated solution trees and allow the heuristic values of related tasks to be updated. Similarly, when either a solution tree is found or the goal is proved to be FALSE, all processors should stop further processing. These pruning information are more complicated than the incumbent in the parallel branch-and-bound algorithm implemented in MANIP. In this case, a bus is necessary to broadcast to all processors a subgoal or clause found to be TRUE or FALSE. To minimize the information broadcast, the subgoal or clause should correspond to the nonterminal node closest to the root in the AND/OR tree. Other processors receiving this information must update all tasks in its Active List by reordering the tasks according to the new heuristic values computed and by eliminating tasks that cannot lead to a solution tree. The complete path from the root to each active task must be maintained to allow the pruning information to be incorporated. The overhead for the propagation of pruning information is extensive and may not be beneficial because the probability-to-cost ratios may be fallible. The no-wait policy is again applied here to continue the evaluation of tasks according to previously computed heuristic values. Information received on subgoals will be used to eliminate unnecessary work when the task is selected.

The last problem on the implementation of a heuristic search lies in the management of the large memory space required. In our study of MANIP, it was found that a direct implementation involving an ordered list of pointers to the subproblems results in poor locality of access, because the subproblems are not ordered by lower bounds in the secondary memory. A specially designed virtual memory that tailors its control strategies to the access behavior of the algorithm was found to be inflexible. The inadequacies of these approaches are due, again, to the strict adherence to the selection rule. A better solution is to use the no-wait policy to implement a modified heuristic search in each processor. In the modified heuristic search, the range of possible lower bounds (in this case, the range of probability-to-cost ratios) is partitioned into b disjoint regions (Figure 6). The subproblems in each region are maintained as a separate list. The top portion of each list

resides in the main memory, and the rest resides in the secondary memory. Due to the high overhead of secondary-storage accesses, subproblems in a list are expanded in a depth-first manner. Only subproblems in the main memory are candidates for selection. The modified algorithm is identical to a depth-first search when one list is used, and is identical to a pure heuristic search when infinity lists are used. In general, as the number of lists increases, the number of subproblems expanded decreases and the overhead of the secondary-memory accesses increases. The number of lists should be chosen to maximize the overlap between computations and secondary-memory accesses. Experience on branch-and-bound algorithms showed that two to three lists are adequate.

5. CONCLUSIONS

In this paper, we have extended the architecture of MANIP for the parallel processing of logic programs. A logic program is assumed to be represented in the form of an AND/OR tree. The results that we have obtained can be summarized as follows.

(1) OR-parallelism and AND-parallelism have been unified into OR-parallelism. The objective of an OR-tree is to select a solution tree and to prove that the goal is TRUE; whereas in an AND-tree search, the objective is to find a set of subgoals to prove that the goal is FALSE. Both types of searches require only one of the correct descendents to be selected and can be considered as OR-tree searches. When the goal is likely to be TRUE, OR-parallelism should be used. In contrast, when the goal is likely to be FALSE, AND-parallelism should be used.

(2) Heuristic information using success probabilities and average overheads of evaluation have been defined to guide the search of logic programs. These information can be generated statically; however, they represent a prior information that do not take into account the query used, the dynamic pruning information obtained, and the values of variables being bound. They are useful to roughly differentiate between tasks that are likely to lead to solution trees and those that might not. Moreover, they define whether the goal is likely to be TRUE or FALSE.

(3) An optimal heuristic search strategy that minimizes the expected overhead of obtaining one solution tree is derived. The search is guided by the probability-to-cost ratios of subgoals.

(4) The architecture of MANIP, proposed earlier for the parallel evaluation of branch-and-bound algorithms, has been extended to implement a heuristic search of logic programs. Problems on selection and virtual-memory support have been considered. The strict adherence to the heuristic search is found to be unrewarding because the probability-to-cost ratios may be fallible, and the overheads of selecting tasks according to these ratios are high. These overheads include the update of the ratios when new pruning information is received, and the selection of tasks from other processors or the secondary memory according to these ratios.

REFERENCES

[Bar83] J. Barnett, "Optimal Searching from AND Nodes," *IJCAI*, pp. 786-788, 1983.

[CiH84] A. Ciepietewski and S. Haridi, "Execution of Bagof on the OR-parallel Token Machine," *Proc. Int'l Conf. on Fifth Generation Computer Systems*, pp. 551-560, 1984.

[ClG83] K. Clark and S. Gregory, "PARLOG: A Parallel Logic Programming Language," Research Report DOC 83/5, Imperial College, March 1983.

[CoK83] J. Conery and D. Kibler, "AND Parallelism in Logic Programming," *IJCAI*, pp. 539-543, 1983.

[DeG84] D. DeGroot, "Restricted AND-Parallelism," *Proc. Int'l Conf. on Fifth Generation Computer Systems*, pp. 471-478, 1984.

[FuN82] K. Furukawa, K. Nitta, and Y. Matsumoto, "Prolog Interpreter Based on Concurrent Programming," *Proc. of First Int'l Conf. Logic Programming*, 1982.

[Gar73] M. Garey, "Optimal Task Sequencing with Precedence Constraints," *Discrete Mathematics*, Vol. 4, pp. 37-56, 1973.

[HaA84] R. Hasegawa, M. Amamiya, "Parallel Execution of Logic Programs Based on Dataflow Concept," *Proc. of Int'l Conf. on Fifth Generation Computer Systems*, pp. 507-516, 1984.

[KKM83] S. Kasif, M. Kohli, and J. Minker, "PRISM: A parallel Inference System for Problem Solving," *Proc. IJCAI*, pp. 544-546, 1983.

[Kow79] R. Kowalski, *Logic For Problem Solving*, Elserier, North Holland, 1979.

[MaM73] A. Martelli and U. Montanari, "Additive AND/OR Graphs," *IJCAI*, pp. 1-11, 1973.

[MaM82] A, Martelli and U. Montanari, "An Efficient Unification Algorithm", *ACM Trans. on Prog. Lang. and Systems*, Vol. 4, pp. 258-282, 1982.

[Mot84] T.Moto-Oka, et al., "The Architecture of a Parallel Inference Engine--PIE," *Proc. Int'l Conf. on Fifth Generation Computer Systems*, pp. 479-488, 1984.

[Nil80] N. J. Nilsson, *Principles of Artificial Intelligence*, Tioga, Palo Alto, CA, 1980.

[PaW78] M.Paterson and M. Wegman, "Linear Unification", JCSS, Vol. 16, pp. 158-167, 1978.

[PaW79] E. Page and L. Wilson, *Introduction to Computational Combinatorics*, Cambridge University Press, 1979.

[Pea84] J. Pearl, *Heuristics*, Addison-Wesley, 1984.

[Sha83] E. Shapiro, *A Subset of Concurrent Prolog and its Interpreter*, ICOT Tech. Report TR-003, Feb. 1983, Tokyo, Japan.

[SiK75] H. A. Simon and J. Kadane, "Optimal Problem-solving Search: All-or-None Solutions," *Artificial Intelligence*, Vol. 6, pp. 235-246, 1975.

[StM84] S. J Stolfo and D. P. Miranker, "DADO: A Parallel Processor for Expert Systems," *Proc. Int'l Conf. on Parallel Processing*, pp. 74-82, 1984.

[WLY84] B. W. Wah, G.-J. Li, and C. F. Yu, "The Status of MANIP--A Multicomputer Architecture for solving Combinatorial Extremum-Search Problems," *Proc. 11'th Annual Int'l Symp. Comput. Architecture*, pp. 56-63, 1984.

[WLY85] B. W. Wah, G.-J. Li, and C. F. Yu, "Multiprocessing of Combinatorial Search Problems," to appear in *IEEE Computer*, June 1985.

[WaM84] B. W. Wah and E. Y. W. Ma, "MANIP--A Multicomputer Architecture for Solving Combinatorial Extremum Search Problems," *IEEE Trans. on Comput.*, Vol. C-33, No. 5, pp. 377-390, May 1984.

[YaN84] H. Yasuhara and K. Nitadori, "ORBIT: A Parallel Computing Model of Prolog," *New Generation Computing*, Vol. 2, pp. 277-288, 1984.

New Generation Computing, 2 (1984) 323-345
OHMSHA,LTD. and Springer-Verlag

Towards a Pipelined Prolog Processor[†]

Evan TICK and David H. D. WARREN

Artificial Intelligence Center, SRI International,
Menlo Park, CA94025, USA

Received 6 August 1984

Abstract This paper describes the design of a Prolog machine architecture and organization. Our objective was to determine the maximum performance attainable by a sequential Prolog machine for "reasonable" cost. The paper compares the organization to both general purpose micro-coded machines and reduced instruction set machines. Hand timings indicate a peak performance rate of 450 K LIPS (logical inferences per second) is well within current technology limitations and 1 M LIPS is potentially feasible.

Keywords: Prolog, Architecture, Microcode, Instruction Set, Pipelining

§1 Introduction

This paper describes the design of a Prolog machine architecture and organization. Our objective was to determine the maximum performance attainable by a sequential Prolog machine for a cost comparable to current high performance Lisp machines. A compiler is used to produce object programs in a high-level stack oriented instruction set. As with most high-level language processors, e.g. ICOT's **PSI**[1] and the Symbolics **3600 Lisp Machine**,[2] the organization is centered around a micro-controller because of the complex nature of the instruction set. In our design, the following criteria are stressed:

- *A lean cycle, i.e. the number of operations on the critical path between the start and end of the cycle is minimized.*
- *Issue one micro-instruction per cycle if interlocks allow.*

The cost of expanding the high-level machine instructions into micro-

---

† Adapted from the paper "TOWARDS A PIPELINED PROLOG PROCESSOR" by Evan Tick and David H.D. Warren appearing in 1984 INTERNATIONAL SYMPOSIUM ON LOGIC PROGRAMMING, February 6-9, 1984, Atlantic City, NJ, pp. 29-40. Copyright © 1984 IEEE.

sequences is offset by overlapping the micro-instructions in a pipelined execution unit. Memory accesses are also overlapped by use of an interleaved memory. A side-benefit of the interleaving is that it makes acceptable the use of slower, and therefore cheaper, memory. This side-benefit is especially important because memory references tend to be more random than in numerical processing, so that caching data is less effective.

The paper falls broadly into three parts. The first part introduces the architecture and instruction set. The second part describes the hardware organization and presents preliminary results in the form of hand timings. In the last part conclusions are drawn and plans for future work are summarized.

§2 Motivation

Japan's Fifth Generation Computer Systems project[3] aims to build highly parallel logical inference machines with prodigious performance, by exploiting advanced circuit technology, and by pursuing research into non-von Neumann architectures. The target is a performance of 100~1000 M LIPS (logical inferences per second).

To attain such a performance, it will be necessary to exploit large-scale parallelism in logic programs, of which the main kinds are AND parallelism (where several goals in a clause are executed concurrently) and OR parallelism (where several clauses matching a goal are processed concurrently). However it remains to be seen whether practical logic programs have enough large-scale parallelism to enable such ambitious performance targets to be achieved. Certainly, there are important examples of logic programs which do not have any inherent large-scale parallelism, e.g. simple list concatenation.

From a machine design standpoint, the problem is analogous to the classical argument between advocates of vector machines and advocates of fast scalar machines for numerical computation. To attain very high performance, a vector capability is necessary; however, performance is bottlenecked by scalar performance. Similarly, *to attain very high performance in logical inference machines, inherent parallelism must be exploited*; *however, performance will be bottlenecked by the speed of sequential inference*.

In view of these concerns, we believe it is important to investigate the maximum performance that can be achieved by a sequential Prolog machine, where only small-scale parallelism (invisible to the programmer) is exploited. It is also our belief that systems relying on radical departures in both hardware and software technology usually achieve less than what is expected. For this reason, we look to conventional pipelining methods to achieve high performance.

Although the processor model discussed here is sequential, the architecture is structured to permit exploitation of *unification* parallelism, by allowing implementations with multiple execution units. We believe AND and OR parallelism can also be successfully implemented around this machine model in tightly coupled multiprocessor system, of say 8 to 16 processors, attaining very high performance.

§3 Architecture

The architecture is very similar to the abstract machine based on DEC-10 Prolog described by Warren,[4] modified to incorporate tail recursion optimization.[5] The main differences are :

- Copying replaces structure-sharing as the means for constructing complex terms; however structure-sharing is still used to represent the goals comprising a resolvent.
- Choice points are separated from environments (local stack frames), and become optional.
- Environments are "trimmed" during execution (if the computation is determinate), by discarding variables no longer needed. This can be viewed as a generalization of tail recursion optimization.
- Potentially "unsafe" variables in the final goal of a clause are made global only if needed at runtime, rather than by default at compile time.

The architecture also has much in common with the abstract machine design of Bowen, Byrd, and Clocksin.[6] It is described in more detail in a separate report.[7]

3.1 Data Objects

A Prolog term is represented by a word containing a value (which is generally an address) and a tag. A large address space is assumed, with values occupying around 32 bits. The tag distinguishes the type of term, and must be at least 2 bits and preferably up to 8 bits. The main types are references (corresponding to bound or unbound variables), structures, lists, and constants (including atoms and integers). An unbound variable is represented by a reference to itself. It is distinguished by a separate tag in the hardware implementation.

Structures and lists are represented in a non-structure-sharing manner, i.e., they are created by explicitly copying the functor and arguments into consecutive words of memory. For efficiency, lists have a separate tag from structures, and so no functor needs to be stored.

3.2 Data Areas

The main data areas are the code area, containing instructions and other data representing the program itself, and three areas operated as stacks, the **stack**, the **heap**, and the **trail**. (There is also a small push-down list (PDL) used for unification). The stacks generally grow with each procedure invocation and contract on backtracking. In addition, **tail recursion optimization** removes information from the local stack when executing the last procedure call in a determinate procedure, and the cut operator excises backtracking information from both the local stack and the trail.

The heap contains all the structures and lists created by unification and procedure invocation. The trail contains references to variables which have been bound during unification and which must be unbound on backtracking. The stack contains two kinds of objects: **environments** and **choice points**. An environment consists of a vector of value cells for variables occurring in the body of some clause, together with a **continuation** comprising a pointer into the body of another clause and its associated environment. In effect, a continuation represents a list of (instantiated) goals still to be executed. A choice point contains all the information necessary to restore an earlier state of computation in the event of backtracking. It is created when entering a procedure if (and only if) the procedure has more than one clause which can potentially match the call. The information that is stored is a pointer to the alternative clauses, plus the values of the following registers (see below) at the time the procedure is entered: H, TR, B, CP, E, and A1 to Am where m is the number of arguments of the procedure.

3.3 Registers and Treatment of Variables

The current state of a Prolog computation is defined by certain registers containing pointers into the main data areas. The main registers are as follows:

P	program pointer (to the code area)
CP	continuation program pointer (to the code area)
E	last environment (on the local stack)
B	last choice point (backtrack point) (on local stack)
A	top of stack (not strictly essential)
TR	top of trail
H	top of heap
HB	heap backtrack point (i.e. the H value corresponding to B)
S	structure pointer (to the heap)

A1, A2, ... argument registers
X1, X2, ... temporary variables

The A registers and X registers are in fact identical; the different names merely reflect different usages. The A registers are used to pass the arguments to a procedure. The X registers are used to hold the values of a clause's temporary variables.

A **temporary** variable is a variable which has its first occurrence in the head or in a structure or in the last goal, and which does not occur in more than one goal in the body, where the head of the clause is counted as part of the first goal. Temporary variables do not need to be stored in the clause's environment.

A **permanent** variable is any variable not classified as a temporary variable. Permanent variables are stored in an environment, and are addressed by offsets from the environment pointer. They are referred to as Y1, Y2, etc. Note that there can be no permanent variables in clauses with less than two goals in the body, and therefore such clauses do not need environments. Permanent variables are arranged in their environment in such a way that they can be discarded as soon as they are no longer needed. This "trimming" of the environment only has real effect when the environment is more recent than the last choice point.

3.4 The Instruction Set

Prolog programs are encoded as sequences of Prolog instructions. In general, there is one instruction for each Prolog symbol. An instruction consists of an operation code (**opcode**) with some operands (typically just one). The opcode generally encodes the type of Prolog symbol together with the context in which it occurs. It need occupy no more than one byte (eight bits). The operands include small integers, offsets, and addresses, which identify the different kinds of Prolog symbol. Depending on the details of the encoding, operands might occupy one, two, or four bytes, or in some cases less than one byte.

The Prolog instruction set can be classified into *get* instructions, *put* instructions, *unify* instructions, *procedural* instructions, and *indexing* instructions. In the descriptions that follow, we will omit discussion of certain details and optimizations which are not essential for understanding the rest of this paper.

The *get* instructions correspond to the arguments of the head of a clause, and are responsible for matching against the procedure's arguments given in the A registers. The main instructions are :

get_variable Yn, Ai	get_variable Xn, Ai
get_value Yn, Ai	get_value Xn, Ai
get_constant C, Ai	get_nil Ai
get_structure F, Ai	get_list Ai

Here (and in the description of other classes of instructions, below) Ai represents the argument register concerned, and Xn, Yn, C, and F represent respectively a temporary variable, a permanent variable, a constant and a functor. The get_ variable instruction is used if the variable is currently uninstantiated (i.e., if this is the first occurrence of the variable in the clause). Otherwise the get_value instruction is used.

The *put* instructions correspond to the arguments of a goal in the body of a clause, and are responsible for loading the arguments into the A registers. The main instructions are :

```
put_variable Yn, Ai          put_variable Xn, Ai
put_value Yn, Ai             put_value Xn, Ai
put_unsafe_value Yn, Ai
put_constant C, Ai           put_nil Ai
put_structure F, Ai          put_list Ai
```

The put_unsafe_value instruction is used in place of the put_value instruction in the last goal in which an **unsafe** variable appears. An unsafe variable is a permanent variable which did not first occur in the head or in a structure, i.e., the variable was initialized by a put_variable instruction. The put_unsafe_ value instruction ensures that the unsafe variable is dereferenced to something other than a reference to the current environment, binding the variable to a new value cell on the heap if necessary, thus "globalizing" the variable.

The *unify* instructions correspond to the arguments of a structure (or list), and are responsible both for unifying with existing structures and for constructing new structures. The main instructions are:

```
unify_variable Yn           unify_variable Xn
unify_value Yn              unify_value Xn
unify_constant C            unify_nil
unify_structure F, Xn       unify_list Xn
```

A sequence of *unify* instructions is preceded by an instruction to *get, put* or *unify* a structure or list. This preceding instruction determines one of two modes, **read mode** or **write mode**, that the following unify instructions will be executed in. In read mode, *unify* instructions perform unification with successive arguments of an existing structure, addressed via the S register. In write mode, *unify* instructions construct the successive arguments of a new structure, addressed via the H register. A nested substructure or sublist is translated by a unify_variable Xn instruction followed, after the end of the current *unify* sequence, by a corresponding unify_structure F, Xn or unify_list Xn instruction.

The *procedural* instructions correspond to the predicates which form the head and goals of the clause, and are responsible for the control transfer and environment allocation associated with procedure calling. The main instructions are:

```
proceed          allocate
execute P        deallocate
call P, N
```

where P represents a predicate and N is the number of variables (still in use) in the environment. The procedural instructions are used in the translation of clauses with zero, one, or two or more goals in the body as follows:

P.	P :- Q, R, S.
get args of P	allocate
proceed	*get args of* P
	put args of Q
	call Q, N
	put args of R
P :- Q.	call R, N1
get args of P	*put args of* S
put args of Q	deallocate
execute Q	execute S

Note that the size of an environment is specified dynamically by the **call** instruction. To optimize instruction fetch in the hardware implementation, each of the **proceed**, **execute** and **call** instructions is in fact replaced by two instructions: a **prefetch** (or **prefetch_continuation**) instruction occurring as early as possible in the clause code, and a **jump** or **invoke** instruction occurring at the point the control transfer is required. This is described in more detail in the section on hardware organization.

The *indexing* instructions link together the different clauses which make up a procedure, and are responsible for filtering out a subset of those clauses which could potentially match a given procedure call. This filtering, or indexing, function is based on a key which is the principal functor of the first argument of the procedure (given in **A1**). The main instructions are:

try_me_else C	try C
retry_me_else C	retry C
trust_me_else fail	trust C

switch_on_term(Cr, Cc, Cl, Cs)
switch_on_constant(N, Table)
switch_on_structure(N, Table)

Here C, Cr, Cc, Cl, Cs are addresses of clauses (or sets of clauses), and **Table** is a hash table of size **N** (the details of which we will not go into).

Each clause is preceded by a **try_me_else**, **retry_me_else**, or **trust_ me_else** instruction, depending on whether it is the first, an intermediate, or the last clause in the procedure. These instructions are executed only in the case that **A1** dereferences to a variable and all clauses have to be tried for a match. The operand **C** is the address of the following clause.

The **switch_on_term** instruction dispatches to one of four addresses, **Cr**, **Cc**, **Cl**, **Cs**, depending on whether **A1** dereferences to a variable, a constant, a list, or a structure. **Cr** will be the address of the **try_me_else** (or **trust_me_ else**) instruction which precedes the first clause in the procedure. **Cl** will be the address of the single clause whose key is a list, or the address of a sequence of such clauses, identified by a sequence of **try, retry,** and **trust** instructions. **Cc** and **Cs** may be the addresses of a single clause or sequence of clauses (as in the case of **CI**), or more generally may be respectively the address of either a **switch_on_constant** or **switch_on_structure** instruction which provides hash table access to the clause or clauses which match the given key.

3.5 Optimizations

Note that, since the argument registers and the temporary registers are identical, certain instructions are null operations and can be omitted :

```
get_variable Xi, Ai
put_value Xi, Ai
```

The compiler takes pains to allocate temporary variables to **X** registers in such a way as to maximize the scope for this optimization.

3.6 Examples of Clause Encoding

As examples of clause encoding, here is the code for the *concatenate* and *quick sort* procedures.

```
concatenate( [] , L, L).
concatenate( [X | L1], L2, [X | L3] ) :-
        concatenate(L1, L2, L3).

concatenate/3 : switch_on_term C1a, C1, C2, fail

C1a:      try_me_else C2a            % concatenate(
C1 :      get_nil A1                 %      [] ,
          get_value A2, A3           %      L, L
          proceed                    % ).

C2a:      trust_me_else fail         % concatenate(
C2 :      get_list A1                %      [
          unify_variable X4          %        X |
          unify_variable A1          %        L1] , L2,
          get_list A3                %      [
          unify_value X4             %        X |
          unify_variable A3          %        L3]) :-
          execute concatenate/3      % concatenate(L1, L2, L3).

qsort( [] , R, R).
qsort([X | L], R0, R) :-
   split(L, X, L1, L2), qsort(L1, R0, [X | R1]), qsort(L2, R1, R).

qsort/3 : switch_on_term C1a, C1, C2, fail

C1a:      try_me_else C2a            % qsort(
```

```
C1 :    get_nil A1                    %    [ ] ,
        get_value A2, A3             %    R, R
        proceed                       %).

C2a:    trust_me_else fail           % qsort(
C2 :    allocate
        get_list A1                   %      [
        unify_variable Y6            %         x |
        unify_variable A1           %         L] ,
        get_variable Y5, A2         %      RO,
        get_variable Y3, A3         %      R) :-
        put_value Y6, A2            % split(L, X,
        put_variable Y4, A3         %      L1,
        put_variable Y1, A4         %      L2
        call split/4, 6              %),
        put_unsafe_value Y4, A1      % qsort(L1,
        put_value Y5,A2             %      RO,
        put_list A3                   %      [
        unify_value Y6               %         x |
        unify_variable Y2           %         R1]
        call qsort/3, 3              %),
        put_unsafe_value Y1, A1      % qsort(L2,
        put_value Y2, A2            %      R1,
        put_value Y3, A3            %      R
        deallocate
        execute qsort/3             %).
```

The following example further illustrates the handling of permanent variables :

```
compile(Clause, Instructions) :-
    preprocess(Clause, C1),
    translate(C1, Symbols),
    number_variables(Symbols, O, N, Saga),
    complete_saga(O, N, Saga),
    allocate_registers(Saga),
    generate(Symbols, Instructions).
```

```
        try_me_else fail             % compile(Clause,
        allocate
        get_variable Y2, A2          %    Instructions) :-
        put_variable Y5, A2          % preprocess(Clause, C1
        call preprocess/2, 5         %),
        put_unsafe_value Y5, A1      % translate(C1,
        put_variable Y1, A2          %    Symbols
        call translate/2, 4          %),
```

408

```
put_value Y1, A1              % number_variables(Symbols,
put_constant O, A2            %     O,
put_variable Y4, A3           %     N,
put_variable Y3, A4           %     Saga
call number_variables/4, 4    %),
put_constant O, A1            % complete_saga(O,
put_unsafe_value Y4, A2       %     N,
put_variable Y3, A3           %     Saga
call complete_saga/3, 3       %),
put_unsafe_value Y3, A1       % allocate_registers(Saga
call allocate_registers/1,2   %),
put_unsafe_value Y1,A1        % generate(Symbols,
put_value Y2, A2              %     Instructions
deallocate
execute generate/2            %).
```

The following two examples illustrate the encoding of nested substructures:

d(U * V, X, (DU * V) + (U * DV)) :- d(U, X, DU), d(V, X, DV).

```
try_me_else ...               % d(
get_structure '*'/2, A1       %     *(
unify_variable A1             %         U,
unify_variable Y1             %         V),
get_variable Y2, A2           %     X,
get_structure '+'/2, A3       %     +(
unify_variable X4             %         SS1,
unify_variable X5             %         SS2),
get_structure '*'/2, X4       % SS1 = *(
unify_variable A3             %         DU,
unify_value Y1                %         V),
get_structure '*'/2, X5       % SS2 = *(
unify_value A1                %         U,
unify_variable Y3             %         DV)) :-
call d/3, 3                   % d(U, X, DU),
put_value Y1, A1              % d(V,
put_value Y2, A2              %     X,
put_value Y3, A3              %     DV
execute d/3                   %).
```

test :- do(parse(s(np, vp), [birds, fly], [ ])).

```
trust_me_else fail            % test :-
put_structure s/2, X2         % do(SS1 = s(
unify_constant np             %         np
```

```
        unify_constant vp            %         vp),
        put_list X4                  % SS2 = [
        unify_constant fly           %         fly |
        unify_nil                    %         []] ,
        put_list X3                  % SS3 = [
        unify_constant birds         %         birds |
        unify_value X4               %         SS2] ,
        put_structure parse/3, A1    %      parse(
        unify_value X2               %         SS1,
        unify_value X3               %         SS2,
        unify_nil                    %         [] )
        execute do/1                 %).
```

The following example illustrates the use of the indexing instructions:

```
call(X or Y) :- call(X).
call(X or Y) :- call(Y).
call(trace) :- trace.
call(notrace) :- notrace.
call(nl) :- nl.
call(X) :- builtin(X).
call(X) :- ext(X).
call(call(X)) :- call(X).
call(repeat).
call(repeat) :- call(repeat).
call(true).
```

```
call/1 : try_me_else C6a
         switch_on_type C1a, L1, fail, L2

L1 :     switch_on_constant 4, $(trace : C3,
                                  notrace : C4,
                                  fail,
                                  nl : C5)

L2 :     switch_on_structure 1, $(or/2 : L3)

L3 :     try C1
         trust C2

C1a :    try_me_else C2a            % call(
C1 :     get_structure or/2, A1     %    or(
         unify_variable A1          %       X, Y)) :-
         execute call/1.            % call(X).

C2a :    retry_me_else C3a          % call(
C2 :     get_structure or/2, A1     %    or(
```

```
            unify_void 1                   %        X,
            unify_variable A1              %          Y)) :-
            execute call/1                 % call(Y).

C3a:        retry_me_else C4a              % call(
C3:         get_constant trace, A1         %     trace) :-
            execute trace/O                % trace.

C4a:        retry_me_else C5a              % call(
C4:         get_constant notrace, A1       %     notrace) :-
            execute notrace/O              % notrace.

C5a:        trust_me_else fail             % call(
C5:         get_constant nl, A1            %     nl) :-
            execute nl/O                   % nl.

C6a:        retry_me_else C7a              % call(X) :-
            execute builtin/1              % builtin(X).

C7a:        retry_me_else L4               % call(X) :-
            execute ext/1                  % ext(X).

L4:         trust_me_else fail
            switch_on_type C8a, L5, fail,L7

L5:         switch_on_constant 2, $(repeat: L6, true: C11)

L6:         try C9
            trust C10

L7:         switch_on_structure 1, $(call/1 : C8)

C8a:        try_me_else C9a                % call(
C8:         get_structure call/1, A1       %     call(
            unify_variable A1              %          X)) :-
            execute call/1                 % call(X).

C9a:        retry_me_else C10a             % call(
C9:         get_constant repeat, A1        %     repeat
            proceed                        %).

C10a:       retry_me_else C11a             % call(
C10:        get_constant repeat, A1        %     repeat) :-
            put_constant repeat, A1        % call(repeat
            execute call/1                 %).

C11a:       trust_me_else fail             % call(
C11:        get_constant true, A1          %     true
            proceed                        %).
```

§4 Hardware Organization

The model described is a single-user, single-pipeline Prolog processor. The memory system, instruction and execution units (I-Unit and E-Unit(s)) and μcontroller are discussed in this paper. Systems issues, e.g. interrupt handling, are not discussed. The model description will set the stage for an answer to the following question (further discussed in the *Conclusion*) :

Instead of designing a special purpose processor, why not emulate the instruction set on a general purpose μcoded machine, e.g. Symbolics 3600, or compile it onto a reduced instruction set machine, e.g. IBM 801[8]?

4.1 Memory

The memory model is an interleaved memory with a four cycle access. Because memory accesses are overlapped, access time is not a critical parameter in the processor model: For a single E-Unit, first-come-first-served (FCFS) module queues prevent the possibility of read-write, write-read and write-write races ; (extension to multiple E-Units will require a more complex solution).

The model can be extended to include a cache in front of memory or in the I-Unit only. If the locality of heap references is minimal, the cache is better used for instructions only, especially in a multiple E-Unit system.

4.2 E-Unit

The basic datapaths of the E-Unit (Fig. 1) form a three stage pipeline :

- **C** stage — Array access of the stack buffer, register file, trail buffer and control counters, latching results into the temporary registers (**T, T1**).
- **E** stage — arithmetic-logic unit (ALU) execution, latching results into the result (**R**), push-down list (**PDL**), memory address (**MAR**) and memory data (**MDR**) registers.
- **P** stage—Putaway into **C** stage arrays.

Many of the high-level Prolog machine instructions make an arbitrary number of passes through the execution pipe. Controlling such complex sequences while minimizing pipeline breaks is well suited for *data-stationary* μcode.[9] The μcontroller function is to supply the execution pipe with μinstructions of the form : "C, E, P control ‖ locks to set ‖ branch control ‖ branch address."

Thus each instruction contains control information for a single pass through the pipe. A μinstruction is joined with the machine instruction operand to form a *control word*. Control words are latched in a series of *control registers* (one per stage). At each stage, the control word is checked against *resource locks*. A control word can proceed to the next stage if no required resources are locked and *subsequent* control words can proceed. If the control word cannot proceed, constituting a pipeline break, the result of stage execution is not

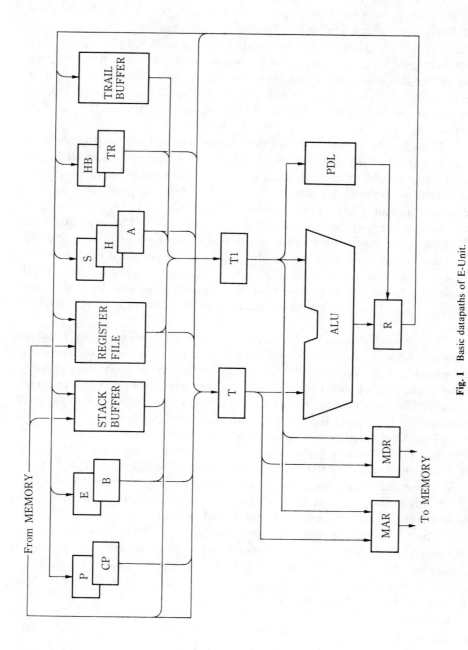

Fig. 1 Basic datapaths of E-Unit.

latched. Resource locks, as indicated in the μinstruction, are initially set when the control word first enters the pipe.

The I-Unit delivers the initial μinstruction address of the μsequence corresponding to each machine instruction. These are queued in the E-Unit. The model assumes distinct μsequences for instructions executed in read and write modes. Because the μinstructions are overlapped, the mode may be selected after subsequent μsequence addresses have been queued. Therefore either the I-Unit must deliver two alternative μaddresses (corresponding to the two modes) from which the E-Unit selects one, or else alternative μsequences are allocated on sufficient boundaries in the μstore to allow concatenating the mode to a single μaddress.

The μstore is a two port read-only memory (ROM) permitting access to the next sequential μinstruction and the target μinstruction indicated by the branch address field of the current μinstruction. The type of μcontrol transfer is indicated by the branch control field. The controller supports μroutine call and return, unconditional and conditional branches, dispatch next machine instruction and n-way branch (via a specialized ROM). The controller can dispatch a new machine instruction every cycle (if the I-Unit can supply them) by virtue of a bypass around the μaddress queue. A conditional branch can be resolved by a logic signal produced early in the cycle, selecting the correct μinstruction late in the cycle. For branch conditions generated too late in the cycle, e.g. by arithmetic comparison, an extra cycle is taken, keeping the cycle lean.

As with other tagged architecture machines, careful consideration must be given to defining an extensive but not excessive set of tags. The tag encoding must permit quick decoding for determining object type, a criterion directly related to the critical path of the μcontroller because conditional branches can be resolved by condition codes set by tag decoding. A benefit of the tagged architecture is the ability to introduce hardware type checking.

The E-Unit datapath includes a stack buffer, general register file, trail buffer and PDL. The trail buffer is used to cache the trail stack segment, and is not strictly necessary. The PDL is used during unification. Both arrays are first-in-last-out stacks which are burst to memory when they fill up. A *multiple E-Unit* organization refers to multiple pipes, each with its own μcontroller and ALU, sharing a single I-Unit, stack buffer and register file.

The register file is modeled as a one input, one output array storing the temporary variables and procedure arguments. Control pointers are implemented in ad hoc registers and counters. The **B**, **E** and **A** (top-of-stack) pointers are needed for managing the stack. The **S** and **H** pointers are kept in counters, reducing interlocks. The **P** and **CP** pointers require access from both the I-Unit and E-Unit(s).

The stack buffer caches the top of stack in a fast array. The stack holds two types of objects: environments and choice points. Each is arbitrary in length. An environment holds permanent variables which are directly referenc-ed. A choice point holds state pointers and goal arguments which require nothing more than sequential referencing, but are accessed directly for design uniformity.

A current environment not contained in the buffer must be copied onto the top of the stack from memory, or the stack must be bypassed in such cases. The former policy increases stack size in an effort to enforce locality of stack references and may cause thrashing. The latter policy simplifies buffer manage-ment and cannot increase thrashing.

Because the stack is a segment in the virtual address space it is conceiv-able to reference the stack directly from memory. If a memory cache is needed anyway, e.g. for the heap and program, the stack reference penalty will be reduced. Such an organization does not differ greatly from a standard (scientific/numerical) processor.[8] However, this approach typically burdens the compiler with performing global allocation of registers. With the stack buffer model, the compiler need only allocate registers locally, clause by clause. A stack buffer becomes even more essential if there are multiple E-Units, which must lock portions of the stack. Setting and testing locks on word units is less expensive in a sequential stack buffer than in a set-associative cache.

Without a general purpose cache, a specialized buffer is needed to decrease the stack reference penalty. The stack buffer design we favor holds a sequential set of locations from the virtual stack segment. The buffer is managed explicitly by the μcontroller. A copy-back policy is instituted, i.e. updates are not immediately reflected in memory. All direct memory references interrogate the buffer and make updates if the virtual address falls between the bounds registers.

Stack references consist of an offset plus a base register. The offset may be specified as a macroinstruction operand. In addition, μinstructions can specify a value or hardware counter (for use when reading and writing choice points). The base register is either the E or B register. Because of the time critical nature of stack address generation, the number of buffer entries must be kept low. The generated address is guaranteed to fall within the valid buffer range by virtue of the following policy. When the **allocate** and **try** instructions update a base register to become the new top of stack and that point is within a certain number of buffer entries from the lowest page, a copy-back is initiated. In the current model, a copy-back cannot proceed in parallel with E-Unit operation, i.e. the pipe is broken.

4.3 I-Unit

The primary function of the instruction unit is to supply instructions to the E-Unit(s). The I-Unit also processes certain control instructions directly from the instruction buffers in an effort to reduce the procedure call penalty.

The Prolog machine instruction set has no conditional branches, only procedure calls which can match one of possibly several clauses. The main design criterion of the I-Unit is to compute clause addresses quickly. To this end, only *indexing on tag* (switch_on_term) is optimized. Control instructions detected and executed in the I-Unit are prefetch and prefetch_continuation. These instructions attempt to prefetch the next clause to be executed into the I-Unit. If the indexing method is not by tag, however, no prefetching is done.

prefetch P is generated by the compiler anywhere before the corresponding jump or invoke instruction. P is the address of a switch_on_term instruction having four operands defining a dispatch table. Each operand, a clause address, corresponds to a different type tag. If the clause has alternatives, they are explicitly defined by try, retry and trust instructions linking the alternatives. The jump instruction is generated by the compiler at the clause end, indicating that the instruction streams should be switched, i.e. it is an unconditional branch to a clause determined in the preceding prefetch.

The I-Unit services prefetch P by using the low order bits of P to address a small *map cache*. This cache holds a set of previously seen switch_on_term instructions. If the entry key matches P, the tag of register A1 (holding the first argument of a procedure call) is used to select which clause is to be executed. The A1 register is treated specially to allow synchronization with the prefetch instruction. A flag (distinct from a register lock) indicates A1's validity. This allows the placement of the prefetch anywhere in the stream. The I-Unit simply retries the mapping if A1 is not valid. If the map entry does not match, the instruction cache is accessed for P. A suitable map cache entry is chosen for replacement by the returning switch_on_term instruction.

There are two interchangable instruction buffers (FCFS queues) in the I-Unit. With each is associated a program counter. At any given time, one is marked "current" and the other "future". The eventual clause address produced by the prefetch mapping is latched into the future program counter. This counter contends with the current counter (and E-Unit(s)) for cache cycles, in an effort to fill up the future instruction buffer.

The jump instruction, executed in the I-Unit, switches the buffers. In clauses requiring even moderate unification of procedure arguments, the I-Unit will be able to at least partially fill the future instruction buffer beneath normal E-Unit operation, if the cache holds the instructions. This gives a one cycle delay for the jump, needed to recognize the opcode and switch streams.

prefetch_continuation is similar to prefetch, but is used in unit clauses and has no operand; the CP register holds the address of a switch_on_term instruction. The invoke instruction is similar to jump, but stores the continuation address in the CP register.

§5 Timing Results

Using the hardware model described, *approximate* μcode translations were written for the machine instruction set. Two simple Prolog programs were expanded from machine instructions to μcode traces. This section presents hand timings of those traces.

5.1 Determinate Concatenate

The first program trace is the determinate execution of *concatenate* :

```
concatenate ( [ ] , L, L).
concatenate ([X | L1], L2, [X | L3] ) :-
            concatenate (L1, L2, L3).
```

For instance, "?-concatenate ([a, b], [c, d, e], X)." instantiates X to [a, b, c, d, e]. The timing considered here is based on the execution of "?-concatenate ([a, b, c,...], [z], X)." To execute this goal, the following machine instructions are executed repeatedly.

```
prefetch concatenate/3
get_list A1
unify_variable X4
unify_variable A1
get_list A3
unify_value X4
```

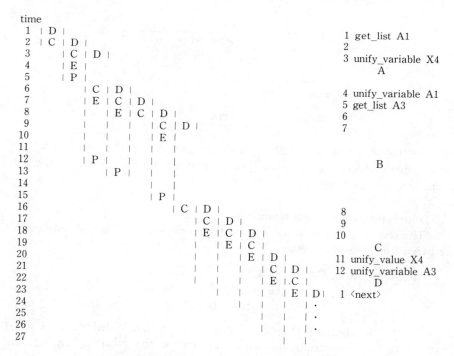

Fig. 2 Determinate concatenate timing.

```
unify_variable A3
jump
```

The second clause is always immediately chosen, i.e. no unification is attempted with the first clause, by virtue of indexing. The 8 machine instructions are dynamically expanded into 12 μinstructions. The timing diagram (Fig. 2) has time, in machine cycles, running vertically and pipe stages running horizontally. The decode (**D**) stages, representing the μstore access, are annotated with the μinstruction number. The start of a μsequence is labelled with the corresponding machine instruction. Memory references are denoted by blank stages extending beyond the execution stage. Memory reads are followed four cycles later by a putaway stage.

It is assumed that the I-Unit can supply an aligned instruction to the E-Unit each cycle within the context of a single clause, i.e., instruction boundary problems are ignored. It is assumed that the heap is not cached. **jump** and **prefetch** are not shown because they are removed from the instruction stream by the I-Unit. The timing indicates 8 instructions execute in 22 cycles, giving 2.8 cycles per instruction. If one procedure call is considered a single logical inference, the performance is 22 *cycles per logical inference* (CPLI).

The following table (Table 1) summarizes the frequency and total penalty of each type of break in determinate concatenate :

Table 1

	# occur.	penalty (cycles)	total (%)
control register dependency	1 A	2	20
memory read	1 B	6	60
micro-control	1 C	1	10
macro-control	1 D	1	10

Micro-control refers to delayed branch resolution due to arithmetic compares. Macro-control refers to **jump** delay. The control register dependency was due to an interlock on the **S** pointer.

5.2 Non-determinate Concatenate

The second program trace is a substring search requiring the non-determinate execution of *concatenate* :

```
substring(Sub, Bef, Aft, Str) :-
                concatenate(Bef, Int, Str),
                concatenate(Sub, Aft, Int).
```

For instance, "?-substring ([a, b], X, Y, [d, a, a, b, c])." instantiates X to [d, a] and Y to [c], indicating the strings delimiting the substring [a, b]. The timing considered here is based on the execution of "?-substring ([z], X, Y, [a, b, c, ...]).'' which repeatedly fails. The machine instructions executed in each iteration are given in Fig. 3 .

The timing[10] was done with assumptions similar to determinate *concatenate*. The failure of unify_value X4 causes the top of stack to be reset to the last choice point. The 19 instructions expand into approximately 89 μinstructions which execute in 165 cycles, giving 8.7 cycles per instruction and 55 CPLI (assuming each iteration corresponds to 3 logical inferences). The pipe breaks are summarized below (Table 2).

prefetch_continuation	⟨succeeding unit clause⟩
try_me_else C1	create choice point
get_nil A1	1 level of indirection on dereferencing A1
	bind A1 (variable) to nil ; trail binding
get_value A2, A3	unify A3 (list ptr) to A2 (variable) ; trail binding
	1 level of indirection on dereferencing A2
	0 levels of indirection on dereferencing A3
jump	
prefetch concatenate/3	⟨failing recursive clause⟩
get_list A1	
unify_variable X4	
unify_variable A1	
get_list A3	
unify_value X4	unify bound to bound : fail so backtrack ; detrail 2 bindings
prefetch concatenate/3	⟨succeeding recursive clause⟩
get_list A1	1 level of indirection on dereferencing A1
	bind A1 (variable) to newly created list ptr ; trail binding
unify_variable X4	
unify_variable X1	
get_list A3	
unify_value X4	unify X4 (variable) to bound argument ; no trailing
	1 level of indirection on dereferencing X4
unify_variable A3	
jump	

Fig. 3 Non-determinate concatenate instruction trace.

Table 2

	# occur.	penalty (cycles)	total (%)
memory read	6	36	49
micro-control			
late branch res.	14	14	19
dispatch via ROM	5	5	7
macro-control			
procedure call	2	2	3
stack tests		10	14
register dependency	3	6	8

ROM dispatches are used by unification μcode for quick n-way branches dependent on the tags of the two terms unified. The *procedure call delay* assumes the prefetching mechanism hid most of the penalty. *Stack tests* refer to stack bounds checks when reading and writing a choice point. In this example, the choice point was always found in the stack buffer by virtue of tail recursion optimization.

5.3 Analysis

Assuming a 100ns cycle time for the model, which seems feasible using circuit technology comparable to the Symbolics 3600, determinate concatenate runs at 450 K LIPS and non-determinate concatenate runs at 180 K LIPS. (A much shorter cycle time, 50ns or less, is conceivable using ECL or other very fast technology). To put these results in perspective,

- We estimate a firmware implementation of the Prolog instruction set on the Symbolics 3600 would run determinate concatenate at 110 K LIPS.
- Determinate concatenate compiled by DEC-10 Prolog compiler,[4] runs on DEC-2060 at 40 K LIPS.
- PSI performance is predicted to be 30 K LIPS.[1]
- We estimate, on the basis of a prototype implementation, that a macrocode emulation of the Prolog instruction set on the VAX/780 would run determinate concatenate at 15 K LIPS.

For determinate concatenate with the heap referenced through a one cycle cache with bypass (and 100% hit ratio), 4 cycles are saved. Compiler optimization can prevent the interlock on S, saving 2 cycles. These modifications combined give the performance of 2.0 cycles/instruction and 16 CPLI, a 27% speed improvement.

For non-determinate concatenate a cached heap would at best save 24 cycles. Removing S interlocks saves 6 cycles. These modifications combined give the performance of 7.1 cycles/instruction and 45 CPLI, an 18% speed improvement.

§6 Conclusions and Future Work

The work completed to date indicates that a sequential Prolog machine with significant performance can be built using conventional design principles for pipelined processors. Assuming reasonable technology, the timing results show the model runs significantly faster than all current or near-future implementations of Prolog. Far more importantly, we feel the sequential pipelined machine will provide the best cost/performance ratio in the just now emerging high-end environment of logical inference processors.

There appear to be several reasons why the pipelined Prolog processor can significantly out-perform a microcode implementation on a more general purpose machine such as the Symbolics 3600. The lean cycle of the Prolog processor permits greater overlapping than the partially overlapped 3600 "fat" cycle. We believe our model would have a cycle time of less than half the 3600, given an equivalent technology. Compared to the 3600, memory accesses are more highly overlapped, allowing a slow memory with less performance degradation. In addition, the specialized hardware support for procedure call, indexing, and unification dispatching enhances Prolog performance. It should be borne in mind, however, that the present processor design is probably somewhat more complex (and costly) than the 3600.

Justifying any advantage over reduced instruction set machines is more difficult. The micro-architecture of the Prolog processor is primitive and permits more parallelism, on the datapath level, than a conventional machine. The object code is more compact, making memory caching more effective. There are no conditional branches in the machine instruction set, only on the μinstruction level, permitting branch target prefetch and "late select". Thus we expect the Prolog macro-instruction prefetch unit to be more efficient than a conventional prefetch unit which must change context more frequently. Were the instruction set compiled into primitive instructions, *many* conditional branches and sub-routine calls would be generated (if only to keep the object program to a reasonable length). Although the dynamic translation of machine instructions into μsequences has a large latency, it is usually hidden when calling procedures by executing certain procedural instructions in the I-Unit concurrently with E-Unit operation. Disadvantages of the Prolog machine include the effectiveness of a directly accessible stack buffer, which is unproved. In addition, the impact of a large μinstruction on hardware cost (and speed) has not been assessed.

Related design problems receiving our attention concern designing a better stack buffer and defining multiple E-Unit operation.

The fundamental problem with non-determinate computation is the burden of saving the complete program history at each choice point. Currently, the stack holds both active environments and backtrack information, consisting of choice points and inactive environments. The creation of a choice point "freezes" all objects below it on the stack because resumption of that choice point must reinstate the machine exactly. This lessens the locality of the stack, i.e. current environments may lie deep within the stack, resulting in degraded stack performance. A primary concern is to increase the stack locality of the computation. Two ideas are being entertained :

- Split the stack into a choice point stack and environment stack.
- Split the stack into two windows, holding the current choice point and the current environment. Note that one of these objects must be at the top of the stack.

Additional E-Unit pipes introduce new problems as well as aggravating old ones. Instruction bandwidth produced by the I-Unit limits the number of pipes, beyond which performance is no longer cost effective. Memory requests from different pipes can cause races. These must be prevented either by careful compiler scheduling of the pipes or, more likely, dynamic synchonization in hardware. An efficient set of interlocks and hardware locking mechanism is needed.

One such multiple pipeline model is described in Tick.[11] Timing results for a program trace of *quick sort* indicated that the benefit of concurrent unifications on multiple pipes rapidly degrades under the influence of complex control instructions (e.g., **allocate, deallocate, try_me_else**). The major control burden is the stack management. Although the management algorithms are simple, the number of control cycles is not less than the number of sequential unification cycles for the program examined. A plausible solution to multiple pipeline inefficiency involves allowing the pipes to freely execute across procedure call boundaries. This scheme, essentially and-parallelism, is itself difficult to implement efficiently.

Acknowledgements

This work was supported by a Digital Equipment Corporation external research grant.

References

1) Nishikawa, H., Yokota, M., Yamamoto, A., Taki, K. and Uchida, S.: "The Personal Sequential Inference Machine (PSI): Its Design Philosophy and Machine Architecture," Logic Programming Workshop '83 (Universidade Nova de Lisboa) (June, 1983) 53-73.

2) "Symbolics 3600 Technical Summary" (Symbolics Inc.,Cambridge, Massachusetts)(1983).

3) Moto-oka, T. (ed.): Fifth Generation Computer Systems (North-Holland) (1982).

4) Warren, D. H. D.: "Applied Logic — Its Use and Implementation as Programming Tool," Ph. D dissertation (University of Edinburgh) (1977). Available as Technical Note, *290* (Artificial Intelligence Center, SRI International).

5) Warren, D. H. D.: "An Improved Prolog Implementation which Optimises Tail Recursion," Research Paper, *156* (Dept. of Artificial Intelligence, University of Edinburgh) (1980) (presented at the 1980 Logic Programming Workshop, Debrecen, Hungary).

6) Bowen, D. L., Byrd, L. M. and Clocksin, W. F.: "A Portable Prolog Compiler," Logic Programming Workshop '83 (Universidade Nova de Lisboa) (June, 1983) 74-83.

7) Warren, D. H. D.: "An Abstract Prolog Instruction Set," Technical Report, *309* (Artificial Intelligence Center, SRI International) (1983).

8) Radin, G.: "The 801 Minicomputer," IBM Journal of Research and Development, *Vol. 27* (May, 1983) 237-246.

9) Kogge, P. M.: The Architecture of Pipelined Computers (McGraw-Hill) (1981).

10) Tick, E.: "An Overlapped Prolog Processor," Technical Report, *308* (Artificial Intelligence Center, SRI International) (1983).

11) Tick, E.: "Towards a Multiple Pipeline Prolog Processor," International Workshop on High-Level Computer Architecture (The University of Maryland) (May, 1984) to be published.

Status and Performance of the Zmob Parallel Processing System[1]

Mark Weiser, Steve Kogge, Michelle McElvany,
Roger Pierson, Rehmi Post, Ashok Thareja
Computer Science Department
University of Maryland
College Park, MD 20742

1. Introduction

The Zmob computing system is an MIMD architecture without shared memory [4] [2]. Some of its unique features are: a large number (256) of general-purpose processors, inexpensive off-the-shelf components, very-high-speed communication ($>$100 Mbits), and a unique communication mechanism combining features of both cross-bar and broadcast media. The use of the well known Z-80 processor permits easy access to readily available software, and extensions to the Unix[2] operating system give easy user access to Zmob's processing power. A 256 processor Zmob is now under construction at the University of Maryland, where several 16 and 32 processor Zmobs are already in use.

2. The Architecture

Zmob's vital statistics are shown in table 1. The Zmob computing environment has 4 components: the conveyor belt, the mail stops, the Z-80 processors, and the host computer (see figure 1). A single conveyor belt is shared among all the Zmob processors, and each Z-80 has a single dedicated mail stop connecting it to the conveyor belt. A Z-80/mailstop pair is called a *moblet*. The host computer can communicate to the conveyor belt through mail stops or though a special interface. Zmob is easily reconfigured to have between 2 and 4096 processors. The figure 256 is a compromise between degree of parallelism and communications delay.

The Zmob conveyor belt allows processors to be connected in unit time as in a cross-bar, but also allows broadcast and broadcast by pattern messages as in a bus or other shared media. Processors experience no communication delay because in the time it takes to read or write from the belt a new free message slot has rotated into position to be used by that processor. Messages may be read from the belt destructively or non-destructively, thus permitting single-destination or broadcast transmission.

The conveyor belt's advantage over a shared medium such as Ethernet [1] is that all Zmob processors can talk simultaneously without interfering with other interprocessor communication. Furthermore, the active nature of the conveyor belt means that a message can be sent by pattern and removed by the first free processor matching that pattern. In a broadcast medium there would be no way to prevent every matching processor from receiving the message.

2.1. Architectural Details

2.1.1. The conveyor belt

The conveyor belt is a 48 bit wide active shift register. The 48 bits constitute a *message*, and are divided into 20 bits for data, 12 bits each for source and destination address, and 4 bits for status. The two status bits under software control are used to indicate broadcast messages and messages sent by pattern.

Each mail stop synchronously shifts 48 bits to its neighbor every 111 nanoseconds[3]. Thus the total number of bits in motion on the belt at any one time is 48*number-of-processors.

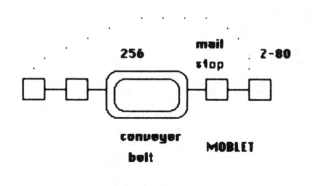

Figure 1. Zmob architecture.

	Per Processor	Total Zmob
Instructions/Sec	4×10^6	10^8
FP Adds/Sec	4×10^4	10^7
Comm. Bytes/Sec	10^5	25×10^6
Secs for moblet load	1.0	1.0

Table 1. Zmob Statistics.

---

1. Performance data on Zmob is still being gathered. It will be presented in the conference talk. People interested in hardcopy of the performance data presented in the talk should write to the first author, preferably by net: mark@maryland or seismo!umcp-cs!mark.

2. Unix is a trademark of Bell Laboratories

---

3. The shift time is dependent on the Zmob master clock cycle. Different Zmob papers give different values for this: the original spec was for 10Mhz, the first Zmob ran at 6 Mhz, and current versions run at 9 Mhz which the numbers in this paper reflect.

Reprinted from *The Proceedings of COMPCON S'85*, 1985, pages 71-73.

For 256 processors this is a total data-in-motion rate of 14 gigabytes/sec. This figure makes it clear that using active shift registers rather than a passive medium gives the potential for much higher bandwidth.

Each group of 48 bits is called a *bin* of the conveyor belt. Bins are dedicated to mailstops. A mail stop may read from any bin except its own and can write only to the bin it owns. Every mail stop has a unique 12-bit address.

2.1.2. The mail stops

A mail stop has two logically independent elements, the writer and the reader. Each is capable of buffering one message to or from the conveyor belt. Normally a message intended for a given mailstop will be removed from the belt as the message shifts past. The exception is messages with the broadcast bit set, which are read from the belt but not removed. If a mail stop's input buffer is full then messages intended for that mail stop are not read but remain on the belt where they can be read on a later rotation. During each rotation the *sender* of an unreceived message may also check that the message has not been received and remove it if desired.

Messages may be sent to all processors or to just one, and may be directed by address or by pattern. A pair of software settable hardware masks in each moblet specify the bit patterns to receive messages sent by pattern.

Selected processors may also send *control messages*. A control message is only 4 bits wide and is received immediately into its own hardware buffer regardless of any other messages pending. Control messages cause Z-80 non-maskable interrupts to the ROM on each processor, and so allow complete control of each processor from the belt.

2.1.3. The z-80a processors

Mail stops are controlled by individual Z-80A microprocessors, each with 62k RAM memory, 2k EPROM (formerly 1k), hardware multiply, floating point processor, and serial and parallel communication ports in addition to the mail stop. All I/O is through memory mapped registers. The Z-80's are quite conventional and run typical Z-80 software. Each Z-80 also controls a set of orange, green, amber, and red LED's which are visible from the front of the Zmob.

The serial ports are used for debugging individual processors. The parallel ports are reserved for future expansion to floppy disks, small Winchester disk drives, D/A converters, or high speed communication equipment.

2.1.4. Operating environment

Because Zmob has no mass storage of its own and each processor is limited to 64k of memory, the host machine plays a vital role in the effective use of Zmob. We currently use a Vax-11/780[4] and a Pyramid 90x as hosts. The host-to-Zmob communications channel could be a severe bottleneck, and several methods for using this channel are planned. The most basic method and the only one now working is to use one or more moblet serial ports to communicate to the host machine. Somewhat faster methods using parallel ports or a direct Vax interface are under development.

The Zmob is physically configured as four 84 inch high racks, each holding four backplane cages, with 16 mailstop

cards and 16 processor cards in each backplane[5]. Each rack has a smoked plexiglas front to allow viewing the LED's on the processor boards. The backplane carries power, clock, and conveyor belt signals. The cages are connected in a ring by sections of 100-wire ribbon cable going from each cage to its neighbor (every other wire is a ground). The operation of the Zmob is independent of the exact number of processors, so it is a simple matter to take one or more backplanes out of the loop to partition into their own little Zmob. The smallest Zmob that is convenient to operate is a single backplane with 8 or 16 processors, with the conveyor belt cable running from one side of the backplane to the other.

The moblets are all cycled by a master clock which insures that they all shift the conveyor belt at the same time. The master clock also sends a *self* pulse once per revolution, which is the signal that a mailstop can now write to the belt.

The 256-moblet Zmob draws approximately 4000 watts of power, including cooling fans. Fabrication of a 256 processor Zmob by a commercial prototyping firm, including PC board layout, computerized board testing, integration, cabinetry, and installation, cost 163,000.

3. The Zmob Simulators

Three simulators were developed for use while waiting for the Zmob hardware. Each is an accurate model of a portion of the Zmob system, and together they cover almost of its functional capabilities. All simulators run on a Vax-11/780 under the Berkeley/Unix operating system.

The first simulator accurately models the Z-80A processor within Zmob, including memory mapped I/O, floating point, and conveyor belt registers. This was the first simulator built, and served to debug basic PROM routines as well as serving as a test bed for porting standalone software to Zmob. For instance, the Zmob versions of Forth and CP/M both were run first on this simulator.

The second simulator accurately models the mailstops and conveyor belts, and is used for low level operating system debugging. A piece of code designed to work with the mailstop is exercised by connecting it to the simulator. The user running the simulator can cause any set of events, with any timing, to happen on the conveyor belt and mailstop. Thus worst case conditions can be explored under complete user control.

The final simulator is an accurate model of the conveyor belt as seen through the Zmob operating system, and is the only simulator which permits running parallel user programs. Subroutine calls read and write the conveyor belt, and programs are written in C. Each Zmob process is modeled by a Unix process, and the conveyor belt is modeled by another Unix process. They communicate using the Inter-Processor-Communication extension to Unix developed by Rashid [3].

Figure 2 shows a 6 processor Zmob as displayed on the Zmob monitor. This monitor can display activity on the conveyor belt and mailstops, and allows a user to play back communications activity single stepped or continuously. The monitor is showing a snapshot of an implementation of the dining philosophers problem running on the Zmob simulator.

---

4. Vax is a trademark of Digital Equipment Corporation.

5. Some of the backplane cages only hold 8 mailstop and processor cards to allow room for debugging probes.

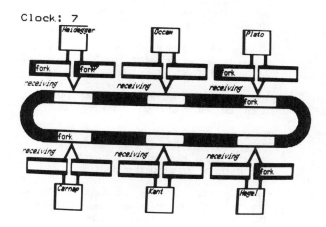

Clock: 7

Figure 2. Zmob Belt Monitor. Z-80 processors are indicated by rectangles with the names of philosophers. Each processor is connected to its input and output buffers, which are in turn connected to the conveyor belt. Messages are seen circulating on the conveyor belt and waiting in various buffers. Source and destination of messages is color coded (not reproduced).

4. Zmob Systems Software

Systems software for using Zmob consists of the usual cross-compilers and assemblers, linker, and loaders. The languages Forth and C, and a version of prolog, currently run on Zmob. Of the layers of system software described below, only the physical channel layer is currently usable. System software for communicating with Zmob is constructed in layers, each hiding more of the detail of Zmob from the user.

The first layer is the *physical channel*. This is the raw communication medium to Zmob and is generally used mostly by the host system device driver. Only the moblets directly connected to the host are immediately accessible. When the Zmob or host machine first comes up the directly accessible moblets are loaded with the appropriate software for implementing the next communication layer (virtual channel). Henceforth these moblets are inaccessible to anything but the host device driver.

The next layer is the *virtual channel*. This is the most general medium for communicating to moblets, and loses very little functionality when compared to the physical channel. Every moblet not directly connected to the host appears to the system to be a separate physical device independently readable and writable. Under the host Unix operating system these physical devices are called /dev/zmob/0 through /dev/zmob/255. When a host process writes to /dev/zmob/x, the message is routed though the host device driver to the directly connected moblets. These moblets distribute the message along the belt to moblet x where it is read as an ordinary message. If moblet x writes to any of the host-connected moblets, the message is routed through the host device driver to /dev/zmob/x where it can be read in the usual way by any Unix process.

The final layer of functionality is the *virtual processor*. This layer hides the identity of individual processors so users can write programs without needing to know which processors are free. It consists of two programs: the allocator and the loader. The allocator keeps a table of moblets that are in one of three states: free, busy, or unallocatable. Moblets in the last category include the host interface moblets and any which are believed to be broken. Busy moblets must eventually be freed by the process which requested them. A free moblet is available for allocation to a process.

The allocator is called by the loader. The loader accepts load modules which contain object code for several moblet processes and associated symbol tables. Object modules are identified in the symbol table by the names ZMOB0, ZMOB1, etc. Any object module may reference these names in its text.

The loader asks the allocator for enough moblets to hold all its object modules. It then loads each moblet with the appropriate object code, changing any references to ZMOBx to refer to the actual moblet address as returned by the allocator. In this way several different groups can share the Zmob without interference as long as the total number of processors needed does not exceed 256.

5. Performance

this space intentionally left blank

6. Summary - Advantages and Disadvantages

Most of the difficulties encountered with Zmob so far relate to the choice of the Z-80 microprocessor. The Z-80 is a powerful computing engine and has become the workhorse of the home computer field. Its instruction set and basic execution speed would be perfectly adequate for general parallel processing research except for two things. First is the inability to address more than 64k of memory without bank switching. This is the same problem encountered by C.mmp [6] so it was not unexpected. Zmob's focus was on higher degrees of parallel programming and it has close to an order of magnitude more processors than any other general purpose MIMD machine yet built (excluding local networks). Only an inexpensive microprocessor could achieve this degree of parallelism, and the most widely available processor during Zmob's design was the Z-80.

The second difficulty with the Z-80 processor is the lack of a privileged mode of instruction execution. If several people wish to use the Zmob at once they should be excluded from ever interfering with one another by accidently writing to one another's moblets. This kind of exclusion is most logically done in system software residing in each moblet. Unfortunately there is no way to protect memory in the Z-80 or to prevent user code from writing any arbitrary message to the belt. Memory protection and privileged instructions for accessing protected memory would solve this problem and make for a much more reliable multi-user machine.

More recent microprocessor designs, such as the Motorola 68000, do not have either of these difficulties. One possible future change to Zmob would be to replace the Z-80 processor boards with a more powerful microprocessor board. Zmob's design intentionally separates mailstop from processor logic so such a replacement would not be difficult either logically or physically.

The conveyor belt design also has certain problems. First is the difficulty of implementing a *promiscuous mode* mailstop. The term *promiscous mode* is borrowed from the Ethernet literature [5], where it refers to a machine which reads every message passing by regardless of its intended recipient. The difficulty of promiscous mode on the conveyor belt is that a message may be removed once it is read, and therefore if moblet A sends a message to moblet B which removes it, a promiscuous mailstop located downstream on the conveyor belt from both A and B will never see any of the message passing between them. This problem can be overcome since messages are not really removed from the belt but only have their *bin full* bit cleared, but the solution still requires considerable special purpose hardware on the belt.

A more serious difficulty occurs in the limitation on processor to processor communication. Although the entire conveyor belt is shifting 48 bits every 111 nanoseconds, any two processors can communicate at a rate determined by the total number of processors on the belt. Thus with 7 processors a message can be exchanged every microsecond, certainly fast enough. But a 4096 processor Zmob (the maximum permitted by the 12 bit moblet addresses) permits a message exchange only once every .4 milliseconds, a data rate of approximately 32kbits/second.

A final problem is really just a lessening of expectations. During the Zmob design it was felt that the pattern matching facilities would be extremely powerful and utilized by almost all Zmob applications. It now appears that 12 bits is just not enough for the kinds of pattern matching that would benefit most applications, so patterns have not received the kind of usage that was anticipated.

However, these disadvantages do not detract seriously from the Zmob's advantages. It has a large number of general purpose processors, more than any other general purpose multiprocessing system. Its processors use distributed memory rather than shared, permitting simpler operating systems. The processors are extremely well-known, permitting easy access to existing software and wizards. The total interprocessor bandwidth is extremely high, the processor-to-processor communication speed is reasonable, and the total price is less than a large midi-computer. Zmob is in use on a daily basis playing music, inverting matrices, solving problems, doing C-language remote procedure calls, and running other experimental applications for its users.

7. Acknowledgements

Zmob was first conceived in Spring 1979 by a group of faculty and graduate students at the University of Maryland, including Chuck Rieger, Azriel Rosenfeld, Pete Stewart, Bob Bane, Randy Trigg, Angela Wu, and Todd Kushner. Detailed design and construction was begun in the Fall of 1979 by Chuck Rieger assisted by Bob Bane and Randy Trigg. A wire-wrapped 2-processor prototype was operational a year later. The first printed circuit boards were tested the following year in Spring 1982, when Mark Weiser began directing the project, and fabrication of the 256 processor version was begun at that time. Performance data courtesy of the Numerical Analysis Laboratory, especially Robert van de Geijn, the Maryland Parallel Problem Solving Laboratory, and the Systems Performance Laboratory, all in the Computer Science Department, University of Maryland.

REFERENCES

[1]   D. R. Boggs and R. M. Metcalfe, "Ethernet: Distributed Packet Switching for Local Computer Networks," *Communications of the ACM* **19**, 7, pp. 395-404, July 1976.

[2]   Todd Kushner, Angela Y. Wu, and Azriel Rosenfeld, "Image Processing on ZMOB," *IEEE Transactions on Computers* **C-31**, 10, pp. 943-951, October 1982.

[3]   Richard F. Rashid, An inter-process communication facility for UNIX, CMU-CS-80-124 June 1980.

[4]   Chuck Rieger, Robert Bane, Craig Stanfill, Randy Trigg, and Mark Weiser, Three ZMOB Papers for the CAPAIDM Hot Springs Conference, Univ.of Md., CSD, TR1099 September 1981.

[5]   J. F. Shoch and J. A. Hupp, "Measured Performance of an Ethernet Local Network," *Communications of the ACM* **23**, 12, pp. 711-721, Dec 1980.

[6]   W. A. Wulf and C. G. Bell, "C.mmp--A Multi-Mini-Processor," *Proceedings of the AFIPS Fall Joint Computer Conference* **41**, pp. 765-777, 1972.

Aquarius -- A High Performance Computing System for Symbolic/Numeric Applications

Alvin M. Despain and Yale N. Patt

Computer Science Division
University of California, Berkeley

ABSTRACT

The Aquarius project at Berkeley is an on-going investigation [1] whose ultimate research goal is to determine how enormous improvements in performance can be achieved in a machine specialized to calculate some very difficult "real" problems in design automation, discrete simulation, expert systems, and signal processing. Our approach can be characterized by three important points: (1) Aquarius is to be a MIMD machine made of heterogeneous processing elements, each of which is tailored to accommodate its own individual processing requirements, (2) it is to exploit parallelism at all levels of execution, and (3) it is to support logic-programming at the ISP level. This paper defines the systems architecture of Aquarius, and describes its key innovative features. The current status of the project and our immediate future plans are delineated. Preliminary measurements which auger well for our goal of massive improvements in performance are included.

1. INTRODUCTION

1.1. The Execution Environment

The objective of the Aquarius project is to determine how a very large improvement in performance can be achieved in a machine specialized to solve some very difficult problems which are characterized by intensive numerical calculations tightly coupled to substantial symbolic manipulations, both within an algorithm that requires computing over a search space. We believe that such an execution environment characterizes the requirements of many expert systems. We also believe, as we described in [1], that such an execution environment models the way humans (e.g., engineers) solve problems. Finally, we believe that an execution environment that embodies the above characteristics can achieve the enormous improvements in performance that we are seeking.

1.2. Design Considerations

We plan to obtain radical improvements in performance in several important ways: (1) Aquarius supports a new style of computing, the use of a variant of logic programming (initially, PROLOG) as the primary control mechanism for the problem solution process. (2) Aquarius is a heterogeneous MIMD machine, tailoring the processing elements to the requirements of the intended set of applications. (3) Aquarius exploits parallelism at several levels of concurrency, from its partitioned memory address space to its use of restricted data flow techniques to implement the architecture.

Aquarius, is driven in the direction of high performance. Cost is very much a secondary consideration. Aquarius believes that very high performance demands tailoring the architecture to the application space. This means different processors for handling logic programming, numerical computations, and I/O processing. It means a high performance interconnect system. It means exploiting VLSI technology, but for performance reasons, not for the cost considerations of replicating chips.

1.3. The Status of Aquarius

While the ideas behind Aquarius have been crystallizing in our minds for some time now, the actual work as a unified project has been going on for about two years. This paper reports the current status of the project, and describes our plans for the immediate future.

Section 2 describes the systems architecture. It is evolving from Aquarius I, an attached logic-programming processor communicating to a host (NCR/32) over NCR's 32-bit PM bus, to Aquarius II, a heterogeneous MIMD machine containing separate tailored logic, numeric, and I/O processors, and a memory partitioned into a small shared synchronization store accessible over a shared bus and a large store accessible by all processing elements via a full cross-bar switch.

Section 3 describes our work with Prolog. A full compiler for Prolog has been written itself in Prolog, and is running on our simulator of Aquarius I. We have also achieved significant speed-ups in the performance of Prolog by identifying (statically, at compile time) AND parallelism, which allows AND sub-goals to be evaluated concurrently, and by introducing intelligent backtracking.

Section 4 describes our work on designing and implementing a logic processor. We are calling our first logic processor, the PLM. It is fully designed, and is in the process of being fabricated. Our simulations, see Table 1, predict that when it is operational (early 1985), it will be the highest performing PROLOG engine available.

Section 5 describes our current attempts at exploiting concurrency at the microarchitecture level. We have defined a new microarchitecture, a restricted data flow engine, which executes the data flow graph of a part of the dynamic instruction stream. We are calling this microengine HPS for high performance substrate. It is a generalization and modification of the floating point unit of the IBM 360/91. We have simulated the implementation of a major part of a complex architecture (the VAX 11), with promising results, as shown in Table 2.

2. SYSTEMS ARCHITECTURE

2.1. Heterogeneous Processors

The systems architecture of Aquarius, see figure 1, is to be a heterogeneous MIMD machine with separate processors tailored to accommodate the specialized requirements of logic programming, numeric computation, and I/O processing. The memory system will be partitioned into a small shared memory to handle synchronization functions, and a large memory for storing the usual instruction streams and data. We expect the ratio of unsynchronized to synchronized memory accesses to be about 100 to 1.

Many of our insights have come from our work on Aquarius I, the first phase of our work. Aquarius I, which is nearing completion (see figure 2), consists of an attached Prolog processor, the PLM, connected to a general purpose host machine, the NCR/32, via the NCR 32-bit PM bus.

The individual processing elements will be, at least initially, one of three kinds: a Parallel Prolog Processor, capable of parallel unification, a floating point arithmetic processor, capable of executing IEEE standard floating point arithmetic, and an I/O processor, capable of optimizing on some of the operating system critical functions.

Reprinted from *The Proceedings of COMPCON '85*, 1985, pages 376-382.

PERFORMANCE ESTIMATES FOR LOGIC-PROGRAMMING SYSTEMS			
DETERMINISTIC CONCATENATE (ONLY).			
Machine	System	Performance	Reference
Berkeley PLM	(TTL)/Compiled	425,000 LIPS	Simulator result
TICK & WARREN	VLSI	415,000 LIPS	Est: Tick&Warren
SYMBOLICS3600	Microcoded	110,000 LIPS	Est: Tick&Warren
DEC 2060	Warren Compiled	43,000 LIPS	Warren
J. 5th Gen PSI	Microcoded	30,000 LIPS	Est: PSI paper
IBM 3033	Waterloo	27,000 LIPS	Warren
VAX-780	Macrocoded	15,000 LIPS	Est: Tick&Warren
SUN-2	Quintus Comp.	14,000 LIPS	Warren
LMI/LAMBDA	Uppsala	8,000 LIPS	Warren
VAX-780	POPLOG	2,000 LIPS	Warren
VAX-780	M-Prolog	2,000 LIPS	Warren
VAX-780	C-Prolog	1,500 LIPS	Warren
SYMBOLICS3600	Interpreter	1,500 LIPS	Warren
PDP 11/70	Interpreter	1,000 LIPS	Warren
Z-80	MicroProlog	120 LIPS	Warren
Apple-II	Interpreter	8 LIPS	Warren
PERFORMANCE ON GENERAL BENCHMARK PROGRAMS			
Machine	System	Performance	Reference
Berkeley PLM	(TTL)/Compiled	205,000 LIPS	Simulator result
LMI/LAMBDA	Micro/Compiled	12,400 LIPS	LMI Corp.
J. 5th Gen PPC	Microcoded	10,000 LIPS(est)	NTIS (#N83-31379)
LM-2	Microcoded	9,500 LIPS	Prolog Digest v2.20
LMI/LAMBDA	Macro/Compiled	6,200 LIPS	LMI Corp.
SYMBOLICS 3600	Microcoded	5,000 LIPS	Prolog Digest v2.20
LMI/LAMBDA	Micro/Interpreter	3,400 LIPS	LMI Corp.
LMI/LAMBDA	Macro/Interpreter	1,700 LIPS	LMI Corp.
Apple-II	Pascal-Interpreter	10 LIPS	Colmerauer
PERFORMANCE ON THE WARREN BENCHMARK			
(list30 list50 times10 divide10 log10 ops8 palin25 query)			
Machine	System	Performance	Reference
Berkeley PLM	(TTL)/Compiled	149,216 LIPS	Simulator result
LMI/LAMBDA	Micro/Compiled	12,400 LIPS	LMI Corp.
DEC 2060	Warren Compiled	12,175 LIPS	Warren Thesis

Table 1: Performance Comparison Among Logic Programming Systems

Measurements	Benchmark				
	1	2	3	4	5
Performance (MIPS, 200ns clock)	6.25	6.16	7.27	6.50	6.37
result distribution network bandwidth	6	6	7	7	6
node table size	35	25	35	35	26

Table 2: Performance of HPS

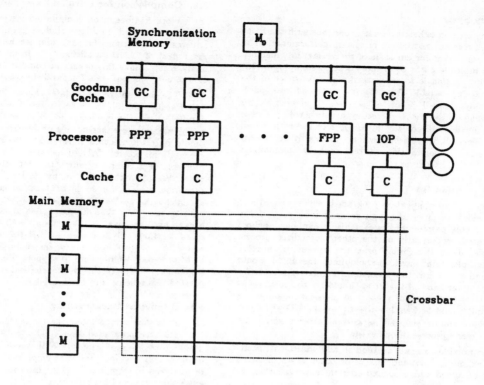

Figure 1: Aquarius Architecture

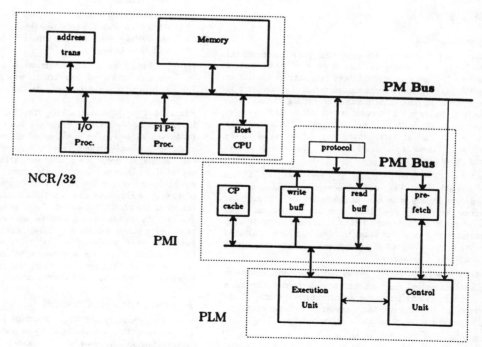

Figure 2: Aquarius-I System Architecture

2.2. The Memory System

The memory partition is based on our experience with the PLM that bus bandwidth was our bottleneck in system performance. The fundamental problem is that for our style of processing, i.e., memory intensive, we need multiple paths to memory when we employ multiple processors. Our solution is to separate the address space of the shared (synchronization) variables from the rest of the address space. Since we expect only about 1 % of the accesses to involve shared variables, we can handle the cache coherency problem with a Goodman cache [2], and the bulk of the memory accesses with a full cross-bar switch. Since VLSI cross-bar switches can easily implement up to about 16 x 16 cross points, this will represent the nominal size of our system.

2.3. Processing on Aquarius

The processing of an application program is supervised by the PLM processor, which executes the logic-programming part of the calculations. It creates parallel processes (this is explained below) that can be executed concurrently on the other, specialized processors. For example, if, in the Prolog program, a numeric, floating point, matrix multiplication should be required, the PLM would create a process and dispatch it to a specialized numeric processor for execution. On the other hand, if the PLM should try to access a virtual memory location that was not present in physical memory, the memory access fault would be handled directly by the I/O processor, and the PLM would simply suspend its current process and begin executing another ready process (if one exists).

This scheme provides a ready method to add additional special processors. For example, front-end image, or other types of signal processors, could be added and brought under the supervision of the PLM, executing a Prolog control program.

3. COMPILER ISSUES

3.1. The Prolog Compiler

One of our accomplishments achieved this year has been the the implementation of a Prolog-to-PLM compiler. The source language is close to C-Prolog and the target language is similar to that defined in [3]. Our goals were to implement the compiler in Prolog in a hierarchical and modular manner according to good program development techniques. The code generated by the compiler was to be highly optimized, both for time and space. Preferably, the compiler was to be fast and as determinate as possible, while at the same time performing these optimizations. We have largely succeeded in most of these goals.

The compiler was designed primarily by Peter Von Roy [4], but extended more recently [5]. The idea of compiling Prolog and of writing a compiler in Prolog was first put forward in [6], and our experience confirms Warren's belief that both are good ideas. The implementation of the compiler showed that it is possible to develop large Prolog programs in a modular manner. Our compiler is divided into separate sections handling files, procedures, and clauses, which interact across a narrow interface.

The compiler generates highly optimized code, and compares favorably with hand-compiled code. A number of register allocation strategies permit environment trimming to minimize the size of the stack and the attempt to minimize the number of register transfers. There is also a large repertoire of peephole optimizations.

Future work on the compiler includes the implementation of assert and retract. These will require built-in predicates to modify the code previously generated by the compiler. A scheme has been designed [7] and will soon be implemented.

Modes have not yet been implemented, but could be used to improve the code further.

3.2. Compilation for Parallel Execution

Work has begun on compilation issues concerning parallel execution of 'standard' Prolog, including parallel unification and parallel streams of execution. In particular we have been able to extract a great deal of 'AND-Parallelism' [8] from a static data dependency analysis [9]. Since this occurs at compile time, it allows the generation of very efficient code for parallel execution.

The alternative candidate clauses in a procedure represent 'OR-Parallelism' [8]. However, while it is simple to execute these in parallel, it may be inefficient to do so, since alternative answers to a query may not be either needed or desired. Thus any 'OR-Processes' should only be executed if there are spare resources available after executing all possible 'AND-Processes'. This presents and interesting problem for a compiler, which (by definition) can only create static code. We solve this problem by 'forking' a process from the main execution stream for each next 'OR-Clause', effectively 'looking-ahead' for the next alternative clause. The new process is assigned a priority one lower than its parent, so all 'OR-Processes' only run in background relative to the main 'AND-Processes'. The system scheduler then only executes an 'OR-Process' when there are otherwise idle resources. Some new instructions have been added to the PLM processor architecture to support this scheme [10]. We are just beginning to explore this approach, and as yet, we have not incorporated this scheme into our compiler.

3.3. Intelligent Backtracking

It is shown in [9] that the static data dependency analysis (of Prolog source programs), can yield a collection of data dependency graphs (one for each clause). With these graphs, a more intelligent form of backtracking than that employed in Prolog interpreters, can be achieved by compilation [11]. In order to achieve this, we distinguish three types of backtracking.

(1) Backtracking which occurs when a literal is called in forward execution and fails.

(2) Backtracking which occurs when a literal is backtracked into during backward execution (backtracking), which is invoked by an initial failure that occurred **inside** the clause of the literal, and then fails.

(3) Backtracking which occurs when a literal is backtracked into during backward execution, which is invoked by an initial failure that occurred **outside** the clause of the literal, and then fails.

For each type of backtracking, the backtrack literal of each body literal can be determined from the data dependency graph. Thus a backtrack table can be constructed at compile time. At run-time, a choice-point table, which records untried clauses for each procedure call, is maintained. Two new instructions, **enter** and **make**, are invented to incorporate this intelligent backtracking into PLM. A **make** instruction is inserted before a procedure call to catch failure of that procedure, so that on failure PLM can use the information stored in backtrack table and choice-point table to backtrack intelligently. An **enter** instruction is inserted after a procedure call so that the untried candidate clauses can be recorded in the choice-point table. It is shown in [11] that, with this scheme, redundant backtracking steps can sometimes be avoided with very little run-time overhead. We are now incorporating this scheme into our PLM processor architecture and the compiler.

4. THE PLM PROCESSOR

The Programmed Logic Machine (PLM) is the first experimental processor that we are building as part of the Aquarius project. It is an attached processor which connects via NCR's 32-bit PM bus to the host NCR/32 processor. We have simulated it at several levels of detail during its design, and have now constructed it in TTL logic. It is composed of about TTL 300 chips, ranging from simple gates to LSI circuits (e.g. PLA's). At the time of this writing, the TTL version of the processor has been constructed, and is being debugged.

The design of the PLM is based on an abstract model for Prolog execution and instruction set architecture (ISA) originally described by Warren [3] and modified by Dobry, Patt and Despain [7]. Under this model, the address space of the PLM is divided into two separate and distinct areas, the Code Space and the Data Space. The Code Space is a pseudo-static area (pseudo-static due to the Prolog predicates **assert** and **retract**). It contains the code constituting the Prolog program and other information used to describe atoms (akin to the property lists of LISP). Items in the Code Space have variable length; addressing is at the byte level. The instruction prefetch unit and some built-in functions have access to the Code Space.

The Data Space contains tagged 32-bit words representing all data items and state information for a running Prolog program. It is addressed as 32-bit words. For data items, of the 32 bits, as few as 4 and as many as 6 bits are used for tags depending on the type of the data item. Four data types are distinguishable by the processor via two primary tag bits. They are **reference** representing Prolog variables, both bound and unbound; **constant** representing various types of constant data; and two forms of compound data, **list** and **structure**. In addition, each data item has a cdr-bit in its tag field to support a cdr-coded representation of compound data, and a garbage collection bit used by an external garbage collection mechanism (via a built-in function). Secondary tag bits (and in the case of constants, possibly tertiary tag bits in the identifier field) may further refine the data types, but these are generally not recognized by the instruction set and are used only by built-in functions.

The Data Space is further divided into three main areas. The Heap contains all of the compound data items generated by the program and possibly global variables (as well as an area for "side-effect" variables used by some built-in functions). It is allocated as a LIFO and only deallocated upon backtracking. It is the area which participates in garbage collection. The Stack contains two forms of frames, environments and choice points. An environment, allocated for an individual clause, contains a small amount of state information associated with the clause and space for all permanent variables (variables not residing in registers) used by the clause. A choice point contains sufficient state information to restore the state of the processor in the event of failure and subsequent backtracking. Environments and choice points are created and removed by explicit instructions in the instruction set. The Stack is allocated and deallocated as a LIFO and is not garbage collected. The Trail contains pointers to the variables in the Stack and Heap which have been bound and must be unbound upon backtracking. It is allocated and deallocated as a LIFO. In addition to the above areas, a small scratchpad area called the PDL is used during unification of nested lists and structures. Though logically part of the Data Space, in the PLM the PDL is physically located in the execution unit.

4.1. Preliminary Measurements

The PLM processor has been extensively simulated [12] using benchmark programs. Table 1 compares the performance of the PLM processor to estimates of other Prolog execution systems. The benchmark programs are mostly from the thesis of Warren [6]. It is interesting to note that the performance of the PLM is expected to be about ten times that of the highest performance operational system, and about the same as the performance estimate for the

processor proposed by Tick and Warren [13]. At the time of this writing, the TTL version of the PLM processor is being debugged, so no actual performance data is available, but preliminary tests have confirmed the simulation results so far.

5. THE MICROARCHITECTURE

5.1. HPS

HPS is a restricted data flow microarchitecture targeted for implementing high performance computing engines. It is an expansion and generalization of ideas originally put forward in the floating point unit of the IBM 360/91. Our approach is to implement the architecture in three tiers, the programming logic level of control at the top (much like what CEDAR [14] proposes), classical control flow in the middle, and fine granularity data flow at the bottom. One can argue that the top layer is algorithm oriented, the middle layer is the classical ISP architecture and that the bottom layer is the microarchitecture.

We are calling the bottom layer HPS (for high performance substrate), reflecting the notion that it can be used to implement very dissimilar middle layer control flow architectures. Our model of the bottom layer (i.e., fine granularity data flow) is not unlike that of Dennis [15], Arvind [16], and others, but with some very important differences, which will be discussed below.

An abstract view of HPS is shown in figure 3. Instructions are fetched and decoded from a dynamic instruction stream, shown at the top of the figure. The figure implies that the instruction stream is taken from a sequential control flow ISP architecture. While that will probably usually be the case, it is not a necessary part of the HPS specification. What is necessary is that, for each instruction, the output of the decoder which is presented to the Merger for handling by HPS is a data flow graph.

A very important part of the specification of HPS I is the notion of the active instruction window. Unlike classical data flow machines, it is not the case that the data flow graph for the entire program is in the machine at one time. We define the active window as the set of ISP instructions whose corresponding data flow nodes are currently being worked on in the data flow microengine.

As the instruction window moves through the dynamic instruction stream, HPS executes the entire instruction stream. Parallelism which exists within the window is fully exploited by the microengine. This parallelism is limited in scope; ergo, the term "restricted data flow."

We have chosen this restricted data flow execution model because our studies have shown that the parallelism available from the middle control flow tier is highly localized. We argue that, by restricting the active instruction window, we can exploit almost all of the inherent parallelism in the program while incurring very little of the synchronization costs which would be needed to keep the entire program around as a total data flow graph.

The Merger takes the data flow graph corresponding to each ISP instruction and, using a generalized Tomasulo algorithm to resolve any existing data dependencies, merges it into the entire data flow graph for the active window. Each node of the data flow graph is shipped to one of the node tables where it remains until it is ready to fire.

When all operands for a data flow node are ready, the data flow node is fired by transmitting the node to the appropriate functional unit. The functional unit (an ALU, memory, or i/o device) executes the node and distributes the result, if any, to those locations where it is needed for subsequent processing: the node tables, the Merger (for resolving subsequent dependencies) and the Fetch Control Unit (for bringing new instructions into the active window). When all the data flow nodes for a particular instruction have been executed, the instruction is said to have executed. An instruction is retired from the active window when it has executed and all the instructions before it have retired. All side effects to memory are taken care of when an instruction retires from the active window. This is essential for the correct handling of precise interrupts [17].

The instruction fetching and decoding units maintain the degree of parallelism in the node tables by bringing new instructions into the active window, which results in new data flow nodes being merged into the data flow node tables.

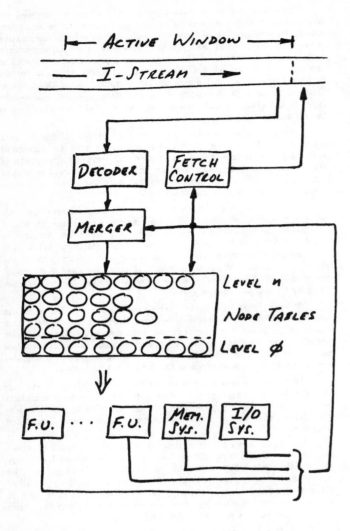

FIGURE 3. HPS. ABSTRACT MODEL

The major characteristics of the simulation model are the following: the maximum active instruction window, the cache, the branch prediction scheme, the node merging rate, and the penalty of branch prediction failure. The model is established to catch the parallelism in the instruction stream which can be potentially exploited by HPS. We implemented the 115 most frequently used opcodes from the VAX instruction set and all the addressing modes.

The instruction window size was set sufficiently high (32) that it should not be a performance limitation for any node merging rate that we experimented with. We expect that for low node merging rates this upper limit of 32 will never be achieved and the window size can be lowered without affecting performance.

Our measurements are presented in Table 2. These measurements assume that the engine has the capability to merge 8 nodes per cycle into the HPS data path. The potential performance was between 6.16 and 7.27 VAX MIPS for the five benchmarks that we tested. The hardware requirements were measured in terms of two critical hardware resources: node table size and distribution network bandwidth. The size of the node table supports our claim on the low synchronization overhead. That is, we can design the node table with fast and expensive logic because the size is so small.

6. CONCLUSIONS

This paper has presented the work going on under the Aquarius project. We have identified the issues that we consider important to tackle if we are to achieve very high performance, and we have reported our preliminary results.

7. ACKNOWLEDGMENTS

As always, we acknowledge first our students, who are very much a part of the Aquarius project: Jung-Herng Chang, Wayne Citrin, Tep Dobry, Barry Fagin, Wen-mei Hwu, Steve Melvin, Carl Ponder, Michael Shebanow, Peter Van Roy (temporarily on leave to serve in the Belgian Army), Jean Wong, and Robert Yung. We also acknowledge the stimulating interactions with R. Fateman, W. Kahan, Richard M. Karp, Eugene Lawler, Alan Smith, and Vason Srini. Finally, we acknowledge the financial support of several institutions. In particular, this work was partially sponsored by the Defense Advanced Research Projects Agency (DOD) under contract no. N00039-84-C-0089 and contract no. N00039-83-C-0107, and by the California MICRO program. We also thank the Digital Equipment Corporation and the NCR Corporation for their generous contributions of equipment, and for funding part of the work done on the project.

References

1. A. M. Despain and Y. N. Patt, "The Aquarius Project," *Digest of Papers, COMPCON Spring 1984*, pp.364-367, IEEE Press (Spring 1984).

2. J.R. Goodman, "Using Cache Memory to Reduce Processor-Memory Traffic," *Computer Architecture Conference Proceedings*, pp.124-131, IEEE Computer Society Press (June, 1983).

3. D. H. D. Warren, *An Abstract Prolog Instruction Set*, AI Center, SRI International, Menlo Park, CA 94025 (1983).

4. Peter Van Roy, "A Prolog Compiler for the PLM," *Masters Report*, Computer Science, University of California (August 1984).

5. Wayne Citrin, Peter Van Roy, and Alvin M. Despain, "A Prolog Compiler," *Submitted to International Symposium on Logic Programming - 1985* (November 1984).

6. D. H. D. Warren, "Applied Logic - Its Use and Implementation as Programming Tool," Ph.D. Thesis, Univ. Edinburgh, Scotland (1977). Available as Tech. Note 290, AI Center, SRI International

5.2. Preliminary Measurements

Our first experiment with HPS was to partially simulate the VAX architecture. We did this for several reasons, not the least of which was to acquire some experience with implementing a complex architecture with which we were familiar. We felt that this experience would we useful when we begin the implementation of a programming logic processor with HPS. In this section, we describe the simulation and report the measurements which we obtained.

We also need to point out (lest anyone take these results out of context) that this was a partial simulation, and did not handle a number of the key aspects of the VAX architecture for which performance penalties would be incurred. We include the (optimistic) data none the less because it gives a first cut at how HPS can be used to implement a very complex ISP architecture.

7. T.P. Dobry, Y.N. Patt, and A.M. Despain, "Design Decisions Influencing the Microarchitecture For A Prolog Machine," *MICRO 17 Proceedings* (Oct. 1984).

8. John S. Conery, "The AND/OR Model for Parallel Interpretation of Logic Programs," Ph.D. Thesis, Dept. Information and Computer Science, Univ. Calif., Irvine (1983).

9. J.-H. Chang, A. M. Despain, and D. DeGroot, "AND-Parallelism of Logic Programs Based on A Static Data Dependency Analysis," *to appear in Compcon Spring 85* (August 15, 1984).

10. T. P. Dobry, Jung-Herng Chang, Alvin M. Despain, and Yale N. Patt, "Extending a Prolog Machine for Parallel Execution," *Submitted to Symposium on Logic Programming - 1985* (November 1984).

11. J.-H. Chang and A. M. Despain, "Semi-Intelligent Backtracking of Prolog Based on A Static Data Dependency Analysis," *to appear* (Sept. 12, 1984).

12. T. P. Dobry, Alvin M. Despain, and Yale N. Patt, "Performance Studies of a Prolog Machine Architecture," *Submitted to Symposium on Computer Architecture - 1985* (November 1984).

13. Evan Tick and David Warren, "Towards a Pipelined Processor," Tech. Report, SRI A.I. Center, Menlo Park, Ca. (Aug. 1983).

14. D. Gajski, D. Kuck, D. Lawrie, and A. Sameh, "CEDAR: A Large Scale Multiprocessor," *Comput. Arch. News* Vol. 11(1), pp.7-11 (Mar 1983).

15. Jack Dennis and David Misunas, "A Preliminary Architecture for a Basic Data Flow Processor," *SIGARCH Newsletter* Vol. 3(4), pp.126-162 (1974).

16. Arvind and Kim P. Gostelow, "A New Interpreter for Data Flow and its Implications for Computer Architecture," Technical Report #72, Dept. Info. & Comput. Sci., Univ.of Calif., Irvine CA (October 1975).

17. D. W. Anderson, F. A. Sparacio, and R. M. Tomasulo, "The IBM System/360 Model 91: Machine Philosophy and Instruction Handling," *IBM J. Res. Dev.* Vol. 11(1), pp.8-24 (1967).

New Generation Computing, 2 (1984) 105-129
OHMSHA,LTD. and Springer-Verlag

Dataflow Computing and Eager and Lazy Evaluations

Makoto AMAMIYA and Ryuzo HASEGAWA

Musashino Electrical Communication Laboratory,

Nippon Telegraph and Telephone Public Corporation,

3-9-11 Midori-cho Musashino-shi, Tokyo 180, Japan

Received 15 December 1983

Abstract   Eager and lazy evaluations in a dataflow model are proposed, Such evaluation enables nonstrict evaluation, structure data manipulation and nondeterminate computation. Several dataflow computation models are discussed from the viewpoint of their by-value and by-reference mechanisms, i. e., their token to data correspondence. It is shown that effective implementation is achieved by unifying both mechanisms. This implies the effective implementation of the lenient cons and lazy cons concept in list manipulation. Nonstrict list manipulation is shown to be useful for stream-oriented processing, and for nondeterminate computation combined with the nonstrict primitive operator, Arbiter. Several sample programs are included to show that concurrent processes and object-oriented programs can be intuitively described in functional language.

Keywords : Dataflow, Demand Driven, Eager/Lazy Evaluation, List Processing, Stream Processing, Lenient Cons, Lazy Cons

§1   Introduction

The dataflow computation model is a promising basis for highly-parallel computer architectures.[4,5,11,13] The reduction-based computation model, on the other hand, also has many good points that support functional and logic programming[10,8,17] because of its computation power, which includes lazy evaluation and higher-order function (partial computation) facilities. However, how to implement the hardware for a highly-parallel machine that realizes the reduction-based computation model has yet to be determined.

There are two ways to implement the reduction model. One is control-flow based ; that is, a number of von Neumann-type sequential processors run concurrently through packet communications. The ALICE[9] machine is considered to be in this category. The other is dataflow based ; that is, a number of dataflow processors are used instead of von Neumann-type control-flow processors. The dataflow-based architecture is more suitable for highly-parallel machine organization, since it can eliminate the gap that appears between intra-processor execution and inter-processor packet communications[21] if von Neumann processors are used.

This paper shows the dataflow model to be effective for implementing a highly-parallel reduction mechanism by discussing eager and lazy evaluation, nonstrict evaluation and their relations to nondeterminacy, based on the dataflow model (Higher-order function execution facilities in the dataflow model are discussed in other literature[18]).

The levels of computational capability in the dataflow model can be set according to the type of data assigned to the tokens flowing in the dataflow graphs. If the tokens are considered to be primitive data values, the model has little power for primitive data-driven computation (This is called a by-value mechanism[22]*). On the other hand, if cells (or pointers to them) that hold values or program codes are assigned to tokens, the model has greater power to support eager and lazy evaluations and higher-order function execution facilities (This is called a by-reference mechanism[22]*).

The eager evaluation mechanism makes it possible for producer processes and consumer processes to work concurrently. This mechanism provides high performance through highly-pipelined concurrent processing. The lenient cons concept[3] is a typical example of such eager evaluation. The lazy evaluation mechanism makes it possible to implement demand-driven control. In this case, the producer process suspends itself and resumes on demand sent from the consumer process. The lazy cons concept[14] is an example of such lazy evaluation.

The eager and lazy evaluations mechanism is very useful in supporting functional programming with the stream concept,[15] since determinate and nondeterminate programs can be described using an infinite recursive structure. This implies that concurrent processes and object-oriented programming can be written in functional style more intuitively.

§2 Reduction and Dataflow Models

After clarifying the relationship between the reduction and dataflow models, several computation structures are discussed from the viewpoints of dataflow control and the data mechanism.

2.1 Reduction Model versus Dataflow Model

There are three important considerations for evaluation of a functional program ; (1) eager and lazy evaluations, (2) call-by-value, call-by-name or call-by-need, and (3) strict or nonstrict evaluation.

Eager and lazy evaluations are a general evaluation-strategy concept. If the evaluation of expressions proceeds innermost, it is called an eager evaluation, and if it proceeds outermost, it is called a lazy evaluation.

When the eager and lazy evaluations concept is applied to a parameter mechanism in a function application, it is termed call-by-value, call-by-name or call-by-need. In a call-by-value mechanism, each argument of a function is evaluated before the function body is evaluated. In a call-by-name mechanism, a parameter that is called by name is not evaluated until it is encountered in the expression of the function body. In a call-by-need mechanism, a parameter is evaluated only the first time its value is actually needed, even if it is encountered several times in the function body. Thus, call-by-need is more efficient than call-by-name.

The strict and nonstrict evaluations concept is coordinate to the eager and lazy evaluations concept. In strict evaluation, all subexpressions, e1, e2,.., en, must be evaluated to specific values in order for the expression e(e1, e2,.., en) to be evaluated to a value. In nonstrict evaluation, on the other hand, the

---

* The terms by-value and by-reference are used with meanings slightly different from those in the literature (Ref. 22)).

expression may be evaluated to a value even if some of the subexpressions have no values. Therefore, only the nonstrict evaluation supports lazy evaluation. If eager evaluation is combined with nonstrict evaluation, it is called nonstrict eager evaluation.

A reduction model, which specifies only reduction (or rewriting) rules, does not explicitly express evaluation control. A dataflow model, on the other hand, can explicitly express execution control using a token-driven control mechanism in which tokens are used as data or control signals. In this sense, the dataflow model can be called an implementation model.

For example, in the conditional expression

$$\textbf{if } p(x) \textbf{ then } f(y) \textbf{ else } g(z), \tag{1}$$

the reduction model specifies only the following rewriting rule,

$$\textbf{if } p(x) \textbf{ then } f(y) \textbf{ else } g(z) \Longrightarrow f(y) \text{ if } p(x) \text{ is true,}$$
$$\textbf{if } p(x) \textbf{ then } f(y) \textbf{ else } g(z) \Longrightarrow g(z) \text{ if } p(x) \text{ is false.} \tag{2}$$

The dataflow model, however, can describe several implementations of evaluation control that satisfies the nonstrictness property of this rewriting rule.

2.2 Dataflow Model

In a dataflow model, programs are represented as a directed graph called the dataflow graph. The graph has several input ports and output ports. Nodes in the graph represent operations. There are two categories of operation : data manipulation and dataflow control. The former includes arithmetic operation, list manipulation and memory read or write while the latter includes switch operation, gate operation and linkage operation.

Node operations are enabled when tokens (called operands) arrive at input arcs, and the operation results are set to their output arcs. The result token on the output arc becomes the operand token for its destination nodes.

Execution starts when initial tokens are put into the input ports of the dataflow graph and is completed when result tokens are output from its output ports. In the course of computation, a number of tokens flow in the dataflow graph.

2.3 Nonstrict Evaluation in the Dataflow Model

Nonstrict evaluation is important for realizing lazy evaluation and nondeterminate computation. Three nonstrict evaluation levels are realized in the dataflow model. They are the function application, expression evaluation and primitive operation levels.

〔1〕 Nonstrictness in the function application

Nonstrictness in function application is implemented as a function linkage mechanism for partial execution.[3] The mechanism is shown in Fig. 1 for function application

$$(u, \ v) = f\ (x, y, z).$$

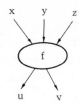

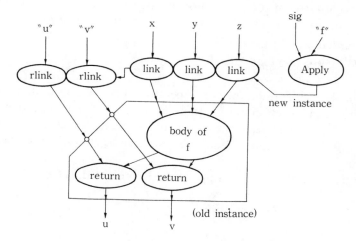

Fig. 1 Function application mechanism.

This graph shows that evaluation of the function body is initiated by signal, and it advances every time the value of x, y or z is received. Thus, if function f has values for u and v independent of whether the value of z is defined or not, then the evaluation can return those values.

〔2〕 **Nonstrictness in expression evaluation**

Nonstrict evaluation in the expression level is represented directly in dataflow graph using control tokens and gate nodes.

The dataflow implementation for conditional expression (1) is shown in Fig. 2, as an example. In this figure, predicate node p generates a Boolean token that controls the switch operation. Figure 2 (a) shows implementation of the

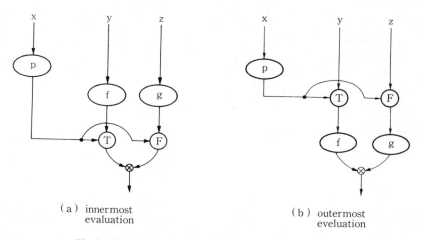

(a) innermost evaluation

(b) outermost eveluation

Fig. 2 Dataflow graph for **if** p(x) **then** f(y) **else** g(z).

innermost (nonstrict eager) evaluation, while Fig. 2 (b) shows implementation of the outermost (nonstrict lazy) evaluation. Both implementations satisfy the reduction rule for expression (1), since when p(x) is true (or false) the result is that of f(y) (or g(z)) independent of whether g(z) (or f(y)) has value or not.

〔3〕 **Nonstrict primitive operator**

In order to support nonstrict eager and lazy evaluations for structure data and nondeterminate computations, two nonstrict primitive operators are necessary.

One primitive is the cons operator for list manipulation.* The cons and car (or cdr) operations for list data are defined by the reduction rules:

$$car\ (cons\ (x, y)\ ) \Longrightarrow x,$$
$$cdr\ (cons\ (x, y)\ ) \Longrightarrow y.$$

In order to satisfy these rules, the cons operation must be nonstrict. That is, the cons operator cons (x, y) should output the result value independent of the evaluation of x or y. This resulting cons value is incomplete structure data with hole in it (Fig. 3). The implementation of this cons operator is described in the next Section.

Arbiter is another nonstrict primitive. Represented as (u, v) = Arb(x, y),

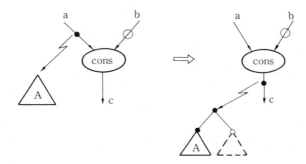

Fig. 3 Nonstrict cons operation.

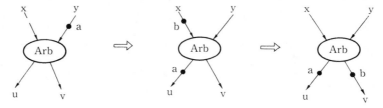

Fig. 4 Arbiter.

---

* Discussions on structure data manipulation are focused on list manipulation in this paper for two reasons. (1) Principal issues on structure data manipulation are inherent in list manipulation, and (2) stream-oriented processing (Ref. 23)) is realized in the framework of list processing.

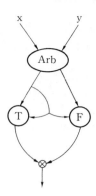

Fig. 5 Realization of nonstrict-or.

it has two inputs (x and y) and two outputs (u and v), as shown in Fig. 4. It outputs the first value to arrive, either x or y, to the left output port u, and outputs the remaining value to the right port, v. Arbiter is inevitable to support nonstrict operations for nondeterminacy, including nonstrict-merge, nonstrict-or, nonstrict-and and the guarded command.[12] As an example, nonstrict-or implementation using Arbiter is shown in Fig. 5. Nonstrict-or returns true when either x or y is true, independent of the other value.

§3 Data Mechanism in Dataflow Models

In a dataflow model, several types of data are assigned to tokens. The most primitive dataflow model assigns the data itself, such as number, Boolean, or structure data to tokens. The computation mechanism built on this assignment is called a by-value mechanism. More advanced dataflow models assign cells, such as variable, list or pointer to program code entry to tokens. The computation mechanism built on this assignment is called a by-reference mechanism. Even more sophisticated dataflow models, those that provide more elaborate computation control, are combination of by-value and by-reference mechanisms.

3.1 By-value Mechanisms

In by-value mechanisms, there is no notion of cells that hold data value, and all operations are directly driven by data. As the computation proceeds innermost by pure data driven control, it implements eager evaluation in principle, as shown in Fig. 6.

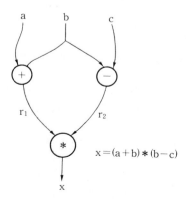

$$x = (a+b)*(b-c)$$

Fig. 6 By-value mechanism.

The by-value dataflow mechanism contains a problem caused by innermost evaluation. Although outermost evaluation is possible for expressions, the by-value mechanism needs complicated control to implement such outermost evaluations as call-by-name for function applications. That is, in the function application, unnecessary arguments may be evaluated, or in the worst case, some evaluation may never stop, since all of the arguments are evaluated before the function body is evaluated. For example, if conditional expression (1) is defined as a function, all its argument, p(x), f(y) and g(z), are evaluated eagerly. To avoid this, sophisticated control is necessary in the by-value mechanism.

3.2 By-reference Mechanisms

The by-reference mechanism assigns cells to tokens. All operations have their own operand value cells and a resulting value cell. Each cell is shared between two operations, i. e., used as the result cell for one operation and as the operand cell for its destined operation. Therefore it is necessary to control read and write accesses between operations. Either of two types of implementation are possible, depending on the read and write access control :

〔1〕 **Cell-driven eager evaluation**

One implementation is called cell-driven control because operations are initiated when operand cells arrive. The initiated operation tries to read-access its operand cell and waits for a value to be written by the preceding operation. A read-ready tag (r) is used to control such concurrent read and write accesses in each cell. A simple example of cell-driven control is shown in Fig. 7.

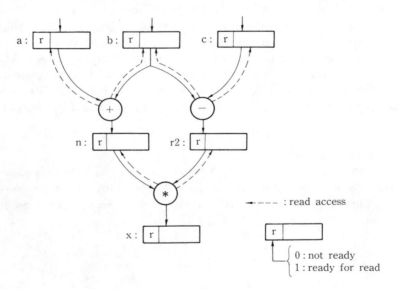

Fig. 7 By-reference mechanism (cell driven).

This mechanism realizes maximal eager evaluation, since all operations are initiated eagerly when their cell tokens arrive. However it causes two problems : the cost of memory management for cell allocation, and explosive operation activation. Still worse, it can not solve the call-by-name problem.

〔2〕 **Demand-driven lazy evaluation**

The other implementation is called demand-driven control because every operation is initiated when its value is required from its destined operation. In the course of execution, demand tokens flow against the direction of arc, then result data are returnd, as shown in Fig. 8. Initially, each cell has pointer to the

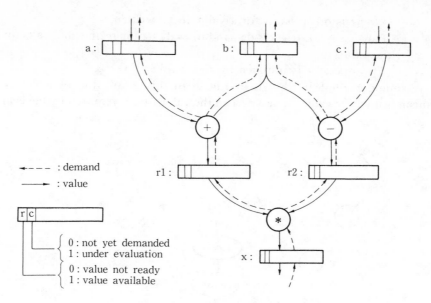

Fig. 8 By-reference mechanism (demand driven).

operation node that generates its value. When an operation is initiated, it reads its operand cell. If the cell contains no value, the read-access triggers a demand to the preceding operation and waits until the value arrives. To control this demand-triggering and value-awaiting mechanism, two tags are used in each cell : the read-ready tag and the demand-trigger tag.

This implementation, which realizes pure lazy outermost evaluation, solves the call-by-name problem, since function arguments are evaluated only when values are required in the function body evaluation.[16] However, this model has two problems in cost effectiveness. First, it is expensive to implement the demand-driven control mechanism. Second, computation takes much more time than data-driven control does because of the double flow of tokens.

3.3 Combined By-value and By-reference Mechanisms

More effective implementation of eager and lazy evaluations selectively uses the by-value and by-reference mechanisms. In this model, cells are allocated only to value names defined by, for example, value definition[1] or function arguments. Each cell has two tags, r and c, which are used for eager and lazy evaluations control. The contents of each cell is either an evaluated value or a pointer to a program code entry called a "recipe". When tag r is on, the cell contains a value and read access is permitted. When tag c is on, the contents of the cell is a recipe.

Five primitive operators, gcell, wrcd, bind, repl and eval, are used for cell-access control :

Gcell(s) : creates a new cell, sets tags r and c of the cell to off and returns the cell.

(This operator is initiated by signal token s.)

Wrcd(x, l) : writes program code entry (node name) n to cell x, sets tag r to on and returns the cell.

Bind(x, v) : writes value v to cell x, sets tag c to on and returns the cell.

Repl(x, v) : replaces cell x with value v and returns the cell.

Eval(x, s) : reads the value of cell x.

If tag r is off, it waits for a value to be written.

If tag c is on, it triggers demand to evaluate the recipe and waits for the value.

(This operator is initiated by signal token s.)

A simple example is shown in Fig. 9. In this graph, the by-reference mechanism is used for value name x. When the value of x is required by the eval

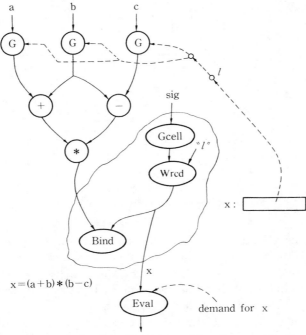

$$x = (a + b) * (b - c)$$

Fig. 9 Typical combined by-value and by-reference mechanism.

operator, a demand signal is triggered from cell x to the gate nodes to pass data a, b and c to the graph. Thus, the expression $(a + b) * (b - c)$ is evaluated by a by-value mechanism.

The function application mechanism for

$$(u, v) = f(g(x), y, h(z))$$

is shown in Fig. 10. In this example, eval operations for values x, y and z are

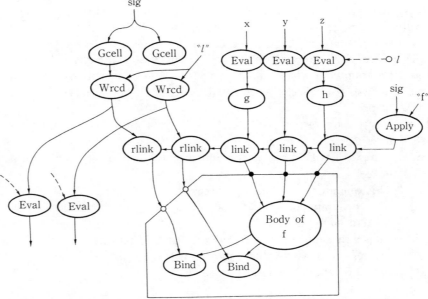

Fig. 10 Function application mechanism for by-value and by-reference combination.

initiated when demands are transmitted from the eval operation for value u or v (It should be noted that the implementation will realize eager evaluation, if the cells do not contain recipes (i. e., tag c is off) and demand signals are used so that the eval operator for each value is immediately initiated when each cell arrives).

3.4 Structure Data Manipulation

Although two by-value and by-reference models may be considered in structure data manipulation, the by-value model in which list data are directly assigned to tokens is not practical.

In the by-reference mechanism, list data are stored in a memory device called a structure memory, and pointers to the data are carried as tokens. Then the cons operator generates a cons cell in the structure memory, and outputs a token that points to the cell. The car (or cdr) operator reads the car (or cdr) field of the cell pointed to by the operand token. This model can implement the nonstrict cons operation, since each cons operator can output cons cell as a resulting value, independent of whether the cell has a car (or cdr) value or not.

The by-reference mechanism also enables two implementations of list processing : innermost eager evaluation (called lenient cons[3]), and outermost lazy evaluation (called lazy cons).[14]

In the lenient cons, cons operations are initiated on the arrival of an initiation signal, and the resulting cons cell is output while car (or cdr) value evaluation is proceeding. In lazy cons, on the other hand, the car (or cdr) value evaluation is initiated only when its value is demanded by the car (or cdr) operation. Two tags, r and c, are used also in car and cdr field of these two implementations, to control read and write accesses. A typical lazy cons implementation is shown in Fig. 11. If x and y are to be evaluated, the eval node will

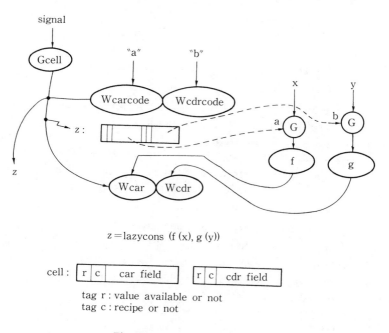

z = lazycons (f (x), g (y))

cell : | r | c | car field | | r | c | cdr field |

tag r : value available or not
tag c : recipe or not

Fig. 11 Lazycons implementation.

be substituted for the gate node. It should be noted that the lenient cons implementation will eliminate Wcarcode, Wcdrcode and two gate nodes from this graph.

§4 Eager and Lazy Evaluations

By selectively using the by-value and by-reference mechanisms, eager and lazy evaluations can effectively be realized in combination with structure data manipulation. In practical implementations, the compiler will eliminate unnecessary value cell allocation and produce an optimized dataflow graph, so that by-reference mechanism will only be used for structure data manipulations and explicitly specified lazy evaluation.

The process of delaying evaluation is specified explicitly by introducing a delay operator in functional language. For instance, delaying evaluation of the expression $E1(x, y, z)$ is specified as

$$E' \,(\textbf{delay } E(x, y, z)) \qquad \text{as an expression,}$$
$$\text{or} \quad E' \,(u) \textbf{ where } u = \textbf{delay } E(x, y, z) \qquad \text{as a value definition.}$$

The dataflow implementation of delaying and demanding the evaluation is shown in Fig. 12. As shown in that figure, delay operators expressed in source

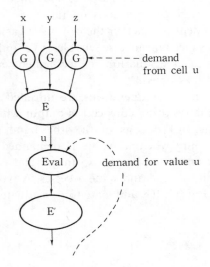

Fig. 12 Dataflow graph for $E'(u)$, $u = \textbf{delay } E(x, y, z)$.

language are represented as gate (or eval) nodes for input values in the compiled code (dataflow graph). Demanding the evaluation of $E(x, y, z)$ passes data x, y and z through the gates, if they are not delayed (If x, y or z is delayed, the eval operator is used in place of the gate operator). If delayed evaluations are nested, the demands to open gates are transmitted to the inner value names.

A typical example of this is conditional expression evaluation. For innermost evaluation like that in Fig. 2 (a),

if $p(x)$ **then delay** $f(y)$ **else delay** $g(z)$

is transformed into the dataflow graph in Fig. 13 (It should be noted that optimization of this graph leads to the graph in Fig. 2 (b)).

Call-by-need is specified using delay operators. For example, when function F is defined as

function $F(u) = E'(u)$,

call-by-need is specified by the formal argument in the function definition, such as

444

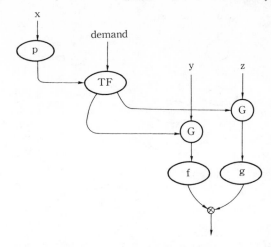

Fig. 13 Dataflow graph for **if** p(x) **then delay** f (y) **else delay** g(z).

function F (**delay** u) = E′ (u),

and by actual arguments in the function invocation, such as

F(**delay** E(x, y, z)).

(The compiler will automatically insert the delay operator for the actual argument.)

If the conditional expression is defined as function ff,

function ff(x, **delay** y, **delay** z) = **if** x **then** y **else** z,

for function application ff (p(x), f (y), g(z)), the evaluation of expressions f(y) and g(z) is delayed until they are demanded during evaluation of the conditional expression of function body ff. The dataflow graph for function ff is shown in Fig. 14 as an example of call-by-need implementation.

The lenient cons operation exploits parallelism maximally due to the nonstrict eager evaluation. That is, by using lenient cons operations, a stream-oriented concurrent program, in which the stream producer and its consumer run concurrently, can easily be described. For example, in the following program, which calculates summation of natural numbers, highly pipelined concurrent processing is realized between the natural number producer intseq(i), and its consumer summ(i, n).

summ(x, 100,0) **where** {x = intseq(1)} . —— top function,

function intseq(i) = cons(i, intseq(i + 1)).

function summ(x, n, a) = **if** n = 0 **then** a

         else summ(cdr(x), n−1, a + car(x)).

Though this program executes in a highly concurrent way, there is a problem in that function intseq is evaluated infinitely ; it never stops.

However, this infinity problem is solved using delayed evaluation. If the function intseq is defined using the delay operator, such as

function intseq(i) = cons(i, **delay** intseq(i + 1)),

function intseq is evaluated only when its value is required by the cdr operation in function summ.

Using the delay operator, lazy cons is formally defined as

lazycons(x, y) = = cons(delay x, delay y).

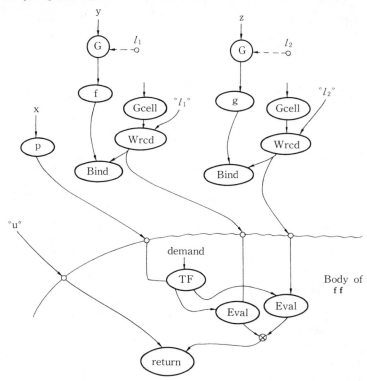

Fig. 14 Dataflow implementation of call-by-need in function ff.

Nondeterminate program implementation makes use of the nonstrict primitive operator, Arbiter. For example, nonstrict merge operation is defined as

$$\textbf{function } merge(x, y) = cons(a, merge(v, w))$$
$$\textbf{where } \{(u, v) = Arb(x, y),$$
$$a = car(u), w = cdr(u)\}.$$

The merge function merges two streams into one. This function realizes nondeterminate execution because the stream element that arrives earlier is put before the stream element arriving later, independent of whether the element has come from x or y.

Another example of nondeterminate computation is an implementation of guard.[12] The case expression

$$\textbf{case } \{Gdl (yl) \rightarrow El(x1),$$
$$Gd2(y2) \rightarrow E2(x2),$$
$$\cdots$$
$$Gdn(yn) \rightarrow En(xn)\}$$

means that one of the guarded expressions, Gdi(yi) -> Ei(x) that satisfies guard condition Gdi(yi), i. e. Gdi(yi) is evaluated to true, is selected and the value of Ei(x) is returned as its value. The dataflow implementation for this expression is shown in Fig. 15. The send node in the graph sends a signal to the node designated by its operand.

§5 Programming Examples of Eager and Lazy Evaluations

Several applications of eager and lazy evaluations are described in this Section. The program examples show that object oriented programming, co-routines and nondeterminacy can be described in functional language based on

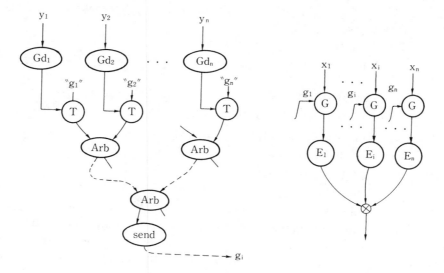

Fig. 15 Implementation of guard.

the stream-oriented concept. The application samples are adopted for comparison of descriptive capability with logic programming.[19,7] The programs are written in the functional language Valid-S, which is an extended version of Valid[1] for symbol manipulation.

5.1 Valid-S

To understand the program examples, it is first necessary to understand Valid-S. The major extension to the original version of Valid has been designed to unify its functional and logic programming features. However, in the following, only a subset is introduced, i. e., pattern matching facilities for both value definition and function invocation.

(1)　Patterns are described in the following list notation for lists a, b, c

$$[a. b] == cons(a, b), (== should be read "is defined to be")$$
$$[\ ] == nil,$$
$$[a, b] == [a. [b. [\ ]]] \ ,$$

Atom includes value names, function invocation, quoted constants, conditional expressions and case expressions.

(2)　Value definition is described as

　　Leftpatterns = Rightpatterns.

Value names to be defined should be included in Leftpatterns, while value names in Rightpatterns must be defined by other value definition in the block encompassing this value definition or by formal argument specification in the function head. Both Leftpatterns and Rightpatterns may be a tuple of patterns. The number of patterns in the tuple must be equal in Leftpatterns and Rightpatterns. If the left- and right-patterns do not match, the value definition is illegal and the execution is aborted. Example

$$[x.y] \ = ['a. 'b] \implies x = 'a, y = 'b,$$
$$['a, 'b. x] \ = ['a, 'b, 'c] \implies x = ['c],$$
$$(['a. x], ['b. y],z) = (['a. 'b], ['b, 'c], ['d, 'a])$$
$$\implies x = 'b, y = ['c], z = ['d, 'a],$$
$$['a, 'b, x] \ = [y,'b,'c] \implies if \ y = 'a \ then \ x = 'c \ else \ Error.$$

If [x | y], instead of [x. y], is used in the Rightpatterns, it means [x. **delay** y].

(3)   Function definition is described as

FunctionHead = Body.

. . .

FunctionHead = Body.,

where FunctionHead is of the form

FunctionName(Pattern, ..., Pattern),

and Body is an Expression.

Function invocation is described as

FunctionName(Pattern, ..., Pattern).

Function activation is pattern directed. That is, patterns in actual arguments are examined for matching to corresponding formal argument patterns in every candidate function head, and only the function with a head that succeeded in matching the all argument patterns is activated.

(4)   Expression is described as

PrimitiveExpression
where {ValueDefinition, ..., ValueDefinition}.

Value names used in PrimitiveExpression can be defined in a **where**{...} block. Value names defined in the block may also be used in the same block. PrimitiveExpression includes Pattern, ArithmeticExpression, TupleExpression, ConditionalExpression, CaseExpression (CaseExpression expresses nondeterminate choice of a guarded expression, as described in Section 4).

(5)   Sequential evaluation of Expressions is specified explicitly as

E2 **after** E1,

which means expression E2 is evaluated after expression E1.

5.2   Realization of the Object in Valid-S

The object, which is an active process that receives messages and performs action on its internal state according to the message received, is realized in functional style. The realization is similar to that of Concurrent Prolog based on the stream concept. Program 1 is a realization of a counter process. The top level function, manycounters(sig), is initiated by signal sig, and evaluates functions, input, umc, ct and output in parallel. The function input reads the commands

```
manycounters(sig)
= output(rs)
     where {rs = umc(msg), msg = input(sig)}
umc( [ [x. nam]. nmsg] )
= if x = 'create then [z. umc(nmsg) ]
          where {s = usc(nam, nmsg), z = ct(s, 0)}
     else umc(nmsg).
usc(nam, [ [naml. op]. nmsg])
= if nam = naml then [op | usc(nam, nmsg)]
     else usc(nmsg).
usc (nam, [ ['delete. nam]. nmsg]) = [].
ct(['clear. nmsg], count) = ct(nmsg, 0).
ct(['up. nmsg],count) = ct(nmsg,count + 1).
ct(['down. nmsg], count) = ct(nmsg, count − 1).
ct([ ['show. v]. nmsg], count)
= [bind(v, count). ct(nmsg, count)].
```

input(sig) = [read(sig) | input(sig)].
output([cs. ns]) = output(ns) **after** print(cs).
bind(x, y) = [x. y].

Program 1 Counter process.

one by one and generates a message stream. The message stream, which is produced using the lazy evaluation mechanism, is an infinite sequence of commands. The function umc picks up the command 'create, and attaches the specified process name, then creates a new counter process, usc. The process usc extracts the message to its own, and transmits it to the own counter object, ct. Counter object ct takes action according to the message, 'clear, 'up, or 'down, and changes its counter value. If ct receives the message ['show. x], it binds the counter value to variable x. Message communications between processes are shown in Fig. 16.

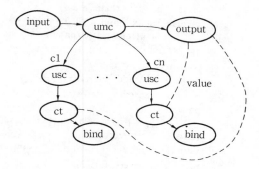

Fig. 16 Communications structure for a many-counter system.

The characteristics of this realization are: (1)History, i. e. status, is dealt with in the form of an infinite stream (stream of status). (2) Interprocess communications are done using the by-reference mechanism. That is, the shared variable cells that comprise the message stream are considered as a communication channel between concurrent processes. (3) Sharing and referring of status among processes is done applicatively through argument passing using the by-reference mechanism.

5.3 Realization of Coroutines

Coroutines, in which processes suspend their own execution and resume on receipt of demand messages, are effectively realized using the eager and lazy evaluations. Program 2 shows an example of coroutine control. The functions fibo, pasc and prim produce a Fibonacci number series, Pascal's triangle number series, and prime number series, respectively. These functions produce an infinite sequence of each number. The function inp is the same as the function input in the counter program. The commands are given in the form [seriesname, count] which means to output the number of elements specified by count in the series number which is specified by seriesname. The function cor only transmits the message to each output function according to the series name. For example, when cor receives the message ['fib, n], the message is handed to the function outfib, which prints n consecutive elements of the Fibonacci series. If cor receives the command ['fib, m] at some time later, outfib will print the next m consecutive elements of the Fibonacci series. The communications structure is shown in Fig. 17.

coroutine(s)
= cor(m, u, v, w)
   where{m = inp(s),
             u = fibo(s),
             v = pasc(s),
             w = prim(s)}.
inp(sig) = [read(sig) | inps(sig)],
cor([['fib, count]. nmsg], u, v, w)
   = cor(nmsg, outfib(u, count), v, w).
cor([['pas, count]. nmsg], u, v, w)
   = cor(nmsg, u, outpas(v, count), w).
cor([['pri, count]. nmsg], u, v, w)
   = cor(nmsg, u, v, outpri(w, count)).
outfib(u, count) = outs(u, count, 'fib).
outpas(v, count) = outs(v, count, 'pas).
outpri(w, count) = outs (w, count, 'pri).
outs([e. x], count, name)
 = **if** count = 0 **then** [e. x]
     else outs(x, count − 1, name)
               after print(e, name)
fibo(s) = [1. [1 | addlist(fibo(s))]].
addlist([e, x1. x])
 = [e + x1 | addlist([x1. x])].
pasc(s) = pastri([1. zeros(s)]).
pastri([v1. v])
 = [[v1. v] | pastri([1. vsum([v1. v],v)])].
zeros(s) = [0 | zeros(s)].
vsum([u. x], [v. y]) = [u + v | vsum(x, y)].
prim(s) = sieve(s, ints(2)).
ints(m) = [m | ints(m + 1)].
sieve(s, [e. m]) = [e | sieve(s, del(e, m))].
del(m, [e. n])
 = **if** remainder(e, m) = 0 **then** del(m, n)
     else [e | del(m, n)].

Program 2 Coroutines.

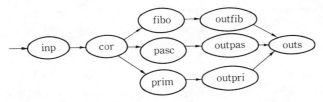

Fig. 17 Communications structure for coroutines.

The characteristics of this coroutines realization are : (1) Using the lazy evaluation mechanism, a conceptually infinite stream can be produced. This concept of infinity makes the programming more intuitive and easier. (2)

—— database = [[flightname. seats],....]
—— commandstream = [[reserve, flightname, seatsnum, varname],
                    [info, flightname, varname],
                    ...]
airlinesystem(sig)
 = (output(respl, 'tty1) **where** {respl = select('user1, resp)},
    output(resp2, 'tty2) **where** {resp2 = select('user2, resp)})
   where {resp = DBsys(cs, database),
            cs = merge(userl(sig), user2(sig))}.

```
select(usnam, [[user. x]. cs])
= if usnam = user then [x. select(usnam, cs)]
    else select(usnam, cs).
userl(sig) = userid('userl, input('tty1)).
user2(sig) = userid('user2, input('tty2)).
userid(id,[c. cs]) = [[id. c]. idcs]
                        where {idcs = userid(id, cs)}.
input (tty) = [read(tty) | input(tty)].
output([cs. ns], tty) = output(ns, tty) after print(cs, tty).
bind(x, y) = [x. y].
DBsys([[usnam, 'info, flight, var]. cs]db)
= [[usnam. ans]. resp]
    where {ans = bind(var, seats(flight, db)),
            resp = DBsys(cs, db)}.
DBsys ([[usnam, 'reserve, flight, stnum, quest]. s], db)
= [[usnam. answer]. resp]
    where {answer = bind(quest, ans)
            resp = DBsys(s, newdb),
            (ans, newdb) = reserve(flight, stnum, db)}.
reserve(flight, stnum, db)
= (ans, newdb)
    where {(ans, newdb) = respond(flight, rsnum − stnum, db)
            rsnum = seats(flight, db)}.
respond(flight, sts, db)
= if sts >= 0 then ('ok, newdb)
                where {newdb = modify(flight, sts, db, db)}
    else ('fail, db).
modify(flight, val, [[flnam. x]. restdb],db)
= if flnam = flight then db after Repl(x, val)
    else modify(flight, val, restdb, db).
seats(flight, [[flnam. x]. rdb])
= if flnam = flight then Eval(x)
    else seats(flight, rdb).
seats (flight, []) = 'error.
```

Program 3 Air line reservation system.

Delaying and demanding the evaluation control the suspension and resumption of message transfer. (3) As the delayed function is forced implicitly when a cell with tag c on is accessed, programmers need not force the evaluation explicitly. (4) The extent of eager evaluation can be controlled using a counter, as described for the function outs. This control method is useful for controlling parallel execution, e. g., avoidance of a combinatorial explosion in or-parallel execution of a logic program.[2]

5.4 Realization of Nondeterminacy

A typical example of nondeterminate readers and writers problem is the airline reservation problem.[6] Program 3 is an implementation for an airline reservation system with two users (The two-user system can easily be extended to a many-user system). The top function, airlinesystem (sig), executes DBsys for the command stream merged from the two user streams, userl and user2. The database is assumed to be initially given. The functions userl and user2 read commands from ttyl and tty2, and attach a user tag to each command. The function select picks up only the responses with the specified user tag. Behavior of DBsys and other functions following DBsys are similar to those of Ref. 6). It should be noted that the primitive operators repl and eval are used in the functions modify and seats for efficiency. The communications structure is shown in Fig. 18.

451

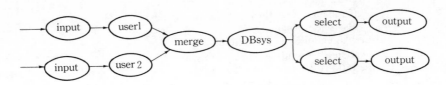

Fig. 18 Communications structure for airlinesystem.

5.5 Other Examples
〔1〕 **Bounded buffer**

Program 4 shows that the generator and consumer use a bounded buffer for communications. The buffer is filled with data produced by the generator,

consumer(x, d) **where** {(x, d) = generator(1, 20)}.

generator(x, n) = **if** n > 0 **then** ([x. y], s)
　　　　　　　　　　　　where{(y, s) = generator(x + 1, n − 1)}
　　　　　　　　else (z, z)
　　　　　　　　　　　　where {z = [x | generatorl(x + 1)]}}.

generatorl(x) = [x | generatorl(x + 1)].

consumer([x1. xx], [dl. dd]) = consumer(xx, dd) **after** print(x1).

Program 4 Bounded buffer.

which is activated every time the consumer takes out data. This is a typical application of eager and lazy executions.

〔2〕 **Constraints** [20,19]

Program 5 is a realization of constraints. The constraints can be effectively implemented using nondeterminate case expression.

p(x, y, z)
　　= **case** { val(x) and val(y) −> bind(z, x + y),
　　　　　　　　val(y) and val(z) −> bind(x, z − y),
　　　　　　　　val(z) and val(x) −> bind(y, z − x)}
　− − Note :　val(x) waits until a value is written x,
　　　　　　　and returns true.

Program 5 Constraint.

§6 Conclusions

Nonstrict, eager and lazy evaluation mechanisms have been described based on a dataflow computation model. Such mechanisms are efficiently implemented by selectively using the by-value and by-reference mechanisms in the framework of a dataflow model.

The examples presented in this paper prove that modular programming with history sensitivity, such as object oriented programming, nondeterminate execution and the coroutine concept, can be intuitively expressed in functional language using the stream concept, and that such stream-oriented processing is effectively supported by the nonstrict eager and lazy evaluation mechanisms described.

There may be some critique on restricting logic program to "don't-care" nondeterminism[17] like Concurrent Prolog and PARLOG, since similar programs are described in functional style, and this suggests a connection between functional languages and logic languages. As for logic programs, the realization of "don't-know" nondeterminism, and therefore the way of implementing or-parallelism, is an important problem. In this sense, the dataflow architecture is promising as a bridge between functional and logic language implementations, because the eager and lazy evaluation mechanisms are also useful for realizing or-parallel execution of a logic program. That is, the eager evaluation is used for or-parallel forking, and the lazy evaluation is used to prevent combinatorial explosion of the or-parallelism.[2]

All primitive operators described in this paper will be realized in the dataflow machine prototype, DFM, which is now under development at Musashino Electrical Communication Laboratory, NTT.

Acknowledgements

The authors would like to thank Dr. Noriyoshi Kuroyanagi, director of the Communication Principles Research Division at Musashino Electrical Communication Laboratory, for his helpful guidance and encouragement. They also wish to thank the members of the dataflow architecture group in the Communication Principles Research Section 2 for their fruitful discussions.

References

1) Amamiya, M.: "A Design Philosophy of High Level Language for Data Flow Machine, Valid." Proc. Annual Conf. of IECE, Japan (1981).

2) Amamiya, M., Hasegawa, R. and Kiyoki, Y.: "Eager and Lazy Evaluation Mechanism in Data Flow Architecture and Its Application to Parallel Inference Machine," Proc. of Work Meeting for Computers, IECE, Japan (1983).

3) Amamiya M., Hasegawa R. and Mikami, H.: "List Processing with Data Flow Machine," Lecture Notes in Computer Science, No. 147 (Springer-Verlag, 1983) 165-190.

4) Amamiya, M., Hasegawa, R., Nakamura, O. and Mikami, H.: "A List-Processing-Oriented Data Flow Machine Architecture," Proc. of the 1982 National Computer Conference, AFIPS (1982) 143-151.

5) Arvind and Kathail, V.: "A Multi Processor Dataflow Machine That Supports Generalized Procedures," Proc. 8th Ann. Sympo. Computer Architecture (1981) 291-302.

6) Bryant, R. E. and Dennis, J. B.: "Concurrent Programming," Lecture Notes in Computer Science, No. 143 (Springer-Verlag, 1982) 426-451.

7) Clark, K.L. and Gregory, S.: "PARLOG: A Parallel Logic Programming Language," Research Report, DOC 83/5 (Imperial College of Science and Technology, Univ., London, 1983).

8) Clark, K. L. and Tärnlund, S.-Å. (ed.): "Logic Programming" (Academic Press, London, 1982).

9) Darlington, J. and Reeve, M. J.: "ALICE: A Multiprocessor Reduction Machine," Proc. Conf. Functional Programming Language and Computer Architecture (ACM, New York, 1981) 65-75.

10) Darlington, J., Henderson, P. and Turner, D. A.: "Functional Programming and its Applications" (Cambridge Univ. Press, 1982).

11) Dennis, J. B.: "Data Flow Supercomputers," IEEE Computer, 13, No. 11 (1980) 48-56.

12) Dijkstra, E. W.: "Guarded Commands, Nondeterminacy and Formal Derivation of Programs," Commun. ACM, 18, No. 8 (1975) 453-457.

13) Gurd, J. and Watson, I.: "Data Driven System for High Speed Computing, Part 1," Computer Design (June, 1980) 91-100.

14) Hasegawa, R. and Amamiya, M.: "On the implementation of Lazy Evaluation with Data Flow Machine," Proc. Ann. Conf. IPSJ, Japan (1982).

15) Kahn, G.: "The Semantics of a Simple Language for Parallel Programming," Proc. IFIP Congress '74 (1974) 471-475.

16) Keller, R. M., Lidstrom, G. and Patil, S. S.: "A Loosely-Coupled Applicative Multiprocessing System," Proc. of the 1979 National Computer Conference, AFIPS (1979) 613-622.

17) Kowalski, R. A.: "Logic for Problem Solving" (North-Holland, 1979).

18) Ono, S., Takahashi, N. and Amamiya, M.: "Partial Computation with a Dataflow Machine," Proc. Fifth Conf. on Mathematical Methods in Software Science and Engineering (Research Institute for Mathematical Science, Kyoto Undversity, 1983).

19) Shapiro, E. and Takeuchi, A.: "Object Oriented Programming in Concurrent Prolog," New Generation Computing, *1, No. 1* (1983) 25-48.

20) Sussman, G. J. and Steel, G. L.: "Constraints — A Language for Expressing Almost Hierarchical Descriptions," Artificial Intelligence, *14* (1980).

21) Takahashi, N. and Amamiya, M.: "A Data Flow Processor Array System: Design and Analysis," Proc. 10th Ann. Sympo. Computer Architecture (1983) 243-250.

22) Treleaven, P. C., Brownbridge, D. R. and Hopkins, R. P.: "Data Driven and Demand Driven Computer Architecture," ACM Computing Survey, *14, No. 1* (1982) 93-143.

23) Weng, K. S.: "Stream-Oriented Computation in Recursive Data Flow Schemas," Technical Memo, *TM-68* (Laboratory for Computer Science, MIT, 1975).

The FAIM-1 Symbolic Multiprocessing System

A. L. Davis
S. V Robison

Fairchild Laboratory for Artificial Intelligence Research, 4001 Miranda Ave., Palo Alto

ABSTRACT

The **FAIM-1** multiprocessing system is an ultra-concurrent symbolic multiprocessor which attempts to significantly improve the performance of AI systems. The system includes a language in which concurrent AI applications programs can be written, a machine which provides direct hardware support for the language, and a resource allocation mechanism which maps the program onto the machine in order to exploit the program's concurrency in an efficient manner at run-time. The architecture is consistent with high performance VLSI implementation and packaging technology, and is easily extended to include arbitrary numbers of processors.

1 Introduction

Our goal is to produce a *High Performance Symbolic Multiprocessor*, one hundred or more times faster than current machines in common use (e.g. Vax 11/780) to meet the voracious computational demands of future Artificial Intelligence applications. This implies a *real* machine — one that works, is affordable and that people can program. Such a machine should entice researchers into the area of distributed AI problem solving and encourage the subsequent widespread use that will be necessary to create the expertise necessary to make sophisticated, cost-effective machine intelligence applications practical. The FAIM-1 is also an architecture which is conveniently extensible, both in terms of scale (number of processors) and for future modifications to incorporate the benefits of new technology and system's ideas.

Our system design strategy is primarily motivated by our goals and top down motivations induced by AI application needs, but restricted by the need to produce a high-performance cost-effective system in the available technology. It is also neccessary to provide a consistent system which is designed from first principles to meet our needs rather than adopting an ad hoc combination of systems ideas and components that were developed for sequential systems. Such a system must also be complete enough to permit viable use and evaluation. It therefore includes a language, programming environment, architecture (and hardware prototype), and a resource allocation strategy. The focus of this paper is to present a brief synopsis of the language and then describe the architecture and resource allocation methodology that supports.

In order to achieve our performance goals for an appreciably higher performance generation of intelligent machine systems based on concurrent multiprocessing, it is necessary to make a significant break with conventional architectural principles. Some of the traditional mechanisms simply are not viable in a highly concurrent environment. On the other hand, a dramatic shift of computational base from sequential to concurrent processing will be difficult after 30 years of highly refined experience with uniprocessing. Programmers are not going to make the difficult shift in practice, if the new systems require a significant change in the style in which they solve problems, or if the speed of the target machine is too slow to motivate the effort. Our approach in satisfying these conflicting constraints is to provide a reasonably small shift in thinking at the programming language level to incorporate concurrency, while making major changes in the structure of both the system software and hardware architecture to achieve the necessary level of system performance.

The design of the FAIM-1 system is based on the exploitation of concurrency at all levels of the system, and to pursue technological performance mechanisms in the implementation of the prototype hardware.

2 The OIL Programming Language

OIL can be viewed both as a high level, concurrent, AI symbolic programming language and as the machine language for the FAIM-1 multiprocessing system. The design of OIL was primarily influenced by current AI programming practices. The proliferation of so-called AI languages is an indication that programmers have not yet found a suitable linguistic mechanism in which to describe their algorithms. LISP has traditionally been the vehicle of choice. A closer look at how programmers use LISP indicates that it is often used to write a collection of functions that subsequently serve as the programming language for the actual solution. This style is found to some extent in much of today's programming activity, but it is ubiquitous in the AI community. The languages commonly used in AI applications fall into four categories:

1. *Object-oriented* languages provide a mechanism that allows task-level subprograms to communicate by passing messages.

2. *Logical* languages permit computation to be expressed declaratively as a set of rules and facts, and evaluation is based upon unification.

3. *Procedural* languages provide traditional serially executed code with function calls, as exemplified by LISP.

4. *Representation* languages are primarily used for structuring knowledge, particularly in database applications, rather than directly for implementing general-purpose algorithms.

A complex AI application may require several (or all) of these programming styles. Emulating one programming style within another is inefficient. There is therefore a need for a better linguistic mechanism that efficiently incorporates all the major styles.

An OIL program is a collection of objects that communicate by sending messages. The nature of the communication structure explicitly indicates the level of concurrency represented by the program. An OIL object consists of some local state information (typically variables) and several *ports* through which messages are sent and received in FIFO order. A *behavior*, associated with each port, describes what the object does in response to a message. The behavior is a program, that may modify the local state and/or send messages to other objects. OIL behaviors are of two distinct types: logical and procedural. Logical behaviors are written in a declarative style similar to a parallel version of Prolog. Procedural behaviors are written imperatively similar to a parallel lexically scoped LISP. Mechanisms are provided for control to pass between logical and procedural behaviors in a single object, and messages can be used to invoke behaviors of any type in other objects.

Our distributed control model does not guarantee that messages arrive in the order that they were sent, therefore there are two kinds of messages: *blocking* and *nonblocking*. When a nonblocking message is sent, the sender continues execution after the transmission of the message. When a blocking message is sent, the sender is suspended until a reply to the message is received.

To permit more sophisticated synchronization and distributed procedure call mechanisms, the notion of an *entry* is defined. An entry is a collection of ports with one behavior associated with the collection. The behavior is triggered only after all the ports in the collection receive messages. When execution of the behavior terminates the ports are emptied and the object is ready to handle new messages.

Procedural behaviors are written in a language which is a modification of an existing lexically-scoped dialect of Lisp called T^{12}. The nature of these modifications has been to introduce parallel control and data structures into the language, and also to provide the interface to the logical and object-oriented components of OIL. For brevity, only a synopsis of the modifications will be presented here.

OIL procedural functions can be evaluated under a number of parallel strategies. The available evaluation modes are: parallel, eager, future, lazy, and sequential. A number of parallel control structures can also be specified, in particular parallel AND, OR, COND, and FORALL. It is possible to define a number of parallel data structures such as bags, sets, and streams. Each of these structures can be manipulated concurrently using the control structures. OIL also contains some of the expected generic functions for conversion between the data structure types, as well as manipulation of those structures. For example, intersection, union, and complement are defined over sets.

Logical behaviors are written in a parallel version of Prolog. The semantics are different from both sequential Prolog[3] and Concurrent Prolog[15]. We view the logical program as a specification of an AND/OR process tree of goals as described by Conery[4]. In order to help the compiler generate efficient code, only ground terms (facts) may be added or deleted during program execution. Most of the decisions on how to execute the logic programs in parallel will be made by the compiler using a careful dataflow analysis of the rules and incorporating the advice of the programmer supplied pragmas. In addition the user will be able to explicitly control the parallelism using features from other logical languages such as read only variables and the commit operator. It is also possible to control subgoal evaluation to be either AND parallel, OR parallel, or sequential.

Since the logical and procedural parts of OIL are separate, a need for a clean interface between the two is required. Each type of code must be able to invoke the other. A natural way to allow the logical behavioral code to invoke procedural code is to allow goals fired on the right side of Horn clauses to actually invoke procedural segments directly. Facilities are provided to permit the procedural segments to be backtracked properly. Procedural segments can invoke logical behaviors by calling them with a clause to be unified and passing a closure to the declaritive section. Results are passed back as the consistent binding set produced by a successful unification if one exists.

The programmer may also annotate OIL code with what amount to hints about the dynamic nature of the program's execution. These pragmas will be used by the resource allocation routines in the compiler. Currently the types of information which the programmer may supply are: the estimated sizes of dynamic data types; the priority of a particular program component for resources if conflict exists; the appropriate buffering capacity of streams; the probabilities of a particular choice at decision points; the lifetime expectancy of objects; and the distributions on type and identity of object creations.

3 Architecture of the FAIM-1 System

The primary purpose of the FAIM-1 architecture is the efficient, high-performance execution of OIL programs. The objective is accomplished by supporting, directly in hardware, the computational model on which OIL is based.

The FAIM-1 is a multiprocessor system consisting of a number of identical processing elements, called *Hectagons*, interconnected by a communication network. Each Hectagon is a complete computer capable of sequentially executing any compiled OIL program that can be stored in its local memory. Hectagons communicate with each other via messages which are sent through communication *ports*. Note the similarity between this model and the organization of an OIL program. Each Hectagon has 6 ports that may potentially be active concurrently. Communication lines run between ports on different Hectagons; the exact configuration of connections is called the *communication topology*.

A Hectagon is composed of 6 self-timed[14] subsystems – named the *FRISC, ISM, CxAM, SPUN, SRAM*, and *Post Office*. Three of these subsystems (ISM, CxAM, SRAM) are specialized memory systems that provide *intelligent* storage, the Post Office supports inter-Hectagon communication, the FRISC element is the processor, and unification support is provided by the SPUN element. Eventually each of these subsystems will be implemented as custom-VLSI devices. In the prototype implementation some of the subsystems will be constructed from off-the-shelf components in order to shorten the design time of the initial prototype.

3.1 Communication Topology

The communication topology chosen for FAIM-1 is divided into two levels. At the bottom level, Hectagon elements are wired together to form a *processing surface*, where each Hectagon is wired to 6 neighboring Hectagons. At the top level an arbitrary number of processing surfaces are connected together to produce a multiple surface instance of a FAIM-1 system. When a connection leaves the surface from a peripheral Hectagon's ports, it is routed to a simple 3-ported switch. One of the remaining ports of the switch is used for connection to an adjacent surface while the other is *wrapped* around to a switch on the opposite edge of the same hexagonal surface. Figure 1 shows an E-3 surface with the switches and wrap lines. This wrapped, hexagonal mesh is a 3-axis variant of a twisted toroidal topology[10]. Three of the wrap lines in this figure have been labelled rather than drawn to improve the clarity of the diagram.

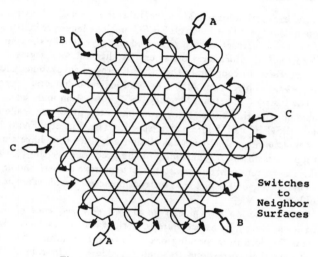

Figure 1: Twisted Hex-Plane Topology

The wrap lines reduce the maximum communication distance between elements on the surface. It is hoped that the resource allocation strategy will be able to allocate tasks onto this surface such that a high degree of communication locality will be achieved. However, it is unlikely that strict locality can be efficiently achieved for highly dynamic AI programs. Therefore reducing worst-case communication times (by reducing communication distance) is also important.

Multiple FAIM-1 surfaces can be logically placed as floor tiles in a planer array, with adjacent Hectagon off-surface switch wires connected together. Figure 2 illustrates this multi-surface interconnection plan. In this figure, Hectagons on the same surface have similar textures. The switches and wrap lines have been omitted for clarity.

The tiling of a plane with several processor surfaces produces a large number of peripheral ports that can be attached to non-Hectagon devices. This is useful for I/O purposes, providing a large number of connections to secondary storage units or host processors. By varying the surface size and the number of surfaces that are connected together it is possible to produce a system containing any desired number of processors.

The primary advantage in using a hex communication topology is that it is easily extensible. The periphery of a processing surface forms a regular hexagon. In the 19 processor instance

each peripheral edge contains 3 processing elements, hence the **E-3** designation. Ignoring the derivation for brevity, an n-edge surface contains $3n(n-1)+1$ processors, of which $6(n-1)$ are on the periphery of the surface. Assuming that only processing elements on the periphery can communicate with the surface's external environment, then the growth rate of the potential processing power of the surface scales as n^2 while the off-surface communication bandwidth scales as n. A secondary advantage is that the on-surface wiring scheme is strictly planer and therefore amenable to wafer-scale packaging, either as a hybrid or a full-wafer integration design.

Fault tolerance is an important aspect of any highly replicated multiprocessor architecture, since the probability of at least one processor being down increases with the number of processors in the system. Koren[9] has developed several fault tolerant strategies for hex plane topologies. In addition, communication fault tolerance is enhanced in a hex mesh topology because each element has a number of paths by which it may send messages to any particular destination.

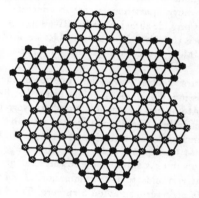

Figure 2: The Tiling of Multiple Surfaces

3.2 Post Office

Run-time program objects communicate by sending messages. The Post Office provides direct hardware support of this activity. The other Hectagon subsystems are not directly involved in communication activities and therefore are left free to concurrently support other activities.

If a message's destination is not one of the sender's 6 neighboring Hectagons then the Post Office will route the message to its destination by sending the message to a neighbor that is "generally" in the direction of the destination. Conceptually, messages may be of arbitrary length. Physically, each message is broken up and sent as a sequence of fixed-length packets. Destinations are specified as relative X-and-Y axis offsets from the originating Hectagon. This inherently provides NEWS (North-East-West-South) routing. Viewing a hex plane as a quad-mesh with one diagonal will give the proper cartesian perspective.

Upon receiving a message, the Post Office determines if its Hectagon is the destination. If it is, the message is handled at that site. Otherwise, the Post Office must pass the message on toward its destination. Using the destination field in the message, the Post Office computes the desired port and forwards the message. If that port is busy, and a secondary port is available that will reduce the Manhattan distance of the message from its final destination, then this secondary port is used. Just before the message is forwarded, the Post Office adjusts the message's destination field according to which output port is used. If the primary and all secondary ports are busy then the Post Office waits until a port is available or until the current time is beyond a *critical time* that is part of the message. If a desired port becomes available then it is used. If the critical time is passed then any port that is available is taken. The critical time concept prevents deadlock by randomizing routing in congested areas. When a packet is finally sent, the receiving Post Office verifies packet integrity based on a CRC check; an error causes retransmission of the packet.

The Post Office design supports a high-level of communication concurrency. While a pair of communicating neighbor processors can send a packet in only one direction at any particular moment, and procedural data structures which are associatively accessed are stored in the CxAM.

In previous systems, hashing schemes of one form or the other have been used in lieu of CAM components. This choice makes sense in traditional architectures where the "smart processor with big, dumb memory" partition is cast in concrete. The typical CAM does not provide sufficient associative support for AI match functions, since they match either tag bits or single word contents. In FAIM-1, the CxAM can match structures as well as slot contents.

The structure of both entries and queries in the CxAM is a LISP S-expression. Each slot therefore can either be a structure or an atom. Atoms can be symbols, numbers, variables, or *don't cares*. Semantically, variables are treated as *don't cares* by the CxAM. The inclusion of variables as atom types for the CxAM is based on FAIM-1's support of logic programming. The binding of variables to values is supported elsewhere in the Hectagon.

The CxAM responds to four commands: *Find Match, Give Match, Delete Structure,* and *Add Structure*. The Find and Give functions are optimized for speed, while the Delete and Add functions are implemented with more concern for minimizing circuit area than performance. The frequency of Find and Give is much higher during program execution than that for Delete and Add. The CxAM also manages its own free space and removes garbage automatically, thereby freeing the FRISC element to process instructions rather than manage storage.

3.5 Reduced Instruction Set Computer and Structure Memory

The FRISC (for Fanatically Reduced Instruction Set Computer) is a specialized processor which supports the operations of OIL and coordinates the other Hectagon subsystems.

The FRISC supports low-level symbol processing in ways similar to uniprocessor "lisp-machines": tagged-memory architectures, stack caches and a tailored instruction set. A significant implementation difference, however, is that we provide direct hardware support for the common cases only and deal with difficult (and rarely used) cases via exception handling. This approach makes complex microprogramming support for the most general case unnecessary, which removes a level of control indirection and improves the overall performance of the FRISC element[11].

Altogether, the FRISC supports 64 basic instructions, corresponding to OIL functions such as UNIFY, CAR, etc. It is also interesting to examine the functions that are not in the FRISC instruction set. Jump and Call opcodes are absent since they are handled directly by the ISM. Also missing are complex string search instructions since they are supported directly by the CxAM. Instructions are formed out of one or two six-bit *packets*. All 0-address operators (both monadic and dyadic stack operations) fit in one packet. Memory/stack operations that require an address offset and operations with immediate data use two packets.

The FRISC views most data structures as objects; a conventional memory with a small finite-state machine attached to it (collectively called the SRAM) provides an object-oriented memory system for the FRISC. The SRAM (Structure RAM) stores all procedural data structures, as well as logical variable bindings it is possible for all 6 of a particular Hectagon's ports to be active simultaneously.

3.3 Instruction Stream Memory

The Instruction Stream Memory (ISM) is a specialized instruction memory unit that holds all FRISC machine language instructions. These instructions are generated and allocated by the compiler from OIL procedural behaviors. Additional code segments are generated to coordinate the other Hectagon subsystems and support OIL object communication and logical behaviors.

The Instruction Stream Memory (ISM) subsystem must be capable of delivering the right instruction to the processor (called the FRISC in FAIM-1) at high speed. Thus, in the FAIM-1 system, the normal address calculation activities that have traditionally been the responsibility of the processor are the ISM's job. The current ISM design attempts to improve its performance by capitalizing on the fact that instruction access patterns are not random.

The instruction stream can be viewed as a sequence of instructions broken by calls or jumps, both of which may be conditional. Modern programming practices tend to produce shorter sequences that correspond to small procedures. The role of either a jump or call is to select a next instruction that is not in lexical order. Since the jump and call instructions exist in the memory, the ISM can predict when one will appear and plan for it in advance. This idea is certainly not new; branch prediction and instruction prefetch have been used to improve performance in many conventional architectures. Most of these systems (for example scoreboards as in the IBM System 360/91[1], translation look aside buffers, and instruction caches[16]) increase speed by interposing a piece of hardware between the memory and the processor.

The ISM takes this approach a step further. It provides a specialized instruction memory rather than merely placing a specialized interface in front of a conventional memory. The obvious disadvantage is that the ISM is only useful for storing instructions, and therefore the ISM cannot serve multiple roles as in conventional systems. The advantages, however are numerous. The ISM can be tuned for its sole function of high-speed instruction delivery, the processor's complexity is reduced, code density can be increased since most jumps and calls can be removed from the code stream, a separate parallel data path for instruction delivery can be used, and a more flexible interrupt and trap structure is permitted.

The calling sequence of the FRISC is a bit different than the conventional *save-state-always* mode. If a called routine makes further calls then the first instruction is to save the ISM state.

This permits a leaf routine to be optimized and avoids delays incurred by saving the machine state.

3.4 Context Addressable Memory

The Context Addressable Memory (CxAM) is a highly parallel associative storage system capable of searching for and retrieving structured data. Pattern matching and associative storage accesses are common operations in many AI programming paradigms. The CxAM provides direct hardware support for this important activity. Rule headers for logical OIL behaviors, and the bodies of logical rules in list form. The SRAM's atomic addressable entity is a word, which is composed of two portions: a 4-bit tag and a 16-bit data field. Multiple-word objects (e.g. simple vectors, bignums, or continuations) are represented as a structure containing one or more header words followed by indexable data fields. The tag bits support the common dynamic data types allowed in many AI languages. Using the data tag bits, the SRAM can (concurrently with other FRISC computation) chase a pointer chain to retrieve an object requested by the FRISC.

The close connectivity between the FRISC and its small SRAM removes the usual performance gap between registers and primary memory. In our case, registers have at most a 2:1 speed advantage over memory, so the complexity of a general register architecture is not easily justified. Stack architectures are a more natural fit as a compiler target, providing improved instruction code density, reduced data path complexity, and faster context switches. The resulting simple data path and simple instruction set is a candidate for straightforward control implementation.

3.6 Streamed Pipeline Unifier

The Streamed Pipelined UNifier (SPUN) provides support for unification of logical OIL behaviors. The CxAM can be used to find the next rule or set of rules to be tried, but the CxAM does not perform full unification since its match function does not consider variable bindings. The SPUN unit takes the query and the streamed set of matched structures, detects which variable bindings still need to be matched, fetches the binding in the current context from the SRAM and completes the unification. This may entail binding a variable, in which case the SPUN unit must post this binding back in the SRAM. It may also entail starting another subgoal unification, in which case the present state must be stacked, and a new query must be presented to the CxAM.

4 Resource Allocation

Given a program that is a collection of concurrent tasks and a machine composed of a number of processors on which to run the program, there is an inherent problem of how to allocate the tasks onto the physical resources in an efficient manner. In systems such as the Cosmic Cube [13] the burden of task allocation is left for the programmer; for certain cases this is neither a complex nor difficult task. In general however, it is important that the task structure reflect the programmer's organization of the solution and be independent of the machine architecture. Efficient task allocation is a critical problem that must be solved if advanced, highly concurrent machine systems are to mature and be truly useful. Several mechanisms have been studied, but generally three options exist:

1. **Programmed** resource allocation relies on a *smart programmer* to write specific load modules for each individual processing element (PE). The disadvantage is that the task may be complex and the solution non-intuitive. The advantage is that in many cases the programmer knows the optimal allocation better than any automatic mechanism.

2. **Dynamic** resource allocation employs a *smart operating system* to observe how load is distributed in the system. If an inefficient allocation exists the OS redistributes some of the load from busy PE's to lightly loaded or idle PE's. The advantage of this mechanism is that if the load changes rapidly then neither the programmed nor the static mechanisms can adapt properly. The drawback is that the overhead of dynamic allocation must be paid at runtime and therefore can decrease system performance.

3. **Static** resource allocation relies on a *smart compiler* to analyze the program text and to partition the resulting object code into a set of cooperating, concurrent subtasks that conform to the grain size of the PE's and their interconnection topology. The primary advantage of this mechanism is that it does not increase the programmer burden and also does not diminish the run-time performance of the system. The primary disadvantages are that the compiler/resource allocator can be very complex, and if the program exhibits highly dynamic behavior the result may be far from optimal.

Since the major goal of the FAIM-1 system is very high performance, the focus for resource allocation strategies is on static methods. The resource allocation decisions are made in a post-compiler process called the *Allocator*. The allocator uses programmer supplied pragmas in the OIL source code to guide allocation decisions. These pragmas can be viewed as programmer hints about the nature of dynamic program behavior, which the compiler cannot extract from the raw program text alone.

The compiled code and pragmas are passed to the allocator by the compiler. The allocator then performs a dataflow analysis on the procedural code, a communication connectivity analysis on the program objects, and an inference connectivity analysis on the logical behaviors to produce a *directed-program (DP) graph*. The nodes of the DP graph are of four types, which indicate decisions, synchronization, parallel fork, and meta. Meta is used to model iterative and recursive structures. Both the arcs and the nodes of the DP graph are labeled with seven parameters that indicate the resource requirements resulting from that node's activation, e.g. amounts of the three special types of storage (ISM, CxAM, and SRAM). The parameters also indicate probable growth, recursion depth, iteration length, and the probability that a certain decision branch will be taken. This last group of parameters is condensed from the pragma information.

The DP graph is then transformed into a *load-cluster graph* by a series of function preserving graph transformations. The cluster graph consists of clusters of code, each of which will fit on a single Hectagon processor. The cluster graph also represents a balance between the maximum number of concurrent tasks and the minimum communication overhead. The problem of finding an optimal cluster graph is provably NP hard. Fortunately a perfect fit is not necessary and our method uses heuristic methods to find an acceptable fit. The algorithm used is of time complexity $O(N^2)$. The cluster graph is then mapped into a hex-connected graph (representing the physical topology of the machine) using a standard simulated annealing technique[8].

5 Conclusions

In this paper, we have presented an overview for the design of a highly parallel symbolic processor known as FAIM-1. In general there have been two approaches taken in the design of similar systems. The first is to build concurrent processing ensembles out of conventional processor and memory components as has been done for the Cosmic Cube[13], Butterfly[5], and DADO[17] systems. In general we feel that to truly achieve a new generation of viable symbolic processors which significantly out-perform traditional systems, it will be necessary to reallocate the transistor budget to tasks which are specific to the domain of symbolic processing. This is not possible by merely assembling old components in new ways. The other approach is to experiment with radical new models of computation which are inherently highly parallel as is the case with the Connection[6] and Boltzmann[7] machines. The problem with this approach is that the ways in which we solve problems must change radically as well, and the incorporation of 30 years of expertise in programming is all but impossible. We feel that both approaches are viable: the first in the short term and the second in the long term. The FAIM-1 design attempts to fill the gap by providing a rather different but specialized architecture for performance, while requiring only a small change in programming practice to incorporate concurrency.

6 Acknowledgements

The FAIM-1 system is the result of a wide variety of ideas from a number of project members, and does not represent the sole effort of the authors. Key contributions have been made by: Judy Anderson, Allan Schiffman, Shimon Cohen, Ken Stevens, Ian Robinson, Mike Deering, Marty Tenenbaum, Don Barch, Dick Lyon, Erik Brunvand, Bill Coates, Bill Athas, Barak Pearlmutter, Bob Hon, John Conery, and Gary Lindstrom.

Bibliography

[1] C. G. Bell and A. Newell. *Computer Structures: Readings and Examples*. McGraw-Hill, 1971.

[2] E. Brunvand. *Context Addressable Memory for Symbolic Processing Systems*. Masters Thesis, University of Utah, Dept. of Computer Science, August 1984.

[3] W. F. Clocksin and C. S. Mellish. *Programming in Prolog*. Springer-Verlag, 1981.

[4] J. S. Conery, D. F. Kibler. *Parallel interpretation of logic programs*. Functional programming languages and computer architecture, October 1981, 163-171.

[5] R. Gurwitz *The Butterfly Multiprocessor*. Talk presented at the 1984 ACM National Convention, San Francisco, October, 1984.

[6] D. Hillis. *The Connection Machine (Computer Architecture for the New Wave*. AI Memo 646, M.I.T. Artificial Intelligence Laboratory, 1981.

[7] G. Hinton, T J. Sejnowski and D. H. Ackley *Boltzmann Machines: Constraint Satisfaction Networks that Learn*, CMU-CS-84-119, Carnegie Mellon University, May 84.

[8] S. Kirkpatrick, C. D. Gelatt, and M. P. Vecchi. it Optimization by simulated annealing. Science 220, 1984, pp. 671-680.

[9] D. Gordon, I. Koren and G. M. Silberman. *Fault-Tolerance in VLSI Hexagonal Arrays*. Preprint.

[10] A. J. Martin. *The Torus: An Exercise in Constructing a Processing Surface*. Proc. of the Second Caltech Conference on VLSI, 1981, 527-538.

[11] D. A. Patterson, C. H. Seguin. *RISC 1: A reduced instruction set VLSI computer*. Proc. Eighth International Symposium on Computer Architecture, 1981, 443-458.

[12] J. A. Rees, N. I. Adams, J. R. Meehan *The T Manual*, Yale University, Fourth Edition, 1984.

[13] C. L. Seitz. *The Cosmic Cube*. To appear CACM.

[14] C. L. Seitz. *System Timing*. In Introduction to VLSI Systems. Chapter 7 , McGraw-Hill,1979.

[15] E. Shapiro. *A Subset of Concurrent Prolog and its Interpreter*. TR-003, Institute for New Generation Computer Technology, , 1983.

[16] A. J. Smith. *Cache Memories*. Computing Surveys 14, 3, 1982, pp. 473-530.

[17] S. J. Stolfo, et al. *Architecture and Applications of DADO, A Large-Scale Parallel Computer for Artificial Intelligence*. Proceedings of the Eighth International Joint Conference on ARtificial Intelligence, Karlsruhe, West Germany, August, 1983, pp. 850-854.

Initial Assessment
of
Architectures for Production Systems

Charles Forgy[1]
Anoop Gupta[1]
Allen Newell[1]
Robert Wedig[2]
Carnegie-Mellon University
Pittsburgh, Pennsylvania 15213

Abstract

Although production systems are appropriate for many applications in the artificial intelligence and expert systems areas, there are applications for which they are not fast enough to be used. If they are to be used for very large problems with severe time constraints, speed increases are essential. Recognizing that substantial further increases are not likely to be achieved through software techniques, the PSM project has begun investigating the use of hardware support for production system interpreters. The first task undertaken in the project was to attempt to understand the space of architectural possibilities and the trade-offs involved. This article presents the initial findings of the project. Briefly, the preliminary results indicate that the most attractive architecture for production systems is a machine containing a small number of very simple and very fast processors.

1. Introduction

Forward-chaining production systems are used extensively in artificial intelligence today. They are especially popular for use in the construction of knowledge-based expert systems [9, 11, 13, 14, 17]. Unfortunately, production systems are rather slow compared to more conventional programming languages. Consequently some computationally intensive tasks that are otherwise suitable for these systems cannot be implemented as production systems. The Production System Machine (PSM) project was created to develop hardware solutions to this problem. The first goal of the project is to understand the space of architectural possibilities for the PSM and the trade-offs involved. This article describes the initial results of the studies performed by the PSM project.

The rest of the paper consists of the following sections. Section 2 provides a brief description of the OPS production systems considered by the PSM project and includes a description of the Rete algorithm that is used to implement them. The Rete algorithm forms the basis for much of the later work. Section 3 elaborates on the need for hardware for production systems. It explains why we do not expect substantial further speed-ups from software techniques. Section 4 presents the results of measurements of some existing production system programs. The measurements enable us to explore the possibility of using parallelism in executing production system programs. Sections 5, 6, and 7 discuss three methods for speeding up the execution of production systems. Section 5 considers the role of parallelism, Section 6 considers processor architectures, and Section 7 considers hardware technology issues. The conclusions are presented in Section 8.

2. Background

The PSM project is concerned with the OPS family of production systems [2, 4, 6]. These languages are for writing pure forward-chaining systems. An OPS program consists of a collection of *production rules* (or just "productions") and a global data base called *working memory*. Each production has a left-hand side which is a logical expression and a right-hand side consisting of zero or more executable statements. The logical expression in the left-hand side is composed of one or more *conditions*. A condition is a pattern; the left-hand side of a production is considered satisfied when every condition matches an element in working memory. The OPS interpreter executes a program by performing the following cycle of operations:

1. **Match:** The left-hand sides of all the productions are matched against the contents of working memory. The set of satisfied productions is called the conflict set.

2. **Conflict Resolution:** One of the satisfied productions is selected from the conflict set. If the conflict set is empty, the execution halts.

3. **Act:** The statements in the selected production's right-hand side are executed. The execution of these statements usually results in changes to the working memory. At the end of this step, the match step is executed again.

In this paper we are primarily concerned with speeding up the match operation. This is because the match operation takes most of the run time of interpreters that are implemented in software on uniprocessors. Moreover, when OPS is run on a parallel machine (which the PSM will be) the three operations can be pipelined, and much of the time required for conflict resolution and act can be overlapped with the time taken for the match. The total run time will consist of the time for the match plus a small amount of start-up time for the other two operations.

The algorithm that will be used in the production system machine is the Rete match algorithm [1, 3]. This algorithm has been used with variations in all the software implementations of OPS. It exploits two basic properties of OPS production systems to reduce the amount of processing required in the match:

- **The slow rate of change of working memory.** It is common for working memory to contain from a few hundred to over a thousand elements. Typically, executing a production results in two to four of the elements being changed. Thus on each cycle of the system, the vast majority of the information that the matcher needs is identical to the information it used on the previous cycle. Rete matchers take advantage of this by saving state between cycles.

- **The similarities among the left-hand sides.** The left-hand sides of productions in a program always contain many common subexpressions. Rete attempts to locate the

---

[1]With the Department of Computer Science.

[2]With the Department of Electrical and Computer Engineering.

common subexpressions, so that at run-time the matcher can evaluate each of these expressions only once.

The Rete interpreter processes the left-hand sides of the productions prior to executing the system. It compiles the left-hand sides into a network that specifies the computations that the matcher has to perform in order to effect the mapping from changes in working memory to changes in the conflict set. The network is a dataflow graph. The input to the network consists of changes to working memory encoded in data structures called tokens. Other tokens output from the network specify the changes that must be made to the conflict set. As the tokens flow through the network, they activate the nodes, causing them to perform the necessary operations, creating new tokens that pass on to subsequent nodes in the network. The network contains essentially four kinds of nodes:

- **Constant-test nodes:** These nodes test constant features of working memory elements. They effectively implement a sorting network and process each element added to or deleted from working memory to determine which conditions the element matches.

- **Memory nodes:** These nodes maintain the matcher's state. They store lists of tokens that match individual conditions or groups of conditions.

- **Two-input nodes:** These nodes access the information stored by the memory nodes to determine whether groups of conditions are satisfied. For example, a two-input node might access the lists of tokens that have been determined to match two conditions of some production individually and determine whether there are any pairs of tokens that match the two conditions together. In general, not all pairs will match because the left-hand side may specify constraints such as consistency of variable bindings that have to hold between the two conditions. When a two-input node finds two tokens that match simultaneously, it builds a larger token indicating that fact and passes it to subsequent nodes in the network.

- **Terminal nodes:** Terminal nodes are concerned with changes to the conflict set. When one of these nodes is activated, it adds a production to or removes a production from the conflict set. The processing performed by the other nodes insures that these nodes are activated only when conflict set changes are required.

3. The Need for Hardware

The previous work on the efficiency of OPS systems has concentrated on software techniques. Over the past several years, improvements in the software have brought about substantial speed increases. The first LISP-based version of OPS was OPS2, which was implemented in 1978 [5]. The widely-used LISP version OPS5 was implemented about 1980 [2]. The improvements in software technology during that time made OPS5 at least five to ten times faster than OPS2. OPS5/LISP has been followed by two major reimplementations: an interpreter for OPS5 written in BLISS (a systems programming language) and the OPS83 interpreter [6]. OPS5/BLISS is at least six times faster than OPS5/LISP, and OPS83 is at least four times faster than OPS5/BLISS.[3] The speed-up from OPS2 to OPS5/BLISS resulted from a number of factors, including changing the representations of the important data structures and putting in special code to handle common cases efficiently. The additional

speed-up of OPS83 resulted primarily from a new method of compiling left-hand sides. In all earlier versions of OPS, the left-hand sides were compiled into an intermediate representation that had to be interpreted at run time; in OPS83, the left-hand sides are compiled into native machine code.

It appears that with the advent of OPS83, further substantial improvements in software techniques have become difficult to achieve. Some amount of optimization of the compiled code is certainly possible, but this is expected to result in rather small increases in speed compared to what has occurred in recent years. The code that the OPS83 compiler produces is fairly good already. A factor of two speed-up due to compiler optimizations might be achieved; a factor of five seems unlikely at this time. Since the importance of achieving further speed increases for OPS is so clearly indicated, we feel that it is essential to investigate hardware support for OPS interpreters.[4]

4. Measurements of Production Systems

One of the first tasks undertaken by the PSM group was to perform extensive measurements of production systems running in OPS5. These measurements were necessary to evaluate the possibilities for speeding up Rete interpreters. Six systems were measured: R1 [13], a program for configuring VAX computer systems; XSEL [14], a program which acts as a sales assistant for VAX computer systems; PTRANS [9], a program for factory management; HAUNT, an adventure-game program developed by John Laird; DAA [11], a program for VLSI design; and SOAR [12], an experimental problem-solving architecture implemented as a production system. The R1, XSEL, and PTRANS programs were chosen because they are three of the largest production systems ever written, and because they are actually being used as expert systems in industry. The DAA program was chosen because it represents a computation-intensive task compared to the knowledge-intensive tasks performed by the previous programs. The SOAR program was chosen because it embodies a new paradigm for the use of production systems. Altogether, the six programs represent a wide spectrum of applications and programming styles. The systems contain from 100 to 2000 productions and from 50 to 1000 working memory elements. A few of the more important results are presented here; more detailed results can be found in [7].

The first set of measurements concern the surface characteristics of production system programs—that is, the characteristics of the programs that can be described without reference to the implementation techniques used in the interpreter. Table 1 shows the results. The first line gives the number of productions in each of the measured programs.[5] The second line gives the average number of conditions per production. The number of conditions in a production affects the complexity of the match for that production. The third line gives the average number of actions per production. The number of actions determines how much working memory is changed when a typical production fires. Together these numbers give an indication of the size and complexity of the productions in the systems. They show that productions are typically simple, containing neither large numbers of conditions nor large numbers of actions.

Feature	R1	XSEL	PTRANS	HAUNT	DAA	SOAR
1. Productions	1932	1443	1016	834	131	103
2. Conds/Prod	5.6	3.8	3.1	2.4	3.9	5.8
3. Actions/Prod	2.9	2.4	3.6	2.5	2.9	1.8

Table 1: Summary of Surface Measurements

---

[3]In absolute terms, a large production system with a large working memory and moderately complex left-hand sides (e.g., R1 [13]) might be expected to run at a rate of one to two production firings per second with OPS5/LISP running on a VAX 11/780; at a rate of six to twelve firings per second with OPS5/BLISS; and a rate of twenty-five to fifty firings per second with OPS83.

[4]The DADO project at Columbia University is also investigating hardware support for production systems [8, 18].

[5]In some cases only a subset of the complete production system program was measured because of problems with the LISP garbage collector. The numbers given in the table indicate the number of productions in the subset of the program that was measured.

462

The second set of measurements relate to the run-time activity of the OPS5 interpreter. Table 2 shows how many nodes are activated on average after each change to working memory. Line 1 shows the number of constant-test nodes activated. Although constant-test node activations constitute a large fraction (65%) of the total node activations, only a small fraction (10% to 30%) of the total match time is spent in processing them. This is because the processing associated with constant-test nodes is very simple compared to the memory nodes and the two-input nodes. Line 2 shows the number of memory nodes activated, and Line 3 the number of two-input nodes. Most of the matcher's time is spent evaluating these two kinds of nodes. Line 4 shows the number of terminal nodes activated. Since these numbers are small, updating the conflict set is a comparatively inexpensive operation. There are two major conclusions that can be drawn from this table. First, except for the constant-test nodes, the number of nodes activated is quite small. Second—and perhaps more significantly—except for the constant-test nodes, the numbers are essentially independent of the number of productions in the system.[6] This is important in the design of parallel production system interpreters (see the discussion of parallelism below).

Node Type	R1	XSEL	PTRANS	HAUNT	DAA	SOAR
1. Constant-test	136.3	105.3	122.1	88.5	35.9	26.5
2. Memory	12.3	8.7	10.7	12.5	4.0	11.1
3. Two-input	47.1	32.4	35.0	36.8	22.2	39.5
4. Terminal	1.0	1.7	1.7	1.5	2.0	4.0

Table 2: Node Activations per Working Memory Change

5. Parallelism

On the surface, the production system model of computation appears to admit a large amount of parallelism. This is because it is possible to perform match for all productions in parallel. Even after the left-hand sides have been compiled into a Rete network, the task still appears to admit a large amount of parallelism, because different paths through the network can be processed in parallel. It is our current assessment, however, that the speed-up available from parallelism in production systems is much smaller than it initially appears.

We are exploring three sources of parallelism for the match step in production system programs: production-level, condition-level, and action-level parallelism. In the following paragraphs we briefly describe each of these three sources, and where possible give the speed-up that we expect from that source.

5.1. Production-level Parallelism

In production-level parallelism, the productions in the system are divided into several groups and a separate process is constructed to perform match for each group. All the processes can execute in parallel. The extreme case for production-level parallelism is when the match for each production is performed in parallel. The major advantage of production-level parallelism is that no communication is required between the processes performing the match, although the changes to working memory must be communicated to all processes. Since the communications requirements are very limited, both shared memory and non-shared memory multiprocessor architectures can exploit production-level parallelism.

The measurements described in Section 4 are useful in determining the amount of speed-up that is potentially available from production-level parallelism. Line 3 of Table 2 shows that on average, each change to working memory causes about thirty-five two-input nodes to be activated. Since the sharing of nodes at this level of the network is limited, the number of two-input nodes activated is approximately equal to the number of productions containing conditions that match the working memory element. Thus, on average, when an element is added to or deleted from working memory, the stored state for thirty-five productions must be updated.[7] The number of affected productions is significant because most of the match time is devoted to these productions. Thus the immediately apparent upper bound to the amount of speed-up from production-level parallelism is around thirty-five. However, it is easy to see that this is a very optimistic upper bound. Measurements show that it is common for a few of the affected productions to require five or more times as much processing as the average production. Thus in a machine that uses substantial amounts of production-level parallelism, the match would be characterized by a brief flurry of parallel activity followed by a long period when only a few processors are busy. The average concurrency would be much lower than the peak concurrency.

5.2. Condition-level Parallelism

In condition-level parallelism, the match for each condition in the left-hand side of a production is handled by a separate process. Condition-level parallelism involves more communication overhead than production-level parallelism. It is now necessary to communicate tokens matching one condition to processes that combine tokens, thus forming new tokens matching several conditions in the left-hand side. This increased communication makes shared-memory multiprocessors preferable to non-shared memory multicomputers. The speed-up expected from condition-level parallelism is quite limited. This is because productions tend to be simple, as Table 1 shows. Since the typical production contains only three to six conditions, even when all the conditions in an left-hand side have to be processed (a rare occurrence) only three to six parallel processes can be run.

5.3. Action-level Parallelism

In action-level parallelism, all the changes to working memory that occur when a production fires are processed in parallel. Action-level parallelism does not require any more data communication overhead than the previous two sources of parallelism, but it does involve a substantial amount of extra synchronization overhead. The speed-up possible from action-level parallelism is also quite limited. A typical production makes two to four working memory changes, so the amount of action-level parallelism available is at most two to four.

5.4. Simulation Results

To gain a more detailed evaluation of the potential for parallelism in the interpreter, a simulator has been constructed, and simulations of the execution of the XSEL, PTRANS, and DAA expert systems have been run. The cost model assumed for the simulation is based on the costs that have been computed for the OPS83 matcher. Since the OPS83 matcher would have to be modified somewhat in order to run in parallel, the costs have been adjusted to take these modifications into account.

The graph in Figure 1 indicates the speed-up that is achieved through the use of production-level, condition-level, and action-level parallelism. As the graph shows, the speed-up obtained is quite limited. This is a combined effect of the facts that (1) the processors must wait for all affected productions to finish match before proceeding to the next cycle, and (2) there is a large variance in the computational requirements of the affected productions. The graphs show that a speed-up of four to six times can be obtained with relatively good processor utilization, but to obtain a larger factor requires much more hardware.

---

[6]There are known methods of reducing the effect of production system size on the number of constant-test node activations (see [1]).

[7]Note that the number thirty-five is independent of the number of productions in the program. An intuitive explanation for this is that programmers divide problems into subproblems, and at any given time the program execution corresponds to solving only one of these subproblems. The size of the subproblems is independent of the size of the overall problem and primarily depends on the complexity that an individual can deal with at the same time.

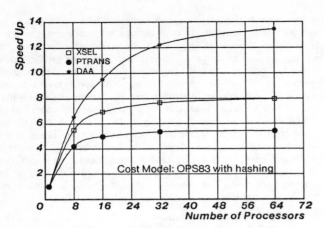

Figure 1: Parallelism in Production Systems

6. Processor Architecture

Because of our experience with the Rete network, we have a good idea of how a machine executing OPS will behave. In the Rete network, there are only a few different types of code sequences to deal with. By calculating the time that a given processor requires to execute these sequences, we can accurately determine how effective the processor is for this task. Typical code sequences from the Rete network are shown in Figures 2 and 3. Figure 2 shows the computation performed by a constant-test node. Figure 3 shows a loop from a two-input node. The loop is executed when the two-input node compares a token from one memory with the tokens in another memory.

```
    load    R1,"active"            ;load the constant
    cmp     R1,1(R.CurWme)         ;compare the value
    jne     L1                     ;if not equal, fail
```

Figure 2: Assembly Code for a Constant Test

```
    move    R0,R.MPtr1             ;test memory pointer
    jeq     L2                     ;exit if nil
10$: load   R.Wme1,WME(R.MPtr1)    ;get the wme
    jsb     L3                     ;goto tests
    load    R.MPtr1,NEXT(R.MPtr1)  ;get next token
    jne     10$                    ;continue if not nil
    jmp     L2                     ;exit
```

Figure 3: Loop from a Two-input Node

As these code sequences illustrate, the computations performed by the matcher are primarily memory bound and highly sequential. Each instruction's execution depends on the previous one's, leaving little room for concurrent execution of the instructions. Consequently, it is not advantageous to develop a processor with multiple functional units able to extract concurrency and simultaneously execute multiple instructions. It is also not worthwhile to design a computer with a large range of complex instructions and addressing modes since the majority of time is spent executing simple operations. We conclude that a machine for executing production systems should have a simple instruction set and should execute the instructions in as few clock cycles as possible. The processor designs that best satisfy these requirements are the reduced instruction set (RISC) machines such as the Berkeley RISC [15], the Stanford MIPS [10], or the IBM 801 [16]. Such a machine could execute most instructions in two machine cycles. We estimate that a complex instruction set machine requires four to eight cycles per instruction, making the simple machine two to four times faster.

7. Device Technology

Since the correct choice for the machine appears to be a RISC-like processor and rather modest levels of parallelism, we are exploring the use of high-speed logic families in its implementation, such as ECL or GaAs. The difficulties inherent in the use of these technologies are offset to a large degree by the fact that the machine will use relatively little hardware. Certainly designing each component will be more difficult than designing a similar component in TTL or MOS; however the machine will be fairly simple so the total design time will not be excessive. In addition, while the processors will be more expensive than processors implemented in slower technologies, the machine will not contain large numbers of them, and the total cost will not be excessive. We estimate an ECL implementation of the machine would be about four times faster than a TTL implementation, provided the processor did not spend too much time waiting on memory.

8. Conclusions

The PSM project is investigating the use of hardware support for production system interpreters. We expect to obtain speed increases from three sources: parallelism, processor architecture, and device technology. Our studies are not complete, but some initial results are available:

- Parallelism: The task admits a modest amount of parallelism. We expect parallelism to contribute a 5 to 10 fold increase in speed.

- Processor architecture: The most attractive architectures for this task are the simple (or so-called RISC) processors. We estimate that a RISC machine would be 2 to 4 times faster than a complex instruction set machine.

- Device technology: Since speed is of paramount importance in this task, and since very simple processors are appropriate, it will be advantageous to use high-speed device technologies. We estimate that using ECL would provide a factor of 4 increase in speed.

In summary then, a machine built along the lines we suggest would be between 5 * 2 * 4 = 40 and 10 * 4 * 4 = 160 times faster than a complex uniprocessor implemented in a slower speed technology. It should be emphasized that these are preliminary results, and are subject to change as the work proceeds.

9. Acknowledgments

H. T. Kung, John McDermott, and Kemal Oflazer contributed substantially to this research.

This research was sponsored by the Defense Advanced Research Projects Agency (DOD), ARPA Order No. 3597, monitored by the Air Force Avionics Laboratory under Contract F33615-81-K-00450.

References

1. Forgy, C. L. *On the Efficient Implementations of Production Systems.* Ph.D. Th., Carnegie-Mellon University, 1979.
2. Forgy, C. L. OPS5 User's Manual. Tech. Rept. CMU-CS-81-135, Carnegie-Mellon University, 1981.
3. Forgy, C. L. "Rete: A Fast Algorithm for the Many Pattern/Many Object Pattern Match Problem." *Artificial Intelligence 19* (September 1982).
4. Forgy, C. L. and McDermott, J. OPS, A Domain-Independent Production System. International Joint Conference on Artificial Intelligence, IJCAI-77.
5. Forgy, C. L. and McDermott, J. The OPS2 Reference Manual. Department of Computer Science, Carnegie-Mellon University, 1978.
6. Forgy, C. L. The OPS83 Report. Department of Computer Science, Carnegie-Mellon University, May 1984.

7. Gupta, A. and Forgy, C. L. Measurements on Production Systems. Carnegie-Mellon University, 1983.

8. Gupta, A. Implementing OPS5 Production Systems on DADO. International Conference on Parallel Processing, August, 1984.

9. Haley, P., Kowalski, J., McDermott, J., and McWhorter, R. PTRANS: A Rule-Based Management Assistant. In preparation, Carnegie-Mellon University

10. Hennessy, J. L., et al. The MIPS Machine. Digest of Papers from the Computer Conference, Spring 82, February, 1982, pp. 2-7.

11. Kowalski, T. and Thomas, D. The VLSI Design Automation Assistant: Prototype System. Proceedings of the 20th Design Automation Conference, ACM and IEEE, June, 1983.

12. Laird, J. and Newell, A. A Universal Weak Method: Summary of Results. International Joint Conference on Artificial Intelligence, IJCAI-83.

13. McDermott, J. R1: A Rule-based Configurer of Computer Systems. Tech. Rept. CMU-CS-80-119, Carnegie-Mellon University, April, 1980.

14. McDermott, J. XSEL: A Computer Salesperson's Assistant. In Machine Intelligence, J.E. Hayes, D. Michie, and Y.H. Pao, Ed.,Horwood, 1982.

15. Patterson, D. A. and Sequin, C. H. "A VLSI RISC." Computer 9 (1982).

16. Radin, G. "The 801 Minicomputer." IBM Journal of Research and Development 27 (May 1983).

17. Stolfo, S. J. and Vesonder, G. T. ACE: An Expert System Supporting Analysis and Management Decision Making. Department of Computer Science, Columbia University, 1982.

18. Stolfo, S. J. and Shaw, D. E. DADO: A Tree-Structured Machine Architecture for Production Systems. National Conference on Artificial Intelligence, AAAI-1982.

Mapping Production Systems into Multiprocessors

M. F. M. Tenorio and D. I. Moldovan
Department of Electrical Engineering - Systems
University of Southern California
Los Angeles, CA, 90089-0781

Index Terms: Artificial Intelligence, Parallel Processing, Expert Systems, Mapping Techniques, Multiprocessors

Abstract

This paper proposes a methodology for mapping production systems (PS) into multiprocessor computer structures. First, a graph grammar model for PS is presented. Using the model, an algorithm is constructed to analyze the interdependencies between rules. The problem of assigning rules to processors is addressed based on the dependencies inherent in PS. First, we study the allocation problem when sufficient processing elements are available and the intercommunication network is given. Second, we study the partitioning problem when the number of rules is greater than the number of processing elements and is necessary to achieve a balanced load. An algorithm is presented for the allocation and partitioning problem. An example of mapping a PS with 32 rules into a multiprocessor system with 8 processing elements and different interconnection networks is presented.

1 Introduction

The size and complexity of PS make it difficult to precisely predict their computational needs. It is commonly agreed that parallel processing is a necessary tool to improve the performance of large systems. In this paper we present techniques for parallel processing of production systems. A production system is a general computational mechanism used in many artificial intelligence applications [DaKi79]. It consists of a set of production rules, a global database and a control scheme. In general the production is a pair of statements called

[1]This research was supported by NSF Grant ECS - 8307258, JSEP Contract No F49620-81- c0070 and DARPA Contract No F-33615-82- k-1786. M. F. M. Tenorio was also supported by the National Research Council of the Federal Republic of Brazil - CNPq #1981.

Reprinted from *The Proceedings of the International Conference on Parallel Processing*, 1985, pages 56-62. Copyright © 1985 by The Institute of Electrical and Electronics Engineers, Inc.

the precondition and the postcondition. If the precondition can be matched against the database, the production is said to be eligible to fire. The control mechanism decides among possible rules, and the one assigned to fire executes its postcondition. The control mechanism then inspects the database for termination conditions and overall synchronization issues.

In section 2 we present a graph grammar model for PS. In section 3 we discuss rule interdependencies. Section 4 presents an algorithm to analyze the presence of these dependencies. In section 5 we present a parallel processing model for PS. In section 6 we introduce the allocation and partitioning algorithm, to improve system performance. Section 7 contains some conclusions and future research.

2 Production System Model

The behavior of a PS can be studied using graph grammar theory. In [Ehri78] and [Nagl78] it is suggested that manipulations database networks can be expressed using graph productions and derivations. In this paper we consider the left hand side and right hand side of production rules are colored graphs and the application of a production is nothing but a graph manipulation. The initial database of a PS is also a colored graph and so are the states of the search space. The nodes represent entities, e.g., constants, attributes and variables, while links represent the relationship among those nodes. The colors represent the relations, types and values, that correspond to nodes and links.

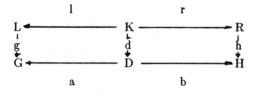

Figure 1: A Production Rule and a Direct Derivation

Let G be a colored graph that represents the initial database. The labels represent constant elements and their relationship. Let p be a production with right hand side R, another colored graph. Similarly, let L be the left hand side of this production, possibly containing variable elements. Let l, r, h and g be morphisms between graphs, that in this case represent graph inclusions as shown in figure 1. Let a direct derivation of H from G via p, $G \Rightarrow H_p$, be the colored graph H obtained by deleting the image of L in G, i.e. gL, thus getting D and adding the image of R in H to D, i.e. hR. In short, a PS can be modelled as a programmable rewriting system, PRS = (GG,CG) where the graph grammar GG contains the starting colored graph, the set of production rules and an alphabet, and the control graph CG includes the starting colored graph, goal graphs and all the paths to be explored by the system in an orderly fashion.

3 Rule Interdependencies

In this section we study the interdependencies which exist between two rules. This is done in order to establish which rules have shared elements that hinder a parallel application. Consider two production derivations as shown in the figure 2.

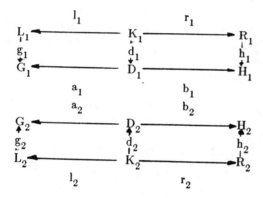

Figure 2: Two Production Derivations

The following dependencies are defined between the rules 1 and 2.

Definition 3.1 - Output Dependency (o-dependency)
Rule p_1 is output dependent on rule p_2, written $p_2\text{->}p_1$, iff

$$(h_1R_1) \bigcap (h_2R_2 - h_2r_2K_2) \neq \emptyset$$

This means that the postcondition of rule 1 and the postcondition of rule 2 less the part that came from the interface graph have common elements. Output dependency does not prevent parallel application of rules.

Definition 3.2 - Input Dependency (i-dependency)
Rule p_1 is input dependent on rule p_2, written $p_2\text{->}p_1$, iff

$$(g_1L_1) \bigcap (g_2L_2 - g_2l_2K_2) \neq \emptyset$$

This means that the precondition of rule 1 and the precondition of rule 2 less the part that comes from the interface graph have common elements. Input dependency prevents parallel application of rules.

Definition 3.3 - Interface Dependency (k-dependency)
Rules p_1 and p_2 are interface dependent iff

$$(g_1l_1K_1 \bigcap g_2l_2K_2) \bigcup$$
$$\bigcup (h_1r_1K_1 \bigcap h_2r_2K_2) \neq \emptyset$$

This means that the morphisms of the interface graphs in the database have common elements. Interface dependency does not prevent parallel application of rules.

Definition 3.4 - Input-Output Dependency (i-o dependency)
Rule p_1 is i-o dependent on rule p_2, written $p_2\text{->}p_1$, iff

$$(g_1L_1) \bigcap (h_2R_2 - h_2r_2K_2) \neq \emptyset$$

This means that the precondition of rule 1 and postcondition of rule 2 less the elements that come form the interface graph have some common elements. This implies strict sequentiality.

The interdependencies between rules are summarized in table 1. The degree of coupling varies from totally independent when rules have no common elements to strictly dependent when only sequential execution is possible. We quantify the degree of interaction between rules with numbers from 0 to 4 as shown in table 1. In the case when two rules are k-dependent or o-dependent it is still possible to process them in parallel.

4 Algorithm For Parallelism Analysis in PS

In this section we describe a technique for analyzing the parallelism between rules in PS. This technique consists of detecting the dependencies between all pairs of rules and eventually constructing a binary matrix which summarizes the parallelism between rules. This analysis is static in the sense that is independent of the initial database and the goal, and can be done before the PS is run. As a result of this analysis the overall search space can be significantly reduced [Teno84]. The information provided by this analysis can be used by the control of the PS to improve efficiency of PS processing. The main steps of the parallelism detection procedure are:

Dependencies				rank	type
i	i-o	o	k		
0	0	0	0	0	Totally independent, parallel.
0	0	0	1	1	Independent, parallel, same context.
0	0	1	X	2	Weakly independent, parallel.
0	1	X	X	3	Dependent, sequential, but composable.
1	X	X	X	4	Strictly dependent, sequential.

Table 1: Degrees of rule interdependencies

Step 1 Construct D matrix. First we form a matrix D of size m x m where m is the number of production rules. In the case when m is large one should group the rules into functional clusters and process one cluster at a time. Each entry d_{kj} in the matrix is a 4-bit binary word defined as

$$d_{kj} = (i, i\text{-}o, o, k)$$

If production pair (k,j) has dependencies of type i, i-o, o, k as defined in the previous section, then the respective bit is "1", otherwise is "0".

Step 2 Construct F matrix. From matrix D we form another m x m matrix, called F, by replacing each 4-bit binary entry with the corresponding decimal number according to table 1. This matrix indicates the degree of coupling between production rules. For some PS it may be possible to permute the rows and columns of the F matrix such that highly coupled rules can be clustered together. This would be helpful in partitioning PS in clusters of dependent rules for parallel execution and in analyzing cluster interaction when the PS is modified.

Step 3 Construct C matrix. It is easy now to form a new binary matrix C which indicates whether or not rules can be executed in parallel. Matrix C is m x m and is constructed as follows:

$$a_{ij} = \{0,1,2\} \quad => \quad c_{ij} = 0$$
$$a_{ij} = \{3,4\} \quad => \quad c_{ij} = 1$$

Clearly, $c_{ij} = 0$ indicates that rules i and j can be applied in parallel. When both $c_{ij} = 0$ and $c_{ji} = 0$ rule i is commutative with rule j. This is important in situations when sequences i,j and j,i are applied to the same database; only one sequence needs to be applied. This result can be extended to more than two rules. Suppose $c_{ij} = c_{ik} = c_{kj} = c_{jk} = c_{ki} = c_{ji} = 0$. Then, all sequences involving rules i,j and k are equivalent. Moreover, rules i, j and k can be processed simultaneously if desired.

Step 4 Construct C' matrix. Matrix C from the previous step can be augmented with all possible composed productions, for the purpose of increasing even further the amount of parallelism. Recall that for every $a_{ij} = 3$, an i-o dependence exists between rules i and j, and a new composed production j•i can be created. Instead of applying rules j and i in sequence, it is faster to apply the composed rule j•i. Matrix C' is defined as

$$C' = \begin{bmatrix} C \\ C'' \end{bmatrix}$$

where C'' is created as follows : for every $a_{ij} = 3$ form a row j•i such that the row vector is

$$\overline{j \bullet i} = (\overline{i} + \overline{j}) \cdot \overline{m}$$

where i and j are row vectors corresponding to the i and j rows and m is a vector whose entries are "1" except in the jth column and + and · are OR and AND operations. Next, we show how the technique described above is applied to a small PS.

Example 1

Consider a 6-rule PS as shown below:

$$D = \begin{bmatrix} (1011) & (0001) & (1000) & (0000) & (0000) & (0000) \\ (0001) & (1011) & (1000) & (0000) & (0000) & (0000) \\ (0000) & (0110) & (1011) & (0011) & (1000) & (0001) \\ (0000) & (0110) & (0011) & (1011) & (1000) & (0001) \\ (0000) & (0100) & (0000) & (0000) & (1010) & (0000) \\ (0000) & (0110) & (0001) & (0001) & (1000) & (0011) \end{bmatrix}$$

$$F = \begin{bmatrix} 4 & 1 & 4 & 0 & 0 & 0 \\ 1 & 4 & 4 & 0 & 0 & 0 \\ 0 & 3 & 4 & 2 & 4 & 1 \\ 0 & 3 & 2 & 4 & 4 & 1 \\ 0 & 3 & 0 & 0 & 4 & 0 \\ 0 & 3 & 1 & 1 & 4 & 2 \end{bmatrix}$$

$$\begin{array}{c} \\ \\ \\ C = \\ \\ \\ \end{array} \begin{array}{c} 1 \\ 2 \\ 3 \\ 4 \\ 5 \\ 6 \end{array} \begin{bmatrix} 1 & 0 & 1 & 0 & 0 & 0 \\ 0 & 1 & 1 & 0 & 0 & 0 \\ 0 & 1 & 1 & 0 & 1 & 0 \\ 0 & 1 & 0 & 1 & 1 & 0 \\ 0 & 1 & 0 & 0 & 1 & 0 \\ 0 & 1 & 0 & 0 & 1 & 0 \end{bmatrix}$$

From matrix D results a matrix F as explained in step 2 of the algorithm

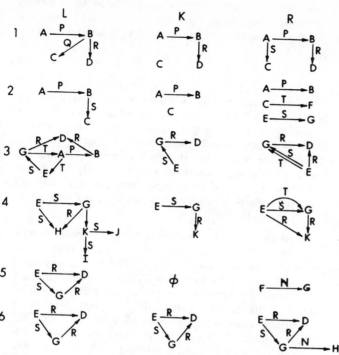

Figure 3: Production Rules

This matrix shows the coupling between rules. Next, we construct matrix C, as explained in step 3 of the algorithm.

This matrix carries information about the possibility of concurrent application of rules in the search space. For example, $c_{3,4} = c_{4,6} = c_{6,3} = c_{3,6} = c_{6,4} = c_{6,3} = 0$; which means that rules 3, 4 and 6 can be applied in parallel, and also their sequential applications in any order are equivalent. For this example, we selected a certain initial database. The search space for this PS with a depth of 4 has 103 nodes. This search space can be reduced to only 34 distinct nodes by using the results from the analysis of parallelism presented above. Parallel rules have zero entries in the C matrix.

5 Processing Model

Algorithms performed in a distributed computer system are partitioned among the components of the system. In our model, the set of rules is partitioned into disjoint subsets, each set allocated to one processor. The database is also partitioned as the intersection of the original database with the union of the precondition of each rule subset. This partitioning does not necessarily lead to disjoint database subsets. These sets of elements are allocated to the same processor as the corresponding rule set.

Furthermore, our model assumes that all processors have the same computational power, which means that the execution time of each rule is independent of the processing element to which it is assigned, and depends only on its size. The processors are connected through an alignment network and communication can only take place through available links. Messages that cannot reach immediately their destination are routed through the shortest paths.

Each processing element (PE) has three local memory modules, program memory, data memory and control memory. Program memory contains the rules assigned to the PE. Data memory contains the corresponding database subset and is comparable in size to the program memory, since each rule has several items and only relevant items to those rules are stored in the data memory. Control memory contains the address of the rules that are i and i-o dependent on each rule (the column of the C matrix), and any variable assignment that takes place during the matching phase. The portion of the database present in each PE_i is equal to:

$$G_i = \cup_j (L_j \cap G)$$

such that rules p_j are assigned to PE_i

In the beginning, the elements of the initial database are distributed among the PE's. Each PE creates a blackboard for each precondition present in its program memory. If an element w is part of the precondition and was initially present in the database, a token is placed in the blackboard to indicate its presence. If w contains a variable, that token is not permanent or unique, and the assignment of that variable is kept in the local memory for future consistency checks from other variable assignments.

As soon as all the precondition elements of a rule have been marked, and consistency among variable assignments was established, a flag is set to indicate to the central control which rule is ready to fire. There, a decision is made about which rule to fire and a record of the firing sequence is kept for future reference. All PE's now reset their flags and the one chosen to fire starts.

This firing procedure requires several phases. First, the tokens of the elements that belong to (L-K) of the rule fired are cleared. The assignments are passed to the postcondition. The (R-K) elements are broadcast simultaneously to PE's that have rules with i-o dependencies on the rule fired. The (L-K) elements whose tokens were cleared are broadcast in form of anti-tokens to all i-dependent rules.

Not all the weakly i-o dependent rules will necessarily match the database, but certainly all their blackboards will be updated, and their respective PE's continue to listen to the items being broadcast.

Then the antitokens are sent to i-dependent rules. Recall that by the construction of the C matrix, if a rule is i and i-o dependent, it is characterized as being i-dependent in its dynamic behavior. The marking (1xxx) in the D matrix and (5) in the F matrix indicate this fact. Because of this, there is no need to update the i-dependent blackboards prior to the broadcast of the (R-K) postcondition elements inserted.

The communication is done in parallel and if no available direct path is found, the elements are then routed. As these elements are received, the updating phase is performed in parallel. An exception to this is when two rules containing the same element are assigned to the same processor. In this case the update of the boards is done serially, first the rule with less elements yet to be matched. An alternative and more efficient way to maintain the state of the database is to create local subRETE networks [Forg79] or criticality lists. Efficiency in communication is achieved from the fact that each message has a preestablished destination without the need for address checking or partial prematches. When a PE receives an element it proceeds to update the state of its rule boards. The selection phase mentioned in [Ofla84], that would be extremely time consuming is then substituted by the analysis algorithm at compiling time.

In [Forg79] it is reported that 90% of the time spent by a production system is in the matching phase. According to [GuFo83] and [Ofla84], 20 to 30 rules are involved in each cycle. One can expect speedups of 7 or more just from the elimination of the matching phase, with the technique presented here. Further speedup can be achieved with the use of antitoken mechanisms overlapped with the updating phase, the use of local RETE nets, criticality lists or content addressable hardware.

If we assume that a single bus is to be used or a completely connected network [Ston77][Pric81], the communication time in the first case and the interconnection cost in the second would override the benefits of a parallel architecture. The design of an optimal network for PS has been addressed in [MoTe85]. Here we want to discuss the partitioning and the allocation problems when the network is given. This is a more realistic case since the PS is frequently updated.

6 Allocation and Partitioning

Consider a PS with m rules to be executed on n PE's. Let E be a (1xm) vector, such that the entry e_i is the execution time (updating time) of rule i in any PE_j. Also, let I be a (nxn) matrix such that each entry $i_{kj} = 1$ if there exists a direct link representing the interconnection network between PE_k and PE_j, and zero otherwise. C is the (mxm) matrix as in the previous algorithm. Now let A represent a mxn matrix called the assignment matrix and a_{ij} is one if p_i is assigned to PE_j. So,

$$\Sigma_j \ a_{ij} = 1$$

Let a nxn matrix S represent the length of the shortest path between any two processors. The allocation problem consists of assigning rules to processing elements such that the overall communication cost is reduced. First, it is assumed that there are as many processors as rules, and the communication cost is the only factor that influences the overall system performance, since all PE's behave similarly. The allocation can be formulated as:

$$\min \{\Sigma_l \Sigma_k \ s_{lk} \}$$

where l and k are the indices of PE's that contain rules that depend on each other and s is the length of the shortest path between the PE's. There is no reason in our architecture to opt for a dynamic rule assignment since those are extremely costly, all the PE's are similar and I is fixed. The partitioning problem consists of assigning m rules to n processors, where $m > n$. Let |bij| be the number of rules assigned to processor j that are i-o dependent on p_i. The partitioning problem to achieve a balanced load can be stated as:

$$\min \{\max |bij|\} \equiv \min \Sigma_k \ e_k$$
$$1 \leq i \leq n \qquad \text{such that} \quad p_k \in bij$$
$$1 \leq j \leq m$$

This does not take into account the geometry of the interconnection network I. Let ε_{ij} be the sum of the execution time of all the rules i-o dependent on p_i assigned to the same processor j, i.e., $\varepsilon_{ij} = \Sigma_k \ e_k$ if $p_k \in$ bij. Let c_{ij} be the communication time between the PE assigned with p_i and the PE_j assigned with i-o dependent rules. The execution time of rule j denoted as e_j is proportional to $|L_j|$ and s_{ij} is proportional to length of the shortest path i,j . Let ν be the time for internal blackboard token deletion. This time is negligible in respect to the other costs. The cost of assigning a rule i to PE_j is then given by:

$$t_{ij} = \max_j (\ \varepsilon_{ij} + c_{ij} \ ) + \nu_i$$

Now we define the overall cost of assigning all the rules to processors as:

$$J(A) = \Sigma_i \Sigma_j \ a_{ij} . t_{ij}$$

The optimal assignment is found by minimizing the above expression over all A matrices. Partitioning of PS with no assumed interconnection network was first reported in [Ofla84]. In the next subsection we will describe an iterative algorithm that will assign the rules to processors, while minimizing both the total execution and communication time, using a given network. An and executes extremely fast, in few iterations for the large majority of PS's. It is guaranteed to achieve local optimum, and conditions for global optimality and a comparison with the results using A^* algorithm are currently under study.

6.1 The Mapping Algorithm

Given C, I and E, let's first define a transformation $\tau: A \rightarrow A'$ such that $J(A) \geq J(\tau(A))$. Such transformation is determined as follows:

1. Each entry ij of the matrix S(nxn) is calculated as the shortest path between i and j in I (nxn).

2. For a given initial assignment A_0 (mxn), calculate the T matrix (mxn) in the following way: for each rule i and processor j,

   - Assign rule i to processor j in the matrix A_0, keeping the rest of A_0 constant.

   - Using the column c_i of the C matrix, for all i-o entries, $c_{i,k} = 1$, calculate the cost of the communication between rule i and all the dependent rules k and add their execution cost, if they are assigned to the same processor.

   - Find the highest cost of all rules. $t_{ij} = \max_k(\varepsilon_{ik} + c_{ik})$

3. Form a new matrix Δ as follows: for each row i of T, calculate the minimum cost $\Delta_{ij} = t_{ij} - \min\{t_{ij}\}$. Let j_{min} be the value of j that gives the minimal t_{ij}.

4. Calculate $\max_{ij}\{\Delta_{ij} \cdot a_{ij}\}$. Let i_{min} be the value of i that gives this maximum.

5. Reassign rule i_{min} to processor j_{min}.

6. In case i_{min} or j_{min} are not unique, choose the transformation that maximizes:
   $$\max[(J(\tau(A)) - J(A)) \cdot (\Delta_{kl})]$$
   all k and l.

7. Calculate $J(\tau(A)) = \Sigma_i \Sigma_j t_{ij} \cdot a_{ij}$. From the definition of this procedure it is guaranteed that $\tau(A) \geq J(\tau(A))$.

In practice, in large expert systems, since C is sparse, $T(\tau(A))$ can be calculated very easily from T(A). It is important to know that this algorithm does not "cycle" indefinitely and that it terminates if a global optimum exists. Proofs for that can be found in [Teno85]. Next, we show an example of the algorithm.

6.2 Example

We studied the mapping of one PS on a multiprocessing system. A 32x32 C matrix was generated using known PS statistics [GuFo83]. A simulator that allowed for different interconnection networks was written. In this example, we set our system to have 8 PE's and we tested the system with a perfect shuffle with exchange, mesh connected and circular interconnection networks.

The overall assignment cost depends on the initial assignment A_0. Using the PSEX - perfect shuffle with exchange network, we executed the assignment with three different initial A matrices. In the first case all the rules were assigned to PE_1. In the second case, m/n rules were assigned to PE_1, and the following group of m/n to PE_2 and so forth. We call this a bucket round robin assignment. In the third case we used the round robin strategy. We found that the best initial assignment is problem dependent but for many problems, the round robin is the best assignment. This is due to the fact that usually context dependent rules, K-dependent, are written in sequence by the programmer. So, theoretically the assignment of context dependent rules performed in a round robin fashion [Ofla84] is the best possible initial assignment. Unfortunately the information about context dependency is not readily available and algorithms to cluster those rules are computationally very intensive [Pric81]. The operation of clustering corresponds to diagonalizing the D matrix. The easiest initial assignment for the algorithm is the round robin technique. Our simulation results are shown in table 2. The numbers indicate overall assignment costs.

	PS-EX		MESH		Circ.	
	INITIAL	FINAL	INITIAL	FINAL	INITIAL	FINAL
PE_1	1530	1325	1530	1315	1530	1325
Bucket	587	580	569	548	587	587
RR	637	600	629	583	648	572

Table 2: Effect of the initial assignment on the final cost using different interconnection networks

We utilized different interconnection networks to execute the algorithm. The choice of the best network is problem dependent as the network has to closely approximate the C matrix [MoTe85].

7 Conclusion

In this paper we presented techniques for analyzing dependencies in production systems and assigning rules to processors to minimize both the communication cost and execution cost. The assignment algorithm converges quickly to a local minimum and cost reductions of 4 to 5 times have been observed for a multiprocessor using 8 PE's over a uniprocessor. Using the method proposed in this paper, it is possible to design efficient parallel computer architectures for PS. Trade offs between processing speeds and interprocessor communications are possible. We are now in the phase of implementing in software this mapping technique for expert system languages. An OPS5 version of a D matrix extractor has been successfully completed and data from practical expert systems is now being studied for the purpose of designing efficient parallel processing systems for PS.

8 References

[DaKi79]- Davis, R. and J. King "An Overview Of Production Systems" - in Machine Intelligence 1979

[Ehri78]- Erhig, H., "Introduction of Algebraic Theory of Graph Grammars", Proc. Int. Workshop on Graph Grammars and Their Application to Comp. Sci. and Biol., Bad Honnef, 1978. Also Lecture Notes in Computer Science, Vol. 73, Springer-Verlag.

[Nagl78]- Nagl, M. - "A Tutorial and Biographical Survey on Graph Grammars", Same as above.

[FeLe77]- Fennell, R.D. and Lesser, V.R. "Parallelism in AI Problem Solving: A Case Study of Hearsay II" - IEEE Transation on Computers, Vol c-26 No 2 Feb. 1977

[Forg82]- Forgy, C.L. "RETE. A fast Algorithm For The Many Pattern/Many Object Pattern Problem". AI Journal 82

[GuFo83]- Gupta, A. and Forgy, C. L. "Measurements on Production Systems". Tech. Report Department of Computer Science, CMU, December 1983.

[Gupt84]- Gupta, A. "Implementing OPS5 on DADO" Proc. of IC on Parallel Processing Aug 84

[MoTe85]- Moldovan, D.I. and Tenorio, M.F. - "Parallel Processing of Production Systems", Submitted to IJCAI 85

[MoTu84]- Moldovan, D.I. and Tung, Y.W. "SNAP - A VLSI Architecture for Artificial Intelligence", Journal of Parallel and Distributed Computing, May 1985 (also Technical Report PPP-84-3, USC, EE Dept.)

[Nils80]- Nilsson, N. "Principles of Artificial Intelligence", Tioga, California 1980.

[Prin81]- Prince, C.C. "The Assignment of Computational Tasks Among Processors in a Distributed System. Proc. of NCC, AFIPS, 1981.

[Ofla84]- Oflazer, K. "Partitioning in Parallel Processing Of Production Systems" Proc. IC on Parallel Processing Aug 1984.

[StSh82]- Stolfo,S.J. and Shaw, D.E. "DADO: A tree Structured Machine architecture for PS" Proc. IJCAI, CMU Pennsylvania, 1982.

[StMi84]- Stolfo,S.J. and Miranker, D.P. "DADO: A Parallel Processor for Expert Systems" Proc. IC on Parallel Processing Aug 84

[Teno84]- Tenorio, M.F.M. "Parallelism in Production Systems" - Thesis Proposal of the Dept. of EE- systems, Univ. of So. California, April 84

[Teno85]- Tenorio, M.F.M. "Parallel Processing Techniques for Production systems" - Ph.D. Thesis - Dept. of Electrical Engineering - systems / University of Southern California - In preparation.

DADO: A Parallel Processor for Expert Systems*

Salvatore J. Stolfo
and
Daniel P. Miranker
Department of Computer Science
Columbia University
New York City, N. Y. 10027

Abstract -- DADO is a parallel, tree-structured machine designed to provide significant performance improvements in the execution of large expert systems implemented in production system form. A full-scale version of the DADO machine would comprise a large (on the order of a hundred thousand) set of processing elements (PE's), each containing its own processor, a small amount (16K bytes, in the current prototype design) of local random access memory, and a specialized I/O switch. The PE's are interconnected to form a complete binary tree.

This paper describes the application domain of the DADO machine and the rationale for its design. We then focus on the machine architecture and detail the hardware design of a moderately large prototype comprising 1023 microprocessors currently under development at Columbia University. We conclude with very encouraging performance statistics recently calculated from an analysis of extensive simulations of the system.

Introduction

Due to the dramatic increase in computing power and the concomitant decrease in computing cost occurring over the last decade, many researchers are attempting to design computing systems to solve complicated problems or execute tasks which have in the past been performed by human experts. The focus of *Knowledge Engineering* is the construction of such complex, knowledge-based expert computing systems.

In general, knowledge-based expert systems are Artificial Intelligence (AI) problem-solving programs designed to operate in narrow "real-world" domains, performing tasks with the same competence as a skilled human expert. Illucidation of unknown chemical compounds [3], medical diagnosis [23], mineral exploration [4] and telephone cable maintenance [30] are just a few examples. The heart of these systems is a *knowledge base*, a large collection of facts, definitions, procedures and heuristic "rules of thumb", *acquired directly from a human expert*. The knowledge engineer is an intermediary between the expert and the system who extracts, formalizes, represents, and tests the relevant knowledge within a computer program.

Just as robotics and CAD/CAM technologies offer the potential for higher productivity in the "blue-collar" work force, it appears that AI expert systems will offer the same productivity increase in the "white-collar" work force. As a result, Knowledge Engineering has attracted considerable attention from government and industry for research and development of this emerging technology. However, as knowledge-based systems begin to grow in size and scope, they will begin to push conventional computing systems to their limits of operation. Even for experimental systems, many researchers reportedly experience frustration based on the length of time required for their operation. Much of the research in AI has focused on the problem of representing and organizing knowledge, but little attention has been paid to specialized machine architectures supporting problem-solving programs.

DADO is a large-scale parallel machine designed to support the rapid execution of expert systems, as well as multiple, independent systems. In the following sections we present an overview of DADO's application domain as well as the rationale for its design. We then detail the hardware design of the *DADO2* prototype, currently under construction at Columbia University, consisting of *1023 microprocessors*. We conclude with a presentation of performance statistics recently calculated from extensive simulations of the system, and an overview of the software systems implemented to date. Based on our studies, a full scale version of *DADO* comprising many thousands of processing elements will, in our opinion, be technically and economically feasible in the near future.

Expert Systems

Current Technology. Knowledge-based expert systems have been constructed, typically, from two loosely coupled modules, collectively forming the *problem-solving engine* (see Figure 1). The *knowledge base* contains all of the relevant domain-specific information permitting the program to behave as a specialized, intelligent problem-solver. Expert systems contrast greatly with the earlier general-purpose AI problem-solvers which were typically implemented without a specific application in mind. One of the key differences is the large amounts of problem-specific knowledge encoded within present-day systems.

Much of the research in AI has concentrated on effective methods for representing and operationalizing human experiential domain knowledge. The representations that have been proposed have taken a variety of forms including purely declarative-based logical formalisms, "highly-stylized" rules or productions, and

*This research has been supported by the Defense Advanced Research Projects Agency through contract N00039-82-C-0427, as well as grants from Intel, Digital Equipment, Hewlett-Packard, Valid Logic Systems, AT&T Bell Laboratories and IBM Corporations and the New York State Science and Technology Foundation. We gratefully acknowledge their support.

structured generalization hierarchies commonly referred to as semantic nets and frames. Many knowledge bases have been implemented in rule form, to be detailed shortly.

Figure 1: Organization of a Problem-Solving Engine.

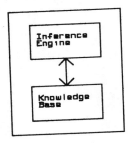

The *inference engine* is that component of the system which *controls* the deductive process: it implements the most appropriate strategy, or *reasoning* process for the problem at hand. The earliest AI problem-solvers were implemented with an iterative branching technique searching a large combinatorial space of problem states. Heuristic knowledge, applied within a static control structure, was introduced to limit the search process while attempting to guarantee the successful formation of solutions. In contrast, state-of-the-art expert systems separate the control strategy from an inflexible program, and deposit it in the knowledge base along with the rest of the domain-specific knowledge. Thus, the problem-solving strategy becomes domain-dependent, and is responsible to a large extent for the good performance exhibited by today's systems. However, a great deal of this kind of knowledge is necessary to achieve highly competent performance.

Within a great number of existing expert system programs, the corpus of knowledge about the problem domain is embodied by a *Production System* program. As has been reported by several researchers, production system representation schemes appear well suited to the organization and implementation of knowledge-based software. Rule-based systems provide a convenient means for human experts to explicate their knowledge, and are easily implemented and readily modified and extended. Thus, it is the ease with which rules can be acquired and explained that makes production systems so attractive.

Production Systems. In general, a *Production System* [6, 17, 18, and 19] is defined by a set of rules, or *productions*, which form the *Production Memory*(PM), together with a database of assertions, called the *Working Memory*(WM). Each production consists of a conjunction of *pattern elements*, called the *left-hand side* (LHS) of the rule, along with a set of actions called the *right-hand side* (RHS). The RHS specifies information that is to be added to (asserted) or removed from WM when the LHS successfully matches against the contents of WM. An example production, borrowed from the blocks world, is illustrated in Figure 2.

In operation, the production system repeatedly executes the following cycle of operations:

1. *Match*: For each rule, determine whether the LHS

Figure 2: An Example Production.

```
(Goal (Clear-top-of Block))
(Isa =x Block)
(On-top-of =y =x)
(Isa =y Block)  -->
                delete(On-top-of =y =x)
                assert(On-top-of =y Table)
```

If the goal is to clear the top of a block,
and there is a block (=x)
covered by something (=y)
which is also a block,
then
remove the fact that =y is on =x
and assert that =y is on top of the table.

— — — — — — — — — —

matches the current environment of WM. All matching instances of the rules are collected in the *conflict set of rules*.

2. *Select*: Choose exactly one of the matching rules according to some predefined criterion.

3. *Act*: Add to or delete from WM all assertions specified in the RHS of the selected rule or perform some operation.

During the selection phase of production system execution, a typical interpreter provides *conflict resolution strategies* based on the *recency* of matched data in WM, as well as syntactic discrimination. Rules matching data elements that were more recently inserted in WM are preferred, with ties decided in favor of rules that are more specific (i.e., have more constants) than others.

Why a specialized PS architecture? One problem facing expert systems technology is efficiency. It should be evident from the above description that large PS programs would spend most of their time executing the match phase requiring an enormous number of primitive symbol manipulation tasks. (Indeed, Forgy [6] notes that some PS interpreters spend 90% of their time in the match phase.) Hence, as this technology is ambitiously applied to larger and more complex problems, the size and concomitant slow speed of execution of production system programs, *with large rule bases*, on conventional machines will most likely doom such attempts to failure. The *R1* program [13], designed to configure Digital Equipment Corporation VAX computers, provides a convincing illustration.

In its current form, *R1* contains approximately 2500 rules operating on a WM containing several hundred data items, describing a partially configured VAX. Running on a DEC VAX 11/780 computer and implemented in OPS5 [8], a highly efficient production system language, *R1* executes from 2 to 600 production system cycles per minute. Configuring an entire VAX system requires a considerable amount of computing time on a moderately large and expensive computer. The performance of such systems will quickly worsen as experts are designed with not only one to two thousand rules, but perhaps with *tens of thousands* of rules. Indeed, several such large-scale systems are currently under development at various research centers. Statistics are difficult to calculate in the absence of specific empirical data, but it is conceivable that such large systems may require an unacceptable amount of computing time for a medium size conventional computer to execute a single cycle of production system execution! Thus, we consider the design and implementation of a specialized *production system machine* to warrant serious attention by parallel architects and VLSI designers.

Much of the experimental research conducted to date on specialized hardware for AI applications has focused on the realization of high-performance, cleverly designed, but for the most part, architecturally conventional machines. (MIT's LISP Machine exemplifies this approach.) Such machines, while quite possibly of great practical interest to the research community, make no attempt to employ hardware parallelism on the massive scale characteristic of our own work.

Thus, simply stated, the goal of the DADO machine project is the design and implementation of a *cost effective* high performance *rule processor*, based on large-scale parallel processing, capable of rapidly executing a production system cycle for very large rule bases. The essence of our approach is to execute a very large number of pattern matching operations on concurrent hardware, thus substantially accelerating the match phase. Our goals do not include the design of a high-speed parallel processor capable of a fruitless parallel search through a combinatorial solution space.

A small (15 processor) prototype of the machine, constructed at Columbia University from components supplied by Intel Corporation, has been operational since April 1983. Based on our experiences with constructing this small prototype, we believe a larger DADO prototype, comprising 1023 processors, to be technically and economically feasible for implementation using current technology. We believe that this larger experimental device will provide us with the vehicle for evaluating the performance, as well as the hardware design, of a full-scale version of DADO implemented entirely with custom VLSI circuits.

The DADO Machine

The System Architecture. DADO is a fine-grain, parallel machine where processing and memory are extensively intermingled. A full-scale production version of the DADO machine would comprise a very large (on the order of a hundred thousand) set of *processing elements* (PE's), each containing its own processor, a small amount (16K bytes, in the current design of the prototype version) of local random access memory (RAM), and a specialized I/O switch. The PE's are interconnected to form a *complete binary tree* (see Figure 3).

Within the DADO machine, each PE is capable of executing in either of two modes under the control of run-time software. In the first, which we will call *SIMD mode* (for single instruction stream, multiple data streams [5]), the PE executes instructions broadcast by some ancestor PE within the tree. (SIMD typically refers to a single stream of "machine-level" instructions. Within DADO, on the other hand, SIMD is generalized to mean a single stream of remote procedure invocation instructions. Thus, DADO makes more effective use of its communication bus by broadcasting

more "meaningful" instructions.) In the second, which will be referred to as *MIMD* mode (for multiple instruction stream, multiple data stream), each PE executes instructions stored in its own local RAM, independently of the other PE's. A single conventional coprocessor, adjacent to the root of the DADO tree, controls the operation of the entire ensemble of PE's.

When a DADO PE enters MIMD mode, its logical state is changed in such a way as to effectively "disconnect" it and its descendants from all higher-level PE's in the tree. In particular, a PE in MIMD mode does not receive any instructions that might be placed on the tree-structured communication bus by one of its ancestors. Such a PE may, however, broadcast instructions to be executed by its own descendants, providing all of these descendants have themselves been switched to SIMD mode. The DADO machine can thus be configured in such a way that an arbitrary internal node in the tree acts as the root of a tree-structured SIMD device in which all PE's execute a single instruction (on different data) at a given point in time. This flexible architectural design supports *multiple-SIMD* execution (MSIMD), as, for example, [24], but on a much larger scale. Thus, the machine may be logically divided into distinct partitions, each executing a distinct task, and is the primary source of DADO's speed in executing a large number of primitive pattern matching operations concurrently.

The DADO I/O switch, which will be implemented in semi-custom gate array technology and incorporated within the 1023 processing element version of the machine, has been designed to support rapid global communication. In addition, a specialized combinational circuit incorporated within the I/O switch will allow for the very rapid selection of a single distinguished PE from a set of candidate PE's in the tree, a process we call resolving. Currently, the 15 processing element version of DADO performs these operations in firmware embodied in its off-the-shelf components.

The Binary Tree Topology. In our initial work, several alternative parallel machine architectures were studied to determine a suitable organization of a special-purpose production system machine. High-speed algorithms for the parallel execution of production system programs were developed for the perfect shuffle [21] and binary tree machine architectures [1]. Forgy [7] proposed an interesting use of the mesh-connected ILLIAC IV machine [12] for the parallel execution of production systems, but recognized that his approach failed to find all matching rules in certain circumstances. Of these architectures, the binary tree organization was chosen for implementation. For the present paper we summarize these reasons as follows:

- Binary trees are efficiently implemented in VLSI technology:

  * Using the well known "Hyper-H" embedding (see [2]), binary trees can be embedded in the plane in an amount of area proportional to the number of processors. Thus, as VLSI continues scaling downward, higher processor densities can be achieved.

  * A design for a single chip type, first reported by Leiserson [11], embeds both a complete binary subtree and one additional PE, which can be used to implement an arbitrarily large binary tree. Thus, binary tree machines have a very low number of distinct integrated parts.

* Pin-out on the Leiserson chip remains constant for any number of embedded PE's.

* The Leiserson chip used with a simple recursive construction scheme produces printed circuit board designs that make optimal use of available area. This single printed circuit board design is suitable for implementing an arbitrarily large binary tree.

- Broadcasting data to a large number of recipients is handled efficiently by tree structures.

- Most importantly, the binary tree topology is a natural fit for production system programs.

We note that binary trees do have certain limitations of practical importance. Although broadcasting a small amount of information to a large number of recipients is efficiently handled by binary trees, the converse is, in general, unfortunately not true. That is, for certain computational tasks (permutation of data within the tree, for example) the effective bandwidth of communication is restricted by the top of the tree. Fortunately, as we shall see shortly, this "binary tree bottleneck" does not arise in the execution of production systems.

Production System execution. In our earlier work, extensive theoretical analyses and software simulations of a high-speed algorithm for production system execution on *DADO* was completed and reported in [25]. In its *simplest* form, the algorithm operates in the following way:

1. By assigning a single rule to each PE, executing in MIMD mode, at a (logically) fixed level within the tree, each rule in PM is matched concurrently. (This fixed level within the tree is referred to as the PM-level, see Figure 3.) Thus, the time to calculate the conflict set of rules on each cycle is independent of the number of productions in the system. Variations of this approach allow for multiple rules to be located at a PM-level PE, thus increasing the time to match a modest degree.

2. By assigning a data item in WM to a single PE executing in SIMD mode, lying below the PM-level, WM is implemented as a true hardware *content-addressable memory*. Thus, the time required to match a single pattern element in the LHS of a rule is independent of the number of facts in WM. (In a manner similar to production storage, more effective use of the WM PE's is made by allowing several WM elements to be present. The WM elements stored at a single PE, however, are "disjoint" in the sense that they may match different condition elements in the LHS of a rule.)

3. The selection of a single rule for execution from the conflict set is also performed in parallel by a logarithmic time binary tree selection executed above the PM-level. Thus, the logarithmic time lower bound of comparing and selecting a single item from a collection of items is achievable on *DADO* as well.

4. Lastly, the RHS actions specified by the selected rule are broadcast to all PM-level PE's which update their respective WM-subtrees in parallel.

Figure 3: Functional Division of the DADO Tree.

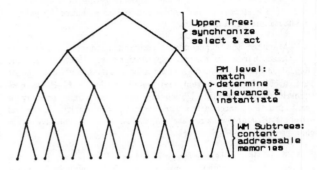

A comparative evaluation of this algorithm with various allocation schemes has been reported elsewhere (see [10, 15, 25, 27, and 28]). It should be noted that although the running time of the basic algorithm is shown to be insensitive to the size of PM and WM, in practice a fixed size machine may not, in general, attain these lower bound results. Thus, in situations where WM and PM are too large to be conveniently distributed in the manner discussed above for a machine of fixed size, some performance degradation will result.

For example, the second DADO prototype will consist of 1023 PE's and is expected to be logically divided with a PM-level consisting of 32 PE's, each rooting a WM-subtree with 31 PE's. To execute a 2500 rule system such as R1 will require partitioning ~75 rules to each PM-level PE. It would appear that the time to match would depend on 75 rules rather than 2500 for this example. However, recent statistics reported indicate that never more than ~30 rules are active on each cycle of execution of R1. Hence, with a suitable partitioning of rules, no more than 1 rule would be processed by each PM-level PE in our example configuration, thus attaining a match time independent of 2500 rules. Note, though, that each PM-level PE can access 31 WM elements in parallel. Thus, in total, 32 X 31 or ~1000 WM elements would be accessed at any one point in time. In the case where a single rule might require access to more than 31 WM elements at a time, performance will degrade gracefully. Hence, 31 elements can be accessed by a single PM-level PE in one time unit, 62 in two time units, 93 in three, etc.

Recently, we have completed a number of reports which detail five related algorithms for the parallel execution of PS programs to account for various differences in PS programs. As noted, some PS programs, (R1, for example) may not have a high degree of "production-level parallelism". That is, on each cycle only a relatively small number of productions may have satisfied LHS's. Other PS programs may have a high degree of production-level parallelism. Many other variations are possible which lead to a variety of related algorithms which attempt to maximize system performance by integrating various rule partitioning schemes with clever "state saving" schemes. The details of the various methods are beyond the scope of this paper, and thus the reader is encouraged to see [15] and [28]. Studies of such situations have been made and the projections of possible performance degradation are summarized in a later section of this paper.

Although analytical studies and software implementations are primary tasks of the *DADO* project, our current efforts have focused on the construction of hardware. Many parallel computing devices have been proposed in the literature, however, often such devices are constructed only on paper. Many scientific and engineering problems remain undetected until an actual device is constructed and experimentally evaluated. Thus, we are actively building a large prototype consisting of 1023 Intel 8751 microcomputer chips. A small 15 PE version of *DADO* is currently operational at Columbia University acting as a development system for the software base of the larger prototype. In the remainder of this paper we concentrate on the details of the hardware for these prototypes as well as the software systems that have been implemented thus far.

The DADO Prototypes

Physical Characteristics. A 15-element *DADO1* prototype, constructed from (partially) donated parts supplied by Intel Corporation, has been operational since April 25, 1983. The two wire-wrap board system, housed in a chassis roughly the size of an IBM PC, is clocked at 3.5 megahertz producing 4 million instructions per second (MIPS)[16]. (The effective usable MIPS is considerably less due to the significant overhead incurred in interprocessor communication. For each byte quantity communicated through the system, 12 machine instructions are consumed at each level in the tree while executing an asynchronous, 4-cycle handshake protocol.) DADO1 contains 124K bytes of user random access storage and 60K bytes of read only memory. A much larger version, *DADO2*, is currently under construction which will incorporate 1023 PE's constructed from two commercially available Intel chips and one semi-custom gate array chip (to be fabricated by LSI Logic). DADO1 does not provide enormous computational resources. Rather, it is viewed as the development system for the software base of DADO2, and is not expected to demonstrate a significant improvement in the speed of execution of a production system application.

DADO2 will be implemented with 32 printed circuit boards housed in an IBM Series I cabinet (donated by IBM Corporation). A DEC VAX 11/750 (partially donated by DEC Corporation) serves as DADO2's coprocessor (although an HP 9836 workstation may be used as well) and is the only device a user of DADO2 will see. Thus, DADO2 is considered a transparent back-end processor to the VAX 11/750.

The DADO2 system will have roughly the same hardware complexity as a VAX 11/750 system, and if amortized over 12 units will cost in the range of 70 to 90 thousand dollars to construct considering 1982 market retail costs. The DADO2 semi-custom I/O chip is planned for implementation in gate array technology and will allow DADO2 to be clocked at 12 megahertz, the full speed of the Intel chips. The average machine instruction cycle time is 1.8

microseconds, producing a system with a raw computational throughput of roughly 570 million instructions per second. We note that little of this computational resource is wasted in communication overhead as in the DADO1 machine.

The Prototype Processing Element. Each PE in the 15-element DADO1 prototype system incorporates an Intel 8751 microcomputer chip, serving as the processor, and an 8K X 8 Intel 2186 RAM chip, serving as the local memory. DADO2 will incorporate a slightly modified PE. The Intel 2187, which is fully compatible with but faster than an Intel 2186, replaces the DADO1 RAM chip allowing the processor to be clocked at its fastest speed. Two such chips will be used (with a 16K X 1 chip for parity), increasing the PE storage capacity to 16K bytes. Further, the custom I/O chip will contain memory support circuitry and thus also replaces several additional gates employed in DADO1.

Although the original version of DADO had been designed to incorporate a 2K byte RAM within each PE, a 16K byte RAM was chosen for the prototype PE to allow a modest degree of flexibility in designing and implementing the software base for the full version of the machine. In addition, this extra "breathing room" within each PE allows for experimentation with various special operations that may be incorporated in the full version of the machine in combinational circuitry, as well as affording the opportunity to critically evaluate other proposed (tree-structured) parallel architectures through software simulation.

It is worth noting though that the proper choice of "grain size" is an interesting open question. That is, through experimental evaluation we hope to determine the size of RAM for each PE, chosen against the number of such elements for a fixed hardware complexity, appropriate for the widest range of production system applications. Thus, future versions of DADO may consist of a number of PE's each containing an amount of RAM significantly larger or smaller than implemented in the current prototype systems.

The Intel 8751 is a moderately powerful 8-bit microcomputer incorporating a 4K erasable programmable read only memory (EPROM), and a 256-byte RAM on a single silicon chip. One of the key characteristics of the 8751 processor is its I/O capability. The 4 parallel, 8-bit ports provided in a 40 pin package has contributed substantially to the ease of implementing a binary tree interconnection between processors. Indeed, DADO1 was implemented within 4 months of delivery of the hardware components. Figure 4 illustrates the DADO1 prototype PE, while figure 5 illustrates DADO2's PE.

Note that the same processor connections exist in the DADO2 PE design as those appearing in the DADO1 design. If in the unlikely event that the planned I/O chip does not function properly, DADO2 will thus remain operational, but will not run as fast as envisaged. Since the DADO1 hardware to date has remained operable, we are convinced that the fully upward compatible DADO2 PE design ensures the successful operation of a 1023 PE version of the machine.

In DADO1 the communication primitives and execution modes of a DADO PE are implemented by a small *kernel system* resident within each processor EPROM. The specialized I/O switch envisaged for the larger version of the machine is simulated in the

Figure 4: The DADO1 Prototype Processing Element.

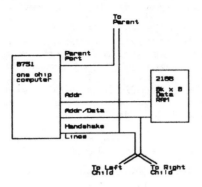

Figure 5: The DADO2 Prototype Processing Element.

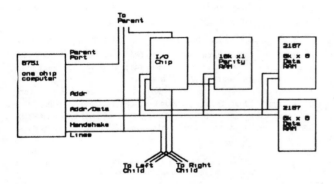

smaller version by a short sequential computation. As noted, the 1023 element prototype would be capable of executing in excess of 570 MIPS. Although pipelined communication is employed in the DADO1 kernel design, it is expected that fewer MIPS would be achieved on DADO2 without the I/O chip, as detailed in the following section. Thus, the design and implementation of a custom I/O chip forms a major part of our current hardware research activities.

It should be noted that, in keeping with our principles of "low-cost performance," we have selected a processor technology one generation behind existing available microcomputer technology. For example, DADO2 could have been designed with 1023 Motorola 68000 processors or Intel 80286 chips. Instead, we have chosen a relatively slow technology to limit the number of chips for each PE, as well as to demonstrate our most important architectural principals in a cost effective manner.

Furthermore, since the Intel 8751 does not press current VLSI technology to its limits, it is surely within the realm of feasibility to implement a DADO2 PE on a single silicon chip. Thus, although

DADO2 may appear impressive (an inexpensive, compact system with a thousand computers executing roughly 600 million instructions per second) its design is very conservative and probably at least an order of magnitude less powerful than a similar device using faster technology. It is our conjecture though that the machine will be practical and useful and many of its limitations will be ameliorated as VLSI continues its downward trend in scaling. (DADO3 may serve to prove this conjecture.)

Performance Evaluation of DADO2.

Design Alternatives. Much of the available computing power in the DADO1 prototype is consumed by firmware executing a four cycle handshake communication protocol. For this reason we investigated the tradeoffs involved with adding a specialized I/O circuit to each PE to handle global communication in DADO2. The current I/O circuit design provides the means to broadcast a byte to all PE's in the tree in less than one Intel 8751 instruction cycle. This efficiency gain does not come free. The I/O circuit increases a PE's component count as well as the total area on a printed circuit board for the system. To decide this issue, we investigated the relative performance of a machine design incorporating the I/O circuit and a design without the I/O circuit, using the available area for additional PE's.

A second but orthogonal issue for the machine design is whether or not it is worthwhile to buffer the instruction stream broadcast to PE's executing in SIMD mode. In a typical SIMD machine a control processor issues a stream of machine level instructions that are executed synchronously in lock step by all of the slave processors in the array. DADO is different. Since each PE of DADO is a fully capable computer, and communication between PE's is generally expensive, we wish to make an instruction as "meaningful" as possible. What is communicated as an instruction in DADO is usually a pointer to a procedure, stored locally in each slave PE. Primitive SIMD DADO instructions are in fact parallel procedure calls and may be viewed as macro instructions.

For example, a common instruction that will be executed by a DADO PE is "MATCH(pattern)", where MATCH is a generalized pattern matching routine local to each processor.

Transmitting pointers to procedures makes effective use of communication links but introduces a difficult problem. A procedure may behave differently depending on the local data. Thus, the same macro instruction may require different amounts of processing time in each PE. In such a device either the PE's must synchronize on every instruction, and therefore potentially lay idle while the slowest PE finishes, or the PE's must be able to buffer the instruction stream to possibly achieve better utilization. However, buffering the instructions requires overhead and may in fact decrease the overall performance.

Evaluation Method. To resolve these two design issues the DADO instruction stream was characterized by studying the code implementing the match phase of the DADO production system algorithm, (roughly 10 pages of PPL/M, detailed in the following section). Queuing models were developed for each configuration representing the 4 possible combinations: a DADO PE with and without the I/O circuit, and with and without buffering. The four models were simulated using the IBM Research Queuing Network Simulation package, RESQ2, [20]. The package has a number of very powerful simulation primitives including generation of job streams with a variety of distributions times, active queues with a variety of queueing service disciplines as well as mechanisms to provide flow control. Complete details of this study can be found in [14].

Evaluation Results. Figure 6 summarizes the relative throughput of the four configurations working on a problem typical of the size we expect a 1023 node *DADO* to handle: 1000 productions and 1000 working memory elements (although for certain PS programs, R1, for example, we will be able to implement nearly 2500 production rules). The simulations show that the I/O circuit can be expected to nearly double the performance of the *DADO* machine. However, the overhead associated with buffering causes a decrease in performance of 27 and 20 percent in configurations with and without the I/O circuit, respectively.

Figure 6: Relative Performance of Four PE Configurations.

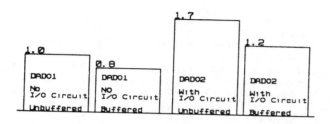

Figure 7 is a comparison of a 5 level *DADO* subtree (comprising 31 PE's) without the I/O circuit, and a 4 level *DADO* subtree, (comprising 15 PE's) with the I/O circuit. The x-axis represents a rough approximation of the number of WM data elements in the system. The graph shows that for a typical size problem a 9 level deep *DADO2* with the I/O circuit will outperform a 10 level deep *DADO1* without the I/O circuit by roughly 15 percent. However, the smaller machine's performance degrades faster than that of the larger machine. The simulations indicate for problems larger than those we anticipate it is worthwhile to dispense with the I/O circuit in favor of additional PE's.

Programming DADO

PL/M [9] is a high-level language designed by Intel Corporation as the host programming environment for applications using the full range of Intel microcomputer and microcontroller chips. A superset of *PL/M*, which we call *PPL/M*, has been implemented as the system-level language for the *DADO* prototypes. *PPL/M* provides a set of facilities to specify operations to be performed by independent PE's in parallel.

Intel's *PL/M* language is a conventional block-oriented language providing a full range of data structures and high-level statements. The following two syntactic conventions have been added to *PL/M* for programming the SIMD mode of operation of *DADO*. The design of these constructs was influenced by the methods employed in specifying parallel computation in the *GLYPNIR* language [12] designed for the *ILLIAC IV* parallel processor. The *SLICE* attribute defines variables and procedures

Figure 7: Performance Comparison of DADO1 and DADO2 on Variable Size Working Memory.

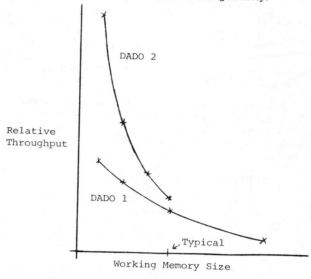

that are resident within each PE. The second addition is a syntactic construct, the *DO SIMD block*, which delimits *PPL/M* instructions broadcast to descendant SIMD PE's. (In the following definitions, optional syntactic constructs are represented within square brackets.)

The SLICE attribute:

DECLARE variable[(dimension)] type SLICE;

name: PROCEDURE[(params)] [type] SLICE;

Each declaration of a SLICEd variable will cause an allocation of space for the variable to occur within each PE. SLICEd procedures are automatically loaded within the RAM of each PE by an operating system executive resident in *DADO*'s coprocessor.

Within a *PPL/M* program, an assignment of a value to a SLICEd variable will cause the transfer to occur within each enabled SIMD PE concurrently. A constant appearing in the right hand side will be automatically broadcast to all enabled PE's. Thus, the statement

X=5;

where X is of type BYTE SLICE, will assign the value 5 to each occurrence of X in each enabled SIMD PE. (Thus, at times it is convenient to think of SLICEd variables as vectors which may be operated upon, in whole or in part, in parallel.) However, statements which operate upon SLICEd variables can only be specified within the bounds of a DO SIMD block.

DO SIMD block:

```
DO SIMD;
   r-statement₀;
   ...
   r-statementₙ;
END;
```

The r-statement is restricted to be any *PL/M* statement *incorporating only SLICEd variables and constants.*

In addition to the full range of instructions available in *PPL/M*, a *DADO* PE in MIMD mode will have available to it a set of built-in functions to perform the basic tree communication operations, in addition to functions controlling the various modes of execution.

Direct hardware support is provided by the semi-custom I/O chip for each of the global communication functions: BROADCAST, REPORT and RESOLVE, other communication primitives are implemented by firmware embedded in the processor EPROM. The interested reader is referred to [26] for the details of these primitives, as well as a complete specification of the *PPL/M* language.

The RESOLVE instruction recently redesigned from studying DADO1's behavior deserves special mention here. The RESOLVE instruction is used in practice to disable all but a single PE, chosen from among a specified set of PE's. In DADO1, first a SLICEd variable is set to one in all PE's to be included in the candidate set. The RESOLVE instruction is then issued by a PE executing in MIMD mode, causing all but one of the flags in descendant PE's, executing in SIMD mode, to be changed to zero. (Upon executing a RESOLVE instruction, one of the inputs to the MIMD PE will become high if at least one candidate was found in the tree, and low if the candidate set was found to be empty. This condition code is stored in a SLICEd variable, which exists within the MIMD PE.) By issuing an assignment statement, all but the single, chosen PE may be disabled, and a sequence of instructions may be executed on the chosen PE alone. In particular, data from the chosen PE may be communicated to the MIMD PE through a sequence of REPORT commands.

In DADO1, the RESOLVE function is implemented using special sequential code, embedded within the EPROM, that propagates a series of "kill" signals in parallel from all candidate PE's to all (higher-numbered) PE's in the tree. In DADO2, the RESOLVE operation has been generalized to operate on 8-bit data, producing the *maximum* value stored in some candidate PE. Repeated use of this max-RESOLVE function allows for the very rapid selection of multiple byte data. This circuit has proven very useful for a number of DADO algorithms which made use of the tree neighbor communication instructions primarily for ordering data within the tree. The use of the high-speed max-RESOLVE often obviates the need for such communication instructions. Consequently, the view of DADO as a binary tree architecture has become, fortuitously, nearly transparent in most of the algorithms written for DADO thus far.

Conclusion

The largest share of our software effort has concentrated on parallel implementations of various AI applications. The most important of these is an interpreter for the parallel execution of production system programs. A restricted model of production systems has been implemented in *PPL/M* and is currently being tested. Our plans include the completion of an interpreter for a more general version of production systems in the coming months.

We have also become very interested recently in *PROLOG*. Since *PROLOG* may be considered as a special case of production systems, it is our belief that *DADO* can quite naturally support performance improvements of *PROLOG* programs over conventional implementations. Some interesting work in this direction has been reported in [31].

Lastly, we note the relationship of *LISP* to *DADO*. Part of our work has concentrated on providing *LISP* with additional parallel processing primitives akin to those employed in *PPL/M*. We have come to use PSL LISP this purpose due to its relative ease in porting to a new processor.

By way of summary, it is our belief that *DADO* can in fact support the high-speed execution of a very large class of AI applications specifically expert systems implemented in rule form. Coupled with an efficient implementation in VLSI technology, the large-scale parallelism achievable on *DADO* will indeed provide significant performance improvements over von Neumann machines. Indeed, our preliminary statistics suggest that the 1023 PE version of *DADO* is expected to execute *R1*, for example, at an average rate in excess of *85 production system cycles per second!* Present statistics for a reimplementation of R1 on a VAX 11/780 project a performance of 30-50 cycles per second. It is interesting to note further that the DADO2 prototype will be comparable in hardware complexity to the DEC VAX 11/750, a smaller, slower and much less expensive version of the VAX 780 used presently to execute *R1*. Hence, DADO2's parallelism achieves a 50% performance improvement over a machine roughly six times its size.

References

[1] Browning, S., "Hierarchically organized machines," In Mead and Conway (Eds.), *Introduction to VLSI Systems*, 1978.

[2] Browning, S., *The Tree Machine: A Highly Concurrent Computing Environment*, Ph.D. Thesis, California Institute of Technology, 1980.

[3] Buchanan, B. G. and Feigenbaum, E. A., "DENDRAL and Meta-DENDRAL: Their applications dimension," *Artificial Intelligence*, 11:5-24, 1978.

[4] Duda, R., Gashnig, J. and Hart, P.E., "Model design in the PROSPECTOR consultant system for mineral exploration," In D. Michie (Ed.), *Expert Systems in the Micro-Electronic Age*, Edinburgh University Press, 1979.

[5] Flynn, M. J., "Some computer organizations and their effectiveness," *IEEE Transactions on Computers*, 1972.

[6] Forgy, C. L., *On the Efficient Implementation of Production Systems*, Ph.D. Thesis, Carnegie-Mellon University, 1979.

[7] Forgy, C. L., "A note on production systems and ILLIAC IV," Technical Report 130, Department of Computer Science,

Carnegie-Mellon University, 1980.

[8] Forgy, C. L., "RETE: A fast algorithm for the many pattern/many object pattern problem," *Artificial Intelligence Journal*, 1982.

[9] Intel Corporation, *PL/M-51 Users's Guide for the 8051 Based Development System*, Order Number 121966, 1982.

[10] Ishida, T. and S. J. Stolfo, "Simultaneous firing of production rules on tree-structured machines," Technical Report, Department of Computer Science, Columbia University, 1984. (Submitted to *Int. Conf. Fifth Generation Computer Systems.*)

[11] Leiserson, C. E., *Area-Efficient VLSI Computation*, Ph.D. Thesis, Department of Computer Science, Carnegie-Mellon University, 1981.

[12] Lowrie, D. D., T. Layman, D. Daer and J. M. Randal, "GLYPNIR-A programming language for ILLIAC IV," *Comm. ACM*, 18-3, 1975.

[13] McDermott, J., "R1: The formative years," *AI Magazine* 2:21-29, 1981.

[14] Miranker, D. P., "The performance analysis of four competing DADO PE configurations," Technical Report, Department of Computer Science, Columbia University, 1983.

[15] Miranker, D. P., "Performance estimates for the DADO machine: A comparison of TREAT and RETE," Technical Report, Department of Computer Science, Columbia University, 1984. (Submitted to *Int. Conf. on Fifth Generation Computer Systems.*)

[16] Miranker, D. P., "The system-level design of the DADO1 prototype," (in preparation).

[17] Newell, A., "Production systems: models of control structures," In W. Chase (editor), *Visual Information Processing*, Academic Press, 1973.

[18] Nilsson, N., *Fundamental Principles of Artificial Intelligence*, Tioga Press, Menlo Park, California, 1980.

[19] Rychener, M., *Production Systems as a Programming Language for Artificial Intelligence Research*, Ph.D. Thesis, Department of Computer Science, Carnegie-Mellon University, 1976

[20] Sauer, Charles H., Macnair, Edward A., Kurose, James F. "The research queueing package, CMS User's Guide," Technical Report RA 139 #41127, IBM Research Division, 1982.

[21] Schwartz, J. T., "Ultracomputers," *ACM Transactions on Programming Languages and Systems* 3(1), 1980.

[22] Shaw, D. E., "The NON-VON supercomputer," Technical Report, Department of Computer Science, Columbia University, 1982.

[23] Shortliffe, E. H., *Computer-Based Medical Consultations: MYCIN*, New York: American Elsevier, 1976.

[24] Siegel, H. J., L. J. Siegel, F. C. Kemmerer, P. T. Mueller, H. E. Smolky and D. S. Smith, "PASM: A partitionable SIMD/MIMD system for image processing and pattern recognition," *IEEE Transactions on Computers*, 1981.

[25] Stolfo, S. J. and D. E. Shaw, "DADO: A tree-structured machine architecture for production systems," *Proc. National Conference on Artificial Intelligence*, Carnegie-Mellon University and University of Pittsburgh, 1982.

[26] Stolfo, S. J., D. Miranker and M. Lerner, "PPL/M: The system level language for programming the DADO machine," Technical Report, Department of Computer Science, Columbia University, 1982. (Submitted to *ACM TOPLAS.*)

[27] Stolfo, S. J., "The DADO parallel computer," Technical Report Department of Computer Science, Columbia University, 1983. (Submitted to *AI Journal.*)

[28] Stolfo, S. J., "Five algorithms for PS execution on the DADO machine," Technical Report, Department of Computer Science, Columbia University, 1984. (Submitted to *AAAI 84.*)

[29] Stolfo, S. J., "On the design of parallel production system machines: What's in a LIP?," Technical Report, Department of Computer Science, Columbia University, 1984. (Submitted to *Int. Conf. on Fifth Generation Computer Systems.*)

[30] Stolfo, S. J., Vesonder, G. T., "ACE: An expert system supporting analysis and management decision making," *Bell System Technical Journal*, (To appear 1984).

[31] Taylor, S., C. Maio, S. J. Stolfo and D. E. Shaw, "PROLOG on the DADO machine: A parallel system for high-speed logic programming," *Proc. Third International Phoenix Conference on Computers and Communication*, 1984.

DESIGN SKETCH FOR A MILLION-ELEMENT NETL MACHINE

Scott E. Fahlman

Carnegie-Mellon University
Department of Computer Science
Pittsburgh, Pennsylvania 15213

Abstract

This paper describes (very briefly) a parallel hardware implementation for NETL-type semantic network memories. A million-element system can be built with about 7000 IC chips, including 4000 64K RAM chips. This compares favorably with the hardware cost of holding the same body of knowledge in a standard computer memory, and offers significant advantages in flexibility of access and the speed of performing certain searches and deductions.

1. Introduction

In [1] I presented a scheme for representing real-world knowledge in the form of a hardware semantic network. In this scheme, called NETL, each node and link in the network is a very simple hardware processing element capable of passing single-bit markers through the network in parallel. This marker-passing is under the overall control of an external serial processor. By exploiting the parallelism of this marker-passing operation, we can perform searches, set intersections, inheritance of properties and descriptions, multiple-context operations, and certain other important operations much faster than is possible on a serial machine. These new abilities make it possible to dispense with hand-crafted search-guiding heuristics for each domain and with many of the other procedural attachments found in the standard AI approaches to representing knowledge. In addition to the difficulty of creating such procedures, and the very great difficulty of getting the machine to create them automatically, I argue that the heuristic systems are brittle because they gain their efficiency by ignoring much of the search space. NETL, on the other hand, looks at every piece of information that might be relevant to the problem at hand and can afford to do so because it does not have to look at each piece of information serially.

NETL has been viewed by many in the AI community as an interesting metaphor and a promising direction for future research, but not as a practical solution to current AI problems because of the apparently impossible cost of implementing a large NETL system with current technology. The problem is not that the hardware for the nodes and links is too costly -- hundreds or even thousands of these elements can be packed onto a single VLSI chip. Rather, the problem is in forming new private-line connections (wires) between particular nodes and links as new information is added to the network. These connections cannot be implemented as signals on a single shared bus, since then all of the parallelism would be lost. Indeed, it is in the pattern of connecting wires, and not in the hardware nodes and links, that most of the information in the semantic network memory resides. A large switching network, similar to the telephone switching network, can be used in place of physical wires, but for a network of a million elements one would need the functional equivalent of a crossbar switch with 4×10^{12} crosspoints. Such a switch would be impossibly expensive to build by conventional means.

In the past year I have developed a multi-level time-shared organization for switching networks which makes it possible to implement large NETL systems very cheaply. This interconnection scheme, which I call a **hashnet** because some of its internal connections are wired up in a random pattern, has many possible uses in non-AI applications; it is described in its general form in another paper [2]. In this paper I will briefly describe a preliminary design, based on the hashnet scheme, for a semantic network memory with 10^6 NETL elements. (An "element" in NETL is the combination of a single node and a four-wire link.) A million-element NETL system is 10-20 times larger than the largest AI knowledge bases in current use, and it offers substantial advantages in speed and flexibility of access. It is an open question whether a knowledge-base of this size will be adequate for common-sense story understanding, but a system of 10^6 NETL elements should hold enough knowledge for substantial expertise in a variety of more specialized domains. In a paper of this length I will be able to sketch only the broad outlines of the design -- for a more complete account see [3].

The NETL machine itself, excluding the serial control computer, requires about 7000 VLSI chips, 4000 of which are commercial 64K dynamic RAM chips. (See the parts list, table 1.) As we will see later, with the same 64K memory technology it would require a comparable number of chips to store the same body of information in a conventional Planner-style data base, assuming that the entire data base is kept in a computer's main memory and not on disk. So, far from being impossibly expensive, this scheme is quite competititve with standard random-access memory organizations. I am about to seek funding to build a million-element prototype machine within the next two or three years. The 64K RAM chips are not available today in sufficient quantities, and may be quite expensive for the next couple of years. The prototype machine will be designed so that 16K RAMs can be substituted if necessary, giving us a 256K element machine to use until the 64K RAM chips are obtained.

2. Requirements of NETL

Figure 1 shows a basic NETL element as it was originally conceived. Commands from the control computer are received over the common party-line bus. The applicability of any command to a given element depends on the element's unique serial number, on the state of 16 write-once flag bits which indicate what type of node or link the element represents, and on

---

[1]This research was sponsored by the Defense Advanced Research Projects Agency (DOD), ARPA Order No. 3597, monitored by the Air Force Avionics Laboratory Under Contract F33615-78-C-1551. The views and conclusions contained in this document are those of the author and should not be interpreted as representing the official policies, either expressed or implied, of the Defense Advanced Research Projects Agency or the US Government.

the state of 16 read-write **marker bits** which indicate the current state of the element. These marker bits represent the short-term memory in the system. Also present are some number (4 in this design) of distinct **link wires**, and a **node terminal** to which link wires from other elements can be connected. Commands typically specify that all elements with a certain bit-pattern should send a one-bit signal across incoming or outgoing link wires, and that any element receiving such a signal should set or clear certain marker bits. It is also possible to address a command to a specific element, or to get any element with a certain marker pattern to report its serial number over the common bus. Using these commands, it is possible to propagate markers through the network Quillian-style or to control the marker propagation in any number of more precise ways. For details, see [1], especially section 2.3 and appendix A.1.

In a million-element design, then, we have 4 sets of 10^6 link wires to connect to 10^6 node terminals, each by a private line. A link wire is connected to only one node terminal, but a node terminal may have any number of link wires attached to it. Unlike the telephone system, this network must support all 4 million connections simultaneously; once a connection is made, it becomes part of the system's long-term memory, and a connection is seldom, if ever, released. As the system learns new information, new links are wired up one at a time, and this must be done without disturbing the connections already in use. If the same network hardware is to be used for different knowledge bases at different times, it must be possible to drop one set of connections and replace them with a new set.

A few additional constraints will help us to separate interesting designs from uninteresting ones. If we want to obtain a roughly human-like level of performance in our knowledge base, the transmission of a bit from one element to another can take as long as a few milliseconds. Since answering a simple question -- for example, determining whether an elephant can also be a cabbage -- takes something like 20 to 60 basic marker-propagation cycles, a propagation time of 5 milliseconds gives a response time of .1 to .3 seconds. This figure is independent of the total size of the network. This means that some degree of parallelism is essential, but that with microsecond-speed technologies there is room for some time-sharing of the hardware as well.

New connections are established individually, and setting them up can take somewhat more time than simple propagations: humans are able to add only a few items to long-term memory per second. If an attempt to create a new connection should fail occasionally, nothing disastrous occurs -- the system simply skips over the link it is trying to wire up and goes on to the next free one.

3. The NETL Machine Design

As mentioned earlier, the key problem here is to build a switching network for connecting link-wires to nodes. Since the four wires of a link are used at different times, we can think of this switch as four separate sub-netowrks, each with 10^6 inputs, 10^6 outputs, and with all 10^6 connections operating at once. This network must be, in the jargon of network theory, a **seldom-blocking network**. It must be possible to add new connections one by one, without disturbing any connections that are already present, but some small chance of failure in establishing new connections can be tolerated. Once established, a connection must work reliably, and must be able to transmit one-bit signals in either direction. Note that by "connection" here I mean a setting of the network switches that establishes a path from a given input to a given output; the pysical wiring of the network is of course not altered during use.

The basic concept used in this design is to build a 960 x 960 seldom-blocking switching network, then to time-share this network 1024 ways. The number 960 arises from packaging considerations; this gives us a total of 983,040 virtual connections, close enough to one million for our purposes. The 1024 time

slices roll by in a regular cycle; a different set of switch settings is used during each slice. There are four sets of 1024 switch settings, corresponding to the four link-wire sub-netowrks. The bits describing the 4096 settings for each switch are stored in random access memory chips between uses. The NETL elements are likewise implemented in a time-shared fashion: 960 element units are implemented in hardware (four to a chip with shared bus decoders), and each of these element devices is time shared 1024 ways. Each NETL element exists in hardware only during its assigned time-slice; most of the time, it exists only as 32 bits of state in a memory chip.

Let us begin by considering the construction of a 960 x 960 hashnet without time-sharing. The basic unit of construction is the 15-way selector cell shown in figure 2a. This cell connects its input to any of its 15 outputs, according to the contents of a four-bit state register. A value of 0 indicates that the cell is currently unused and that its input is not connected to any output. A single integrated circuit chip can easily hold 15 of these selector cells; the corresponding outputs from each cell are wired together internally, as shown in figure 2b. With assorted power and control lines, this 15 x 15 switching element requires a 48-pin package.

To build a 960 x 960 seldom-blocking network out of these elements, we arrange them in four layers with 1920 selector cells (128 chips) in each. (See figure 3.) The outputs of each layer are wired to the inputs of the next layer with a fixed but randomly chosen pattern of wires. Each of the input terminals of the hashnet is wired to 2 selector cells in the first layer; each of the outputs of the hashnet is wired to 2 outputs lines from the last layer of cells. Initially all of the selector cells are in the non-busy state. As paths through the network are set up, each one uses up one of the selector cells in each layer. Note, however, that half of the selector cells remain unused even when all 960 connections are in place; this spare capacity ensures that the network will have a low chance of blocking even for the last few connections.

To set up a new connection from a given input to a given output, we first broadcast a marking signal through the network from the input to all of the selector cells and outputs that can be reached. Only non-busy cells play a role in this process. If this signal reaches the desired output, one of the marked paths is traced back toward the source, with the selector cells along the way being set up appropriately. These cells become busy and will not participate in any other connections. Since the inter-layer wiring of the network is random, and since we are using many fewer switches than are needed for a strictly non-blocking network, we cannot guarantee that a desired connection can be found. We can guarantee that the probability of being unable to find a desired connection is very small. In simulation tests of this design, 100 complete sets of connections were attempted -- 10,000 connections in all -- with only 2 failures. As noted earlier, an occasional failure to find a connection is not disastrous in the NETL application; we just try again with a different link.

Instead of using four layers of selector cells, it is possible to get the same effect using only one layer. The output wires of this layer are randomly shuffled and fed back to the inputs; these wires also go to the network's ouput terminals. Four sets of switch settings are used, corresponding to the four layers of the original network. The signal bits are read into this layer of cells and latched. Using the first-layer switch settings, they are sent out over the appropriate output wires and shuffled back to the inputs where these bits are latched again. Then the second layer setup is used and the signal bits are shuffled again. After four such shuffles, the bits are in the right place and are read from the network's outputs. We have traded more time for fewer switches and wires; the same number of setup bits are used in either case.

To go from a thousand connections to a million, we time-share this network 1024 ways. This requires two modifications to the network. First, instead of having only 4 bits of state for each selector cell (or 16 bits if the shuffling scheme is in use), we need a different set of bits for each time slice. These bits are read from external memory chips; 4 bits of setup are read in through each selector cell input, followed by the signal bit. Second, since the NETL elements are permanently tied to their assigned time-slices, we need some way to move the signal bits from one time-slice to another. This operation is carried out by time-slice shifter chips. Each of these devices is essentially a 1024-bit shift register. During one cycle of time-slices this shift register is loaded: during each slice, a signal bit is received along with a 10-bit address indicating the slice that the signal bit is to go out on. The address governs where in the shift register the signal bit is loaded. On the next cycle of slices, the bits are shifted out in their new order. An entire layer of 1920 time-shifters is needed (packed 5 to a chip), along with memory chips to hold the 10-bit time-slice addresses. The chance of blocking is minimized if these are placed in the center of the network, between the second and third layers of cells. Some additional chance of blocking is introduced by addition of the shifters to the network, but not too much. In our simulations of an almost-full network with time sharing, we encountered 37 blocked connections in 110,000 attempts.

4. Cost and Performance

As can be seen from the parts list, most of the cost of the NETL machine is in the memory chips. In order to keep the number of chips below 10,000 -- a larger machine would be very hard to build and maintain in a university research environment -- 64K dynamic RAM chips have been used wherever possible in the design. The memory associated with the element chips must be either 2K x 8 static RAMS or fast 16K dynamic RAMS for timing reasons. In fact, the limited bit-transfer rate of the memory chips is the principal factor limiting the speed of the network; if 16K x 4 chips were available, the system could be redesigned to run four times as fast.

As it currently stands, the system has a basic propagation time of about 5 milliseconds. This is the time required to accept 10^6 bits and to steer each of these to its independent destination. This assumes the use of 2K x 8 static RAMs for the element memories and allows for a rather conservative page-mode access time of 200 nanoseconds for the 64K RAM chips. (In page mode, half of the address bits remain constant from one reference to the next.) The 256K element version, using 16K RAM chips, should have a propagation time of 1.25 milliseconds.

Since the million-element machine contains 4000 64K RAM chips, the parts cost of the machine is tied closely to the price of these chips. Currently, if you can get 64K RAMs at all, they cost over $100, but the price is likely to drop rapidly in the next two years. If we assume a price of $20 for the 64K RAMs and $10 for the 2Kx8 RAMs, we get a total of roughly $100,000 for the memory chips in the machine. It is also hard to know what price to assign to the three custom chips in the design. An initial layout cost of $150,000 for all three would probably be reasonable, but this cost would occur only once, and the chips themselves should be easy to fabricate. We have not yet thought hard about board-level layout, but rough calculations suggest that the machine would fit onto about 52 super-hex boards of two types. Two standard equipment racks ought to be sufficient for the whole machine.

For comparison, it might be worthwhile to calculate the cost of storing the same information in a Planner-style data base in the memory of a serial machine. To make the comparison fair, let us assume that the entire data base is to be kept in main memory, and not paged out onto disk. To store the information in the network itself, in the simplest possible form, would require 80 million bits of memory: 4 million pointers of 20 bits each. This would require 1250 64K RAM chips. A simple table of pointers, of course, would be very slow to use. If we add back-pointers, the figure doubles. If we add even the most limited sort of indexing structure, or store

the entries in a hash table or linked list, the amount of memory doubles again. At this point, we have reached 4000 64K RAM chips, the same number used in the NETL machine. The moral of the story would seem to be that the greater power and flexibility of the NETL organization can be had at little, if any, extra cost.

Acknowledgements

Ed Frank and Hank Walker provided me with much of the technical information required by this design. The network simulations were programmed and run by Leonard Zubkoff.

References

[1] Fahlman, S. E.
     NETL: A System for Representing and Using Real-World Knowledge.
     MIT Press, Cambridge, Mass., 1979.

[2] Fahlman, S. E.
     The Hashnet Interconnection Scheme.
     Technical Report, Carnegie-Mellon University, Department of Computer Science, 1980.

[3] Fahlman, S. E.
     Preliminary Design for a Million-Element NETL Machine.
     Technical Report, Carnegie-Mellon University, Department of Computer Science, 1980.
     (forthcoming).

Table 1: Parts List

Device Type	Number
Custom 15 x 15 Selector (48 pin)	128
Custom 5x 1K Time Shifter (16 pin)	384
Custom 4x NETL Element Chip (48 pin)	240
64K Dynamic RAM (for selectors)	2176
64K Dynamic RAM (for shifters)	1920
2Kx8 Static RAM (for elements)	2160
Total Device Count	**7008**

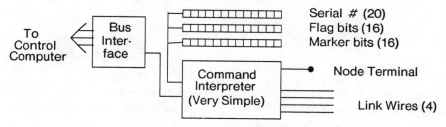

Figure 1: NETL Element

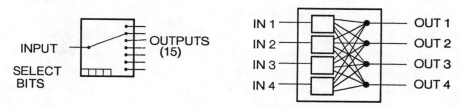

Figure 2A: The Selector Cell

Figure 2B: Selectors on 15x15 Chip
(Drawn as 4x4 chip.)

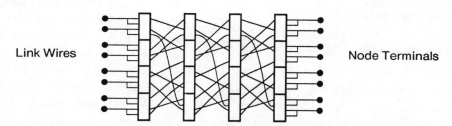

Figure 3: The Basic Hashnet Arrangement (simplified)

MASSIVELY PARALLEL ARCHITECTURES FOR AI:
NETL, THISTLE, AND BOLTZMANN MACHINES

Scott E. Fahlman & Geoffrey E. Hinton
Computer Science Department, Carnegie-Mellon University
Pittsburgh PA 15213

Terrence J. Sejnowski
Biophysics Department, The Johns Hopkins University
Baltimore MD 21218

ABSTRACT

It is becoming increasingly apparent that some aspects of intelligent behavior require enormous computational power and that some sort of massively parallel computing architecture is the most plausible way to deliver such power. Parallelism, rather than raw speed of the computing elements, seems to be the way that the brain gets such jobs done. But even if the need for massive parallelism is admitted, there is still the question of what kind of parallel architecture best fits the needs of various AI tasks.

In this paper we will attempt to isolate a number of basic computational tasks that an intelligent system must perform. We will describe several families of massively parallel computing architectures, and we will see which of these computational tasks can be handled by each of these families. In particular, we will describe a new architecture, which we call the Boltzmann machine, whose abilities appear to include a number of tasks that are inefficient or impossible on the other architectures.

FAMILIES OF PARALLEL ARCHITECTURES

By "massively parallel" architectures, we mean machines with a very large number of processing elements (perhaps very simple ones) working on a single task. A massively parallel system may be complete and self-contained or it may be a special-purpose device, performing some particular task as part of a larger system that contains other modules of a different character. In this paper we will focus on the computation performed by a single parallel module, ignoring the issue of how to integrate a collection of modules into a complete system.

One useful way of classifying these massively parallel architectures is by the type of signal that is passed among the elements. Fahlman (1982) proposes a division of these systems into three classes: marker-passing, value-passing, and message-passing systems.

Message-passing systems are the most powerful family, and by far the most complex. They pass around messages of arbitrary complexity, and perform complex operations on these messages. Such generality has its price: the individual computing elements are complex, the communication costs are high, and there may be severe contention and traffic congestion problems in the network. Message passing does not seem plausible as a detailed model of processing in the brain. Such models are being actively studied elsewhere (Hillis, 1981; Hewitt, 1980) and we have nothing more to say about them here.

Marker-passing systems, of which NETL (Fahlman, 1979) is an example, are the simplest family and the most limited. In such systems, the communication among processing elements is in the form of single-bit markers. Each "node" element has the capacity to store a few distinct marker bits (typically 16) and to perform simple Boolean operations on the stored bits and on marker bits arriving from other elements. These nodes are connected by hardware "links" that pass markers from node to node, under orders from an external control computer. The links are, in effect, dedicated private lines, so a lot of marker traffic can proceed in parallel.

A node may be connected to any number of links, and it is the pattern of node-link connections that forms the system's long-term memory. In NETL, the elements are wired up to form the nodes and links of a semantic network that represents some body of knowledge. Certain common but computation-intensive searches and deductions are accomplished by passing markers from node to node through the links of this network. A key point about marker-passing systems is that there is never any contention due to message traffic. If many copies of the same marker arrive at a node at once, they are simply OR'ed together.

Value-passing systems pass around continuous quantities or numbers and perform simple arithmetic operations on these values.

---

* Scott Fahlman is supported by the Defense Advanced Research Projects Agency, Department of Defense, ARPA Order 3597, monitored by the Air Force Avionics Laboratory under contract F33615-81-K-1539. The other two authors are supported by grants from the System Development Foundation. The views and conclusions contained in this document are those of the authors and should not be interpreted as representing the official policies, either expressed or implied, of the Defense Advanced Research Projects Agency or the U.S. Government.

Traditional analog computers are simple value-passing systems. Like marker-passing systems, value-passing systems never suffer from contention. If several values arrive at a node via different links, they are combined arithmetically and only one combined value is received. Many of the iterative relaxation algorithms that have been proposed for solving low-level vision problems are ideally suited to value-passing architectures, and so are spreading-activation models of semantic processing (Davis and Rosenfeld, 1981; Anderson, 1983).

At CMU we have done some preliminary design work on a machine that we call Thistle. This system combines the marker-passing abilities of NETL with value-passing. Each element of the Thistle machine has storage for 16 single-bit markers and 4 eight-bit values. The values can be added, multiplied, scaled, and compared to one another. Links in the Thistle system pass a value from one node to another, perhaps gated by various markers and multiplied by a "weight" associated with the link. In Thistle, the values converging on a node can be summed or combined by MIN or MAX.

Both NETL and Thistle use a *local* representation for their knowledge: each concept or assertion resides in a particular processing element or connection. If a hardware element fails, the corresponding knowledge is lost. It has been suggested many times that a *distributed representation*, in which a concept is represented by some pattern of activation in a large number of units, would be more reliable and more consistent with what is known about the workings of the brain. Such systems are harder to analyze, since the behavior of the system depends on the combined action of a large number of elements, no one of which is critical. However, distributed systems offer certain computational advantages in addition to their inherent reliability. The Boltzmann architecture, described in the next section, is a variant of the value-passing architecture that uses distributed representations and probabilistic processing elements. The randomness is actually beneficial to the system, allowing it to escape from local minima during searches.

THE BOLTZMANN MACHINE

The Boltzmann architecture is designed to allow efficient searches for combinations of "hypotheses" that maximally satisfy some input data and some stored constraints. Each hypothesis is represented by a binary unit whose two states represent the truth values of the hypothesis. Interactions between the units implement stored knowledge about the constraints between hypotheses, and external input to each unit represents the data for a specific case. A content-addressable memory can be implemented by using distributed patterns of activity (large combinations of hypotheses) to stand for the kinds of complex items for which we have words. New items are stored by modifying the interactions between units so as to create new

stable patterns of activity, and they are retrieved by settling into the pattern of activity under the influence of an external input vector which acts as a partial description of the required item.

A good way to approach the best-fit problem is to define a measure of how badly the current pattern of activity in a module fits the external input and the internal constraints, and then to make the individual hardware units act so as to reduce this measure. Hopfield (1982) has shown that an "energy" measure can be associated with states of a binary network, and we generalize this measure to include sustained inputs from outside the network:

$$E = -1/2 \sum_{ij} w_{ij} s_i s_j - \sum_i (\eta_i - \theta_i) s_i \qquad (1)$$

where η_i is the external input to the ith unit, w_{ij} is the strength of connection (synaptic weight) from the jth to the ith unit, s_i is a boolean truth value (0 or 1), and θ_i is a threshold.

A simple way to find a *local* energy minimum in this kind of network is to repeatedly switch each unit into whichever of its two states yields the lower total energy given the current states of the other units. If hardware units make their decisions at random, asynchronous moments and if transmission times are negligible so that each unit always "sees" the current states of the other units, this procedure can only decrease the energy, so the network must settle into an energy minimum. If all the connection strengths are *symmetrical*, which is typically the case for constraint satisfaction problems, each unit can compute its effect on the total energy from information that is locally available. The difference between the energy with the kth unit false and with it true is just:

$$\Delta E_k = \sum_i w_{ki} s_i + \eta_k - \theta_k \qquad (2)$$

So the rule for minimizing the total energy is to adopt the true state if the combined external and internal input to the unit exceeds its threshold. This is just the familiar rule for binary threshold units.

It is possible to escape from poor local minima and find better ones by modifying the simple rule to allow occasional jumps to states of higher energy. At first sight this seems like a messy hack which can never *guarantee* that the global minimum will be found. However, the whole module will behave in a useful way that can be analyzed using statistical mechanics provided that each unit adopts the state with a probability given by

$$p_k = \frac{1}{1 + e^{-\Delta E_k / T}} \qquad (3)$$

where T is a scaling parameter that acts like the temperature of a physical system.

This rule, which resembles the input-output function for a cortical neuron (Hinton and Sejnowski, 1983a), ensures that when the system has reached "thermal equilibrium" the relative probability of finding it in two global states is a Boltzmann distribution and is therefore determined *solely* by their energy difference:

$$\frac{P_\alpha}{P_\beta} = e^{-(E_\alpha - E_\beta)/T} \qquad (4)$$

If T is large, equilibrium is reached rapidly but the bias in favor of the lower energy states is small. If T is small, the bias is favorable but the time required to reach equilibrium is long. One way to beat this trade-off is to start with T large and then reduce it (Kirkpatrick, Gelatt, & Vecchi, 1983).

An important consequence of achieving a Boltzmann distribution is that it allows several simple learning rules which modify the probability of a global state by modifying the individual connection strengths. At equilibrium, the probability of a state is a simple function of its energy (Eq. 4), and the energy is a linear function of the weights between pairs of units that are active in that state (Eq. 1). This allows us to compute the derivative of the probability of a global state with respect to each individual weight. Given this derivative, the weights can be changed so as to make the probabilities of global states approach any desired set of probabilities, and so it is possible to program a Boltzmann machine at the level of desired probabilities of states of whole modules, without ever mentioning the weights (Hinton & Sejnowski, 1983a). This kind of deliberate manipulation of probabilities requires a "programmer" who specifies what the probabilities should be. A more powerful learning procedure that does not require a "programmer" is also possible in these networks. The procedure modifies the weights so as to generate good internal models of the structure of an environment. There is not space here to describe this procedure (see Hinton & Sejnowski, 1983b for details).

COMPUTATIONAL PROBLEMS

One recurrent theme in the history of AI is the discovery that certain aspects of intelligence could be modeled in some elegant way, if only we had enough computing power. Once a task is understood in these terms, the search begins for ways to provide that power or to come up with tricks that reduce the amount of computation required. Massive parallelism provides us with a new tool for attacking some of these computational problems. In this section we will identify some fundamental computational abilities that any truly intelligent system will have to possess, and we will see how well the parallel architectures described above can handle each of these tasks.

In what follows, we will focus on tasks that have to do with recognition and search in a very large space of stored descriptions, but a key point is that these abilities are also important in planning and inference. For example, the various recognition processes described here may be used to select rules and actions in some sort of production system. In such systems, sequential behavior would be driven by a series of massively parallel recognition steps.

Set Intersection

Recognition can be viewed as the process of finding, in a very large set of stored descriptions, the one that best fits a set of observed features. In its simplest form, this can be viewed as a set-intersection problem. Each observable feature is associated with a set of items that exhibit that feature. Given a number of observed features, we want to find the item or items in memory that exhibit *all* of these features; that is, we must intersect the sets associated with the observed features to find the common members.

This set-intersection operation is discussed at length in Fahlman (1979). It is a well-defined operation that comes up very frequently in AI knowledge-base systems. On a serial machine, set-intersection takes time proportional to the size of the smallest of the sets being intersected, but frequently all of the sets are quite large. In a parallel marker-passing system such as NETL, such set intersections are done in a single operation, once the members of each set have been marked with a different marker. The system simply asks (in a single cycle) for elements that have collected all of the markers. Value-passing systems can do as well by marking the members of each set with one unit of activation and then looking for units whose activation is over some threshold.

The Boltzmann machine can also intersect sets in a single settling, at least in simple cases. Consider, for instance, a representational scheme in which each active hardware unit represents a very large set -- the set of all items whose patterns have that unit active. A more specific set is represented by a combination of active units, and the intersection of several specific sets is represented by the union of these combinations. The union of the active units acts as an intensional representation of the intersection -- it can be formed even if no known item lies in all the sets. Given this intensional description, the problem of finding the item that fits it is just the problem of activating the additional units in the pattern for that item. This is the kind of pattern completion task which the Boltzmann machine can solve in a single settling (Hinton, 1981a).

Transitive closure

In knowledge-base systems it is frequently necessary to compute the closures of various transitive relations. For example, we might need to mark all of the animals in the data base, perhaps because we want to intersect this set with another. If the "is a" relation is transitive, a reptile is an animal, and a lizard is a reptile, then lizards are animals. We must therefore mark not only those items whose membership in the animal class is explicitly stated, but also those that inherit this membership through a chain of "is a" statements. The "is a" relation is the most important of the transitive relations in most data bases, but we might also want to compute closures over relations such as "part of", "bigger than", "later in time", etc.

In a serial machine, the computation of a transitive closure requires time proportional to the size of the answer set. In a marker-passing machine, it takes time proportional to the length of the longest chain of relations that has to be followed. If the relations form a single long chain these times are identical, but if they form a short bushy tree, the marker-passing system can be very much faster. Value-passing systems that use local representations can simulate marker-passing systems on this task, and so get the same sort of performance.

The Boltzmann architecture does not handle this task so cleanly. Closure over the "is a" relationship can be handled by making the pattern of active units for an item include the patterns for all items above it in the type hierarchy. By starting with a part of this pattern and completing it (that is, dropping into an energy minimum in which additional units are turned on) we can in effect compute the closure of "is a". However, it is not yet known whether this technique will work for data bases with very large, tangled type hierarchies, and it cannot be simply extended to handle additional transitive relations such as "part of". Hinton (1981b) describes an encoding of "part of" hierarchies in a Boltzmann-like system, but in that model the "part of" hierarchy must be traversed sequentially.

Contexts and partitions

Some information in a knowledge base is universal, but much of it is valid only in certain contexts: times, places, imaginary worlds or hypothetical states. At any given time, the system is working within some set of nested and overlapping contexts; it must have access to the bundle of information associated with each of those contexts and to the universal information, but not to information that is only valid in other contexts. Each context acts like a transparent overlay to the knowledge base, adding a bundle of new facts or occasionally covering something up.

In the presence of multiple overlapping partitions, a serial machine must check each assertion for membership in one of the active partitions before that assertion can be used. This can be a time-consuming task. Marker-passing systems handle this easily. The tree of active contexts is marked using the transitive closure machinery. This mark is then propagated to all of the assertions associated with these contexts, activating them; assertions without this mark are inactive in subsequent processing. In effect, we are using one set of markers to gate the passage of other markers: many simple Boolean operations are performed during each cycle. The value-passing and Boltzmann architectures have similar abilities: the state of some units can cause other units to behave normally or turn off. In these systems we can also fade contexts in and out gradually, if that is what the problem requires. (See Berliner, 1979)

Best-match recognition

The set-intersection computation described above is sufficient if the features are discrete, noise-free, and if every member of a class exhibits all of the associated features. Few real-world recognition tasks approach this ideal. More often, the task is to find the stored description that best matches a set of features, even if the match is imperfect. Some of the features may be observed with high confidence, while others are weak. Some observations my fall on the boundary between two features or may be smoothly continuous.

Marker-passing systems are very poor at handling imperfect matches of this sort. Value-passing systems like Thistle are ideal for this: there can be a very large number of observations, each sending some amount of activation to a number of hypotheses; the size of this activation depends on the confidence level of the observation and the strength of the connection between the feature and the hypothesis. Hypotheses may also be given some extra activation on the basis of top-down expectations. After all of these votes have been collected, the system simply asks for the element with the most activation to identify itself -- this is our best match. The Boltzmann machine does almost as well as Thistle in cases like this: in clear-cut cases it finds the global energy minimum corresponding to the description that best fits the weighted combination of observed features and expectations. If there are several good descriptions it is biased towards the best.

Gestalt recognition

In the preceding paragraphs we looked only at bottom-up recognition, perhaps modified by a bit of top-down priming to help expected answers. Real-world recognition problems present a more complicated picture: the whole object can only be identified on the basis of its features, but the features can only be identified in relation to one another and to the emerging picture of the whole; if taken out of context, each feature is ambiguous (Palmer, 1975). There is usually a single answer -- a set of identities for the whole and for each of the parts -- that is much better than any other, but this cannot be found by pure bottom-up or pure top-down processing; instead, like the solution of a set of simultaneous equations, it must either emerge as a whole or be found by laborious iteration. There may be many levels of features and sub-features, with a complex network of inter-level constraints.

Here the Boltzmann machine is in its element. The observations and expectations provide the inputs to the network. The knowledge about the plausibility of each possible interpretation is stored in the weights within the network. The problem is to combine these sources of information rapidly and correctly. The inputs define one potential energy function over possible states of the network, and the weights define another. The statistically optimal solution can be found by adding the functions together and finding the global minimum (Hinton and Sejnowski, 1983b). This is exactly what the Boltzmann machine does. On paper, then, the Boltzmann machine looks very promising for recognition tasks of this sort, but more analysis and some large-scale simulations are needed in order to determine whether this promise is realistic. A deterministic value-passing machine like Thistle might be able to get comparable results, but programming it to do so would be a very difficult task because there is no known learning procedure, and great care would have to be taken to avoid local minima that would trap a deterministic iterative search. Marker-passing systems exhibit the same limitations here that we saw in best-match recognition; they are inappropriate for this sort of task.

Recognition under transformation

Sometimes the problem is not just to recognize a whole object and its features at once, but to do this even though the object has undergone a complex transformation. In vision, for example, we must match the image against a set of stored, viewpoint-invariant shape descriptions and to do this we must apply transformations like translation, rotation, scaling, and perhaps other, non-rigid transformations (Hinton, 1981c). Once again, we are trying to make many choices at once in order to find a combination of choices that gives us the best match. Some of the choices are made over smooth continuous domains (the transformations) and some are discrete choices (the description chosen from memory). Once again, the Boltzmann machine should excel at this task, but must be tested; the Thistle machine might be able to do the job but would require tricky programming; the NETL machine is out of the game.

Many other computational tasks could be added to the list, but these are the ones that currently seem most important to us. None of the architectures we have explored can do a good job on *all* of these tasks. This analysis suggests two goals for the immediate future: first, to explore more thoroughly the computational properties of the Boltzmann architecture, especially when applied to large real-world tasks; second, to try to find some way to combine, in a single system, the "gestalt recognition" of the Boltzmann machine, the precise set operations of NETL-style marker passing, and the flexible sequential behavior of the traditional von Neumann architecture.

Acknowledgements

We thank the members of the Parallel Models group at CMU and the Parallel Distributed Processing group at UCSD for helpful discussions.

References

Anderson, J. R. *The Architecture of Cognition*. Harvard University Press, 1983.

Berliner, H. J. On the construction of evaluation functions for large domains. In *Proceedings of the 6th International Joint Conference on Artificial Intelligence*. Tokyo, Japan, August 1979.

Davis, L. S. & Rosenfeld, A. Cooperating processes for low-level vision: A survey. *Artificial Intelligence*, 1981, 3, 245-264.

Fahlman, S. E. *NETL: A system for representing and using real-world knowledge*. Cambridge, Mass.: MIT Press, 1979.

Fahlman, S. E. Three flavors of parallelism. In *Proceedings of the Fourth National Conference of the Canadian Society for Computational Studies of Intelligence*. Saskatoon, Saskatchewan, May 1982.

Hewitt, C. E. The apiary network architecture for knowledgeable systems. In *Proceedings of the Lisp conference*. Stanford, August 1980.

Hillis, W. D. The connection machine. T. R. 646, Cambridge Mass: MIT A.I. Lab. 1981.

Hinton, G. E. Implementing semantic networks in parallel hardware. In G. E. Hinton & J. A. Anderson (Eds.) *Parallel Models of Associative Memory*. Hillsdale, NJ: Erlbaum, 1981a.

Hinton, G. E. Shape representation in parallel systems. In *Proceedings of the Seventh International Joint Conference on Artificial Intelligence*, Vol 2. Vancouver BC, Canada. August 1981b.

Hinton, G. E. A parallel computation that assigns canonical object-based frames of reference. In *Proceedings of the Seventh International Joint Conference on Artificial Intelligence*, Vol 2. Vancouver BC, Canada. August 1981c.

Hinton, G. E. & Sejnowski, T. J. Analyzing Cooperative Computation. In *Proceedings of the Fifth Annual Conference of the Cognitive Science Society*, Rochester NY, May 1983a.

Hinton, G. E. & Sejnowski, T. J. Optimal perceptual inference. In *Proceedings of the IEEE conference on Computer Vision and Pattern Recognition*, Washington DC, June 1983b.

Hopfield, J. J. Neural networks and physical systems with emergent collective computational abilities. *Proceedings of the National Academy of Sciences USA*, 1982, 79, 2554-2558.

Kirkpatrick, S. Gelatt, C. D. & Vecci, M. P. Optimization by simulated annealing. *Science* 1983, 220, 671-680.

Palmer, S. E. Visual perception and world knowledge: Notes on a model of sensory-cognitive interaction. In D. A. Norman & D. E. Rumelhart (Eds.) *Explorations in Cognition*. San Francisco: Freeman, 1975.

Physica 10D (1984) 213–228
North-Holland, Amsterdam

THE CONNECTION MACHINE: A COMPUTER ARCHITECTURE BASED ON CELLULAR AUTOMATA

W. Daniel HILLIS

MIT Artificial Intelligence Laboratory, Cambridge, MA 02139, USA

and

Thinking Machines Corporation, 577 Beaver St., Waltham, MA 02154, USA

This paper describes the Connection Machine, a programmable computer based on cellular automata. The essential idea behind the connection machine is that a regular locally-connected cellular array can be made to behave as if the processing cells are connected into any desired topology. When the topology of the machine is chosen to match the topology of the application program, the result is a fast, powerful computing engine. The Connection Machine was originally designed to implement knowledge retrieval operations in artificial intelligence programs, but the hardware and the programming techniques are apparently applicable to a much larger class of problems. A machine with 100,000 processing cells is currently being constructed.

1. Introduction

The connection machine was designed to concurrently manipulate knowledge stored in semantic networks. This application needs the connection machine because conventional serial computers cannot move through such networks fast enough. The connection machine attacks the speed problem by providing processing power proportional to the size of the network. Each node and link in the network has its own simple processor. These connect to form a uniform locally-connected network of perhaps a million processor/memory cells.

The connection machine was not originally intended to be a general-purpose parallel computer. It was designed to be fast at a few simple operations that are important for artificial intelligence, such as property lookup in a semantic inheritance network. As it turns out the resulting machine seems to be quite general, and we are only beginning to understand how to apply it to many other problems. The paper describes the need for such a machine in artificial intelligence research, what it will do, and how it will work. It also summarizes progress already made toward its design and a plan to actually build a hundred-thousand-cell prototype.

2. Our machines are too slow

A semantic network is one of the basic tools used in artificial intelligence research to represent knowledge. (For examples see [2] and [6].) In a semantic network each "object" is represented as a node in a network, with the links in the network representing relationships between those objects. On a serial machine, the time required to retrieve information from a network often increases with size of the network. Thus paradoxically, programs become slow as they become smart. Today, we write artificial intelligence programs that use a few hundred facts. We would like to increase this to a few million, but the programs already take minutes to make decisions that must be made in seconds. Scaled up, they would take years. Von Neumann machines, even if they are built of exotic ultrafast components, are unlikely candidates for solving

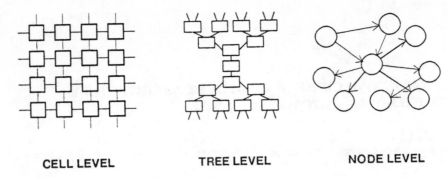

CELL LEVEL   TREE LEVEL   NODE LEVEL

Fig. 1.

these problems, since they are limited by the speed of light. A supercomputer inside a six-inch cube would take one nanosecond to send a single signal from one corner to the other. A nanosecond cycle time is less than a factor of a hundred better than currently available machines, not nearly enough to solve our million-scaled artificial intelligence problems.

3. The potential solution is concurrency

The light at the end of the tunnel is concurrency. Integrated-circuit technology makes it economically feasible to produce millions of computing devices to work on our problems in parallel. Artificial intelligence mechanisms have been proposed that are suitable for such extreme parallel decomposition [Fahlman, Minsky, Shank, Rieger, Winston, Steels, Steele, Doyle, Drescher, etc.]. These systems represent information as networks of interconnected nodes. Many of their operations are dependent only on local information at the nodes. Such operations could, potentially, be performed in parallel on many nodes at once, making the speed of the system independent of the size of the network.

Unfortunately, the word-at-a-time von Neumann architecture is not well suited for exploiting such concurrency. When performing relatively simple computations on large amounts of data, a von Neumann computer does not utilize its hardware efficiently; the number of interesting events per

second per acre of silicon is very low. Most of the chip area is memory and only a few memory locations are accessed at a time. The performance of the machine is limited by the bandwidth between memory and processor. This is what Backus [1] calls the *von Neumann Bottleneck*. The bigger we build machines, the worse it gets.

The bottleneck may be avoided by putting the processing where the data is, in the memory. In this scheme the memory becomes the processor. Each object in memory has associated with it not only the hardware necessary to hold the state of the object, but also the hardware necessary to process it.

4. A few specific operations must be fast

Knowledge retrieval in Artificial Intelligence involves more than just looking up a fact in a table. If the knowledge is stored as a semantic network, then finding the relevant information may involve searching the entire network. Worse yet, the desired fact may not be explicitly stored at all. It may have to be deduced from other stored information.

When retrieving knowledge, programs often spend most of their time repeating a few simple operations. Here are some operations that we want to be fast:

i) We need to *deduce* facts from semantic inheritance networks, as in KLONE [2], NETL [6], OWL [22] or OMEGA [9].

ii) We need to *match* patterns against sets of

assertions, demons, or productions. If there is no perfect match we may need the best match.

iii) We need to *sort* a set according some parameter. For instance, a program may need to order goals in terms of importance.

iv) We need to *search* graphs for sub-graphs with a specified structure. For instance, we may wish to find an analogy to a situation.

Tools have already been developed for describing for these operations in terms of concurrent processes. In Codd's relational database algebra, [4] database queries are specified in terms of a few simple, potentially-concurrent primitives. Another example, more directly connected to artificial intelligence, is Fahlman's [6] work on marker propagation. Fahlman has shown that many simple deductions, such as property inheritance can be expressed in terms of parallel operations. Schwartz [18] has developed a language based on set operations. Woods has developed a more powerful extension of marker propagation. By providing a few powerful primitives that can be evaluated concurrently, each of these descriptive systems allows a programmer to express concurrent algorithms naturally. The connection machine is designed to exploit the parallelism inherent in these operations.

5. Marker propagation was a good first step

In 1968, Quillan [27] proposed that information stored in a semantic network could be manipulated by concurrently propagating markers through the network. Such a system would be able to retrieve information in a time that was essentially independent of the size of the network. This basic idea was extended considerably in the late 1970's by Fahlman [6] and by Woods, [25] who worked out ways of controlling the marker propagation to perform deduction and retrieval operations on inheritance networks. Fahlman also proposed hardware for actually implementing his system concurrently.

Unfortunately, many of the marker propagation strategies are just heuristic. In complicated cases

they give the wrong answers [6, 13]. Systems with well-defined semantics, like OWL [22] and OMEGA [8], have never been successfully expressed in terms of markers. I believe that marker propagation systems, while on the right track, are not sufficiently powerful to implement these systems.

6. The connection machine

The connection machine architecture captures many of the positive qualities of marker propagation, without some of its weaknesses. It is a way of connecting together millions of tiny processing cells so that they can work on a problem together. Each cell can communicate with a few others through a communications network. *The communication connections are configured to mimic the structure of the specific problem being solved.* For a particular semantic network, the cells are connected in the same way as the data in the network. Thus, each chunk of data has its own processor, connected to processors of related data.

If the connections were physical wires, the machine would have to be rewired for every problem. Since this is impractical, the processing cells are connected through a switching network. They communicate by sending messages. Receiving a message causes a cell to change its state, and perhaps to transmit a few more messages. As in Hewitt's *actor systems*, all computation takes place through the exchange of messages.

Below I describe how this all works: the communication network, the algorithms for computation and the formation of connections, and the operation of the cells. The most important features of the connection machine are:

i) It is fast. Most of the chip area is usefully active during a computation. The system may execute several million operations at a time.

ii) It is wireable. The communication network is locally connected. All wires are short and pack efficiently into two dimensions. The ratio of wires to active elements can be independent of the size of the system.

iii) It is useful. The connection machine seems to be able to implement all of the operations of the relational algebra, as well as structured inheritance networks such as KLONE [2], OMEGA [8], and OWL [22].

7. All comunication is local

At the lowest level, the connection machine is a uniform array of *cells*, each connected by physical wires to a few of its nearest neighbors. Each cell contains a few words of memory, a very simple processor, and a communicator, fig. 2. The communicators form a packet-switched communications network. Cells interact through the network by sending messages. Each cell knows the addresses of a few other cells. When two cells know each other's addresses, they can communicate. This establishes a virtual *connection* between the cells. Connected cells behave as if they were linked by a physical wire, although messages actually pass through the network.

Since the physical wires are all short, messages must reach their destinations in incremental steps, through intermediate communicators. A cell addresses a message by specifying the relative displacement of the recipient (example: up two and over five). This does not specify the route the message is to take, just its desination. When a communicator receives a message it decides on the basis of the address and local information which way the message should go next. It modifies the address and sends it to the selected neighbor. For

example, a communicator receiving a message addressed "up two and over five" can change it to "up one and over five" and send the message to the communicator above. When the address is all zeros, the message is at its destination and can be delivered. A single message step is illustrated in fig. 3.

8. Cells are simple

Most of the hardware in a cell is memory. Each cell has a few registers, a state vector, and a rule table. The registers and state vector are duplicated for each cell, but the rule table is identical for all cells, so a single table can be shared among several cells on a chip. Registers hold relative addresses of other cells. A cell normally has three virtual connections, so three registers are needed. There are also two or three extra registers for temporary storage of addresses and numbers. The state vector is a vector of bits. It stores markers, arithmetic condition flags and the type of the cell. A cell may have 10 to 50 bits of state vector. Addresses in a million word machine are 20 bits long, so there will be a total of about 150 bits per cell, not including the shared rule table.

The rule table tells the cell how to behave when it receives a message. Each message contains an address or number and a type field. The way a cell responds to a message depends on the state of the cell and the type of the message. When a message is received, the state and the message type are combined and used as an index into the rule table. The appropriate response is determined from the table entry. It may involve changing the cell's state

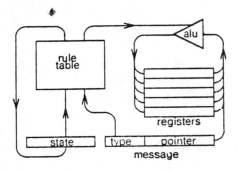

Fig. 2.

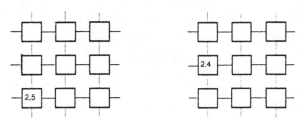

Fig. 3.

vector, originating new messages, or performing an arithmetic operation, or some combination of these operations. The cell's state vector usually changes as a result of receiving a message.

Each message has two parts, a type and a pointer. The pointer is either a number, or the address of another cell. If a cell is to transmit a message, the rule table must indicate the type of the message, the pointer of the message, and the address of the recipient. The pointer and the address normally come from the registers, although they may also be loaded with numerical constants, such as the cell's own address. Since the addressing scheme is relative, the cell's own address is always zero. The addresses of immediate neighbors are also simple constants.

Arithmetic operations take place on the contents of the pointer registers, and the result can be stored back into a register. The state vector has condition-code bits which are set according to the result. For instance, there are bits indicating a zero result, a negative result, and a carry overflow. Since these bits are treated as part of the state vector, they can influence the future behavior of the cell. This is useful for numerical sorting operations.

9. Storage is allocated locally

Data in the connection machine is stored as the pattern of connections between cells. This is similar to Lisp [26], where data is stored as structures of pointers. The connections represent the contents of the memory.

Unconnected cells can establish a connection by a mechanism called *message waves*. Assume cell JOHN wants to get a point to cell MARY, but has no idea where cell MARY is. JOHN can get such a point by broadcasting a message wave through the network, searching for MARY. Each message in the wave contains the address of the cell that originated the wave. The wave is propagated by the individual cells, each cell forwarding the wave to its neighbors, incrementing or decrementing the back-pointer appropriately. This is illustrated in fig. 4. When the wave reaches cell MARY, MARY sends her address back to JOHN, using JOHN's address as specified in the wave. JOHN then sends out a second wave to cancel the still spreading request. The cancel wave travels at twice the speed of the request wave, so it overtakes the request and prevents it from propagating further.

A similar technique may be used to connect to a cell of a particular type, rather than to a specific cell. This happens most often when building new structures from unused cells. In this case handshaking is necessary to insure that only a single cell is found, even though several satisfactory cells may have replied to the request before it was canceled. An unused cell which sees a request wave transmits an AVAILABLE message back to the originator.

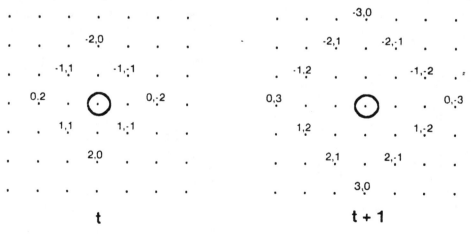

Fig. 4.

The originator replies to the first such message with an ACCEPT, and to all subsequent messages with REJECT messages.

It is possible to calculate just how far the request message travels before the cancel wave catches up. The space-time diagram in fig. 5 shows how far each message must travel. If the request wave propagates at half the rate of the other messages, it will travel three times the necessary distance before it is canceled. This means that when connecting to an unused node, if we assume that the free nodes are uniformly distributed, it will be necessary to refuse about three AVAILABLE messages per connection.

This method of allocating storage may allow the machine to continue to operate with defective cells. Cells are connected on the basis of availability, not address, so bad cells need never be built into the network. Assume each cell has some way of knowing which of its neighbors are functioning properly. Since a cell only interacts with the system through its neighbors, a malfunctioning cell can be cut off from the rest of the system. The neighbors never route a message through the bad cell and ignore any messages it tries to transmit. None of the connection machine's algorithms depend on a cell existing at specific addresses. A system with a few faulty cells could continue to function, with a slight degradation in performance. This defect-tolerance will become important if we ever need to build very large machines.

10. Trees represent nodes

A node in a semantic network can be linked to an arbitrary number of other nodes. A physical cell, on the other hand, can only connect to a few other cells. Since the network is to be represented as a structure of connected cells, there must be some way of representing nodes with an arbitrary number of connections. This is accomplished by representing each node as a balanced binary tree of cells.

In this scheme, each cell only needs three connections. One connection links the cell to those above it in the tree and the other two connections link to the subtrees below. Each node is a tree of cells. The depth of the tree is equal to the logarithm of the number of connections to the node. The total number of cells required to represent a node is equal to the number of connections minus one.

The links in the network are also represented as connected cells. In this case, there is no fanout problem. Each link connects to exactly three nodes: the two linked nodes, plus the type of the link. Thus, a link can be represented by a single cell, that connects leaves of the appropriate node trees. The representation of a small net is shown in fig. 6.

Operations which add connections to the node three must leave it balanced. To help with this, each cell carries a bit indicating if new connections should be added to the left or right side of the cell. This bit is set if the three below the cell is left-heavy, clear if it is right-heavy, and may be either

Representing Nodes in terms of Cells.

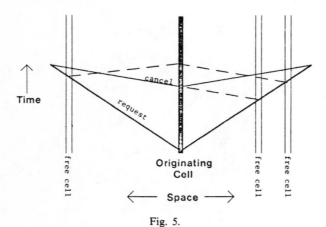

Fig. 5.

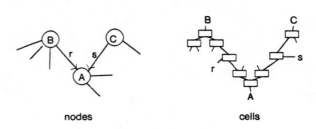

nodes   cells

Fig. 6.

if it is perfectly balanced. When adding a new connection, a message starts at the top of the tree and moves left or right as it goes down according to the balance bit. As it passes though, it complements the bit, as shown in fig. 7. This operation not only selects the correct terminal of the tree, but also leaves the balance bits in a consistent state, ready for the next insertion. A similar algorithm must be used for deletion. (This elegant algorithm was invented by Carl Feynman and independently by Browning at the California Institute of Technology.)

The algorithm can be generalized to make a number of connections simultaneously. To do this, we send the number of connections to be made to the top cell of the tree. The cell divides this number by two and passes the result to the left and right sub-cells. If the number does not divide evenly the extra count is passed to the lean side of the tree. If each node repeats this process the numbers that reach the terminal nodes will indicate how many connections are to be made to those points. Again, the balance bit must be toggled as the numbers pass through.

11. Objects can move to shorten distances

It is sometimes useful to make a distinction between the hardware of a cell and the computational object that is stored in a cell. I will call the object a *cons*, by analogy to Lisp. A cell with no cons is *free*, and may be used to build new structures.

Connections are all bidirectional, so each cons knows the address of all conses that know its

address. Knight has pointed out that a cons is free to move from cell to cell, as long as it informs its acquaintances where it is moving. This would allow conses with frequent communication to move nearer. Conses in the configuration shown in fig. 8 could swap places. Conses that do not wish to swap could act as intermediaries, negotiating swaps between conses on either side (fig. 8c).

If conses keep track of their utilization, an often used cons may force a swap even if it is to a less-used cons's disadvantage. This would allow implementation of a *virtual network*, analogous to virtual memories on conventional computers. Little used conses would gradually be pushed away from the center of activity and eventually fall off into a secondary storage device. As in virtual memory, there could be several layers of successively slower and less expensive memories, say NMOS, magnetic bubbles, and disk.

I have not yet studied these migration schemes in detail. Whatever system we use, memory management in a connection machine should be easier than in conventional systems because each object is referenced only by a small, well-defined set of acquaintances. It can be safely moved after informing those acquaintances.

12. The Connection Machine operates on sets

In this section I present a register-machine description of the connection machine. This is only one possible interface between the connection machine and the outside world. It is included here because it shows specifically how the connection machine can perform certain retrieval operations. This model does not capture the full power of

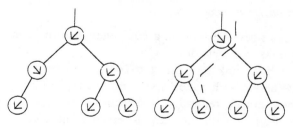

Fig. 7.

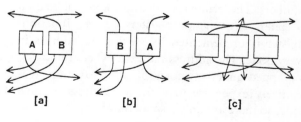

Fig. 8.

the connection machine. The instructions described below are implemented by loading the rule tables of the cells, starting the machine, and waiting for the calculation to complete. This mode of operation fails to take full advantage of the memory's parallelism.

The connection machine is connected to a conventional computer in the same way as any other memory. Its contents can be read and written with normal array-like read and write operations. There are also other ways of accessing and modifying the contents. To take advantage of these additional functions, the programmer must follow certain conventions for the format of stored data. The machine treats the data as a set of named nodes, connected by named links. In artificial intelligence programs the nodes of such a network usually represent concepts and the links represent relations between those concepts. The connection machine, however, knows nothing about the semantics of networks, only their structure.

The abstract machine has several registers. Unlike the registers of a serial machine, which hold numbers or pointers, the connection machine registers hold sets or functions.

Set-registers contain sets of nodes in the network. These sets can be arbitrarily large. The basic operations of the machine take place on every member of a set simultaneously, which accounts for most of the machine's concurrency. The letters A, B, C, and so on, will refer to set-registers. Each set-register is implemented using one bit in the state vector of every node. A set-register contains exactly those nodes that have the corresponding bit set.

There are also function-registers. These contain functions mapping nodes to nodes, or nodes to numbers. The letters F, G, H, and so on will be used to refer to function-registers. Each function-register is implemented by storing an address in every node. The address indicates where that node is mapped under the corresponding function. It is relatively expensive to store an address at each node, so there are only a small number of function-registers.

The instructions of the register machine fall roughly into four groups: set operation, propagation, function manipulation and structure modification, and arithmetic. Instructions in the first two groups give the machine the power of a parallel marker propagation machine such as Fahlman's. The other instructions give the machine additional capabilities involving function manipulation, pointer passing and arithmetic. Each instruction group will be discussed separately below.

Group I: set operations

Since the set-registers of the connection machine hold sets of objects, natural register-to-register operations are the standard set operations. In the connection machine,

A ← INTERSECT (B, C)

represents a single instruction, where "←" indicates that the value on the right is deposited into the register on the left. This particular instruction intersects the contents of two set-registers and loads the result into a third. The other standard set operations (UNION, DIFFERENCE, COMPLEMENT) are also single instructions. "Complement" in this case means complement with respect to the set of all of the nodes in the network.

Registers may be initialized to the empty set with the CLEAR instruction.

These set instructions all operate simply by performing the appropriate Boolean operations on the state vectors of all the nodes in the network. No messages need to be sent.

Group II: propagation

Consider the following equivalent descriptions of links in a network:
i) Each link is a directed connection between two nodes, with a label specifying the type of link. There are no redundant connections, i.e. no two connections with the same label start and end at the same nodes.

ii) Each link type is a predicate on pairs of node, selecting pairs that bear the specified relationship.

iii) Each link type is a relation which maps each node to a (possibly empty) set of nodes. Specifically it maps a node into the nodes to which it is connected by a link of that type.

iv) Each link type is a function that maps sets of nodes into sets of nodes connected by that type of link. The function is additive in the sense that if $A = B \cup C$ then $F(A) = F(B) \cup F(C)$. Thus, the function is defined by its behavior on the singleton sets.

These descriptions are all equivalent, in that they all describe the same mathematical object: an arbitrary set of ordered pairs of nodes. Let us call such an object a *relation*, but when we speak of applying a relation to a set, the last description is most useful in understanding what is really happening. I will be careful to *not* call this object a *function*, because that would confuse it with the things kept in function registers.

As an example, assume that the network contains nodes representing physical objects and nodes representing colors. Each object node has a color-of link connecting to the node that represents the object's color. Given such a network, we may find the color of an object by applying the color-of relation to a set containing the object. When we apply a relation we are treat it as a function from sets to sets, as in the last viewpoint above. For instance, if register A contains the singleton set {apple} then,

B ← APPLY-RELATION (color-of, A)

will load register B with {red}. Of course, the registers do not need to be loaded with singleton sets. If A had contained {apple, banana, cherry} the same instruction would have put {red, yellow} into B. Here both apples and cherries are red, so both nodes would map into the same color node.

The applied relation may map several sets into one. color-of for example, will map both {apple} and {cherry} into {red}. This means that the relations do not always have inverses when viewed as functions. There is however always a *reverse*,

which corresponds to moving backwards along the link in the same way that the standard relation corresponds to moving forward along the link. For example, if A contains {red} then

B ← APPLY-REVERSE-RELATION (color-of, A)

will load B with set of all red things. The inverse relation has the property that it will always get back at least what you started with:

A ⊂ APPLY-REVERSE-RELATION (relation, APPLY-RELATION (relation, A)) .

Another useful associated relation is the transitive closure. This does not make much sense with respect to the color-of relation, so instead imagine a genealogy network in which nodes representing individual people are connected by parent-of links. In such a network, if register A contained {John},

B ← APPLY-RELATION-CLOSURE (parent-of, A, U)

would load B with the set of all of the ancestors of John. The third argument U, specifies the set over which the relation is closed. In this case, U specifies the set of all nodes. If we are interested only in John's matriarchal ancestry, this third argument would be the set of females. There is also an APPLY-REVERSE-RELATION-CLOSURE instruction, which would find all of John's descendants. All of the instructions in this section work by transmitting messages from node to node containing selected bits from the node's state vector. Thus, for example, the APPLY-RELATION instruction works by having all nodes in the specified set (that is, all nodes with a specific bit in their state vector set) transmit messages to this effect through color-of links. Nodes receiving such messages can then set the appropriate bit indicating that they are a member of the answer set.

Example: *property inheritance in a virtual-copy hierarchy*

Assume that colors and types of objects are represented in a network. There are two types of links in this network, color-of links and virtual-copy links. The virtual-copy links represent class membership. This is a transitive property: crab-apples are a kind of apple, apples are a kind of fruit, so crab-apples are fruit. The color-of links connect an object to its color. If there is no explicitly stored color-of link then the color is inherited though the virtual-copy hierarchy; crab-apples are red because crab-apple is a virtual copy of apple.

Here is a sequence of connection machine operations that finds all of the red things stored in such a virtual copy network

A ← APPLY-REVERSE-RELATION (color-of, {red}); A is all explicitly red things ,

B ← COMPLEMENT ({red}) ,

B ← APPLY-REVERSE-RELATION (color-of, B); B is all explicitly non-red things ,

B ← COMPLEMENTS (B)

C ← APPLY-REVERSE-RELATION-CLOSURE (virtual-copy, A, B); C gets all red things .

This code will properly inherit the color of all super-types. It will also allow inherited properties to be explicitly overridden.

Group III: *instructions for manipulating functions*

The instructions mentioned so far, allow the machine to do anything that can be done with a counter-addressable memory or a marker-propagation machine. Marker programs that use *n* marks can always be translated into a connection-machine programs using *n* set-registers. Unfortunately, not all easy-to-partition algorithms can be expressed in terms of set operations. For example, in the genealogy network above it would be impossible to find every man who is his own father. To compute this function the machine must consider each node independently. A marker-propagation machine would require a separate marker for each individual. In relational database terms, a marker propagation or a set machine can concurrently compute projections and restrictions, but not joins.

This motivates the introduction of the next group of instructions, which give the connection machine additional power for handling these sorts of problems. The source of this additional power is the connection machine's ability to manipulate arbitrary functions. Such functions, from nodes to nodes, are held in the function-registers. In the sample instructions below, the letters F, G and H represent function registers.

The easiest way to load a function register is from a relation stored in the network. Since functions must be single valued and a relation can be multiple valued, they cannot always a loaded directly. The connection machine handles the problem by selecting among the multiple values by an "indexing" operation. For example, if r is a single-valued relation, then

$$F ← FUNCTION (r, 1)$$

will load function register F with the function that maps each node onto its r-related node, if there is one. If there is more than one, it will choose a single value according to the index. This second argument indexes the choice among the multiple values by using it to determine a unique path through the various fan-out trees in the representation of the network. The exact details of this algorithm are unimportant, except in that it guarantees that the FUNCTION instruction executed twice with the same index will return the same result. This allows a *k*-valued relation to be treated as a *k*-long vector of functions.

One thing to do with a function is to apply it, so there are APPLY-FUNCTION and APPLY-FUNCTION-CLOSURE, which are analogous to the APPLY-RELATION and APPLY-RELATION-CLOSURE instructions for applying relations.

A function may also be used to modify the structure of the network. This is the only available mechanism for building structure concurrently. For any relation r, the instruction

INSERT (F, r)

will add to r all pairs in the contents of function-register F. Similarly DELETE will delete pairs from a relation.

Since functions can be viewed as sets of ordered pairs, they may also be combined using INTERSECT-FUNCTIONS and DIFFERENCE-FUNCTIONS. UNION-FUNCTIONS may also be used if the result is actually a function, as in the union of functions with disjoint domains.

The COMPOSE instruction can be used to compose a relation with a function. Since such a composition is multiple valued in general, it too takes an index like the FUNCTION instruction:

G ← COMPOSE (r, F, n)

composes the relation r with the function F and chooses a function from the result using the index n.

The instructions in this section are the first ones that require nodes to send pointers in messages. An instruction like COMPOSE, for example, works by passing the contents of one register in each node backwards through selected links. Other instructions, such as INSERT, must actually allocate new cells and splice them into the existing network, by the message-wave mechanism described earlier.

Instructions like UNION-FUNCTIONS which do not send messages at all. Instead, they are implemented by register-to-register operations *within* each node. These instructions are similar to those in the first group (set operations).

Example: relational join

Given a genealogy network with parent-of and sex-of links, we wish to insert grandfather-of links between appropriate nodes. We assume that each person has only one sex and two parents (one of each sex).

```
A ← APPLY-REVERSE-RELATION (sex-of, {male}); A gets the set of all males .
F ← IDENTITY-FUNCTION (   )
F ← RESTRICT (F, A); F is the identity function for males only .
F ← COMPOSE (parent-of, F, 1); F is now the father function .
G ← COMPOSE (parent-of, F, 1); G is one of the grandfather functions .
INSERT (G, grandfather-of); build G into the network .
G ← COMPOSE (parent-of, F, 2); G is now the other grandfather function .
INSERT (G, grandfather-of); build your other grandfather into the network .
```

The final way to create one function from another is to delete portions of it with the RESTRICT instruction. This instruction restricts the domain of function to a set contained in one of the set registers. For example,

F ← RESTRICT (G, A)

will load F with the portion of the function in G that maps from the contents of A.

A function register may be initialized to the null function with the CLEAR-FUNCTION instruction, or to the identity function with the IDENTITY-FUNCTION instruction.

This example is a special case of the relational database equi-join operation. The code takes advantage of the fact that grandfather-of is a two-valued relation. Join on an *n*-valued relational would require repeating an operation *n* times. This is to be expected, since in the worst case the equi-join operation produces the Cartesian product of its inputs.

Group IV: arithmetic instructions

The arithmetic instructions manipulate functions from nodes to numbers. Numbers are just special nodes. The only thing that distinguishes them from ordinary nodes is that they are recognized by the arithmetic instructions. Thus node-to-number functions can be held in function-registers and manipulated by all of the function manipulation instructions mentioned above. They can also be manipulated by the arithmetic instructions.

The first set of arithmetic instructions are similar to the FUNCTION instruction. Like FUNCTION, they load a specified function register from a relation. The function instruction derives a single value from the potentially many-valued relation by choosing among them according to its index argument. The arithmetic instructions derive a single value by combining the values with an arithmetic operation. Thus,

$$F \leftarrow \text{SUM} (r, I)$$

will load F with the function that maps each node into the sum of all its r-related nodes. Another way of saying this is that it associates with each node a number, which is the sum of the nodes that can reached from it over r-links. The second argument to SUM indicates how to get a number from the node. In the example, I (for identity) indicated that the node itself is to be used as the value. This makes sense, of course, only if these nodes are numbers. Otherwise an error condition would be flagged.

MAXIMUM and MINIMUM are two other instructions that require the r-mapped nodes to be numbers. These instructions have the same format as SUM, but instead of adding the numbers, they reduce the set to a single value by choosing either the largest or the smallest value.

AND and OR are classified as arithmetic instructions because they operate on and produce numbers. These instruction perform bit-wise logical operations on the binary representations of numbers. They have the same format as SUM, and produce a function in a similar manner.

These five instructions (SUM, MINIMUM, MAXIMUM, AND, OR) are just examples of plausible arithmetic instructions. Any function which turns a set of objects into a single number would make

sense as an instruction. Any symmetric and associative arithmetic operation will do. There could be a MULTIPLY instruction, for instance. Asymmetric functions, like subtract, do not make sense in this context because it would not be obvious what should be subtracted from what.

This first class of arithmetic instructions operate by utilizing the fan out trees to actually perform the required arithmetic. They are thus similar to the pointer passing functions of the last section, except instead of selecting a single answer from those arriving at a fan out tree based on an index, the answers are all combined in some manner.

There is a second class of arithmetic instruction for which asymmetric operations make sense. These instructions combine two functions into a single function, or to put it another way, they associate with each node a value that depends on other values already associated with the node. So, for example,

$$F \leftarrow \text{FUNCTION-SUBTRACT} (G, H)$$

with load F with the function that maps each node to the difference of the values of the G and H functions applied to that node. Similar instructions are FUNCTION-SUM, FUNCTION-MAXIMUM, FUNCTION-MINIMUM, FUNCTION-AND, and FUNCTION-OR.

This class of arithmetic instruction involves no message passing. These instructions are all executed as register-to-register operations at each node.

13. How to connect a million processors

The most difficult technical problem in constructing a connection machine is the communications network. The machine's speed is limited by the bandwidth of the network. This bandwidth depends on the topology of the network, which is limited by physical layout and wiring constraints. Highly connected structures, such as the Boolean n-cube, are difficult or impossible to wire for such large numbers of nodes. Constraints on wiring density suggest simple tessellated structures, such as the grid or the torus. These grid-like structures are easy to wire, but the large average distance between nodes slows communication.

Instead of choosing either of these extremes, I have developed a compromise that allows us to take best advantage of the available wiring density. It is a family of connection patterns that spans the gap between the low-performance grid, and the unwireable n-cube. Given a set of engineering numbers, such as the number of pins on available connectors or the maximum wire density, we can choose from the family the highest performance connection pattern that satisfies the constraints.

A method for generating the family connection patterns is shown in fig. 9. I illustrate here only the one-dimensional case. The two or three-dimensional layout is generated by repeating this pattern in each dimension independently. The first member of the family is the torus. In two dimensions this is just a grid with opposite edges connected, as in the ILLIAC IV [20]. This pattern can easily be projected into a line, as shown. The second member of the family is generated from the torus by connecting each node to the node farthest away as shown. The nodes may be rearranged for efficient wiring by first twisting the torus and then folding it, so that each node is adjacent to the node half-way around the torus from itself. This pattern may now be projected into a line as shown.

This operation of connecting, twisting and fold-

ing results in a connection pattern with one half the maximum distance and twice the density of wires. The procedure may be repeated as many times as necessary to achieve an optimal tradeoff between performance and wireability. If the torus is twisted $\log(n)$ times, where n is the number of nodes, the resulting structure will be an augmented Boolean n-cube. The number of parallel wires in the connecting buses may also be varied, generating a two-parameter family of interconnection patterns.

The resulting connection pattern has the following desirable properties:

○ *Uniformity*. The network looks similar from the viewpoint of each node.
○ *Extensibility*. More nodes can be added by plugging more cells on at the edges.
○ *A maximum wire length*. Short wires allow synchronous operation.
○ *A maximum wiring density*, chosen to match available technology.
○ *A maximum number of pins per module*, chosen to match available technology.

For an integrated circuit or a printed-circuit board the pattern would be repeated in two dimensions. It is also extendable to three dimensions if such a technology becomes available.

According to our initial calculations, the maximum performance network built with off-the-shelf 1981 components is a twice-folded torus with five-bit data paths.

14. What can the machine do?

One goal of the proposed research is to formalize just what the connection machine can and cannot do. There already exists one well-worked-out formalism for describing retrieval operations: relational database theory. Codd's *relational calculus* allows queries to be described in the form of a predicate calculus. The *relational algebra* provides a set of operations for computing these queries [4]. We do not expect to convert artificial intelligence

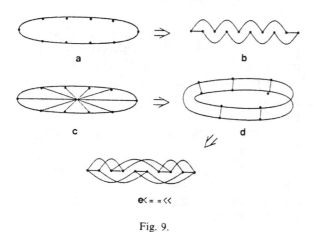

Fig. 9.

knowledge representations to relational databases, because they do not provide a natural way of expressing artificial intelligence knowledge manipulation. But relational database theory does address a well-specified set of problems that are similar to those that we must solve for semantic networks. I believe that relational database formalisms will provide theoretical tools for describing the operations of the connection machine.

The notion of *relational completeness*, for example, provides a measure of the expressive power of a retrieval language. If a machine can concurrently process all of the operations of the relational algebra, which is relationally complete, we know that it can compute any query that is expressible in the relational calculus. This gives us confidence that our system has no hidden weaknesses.

15. Comprison with other concurrent architectures

The connection machines differs from most cellular automata in its mechanisms for arbitrary communication. It is useful to contrast the connection machine with other parallel computing mechanisms. Here is a list of some of these machines, that is, a list of some of the things which a connection machine is not.

○ It is not a way of hooking together a collection of general-purpose computers as in [20, 7, 11, 3, 21, 24, 19, 8]. The connection machine shares many features with these systems, such as extensibility, concurrency, and uniformity, but the individual processing elements in the connection machine are smaller. Since each connection-machine cell contains only a few dozen bytes of memory there can be many more of them, allowing for a higher degree of concurrency. The penalty is that the connection machine is less general-purpose; it must be used in conjunction with a conventional machine.

○ It is not a marker-propagation machine, as proposed by Fahlman [6]. The connection machine is able to execute marker-type algorithms, but its pointer manipulation capabilities give it additional power.

○ It is not a simple associative memory [16]. The elements in content addressable memories are comparable in size to connection machine cells, but the connection machine's processing operations are far more general, due to its ability to communicate between cells.

○ It is not a systolic array [15, 14]. In the connection machine, cells may operate asynchronously. Uniformity is not critical; some cells may be defective or missing. The connection machine is also more flexible than a hard-wired systolic-array, although for problems that can be done on both it is likely to be slower. Systolic array algorithms can all be executed efficiently on the connection machine.

○ It is not a database management machine like RAP [17] or CASSM [5]. They are designed to process a more restricted class of queries on a much larger database.

The machine is designed for symbol manipulation, not number crunching. It does have limited parallel arithmetic capabilities because they are often useful in symbol manipulation, for example, in computing a score for a best-match retrieval. Similar architectures may have application in numeric processing, but we do not at this time plan to investigate these possibilities.

16. We plan to build a prototype

In 1967 the MIT Artificial Intelligence Laboratory commissioned the construction of the world's first 256 K-word core memory. The cost was approximately half a million dollars, or about two dollars a word. The "old moby" is actually still in use, although it is now flanked by 256 K words of semiconductor memory that cost literally one hundredth as much.

The proposed 128 K connection machine will cost about as much per processor as the core cost per word. Part of this represents a one-time tooling cost, but by far the largest expense is the fabrication of the chips. These fabrication estimates assume the low yields and short runs appropriate for a first-time project. If the architecture proves successful and is duplicated on a larger scale, the per-cell costs would drop dramatically. Fundamentally, a connection machine should only cost a constant factor more than a similar-sized semiconductor random access memory. If, say, half of the area of a connection machine chip is pointer memory, then storing a given amount of data would take twice as many connection machine chips as RAM chips. The RAM, of course, would only store the data, not process it.

At the MIT Artificial Intelligence Laboratory, we have designed a prototype connection machine, which it is currently being built by Thinking Machines Corporation, of Cambridge Massachusetts. The machine will start with 131,071 (128 K) processing cells. The machine is expandable 1024 K cells. It is built almost entirely out of custom large-scale integrates circuits, with approximately 100,000 transistors per package. The 128 K-machine will have more than two thousand of these integrated circuits. Because the connection machine is incrementally extendable, like ordinary memory, it will be possible to build a million element machine by simply plugging together eight duplicated sections, although we will probably never actually do this with this first machine. We expect the first prototype to begin operating by the end of 1984.

Acknowledgments

This report describes research done at the Artificial Intelligence Laboratory of the Massachusetts Institute of Technology. Support for the Artificial Intelligence Laboratory's artificial intelligence research is provided in part by the Advanced Research Projects Agency of the Department of Defense under contract with the Office of Naval Research contract N00014-80-C-0505. The author is supported by a fellowship provided by the Fannie and John Hertz Foundation. An earlier version of this report may be found in [12].

References

[1] J. Backus, "Can programming be liberated from the Von Neumann style?", Communication of the ACM 21 (1978) 613–641.
[2] R.J. Brachman, On the Epistemological Status of Semantic Networks, Report No. 3807 (Bolt Beranek and Newman Inc., Cambridge, MA, April 1978).
[3] S.A. Browning, "A tree machine", Lambda Magazine 1 (1980) 31–36.
[4] E.F. Codd, "Relational Completeness of Data Base Sublanguages", in: R. Rustin, ed., Database Systems, Courant Computer Science Symp. Series, vol. 6 (Prentice Hall, London, 1972).
[5] G.P. Copeland, G.J. Lipovski and S.Y.W. Su, "The Architecture of CASSM: A Cellular System for Non-numeric Processing", Proc. 1st Annual Symp. Com. Arch. 1973, pp. 121–128.
[6] Scott Fahlman, NETL: A System for Representing and Using Real-World Knowledge (MIT Press, Cambridge, 1979).
[7] E.C. Gritton et al., "Feasibility of a Special-Purpose Computer to Solve the Navier–Stokes Equations", Rand Corp. r-2183-RC (June 1977).
[8] C.E. Hewitt, "The Apiary Network Architecture for Knowledgeable Systems", Proc. Lisp Conf. Stanford (August 1980) pp. 107–118.
[9] C. Hewitt, G. Attardi and M. Simi, "Knowledge Embedding in the Description System Omega", Proc. First Nation Conf. on A.I. (August 1980) pp. 157–164.
[10] John H. Holland, "A Universal Computer Capable of Executing an Arbitrary Number of Sub-Programs Simultaneously", Proc. 1959 E.J.C.C. pp. 108–113.
[11] R.H. Halstead, "Reference Tree Networks: Virtual Machine and Implementation", MIT/LCS/TR-222 (MIT Laboratory for Computer Science, Cambridge, MA, June 1979).
[12] W. Daniel Hillis, "The Connection Machine, Computer Architecture for the New Wave", MIT AI Lab Memo 646, September 1981.
[13] P.A. Koton, "Simulating a Semantic Network in LMS", Bachelor Thesis, Dept. of Electrical Engineering and Computer Science, MIT, Cambridge, MA (January 1980).
[14] H.T. Kung and P.L. Lehman, "Systolic (VLSI) Arrays for relational database operations" Int. Conf. on Management of Data, May 1980.
[15] H.T. Kung, and C.E. Leiserson, "Systolic Arrays", In Itro. to VLSI Systems by C.A. Mead and L.A. Conway (Addison-Wesley, New York 1980) section 8.3.
[16] C.Y. Lee and M.C. Paul, "A Content-Addressable Distributed-Logic Memory with Applications to Information Retrieval", IEEE Proc. 51:924-932, June 1963.
[17] S.A. Ozkarahan, S.A. Schuster and K.C. Sevcik, "A Data Base processor", Tech. Rep. CSRG-43, Comp. Sys. Res. Group, U. of Toronto, Sept. 1974.
[18] J.T. Schwartz, "On Programming, An Interim Report on the SETL Project", Computer Science dept., Courant Inst. Math. Science., New York University (1973).

[19] C. Rieger, "ZMOB: A mob of 256 Cooperative Z80a-based Microcomputers", Univ. of Maryland C.S. TR-825, College Park, MD (1979).

[20] D. L. Slotnick et al., "The ILLIAC IV Computer", IEEE Transactions on Computers. vol. C-17, No. 8 (August 1978), pp. 746–757.

[21] R.J. Swan, S.H. Fuller and D.P. Siewiorek, "Cm*–A Modular, Multi-Microprocessor", AFIPS Conf. Proc. 46 (1977).

[22] P. Szolovitz, L. Hawkinson and W.A. Martin, "An Overview of OWL, a Language for Knowledge Representation", MIT/LCS/TM-86, MIT Laboratory for Computer Science, Cambridge, MA (June 1977).

[23] Tommaso Toffoli, "Cellular Automata Mechanics," Tech. Rep. No. 208, Logic of Computers Group, CCS Dept., The University of Michigan (November 1977).

[24] S.A. Ward, "The MuNet: A Multiprocessor Message-Passing System Architecture", Seventh Texas Conf. on Comp. Syst. Houston, Texas (October 1978).

[25] W.A. Woods, "Research in Natural Language Understanding, Progress Report No. 2", Report No. 3797 (Bolt Beranek and Newman, Cambridge, MA, 1978).

[26] Patrick H. Winston and Berthold K.P. Horn, Lisp (Addison-Wesley, New York, 1981).

[27] M. Quillian, "Semantic Memory," in: Minsky, ed., "Semantic Information Processing" (MIT Press, Cambridge, 1968).

THE USE OF META-LEVEL CONTROL FOR COORDINATION IN A DISTRIBUTED PROBLEM SOLVING NETWORK

Daniel D. Corkill and Victor R. Lesser

Computer and Information Science Department
University of Massachusetts
Amherst, Massachusetts, 01003

ABSTRACT

Distributed problem solving networks provide an interesting application area for meta-level control through the use of organizational structuring. We describe a decentralized approach to network coordination that relies on each node making sophisticated local decisions that balance its own perceptions of appropriate problem solving activity with activities deemed important by other nodes. Each node is guided by a high-level strategic plan for cooperation among the nodes in the network. The high-level strategic plan, which is a form of meta-level control, is represented as a network organizational structure that specifies in a general way the information and control relationships among the nodes. An implementation of these ideas is briefly described along with the results of preliminary experiments with various network problem solving strategies specified via organizational structuring. In addition to its application to Distributed Artificial Intelligence, this research has implications for organizing and controlling complex knowledge-based systems that involve semi-autonomous problem solving agents.

I INTRODUCTION

Cooperative distributed problem solving systems are distributed networks of semi-autonomous processing **nodes** that work together to solve a *single* problem. Each node is a sophisticated **problem solving system** that can modify its behavior as circumstances change and plan its own communication and cooperation strategies with other nodes. Our research has emphasized applications where there is a natural spatial distribution of information and processing requirements among the nodes but insufficient local information for any node to make completely accurate processing and control decisions without interacting with other nodes. An example of this type of application is a distributed sensor network [13, 20, 14]. Our approach for implementing these applications is to have the nodes cooperate via an iterative, coroutine exchange of partial and tentative high-level results. In this way, the system as a whole can function effectively even though the nodes initially have inconsistent and incomplete views of the information used in their computations [15, 16, 17, 1, 2].

A key problem in cooperative distributed problem solving networks is obtaining sufficient global coherence for effective cooperation among the nodes [21]. If this

This research was sponsored, in part, by the National Science Foundation under Grant MCS-8006327 and by the Defense Advanced Research Projects Agency (DOD), monitored by the Office of Naval Research under Contract NR049-041.

coherence is not achieved, then the performance (speed and accuracy) of the network can be significantly diminished as a result of:

- lost processing as nodes wait for something to do;

- wasted processing as nodes work at cross-purposes with one another;

- redundantly applied processing as nodes duplicate efforts;

- misallocation of activities so that important portions of the problem are either inaccurately solved or not solved in timely fashion.

These problems have been observed in our experiments with three-to-five node networks [15, 17]. We expect these problems will become even more significant as we move to networks containing larger numbers of nodes operating in changing environments.

In this paper we describe a decentralized approach to network coordination that relies on each node making sophisticated local decisions that balance its own perceptions of appropriate problem solving activity with activities deemed important by other nodes. Each node is guided by a high-level strategic plan for cooperation among the nodes in the network. This strategic plan, which is a form of meta-level control, is represented as a network organizational structure that specifies in a general way the information and control relationships among the nodes.

In the next section we expand on the use of organizational structuring as a meta-level network coordination technique. In Section 3, we briefly describe the local control component of a node and how organizational structuring decisions influence this component. Section 4 presents the results of preliminary experiments with various network problem solving strategies specified via organizational structuring. Section 5 discusses the prospects of more complex forms of meta-level control using organizational structuring. We conclude by comparing this approach to recent applications of meta-level control in knowledge-based Artificial Intelligence systems.

II NETWORK COORDINATION VIA ORGANIZATIONAL STRUCTURING

Network coordination is difficult in a cooperative distributed problem solving network because limited internode communication restricts each node's view of network problem solving activity. In addition, network reliability issues (which require that the network's performance degrades gracefully if a portion of the network fails) preclude the use of a global "controller" node. It is important that the network coordination policies do not consume more processing and communication resources than the benefits derived from the increased problem solving coherence. We believe that in networks composed of even a small number of nodes, a complete analysis to determine the detailed activites at each node is impractical. The computation and communication costs of optimally determining the activities far outweigh the improvement in problem solving performance. Instead, coordination in distributed problem solving networks must sacrifice some potential improvement for a less complex coordination problem.

What is desired is a balance between problem solving and coordination so that the combined cost of both activities is acceptable. The emphasis is shifted from optimizing the activities in the network to achieving an acceptable performance level of the network as a whole. These policies must also have enough flexibility to provide sufficient system robustness and reliability to respond to a changing task and hardware environment. In order for network control to satisfy these requirements, it must be able to tolerate the lack of up-to-date, incomplete, or incorrect control information due to delays in the receipt of information, the high cost of acquisition and processing of the information, and errors in communication and processing hardware.

We feel that the balance between local node control and network-wide control is a crucial aspect of the design of such decentralized network control policies. It is unrealistic to expect that network control policies can be developed which are sufficiently flexible, efficient, and require limited communication, while simultaneously making all the control decisions for each node in the network. We believe a node needs a sophisticated form of local control that permits it to plan sequences of activities and to adapt its plan based on its problem solving role in the network, on the status and role of other nodes in the network, and on self-awareness of its activities.

An **organizational structure** is used to provide each node with a high-level view of problem solving in the network. It specifies a general set of node responsibilities and node interaction patterns that is available to all nodes. Included in the organizational structure are control decisions that are not quickly outdated and that pertain to a large number of nodes. The sophisticated local control component of each node is responsible for elaborating these relationships into precise activities to be performed by the node. In this way we have split the network coordination problem into two concurrent activities [5]:

1. construction and maintenance of a network-wide organizational structure;

2. continuous local elaboration of this structure into precise activites using the local control capabilities of each node.

The organizational structure provides a control framework which reduces the amount of control uncertainty present in a node (due to incomplete or errorful local control information) and increases the likelihood that the nodes will be coherent in their behavior by providing a general and global strategy for network problem solving. The organizational structuring approach to limiting control uncertainty still preserves a certain level of control flexibility for a node to adapt its local control to changing task and environmental conditions.

In order for any network coordination policy to be successful, it must achieve the following conditions:

coverage – any given portion of the overall problem must be included in the activities of at least one node;

connectivity – nodes must interact in a manner which permits the covering activities to be developed and integrated into an overall solution;

capability – coverage and connectivity must be achievable within the communication and computation resource limitations of the network.

The organizational structure specifies a range of possible coverages and connectivity patterns that can potentially satisfy the capability condition. Using the coverage and connectivity guidelines specified in the organizational structure, the local control component of each node selects a problem solving strategy based on the dynamics of the specific local problem solving situation.

III AN IMPLEMENTATION OF ORGANIZATIONAL STRUCTURING

To provide a framework for studying the use of organizational structuring in coordinating the local activity decisions of the nodes in a cooperative distributed problem solving network, we have constructed the Distributed Vehicle Monitoring Testbed [17]. The testbed simulates a network of problem solving nodes attempting to identify, locate, and track patterns of vehicles moving through a two-dimensional space using signals detected by acoustic sensors. By varying parameters in the testbed that specify the accuracy and range of the acoustic sensors, the acoustic signals that are to be grouped together to form patterns of vehicles, the power and distribution of knowledge among the nodes in the network, and the node and communication topology, a wide variety of cooperative distributed problem solving situations can be modelled.

Each problem solving node is an architecturally-complete Hearsay-II system [7] (with knowledge sources appropriate for the task of vehicle monitoring). The basic Hearsay-II architecture has been extended to include more sophisticated local control and the capability of communicating hypotheses and goals among nodes [3, 4]. In particular, a planning module, a goal blackboard, and communication knowledge sources have been added (Figure 1). Goals are created on the goal blackboard to indicate the node's intention to abstract and extend hypotheses on the data blackboard. The planner can adapt the node's local activities in response to the potential processing activities of the node (based on the goals created from the node's hypothesis structure) and to externally-directed requests from other nodes (communicated goals).

Meta-level control via organizational structuring is introduced into this node architecture through the use of a nonprocedural and dynamically variable specification of the behaviors of each node's planner, its scheduler, and its communication knowledge sources. These data structures,

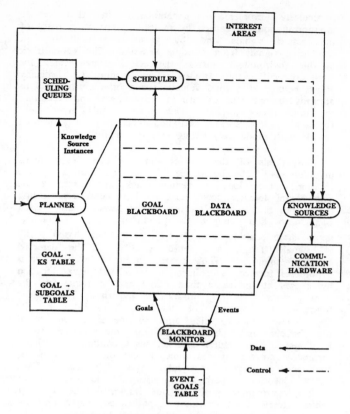

Figure 1: Testbed Node Architecture.

the minimum rating needed for a goal to be subgoaled are also specified.

Hypothesis transmission interest areas and goal transmission interest areas influence the behavior of the hypothesis and goal transmission knowledge sources at the node. Transmission interest areas are specified for one or more lists of nodes that are to receive information from the node. Each transmission interest area has a weight specifying the importance of transmitting hypotheses or goals from that area (to nodes specified in the node-list) and a threshold value specifying the minimum hypothesis belief or goal rating needed to transmit from that area.

Hypothesis reception interest areas and goal reception interest areas influence the behavior of the hypothesis and goal reception knowledge sources at the node. Reception interest areas are specified for lists of nodes that are to transmit information to the node. Each reception interest area has a weight specifying the importance of receiving a hypothesis or goal in that area (from a node specified in the node-list), a minimum hypothesis belief or goal rating needed for the hypothesis or goal to be accepted, and a credibility weight. The credibility weight parameter is used to change the belief of received hypotheses or the rating of received goals. A node can reduce the effect of accepting messages from a node by lowering the belief or rating of messages received from that node. Each hypothesis reception interest area also has a focusing weight parameter that is used to determine how heavily received hypotheses are used in making local problem solving focusing decisions. This is accomplished by modifying the rating of local processing goals indicating potential work on these received hypotheses.

There are also additional parameters associated with the interest areas of each node that specify the relative weighting a node gives to performing activities it perceives as important versus activities proposed by other nodes. The settings of these parameters control the various authority relationships among the nodes in the network.

These interest area and authority specifications provide the interface between the activity decisions made by a node and organizational structuring decisions. They can be used to control the amount of overlap and problem solving redundancy among nodes, the problem solving roles of nodes (such as "integrator", "specialist", and "middle manager"), the authority relations between nodes, and the potential problem solving paths in the network. These data structures can be viewed as rudiments of a third blackboard – an **organizational blackboard** containing the organizational roles and responsibilities for the node. A node's organizational responsibilities can be established and changed by simply modifying these data structures. The specification data structures themselves do not provide an explicit, high-level representation of these organizational roles and responsibilities (this will involve future work), but instead serve as a low-level "job description" of those activities a node should be performing and those activities a node should be avoiding.

IV TESTBED EXPERIMENTS WITH ORGANIZATIONAL STRUCTURING

In this section we show how different organizational strategies for network problem solving can be achieved by

called **interest areas**, are used to implement particular network configurations and coordination policies. Each interest area is a list of regions and levels of the data or goal blackboard. Associated with each interest area are one or more parameters that modify the behavior of the node. There are five sets of interest areas for each node in the testbed:

Local processing interest areas influence the local problem solving activities in the node by modifying the priority ratings of goals and knowledge source instantiations and the behavior of the node's planner and scheduler. Each local processing interest area has a single parameter associated with it: a weight specifying the importance of performing local processing within the interest area. By changing the blackboard regions and their weights, problem solving can be restricted to particular blackboard regions and levels, and problem solving on particular regions and levels can be given priority (changing the characteristics of the search performed at a node). Knowledge sources are scheduled based on the confidence of their input data, the priority of the type of problem solving performed by the knowledge source, and the rating of processing goals. The goal rating is determined directly from the interest area weight and indirectly from the goal's relation to higher-level processing goals. Each node's local processing interest area specification also includes a subgoaling specification. This data structure lists the blackboard levels and regions where processing goals are to be subgoaled and the levels, sizes, and ratings of the subgoals.[*] Threshold values indicating

---

[*] The size and rating of a subgoal are specified in terms of the size and rating of the original processing goal.

appropriate settings of the interest area specifications at each node and how these different strategies perform in a specific distributed problem solving situation. Characteristics that were varied included:

- whether communication is **voluntary** (a node transmits hypotheses at its pleasure), **requested** (a node transmits hypotheses only when that information is requested by another node), or a **mixed initiative** combination of voluntary and requested hypotheses (a node volunteers only its highest rated hypotheses and awaits requests before transmitting any other hypotheses);

- whether a node is **self-directed** or **externally-directed** in its activities (or a combination of both);

- whether hypotheses, goals, or both hypotheses and goals are used for internode coordination.

The organizational strategies were evaluated using two different network architectures: a laterally-organized, four-node network with broadcast communication among nodes and a hierarchically-organized, five-node network in which the fifth node acts as an integrating node. In both architectures, the network is structured so that the nodes cooperate by exchanging partial and tentative high-level hypotheses.

The sensor configuration and input sensory signal data used in these experiments is shown in Figure 2. Four sensors with identical characteristics and slightly overlapping ranges cover the monitoring area. This environmental scenario was designed to test the network's ability to use prediction to extend strongly sensed portions of an actual vehicle track through weakly sensed portions in the presence of a moderately sensed "ghost" track. Ghost tracks are a

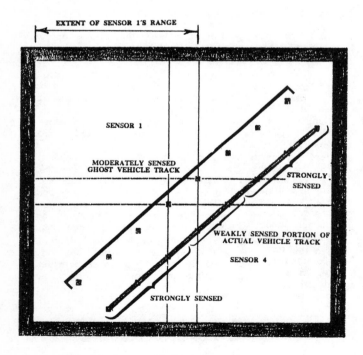

Figure 2: Sensor Configuration and Input Data.

particularly problematic phenomenon in the vehicle monitoring domain, caused by multiple propagation paths of the actual signals and by geometrical ambiguity in combining signals from multiple vehicles. The ghost track in this environment mirrors the actual vehicle track for eight consecutive time frames. This is unusual. Typically ghosts behave as normal vehicles for a brief period only to abruptly disappear or to turn at sharp angles and accelerate to infinite velocity [10]. The ghost in this environment represents a "worst-case" situation, appearing as a normal vehicle with moderately strong sensory support.

Synthesis of the answer map in these experiments involves five blackboard levels: signal location, group location, vehicle location, vehicle track, and pattern track. The **Signal location** level contains hypotheses representing the output of low-level analysis of the sensory data. Each signal location hypothesis includes the frequency, approximate position, time frame,* and belief (based partly on signal strength and sensor quality) of the detected acoustic signal. The **group location** level contains hypotheses formed from harmonically-related signal location hypotheses at the same time frame and approximately the same position. Each group location hypothesis includes the fundamental frequency of the related signals and its approximate position, time frame, and belief (a function of the beliefs and characteristics of the related signal locations). The **vehicle location** level contains hypotheses formed from group location hypotheses that can be combined to form a particular type of vehicle. Each vehicle location hypothesis includes the identity of the vehicle, approximate position, time frame, and belief. The **vehicle track** level contains hypothesized movements of vehicles over time. Each vehicle track hypothesis includes the identity of the vehicle, its approximate position at successive time frames, and belief. The **pattern track** level contains hypotheses formed from vehicle track hypotheses of specific vehicle types that maintain a particular spatial relationship among themselves. Pattern tracks were included in the testbed to investigate the effect of strong constraints between distant nodes.

In the four-node network each node is positioned near one of the sensors and receives signal location hypotheses from that sensor only. The interest areas on the organizational blackboard of each node specify that it is to synthesize its sensory data to the vehicle track level and transmit any of these vehicle track hypotheses that can be extended into the sensory area of another node to that node. Each node is also directed to attempt to generate hypotheses at both the vehicle track and pattern track levels which span the entire monitoring area. This means that each node is in a race with the other three to generate the complete answer map.

In the five-node network four of the nodes are positioned near one of the sensors and receive signal location hypotheses only from that sensor. (Their signal location input is identical to the four-node network.) The fifth node receives no sensory data. Instead, it is instructed through interest areas on the organizational blackboard to work only at the vehicle track and pattern track levels with vehicle track hypotheses received from the other four nodes. The four nodes with sensory data are assigned the role of synthesizing their signal location hypotheses to the vehicle

---

* The environment is not sensed continuously. Instead, it is sampled at discrete time intervals called **time frames.**

track level and transmitting them to the fifth node. In the five-node network configuration, these four nodes do not work outside the area of their sensory data at any blackboard level and do no work at the pattern track level.

In the four-node configuration, voluntary communication is obtained by providing each node with hypothesis transmission interest areas specifying transmission of vehicle track hypothesis to nodes with sensors in the area of possible extension of these hypotheses. To keep the node entirely self-directed in its local activity decisions, each node is instructed not to generate processing goals from hypotheses received from other nodes. The beliefs of the received vehicle track hypotheses, however, are not reduced. This means that the node can use received information in extending its own hypotheses without having to find local information that can be combined with the received hypotheses. This separation of belief in the data from focusing priority fits nicely into the integrated data- and goal-directed architecture. Externally-directed control is obtained by instructing each node to create goals from hypotheses received from other nodes and to use only those goals in its local activity decisions. In this strategy, the receipt of a highly-believed hypothesis from another node causes the receiving node to try its best to find something that can be combined with the received hypothesis. Combined self-directed and externally-directed control is obtained by instructing each node to use goals generated from both internal and received hypotheses in its activity decisions.

The requested communication strategy is obtained by instructing each node to process its local sensory data to the vehicle track level, but rather than voluntarily transmitting vehicle track hypotheses, any vehicle track extension goals that are within the sensory area of another node are sent to that node. When a node creates a vehicle track hypothesis that satisfies one of these received goals it transmits the hypothesis to the originator of the goal. Within the requested communication strategy, self-directed, externally-directed, and combined control strategies are obtained by instructing each node to use goals generated from internal hypotheses, goals received from other nodes, or both in its local activity decisions, respectively.

In the five-node configuration, mixed-initiative communication is obtained by having the worker nodes transmit only highly rated hypotheses to the integrating node. The integrating node transmits goals to the worker nodes informing them of its need for additional data. If the received goals are not used for focusing, the worker nodes remain self-directed in their local activity decisions, only responding to those goals that are achieved as a result of self-directed processing activity. If the received goals are used for focusing, the worker nodes become externally-directed and attempt to achieve the received goals. Again, a combined self- and externally-directed approach can also be specified.

A. Results of the four-node network experiments

Each of the organizational problem solving strategies were run on the environment of Figure 2. The network was stopped when the complete actual pattern track hypotheses was formed at one of the four nodes. The results are shown in Table 1. Whether the network used voluntary or requested communication of hypotheses had

FOUR-NODE EXPERIMENTS

Problem Solving Strategy	Network Cycles	Sent Hyps	Sent Goals
VH/SD	33	23	0
VH/ED	86	39	0
VH/S&ED	79	45	0
RH/SD	32	32	80
RH/ED	83	35	133
RH/S&ED	75	40	78

FIVE-NODE EXPERIMENTS

Problem Solving Strategy	Network Cycles	Sent Hyps	Sent Goals
VH/SD	27	20	0
MH/SD	25	18	14
MH/ED	40	33	30
MH/S&ED	29	22	18

Table 1: Summary of Network Experiments.

Strategies:

VH	Voluntary Hypothesis Communication
RH	Requested Hypothesis Communication
MH	Mixed-Inititive Hypothesis Communication
SD	Self-Directed Control
ED	Externally-Directed Control
S&ED	Combined Self- and Externally-Directed Control

little effect on the number of network cycles[*] required to generate an answer. Whether the strategy was self-directed or externally-directed had a much greater effect on network performance. The completely externally-directed strategies performed much worse than the completely data-directed strategies, with the combined strategies in between.

Why does externally-directed control perform so poorly in these experiments? A closer inspection reveals why. Node 1 (the node associated with Sensor 1) senses signal location hypotheses in only two time frames. Its signal location hypotheses are associated with the false ghost track. It does not sense the actual vehicle track at all. Having no other work to perform Node 1 quickly forms a two time-frame segment of the ghost track and transmits it to the other three nodes. This hypothesis is rated higher than the strongly sensed signal location hypotheses because it is at a higher blackboard level and appears to be a reasonable vehicle track from Node 1′s perspective. Due to their bias to external direction the other three nodes suspend work on the strongly sensed lower level hypotheses of the actual track and attempt to extend the ghost track, resulting in inappropriate knowledge source activities and lost time. This is a prime example of distraction [15].

To verify that distracting information received from Node 1 is indeed the cause of the poor performance of the externally-directed strategies, the requested communication with both self-directed and externally-directed control

---

[*] A **network cycle** is the execution of one local processing knowledge source at each node in the network. If a node has no work to perform during a cycle, its potential knowledge source execution is lost.

experiment was rerun with Node 1 disabled. The number of network cycles was reduced from 75 with Node 1 to 38 without Node 1. The network actually performs much better without Node 1, even though the remaining nodes still receive all signal location hypotheses associated with the ghost track.

B. Results of the five-node network experiments

The results of the five-node experiments are also shown in Table 1. In this case the network was stopped when the complete actual pattern track hypothesis was formed at the integrating node. Whether the network used voluntary or mixed-initiative communication of hypotheses again had little effect on the number of network cycles required to generate an answer. As with the four-node network experiments, whether the strategy was self-directed or externally-directed had a much greater effect on network performance. The completely externally-directed strategies performed much worse than the completely data-directed strategies, with the combined strategies in between.

In this case the information received by the integrating node (Node 5) from Node 1 causes it to make inappropriate coordination decisions for the other three worker nodes. In place of distracting hypotheses received directly from Node 1, distraction of the worker nodes takes the indirect form of distracting goals received from Node 5.

The mixed-initiative communication with externally-directed control experiment was rerun with Node 1 disabled. Again the loss of Node 1 improved the performance of the network by eliminating its distracting influence. The number of network cycles was reduced from 40 with Node 1 to 29 without Node 1. The network again performed much better without the distractions from Node 1.

C. Comparing the four-node and five-node experiments

When the additional processing provided by the fifth node is taken into account, the performance of the lateral four-node network was basically identical with the performance of the hierarchical five-node network in comparable self-directed experiments (Table 2). The five-node network does appear to perform better than the four-node network in the externally-directed strategies. When a node in the four-node network receives distracting

Problem Solving Strategy	Normalized Four-Node Network Cycles	Five-Node Network Cycles
VH/SD	26.4	27
R-MH/SD	25.6	25
R-MH/ED	66.4	40
R-MH/S&ED	60.0	29

Table 2: Network Cycle Comparison of the Four- and Five-Node Experiments.

Strategies:

VH	Voluntary Hypothesis Communication
R-MH	Requested or Mixed-Initiative Hypothesis Communication
SD	Self-Directed Control
ED	Externally-Directed Control
S&ED	Combined Self- and Externally-Directed Control

information it generally processes it to the pattern track level before resuming work on its own lower level hypotheses (due to the generally higher belief associated with higher abstraction levels). A worker node in the five-node network only processes distracting information to the vehicle track level, and then sends the information on to the integrating node. Thus the worker node can resume its activities sooner than a node in the four-node architecture. The integrating node, while distracted, is not synthesizing low level data and is therefore less affected by the distracting information. By dividing the additional work caused by the distracting hypotheses between nodes with different problem solving responsibilities, the overall effect of distraction is reduced.

While the experiments reported in this section indicate that different network problem solving strategies specified via organizational structures have different problem solving characteristics, they do not provide sufficient data for drawing any conclusions on the particular benefits of particular organizational strategies. These experiments were performed with a single environmental scenario with fairly unrestricted communication. Different problem solving characteristics may favor different organizational strategies. Particularly important is exploration of larger networks. (These experiments are just beginning.) A four or five node network simply has too few nodes for organizational structuring decisions to have a significant impact. Experiments with tens or even hundreds of nodes are needed before the full effect of organizational structuring will be seen.

V MORE COMPLEX META-LEVEL CONTROL

While organizational structuring could be performed by directly changing the interest areas of each node (the approach used in the experiments reported here), an indirect approach allows the node to adopt or reject its organizational roles.

Instead of modifying the specifications directly, a second, separate set of node activity specification data structures is kept at each node. The original interest areas remain as the behavioral command center of the node. Their settings directly influence the node´s activities. The second specifications set forms the lowest level of the full-fledged organizational blackboard. They are the result of elaborating higher-level organizational roles and responsibilities into an "organizational job description". The complete structure of this organizational blackboard, and the processing needed to perform the elaboration, remain an open research issue. What is important here is that the specifications directly controlling the behavior of a node and the behavior suggested by the organizational structure are *separated*. The node undertakes its organizational activities only by transferring organizational specifications into its interest areas.

The activities of a node should also be influenced by its potential for performing them. A node is continually receiving sensory data and hypotheses from other nodes. This information provides numerous opportunities for local node activities. However, the node´s interest areas (possibly set from the organizational blackboard) may be strongly opposed to performing these activities. The node´s potential for work is represented on a fourth blackboard, the **local node focusing blackboard**. This blackboard specifies where the node perceives there is substantial work it is able to perform. As with the organizational specifications, these focusing specifications can be transferred to the node's interest areas, at which point the node will actively pursue these activities.

When the roles and responsibilities represented in the organizational blackboard are in conflict with the criteria on the local node focusing blackboard, an arbiter for determining the actual interest areas is needed (Figure 3). Favoring the specifications on the organizational blackboard make the node's behavior more in line with the organizational structuring decisions (more of a "company node"), while favoring the local node focusing specifications make the node more responsive to its ability to immediately perform work on quality data. Such **node skepticism** is an important source of network robustness when organizational structuring decisions are made using incomplete and inaccurate information. A skeptical node's local activity decisions are constantly pulled in two directions: toward the responsibilities specified by the organizational structure and toward the activities suggested by its local data and interactions with other nodes. The tension between these two directions can lead to an increase in the network's ability to tolerate organizational control errors. If a node's organizational responsibilities are inappropriate to its potential activities, the node can proceed with locally generated activities. Similarly, organizational responsibilities can be ignored by nodes which possess strong information to the contrary; a node with a unique perspective is not necessarily stifled by an uninformed majority. The degree of node skepticism exhibited by a node should dynamically change according to the node's perception of the appropriateness of the organizational structure. If a node has no reason to doubt the organization structure it should be receptive to organizationally-specified activities. As a

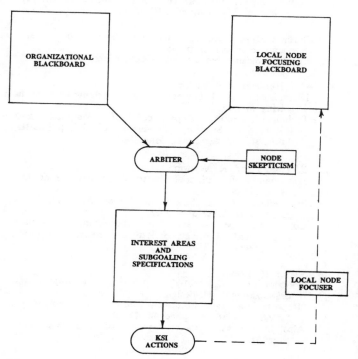

Figure 3: The Organizational and Local Node Focusing Blackboards and Node Skepticism.

node becomes skeptical of the organizational structure, it should switch to its own local activities, and disregard organizational activities which are in conflict with its local activities [5].

The existence of the organizational and local node focusing blackboards also help indicate when the portion of the network organizational structure relating to the node needs changing. A strong mismatch between the two blackboards is a sign of trouble, and the information contained in the focusing blackboard can be a valuable aid in determining new roles and responsibilities.

Three additional components are relevant to the organizational structuring approach to network coordination:

1. A **distributed task allocation** component for deciding what dynamic information and processing goals should be transmitted among the nodes. Given the high-level strategic plan for the allocation of activities and control responsibilities among nodes (the organizational structure) there is still a need to make more localized, tactical decisions that balance the activities among the nodes based on the dynamics of the current problem solving situation [19].

2. A **knowledge-based fault-diagnosis** component for detecting and locating inappropriate system behavior. We are looking to not only isolate problems caused by hardware errors, but also inappropriate settings of the problem solving parameters that specify strategic and tactical network coordination [12].

3. An **organizational self-design** component for initially developing an organizational structure and for modifying that structure to reduce the effect of hardware errors or an inappropriate organizational structure (both recognized by the fault-diagnosis component). When a hardware error is detected, the the network coordination policy needs to be modified so that the offending hardware and resulting incorrect processing does not distract problem solving in other parts of the network and to establish alternative paths for generating a more accurate version of the needed information wherever possible. When the organizational structure becomes inappropriate (due to changes in the internal or external environment of the distributed problem solving network) plausible alternative structures need to be determined and evaluated as potential candidates for network reorganization [5].

VI CONCLUSION

Distributed problem solving networks provide an interesting application area for meta-level control through the use of organizational structuring. The organizational structure provides each node with a high-level view of problem solving in the network. The sophisticated local control component of each node is responsible for elaborating these relationships into precise activities to be performed by the node, based on the node's problem solving role in the network, on the status and organizational roles of other nodes in the network, and on self-awareness of the node's activities. The balance between local node control and organizational control is a crucial aspect of this approach.

We have implemented this approach in the Distributed Vehicle Monitoring Testbed [17]. Our preliminary experiments using the testbed indicate that by adjusting the organizational structure different network problem solving strategies can be obtained. The next step in this research is experimentation with larger distributed problem solving networks where the effects of organizational structuring decisions will become increasingly significant.

It is interesting to note that the themes of this research, which advocate the interplay between organizational control and sophisticated local node control, are close in emphasis to recent trends emphasizing meta-level control and sophisticated planning in knowledge-based Artificial Intelligence systems [11, 6, 9, 22, 8]. The introduction of an organizational-level of control into distributed problem solving is an example of the use of meta-level control to coordinate activity in a complex system. As Nilsson has noted, the field of distributed Artificial Intelligence serves to illuminate basic Artificial Intelligence issues [18]. In this case, the need to control the uncertainty inherent with semi-autonomous problem solving agents possessing only a local and possibly errorful view of the global state of problem solving is very similiar to the control problems that are being faced in the development of the new generation of knowledge-based problem solving systems which have significantly larger and more diverse knowledge bases.

Our use of meta-level control with its emphasis on providing general guidelines for acceptable problem solving behavior differs from the work of Hayes-Roth, Davis, and Stefik which uses meta-level control to make specific strategic problem solving decisions [11, 6, 22]. In our approach the specific strategy decisions are made by the local control component of a node using the guidelines provided by the meta-level organizational structure.

REFERENCES

1. Richard S. Brooks.
   A balance principle for optimal access control.
   Technical Report 80-20, Department of Computer and Information Science, University of Massachusetts, Amherst, Massachusetts, November 1980.

2. Richard Samuel Brooks.
   Experiments in Distributed Problem Solving with Iterative Refinement.
   PhD Thesis, Department of Computer and Information Science, University of Massachusetts, Amherst, Massachusetts, February 1983.
   Available as Technical Report 82-25, Department of Computer and Information Science, University of Massachusetts, Amherst, Massachusetts, October 1982.

3. Daniel D. Corkill and Victor R. Lesser.
   A goal-directed Hearsay-II architecture: Unifying data and goal directed control.
   Technical Report 81-15, Department of Computer and Information Science, University of Massachusetts, Amherst, Massachusetts, June 1981.

4. Daniel D. Corkill, Victor R. Lesser, and Eva Hudlicka.
   Unifying data-directed and goal-directed control: An example and experiments.
   In *Proceedings of the Second National Conference on Artificial Intelligence*, pages 143-147, August 1982.

5. Daniel David Corkill.
   A Framework for Organizational Self-Design in Distributed Problem Solving Networks.
   PhD Thesis, Department of Computer and Information Science, University of Massachusetts, Amherst, Massachusetts, February 1983.
   Available as Technical Report 82-33, Department of Computer and Information Science, University of Massachusetts, Amherst, Massachusetts, December 1982.

6. Randall Davis.
   Meta-rules: Reasoning about control.
   Artificial Intelligence 15(3):179-222, December 1980.

7. Lee D. Erman, Frederick Hayes-Roth, Victor R. Lesser, and D. Raj Reddy.
   The Hearsay-II speech understanding system: Integrating knowledge to resolve uncertainty.
   Computing Surveys 12(2):213-253, June 1980.

8. Lee D. Erman, Philip E. London, and Stephen F. Fickas.
   The design and an example use of Hearsay-III.
   Proceedings of the Sixth International Joint Conference on Artificial Intelligence, pages 409-415, August 1981.

9. Michael R. Genesereth and David E. Smith.
   Meta-level architecture.
   Stanford Heuristic Programming Project Memo HPP-81-6 (working draft), Computer Science Department, Stanford University, Stanford, California, December 1982.

10. Peter E. Green.
    Distributed acoustic surveillance and tracking.
    In *Proceedings of the Distributed Sensor Networks Workshop*, pages 117-141, January 1982.
    Copies may be available from MIT Lincoln Laboratory, Lexington, Massachusetts, 02173.

11. Barbara Hayes-Roth and Frederick Hayes-Roth.
    A cognitive model of planning.
    Cognitive Science 3(4):275-310, October-December 1979.

12. Eva Hudlicka and Victor R. Lesser.
    Diagnosing the behavior of a distributed problem solving system.
    Technical Report, Department of Computer and Information Science, University of Massachusetts, Amherst, Massachusetts, May 1983.

13. R. Lacoss and R. Walton.
    Strawman design of a DSN to detect and track low flying aircraft.
    Proceedings of the Distributed Sensor Nets Workshop, pages 41-52, December 1978.
    Copies may be available from the Computer Science Department, Carnegie-Mellon University, Pittsburgh, Pennsylvania, 15213.

14. Victor R. Lesser.
    Cooperative distributed problem solving and organizational self-design.
    "Reports on the MIT Distributed AI Workshop", *SIGART Newsletter*, page 46, October 1980.
    Also in the same issue: "Models of problem-solving," page 51.

15. Victor R. Lesser and Lee D. Erman.
    Distributed interpretation: A model and experiment.
    IEEE Transactions on Computers, C-29(12):1144-1163,
    December 1980.

16. Victor R. Lesser and Daniel D. Corkill.
    Functionally-accurate, cooperative distributed systems.
    IEEE Transactions on Systems, Man, and Cybernetics,
    SMC-11(1):81-96, January 1981.

17. Victor Lesser, Daniel Corkill, Jasmina Pavlin, Larry
    Lefkowitz, Eva Hudlicka, Richard Brooks, and Scott
    Reed.
    A high-level simulation testbed for cooperative
    distributed problem solving.
    *Proceedings of the Third International Conference on
    Distributed Computer Systems*, pages 341-349, October
    1982.

18. Nils J. Nilsson.
    Two heads are better than one.
    SIGART Newsletter (73):43, October 1980.

19. Jasmina Pavlin and Victor R. Lesser.
    Task allocation in distributed problem solving systems.
    Technical Report, Department of Computer and
    Information Science, University of Massachusetts,
    Amherst, Massachusetts, May 1983.

20. Reid Garfield Smith.
    *A Framework for Problem Solving in a Distributed
    Processing Environment*.
    PhD Thesis, Stanford University, December 1978.
    Available as Technical Report STAN-CS-78-800,
    Computer Science Department, Stanford University,
    Stanford, California.

21. Reid G. Smith and Randall Davis.
    Frameworks for cooperation in distributed problem
    solving.
    IEEE Transactions on Systems, Man, and Cybernetics
    SMC-11(1):61-70, January 1981.

22. Mark Jeffery Stefik.
    Planning with Constraints.
    PhD Thesis, Stanford University, January 1980.
    Available as Technical Report STAN-CS-80-784,
    Computer Science Department, Stanford University,
    Stanford, California.

A FRAMEWORK FOR DISTRIBUTED PROBLEM SOLVING

Reid G. Smith

Defence Research Establishment Atlantic
Box 1012
Dartmouth, Nova Scotia, Canada, B2Y 3Z7

Abstract

The contract net framework for distributed problem solving is discussed. Task distribution is viewed as a mutual selection process, a discussion carried on between a node with a task to be executed and a group of nodes that may be able to execute the task. This leads to the use of a control formalism based on a contract metaphor, in which task distribution corresponds to contract negotiation.

The three primary components of the framework are described: communication, control, and knowledge organization. The use of the framework is illustrated for a distributed sensing system. We then discuss suitable applications and limitations of the framework.

1   Distributed Problem Solving

Distributed Problem Solving is the cooperative solution of problems by a decentralized and loosely coupled collection of knowledge-sources (KSs), each of which may reside in its own distinct processor.[1] Decentralized means that both control and data are logically, and sometimes geographically, distributed--there is neither global control nor global data storage. The KSs cooperate to solve problems by sharing tasks and/or results. Loosely coupled means that individual KSs spend the great percentage of their time in computation as opposed to communication. Such problem solvers offer advantages of speed, reliability, extensibility, the ability to handle applications with a natural spatial distribution, and the ability to tolerate errorful data and knowledge. In addition, as a result of their modularity, they offer conceptual clarity and simplicity of design.

---

[1] This work was supported in part by the Advanced Research Projects Agency under contract MDA 903-77-C-0322, and the National Science Foundation under contract MCS 77-02712. It was carried out on the SUMEX-AIM Computer Facility, supported by the National Institutes of Health under grant RR-00785. This paper is based on work done as part of a Ph.D. dissertation at Stanford University. The contributions of Randall Davis, Bruce Buchanan, and the rest of the staff and students of the Heuristic Programming Project are gratefully acknowledged.

2   The Contract Net Framework

The central result of the research reported here is the contract net framework for problem solving in a distributed processing environment. The framework has three major conceptual components: a control component that specifies the possible modes of interaction between processor nodes; a knowledge organization component that specifies how knowledge is organized in individual nodes and distributed throughout the collection of nodes; and a communication component that provides the basis for node interaction.

2.1   Communication And Control

2.1.1   Connection And Contract Negotiation

In the design of the communication and control components of the framework, our emphasis to date has been placed on facilitation of task-sharing as a means of cooperation for problem solving. The computational load for execution of subtasks of the overall problem is distributed among the nodes. To enable this distribution, there must be a means whereby nodes with tasks to be executed can find other idle nodes with KSs capable of executing those tasks. We call this the connection problem. (In centralized problem solvers it is called the invocation problem; that is, which KS to invoke at any given time for the execution of a task.) In a distributed problem solver, both sets of nodes can proceed simultaneously, engaging each other in a process of negotiation to solve the connection problem. Task distribution can thus be considered as a process of contract negotiation, or mutual selection based on a two-way transfer of information. This process gives rise to the name--the **contract net framework** [Smith, 1978b].

The collection of nodes is referred to as a contract net and the execution of a task is dealt with as a contract between two nodes. Thus, each node in the net takes on one of two roles related to the execution of an individual task: manager or contractor. A **manager** is responsible for monitoring the execution of a task and processing the results of its execution. A **contractor** is responsible for the actual execution of the task. Individual nodes are not designated a priori as managers or contractors. These are only roles, and any node can dynamically take on either role. During the course of problem solving, a particular node normally takes on both roles (perhaps even simultaneously for different contracts).

The normal method of negotiating a contract is for a node that generates a task to advertise the existence of that task to other nodes in the net with a **task-announcement** message. It then acts as the manager of that task for its duration. Many such announcements are made over the course of time as tasks are generated for execution.

Nodes in the net have been listening to the task announcements and have been evaluating their own level of interest in each task with respect to their specialized hardware and software resources. When a task of sufficient interest is found, a node submits a bid. A bid message indicates the capabilities of the bidder that are relevant to execution of the announced task. A manager may receive several such bids in response to a single task announcement; based on the information in the bids, it selects one (or several) node(s) for execution of the task. The selection is communicated to the successful bidder(s) through an **award** message. These selected nodes thus become contractors for that task.[1]

_____

[1] This is a simplified version of the actual process (and does not work, for example, in the case of a task that cannot be executed due to insufficient data). We have also ignored the use of focused addressing and more specialized interactions like directed contracts. See [Smith, 1978b] for the

2.1.2   The Contract Net Protocol

The use of communication protocols in networks of resource-sharing computers, such as the **ARPAnet**, is by now quite familiar. The primary function of these protocols is to effect reliable and efficient communication between computers. Such low-level protocols are, however, only a start--a prerequisite for distributed problem solving. They enable bit streams to be passed between nodes but do not consider the semantics of the information being passed. We require a high-level protocol, which we call a **problem-solving protocol (PSP)**, to assign problem-solving interpretations to the bit streams--to control the processes used to solve problems as opposed to the processes used to effect communication. This enables the applications programmer to focus on **what** the nodes must say to each other, as opposed to **how** to say it.

The contract net protocol is the PSP that governs all problem-solving interactions between nodes in a contract net. Task-dependent information is placed in typed slots in the messages of the protocol and is encoded in a **common internode language**. Task-independent information is encoded directly in the protocol; that is, in the specification of message types and their associated slots.

A task announcement message, for example, has four slots for task-dependent information. The **eligibility specification** is a list of criteria that a node must meet to be eligible to submit a bid. It enables a node receiving the message to decide whether or not it is able to execute the task. The **task abstraction** is a brief description of the task to be executed. It enables a node to rank the announced task relative to other announced tasks. The **bid specification** is a description of the expected form of a bid. It enables a node to include in a bid only the information about its capabilities that are relevant to the announced task. Finally, the **expiration time** is a specification of the time period during which the announcement is valid.

The common internode language provides the primitive elements for encoding task-dependent information in the task abstraction, eligibility specification, bid specification, and so on. The implemented language enables

_____

specification of the full set of message types in the protocol and a complete discussion of the processing associated with each of the message types.

statements of the form Respond with <value> of <attribute> of <object> to be encoded, where some of the objects are **node**, **task**, **procedure**, and **contract**. Objects are linked together by attributes, each of which has a value (which may be another object). A **contract** object, for example, has a **manager** attribute whose value is a **node** object. The language has a grammar and a core vocabulary of terms that appear to be of use in a wide variety of applications. The vocabulary is also extensible; that is, new terms can be added for specific applications.

2.2   Example

The following is an example of the negotiation for a task that involves gathering of sensed data and extraction of signal features. It is taken from an **INTERLISP** simulation of a distributed sensing system (DSS) [Smith, 1978a].

The managers for this **signal** task attempt to find a set of sensor nodes such that the set has an adequate spatial distribution about the surrounding area and has an adequate distribution of sensor types. Sensor nodes, on the other hand, attempt to find managers for the signal task that are closest to them.

The eligibility specification in the signal task announcements indicates that only those nodes located in the same area as the announcer and having sensing capabilities should bid on this task. This helps to reduce extraneous message traffic and bid processing. The task abstraction indicates the type of task and the position of an individual signal group contractor. It enables a potential contractor to determine the manager to which it should respond. The bid specification indicates the information that a manager needs to select a suitable set of sensor nodes--the position of the bidder and the number of each of its sensor types.

The potential contractors listen to the task announcements from the various managers. They respond to the nearest manager with a bid that contains the information specified in the task announcement. The managers use this information to select a set of bidders and then award signal contracts. The award messages specify the sensors that each contractor is to use to provide raw data to its manager.

Sample messages that are transmitted during negotiation of the signal contracts are shown below. Terms written in upper case are included in the core common internode language, while terms written in lower case are specific to the DSS problem. The "*" indicates a broadcast message.

```
To: *                    <Managers make announcements
From: 25                          of this form.>
Type: TASK ANNOUNCEMENT
Contract: 22-3-1
Message:
    Task Abstraction:
      TASK TYPE 'signal
      NODE NAME '25 POSITION 'p
    Eligibility Specification:
      MUST-HAVE DEVICE TYPE 'sensor
      MUST-HAVE NODE NAME 'SELF POSITION area 'A
    Bid Specification:
      NODE NAME 'SELF POSITION
      EVERY DEVICE TYPE 'sensor TYPE NUMBER
```

```
To: 25                   <Sensor nodes respond to
From: 42                        the nearest manager.>
Type: BID
Contract: 22-3-1
Message:
    Node Abstraction:
      NODE NAME '42 POSITION 'q
      sensor TYPE 'S NUMBER '3
      sensor TYPE 'T NUMBER '1
```

```
To: 42                   <Several similar awards
From: 25                         are transmitted.>
Type: AWARD
Contract: 22-3-1
Message:
    Task Specification:
      sensor NAME 'S1
      sensor NAME 'S2
```

2.3   Knowledge Organization

The knowledge organization component of the framework specifies mechanisms for **retrieval** and **distribution** of knowledge in a distributed problem solver. Retrieval can be further broken down into two parts: **partitioning** and **indexing**. Partitioning indicates the ways in which the knowledge is broken up into modules; indexing indicates the handles placed on the knowledge modules so that they can be accessed.

2.3.1 Partitioning

It is common in AI problem solvers to partition expertise into domain-specific **knowledge-sources** (KSs), each of which is expert in a particular part of the overall problem. KSs are typically formed empirically, based on examination of different types of knowledge that can be brought to bear on a particular problem. In a speech-understanding problem, for example, knowledge is available from the speech signal itself, from the syntax of the utterances, and from the semantics of the task domain [Erman, 1975]. The decisions about which KSs are to be formed is often made in concert with the formation of a data hierarchy for a problem. KSs are typically chosen to handle data at one level of abstraction or to bridge two levels (see, for example [Erman, 1975] and [Nii, 1978]).

In a distributed processor there is an additional consideration: The KSs themselves will likely be distributed to different nodes, and their interactions will therefore often be more expensive than in a uniprocessor. As a result, the kernel size of the KSs must be chosen carefully, based on the characteristics of the distributed processor. KSs that are too small will result in a large amount of communication between nodes, thus reducing the speedup that can be achieved via a distributed approach. Matching of kernel size to distributed processor characteristics must at present be done via trial and error by the applications programmer.

2.3.2 Indexing

In the contract net framework, the main issue in indexing of knowledge is connecting nodes with tasks to be executed to nodes with KSs that are appropriate to execute those tasks. Two major types of knowledge are recognized for indexing: **task-centered knowledge** and **knowledge-source-centered knowledge** (KS-centered knowledge). Task-centered knowledge is useful for finding nodes capable of executing tasks and KS-centered knowledge is useful for finding tasks to be executed by a node. The contract net appears to be the first use of both kinds of knowledge at the same time.

In the DSS, for example, the task-centered knowledge used by the manager for the signal task specifies that contracts should be awarded so that the area surrounding the manager is covered with an adequate distribution of sensor types. The KS-centered knowledge used by a sensor node specifies that a signal task should be selected from the closest manager that offers such a task.

2.3.3 Distribution Of Knowledge

Distribution also has two aspects: **static distribution**, how knowledge is initially loaded into the nodes, and **dynamic distribution**, how knowledge is transferred between nodes as work on the overall problem proceeds.

The criteria for a good static distribution of knowledge are minimization of message traffic and avoidance of critical function nodes that could reduce processing speed and create reliability problems. In the DSS, for example, KSs with expertise at a particular level of the data hierarchy were placed in different nodes. This enabled nodes to carry on simultaneously with computation specific to those levels of the data hierarchy that concerned them (without the need for frequent interactions with nodes operating at different levels of the hierarchy).

In the contract net framework, dynamic distribution of knowledge can be effected in three ways. First, a node can transmit a request directly to another node for the transfer of the required knowledge. The response is the knowledge requested (e.g., the code for a procedure). Second, a node can broadcast a task announcement in which the task is a transfer of knowledge. A bid on the task indicates that another node has the knowledge and is willing to transmit it. Finally, a node can note in its bid on a task that it requires particular knowledge in order to execute the task. The manager can then send the required knowledge in the contract award if the bid is accepted. Each of these interactions is simplified by the use of a common internode language.

Dynamic distribution enables effective use of available computational resources: A node that is standing idle because it lacks information required to execute a previously announced task can acquire that information as indicated above. Dynamic knowledge distribution also facilitates the addition of a new node to an existing net; the node can dynamically acquire the procedures and data necessary to allow it to participate in the operation of the net. This is especially useful in the DSS application.

3 Discussion

There are several reasons for adopting a distributed approach to problem solving. These include speed, reliability, extensibility, and the ability to handle applications that have a natural spatial distribution. The design of the contract net framework has taken into account each of these considerations. We relate here design choices made in the framework to their underlying motivations.

In order to achieve high speed we wish to avoid bottlenecks. Such bottlenecks can arise in two primary ways: by concentrating disproportionate amounts of computation or communication at central resources, and by saturating available communications channels so that nodes must remain idle while messages are transmitted.

To avoid bottlenecks we facilitate the distribution of control and data. This is a major motivation for the use of local contract negotiation to achieve connections and task distribution and to provide a means for dynamic distribution of procedures and other data. System concurrency is also enhanced because both managers and contractors simultaneously seek each other out, finally achieving connections by mutual selection.

To avoid communications channel saturation we attempt to maintain loose-coupling. The framework is well-suited to loosely coupled systems in three respects. First, it provides a very general form of guidance in determining appropriate partitioning of problems: the notion of tasks executed under contracts is appropriate for a kernel size larger than that typically used in parallel systems. Second, the framework attempts to be efficient with respect to its use of communications channels by reducing the number and length of messages. The information in task announcements, for instance, helps minimize the amount of channel capacity consumed by communications overhead. Extraneous traffic is eliminated by the eligibility specifications of the task announcements and the bid messages are reduced in length because of the bid specifications. Finally, the framework enables dynamic distribution of procedures and other data. Thus the option exists to distribute information only when required.

Reliability is also enhanced by the distribution of control and data, together with shared responsibility for tasks (by managers and contractors). The failure of a contractor,

for example, is not fatal, since its manager can re-announce the appropriate contract and recover from the failure. This strategy allows the system to recover from any node failure except that of the node that holds the original top-level problem.[1]

Extensibility is facilitated by the use of a common internode language and dynamic distribution of knowledge.

The ability to handle applications with a natural spatial distribution is facilitated by the use of local contract negotiation to achieve connection and task distribution.

4 Suitable Applications

The framework is particularly well-matched to problems that use a hierarchy of tasks and levels of data abstraction. Heuristic search problems are examples of the former, and applications that deal with sensed data (e.g., audio or video signals) are examples of the latter.

The manager-contractor structure provides a natural way to effect hierarchical control and the managers at each level in the hierarchy are an appropriate place for data integration and abstraction. The contract links between nodes assist in coordination of KSs (i.e., a manager can coordinate the actions of contractors working on related subtasks).

It also follows that the framework is primarily applicable to domains where the subtasks are large (in the loose-coupling sense) and where it is worthwhile to expend a potentially nontrivial amount of computation and communication to invoke the best KSs for each subtask. (The same basic mechanism can, however, be used simply as a means of task distribution with distributed control and shared responsibility for tasks to maintain reliability and avoid bottlenecks.)

The framework has also been designed to

---

[1] At the top level, contracting can distribute control almost completely, hence removing the bottlenecks that centralized controllers create. There still remains, however, the reliability problem inherent in having only a single node responsible for the top-level problem. Since this cannot be handled directly by the manager-contractor links, standard sorts of redundancy are required.

provide a more powerful mechanism for transfer of control than is available in current problem-solving systems (see [Smith, 1978b] for a complete discussion). The announcement-bid-award sequence of contract negotiation enables more information and more complex information to be transferred in both directions (between caller and respondent) before KS-invocation occurs. In addition, information about the complete collection of candidate KSs is available before a final selection is made. The computation devoted to the selection process, based on the information transfer noted above, is more extensive and more complex than that used in traditional approaches, and is local in the sense that selection is associated with and specific to an individual KS (rather than embodied in, say, a global evaluation function). As a result, the framework is most useful when the specific KS to be invoked at any time is not known a priori and when specific expertise is required.

5   Limitations And Extensions

We have proposed a framework that offers some ideas about what information is useful for distributed problem solving and how that information can be organized. There is still a considerable problem involved in instantiating the framework in the context of a specific task domain. The contract net protocol provides a site for embedding particular types of task-dependent information (e.g. an eligibility specification), but does not specify, for a particular problem, the content, nor how to instantiate it in a particular domain. We require more experience with the framework to better understand its utility as a mechanism for helping a user structure and understand distributed problems.

We have emphasized task-sharing as a means of internode cooperation and have attempted to provide some structured mechanisms for the communication required to effect this mode of cooperation. We have, however, not yet adequately studied **result-sharing** as a means of cooperation; that is, nodes assisting each other through sharing of partial results, based on somewhat different perspectives on the overall problem. Different perspectives arise because the nodes use different KSs (e.g., syntax vs acoustics in the case of a speech understanding system) or different data (e.g., data that is sensed at different locations in the case of a DSS). This type of cooperation appears to be of use in dealing with problems where errorful data or knowledge lead to conflicting views of the problem at individual nodes (see [Lesser, 1978] for a preliminary discussion). It is our intention to examine the structure of communication for this mode of cooperation with a view to extending the contract net framework so that a synthesis of the two approaches to distributed problem solving can be attempted.

References

[Erman, 1975]
    L. D. Erman and V. R. Lesser, A Multi-level Organization For Problem Solving Using Many, Diverse, Cooperating Sources of Knowledge. IJCAI4, 1975, pp. 483-490.

[Lesser, 1978]
    V. R. Lesser, **Cooperative Distributed Processing.** COINS TR 78-7, Dept. of Computer and Information Science, University of Massachusetts, May 1978.

[Nii, 1978]
    H. P. Nii and E. A. Feigenbaum, Rule-Based Understanding Of Signals. In D. A. Waterman and F. Hayes-Roth (Eds.), **Pattern-Directed Inference Systems.** New York: Academic Press, 1978. Pp. 483-501.

[Smith, 1978a]
    R. G. Smith and R. Davis, Applications Of The Contract Net Framework: Distributed Sensing. **Proceedings of the ARPA Distributed Sensor Net Symposium,** Pittsburgh, PA, December 1978, pp. 12-20.

[Smith, 1978b]
    R. G. Smith, **A Framework For Problem Solving In A Distributed Processing Environment.** Ph.D. Dissertation, STAN-CS-78-700 (HPP-78-28) Dept. of Computer Science, Stanford University, December 1978.

THE LOCO APPROACH TO DISTRIBUTED TASK ALLOCATION
IN AIDA BY VERDI

V. M. Milutinović, J. J* Crnković, L.-Y. Chang, and H. J. Siegel
School of Electrical Engineering
Purdue University
West Lafayette, Indiana 47907
(317)-494-3530

ABSTRACT

A system of special purpose processing resources shared by a number of general purpose processing resources is considered. We assume that special purpose processing resources are dedicated to different tasks typical of complex artificial intelligence multitask jobs. Possible types of special purpose processing resources include pipelined array processors, SIMD parallel processor systems, or MIMD multiprocessor systems, with associated data bases or knowledge bases, for numeric or symbolic computing. Each specific type may be represented by several units. Such a structure may be found in the large local area networks of the 1990s which are used predominantly for artificial intelligence, or in high-end computers of the 5th generation. Given such a processing environment, in this paper an approach for efficient distributed task allocation is introduced. It is referred to as the LOCO approach, because an analogy with a locomotive engine (and appended wagons) is used to describe it. An analytic model of the LOCO approach is developed and used for performance analysis. Results of the performance analysis are presented comparatively with those of load balancing applied to the same processing environment. Although our primary concern is a processing environment for artificial intelligence, we find that the LOCO approach can be used efficiently in other types of processing environments, as well.

KEYWORDS: *Distributed Task Allocation, Loosely Coupled Multiprocessor Systems, Artificial Intelligence Oriented Systems.*

I. INTRODUCTION

Conventional general purpose (*GP*) computers are not able to meet the complex computational requirements typical of artificial intelligence (*AI*). However, the overall processing power of the conventional GP computers can be considerably enhanced if appropriate special purpose processing resources (*SPPRs*) are attached to them. In that case, the GP computers serve as the hosts and the SPPRs as their computational enhancements. In such a processing environment, the SPPRs are oriented to various specialized tasks typical of complex multitask AI jobs. These tasks may be signal processing [e.g., RabGo75], natural language processing/understanding [e.g., Grosz82], vision processing/understanding [e.g., Brady82], intelligent retrieval from knowledge bases within the expert systems [e.g., HaWaL83, etc. Internally, the SPPRs may be organized as special function processors, systolic arrays, pipelined array processors, SIMD machines [Flynn72], or MIMD machines [Flynn72]. Each SPPR will have an associated data base or knowledge base, and will be oriented to numeric or symbolic processing. We have many examples of internal organizations oriented to dedicated control [e.g., MilWa83, Milut83], signal processing [e.g., McDMa82], speech processing/understanding [e.g., Lerne80], image processing/understanding [e.g., SiSiK81], efficient retrieval from relational data bases [e.g., MuKaM83], combinatorial search [WahMa84], inference [Ushid83, SuHoS81], etc. A single SPPR may consist of a large number of processing elements (*PEs*). As an example, the MPP processor for image processing [Batch80] includes 2^{14} PEs. The DADO production system is supposed to include on the order of magnitude of a hundred thousand PEs [StoSh82]. A large number of PEs is used to speed up a special-purpose computation, and not to acquire general processing power.

*J. J. Crnković is now with the Department of Mathematical and Computer Sciences, University of Miami, Coral Gables, Florida 33124.

This research was partially supported by the U.S. Army Research Office, Department of the Army, under contract DAAG29-82-K0101, and the School of Electrical Engineering, Purdue University.

Proceedings of the 5th IEEE International Conference on Distributed Computing Systems, Denver, Colorado, May 13-17, 1985.

As the application requirements are getting more and more complex, the overall computational capabilities can be further increased by adding more SPPRs to a GP host. Several experiments of this type were reported [MarBr81]. This trend is very likely to continue, especially given the great importance and massive computational requirements typical of the general area of AI. Consequently we expect that in the 1990s systems oriented to AI will consist of hundreds of SPPRs. As the SPPRs will still be costly, it will make sense to share them among a number of GP hosts. It is very unlikely that all SPPRs in such a system will be of the same type, and it is even more unlikely that each one will be different from the others. We expect that they will be of a variety of different types where each type is represented by an appropriate number of units. Different SPPRs will be of different levels of specialization. It is reasonable to expect that the whole system of GP hosts and SPPRs will span an area the size of a typical university campus or military base (up to about 1 mile in radius).

A similar type of processing environment may also be found in high-end computers of the 5th generation. Input/output (in the wide sense) will include natural language processing and computer vision. Memory (in the wide sense) will incorporate a variety of data bases and knowledge bases. The processor (in the wide sense) will incorporate the capabilities for both information and knowledge processing [TreLi82].

In both cases it will be extremely important to have an efficient mechanism for the dynamic allocation of different tasks belonging to complex AI jobs [Davis83]. For a number of reasons, this mechanism must be distributed in nature. It might exist as distinct and identifiable blocks of code, or only as a design philosophy [Enslo78, JenPl84]. The complexity of the problem is higher than what may initially be expected, as most of the hosts may be working in a multiprogramming environment, where different processes running on the same host will have jobs with tasks oriented to different SPPRs. Also, the allocation requirements will change in time. Obviously, the solution of this problem should involve the following two basic aspects:
(a) System architecture that supports an efficient task allocation
(b) Dynamic task allocation procedure which is distributed in nature.
With all that in mind, in this paper a system architecture is considered which consists of GP hosts and logically clustered SPPRs, all connected by a shared multiple access bus, possibly but not necessarily of the CSMA/CD type [e.g., ShDaR82]. Such a structure is well suited to the execution of complex multitask jobs typical of AI and will be referred to as *AIDA* (Artificial Intelligence Directed Architecture). For this type of system architecture an efficient approach to dynamic and distributed task allocation is introduced and analyzed. It is referred to as the *LOCO* approach, because an analogy with a locomotive engine (and appended wagons) is used to describe it [MilSi84]. As will be seen later, this approach is quite general in nature, and can be applied to processing environments other than the one described here.

It should be noted that the emphasis here is on a system that consists of a large number of heterogeneous classes of SPPRs, made accessible to a very large number of users through a large number of hosts. Furthermore, due to the variety of SPPRs, the types of computations to be performed are unlimited — the system is not restricted to any single task domain. This makes it very appropriate for environments, such as AI, that require many different types of tasks to be executed. This can be contrasted to a parallel processing system like PASM [SiSiK81] in the following ways: (1) PASM's computation engine consists of a set of homogeneous processors, (2) the PASM processors are interconnected by a multistage network [Siege84], rather than a network of shared busses, (3) when operating in SIMD mode, the PASM processors exploit instruction level parallelism, while the inter-SPPR parallelism is on the task level, (4) PASM is intended for image understanding [KuSiA84], where LOCO/AIDA is much more "general purpose" in nature, (5) PASM is intended to support a much smaller set of users than LOCO/AIDA, and (6) PASM itself could be an SPPR in LOCO/AIDA.

One excellent study of distributed resource sharing is given in [Wah84]. According to it, AIDA can be treated as a resource sharing network architecture based on a single shared bus, and LOCO as a procedure with an addressing mechanism distributed in the network. Also, the LOCO/AIDA environment is characterized by a number of elements typical of the data flow environment [GaPaK82].

This paper is organized into six sections. Assumptions of the analysis are addressed in Section II. The system architecture (AIDA) is introduced in Section III. The distributed procedure for dynamic task allocation (LOCO) is introduced in Section IV, first through an example and then generalized. A model of the LOCO approach based on AIDA architecture is introduced in Section V. For comparison purposes, in the same section, a model of load balancing (LB) applied to the same system architecture is introduced, as well. Performance analysis of the LOCO approach and its comparison to the LB approach are given in Section VI.

II. BASIC ASSUMPTIONS OF THE ANALYSIS

The presentation to follow will be based on the following assumptions:

1. A task is the monolithic complex of computation that can be performed by an SPPR without any intermediate interaction by the host. In other words, once an SPPR is loaded with the program, its parameters, and the data, it can autonomously execute the task until its completion. The tasks are highly specialized. Consequently, a great variety of different SPPR types is necessary. For the number of different SPPR types (N_C) we assume $N_C \gg 1$.

2. Each task (T) is part of the job (J) that belongs to a process (P) running in one of the hosts (H). A number of processes can run concurrently in the same host. A single process may include a number of jobs (running sequentially or concurrently). A single job consists of a number of different tasks (running sequentially or concurrently). This fact can be symbolically represented as in the example of Fig. 1. Con-

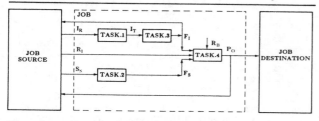

Figure 1.   Example of a Complex Multitask AI Job.

I_R –	Rough image	F_S –	Signal features
I_T –	Transformed image	R_I –	Input rules
F_I –	Image features	R_B –	Built-in rules
S_S –	Signal (seismic or EEG)	P_O –	Output predicates

nection lines indicate the intertask data dependency. In the example of Fig. 1, TASK.1 and TASK.2 can run concurrently on two different SPPRs, while TASK.3 must wait for TASK.1 to be completed, since it needs TASK.1's output data. The same task may exist in various concurrent jobs. As the number of jobs can be very large, it may help if each SPPR type is represented by more than one unit. For the number of units per SPPR type* (N_U) we assume $N_U \gg 1$.

3. The total number of SPPRs in the system (N_S) is given by $N_S = N_U * N_C$. We anticipate that in real systems of the 1990s this number may get to be on the order of several hundreds. The number of hosts acting as job generators is assumed to be of the same order of magnitude. These facts justify the use of an infinite population model in the analysis to follow.

4. As stated earlier, the SPPRs may be more or less specialized. A specific task can run on one SPPR type only, or on one of a number of different SPPR types. In the second case, however, one of the SPPR types will be the most suitable. In the presentation to follow, a task will always be associated with one SPPR type, regardless of if it is the only possibility, or the most suitable possibility. This assumption simplifies the presentation without affecting its generality.

---
*Unless otherwise noted, we assume that each SPPR type is represented by the same number of units. This will simplify the notation without affecting the generality of our analysis.

5. The duration of a task execution is considerably longer than the time needed to transfer data to the SPPR that will execute the task. The transfer time includes the time to access the communications medium and to exchange control data. This assumption is quite realistic. On one hand, advanced fiber optic technology is enabling local area communications to reach gigabit/second speeds [e.g., PoCoS83]. On the other hand, the execution time of AI tasks may be extremely high. This is due to extensive data quantities (tasks with 2^{14} pixels and/or 2^{10} logic rules are not uncommon) and extensive computational intensity (for both numeric processing and logic search). As known from previous work [e.g., Wah84], if the task transmission time is small compared to the task service time, the single bus approach is the best approach. This was the justification for us to concentrate in our research on the single bus system architecture for support of the task allocation.

6. Each task in execution can be treated as a secondary process (running on the SPPR) that can generate a number of secondary jobs, each one consisting of a number of secondary tasks. The nesting can continue as necessary. We treat this issue as a VERtically Distributed Intertasking, or simply VERDI. Consequently, the system architecture is referred to as the AIDA by VERDI. We mention this nesting as an interesting property of the LOCO approach. However, that issue will not be further analyzed in this work.

7. AI tasks (both those predominantly oriented to numeric and symbolic processing) are characterized by large execution time variations [Brady82, Grosz82]. The same conclusion has been derived by a recent study [Rober84]. Consequently, the correlation between past experience on execution time for a given type of task and its future execution time is low. This fact represents one of the essential differences between typical AI tasks, and the tasks typical of the "conventional" GP processing environment. *It is of crucial importance for the analysis to follow.* As will be seen later, this fact has a major influence on our choice of the task allocation procedure, and the underlying system architecture.

8. Programming of the SPPRs is very complex. Although the user can develop its own software, typically parametric library routines are used. The user's major effort is to specify the software parameters. The library routines are assumed to be relatively short, as they control specialized processing resources. These facts influence the choice of the system architecture for the efficient support of task allocation.

9. The area over which the system is spanned, as well as the bandwidth of the communications medium, ensure that the propagation time between any two points in the system is negligible in comparison with duration of the shortest possible message. We assume that enough bandwidth is available, so that computation and not the communication is a system bottleneck. This assumption permits us to neglect the media access and handshaking effects in the analysis to follow.

10. This paper concentrates on the case when SPPRs are the bottleneck in the system. The case when both SPPRs and interconnection network are the bottleneck in the system is not considered as a part of this work.

Unless otherwise noted, all these assumptions will be used throughout the presentation to follow.

III. SYSTEM ARCHITECTURE

One possible approach to a system architecture for the processing environment treated here implies connecting of SPPRs to the backends of the hosts and connecting of hosts into a single shared bus network, as indicated in Fig. 2a. This approach permits load balancing [e.g., HwCrG82], but reliability and expandability may be problematic. We follow here another approach according to which the SPPRs are moved into the front-end and share the same bus with the hosts, as indicated in Fig. 2b. This approach has good reliability and expandability. It supports load balancing and several good papers exist on that topic [e.g., WahJu83, WahHi82]. Load balancing is very efficient if execution times of the tasks waiting for processing can be precisely estimated. This estimation may not be possible or may require intensive computation [TanTo84]. So allocation typically relies on past experience about the execution time for a given type of task. If the correlation between past and future execution time is relatively high, the load balancing proves to achieve a very good performance [e.g., NiHwa81, ChoKo79]. Unfortunately, this assumption is not satisfied in our case and we cannot use the existing results. We were forced to search for appropriate task allocation procedure and a system architecture that are *efficient without any knowledge about task execution times.*

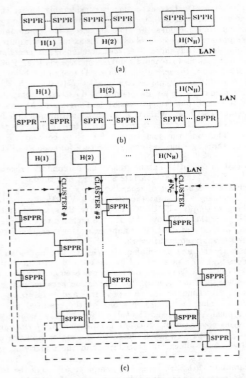

Figure 2. Some Possible System Architectures for Distributed Processing on a LAN (Local Area Network).

(a) The SPPRs in back-end of the hosts, with load balancing.

(b) The SPPRs directly appended to the LAN, with load balancing.

(c) Logical clustering of physically remote SPPRs. The SPPRs are assumed to be physically remote. However, they are connected by a high-speed link, and they behave as if they were locally clustered, i.e., logically clustered.

Fortunately, *the existence of a high-speed communications medium gives an important new dimension to distributed processing*. It enables the introduction of the concept of logical clustering of physically remote SPPRs of the same type. Consequently, given a fast enough communications medium and a small enough local area, it makes sense to interconnect all SPPRs of one type into a single logical cluster, as indicated in Fig. 2c. Although physically remote, these SPPRs behave as if they were logically local to each other. Consequently, we have N_C logical clusters, with N_U SPPRs of the same type in each.

Logical clustering means that all SPPRs of the same type are treated as a single multiple-server service station. No load balancing is needed any more as it implies the environment characterized by multiple single-server service stations. Also, the lack of correlation between past and future is of no importance any more. The task is simply sent to a logical cluster that consists of all SPPRs which are best suited to its efficient execution. It waits in the queue associated to the logical cluster until after all the previously arrived (in the case of FIFO disciplines) or higher priority tasks (in the case of priority disciplines) have been served. Note that the concept of clusters in our approach is considerably different compared to the concept of clusters in Cm* [SwFuS77], Ultracomputer [GoGrK83], or Cedar [GaLaK84].

Now we will describe the Artificial Intelligence Directed Architecture (AIDA), which is based on the above described principle of logic clustering. It is given in Fig. 3. The system consists of N_H hosts and N_S SPPRs organized into N_C clusters with N_U SPPRs per cluster. Each cluster is associated with a mass storage unit $M(j)$; $j=1,...,N_C$. This is where the software (parametric library routines) for all SPPRs

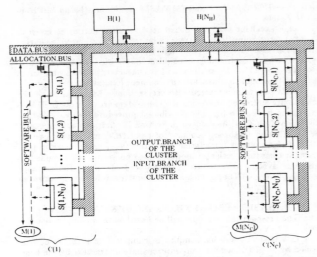

Figure 3. The AIDA: An Architecture for Efficient Support of the LOCO Approach to Distributed Task Allocation.

in that cluster is stored. Knowledge bases and data bases can exist within SPPRs, in the mass storage units associated with the cluster, or in any other suitable form. The SPPRs are interconnected by a system of buses. Separate buses are used for task allocation, for data and parameter transfer, and for the transfer of the library routines. These buses will be referred to as the allocation, data, and software bus, respectively. The allocation bus is a single-line bus (bit transfer). It connects the hosts, the SPPRs, and the mass storage units, as the software libraries have to be updated occasionally. It includes the cluster branches. Each cluster branch is separated into the INPUT.BRANCH and the OUTPUT.BRANCH. The INPUT.BRANCH is daisy chained, as indicated in Fig. 3. Given assumption #8, the software bus can also be a single-line bus (bit transfer). We assume one software bus per logical cluster. The software buses connect the SPPRs of the cluster with the corresponding mass storage unit. Given assumption #5, the data bus should be a multiple-line bus (word transfer). It connects the hosts and the SPPRs. An identification number (ID) is assigned to each host ($H.ID$), process ($P.ID$), job ($J.ID$) and task ($T.ID$). Identification numbers are also associated to the clusters ($C.ID$), SPPRs ($S.ID$), mass storages ($M.ID$), and library routines ($L.ID$). All these identification numbers act as processing environment specifiers. The way they are used is indicated in Table 1. The short specification can be used only if the missing specifiers are known from the context.

Table 1. Processing Environment Specifiers

Item:	Mnemonic:	Full specification:	Short specification:	Example:
CLUSTER	C	C(C.ID)	C(C.ID)	C(4)
HOST	H	H(H.ID)	H(H.ID)	H(7)
JOB	J	J(H.ID,P.ID,J.ID)	J(J.ID)	J(7,5,3) or J(3)
LIBRARY ROUTINE	L	L(C.ID,L.ID)	L(L.ID)	L(28,4) or L(4)
MASS STORAGE	M	M(C.ID)	M(C.ID)	M(4)
PROCESS	P	P(H.ID,P.ID)	P(P.ID)	P(7,5) or P(5)
SPPR	S	S(C.ID,S.ID)	S(S.ID)	S(12,4) or S(4)
TASK	T	T(H.ID,P.ID,J.ID,T.ID)	T(T.ID)	T(7,5,3,1) or T(1)

The following identification numbers and related pieces of information are needed to allocate and run the task: cluster ID (C.ID), library routine ID (L.ID), program parameters (or their locations), and the data (or their locations). Data for a task reside either in a single memory block of one of the system resources (host or SPPR), or in a number of memory blocks, possibly some in the hosts and others in the SP processors. Each system resource containing a data block keeps a list of all tasks that will need or that might need that data block (until permission is given to delete that data block). So, if a task needs a data block it must know the ID of the system resource currently holding that data block. When requesting the data block, the task has to specify its own ID (T.ID). Each task is associated with a vector ($\vec{D}$), the elements of which define the sources of input data for that task. A scalar E is also associated with each task. Its form is either $E = X$ or $E = [C.ID.S.ID]$. It specifies which SPPR executed that task. Initially the value of E is undefined, i.e., E = X. When a task is assigned to an SPPR, this processor will set the value of E to point to itself, i.e., E = [C.ID,S.ID]. Once a task is executed, the output data will be stored in the local memory of the SPPR that executed that task.

Each host and SPPR has attached to it a task allocation controller. This controller is a hardware device which executes special purpose dedicated software to interface the host or SPPR to the interconnection network and to the rest of the system. The controllers are inserted between the host or SPPR and the network. The controller can be implemented as a VLSI chip and will be, hereafter, referred to as *the LOCO station*. The LOCO station controls the access to all the buses and executes the task allocation procedure. So hosts and SPPRs are free of these activities, which has a number of positive implications on system expandability, reliability, and compatibility of various heterogeneous SPPRs. Different access schemes can be used on the buses. The concept of the carrier sense multiple access with collision detection (CSMA/CD) seems to be the most suitable. However, the analysis of possible access schemes will not be presented as a part of this work. When the station acquires a bus, it broadcasts the message with the destination address in its heading. The message is accepted only by the station that matches the address from the message header. On the data and software buses, the station responds only if it recognizes its own address in the message heading. On the allocation bus, each station is responding to three types of addresses: (a) cluster address (C.ID), (b) station address, i.e., SPPR address (C.ID,S.ID), and (c) the address of the train (to be defined later) currently located at that station (H.ID,P.ID,J.ID). If the address in the message header consists of a C.ID only, the message will be accepted by the station associated with the first idle SPPR in the chain of the cluster C.ID (this can be ensured by appropriate daisy chaining). If the address in the message header consists of both a C.ID and S.ID, the message will be accepted by the specified SPPR. If the address in the message header consists of a H.ID, P.ID, and J.ID, the message will be accepted by the SPPR currently in possession of the train (to be defined later).

IV. TASK ALLOCATION PROCEDURE

The basic idea in the LOCO approach to distributed task allocation is to use the processing environment specifiers (see Table 1) in competition among different tasks for the SPPRs they need. The specifiers define which job is competing for which SPPR type (indicated by the C.ID). Once the SPPR is assigned to a job, in order to execute one of its tasks, the SPPR is loaded with the necessary library routine, its parameters and data, and the execution of the task can start. When the execution of the task is completed, the job will compete for the next SPPR that it needs, and so on.

The LOCO procedure will be first presented through an example and then it will be generalized. Assume that the host H(H.ID)=H(7) is running a process P(H.ID,P.ID)=P(7,5) or abbreviated P(5), with a job J(H.ID,P.ID,J.ID)=J(7,5,3) or abbreviated J(3). Assume that J(3) consists of four tasks interrelated as in Fig. 1 and abbreviated as: T(1), T(2), T(3) and T(4). Assume that task T(1) has to be executed in cluster C(2) under the control of the library routine L(5), T(2) in C(4) under L(15), T(3) in C(2) under L(115), and T(4) in C(1) under L(135). From Fig. 1 it follows that data for task T(1) reside in host H(7), for T(2) in H(7), for T(3) in the SPPR that executed T(1), and for T(4) in H(7) as well as in the SPPRs that executed T(2) and T(3). The final data produced by job J(3) reside in the SPPR that executed T(3) and T(4).

One possible interpretation of the above specified job may be as follows: T(1) refers to the transformation of a flying object image and needs the appropriate SPPR of the SIMD type; T(2) refers to processing of the seismic signal (that may contain some information corresponding to the object launching) and is best executed on a specialized pipelined array processor; T(3) refers to image understanding and requires the appropriate SPPR of the MIMD type. Output data from this task are for some reason needed by the job source. Finally, T(4) refers to intelligent retrieval from a knowledge base within an expert system which is oriented to identification of flying objects. The expert system needs input data from T(2), T(3), and the job source. Its output data are needed in the job destination (same or another host), and also in the job source, e.g., for updating of relevant information. Another possible interpretation may be in the domain of the medical experiment, where T(1) and T(3) refer to processing and understanding of the scanner image, T(2) to processing of an EEG signal, and T(4) to intelligent retrieval from appropriate knowledge base within an expert system for medical diagnosis.

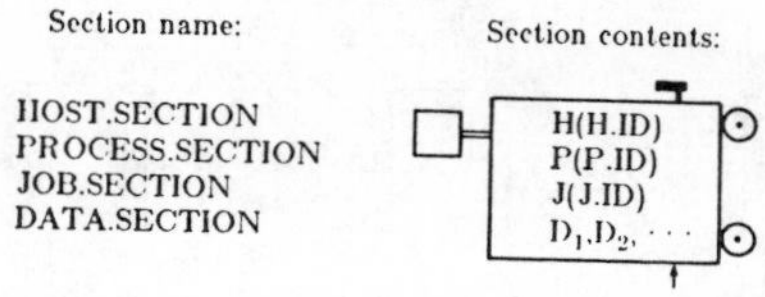

Section name: Section contents:

HOST.SECTION
PROCESS.SECTION
JOB.SECTION
DATA.SECTION

Figure 4.   Structure of the Locomotive and Contents of Different Locomotive Sections.

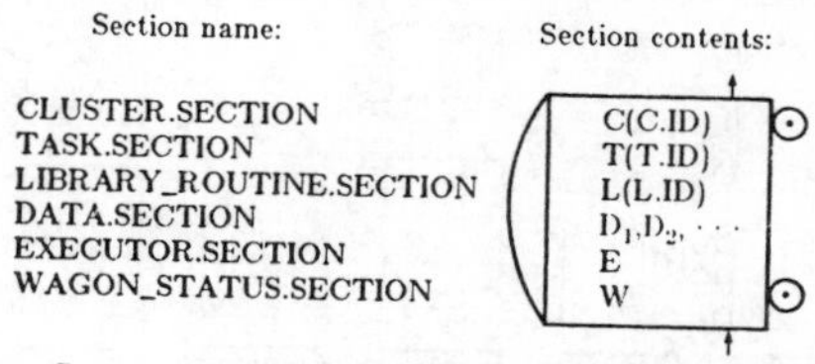

Section name: Section contents:

CLUSTER.SECTION
TASK.SECTION
LIBRARY_ROUTINE.SECTION
DATA.SECTION
EXECUTOR.SECTION
WAGON_STATUS.SECTION

Figure 5.   Structure of the Wagon and Contents of Different Wagon Sections. Depending on the LOCO version, the DATA.SECTION may contain either data or pointers to data.

Now we describe the way in which the LOCO procedure will treat the above specified job. Once the job J(3) is defined in the process P(5), the host's station corresponding to H(7) will create the message (train) that consists of a number of submessages. One of them is dedicated to the job J(3) as a whole *(the LOCOmotive)*. The others are dedicated to different tasks *(the wagons)*.

The structure of the locomotive is shown in Fig. 4. It consists of four sections. Sections HOST.SECTION, PROCESS.SECTION, and JOB.SECTION define the processing environment of the corresponding job. Section DATA.SECTION defines the tasks that produce the final data needed by this job (other tasks are producing the intermediate data only). Since the locomotive is playing the vital role in the task allocation approach under consideration here, it is referred to as the LOCO approach. Note that the above description of the locomotive implies the case when the job source and the job destination are the same. For the case when job source may be different than the job destination, only a minor modification of the locomotive is required.

The structure of the wagon is shown in Fig. 5. Each wagon W(k), k=1,2,..., consists of six sections. Section CLUSTER.SECTION specifies the cluster in which the task corresponding to that wagon has to be executed. Section TASK.SECTION specifies the task corresponding to the wagon. Since the wagon is always appended to the locomotive, the short specification of the task can be used. The full specification can be obtained by combining this section and the first three sections of its locomotive. The LIBRARY_ROUTINE.SECTION specifies the library routine to be used in the task execution. Typically, this section will also contain the parameters to be passed to the routine, or at least, the pointers to these parameters. The DATA.SECTION specifies the tasks that produce data for the task corresponding to the wagon. The EXECUTOR.SECTION specifies the particular SPPR that executed the task corresponding to that wagon. Before the execution of the job starts, it is not known which SPPR will do the execution of which task. So, as indicated earlier, the contents of this section is initially E=X, as mentioned earlier. The WAGON_STATUS.SECTION contains the specifier W that indicates if the task corresponding to this wagon is currently under execution somewhere in the system (W=IMAG) or not (W=REAL). If W = REAL and the wagon is behind the locomotive, its execution is completed. If W = REAL and wagon is in the front of the locomotive, its execution did not start yet.

For the particular case of Fig. 1, the initial form of the train is given in Fig. 6a. Initially, the locomotive is pushing the train. The front wagon corresponds to T(1), the next one to T(2), etc. Of course, the appropriate preamble should be appended to the front, and the appropriate cyclic redundancy check (CRC) for error detection purposes to the end of the train. Once the train is created, the host's station will compete for the allocation bus and after accessing it, the station will broadcast the train. The CLUSTER.SECTION of the front wagon (now W(1)) has the function of the train destination address, and the train will end up in the first currently idle SPPR of the cluster C(2). When the train is accepted an acknowledgement will be sent to the train transmitter. The ID of the train transmitter can be found by

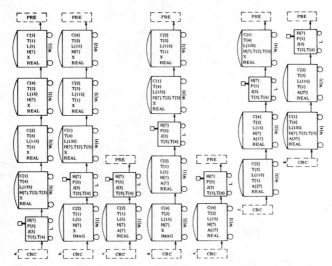

Figure 6. Different Forms of the Train During Execution of the Job from Figure 1.

PRE – Preamble   CRC – Cyclic redundancy check

examining the contents of the locomotive. If the first SPPR in the chain is currently busy, it will pass the train to the next SPPR in the chain. If none is available, the train will "wait" in the queue until the first SPPR becomes available. This "queue" may physically exist in the form of the closed cluster-dedicated loop within which the train is propagated until allocated. This is indicated by dashed lines in Fig. 2c. The station that transmitted the train will wait for the acknowledgement. When the acknowledgement is received it will clean up the buffer in which the train was stored and will use it for the other purposes. Here an error-free channel is assumed.

Assume one of the SPPRs is free (e.g. S(7)). Using the allocation bus, the SPPR S(7) will acknowledge the receipt of the train and at the same time it will request data from all the sources specified in the DATA.SECTION of W(1), i.e., from P(7,5). Using the software bus, the SPPR S(7) will request the library routine specified in the program section of W(1), i.e., L(5). In the meantime, before the data and program arrive, the SPPR S(7)'s station will examine W(2) to see if T(2) can run concurrently with T(1). This is indicated by the contents of the DATA.SECTION of W(2). In this example, concurrency is possible. Note that the wagon must be in the station while the SPPR works on its load. It will have W=IMAG during that time. So, W(1) will be removed and the imaginary copy of W(1) will be appended to the back of the train. A copy of the locomotive will be saved at the station along with the wagon. The train (see Fig. 6b) will now be broadcast and hopefully accepted by one of the stations in C(4), e.g., S(17). The station S(17) will acknowledge the receipt of the train, will request its data and program and will examine W(3) for possible concurrency. This time concurrency will not be possible, since T(3) needs data from T(1) and the wagon corresponding to T(1) is imaginary which means that T(1) is not yet completed. So, the train will sit in the station S(17) for some time. So far, our example clearly points to the ability of the LOCO procedure to exploit maximally the existing parallelism on the task level. Other more sophisticated forms of parallelism could be handled by the LOCO procedure equally well.

After some time, T(1) will be completed. The station S(7) will place the output data into its local memory and will "remember" that the data will be needed by T(7,5,3,3). That information is obtained from the train while it is at the station. The station S(7) will set up E=S(7) in the wagon W(1), will append W(1) to the train, and will broadcast it (see Fig. 6c).

The message from Fig. 6c will be accepted by the station which is currently in the position of the train, i.e., S(17). The station S(17) will now exchange the imaginary wagon with the real one, and will reexamine if T(3) can run concurrently. Since now it can, the train of the form indicated in Fig. 6d will be broadcast. Assume that this train will be accepted by S(2,27) and that T(4) will be executed in S(1,37). In that case, the train will have the forms indicated in Figs. 6e, 6f, and 6g.

Note that a wagon will be destroyed when it is not needed any more. Finally, the locomotive is pulling the wagons. Once the train from Fig. 6g is accepted by P(7,5) it will request the final data from S(2,27) and S(1,37). At last, P(7,5) will broadcast the permission to delete all memory blocks corresponding to J(7,5,3).

Our example described the basic idea of the LOCO approach. A more rigorous definition can be easily derived from this example. However, note that the LOCO approach is more powerful than indicated by the example. Instead of the topology from Fig. 1, any topology can be used. Next, in the example used here, the schedule of the train and its load (i.e., which type of SPPRs will be visited and what will be the data sources) is set up at the time when the train was created. However, each task can be given the possibility to change the contents of all the wagons corresponding to the tasks not yet executed. In that case the task execution is made conditional, as well as the data to be used. Also, as indicated earlier, each SPPR can be given the possibility to treat each accepted task as a secondary process which can generate secondary jobs and secondary tasks, where a new secondary train has to be associated with each secondary job. Also, it is very important to note that, under assumption #5, *all possible parallelism on the task execution level can be fully exploited by the LOCO procedure.* The actual extent to which the parallelism will be exploited depends upon how the train is composed when it is generated, i.e., the way in which the job is decomposed into tasks and the way in which the wagons are ordered.

Note that the LOCO procedure can exist in various versions. In one version, the train first competes for the appropriate SPPR and then collects the input data (specified by the pointers in the train). In a variation, the train first collects the data needed for the task and then competes for the appropriate SPPR. The former version was explained in the example, since we feel it is simpler. It needs a smaller queueing buffer in each cluster, but is less time-efficient. The latter version will be treated in the performance analysis to follow. It needs a larger queueing buffer in each cluster, but is more time-efficient.

V. MODELLING

We first develop a model of complex multitask job (intertask model) which is applicable to both the LOCO and LB approaches. Then we develop the models of the task execution time (intratask model), separately for the LOCO and LB approaches. Load balancing has attracted a lot of research interest, and some very good work has been reported recently [e.g., ChoAb82, NiHwa81, TanTo84, WahJu83]. However, here under the term LB approach we consider the approach which is obtained by applying the principles of load balancing to the system architecture of Fig. 2b.

A. Model of the Multitask Job (Intertask Model)

We assume a complex multitask job that consists of J tasks (running serially and/or concurrently). Each task is serviced by a generalized service station (*GSS*). Activities of the GSS include allocation of the task to one of the appropriate SPPRs, collection of input data from appropriate data sources, collection of the library routine from the appropriate mass storage unit, and execution of the task. The only difference between the GSS for the LOCO and LB approaches is in the allocation of the task to one of the appropriate SPPRs. So the differences are within the GSS and are not visible on the level of the intertask model. Consequently, both procedures can be represented by the same open queueing network model [Kobay78], as indicated in Fig. 7.

Our analytical model based on queueing theory incorporates only the most essential parameters of two procedures under consideration. We are forced to such an approach by the inherent limitations of queueing theory.

We assume an infinite population queueing network. Task generation does not depend on the number of tasks currently existing in the network. Task generation is governed by the Poisson process. Routing of tasks abides by a first-order Markovian chain. Queueing discipline at each GSS can be any work-conserving one. Service time is exponentially distributed. The task destination is capable of absorbing all tasks departing from the system. The observation interval is long enough so that the system can reach a steady state. Under these conditions, Jackson's decomposition theorem [Kobay78] holds, and the steady-state distribution of the probability that the network is in state $\bar{\mathbf{n}}$ is given by:

$$P[\bar{\mathbf{n}}] = \prod_{i=1}^{N_S} p_i(n_i)$$

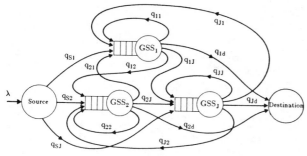

Figure 7. Open Queueing Network Model of a Multitask Job for the LOCO and LB Approaches.

$q_{i,j}$ – Branching probabilities for different tasks within the job
G_{SS} – Generalized service station
J – Number of tasks in the job
i,j = S(Source), 1,2,...,J,d(Destination).
λ – Poisson arrival rate at the source node.

where $p_i(n_i)$ is the marginal distribution of the variable n_i $(i=1,...,N_S)$, and N_S refers to the number of possible states [Kobay78]. Elements of the vector $\vec{n}$ refer to the number of tasks in each of N_S SPPRs of a given cluster. This conclusion implies that execution of different tasks within a complex multitask job can be analyzed independently one from another, regardless of the intertask data dependency and other relevant parameters. The same holds for both the LOCO and LB approaches. On the basis of this conclusion, in the next subsection the intratask models for the LOCO and LB approaches are introduced and used later for their comparative performance analysis.

B. Model of the Task Execution (Intratask Model)

We consider a task which belongs to a complex (multitask) job, and its execution in the GSS. In general, input data for the task reside in one or more of the hosts or SPPRs. Now we assume that input data reside in a given host. Also, we assume that when the task is ready for execution, before its allocation, first the input data have to be requested from the host. The same applies for both the LOCO and LB approaches. The model of the host as a source station for data retrieval is given in Fig. 8a. The FIFO queueing discipline is assumed. If the data request at the host i $(i=1,...,N_H)$ is a Poisson process characterized by the arrival rate $\lambda_{H,i}$, the probability density function $(p.d.f.)$ of the data request interarrival intervals is given by:

$$f_A^{H,i}(t) = \lambda_{H,i}e^{-\lambda_{H,i}t} \quad ; \quad t \geq 0$$

The value of $\lambda_{H,i}$ can easily be measured as:

$$\lambda_{H,i} = \lim_{t\to\infty} \frac{\text{number of data requests}}{t}$$

If the service (i.e., data retrieval) at the host i $(i=1,...,N_H)$ is an exponential process characterized by the service rate $\mu_{H,i}$, then the p.d.f. of the service time is given by:

$$f_s^{H,i}(t) = \mu_{H,i}e^{-\mu_{H,i}t} \quad ; \quad t \geq 0$$

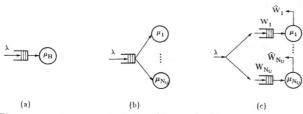

(a)   (b)   (c)

Figure 8. Elements of the Task Execution Model.

(a) The host as a service station for data retrieval
(b) The LOCO approach
(c) The LB approach
$\hat{W}_i(i=1,...,N_U)$ – Estimated waiting time
$W_i(i=1,...,N_U)$ – Real waiting time

The value of $\mu_{H,i}$ can easily be measured as:

$$\mu_{H,i} = \frac{\overline{C}_{H,i}}{\overline{D}_{H,i}}$$

where $\overline{D}_{H,i}$ refers to the average number of instructions executed during data retrieval, and $\overline{C}_{H,i}$ to the average number of instructions executed in a unit of time. The utilization factor is given by:

$$\rho_{H,i} = \lambda_{H,i}/\mu_{H,i}$$

The waiting time p.d.f. at the host is given by:

$$f_w^{H,i}(t) = \mu_{H,i}\rho_{H,i}(1-\rho_{H,i})e^{-\mu_{H,i}(1-\rho_{H,i})t} \quad ; \quad t \geq 0$$

Finally, the response time p.d.f. at the host is given by:

$$f_T^{H,i}(t) = f_s^{H,i}(t) \otimes f_w^{H,i}(t) = \mu_{H,i}(1-\rho_{H,i})e^{-\mu_{H,i}(1-\rho_{H,i})t} \quad ; \quad t \geq 0$$

where $\otimes$ stands for convolution. The average response time for data retrieval at the host is given by:

$$\overline{T}^{H,i} = \int_{-\infty}^{\infty} t \cdot f_T^{H,i}(t)dt$$

Next, after the data are requested and obtained, the task is allocated to a SPPR according to the existing task allocation procedure. Note that our model of the LOCO procedure concentrates on a single cluster. So the parallel execution of different tasks in different clusters is incorporated only indirectly.

In the case of the LOCO approach, the task is sent to the queue corresponding to the appropriate logical cluster. As indicated earlier, this queue may physically exist in the form of the closed cluster-dedicated loop within which the train is propagated until allocated (see Fig. 2c). So the logical cluster can be modelled as a single multiple server service station. The FIFO queueing discipline is assumed. We assume a Poisson arrival of the tasks (due to the decomposition of the complex multitask jobs with Poisson arrivals) with the arrival rate at cluster j $(j=1,...,N_C)$ equal to $\lambda_{c,j}$. We assume an exponential service at each SPPR in the cluster, with the service rate equal to $\mu_{c,j}$. Thus, an M/M/m queueing system is assumed, where m = N_U. Both $\lambda_{c,j}$ and $\mu_{c,j}$ can easily be measured in real systems. The traffic intensity of the cluster is given by $a_{c,j} = \lambda_{c,j}/\mu_{c,j}$ and the utilization factor by $\rho_{c,j} = \lambda_{c,j}/(m_j \cdot \mu_{c,j}) = a_{c,j}/m_j$, where m_j is the number of SPPRs in the cluster j. Note that $m_j = N_U$ under the assumption that each cluster contains the same number of SPPRs. Now we are temporarily removing that assumption in order to make the results more general. The response time p.d.f. at the cluster j is given by convolution of the appropriate service time p.d.f. and waiting time p.d.f.:

$$f_T^{c,j}(t) = f_s^{c,j}(t) \otimes f_w^{c,j}(t)$$

In expanded form this reads:

$$f_T^{c,j}(t) = \begin{cases} m_j\mu_{c,j}(1-\rho_{c,j})E_2(m_j;j)\dfrac{e^{-m_j\mu_{c,j}(1-\rho_{c,j})t}}{1-m_j(1-\rho_{c,j})} ; \ t\geq 0; \ \rho_{c,j} > \dfrac{m_j-1}{m_j} \\ \\ m_j\mu_{c,j}(1-\rho_{c,j})E_2(m_j;j)\dfrac{e^{-\mu_{c,j}t}}{m_j(1-\rho_{c,j})-1} ; \ t\geq 0; \ \rho_{c,j} < \dfrac{m_j-1}{m_j} \end{cases}$$

where:

$$E_2(m_j;j) = \left[\frac{a_{c,j}^{m_j}}{m_j!(1-\rho_{c,j})}\right] / \left[\sum_{k=0}^{m_j-1}\frac{a_{c,j}^k}{k!} + \frac{a_{c,j}^{m_j}}{m_j!(1-\rho_{c,j})}\right]$$

Finally, the average response time for task execution in the logical cluster is given by:

$$\overline{T}^{c,j}(LOCO) = \int_{-\infty}^{\infty} t \cdot f_T^{c,j}(t)dt$$

Note that $\overline{T}^{c,j}(LOCO)$ refers to the average time that a task spends in the LOCO cluster, after the data are retrieved.

As already mentioned, we consider a task which is part of a complex multitask job. So the model has to incorporate both the response time for data retrieval and response time for task execution. Passing the output data, from the task under consideration, to the following task, is incorporated into the model of the following task.[*] In conclu-

---
[*]Note that final data have to be forwarded to the job destination. However, this can be neglected if the number of serially executed tasks is large enough.

sion, the GSS in the case of the LOCO approach can be modeled as a cascade of the models from Figs. 8a and 8b. This issue will be addressed in Section VI.

In the case of the LB approach, the source of the task first inquires about the load of different SPPRs appropriate for that task. After that information is obtained, the data for the task are requested and obtained and the task is sent to the queue of the SPPR which reported the minimal load (in terms of the total estimated execution time of all tasks currently waiting in its queue). Note that the reported load represents the estimated value ($\hat{W}$), and not the real value (W). The minimal reported value is not necessarily the absolute minimal value. This is indicated in Fig. 8c. In conclusion, the GSS for the case of the LB approach can be modelled as a cascade of the models from Figs. 8a and 8c. Under the same conditions as in the case of the LOCO approach, if the load estimation is ideal, the average task response time at the SPPR should be given by the same equation for both approaches:

$$\overline{T}_j(LB;IDEAL) = \overline{T}_j(LB;\sigma=0) = \overline{T}^{c,j}(LOCO)$$

where σ refers to the standard deviation of the task execution time estimate. In this case, the LOCO and LB approaches are characterized by the same performance.

For fair comparison of the LOCO and LB approaches, a model for the LB approach has been chosen which maximally favors the LB approach. Consequently, a multiserver model has been chosen, with information on the standard deviation of the task execution time estimate incorporated into the service time p.d.f.

According to the Kingman-Kollerstrom approximation [Klein76], the waiting time distribution in a G/G/m system is given by:

$$W(t) = 1 - e^{-\frac{(2/(m\mu))(1-\rho)}{\sigma_a^2+\sigma_b^2/m^2}t}$$

where σ_a^2 refers to the variance of the interarrival time, and σ_b^2 to the variance of the service time. The waiting time p.d.f. $f_w(t)$ is a derivative of the above given W(t). Using this approach we evaluate $\overline{T}_j(LB)$ for the M/G/N_U system. Note that the LB approach is characterized by: $m_j = N_U = m$, $\mu_{c,j} = \mu$, and $\lambda_{c,j} = \lambda$. For G we select the gamma distribution defined by:

$$f_g(t) = \begin{cases} \dfrac{\alpha(\alpha t)^{\beta-1}e^{-\alpha t}}{\Gamma(\beta)} & ; \ t \geq 0 \\ 0 & ; \ t < 0 \end{cases}$$

with $\beta = 3$ and $\alpha = A\mu$. We have chosen an integer β to simplify the analysis, without affecting its generality. The value $\beta=3$ has been chosen as it is the case when the gamma distribution closely corresponds to the normal distribution [Klein76]. Parameter A has been incorporated to enable more flexible variations of the mean and the variance. For the gamma distribution, the mean and variance are equal to β/α and β/α^2, respectively [Kobay78]. For selected values of α and β, the service time p.d.f. is given by:

$$f_s(t) = \begin{cases} \dfrac{(A\mu)^3 t^2 e^{-A\mu t}}{2} & ; \ t \geq 0 \\ 0 & ; \ t < 0 \end{cases}$$

with the mean equal to $\dfrac{3}{A\mu}$, and the variance equal to $\dfrac{3}{A^2\mu^2}$. Note that $\int_0^{\beta/\alpha} f_g(t)dt = 0.575$, and for the exponential distribution we have: $\int_0^{1/\mu} \mu e^{-\mu t}dt = 0.63$. This approach allows us to evaluate the LB system performance for different values of σ (σ was defined earlier), and for various appropriate values of A.

The response time p.d.f. for LB system is given by convolution of appropriate service time p.d.f., and waiting time p.d.f.:

$$f_t^j(t) = f_s^j(t) \otimes f_w^j(t)$$

where $j = 1,...,N_U$ (number of SPPRs in a cluster). In expanded form this reads:

$$f_t^j(t) = \begin{cases} \dfrac{A^3\mu^3 C}{(A\mu-C)^3}e^{-Ct} & ; \ C < A\mu \\ \dfrac{A^3\mu^3 C[t^2(C-A\mu)^2-2t(C-A\mu)+2]}{2(C-A\mu)^3}e^{-A\mu t} & ; \ C > A\mu \end{cases}$$

where:

$$C = \frac{2A^2m\mu(1-\rho)}{A^2\rho^2+3}$$

Finally, the average response time for task execution (after the data are retrieved) is given by:

$$\overline{T}_j(LB) = \int_{-\infty}^{\infty} tf_t^j(t)dt$$

Another possibility for dealing with LB approach is by using the following assumption: If the load estimation is nonideal ($\sigma\neq0$), then the average task execution time for the LB approach should be given by:

$$\overline{T}_j(LB;\sigma\neq0) = \overline{T}^{c,j}(LOCO) * \Omega(\sigma;m_j)$$

where $\Omega(\sigma;m_j)$ is the modification function for the LB approach, in the case when the data retrieval time is not taken into consideration. The function Ω characterizes the load estimation. The form of function $\Omega(\sigma;m_j)$ depends on the type of estimation. We assume that statistical characteristics of the estimation error $\rho_i = W_i-\hat{W}_i$ (i=1,...,m_j) at each station are the same and given by the zero-mean Gaussian distribution of the form:

$$\omega(\rho_i) = \frac{1}{\sqrt{2\pi\sigma^2}} e^{-\frac{\rho_i^2}{2\sigma^2}}; \quad -\infty < \rho_i < +\infty$$

As already indicated, σ is equal to the standard deviation of the load estimation. It is very difficult to obtain an analytic form of the function $\Omega(\sigma;m_j)$. The family of curves in Fig. 9 is obtained by simulation. In this figure, the value of σ is treated relatively to the average execution time of all tasks involved in the simulation ($\overline{T}$). The level of detail in our simulation model was chosen to correspond to the level of detail in our analytical model.

Using the method of empirical-functions smoothing and applying it to Fig. 9, it is possible to derive analytical expression for $\Omega(\sigma/\overline{T};m_j)$. We assume that the function Ω could be given by the following analytical formula:

$$\Omega(x) = K \cdot e^{-(x-2)**2} + 1$$

Coefficient K depends on m_j. It has been determined that it is equal to 0.77, 1.53, 2.24, and 2.83, for m_j equal to 2, 4, 8 and 16, respectively. The standard deviation is less than 2.1% in all cases. Using these results, we get an estimation for coefficient K which is characterized by a standard deviation less than 5%, for all selected cases. This value reads:

$$K = \frac{m_j-1}{m_j} \cdot \frac{\log_2(m_j)+2}{2}$$

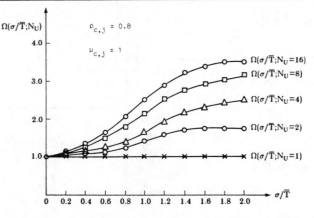

Figure 9.   Modification Function for the LB Approach, obtained from the Simulator.

σ –   Standard deviation of the task execution time estimate

$\overline{T}$ –   Average task execution time (execution only, no waiting)

N_U –   Number of units in the cluster

It is possible to use this approximation only in the cases when we have values for the LOCO approach and we need to generate the values for the LB approach, under the conditions of our simulation. Our simulator is of the "self-driven" type [Kobay78], and is implemented in the SLAM language. We have fully followed the methodology of [Kobay78] for simulation model formulation, simulator implementation, design of the simulation experiments, validation of the simulation model, and analysis of the simulation data. *Throughout the simulation, the traffic of individual SPPRs was kept constant.*

VI. PERFORMANCE ANALYSIS

We consider first the model of the LOCO approach developed in the previous section (Figs. 8a and 8b). According to [Kobay78], the average time that a task spends in the system is given by:

$$\overline{T}_{i,j}(LOCO) = \int_0^\infty t\, f_{T(i,j)}(t)dt$$

where:

$$f_{T(i,j)}(t) = f_T^{H,i}(t) \otimes f_T^{c,j}(t)$$

We assume that the input data reside in the host i ($i=1,...,N_H$), and that the task is executed in cluster j ($j=1,...,N_C$). After applying a series of transformations we get:

$$\overline{T}_{i,j}(LOCO) =$$

$$\frac{m_j\mu_{c,j}(1-\rho_{c,j})E_2(m_j;j)}{\mu_{H,i}(1-\rho_{H,i})[1-m_j(1-\rho_{c,j})][m_j\mu_{c,j}(1-\rho_{c,j})-\mu_{H,i}(1-\rho_{H,i})]} \; ; \; \left\{ \begin{array}{l} \rho_{c,j} > \dfrac{m_j-1}{m_j} \\ m_j\mu_{c,j}(1-\rho_{c,j}) > \mu_{H,i}(1-\rho_{H,i}) \end{array} \right\}$$

$$\frac{\mu_{H,i}(1-\rho_{H,i})E_2(m_j;j)}{-m_j\mu_{c,j}(1-\rho_{c,j})[1-m_j(1-\rho_{c,j})][m_j\mu_{c,j}(1-\rho_{c,j})-\mu_{H,i}(1-\rho_{H,i})]} \; ; \; \left\{ \begin{array}{l} \rho_{c,j} > \dfrac{m_j-1}{m_j} \\ m_j\mu_{c,j}(1-\rho_{c,j}) < \mu_{H,i}(1-\rho_{H,i}) \end{array} \right\}$$

$$\frac{m_j\mu_{c,j}(1-\rho_{c,j})E_2(m_j;j)}{\mu_{H,i}(1-\rho_{H,i})[m_j(1-\rho_{c,j})-1][\mu_{c,j}-\mu_{H,i}(1-\rho_{H,i})]} \; ; \; \left\{ \begin{array}{l} \rho_{c,j} < \dfrac{m_j-1}{m_j} \\ \mu_{c,j} > \mu_{H,i}(1-\rho_{H,i}) \end{array} \right\}$$

$$\frac{\mu_{H,i}(1-\rho_{H,i})m_j(1-\rho_{c,j})E_2(m_j;j)}{-\mu_{c,j}[m_j(1-\rho_{c,j})-1][\mu_{c,j}-\mu_{H,i}(1-\rho_{H,i})]} \; ; \; \left\{ \begin{array}{l} \rho_{c,j} < \dfrac{m_j-1}{m_j} \\ \mu_{c,j} < \mu_{H,i}(1-\rho_{H,i}) \end{array} \right\}$$

where:

$$a_{c,j} = \frac{\lambda_{c,j}}{\mu_{c,j}} \quad \& \quad \rho_{c,j} = \frac{\lambda_{c,j}}{m_j\mu_{c,j}}$$

and $E_2(m_j;j)$ was defined earlier in the text. The first two formulas apply to the case: $m_j = 1$. The dependence of the $\log_{10}[\overline{T}_{i,j}(LOCO)]$ on m_j is presented in Fig. 10 for the case when $m_j=N_U$, and for different values of $\mu_{H,i}$ and $\rho_{H,i}$. *Note that the total traffic in Fig. 10 is kept constant, regardless of the value of N_U. Consequently, when N_U increases, the individual traffic of each SPPR decreases.* Variance of the total time that a task spends in the LOCO system is given by:

$$\sigma_T^2(LOCO) = \int_0^\infty t^2 f_{T(i,j)}(t)dt - \overline{T}_{i,j}^2(LOCO)$$

After a series of transformations we get:

$$\sigma_T^2(LOCO) =$$

$$\frac{m_j\mu_{c,j}(1-\rho_{c,j})E_2(m_j;j)\{2[1-m_j(1-\rho_{c,j})][m_j\mu_{c,j}(1-\rho_{c,j})-\mu_{H,i}(1-\rho_{H,i})]-m_j\mu_{c,j}(1-\rho_{c,j})E_2(m_j;j)\}}{\mu_{H,i}^2(1-\rho_{H,i})^2[1-m_j(1-\rho_{c,j})]^2[m_j\mu_{c,j}(1-\rho_{c,j})-\mu_{H,i}(1-\rho_{H,i})]^2} \; ;$$

$$(\rho_{c,j} > \frac{m_j-1}{m_j}; \; m_j\mu_{c,j}(1-\rho_{c,j}) > \mu_{H,i}(1-\rho_{H,i}))$$

$$\frac{\mu_{H,i}(1-\rho_{H,i})E_2(m_j;j)\{2[1-m_j(1-\rho_{c,j})][\mu_{H,i}(1-\rho_{H,i})-m_jC_{u,j}(1-\rho_{c,j})]-\mu_{H,i}(1-\rho_{H,i})E_2(m_j;j)\}}{m_j^2\mu_{c,j}^2(1-\rho_{c,j})^2[1-m_j(1-\rho_{c,j})]^2[\mu_{H,i}(1-\rho_{H,i})-m_jC_{u,j}(1-\rho_{c,j})]^2} \; ;$$

$$(\rho_{c,j} > \frac{m_j-1}{m_j}; \; m_j\mu_{c,j}(1-\rho_{c,j}) < \mu_{H,i}(1-\rho_{H,i}))$$

$$\frac{m_j\mu_{c,j}(1-\rho_{c,j})E_2(m_j;j)\{2[m_j(1-\rho_{c,j})-1][\mu_{c,j}-\mu_{H,i}(1-\rho_{H,i})]-m_j\mu_{c,j}(1-\rho_{c,j})E_2(m_j;j)\}}{\mu_{H,i}^2(1-\rho_{H,i})^2[m_j(1-\rho_{c,j})-1]^2[\mu_{c,j}-\mu_{H,i}(1-\rho_{H,i})]^2} \; ;$$

$$(\rho_{c,j} < \frac{m_j-1}{m_j}; \; \mu_{c,j} > \mu_{H,i}(1-\rho_{H,i}))$$

$$\frac{m_j\mu_{H,i}(1-\rho_{H,i})(1-\rho_{c,j})E_2(m_j;j)\{2[m_j(1-\rho_{c,j})-1][\mu_{H,i}(1-\rho_{H,i})-\mu_{c,j}]-m_j\mu_{H,i}(1-\rho_{H,i})(1-\rho_{c,j})E_2(m_j;j)\}}{\mu_{c,j}^2[m_j(1-\rho_{c,j})-1]^2[\mu_{H,i}(1-\rho_{H,i})-\mu_{c,j}]^2} \; ;$$

$$(\rho_{c,j} < \frac{m_j-1}{m_j}; \; \mu_{c,j} < \mu_{H,i}(1-\rho_{H,i}))$$

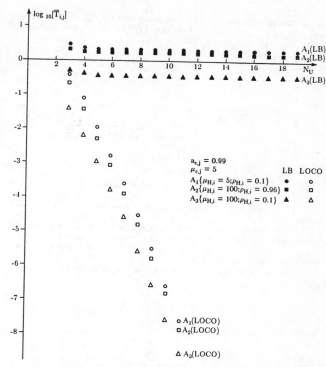

Figure 10. Average Time that Task Spends in the LOCO and LB Systems.

N_U – Number of units in the cluster

Average total time spent in the system, averaged over all possible data sources and task types, is given by:

$$\overline{T}(LOCO/SYSTEM) = \sum_{i=1}^{N_H}\sum_{j=1}^{N_C} \overline{T}_{i,j}(LOCO)p_{i,j}$$

where $p_{i,j}$ refers to the probability that input data reside in the host i and the task is executed in cluster j. Average queue length of the cluster j ($j=1,...,N_C$) in terms of the number of tasks waiting in the queue associated to cluster j is given by [Kobay78]:

$$\overline{Q}_j = \sum_{n=m_j}^\infty (n-m_j)p_n = \frac{a_{c,j}^{m_j}}{m_j!}\frac{\rho_{c,j}}{(1-\rho_{c,j})^2}\cdot p_0$$

where:

$$p_0 = \left[\sum_{n=0}^{m_j-1} \frac{a_{c,j}^n}{n!} + \frac{a_{c,j}^{m_j}}{m_j!}\frac{1}{1-\rho_{c,j}} \right]^{-1}$$

The variance of the queue length is given by:

$$\sigma_{Q_j}^2 = \sum_{n=m_j}^\infty (n-m_j)^2 p_n - \overline{Q}_j^2 = \frac{a_{c,j}^{m_j}}{m_j!}\cdot\frac{1-\rho_{c,j}+2\rho_{c,j}^2}{(1-\rho_{c,j})^3}\cdot p_0$$

where p_0 is defined above, and p_n is the probability of having n tasks in the cluster.

We consider now the model of the LB approach developed in the previous section (Figs. 8a and 8c). According to queueing theory, the average time that a task spends in the system is given by:

$$\overline{T}_{i,j}(LB) = \int_0^\infty t\, f_{T(i,j)}(t)dt$$

where:

$$f_{T(i,j)}(t) = f_T^{H,i}(t) \otimes f_T^j(t)$$

We assume that the input data reside in the host i ($i=1,...,N_H$), and the task is executed in the SPPR of the type j ($j=1,...,N_U$). After applying a series of transformations we get:

$$
\overline{T}_{i,j}(LB) =
\begin{cases}
\dfrac{A^3 D \mu^2}{(A\mu - C)^2 \cdot (D-C) \cdot C} & \begin{array}{l} C < A\mu \\ D > C \end{array} \\[2em]
\dfrac{A^3 C \mu^3}{(C - A\mu)^2 (D-C) D} & \begin{array}{l} C < A\mu \\ D < C \end{array} \\[2em]
\dfrac{A^3 C \mu^3 [(C - A\mu)^2 + (C - A\mu)(D - A\mu) + (D - A\mu)^2]}{(C - A\mu)^2 (-D + A\mu)^2 \cdot D} & \begin{array}{l} C > A\mu \\ D < A\mu \end{array} \\[2em]
\dfrac{CD \{ 3(C - A\mu)^2 (D - A\mu)^2 - 2A\mu(C - 2A\mu + D)(C - A\mu)(D - A\mu) + A^2\mu^2[(D - A\mu)^2 + (C - A\mu)(D - A\mu) + (C - A\mu)^2] \}}{(C - A\mu)^2 (D - A\mu)^2 \cdot A^2 \cdot \mu} & \begin{array}{l} C > A\mu \\ D > A\mu \end{array}
\end{cases}
$$

where:

$$
C = \frac{2A^2 m \mu(1 - \rho)}{A^2 \rho^2 + 3} \quad \text{and} \quad D = \mu_{H,i}(1 - \rho_{H,i}).
$$

The dependence of the $\log_{10}[\overline{T}_{i,j}(LB)]$ on m_j is presented in Fig. 10 for various values of $\mu_{H,i}$ and $\rho_{H,i}$. The plotting is provided for $A = 1.75$. Note that total traffic in Fig. 10 is kept constant, regardless of the value of N_U. This is the same as in the case of Fig. 10, but different compared to Fig. 9. When N_U increases, the individual traffic of each SPPR decreases, but slower (Fig. 10).

Variance of the total time that a task spends in the LB system is given by:

$$
\sigma_T^2(LB) = \int_0^\infty t^2 f_{T(i,j)}(t)dt - \overline{T}_{i,j}^2(LB)
$$

After a series of transformations we get:

$$
\sigma_T^2(LB) =
$$

$$
\frac{A^3 \mu^2 D |2(C - A\mu)^2(C - D) - A^3 \mu^2 D|}{C^3(C - A\mu)^2(D - C)^2} \quad ; \quad \begin{array}{l} C < A\mu \\ \mu_{H,i}(1 - \rho_{H,i}) > C \end{array}
$$

$$
\frac{A^3 \mu^2 C |2(C - A\mu)^2(D - C) - C|}{(C - A\mu)^2(D - C)^2 D^2} \quad ; \quad \begin{array}{l} C < A\mu \\ \mu_{H,i}(1 - \rho_{H,i}) < C \end{array}
$$

$$
\frac{A^3 \mu^2 C [(C - A\mu)^2 + (C - A\mu)(D - A\mu) + (D - A\mu)^2][2(C - A\mu)^2(D - A\mu)^2 + CDA^2\mu^2((C - A\mu)^2 + (C - A\mu)(D - A\mu) + (D - A\mu)^2)]}{(C - A\mu)^3 \cdot (A\mu - D)^3 \cdot D^2} \quad ; \quad \begin{array}{l} C > A\mu \\ \mu_{H,i}(1 - \rho_{H,i}) < A\mu \end{array}
$$

$$
\frac{CD}{(C - A\mu)^6(D - A\mu)^6 \cdot A^2 \cdot \mu^2} \Big\{ 2(C - A\mu)^3(D - A\mu)^3[6(C - A\mu)^2(D - A\mu)^2 - 3(C - A\mu)(D - A\mu)(C - 2A\mu + D)A\mu
$$
$$
+ ((D - A\mu)^2 + (C - A\mu)(D - A\mu) + (C - A\mu)^2)A^2\mu^2] - CD \cdot [3(C - A\mu)^2(D - A\mu)^2
$$
$$
- 2(C + D - 2A\mu)(C - A\mu)(D - A\mu)A\mu + ((D - A\mu)^2 + (C - A\mu)(D - A\mu) + (C - A\mu)^2)A^2\mu^2] \Big\} \quad ; \quad \begin{array}{l} C > A\mu \\ \mu_{H,i}(1 - \rho_{H,i}) > A\mu \end{array}
$$

where $D = \mu_{H,i}(1 - \rho_{H,i})$, while C and A were defined earlier.

Average total time spent in the system, averaged over all possible data sources and SPPR types, is given by:

$$
\overline{T}(LB/SYSTEM) = \sum_{i=1}^{N_H} \sum_{j=1}^{N_U} \overline{T}_{i,j}(LB) \cdot p_{i,j}
$$

where $p_{i,j}$ refers to the probability that input data reside in the host i and the task needs the SPPR of the type j. The formulas for $\overline{T}(LB)$ and $\overline{T}(LOCO)$ match each other very closely for $N_U = 1$. Numerical values differ only in the third decimal digit.

For the LB approach, average queue length $\overline{Q}_j(LB)$ could be evaluated using Little's formula [Klein 76]:

$$
\overline{Q}_j(LB) = \lambda(\overline{T}_j(LB) - \frac{m\rho}{\lambda}) = \lambda \overline{T}_j(LB) - m\rho
$$

where $\overline{T}_j(LB)$ was defined earlier, and index i is omitted. After a series of transformations, we get:

$$
\overline{Q}_j(LB) =
\begin{cases}
\dfrac{\lambda A^3 \mu^3}{(A\mu - C)^3 \cdot C} - m\rho & ; \; C < A\mu \\[1.5em]
\dfrac{\lambda C[(C - A\mu)^2 - (C - A\mu)A\mu + A^2\mu^2]}{(C - A\mu)^3} - m\rho & ; \; C > A\mu
\end{cases}
$$

where C and A were defined earlier.

Some conclusions may be derived from Figs. 9 and 10. The higher the value of σ (implies $A < 3$), the larger the performance difference between the LOCO and LB approaches, which is expected.

In the environment under consideration, as already mentioned in Section II, the values of σ are relatively large due to the fact that, in the AI environment, the correlation between past values and future values of execution times for the same type of task may be very low. This indicates that, for realistic values of σ, the performance difference between the LOCO and LB approaches can be relatively high. For example, according to our simulation, for $\sigma/\overline{T} = 1$ (standard deviation of the estimation is equal to the average task execution time), and $N_U = 8$ (case of eight SPPRs in each cluster), the total time that the task spends in the system is 2.6 times shorter for the LOCO approach, compared with the LB approach. Note that our simulator neglects the time needed in the LB approach for the inquiry and processing of the information about the load of different SPPRs.

A number of observations have been derived from our analysis. For example, with the given conditions, the higher is the value of N_U, the larger is the performance difference between the LOCO and LB approaches. However, the step of the performance increase is smaller for the higher values of N_U.

VII. CONCLUSION

In this paper a problem was recognized, one of having a large number of special purpose processing resources (SPPRs) shared by a number of hosts. Processing structures of this type will arise in 1990s around AI and other computationally massive applications. Similar processing structures may arise in the high-end computers of the 5th generation. In such a processing structure, it is of crucial importance to have an efficient procedure for the distributed allocation of different tasks among different SPPRs.

Under the assumptions that affect the above described processing structure, a distributed task allocation procedure was introduced which is efficient in a large range of circumstances. Both the task allocation procedure (LOCO) and the underlying system architecture (AIDA) were presented and analyzed.

One of the most desirable features of this approach is that the task allocation controller (the LOCO station) can easily be implemented in a single VLSI chip. The LOCO station acts as an interface between the SPPR and the tasks to be executed by it. The LOCO station enables SPPRs of different types to be incorporated into a monolithic task allocation scheme.

Acknowledgments
The authors thank Professors E. J. Coyle, C. E. Houstis, and B. W. Wah of Purdue University for their creative suggestions.

References

Batch80
Batcher, K. E., "Design of a Massively Parallel Processor," *IEEE Transactions on Computers*, Vol. C-29, No. 9, September 1980, pp. 836-840.

Brady82
Brady, M., "Computer Vision," *Artificial Intelligence*, Vol. 19, 1982, pp. 7-16.

ChoAb82
Chou, T. C. K., Abraham, J. A., "Load Balancing in Distributed Systems," *IEEE Transactions on Software Engineering*, Vol. SE-8, No. 4, July 1982, pp. 401-412.

ChoKo79
Chow, Y.-C., Kohler, W. H., "Models for Dynamic Load Balancing in a Heterogeneous Multiple Processor System," *IEEE Transaction on Computers*, Vol. C-28, No. 5, May 1979, pp. 354-361.

Davis83
Davis, A. L., "Computer Architecture," *IEEE Spectrum*, Vol. 20, No. 11, November 1983, pp.94-99.

Enslo78
Enslow, P. H., "What is a Distributed Data Processing System," *IEEE Computer*, Vol. 11, No. 1, January 1978, pp. 13-21.

Flynn72
Flynn, M. J., "Some Computer Organizations and Their Effectiveness," *IEEE Transaction on Computers*, Vol. C-21, 1972, pp. 948-960.

GaLak84
Gajski, D. D., Lawrie, D. H., Kuck, D. J., Sameh, A. H., "Cedar," *Proceedings of the IEEE Spring Compcon 84*, San Francisco, CA, February/March 1984, pp. 306-309.

GaPaK82
Gajski, D., Padua, D. A., Kuck, D. J., Kuhn, R. H., "A Second Opinion on Data Flow Machines and Languages," *IEEE Computer*, Vol. 10, No. 2, February, 1982, pp. 58-69.

GoGrK83
Gottlieb, A., Grishman, R., Kruskal, C. P., McAuliffe, Rudolph, L., Snir, M., "The NYU Ultracomputer - Designing an MIMD Shared Memory Parallel Computer," *IEEE Transactions on Computers*, Vol. C-32, No. 2, February 1983, pp. 175-189.

Grosz82
Grosz, B. J., "Natural Language Processing," *Artificial Intelligence*, Vol. 19, 1982, pp. 131-136.

HaWaL83
Hayes-Roth, F., Waterman, D. A., Lenat, D. B., (editors), *Building Expert System*, Addison-Wesley, 1983.

HwCrG82
Hwang, K., Croft, W., Goble, G., Wah, B., Briggs, F., Simmons, W., Coates, C., "A UNIX-Based Local Computer Network with Load Balancing," *IEEE Computer*, Vol. 10, No. 4, April 1982, pp. 55-66.

JenPl84
Jensen, E. D., Pleszkoch, N., "ArchOS: A Physically Dispersed Operating System," *IEEE Distributed Processing Technical Committee Newsletter*, Vol. 6, No. SI-2, June 1984, pp. 15-24.

Klein76
Kleinrock, L., *Queueing Systems* (Vol. I and II), John Wiley and Sons, New York, 1976.

Kobay78
Kobayashi, H., *Modeling and Analysis: An Introduction to System Performance Evaluation Methodology*, Addison-Wesley, 1978.

KuSiA84
Kuehn, J. T., Siegel, H. J., Adams, G. B., Tuomenoksa, D. L., "The Use and Design of PASM," in *Image Processing: From Computation to Integration*, Levialdi, S., ed., Academic Press, London, 1984.

Lerne82
Lerner, E., "Understanding Speech Proves Tough Task for Machine," *Computer Design*, September 1982, pp. 41-44.

MarBr81
Maron, N., Brengle, T., "Integrating an Array Processor Into a Scientific Computing System," *IEEE Computer*, Vol. 9, No. 9, September 1981, pp. 41-44.

McDMa82
McDonough, K. C., Magar, S. S., "A Single Chip Microcomputer Architecture Optimized for Signal Processing," *Proceedings of the IEEE International Conference on Acoustics, Speech and Signal Processing*, Paris, France, May 1982, pp. 1-5.

MilSi84
Milutinović, V., Siegel, H. J., "The LOCO Approach to Distributed Task Allocation in AIDA by VERDI," *Purdue University Technical Report*, TR-EE 84-49, November 1984.

Milut83
Milutinović, V., "A High-Level Language Architecture: Bit-Slice Based Processor and Associated System Software," *Microprocessing and Microprogramming*, Vol. 12, Nos. 3 and 4, October/November 1983, pp. 142-151.

MilWa83
Milutinović, V., Waldschmidt, K., "A High-Level Language Architecture for Time-Critical Dedicated Microprocessing," *Microprocessing and Microprogramming*, Vol. 12, No. 1, August 1983, pp. 33-42.

MuKaM83
Murakami, K., Kakuta, T., Myazami, N., Shibayama, S., Yokota, H., "A Relational Data Base Machine: First Step to Knowledge Base Machine," *Proceedings of the ACM International Symposium on Computer Architecture*, Stockholm, Sweden, June 1983, pp. 423-425.

NiHwa81
Ni, L. M., Hwang, K., "Optimal Load Balancing Strategies for Multiple Processor Systems," *Proceeding of the IEEE/ACM International Conference on Parallel Processing*, Bellaire, MI, August 1981, pp. 352-357.

PoCoS83
Porter, D. R., Couch, P. R., Schelin, J. W., "A High-Speed Fiber Optic Data Bus for Local Data Communications," *IEEE Journal on Selected Areas in Communications*, Vol. SAC-1, No. 3, April 1983, pp. 479-488.

RabGo75
Rabiner, L. R., Gold, B., *Theory and Applications of Digital Signal Processing*, Prentice-Hall, 1975.

Rober84
Roberts, D., "A Study of the Artificial Intelligence Software Environment," *Purdue University Internal Report*, EE 496-84, August 1984.

ShDaR82
Shoch, J., Dalal, Y., Redell, D., Crane, R., "Evolution of the Ethernet Local Computer Network," *IEEE Computer*, Vol. 10, No. 8, August 1982, pp. 10-27.

Siege84
Siegel, H. J., *Interconnection Networks for Large-Scale Parallel Processing: Theory and Case Studies*, Lexington Books, Lexington, Ma 1984.

SiSiK81
Siegel, H. J., Siegel, L. J., Kemmerer, F., Mueller, P. T., Smalley, H. E., Smith, S. D., "PASM: A Partitionable SIMD/MIMD System for Image Processing and Pattern Recognition," *IEEE Transactions on Computers*, Vol. C-30, No. 12, December 1981, pp. 791-801.

StoSh82
Stolfo, S. J., Shaw, D. E., "DADO: A Tree-Structured Machine Architecture for Production Systems," *Proceedings of the AAAI National Conference on Artificial Intelligence*, Pittsburgh, PA, 1982.

SuHoS81
Sussman, G. J., Holloway, J., Steel, G. L., Bell, A., "Scheme-79 — Lisp on a Chip," *IEEE Computer*, Vol. 14, No. 7, July 1981, pp. 10-21.

SwFuS77
Swan, R. J., Fuller, S. H., Siewiorek, D. P., "Cm* - A Modular Multi-Microprocessor," *Proceedings of the National Computer Conference*, Dallas, TX, June 1977, pp. 637-644.

TanTo84
Tantawi, A. N., Towsley, D., "Optimal Load Balancing in Distributed Computer Systems," *University of Massachusetts Technical Report*, RC-10346, January 1984.

TreLi82
Treleaven, P. C., Lima, I. G., "Japan's Fifth-Generation Computer Systems," *IEEE Computer*, Vol. 15, No. 8, August 1982, pp. 79-88.

Uchid83
Uchida, S., "Inference Machine: From Sequential to Parallel," *Proceedings of the ACM International Symposium* on Computer Architecture, Stockholm, Sweden, June 1983, pp. 410-416.

Wah84
Wah, B. W., "Comparative Study of Distributed Resource Sharing on Multiprocessors, *IEEE Transactions on Computers*, Vol. C-33, No. 8, August 1984, pp. 700-711.

WahHi82
Wah, B. W., Hicks, A., "Distributed Scheduling of Resources on Interconnection Networks," *Proceedings of the National Computer Conference*, AFIPS Press, pp. 697-709, 1982.

WahJu83
Wah, B. W., Juang, J.-Y., "An Efficient Protocol for Load Balancing on CSMA/CD Networks," *Proceedings of the IEEE Conference on Local Computer Networks*, Minneapolis, MN, October 1983, pp. 55-61.

WahMa84
Wah, B. W., Ma, Y. W., "MANIP: A Multicomputer Architecture for Solving Combinatorial Extremum Search Problems," *IEEE Transactions on Computers*, Vol. C-33, No. 5, May 1984, pp. 377-390.

Chapter 8: Fifth-Generation Computer System

The Fifth-Generation Computer System, or FGCS, Project was a project started in Japan in 1982 to further the research and development of the next generation of computers. It was conjectured that computers of the next decade will be used increasingly for nonnumeric data processing such as symbolic manipulation and applied AI. The goals of the FGCS project are (1) to implement basic mechanisms for inference, association, and learning in hardware; (2) to prepare basic AI software to utilize the full power of the basic mechanisms implemented; (3) to implement the basic mechanisms for retrieving and managing a knowledge base in hardware and software; (4) to use pattern recognition and AI research achievements in developing user-oriented man-machine interfaces; and (5) to realize supporting environments for resolving the "software crisis" and enhancing software production.

The FGCS project is a marriage between the implementation of a computer system and the requirements specified by applications in AI, such as natural-language understanding and speech recognition. Specific issues studied include the choice of logic programming over functional programming, the design of the basic software systems to support knowledge acquisition, management, learning, and the intelligent interface to users, the design of highly parallel architectures to support inferencing operations, and the design of distributed-function architectures that integrates VLSI technology to support knowledge databases [1-6].

A first effort in the FGCS project is to implement a sequential inference machine, or SIM.[7,8] Its first implementation is a medium-performance machine known as a personal sequential inference, or PSI, machine [9,10]. The current implementation is on the parallel inference machine, or PIM [11-17], with a dataflow version [17] and using the reduction approach, PIM-R [36]. Another architectural development is on the knowledge-base machine, Delta [11,12,18-20]. Last, the development of the basic software system acts as a bridge to fill the gap between a highly parallel computer architecture and knowledge information processing [21-23]. Currently, all the projects are progressing well; however, the struggle is still far from over [24].

The Japanese FGCS project has stirred intensive responses from other countries [25-35], and some papers contained in this tutorial text represent a sample of these efforts. The British project is a five-year $550 million cooperative program between government and industry that concentrates on software engineering, intelligent knowledge-based systems, VLSI circuitry, and man-machine interfaces. Hardware development has focused on ALICE, a multiprocessor reduction machine based on extended graph reduction and implementing Hope, Prolog, and Lisp. [29-34]. The European Commission has started the $1.5 billion 5-year European Strategic Program for Research in Information Technologies (Esprit) in 1984 [26]. The program focuses on microelectronics, software technology, advanced information processing, computer integrated manufacturing, and office automation. In the United States, the most direct response to the Japanese FCGS project was the establishment of the Microelectronics and Computer Technology Corp. in 1983 [35]. The project has an annual budget of $50 to $80 million per year. It has a more evolutionary approach than the revolutionary approach of the Japanese and should yield technology that the corporate sponsors can build into advanced products in the next 10 to 12 years. Meanwhile, other research organizations have been formed to develop future U.S. computer technologies in a broader sense. These include DARPA's Strategic Computing and Survivability, the semiconductor industry's Semiconductor Research Corporation, and the Microelectronics Center of North Carolina [35].

Seven papers are included in this chapter. The first paper, (Moto-oka and Stone) provides general descriptions and goals of the FGCS project [2]. The next four papers (Taki et al., Goto et al., Ito et al., Shibayama et al.) describe the PSI, PIM, dataflow execution of logic programs, and Delta [9,14,17,18]. The paper on the software system [21] is not included here because of the orientation of this tutorial text toward the architectural aspects of AI architectures. The last two papers present ALICE, a graph-reduction computer architecture [30,31]. Readers may also refer to the article on Esprit for the research efforts in Europe [26] and the special issue in the IEEE Spectrum on the research efforts in the United States [35]. These papers are not included here because they are not directly related to architectures for AI.

References

[1]   K. Fuchi, "The Direction the FGCS Project Will Take," *New Generation Computing*, vol. 1, no. 1, pp. 3-9, 1983.

[2]   T. Moto-oka and H.S. Stone, "Fifth-Generation Computer Systems: A Japanese Project," *Computer*, vol. 17, no. 3, pp. 6-13, March 1984.

[3] K. Kawanobe, "Current Status and Future Plans of the Fifth-Generation Computer System Project," *Proceedings of the International Conference on Fifth-Generation Computer Systems*, pp. 3-36, ICOT, Tokyo, Japan, and North-Holland, Amsterdam, The Netherlands, 1984.

[4] P.C. Treleaven and I.G. Lima, "Japan's Fifth-Generation Computer Systems," *Computer*, vol. 15, no. 8, pp. 79-88, Aug. 1982.

[5] T. Moto-oka, "Overview to the Fifth Generation Computer System Project," *Proceedings of the 10th Annual International Symposium on Computer Architecture*, pp. 417-422, IEEE Computer Society, Washington, D.C., June 1983.

[6] L. Bic, "The Fifth Generation Grail: A Survey of Related Research," *Proceedings of the ACM'84 Annual Conference*, pp. 293-297, ACM, New York, N.Y., Oct. 1984.

[7] S. Uchida and T. Yokoi, "Sequential Inference Machine: SIM Progress Report," *Proceedings of the International Conference on Fifth-Generation Computer Systems*, pp. 58-81, ICOT, Tokyo, Japan, and North-Holland, Amsterdam, The Netherlands, 1984.

[8] T. Yokoi, S. Uchida, and ICOT Third Laboratory, "Sequential Inference Machine: SIM—Its Programming and Operating System," *Proceedings of the International Conference on Fifth-Generation Computer Systems*, pp. 70-81, ICOT, Tokyo, Japan, and North-Holland, Amsterdam, The Netherlands, 1984.

[9] K. Taki, M. Yokota, A. Yamamoto, H. Nishikawa, S. Uchida, H. Nakashima, and A. Mitsuishi, "Hardware Design and Implementation of the Personal Sequential Inference Machine (PSI)," *Proceedings of the International Conference on Fifth-Generation Computer Systems*, pp. 398-409, ICOT, Tokyo, Japan, and North-Holland, Amsterdam, The Netherlands, 1984.

[10] M. Yokota, A. Yamamoto, K. Taki, H. Nishikawa, and S. Uchida, "The Design and Implementation of a Personal Sequential Inference Machine: PSI," *New Generation Computing*, vol. 1, no. 2, pp. 125-144, 1983.

[11] K. Murakami, T. Kakuta, R. Onai, and N. Ito, "Research on Parallel Machine Architecture for Fifth-Generation Computer Systems," *Computer*, vol. 18, no. 6, pp. 76-92, June 1985.

[12] K. Murakami, T. Kakuta, and R. Onai, "Architectures and Hardware Systems: Parallel Inference Machine and Knowledge Base Machine," *Proceedings of the International Conference on Fifth-Generation Computer Systems*, pp. 18-36, ICOT, Tokyo, Japan, and North-Holland, Amsterdam, The Netherlands, 1984.

[13] T. Moto-oka, H. Tanaka, H. Aida, K. Hirata, and T. Maruyama, "The Architecture of a Parallel Inference Engine (PIE)," *Proceedings of the International Conference on Fifth-Generation Computer Systems*, pp. 479-488, ICOT, Tokyo, Japan, and North-Holland, Amsterdam, The Netherlands, 1984.

[14] A. Goto, H. Tanaka, and T. Moto-oka, "Highly Parallel Inference Engine PIE—Goal Rewriting Model and Machine Architecture," *New Generation Computing*, vol. 2, no. 1, pp. 37-58, 1984.

[15] S. Uchida, "Inference Machine: From Sequential to Parallel," *Proceedings of the 10th Annual International Symposium on Computer Architecture*, pp. 410-416, IEEE Computer Society, Washington, D.C., June 1983.

[16] N. Ito and H. Shimizu, "Dataflow Based Execution Mechanisms of Parallel and Concurrent Prolog," *New Generation Computing*, vol. 3, no. 1, pp. 15-41, 1985.

[17] N. Ito, H. Shimizu, M. Kishi, E. Kuno, and K. Rokusawa, "Data-Flow Based Execution Mechanisms of Parallel and Concurrent Prolog," *New Generation Computing*, vol. 3, no. 1, pp. 15-41, 1985.

[18] S. Shibayama, T. Kakuta, N. Miyazaki, H. Yokota, and K. Murakami, "A Relational Database Machine with Large Semiconductor Disk and Hardware Relational Algebra Processor," *New Generation Computing*, vol. 2, no. 2, pp. 131-155, 1984.

[19] K. Murakami, T. Kakuta, N. Miyazaki, S. Shibayama, and H. Yokota, "A Relational Data Base Machine: First Step to Knowledge Base Machine," *Proceedings of the 10th Annual International Symposium on Computer Architecture*, pp. 423-425, IEEE Computer Society, Washington, D.C., June 1983.

[20] H. Sakai, K. Iwata, S. Kamiya, M. Abe, A. Tanaka, S. Shibayama, and K. Murakami, "Design and Implementation of Relational Database Engine," *Proceedings of the Fifth-Generation Computer Systems*, pp. 419-426, ICOT, Tokyo, Japan, and North-Holland, Amsterdam, The Netherlands, 1984.

[21] K. Furukawa and T. Yokoi, "Basic Software System," *Proceedings of the International Conference on Fifth-Generation Computer Systems*, pp. 37-57, ICOT, Tokyo, Japan, and North-Holland, Amsterdam, The Netherlands, 1984.

[22] C.D. McCrosky, J.J. Glasgow, and M.A. Jenkins, "Nial: A Candidate Language for Fifth Generation Computer Systems," *Proceedings of the ACM'84 Annual Conference*, pp. 157-166, ACM, New York, N.Y., Oct. 1984.

[23] D. Michie, "Inductive Rule Generation in the Context of the Fifth Generation," *Proceedings of the International Machine Learning Workshop,* pp. 65-70, University of Illinois, Urbana, Il., June 1983.

[24] T. Maneul, "Cautiously Optimistic Tone Set For 5th Generation," *Electronics Week,* vol. 57, no. 34, pp. 57-63, Dec. 3, 1984.

[25] K.G. Wilson, "Science, Industry, and the New Japanese Challenge," *Proceedings of the IEEE,* vol. 72, no. 1, pp. 6-18, Jan. 1984.

[26] "ESPRIT: Europe Challenges U.S. and Japanese Competitors," *Future Generation Computer Systems,* vol. 1, no. 1, pp. 61-69, 1984.

[27] M. van Emden, "Towards a Western Fifth-Generation Computer System Project," *Proceedings of the ACM'84 Annual Conference,* pp. 298-302, ACM, New York, N.Y., Oct. 1984.

[28] *Proceedings of the ACM'84 Annual Conference: The Fifth-Generation Challenge,* ACM, New York, N.Y., 1984.

[29] J. Darlington and M. Reeve, "ALICE: A Multi-Processor Reduction Machine for the Parallel Evaluation of Applicative Languages," *Proceedings of the Conference on Functional Programming Languages and Computer Architecture,* pp. 65-74, ACM, New York, N.Y., 1981.

[30] K. Smith, "New Computer Breed Uses Transputers for Parallel Processing," *Electronics,* vol. 56, no. 4, pp. 67-68, Feb. 24, 1983.

[31] J. Darlington and M. Reeve, "ALICE and the Parallel Evaluation of Logic Programs," *Preliminary Draft,* Department of Computing, Imperial College of Science and Technology, London, England, June 1983.

[32] I.W. Moor, "An Applicative Compiler for a Parallel Machine, *Research Report DoC83/6,* Imperial College, London, England, March 1983.

[33] J. Darlington, A.J. Field, and H. Pull, The Unification of Functional and Logic Languages, *Technical Report,* Imperial College, London, England, Feb. 1985.

[34] M. Dawson, "A LISP Compiler for ALICE," *Technical Report,* Imperial College, London, England, 1985.

[35] "Special Issue on Tomorrow's Computers," *IEEE Spectrum,* vol. 20, no. 11, pp. 51-58, 69, Nov. 1983.

[36] R. Onai et al., "Architecture of a Reduction-Based Parallel Inference Machine: PIM-R," *New Generation Computing,* vol. 3, no. 2, pp. 197-228, 1985.

Reprinted from *Computer*, Volume 17, Number 3, March 1984, pages 6-13.
Copyright © 1984 by The Institute of Electrical and Electronics Engineers, Inc.

A new generation of computers should evolve from the current research and development of nonnumeric data processors such as problem-solving, inference, and knowledge-base systems.

Fifth-Generation Computer Systems: A Japanese Project

Tohru Moto-oka, University of Tokyo

Harold S. Stone, University of Massachusetts

In recent years, there has been a great deal of discussion on the growing need for a new generation of computers. In 1982, a research project known as the fifth-generation computer systems, or FGCS, project, was started in Japan to further the research and development of the next generation of computers.

As observers of this project, we conjecture that the computers of the next decade will be used increasingly for nonnumeric data processing such as symbol manipulation and applied artificial intelligence. Moreover, it appears that conventional systems applications—such as scientific calculations—will be performed by the evolving supercomputers and that current database and mainframe systems will be improved for use in national and worldwide network systems. In this article, we discuss the current directions and eventual goals of the FGCS project,[1] the structure of the research, and some of the accomplishments since the project's beginning. Particular emphasis is placed on three specific areas of research: (1) parallel inference systems, (2) the relational database research that will support knowledge-base systems, and (3) personal sequential inference, or PSI, systems.

Goals of the FGCS project

Fundamental changes in computer architecture and software are now required to support computers of the 1990's. To carry out nonnumeric computations, these machines must evolve according to the following technical goals:

(1) Implementation of basic mechanisms for inference, association, and learning in hardware, making these capabilities the core functions of fifth-generation systems.
(2) Preparation of basic artificial intelligence software in order to utilize the full power of the functions just mentioned (goal 1).
(3) Implementation of the basic mechanisms for retrieving and managing a knowledge base in hardware and software.
(4) Advantageous use of pattern recognition and artificial intelligence research achievements in developing user-oriented man-machine interfaces.
(5) Realization of supporting environments for resolving the "software crisis" and enhancing software production.

Developing viable products from these goals is dependant upon the continued evolution of current VLSI technology, software engineering, and artificial intelligence. Consequently, interim achievements of the project should be applied to these technologies to ensure their necessary advancement.

FGCS project structure

ICOT. At the beginning of the 10-year FGCS project, the Institute for New Generation Computer Technology, or ICOT (Japanese abbreviation), was formed with the support of both the Ministry of International Trade and Industry, or MITI, and eight leading electronic manufacturers in Japan. This institute, consisting of 40 researchers on leave from industry with support from advisory groups from universities and research institutes, has been subsequently organized to conduct research in three major areas:

- problem-solving and inference machines,
- knowledge-base management systems, and
- intelligent man-machine interfaces.

These areas of research are shown in Figure 1. The right-hand circle shows two new types of computing devices now underway at ICOT—the knowledge-base machine and the problem-solving and inference engine. The central circle shows the component that deals with software and algorithms; critical problems in this sphere

EH0242-8/86/0000/0536$01.00 © 1984 IEEE

of research include knowledge representation and manipulation. The left-hand circle shows the intelligent man-machine interfaces. This activity has focused on the design of an intelligent work station that uses an inference engine as its core processing facility.

Three phases of completion. The three areas of research form the basis of the first phase of a 10-year project to be completed in three phases. In the first phase, the intermediate research goals are

- to investigate architectures suitable for logical inference and database operations, particularly parallel architectures that can achieve extremely high performances,
- to design a Prolog-based language that is suitable for knowledge representation and inferencing, and
- to design a workstation containing a sequential inference machine that can be used as a major tool during the second phase of the project.

During the first phase of the project, the foundations for the remainder of the project will be established, and the basic tools to be used in the second phase will be built. While the research is to be directed at techniques for building parallel inference machines and parallel database machines, the workstation available at the end of the first stage will be a sequential, not parallel, inference machine. During the second phase, the ideas produced during the first phase will be prototyped, and during the third phase, the research of the second phase will be integrated and evaluated.

Logic programming and inference machines

The design and development of a problem-solving machine is contingent upon the development of hardware that supports the kernel language used for writing the inference-based algorithms. The hardware mechanism used for inferencing will eventually be integrated with the hardware used for dealing with (1) a knowledge base (the goal of the knowledge-base research), and (2) intelligent interfaces (the goal of the high-performance interface equipment research). The final result should be a prototype of a fifth-generation computer system.

Performance of the inference engine is measured in logical inferences per second, or lips. One inference is roughly equivalent to one rule firing in a rule-based expert system. An inference machine for the 1990's should have a maximum performance of 100M lips to 1G lips. In terms of conventional von Neumann architecture, 1 lips is roughly equivalent to the execution of 100 to 1K ips, so that an inference engine running at 1G lips in some sense has the performance of a conventional machine operating at 10^{11} to 10^{12} ips.

High-performance architectures. Clearly, at speeds such as these it is not likely that a purely sequential implementation will do; parallel execution is the key to realizing this level of performance. Consequently, one primary focus of the FGCS project is to research architectures that are suited both to highly parallel inferencing and to manipulation of abstract data-types. The FGCS research is working toward a target goal of 1000

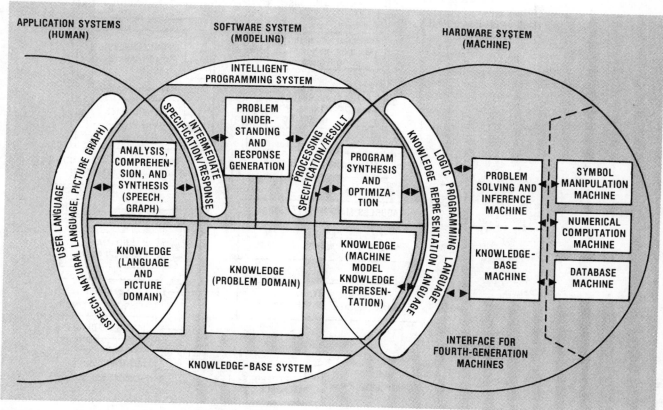

Figure 1. A conceptual diagram of a fifth-generation computer system from the programmer's standpoint.

processing elements. Among the tools being developed in the course of the research are VLSI-CAD tools to support the design of such hardware.

A Prolog-like language. The inference-machine architecture should be capable of using rules and assertions to process knowledge information. Existing artificial intelligence technology has been based primarily on Lisp, which has a sequential, functional character. Prolog seems to be a more appropriate language because its logic programming character provides for greater power of expression and for several different types of parallel execution. Consequently, a Prolog-like language is being designed for the interface between FGCS hardware and software, and the FGCS hardware architecture should provide direct support for Prolog-like inferencing. In the initial phase of the project a sequential inference language, Kernel Language 0, or KL-0, has been the sub-

ject of study and the corresponding architecture is the sequential inference machine, or SIM. In the second phase of the research, parallelism will be a major focus that will appear in the successor language KL-1 and in the successor architecture known as a parallel inference machine, or PIM.

PSI. The design of the inference machine is being done in stages. The first implementation of a SIM is a medium performance machine known as a personal sequential inference, or PSI, machine, which has been delivered to ICOT in prototype form. The next phase will be to extend this machine to a "super PSI" with several times the performance of the PSI. The PSI is intended to be a powerful personal workstation that can be a major tool for subsequent phases of the project. Its performance is roughly 20 to 30K lips, and the super PSI should reach 100K to 1M lips.

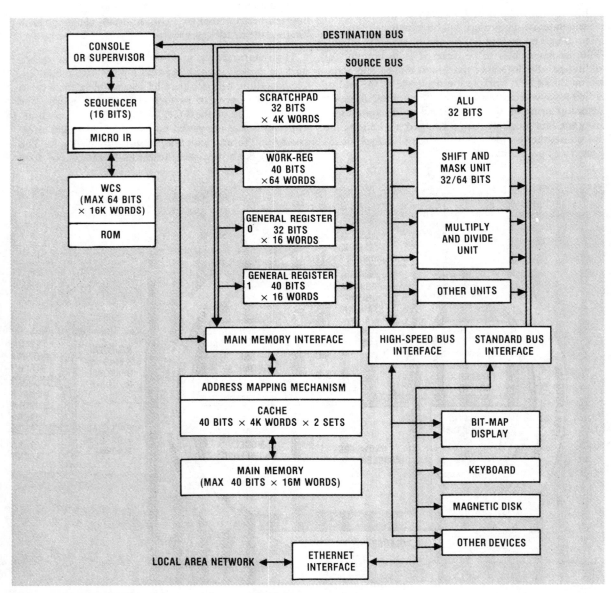

Figure 2. A block diagram of a personal sequential inference system.

A block diagram of the PSI appears in Figure 2. Some of the principal characteristics of the architecture are

- efficient support for logic programming in hardware and firmware,
- sophisticated man-machine communications including a high-resolution, bit-mapped display and pointing device,
- local-area network interface,
- architectural support for process switching for a single-user multiprocess system,
- three machine modes—kernel, supervisor, and user,
- microprogrammed control and a tagged-data architecture,
- hardware support for the logic programming processes of unification and resolution,
- a cache memory for speed enhancement,
- address-translation hardware to provide multiple virtual stacks in main memory, and
- hardware and firmware support for collecting performance statistics such as the number of variables per unification, the mean time for one resolution, the cache-hit ratio, and the locality of addressing patterns.

Virtual memory support and parallel inferencing are extensions not present in PSI that may be implemented in the super PSI.

The logical address for PSI is 32 bits. Eight bits of the address designate 256 different areas of the logical-address space. Each area can be used as an independent stack or heap. KL-0 uses four independent stacks, one each for control, local variables, global variables, and a trail. These stacks can be shared among processes.

Knowledge-base systems

A knowledge base is an extension of a database. If one views a database as a collection of facts and relations among facts, a knowledge base is a database plus a collection of rules from which it is possible to manipulate the database to infer new facts and relations not explicitly stored. Knowledge-base management is built upon techniques for representing, storing, retrieving, updating, and acquiring knowledge. Key to the implementation of a knowledge-base machine is the underlying database machine architecture. Consequently, a parallel relational database machine architecture is an appropriate starting point for a knowledge-base machine.

Delta. The FGCS is designing a relational database machine called Delta, shown in Figure 3. In this system a query generated in a PSI (tied to Delta through a network) is translated into a command string sent to Delta. Commands received are interpreted into a sequence of relational algebra primitives that activate the remainder of the processor (see Figure 3). At the cost of a potentially high performance burden, the relational model has been selected because of its high data independence, simplicity, and the uniformity of the operator set. FGCS researchers are investigating ways to achieve the necessary performance while retaining the major advantages of relational databases.

Grace. One of the major bottlenecks in relational database machines is the "join" operation. When a join operation is executed on two relations, the size of the resulting relation in the worst case may be as large as the

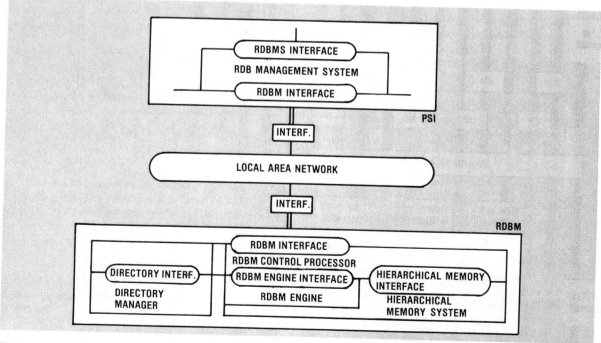

Figure 3. System organization of the Delta, a relational-database machine, or RDBM, at the Institute for New Generation Technology. The directory manager controls access to the database, the relational engine for manipulating data, and the hierarchical memory for storing the data. The data produced by a query are collected and reformatted as necessary in the control processor and then returned to the PSI that initiated the query.

March 1984

539

product of the sizes of the two relations. Even in the best case, efficient implementations of the join operator usually sort each of the two relations being joined before the join itself is done. Sorting time grows as $N \log N$ for relations of size N. Consequently, as the size of a relational database grows, the processing power required to do join operations must grow faster than the size of the data.

A number of research projects have looked into architectures for high-performance joins.[2-7] One of the more promising approaches is that of Babb[6] which uses a hashed bit array for the join. The purpose of the bit array is to filter out data that cannot be joined, and thereby reduce the processing load by manipulating only the data that participates in the join. While it may not be possible to filter out all useless data, the reduction actually achieved might be large enough to make this method quite attractive for implementation.

At the University of Tokyo, a relational algebra machine that makes use of joinability filters is currently being investigated.[8] This machine, known as Grace, uses hash and sort techniques to organize data into clusters. Hashing distributes data into "buckets." The idea is that data in different buckets cannot be joined together, and the actual work involved in joining data reduces to joining data that are hashed to the same bucket. This method of filtering data is independent of the joinability filter used by Babb[6] and McGregar.[7] Therefore, it may be possible to use the joinability filter in conjunction with

the hash and sort technique to reduce substantially the total amount of data processed. Since the buckets produced by the hashing algorithm are independent of each other, they can be processed in parallel, and the architecture is therefore quite suitable for a parallel implementation. However, there are several open questions being treated in the current study regarding impediments to fully parallel execution. A more complete discussion of the architecture of Grace and its operation is given by Kitsuregawa.[8,9]

Parallel inferencing

At the University of Tokyo, a language known as Paralog (from parallel Prolog) has resulted from a recent study on parallelism in logic programming. Except for the inclusion of special operators that take advantage of sequential execution, Prolog could be viewed as a parallel language. In Paralog, such operators have been eliminated, and parallelism is achieved through parallel execution of the OR alternatives. Goal statements, therefore, are executed in a breadth-first manner as opposed to Prolog's sequential depth-first manner. The language has been tested and measured on the Topstar II experimental data-flow machine,[10] and it has become clear that there are yet more opportunities for parallelism than just the OR parallelism captured in this experiment.

The parallel inference-machine model currently being investigated appears in Figure 4. It is able to execute

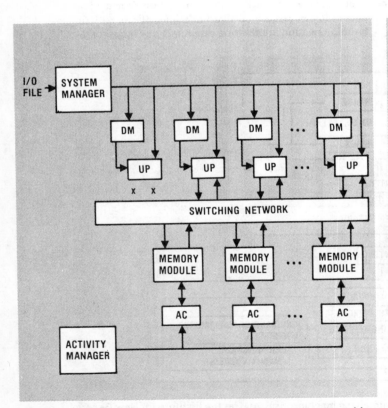

Figure 4. The system organization of the parallel inference machine at the University of Tokyo (UP = unify processor, DM = definition memory, and AC = activity controller).

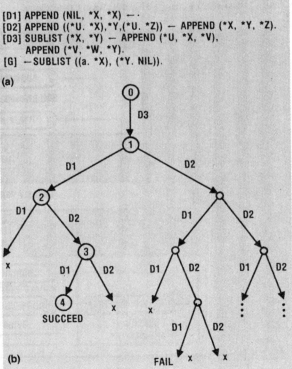

Figure 5. An example of Prolog programming (a) and the search tree in the case of left-first unification of literals (b).

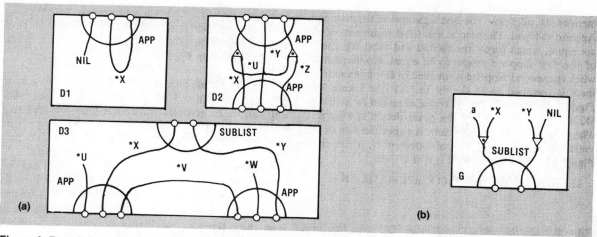

Figure 6. Templates to corresponding statements (see Figure 5) constituting a proof diagram. The list notation of Figure 5 is represented by an operator depicted as a triangle with a dot. Statements are represented by templates in (a) and the goal clause G is represented in (b). Each term in a statement is indicated by a half circle; an upper half circle indicates the goal of a statement and a lower half circle indicates a clause on the right-hand side of a statement. The small circles along the perimeter of each template represent the arguments supplied to the corresponding clause or goal. Links between arguments show how arguments of clauses and goals are related.

Paralog directly; individual processors are included for unification operations and activity control, while data are held in definition memories and main memory. In addition, the simple example in Figure 5 illustrates how Prolog is directly executed on this architecture.

Program statements. The Prolog program in the example consists of four statements. The first two define the Append operation. To the left of the arrow is the statement head and to the right is the condition under which the head is true. The first statement may be read as "when any variable $*X$ is appended to the empty list (nil), the resulting list is the variable $(*X)$." Since the right-hand side is empty, the statement is true for all conditions. The second statement indicates that the list obtained by appending the variable $*Y$ to the list $(*U.*X)$ is the list $(*U.*Z)$, provided that $*Z$ is the list obtained by appending $*Y$ to $*X$. In Prolog, a variable is indicated by a prefixed asterisk; if some Prolog construct is substituted for a variable in any statement, the same construct must be substituted for every instance of that variable in that statement. The two statements for Append not only define Append but give a constructive algorithm for appending one list to another when they are executed in a Prolog environment.

The Sublist statement says that $*X$ is a sublist of $*Y$ under one condition: there is a list $*V$ composed of $*X$ appended to $*U$ such that the list $*Y$ is composed of some list $*W$ appended to $*V$ (that is, the list $*Y$ consists of $*U$ followed by $*X$ followed by $*W$). Either or both of the lists $*U$ and $*W$ may be empty.

The last line of the program has no left-hand side. This is an executable statement that asks if the list $(a.X)$ is a sublist of $*Y$. We call this type of construction a *goal clause* of the program. Figure 5 also shows the decision tree that outlines how the statement is executed. At the root node of the tree is the initial goal, G. To evaluate G we must evaluate Sublist (arc D3). The Sublist statement results in the invocation of the Append statement. But

there are two choices, and the decision tree shows that both D1 and D2 will be executed while seeking a condition that satisfies statement G. The machine model that executes the statements is shown in Figure 6.

An example of the execution of the program is given in Figure 7; as illustrated, statement D3 is invoked initially and, in turn, invokes D1 (see Figure 7a). The first argu-

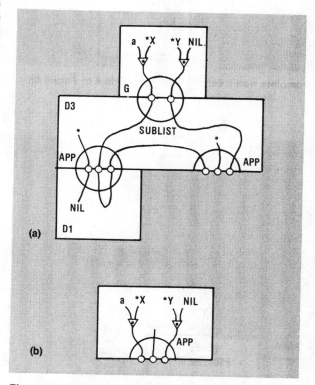

Figure 7. Examples of goal frames including the goal frame of node 2 in the search tree in Figure 5b (a) and the reduced form of the same goal frame (b).

ment of D1, nil, forces the first argument of the matching Append to be nil. The second and third arguments of D1 are equal, which forces the second and third arguments of the first Append clause to be equal. Consequently, when the second Append is invoked in D3, its first argument is specified to be the list $(a.*X)$ (see Figure 7b). Figure 8 shows a completed frame obtained by invoking D2 and D1 after reaching the point shown in Figure 7. The result returned by this frame is a specification of the variables $*X$ and $*Y$ in the goal statement G. In this case, Figure 8 shows that the goal is true if

$$(a. *X) = (*U. \text{nil}), \text{ and } (*Y. \text{nil}) = (*U. *W)$$

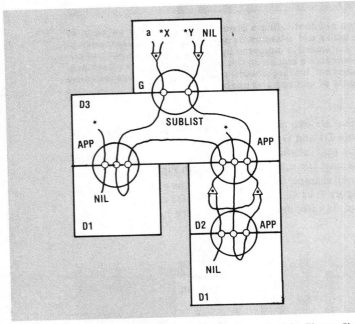

Figure 8. A complete frame corresponding to node 4 in Figure 5b.

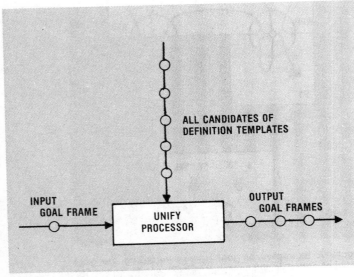

Figure 9. The basic concept for a unify processor.

In other words, $(a. *X)$ is a sublist of $(a. *X. *W)$. Of course, this answer is not unique and other answers will be produced as the inference engine traverses the execution tree shown in Figure 6.

Types of parallelism. In this article, the process of matching up input and output parameters has been called *unification*. In general, unification does not lead to a single solution and could, in fact, fail when there is no consistent way to assign argument values to a goal or produce many results when multiple possibilities exist.

As shown in Figure 8, any collection of templates arranged consistently could constitute a proof diagram. By examining the data flow in the proof diagrams, we can estimate where the parallelism might be. There are at least three types of parallelism revealed by the proof diagrams:

- OR parallelism,
- AND parallelism, and
- unification parallelism.

In the case of Figure 6, Append can be evaluated in more than one way; any goal that has multiple right-hand sides can have all right-hand sides evaluated concurrently. This is an example of OR parallelism. In the template view of the machine, OR parallelism is implemented by increasing the number of goal frames so that each goal frame may be associated with a different definition template.

Parallel implementation of OR parallelism is achieved easily by using many copies of inference engines, each capable of processing an independent goal.

Rule D3 has two clauses joined by an AND operator (see Figure 6); the two clauses can be evaluated concurrently in some instances and therefore produce AND parallelism. However, the rules of unification force us to assign arguments consistently across the several clauses of an AND construction; consequently, AND parallelism is more difficult to control. The template model of an inference machine provides for AND parallelism by applying simultaneous matchings to several clauses of a template.

AND parallelism is rather difficult to implement if it must maintain consistency. Additional research in this area is necessary to determine how best to implement AND parallelism.

The last type of parallelism, unification parallelism, is best exhibited through Figure 8. The templates in Figure 8 identify one of many possible ways to unify the goal arguments by matching arguments consistently within the templates, and parallelism is achieved by finding many of the possible unifications concurrently.

Unification parallelism presents an interesting opportunity for capturing some parallelism of execution, but it probably requires special hardware support that is not well understood at this time. Figure 9 shows a unification processor, suggesting how it might perform the unification. For parallelism, a system would use many unification processors; a goal frame is sent from a memory module to a unify processor through a switching network. The unify processor executes a unification operation by matching the initial goal frame to definition templates (the figure shows definition templates streaming into the unification processor.) Each template is matched with the goal to determine if one or more variables unify. Parallelism might be provided internally in the unification processor through pipeline techniques, but we may also achieve parallelism by running many independent unifications on different unification processors.

The research and development targets of the FGCS project are central functions of knowledge information processing such as problem-solving systems, inference systems, and knowledge-base systems. These functions may be handled more efficiently in FGCS architectures than in conventional computer systems.[11] FGCS is therefore obliged to move toward the target systems through a 10-year process of trial and error, encompassing approximately three years for the initial stage of idea development, four years for the middle stage of prototyping, and three years for the final stage of evaluation. FGCS hopes not only to conduct creative computer research, but also to make substantive contributions in the form of a new generation of computers. ∎

References

1. T. Moto-oka, ed., *Fifth-Generation Computer Systems,* North-Holland, New York, 1982.

2. H. T. Kung and P. L. Lehman, "Systolic (VLSI) Arrays for Relational Database Operations," in *Proc. ACM SIGMOD,* May 1980, pp. 105-116.

3. S. W. Song, "A Highly Concurrent Tree Machine for Database Applications," in *Proc. Int'l. Conf. Parallel Processing,* 1980, pp. 259-268.

4. Y. Tanaka et al., "Pipeline Searching and Sorting Modules as Components of Data Flow Database Computers," *Proc. IFIP,* North-Holland, New York, 1980, pp. 427-432.

5. Y. Oda, "Database Machine Architecture Using a Data Partitioning Network," in *Institute of Electronics and Communication Engineers of Japan, Tech. Group Meeting,* tech. report EC80-72, IECE Japan, 1981 (in Japanese).

6. E. Babb, "Implementing a Relational Database by Means of Specialized Hardware," *ACM Trans. Database Systems,* Vol. 4, No. 1, 1979, pp. 1-29.

7. D. R. McGregar et al., "High Performance Hardware for Database Systems," in *Systems for Large Data Bases,* North-Holland, New York, 1976, pp. 103-116.

8. M. Kitsuregawa et al., "Application of Hash to Database Machine and Its Architecture," *New Generation Computing,* Vol. 1, No. 1, Springer-Verlag, New York, 1983, pp. 63-74.

9. M. Kitsuregawa et al., "GRACE: Relational Algebra Machine Based on Hash and Sort—Its Design Concepts," *JIP,* Vol. 6, No. 3, 1983, pp. 148-155.

10. H. Aida and T. Moto-oka, "Performance Measurement of Parallel Logic Programming System—Paralog," *Proc. Prolog Environment Workshop,* 1982.

11. T. Moto-oka, and K. Fuchi, "The Architectures in the Fifth-Generation Computers," *Proc. IFIP,* North-Holland, New York, 1983, pp. 589-602.

Tohru Moto-oka, a professor of electrical engineering in the University of Tokyo, is the chairman of the promoting committee for the fifth-generation computer systems project. His current activities include research on computer architectures, inference machines, database machines, parallel processing, and computer-aided logic design systems.

He received both his bachelor and doctor of engineering in electrical engineering from the University of Tokyo.

Harold S. Stone is the author of "Computer Research in Japan." For his biography, see p. 32.

Comments or questions about this article can be addressed to Moto-oka at the Electrical Engineering Department, University of Tokyo, 7-3-1 Hongo, Bunyko-ku, Tokyo 113, Japan. (In the US, Harold Stone, 64 Morgan Circle, Amherst, MA 01002.)

PROCEEDINGS OF THE INTERNATIONAL CONFERENCE
ON FIFTH GENERATION COMPUTER SYSTEMS 1984,
edited by ICOT. © ICOT, 1984

HARDWARE DESIGN AND IMPLEMENTATION OF
THE PERSONAL SEQUENTIAL INFERENCE MACHINE (PSI)

Kazuo Taki, Minoru Yokota, Akira Yamamoto,
Hiroshi Nishikawa, and Shunichi Uchida

and

Hiroshi Nakashima, and Akitoshi Mitsuishi

ICOT Research Center
Institute for New Generation Computer Technology
Tokyo, Japan

Information Systems and
Electronics Development Laboratory
Mitsubishi Electric Corp.
Kamakura, Japan

ABSTRACT

The Personal Sequential Inference Machine (PSI) is a personal computer designed as a tool for software and hardware development in Japan's Fifth Generation Computer Systems (FGCS) project. This paper describes PSI's hardware systems and the unique features of its data processing and sequence control units.

The PSI system adopts a logic programing language as its primary language. It consists of a large main memory (16 mega words), interactive I/O devices, and operating system support and language support hardware. PSI's machine language is a high-level language based on logic programming, and its description level is very similar to that of Prolog. It is called Kernel Language Version 0 (KL0). Unification and backtracking, the principal operations of KL0, are performed by the KL0 firmware interpreter in cooperation with several dedicated hardware components. These include branch and dispatch facility testing tags, a cache memory designed for stack access, and a high-speed local memory (called a work file) designed for use in tail recursive optimization.

Commercially available high-speed Schottkey TTL ICs are used in the CPU. Printed circuit boards for the CPU, main memory, and I/O controllers are mounted in a single cabinet along with secondary storage devices. A prototype machine has been manufactured and microprogram development is nearly complete.

1 INTRODUCTION

Japan's Fifth Generation Computer Project has started using a new logic-based programming language as its primary language for both software and hardware research and development. However, programming environments for such languages have not been sufficiently developed in conventional computer systems in terms of their processing speed, memory space, language support, and flexibility for experimentation. In order to build a research and development tool fulfilling these requirements, a high-level language machine specialized for logic programming is under development at ICOT and supporting companies [Uchida 83], [Yokota 83], [Nishikawa 83]. The machine is called the Personal Sequential Inference Machine (PSI), reflecting its machine features and functions.

To develop a viable programming environment for

logic programming, several targets have been established for PSI, as follows:

(a) Efficient execution of logic programming language KL0 (Kernel Language version 0), which is the machine language of PSI [Chikayama 84-1]

(b) A machine architecture that supports the SIMPOS operating system developed for PSI [Hattori 83]

(c) Memory size and execution speed sufficient for executing large application programs. Specifically, as compared with the compiler version of Dec-10 Prolog [Bowen 81] on the Dec-2060, PSI will have a maximum of 16M words of memory, which is 64 times larger than that of Dec-10 Prolog, and will attain approximately 30K LIPS (logical inferences per second) in processing speed, which is almost equivalent to the Dec-10 Prolog on the Dec-2060.

(d) Highly interactive I/O devices, such as a bit-mapped display, mouse, etc.

(e) A local area network (LAN) system for inter-PSI communication and resource sharing

(f) Reasonable physical size for personal use and practical cost-effectiveness

(g) Reliability as a research and development tool

(h) Early availability

Other target specifications are listed below. These involve the plan to use PSI as a tool for architectural research into efficient execution mechanisms for logic programming.

(a) The adoption of hardware mechanisms resulting from ICOT research that increase unification speed

(b) A flexible microprogrammed sequence controller with large writable control storage

(c) Hardware and firmware evaluation facilities for measuring dynamic characteristics and collecting statistical data

To satisfy these specifications, we have proceeded with the designs for the architecture and the hardware. In this paper, PSI's hardware system and its unique features will mainly be described. The PSI architecture is presented first, then the hardware configuration and the detailed specifications for the specially designed part of the PSI CPU are described. The action and usage of each hardware component of the CPU at the time of program execution are also mentioned.

2 PSI ARCHITECTURE

In this chapter, we summarize the hardware architecture of PSI mainly from the machine-language level, i.e., from the system programmer's point of view.

2.1 Word format

A word consists of 40 bits, as shown in Fig.1. Eight bits are used for a tag and 32 bits for data. The tag contains two mark bits for garbage collection (GC tag) and six bits for a data tag that represents one of the following data types:

    undefined, symbolic atom,

    integer, floating point number,

    stack/heap vector, string, code, built-in code,

    local/global variable, local/global reference,

    hooked variable, control marks, etc.

2.2 Machine instructions

KL0, a logic programming language whose specifications are almost equivalent to those of Dec-10 Prolog, is designed to define the functions of the PSI machine instructions. The representation of the machine instruction, shown in Fig.2, is a simple converted form of the KL0 source program. Each instruction code can correspond to each component of the source program. The machine instruction is executed by the firmware interpreter, by which unification and backtracking are also performed. The reason for the adoption of high-level machine instructions is discussed in section 4.1.

The representation of the machine instruction of a KL0 clause contains a clause header, head arguments and some body goals (cf. Fig.2). These body goals include user-defined predicates (which are actually pointers to the instruction representation of the clause and arguments) and built-in predicates. Most built-in predicates have a compact format that contains one operation code and at most three arguments in one word. Each of the arguments has a 3-bit tag and 5-bit data. When the built-in predicate is executed, a corresponding firmware subroutine is called directly according to the operation code. If integers or variable numbers appearing as arguments are small enough to represent in five bits, most built-in predicates can be packed in one word. This representation is quite effective in saving memory space and shortening the execution time.

2.3 KL0

The specification of KL0 is summarized as follows:

(a) It is based on a subset of Dec-10 Prolog.

(b) It has extended control structures.

(c) It has hardware control functions.

"Subset of Dec-10 Prolog" means that KL0 does not include built-in predicates compatible with those of Dec-10 Prolog for internal data base management, such as Assert or Retract, and I/O predicates, such as Read or Write. These predicates are replaced by user-defined predicates using primitive built-in predicates of the hardware control functions.

The hardware control functions correspond to direct hardware operations to handle hardware registers, memory, and the I/O bus.

The extended control structures [Takagi 83] contain such functions as Bind-hook, On-backtrack, Extended-cut, etc. Bind-hook is a special function for procedure invocation, which calls a previously registered procedure when a specified variable is unified to a value. On-backtrack is a function that invokes a previously registered procedure only when backtracking occurs and control returns to the registration point of the procedure. Extended-cut specifies the level of a predicate's call to cut the or nodes of that level. These extended control structures enhance the descriptive power of the language, but require many run-time supports (operations that can not be determined during compilation).

p1(X,Y,test) :- p2(X,Z), add(Z,5,A), p3(A,256,Y)

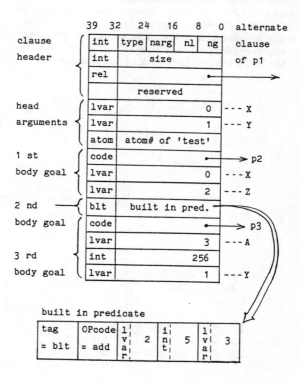

Fig.2   Representation of Machine Instructions

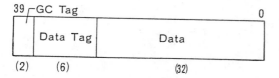

Fig.1   Word Format

All the system programs and the user programs are written in logic programming language ESP (Extended Self-contained Prolog) [Chikayama 83-2] [Chikayama 84-2], which is the system description language and user language of PSI. These programs are compiled into KL0 for execution.

2.4 Execution environment for KL0

To execute KL0 programs, the interpreter uses four stacks, namely, local, global, control, and trail stacks, and one heap area. The heap area is used to store machine instructions and vectors (vectors include usual structured data such as lists and arrays). For representing structured data, the structure-sharing method [Warren 77] is used. The utilization of the stacks and execution control mechanisms are basically the same as in Dec-10 Prolog [Bowen 81][warren 77]. However, Dec-10 Prolog's local stack is separated into control and local stacks in PSI, because an independent control frame is needed for extended control structures.

Fig.3 shows the execution environment of KL0 during unification. There are machine instructions for the clauses of 'caller' and 'callee' in the heap area, and instruction pointers for each. As in Dec-10 Prolog, a group of variable cells, called a frame, is made corresponding to caller or callee. These frames are placed on the local stack for variables and on the global stack for variables in the structured data. To access a variable cell, the relative distance from the frame base that is pointed to by a frame-base pointer is used. The control stack is used to store frames containing information of the return chain and the backtrack chain, as well as pointers to the environment for continuing execution at the return point. The trail stack is used for storing cell addresses that must be recovered to the initial state on backtracking and is accessed using

its stack-top pointer. These pointers, namely, instruction pointers, frame-base pointers, and stack-top pointers, constitute the execution environment of KL0.

2.5 Address representation

To execute KL0 programs, four stacks and a heap area are required. Concurrent execution of multiple processes is necessary for PSI, and sharing of instruction codes and variable spaces among the processes are also required. To satisfy these requirements, the address space is divided into independent logical spaces, called 'areas', and each is identified by an area number. An area can be assigned to one of four stacks of a process, or to a heap area shared among processes for code storage and common variable spaces. Thus, the address representation of PSI, shown in Fig.4, contains an 8-bit area number and a 24-bit inner area address. This means that there can be up to 256 areas, each of which can be assigned physical memory up to 16M words.

2.6 Address translation

PSI can have up to 16M words of physical memory. To allocate and relocate physical memory more efficiently to each area, an address translation mechanism is introduced. Physical memory is managed in 1K-word pages. Pages are allocated to each area on demand, and deallocation is performed by a garbage collector. Fig.5 illustrates the address translation mechanism, which is performed using two tables, one for the page map base and another for the page map.

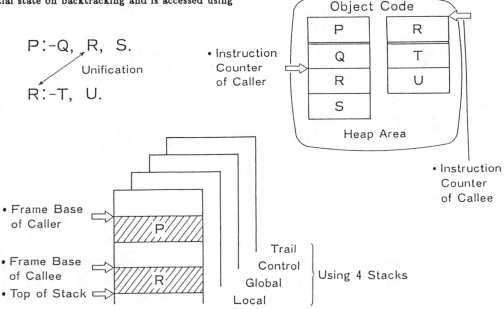

Fig.3   Execution Environment for KL0

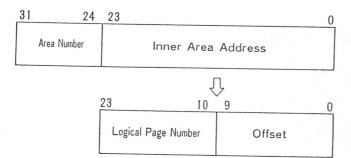

31	24	23	0
Area Number		Inner Area Address	

⇩

23	10	9	0
Logical Page Number		Offset	

An Area: A Logical Address Space of
Maximum 16 M Words
Whole Address Space (32 Bits):
Consisting of Independent 256 Areas

Fig.4   Address Representation

2.7 Multiple processes

Many programs, such as the editor, compiler, device handlers, and user programs, are executed as different processes in PSI. Each of these processes has a process status that includes KL0 execution environment and hardware control information, such as processor priority for interrupt processing. This environment and information is collected in a table, called a process control block (PCB).

The PCB of an inactive process is stored in a local memory in the CPU, whereas the PCB of an active process (current PCB) is distributed in CPU registers. The contents of the current PCB are swapped by the firmware when process switching occurs. Process switching is initiated by an interrupt or various built-in predicates. The maximum number of processes is 63 due to the limitation on the number of areas. However, this is sufficient for the operating system and most user programs.

2.8 Interruption

A vectored interrupt system is adopted in PSI. An interrupt vector is prepared for each interrupt source (e.g., an I/O device) and a registered process identifier is assigned to each vector. When an interrupt occurs, a process is switched to the corresponding registered process by the firmware. There are eight interrupt levels, two for external and six for internal interrupts. PSI also has a non-maskable trap system to deal with errors that occur during program execution.

Garbage collection (GC) is performed as an independent process in PSI and is invoked by a GC trap. However, some interrupts, such as hardware errors and urgent interrupts from I/O devices, may take priority over garbage collection. These urgent interrupts are handled by special processes, called supra-GC processes, that use some special areas for stacks and a heap. These areas, called GC-less areas, are not subject to garbage collection.

3 SYSTEM CONFIGURATION

3.1 Configuration of the total system

Fig.6 shows the system configuration of PSI. The PSI CPU contains a sequence control unit, a data processing unit, a memory module, which includes a cache and an address translation unit, and an I/O bus interface unit. These are connected to each other by internal buses. The PSI I/O system contains a IEEE-796 standard bus and several I/O devices. A console processor is connected to the CPU for maintenance, initialization, and debugging support. A mini-computer (PDP11/23plus) can also be connected to the CPU instead of the console processor as a more powerful debugging aid.

3.2 I/O devices

PSI has the following I/O devices:

a bit-mapped display (1200 x 900 pixels),

an optical mouse, a keyboard,

hard disk drives (37M bytes x 2),

floppy disk drives (1M bytes x 2),

a local area network (LAN),

and a serial printer

Some commercially available devices that have IEEE-796 standard interfaces can also be connected. There is a 512K-byte buffer memory on the I/O bus, which is used for data transfer to secondary storage devices and the LAN. The buffer memory is also managed as a disk cache by the software. The bit-mapped display controller has raster operation functions and independent image memory. The image memory can store more than ten full screen images and character fonts. Window images are normally stored here to decrease the load on the I/O bus.

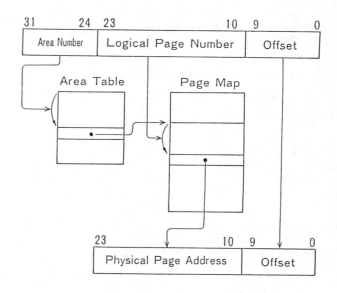

Fig.5   Address Translation Mechanism

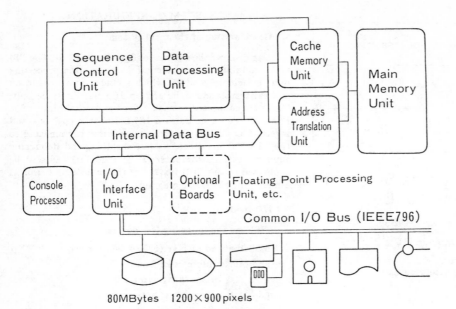

80MBytes   1200×900 pixels

Fig.6   System Configuration

4 HARDWARE DESIGN

4.1 Basic design concepts

In the PSI hardware design, priority was given to sufficient execution speed and large memory space, while keeping reasonable physical size and early availability. To satisfy these requirements, the design philosophy called for avoiding hardware complexity and for utilizing microprogram techniques. However, the PSI CPU has adopted some specialized hardware mechanisms concentrating on speedup of the KL0 firmware interpreter, especially of unification and execution controls. To satisfy the requirement for fast development, it was decided to utilize commercially-available LSIs and time-tested implementation techniques. In this section, the basic design concepts that determine PSI hardware architecture are discussed.

(1) Machine instruction level and CPU architecture

Two different design methods were considered concerning the machine instruction and CPU architecture designs. The first method takes high-level machine instructions, whose level is nearly the same as the source language level, like those of PSI. The representation of the machine instructions can closely correspond to the source program; thus, the size of the instruction code is held down. In this method, machine instructions are executed by the firmware interpreter. For interpretive execution, it is useless to adopt such heavy hardware as an instruction pre-fetch unit or a pipelined execution unit because microprogram branch occurs very frequently and it breaks the execution pipes. The second method is to choose low-level machine instructions. In this method, source programs are compiled into machine instructions, fetched by an instruction pre-fetch unit and executed less interpretively (determinately) by a pipelined execution unit (for example, [Tick 84]). In this method, the determinate instruction execution mechanism makes the hardware easy to optimize; thus, it is more suitable for high-speed execution. However, the complexity and the amount of the hardware will increase.

The extended control structures of KL0 [Takagi 83] require several run-time supports (operations that can not be determined during compilation). These run-time supports are easily realized by the interpretive execution method which doesn't require complex hardware. And translation cost between source programs and machine instructions is very low for the method. For these reason, PSI has chosen the interpretive execution method. Since the method doesn't require frequent memory access to the instruction codes, because of the small instruction code size, the instruction pre-fetch unit or the instruction cache memory can be omitted. The interface between the CPU and the main memory is then simplified to a single connection between the CPU and one cache memory. As a result, PSI has adopted a simple hardware architecture. However, several hardware components are specially designed to enhance the performance of the KL0 firmware interpreter.

(b) Speeding up stack access

In executing a language like Dec-10 Prolog, information for backtracking is often pushed and left on the stack, and thus the frame of the caller clause is often buried deep in the stack. Because of this, the stack accesses scatter both to the top and to the inner part of the stack. Hence, a stack cache that has only a copy of the stack-top data in high-speed memory doesn't work efficiently. An independent hardware stack is also unsuitable because it is not large enough to be used for the global stack KL0 requires. Accordingly, a cache memory that is a more general hardware facility has been chosen to speed up PSI and a few functions suited to stack access have been adopted for the cache memory.

(c) Specialized hardware

Data paths and the basic CPU control timing have been kept as simple as possible. However, branch mechanisms for micro instructions, such as conditional branch and dispatch, which are often used in the firmware interpreter, and a register file used for the tail recursion optimization [Warren 80] are specially designed for the efficient execution of KL0. These are described in detail in following sections.

4.2 Micro instructions

4.2.1 Control features

A very simple pipelined control is used to fetch the next micro instruction in parallel with execution of the current micro instruction. The branch control circuit is designed so that the execution result of a micro instruction, such as an ALU flag or a register value, can be used in the immediately subsequent micro instruction as a jump condition or as dispatch source data. These simplify microprogram coding and increase the execution speed of unification, which uses many branches and dispatch operations.

4.2.2 Micro instruction format

As shown in Fig.7, a micro instruction has a 64-bit word length and has a field assignment that enables effective parallel control of hardware resources. There are three micro instruction types. They have common fields between bit 63 to 22. These fields mainly specify data operations. Bits 21 to 0 have different meanings in each instruction type and mainly specify branch controls and ALU operations.

Type 1 instructions specify various conditional branches and dispatch operations. Relative addresses (up to $\pm$ 256) are used for conditional branches. Arithmetic operations are available in type 1. Type 2 instructions specify absolute jump, logical operations, and bit rotation of the barrel shifter. Type 3 instructions specify various opera-

tions, such as arithmetic and logical operations, bit rotation, tag replacement with immediate data, I/O bus controls, etc. However, jump operations are limited to indirect jumps using the jump register.

The three-operand operation is specified by the data operation fields. Namely, two operands specified by the SC1F and SC2F fields are processed by the ALU and stored in a register specified by DSTF field in one micro instruction cycle. One of frequently used registers can also be specified as an destination register by the multi-destination field. Data specified by the SC2F field can be shifted and masked by the barrel shifter and field extractor before the ALU operation. Memory access control is specified by the cache control field (CCF) independent of the data operations mentioned above. DRF and LARF fields specify the selections of the data register and the logical address register used in memory access from PDR and CDR, and PLAR and CLAR. LAIF specifies the automatic increment of the logical address register.

4.3 Data processing unit

4.3.1 Configuration of the data processing unit

Fig.8 shows the configuration of the data processing unit. A register file, called a work file, the ALU for 32-bit operation with barrel shifter and field extractor at its entrance, address and data registers for memory interface, and tag circuits are connected to each other by internal buses. There are three such buses; two are source data busses and one is a destination bus. Each is 40-bits wide; 8 bits are for tag transfer and 32 bits are for data transfer. These internal buses also connect other units that are shown in Fig.6. The work file (which has many addressing modes), pairs of memory interface registers, and tag operation circuits are special hardware for KL0 execution.

4.3.2 Treatment of tags

Tag processing (which doesn't contain branch and dispatch using tags) rarely appears in usual microprograms with the exception of tag replacement and tag comparison.

60	50	40	30	20	10	0

| RSVF | DBGF | DRRF | LARF | LAIF | MDF | DSTF | SC1F | SMF | SC2F | CCF | BYRF | FF1F | O11F / 0 / 1 | IALF / ALF / ALF | CNDF / BIRF / BIRF | RAF / AAF | / / EALFF,SIF22F,FJ2F,BCF,TEF / TVF | Type 1 / Type 2 / Type 3 |

Fig.7   Micro Instruction Format

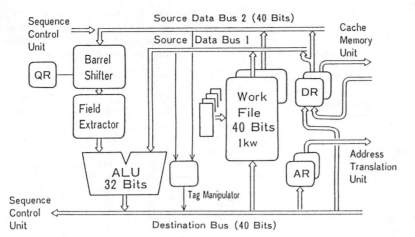

Fig.8   Configuration of the Data Processing Unit

When data processing or data transfer is performed, tag data from one source bus is transferred directly to the destination bus or completely replaced by immediate tag data and transferred. Tags on two source buses are compared in parallel with the data processing and an equality flag is set. This can be tested in a conditional branch instruction. Only the garbage collection microprogram requires tag processing. Bit operation of the GC tag is performed by the same ALU for the data processing. The tag usage in the microprogram sequence control is described in section 4.4. Only the data registers of the memory interface and the work file have tags.

4.3.3 Barrel shifter and field extractor

The barrel shifter can perform up to 32 bits of rotating shift. It can also perform left/right shift of 1 bit combined with the Q register, which is used for multiplication and division as specified by the ALU control field.

The field extractor is a masking circuit that has three different types of masking operations, namely, the low most 5 bit through, the lowest byte through and the lower double byte through operations. These masking operations are often used for extracting operands of built-in predicates, string data, and packed information of machine instructions in combination with the barrel shifter.

4.3.4 ALU and a swap circuit

The ALU is constructed from commercially available ALU LSIs. The ALU control field of the micro instruction has an encoded format that controls only the required functions of the ALU. Arithmetic operations include addition, subtraction, those with carry or borrow, multiplication and division combined with the shift and Q-register operations, and the 24-bit operations for inner area address calculation mentioned in section 2.5. Some flags, such as carry, overflow, and zero, are set for use in conditional branches when flag setting is enabled by micro instruction FF1F field. Logical operations include THROUGH, AND, OR, EXCLUSIVE-OR, AND with SWAP, and OR with SWAP. 'With SWAP' means

that bytes are exchanged between byte 0 and 3, and between 1 and 2. The swap circuit is positioned at the exit of the ALU. It is used for re-directing numerical byte data and byte string data; these have the opposite byte order. This circuit is also used to re-direct bytes in the I/O bus access.

4.3.5 Address registers and data registers

There are pairs of memory interface address registers and data registers called PLAR, CLAR, PDR and CDR. LAR means logical address register; P and C mean parent and current of predicate call respectively. When unification is performed, machine instructions and data of both the parent clause (caller) and the current clause (callee) must be fetched from memory. Registers prefixed P and C are used for memory access for the parent clause and the current clause respectively. Tags of PDR and CDR are used for tag dispatch and the least-significant 5 bits of PDR and CDR are used for addressing the work file, as described in later sections. PLAR and CLAR are automatically incremented when contiguous data is being read or written.

4.3.6 Work File

The work file (WF) is a multi-purpose register file most frequently used in the data processing unit. The work file has a 40-bit x 1K-word capacity and has many addressing modes. The WF can be read from and written to different arbitrary addresses in a single micro cycle. That is, data read from the WF is sent to the ALU and the result is rewritten to different WF addresses in one micro cycle. The first 16 words of the WF are designed as dual-port registers for use as general registers. Fig.9 shows the following WF addressing modes.

(a) Direct addressing

The first and last 64 words of the WF constitute an area directly addressable by micro instructions. The first 16 words are used as general registers and the subsequent 48 words are mainly used as logical registers containing information of the current KL0 execution environment. The last 64 words are called the constant area because the mask patterns and constants used by the firmware interpreter are stored there.

(b) Indirect addressing

WFAR1 and WFAR2 are address registers of WF. The WF can be indirectly accessed by any address using these registers. These registers have auto-increment and auto-decrement, and boundary detection functions. The latter means that flags are set when the contents of the register points to the 32-word or 256-word boundary of WF. These functions enable a part of the WF to be used as a stack area. In practice, they are used to access the local frame buffer and trail buffer, described later.

(c) Indirect addressing using PDR and CDR

In this addressing mode, a WF address is generated by concatenating the content of WFBR and the least-significant 5 bits of PDR or CDR (whichever is specified by the DRF field). This is used to access a local variable cell on the local frame buffer (LFB). WFBR points to the base of LFB, and PDR or CDR holds the cell number of a local variable that is a part of the machine instruction code fetched from memory.

(d) Direct addressing using a base register

In this addressing mode, a WF address is generated by concatenating the contents of WFCBR and a 5-bit direct address specified by the micro instruction. WFCBR is used to point to the base of the extended constant area or work area.

(e) Local frame buffer

The local frame buffer (LFB) is a temporary local frame for a current clause (corresponds to a current frame on a local stack, as shown in Fig.3) created in the WF, not on the local stack in main memory. In the unification using LFB, the local variables of the parent clause that are required for unification are first copied to LFB, then unified with the arguments of the clause head of the current clause. The LFB then temporarily becomes a current local frame. When the execution proceeds to the first body goal of the current clause, if it is a user-defined clause, LFB is pushed onto the local stack and a new temporary local frame for the new current clause is created in the WF. However, if the first body goal is a built-in predicate and the following body goals are also built-in predicates, LFB continues to be used as the current local frame, and is not pushed onto the stack until a user-defined predicate appears. When a user-defined predicate is called, if it is the last body goal and it has no alternative clause, LFB is over-written to new local variables used in the new current clause instead of being pushed onto the stack. This means that the last body goal that has no alternative clause is not called, but invoked through jumping. This corresponds to tail recursive optimization [Warren 80]. This method of using the LFB often leaves local variable cells in the WF and decreases stack access in the main memory.

LFB has fixed size of 32 words. Physically, two LFBs are used alternately by firmware control. In unification, the information to be pushed onto the trail stack is also temporarily stored in a WF area, called the trail buffer.

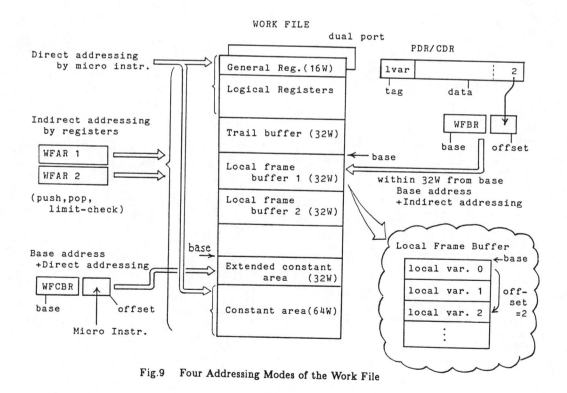

Fig.9   Four Addressing Modes of the Work File

4.3.7 WCS as a register file

The writable control storage (WCS) is used for fetching micro instruction in the latter half of the micro instruction cycle. WCS is designed to be accessible from the internal bus in the first half of the micro cycle. This enables read and write access to WCS under micro program control. Using this function, the last 1K-word area of WCS is assigned as a save area for the process control block. This increases the speed of process switching.

4.4 Sequence control unit

4.4.1 Configuration of the sequence control unit

Fig.10 shows the configuration of the sequence control unit. A micro program control system is used in PSI. A 64-bit x 16K-word WCS is implemented. The first half of the micro instruction cycle generates the address of the next micro instruction, and the second half fetches it. There are several address generation methods, such as absolute branch, relative branch, continuation, OP code dispatch, tag dispatch, multi-way branch using operand tags, conditional branch using a relative address, micro subroutine call, subroutine return, and indirect branch through a jump register. The specialized features of this machine are tag dispatch, multi-way branch and variations on the branch conditions.

4.4.2 OP code dispatch

The instruction code for a built-in predicate contains an operation code (OP code), as shown in Fig.2. This instruction code is transferred to the instruction register (IR) and the OP code is extracted and fed to the dispatch memory. The dispatch memory translates the OP code into the start address of the firmware subroutine corresponding to the operation in a half micro cycle, and this is used for fetching the next micro instruction. The dispatch memory has 256 x 14-bit entries that can be used for up to 256 built-in predicates.

4.4.3 Tag dispatch

The operation for testing the tag is frequently required in the firmware interpreter. The tag dispatch circuit is introduced to increase the speed of tag testing and branch address generation. Address generation is performed in a half micro cycle using the tag of the data read into PDR or CDR from memory. In contrast to OP code dispatch, tag dispatch is a multi-way branch using a base address specified by a micro instruction and an offset generated by the dispatch memory.

There are 64 types of tags in PSI. However, only up to 16 branch targets for multi-way branches are required in practical firmware coding. One of the firmware routine needs a five-way branch, an other needs an eight-way branch, etc. A PDR or CDR tag is translated into a code of three or four bits by the dispatch memory. The code is then concatenated with the base address and used for the next micro instruction address. Twelve translation patterns, from the tag to the code, can be stored in the dispatch memory. Nine are used. The pattern to be used is specified by the micro instruction. As one to several steps of the operation must be executed at the branch destination, the translation pattern is designed to generate multi-way branch addresses in one-, two-, four- or eight-word intervals, according to the request.

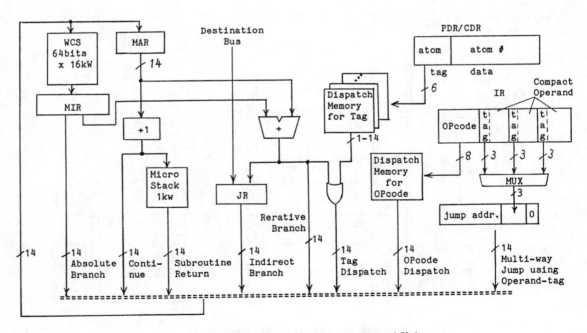

Fig.10   Configuration of the Sequence Control Unit

The dispatch memory consists of 14 bits x 1K words of RAM and is shared for OP code dispatch and tag dispatch.

4.4.4 Multi-way branch using operand tag

The built-in predicate takes up to three compact operands, as shown in Fig.2. Each operand has three bits of compact tag. The instruction register extracts these tags. They are then shifted to the left by one bit and concatenated with the base address of the multi-way jump. Thus an 8-way branch with a two-word address interval is achieved.

4.4.5 Conditional branch

The wide variety of branch conditions is one of the special features of the system. True and the false branches can be specified for each of 64 branch conditions. A conditional branch testing the equality between a register tag (in PDR, CDR, or WF) and an immediate tag data is also available. The major flags used for branch conditions are listed below.

(a) 10 types of ALU flags
(b) Universal flags that can be set and reset independently through FF1F of micro instructions.
(c) Each bit of a register tag of PDR, CDR, or WF
(d) Interrupt request flags
(e) A flag indicating that jump register is equal to zero
(f) I/O bus condition flags

Among these conditions, (b) is frequently used for the interface between firmware modules. These 'switches', which can be easily set and reset, are a valuable asset for a system with so many firmware modules.

4.4.6 Subroutine call and return

Microprogram subroutine call and return are available. The return address is automatically pushed onto and popped from the micro address stack (MSTK). MSTK can be also read from, and written to by the internal bus, so it can be saved and restored when process switching occurs. The MSTK is 1K-word deep but it uses less than 16 words in current coding.

4.4.7 Indirect branch using jump register

The branch address can be set to the jump register (JR) in two ways: from the destination bus, and from the calculated result of the relative address specified by RAF of the micro instruction. An indirect JR branch is available in type 1 and type 3 micro instructions.

JR is also used as a loop counter. Decrementing is specified by the MDF field and zero testing is performed by the function of (e) described in section 4.4.5.

4.5 Memory module

4.5.1 Configuration of the memory module

Fig.11 shows the configuration of the memory module. It contains the cache unit, address translation unit, main memory, and cache control unit. All memory access is performed using the cache order given in the micro instruction. Only when the cache misses an actual memory access is initiated by the cache control unit. The cache memory is accessed through a logical address. The logical-to-physical address translation is performed in parallel with the cache access and the result of the translation is used only when the cache misses. The cache control unit has an independent sequence controller and controls the address translation unit, memory access timing, and memory refresh. Once the cache order is executed, the cache unit works independently from the main sequence control unit. The CPU works in parallel with the cache until completion of the cache order.

4.5.2 Cache unit

The cache memory has a 40-bit x 8K-word capacity, it is constructed from two sets of 4K words. The access time is equivalent to one micro cycle for hit and four micro cycles for miss-hit. The set-associative method is used for cache management and the LRU method is used for the replacement algorithm. The block size is four words and the contents of a block are replaced when the cache misses.

The write-swap method is used in write operations in which write data is only written to the cache instead of to main memory when a write order is executed. When the cache misses, the old data in a cache block is actually written back to main memory. Although the method necessitates writing back old data and reading in required data when the cache misses, it enhances performance when data must be frequently pushed onto and popped from stacks, because there is less overhead for write access to the cache. The write-swap cache is easier to design if the memory has no DMA paths with the I/O devices, as in PSI.

4.5.3 Address translation unit

The address translation mechanism is shown in Fig.5. The page map uses a valid bit that is set during page allocation and tested during address translation. This unit has another memory, called page map size memory, which holds the page size allocated to each area.

4.5.4 Main memory

The word length of the main memory is 40 bits. Up to 16M words of main memory can be installed in PSI. There is an error detection and correction circuit in the cache unit, that can correct single-bit errors and detect double-bit errors. A four-word block transfer is used to transfer data between the main memory and the cache memory. This is performed using the nibble-mode of a dynamic RAM to increase the transfer speed.

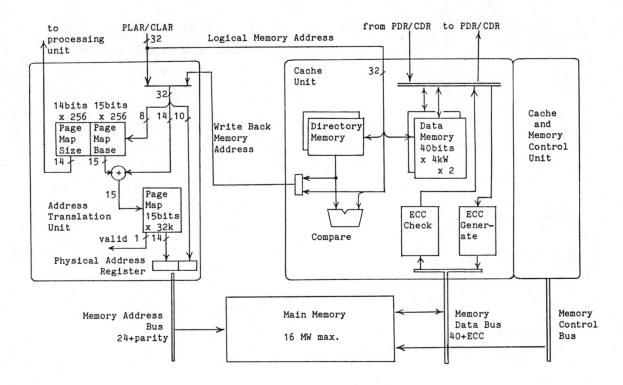

Fig.11   Configuration of the Memory Module

4.6 Hardware implementation

High-speed Schottkey TTL ICs and highly-integrated MOS RAM chips are mainly used in the hardware implementation, because of their commercial availability and small size. The machine cycle time is 200 nano seconds. The CPU is constructed from 12 printed circuit boards, each of which contains about 160 ICs; the main memory is constructed from 16 boards of the same size when 16M words are installed. The CPU boards, the memory boards, 10 or more controller boards for I/O devices, Winchester hard disk drives, and floppy disk drives are all installed in one cabinet.

5   FIRMWARE DEVELOPEMENT

The firmware contains three groups of micro programs, such as the interpreter kernel, built-in predicates, and OS supports such as interrupt handling. Total code size of the firmware is approximately 12K steps.

The interpreter kernel contains routines for basic execution control and unification; both have about same code size, that is, 1.6K steps in total. There are approximately 160 built-in predicates, each of which have from 50 to 100 steps of code; the total code for the built-in predicates is 9K steps. The OS support micro program contains routines for interrupt handling, process switching and memory management, for which the total code size is 1.5K steps.

6   CONCLUSION

In this paper, we presented the machine architecture and hardware design of the personal sequential inference machine, PSI. We also described the system configuration and the basic hardware design philosophy: to design basically simple but partially specialized hardware using microprogram techniques to enhance the efficiency of interpretive execution of high-level machine instructions. We also described the detailed specifications of the hardware components, particularly the register file, which has special functions for tail recursive optimization, and microprogram dispatch facilities using tags.

The experimental hardware development of PSI is already complete, as is testing of the basic firmware modules. An operating system and a programming system for PSI are being developed; tests and debugging are underway on a real machine.

We plan to precisely measure PSI's processing speed using some bench mark programs, and to evaluate the design of hardware components and the firmware interpreter by measuring the dynamic action of the hardware system during program execution. We also plan to compare the architecture of PSI with a machine having determinate instruction execution (not interpretive) and pipelined execution mechanisms (for example, [Tick 84]), and to analyze the strengths and weaknesses of the architecture.

ACKNOWLEDGMENTS

We would like to thank to Mr.Kazuhiro Fuchi, Director of the ICOT Research Center, and Dr.Toshio Yokoi, Chief of the Third Research Laboratory for their continuous encouragement. Thanks are also due to Dr.Takashi Chikayama for his valuable advice, and to other members of ICOT for useful suggestions and discussion. We would also like to extend our thanks to Dr.David Warren for his advice on the tail recursive optimization method.

REFERENCES

[Bowen 81] D.L.Bowen : DEC system-10 PROLOG USER'S MANUAL, Dec.15 1981 Department of Artificial Intelligence, University of Edinburgh

[Boyer 72] R.S.Boyer, and J.S.Moor : The Sharing of Structure in Theorem Proving Programs, Machine Intelligence Vol.1-7, Edinburgh Up (1972)

[Chikayama 83-1] T.Chikayama : Fifth Generation Kernel Language, Proc.of the logic Programming Conference '83, in Tokyo, March 22-24 1983 pp.7.1 1-10

[Chikayama 83-2] T.Chikayama : ESP—Extended Self Contained Prolog—as a Preliminary Kernel Language of Fifth Generation Computers, New Generation Computing Vol.1 No.1 1983, Ohmsha,Ltd.

[Chikayama 84-1] T.Chikayama : KL0 Reference Manual, ICOT Technical Report (to appear)

[Chikayama 84-2] T.Chikayama : ESP Reference Manual, ICOT Technical Report TR-044, Feb. 3 1984

[Cohen 81] J.Cohen : Garbage Collection of Linked Data Structures, ACM Computing Serveys, Vol.13 No.3 1981

[Hattori 83] T.Hattori, and T.Yokoi : Basic Constructs of the SIM Operating System, New Generation Computing Vol.1 No.1 1983, Ohmsha,Ltd.

[Morris 79] F.L.Morris : A Time- and Space-Efficient Garbage Compaction Algorithm, CACM Vol.22 No.10 1979

[Nishikawa 83] H.Nishikawa, M.Yokota, A.Yamamoto, K. Taki, and S.Uchida : The Personal Sequential Inference Machine (PSI)—Its Design and Machine Architecture, Proc.of Logic Programming Workshop, Algrave / PORTUGAL, June 1983, pp.53-73

[Takagi 83] S.Takagi, T.Chikayama, M.Yokota, and T. Hattori : Introducing Extended Control Structures into Prolog, Proc.of 26th Inter- Domestic Conference of IPSJ, March 1983, No.4D-11, in Japanese

[Tick 84] E.Tick, and D.H.D.Warren : Towards a Pipelined PROLOG Processor, Proc.of the International Symposium on Logic Programming, in USA, Feb. 6-9 1984, pp.29-40

[Uchida 83] S.Uchida, M.Yokota, A.Yamamoto, K.Taki, and H.Nishikawa : Outline of the Personal Sequential Inference Machine—PSI, New Generation Computing, Vol.1 No.1 1983, Ohmsha,Ltd.

[Warren 77] D.H.D.Warren : Implementing Prolog—compiling predicate logic programs, Vol.1,2, D.A.I Research Report No.39,40, Univ. of Edinburgh, 1977

[Warren 80] D.H.D.Warren : An Improved Prolog Implementation which optimizes Tail Recursion, Proc.of the Logic Programming Workshop, in Hungary, July 1980

[Yokota 83] M.Yokota, A.Yamamoto, K.Taki, H.Nishikawa, and S.Uchida : The Design and Implementation of a Personal Sequential Inference Machine : PSI, New Generation Computing, Vol.1 No.2 1983, Ohmsha,Ltd.

[Yokota 84] M.Yokota, A.Yamamoto, K.Taki, H.Nishikawa, S.Uchida, K.Nakajima, and M.Mitsui : A Microprogram Interpreter of the Personal Sequential Inference Machine, Proc.of International Conference on FGCS '84, Nov. 6-9 1984, in Tokyo

New Generation Computing, 2 (1984) 37-58
OHMSHA,LTD. and Springer-Verlag

Highly Parallel Inference Engine PIE
— Goal Rewriting Model and Machine Architecture—

Atsuhiro GOTO, Hidehiko TANAKA and Tohru MOTO-OKA

Department of Electrical Engineering, Faculty of Engineering,
The University of Tokyo,
3-1 Hongo 7-chome, Bunkyo-ku, Tokyo 113, Japan

Received 2 December 1983
Revised manuscript received 12 January 1984

Abstract Logic programming is expected to make knowledge information processing feasible. However, conventional Prolog systems lack both processing power and flexibility for solving large problems. To overcome these limitations, an approach is developed in which natural execution features of logic programs can be represented using Proof Diagrams. AND/OR parallel processing based on a goal-rewriting model is examined. Then the abstract architecture of a highly parallel inference engine (PIE) is described. PIE makes it possible to achieve logic/control separation in machine architecture. The architecture proposed here is discussed from the viewpoint of its high degree of parallelism and flexibility in problem solving in comparison with other approaches.

Keywords: Parallel Inference Machine

§1 Introduction

Logic programming[10] is expected to find new applications in Knowledge Information Processing Systems (KIPS).[11] However, these are several problems with the present state of the art. First, applications in Knowledge Information Processing Systems require exponential time on a conventional deterministic machine. Second, although complete separation of logic (the specification of the problem) and control (the method of solving the problem) allows a great amount of flexibility during execution, conventional implementation schemes for sequential Prolog[15] sacrifice this flexibility for efficiency in sequential machines.

Logic programming is assumed to be capable of providing a convenient mechanism for problem solving in a parallel processing environment. Recently, several interesting ideas related to the parallel processing of logic programs have been proposed.[3,6,14] However, none of them has clarified the total system organization and its realizability.

The aim of this research is to develop a highly parallel inference engine (PIE) for super computers utilized in KIPS. This paper proposes an abstract machine architecture for PIE based on a goal-rewriting model to meet this goal. PIE pursues, (1) highly parallel processing for both high performance and natural execution of logic programs, (2) realization of logic/control separation features in machine architectures, and (3) flexible and efficient problem solving strategies.

First the various approaches to parallel processing of logic programs are examined and Proof Diagram representation of pure Prolog programs introduced. Then, an abstract architecture for PIE is proposed and compared with other approaches.

§2 Proof Diagram

In this section a Proof Diagram, which is a modified Ferguson diagram,[8] is first introduced to help in the discussion on parallel processing of logic programs. Parallelism in logic programs is then examined.

A Proof Diagram is a useful representation for discussing the computation of Prolog-like logic programs. This is illustrated in the following simple example written is pure-Prolog.

⟨Program 1⟩

[D1] append (nil,*x, *x).
[D2] append ([*u | *x],*y,[*u | *z]) :- append (*x, *y, *z).
[D3] sublist (*x, *y) :- append (*u, *x, *v), append (*v, *w, *y).
[G]   ?-sublist ([a | *x],[*y | nil]).

2.1 Template Representation of Horn Clauses in Proof Diagrams

An initial goal [G] in the pure-Prolog program is an AND-connective of goal literals in general. Definition clauses [D1~D3] are rewriting rules indicating that a head literal can be rewritten by corresponding body goal literals (or null as in [D1]). There can be plural definition clauses with the same predicate name of head literals like [D1] and [D2].

In Proof Diagrams, these Horn clauses are represented by an initial goal template and definition templates as shown in Fig. 1. Half-circles in each template represent literals. Each half circle includes the corresponding predicate symbol and argument-ports (shown by small cirles) corresponding to its arguments.

When an argument is bound to a certain value, the argument-port is connected to a function value or a constant by a link in the diagram. On the other hand, when arguments of literals or functions in a clause are unbound variables, they are connected with each other by a continuous link for each

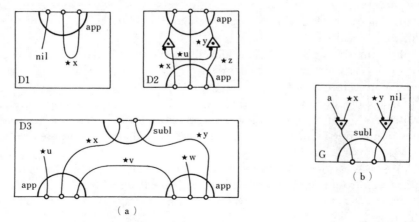

Fig. 1 Definition templates and a goal template corresponding to program 1.

variable's name in the clause.

2.2 Goalframes and their Resolution in Proof Diagrams

The execution of a pure-Prolog program using input resolution can be shown as a search tree, as illustrated in Fig. 2.

The intermediate result in each node of a search tree is defined as the combination of an intermediate goal clause and its environment of unifications.

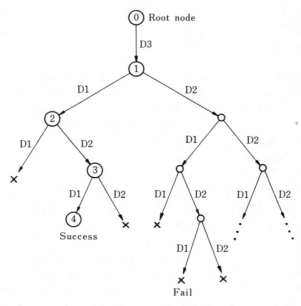

Fig. 2 The search tree in the case of left first unification of literals.

The word "environment" means the substitutions of terms for variables produced by the previous unifications. This intermediate result is called a **goalframe** and is represented by the combination of templates in the Proof Diagram. For example, an intermediate goal derived from two contiguous resolutions among initial goal [G] and definition clauses [D3] and [D1] is shown in Fig. 3(a). This goalframe corresponds to node-2 of search tree in Fig. 2.

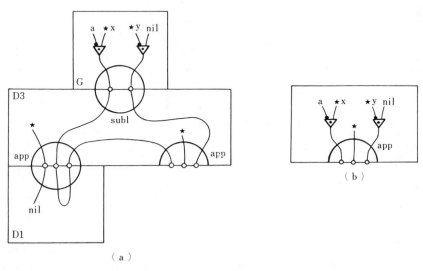

Fig. 3 Example of a goalframe : (a) The goalframe of node-2 in the search tree of Fig. 2, (b) Reduced form of (a).

A unification operation in resolution is the matching operation between arguments of two concerned literals. This corresponds, in the Proof Diagram, to connecting an upper half-circle in a goal template with a lower half-circle in a definition template, tracing links from joined argument-ports in both directions and checking whether they can combine consistently. If both ends of the traced links are inconsistent, this unification ends in failure. If unification ends in success, the whole templates becomes the next intermediate goal. In the Proof Diagram, this successful unification is shown by a full circle. There remain goal literals which need further unification as upper half-circles. In other words, a unification is described as connecting an appropriate definition template with the goal literal of a goalframe.

A goalframe corresponding to a successful leaf node (null clause) is called a **complete-frame**. The complete-frame corresponding to node-4 in Fig. 2 is shown in Fig. 4. A complete-frame represents one of the solutions of the given problem.

As described above, successful computation of a pure-Prolog program involves producing a complete-frame by combining the initial goal template

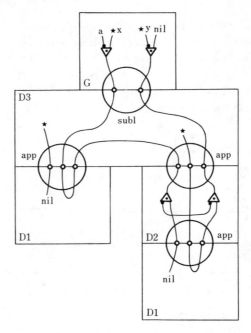

Fig. 4 A complete-frame corresponding to the node-4 of Fig. 2.

with definition templates. A complete-frame represented in the Proof Diagram corresponds to a sequence of derived goal clauses ending with a null clause.

2.3 Reduction of Goalframes

In this section, the operation for reducing goalframes is introduced. Reduction means removing from a goalframe information unnecessary for later resolution. For example, the goalframe shown in Fig. 3(a) includes unnecessary information, such as that which cannot be traced from the argument-ports of upper half-circles (goal literals) and information on successful unifications shown by full circles. A reduced form of the goalframe is shown in Fig. 3(b).

In sequential execution of conventional Prolog, it is necessary to store in a stack mechanism information on how templates are connected and argument-ports combined, because backtracking is a dominant function. To this end, sequential execution cannot reduce goalframes completely. Thus, repeated dereferencing is required when the ends of certain links are referred to. On the other hand, the execution model described later in this paper needs no backtracking, since all definition template candidates are applied at the same time. Therefore, goalframes can be completely reduced.

2.4 Parallelism in Logic Programs

In discussions on parallelism in logic programs, the terms 'AND-parallelism' and 'OR-parallelism' are usually used and refer to the AND/OR division of a given problem.[12] Here parallelism is reviewed from the viewpoint of Proof Diagram representation. There are four types of parallelism in the execution process of logic programs, as shown in Fig. 5.

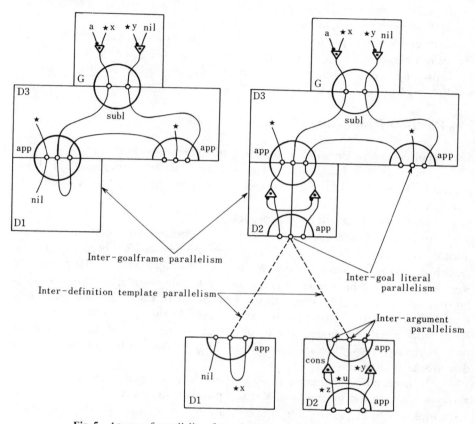

Fig. 5 4-types of parallelism from the viewpoint of Proof Diagram.

(1) **Inter-Argument Parallelism**
Multiple argument-ports in the matching operation of two literals can be matched in parallel.
(2) **Inter-Definition Template Parallelism**
If there are multiple definition template candidates* in a matching operation of a certain goal literal in a goalframe, each matching operation between the goal literal and the definition template candidate can be executed in parallel.

---

* a definition template candidate: a definition template whose head literal has the same predicate name as the concerned goal literal.

561

(3) **Inter-Goal Literal Parallelism**

If there are multiple goal literals in a goalframe, unification operations for each goal literal can be executed in parallel.

(4) **Inter-Goalframe Parallelism**

If there are multiple goalframes in the system, the rewriting operations for these goalframes can be executed in parallel.

Inter-argument parallelism should be thought of as parallelism in the matching operation rather than parallelism of logic program execution. Thus, the following sections will concentrate mainly on the other three types of parallelism.

§3 Parallel Processing of Logic Programs

3.1 Approaches to Parallel Processing of Logic Programs

There are various approaches to the parallel processing of logic programs. These approaches can be characterized mainly in terms of interpretation of clauses.

〔1〕 **Logical formula oriented approach**

In this approach, each clause itself is the operational object just as in the resolution of logical formulas. This approach can be classified broadly into two model categories: goal-rewriting models and knowledge-rewriting models. Roughly speaking, the former oriented toward top-down inference and the latter bottom-up inference. The PIE approach proposed in the following sections is regarded as a goal-rewriting model, as are several other pertinent proposals.[3,9] Knowledge-rewriting models try to derive convenient knowledge from given one. However, they can also cooperate with goal-rewriting models for bi-directional inference.

In both models a clause (goal or knowledge) is rewritten to a new one through a resolution mechanism. Various proof strategies can be introduced as selections of input clauses for the resolution mechanism. In this approach, flexible proof strategies can be developed naturally.

〔2〕 **Procedure-oriented approach**

Procedure-oriented approaches can be thought of in terms of top-down inference. This approach focuses on instances of logical variables generated through unification operations and regards clauses as descriptions of processes that execute unification operations. Proposals based on procedure-oriented approaches can be found in Ref. 6) and 14).

Conery and Kibler have proposed an AND/OR model.[6] This approach is a parallel processing model based on the concept of independent processes communicating via messages. It utilizes both AND processes and OR processes. These processes are invoked one after another in a tree form, and parallel processing proceeds, sending and receiving success, failure, and redo messages. Such an AND/OR model is certainly simple and clear theoretically. However, procedure-oriented approaches like this have several shortcomings in implementation. First, each process must wait for return messages from parent/son processes, so that processes reside for long periods in the system. Second, each process merges the values returned from son processes, so that parent processes tend to be very busy.

Umeyama and Tamura have proposed an OR-parallel processing model,[14] which can be regarded as one of more concrete models of the AND/OR model adopting the principle of data flow execution. The overall processing is done by the flows of tokens among process graphs consisting of five kinds of function units. However, there still remain the above problems.

Several concurrent programming languages for logic programming have been proposed.[5,13] These languages are somewhat restricted in their language specifications. Their main features are as follows:

(1) literals have a producer/consumer relation with respect to shared variables, (e.g., read-only annotations);

(2) guards are introduced to permit a limited amount of computation so that a choice can be made between alternative solutions (not "don't know non-determinism" but "don't care non-determinism").

These language features are assumed to be approaches to parallel processing. However, their areas of application areas seem to be different from those of goal-rewriting models.

〔3〕 **Relational table oriented approach**

This approach is exactly like the relational data base approach, representing a set of facts through a table.[2] This approach seems to be important for set operations and for interfacing mechanism with large data bases. However, it is not sufficiently developed for inference machines and will not be mentioned further in this paper.

3.2 Parallel Processing Based on Goal-Rewriting Models

As can easily be understood from Proof Diagram representation, it is natural to approach parallel processing of logic programs from the viewpoint of rewriting the goalframes themselves. Therefore, the inference machine envisioned here is based on a goal-rewriting model. In this model, parallel processing of goalframes is the first step, and inter-goal literal parallelism and inter-definition template parallelism are regarded as the sources of its parallel activities (goalframes) for inter-goalframe parallel processing.

〔1〕 **OR-parallel processing in goal-rewriting models**

With inter-definition template parallelism, OR-parallel processing of goalframes can easily be set in motion by introducing OR-parallel unify processes (OR-UP for short), which produce a new goalframe from each successful matching pair, as shown in Fig. 6.

A goalframe is consumed by an OR-UP, and a plural number of goalframes may be newly generated in the process. These goalframes have an OR-

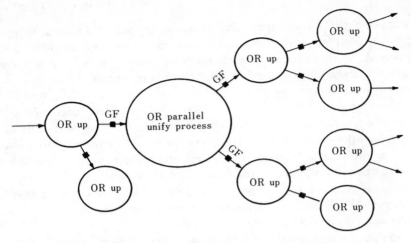

Fig. 6 Inter-goalframe parallel processing by OR-parallel unify processes.

relation in a non-deterministic sense. Each of them can invoke another OR-UP, so that OR-parallel processing can naturally be induced by repeating the same executions for these newly generated goalframes. As a whole, many processes are born and disappear, handing over the goalframes from one to another.

Generally, OR-parallel processing like the above may have the following problems :
(1) Different goalframes may reach the same complete-frame.
(2) One goalframe reaches a special case of another complete-frame.
The causes of these redundant executions and solutions are :
(1) There are pairs or sets of definition templates with the same reduced forms.
(2) There are certain redundant definition templates, e.g., one is a special form of another.
(3) The initial goal template has a special form.
The cost of identifying and eliminating these redundancies could be enormous. If there were n-goalframes, the cost of these redundancy checks would be roughly $O(_nC_2)$. Although redundant execution may not affect the processing function itself, this problem should be taken into consideration from the viewpoint of processing efficiency.

〔2〕 **AND-parallel processing in goal-rewriting models**
Inter-goal literal parallelism is AND-parallelism. When there are no shared variables among the goal literals in a goalframe, or when the goalframes can be divided into several groups of literals with no shared variables, the goalframe can be AND-divided into several sub-goalframes, and AND-parallel processing easily started. In this case, AND-divide processes are added to the parallel processing through OR-UPs.

However, if there are any shared variables among the literals, AND-parallel processing is very difficult. The first problem is the collision of bindings for the shared variables. When the goal literals with shared variables are forcedly divided, the binding values for shared variables must be checked for consistency. The second problem is non-termination of execution. In many cases, forcible AND-division of goalframes may produce sub-goalframes which cannot be brought to complete-frames.

§4 An Abstract Machine Based on Goal-Rewriting Model

This section discusses an abstract machine, concentrating mainly on OR-parallel processing in a goal-rewriting model. A look is first taken at how the internal structure of goalframes should be represented in a highly parallel environment. The abstract architecture of PIE is then proposed.

4.1 Primary Considerations in the Internal Structure of Goalframes

The conceptual view of goalframes has already been given in Section 2.2. This view can be summarized as follows :

a goalframe =

{templates (definitions, an initial goal) + an environment}

where "an environment of a goalframe" is linkage information among constituting templates. The linkage information specifies substitutions of variables in each unification $U(GF_i, DT_j)$ between goalframe GF_i and definition template DT_j. An example of linkage information for a resolvent goalframe is shown in Fig. 7. $\{X', Y'\}$ and $\{X, Y, U, V, W\}$ are the variables in GF_0 and DT_j.

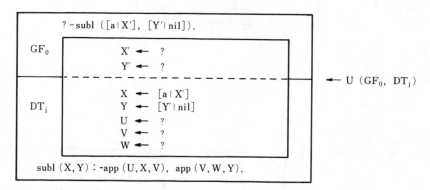

Fig. 7 An example of a goalframe with the linkage information.

In conventional implementations of sequential Prolog, the following two items are mainly required in the internal representation of goalframes :

(1) an efficient structure for the resolution mechanism ;

(2) a space-saving structure for the goalframe memory.

However, the aims of PIE are different from conventional approaches.

The main concerns are the realization of highly parallel processing for high performance and the realization of flexible control strategies for natural execution of logic programs. Therefore, the third requirement, for independence and locality of run-time structures, becomes the most significant. The following alternatives are examined from this point of view.

〔1〕 **Structure sharing or copying**

In implementations of Prolog-like languages, the first question has been whether the structures should be shared or copied.

Structure sharing[1] aims to avoid redundancy in the representation of different instances (constituting a goalframe) of the same definition template by representing each instance through a pair consisting of a pointer to the definition template in the program (skeleton) and a pointer to its linkage information (an environment of a definition template). However, in structure sharing pointer linkages are apt to be long, making repeated dereferencing necessary to get the binding value of a variable. This causes non-locality of run-time structures.

〔2〕 **Environment sharing or copying**

The next alternatives are sharing or copying the environment of a parent's goalframe. In inter-goalframe parallel processing using OR-parallel unify processes, a plural number of goalframes may be born from one parent goalframe. In this case, the environment of a parent goalframe, such as PGF in Fig. 8, is commonly inherited by son goalframes, SGF_1 and SGF_2.

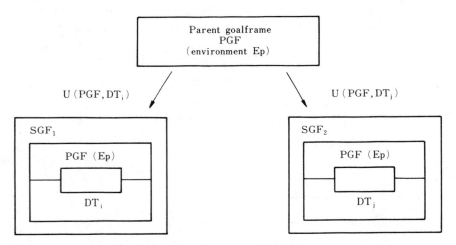

Fig. 8 Inheriting the parent environment.

In environment sharing, environment Ep of PGF is shared among sons SGF_1 and SGF_2, in order to economize on copying operations in generating each new environment. In many cases, however, it is not necessary for sons to inherit all of the parent environment. Moreover, the variables remaining unbound in the parent environment must be copied when son environments are newly generated.

In environment copying, each son inherits a copy of the parent environment. More practically, only the necessary environment for each is copied. In this case, independency and locality of goalframes can be enhanced, making it easy to achieve flexible task distribution in highly parallel processing.

4.2 Inter-Goalframe Parallel Processing in PIE

The preceding discussion supports the following principal directions for the internal representation of goalframes in PIE.

(1) Independent structure

Each goalframe is principally an independent structure in the sense of environment copy and structure copy.

(2) Reduced form

Instead of storing linkage information (binding of variables) as a binding environment, a term to which a variable becomes bound are literally substituted for all occurrences of the variable in a goalframe.

These directions have several advantages in a highly parallel processing environment. This is discussed in later sections.

With the above directions for internal structures of goalframes, parallel processing using OR-UPs can be represented as shown in Fig. 9.

OR parallel unify process

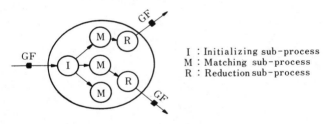

I : Initializing sub-process
M : Matching sub-process
R : Reduction sub-process

Fig. 9 OR-parallel unify process in PIE.

An OR-UP consists of three types of sub-processes :

(1) Initializing sub-process

This process inputs one goalframe and selects one literal from it, then invokes matching sub-processes for each definition template candidate.

(2) Matching sub-process

Each matching sub-process executes a pair matching operation :

{an input goalframe copy, one definition template candidate}.

If successful, the matching sub-process generates substitution between them and invokes a reduction sub-process.

(3) Reduction sub-process

The reduction sub-process generates a new goalframe from

{an input goalframe copy, definition template, substitutions}.

The OR-parallel unify processes are mapped into the processing modules of PIE, called Unify Processors (UPs), as shown in Fig. 10. A Unify Processor inputs one goalframe, then selects one goal literal from the goalframe and inputs all definition template candidates from the Definition Memory (DM). The Unify Processor repeatedly executes unification operations between the input goalframe and all candidates of definition templates, then generates new goalframes for all successful unifications.

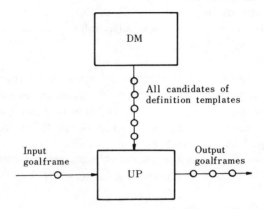

Fig. 10 The basic concepts of the unify processor of PIE.

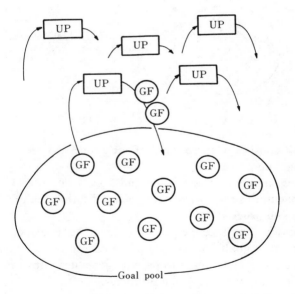

Fig. 11 Inter-goalframe parallel processing feature of PIE.

The overall parallel processing mechanism of PIE consists of many Unify Processors and a goal-pool storing a lot of goalframes, as shown in Fig. 11. Each Unify Processor repeatedly inputs goalframes from the goal-pool and returns the new goalframes (or none) to it. In this execution, each Definition Memory is regarded as having whole definitions.

4.3 Activity Control Features of PIE

In this section, activity control mechanisms for problem solving in inter-goalframe parallel processing are examind.

〔1〕 **The role of activity control mechanisms**

An unlimited number of OR-UPs, as illustrated in Fig. 6, are now mapped onto the finite number of Unify Processors. Usually the degree of parallelism in such OR-parallel processing is enormous, because it is equivalent to the width of the search tree. In practice, however, not all of the computations succeed, and many of them fail. Generally, logic programs can be executed employing different problem solving strategies without changing their semantics. Moreover, efficiency may differ radically, depending on the strategy used. On the other hand, logic programming languages are now maturing. Some extensions include control structures such as meta-logicals like 'not' and 'guard'. Therefore, the main role of activity control mechanisms is regarded as being to control the activation of OR-parallel unify processes according to both the problem solving strategies and the extended language features involved.

The first question in establishing the above mechanisms is how to manage the parallel activities : the goalframes in a goal pool.

〔2〕 **The relation tree and node control commands**

In OR-parallel processing, goalframes have, within the scope of pure-Prolog, an OR-relation to each other in a non-deterministic sense. When additional meta-logical predicates are introduced in logic programs, or when restrictive AND-parallel processing is introduced, goalframes take on various other relations among one another.

It is difficult to record the relations in goalframes themselves, because goalframes are consumed by OR-UPs one after another. Therefore, a tree-form structure, called a "relation tree", is established to represent relations between goalframes, as shown in Fig. 12, and various operations using node control commands are then carried out. Node control commands have the following form :

        〈destination node id., command name, argument list .....〉.

The operations of node control commands are determined by both the commands themselves and the attributes of the destination nodes.

The relation tree consists of a root-node, relay-nodes, and expanded-nodes. The root-node is regarded as the input process of an initial goal, and relay-nodes principally correspond to resolutions of OR-UPs. A relay-node (non-terminal) records the relationship between its son-nodes as a node at-

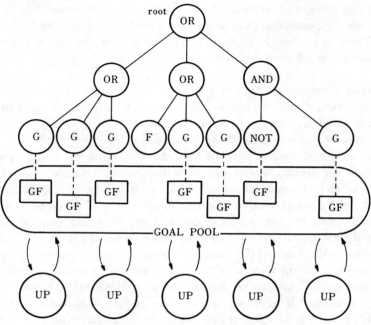

Fig. 12 Activity control feature of PIE.

tribute, as shown in Fig. 13. This is because relations between goalframes are given when the goalframes are generated by OR-UPs. In other words, each OR-

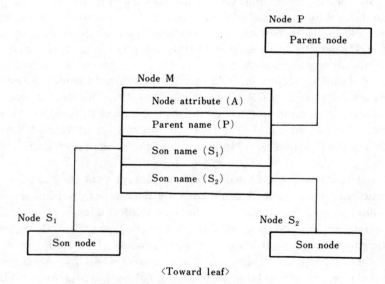

⟨Toward leaf⟩

Fig. 13 A node of the relation tree.

UP specifies the relation among its son goalframes.

All goalframes existing at a certain time of execution can correspond to particular terminal nodes on the relation tree, called goal-nodes. Each goal-node has a node attribute representing the corresponding goalframe status (active, suspended) or any other attribute caused by meta-logical predicates. When the resolutions of a goalframe with all definition template candidates end in failure, the goal-node for this goalframe takes the place of an expanded-node having the attribute "failure" (called a failure-node). These expanded-nodes are pruned, and ⟨failure⟩ commands are sent to their parent nodes. A relay-node with all of its son-nodes pruned as failure-nodes also becomes a failure-node. Then, the fully expanded branches of the relation tree are dynamically pruned, sending ⟨failure⟩ commands upward in the relation tree. When one of the goalframes reaches a complete-frame, a success-node is temporally generated and then soon pruned, sending a ⟨success⟩ command to its parents. If only one solution is required, other goalframes are inactivated by propagating ⟨success⟩ commands upward and ⟨stop⟩ commands downward over the relation tree.

When new goalframes are generated, the goal-node is replaced by a sub-tree consisting of a relay-node (usually with an OR attribute) and the goal-nodes corresponding to the new goalframes, as shown in Fig. 14. In this case, ⟨son⟩ commands are used to link the new goal-nodes to their parent-node(M).

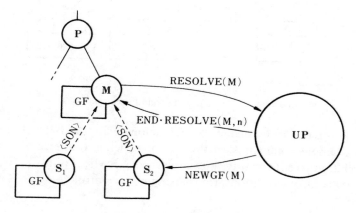

Fig. 14 Expanding the relation tree.

By introducing the above relation tree, on which all goalframes in execution are arranged as terminal nodes, various control facilities can be established, such as killing or inactivating the execution of a certain goalframe and reactivating it according to an other goalframe's status.

〔3〕 **An example of meta-logical predicate execution**

The following, more concrete example illustrates how the meta-logical-predicate "not" can be realized. It is assumed that in the goalframe including "not"

$$?- not(goal_1), goal_2.$$

There are no shared variables between "goal$_1$" and "goal$_2$". In this case, the goalframe is divided into two sub-goalframes executable in parallel. On the relation tree, the goal-node is replaced by a not-node, a goal-node and an and-node as shown in Fig. 15(a).* A not-node is a special goal-node. It becomes a failure-node when a null clause (complete-frame) is resolved by an OR-UP, and a success-node when the OR-UP fails. When the OR-UP generates new goal-frames, the not-node is replaced by an and-node and not-nodes corresponding to the new goalframes, as shown in Fig. 15(b). An and-node becomes a success-node when all of its son-nodes have become success-nodes. When one of them becomes a failure-node, the and-node sends ⟨stop⟩ commands to its other son nodes to inactivate unnecessary goal-nodes.

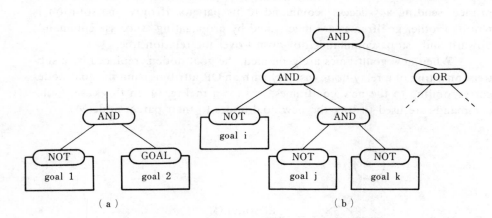

Fig. 15 An execution feature of meta-logical predicate 'NOT'.

The relation tree is divided and stored among many Activity Controllers. In the above example, commands are thought of as being transferred among the nodes of a relation tree. In reality, however, each Activity Controller executes various activity control operations, transferring node control commands among them.

§5 Discussion on PIE Architecture

5.1 Independence Enhancement of Parallel Activities

The most important problem in general in achieving highly parallel processing is the independence of each task unit. There is necessarily some relationship among task units making up the given problem, restricting the

---

* This example is different from practical implementations for the sake of simplicity.

independency among them to a certain extent. However, the processing system itself is apt to over-restrict their independence.

The abstract machine architecture for PIE enhances this independence and locality.

[1] Structure/environment sharing approach

One approach can be found in the OR-parallel token machine[3,4] and ALICE.[7] These machine models are based on structure sharing representations for the run-time structures of goalframes. This structure sharing approach in an OR-parallel processing environment can be also considered an environment sharing approach. In this model, goalframes are divided into templates and environments based on structure sharing concepts. They are then stored in a static memory (a program memory) and a dynamic memory (an environment memory). A token corresponding to each goalframe is used to refer to these two memories.

In a structure/environment sharing approach, the required capacity is smaller, and traffic in the switching network decreases because data sent to unify-processors are limited to data necessary for unification. However, management of the shared environment is the most important consideration.

In a parallel processing environment, even in structure sharing, the environment for unbound variables, called "uncommitted contexts[3]", cannot be shared but must be copied. The investigation needed to decide whether the context can be shared or must be copied constitutes a significant drawback. Haridi et al. have proposed an interesting technique for accomplishing this requirement,[3] using linked directories. However, a complex garbage collection problem remains. Also, it is questionable whether this management of environments can be executed in a highly parallel processing environment, because goal memories are in danger of becoming a bottle-neck in the machine. Therefore, models like the above should be considered excellent medium scale machines only.

[2] Preliminary evaluations

A software simulator was made up to examine the parallelism of certain program examples. The results of these simulations confirm that the machine model is suitable for highly parallel processing.

The parallelism of the sample programs[16] is shown in Fig. 16. "Depth" on the horizontal axis indicates the number of invocations of processes, i.e., the depth of the search tree, and "the number of successful unifications" on the vertical axis means the number of processes invoked next, i.e., the parallelism of each depth.

It becomes clear that the size of each goalframe can be kept small through reduction operations, as shown in Fig. 17. This indicates that invoking an OR-UP with a whole goalframe is not a burden on this system. However, it may be necessary to consider the structure memory in machine organization to insure efficient processing of large data structure objects.

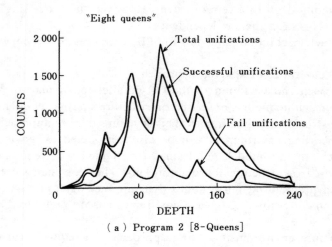

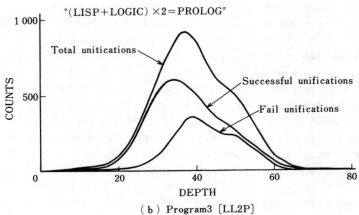

Fig. 16 Parallelism of sample programs.

5.2 Flexibility in Problem Solving Strategies

Conventiolal Prolog implementation can efficiently execute resolution operations on sequential machines through a backtrack mechanism. However, this implementation results in oversequencing in the execution order of literals and in the selection order of definition clauses.

In contrast, in the parallel processing model of PIE, each process handles the whole goalframe, keeping the execution order of literals in the goalframe free from the resolution mechanism and allowing the initialization sub-process to select a suitable literal.

In execution through OR-UPs, backtracking is not necessary, making the various execution strategies, for example, depth-first, breadth-first or their

574

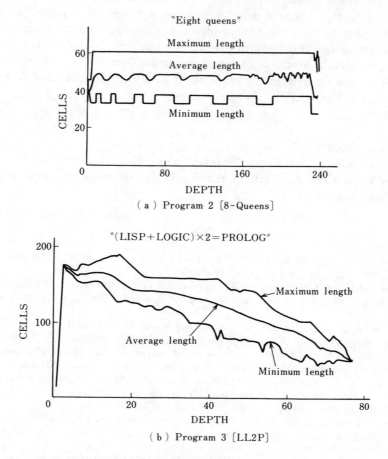

"Eight queens"

(a) Program 2 [8-Queens]

"(LISP + LOGIC) × 2 = PROLOG"

(b) Program 3 [LL2P]

Fig. 17 Length of reduced form goalframes.

amalgamation, possible through selection of the goalframes to be resolved.

5.3 Powerful Activity Controlling

The inter-goalframe relationship is stored in the naming scheme of tokens in an OR-parallel token machine[4] and in a goal tree in PRISM.[9] These methods are thought not to be powerful and not yet useful in practical application. In the model presented here, the relationship among goalframes is separated as a relation tree from the resolution mechanism, permitting a powerful control mechanism to be realized. To this end, when extended language features are introduced over the Horn clause logic, certain attributes will be given to the nodes, and commands to operate on the relation tree will be incorporated.

§6 Conclusion

As described above, the abstract architecture of the highly parallel inference engine PIE features parallel processing based on a goal-rewriting model, enhancing locality and independence of run-time structures, i.e., goal-frames. Execution is controlled using a relation tree and various node control commands, separate from the resolution mechanism. This realization of logic/control separation features in the machine architecture have resulted in high performance and flexibility in problem solving.

Acknowledgements

The authors would like to thank Hitoshi Aida, Tsutomu Maruyama, Masanobu Yuhara and Keiji Hirata, the members of the research group SIGIE, for their help in this work.

References

1) Boyer, R. S. and Moore, J. S.: "The Sharing of Structure in Theorem-proving Progams", Machine Intelligence, 7 (1972) 101-116.
2) Chakravarthy, U.S., et al.: "Interfacing Predicate Logic Languages and Relational Databases", Proc. of First International Logic Programming Conference (Sept., 1982) 91-98.
3) Ciepielewski, A. and Haridi, S.: "A Formal Model for Or-Parallel Execution of Logic Programs", Information Processing 83 (Sept., 1983) 299-306.
4) Ciepielewski, A. and Haridi, S.: "Control of Activities in an OR-Parallel Token Machine", Proceeding of Logic Programming Workshop '83 (July, 1983) 536.
5) Clark, K. L. and Gregory, S.: "A Relational Language for Parallel Programming", Proc. of the 1981 Conf. on Functional Programming Languages and Computer Architecture (Oct., 1981).
6) Conery, J. S. and Kibler, D. F.: "Parallel Interpretation of Logic Programs", Proc. of the 1981 Conf. on Functional Programming Languages and Computer Architecture (Oct., 1981) 163-170.
7) Darlington, J. and Reeve, M.: "ALICE: A Multi-Processor Reduction Machine for the Parallel Evaluation of Applicative Languages", Proc. of the 1981 Conf. on Functional Programming Languages and Computer Architecture (Oct., 1981) 65-76.
8) van Emden, M. H.: "An Algorithm for Interpreting Prolog Programs", Proc. of First International Logic Programming Conference (Sept., 1982) 56-64.
9) Kasif, S., Kohli, M., and Minker, J.: "PRISM: A Parallel Inference System for Problem Solving", Proceeding of Logic Programming Workshop '83 (July, 1983) 123-152.
10) Kowalski, R.: "Logic Programming", Information Processing 83 (Sept., 1983) 133-146.
11) Moto-oka, T. (ed.): Proceeding of International Conference of Fifth Generation Computer System (Oct., 1981).
12) Nilsson, N. J.: Principle of Artificial Intelligence (Tioga Publishing Company, 1980).
13) Shapiro, E. Y.: "A Subset of Concurrent Prolog and its Interpreter", ICOT Technical Report, TR-003 (ICOT, 1983).
14) Umeyama, S. and Tamura, K.: "A Parallel Execution Model of Logic Programs", The 10th Annual International Symposium on Computer Architecture, ACM (June, 1983) 349-355.
15) Warren, D. H. D.: "Implementing Prolog — compiling predicate logic programs", D. A. I. Research Report, 39-40 (1977).
16) Goto, A., et al.: "On the Efficient Parallel Processing of the Highly Parallel Inference Engine — PIE", IECEJ Technical Group Meeting, EC83-9 (May, 1983) [in Japanese].

New Generation Computing, 3 (1985) 15-41
OHMSHA,LTD. and Springer-Verlag

Data-flow Based Execution Mechanisms of Parallel and Concurrent Prolog

Noriyoshi ITO, and Hajime SHIMIZU
Institute for New Generation Computer Technology, 1-4-28 Mita, Minato-ku, Tokyo 108, Japan.

Masasuke KISHI, Eiji KUNO, and Kazuaki ROKUSAWA
Oki Electric Industry Co., Ltd., 4-10-12 Shibaura, Minato-ku, Tokyo 108, Japan

Received 30 July 1984
Revised manuscript received 28 December 1984

Abstract   Study attempts to show that our machine architecture based on the data flow model is suitable for two types of logic programming languages with different aims: one is Parallel Prolog and the other is Concurrent Prolog. The data flow model can naturally implement parallel computation, and it has close similarity to these languages. Unification and nondeterministic control, two basic functions of these languages, are represented by data flow graphs and interpreted by the machine. Several representations of variables, that facilitate the development of parallel unification and nondeterministic control mechanisms for these languages, the unification and control primitives needed to execute these languages on this architecture are presented.

Keywords : Parallel Processing, Data Flow Model, Logic Programming Language, Unification, Nondeterminism

§1   Introduction

Recently, a number of parallel inference machines have been proposed by various institutes and researchers to be used in the execution of Prolog, a logic programming language based on first-order predicate logic. Prolog is a simple language possessing strong descriptive capabilities and intrinsic potential for parallel processing.[15] Most of these parallel Prolog interpreters focus on OR parallelism or independent AND parallelism, even if AND-parallel execution is implemented. Their target is to solve all-solution problems in a highly-parallel execution environment. Such Prolog language is called Parallel Prolog.

Concurrent Prolog[18,19] has been proposed as one of languages enabling interactive control of AND processes. Concurrent Prolog is a successor to the Relational Language by K. Clark and S. Gregory,[6] who have further extended the Relational Language to PARLOG.[7] A common feature of these languages is that they facilitate interactive communication of partial bindings, or messages, among AND processes. Of these, Concurrent Prolog has been chosen for the parallel inference machine because it provides more flexible input/output annotation than other languages.

Both Parallel and Concurrent Prolog consist of Horn clauses based on first-order predicate logic; however their aims are somewhat different. The former's aim is to find all solutions, while the latter's prime aim is object-oriented programming.

The authors have been engaged in research on a parallel inference machine and have evaluated it for Parallel Prolog programs using a detailed software simulator.[13,14] Simulation results indicate that machine performance can be significantly improved by exploiting parallelism. The machine is based on the data flow model, which is closely related to functional languages and is naturally well suited to parallel processing.[2,4,11] Programs in the data flow model is represented by data flow graphs, where nodes correspond to operators and directed arcs correspond to data paths along which operands are sent. An operator in the graphs is driven by arrivals of the operands from its input arcs and outputs the result operands to its output arcs without affecting the other operators' executing in parallel. This functionality of the operators has close similarity to the functional languages.

The data flow model has also similarity to the logic programming languages described above. Execution of logic programs is performed in a goal driven manner: a clause in the programs is initiated when a goal is given, and returns the results (solutions) to the goal. If multiple clauses are given, their unification with the goal can be initiated in parallel, by representing these clauses by data flow graphs.

These logic programming languages both make use of the unification operation, which is one of their basic functions. Nondeterminism is another basic feature of these languages; the control of 'don't-know nondeterminism' is required for Parallel Prolog, While the control of 'don't-care nondeterminism' is required for Concurrent Prolog.[7,17] Details of the execution mechanisms for both languages are described in this paper.

Parallel Prolog and Concurrent Prolog are outlined in Section 2. Section 3 describes an abstract machine architecture. Section 4 discusses variables in both languages and their representation on our machine. Section 5 and 6 describe the primitive operators required to implement unification and non-deterministic control for both languages.

§2 Parallel Prolog and Concurrent Prolog

The Parallel Prolog programs can be interpreted in a sequential manner by using backtracking. If problems to be solved are very complex, however, it is necessary to solve the problems by exploiting parallelism instead of using the sequential interpreters, because they may need much more time than we can stand.

A Parallel Prolog program consists of a set of clauses as shown below:

$$H1 \leftarrow B1.$$
$$H2 \leftarrow B2.$$
$$\cdots$$
$$Hn \leftarrow Bn.$$

Here, Hi and Bi denote a head literal and a body, respectively (where $1 \leq i \leq n$). The symbol '$\leftarrow$' represents an implication: if its right side (the body) is satisfied, the left side (the head) is also satisfied. The body can consist of an arbitrary number of body literals connected by ANDs. A literal has the form, $p(t1, t2, \ldots, tm)$, where p is a predicate, and ti $(1 \leq i \leq m)$ is a term. A term may be a non-structured data item such as a variable, symbol, or numeric number, or a structured data item such as a list or compound term. A clause without body literals is called a unit clause.

Unification is initiated when a set of clauses and a goal statement (a clause consisting of an arbitrary number of body literals with no head) are given. One literal is selected from the goal statement; this is called a goal literal. A clause in which the predicate of the head literal is identical with that of selected goal literal is a candidate for unification. The subset of clauses that share the same head predicate is called the definition of the predicate.

When a goal literal, G, is given, the definition of G is invoked. A clause is then selected from the definition, and unification of G and the head literal of the clause, Hi, is attempted. Generally, when multiple clauses exist in the definition, unification of G and each Hi can be executed in parallel. This parallelism among clauses is called OR parallelism, and each process executing a clause is called an OR process. A unit clause that is successfully unified with G returns the result (solution). A non-unit clause initiates the next unification treating the body as a new goal statement.

If multiple literals exist in the goal statement, they are connected by logical ANDs. That is, the goal statement is satisfied (the solutions are found for the body) only when solutions are found for all the literals and there is no inconsistency between these solutions. The literals in a goal statement can be executed in parallel. The machine can exploit this parallelism efficiently in cases where the goal literals have no shared variables, or shared variables are bound to the ground instances before invocation of these literals, because consistency checking is easy or unnecessary.

In AND parallelism, however, the search space may be expanded in some cases, or the overhead for consistency checking between the solutions returned from the literals may be increased if these goal literals have shared variables.

Therefore, syntactical operators were introduced for specifying whether sequential or parallel execution is to be used for these AND-connected literals. In this paper, the symbol '&' represents an operator that specifies sequential execution of the literals on both sides of the operator in left-to-right order. The symbol '//' represents an operator that specifies parallel execution of the literals on both sides of the operator. Processes dedicated to solving goal literals are called AND processes.

A Concurrent Prolog program is given as a set of guarded clauses, as in the following:

$$H1 \leftarrow G1 \mid B1.$$
$$H2 \leftarrow G2 \mid B2.$$
$$\cdots$$
$$Hn \leftarrow Gn \mid Bn.$$

Here, Hi, Bi, and the symbol '$\leftarrow$' are the same as in Parallel Prolog, and Gi denotes a guard (where $1 \leq i \leq n$). The guard can consist of an arbitrary number of literals as in the body. The symbol '$\mid$' is called a guard bar or commit operator, and is regarded as one of the sequential control operators that perform exclusive control, as in Dijkstra's guarded command.[10]

In the above program, the head literal and the guard are executed as in Parallel Prolog. That is, OR-parallel and AND-parallel execution can be implemented. In the OR-parallel execution environment of Concurrent Prolog programs, only one clause for which head unification and guard invocation have been successfully completed is able to proceed to the execution of the body. The results derived from other clause are discarded at that time. This exclusive control is implemented by the guard control mechanism, as described in Section 6.

Another role of the commit operator is to make available (i. e. export) the bindings of the variables of the goal literal, G, to other processes. That is, if processes share variables, the bindings for the variables are made available to these processes by the guard control primitives. This function enables AND processes to communicate bindings or messages interactively. On the other hand, in the all-solution searching program, AND processes may be executed independently: AND processes sharing unbound variables may generate the bindings for these variables, which are then used to check consistency of their bindings.

Another feature of Concurrent Prolog is read-only annotation, in which tags are appended to variables. If an attempt is made to unify a variable having a read-only tag with a non-variable term, the unification is suspended until this variable is bound to a non-variable term by another unification. This mechanism can be implemented by adding tag bits to the memory cells used for these variables, as described in the following section.

§3 Abstract Machine Architecture

The machine can exploit OR and AND parallelism as described above, as well as parallelism in unification. When a goal literal and its definition are given, the goal literal is unified with a head literal of each clause in the definition. This operation is called head unification. In head unification, if both literals consist of multiple arguments, or if both arguments are structured data, the unification of these arguments or their substructures can be executed in parallel. The machine is constructed from multiple processing elements and multiple structure memories interconnected by networks as shown in Fig. 1[12]; it is based on the data flow model and can exploit this type of low-level parallelism.

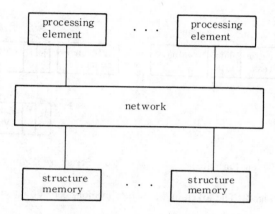

Fig. 1 The abstract machine architecture.

The parallel inference machine uses a tagging scheme, in which each operand has a value field and a tag field, which specifies the data type of the operand. If the operand is a structured data, the value field has a pointer to the structure memory, and the tag field is further divided into two subfields: a data type subfield, which specifies the data type of structure, such as a list or a vector; and an attribute subfield. The attribute subfield contains a non-ground flag, which indicates whether the structure has any simple variables. The attribute subfield also contains a shared flag, which indicates whether the structure has any shared-type variables (i. e., shared variables, global variables, or read-only variables). These variable types are described in detail at Section 4. The machine recognizes the tag field of the operand and transfers control to the appropriate firmware routine.

When a goal literal is given, unification is initiated by invoking the compiled clauses of its definition. The clauses are represented by data flow graphs, which correspond to the machine language of the parallel inference machine. Each node and each directed arc in a data flow graph respectively corresponds to an operator and a data path along which an operand is sent. A node in the graph can be executed when operands have arrived from all its input arcs. The machine is based on the unfolding interpreter,[4] which provides procedure invocation primitives that allocate a unique identifier to each procedure instance and maintain the history of the procedure invocations. The identifier, as well as an operator address, is added to each token carrying arguments (operands), and is used to distinguish among activities (operators). All the operators, therefore, can be executed independently. The token format is shown in Fig. 2 (a).

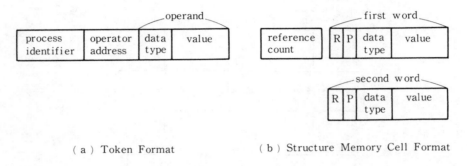

(a) Token Format   (b) Structure Memory Cell Format

Fig. 2 The token and structure memory cell format.

Structured data is stored in and distributed to the structure memories and is shared among processing elements instead of being locally copied to each processing element; the contents of the structured data can be referred to on demand. One advantage of this method is that it minimizes the overhead caused by copying of the structured data. The other is that it eliminates redundant storage for locally copied structured data. There may prove to be significant advantages in the manipulation of complexly structured data such as is required in natural language processing applications.

A problem in sharing structured data among processes is latency in accessing the structured data. Latency may be increased as the number of processing elements increases. In order to exploit parallelism, the processing element must issue multiple memory requests without waiting for responses. In such an environment, requests and responses must be managed by their identifiers since responses may not be returned to the processing element in the order in which the requests were issued. The data flow model implements this type of control in a natural way, and exploits low-level parallelism because it is assured of independence among operations or instructions.[3,5]

Structured data is stored in structure memory cells. Each cell consists of two words and each word has a data type tag field, a value field, and two flags: R (ready) flag and P (pending) flag. These flags are used for providing asynchronous communication between read and write operations to the memory word. R flag shows whether or not the contents of the data type tag and value fields are valid (i. e., whether or not a write operation to the memory cell is performed). P flag shows whether or not some read operations are linked to the value field. A read operation to a memory word, whose R tag is OFF, is suspended and linked to the memory word until a write operation to the memory word is issued. In order to implement a garbage collection of the structure memories, the reference count tags are appended to every memory cell,[1,8,16] which also used for stream control as described in Section 5. Figure 2 (b) shows a structure memory cell format.

§4　Variables and Their Representation

A variable can be unified with, and bound to, any type of term. When a variable has multiple occurrences in a clause, however, the same term must be bound to each occurrence of the variable. If a variable is shared among unification processes being executed in parallel, it is called a shared variable. It is called a simple variable if it appears in a clause only once, or if unification affecting the variable is executed sequentially even if it appears more than once. Shared variables are distinguished from simple variables by their data type.

When a simple variable is unified with any term, the variable can be directly replaced by the term and no binding are generated. However, when a shared variable is unified with a term other than a simple variable, the substitution information for the shared variable is output by unification. This substitution information is called the binding environment of the shared variable. The binding environment, represented as a list of shared variables and their instances, is used to check whether the bindings of the shared variables are consistent among the parallel unification operations. It is also used to substitute terms for shared variables.

Shared variables are created dynamically and represented by unique identifiers in Parallel Prolog. A shared variable in the unification of the head and guard of a guarded clause (i. e., a clause in Concurrent Prolog) is treated in the same manner as in Parallel Prolog. However, when a goal literal is given, only one clause can commit the binding information for the shared variables. Thus, shared variables can be represented by pointers to global memory cells. We call such shared variables global shared variables, or simply global variables.

The commit operator can be regarded as a write command to the memory cells pointed to by the global variables, and the read-only tag can be regarded as a read command to the memory cell. A variable with a read-only tag is called a read-only global variable, or simply a read-only variable. It is also represented as a pointer to the same memory cell to which the global variable points.

If the guard has multiple literals with global variables and these literals are executed in parallel, child processes invoked from these guard literals may communicate bindings via the global variables. Bindings are localized in this guard, i. e., information about these bindings is unavailable to the parent clause that invoked this guard until the guard is successfully terminated (i. e., the commit operation is issued). The guard acts like a *mirror* in which bindings are reflected from one child to another.

On the other hand, the children invoked from the body must "see" the bindings of their ancestors through the body. That is, the body acts like a *window* through which the bindings can be "viewed" by the children.

The relationship between a parent clause and its invoked children is illustrated in Fig. 3. The two ovals in the figure correspond to the guard and body of the clause; the left oval represents a guard, the right one represents a body, and the junction of these ovals corresponds to a commit operator. The guard and body are executed from left to right. The bottom surface of the guard reflects bindings from its children, but the body allows the bindings to pass through.

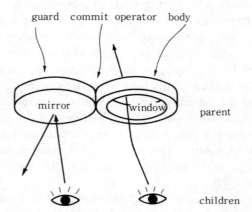

Fig. 3 Relationship between a guarded clause and its children.

Figure 4 depicts this relationship when the following clauses are given:

$$p0(X) \leftarrow q1(Y) \,//\, q2(Y) \mid \ldots$$
$$q1(Z) \leftarrow r1(Z) \,//\, r2(Z) \mid r3(Z) \ldots$$
$$r1(W) \leftarrow s1(w) \mid \ldots$$
$$r2(U) \leftarrow \ldots$$

In the above example, it is assumed that the clause with head predicate p0 (clause p0) is initially called. Because two parallel guard literals q1(Y) and q2(Y) of clause p0 share the variable Y, and Y is unbound before these literals are called, a new global variable, Yg, is created. Yg is sent as an argument of clauses q1 and q2, which are executed in parallel and share the global variable Yg. Clause q1 invokes clauses r1 and r2 from its guard; it also invokes clause r3 from its body if the invoked clauses r1 and r2 succeed. The binding for Yg is hidden from the clauses r1 and r2, and transparent to the clause r3.

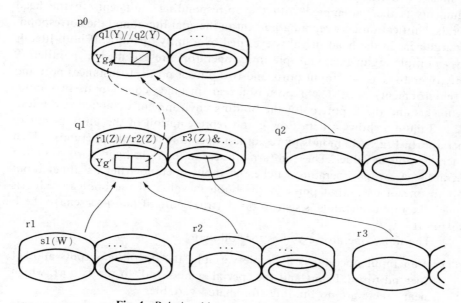

Fig. 4 Relationships among guarded clauses.

In order to hide the bindings of guard literals, local copies of global variables included in a guard must be created before the guard is invoked. We call this method local copying of shared variables. A local copy of Yg, which is represented by Yg′, is created when clauses r1 and r2 are invoked from the guard of clause p1, as shown in Fig. 4. The local copy can be represented as a memory cell having two words: (1) a slot for a local instance of the global variable, and (2) a pointer to its parent guard, which is used to send the local instance to the original global variables in the parent when the commit operator is issued. The latter may be regarded as the binding environment for the locally copied variable.

However, if it is guaranteed that all the clauses invoked by a guard literal does not affect the arguments of the guard literal (i. e., if all the clauses does not bind any instance to the arguments), it is unnecessary to create local copies of global variables.

§5 Primitives for Parallel Prolog

This section describes the basic unification primitives, nondeterministic control primitives, and AND sequential/parallel control mechanisms for goal literals in Parallel Prolog.

5.1 Basic Unification Primitive Operators

The operators in the invoked clauses are initiated by passing goal arguments via the procedure invocation primitives; unification of the goal arguments is then attempted with the corresponding arguments in the head literals. Unification between an argument in the goal literal and the corresponding argument in the head literal is executed by a unify operator. If both literals have multiple arguments, multiple unify operators are executed in parallel. A unify operator has two input ports and two output ports: I (instance) port and E (environment) port. The I port is for an instance common to two input arguments and the E port is for the binding environment of shared variables.

Figure 5 shows a data flow graph representation of the unify primitive operator. In Fig. 5, diamonds represent test operators for input operands, which generate boolean values. These in turn are sent to the right-hand ports of switch operators. A switch operator switches an input operand from its upper input port to one of its output ports by the boolean value: if the boolean value is "true", the input operands is sent to the T (true) port; if not, it is sent to the F (fail) port.

The unify operator executes the following sequence:

(1) If an input operand is a simple variable, the operator outputs another operand to the I port and the special symbol 'nil' to the E port, which means there are no bindings for shared variables.

(2) If one is a shared variable and the other is a term other than a simple variable, the operator outputs the shared variable to the I port and outputs a newly constructed list consisting of the shared variable and its instance (i. e. the term) to the E port.

(3) If both operands are atomic terms (i. e., symbols or numeric numbers) and if their unification succeeds (i. e., if both terms are same), the operator outputs one of the terms to the I port and 'nil' to the E port; it outputs special 'fail' symbols to its two output ports, if the unification fails.

(4) If both operands are structured data, a structure-unify procedure, shown by the rectangular box in Fig. 5, is invoked. This procedure decomposes two input structures into their substructures and recursively invokes unify operators for these substructures. In this procedure, all the outputs from the E ports of the unify operators are used to check consistency, and all the outputs from the I ports are used to reconstruct a new instance. In order to reduce overhead in reconstructing a new structured data, if one

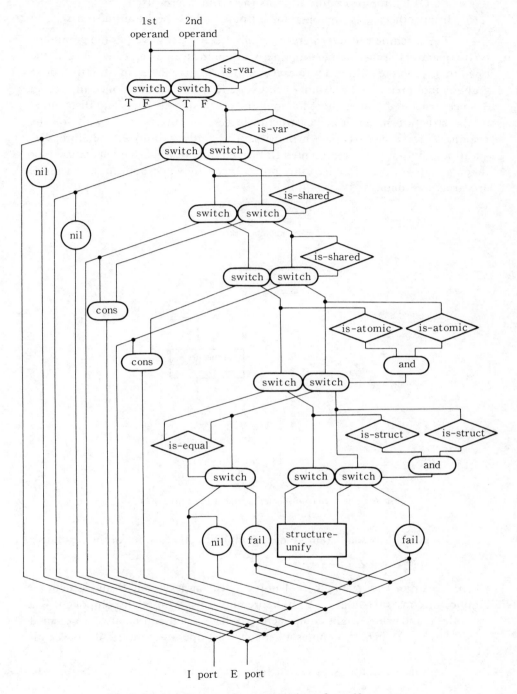

Fig. 5 A data flow graph representation of a unify operator.

of the operands is a ground term (i. e., its non-ground flag and shared flag are OFF), the procedure outputs the ground term itself.

(5) In all other cases, the operator outputs 'fail' to both output ports.

The machine can interpret this graph directly. However, as the granularity of operators seems to be too fine, communication overhead between the operators is too great. In order to execute this primitive faster, most of the above graph is interpreted by hardware or firmware routines. As mentioned in Section 3, since structured data is shared among the processing elements and distributed to the structure memories, the structure access primitives must wait for the responses from the structure memories. The unify primitive, therefore, has additional output ports, represented by broken lines in Fig. 6, which are used for token passing to the structure-unify procedure, only when both input operands are structured data.

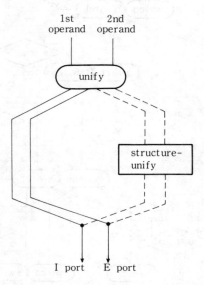

Fig. 6   The actual implementation of the unify operator.

Figure 7 shows an example of a compiled code for the following clause:

$$p([Y, b], Z, c) \leftarrow \ldots$$

where a pair of square brackets denotes a list, and symbol b and c denotes atomic (or constant) values. [Y, b] represents a list whose left component is a variable Y and whose right component is a list [b]: it can be also represented as [Y|[b|[]]], where '|' denotes a list construct operator and '[]' denotes a nil list.

A unify operator is provided for each of the three arguments of head

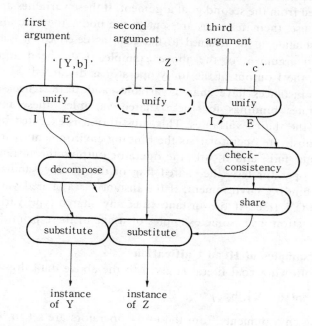

Fig. 7 Data flow graph of clause p([Y, b], Z, c) ← ...

predicate p; these are executed in parallel. A variable can be unified with any term and the unify operator outputs the term itself for the common instance. Therefore, when the clause head argument is a variable, as in the second argument in the example, the unify operator can be omitted, as shown by the broken lines in the figure.

Two outputs from the E ports of the unify operators are sent to a check-consistency operator. The check-consistency operator checks for consistency among the binding environments of the shared variables. This operator generates a new binding environment for the shared variables if their bindings are consistent, and the symbol 'fail' if they are not. In this consistency checking, if substitution information for the shared variable is included in both its two input environments, the check-consistency operator calls a unify operator; the invoked unify operator tries to unify the two instances bound to the same shared variable. A new common instance obtained by this unify operator is output in the form of a binding environment, as described above. If simple variables are included in the new instance, they are changed to shared variables. This is done by a share operator.

In the above example, the head literal has two variables, Y and Z: Y is the left list component of the first argument and Z is the second argument. The instance of Y is obtained by the left output from the decompose-list operator, whose input is the I port output of the first unify operator. The instance of Z is directly obtained from the second goal argument. If these variables appear in the body of the clause, their instances are sent to the body; they are also used for constructing a solution to be returned to the goal, as described in Subsection 5.4. As in the third argument of the above example, if the head argument is a constant value, the I output of the unify operator is discarded.

If these instances have shared variables and if the check-consistency operator generates bindings for these shared variables, these instances are substituted for the shared variables. This substitution is executed by substitute operators. A substitute operator tests the binding environment; if it is 'fail' the operator outputs 'fail', and if 'nil', the operator outputs the instance directly; otherwise, the operator tests the shared flag of the instance and replaces the instance with binding environment, if the instance is a shared variable or its shared flag is ON (i. e., if the instance has any shared-type variables). The following subsection gives some examples of usage of these primitives.

5.2 Some Examples of Head Unification

If the following goal literal is given to the above data flow graph:

← p([a | X], b, c).

all the binding environments from the unify operators are set to 'nil' or 'fail', since there is no shared variable in the goal and head literals. The check-consistency operator, thus outputs 'nil' or 'fail' to the substitute operators. The substitute operators then simply pass the common instances from the unify operators or outputs 'fail', according to the binding environment. These outputs constitute the result of the head unification of the clause.

The following is another example in which a goal literal including shared variable is given:

← p([a | X], X, c) & . . .

where variable X occurs twice in the literal. In this case, the compiled code of the goal invocation is as shown in Fig. 8.

The share operator tests the non-ground flag of the instance for X and, if the non-ground flag is ON, it changes all the simple variables in the instance into the shared variables; if not, it outputs the instance itself. If X is unbound before calling p([a|X], X, c) as in the above example, X is changed to a shared variable, Xs. The subscript 's' indicates that the variable is shared. Xs constitutes the first and second arguments of the goal literal. These arguments are sent to the head literals of the clauses in the definition. Assume that the same clause as shown in Fig. 7 is given in the definition. In head unification, the unify operator of the first argument generates a binding environment [(Xs = [b])], which shows the instance for Xs is [b], and the unify operator of the last argument generates a binding environment 'nil'. These two environments are sent to the check-consistency operator, which outputs the final environment [(Xs = [b])] .

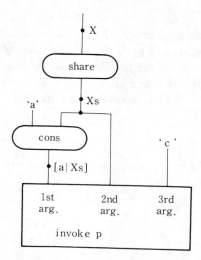

Fig. 8 Data flow graph of goal
← p([a | X], X, c) & ....

The substitute operators replace the instances from the unify operators according to this final environment.

If another clause, such as the following, is given for the same goal literal:

p([Y, b | Z], [b, c | W], c) ← ...

three unify operators are used for three head arguments. The binding environments from these unify operators become [(Xs = [b | Z])], [(Xs = [b, c | W])], and 'nil'. The result of consistency checking will output the final environment [(Xs = [b, c | W])], which is sent to the share operator and is then changed to [(Xs = [b, c | Ws])], as described above. The final instances of three arguments, therefore, become [a, b, c | Ws], [b, c | Ws], and c, where the first and second instances share the variable, Ws.

When a variable occurs two or more times in the head literal, the compiler can also generate codes described above: the codes in which share operators are executed before head unify operators are executed. However, in order to reduce the overhead of consistency checking, lazy execution of the share operator can be implemented as shown in the following example. Assume that a goal literal and a clause are given:

← p([a | X], [W], c) & ...
p([Y, Z], Z, c) ← ...

A compiled graph of the clause and tokens on the arcs are shown in Fig. 9. In this case, instead of updating the variable Z appearing in the clause head to a shared variable Zs before executing the unify operators, a unify operator is executed to assure that the multiple occurrences of Z are bound to the same instance. That is, both instances of Z (the first one is obtained from the unify operator of the first head argument and the second one is directly obtained from the second goal argument) are unified again by another unify operator. This final unify operator produces the list [W] as an instance for Z; the list [W] is then sent to the share operator and changed to [Ws], before it is returned to the goal. The goal literal will receive this shared structure as the instances of its variables X and W.

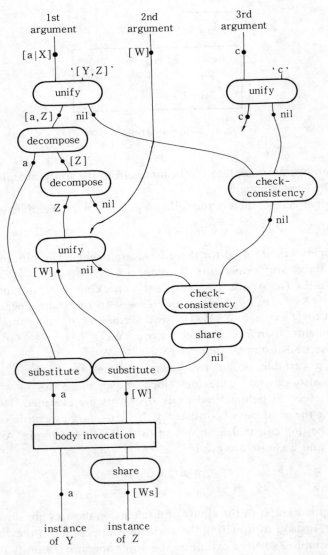

Fig. 9 Data flow graph of clause p([Y, Z], Z, c) ← . . . and its tokens.

If there is a body in the clause and the instance of Z is used in the body literal, the variable W may be bound to another term by calling the body literal. If this share operator is executed after the body literal is invoked instead of just after head unification, the body unification treats the variable as a simple variable. Therefore, the unify operators in this unification do not produce the binding environment of Ws. This lazy execution of the share operator reduces the overhead of consistency checking.

5.3 Nondeterministic Merge Primitives

If unification succeeds and one of the solutions is obtained, it is returned to the goal statement. A solution is a list constructed from final instances of the head arguments followed by a binding environment, or 'fail'; a construct operator of the solution tests all of its operands, and if all of them are not 'fail' it generates a new list; otherwise, it returns 'fail'. In the OR-parallel environment, multiple solutions may be obtained in a nondeterministic manner. That is, solutions may be returned to the goal in the order in which they are obtained. This nondeterminism is called 'don't-know nondeterminism'. We introduced a non-strict data structure called a stream to implement this nondeterministic control. Solutions are merged into a stream by stream merge primitives, as shown in Fig. 10.[4,12]

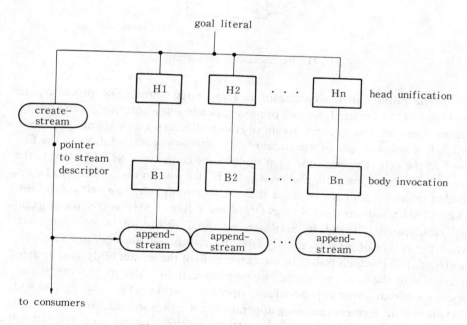

Fig. 10 Stream merging primitives.

When a goal literal calls its definition, an empty stream is created by a create-stream operator, which generates a stream descriptor as shown in Fig. 11. A stream descriptor cell consists of two pointers: a Stream Head Pointer (SHP) and a Stream Tail Pointer (STP). R(ready) and P(pending) flags of the cell words to be stored these pointers are initialized to OFF (empty). The pointer to the stream descriptor is returned immediately to the goal, the consumer of the stream, which in turn reads the contents of SHP by this pointer if the R flag of SHP is ON. The goal waits for a solution (i. e., sets its P flag ON and chains the read request to SHP) if the stream is still empty (i.e., if its R flag is OFF).

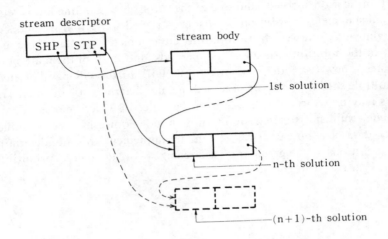

Fig. 11 Representation of a stream.

The pointer to the descriptor is also shared among OR processes, the producers of the stream. Each OR process appends a new solution by an append-stream operator. The append-stream operator allocates a new stream body cell, which is a new tail cell of the stream body, and writes the solution to the first word of the cell. The operator then updates the contents of STP to point to the new cell by testing its R flag: when it is OFF (i. e., when the solution to be appended to the stream is a first one), the operator writes the new cell address into STP and SHP, and sets their R flags ON (if the P flag of SHP is ON, the consumers' read requests linked to SHP are activated before this write operation); when the R flag of STP is already ON, the append-stream operator reads the contents of STP, which points to the current tail of the stream body, and updates it to point to the newly allocated stream body cell. In order to lock the stream descriptor from other append-stream operators while STP is being updated, the processing element executing append-stream operator sends an uninterruptable command, which contains the stream descriptor address and new tail cell address, to the structure memory pointed by the stream descriptor. The structure memory then performs this read-and-write cycles without interruption from other memory operations. Finally, the operator writes the new cell address into the second word of the current tail cell, previously pointed to by the STP, also by testing its P flag: if it is ON, the suspended read requests are activated. Thus, every second word of the stream body cells points to the rest of the stream. This update is indicated by the broken line in Fig. 11.

A failed OR process does not affect the stream; the append-stream operator checks whether solution is 'fail', before appending the solution.

In order to signal the goal statement that all the OR processes have terminatad, the stream descriptor has a reference count of active OR processes. The reference count is initialized to the number of OR clauses invoked. It is decremented by one each time an append-stream operator is executed; it is incremented by the number of the newly created OR processes each time an AND process calls its body literal.

If the reference count reaches zero by decrementing, the append-stream operator writes 'fail', which signals the end-of-stream, into the second word of the cell pointed to by STP, and the descriptor becomes a garbage cell. If all the OR processes fail (i. e., if the stream is still empty when the reference count is zero), the SHP is set to 'fail'; otherwise, it is set to the pointer of the first word in the stream body. A waiting goal literal reads SHP, accesses the stream body cell, and decomposes it into a solution and the rest of the stream body. This stream reading operation can be executed recursively, until the rest of the stream becomes 'fail'.

5.4 Execution of AND Literals

As a solution consists of instances for goal literal arguments and a binding environment, AND-sequential and AND-parallel execution can be achieved. In this subsection, both execution mechanisms will be shown.

[1] AND-sequential execution

Assume the following clause is given in the definition of predicate p:

$$p([a \mid X], Y) \leftarrow q(X, Z) \& r(Z, Y).$$

In this example, two body literals $q(X, Z)$ and $r(Z, Y)$ are executed sequentially. Connection paths between the instances of the variables are shown as in Fig. 12.

In this figure, Eh is the created binding environment by head unification, Eq is the environment returned from the definition of q, Er is the environment returned from the definition of r, and Ep is the final environment of the clause p to be returned to the goal statement. The additional literal, apply-append([a| X], Y, Ep), represents a creation of the solution and execution of the append-stream operation described above. The solution to be returned is a list of final instances for the arguments in the head literal followed by Ep. The input/output modes for the literal arguments can be specified in the compiler. When these

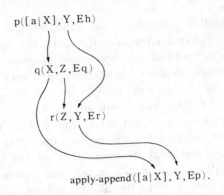

Fig. 12 Connection paths of clause
$$p([a|X], Y) \leftarrow q(X, Z) \& r(Z, Y).$$

modes are specified, the arguments to be returned can be a subset of those contained in the clause head to improve performance.

The compiler generates complete data flow graph procedures, which is shown as Fig. 13 (a), (b), and (c), according to the connection paths shown in Fig. 12. When a goal literal, whose predicate is p, is given, its arguments are passed to head unification of the clause shown by Fig. 13(a). The instances of variables X and Y are obtained if head unification succeeds. Succeeded head unification invokes the definition of the first body literal $q(X, Z)$, whose first argument is the obtained instance X and second instance is an unbound variable Z. If head unification fails, the invocation of $q(X, Z)$, is suppressed: the procedure invocation primitives do not invoke the procedure and decrement the reference count of the stream descriptor if its input argument is 'fail'. The instance of Y, which is not used in $q(X, Z)$, is sent to the next stage by bypassing this literal.

The invocation of the literal $q(X, Z)$ may return the stream of solutions $\{(X_i, Z_i, E_{q_i})\}$, where X_i and Z_i are i-th instances of X and Z, respectively, and E_{q_i} is an i-th environment obtained. The recursive procedure apply-r shown as Fig. 13(b) is then invoked, reads the stream, and divides it into the first solution (X_1, Z_1, E_{q_1}) and the rest of the stream $\{(X_i, Z_i, E_{q_i})\}$, which is used as the argument of the recursive call of the apply-r (where, $i = 2, 3, \ldots$). If the stream is still empty, the read request is suspended as described in Subsection 5.3. When no successful solutions are obtained, or when the rest of stream is 'fail' (i. e., no more solutions are exist), the invocation of the procedure is suppressed.

The body of apply-r further decomposes the solution into the instances of X and Z, and the environment E_q, which is used to check consistency with the environment of head unification Eh to produce a new environment E_q'. The bypassed instance of Y is replaced by this new environment (the result of check-consistency primitive).

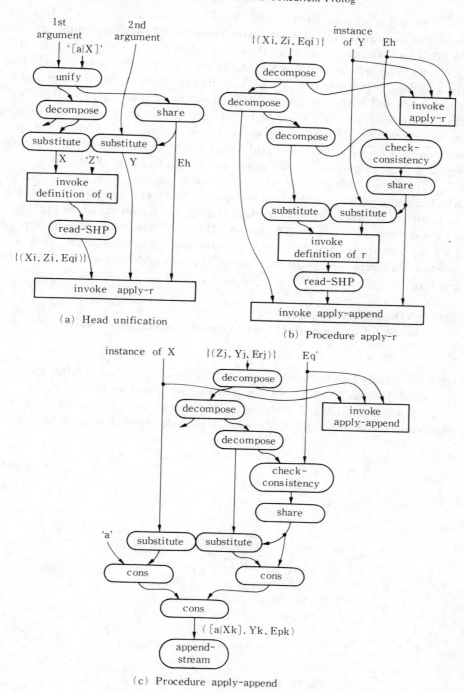

Fig. 13   The complete data flow graphs of clause p([a | X], Y) ← q(X, Z) & r(Z, Y).

In this procedure, when a goal literal has shared variables in its first and second arguments, the instances of X and Y, obtained by the substitute operators in Fig. 13(a), will share these variables. For example, if the given goal literal is p(Ws, Ws), the instances of X and Y are Xs and [a | Xs], respectively, and share the variable Xs (where Ws = [a | Xs]). If the execution of the first literal q(X, Z) succeeds and binds any term to the instance of X (the shared variable Xs), the same substitution for Xs must be applied to that of Y. The substitution information for Xs is given by Eq and will be used to produce the new environment Eq'. The shared variable Xs in the bypassed instance of Y is then replaced according to Eq' by the substitute operator in Fig. 13(b).

The consistent solution set, then, invokes the next body literal r(Z, Y), which again generates another stream {(Zj, Yj, Erj)}. The new stream is used as an argument of the next recursive procedure apply-append shown in Fig. 13(c). As the instance of X obtained from q(X, Z) is also transferred to apply-append ([a | X], Y, Ep) by bypassing r(Z, Y), the same consistency checking and substitution operations as in the case of the bypassed instance of Y must be executed.

[2] AND-parallel execution

In the following example, AND-parallel execution is specified:

$$p([a \mid X], Y) \leftarrow q(X, Z) \;//\; r(Z, Y).$$

Here, both body literals q(X, Z) and r(Z, Y) are executed in parallel. Connection paths between instances of the variables are shown in Fig. 14.

Since the variable Z is shared by two literals and is uninstantiated, it is changed to the shared variable Zs by the share operator before these literals are

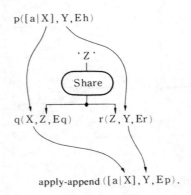

Fig. 14 Connection paths of clause
p([a | X], Y) ← q(X, Z) // r(Z, Y).

called. The two AND processes of the body obtain streams having as their i-th and j-th elements (Xi, Zi, Eqi) and (Zj, Yj, Erj), respectively. This clause should obtain all combinations of these two solutions and check consistency between the two binding environments Eqi and Erj, the results of which are the final binding environments and are used for substitution of the instances of Xi and Yj. In this case, the procedure apply-append is defined as a duplicated recursive procedure, in order to divide two streams into their solutions.

§6 Primitives for Concurrent Prolog

Processing of the clause head and the guard in Concurrent Prolog is almost the same as in Parallel Prolog, as described in Section 5. The major difference is that create-global-variable operators are used instead of share operators, and copy-global-variable operators are issued for every argument passed from the head to the guard before the guard consisting of multiple literals are called.

When the input operands of the create-global-variable operators are simple variables or structured data including simple variables, the operators allocate memory cells to all simple variables and change them into global variables. The copy-global-variable operators create a local copy for each global variable in their input operands. These outputs are passed to the clauses invoked by guard literals as their arguments.

Another difference from Parallel Prolog is the existence of a commit operator and read-only annotation.

6.1 Read-only Annotation

When a read-only tag is postfixed to a variable appearing as an argument in the goal literal, the set-read-only-tag operator is executed. This operator changes an instance of a variable to a read-only variable only when it is a global variable, as described in Section 4. When the input operand is other than a global variable, the operator outputs the input operand itself.

In the head unification of a clause, if the input argument from the goal literal is a read-only variable and if the corresponding head argument is a non-variable term, the unify operator tries to read the contents of the memory cell, which is pointed to by the read-only variable, before unification is performed. If the instance of the variable (contained in the memory cell) is not a non-variable term, the read request is suspended until the variable is bound to a non-variable term. The memory cell will be written by a guard operation mechanism, described below. In all other cases, the action of the unify operator is the same as in Parallel Prolog.

6.2 Guard Operation Mechanism

As described in Section 4, a commit operator has two functions: one for exclusive control and another for commitment of the binding environment for the global variables obtained by unification of the head and guard of the clause.

Exclusive control is nondeterministic, in that only one process which has executed the commit operator first can continue to a subsequent process. This nondeterminism is called 'don't-care nondeterminism'. To perform exclusive control, semaphore operators are provided. When a definition consisting of multiple guarded clauses is invoked, a create-guard operator is executed, as shown in Fig. 15. This operator generates a semaphore flag to be shared between OR processes, initializes the flag to OFF, and sends its pointer to these OR processes.

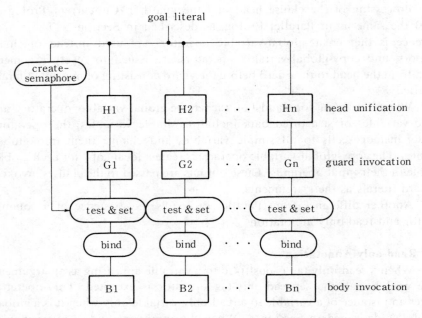

Fig. 15 The guard control primitives.

An OR process executing a guarded clause activates a test & set operator of the semaphore flag when unification of the clause head and the guard succeeds. The test & set operator reads and returns the contents of the semaphore flag, which shows whether or not it is the first OR process that passed the commit operator, and sets the semaphore flag to ON.

If the result of this test operation is OFF, the bind operator tests the binding environment for global variables; if it is not 'nil' or 'fail', the operator tries to unify an old instance previously written into the memory cell with a new instance of each global variable in the environment. That is, the bind operator obtains a pair consisting of a global variable and an instance from the binding environment, and executes the following sequence for all the pairs in the binding environment: it reads the contents of the memory cell pointed to by the global variable, attempts to unify the instance from the binding environment with the contents of the memory cell (i. e., the old instance for the global variable), then writes their common instance into the memory cell if the unification succeeds. While the memory cell is being written, it is locked to any other accesses. Finally, the written instances are made available to other processes and a trigger token is returned to the parent literal, that may initiate the next literal or the commit operator in the parent clause.

§7 Conclusion

Execution mechanisms on a data flow machine for Parallel and Concurrent Prolog have been presented and primitive operators for supporting these two languages described. It has been shown that two types of logic programming languages with different aims can be supported on this machine.

There are two basic functions embedded in these languages: one is unification, and the other is nondeterminism. Several primitives for performing these functions are introduced and programs written by these languages are compiled into data flow graphs, which corresponds to the machine language. Thus, parallelism in the programs can be exploited naturally.

In order to exploit AND parallelism efficiently, unification primitives being executed in parallel generate bindings only for undefined shared variables. Check-consistency primitives of these bindings, therefore, are rather simplified and performance by exploiting this parallelism significantly increases.

Control of nondeterminism is related to OR parallelism: 'don't-know nondeterminism' is necessary in Parallel Prolog, while 'don't-care nondeterminism' is necessary in Concurrent Prolog. Stream merging primitives realize 'don't-know nondeterminism', where OR processes executing independent clauses share a stream tail pointer and append new solutions to the tail of the stream, while stream consumer processes obtain the solutions by traversing the stream from its head pointer. Semaphore primitives and exporting mechanism of bindings for shared variables realize 'don't-care nondeterminism', as in Dijkstra's guarded command. The guard, which succeeds first, makes its local bindings available to other processes sharing the variables.

Detailed designs for the machine are presently being developed; its simulation to Parallel Prolog programs indicates that performance can be significantly improved by exploiting parallelism.[14] Future efforts will involve the development of a Concurrent Prolog simulator and prototype hardware to serve as the basis for a highly-parallel inference machine.

Acknowledgements

The authors extend their thanks to Director, Kazuhiro Fuchi, in ICOT, who afforded them the opportunity to pursue this research. Also much appreciated are the valuable advice and comments of Dr. Kunio Murakami,

Chief of the First Research Laboratory in ICOT, Mr. Rikio Onai, Senior Researcher, and other ICOT research members.

References

1) Ackerman, W. B., "A Structured Processing Facility for Data Flow Computers," *Proceeding of International Conference on Parallel Processing*, 1978.

2) Amamiya, M. and Hasegawa R., "Data Flow Machine and Functional Language," *AL81-84, PRL81-63*, IECE Japan, Dec., 1981 [in Japanese].

3) Amamiya, M., Hasegawa, R., Nakamura, O. and Mikami, H., "A List-processing-oriented data flow architecture," *National Computer Conference 1982*, pp. 143-151, June, 1982.

4) Arvind, Gostelow, K. P. and Plouffe, W. E., "An Asynchronous Programming Language and Computing Machine," *TR-114a*, Dept. of ICS, University of California, Irvine, Dec., 1978.

5) Arvind and Innucci, R. A., "A Critique of Multiprocessing von Neumann Style," *Proceedings of 10th International Symposium on Computer Architecture*, June, 1983.

6) Clark, K. and Gregory, S., "A Relational Language for Parallel Programming," *Research Report DOC 81/16*, Imperial College of Science and Technology, July, 1981.

7) Clark, K. and Gregory, S., "PARLOG : Parallel Programming in Prolog," *Research Report DOC 84/4*, Imperial College of Science and Technology, April, 1984.

8) Cohen, J. "Garbage Collection of Linked Data Structures," *Computing Surveys, Vol. 13, No. 3*, Sept., 1981.

9) Conery, J. S. and Kibler, D., "Parallel Interpretation of Logic Programming," *Proceedings of Conference on Functional Programming and Computer Architecture*, ACM, Oct., 1981.

10) Dijkstra, E. M., *A Discipline of Programming*, Prentice-Hall, 1976.

11) Gurd, J. R. and Watson, I., "Data Driven System for High Speed Parallel Computing," *Computer Design*, July, 1980.

12) Ito, N., Masuda, K. and Shimizu, H., "Parallel Prolog Machine Based on the Data Flow Model," *ICOT Technical Report, TR-035*, Institute for New Generation Computer Technology, Tokyo, Japan, 1983.

13) Ito, N. and Kuno, E., "Simulation of a Parallel Prolog Machine," *Proceedings of 28th National Conference of Information Processing Society of Japan*, Tokyo, Japan, March, 1984 [in Japanese].

14) Ito, N. and Masuda, K., "Parallel Inference Machine Based on the Data Flow Model," *International Workshop on High Level Computer Architecture 84*, Hyatt International Hotel, Los Angeles, California, May, 1984.

15) Kowalski, R., "Predicate Logic as Programming Language," *IFIP 74*, North-Holland, 1974.

16) Nakamura, O., Hasegawa, R. and Amamiya, M., "The Design and Evaluation of the Structure Memories for a List Processing Oriented Data Flow Machine," *EC 81-32*, IECE Japan, 1981 [in Japanese].

17) Onai, R. and Asou, M., "Control Mechanisms of the Guard and Read-Only Annotation in Parallel Inference Machine," *Proceedings of 27th National Conference of Information Processing Society of Japan*, Nagoya, Japan, Oct., 1983 [in Japanese].

18) Shapiro, E. Y., "A Subset of Concurrent Prolog and its Interpreter," *ICOT Technical Report, TR-003*, Institute for New Generation Computer Technology, Tokyo, Japan, Jan., 1983.

19) Shapiro, E. Y., "System Programming in Concurrent Prolog," *ICOT Technical Report, TR-034*, Institute for New Generation Computer Technology, Tokyo, Japan, Nov., 1983.

New Generation Computing, 2 (1984) 131-155
OHMSHA, LTD. and Springer-Verlag

A Relational Database Machine with Large Semiconductor Disk and Hardware Relational Algebra Processor

Shigeki SHIBAYAMA, Takeo KAKUTA, Nobuyoshi MIYAZAKI,
Haruo YOKOTA, and Kunio MURAKAMI

ICOT Research Center,
Institute for New Generation Computer Technology,
Mita Kokusai Bldg. 21F, 4-28 Mita 1-chome, Minato-ku, Tokyo 108, Japan

Received 19 December 1983

Abstract   This paper describes the basic concepts, design and implementation decisions, standpoints and significance of the database machine Delta in the scope of Japan's Fifth Generation Computer Project. Delta is planned to be operational in 1985 for researchers' use as a backend database machine for logic programming software development. Delta is basically a relational database machine system. It combines hardware facilities for efficient relational database operations, which are typically represented by relational algebra, and software which deals with hardware control and actual database management requirements. Notable features include attribute-based internal schema in accordance with the characteristics found in the relation access from logic programming environment. This is also useful for the hardware relational algebra manipulation algorithm based on merge-sorting of attributes by hardware and a large capacity Semiconductor Disk for fast access to databases. Various implementation decisions of database management requirements are made in this novel system configuration, which will be meaningful to give an example for constructing a hardware and software combination of a relational database machine. Delta is in the stage between detailed design and implementation.

Keywords: Database Machine, Relational Database, Sorter, Disk Cache, Logic Programming

§1   Introduction

Delta is a hardware-oriented relational database machine which is in the detailed design stage and will be operational in 1985. Delta is planned to be one of the software development tools in Japan's Fifth Generation Computer

Project.[13] Another piece of new hardware which will also be finished in the first stage Project is the Sequential Inference Machine (SIM), which is constructed in order to support efficient logic programming language processing.[22] Delta will be used as a backend database machine in a local area network environment. A number of SIM's will be connected to the Ethernet-like network as the hosts of Delta.

§2 Delta Architecture

Delta's global architecture[16] is shown in Fig. 1. This figure, however, does not show the implementation details of an actual machine. In that sense, Fig. 1 shows the conceptual function distribution of a database machine. The

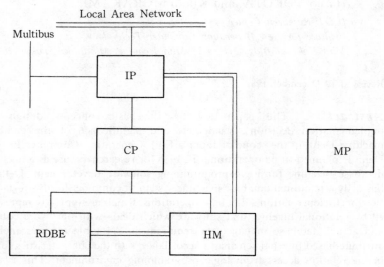

Fig. 1 Delta global architecture.

concept behind the architecture is that functions needed for a database machine should be distributed to efficiently construct a full system. Important functions which are mapped on Delta subsystems are described in the following chapters by means of subtystem descriptions.

2.1 Interface Processor

The Interface Processor (IP) manages interfacing functions to connect a database machine to the overall computing environment such as host machines or local area notworks. This portion should be independent of the control portion for flexible interface requirements. Some interruption type database commands could be analyzed here to avoid the rather time-consuming command analysis process performed in the control portion and make it responsive for users.

2.2 Control Processor

As the functionally distributed database machine is comprised of several separately working processors, a certain central control function which manages the coordination of each subsystem is needed. Distribution of control as well as distribution of operation is required for a regularly-structured highly-parallel machine. However, database operations include not only data intensive operations (join operation is the typical one) but database management facilities such as recovery functions, security control and transaction management to maintain data consistency. These should be fulfilled in a working database management system and also in a database machine once it begins to be actually used. Proposed highly parallel architectures perform these functions poorly and in some cases do not even consider them. Query analysis or command compilation are also time-consuming jobs for a database machine if it receives a high-level user language as SQL.[4] Considering these functions, database machines which are constructed only of data intensive operation-oriented resources are unlikely to tolerate real-life database manipulations. To perform these tasks, a control portion, which is constructed upon a general-purpose computer, is needed. What kind of processor can complete these jobs efficiently is a subject for debate in future database machine research. This could be a conventional von Neumann machine or an inference-based new architecture machine.

2.3 Relational Database Engine

Relational database operations pose a heavy computational burden on conventional von Neumann architecture. This is particularly true when symmetrical accesses to database are required. Indexed internal schemata will perform well only when indexed keys (attributes) are handled. To perform full-range relational algebra operations in a reasonable time, some dedicated hardware is needed. But the use of dedicated hardware without considerations for storage portion architecture will hardly produce a good result. Relational database engine (RDBE), the dedicated hardware for performing relational algebra and other Delta commands, should be considered in conjunction with the Hierarchical Memory subsystem which supplies attribute data to RDBE in a stream at a high bandwidth. There are various kinds of hardware proposed for relational database operations.[1,14,19,7,6] We think that the following points are the properties required for a database engine :

- ○ Stream synchronous processing (does not disturb the data stream flow)
- ○ Processing a stream on-the-fly (pipeline processing)
- ○ Processing a stream in one scan (repeated stream transfers should be minimized.)
- ○ Regular architecture to exploit the use of VLSI technologies
- ○ Applicable for a wide range of database commands

By on-the-fly we mean an operation in which overlapping of data processing and the data transfer is carried out. A database engine should be designed to exploit high bandwidth data transfer from the storage portion. Processing-bound database query execution should be avoided as much as possible, enabling the data to flow smoothly from storage. This means that we expect a high-speed data transfer between the engine portion and the storage portion (possibly from the cache and not from the moving-head-disk) *and* processing the transferred data without delay. An engine should perform better than the transfer rate if the storage subsystem becomes fast with architectural enhancement. This feature requires the capability of processing a data stream on-the-fly from storage, in combination with a high-bandwidth storage hierarchy. And the other factor to make query execution fast is that stream data should not be transferred repeatedly to fulfill an operation. For example, if a database engine can perform a single condition selection at a time, the SQL query :

    SELECT employee_name, age
    FROM employee_list
    WHERE age BETWEEN 25 AND 35

will need to scan the age attribute twice to get the result. There are two solutions to this problem. One is to make the database engine cascadable and flow one data stream into cascaded engines so that each of them can operate on the stream differently. The other is to make a single database engine perform multiple-condition operations, like the example shown above. In our database engine algorithm, multiple-condition queries can be handled (see Section 3 for details), succeeding in suppressing the data trasfer frequency.

The other requirement for an engine is that it should be designed to exploit the benefits of future VLSI technology. This means that if the basic architectural features include some kind of regular structure, it can be manufactured in mass quantity, hence lowering the cost and justifying the use of special purpose hardware. The last requirement is that RDBE should support a wide range of database manipulation operations. This is somewhat contradictory to the requirement detailed just above. As the engine becomes sophisticated enough to support a wide range of database manipulations, it will become complicated in design and difficult to be implemented with VLSI technologies. However, if a database engine performs aggregate operations poorly, for example, these should be done somewhere in the database machine, presumably at a slow speed. This will result in uneven execution times in the database machine's command set, which will be unpleasant for users. Therefore, to attain this feature, the database engine is expected to have some kind of general-purpose processing capability such as incorporation of microprogrammed architecture or a general-purpose processing portion. In our design, the hardware-intensive portion of the RDBE is implemented in a regular form to be implemented using VLSI, while operations which need flexible data manipulation are delegated to a general-purpose processor which also takes care of detailed control of the hardware portion.

2.4 Hierarchical Memory

The database storage portion is a most essential one in a database machine. Conventionally, a one-level collection of moving-head-disk devices constitutes a database storage. Currently, incorporation of layers in storage are considered to be promising for efficient database processing. The idea follows the technology of cache memories first considered and implemented to enhance the processing power of CPU by compensating a main memory access gap. The disk cache is the counterpart of the CPU cache, assuming the locality of reference using replacement algorithms derived mainly from LRU (Least Recently Used) strategy. In a database operation, however, data access patterns sometimes fit LRU poorly. A database has the sequential access property in its nature because database data often needs to be scanned for search. One somewhat artificial but possible example where LRU performs poorly is as follows :

i)   Scan a (part of) relation which overflows the total cache size by one page. By this, the cache is filled up with the relation, the first page of which is replaced with the last page.

ii)   Re-scan the relation once again for another purpose
Cache control looks for the first page in the cache, recognizing the cache miss and then fetching it from a secondary device. The fetched page replaces the second page (next to be searched in cache !) with it.

Thus this process is repeated through the last page. In this situation, apparently, it does no good to have a cache, however large it might be. We have to introduce a cache or a hierarchy of caches to enhance the performance. The algorithm should be carefully chosen to fit the database access properties. One candidate for a wise cache replacement algorithm is the object-oriented cache[15] or an algorithm which makes use of some kind of semantic information. That a (part of) relation is needed likely means the whole of it and not random subparts of it.

The lowest layer storage device should be constructed on moving-head-disks. This is today's most popular technology (it has the best storage/cost factor with acceptable access speed for on-line database use) and is widely accepted as a non-volatile data storage. Other cost-effective devices, such as optical disks could be accommodated in a database machine storage, in the sense discussed above, when they have gained good reliability and become commercially available. Mass storage system (MSS) is a current technology and offers a huge amount of on-line storage using a tape-based technology. It can also be used as a low-end storage, but MSS is somewhat special with its properties of the amount of storage space and access time. When it is used, it should be used as a kind of loading device which is activated when the user needs a large new relation for a possibly new transaction. MSS will poorly perform if it is used like a disk.

As has been pointed out,[2] the major bottleneck which exists in the database operation is disk access time. To overcome this, one idea is to have a fairly large amount of cache storage which can contain *all* the relations which are used during a transaction. This is virtually impossible for every query. However, by giving a large capacity fast storage space with a wise replacement algorithm, most database transactions can be carried out within the fast storage. This is an expectation and not a proven fact as yet. But we think that lowered storage costs will justify the use of a very large semiconductor cache in future.

2.5 Maintenance Processor

As Delta is comprised of several subsystems, some care has to be taken to maintain reliability and serviceability. A supervisory processor in a conventional large computer system has a similar role. In Delta we prepared a Maintenance Processor (MP) for this purpose. MP has communication channels to each of Delta's subsystems. When an error occurs in a processor, it reports the status to MP, and MP will judge the state of the entire system and determine whether to continue operation by isolating the error or to shut the system down.

§3　Relational Algebra Processing Algorithm

3.1　Merge-Sort Relational Algebra Algorithm

There have been numerous algorithms to implement relational algebra by hardware. We have chosen a merge-sort algorithm for Delta's hardware algorithm. The hardware portion for the relational algebra execution is provided in RDBE. The basic RDBE command set concept is related to the fundamental RDBE processing hardware algorithm. Unless the command set is closely associated with the hardware implementation algorithm, efficient processing of that command set will be difficult.

Merge-sort is a well-known algorithm to efficiently manipulate the strings of two or more pre-sorted strings to form a longer sorted string. Logically, there are two or more FIFO memories which contain pre-sorted shorter streams. In the ascending sort, a processor compares the top elements of those FIFO's and outputs the smaller element, at the same time advancing the FIFO which contains the smaller element. This algortithm only outputs each string top as the compared result to form a longer sorted string. If the output is properly controlled by another criterion, most relational algebra operations can be implemented using this algorithm. For example, in two-way merge-sort, if one string is a selection criterion and the other string output is controlled such that those values which match at least one element of the upper string is output (note that the two strings are both sorted), selection to the criterion is accomplished.

As shown in this example, if proper output control is accommodated in the course of the merging process, various useful selection and join algorithms can be realized.

3.2 Merger Algorithm

The merger unit in the RDBE is the portion which performs the algorithm described in the previous chapter. The merger is, basically, similar to a merge sorter, as the algorithm inherently contains the merging process. The merger has two stream buffers which are placed before the comparator unit, and performs two-way merge-sorting. The comparator unit must have several fundamental commands to perform classes of relational algebra operations. We will briefly describe the principal merger functions in the following chapters.

〔1〕 **Simple selection**

A simple selection is defined as a selection against a single criterion, for example, selecting all attribute items by the qualification of "greater than C." This operation is done by placing the constant value in the top of the first FIFO, flowing the stream through the second FIFO and outputting those items which satisfy the criterion. The time required to perform this is NT where N is the length of the attribute and T is the transfer unit time. Criteria such as "less than" and "equal" are easily carried out by simple modification of the output control.

〔2〕 **Range selection**

Range selection is a little more complex than simple selection. Range selection is defined as selection of attribute items by the range specified by two values $C1$ and $C2$. First FIFO contains the two values in sorted order ($C1$ at the top if it is smaller). The process is as follows :

(1) Flows the target attribute items in the second FIFO
(2) Discards the items until the top element exceeds $C1$
(3) Advances the first FIFO to make $C2$ appear at the top
(4) Outputs the stream until the top element exceeds $C2$

It is obvious that range selection which has the form $((X < C1)$ or $(X > C2))$, where $C1 < C2$, is easily done by modifying the control in a reversed manner.

〔3〕 **List selection**

List selection is an operation in which qualified attribute items are selected against a list of constant values. Sorted constant values $C1, C2,.., Cn$ are stored in the first FIFO. The operation is carried out by the following procedure :

(1) Target attribute items in the second FIFO are forwarded
(2) Items they are smaller than the top element in the first FIFO are discarded
(3) If a match is found, the attribute item (at the top of FIFO) is output
(4) If the top element in the second FIFO exceeds the top element in the first FIFO, the first FIFO is advanced.

〔4〕 **Synchronous comparison**

Synchronous comparison is an operation where both the first FIFO and second FIFO are advanced synchronously and the top two items are compared with each other. This is useful when selecting attribute items which have a value which is greater or smaller than the other attribute items. The two streams should be sorted beforehand by tuple-identifier (see Section 5) to correctly correspond the attribute item values.

[5] **Join**

Equi-join operation is performed by the following procedure :

(1) The first FIFO is filled with sorted attribute items
(2) The second FIFO is forwarded with the other sorted attribute items
(3) The top two items in both FIFO's are compared
(4) If the first FIFO top is greater than the second one, the first one is advanced
(5) If the second FIFO top is greater than the first one, the second one is advanced
(6) If a match is found between two items, both are output or, in the case of a natural join, only one of them is.

A general join can be performed by modifying the control of the FIFO advances. There is a problem here that when there are duplicate items in an attribute stream, all the possible combinations should be obtained in join operations. This is solved by the tag field in the attribute items. If there are duplicate values, the tag field of the duplicate items are set by the sorter. The merger portion recognizes duplicates, controls FIFO advances and produces all possible combinations in join operations.

There are other commands in addition to the relational algebra operations. However, they all fall into one of these categories.

§4 Delta Command Set

The Delta's command set is shown in Fig. 2. It consists of several classes of commands. Host software is responsible for converting user queries to the Delta command sequence. We named the sequence a command-tree, because a set of relational database query commands forms a tree structure of Delta commands. In the next Section, command-tree and the transaction concept provided in Delta are described. The following Sections are brief descriptions of the categorized Delta commands.

4.1 Command-Tree and Transaction

A command-tree is a set of Delta commands which represents a meaningful query. A command-tree example is shown in Fig. 3. In this example, the permanent relation 1 and the permanent relation 2 are semi-joined to produce the temporary relation 1 from the permanent relation 1, while the temporary relation 2 is selected from the permanent relation 3. The temporary relations 1 and 2 are then natural-joined to produce the intermediate relation 1, which is the result relation of this command-tree. According to Delta's terminology,

A Relational Database Machine

Relational Algebra Commands	Aggregate Function Commands
Projection Selection Natural-Join θ-Join Semi-Join	Count Summation Maximum Minimum Average
Set Operation Commands	**Set Comparison Commands**
Union Difference Intersection Cartesian-Product	Equal Contain
Update Commands	**Input/Output Commands**
Delete Update Insert	Get Get-Next Get-End Put Put-Next Put-End
Definition Commands	**Transaction Control Commands**
Create-Relation Purge-Relation Rename-Relation Append-Attribute Drop-Attributes	Start-Transaction End-Transaction Abort-Transaction Commit-Transaction
Arithmetic Commands	**Miscellaneous Commands**
Add Subtract Multiply Divide	Sort Unique Group-by Select-Group Copy Classify
Asynchronous Commands	
Sense-Status Abort-Processing	

Fig. 2 Delta command set.

temporary relations are erased when the command-tree has produced a result relation (intermediate relation). Intermediate relations are given a name and can be used across the command-trees. They are, however, erased at the end of the transaction.

There is a notion of transaction in Delta. A transaction is composed of a set of command-trees which are enclosed by a start-transaction command and an end-transaction command. The command pair groups a set of command-trees in between as a transaction. Delta will support update consistency by user's specification of these transaction control commands. This means that updates to the database can be undone by aborting the transaction (abort-transaction command) in which the updates took place, or can be committed also by committing the transaction (commit-transaction command). For read-only database accesses, committing a transaction means that the result relation can no

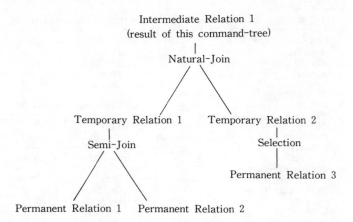

Fig. 3 A command-tree example.

more be used as an intermediate relation, inhibiting subsidiary queries. The only exception to this is when it is used for output. Before a commit-transaction command, intermediate relations can be used as source relations of the command-trees to follow.

4.2 Relational Algebra

Relational algebra-type commands come directly from the original relational algebra. Usually duplicate tuples are not eliminated automatically. Duplicate elimination can be explicitly specified by unique command (see Section 4.12 Miscellaneous Commands). Relational division is not included in the command set because it can be done by a combination of other commands and the frequency of the divide command is not very large. We provide three types of join commands ; natural-join which is considered to be most useful, theta-join for general classes of join and semi-join for efficient use of Delta.

4.3 Set Operation

Set operations between two relations are fully implemented. We have decided to implement Cartesian product command for optimization reasons. Relational algebra queries with some specific execution ordering are sometimes more elegantly represented using Cartesian product operation. In union command, resultant duplicates of tuples are automatically eliminated in contrast to the other commands. If duplicate elimination is not required in union command, it is no more than an append operation of one relation to another. Specification of union command is considered to be an explicit duplicate elimination intention.

4.4 Set Comparison

Set comparison commands are useful when checking two sets of objects. In Prolog language, meta-predicates such as set-of or bag-of are provided. These predicates are useful for interfacing logic programming language and relational database.[10] Set comparison can operate on those set results. Contain command can also be used to perform least-fixed-point operations. By explicitly checking the set equality between source relation and result relation after a join operation, a least-fixed-point set can be obtained.

4.5 Aggregate Function

Aggregate functions are often needed in an actual database operating environment. They are also useful for obtaining statistical database characteristics. Of course, this can be done by selecting all the tuples, sending them to the host, and letting the host calculate the aggregate values. However, communication between host and Delta is done via a local area network, so it would be costly to send all the tuples every time when such aggregate operations are issued. Furthermore, the hosts are logic programming based inference machines, which are not very good at arithmetic speed. This is the reason why Delta supports aggregate type commands internally.

4.6 Arithmetic Operation

Arithmetic operations on numerical values are not essential for a database machine. However, there is certainly a class of update queries, for example, increasing the salary for all of the employees by 20 %, which needs calculation throughout the attribute values. Because of local area network transfer overhead, we also provided this command set (Note that the arithmetic type update shown in the example requires the attribute transfer twice).

4.7 Definition

Definition-type commands are classified into two categories. One deals with definition and deletion of relations and the other deals with attribute appending and dropping. The latter is added to easily manipulate relation schemata.

4.8 Update

Update type commands are "delete", "insert" and "update" commands. The format and syntax of update commands are somewhat specific. The following is the delete command syntax :

[CN, del, TRN1, TRN2]

CN stands for command number, the identifier of a Delta command. The 'del' specifies the command and TRN1 specifies a target relation (the relation from which tuples are deleted) and TRN2 specifies another relation which contains the tuples (derived from TRN1) to be deleted. There is an alternative way to specify the criterion in the command to delete tuples like this:

$$[CN, del, TRN1, attribute1 < 300].$$

In this case, only those tuples which can be specified by the condition field of the command can be deleted. We decided to choose the former syntax to enhance the power for specifying the update criteria.

4.9 Transaction Control

Transaction control-type commands are used to control the update consistency as well as freezing the result relations. Freezing means that the transaction can no more issue commands to Delta except Input/Output commands, in effect, guarding the intermediate relation from further modifications. This is done by commit-transaction command as well as the update commitment. Abort-transaction command means the rollback of updates done previously in that transaction scope. Concurrency control is also done behind the transaction control command. Delta adopts a two-phase lock method to maintain concurrency control. The user can specify a relation list to lock during the transaction in start-transaction command, or the system automatically locks the concerned relation when it is needed to keep the consistency of updates in a transaction. All the locks are undone upon the receipt of commit-transaction or end-transaction command.

4.10 Input/Output

Input/Output commands are used to transfer relations between hosts and Delta. These commands form a command-tree in one command. Only Input/Output commands are valid after commit-transaction command (Of course, Input/Output commands are good anywhere in a transaction). The "get" command has the effect of retransferring the result more than once.

4.11 Asynchronous Commands

Asynchronous-type commands are used to interrupt Delta. These commands expect a fast response from Delta. One of these is the abort-processing command which terminates the current command execution. The other is the sense-status command to sense Delta's execution status. Normally, Delta commands are executed by the arrival order. However, asynchronous-type commands are executed as soon as they arrive at Delta. Abort-processing provides users a facility like Control-C or Break in a usual program run. However, if an update-type command has been executed in the transaction to which the abort-processing is issued, the host has to command Delta to abort that transaction. This is because abort-processing terminates a command execution at a point where data might be inconsistently dirtied.

4.12 Miscellaneous Commands

Miscellaneous-type commands are a collection of utility-type database commands. One very important command here is the sort command, which is often used for output. The unique command is used in combination with other commands when the user wants a duplicate-free relation. Group-by type commands are provided to perform functions known by SQL's group-by operation.

§5 Internal Schema

5.1 Tuple-Based Schema and Attribute-Based Schema

The method of choosing physical or internal schema influences a database machine's performance as much as its internal configuration does. There are two major methods on how to physically store a relation. One is to store it in tuple- or row-based form and the other is to store it in attribute- or column-based form. In Delta we have chosen the attribute-based schema as the internal representation of relations. There are merits and demerits in each schema.

⟨**Merits of tuple-based schema**⟩
- Fits original relational database (set theory) concept
- Read-out of tuples is smooth from sequential storage device

⟨**Demerits of tuple based schema**⟩
- Needs to access extra information such as unnecessary attributes in a query
- Symmetrical access to attributes is difficult (secondary indices to many attributes are hard to make and maintain)

⟨**Merits of attribute-based schema**⟩
- Only concerned attributes should be read
- Symmetrical manipulation of attributes can be easily done

⟨**Demerits of attribute-based schema**⟩
- Needs tuple reorganization (tuple reconstruction) for output
- Needs tuple identifier (extra storage space) for tuple reconstruction

As mentioned in the first chapter, Delta will be used in a logic programming language environment. It is highly desirable to handle almost every attribute in a symmetrical way. In other words, a system can not guess a predetermined access path to a relation. This is closely related to the nondeterministic behavior of logic programming language execution, typically when backtracking of literals occurs. This fact made us select the attribute-based schema. The other strong reason why we chose it is that the schema is appropriate for our RDBE's merge-sort hardware algorithm. We did not want to flow unnecessary attributes through RDBE, which would result in an increase of data transfer time between RDBE and HM. We also considered the difficulty RDBE has in recognizing the boundaries between a field to be sorted and compared and other trailing attribute(s) in RDBE. Later, however, the latter reason proved to be of little significance. There still exist reasons for RDBE to recognize the field boundaries even if we had chosen the attribute-based schema. One obvious example is the existence of tid (tuple identifier) field and the other is the fact that at times RDBE still has to handle some tuple-like streams called concatenated attribute class data which is considered as a part of a relation projected on some attributes. In the case of tid field, the situation is better because there are only two distinct fields in a data stream (like binary relation) and it makes the hardware design much simpler. However, to perform set operations, the tuples should be reconstructed before processing by RDBE. In this case, a usual tuple-based relation is forwarded through RDBE. Unnecessary attributes, however, need not be transferred.

5.2 Clustering

A naive relational database machine design might scan a relation (or attributes in attribute-based schema) every time a query is issued. Certain clustering is necessary for narrowing the search space before brute-force searching takes place. This is particularly true in an environment where a storage hierarchy is accommodated in a database machine system. If a cache (or a similar smaller but faster storage) is filled up with relations, most of which are only staged up to be disposed, the significance of that expensive storage can not be justified. Much work has recently been done on efficient clustering of relations.[20] In Delta, however, we decided to use an attribute-based schema. In a tuple-based schema, it might be difficult to access several attribute values evenly (This is the reason why a smart indexing method is needed). An attribute-based schema has only to consider two fields, namely attribute value field and tid field, for clustering. We therefore adopted a simple two-level clustering method. An example of this clustering is shown in Fig. 4. First, the attribute is sorted according to the attribute's value, divided in multiple first-level clusters according to the range of values. Secondly, the first-level clusters are separately sorted according to tid values in each item (An item, in our terminology, is a pair of tids and a value of attribute). Thus one leaf of this schema (which corresponds to a physical page in storage) contains items the values of which are in a certain attribute value range and also tid values which are in a certain tid value range. Though the access patterns are dominant in deciding the effectiveness of a clustering scheme, we observed that this clustering is effective in symmetrical access pattern queries.[11]

§6 Relational Database Engine (RDBE) Details

RDBE is the key component for the processing of relational algebra in Delta (Fig. 5). RDBE incorporates the basic merge-sort algorithm described in the former Section. In a word, RDBE is a hardware implementation of the merge-sort software algorithm. However, to implement it to work in the actual processing stage in a database machine, various difficult problems must be

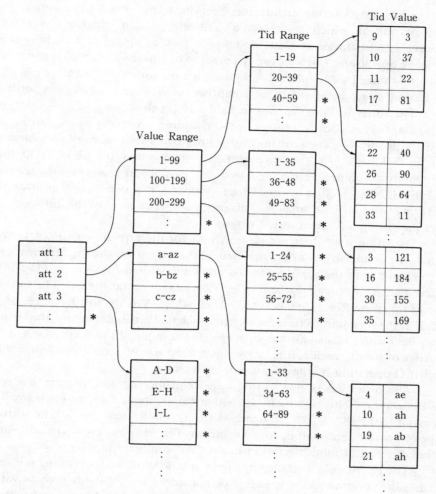

Note : An asterisk indicates pointer abbreviation

Fig. 4 Internal schema of Delta.

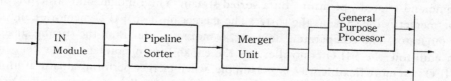

Fig. 5 RDBE schematic configuration.

solved.

As discussed in the architecture Section, RDBE has a general-purpose processor portion which controls the hardware portion (Engine Core) and processes certain classes of Delta commands such as aggregate functions and arithmetic operations. Engine Core is a piece of new hardware which is comprised of a first stage IN Module, second stage pipeline sorter and last stage merger. The second stage sorter is further comprised of smaller stages called sorting stages. The sorter follows the idea of hardware pipeline merge-sorting by.[21] A sorting stage is cascaded to another one, forwarding a partially sorted stream to it. An N-th sorting stage (starting with 1) has two FIFO memories which can contain 2^{N-1} items. The first sorting stage sorts one item from one FIFO and one item from another, producing a two-item partial sort result into the second stage FIFO. The second sorting stage compares the two two-item streams, producing two four-item streams. This process is repeated until the last stage, in effect producing a 2^N-item sorted stream.

A sorting stage does not have to wait for the arrival of two completed streams. Upon the arrival of the first item in the second stream, the first item can be compared with the top item in the previously stored first stream (The first item of the second stream is the smallest item in the second stream). The sorting time of this sorter for 2^N items is $(N+2^N)T$ where N is the sorting stage count and T is the time unit to transfer an item. In actual attribute sorting, the length of an item varies in magnitudes of range (for example, 2B to 2KB). To handle varieties of length, each sorting stage has a fixed size of memory and simulates the FIFO operation by the use of pointer registers.

The sorter has twelve sorting stages and the last sorting stage has two 64KB-memories. This sorter can sort either (1) 4K items if each item is smaller than 16B (64K/4K) or (2) $2N$ items where N is 64K/item-length. The sorting stage comparator part will be implemented by discrete components initially and replaced with LSI implementation in the final configuration.

The IN Module rearranges the field orders before a stream of items is sent to the sorter portion. As a stream is composed of several fields such as value fields and tid fields, the fields should be rearranged so that the sorting key field will appear at the top of each item to match the sorting algorithm. The last stage merger, after performing the proper operation, arranges them back to the right fields order.

The merger is a unit which performs relational algebra and other Delta-command-related operations on a sorted stream. The fundamental structure of the merger is the same as the sorter. The merger has two FIFO memories and a comparator. The comparator, however, is more complex than the sorting stage. In addition, the FIFO controller has the capability to point to some item in FIFO in a more flexible way. For example, when merger performs a natural-join operation, the control procedure proceeds as follows (here, no duplicates are assumed in joined attributes for simplicity):

(1) Repeat unitil the first attribute is exhausted
(2) Send a bufferful of the first attribute to RDBE
(3) Sort the first attribute and load the merger's first FIFO with it
(4) Continue until the second attribute is exhausted
(5) Sort a bufferful of the second attribute and supply it to the merger's second FIFO
(6) First FIFO rewind (set to originally loaded state)
(7) Continue until a bufferful of the second attribute is exhausted
    if top of second FIFO is greater, then pop second FIFO
    if top of second FIFO is equal, then output it and pop second FIFO
    if top of second FIFO is less, then pop first FIFO

The time required to perform this operation is as follows (no clustering effect is assumed here):

$$M/B(2B + \log_2 B + N)T$$

where M is the size of the first attribute, N is the size of the second attribute, B is the merger FIFO size and T is the unit item transfer time. Note that if M is smaller than B, the join can be accomplished by flowing the second attribute once through the merger. This does not depend on the size of the second attribute, because the second attribute can be divided in the merger and the divided subparts can be continuously joined without disturbing the stream flow.

The merger unit is associated with a general-purpose processor for performing aggregate functions, arithmetic operations, complex condition selections and a subset of set operations. Dedicated pieces of hardware for performing these operations are required for higher performance. However, time did not allow us to design those ones. We decided to concentrate on the Engine Core to perform relational algebra. When RDBE is commanded to perform an operation which should be done in the general-purpose processor, the data stream is forwarded to the processor after the stream flows through the merger. In this case the stream flow speed is limited by the processor's processing speed.

§7 Hierarchical Memory Subsystem

The Hierarchical Memory subsystem (HM) is responsible for storing, accessing, clustering and maintaining relations. HM's configuration is shown in Fig. 6. The lowest storage device is state-of-the-art moving-head-disks, the total capacity of which will be 20 GB in the final Delta configuration. HM is provided with a large capacity Semiconductor Disk (SDK), the capacity of which will be 128 MB also in the final configuration. SDK is a semiconductor RAM memory system which is protected against power failure and hence appears to be non-volatile. When power failure is detected, emergency power is supplied from the battery of the power supply system until dumping of SDK content to MHD is finished. The controller of HM is a general-purpose computer named HMCTL. HMCTL is the brain in HM and it performs the tasks assigned to HM. HMCTL's roles are as follows:

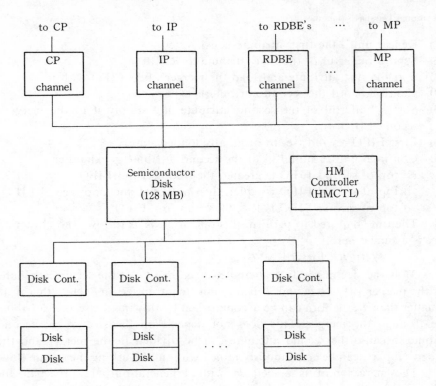

Fig. 6 HM schematic configuration.

o Memory management in SDK and MHD
   · SDK and MHD data staging and destaging
   · CP directory area management
   · SDK power failure management (non-volatility)
o Stream preparation for RDBE
   · Buffer assignment in SDK
   · Clustering search
   · Stream arrangement (page fragment elimination)
o Stream transfer between HM and RDBE
   · Channel activation
   · Multiple stream management
o Transaction rollback
   · Shadow management
   · Update logging
o Tuple and attribute transposing
   · Transposing to tuple
   · Transposing to attribute
   (For bidirectional tuple and attribute conversions)

A general procedure where HM prepares and forwards streams to RDBE is as follows :

(1) Buffers (output qualified buffers and result receiving input buffers for RDBE) are prepared.

(2) The stream (data in the output buffers) is forwarded to RDBE

(3) The input stream from RDBE (result of the RDBE processing derived from output stream) is received

(4) Buffers no longer usable are released

These are directed by CP or RDBE via HM subcommands. Usually HM subcommands are the principal command communication means between HM and other Delta subsystems. HM is almost always passive in the sense that it is directed by other subsystems. HM's most principal role is the stream preparation and transfer.

In the stream preparation process, HM is typically commanded by the prepare-qualified-buffer subcommand. This subcommand means that HM should prepare an attribute in a stream buffer using the qualification specified in the subcommand. The qualification example is value range specification like "greater than 1000". As is described in the clustering chapter, HM maintains a two-level clustering directory and looks for qualified pages when it receives the subcommand. It is not required that HM should filter out attribute items which do not satisfy the qualification. This qualification is a static one and HM fetches such pages which may contain attribute items satisfying the qualification.

Another important role of HM is the data recovery function. HM is the central portion for storing databases, it makes shadows of the update pages directed by CP for later possible transaction rollback specification. HM is further responsible for transposing tuples to attributes and vice versa. Sending result tuples to the host is done by making buffers which contain necessary attributes to constitute the tuple, transposing them into a tuple buffer and transferring it via IP to the host. The transposing, in either direction, is done as much as possible in SDK to reduce the overhead associated with the attribute-based schema.

§8 Implementation Designs[17]

Delta has adopted new pieces of hardware in its architecture. The most notable ones are RDBE and non-volatile large capacity Semiconductor Disk. Other subsystems are basically built up with off-the-shelf components such as minicomputers or general-purpose computers. The Interface Processor will be implemented using a one-board minicomputer with 1 MB main memory. The Control Processor will also be implemented by the same minicomputer with 1 MB main memory. The Relational Database Engine (RDBE) is a new piece of hardware, our idea being based on an algorithm using the hardware supported merge-sorting implemented by the RDBE. Most hardware intensive efforts are being done for the implementation of RDBE, in the sense that it will become the first practical hardware relational database engine. RDBE will also use a minicomputer to control the RDBE's hardware resources. In order to manipulate various relational database processing requirements, for instance, floating-point data calculations, RDBE could not help but become a little sophisticated.

The Hierarchical Memory (HM) subsystem is implemented using a general-purpose computer as a controller (HMCTL), a large amount of fast semiconductor random access memory in the form of a semiconductor disk (SDK) and large capacity moving head disks. The SDK is used for temporarily storing classes of relations generated and managed in Delta. The SDK will be non-volatile (at least from a software point of view) to avoid disk accesses invoked by write-through storage management. We realize there remains a lot to be investigated and researched to make a real hardware-oriented HM. So we decided to simulate the HM using a general-purpose computer system for collecting performance data and making the points to be improved clear in this research. One of the most decisive factors in choosing a general-purpose computer as the HM is that it provides an operating system containing control software on state-of-the-art disks, the capacity of which is over 2GB per unit.

§9 Performance Estimation

The performance of a database machine or a database management system is greatly affected by usage patterns, or how the database is accessed by users. Our preliminary assumptions for the accesses which will be made in a logic programming environment are as follows:

(1) Relations are of only a few attributes. This is because the databases are closely associated with the *facts* of logic programming languages. Usually logic programming language programs contain only a small number of arguments.

(2) Attributes are accessed in a non-deterministic manner. This is a property of logic programming languages. Especially when backtracking takes place, we can not tell which one of the arguments is instantiated. There are classes of arguments which are only subsidiarily accessed. However, compared with usual key-based accesses to databases, there may be a lot of attributes from which the accesses are made. This is one of the reasons why we adopted an attribute-based schema.

(3) Databases are divided into two usage categories. As the environment is research oriented, the usage categories include personal database usage as well as shared database.

(4) High degree of concurrency may manifest when the total system (SIM's, local area network and Delta) are used in a TSS-like manner.

(5) Select, Join and Project are the high frequency commands. Because they are frequently found in our interfacing method between logic programming languages and relational databases.

Apparently, the local area network does not have a very high-bandwidth. We will have a transfer rate around 10 Mbit per second. This can be a bottleneck if heavy query traffic is always flowing through this path. We will not discuss the local area network problem further here. It has to be taken account of in the total system configuration.

9.1 A Delta Performance Estimation

Delta's command-tree execution steps are divided into the following substeps neglecting the host-to-IP command-tree and response transfer time:

(T1)   IP software overhead to invoke IP-to-CP command-tree transfer
(T2)   IP-to-CP command-tree transfer
(T3)   CP software overhead to invoke command-tree analysis
(T4)   Command-tree analysis, generating subcommand sequences
(T5)   Subcommand sequence execution
(T6)   CP software overhead to invoke response transfer to IP
(T7)   CP-to-IP response transfer
(T8)   IP software overhead to invoke response transfer to host

Among these, T5 is the actual database access operation. So T5 is further divided into the following procedures:

(T5.1)   RDBE subcommand execution
(T5.2)   HM subcommand execution
(T5.3)   CP to RDBE subcommand transfer overhead and transfer time
(T5.4)   CP to HM subcommand transfer overhead and transfer time

There is no HM-to-RDBE data transfer time included here. This is because it is hidden in RDBE subcommand execution time, a processing scheme we adopted. Besides the transfer time, some of these substeps are partially done in parallel. So the mere amount of execution times of these substeps will give us an underestimate performance figure. But as the details of these substeps are not sufficiently clarified, it will suffice to have a simple sum for rough estimation.

9.2 Selection Example

We now consider an example selection query in SQL form:

SELECT $a_1, a_2,..., a_n$
FROM A
WHERE a_i IN [value list]

where A is a relation composed of 10 attributes, having 10000 tuples. The a_1, a_2 and so on are the attributes among the 10 attributes. We assume 10B for each attribute here.

The execution time characteristic for selectivity according to a deterministic simulation is shown in Fig. 7. This figure assumes a high semiconductor disk hit ratio. For certain ranges of selectivity, there are different dominating factors. For the selectivity range between 0.01 % and 1 %, the dominating factor is the increasing tid join time. Buffer preparation in semiconductor disk is not

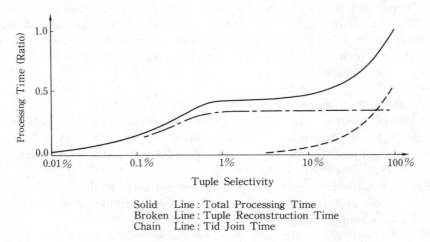

Solid   Line : Total Processing Time
Broken Line : Tuple Reconstruction Time
Chain   Line : Tid Join Time

Fig. 7 A simulation result.

so time-consuming, because the intra-semiconductor disk transfer is fairly fast compared with tid joins. For selectivity factors between 1% and 10%, the estimation curve shows a plateau. In this area, the processing time is dominated by the full tid joining. All the attributes should be scanned for tid join in this area. For the selectivity range between 10% and 100%, along with the tid join time which forms the plateau, tuple reconstruction time becomes influential. The effect of tuple reconstruction rapidly becomes great.

This result, though still not sufficiently quantitative, indicates that the incorporation of a large capacity semiconductor disk is effective for a high performance database machine. The effort to increase the hit ratio by the wise replacement algorithm is the key to effectively utilize the semiconductor disk. We assume that the performance of Delta in the high hit ratio range will be around several hundred milliseconds in the selection example.

§10 Towards a Knowledge Base Machine

The final goal towards which Delta's research line aims is knowledge base machine construction. The Fifth Generation Computer Project has adopted logic programming language as a kernel programming language. This will be the basis for all the research to be carried out during the Project. We think that the knowledge representation problem is the key to construct a knowledge base machine. Relational model has a good affinity to logic programming language because both of them have logic in their foundation. Some attempts have been made to combine relational database and logic programming language.[3, 18] We have presented a compiled approach which defers the evaluation of literals in Prolog when the literal has alternatives in the external database (database machine) in the form of facts.[25] Besides this approach, there may be various other approaches towards attainment of the final goal of a knowledge base machine. Our standpoint is based on the amalgamation of logic programming language and relational database. We do not think that relational database is sufficient for a general class of knowledge base machine achievement. However, the combination of a relational database machine and inference mechanism is a good candidate for a future knowledge base machine.[12] To more closely combine the database and logic programming language, *rules* (unit clauses with variables and non-unit clauses) should be manipulated in database machines. This implies that the database machines should be able to handle structured data in general and have the mechanism to perform a unification operation as a relational algebra level database operation.[24] A unification engine, which operates on a data stream which represents a set of structures instead of an attribute, is one method of performing efficient knowledge base unification. This is easily applicable in Delta's architecture; all that is needed is to place a unification engine along the RDBE. In this case also, some knowledge clustering technique should be accommodated for the efficient use of knowlege space, which is still in the elementary research stage. We think that, like the relational database case, semantic information should be used in the clustering of knowledge bases. For research purposes, Delta will be connected to a sequential inference machine via a shared communication memory. This will provide a powerful research tool for the pursuit of a knowledge base machine.

§11 Conclusion

We have described the architecture of Delta, its commands, subsystem roles, and to some extent RDBE and HM detailed considerations. Delta's new architecture and major decisions such as pipeline relational algebra processing, incorporation of a large capacity non-volatile Semiconductor Disk, and semantics-based clustering will enable it to operate efficiently in relational algebra-based commands processing, particularly when symmetrical accesses to the database are frequent. From a database management viewpoint, Delta has many features which current software database management systems have. More detailed implementation decisions are now being made in the course of the detailed software design and manufacturing steps. When completed, experiment and collection of performance data in actual usage, not only as a database machine but also as a research tool for a knowledge base machine, will be the next research step.

Acknowledgements

The authors would like to express their appreciation to Mr. K. Fuchi, director of ICOT, who provided the opportunity to conduct this research, and offer special thanks to the Toshiba and Hitachi researchers and engineers who are engaged in the implementation of Delta. Many decisions in this paper were made through discussions with them.

References

1) Bancilhon, F. et al.: "VERSO: A Relational Back-End Data Base Machine," Proc. Int'l. Workshop on Database Machines (August, 1982).

2) Boral, H. and Dewitt, D.: "Database Machines: An Idea Whose Time has Passed? — A Critique of the Future of the Database Machines," Proc. Int'l. Workshop on Database Machines (Sept., 1983).

3) Chakravarthy, U. et al.: "Interfacing Predicate Logic Languages and Relational Databases," Proc. First Int'l. Logic Programming Conference (Sept., 1982).

4) Chamberlin, D. et al.: "SEQUEL 2: A Unified Approach to Data Definition, Manipulation, and Control," IBM Journal of Res. and Develop. (1976).

5) Codd, E.: "A Relational Model for Large Shared Data Banks," Commun. ACM, *13* (June, 1970) 377.

6) Dewitt, D.: "DIRECT—A multi-processor organization for supporting relational database management systems," IEEE Trans. Comput., *C-28, No. 6* (1979).

7) Kitsuregawa, M. et al.: "Application of Hash to Data Base Machine and Its Architecture," New Generation Computing, *1, No. 1* (1983) 63-74.

8) Kakuta, T., Miyazaki, N., Shibayama, S., Yokota, H. and Murakami, K.: "A Relational Database Machine "Delta" (I), (II), (III)," Proc. 26th National Conference, Information Processing Society of Japan, *4F-6, 4F-7, 4F-8* (1983).

9) Kunifuji, S., Yokota, H. et al.: "Interface between Logic Programming Language and Relational Database Management System (1)—Basic Concepts—," Proc. 26th National Conference, Information Processing Society of Japan, *5C-9* (1983).

10) Kunifuji, S. and Yokota, H.: "PROLOG and Relational Databases for 5th Generation Computer Systems," ICOT Technical Report, *TR-002* (1982). (revised version 1983)

11) Miyazaki, N. et al.: "On Data Storage Schemes in Database Machines," Proc. 27th National Conference on Information Processing, *2K-5* (Oct., 1983). [in Japanese, English version to appear as ICOT Technical Memorandum]

12) Murakami, K. et al.: "A Relational Database Machine: First Step towards a Knowledge Base Machine," ICOT Technical Report, *TR-012* (1983).

13) Moto-oka, T.: "Overview to the Fifth Generation Computer System Project," Proc. 10th Int'l. Sympo. on Computer Architecture (June, 1983).

14) Schweppe, H. et al.: "RDBM—A Dedicated Multiprocessor Systems for Data Base Management," Proc. Int'l. Workshop on Database Machines (August, 1982).

15) Schweppe, H.: "Some Comments on Semantical Disk Cache Management for a Knowledge Base System," to appear as ICOT Technical Report (Oct., 1983).

16) Shibayama, S., Kakata, T., Miyazaki, N., Yokota, H. and Murakami, K.: "A Relational Database Machine "Delta"," ICOT Technical Memorandum, *TM-0002* (1982).

17) Shibayama, S. et al.: "On RDBM Delta's Relational Algebra Processing Algorithms," Proc. 27th National Conference, Information Processing Society of Japan, *2K-5* (Oct., 1983).

18) Tanaka, Y. Horiuchi, K., and Tagawa, R.: "Combining Inference System and Data Base System by a Partial Evaluation Mechanism," Proc. First Knowledge Engineering Symposium (Tokyo, March, 1983). [in Japanese]

19) Tanaka, Y.: "A Data Stream Database Machine with Large Capacity," Proc. Int'l. Workshop on Database Machines (August, 1982).

20) Tanaka, Y.: "Adaptive Segmentation Schemes for Large Relational Database Machines," Proc. Int'l. Workshop on Database Machines (Sept., 1983).

21) Todd, S.: "Algorithm and Hardware for a Merge Sort Using Multiple Processors," IBM Journal of Res. and Develop., *22* (1978).

22) Uchida, S. et al.: "The Personal Sequential Inference Machine—Outline of Its Architecture and Hardware System," ICOT Technical Memorandum, *TM-0001* (Nov., 1982).

23) Yokota, H., Kunifuji, S. et al.: "How Can We Combine a Relational Database and a Prolog-Based Inference Mechanism?," Proc. Meeting of WGAI, Information Processing Society of Japan (Tokyo, Nov., 1983). [in Japanese]

24) Yokota, H. et al.: "An Investigation for Building Knowledge Base Machines," ICOT Technical Memorandum, *TM-0019* (1983). [in Japanese]

25) Yokota, H., Kunifuji, S. et al.: "Interface between Logic Programming Language and Relational Database Management System (2)—Implementation—," Proc. 26th National Conference, Information Processing Society of Japan, *5C-10* (1983). [in Japanese]

Electronics international

Significant developments in technology and business

New computer breed uses transputers for parallel processing

by Kevin Smith, Senior editor

Without separate stores for data and instructions, machine will be able to run fifth-generation languages

Computer researchers are beginning to break out of the serial-processing straitjacket of von Neumann architecture with its instructions and data rigidly separated. They are devising machines with a high degree of parallel processing achieved by combining discrete chunks of data and associated instructions into packets that can be processed simultaneously by a group of processor elements.

One such computer, called Alice for applicative language idealised computing engine, is taking shape at Britain's Imperial College. It is being developed by a team headed by Mike Reeve and John Darlington, an expert in the theory of computation, to run Darlington's own high-level language, Hope.

But Alice is sufficiently flexible to support other such fifth-generation declarative languages as Prolog and Lisp, says Darlington. These powerful languages are conceived without regard to the limitations of the machines on which they are to run (see "Why fifth-generation languages," p. 68). Alice also could support conventional von Neumann software.

The prototype Alice will be a desktop unit capable of running fifth-generation languages. On problems exhibiting a high degree of parallelism, it promises to be about 100 times faster than a von Neumann machine of comparable complexity. Alternatively, it will offer an order-of-magnitude improvement in running a von Neumann program. Once proved, the architecture could be applied to systems with many thousands of processors instead of the prototype's 16, states Reeve.

Transputer customer. Alice will be one of the first systems to use Inmos Corp.'s transputer [*Electronics*, Sept. 22, 1982, p. 86], billed by the company as a fifth-generation building block because of its efficiency at handling large data flows. When samples become available, 112 transputer chips will be used in the construction of Alice (see figure).

Also under development is a custom high-speed emitter-coupled-logic chip containing a 4-by-4 crossbar switch. An array of these chips will connect each of Alice's 16 processors to any of 16 memory segments.

Until the hardware can be com-

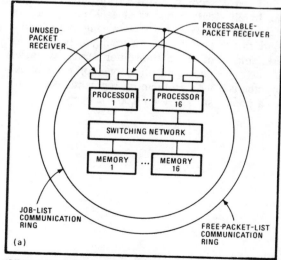

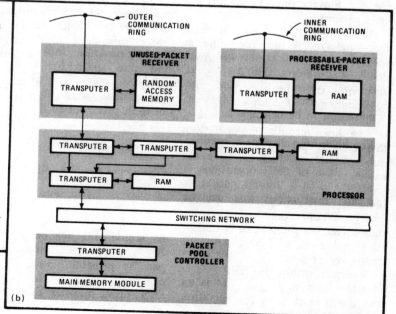

Alice lives here. The prototype Alice (a) will use 16 processors linked by two rings that oversee packet traffic. Each processor (b) combines multiple transputers and memory.

Why fifth-generation languages?

Declarative languages such as Prolog and Lisp allow a programmer to define a desired result without concerning himself about the detailed instructions of how it is to be computed. Unlike conventional languages such as Fortran and Pascal, they are well-suited to parallel-processing machines because program evaluations can be run in any order without regard to sequence.

Aside from the performance advantages of parallel processing, declarative languages offer a solution to the software crisis. They are shorter and more concise, more powerful and understandable than present-day languages, say their proponents. Furthermore, programs can be first written for clarity, then greatly speeded up by program transformation, a task that can be mechanized.

Prolog is best known in Europe as the language Japan chose for its fifth-generation computer project. It is derived from formal deductive logic, the groundwork for which was first laid by Aristotle with his syllogisms. In a more modern guise, such deductive logic is the basis of set theory.

But there is another class of declarative languages of which Lisp and Imperial College's Hope are examples. These languages comprise sets of equations by means of which a required function can be defined in terms of simpler, more primitive functions. The idea is to decompose the original statement into simpler tasks that can be easily executed in parallel by the computer.

To determine factorial n, for example, all its product terms (n, n−1, n−2 . . .1) are first generated, then product pairs are successively multiplied until the expression has been reduced to a single term. Any such reduction process can be expressed as a tree network, each node of which represents a computation. In Alice, there is a data packet for every node in this network.

That is the way is it supposed to work. However, there are many problems that are still to be overcome. One is the need for suitable hardware, because these languages run slowly on a conventional machine. Another problem is how to interface such languages—which have no sense of time and sequence—with a real world dominated by both. **—Kevin Smith**

pleted, compilers have been written for Hope to run on existing machines. Simulations have already been performed.

A unique feature of such declarative languages is that the order in which instructions are performed does not matter at all. Of course, the arguments must be present for the computation to be completed.

Within Alice, the program task is broken down into discrete operations that can be performed in any sequence. Each of these operations is encapsulated in a 256-bit packet of data and instructions that can be handled by the machine as a single entity. Computation is, therefore, data-driven—a packet can be executed at any time, so long as its arguments are present.

Wrapped within the packet is an identifier and a program operation and the data it is to act on, represented symbolically or as a numerical value. There are also four secondary fields used by Alice to track and control the program's execution. In all there are eight fields, each of 32 bits: three primaries, four secondaries, and one spare for experimental purposes.

The idea of a parallel computer is for each processor to dip into a pool of packets held in the common memory whenever it needs work. It returns the processed packet to the pool ready for the next stage of the computation.

The progress of the computation is tracked by the secondary fields in the data packet. For example, a status flag is raised when a packet is "sleeping" as it waits for data to be inserted. Another flag is raised in the reference count when a packet has served its purpose and should be destroyed.

Rings of control. Individual processors are told what packets to process and where to put the results by means of communications rings. The addresses of all processable packets circulate on one ring, and empty memory locations are found on a second ring.

The ring layout is similar to Manchester University's Data-Flow computer—and with good reason, as it formed the starting point for Darlington's design. But whereas the Manchester machine moves data packets around the ring, Alice moves only address pointers around. The packets and messages are moved from memory to processor and back by the ECL cross-bar matrix.

Alice's intelligence derives from the many transputer chips used in its design. Three are in each processor, which can process 150,000 packets a second. Also, transputers control data transfers at each processor's interface ports: two ring ports and a port to the switching network. Last of all, a transputer serves as packet pool controller, one for each of Alice's 16 memory segments, each with storage for 64,000 packets.

ALICE and the Parallel Evaluation of Logic Programs

John Darlington and Mike Reeve

Department of Computing
Imperial College of Science and Technology
180 Queens Gate
London SW7 2BZ   England

(Preliminary Draft)

June 8, 1983

Abstract

This paper outlines several schemes by which logic programs may be evaluated in parallel on an extended graph reduction machine such as Alice.

INTRODUCTION

ALICE (Applicative Language Idealized Computing Engine) is a general purpose multi-processor parallel computer system being developed at Imperial College by John Darlington and Mike Reeve [DaR81]. ALICE is based on an extended graph reduction model of computation and may be viewed as a parallel production system [DaK77].

This paper provides a brief outline of how ALICE might be employed for the parallel evaluation of logic programs. It consists of two parts: the first outlines how ALICE operates; the second describes several schemes by which logic programs can be evaluated in parallel on an extended graph reduction machine such as ALICE.

AN INTRODUCTION TO ALICE

It is now widely accepted that the conventional (von Neumann) style of programming is inadequate for the development of clear, correct and easily modified programs. Many of those seeking to alleviate this "software crisis" have discovered that the clean mathematical semantics of the declarative (side-effect free) programming languages (be they functional or relational) lead to equally clean programs. Thus the declarative languages promise to make programming and program understanding much more straightforward; a point argued eloquently by Backus in his ACM Turing Award Lecture [Bak78].

A variety of declarative languages are used by the academic community (e.g., HOPE [BMS80], KRC [Tur80], PROLOG [Rou75]). Unfortunately the commercial world has been slow to adopt them because their natural mode of evaluation, expression substitution, is far removed from the von Neumann model of computation and as a result they suffer from poor run-time performance on conventional (von Neumann) machines.

ALICE is an attempt to provide a computer architecture that directly implements the expression substitution model of computation associated with the declarative languages. Despite being optimized for the evaluation of declarative languages, ALICE readily supports the conventional (von Neumann) languages. The way the system operates may be understood by considering the evaluation of Factorial(5) according to the following program (written in a functional recursion equation language loosely based on HOPE).

```
Factorial : Integer -> Integer
     Factorial(n) = FactB(0, n)
FactB : Integer x Integer -> Integer
     FactB(i, j) =        1 if i = j
                   else j if j = i + 1
                   else FactB(i, mid) * FactB(mid, j)
                        where mid == Round((i + j)/2)
```

The value of the expression Factorial(5) may be computed by employing the above equations as directed rewrite rules to successively reconfigure its associated expression graph. The computation is illustrated in Figure 1. Note how the independence of sub-expressions resulting from the lack of side-effects permits all available sub-parts of the graph to be rewritten in parallel (e.g., the two expressions at the leaves of the graph during step 3, and the four during step 4).

In ALICE an expression graph is modelled by a collection of packets, one per node. Each packet contains the function present at the associated node and pointers to the packets representing its arguments. It also contains the control information required by the evaluation mechanism when that node is processed. The format of a packet is shown in Figure 2; the primary fields contain the information required to represent a node and the secondary fields hold the control information.

The information held in the three primary fields is as follows:

i) Identifier
    This field contains an identifier unique to the packet and provides a name by which the packet may be referenced.

ii) Function
    This field contains the function which appears at the node represented by the packet.

iii) ArgumentList
    This field contains the identifiers of the packets that represent the arguments of the function. When the packet is employed to represent a literal value the ArgumentList field is replaced by the Value field which contains the binary representation of the value.

The SignalList field and a sub-part of the Status field are used to implement a scheme that ensures that no attempt to rewrite a packet is made until its arguments are in the form required to accomplish the rewrite. A packet that is waiting for

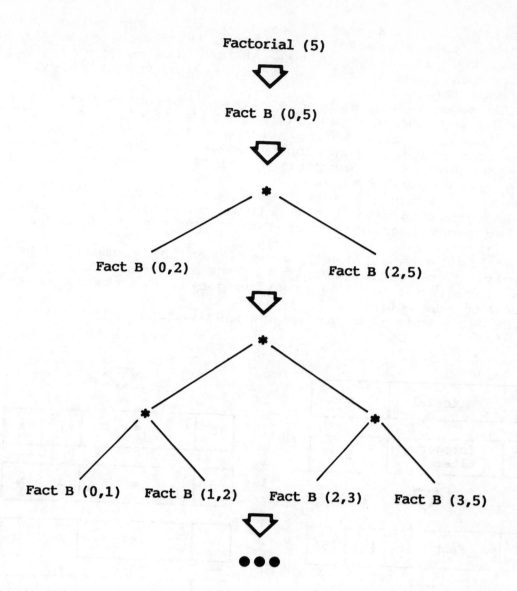

Figure 1: Evaluation of Factorial (5)

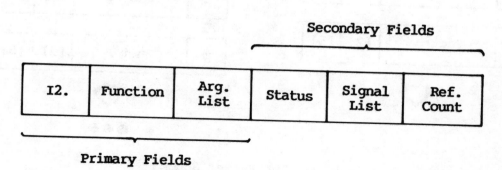

Figure 2: A Packet

its arguments in this manner is said to be "asleep." The process by which an "asleep" packet is notified that such arguments have been evaluated is known as "waking up." The remainder of the information contained in the secondary fields is not relevant to this introduction.

ALICE models the parallel evaluation of an expression graph by replacing any packet representing a node at which a rewritable function (i.e., a data manipulating function rather than a data forming, constructor, function) appears by the collection of packets representing the suitably instantiated right hand side of the appropriate rewrite rule.

Figure 3 shows the packet equivalent of the evaluation in Figure 1 (in some places the shorthand notation [N] is used to denote the identifier of a packet representing the integer value N).

Note that when a packet is rewritten the topmost packet of the resulting collection adopts the identifier of the rewritten packet, since the sub-expression the packet represents is referenced by that identifier.

ALICE provides for both eager evaluation (in which each

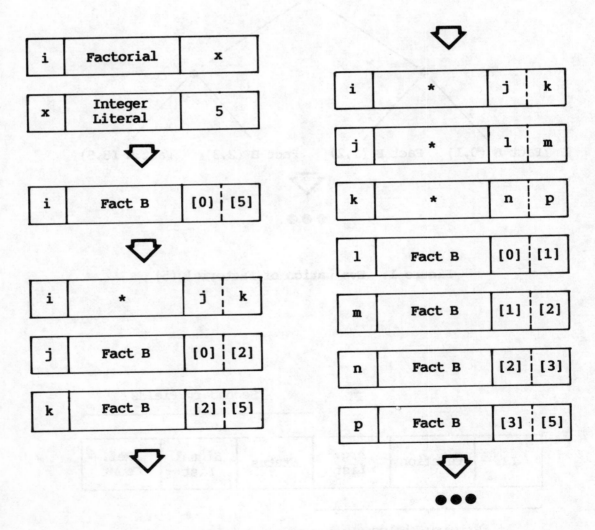

Figure 3: The Packet Scheme

632

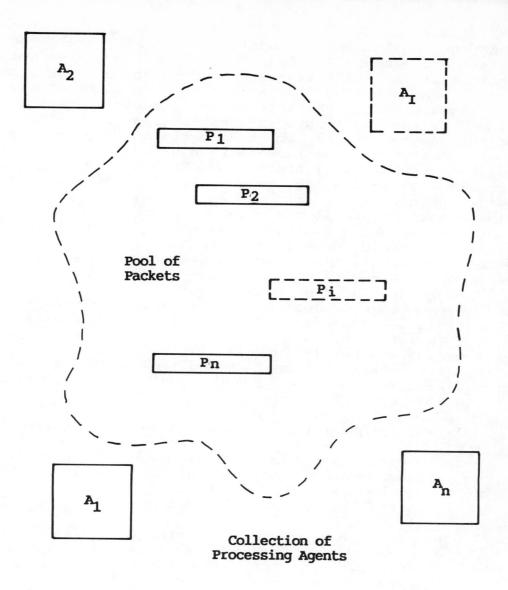

Figure 4: The Abstract Architecture

expression is evaluated as soon as possible) and lazy evaluation (where an expression is only evaluated when its value is explicitly demanded; see [FrW76], [HeM76]). The mode of evaluation may be specified explicitly for each expression evaluated.

One of the extensions that the ALICE scheme makes to the graph reduction model of computation on which it is based, is to introduce a facility that allows the evaluation of an expression to be explicitly suspended until it is explicitly activated as a side-effect of some rewrite rule. This feature provides for explicit sequencing in an otherwise unordered computation. Input/output is an example of an activity that makes use of this feature.

When rewrite rules overlap, ALICE provides a variety of mechanisms for deciding which rule to apply (e.g. most specific/least specific, availability of arguments). Implementations of the languages which support committed ("don't care") nondeterminism (see for example [CIG81]) make use of this feature.

Another of the ALICE extensions to the graph reduction model of computation provides for a rewrite rule to have the side-effect of assigning new contents to any argument packets. Implementations of the logic based programming languages [Kow74] make use of this feature to implement directly the logical variable. It is also employed by implementations of the single assignment applicative languages (c.f. Data Flow [GWG80]) and, together with the facility for sequencing the computation, by implementations of the conventional languages.

At the abstract level the machine required to implement the scheme described above can be envisaged as a pool of packets and a collection of packet processing agents (Figure 4).

An agent executes the following sequences of steps to model the rewriting of a node:

1. Remove some processable packet from the packet pool; i.e., a packet whose Function field contains a rewriteable function.

2. Decide whether it is rewriteable; i.e., check whether the packets associated with any arguments required to be constructor functions are of the correct form.

   If any argument packets are not of the required form:

   a) Arrange for the processing of this packet to be resumed when the required arguments have coalesced to constructor functions.
   b) Restore this packet to the packet pool.
   c) goto 1

3. Determine the appropriate rewrite rule; i.e., match this packet and its argument packets (if any) with the left hand side of some rewrite rule.

4. Generate the packets representing the right hand side of the rule and deposit them in the packet pool; i.e., for each,

   a) Acquire an unused identifier (except in the case of the packet representing the outermost function on

$$P \quad \leftarrow \quad C_1, C_2, \ldots, C_n$$

$$C_1 \quad \leftarrow \quad C_{11}, C_{12}, \ldots, C_{2n}$$

$$C_1 \quad \leftarrow \quad C_{11}, C_{12}, \ldots, C_{1n}$$

. . .

. . .

$$C_n \quad \leftarrow \quad C_{n1}, C_{n2}, \ldots, C_{np}$$

Figure 5: A Logic Program

Grandparent (x,y) ◁ Parent (x,z), Parent (z,y)

Figure 6: The Shared Variable

  the right hand side which adopts the identifier of
  this packet).
  b) Form the contents of the packet body.
  c) Deposit the packet in the packet pool.
5. goto 1

  All the agents operate concurrently, thus the system models
the parallel evaluation of an expression graph.
  To ensure that continuing research at the implementation
level does not affect the applications programming level, an
implementation-independent assembly code has been developed to
provide a stable base for software projects [Ree81]. Known as the
ALICE Compiler Target Language (ALICE CTL) it is intended to be
the code produced by compliers or written directly by programmers
wishing to exploit ALICE facilities not available in the high
level languages. It is designed so that only a simple translator
is required to convert it to the form specific to any particular
implementation.
  At present an ALICE simulator (written in Pascal) permits
the execution of programs writted in the ALICE Compiler Target
Language.
  A prototype ALICE is currently under construction. It will
have 16 processing agents and the packet pool will hold 512K
packets. Physically the machine will be personal work station
sized (c.f. the ICL PERQ). Simulation results indicate that it
will be capable of processing 150K packets per second. Comparisons with declarative language implementations on von Neumann
machines suggest that this is equivalent to 5 Mips. It is expected that the prototype will be operational by summer 1985.

  THE PARALLEL EVALUATION OF LOGIC PROGRAMS ON ALICE

  There is, potentially, a high degree of parallel computation
to be exploited in the evaluation of logic programs. Figure 5
illustrates how this parallelism arises. To solve P all of the
conjuncts C1 and C2 through Cn must be solved. Potentially all
may be solved in parallel. This type of parallel evaluation is
kown as AND-parallelism. In general there will be a number of
ways in which any Ci might be solved. Again all the possible
solutions may be investigated in parallel. This type of parallelism in known as OR-parallelism.
  A major problem arises in attempting to fully exploit AND-
parallelism. Conjuncts may share a variable, so when they are
being solved in parallel each may wish to bind the variable in a
different way. Figure 6 illustrates a program in which this
problem arises.
  Three ways of overcoming this problem have been investigated
at Imperial College. They are as follows:

1. Restrict the language to ensure that each variable is bound by only one cunjunct at any one time.
2. Limit the degree of parallelisms exploited to avoid conflicts.
3. Develop mechanisms to reconcile conflicts.

Restricting the Language

This is the approach taken by Clark and Gregory in their language PARLOG [ClG81]. In PARLOG each shared variable is annotated to indicate which conjunct is allowed to bind the variable. Thus conjuncts have a producer/consumer relation with respect to shared variables. Furthermore, PARLOG does not permit backtracking. Once a choice between solutions has been made the evaluation is committed to that choice. However, guards on each solution permit a limited amount of computation (<u>not</u> involving unification) to be performed in order to choose between alternative solutions. The language may be viewed as a relational analogue of Hoare's Communicating Sequential Processes or Kahn and MacQueen's Streams.

PARLOG may be directly implemented on ALICE. The implementation methodology will be illustrated with a small example. Consider the network of four processes shown in Figure 7. One produces files for printing, two print such files, and the fourth receives the files from the producer and directs them to a non-busy printer.

The network is described in the following PARLOG program.

```
Files(z↑) // <x↑,y↑> Merge-To z // Printer(x) // Printer(y)
where
        Files(x) if. . .
        Printer(x) if. . .
        <u.x, y> Merge-To u.z if <x, y> Merge-To z
        <x, u.y> Merge-To u.z if <x, y> Merge-To z
```

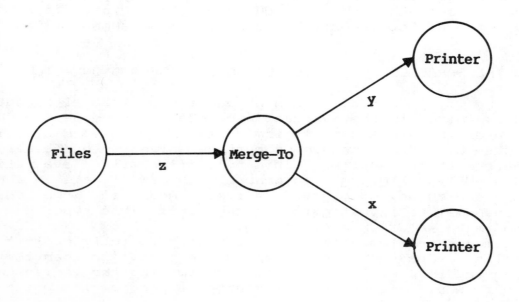

Figure 7: A Printer Spooler

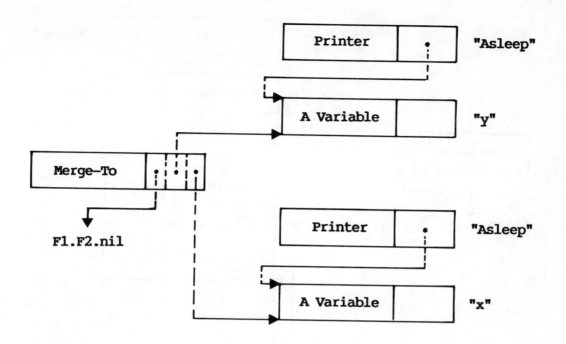

Figure 8: The Initial State

Notice that Merge-To is being used "backwards" to split one stream into two streams.

To simplify the description the Files process will be replaced by the list of files F1.F2.nil. Figure 8 shows the initial state of the system in the ALICE packet representation. x and y are modelled directly by variable packets. The Merge-To and Printer processes are modelled by rewriteable packets. Each Printer is "asleep" pending the instantiation of its associated variable.

Figure 9 shows the system after Merge-To has sent file F1 along the channel x to one of the Printers. This is modelled by instantiating the variable packet associated with x as F1 joined onto another variable packet. Instantiating x causes its associated Printer to be "woken-up." The now active Printer consumes F1 and returns to "sleep" as shown in Figure 10.

The "putting to sleep" and "waking up" of the Printer packets is handled automatically by ALICE.

Steve Gregory has developed a compiler from PARLOG to ALICE CTL (writted in PARLOG).

Limiting the Degree of Parallelism

Broda, Darlington and Reeve have developed a scheme that fully exploits OR-parallelism but ignores AND-parallelism. Its operation is as follows:

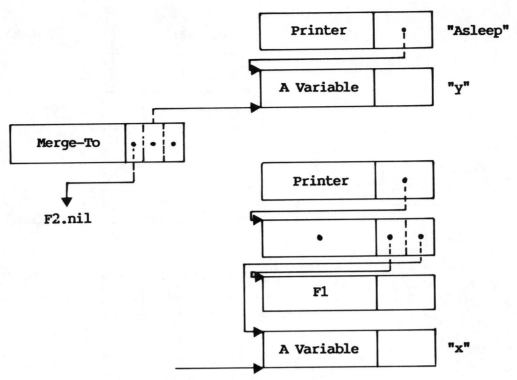

Figure 9:   Evaluating Merge–To

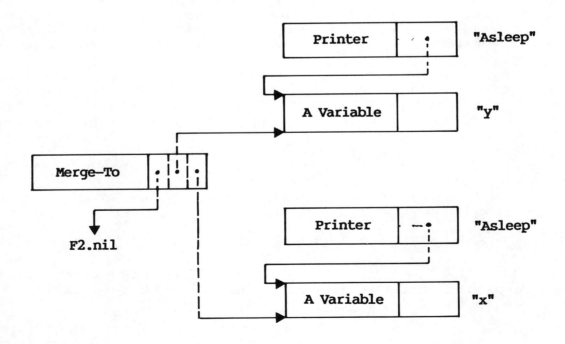

Figure 10:   Evaluating Printer

Fallible (x) & Greek (x)

Human (x) & Greek (x)

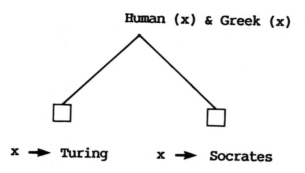

x ➤ Turing   x ➤ Socrates

Greek (Turing)   **Greek (Socrates)**

X

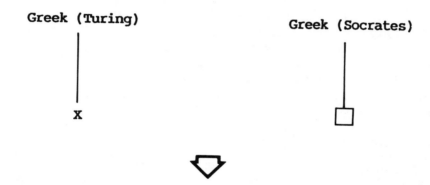

True X ➤ **Socrates**

Figure 11: An OR–Parallel Scheme

i)   Choose the leftmost conjunct,
ii) Solve the conjunct in OR-parallel,
iii) Pass the variable bindings associated with each solu-
     tion through the remaining conjuncts and solve the
     resulting set of alternatives in parallel by a recur-
     sive call to the evaluator.

The following example illustrates the operation of this
scheme. Given

```
Fallible(x) <- Human(x)
Human(Turing)          <-
Human(Socrates)        <-
Greek(Socrates         <-
```

consider the evaluation of the query

    x : Fallible(x) & Greek(x)

   This scheme searches for solutions as follows. First the
solutions to Fallible(x) are found. Thus Fallible(x) is reduced
to Human(x) which is then solved in OR-parallel to yield that x
can be either Turing or Socrates. Next Greek(x) is instantiated
with each of the alternatives for x. Finally Greek(Turing) and
Greek(Socrates) are solved concurrently. Figure 11 illustrates
these steps.
   Rather than finding all of the possible bindings for a
variable in a conjunct before passing them to the right, each
binding should be passed on as it is found to exploit the maximum
degree of parallelism.
   A point to note is that if lazy evaluation is employed this
scheme mimics the left-to-right depth first search of PROLOG.
   Krysia Broda has implemented an interpreter (written in
HOPE) which takes logic programs written in the micro-PROLOG
syntax [CEM81] and evaluates them according to the above scheme
[Bro82].
   A conjunct may be instantiated for a particular set of
variable bindings in two ways. It may either be copied and the
bindings incorporated during the copying or it may be structure
shared. In the structure sharing approach, each instantiation is
represented by a pointer to the skeleton of the conjunct and an
environment which specifies the variable bindings for the particular instantiation. Copying results in a high storage turnover
but gives a highly distributed computation. Conversely structure
sharing requires a minimum of store but leads to a highly centralized computation. In general ALICE would seem to be more
suited to copying because of the resulting distribution of computation. However, if the structures are large and there is little
store available, or there are very few processors available to do
the copying, then structure sharing becomes more attractive.
Krysia Broda's interpreter is transparent to which of the mechanisms is employed. She is currently investigating methods for
dynamically changing between the two according to the availability of store and processors.
   One disadvantage that this scheme shares with conventional
Prolog implementations is that if a goal identical to some previously solved goal occurs during a computation none of the
previous work can be re-used. ALICE permits rewrite rules to be
added, removed, or updated dynamically during a computation. This
feature provides for a straightforeward implementation of the
Prolog ASSERT and RETRACT statements. It would seem useful to use
this feature to remember important lemmas and thereby save their
repeated computation. The critical point is, of course, how to
decide what is relevant and avoid remembering useless information. We plan to investigate several schemes that would allow
these decisions to be made.

Reconciling Conflicting Unifications

   This scheme exploits both AND-parallelisms and OR-parallel-
isms. Conjuncts are solved in parallel and in isolation (i.e.,
full AND-parallelism). Also any OR-parallelism associated with
each conjunct is exploited. The overall solutions are found by

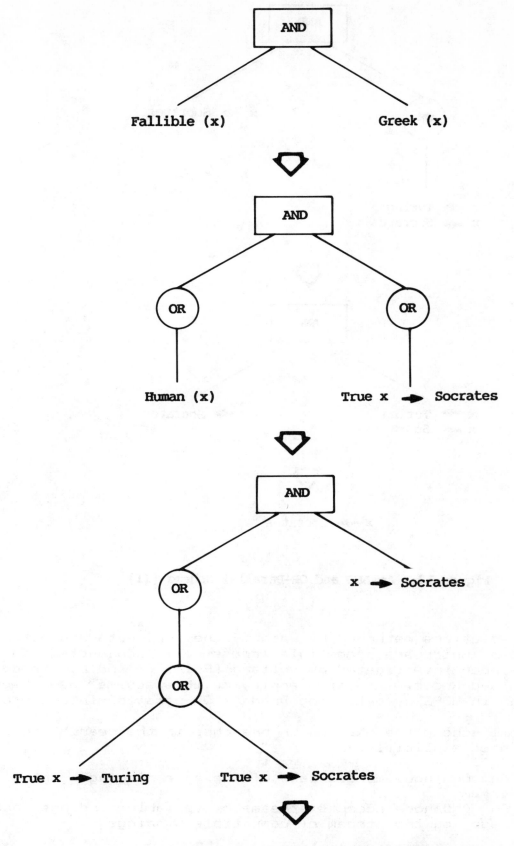

Figure 12: An AND and OR-Parallel Scheme (I)

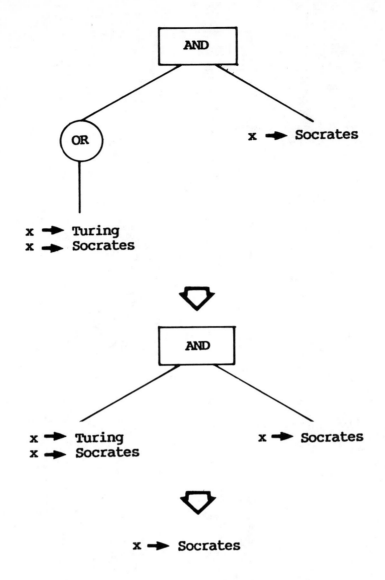

Figure 13: An AND and OR-Parallel Scheme (II)

taking the solutions returned by each of the conjuncts and determining those which are compatible across all conjuncts. This
scheme has been investigated by Pollard [Pol81], and by Broda,
Darlington and Reeve. A system employing this scheme has been
implemented in HOPE by extending Broda's OR-parallel interpreter
[Sim83].

In this scheme the AND and OR branches in the search space
are represented explicitly.

o   An OR node merges sets of variable bindings into a
       stream
o   An AND node accepts streams of variable bindings and
       passes on the stream of compatible bindings

Figures 12 and 13 illustrate the steps involved when the
query x : Fallible(x) & Greek(x) is evaluated according to this
scheme.

Although this scheme offers vast amounts of parallelism, it has two disadvantages in any practical implementation. Firstly it will generally produce more parallelism than is useful (particularly when it is acknowledged that much of the computation will be discarded). Secondly the overheads of reconciling the solutions from each of the conjuncts may well outweigh the benefits gained from the AND-parallelism.

CONCLUSIONS AND FUTURE RESEARCH

The results obtained so far would seem to indicate that scheme which fully exploits OR-parallels and only employs AND-parallelism when there is a definite producer/consumer relation for any shared variable (or no shared variable at all) offers the best compromise between the advantages (faster execution) and the disadvantages (memory and processor requirements) of parallel evaluation. We are currently investigating methods of analyzing logic programs to be able to detect when employing AND-parallelism would be beneficial and when it is wiser to delay the evaluation of a conjunct until more of its variables are bound.

ALICE would be an ideal vehicle on which to implement implosive problem solving algorithms of the kind outlined in [Kor82]. If such techniques could be applied to a logic program interpreter, its performance should be far superior to that of AND/OR graph manipulation systems of the kind described above. We intend to explore this area.

ACKNOWLEDGMENTS

The comments and suggestions of our colleagues in the Department of Computing at Imperial College, in particular those of Krysia Broda, were of great benefit.

The authors gratefully acknowledge the support of the Science and Engineering Research Council of Great Britian.

REFERENCES

Bac78   Backus J. Can Programming be Liberated from the von Neumann Style 1. ACM Turing Award Lecture. CAAM Vol. 21 No. 8, Aug. 1978.

Bro82   Broda K. An OR Parallel PROLOG Interpreter in HOPE. Internal Report, Dept. of Computing, Imperial College, London, 1982.

BMS80   Burstall R.M., MacQueen D.B. and Sanella D.T. HOPE: An Experimental Applicative Language. Internal Report, Dept. of Computer Science, University of Edinburgh, 1980.

CEM81   Clark K.L., Ennals J.R. and McCabe F.G. A Micro-PROLOG Primer. Logic Programming Associates Limited, 1981.

ClG81   Clark K.L. and Gregory S. *A Relational Language for Parallel Programming*. Proceedings of the 1981 ACM/MIT Conference on Functional Programming Languages and Computer Architecture, 1981.

DaK77   Davis R. and King J. *An Overview of Production Systems*. Memo AIM-271, Stanford A.I. Laboratory, 1977.

DaR81   Darlington J. and Reeve M.J. *ALICE: A Multi-Processor Reduction Machine for the Parallel Evaluation of Applicative Languages*. Proceedings of the 1981 ACM/MIT Conference on Functional Programming Languages and Computer Architecture, 1981.

FrW76   Friedman D.P. and Wise D.S. *CONS Should Not Evaluate Its Arguments*. In 'Automata, Languages and Programming', eds. Michaelson S. and Milner R., Edinburgh University Press, 1976.

GWG80   Gurd J.R., Watson I. and Glauert J.R.W. *A Multilayered Data Flow Computer Architecture (3rd Issue)*. Internal Report, Dept. of Computer Science, University of Manchester, 1980.

HeM76   Henderson P. and Morris J.H. *A Lazy Evaluator*. Proc. Third Annual ACM SIGACT-SIGPLAN Symp. on Principles of Programming Languages, 1976.

Kor82   Kornfeld W.A. *Combinatorially Implosive Algorithms*. CACM Vol. 25 No. 10, Oct. 1982.

Kow74   Kowalski R.A. *Logic as a Programming Language*. Proc. IFIP Congress 74, North Holland Publishing Co., 1974.

Pol81   Pollard G. *Parallel Evaluation of Horn Clauses*. Ph.D. Thesis, Dept. of Computing, Imperial College, London, 1981.

Ree81   Reeve M.J. *An Introduction to the ALICE Complier Target Language*. Internal Report, Dept. of Computing, Imperial College, London, 1981.

Rou75   Roussel P. *PROLOG: Manuel de Reference et d'Utilisation*. Groupe d'Intelligence Artificielle, Universite d'Aix-Marseille, Luminy, 1975.

Sim83   Simpson K.E. *An AND/OR Parallel PROLOG Interpreter in HOPE*. Internal Report, Dept. of Computing, Imperial College, London, 1983.

Tur80   Turner D.A. *Programming Language -- Current and Future Developments*. Proc. of Infotech State of the Art Conference, Software Development Techniques, London, 1980.

Chapter 9: Computer Systems For Specialized Artificial Intelligence Applications

Intelligent computer systems for AI applications such as natural-language understanding, speech recognition, and vision require capabilities like monitoring a huge number of sensors, coding, pattern recognition, searching, knowledge base management, dynamic planning, and scheduling. Despite attention given to speeding up high-level symbolic computations, the major bottleneck in some AI applications lies in the processing of some fundamental operations. For example, in many vision systems, 90 percents or more of the computational time may be incurred in the initial segmentation of the visual scene from pixels to low-level symbolic constructs [1]. Similar problems also arise in speech processing. A viable approach is to design special-purpose computers or task-oriented computers to process specialized tasks in a more efficient way [2,3].

Natural-language processing involves the development of computer programs and architectures that can analyze natural language and act appropriately on the information contained in the text or utterance.[4-6] It can be used in applications such as machine translation [7], natural-language interface (question-answering system) [8,9], text analysis, text generation, and speech understanding [10-13]. Early work on natural-language understanding was done mainly in universities. Example systems include ELIZA [14], STUDENT [15], SHRDLU [16], Wilks' Machine Translation system [17], LUNAR [18], MARGIE [19], REQUEST [20], GUS [21], SAM and PAM [22], LIFER [23], ORB1 [24], and TEAM [25]. Recently, some natural-language systems have been commercially available. The first commercial product, INTELLECT, was developed by the Artificial Intelligence Corp. in 1982 [26]. Several other products, such as Themis, Savvy, Straight Talk, Natural link, Logos, Pearl, and Supernatural, are or will be appearing soon for use on various small computers. In West Germany, a government-sponsored project, Ham-Ans, is being developed for hotel-reservation, fisheries data bank, and picture-sequence analysis.

Considerable progress toward practical speech-understanding systems was made in the 1970s. The ARPA Speech Understanding Project developed important ideas about the architecture and control of large AI systems (e.g., HEARSAY's black-board organization) that have been applied in domains besides speech processing [27]. HEARSAY-II [28,29], HARPY [30], HWIM [31], SRI/SDC [32], and Bell's Speech-Understanding System [33] are well-known existing speech-understanding systems. As a topic of interest in natural-language processing, techniques for constructing natural-language interfaces have been developed and are being used [8,34,35]. Special VLSI chips for acoustic processing that includes tasks such as digital filtering, FFT's, linear predictive, and coding are available. Parallel and distributed processing have also been applied in designing speech-understanding systems [3,36-38].

Computer vision is the task of comprehending a sense from the projected image [39-47] and includes areas such as picture processing, image processing, pattern recognition, scene analysis, image interpretation, optical processing, video processing, and image understanding. These fields can roughly be classified into three levels: signal processing, pattern recognition, and image understanding. A large number of computer systems for vision, ranging from low level to high level, have been designed and developed. Examples include CLIP [48], STARAN [49], DPA [50], BAP [51], FLIP [52], PASM [53], PICAP [54], PUMPS [55], STAR [56], MPP [57], TOPPSY [58], REPLICA [59], ZMOB [60], LOCO [61], CONSIGHT-I [62], SRI Vision Module [63], Multiband Aerial-Photo Interpretation System [64], VISIONS [65], Query-Oriented Vision System [66], and ACRONYM [67]. The Department of Defense is currently supporting a number projects to analyze both the processing requirements and machine organizations for computer vision. Owing to the enormous amount of information that must be processed in a computer-vision system, it appears that the issues in computer vision will be one of the major beneficiaries of the new VLSI and VHSI technologies [68-70].

Robotics, especially robot vision and robot programming, is another important application of AI that deals with real objects in the real world [71-77]. Robots have been used in a variety of industrial applications [78,79]. To control robotic systems in complex industrial operations, powerful and intelligent computers are required [80-82].

Yet another good example of illustrating the transfer of intelligence from software to hardware with new advances in hardware technologies and microelectronics is computer chess. High-performance chess hardware and systems are now available [83-87].

Because of space limitations, no paper is selected for inclusion in this chapter.

References

[1] W. Perkins, "A Model Based Vision System for Industrial Parts," *IEEE Transactions on Computers*, vol. C-27, no. 2, pp. 126-143, 1978.

[2] A.P. Reeves, "Parallel Computer Architectures for Image Processing," *International Journal of Computer Vision, Graphics, and Image Processing,* vol. 25, no. 1, pp. 68-88, Academic Press, 1984.

[3] R. Bisiani, H. Mauersberg, and R. Reddy, "Task-Oriented Architecture," *Proceedings of the IEEE*, vol. 71, no. 7, pp. 885-896, July 1983.

[4] T. Winograd, *Language as a Cognitive Process*, Addison-Wesley, Reading, Mass., 1982.

[5] H. Tennant, *Natural Language Processing*, Petrocelli Books, New York, N.Y., 1981.

[6] B.J. Grosz, "Natural Language Processing," *Artificial Intelligence,* vol. 19, no. 2, pp. 131-136, 1982.

[7] A.B. Tucker Jr., "A Perspective on Machine Translation: Theory and Practice," *Communications of the ACM,* vol. 27, no. 4, pp. 322-329, April 1984.

[8] D.L. Waltz, "Natural Language Interfaces," *SIGART Newsletter,* no. 61, pp. 16-64, ACM, New York, N.Y., 1977.

[9] W.A. Woods, "Semantics and Quantification in Natural Language Question-Answering," *Advances in Computers,* edited by M. Yovits, vol. 17, pp. 1-87, Academic Press, Orlando, Fla., 1978.

[10] W. Lea, ed., *Trend in Speech Recognition*, Prentice-Hall, Englewood Cliffs, N.J., 1980.

[11] H.L. Andrews, "Speech Processing," *Computer,* vol. 17, no. 10, pp. 315-324, Oct. 1984.

[12] G.R. Doddington and T.B. Schalk, "Speech Recognition: Turning Theory to Practice," *IEEE Spectrum,* vol. 18, no. 9, pp. 26-32, Sept. 1981.

[13] D.L. Lee and F.H. Lochovsky, "Voice Response Systems," *Computing Surveys,* vol. 15, no. 4, pp. 351-374, Dec. 1983.

[14] J. Weizenbaum, "ELIZA—A Computer Program for the Study of Natural Language Communication between Man and Machine," *Communications of the ACM,* vol. 9, no. 1, pp. 36-45, Jan. 1966.

[15] D.G. Bobrow, "Natural Language Input for a Computer Problem-Solving System," *Semantic Information Processing*, edited by M. Minsky, pp. 146-226, MIT Press, Cambridge, Mass., 1968.

[16] T. Winograd, *Understanding Natural Language,* Academic Press, Orlando, Fla., 1972.

[17] Y.A. Wilks, "An Artificial Intelligent Approach to Machine Translation," *Computer Models of Thought and Language*, edited by R. Schank and K. Colby, pp. 114-151, Freeman, San Francisco, Calif., 1973.

[18] W.A. Woods, "Progress in Natural Language Understanding: An Application to Lunar Geology," *Proceedings of the National Computer Conference,* vol. 42, pp. 441-450, AFIPS Press, Reston, Va., 1973.

[19] R.C. Schank, *Conceptual Information Processing,* North-Holland, Amsterdam, The Netherlands, 1975.

[20] W.J. Plath, "REQUEST: A Natural Language Question-Answering System," *IBM Journal of Research and Development,* vol. 20, no. 4, pp. 326-335, 1976.

[21] D.G. Bobrow, R.M. Kaplan, M. Kay, D.A. Norman, H. Thompson and T. Winograd, "GUS, A Frame-Driven Dialog System," *Artificial Intelligence.* vol. 8, no. 2, pp. 155-173, 1977.

[22] R.C. Schank and R.P. Abelson, *Scripts, Plans, Goals, and Understanding,* Lawrence Erlbaum Press, Hillsdale, N.J., 1977.

[23] G.G. Hendrix, "Human Engineering for Applied Natural Language Processing," *Proceedings of the 5th International Joint Conference on Artificial Intelligence,* pp. 183-191, William Kaufmann, Los Altos, Calif., 1977.

[24] L.M. Pereira, P. Sabatier, and E. Oliveria, "ORB1—An Expert System for Environmental Resource Evaluation Through Natural Language," *Proceedings of the 1st International Logic Programming Conference,* Faculte des Sciences de Luminy, Marseille, France, 1982.

[25] B.J. Grosz, "TEAM: A Transportable Natural Language Interface System," *Proceedings of the Conference on Applied Natural Language Processing,* pp. 39-45, Association for Computational Linguistics, New York, N.Y., 1983.

[26] L.R. Harris, "Experience with ROBOT in Twelve Commercial Natural Language Data Base Query Applications," *Proceedings of the 6th International Joint Conference on Artificial Intelligence,* pp. 365-368, William Kaufmann, Los Altos, Calif., 1979.

[27] D.H. Klatt, "Review of the ARPA Speech Understanding Project," *Journal of the Acoustical Society of America,* vol. 62, pp. 1345-1366, Dec. 1977.

[28] V.R. Lesser and L.D. Erman, "A Retrospective View of the Hearsay-II Architecture," *Proceedings of the 5th International Joint Conference on Artificial Intelligence,* pp. 790-800, William Kaufmann, Los Altos, Calif., 1977.

[29] L.D. Erman, F. Hayes-Roth, V.R. Lesser, and D.R. Reddy, "The Hearsay-II Speech-Understanding System: Integrating Knowledge to Resolve Uncertainty," *Computing Surveys,* vol. 12, no. 2, pp. 213-253, June 1980.

[30] R. Bisiani, "The Harpy Machine: A Data Structure-Oriented Architecture," *Proceedings of the 5th Work-*

shop on Computer Architecture for Non-Numeric Processing, pp. 128-136, ACM, New York, N.Y., March 1980.

[31] J. Wolf and W. Woods, "The HWIM Speech Understanding System," *Trends in Speech Recognition,* edited by W. Lea, Prentice-Hall, Englewood Cliffs, N.J., 1980.

[32] J. Barnett, M. Bernstein, M. Gillman, and I. Kameny, "The SDC Speech Understanding System," *Trends in Speech Recognition,* edited by W. Lea, Prentice-Hall, Englewood Cliffs, N.J., 1980.

[33] S.E. Levinson and K.L. Shipley, "A Conversational-Mode Airline Information and Reservation System Speech Input and Output," *Bell System Technical Journal,* vol. 59, no. 1, pp. 119-137, Jan. 1980.

[34] E. Rich, "Natural-Language Interfaces," *Computer,* vol. 17, no. 9, pp. 39-47, Sept. 1984.

[35] R. Wilensky, Y. Arens, and D. Chin, "Talking to UNIX in English: An Overview of UC," *Communications of the ACM,* vol. 27, no. 6, pp. 574-593, June 1984.

[36] J.B. Pollack and D.L. Waltz, "Parallel Interpretation on Natural Language," *Proceedings of the International Conference on Fifth-Generation Computer Systems,* pp. 686-691, ICOT, Tokyo, Japan, and North-Holland, Amsterdam, The Netherlands, 1984.

[37] E.C. Bronson and L.J. Siegel, "A Parallel Architecture for Acoustic Processing in Speech Understanding," *Proceedings of the International Conference on Parallel Processing,* pp. 307-312, IEEE Computer Society, Washington, D.C., 1982.

[38] J.W. Smith and A.L. Tharp, "A Microcomputer System for Processing Natural Languages," *IEEE Transactions on Pattern Analysis and Machine Intelligence,* vol. PAMI-4, no. 2, pp. 221-223, March 1982.

[39] D.H. Ballardi and C. Brown, *Computer Vision,* Prentice-Hall, Englewood Cliffs, N.J., 1982.

[40] D. Marr, *Vision,* Freeman, San Francisco, Calif., 1982.

[41] M. Brady, ed., "Special Issue on Computer Vision," *Artificial Intelligence,* vol. 17, no. 1-3, Aug. 1981.

[42] A. Rosenfeld, "Picture Processing: 1983," *International Journal of Computer Vision, Graphics and Image Processing,* vol. 26, pp. 347-393, 1984.

[43] R.T. Chin and C.A. Harlow, "Automated Visual Inspection: A Survey," *IEEE Transactions on Pattern Analysis and Machine Intelligence,* vol. PAMI-4, no. 6, pp. 557-573, Nov. 1982.

[44] P.E. Danielsson and S. Levialdi, "Computer Architectures for Pictorial Information Systems," *Computer,* vol. 14, no. 11, pp. 53-67, Nov. 1981.

[45] K.S. Fu and T. Ichikawa, ed., *Special Computer Architecture for Pattern Processing,* CRC Press, Boca Raton, Fla., 1982.

[46] M. Kidode, "Image Processing Machines in Japan," *Computer,* vol. 16, no. 1, pp. 68-80, Jan. 1983.

[47] G.R. Nudd, "Image Understanding Architectures," *Proceedings of National Computer Conference,* pp. 239-252, AFIPS Press, Reston, Va., 1980.

[48] M. Duff, "CLIP4: A Large Scale Integrated Circuit Array Parallel Processor," *Proceedings of the 3rd International Joint Conference on Pattern Recognition,* pp. 728-732, William Kaufmann, Los Altos, Calif., 1976.

[49] J.L. Potter, "The STARAN Architecture and Its Application to Image Processing and Pattern Recognition Algorithms," *Proceedings of the National Computer Conference,* pp. 1041-1047, AFIPS Press, Reston, Va., 1978.

[50] S.F. Readaway, "The DAP Approach," *Infotech State of the Art Report on Supercomputers,* vol. 2, pp. 836-840, Infotech International, London, England, 1979.

[51] A.P. Reeves, "A Systematically Designed Binary Array Processor," *IEEE Transactions on Computers,* vol. C-29, pp. 278-287, 1980.

[52] K. Luetjen, P. Gemmar, and H. Ischen, "FLIP—A Flexible Multiprocessor System For Image Processing," *Proceedings of the 5th International Conference on Pattern Recognition,* pp. 326-328, IEEE Computer Society, Washington, D.C., 1980.

[53] H.J. Siegel, et al., "PASM: A Partitionable SIMD/ MIMD System for Image Processing and Pattern Recognition," *IEEE Transactions on Computers,* vol. C-30, no. 12, pp. 934-947, Dec. 1981.

[54] D. Antonsson, et al., "PICAP—A System Approach to Image Processing," *Proceedings of the Workshop on Computer Architecture for Pattern Analysis and Image Database Management,* pp. 35-42, IEEE Computer Society, Washington, D.C., 1981.

[55] F.A. Briggs, K.S. Fu, K. Hwang, and B.W. Wah, "PUMPS Architecture for Pattern Analysis and Image Database Management," *IEEE Transactions on Computers,* vol. C-31, no. 10, pp. 969-983, Oct. 1982.

[56] C.L. Wu, T.Y. Feng, and M.C. Lin, "Star: A Local Network System for Real-Time Management of Imagery Data," *IEEE Transactions on Computers,* vol. C-31, no. 10, pp. 923-933, Oct. 1982.

[57] J.L. Potter, "Image Processing on the Massively Parallel Processor," *Computer,* vol. 16, no. 1, pp. 62-67, Jan. 1983.

[58] A. Engbersen, "TOPPSY: A Time Overlapped Parallel Processing System," *International Journal of Computer Vision, Graphics and Image Processing,* vol. 24, pp. 97-106, 1983.

[59] Y.W.E. Ma and R. Krishnamurti, "REPLICA—A Reconfigurable Partitionable Highly Parallel Computer Architecture for Active Multi-Sensory Perception of

3-Dimensional Objects," *Proceedings of the 11th Annual International Symposium on Computer Architecture,* pp. 30-37, IEEE Computer Society, Washington, D.C., 1984.

[60] M. Weiser, S. Kogge, M. McElvany, R. Pierson, R. Post, and A. Thareja, "Status and Performance of the ZMOB Parallel Processing System," *Proceedings of COMPCON S'85,* pp. 71-73, IEEE Computer Society, Washington, D.C., Feb. 1985.

[61] V.M. Milutinovic, J.J. Crnkovic, L.-Y. Chang, and H.J. Siegel, "The Loco Approach to Distributed Task Allocation in Aida by Verdi," *Proceedings of the 5th International Conference on Distributed Computing Systems,* pp. 359-368, IEEE Computer Society, Washington, D.C., May 1985.

[62] S.W. Holland, L. Rossol, and M.R. Ward, "CONSIGHT-I: A Vision-Controlled Robot System for Transferring Parts from Belt Conveyors," *Computer Vision and Sensor Based Robot,* edited by G. Dodd and L. Rossol, pp. 81-100, Plenum Press, 1979.

[63] G.J. Gleason and G.J. Agin, "A Modular System for Sensor-Controlled Manipulation and Inspection," *Proceedings of the 9th International Symposium of Industrial Robots,* pp. 57-70, Society of Manufacturing Engineers and Robot Institute of America, Dearborn, Mich., 1979.

[64] M. Nagao, T. Matsuyama, and Y. Ikeda, "Structural Analysis of Complex Aerial Photographs," *Proceedings of the 6th International Joint Conference on Artificial Intelligence,* pp. 610-616, William Kaufmann, Los Altos, Calif., 1979.

[65] A.R. Hanson and E.M. Riseman, "Segmentation of Natural Scenes," *Computer Vision Systems,* edited by A. Hanson and E. Riseman, pp. 129-163, Academic Press, Orlando, Fla., 1978.

[66] D.H. Ballardi, C.M. Brown, and J.A. Feldman, "An Approach to Knowledge-Directed Image Analysis," *Computer Vision Systems,* edited by A. Hanson and E. Riseman, pp. 271-281, Academic Press, Orlando, Fla., 1978.

[67] R.A. Brooks, "Symbolic Reasoning among 3-D Model and 2-D Images," *Artificial Intelligence,* vol. 17, no. 1-3, pp. 285-348, 1981.

[68] B.P. Treleaven and C. Philip, eds., *VLSI Architectures,* Prentice-Hall, Englewood Cliffs, N.J., 1983.

[69] J.L. Hennessy, "VLSI Processor Architectures," *IEEE Transactions on Computers,* vol. C-33, no. 12, pp. 1221-1246, 1984.

[70] C.L. Seitz, "Concurrent VLSI Architectures," *IEEE Transactions on Computers,* vol. C-33, no. 12, pp. 1247-1265, Dec. 1984.

[71] M. Brady, "Artificial Intelligence and Robotics," *Robotics and Artificial Intelligence,* edited by M. Brady, L.A. Gerhardt, and H.F. Davidson, Springer-Verlag, New York, N.Y., 1984.

[72] J.F. Jarvis, "Robotics," *Computer,* vol. 17, no. 10, pp. 283-292, Oct. 1984.

[73] T. Lozano-Perez, "Robotics," *Artificial Intelligence,* vol. 19, no. 2, pp. 137-143, 1982.

[74] T. Lozano-Perez, "Robot Programming," *Proceedings of the IEEE,* vol. 71, no. 7, pp. 821-841, July 1983.

[75] M. Togai, "Japan's Next Generation Robots: A Preview," *Technical Report,* AT&T Bell Laboratories, Holmdel, NJ, 1983.

[76] A.P. Ambler, "Languages for Programming Robots," *Robotics and Artificial Intelligence,* edited by M. Brady, et al., pp. 219-227, Springer-Verlag, New York, N.Y., 1984.

[77] B.E. Shimano, C.C. Geschke, and C.H. Spaulding, "VAL II: A Robot Programming Language and Control System," *Proceedings of the International Symposium on Robotics Research,* MIT Press, Cambridge, Mass., 1984.

[78] J.F. Engelberger, *Robotics in Practice: Management and Application of Industrial Robots,* Kogan Page, London, England, 1980.

[79] W.B. Thompson, ed., *Computer,* vol. 13, no. 5, pp. 7-63, May 1980.

[80] R.H. Taylor and D.D. Grossman, "An Integrated Robot System Architecture," *Proceedings of the IEEE,* vol. 71, no. 7, pp. 842-856, July 1983.

[81] C.A. Klein and W. Wahawisan, "Use of a Multiprocessor for Control of a Robotic System," *International Journal of Robotics Research,* vol. 1, no. 2, pp. 45-59, Summer 1982.

[82] D. Sneed and J. Roach, "A Lisp-Based Robot Control System—Part I: Basic Functions," *Robotics Age,* pp. 8-12, Nov. 1984.

[83] M.M. Newborn, "Recent Progress in Computer Chess," *Advances in Computers,* edited by M.C. Yovits, vol. 18, pp. 59-117, Academic Press, Orlando, Fla., 1979.

[84] J.H. Condon and K. Thompson, "Belle," *Advances in Computer Chess III,* edited by M.R.B. Clarke, pp. 45-54, University of Edingburgh Press, Edingburgh, England, 1981.

[85] C. Ebeling and A. Palay, "The Design and Implementation of VLSI Chess Move Generator," *Proceedings of the 11th Annual International Symposium on Computer Architecture,* pp. 74-80, IEEE Computer Society, Washington, D.C., 1984.

[86] J. Schaeffer, et al., "A VLSI Chess Legal Move Generator," *Proceedings of the 3rd Caltech Conference on Very Large Scale Integration,* pp. 331-350, Computer Science Press, Rockville, Md., 1983.

[87] D.R. Hofstadter, "The Architecture of Jumbo," *Proceedings of the International Machine Learning Workshop,* pp. 161-170, University of Illinois, Urbana, Il., June 1983.